# EUROPEAN WRITERS

Selected Authors

# EUROPEAN WRITERS

## Selected Authors

*GEORGE STADE*
*EDITOR IN CHIEF*

Volume I

**HANS CHRISTIAN ANDERSEN**

**TO**

**JOHANN WOLFGANG VON GOETHE**

CHARLES SCRIBNER'S SONS
NEW YORK

MAXWELL MACMILLAN CANADA
TORONTO

MAXWELL MACMILLAN INTERNATIONAL
NEW YORK OXFORD SINGAPORE SYDNEY

**Library of Congress Cataloging-in-Publication Data**

European writers. Selected authors / George Stade, editor in chief.
v. cm.
Comprises 68 unabridged essays selected by the publisher from its fourteen-volume set of "European writers" edited by George Stade, with W.T.H. Jackson and Jacques Barzun.
Includes bibliographical references and index.
Contents: v. 1. Hans Christian Andersen to Johann Wolfgang von Goethe—v. 2. Maxim Gorky to Marcel Proust—v. 3. Alexander Pushkin to Emile Zola.
ISBN 0–684–19583–6 (set):
1. European literature—History and criticism. I. Stade, George. II. Charles Scribner's Sons.
PN501.E9 1992
809'.894—dc20

# PUBLISHER'S NOTE

*European Writers: Selected Authors* comprises 68 unabridged essays chosen by the publishers from Scribners' fourteen-volume *European Writers,* edited by George Stade, with W. T. H. Jackson and Jacques Barzun. The selection is based on a survey of American libraries with a view toward including those authors and themes most often studied by high school students and undergraduates. No esthetic or cultural claims are advanced for the choices; these are simply the most often requested writers in the early 1990s.

The need to make an affordable set has limited the selections, but we hope that readers wishing to explore the house of European literature more fully will seek out the original *European Writers* in larger research libraries. A list of the 261 essays in that set appears in volume 3.

British authors are treated separately in the ongoing *British Writers* (9 volumes to date; 1979–1991). The Scribner World Literature series also includes *The Books of the Bible* (2 vols.; 1989), *Ancient Writers: Greece and Rome* (2 vols.; 1982), *American Writers* (10 vols.; 1978–1991), and *Latin American Writers* (3 vols.; 1990).

# CONTENTS

## Volume I

# CONTENTS

## Volume II



## Volume III

# CONTENTS

# HANS CHRISTIAN ANDERSEN
## *(1805–1875)*

### *LIFE*

HANS CHRISTIAN ANDERSEN spent his life pursuing fame. In this respect the famous fairy-tale writer was a crazed lover. At a very early age he declared himself willing to suffer all kinds of humiliation and denigration to fulfill what he felt to be his divine destiny, to be a writer. Egocentric to the core, persistent and patient, he denied himself so that destiny would not be denied.

Andersen's perseverance was astounding. Yet his narcissistic striving to succeed as a great writer was also profoundly sad. The strain he placed himself under to produce was so great that he often succumbed to bouts of hypochondria, melancholy, and depression. His nerves became like volatile wires, frayed and tattered. By the time he finally forced fame to turn and smile on him, he was a desperate man. Not only did he question whether he was worthy of fame, but he demanded even more admiration and applause than he had already gained. He licked the boots of the aristocracy to obtain support, and he complained when the Danish nation did not continually crown his head with laurels. He perfected his dress and manners to conceal his desperation. He undertook numerous trips abroad to seek peace of mind. But he could not escape the fact that his life had become an aborted fairy tale and that fame had a Medusa's head.

Whenever he took pen in hand, it was to shield himself from his fears and to vent his anger. His fairy tales were the life he did not lead, what he wanted to say publicly but did not dare. His writings were majestic acts of self-affirmation and self-deception. They did indeed bring him fame, and he did indeed become one of the most famous writers of his day, as he had hoped; but they also prevented the world from knowing him. Even today the world-famous Hans Christian Andersen is really unknown.

The public image of Hans Christian Andersen still prevalent is one fed by the lies and myths he created. For instance, most of the photographs and portraits of Andersen reveal a man at ease with himself, a gentle, composed man often telling stories benevolently to children. He is always well dressed and appears in poses of perfect propriety. He is tall, gaunt, and not particularly handsome. Like the photographers and painters, most biographers have contributed to the deception of the public by emphasizing the quaint and gentle composure of the imaginative writer. They have associated him with the ugly duckling and sketched his life as the poor, gifted son of a cobbler who transformed himself into a successful, "beautiful" writer through his magical, innate talents: Hans Christian Andersen as fairy tale. His name has become virtually synonymous with the genre.

Yet to see him and his work as fairy tale is to do him an injustice. Andersen wrote over thirty plays, six novels, three autobiographies, and several travel books and volumes of poetry, aside from numerous essays, tales, and stories. He was respected and revered during his lifetime as an avant-garde writer. He was a gifted orator and performer, at home in all social classes, one of the most widely traveled men of letters in Europe, and personally acquainted with most of the prominent authors of the nineteenth century. These features of his life and work tend to be forgotten or neglected. The fame of the fairy tales has dwarfed both his total artistic achievement and his pathetic personal history.

One of the difficulties in writing about Andersen as Denmark's most versatile and famous writer is that he himself wrote three autobiographies, all of which tend to distort facts. His first attempt to document his life was *H. C. Andersens Levnedsbog 1805–1831,* written in 1832. It was not discovered until 1926, when it was published in Danish. His second endeavor, *Märchen meines Lebens ohne Dichtung,* completed in 1847 and revised in 1871, was translated into English as *The True Story of My Life.* The third account, *Mit Livs Eventyr* (1855), was translated as *The Fairy Tale of My Life;* this title indicates how Andersen continually sought to portray himself in all his autobiographical writings as a type of romantic hero, a poor swineherd turned into a prince. For instance, the 1847 version begins as follows:

> My life is a beautiful fairy tale, rich and glorious. If I had gone out into the world as a poor and lonely boy and had met a powerful fairy, and if she had said, "Choose your own course and goal in life, then I shall protect and lead you according to the development of your mind and the way things must reasonably happen in this world," then my destiny could not have been happier, nor more cleverly or better guided than the case has been. The story of my life will tell the world what it has told me: there is a loving God who directs everything for the best.
>
> In 1805 there was a newly married couple, a cobbler and his wife, who lived in a small impoverished room in Odense. They loved each other dearly and deeply. He had just turned twenty-two, a remarkably talented man with a genuine poetic nature. She was somewhat older, ignorant about things concerning the world and life, but kind and generous. The man had recently become a guild master and had built his own shoemaker shop and wedding bed. For this purpose he had used the wooden frame on which the coffin of the dead Count Trampe had recently rested. The shreds of the black sheet, which were always to be found on the bed frame later, were souvenirs of this event. Then, on April 2, 1805, instead of the count's corpse, there was a live, crying child on this bed surrounded by flowers and candelabras. That was me, Hans Christian Andersen.

About the only thing true here is the date of Andersen's birth. The fact is that nobody knows exactly where Andersen was born. His parents had been married only two months before his birth and had no permanent residence. His father, Hans Andersen, who was born in 1782, became a journeyman shoemaker. In other words, he belonged to the lowest class of artisans and barely made enough to support himself and his family. He liked to read, take walks in the countryside, and make toys for his son. This was his talented or poetic side. Otherwise he was known to be a skeptical thinker, inclined to doubt the tenets of traditional Christianity. He died in 1816 after a desperate attempt to make money for the family by enlisting as a soldier in Napoleon's army.

Andersen's mother, Anne Marie Andersdatter, was born in 1775 and worked as a servant in various houses in Odense. In 1799 she gave birth to an illegitimate daughter. Later, after Andersen was born, she worked as a laundress and took other menial jobs. Far from being ignorant of the world, she knew real social conditions only too well. When Andersen refers to her as "ignorant," he means that she was illiterate, coarse, and superstitious. Such were Andersen's parents, and the noted Andersen biographer Elias Bredsdorff paints a more accurate picture of the writer's beginnings than the writer himself when he notes:

> Andersen's background was, from a social point of view, the lowest of the low: grinding poverty, slums, immorality and promiscuity. His grandmother was a pathological liar, his grandfather insane, his mother ended by becoming an alcoholic, his aunt ran a brothel in Copenhagen, and for years he was aware that somewhere a half-sister existed who might suddenly turn up and embarrass him in his new milieu—a thought which haunted his life and dreams.
>
> (*Hans Christian Andersen,* p. 16)

Thus Andersen's life was anything but a fairy tale. Though his parents doted on him, there was little they could offer him. Overly sensitive about his family's poverty and his own homely appearance, Andersen kept to himself. He had few friends and preferred to stay at home, where he would play with pictures, puppets, and dolls. By the time he was five, he was sent to school. His memories of his youth reveal a special fascination with the Odense jail and insane asylum, which were joined under a single roof. Given the history of insanity and immorality in his family, he feared going insane and being confined. At the same time he was also intrigued and attracted by the strange people in the jail and asylum. But more important than this attraction was his budding love for the theater.

Odense, a tiny city of eight thousand inhabitants, boasted a municipal theater that produced comic operas, operettas, and plays. When he was seven, his parents took Andersen to the theater, and a new, fantastic world exploded before his eyes: from this point on theater life came to represent a glorious realm of freedom from the misery of his life, and he hoped to become a great writer involved with the stage. At home, he began dressing up in costumes, acting out roles, and writing plays. As soon as he was able he read Shakespeare, and he gave recitals of his own plays to anyone he could attract. His mother became upset by her son's theater mania, but her threats of punishment had no effect. And after the death of her husband in 1816, she was rarely at home to keep an eye on him. In fact she had become so poor that she sent her eleven-year-old son to work against his will. Engaged as an apprentice in a cloth mill, Andersen did not last long there. He could not bear the obscenity and rough treatment of the journeymen, and he left after he was ridiculed and manhandled during a recitation of songs for his fellow workers. His next job was in a tobacco factory, where he worked until his lungs became slightly damaged. His mother then had no choice but to allow him to remain at home, where he devoted himself once again to books and playacting.

In July 1818 Andersen's mother remarried. Her new husband was another journeyman cobbler, but the financial situation of the family improved. Andersen could now attend the local church school, where he was expected to forget theater and poetry and submit to rigorous religious training. Yet Andersen's obsession with the theater was stronger than the school's discipline. Upon his confirmation, in 1819, he was willing to risk anything for a chance to pursue his calling as an artist, although his mother tried to convince him to learn a trade. Finally, knowing how superstitious his mother was, Anderson persuaded her to visit a fortuneteller, who predicted that her son would achieve fame in Copenhagen. And in the fall of 1819 the fourteen-year-old Andersen set out for the city.

Copenhagen destroyed many of his illusions, and the period 1819–1822 was one of trial and hardship. At that time the capital was a relatively small port city of 120,000 inhabitants, and Danish society, dominated by the aristocracy and upper-middle classes, was highly stratified. Though there were increasing signs of liberalism and possibilities for social advancement as Denmark underwent a transition from late-feudal absolutism to a form of constitutional monarchy, the king and his close advisers played an enormous role in all decisions pertaining to government, economy, and the arts. Most of the leading writers of the day, such as Adam Oehlenschläger and Johan Ludvig Heiberg, were dependent on patronage. Almost all the major cultural institutions, such as the theater, ballet, opera, and symphony, benefited from royal subsidies and private contributions. It was practically impossible for a member of the lower classes to establish himself socially, for success did not require "genius" as much as manners, breeding, formal training, and connections. Andersen had none of these. Instead he was helped by the fact that he was naive and foolhardy, entirely unaware that he was pursuing the impossible.

Certainly he was not prepared for the Copenhagen he encountered in 1819. He arrived during vicious anti-Semitic riots that raged for more than ten days, and rented a tiny room in a poor district of the city. He then experienced a series of setbacks that almost caused him to return to Odense. Armed with a letter of introduction to a famous solo dancer at the Royal Theater, he made the first of numerous attempts to impress important people with his talent. During his first interview he took off his shoes to demonstrate how well he could dance. Given his awkwardness, this was a catastrophic sally, and he was obliged to leave as soon as he could find his shoes. Similar catastrophes followed; soon he began to feel that he would find neither employers nor patrons to back his artistic career. Yet Andersen's determination and unusual capacity for improvisation eventually did make an impression on various philanthropic gentlemen, who collected money for him to attend ballet school and later to take singing lessons. He even appeared in some small roles at the Royal Theater. Nevertheless, despite such training and experience, Andersen was never able to cut a gracious figure onstage; and the plays and poems that he began producing were either imitative or pretentious.

This pretentiousness was evident in the way he signed his first book, *Ungdoms-Forsøg* (*Youthful Attempts*, 1822). He chose the nom de plume Villiam Christian Walter out of admiration for William Shakespeare and Sir Walter Scott, and he filled the book with stereotypes, stilted verse, and melodramatic scenes copied from his masters. Indeed, it became evident to all concerned (even to himself) that Andersen needed more formal schooling if he was to attain a measure of success as a writer or performer. Fortunately for him, the board of directors at the Royal Theater decided to offer him a three-year scholarship to attend a private school in Slagelse, a town fifty-six miles west of Copenhagen. Even more important was the choice of Jonas Collin, director of the board and a prominent legal administrator, as Andersen's prime adviser. A sober, highly intelligent, and sensitive man, Collin became Andersen's major benefactor and acted as his father for most of the writer's life. But Andersen had to endure five years of strict schooling before he was entirely accepted into the Collin home as an "adopted" son.

Although Andersen was seventeen when he entered the school at Slagelse, he had to be placed among the eleven-year-olds. This situation was humiliating for him, but he knew practically no Latin, Greek, geometry, geography, or history. Though he read voraciously, his grammar and style were faulty, and he remained an atrocious speller to the end of his life. Bothered by his deficiencies, Andersen pursued his studies with a vengeance. Despite his zeal, however, there were problems. The headmaster, Dr. Simon Meisling, was a moody, dissatisfied person who was apt to belittle the young man when he least expected it. For the next five years Andersen had to contend with Meisling's disparaging treatment in addition to the attempts of Meisling's wife to seduce him. Since he had few friends at school, he was often despondent, depending on letters and contacts from outside to encourage him in his studies. Andersen felt plagued by self-doubt and regarded the regimentation of school as stifling to a prospective writer with great imaginative powers. Meisling discouraged him from following his artistic leanings, and even Collin forbade him to write poetry for some time. Nevertheless, he was not to be deterred from pursuing his chosen destiny. In the spring of 1823 he wrote in a letter: "If anyone can become a poet [*Digter*] through the events of his childhood, then I will become one. Not a minor one, however, there are plenty of those. If I cannot become a great one, I shall strive to become a useful citizen in the community" (Bredsdorff, p. 54).

All or nothing—this was typical of Andersen. His use of the Danish word *Digter* is significant. Like the German term *Dichter,* it implies more than just "poet": it is often used to designate a great writer. And as Andersen's diary entries testify, he yearned to be nothing more and nothing less than a *Digter:*

> What can become of me, and what shall I become? My strong imagination may now land me in an insane asylum. My turbulent feelings may turn me into a suicide. In early days, these two drives both united would have made me into a *Digter.* Oh Lord, are these really your ways here on earth?—Forgive me, Lord, for my shamelessness toward You, You who have done so unspeakably much good for me. Oh, forgive me, Lord, and continue to help me.
>
> (20 September 1825)

> Everything is guided by God. There is destiny. Man is free like the horse on a rocky island who can roam freely, but there are certain limits: it cannot go beyond them! You want the best for yourself by obtaining faith in yourself. So I seek my destiny, all bountiful God!—May the Lord arrange things so that good fortune accompanies me! If it is Your will that I become a *Digter,* You will not weaken my courage and rob me of my talents. My soul lives only for poetry. I believe to have felt Your hand as destiny has taken its course. Do not rob me of Your faith, my Lord, my Father, my one and only. Hear your weak child!
>
> (27 September 1825)

It was not God who came to the rescue, though he would have liked to have believed this. Rather it was Jonas Collin, who interceded on Andersen's behalf whenever he had disputes with Meisling. By 1826, after the headmaster and Andersen had both been transferred to a school in Helsingör, it became clear to Collin that his sensitive ward could no longer endure Meisling's harshness. So he gave Andersen permission to move to Copenhagen to prepare for his final examinations, which he passed in 1828. The next year Andersen recorded another success when he took his university admission tests. However, he had no intention of attending the university, for he had already drawn attention to himself as writer. His second book, *Journey on Foot from Holmens Canal to the East Point of Amager,* written in imitation of E. T. A. Hoffmann, his literary idol at that time, was published in 1829; and his first play, *Love on St. Nicholas Tower,* was produced that same year at the Royal Theater. In 1830 a volume of poetry, *Digte* (*Poems*) appeared containing "You My Thought" ("Min Tankes Tanke ene Du er vorden"), which Edvard Grieg later set to music. Ten years after Andersen had arrived in Copenhagen, he began to be noticed by society.

From 1830 to 1835 Andersen sought to establish himself as one of the most promising writers, if not the most promising writer, in Denmark. He wrote plays, poems, travel books, and stories. He took trips outside Denmark to seek fresh impulses for his writing. In 1831 he journeyed to Germany, Bohemia, and Switzerland, and in each country he tried to advance his career by making the acquaintance of prominent people and leading writers of the time. In particular he was drawn to the German romantics Ludwig Tieck in Dresden and Adalbert von Chamisso in Berlin, who was the first translator of his poems into German. In 1833 Andersen received a two-year travel grant from King Friedrich VI, and he used it to visit the major cities of France, Italy, Switzerland, and Germany. In Paris he met Victor Hugo and Heinrich Heine. In Italy he spent most of his time with the sculptor Bertel Thorvaldsen, the writer Henrik Hertz, and other Scandinavian artists. During these trips he completed another volume of poetry and the long dramatic poem *Agnete and the Merman.* He also kept a personal diary in which he often complained about sickness and melancholy, and described people, cities, and landscapes as though he were writing for posterity.

When one reads Andersen's diaries and letters, it is evident that he felt most at home after he left Denmark. His constant journeys gave him a sense of freedom and an opportunity to mix with extraordinary and influential people. He rarely referred to his family background, and visited his mother only two or three times after leaving Odense. At the time of her death, in 1833, he was in Rome and wrote in his diary:

> A letter arrived from old Collin. My mother is dead, he reported. Thank God! These were my first words. Her sufferings, which I could not relieve, have now come to an end. But I cannot accustom myself to the thought that I am now so completely alone, without one single person who must love me because of blood ties!
>
> (16 December 1833)

These remarks reveal key features of narcissism and self-deception in Andersen's thinking. His diaries and letters show that he was inclined to pity himself, and it appears that his egoism prevented him from realizing a deep filial love and from experiencing either a fulfilling heterosexual or homosexual love. His chronic psychological problems stemmed largely from his incapacity to fulfill his sexual fantasies and erotic wishes, to assert himself as he wished to be understood. Andersen never married and never had sexual intercourse. For a long time literary historians and psychologists speculated that he was homosexual, but recent scholarship suggests that he was heterosexually inclined. The question of his sexual preference, however, is a side issue. He appears to have been an emotional cripple who failed to satisfy his desires and needs in intimate relationships of any kind.

During the 1830's Andersen was attracted to three women: Riborg Voigt, the sister of a friend; Mathilde Örsted, the daughter of the prominent physicist H. C. Örsted; and Louise Collin, the youngest daughter of Jonas Collin. In all three instances he avoided making a firm proposal of marriage, because he feared commitment and was uncertain about his "manliness." His letters and diaries reveal that he felt socially and psychologically inferior to women. Lack of money, low social origins, ugliness, repressed hatred of his mother, the need for privacy—these were some of the factors that drove him to reject himself before he could be rejected by women. There was a strong element of masochism in his relations with women, which also manifested itself in his relations with men. But despite his suffering, Andersen enjoyed the "romantic" role of the rejected lover, a role that was to figure prominently in almost all of his novels and many of his tales.

Aside from the tentative relationships with Riborg, Mathilde, and Louise, Andersen developed a close friendship with Henriette (Jette) Wulff, with whom he shared his most intimate thoughts. A forthright, intelligent woman and champion of revolutionary causes, Jette Wulff was the daughter of the Danish admiral Peter Wulff, who had made Andersen a welcome guest in his home during the 1820's. A semi-invalid, Jette Wulff was one of the few women who did not threaten him sexually. Andersen took her criticism and concern to heart because he felt she supported him in his endeavors and rarely flattered him without good cause. If not for her tragic death off the coast of America in 1853, Andersen might have come to the United States. It had been her dream to settle in America, and she had encouraged her friend, who often made disparaging remarks about Denmark, to think about emigration.

The only other woman who figured prominently in Andersen's life as an "amour" was the famous singer Jenny Lind, who was known as the "Swedish Nightingale." He met her in 1840 and actually courted her for a short period, until it became apparent that she was not interested in marriage, only in a romantic affair. For Andersen, who shunned illicit relationships and brothels, an amorous relationship could be sanctified only through marriage. That he repressed his sexual drive so severely may have led to psychosomatic disturbances and account for his extraordinary vanity. Andersen sought outlets for his repressed sexuality in masturbation (as he records in his journals) and in performing his works (perhaps subconsciously an act of public masturbation). Moreover, his writings were part of a complex process of sublimation. His creative efforts became a necessity; what he referred to as his calling was his compulsive and therapeutic need to contend with neurosis. The more Andersen denied himself, his social background, and his sexual drives, the more he felt called upon by "God" to express his "genius."

As was customary in those days, Andersen formed close male friendships that were marked by homoeroticism. He studied with boys, was looked after by men, traveled exclusively with male peers, moved in male-ordained social circles, and explored realms open primarily to men. It is thus no wonder that Andersen placed men on a pedestal and glorified the male condition in a traditional, chauvinist manner. For instance, at the beginning of his novel *O. T.* (1836) he states:

> There is a condition of happiness which no poet has yet properly sung, which no lady-reader, let her be ever so amiable, has experienced or ever will experience in this world. This is a condition of happiness which alone belongs to the male sex, and even then alone to the elect. . . .
>
> Happy moment, which no woman, let her be ever so good, so beautiful, or intellectual, can experience—that of becoming a student, or, to describe it by a more usual term, the passing of the first examination!
>
> The cadet who becomes an officer, the scholar who becomes an academic burgher, the apprentice who becomes a journeyman, all know, in a greater or less degree, this loosening of the wings, this bounding over the limits of maturity into the lists of philosophy.

Whereas he feared women and gave voice to his fear by rejecting them or getting them to reject him, he felt more free to express his love for men—albeit a masochistic love—in letters and in conversation. His lifelong friendship with Edvard Collin is perhaps the best example of the kind of amorous relationship he had with men. The oldest son of Jonas Collin, somewhat younger than Andersen, Edvard Collin became the legal administrator who managed Andersen's literary and business affairs. Though Collin, like Jette Wulff, was critical of Andersen's melodramatic, egocentric tendencies and fierce ambition, he remained a devoted friend and adviser.

At one time he hurt Andersen deeply by refusing to address him with the familiar "you," or *du* in Danish, and he reprimanded him often because of the writer's excessive public displays—which went against the Calvinist grain of this prudent Danish bureaucrat. But Andersen desired and actually needed to establish a master-servant relationship with Collin. Generally speaking, Andersen placed himself in Collin's control by seeking his approval for everything he wrote and putting his business affairs in his hands. Whenever Collin became severe or critical, Andersen would play the role of the spurned servant-lover, feeling comfortable and productive in this situation. He re-created it time and again in other male relationships. Whether in quest of male or female love, Andersen generally adopted the obsequious attitude that suited his neurotic temperament. It was through portraying this dubious social and psychological situation in his writings that he achieved a measure of stability.

By the early 1830's, Andersen had drawn attention to himself in Copenhagen as a gifted writer, but not until 1835 did he achieve a major breakthrough and taste fame. On returning from Italy he published his novel *Improvisatoren* (*The Improvisatore,* 1835), the first Danish experimental novel of social realism. At the same time he collected five stories for children in his first volume of fairy tales, and with each successive volume his reputation spread throughout Europe. Actually fame came to Andersen more slowly in Denmark than in Germany, England, and France, and he continually complained about the devastating attacks on his works by leading Danish writers. Sören Kierkegaard wrote an entire book ridiculing *The Improvisatore,* and other writers were no less cruel, especially in their reviews of his sentimental plays. Andersen, however, was not singled out for unusual treatment; it had become fashionable for Danish critics to write with a barbed pen. Moreover, he had his fair share of a good press. After publishing the novels *O.T.* and *Kun en Spillemand* (*Only a Fiddler,* 1837), two additional collections of fairy tales, and several plays, Andersen had no cause to complain, especially after King Friedrich VI granted him an annual poet's pension of 400 rixdollars for the rest of his life, a sum augmented at different times later in his career. Thus by 1838 Andersen could feel financially secure, and he was recognized by Danish royalty as one of the kingdom's finest artists.

Unfortunately, he never felt emotionally secure. In Copenhagen his vanity was so well known that he became an easy target for criticism, some of it justified, some of it malicious. Andersen was like a child who cannot control his urge to be the center of attraction. He continually baffled himself and others because he could not restrain his urge to act out his eccentricities in public. For example, he seized every opportunity to recite his poems and stories. Once, in Rome, he intruded on a dinner party in a small restaurant and insisted on reading "The Ugly Duckling" to a group of people he barely knew. When they politely suggested that he might enjoy himself more by sightseeing than by reading stories in a restaurant, he answered that he would prefer to entertain them in this way. Then without further ado he pulled a manuscript from his pocket and read.

This does not mean he was always overbearing. On the contrary, he tried to conceal his ambitious and competitive nature with his will to please and his desire to perform. Georg Brandes, the renowned Danish literary critic and a close friend of Andersen's, remarked astutely of the writer:

> Indeed, he did become a great man. But he did not become a man. There was not the slightest glimmer of manliness in the soul of this child, son of the common people. Much later he developed self-confidence. He developed it from the praise he received abroad but never manly vigor and courage. He lacked an aggressive spirit entirely, nor did he have the means to take the offensive. Never in his life did it occur to him to attack a powerful person for a good cause. He himself had been a poor devil much too long and needed love, kindness, goodwill, and especially recognition. If he used a weapon, then it was for self-defense and always in poetic form: his pen had a blunted point.
>
> (*Skandinavische Persönlichkeiten,* pp. 104–105)

Heinrich Teschner recorded Heinrich Heine's perceptive appraisal of Andersen's character:

> He seemed to me like a tailor. This is the way he really looks. He is a haggard man with a hollow, sunken face, and his demeanor betrays an anxious, devout type of behavior that kings love. This is also why they give Andersen such a brilliant reception. He is the perfect representation of all poets just the way kings want them to be.

Andersen as child and tailor. This childlike "tailor" was to impress the Western world with his talents from 1840 to 1875, and it should be stressed that he was like a *wander-*

*ing* tailor who put his skills to use making fine ornaments and clothes for "emperors." Characteristic of Andersen is the fact that even though he eventually could have afforded to establish a permanent residence in Copenhagen, he never did so. He traveled extensively every year and generally left Denmark whenever he could. Soon after the success of his play *Mulatten* (*The Mulatto*) in 1840, he embarked for Germany and Italy on his first train ride, and he wrote enthusiastically about the railroad, which added a new dimension to his view of people and the countryside. He knew he was always welcome in foreign countries, where he was wined, dined, and feted by the aristocracy, and received with honor in the best of the bourgeois homes and literary salons. In Denmark he was also given generous invitations to visit the estates of friends. Of course it was expected that Andersen would perform for his hosts, display his genius; and he did, often without their asking.

Andersen's rate of artistic production was astounding. Between 1840 and 1850 he finished several plays, wrote the travel book *En Digters Bazar* (*A Poet's Bazaar,* 1842), published poetry, and edited a new volume of fairy tales practically every year. The revolutionary upheavals of 1848–1850 were reflected in some of his stories, but Andersen, who basically supported the cause of enlightened monarchy, avoided direct involvement in political affairs. By 1850 he himself had become a kind of Danish institution.

During the 1850's and 1860's Andersen concentrated more and more on his fairy tales, which were no longer written exclusively for children. He also published the second version of his autobiography and made a trip to Zurich, where he met Richard Wagner. Andersen appreciated Wagner's imaginative use of folklore and was one of the first writers to recognize the composer's radical attempt to transform opera into a total artwork for all classes. By 1860 Andersen's annual pension had been raised to one thousand rixdollars, and he could afford extended journeys, such as the one he took to France, Spain, and North Africa, recorded in travel books such as *In Spain* (1863). When the war between Denmark and Prussia broke out in 1864, he was deeply torn, especially since he had numerous friends in Germany, where he had always been prized as a great *Dichter.* In fact the king of Prussia had presented him with his first royal medal in 1846. However, Andersen's loyalties were clearly with Denmark; he remained in Copenhagen and devoted himself to writing new plays and fairy tales. In 1866, after the war, he resumed his travels and took the opportunity to visit Paris, where he received a special decoration. In 1869 he was honored with the Commander Cross in Copenhagen.

Sensing he was coming to the end of his career, Andersen wrote another autobiographical novel, *Lykke-Peer* (*Lucky Peter*), in 1870. Even in old age the desire to transform his youth into a fairy tale did not abate, and he remained as active as ever during the last five years of his life. By the summer of 1875 it became apparent that Andersen had cancer of the liver, yet he did not give up hope that a miracle would bring about a complete recovery. Indeed, after recuperating from an attack that had kept him bedridden, he made plans for another trip abroad. But his hopes for recovery were illusory, and he died on 4 August 1875.

## *WORKS*

In the English-speaking world, the critical evaluation and general reception of Andersen's creative works have been confined to his fairy tales. Yet, as we have seen, such exclusive focus on the tales has contributed to a misunderstanding of the man and a neglect of his full literary achievement. To grasp the total significance of this remarkable man—"the tailor as romantic"—he must be viewed in the context of Danish culture and the changing literary scene in Europe.

Denmark experienced a major cultural shift at the beginning of the nineteenth century, from the universality of classicism to the romantic cult of genius and individualism. In part this was brought about by the lectures of Henrik Steffens. He introduced the German romantic writers and philosophers to the Danish intelligentsia, in particular to Oehlenschläger and N. F. S. Grundtvig, who in turn forged new paths in the arts and education for further generations of Danish writers.

An impressionable and voracious reader, Andersen benefited from the exciting cultural changes. He was particularly fond of German fairy-tale writers such as Tieck, Novalis, Hoffmann, Friedrich de La Motte-Fouqué, and Chamisso. In addition, he was attracted to the writings of Jean Paul Richter, Friedrich von Schiller, and Johann Wolfgang von Goethe, and was influenced by Shakespeare, Scott, and Washington Irving. But most important for his development was the peculiar form assumed by the Danish romantic movement, which was, as W. Glyn Jones notes,

> accompanied by what is known as the Aladdin motif, after the idea which Oehlenschläger expresses in his play *Aladdin.* This deals with the theory that certain people are chosen by nature, or God, or the gods, to achieve greatness, and that nothing can succeed in stopping them, however weak and ill-suited they may otherwise seem. . . . The twin themes of former national greatness and of the possibility of being chosen to be great, despite all appearances, assumed a special significance for Denmark after 1814.
>
> (*Denmark,* pp. 66–67)

It was Oehlenschläger who signaled the coming of the golden age of Danish literature with his poem *The Golden Horns* (1802), written after a famous encounter with Steffens. This work celebrates Denmark's pagan past and recounts how the gods took back their great gift to the Danes because greed had made them unworthy of their heritage. This national ballad, Oehlenschläger's other poems, and his drama *Aladdin* (1805) instilled a new sense of hope and confidence in Danish social leaders, who had lost political and economic power during the Napoleonic wars. In order to regain national pride after 1814, the aristocracy and the prosperous middle classes were more willing than ever to encourage and support creative and scientific experimentation: tiny Denmark was to show its greatness.

Aside from Oehlenschläger, numerous other talented writers and artists began to make names for themselves. Grundtvig produced significant works in the fields of theology, history, politics, and education. B. S. Ingemann glorified the Danish Middle Ages in his epic poems and novels. H. C. Örsted became one of the founders of electromagnetics and espoused a philosophy of the immortality of the soul that was to influence Andersen. Thorvaldsen became one of the leading sculptors in Europe. C. W. Eckersberg established himself as one of the finest romantic painters in Denmark, and Steen Steensen Blicher had a major impact on the theater as a writer of poetic tragedies. Not only did Andersen absorb and learn from the works of these Danish writers, artists, and intellectuals, but he also came in contact with them: they served as both inspiration and point of departure for his writing.

Of all the Danish writers, the great dramatist and literary critic Johan Ludvig Heiberg played an immense role in Andersen's development. Heiberg was the pioneer of vaudeville in Danish theater. More important, the caustic criticism and sharp wit of the *Kjøbenhavns flyvende Post* (Copenhagen Flying Post), the literary journal he edited, elevated him to the position of cultural arbiter in Copenhagen. Some of Andersen's early poems and stories were printed by Heiberg, who first encouraged and later demoralized him. With his modern ironic sensibility and training in Hegelian dialectics, Heiberg influenced and judged almost all the prominent young Danish intellectuals of his time: Kierkegaard, who began writing his great philosophical works in the 1830's and 1840's; Hertz, who became one of the leading dramatists of this period; and Hans Peter Holst, who was active as a novelist, poet, and dramatist. These three writers and others competed with Andersen for Denmark's laurels and patronage. In an era of growing individualism, when the middle classes were seeking more power in central and northern Europe; when industrialism and urbanization were bringing rapid changes in cultural life and social mobility; when revolutions were changing the maps, mentalities, and hegemonies of European nations; when Denmark was forced to open its tight-knit society slightly to outside influences, it is not surprising that Andersen felt there was also a possibility for a talented young man to establish his claim to genius. The challenge was there. Andersen was imaginative, enterprising, and ingratiating.

Andersen's versatility as a writer needs to be addressed before we examine his fairy tales and consider how and why they have so completely overshadowed his other works in the twentieth century. Here we must bear in mind that Andersen desired to make a name for himself first as a dramatist, novelist, poet, and travel writer, not as a writer of fairy tales, and especially not as a writer for children. Although from the beginning of his career he worked with fairy-tale motifs, and saw his own life as a type of fairy tale, short narrative form was not at first his favorite means of embodying his ideas and dreams.

Andersen's greatest love was unquestionably the theater. Ever since his first visit to the Odense theater in 1812, he had dreamed of performing and writing plays. In the course of his life he composed over thirty dramatic works, and twenty-five of his original pieces, consisting of vaudevilles, opera librettos, romantic dramas, and comedies, were given more than a thousand performances. Today these works are largely forgotten, both in Denmark and abroad; but in Scandinavian theater history Andersen is significant for introducing many foreign styles, such as the French opéra comique and the Austrian folk play, into the Danish theater. Moreover, his experience with the theater influenced the way he shaped many of his stories and fairy tales, for it was through an appreciation of the stage that he developed his keen senses of observation and drama.

Frederick Marker states that Andersen

> belonged among the younger exponents of romanticism but at the same time points ahead toward the realism which eventually triumphed in the 1870's. The production history of his plays provides a microcosm of the exotic, historical, idyllic, and topical elements that were the popular components of the colorful, romantic stage picture.
>
> (*Hans Christian Andersen and the Romantic Theater*, p. 31)

Though it was through the theater that Andersen wished to claim ultimate recognition for his genius, the theater occasioned his most disastrous failures and the most bitter attacks against him. In turn, these caused him to react vociferously against the entire Danish nation, albeit in letters, journals, and private conversations, rarely in public.

Andersen's early notable plays were in the style of vaudeville, which he, along with Heiberg, helped make respectable in Denmark. Most of these light dramas feature plots about love and intrigue, often written in verse and incorporating well-known songs and music. Andersen tended to blend folk figures with situations typical of serious drama to poke fun at the foibles of high and low characters. His first production, *Love on St. Nicholas Tower*, parodied the romantic tragedy of the times by having a tailor and a watchman speak high verse and fight over the hand of a sweet maid of the lower classes. Though Andersen became less satirical in his vaudevilles over the years, most of his other successful plays, such as *The Invisible Man on Sprogø* (1839) and *The Bird in the Pear Tree* (1842), as well as his adaptations of Johann Nestroy's and Ferdinand Raimund's Austrian folk plays, follow the same pattern of parodying social customs of Danes involved in a scandal or delicate love affair.

During the 1830's and 1840's Andersen also wrote librettos. His themes were often taken from romantic novels such as *The Festival at Kenilworth* (1836), based on a work by Scott. When he adapted his own dramatic poem *Agnete and the Merman* for the opera in 1843, it was a monumental flop, and the negative reaction by the public prompted a typically violent response by Andersen, who was in Paris at the time and wrote the following to Jette Wulff:

> This evening I learned—not from my friends since I didn't receive a letter, but from Berling's paper—that *Agnete* was performed and hissed off the stage. That had to happen. At the next performance there will be booing! But my work doesn't deserve this. It is the creation of a poet!—May my eyes never lay rest on this house that has only eyes for my mistakes, but no heart for that gift that enables me to create great things! I hate whatever hates me. I curse whatever curses me! As always, a cold draft of wind comes from Denmark that will turn me into stone abroad! They spit at me, trample me in mud! However, I'm a poet by nature, and God has granted them only one like me. But when I die, I shall ask the Lord never again to grant them such a poet!
>
> (29 April 1843)

The hurt and conceit expressed here were reiterated time and again in Andersen's letters and journals. Andersen was unwilling to recognize that he was capable of writing poor works, and he expected to be flattered as he flattered others. Though he repeatedly asserted that he hated Denmark and the cultivated Danish society, he slavishly sought to shine in his countrymen's eyes. Nor did he accept defeat. In 1846 he composed the libretto for J. P. E. Hartmann's *Liden Kirsten* (*Little Christina,* 1846), based on the true story of a princess who became a nun, and this "comeback" was a resounding success.

His most renowned play, however, was not an opera but a melodrama, *The Mulatto,* which showed the strong influence of French romantic drama, especially that of Hugo. Based on the story *Les épaves* (The Waifs, 1838), by Fanny Reybaud, the drama concerns a young, sophisticated mulatto named Horatio who writes poetry and runs his own plantation in Martinique. He rescues Cecille, the ward of a white plantation owner named La Rebellière, and La Rebellière's wife. Both women are captivated by Horatio's noble nature, and their esteem for the mulatto infuriates La Rebellière. So he contrives to have Horatio declared a slave and sold at auction. But Cecille comes of age at this point, declares her independence, and rescues Horatio by offering to marry him. The mulatto is thus vindicated in the eyes of society. As in the best of Andersen's plays and other works, this compelling social drama emphasizes his favorite fairy-tale themes, or what might be called his Aladdin-and-Cinderella syndrome: the gifted pariah, a neglected genius, shunned and persecuted by society, manages to overcome adversity and shine in the eyes of the world. This theme of emancipation appealed to the rising middle and lower classes in Denmark and reflected the dreams of glory shared by the people in this tiny nation as a whole. To this extent, Andersen often acted as the spokesman of Denmark, even though he was criticized for being inept.

The attacks on Andersen as a playwright ultimately drove him to assume a pseudonym in the 1840's. By producing his plays pseudonymously he hoped to avoid the vitriolic barbs of his critics. From 1845 until his death in 1875 he wrote for the Royal Theater and the Casino Theater, where vaudevilles were staged. It was during this period that he turned more toward fairy-tale dramas and comedies. For example, he wrote *The Blossom of Happiness* (1845), about a forester who wishes to become a great person, such as a prince or a poet. This wish is granted by an elf, but the forester learns that the prince and the poet lead extremely difficult lives because of the responsibilities of their positions. So he is overjoyed when given the chance to return to his former, humble occupation. Another play, *Pearls and Gold* (1849), was an adaptation of Raimund's *Der Diamant des Geisterkönigs* (The Diamond of the King of Spirits, 1824). Here a young man is promised a statue of diamonds if he can find a young woman who has never lied. But once he finds her, he no longer wants to have the statue: she alone is worth more to him than all the riches in the world.

Andersen failed as a dramatist but, to his credit, he did stimulate many of his contemporaries to employ folk motifs, vernacular idioms, and fantasy in their plays. He may have had an influence even on Henrik Ibsen, whom he met. Whether this is the case or not, Andersen was clearly a forerunner in the Scandinavian movement that produced both Ibsen and August Strindberg. Throughout his life he occupied himself with the fantastic "other world" of the stage, but his plays never matched the artistry and luster of his fairy tales.

Nor did his novels, although he was at first recognized as one of Denmark's most promising novelists. When *The Improvisatore* appeared, it was an immediate success at home and highly praised thereafter in Germany and England. The impetus for the novel was Andersen's trip to Italy, where the action takes place. Antonio, a poor orphan with an amazingly poetic nature, has the good fortune to come under the patronage of a rich patrician family in Rome. He is sent to a Jesuit school, where he excels as a student and makes the acquaintance of the handsome and wild Bernardo, who leaves the school to become an officer. In the meantime, despite the severe discipline of the school and the criticism of his benefactors, Antonio develops his artistic skill as an improvisator. After a reunion with Bernardo, he makes the acquaintance of Annunziata, a great Spanish-Italian singer. Both Bernardo and Antonio fall in love with her, and naturally they fight a duel over her. After the first shot Antonio thinks mistakenly that he has killed his friend. He flees to the south of Italy, joins a band of robbers, leaves the robbers, and continues to have many adventures until he establishes a name for himself as an improvisator in the theater. Eventually he learns that Bernardo is alive, and he can return to the patrician society of Rome as a success. Indeed he even marries an ethereal young woman named Maria, whom he had once believed to be blind.

This autobiographical romance is based on the structure of the German *Künstlerroman,* in which a young man rebels against society to develop his skills independently as an artist. The artist remains a rebel, and often he makes his way to a type of paradise or dies in the attempt. This is the pattern in Tieck's *Franz Sternbalds Wanderungen* (*Franz Sternbald's Wanderings,* 1798), Novalis' *Heinrich von Ofterdingen* (1802), and Hoffmann's *Der goldene Topf* (*The Golden Pot,* 1814). Andersen broke with the general romantic pattern somewhat by having his artist return to the fold of society, where he obliges his benefactors to recognize his particular greatness as artist. Obviously, Andersen's work was a thinly veiled depiction of his own life and problems. In fact, he had once been criticized by Heiberg for being too much of a lyrical improvisator, and there is no doubt but that Andersen was clearly bent on responding to Heiberg by showing the positive aspects of versatility and improvisation. Though he impressed his contemporary readers by blending romance and adventure with surrealistic descriptions of the Italian landscape, the melodrama and bombastic language make the book difficult to read today. Like all his longer prose narratives, the novel is pretentious and derivative. By endeavoring to resemble the great German novelists he admired, Andersen became nothing but their pale shadow.

However, he did have success in his own day, and this success moved him to write other romances. He followed *The Improvisatore* with *O.T.* and *Only a Fiddler,* both set in Denmark. Again he mixed obvious autobiographical elements with fictional projections to illustrate his philosophy of genius. Andersen was intrigued by the character of the moody Byronic hero and thought of himself in these terms. In *O.T.,* his protagonist, Otto Thostrup, a brooding, mysterious character, has his initials tattooed on his shoulder. They stand for his name and for the Odense jail, in which his mother had been imprisoned. Otto and a twin sister were born in the Odense jail. When his mother died, he was adopted by a rich baron while his unknown sister was left to drift among the dregs of society. Haunted by this past, Otto seeks to clear his mother's name and find his sister. All this is accomplished with the help of his close friend Wilhelm. In the end Otto is no longer sullen and strange, and he looks forward to marriage with one of Wilhelm's sisters.

In *Only a Fiddler* the ending is not so happy. Here Andersen depicts the tragicomic lives of a poor boy named Christian and a rich Jewish girl named Naomi. They are drawn to each other as children but are separated by events. Naomi is raised in Copenhagen, becomes spoiled, snubs Christian, runs away with a Polish riding master, and eventually marries a French count, with whom she is unhappy. Christian does not lead such an adventurous life. Though a gifted musician, he plods along, never receiving the help he needs to realize his genius. He dies as a village musician in humble circumstances.

In both novels Andersen portrays the mores and manners of Danish society and shows how young men of genius from the lower classes must overcome obstacles to gain recognition. Though Christian never realizes his genius, it is clear that he is gifted, and that if he were helped in the right way by the upper classes he might achieve greatness and happiness. Otto's case in *O.T.* is different because he is aided by influential people, and success is guaranteed.

The social mobility and immobility of talented people intrigued Andersen, and he turned to this theme again in *De to Baronesser* (*The Two Baronesses,* 1848). This novel, filled with one incredible event after another, demonstrates that honest Hermann, the grandson of an eccentric old baroness who has worked her way up from the lower classes, deserves to marry a poor girl who has braved misfortune to keep her virtue. Both young people display the diligence necessary for success; theirs is a marriage of noble minds.

In later years Andersen attempted to write a philosophical novel about genius triumphing over agnosticism and despair. In *To Be or Not to Be?* (1857) Niels Bryde, the moody protagonist, succumbs to the temptation of evolutionary and materialist theories based on the ideas of the German philosophers David Friedrich Strauss and Ludwig Feuerbach. He loses his Christian faith, only to recover it when he realizes there is an immortality of the soul that manifests itself in every particle of life.

In *Lucky Peter,* Andersen's last novel, he returns to the structure of the *Künstlerroman* to reflect on his own life and genius. Again we have the rise to fame of the chosen son of common people. Peter, the poor but talented son of a coachman, is born in the same house as Felix, a rich merchant's son, and their lives are contrasted. Felix amounts to nothing more than a mediocre but rich merchant; Peter achieves greatness because he pursues his destiny with unerring zeal. When he is only a boy, his musical talent is recognized and he is given schooling that enables him to enjoy a meteoric career. Eventually he writes an opera appropriately entitled *Aladdin,* and after receiving a thunderous ovation for singing the title role at the premiere, he collapses and dies. This melodramatic novel appears to be based on Wilhelm Wackenroder's story "Der Tonkünstler Joseph Berglinger" ("The Musical Artist Joseph Berglinger," 1796), in which the hero dies at the greatest moment of his career. Andersen tries to enhance this familiar success story with colorful portraits of Danish social life, but the novel suffers from a contrived plot and didactic commentary. The more he repeats the same plot and ideas, the more trite and unconvincing they become.

Andersen was never really able to master long narrative prose. He was overly conscious of his models in Tieck, Jean Paul, Goethe, Hoffmann, and Scott, and he lacked their humor, subtlety of thought, and variety of theme. At times there are remarkable passages in his novels, especially passages describing country life and customs, but they are generally undercut by an insistent moralistic tone. Only when he forgets that he must follow a prescribed form to justify his life and ideas or to match the work of a famous novelist is he capable of introducing extraordinary chapters that come alive through closeness of observation and penetrating insights.

Andersen's poetry and travel books are similarly uneven. His initial book of poetry, *Digte,* was followed quickly by *Phantasier og Skizzer* (*Fantasies and Sketches*) in 1831. The first contains humorous poems for the most part; the second, melancholy love poems and occasional verse. Andersen could write all types of poetry with great facility. He composed most of his plays and librettos in verse and continued to publish volumes of poetry throughout his life, but he failed to break new ground as a poet because of his derivative styles. His best poems by far are the personal love lyrics; these are deeply felt expressions of longing and despair. In his other lyrical endeavors, he covers a broad range of topics, from folklore and national history to subjects pertaining to children. But though he always satisfies formal requirements of meter and rhythm, he brings nothing new to the themes and forms he employs.

Andersen was at his best when he could experiment with personal experience in his own idiom. This is evident in his first travel book, *Journey on Foot from Holmens Canal to the East Point of Amager,* a humorous and fantastic depiction of a journey, similar to Hoffmann's *The Golden Pot.* Andersen weaves together dream elements, literary references to Tieck, Jean Paul, A. W. Iffland, August Kotzebue, Chamisso, and Goethe, and vivid depictions of landscape to create an intoxicating effect. In his other travel books, such as *A Poet's Bazaar, In Sweden* (1851), *In Spain* (1863), and *A Visit in Portugal* (1866), Andersen mixes impressions, anecdotes, observations, stories, and literary topics with descriptions of the countries and peoples he visited. In addition he includes comments on the changing times. As he was perhaps the most widely traveled author in the nineteenth century, Andersen's notes on customs, portraits of prominent people, and depictions of his own experiences were illuminating for readers of his own time and are still fascinating today. In particular, *In Sweden* contains a highly significant chapter entitled "Poetry's California," in which he argues that literature must keep pace with modern technological developments. If the future belongs to the sciences, then literature must adjust and reflect the new inventions in order to point out the miraculous aspects of life:

> The sunlight of science must penetrate the poet; he must perceive truth and harmony in very tiny things as well as in the immensely great with a clear eye. This perception will purify and enrich his understanding and imagination and show him new forms that will make his words even more alive. Even individual discoveries will inspire us to new heights. . . . Our world is the time of discoveries—poetry, too, has its California.

Certainly Andersen thought of himself as a poetic harbinger of truth and wisdom, a prophet whose versatility should be acclaimed and respected. He sought to stamp his times with his plays, novels, and travel books, and to a certain extent he succeeded. But he made his lasting contribution to art in a form in which he least expected to achieve immortality.

## *THE TALES*

Although Andersen knew he was a simple "tailor" of humble origin, he pretended to be a "romantic" fairy-tale hero, a misunderstood genius or Aladdin. He suspected, however, that audiences and critics saw him differently and might even despise him. The more he tried to dismiss his suspicions and fears, the more he was troubled by nervous disorders and psychic disturbances. To contend with and perhaps rationalize his existence, he eventually made use of Örsted's ideas in *The Soul in Nature* (1850) and combined them with his own animistic belief in Christianity. An early mentor as well as substitute father for Andersen, Örsted argues that the laws of nature are the thoughts of God, and, as the spirit of nature becomes projected, reality assumes the form of miracle. Such views were readily accepted and adopted by Andersen, who felt that if life was divinely miraculous, then God also protected his "elect" and provided help when they needed it. Power is located in the hands of God, and only before Him does one have to bow. In truth, however, Andersen submitted more to a temporal, social system based on aristocratic-bourgeois hegemony than to God, and he had to rationalize the social relations of domination so that he could live with himself. As we know, he tried to deny his class origins and repress his rebellious feelings in order to gain money, comfort, praise, and freedom to exercise his occupation as writer. And as aspiring *Digter* he endeavored both to imitate great poets and to find his own voice and style to depict the social contradictions he had difficulty resolving for himself. Such a situation meant a life of self-doubt and anxiety.

It was not, therefore, from joy and exuberance that Andersen wrote his fairy tales; it was more from a sense of profound suffering, disappointment, chagrin, and resentment. Obviously he also derived great pleasure in composing these stories, and he retained a naive appreciation of his immediate surroundings and experiences that served to inspire his writing. Yet he was fundamentally driven to write most of his tales to quell the anguish he felt as he made his daily compromises to become a great *Digter.*

Altogether he wrote 156 tales. The first collection, *Eventyr fortalte for Børn (Fairy Tales Told for Children,* 1835), consisted of "The Tinder Box," "The Princess and the Pea," "Little Claus and Big Claus," "Little Ida's Flowers," and "Thumbelina." For the most part these were adaptations of folk tales expressly designed for a young audience. In 1837 he added "The Little Mermaid," "The Naughty Boy," "The Traveling Companion," and "The Emperor's New Clothes," and in each subsequent edition until 1843 he dedicated the tales to children. Thereafter the title of his fairy-tale anthologies was changed to *Nye Eventyr* (*New Fairy Tales*), a more accurate indication of the direction Andersen was taking: he no longer wrote exclusively for young audiences (if he ever had), and many of his compositions even broke away from the fairy-tale genre.

Andersen wrote fables, allegories, anecdotes, legends, satires, farces, philosophical commentaries, and didactic stories. In general he developed and revitalized the German genre of the *Kunstmärchen,* or literary as opposed to oral tales, which had become popular in Europe by the beginning of the nineteenth century. Such various writers as Tieck, Wackenroder, Novalis, Clemens Brentano, Achim von Arnim, Joseph von Eichendorff, La Motte-Fouqué, Chamisso, Hoffmann, and Wilhelm Hauff had reworked folklore and introduced fantastic events and characters, together with complex ideas and subtle styles, into their tales. Their compositions were conceived to meet the tastes and needs of a middle-class reading public, whereas the oral folk tales catered to the taste of the lower classes and peasantry. Stimulated by the German romantics, Andersen gradually developed his own peculiar themes, a refreshing, humorous style, and lively colloquial dialogue. Many critics in his day frowned on his idiosyncratic use of Danish as vulgar, but it was just this unconventional colloquial quality that made his appeal unique. Moreover, like the German romantics, Andersen demonstrated how fantastic literature could be devastatingly realistic in its symbolic allusion to social contradictions.

In his autobiography, Andersen remarks that

> the fairy tales became reading matter for children and adults. . . . They found open doors and open hearts in Denmark. Everyone read them. Then I eliminated the phrase "told for children" and followed this with three books of "new tales," which I created myself, and which were highly praised. I could not have wished for anything better. I felt anxious, afraid that I could not justify so much honor in my time. My heart was invigorated by the rays of sunshine. I gained courage and was greatly motivated to develop myself more in this direction and to pay more attention to the rich source from which I had to create. There is definitely progress to be found when one follows the order in which I wrote my fairy tales. One can notice my ideas taking clearer shape, a greater restraint in the use of my medium, and, if I may say, more healthy qualities and a natural freshness.
>
> (*Märchen meines Lebens ohne Dichtung,* pp. 145–146)

It is difficult to know exactly what the "healthy qualities" in his tales are. If for Andersen "healthy" meant greater control over disquieting feelings, masterly sublimation, greater adaptation to frustrating conditions, and artful self-deception, then the tales do reflect "healthy qualities." Yet these same qualities conceal often-overlooked "unhealthy" ideas about social conditions and personal problems that were woven into his narratives. Too many readers regard Andersen's works unhistorically and universalize the symbolic formations of his tales as though the author and his social context were insignificant. They lose sight of the artist, his struggles, and his contribution to the evolution of the fairy-tale genre. In Andersen's case, a critical, historical approach to his tales raises some interesting questions about their contradictory features and their reception in English-speaking countries.

Elias Bredsdorff has noted that only thirty of Andersen's 156 tales have been reprinted—in many translations, some accurate, many not. The tales that have been printed and circulated most in the United States and Great Britain are: "The Tinder Box," "Little Claus and Big Claus," "The Princess and the Pea," "Little Ida's Flowers," "Thumbelina," "The Traveling Companion" (1835); "The Little Mermaid," "The Emperor's New Clothes" (1837); "The Steadfast Tin Soldier," "The Wild Swans" (1838); "The Garden of Eden," "The Flying Trunk," "The Storks" (1839); "Willie Winkie," "The Swineherd," "The Buckwheat" (1841); "The Nightingale," "The Top and the Ball," "The Ugly Duckling" (1843); "The Fir Tree," "The Snow Queen" (1844); "The Darning Needle," "The Elf Hill," "The Red Shoes," "The Shepherdess and the Chimney Sweep," "The Little Match Girl" (1845); "The Shadow" (1847); "The Old House," "The Happy Family," "The Shirt Collar" (1848). Given the fact that these are the "classic" Andersen tales in English, it is worth commenting on their general features before evaluating other tales.

Although Andersen's tales have suffered from the clumsy hands of censors and poor translators up through the 1940's, two fairly reliable editions of his complete short prose narratives have made his entire canon accessible to the English-reading public, one translated by Jean Hersholt, the other by Erik Christian Haugaard. Despite these fine translations, it must be admitted that the full flavor of Andersen's unusual use of the Danish language is difficult to capture. Folk rhythms and colloquialisms, childlike humor and startling puns, topical and historical references, local color and cultural associations—all these have given him a special reception in Denmark, where he is considered distinctively

Danish, the spokesman of the common people, the representative of a vigorous nineteenth-century cultural force. But he is also one of the key figures in the development of the literary fairy tale in the world at large, primarily as the genre has been cultivated for children in the West.

Andersen's tales were among the first considered suitable and proper enough for the nurseries and households of respectable nineteenth-century middle-class families. It must be remembered that in both Great Britain and the United States the fairy tale had been stamped as subversive and suspect from the eighteenth century to the middle of the nineteenth century. It was not regarded as moral and instructive enough for the emerging bourgeois sensibility, which stressed utilitarian values, obedience, sexual abstinence, and Christian virtues. This is not to say that fairy tales for children were banned. Rather there was a limited market for them, since most educators, religious writers, and publishers waged a war against the pagan, superstitious, and irrational features of folk and fairy tales. Such a campaign made middle-class families wary of purchasing the tales. Yet by the 1840's there was a successful counter-campaign in England and America. First the romantics, and later such major Victorian writers as John Ruskin, Charles Dickens, William Makepeace Thackeray, George Macdonald, and Lewis Carroll, wrote fantastic tales for children and spoke out in defense of this imaginative literature.

It was exactly at this point that Andersen himself, influenced by the German romantics, Dickens, and the Danish romantic movement, began to insert himself into the debate. His participation in the literary discourse on fairy tales was not a deliberate critical act, but rather the outcome of his naive interest and predilection. Andersen had always been captivated by fairy tales as stories and dramas, and in 1834–1835 he began to concoct a recipe for the fairy tales that were to bear his imprint: he rewrote folk tales, added a dose of Christian moralism mixed with bourgeois individualism, stirred the ingredients with folk humor, and ladled everything out in a vernacular style. His aim was to please and, at times, to provoke children and adults of all classes.

If we look at those tales that made Andersen famous in England and America (and are still the most popular), it is striking that they are the ones written primarily from 1835 to 1848, the tales Andersen composed mainly for children. These thirty tales are serious and colorful variations on a few personal themes. The major ideas concern the recognition of artistic genius, nobility of mind versus nobility of blood, the exposure of class injustice and hypocrisy, the master-servant relationship, the immortality of the soul, and the omnipotence and omnipresence of God. Almost all the tales touched on Andersen's private desires and functioned psychologically to provide him with secret revenge or to justify his dubious actions to himself. The focus in this necessarily limited discussion will be on the hidden, ambivalent features of "The Tinder Box," "The Princess and the Pea," "The Emperor's New Clothes," "The Nightingale," "The Ugly Duckling," and "The Red Shoes."

"The Tinder Box" reveals how closely Andersen at first adhered to the patterns of the folk-tale tradition when he began writing fairy tales. Characteristic in a number of the magic folk tales *(Zaubermärchen)* is the rise of an adventurous hero who depends on his own talents and gifts from strangers to attain wealth and happiness. Generally speaking the protagonist is downtrodden, oppressed, the youngest member of a family, or a small person; but he is always clever and knows how to make use of his abilities. Once the protagonist is assigned a task or cast into the world, he usually has three encounters with gift-bearing creatures (giants, dwarfs, animals, fairies) and it appears that he will triumph easily. At the peak of his first rise in fortunes, however, there is a sudden fall, or peripetia, and the hero must call on friends and his own resources to renew his rise to power and riches.

As oral stories, the magic folk tales were transcribed in simple, blunt language by Jacob and Wilhelm Grimm and other collectors at the beginning of the nineteenth century. Description and characterization were kept to a minimum. The paratactic sentences were built up with careful transitions so that clearly defined binary oppositions of good and evil could be immediately observed. From the outset the reader or listener of a folk tale knows that the narrative perspective is partial to the hero, who is bound to succeed; the question is always how. The magic of the oral tale depends not so much on the miraculous in the tale itself as on the ingenuity of the narrator in using the arsenal of folk motifs to vary well-known schemes so that they will touch on the dreams and needs of the audience.

In writing "The Tinderbox," Andersen employs the folk motif of the disgruntled soldier who, after years of loyal service, is discharged without due compensation by an ungrateful king. This lowly soldier seeks revenge and wins the hand of a princess. Andersen transforms this plot into a tale that mirrored the wishes of many maltreated, smart young men of the lower and middle classes. The rags-to-riches theme is central to his witty narrative about a young soldier, who by chance meets a disgusting witch whose lower lip hangs all the way down to her chest. He agrees to help her haul money and a tinderbox from a hole in the ground but then chops off her head when she will not tell him why she wants the tinderbox. He goes to town, takes quarters at an inn, lives sumptuously and merrily. He attends the theater, goes for drives in the king's park, and gives money to the poor because he remembers what it felt like not to have a penny in his pocket. When his "luck" runs out, however, he falls as quickly as he had risen in social esteem, and his fair-weather friends abandon him. A type of Aladdin figure, he accidentally discovers the magic of the tinderbox and the power of the three dogs who can provide him with anything he needs. Here Andersen subconsciously concocts a sociopolitical formula that was the keystone of bourgeois progress and success in the nineteenth century: use talents to acquire money and perhaps a wife, establish a system of continual recapitalization (tinderbox and three dogs) to guarantee income and power, and employ money and power to maintain social and political hegemony. The soldier is justified in his use of power and money because he is *essentially* better than anyone else—chosen to rule. The king and queen are dethroned, and the soldier rises to assume control of society through the application of his innate talents and good fortune.

The ironic tone of Andersen's writing, the melodious rhythms, the terse, delightful descriptions, and the dramatic sequences transform an oral folk tale into a colorful literary fairy tale that glimmers with hope. Instead of "once upon a time," Andersen begins the tale on an unusual note: "A soldier came marching down the road: . . . right! Left . . . right! He had a pack on his back and a sword at his side. He had been in the war and he was on his way home."[1] The witch admires his sword and knapsack and, convinced that he is a *real* soldier, willingly gives him all the money he wants. On a psychological level, the killing of the witch followed by the dethronement of the king and queen and the soldier's triumph as "true prince" are the sublimated artistic means Andersen uses to gain revenge on his mother, benefactors, and critics. All this is done with humor throughout the narrative, and there is a delightful picture of Andersen's wish fulfillment at the end of the tale once the king and queen are sent flying into the air:

> The royal guards got frightened; and the people began to shout: "Little soldier, you shall be our king and marry the princess."
>
> The soldier rode in the king's golden carriage; and the three dogs danced in front of it and barked: "Hurrah!"
>
> The little boys whistled and the royal guards

1. All quotations from the fairy tales are from the Haugaard translation.

presented arms. The princess came out of her copper castle and became queen, which she liked very much. The wedding feast lasted a week; and the three dogs sat at the table and made eyes at everyone.

Andersen must have derived immense personal satisfaction in writing this "radical" tale of role reversals, for underneath the humor is dead seriousness, an urge to express his social hostility and to prove himself at all costs. On another level, the tale can be read by children (and adults, of course) as a tale of the sexual and social maturation of a young person in a "dog-eat-dog" world. The soldier has a knapsack (mind, talents) and sword (power, phallus), and in confrontation with the outer world he learns not to waste his sexual and mental powers but to control and direct them to gain happiness. The psychological impulse of the tale is connected to Andersen's obvious criticism of the hypocrisy and injustice of the aristocracy. Throughout the tale, he depicts their artificiality, which is supplanted by the "true nobility" of his young, lower-class soldier.

"The Princess and the Pea" is also a tale about "true nobility," but told with tongue in cheek. A princess proves to be genuine when she feels a pea placed under twenty mattresses. This pea is then exhibited in the royal museum after her happy marriage with the prince, who had been seeking an authentic princess. Obviously Andersen was poking fun at the curious and ridiculous measures taken by the nobility to establish the value of bloodlines. On the other hand, he makes an argument for sensitivity as the decisive factor in determining the authenticity of royalty.

Andersen never tired of glorifying the sensitive nature of an elite class of people. This sensitivity is spelled out in different ways in other tales of 1835, such as "Little Ida's Flowers," "Thumbelina," and "The Traveling Companion." In all these stories "small" or oppressed people cultivate their special talents and struggle to realize their goals despite the forces of adversity. Ida retains and fulfills her dreams of flowers by resisting a crass professor's vicious attacks. Thumbelina survives many hazardous adventures to marry the king of the angels. Johannes, a poor orphan, promises to be good so that God will protect him, and indeed his charitable deeds lead to a marriage with a princess. All the gifted but disadvantaged characters, who are God-fearing, come into their own in Andersen's tales. In contrast, the rich and privileged are either ridiculed or exposed as insensitive, cruel, and unjust.

Perhaps the most amusing and famous of Andersen's tales about "false nobility," a story that has been adapted for film, television, and the radio many times, is "The Emperor's New Clothes." Here a king is literally robbed and denuded in front of our eyes because he wasted his time and money on beautiful new clothes instead of carrying out his responsibilities. Andersen quickly sets the tone of the narrative by taking his readers into his confidence and relating how two swindlers plan to trick the king and the parasites at court. We laugh at the foolish king as the plot develops, and then Andersen aptly introduces the courageous small child who cries: "But he doesn't have anything on!" By having a child speak the truth, Andersen emphasizes a learning process that relies on common sense and a perception of the contradictions in society. Seeing is depicted in this tale as the courage of one's convictions, and this depiction may be a major reason for the narrative's appeal for young readers, who are too often told "to see with your eyes and not with your mouth." For Andersen, sight must become insight, which in turn demands action.

Yet Andersen cannot be considered an antiauthoritarian writer, a champion of emancipatory children's literature. The courageous acts of his heroes are often undercut by their self-denial, humility, and willingness to sacrifice themselves in the service of a benevolent king. One of the classic examples of this type of tale is "The Little Mermaid," which harks back to the folk stories of a water urchin desirous of obtaining a soul so she can marry the human being she loves. Andersen also knew Goethe's "Die neue Melusine" (1819) and Fouqué's *Undine* (1811), stories of the ennobled aspirations of pagan water sprites. However, his tale about the self-sacrificing mermaid is distinctly different from the narratives by Goethe and Fouqué, who, perhaps out of their own sense of guilt for the tendency of upper-class men to seduce and abandon lower-class women, punished their noblemen for forgetting their Christian manners.

Andersen's perspective focuses on the torture and suffering that a member of the "lower species" must undergo to gain a soul. Characteristically he allows the mermaid to rise out of the water and move in the air of royal circles only after her tongue is removed and her tail transformed into legs, described as "sword-like" when she walks or dances. Voiceless and tortured, the mermaid serves a prince who never fully appreciates her worth. Twice she saves his life. The second time is most significant: instead of killing him to regain her identity and rejoin her sisters and grandmother, the mermaid forfeits her own life and becomes an ethereal figure blessed by God. If she does good deeds for the next three hundred years, she will be endowed with an immortal soul. Her divine mission consists of flying through homes of human beings as an invisible spirit. If she finds a good child who makes his parents happy and deserves their love, her sentence will be shortened. A naughty and mean child can lengthen the three hundred years she must serve in God's name.

But the question remains whether or not the mermaid is really acting in God's name. Her falling in love with royalty and all her subsequent actions involve self-denial and rationalization. The mermaid's sense of herself becomes divided and diminished because she is attracted to a class of people who will never accept her on her own terms. To join her supposed superiors she must practically slit her own throat, and though she realizes that she can never truthfully express who she is and what she wants, she is unwilling to return to her own species. Thus she must somehow justify her existence to herself through abstinence and self-abnegation—a behavior preached by the bourgeoisie of the time and certainly not characteristically practiced by the nobility and upper classes.

Paradoxically Andersen seems to be arguing that true virtue and self-realization can be obtained through self-denial. The artistic conception of this paradox emanated from his own experience as a gangly, lower-class youngster who sought to cultivate himself through constant compromise and subjugation to external laws. By becoming voiceless, walking with legs like knives, and denying one's own needs, one will allegedly gain divine recognition for one's essential genius, a metaphor for the educated nod of approval from the dominant class. Nobility is indeed of the mind, but it also needs connections with nobility of the blood to succeed in the real world.

Andersen consistently defended notions of self-abandonment and self-deprivation in the name of aristocratic-bourgeois laws and standards designed to make members of the lower classes into tractable, obedient citizens. Such conformist thinking stemmed from the obsequious, "tailor" side of his personality. As eager as he was for his genius to shine, he was just as eager to please, and just as ready to humiliate himself before wealthy, powerful patrons. Both "The Nightingale" and "The Ugly Duckling," two of Andersen's most finely wrought tales, reveal how he sought to master his dilemma by turning it into a type of success story.

"The Nightingale" can be considered a metaphorical treatise about art, genius, and the role of the artist. It involves a series of transformations in power relations and service. First, the Chinese emperor, a benevolent patriarch, requests that a nightingale be brought to his court because he has heard so much about the bird's priceless art. When the chief courtier finds the nightingale, he exclaims: "I had not imagined it would look like that. It looks so common! I think it has lost its color from shyness and out of embarrassment at seeing so many noble people at one time." Because the common-looking bird (an obvious reference to Andersen himself) possesses an inimitable artistic genius, he is engaged to serve the emperor. Yet when the emperor is given a jeweled mechanical bird that never tires of singing, the nightingale is neglected. So he escapes from the artificial court society and returns to the forest. Later, when the mechanical bird breaks down and the emperor is on the verge of dying, the nightingale returns to serve the autocrat loyally as a natural genius with innate healing powers:

> "And my song shall make you happy and make you thoughtful. I shall sing not only of those who are happy but also of those who suffer. I shall sing of the good and of the evil that happen around you, and yet are hidden from you. For a little songbird flies far. I visit the poor fishermen's cottages and the peasant's hut, far away from your palace and your court. I love your heart more than your crown, and I feel that the crown has a fragrance of something holy about it. I will come! I will sing for you!"
>
> (p. 215)

Though Andersen intended to show in this tale how the health of an emperor—that is, the spirit of an empire—is dependent on true art, he also made it clear that art *wants* to be the devoted servant of an autocrat. Such was Andersen's private resolution of the artist's dilemma. He proclaimed the cult of genius and yet relegated the artist to the humble role of servant because he feared the loss of patronage and social prestige.

In "The Ugly Duckling" genius again assumes an admirable shape, but unlike the nightingale, the swan cannot fly on its own. This tale has generally been interpreted as a parable of Andersen's own success story, because the naturally gifted underdog survives a period of "ugliness" to reveal its innate beauty. But more attention should be placed on Andersen's thesis about the servility of genius. The clumsy young swan, who is chased by coarse, lower-class animals from the henyard, must experience various arduous ordeals before he realizes his essential greatness. This self-realization is ambivalent, for just before he perceives his true nature he is ready to kill himself:

> I shall fly over to them, those royal birds! And they can hack me to death because I, who am so ugly, dare to approach them! What difference does it make? It is better to be killed by them than to be bitten by the other ducks, and pecked by the hens, and kicked by the girl who tends the henyard; or to suffer through the winter.
>
> (pp. 223–224)

These are not the words of an independent genius who can stand on his own. On the contrary, Andersen conveys his secret disdain for the masses and his longing to be accepted by court society. The young swan does not return "home" but lands in a beautiful garden where he is admired by children and adults. Beauty for the swan is measured by the "royal" swans and by the well-behaved children and people in the garden. In the end the swan's growth and flight become an apology for Andersen's escapist and elitist thinking.

Still, the tale has positive psychological features. As a fairy tale for children, the narrative suggests that each child has the potential to liberate himself from oedipal ties, to overcome social obstacles, to gain recognition. The transformation of the ugly duckling into a beautiful swan can thus be interpreted as the confirmation of dreams experienced by numerous children, regardless of class. Yet the swan, like the nightingale, becomes a tame bird—Andersen, who loved to travel and wander like a bird, constantly used this metaphor for himself. It is also interesting that, unlike most folk tales in which the hero becomes independent and omnipotent, Andersen's birdlike geniuses soar high only to return to earth.

Although docile and kind on the surface, Andersen was often merciless in his tales, especially when it came to curbing the pride of rebellious figures who need to be taught a lesson. In "The Red Shoes," Karen, a poor orphan, mistakenly believes she is adopted by a generous old woman because she wears red shoes (a symbol of vanity and sin). Although Karen tries to abandon the shoes, she cannot resist their allure. So she must be taken to task by a stern angel, who pronounces sentence on her:

> You shall dance . . . dance in your red shoes until you become pale and thin. Dance till the skin on your face turns yellow and clings to your bones as if you were a skeleton. Dance you shall from door to door, and when you pass a house where proud and vain children live, there you shall knock on the door so that they will see you and fear your fate.
>
> (p. 292)

The only way Karen can overcome the angel's curse is by requesting the municipal executioner to cut off her feet. Thereafter she does charitable work for the local minister. Upon her death, Karen's soul "flew on a sunbeam up to God." This ghastly tale—reminiscent of the gory, pedagogical best-seller of Andersen's time and later, the German Heinrich Hoffmann's *Struwwelpeter* (1845)—is a detailed description of the punishment that awaits anyone who dares to oppose authority. Andersen stressed that acceptance into God's kingdom depends on obedience, service, and self-restraint. In actuality he spoke not for God but for the standards of discipline and punishment instituted in Danish society. Pedagogically, the themes of Andersen's fairy tales for children comply with the norms and values of traditional Christian education. Needless to say, his classical status today is based on his acceptance of norms that still prevail in the realms of children's literature.

Yet Andersen's fame in English-speaking countries does not rest solely on his fairy tales for children. Such an intriguing, subtle story as "The Shadow" reveals Andersen as a significant precursor of surrealist and existentialist literature. As many critics have noted, this haunting narrative is highly autobiographical; it stems from the humiliation Andersen suffered when Edvard Collin adamantly rejected his proposal to use the familiar "you" *(du)* in their discourse—and there was more than one such rejection. By retaining the formal "you" *(De)*, Collin was undoubtedly asserting his class superiority, and this was meant to remind Andersen of the social distance that separated them. Though they had come to regard each other as brothers during their youth, Collin held firmly to propriety. He controlled a certain portion of Andersen's life—something that the writer actually desired, but also resented.

In "The Shadow," Andersen clearly sought to avenge himself through his tale about a philosopher's shadow that separates itself from its owner and becomes immensely rich and successful. When it becomes a person in its own right and returns to visit the scholar, the shadow/Andersen puts the philosopher/Collin in his place by refusing to use the familiar *du,* and then he explains that it was poetry that made a human being out of him. Not only does the shadow become humanlike, but he gains power over other people through his ability to see evil. Ironically, the shadow's sinister talents allow him to improve his fortunes, whereas the philosopher, who can only write about the beautiful and the good, becomes poor and neglected. Eventually the philosopher is obliged to travel with his former shadow—the shadow now as master, and the master as shadow. When the shadow deceives a princess to win her hand in marriage, the philosopher threatens to reveal the truth about him. The crafty shadow, however, convinces the princess that the philosopher himself is a deranged shadow, and she decides to have him killed to end his misery.

The reversal of fortunes and power relations is not a process of liberation but one of revenge. Andersen's wish fulfillment was directed not only at Collin but at all his superiors, whether they were benefactors or enemies. Yet to see "The Shadow" merely as the product of a personal grudge is to do it an injustice. Andersen ingeniously reworks the folk motif of Chamisso's *Peter Schlemihls wundersame Geschichte* (1814), in which a young man sells his shadow to the devil to become rich; and he also explores the Hegelian notion of master-servant in a fascinating way. The shadow-servant, who is closer to the material conditions of life than the intellectual owner of his services, is able to take advantage of what he sees and experiences—the basic conditions of social life—to overthrow his master; whereas the master, who has been able to experience reality only through the mediation of his shadow, is too idealistic to defend himself.

From a philosophical viewpoint Andersen questions the idea of autonomous identity; from a psychological viewpoint he studies the manifestations of a split personality, a version of the doppelgänger motif common in nineteenth-century literature. The ironic reversal of roles appears at first to be a harmless joke, but Andersen convincingly depicts how the subconscious can subdue both conscience and consciousness. The final effect is a chilling picture of those dark and irrational undercurrents in human experience that continue to surface no matter how people try to repress them.

Written in 1847, "The Shadow" shows Andersen at the height of his powers as a fairytale writer. By now mature in his art, he no longer confined himself to writing stories just for children, and he exploited all types of sources and material for his tales, not just folklore. The length and style of the tales vary considerably. Some are a few pages in length, others are over thirty pages. Some are overly didactic and sentimental; others are ironic, complex, and bitter.

In "A Drop of Water" (1848) Andersen creates a philosophical allegory based on social Darwinism to convey a sardonic view of the cutthroat life and class struggles in Copenhagen. "The Story of a Mother" (1848) is a slightly veiled rendition of his mother's life and the trials and tribulations she endured. "There Is a Difference" (1855) concerns a haughty apple tree and a common dandelion, Andersen's point being that both are children of beauty blessed by God. "Everything in Its Right Place" (1853) and "The Pixy at the Grocer's" (1853) are political fantasy narratives that illustrate the influence of the 1848–1850 revolutionary years on Andersen. In the first story he depicts the rise to power of diligent, hardworking peasants and middle-class people over the aristocracy. In the other he pokes fun at a pixy who cannot make up his mind whether to fight for his ideals or to make a compromise with a grocer so he can have bread and security. Such is Andersen's metaphorical comment on people as reluctant revolutionaries.

*Lovely* (1859) is a brilliant satire on sentimental love and the false appreciation of art. Here a young sculptor is deceived by the outward appearance of a beautiful woman, marries her, and leads a banal life until her death frees him to pursue true art. *On the Last Day* (1852) is a short religious tract about the immortality of the soul. In *The Two Maidens* (1861) Andersen plays superbly with a change in the Danish language concerning gender to comment on the prospects of female emancipation. "The Puppeteer" (1861) is a fantasy story in which the dream of a puppeteer becomes a nightmare when he must contend with conceited actors in a theater instead of with his dolls.

In "The Dung Beetle" (1861) Andersen uses the fable form to write a humorous self-parody. A conceited beetle rises from a dung heap, travels around the world, and mistakenly believes he is honored everywhere without realizing how foolish and pompous he is. "In the Duckyard" (1861) is also a satirical parable, but here Andersen is concerned with attacking the pettiness and arrogance of Danish critics.

His more positive ideas about literature are elaborated in the philosophical piece "The Muse of the Twentieth Century" (1861), in which he argues that poetry can benefit from the inventions of the modern industrial world—ideas that correspond to his essay "Poetry's California." Such optimism is modified in "The Snail and the Rosebush" (1861), a Socratic dialogue in which cynicism is matched against creative naiveté. In an amusing realistic anecdote, "Auntie" (1866), Andersen portrays an eccentric spinster obsessed with the theater, and he uses the occasion to reflect on the fanatic nature of theatergoers and practitioners.

"The Rags" (1868) is another of Andersen's amusing allegorical dialogues; two rags, one Norwegian and one Danish, assert the virtues of their respective cultures. When they are made into paper, their claims to greatness are gently mocked. The Norwegian rag becomes a piece of stationery on which a young Norwegian writes a love letter to a Danish girl, while the Danish rag becomes a sheet of paper on which a Danish poet composes an ode in praise of the loveliness and strength of Norway. "The Cripple" (1872), one of Andersen's final commentaries on art, is a fairy tale within a fairy tale about the social and moral value of the genre. A bedridden cripple named Hans reads tales to his parents, who reject them as worthless. Gradually, however, the adults learn to broaden their horizons and appreciate life through the stories. Hans himself makes a miraculous recovery because of them. Aided by the book of tales and the patronage of the rich family that has given it to him, he makes his way through life as one of Andersen's typical Aladdin figures.

The foregoing summary of Andersen's late and neglected tales can only indicate the broad spectrum of his interests. Many of these stories and others fall flat because they are obvious diatribes or homilies, blunt or too quaint. But the best fuse the tensions of his personal experience with folklore and literary motifs to create vivid symbolic narratives that can be appreciated and interpreted in manifold ways. Two examples of his late period worth discussing in more detail are "The Ice Maiden" (1861) and "The Gardener and His Master" (1871); they represent major tendencies in his work as a whole.

"The Ice Maiden" comes from a legend that inspired Johann Peter Hebel to write *Unverhofftes Wiedersehen* (The Unanticipated Reencounter, 1811) and E. T. A. Hoffmann to create *Die Bergwerke zu Falun* (*The Mines of Falun,* 1819). Based on an actual event, the original story concerns a man who disappears on his wedding day and is found petrified in stone many years later. Hebel retold the story as a short, vividly realistic anecdote. Hoffmann expanded and transformed it into a mysterious, romantic fairy tale about a young man who must decide whether he will serve the queen of crystals in the underworld—which represents erotic and seductive art—or whether he will marry the wholesome daughter of a miner—who represents solid and virtuous middle-class life. Torn between two worlds, the young man ultimately disappears and dies in the mines. Many years later he is found and reunited with his wife in death. This theme is also touched on by Tieck in *Der Runenberg* (1802), and since Andersen was drawn to the German romantics, it is no wonder that he, too, was captivated by this story.

Composed in fifteen chapters, "The Ice Maiden" is one of Andersen's longer tales directed at both children and adults. The setting is Switzerland, which Andersen had recently visited. His hero is a young, talented orphan named Rudy who escapes the clutches of the "Ice Maiden" after she kills his mother. But she threatens to catch him too:

> Mine is the power! . . . I crush anything that comes within my grasp and never let it go! A lovely boy was stolen from me. I had kissed him but not so hard that he died from it. Now he is

> again among human beings. He herds goats in the mountains. Upward, ever upward, he climbs, away from everyone else, but not from me. He is mine and I claim him.
>
> (p. 739)

While the Ice Maiden pursues Rudy single-mindedly, he pursues his destiny and becomes the most skilled hunter and mountain climber in the region. Moreover, his noble character and perseverance enable him to win the hand of Babette, the daughter of a rich miller. On the day before their wedding, however, Rudy drowns while trying to retrieve a rowboat that has drifted from the island where he and Babette have been spending a quiet afternoon. The Ice Maiden was waiting for him and pulled him under. Babette, who had previously had a warning vision of their married life and of a sin committed against Rudy and God, is relieved by his death since it will prevent her from committing this sin. She spends the rest of her life alone, and Andersen ends his bittersweet tale by describing her situation as follows: "The snow on the mountainside has a rose luster, and so does the heart who believes that 'God wills the best for us all.' But few are so fortunate as Babette, who had it revealed to her in a dream."

Unlike the romantics, Andersen is not concerned with the problem of art and the artist in this story. Nor does he argue that society is too philistine and destructive for the creative artist, who must either devote himself to art or die. Andersen takes a more conservative position. He portrays the struggles of a poor, gifted boy who prospers because he is receptive to the natural wonders of divine creation. Such was Andersen's customary self-depiction in fictional form. Genius can be found in the lower classes, and given the proper conditions, it can flourish. Rudy's "nobility" is glorified, but Andersen also added a melodramatic ending that reflected his attitude toward unobtainable women, unrequited love, and Christian salvation.

Through careful description of the Swiss locale and humorous sketches of the miller's household, Andersen transforms the common events and everyday routine of country people into a miraculous adventure story. Despite the unhappy ending, Andersen sought to convince his readers that everyone is actually fortunate because God's intentions are good. The religious and utopian elements of his thinking endow the tale with its powerful social appeal. Miracles can occur. The rise from rags to riches in accord with God's will is possible. Even though evil lurks in the world in the form of the Ice Maiden, spiritual happiness cannot be denied if one is true to one's God-given gifts.

This was Andersen's optimistic outlook. Yet he was also somewhat skeptical as to whether true genius could receive its just reward or be entirely happy, especially in Denmark. In one of his most scintillatingly critical tales, "The Gardener and His Master," written toward the end of his life, this skepticism is given full expression—as usual in a succinct, brilliantly ambivalent manner. The plot is familiar in its broad outlines. A haughty aristocrat possesses an excellent, humble gardener named Larsen, who tends his estate outside of Copenhagen. But the master never trusts the advice of the gardener, nor does he appreciate what his servant produces. He and his wife believe that the fruit and flowers grown by other gardeners are better. When they constantly discover, to their chagrin, that their very own gardener's work is considered the best by the noble families in the region, they hope he will not think too much of himself. Then Andersen comments:

> He didn't; but the fame was a spur, he wanted to be one of the best gardeners in the country. Every year he tried to improve some of the vegetables and fruits, and often he was successful. It was not always appreciated. He would be told that the pears and apples were good but not as good as the ones last year. The melons were excellent but not quite up to the standard of the first ones he had grown.
>
> (p. 1018)

The gardener must constantly prove himself, and one of his great achievements is his use of an area to plant "all the typical common plants of Denmark, gathered from forests and fields," which flourish because of his nursing care and devotion. So, in the end, the owners of the castle must be proud of the gardener because the whole world beat the drums for his success: "But they weren't really proud of it. They felt that they were the owners and that they could dismiss Larsen if they wanted to. They didn't, for they were decent people, and there are lots of their kind, which is fortunate for the Larsens."

In other words, Andersen himself had been fortunate, or, at least this was the way he ironically viewed his career at the end of his life. Yet there is something pathetic about the story. The gardener Larsen is obviously the storyteller Andersen, and the garden with all its produce is the collection of literary works he cultivated and improved throughout his life. The owners of the garden are Andersen's patrons and may be associated with the Danish royalty, the Collin family, and other upper-class readers in Denmark. We must remember that the Collin family and other aristocrats never came to recognize Andersen as *Digter* but thought of him as a fine, gifted popular writer. Andersen, whose vanity was unquenchable, petulantly complained that he was unappreciated in Denmark although other European countries recognized his genius. Such treatment at home, whether real or imagined, he symbolized in this tale.

The reference to the "common plants" that the gardener cultivates pertains to the folklore he adapted and enriched so that it would bloom aesthetically on Danish soil. Andersen boasts that he, the gardener, has made Denmark famous; pictures are taken of this garden and circulated throughout the world. Yet the gardener works within the confines of servitude and patronage, and the voice of the narrator Andersen, even though ironic, rationalizes the humiliating ways in which his masters treat Larsen: they are "decent" people. But we must wonder—and the tension of the narrative compels us to do so—why, if the gardener is superb and brilliant, he does not rebel and quit his job. Why does the gardener suffer such humiliation and domination?

Andersen pondered these questions time and again and presented them in different symbolic forms, as though he hoped his private problems as a "common" artist blessed with genius might be resolved through his different approaches. The result is an immense, rich canon of fairy tales that reflects the social situation of art and the artist as well as social injustices in the nineteenth century. Andersen tried desperately to give his life the form and content of a fairy tale, precisely because he was a troubled, lonely, and highly neurotic artist who sublimated in literary creation his failure to fulfill his wishes and dreams in reality. His literary fame rests on this failure, for what he was unable to achieve for himself he created for millions of readers, young and old, with the hope that their lives might be different from his. Ironically, to read the fairy tales of Andersen today and gain hope means that we must understand the despair of the writer, that we no longer neglect the disquieting features in his life and work.

## Selected Bibliography


INDIVIDUAL WORKS

Note: In all instances place of publication is Copenhagen.

AUTOBIOGRAPHY

*H. C. Andersens Levnedsbog, 1805–1831.* 1832.

*Märchen meines Lebens ohne Dichtung (The True Story of My Life).* 1847.

*Mit Livs Eventyr (The Fairy Tale of My Life).* 1855.

DRAMA

*Ungdoms-Forsøg (Youthful Attempts).* 1822. Includes prose pieces.

*Kjaerlighed paa Nicolai Taarn (Love on St. Nicholas Tower).* 1829.

*Den Unsynglige paa Sprogø (The Invisible Man on Sprogø).* 1839.

*Mulatten (The Mulatto).* 1840.

*Fugelen i Paeretraeet (The Bird in the Pear Tree).* 1842.

*Lykkens Blomst (The Blossom of Happiness).* 1845.

*Meer end Perler og Guld (Pearls and Gold).* 1849.

LIBRETTOS

*Festen paa Kenilworth (The Festival at Kenilworth).* 1836.

*Agnete og Havmanden (Agnete and the Merman).* 1843. First published in 1833 as a dramatic poem.

*Liden Kirsten (Little Christina).* 1846.

POETRY

*Digte (Poems).* 1830.

*Phantasier og Skizzer (Fantasies and Sketches).* 1831.

NOVELS

*Improvisatoren (The Improvisatore).* 1835.

*O.T.* 1836.

*Kun en Spillemand (Only a Fiddler).* 1837.

*De to Baronesser (The Two Baronesses).* 1848.

*At være eller ikke være (To Be or Not To Be?).* 1857.

*Lykke-Peer (Lucky Peter).* 1870.

STORIES

*Eventyr fortalte for Børn (Fairy Tales Told for Children).* 1835.

*Billedbog uden Billeder (Picture Book Without Pictures).* 1839.

"Den grimme Aelling" ("The Ugly Duckling"). 1843.

*Nye Eventyr (New Fairy Tales).* 1843.

"Vanddrabben" ("A Drop of Water"). 1848.

"Historien om en Toder" ("The Story of a Mother"). 1848.

*Paa den yderste Dag (On the Last Day).* 1852.

"Alt paa sin rette Plads!" ("Everything in Its Right Place!"). 1853.

"Nissen has Spekhokeren" (The Pixy at the Grocer's"). 1853.

"Der er Forskjel" ("There Is a Difference"). 1855.

*Deilig (Lovely).* 1859.

*To Jomfruer (The Two Maidens).* 1861.

"Marionetspilleren" ("The Puppeteer"). 1861.

*"Karnbassen"* ("The Dung Beetle"). 1861.

"I Andegaarden" ("In the Duckyard") 1861.

"Det nye aarhundredes Musa" ("The Muse of the Twentieth Century"). 1861.

"Snglen og Rosenhaekken" ("The Snail and the Rosebush"). 1861.

"Isjomfruen" ("The Ice Maiden"). 1861.

"Moster" ("Auntie"). 1866.

"Laserne" ("The Rags"). 1868.

"Garneren og Herskabet" ("The Gardener and His Master"). 1871.

"Kroblingen" ("The Cripple"). 1872.

TRAVEL

*Fodrejse fra Holmens Kanal til Østpynten of Amager i aarene 1828 og 1829 (Journey on Foot from Holmens Canal to the East Point of Amager).* 1829.

*En Digters Bazar (A Poet's Bazaar). 1842.*

*I Sverige (In Sweden).* 1851.

*I Spanien (In Spain).* 1863.

*Et besøg i Portugal (A Visit in Portugal).* 1868.

## TRANSLATIONS

*Andersen's Works.* 10 vols. Boston, 1869–1871. Author's edition.

*The Andersen-Scudder Letters.* Edited and translated by Waldemar Westergaard. Introduced by Jean Hersholt. Essay by Helge Topsoi-Jensen. Berkeley, Calif., 1949.

*The Complete Fairy Tales and Stories.* Translated by Erik Christian Haugaard. New York, 1974.

*The Complete Stories of Hans Christian Andersen.* Translated by Jean Hersholt. 3 vols. New York, 1949.

*The Fairy Tale of My Life.* Translated by W. Glyn Jones. New York, 1954.

*Hans Christian Andersen's Fairy Tales.* Translated by R. P. Keigwin. Introduced by Elias Bredsdorff. New York, 1950.

*The Improvisatore; or, Life in Italy.* Translated by Mary Howitt. London, 1847.

*Lucky Peter.* Translated by Horace E. Scudder. *Scribner's Monthly* (March and April 1871).

*Only a Fiddler.* Translated by Mary Howitt. London, 1845.

*Pictures of Sweden.* Translated by Charles Beckwith. London, 1851.

*A Poet's Bazaar.* Translated by Charles Beckwith. 3 vols. London, 1846.

*Rambles in the Romantic Regions of the Hartz Mountains.* Translated by Charles Beckwith. London, 1848.

*In Spain.* Translated by Mrs. Bushby. London, 1864.

*The Story of My Life.* Translated by Horace E. Scudder. Boston, 1871.

*To Be or Not to Be?* Translated by Mrs. Bushby. London, 1857.

*The True Story of My Life.* Translated by Mary Howitt. London, 1847.

*The Two Baronesses.* Translated by Charles Beckwith. 2 vols. London, 1848.

*Wonderful Stories for Children.* Translated by Mary Howitt. London, 1846.

## BIOGRAPHICAL AND CRITICAL STUDIES

Atkins, A. M. "The Triumph of Criticism: Levels of Meaning in Hans Christian Andersen's *The Steadfast Tin Soldier.*" *Scholia Satyrica* 1: 25–28 (1975).

Bain, R. N. *Hans Christian Andersen.* London, 1895.

Barüske, Heinz. "Hans Christian Andersen—Der Mensch und seine Zeit." In *Aus Andersens Tagebüchern.* Vol. 1. Frankfurt, 1980. Pp. 9–29.

Berendsohn, W. A. *Phantasie und Wirklichkeit in den "Marchen und Geschichten" Hans Christian Andersens: Struktur- und Stilstudien.* Wiesbaden, 1973.

Böök, Fredrik. *Hans Christian Andersen: A Biography.* Translated by C. Schoolfield. Norman, Okla., 1962.

Born, Ann. "Hans Christian Andersen: An Infectious Genius." *Anderseniana* 2:248–260 (1976).

Brandes, Georg. "Hans Christian Andersen." In *Eminent Authors of the Nineteenth Century.* Translated by R. B. Anderson. New York, 1886.

Braude, L. Y. "Hans Christian Andersen and Russia." *Scandinavica* 14:1–15 (1975).

Bredsdorff, Elias. *Hans Andersen and Charles Dickens: A Friendship and Its Dissolution.* Copenhagen, 1956.

———. *Hans Christian Andersen: The Story of His Life and Work, 1805–75.* London, 1975.

Browning, George. *A Few Personal Recollections of Hans Christian Andersen.* London, 1875.

Burnett, C. B. *The Shoemaker's Son: The Life of Hans Christian Andersen.* London, 1941.

Dal, Erik. "Hans Christian Andersen's Tales and America." *Scandinavian Studies* 40:1–25 (1968).

Duffy, Maureen. "The Brothers Grimm and Sister Andersen." In *The Erotic World of Faery.* London, 1972. Pp. 263–284.

Grønbech, Bo. *Hans Christian Andersen.* Boston, 1980.

Haugaard, Erik C. "Hans Christian Andersen: A Twentieth-Century View." *Scandinavian Review* 14:1–15 (1975).

Heltoft, Kjeld. *Hans Christian Andersen as an Artist.* Translated by Reginald Spink. Copenhagen, 1977.

Jan, Isabelle. *Andersen et ses contes: Essai.* Paris, 1977.

Johnson, Spencer. *The Value of Fantasy: The Story of Hans Christian Andersen.* La Jolla, Calif., 1979.

Jones, W. Glyn. *Denmark.* New York, 1970.

Manning-Sanders, Ruth. *Swan of Denmark: The Story of Hans Christian Andersen.* London, 1949; New York, 1950.

Marker, J. *Hans Christian Andersen and the Romantic Theater: A Study of Stage Practices in the Prenaturalistic Scandinavian Theater.* Toronto, 1971.

Meynell, Esther. *The Story of Hans Andersen.* New York, 1950.

Mishler, William, "H. C. Andersen's 'Tin Soldier' in a Freudian Perspective." *Scandinavian Studies* 50: 389–395 (1978).

Mitchell, P. M. *A History of Danish Literature.* Copenhagen, 1957. Pp. 150–160.

Nielsen, Erling. *Hans Christian Andersen in Selbstzeugnissen und Bilddokumenten.* Hamburg, 1958.

Reumert, Elith. *Hans Christian Andersen the Man.* Translated by Jessie Bröchner. London, 1927.

Robb, N. A. "Hans Christian Andersen." In *Four in Exile.* New York and London, 1948; Port Washington, N.Y., 1968. Pp. 120–151.

Spink, Reginald. *Hans Christian Andersen and His World.* London, 1972.

Stirling, Monica. *The Wild Swan: The Life and Times of Hans Christian Andersen.* New York and London, 1965.

Svendsen, H. M., and Werner. *Geschichte der dänischen Literatur.* Neumünster, 1964.

Teschner, Heinrich. *Hans Christian Andersen und Heinrich Heine: Ihre literarischen und persönlichen Beziehungen.* Münster, 1914. Ph.D. dissertation.

Toksvig, Signe. *The Life of Hans Christian Andersen.* London, 1933.

JACK ZIPES

# JEAN ANOUILH

## *(1910–1987)*

IN OCTOBER OF 1969, Jean Anouilh's play *Cher Antoine* (*Dear Antoine*) opened in Paris. The first-night audience was extremely enthusiastic; many clearly thought what several critics who attended the performance later wrote: that the play was a masterpiece and the author among the greatest of contemporary French playwrights. It was time for the curtain call, for the author to come forward to receive the audience's acclaim. But to the confusion of all, even the embarrassment of some, the author had left. Simply left, vanished into the Parisian night as though he had nothing to do with the play.

This refusal to acknowledge the plaudits of the audience baffled the spectators. It almost seemed to some as though the playwright was trying to prolong the spell he had cast on his audience. To the public, still caught up in the death of the leading character, Anouilh's double, the presence of Anouilh on stage would have seemed tantamount to a resurrection.

In the final scene the house of the now-defunct Antoine was being boarded up as a handful of acquaintances recalled his admiration for the ending of Chekhov's *The Cherry Orchard*. In that play, too, a house that once had sheltered a happy family is boarded up while its soul remains in it forever. The question left unanswered was whether it was Antoine or Anouilh who had chosen such a nostalgic finale. The presence of this doubt meant that Anouilh had reached the high point in the role of mystifier he had conceived for himself some forty years before. By playing on appearances, he had not intended to perform a dramatic unveiling of his soul but to lead the spectators up yet another rung of his ladder of pretending. Through a clever game of make-believe, which never ceased to be his first rule, he had achieved a fusion of illusion and reality in the spectators' minds. He had convinced them that, although he had formerly remained mute about private matters, he had stepped on stage that night to expose a large part of his emotional life.

Yet Anouilh was caught at his own game. The leitmotiv in *Dear Antoine* dealt with the solitude and disenchantment that overcame a playwright who, absorbed in his craft, let love pass him by. Like his greasepainted counterpart, Antoine de Saint-Flour, Anouilh felt too alienated to relieve his loneliness by accepting the acclaim of an excited crowd.

While delighting the spectators, who believed themselves to be in full command of the situation, the playwright was reveling in the ultimate theatrical trick. He had succeeded in enmeshing them in such a mixture of reality and dramatic fiction that they could not distinguish one from the other. Thus Anouilh had brilliantly resolved the essential polarity of his art and fulfilled his wish to "detheatricalize" the stage, that is, to reduce the distance between the spectator and the stage, so that the spectator becomes an integral part of the play and does not know the difference between make-believe and reality.

Ever since he set out to make the French theater his with *L'Hermine* (*The Ermine*) in 1931, Jean Anouilh has aroused great curiosity, and sometimes ire, among critics and public alike. The controversies that arise about his plays stem from the fact that he escapes clear-cut identification. This is due not to obscurity in his work or deviousness on his part but simply to the protean aspect of his plays. They are variations on given themes, and as such they give the impression that they constitute contradictions. This apparent inconsistency may originate in the ambiguous behavior of the protagonists. But it is simply a fact of life that ambiguity is an integral component of man's plight in relation to himself and to others; thus, to ask that an image of man be in clear and unambiguous focus is to ask for comforting falsehood. Besides, if man is a "disconsolate but gay animal," as Anouilh asserts, won't he be a paradox to himself?

The isolated works of some authors give evidence of those authors' characteristics, but a particular play of Anouilh's reveals at best only a few elements of his work, never his total makeup. Any one of his plays can be judged as only one hue in the spectrum of his work. It is interesting to discover that a reading of all of Anouilh's plays reveals a yearning on the author's part to treat each piece as a step in a progression. This interpretation is supported by the presence in newer plays of lines quoted from preceding plays. And as one notes in the novels of Balzac or Faulkner, mere names in earlier works by Anouilh appear as full-fledged characters in later plots.

Over the years Anouilh has been recognized as one of the world's leading dramatists: his works are among the most frequently performed everywhere. Theaters, repertory companies, drama schools, and avid readers constantly seek out his plays. He is best known in the United States for the success on Broadway of *L'Alouette* (*The Lark,* 1952) and *Beckett ou l'honneur de Dieu* (*Becket; or, The Honor of God,* 1959), and for the innumerable revivals of the irrepressible *Le bal des voleurs* (*Thieves' Carnival,* 1932), as well as *L'Invitation au château* (*Ring Round the Moon,* 1947) and *Antigone* (1942). *The Lark,* Anouilh's version of Joan of Arc's martrydom, received such acclaim that two English translations of it appeared the year it was performed. *Becket* has been transposed into a remarkable motion picture.

Throughout his long career Anouilh's fame was quite solid. Proclaimed a young avant-gardist in the 1930's, he showed great promise in competition for renown with a constellation of stage directors such as Georges Pitoëff, Charles Dullin, André Barsacq, Jacques Copeau, and Louis Jouvet, who were steering the French stage away from realism, toward stylization, classicism, and poetry. In the 1940's and early 1950's, the decades of the existentialist dramatists, Anouilh continued to attract audiences with the contemporary interpretation of a Greek theme in *Antigone* and the dramatization of man's sense of dedication in *Becket.* In 1959 he boldly endorsed the brash antiplays of Eugène Ionesco, Arthur Adamov, and Samuel Beckett. He went so far as to urge his public to go down the street from the theater where one of his plays was being performed to see Ionesco's *Les chaises* (*The Chairs*), and he unreservedly praised *Waiting for Godot* when Samuel Beckett was virtually unknown. Strangely enough, the birth of the antitheater may well be the reason for a six-year silence on his part. At any rate, he created nothing of his own between *L'Orchestre* (1962) and *Le boulanger, la boulangère et le petit mitron* (The Baker, His Wife, and His Apprentice, 1969), the success of which placed him again in the forefront of contemporary drama. Six years was a long silence for a man who in thirty-eight years had published thirty plays, had adapted works varying from Shakespeare to Oscar Wilde, had created scenarios, made records, written newspaper articles, and even produced a book of scathing fables. But between October 1969 and the following February, Anouilh presented two plays, *Dear Antoine* and *Les poissons rouges,* which provoked wild raves and renewed his love affair with his public. Thus time has shown that "The Great Anouilh," as he is called in France, who once said that a playwright is a gentleman who seduces a lady—the lady in question being the public—can lay claim to the place of Don Juan in the field of drama.

Jean Anouilh was born on 23 June 1910, in the Atlantic port of Bordeaux. His father was a tailor noted for the scrupulousness with which he exercised his skill. Stage directors who feel too restricted by Anouilh's minute descriptions of his characters' stances bemoan the fact that he inherited this particular trait. His mother, a violinist, often played in the orchestra of the casino of Arcachon, a seaside resort forty-five minutes from Bordeaux on the adorably lackadaisical shuttle train. It was in Arcachon that Anouilh's fascination for theatrics was nurtured, for as a little boy he had the privilege of gazing, baffled, at the operettas performed night after night for vacationers. If the actors were second-rate, they nevertheless mesmerized his imagination through their magic ability to play specific, well-defined roles. Orchestra members and struggling actors kept a unique place in his heart, appearing with various traits in *The Ermine, Eurydice* (*Legend of Lovers; Point of Departure,* 1941), *La sauvage* (*Restless Heart,* 1934), and *Le rendez-vous de Senlis* (*The Rendezvous at Senlis; Dinner with the Family,* 1941).

When he was nine, Anouilh moved to Paris with his parents; they lived in the Montmartre district, where some of his plays would be produced later on. At the age of thirteen he precociously wrote in verse what he calls "false plays" (or closet dramas) that he acted out for friends and relatives. After elementary schooling at the École Colbert, he pursued traditional studies at the Collège Chaptal. Jean-Louis Barrault, a classmate, recalled Anouilh as a distant, nattily attired young man, difficult to get to know. Thirty years later, in 1959, the two were to create *La petite Molière,* starring Anouilh's daughter Catherine. Going to law school after he finished at Chaptal must have seemed drab to the aspiring dramatist, especially after a balmy spring evening in 1928 when he was captivated by Jean Giraudoux's *Siegfried.* (It was from Giraudoux, Anouilh declared, that he learned the sense of stylization that characterized all his theater.) Soon after, he created *Mandarine* (1929). *Humulus le muet* (*Humulus the Mute,* 1929) was written the same year in collaboration with Jean Aurenche, whom Anouilh met when he gave up the law and started working in an advertising agency. The same pair wrote four film scenarios between 1936 and 1939. About his training in publicity Anouilh confides that, in lieu of poetic studies, slogans taught him the precision and timing essential to dialogue. In 1930, while awaiting the call to military service, he became Louis Jouvet's secretary general at the Comédie des Champs-Elysées, where most of his plays have been performed. Receiving, in effect, no guidance from the famous actor-director largely responsible for the success of the *Siegfried* he so idolized, Anouilh found the position disappointing and lonely. Still undaunted, he wrote *The Ermine,* which was presented at the Théâtre de l'Oeuvre by Pierre Fresnay in 1932. Acclaimed as a promising young dramatist, Anouilh resolved to dedicate his life to the theater. When in 1935 he sold to Metro-Goldwyn-Mayer the rights to *Y'avait un* prisonnier (*There Was a Prisoner,* 1935) he gained the financial independence that enabled him to start devoting his life to writing.

Although Anouilh's work seems effortless at times, it betrays the thirst for growth and renewal of a playwright acutely engaged in the present, a man of letters not likely to admit that he never forgot the classicist Nicolas Boileau's admonition to polish and repolish one's creations. His desire for constant improvement is illustrated by the various collections of his plays.

Anouilh said that his grouping of plays under the headings of *pièces noires, nouvelles pièces noires, pièces roses, pièces brillantes, pièces grinçantes,* and *pièces costumées* (black plays, new black plays, rosy plays, shining plays, grating plays, and costume plays) aimed to satisfy the public's need for classifications. As he indicates, we must consider such divisions to be somewhat arbitrary, since he did not write all the plays included in a collection at one time. But the groups nevertheless represent the different phases of his evolution.

The *Pièces noires* are not tragedies in the classical sense of the word, but they are dramas in the sense that they display the defeat of individuals in their quest to live within the framework of society and humanity, while at the same time preserving the self. The term "tragedy" would seem too formal to the unpretentious Anouilh, who at the outset of his vocation aspired to nothing more than the role of a man of the theater in the manner of Molière, the writer capable of distracting men from their cares. The volume of *pièces noires* includes *The Ermine, Restless Heart, Le voyageur sans bagage* (*Traveler Without Luggage,* 1936), and *Legend of Lovers.* These names evoke a gallery of portraits, for Anouilh intends to act as portraitist. Each painting represents the stylization of an individual with his past, his present dilemma, his interior climate. But while *The Ermine, Restless Heart,* and *Traveler Without Luggage* take place in a post–World War I setting, *Eurydice* moves in the timelessness of myth. Because all the characters have the same choice to make, they may be put into identical frames. In order to find serenity, each must decide whether to reject or acquiesce in his destiny, as it is assigned to him either by society or by more obscure forces.

Consider *The Ermine.* In a society dominated by the bourgeoisie, Frantz, a young man without money, loves the rich Monime. Her aunt opposes their marriage and a prosperous man thwarts Frantz's attempt to acquire the sum he needs. The young man must renounce Monime, or marry her and condemn her to a humiliating life of lowly prospects. Convinced that old women serve no purpose, he kills the rich aunt in order to use her money "to build an indestructible barrier around his love." Blind with rancor at seeing man's laws bar the way to his will to be happy, he defies those laws and stands alone as the monster-martyr born from the monetary shackles invented by man. He can survive only if he rejects the society that threatens to deprive him of the right to acquire happiness. His situation recalls Rousseau's image of man as enslaved by the merciless social organization men have devised.

Anouilh created Thérèse, the main character of *Restless Heart,* from his memories of the second-rate musicians who played in European cafés in the 1930's. His sympathy for these somewhat grotesque figures grew from an understanding of the tragedy inherent in their lives. They provided him with many a character for the *pièces noires,* since the gap between the life they led and the one to which they aspired was so wide. They lived under the illusion that because of their talent they deserved applause and the finer things of life, but in reality they received less and less of both each day. For Anouilh they symbolized in a stylized manner the fate of the common man, trying to find permanence in a world reduced to shambles by the financial depression of the early 1930's, a world moving inexorably toward World War II.

Thérèse is young, like all the principal characters in the *pièces noires,* and she represents the re-examination of accepted values to which the young have proceeded throughout history. Born to shabby musicians who are on the watch for the stroke of luck that will change their fate, she represses her love for Florent, a talented pianist with whom life would mean wealth and happiness. Her obstinate efforts to show him the sordidness of her background, so as to repel him, appear masochistic. In

Anouilh's terms, however, she accepts her true condition, which is one of suffering, deeming her action more worthy of a human being than giving in to happiness, which for her would be the same as to accept living a lie.

Gaston, in *Traveler Without Luggage,* betrays a yearning for the innocence of a child. He seeks the "noble savage" in himself. As a former amnesiac looking for his past, he is distressed to discover that his family created a jungle instead of a home and, worse yet, that he, too, behaved in a despicable manner. Destiny provides him with an escape from his family, but he has to kill his past, even in this escape, and killing anything is sad. Here the play intimates that a man must cut his ties with other human beings in order to acquire the freshness of spirit and nobility of character he desires.

The heroine in *Eurydice* moves within the pitiful circle of second-rate actors, attached to a mother for whom life is the series of clichés she has heard in bad plays. Like all the young heroines in Anouilh's theater, she emerges out of the playwright's boyish love affair with the ingenues he saw at Arcachon. Although his instinct taught him that they had been touched by many male hands, he has etched them throughout his work as abused but innocent females of the species whose hearts remain as pure as Iphigenia's. They receive nicknames such as "The Wild One" (La Sauvage), "The Dove" (Colombe), and "The Lark" (l'Alouette). With their strong libidos hidden by a rough beauty that nothing mars, they remain his porcelain dolls.

Eurydice's past takes the physical aspect of men's fingerprints left all over her body. She no longer remembers how they came to be there, but Orpheus sees them as so many disgusting tattoos. He knows they are part of her experience of life. When she slips confidently into the euphoria of love, and pictures her future relationship with Orpheus, she remembers that because of her past she lacks the virginity of soul she wishes she could offer to him. Unable to remove the marks, she chooses to die and thus redeem herself. Even Orpheus cannot save her, for when she is given a chance to return to life, he unwittingly lets her die again by indulging his own jealousy. Eventually he, too, chooses death, which seems to be the only realm where one may find gentle peace, beauty, pure love, and the cleansing of one's soul.

As we look at these plays as a whole, it is clear that the yearning for complete freedom and integrity drives all the protagonists to despair, although the circumstances vary. In Anouilh's vision every sight, every touch, every experience, every moment of time leave their imprint on the human soul and preclude any rebirth of interior freshness, of innocence. Man seems to resemble a sheet of blotting paper that can never be cleansed of its spots, even though he wishes to regain his purity.

In addition, according to their heredity, their past history of poverty or wealth, pain or pleasure, people are divided into two races that cannot communicate: as Charles Baudelaire expressed it, the race of Cain and the race of Abel. When the protagonists can be saved by redeemer-like characters who graciously give of themselves to prevent their beloveds' fate, they respond with a sardonic but melancholy refusal. In *Restless Heart,* for example, when Florent pleads with Thérèse to take his love and the serenity he promises, she refuses, and as he stands bewildered, she tells him that he must accept the role of a stranger on earth, the role of a king who possesses all without having suffered for it. Florent feels unjustly accused of some sort of crime, while Thérèse implies that she will remain in a brotherhood based on destitution. Neither of the two seems to have a real freedom of choice. Yet they must find a bearable stance in a world that holds them accountable for what is actually imposed on them by pure chaos.

As he developed the cycle of *pièces noires,* Anouilh was accused of treating only one subject. Actually, these four plays constitute variations on the dilemma of life. As such, they tend to show the pride, the yearnings, and the frustrations of certain characters rather than to expose the definitive philosophy of the dramatist. At this point in his career the young playwright was primarily concerned with the creation of characters, not with the growth of plot; hence the enigmatic quality of the characters' rejection. From the debates the characters engage in, however, one can deduce general trends of thought that Anouilh elaborates more fully in later plays. What mainly stands out in his early work is an interest in the complexity of human motives and the difficulty of making a lucid choice in the chaotic modern world, which pulls people in opposite directions.

Many interpretations of Anouilh's use of the money theme have been developed. Actually, his basic design, which is that of a moralist studying visible responses to social stimuli, is similar to that in works of fiction showing men adjusting to love, family, politics, and money. He explains that he observes men from the "moral" point of view, which to him means dealing with a choice of behavior that either does or does not conform to accepted standards, not only of ethics but also of custom and taste. He does not aim to create purely psychological or metaphysical plays, but attempts to hold a mirror up to his fellow men. However, even though he is not conscious of the fact, his astute studies of their conduct slip into meditations on the human psyche and the human condition, especially in the serious plays. For instance, the murder perpetrated by Frantz in *The Ermine* changes into a symbolic triumph over frustration. The old aunt, who personifies money, becomes the victim of Frantz's anxiety. He is afraid of his possible inability to love forever, of his desires, of his vulnerability. The girl he loves has the purity of a lily. To deserve her, he dreams of possessing a crystal-clear soul, cleansed of all the blemishes that living as a poor man has left.

Once the case of each hero in the *pièces noires* is examined, one realizes that the premise given at the very beginning of the play, involving only the way in which he will find serenity or happiness, becomes an academic question: Does the order of life, the makeup of humanity, the nature of the world, allow any one to achieve happiness or peace within oneself? In Anouilh's kaleidoscope, at this point, the answer is negative. For life transforms and erodes both the subject and the object of happiness in different degrees; it may be impossible for man to accept serenity, although he keeps thinking that he desires it above all things; at the same time society nullifies man's effort toward his own fulfillment by enslaving him through mass-produced rules. In *Antigone,* Anouilh will go so far as to advance the theory that happiness is only a human fabrication.

These dramas appeal by the fact that they enrich us with unconventional images of young individuals in search of a modus vivendi. The characters cannot be placed in neatly labeled boxes, for they fit into no system except the one created by their own identities and Anouilh's stylization. As he makes them define themselves in lucid, realistic dialogue ranging from the virulent to the pathetic, he puts us in the presence of men and women who manage to remain unforgettable. From their original expression of universal misery emanates a certain poetry associated with our vision of the young romantic making a stand in a harsh, absurd world. Finally, it is interesting to see how, while portraying the painful awakening of youth to the inequities brought by life lived among others, Anouilh casually slips into philosophical metaphors, refreshingly stripped of tendentious pronouncements.

The *nouvelles pièces noires* (new black plays) are *Jézabel* (1932), *Antigone* (1942), *Roméo et Jeannette* (*Romeo and Jeannette; Fading Mansions,* 1945), and *Médée* (*Medea,* 1946). It is logical that Anouilh, who avoided realism in his early plays, should turn to myth for the creation of two of these plays, *Antigone* and *Medea.* He was attracted by myth on several grounds. First, the successful modernization of myth accomplished by Giraudoux and Jean Cocteau proved justifiably inspiring. Second, the themes treated in myth fitted in with

Anouilh's penchant for examining the struggle to escape from social, psychological, or metaphysical bondage. Finally, the rejuvenation of mythical characters posed a challenge to Anouilh's capacity for developing the personalities of his protagonists, a development that must be carefully done if re-creation of myth is to be persuasive.

Although not literally mythical, *Jézabel* and *Romeo and Jeannette* fit into the *nouvelles pièces noires* because the fates of their title characters are as well known as those of Antigone and Medea: they are part of literary history. The fact that the shadow of death grows inexorably larger with each swing of the pendulum, while the spectator helplessly watches the hero or heroine being engulfed, gives these plays an atmosphere of tragedy. And the stylistic restraint in *Antigone, Romeo and Jeannette,* and *Medea* contributes to the timeless classical quality of their development and resolution.

As the generic title indicates, the *nouvelles pièces noires* are closely linked to the *pièces noires;* all the plays together form a progression, each gaining a larger degree of impact. In *The Ermine, Restless Heart,* and *Traveler Without Luggage* the prime origin of fate rests in the inflexibility of the characters. Though they represent extremes, they deserve understanding, even sympathy, for we share a slight kinship with them. Jézabel's fate arises from weakness, and it awakens fear that we, like her, may succumb to our own flaws; hence identification grows stronger. The fates of Frédéric and Jeannette fall upon them from unknown causes. We pity these lovers, who mysteriously disintegrate, as if eaten by a baffling disease of the mind. In the case of Antigone and Médée, destiny depends on the whims of the gods, regardless of the characters' own innocence or guilt. Their situation takes on awesome proportions, for it arbitrarily deprives the individual of the chance to save himself through any sort of ascetic withdrawal, no matter how hard the attempt may be. So we wonder whether our freedom, like theirs, is illusory, for we know that we, too, struggle and don't always succeed; complete empathy follows. In Anouilh's view our emotional reaction means that he has accomplished the feat of bringing the theater back to its essence, which is communion: he has succeeded in shocking the public out of its callous attitude toward its fellow beings. We see that as he has patiently humanized his characters to a greater extent with each play, the intensity of the impact on the audience has increased. All the while he continues to exploit the same general themes. Each play mixes the elements of choice and alienation; each plot develops within the narrow social confines of a couple or a family, except *Antigone,* which widens to include the political circle. Generally (*Jézabel* being the exception) the *nouvelles pièces noires* offer an ennobling picture of human courage.

*Jézabel,* a disturbing play, opens this collection, opposing its darkly grotesque atmosphere to the sublime beauty of the rest of the plays. As the title forecasts, the Jézabel of Anouilh, a counterpart of the one who slew the Lord's prophets, must indeed be eaten by dogs: she is an aging woman who poisons her husband to get his money and give it to her lover. Her son, Marc, is in love with a rich young lady from a good family. After he begs his mother to accept the fact of her age and to behave respectably so that he may marry Jacqueline, the play assumes naturalistic overtones. Jézabel vulgarly displays her drinking, her sexual urges, her slovenly appearance. Responding to criticism aimed at the appearance of this facile naturalism, Anouilh later defended the rightness of its use. On the occasion of his adaptation of Roger Vitrac's *Victor,* in 1962, he said that naturalism is actually "not a photograph of reality, but a careful reproduction of that accepted notion of life which has become life itself"; in other words, it is the stylization of an already stylized reproduction of life, and therefore not the result of facility. In truth, *Jézabel,* despite its unevenness, rises beyond its naturalistic level and deserves a reappraisal. Its central character, in all her pitifully abhorrent aspects, resembles many a human being in the courts, prisons, and drug rehabilitation centers. Her condition provokes meditation about the fall of humanity. Unlike Antigone or Medea, Jézabel lacks a personal identity and searches for it in men's arms, only to find herself completely bewildered by their animal responses. She rejects life in the sense that she cannot accept what it has done to her husband, now a man deprived of all enthusiasm. She recalls Eurydice and Antigone when she seems to say that death is indeed preferable to old age and the day-to-day deprivations entailed by the passing of time.

Written in 1932, this play has the obsessive quality and force of Sartre's *No Exit;* Jézabel and her son become each other's hell. He is her hell because no matter how she explains her sordidness, he judges her on his own terms; she is his hell because he knows he is like her and he tries desperately to change her image so that he can be saved.

Besides its philosophical implications *Jézabel* offers a somber comment on motherhood. It becomes a farce in which a woman requires a commitment from her husband and children on the ground that she is a mother, but then concerns herself solely with her beauty creams, her obsession with youth, and her lovers. Her husband, in this burlesque ballet, invariably retreats to the status of a nonentity, allowing himself to be overwhelmed by his wife's selfish recriminations. Instead of acting as the revered legendary head of the family, he turns out to be a beggar who hangs onto his children's coattails for sympathy and even for financial support.

In *Antigone,* as the Chorus remarks, we should enjoy a measure of serenity. We are told that we are among equals, for "we all are innocent." Our roles are interchangeable: one day we play the victim and another the spectator. When the Prologue takes us into the author's confidence by introducing the actors and explaining the casting, we feel like actors ourselves, taking a busman's holiday for the evening. As we settle back calmly into our seats to observe the unfolding of the action, we are quickly snapped out of our complacency by the reminder that we are so tranquil only because tonight it is not our turn to die. We are forced into the awareness that our death is but a question of time, and the play becomes not an individual story but a universal one. In this manner Anouilh, who states in *La grotte* (*The Cavern,* 1961) that the public makes the play and hence should be made to rehearse with the actors, legitimizes the presence of the Prologue in his modernization of the myth by using it to manipulate the spectator. Thus he provides the audience with the necessary distance to bear the sorrows they will witness and, at the same time, the closeness that will enable them to share in the catharsis.

*Antigone* is the masterpiece that brought international fame to Anouilh when it was first published. Written in 1942, and performed in 1944 during the Nazi occupation of France, it aroused the most heated controversy by its double aspect of myth and political satire, for Antigone clearly symbolizes the Resistance, whereas Créon's motives were interpreted by some as an approval of the Vichy government, and by others as a veiled satire of it. As an artist Anouilh did not have to choose sides. He meant to awaken people's consciousness to the concept of revolt. Were Créon's motives weaker than Antigone's, the play would become a clear-cut case of the triumph of good over evil, which would satisfy the emotions but not the intellect, for it would provide too simplistic a view of human dilemmas.

At the time it was particularly daring of Anouilh to modernize a myth embodying a political conflict. The French suffered daily from increasing restrictions that seemed the more arbitrary because they were dictated to the Vichy government by the Nazis. The nation was divided into a camp advocating revolt and a camp accepting the occupation as inevitable. By giving the tragedy an enigmatic meaning that does not exist in the original Sophocles play, Anouilh was offering the partisans in the Resistance the opportunity of interpreting Antigone's gesture as one of support for them, while the Nazis were unable to censure the play because Créon made such a good case for civic obedience. Nevertheless, the presence of this doubt resulted in strong abuse of Anouilh by those who misinterpreted his purpose. In *Pauvre Bitos* (*Poor Bitos,* 1956), published after the liberation, the playwright squelched those excessive and unfounded attacks.

Antigone, a skinny girl no one takes seriously, decides to challenge the so-called order of the world, knowing full well that she will be condemned to die for her boldness. In this she resembles her Greek counterpart but, unlike the classical Antigone, this young girl shows far more vulnerability and hardly conveys the notion that she is a heroic figure. After she attempts to bury Polynice, she runs promptly to her nurse's arms for warmth and security; she admits on several occasions that she is afraid; and while waiting to be entombed, she asks the guard what it is like to die.

As Antigone becomes increasingly shaken by Créon's arguments, she expresses her motives less and less clearly. Whereas she starts by asserting that she has to bury her brother out of fraternal love, she ends up sighing that she does not know anymore why she has chosen to die. This baffling response confers a seemingly insoluble ambiguity to the play. But the very evolution of her moral purpose eventually explains the mystery and removes some of its enigma.

As she talks to her sister, Ismène, at the outset of the action, Antigone appears to be a melancholy instrument of fate, regretting her role, saying that Créon's part is to decree her death, while hers is to bury her brother and accept that death as the consequence. Her action at this stage takes on the value of a clearly defined duty. Her disobedience stems from a fatal necessity dictated by the customs which advocate that the dead must be symbolically laid to rest by the living to escape the penalty of wandering forever in pain over the face of the earth.

When Ismène pleads for an "understanding" of the complexity of the situation and tries to explain the impossibility of making the right choice and the frightful consequences of disobedience, Antigone's anger flares up. The concept of "understanding" strikes Antigone as a cowardly escape from responsibility, as fear of unrestrained life. If Antigone chooses to die, does it mean that she does not feel like living? asks Ismène. Antigone answers by nostalgically reviewing her awareness of the value of life. She recalls the contemplation of a garden in the solitude of daybreak, the sense of wonder one has at the sight of millions of insects endowed with life, running through an incalculable number of living blades of grass. Later she indicates that living could also gain meaning through her love for Hémon, through procreation out of that love, through the relationship shared by members of a family. It becomes clear then that so complete is her knowledge of the value of life that the prospect of suffering or dying does not constitute enough of a deterrent to prevent her from living independently of any restriction, if only once, and even if the penalty for it is annihilation. At that point her original moral purpose is reinforced by her need to live in the absolute sense of the word, to commit herself completely to living.

Antigone's crucial confrontation with Créon takes her a step further. As he accuses her of being guilty of extreme pride, of making a display of personal pathos, of following in Oedipus' footsteps, of engaging in a contest with destiny and death—in a word, of showing "hubris"—he strengthens her decision to do "what she can" regardless of the consequences, as a simple human being, not a king's daughter, and because it is her duty to do so. At the beginning she was going to bury her brother because it was expected of her; now she wills it, as the one act that is in her power to perform, the act that gives her an identity.

When Créon describes the funeral rites as a sham, a series of pharisaical gestures that even she should be ashamed of, Antigone is submerged by a sudden awareness of the absurdity of customs. She resents the hodgepodge of fallacious constraints and the artificial, senseless, and arbitrary nature of any limitation that man allows to impede his right to live as he wants. She visualizes a complete revenge on this absurdity. Her act will be carried out in total freedom, as she desires. In the face of arbitrariness, there does not have to be any necessity to her act other than that which she imposes on it. She sarcastically tells Créon that she will accomplish her mission "for herself." In so doing she will commit an absurdity to limit the absurdity that limitations impose upon man; customs, rules, the state, the human condition will hem in life only so far as it wants to be hemmed in; she transcends the human condition, just as she decides to transcend pain when Créon twists her arm and she blurts out that it does not hurt, since for all intents and purposes she has no arm. Inasmuch as she chooses to impose her own rules and meaning on what happens to her, she can scorn Créon and declare that it is she who has become the queen, while he has become the slave of events. Antigone's solution is to impose her own absurdity on the universal absurdity as a means of conquering it.

Her moment of glory is temporarily reversed, however, when Créon discloses the sordidness of both brothers' characters and the consequent meaningless of his choice to bury one and desecrate the other. After this blow Antigone considers repudiating her decision; in a daze she mumbles, "Yes," when Créon tells her to go home and marry Hémon. But as the knot of the action tightens and Créon, on the threshold of victory, equates life and happiness, Antigone's moral purpose crystallizes in a flash. Men use "filthy happiness" to cover up their hypocrisy. Happiness serves to mask the lies, the compromises, the calculations that men cowardly accept so that they may go on living, so that they may avoid danger and death. Happiness is a masquerade of life itself, and she will not settle for living on those terms. She wants a full life even if it holds no hope of lasting. Therefore, she subscribes completely to her fate, proud to carry out the pursuit of truth begun by her father, Oedipus.

Yet Antigone becomes distraught despite her resolve. The world has turned into a void. As she dictates a letter to Hémon just before her death, she sighs that she does not know anymore why she dies. And neither do we. Her choice starts out as a moral necessity, changes into the rejection of the human condition, then to an endorsement of absurdity, and finally disintegrates into nothingness. In the end she is committing a totally gratuitous act, thereby illustrating the inexplicability of our actions. To the Chorus, which begs him not to let Antigone die, Créon answers that Polynice was a pretext for her and that, when she renounced her first premise, she found another, for what mattered was that she die. It appears that what actually mattered was that she act.

The Chorus concludes the play with a low-keyed wail over the scheme of humanity that augments our bewilderment. It chants that men get caught and die in the struggle of opposite beliefs, whether they themselves have strong beliefs or not. Once dead, their names are soon forgotten by the living. Occasionally one person creates havoc in the consciousness of some of his fellow men. They forgive him for it, as a sad lethargy overtakes them. As for the rest of men, they continue to play cards, oblivious to it all, suggesting that an act like Antigone's cannot change the machinelike indifference of life.

So this play ends with a disturbing lack of hope for the discovery of a rational meaning to our constant strife; yet it consoles us through its existence as a moving work of art. A brilliant handling of dramatic elements gives it a satisfying homogeneity that never falls into dullness. The character development and the organization of the plot impart complete plausibility to the action. The play maintains a smooth, dynamic rhythm thanks to the perfect balance of moods. The moments of intense emotion and those of banter or trivial discussion fit carefully together with the help of the classical restraint of the language. Whereas Sophocles' play is forbidding, Anouilh's work touches the whimsical at times, allowing the modern spectator necessary respite from its strong emotional content. In the scenes involving the nurse and the guards, the playwright not only aims at the comic relief often encountered in Shakespeare but also satirizes contemporary society by introducing the notions of pieces of toast and pensions. Anouilh is irrepressible at heart, and he admitted that he played such tricks to amuse himself.

He remains a master of dialogue by skillfully mixing humor with the poetic lines of Antigone as she evokes her childhood, her love for Hémon, her awe at disturbing the peace of the road in the morning light. As a result of these intricate combinations, Anouilh presents a very human though heroic Antigone who elicits curiosity, fear, pity, compassion, amusement, sorrow, and reflection; she provokes not only admiration but also attachment, as if she were a real person.

Continuing his voyage through man's tragic history, Anouilh turned next to the theme of the doomed lovers. To create *Romeo and Jeannette,* he grafted that theme onto the stifling situation displayed in the *pièces noires.* The plot does not appear very logical, for Frédéric's and Jeannette's characters make them unlikely lovers. But the plausibility of their love resides in its quality. Love befalls the two, as it befell Tristan and Isolde after they drank the love philter. When it has cast its spell, the lovers resemble two prisoners trapped in the same cage, desperately trying to understand why they are enslaved; at the same time they treasure gloomily what ties them, even in the face of a presentiment that it will cause their death.

This play offers a good occasion to examine Anouilh's ideas on love. Never did he present love as a salutary tie between man and woman. It can be sublime for a while, and then it leads to death; sometimes it appears to be a grotesque masquerade among caricatures; at other times it is what people talk about in make-believe, a kind of fairy tale resembling the *pièces roses;* in *Dear Antoine,* Anouilh presents it as a miracle, blessing very few chosen people. As Lucien, Jeannette's brother, warns, a promising love must be craftily hidden from "that one up there," who is jealous and will coldly steal it away. In other words, what we view as one of our few consolations on earth may be merely a myth.

The deaths of Frédéric and Jeannette in a purifying sea do not come as a surprise; this hero and heroine needs redemption for the sin of carnal knowledge as much as did Eurydice. The play, meant by its title to remind us of *Romeo and Juliet,* recalls more *Tristan and Isolde,* or better still Maurice Maeterlinck's *Pelléas et Mélisande,* simply because its rhythm plunges the spectator into the sort of mystic wasteland one finds in the Maeterlinck play. Inasmuch as the central characters keep groping for a way to express their predicament, they seem far removed from Romeo and Juliet, who can elucidate their situation so well.

While the style in *Antigone* showed the firmness befitting a grandiose subject, *Romeo and Jeannette* reveals a controlled poetic fluidity that testifies to Anouilh's amazing versatility. He explained that he first visualized a play before he captured it on paper. Like the later *Léocadia* (*Time Remembered,* 1939), this play has been invested with an aura of unreality. It offers the charms of an elegy, for the dialogue possesses a contemplative tone that puts one in a mood of gentle mourning.

Euripides emphasized a woman's potential for evil in his *Medea;* in his *Medea,* Anouilh redirected the Medea myth to his outlook, making it a confrontation of absolute love and life. As long as man and woman remain—according to Anouilh's favorite metaphor—two little soldiers fighting the battle of life side by side, love can last. Once circumstances transform the woman into a female unaware of the man's need to merge into the stream of life and compete with other men, he reverts to being a male, and the love act becomes a somber struggle in which each partner tries to subjugate the other. Médée does not escape Anouilh's rule of life; she is transformed by her blind passion and refuses to accept any limitation of her powers. Jason also has changed; he pleads for compromise with love, with life, with men, with the world. He is ready to find a purpose in the human condition such as other men have done and acquiesce in the form they have given the world around them. Quite often in Anouilh's work the characters who revolt against the inescapable barriers to their freedom and seem to think that courage lies in accepting death are enjoined to choose to live. For living takes a great deal of courage, too, says the author, the courage of the stoic, since every day brings new suffering. Jason knows this; however, he wants to go on living, to become a man who takes pride in being himself in his totality, not with complacency but with the recognition of his potential for humble acts as well as noble ones. Médée adheres to the identity of proud outcast she chose when she betrayed father, brother, and country to favor absolute love; she demands that commitment to her be absolute on Jason's part. At that point love is no longer possible between them; Médée can only choose death. She also needs to take revenge on a world that she rejects, so she kills her children. Yet we cannot help feeling pity for her, for she is a victim of fate.

The play marks an important step in Anouilh's development: for the first time in his work, the author paints in Jason a character who, having first rejected men's rules for the sake of an absolute, comes to terms with the imperfections inherent in man's condition.

To feel a moment of joy, the spectator of the *pièces roses* is invited to join Anouilh in unadulterated fantasy. In order to create vehicles for amusement, Anouilh delves into all the resources of his imagination as well as into his experience as a stage director, for the complicated physical activity in these plays necessitates a great deal of organization. In his comedies Anouilh resembles a cross between Molière choreographing ballet-comedies and Georges Feydeau compounding quid pro quos. For, like Molière when he had to provide entertainment for Louis XIV's court, Anouilh makes his comedy a spectacle, and like Feydeau he bases the laughter on multiple plots.

In *Humulus the Mute* he turns the tragic impediments of a mute young man and a deaf young girl into a hilariously funny skit. In *Thieves' Carnival* (1932) he enchants by showing the improbable gymnastics performed by thieves who try to hide their tricks from their benevolent victims. The antics executed by the characters have reminded many a critic of the spontaneity of the commedia dell'arte, although the apparent pell-mell of the action has been minutely timed by Anouilh. Had the play first been staged on this side of the Atlantic, *Thieves' Carnival* might well have evolved as a comedy in the manner of the Keystone cops. Anouilh, however, transforms his thieves into characters who move across the stage with the grace of ballet dancers. In this entertainment we again meet the familiar figure of the duchess, in this case Lady Hurf. Unlike her counterpart in *The Ermine,* however, she no longer represents the agent of evil fate, the obstacle to fulfillment; instead, continuing the generous work started by the Duchesse Dupont-Dufort in *Traveler Without Luggage,* she conducts herself as a benefactor bringing together the elements of happiness.

Lady Hurf, realizing that she has never really lived, amuses herself by assisting the thieves who intend to rob her. Though she penetrates their disguise as Spanish dukes, she pretends to recognize them as the real dukes. Everyone moves around her like amiable puppets, for she is the only character who seems to exist in a concrete way; since she is the real culprit of the situation, the action centers on her and she has to explain more forcefully than the other characters her system of values.

The action reveals Anouilh at his best as a showman manipulating the strings of his creations. As for the comedy, it goes beyond slapstick to elaborate a sort of intricate dance of pixielike but bungling thieves who at times steal from each other.

The decidedly tongue-in-cheek make-believe

of *Thieves' Carnival* bears no hint of the desperation that characterized the *pièces noires.* Gone is the need for the poor young man to commit a crime in order to deserve the rich girl he loves. The ludicrous Lord Edgar provides the hopeful suitor of the tale with the proper status by recognizing him as his once-stolen son. Quite a deus ex machina! In the *pièces roses* Anouilh seems to say that all is well that ends well. If man wants to be happy, he must accept all the rules of illusion; the best formula for survival may be to choose the rosiness of illusion instead of the blackness of reality.

*Time Remembered,* a *Sleeping Beauty* for grown-ups, is a glorious exercise in fantasy. In this fairy tale it is the girl Amanda, a little milliner portrayed as a variant of the Thérèse character in *Restless Heart,* who brings the prince to life and love after he has lost interest in both because of the death of his beloved diva. Though the theme is uncomplicated, the love story captivates, thanks to Anouilh's gift for characterization and plot construction. The happy ending of the story arises from the complementary attributes of the characters: with good-natured eccentricity the giddy duchess, hoping to create the atmosphere for love, reconstructs on her estate the setting of the prince's memories; at the same time the tenderness and goodwill of the girl interact perfectly with the ethereal romanticism of the prince.

As one considers the surrealistic decor that reproduces the park where Prince Troubiscoi had met the diva, one realizes how much of the freshness of the child remains in Anouilh. The juxtaposition of the ice-cream booth, the sleepy inn awakened by the sound of violins, and the legs hanging out of an old ivy-covered taxi now inhabited by rabbits seems to jumble together a series of adolescent dreams. One can understand why Anouilh's favorite characters remain Antigone, Eurydice, Thérèse—heroines possessing the qualities of children, marching to danger like child crusaders fiercely fighting the evil powers that threaten to tarnish their innocence.

In *Time Remembered,* as in all the *pièces roses,* Anouilh pleads with men to abandon their futile harshness: he shows them how easy it is to have fun and how, with a little laissez-faire, the world becomes a tenable place in which to live.

During the early part of his career, Anouilh alternated between writing *pièces noires* and *pièces roses.* Then, after effecting a kind of personal catharsis through the creation of three *nouvelles pièces noires* in a row, he immersed himself in art for art's sake with the *pièces brillantes,* and in black humor with the *pièces grinçantes.*

The collection of *pièces brillantes,* "brilliant" connoting brio, sophistication, and polish, includes *Ring Round the Moon* (1947), *Colombe* (*Mademoiselle Colombe,* 1951), *La répétition ou l'amour puni* (*The Rehearsal,* 1950), and *Cécile ou l'école des pères* (*Cécile; or, The School for Fathers,* 1954). *Ring Round the Moon* attests to one aspect of Anouilh's virtuosity that could easily occupy an entire article. In this play he accomplishes the feat of lending plausibility to the exits and entrances of identical twins played by the same actor. As a result of this achievement, he succeeds in so evenly distributing the action among the various characters that most of them spend an equal time on the stage. The result is that each character's situation is equally important and one cannot guess the outcome of the action. Here the ending is a happy one, achieved by Anouilh when he combines the themes previously exploited in the *pièces noires,* so that money and love can exist side by side in harmony. A delight for stage directors, *Ring Round the Moon* is the Anouilh work most performed throughout the world in drama schools and by amateur theater groups.

To further exercise his theatrical boldness, Anouilh turned to the eighteenth-century French dramatist Pierre de Marivaux, whose originality in plot construction and minute analysis of budding love is such that hardly any playwright has dared to imitate him. In *The Rehearsal* Anouilh superimposes the technique of the play-within-a-play, as in Luigi Pirandello, on the framework of Marivaux's love comedy *La double inconstance.* He makes the blasé aristocrat and the delicate young teacher who are falling in love rehearse scenes of the Marivaux play, so that it is Marivaux's dialogue that serves to explain their feelings. At the same time he weaves his own version of *La double inconstance* into the original in order to establish a striking contrast between the cruel monsters of cynicism who make their appearance in the *pièces brillantes* and the valiant, innocent young girls found in both his and Marivaux's works as symbols of idealistic love. The play was so unanimously acclaimed in France that it was published in the Classiques Larousse collection as an example of a dazzling replica of Marivaux's comedy.

To top it all, Anouilh tried his hand at a faithful pastiche of another psychological comedy of Marivaux's in *Cécile; or, The School for Fathers.* Called a jewel, this play was performed for the first time at the wedding of Anouilh's eldest daughter, Catherine. It deals with the relationship of a gracious father, as Anouilh was reputed to be, and his young daughter when she falls in love. As in previous *pièces brillantes,* here Anouilh is concerned with mastering yet another aspect of style. The play effortlessly re-creates the accents of the subtle manners and speech of the French classical era.

It is doubtful that these last two works would be enjoyed by a public outside France, for their charm originates in the very special tradition of the French theater in the seventeenth and eighteenth centuries, which even a Frenchman must have studied to appreciate fully.

The key to the cycle of *pièces grinçantes* lies in the scene in *La valse des toréadors* (*The Waltz of the Toreadors,* 1951) during which General Saint-Pé becomes desperate at the thought that life is not at all what he had believed it to be. Perplexed, he turns to the doctor and asks him the meaning of all he has read in books: the grandiose loves, the prodigious revelations, the tender young girls who love men forever, the joy one feels at having at one's side a little "brother in arms" who changes into a lovable woman at night. The doctor answers calmly that these things represent the dreams of authors who must have been poor devils just like the general, and they both agree that such authors should be prevented from spreading false notions of this kind. The fabrications enumerated by the general are obvious references to Anouilh's themes in the *pièces noires.* Anouilh suddenly seems to be turning his back on the idealism expressed in his earlier work.

In the *pièces grinçantes* he no longer divides the world between idealists and realists, but fills it with ludicrous puppets and cynical hypocrites. He once praised Molière for having written the blackest form of theater in a manner that made men laugh at their own misery and hideousness. As the use of the term "grinçantes" shows, Anouilh intended to do something similar in this new collection of plays. The word "grinçantes" implies, first, the interrupted motion of something that hits a snag. As such it can be applied to laughter interrupted by the awareness that one probably should cry. Second, it refers to the unpleasant sound of something that crushes or grinds, thus recalling the sound of things one does not really want to hear. It follows, then, that the laugh Anouilh wishes to extract must be brought about by a special brand of black humor. It is no surprise, therefore, that he introduces his first antihero, General Saint-Pé, in the first two *pièces grinçantes, Ardèle* (1948) and *The Waltz of the Toreadors.* As the first part of the general's name implies, he may wear the halo of the martyr, but as the second part ironically indicates, he will emerge from the plays as unwanted as a putrid bubble of human gas.

Although in *Ardèle* the action does not directly affect the general, it revolves around him. He starts out by leading a sort of burlesque ballet of people pursuing their personal visions of love. What they call love turns out to be an amalgam of infantile sexuality, pathological fixation, and insolent mimicry. For a time he thinks he is conducting a family council, gathered to decide the fate of an aunt who is a hunchback and is in love with another hunchback; in reality he is accepting with a disturbing complacency the monstrous pronouncements of caricatures who indulge in a ludicrous masquerade of love. Unfortunately, he is too flighty to recognize the pathology hidden in their decision that hunchbacks have no right to love, and he chatters away unaware of the urgency of the situation he has created. But Anouilh soon destroys the mood of light banter with a brutal cascade of bullets. The shock of the incident reminds everyone that human souls are at stake, but it is too late. The poor hunchbacks have been left only one escape, suicide. Not one person has really cared about them. The voice of the young man who encouraged his aunt Ardèle to love, despite her relatives' advice, has gone unheard. Only the cackle of the caricatures Anouilh has painted still rings in our ears. He evidently wants to convince us that idealism is destined to be drowned in the empty gibberish of the wicked and the futile. The general is totally inadequate to meet the responsibility he assumes when he locks up his sister, so he lets the hypocrites decide her fate. Thus he is just as guilty as they are of the ugly act that causes the death of the two innocents. And ugly acts have a way of propagating, as Anouilh points out in the last scene: the young children of the household are pretending to "be in love," so they imitate what they have seen their elders do; they fight like cats and dogs. With this conception of love, we can envision that some day they will also decide on someone's right to love. Somehow the scene is so ludicrous that we smile, but from embarrassment, at the mere sight of such illogical behavior. Our smile is "grinçant" (a gnashing of teeth) and cannot last long, for we realize that there is a serious lesson hidden in that spectacle.

*The Waltz of the Toreadors* sketches another episode in the life of General Saint-Pé. As it happens, he does not handle his own affairs any better than those of others. He continues to wait for someone or something, for "the right circumstances" to decide what he must do, for he is confused by the contradictions between what he is told and what he vaguely discovers to be true. But no one shows him the way. He is like Estragon and Vladimir waiting for Godot. He has not understood that man must jump at the slightest opportunity for fulfillment. Since life is a "ball that lasts only one night," he should dance as much as he can "before the colored lights go off." The moral of the play recalls the "Gather ye rosebuds while ye may" theme. But the general may have missed his chance out of fidelity to his wife; the moral may then be, as the doctor tells him, not to try to know "one's enemy, especially if it is a woman." The doctor implies that the general should not have postponed his happiness out of pity for his wife when he fell in love with Ghislaine, for, women being unpredictable, his sacrifice may prove to have been wasted. Although Anouilh exaggerates the play's cynicism for all its shock value, in reality he is asking whether it is worthwhile for the individual to cast aside his own happiness out of consideration for others who are themselves selfish. The general did not run away with Ghislaine the night he met her at the Saumure ball because he thought that his wife was deeply in love with him. Seventeen years later, while he still foolishly cherishes Ghislaine, his wife reveals to him that on that very night she left the ball and slept with a young officer. For having compromised and thought of others before reaching for his own happiness, General Saint-Pé ends up as a downtrodden buffoon who wears a shiny uniform as if he were ready for a gala but has to find pitiful solace in his kitchen maid's skirts. Anouilh has provided the forbidding answer to his own question: at this point in his plays, ethics have disappeared into the realm of dreams.

There is no obvious tie between *Ardèle* and *The Waltz of the Toreadors* other than the reappearance of General Saint-Pé. He emerges from both plays as an especially well-defined antihero who deserves close scrutiny. He represents especially the confused modern individual desperately trying to keep from drowning in the maze of contradictory forces that rule the world. He is made dizzy by the sweep of changing values in modern society, so he waits for a miraculous inspiration to move him in one direction or another. Since none materializes, he freezes into inaction. Face to face with evil, he does not recognize it or does not dare to acknowledge it. He struggles to find an ethic, although he is fallible enough to expect it to be easy to follow. A little cowardly, incredibly patient, he has been put on earth to be a victim, not a victor. He survives by sinking into sexual gratification and by wearing a uniform that becomes a kind of crutch. When he wears the uniform, others think he is strong and brave. He knows that deep inside he is a lonely, frightened man, but appearances are good enough for him. He is Anouilh's image of today's man.

Ornifle, in *Ornifle ou le courant d'air* (Ornifle; or, The Draft, 1955), is not a frightened man. He discovers, as does General Saint-Pé, that there can be no happy medium between honor and happiness. So he opts for happiness and then proceeds to laugh his way through life, often at the expense of those who are foolish enough to be gullible. Why should man, who does not ask to be born, spend his life surpassing himself? Society proves that any sort of self-denial is futile. Those who practice it are shy weaklings who deserve being used, or people who are possessed by an indecent brand of wickedness because they hide behind a mask of morality. So Ornifle will live for pleasure only.

This play succeeds in offering an interesting modern version of Molière's *Don Juan.* But Anouilh's motives when he created it were not entirely those of Molière. Whereas the action remains forbidding in both plays, Anouilh lends a more airy, flippant tone to his hero, the better to allow him to flaunt his views. Furthermore, when Ornifle collapses of a heart attack as he is about to betray another weakling, the suddenness of his death does not imply punishment, as it does in the Molière play, for Anouilh does not show that his death is inflicted by a mystic supernatural power stronger than he, as is the case with Don Juan. In this instance Ornifle falls dead as if struck by lightning; thus Anouilh bestows on him an almost painless death, such as we think only innocent creatures deserve. Anouilh is saying that Ornifle was an innocent creature, for he did not hide his wickedness.

*Ornifle* represented a first shot at a specific target, since Anouilh, who usually alternated writing at least two different types of plays, doggedly pursued his course, and the following year, with *Poor Bitos,* published what appears to be the sequel to *Ornifle.*

In truth, the political events that provoked his anger coincided with the point of development reached in his work that led him to write satires. In the early days of his vocation Anouilh had looked kindly upon idealism in play after play. Then, as years passed and he looked more closely at the world, he discovered after World War II that more often than not, idealism was a subterfuge used to cover the proverbial multitude of sins. He laughed in disenchantment at what might have been considered his naïveté. He was not certain whether it might not be that the world had changed so much that purity could no longer survive in it, so he seemed to ask those who had believed in his beautiful images of purity not to take him too seriously. At times it appeared that those who were pure enough to believe in tales of idealism were victimized either by life or by other men. Anouilh already knew the harsh rules of life; he now started to look at those who exploit men and distinguished two kinds of opportunists: the Don Juan type, who openly join the forces of evil but can be recognized, and the more dangerous variety, who wrap their wickedness in all sorts of beautiful trappings. In *Poor Bitos* the latter are the ones he pursues, while in *Ornifle* he shows how harmless openly wicked individuals actually may be.

After the liberation of France, a political purge took place. The entire odious episode was based on finger-pointing and summary accusations, and sometimes it led to the executions of those who appeared to have collaborated with the Germans. Naturally there were a number of unjust condemnations, and many people were revolted by the situation. Against this background Anouilh, who was already tormented by various forms of rampant hypocrisy and who had never wanted to judge others, wrote his first brilliant satire, *Poor Bitos.*

As might be expected, the play's strong impact derives from Anouilh's daring frankness and the clever device he chooses to denounce the true character of the *Épuration* (the Purge). By allowing the participants in the debate between Bitos and his tormentors to wear the headdresses of French Revolutionary leaders, he makes them express their motives more forcefully, for they can act safely behind what amount to masks. Since Anouilh wants to show the French their unfortunate tendency to repeat mistakes, the parallelism with the Terror initiated by Robespierre during the Revolution serves to concretize and reinforce his theory.

The indictment is a very severe one, for Anouilh lashes out not only at Bitos, the righteous self-appointed "defender of the people," but also at his tormentors. Bitos, the spokesman for those who hunted the "collaborators," turns out to be a narrow-minded little man for whom education is a dangerous thing. He retains only the cold theory of education, and resents those who teach him anything and those who exert any authority over him. He is a demagogue who hates men and who has been biding his time until he could revenge himself upon all those with more talent, more wealth, or more graciousness than he has. Because he has suffered, he has to make others suffer by submitting them to rigid rules that he can justify only in abstract terms. Most scathing of all is the fact that he will come to terms with those whose ideas he despises in order to serve his personal needs. The provocation of Bitos's obnoxious behavior shows Anouilh's irresistible urge to stylize the humiliating image of a man "caught with his pants down"; hence the scene when Bitos splits his pants and has to bend over to have them sewed up while still wearing them.

More repugnant than Bitos himself is the fact that such creatures have been used from time to time in France by government leaders who did not want to do the dirty work themselves but found a way to be accommodating to those who did. One of the characters, Brassac, points this out when he says that in France one can always find a general to sign a decree, and then add a retroactive clause if need be. The satire reaches its height when Anouilh turns the table on the tormentors of Bitos. They are rich bourgeois or aristocrats who think they belong to an elite that can sit in Olympian fashion and laugh at those who at least try to perform some social service; they do not possess courage enough to roll up their sleeves and serve their country. As Deschamps, the only moderate character in the play besides Victoire, gently reminds them, their motives are no more admirable than those of Bitos, for all they do is take from society and never give in return if they can help it.

Strangely enough, many critics reacted to *Poor Bitos* by lamenting that Anouilh hated humanity. But the play is precisely an indictment addressed to those who treat humanity with cold, mechanized methods instead of indulgence, compassion, and love. Anouilh enjoins those who see man as an abstraction to open their eyes and see that men are made of flesh and blood.

When asked in August 1969 what his favorite play was, Anouilh replied that it was *Poor Bitos:* first, because he had created a new character, which is always a "rosy" event in his life, and second, because he had dared to tell the French, at a time when it was unthinkable to do so, the things they needed to hear. What must be added is that satire was his natural medium of expression. The sweep of the discussion in *Poor Bitos* attests to that; so does the fact that in this form of drama his targets have no way of escaping his unrelenting scrutiny. Since he had the eye of Strindberg, the tongue of Shaw, and the aspirations of Molière, it has been hard for him not to choose exclusively to mock men for their weaknesses. There are signs that he may have come to acknowledge his talents in that field, for his widely acclaimed late plays, *Dear Antoine* and *Les poissons rouges ou mon père ce héros* (The Goldfish; or, My Father, That Hero, 1970), are primarily satires.

Anouilh's propensity for lampooning does not mean that he necessarily looks for objects to blame. If possible, he would just as soon encounter moral beauty of the quality seen in *The Lark* or *Becket*. These two *pièces costumées* are his only serious yet optimistic plays. (The third *pièce costumée* is *La foire d'empoigne* [*Catch as Catch Can*, 1962]).

*The Lark* retells the martyrdom of Joan of Arc. In the Anouilh play, however, "The Lark," as he calls Joan of Arc, remains in full control of her trial except in one instance of weakness, from which she quickly recovers. As for Becket, the archbishop of Canterbury, he forces Henry Plantagenet to reckon with the honor of the Church of England and the Saxons. Thus, as is expected of martyrs, both Joan and Becket emerge triumphant in death.

It would seem that at last, in these two plays, Anouilh found the pure idealism that he had searched for in his earlier plays. By contrast with the heroes of the *pièces noires,* the heroine and hero of *The Lark* and *Becket,* respectively, give their lives for a cause that goes beyond the self. They refuse the ways of materialism for definite reasons instead of ambiguous ones, as was the case with Gaston, Thérèse, and Antigone. Jeanne dies to protect the truth and to preserve the honor of the saints whose voices she heard. Becket accepts his own assassination in order to defend the honor of the Church of England, which he undertook to serve.

At the same time these champions of idealism remain human and accessible instead of becoming alienated from humanity, as did the protagonists of the *pièces noires.* Jeanne continues to sympathize with her soldiers and never answers her tormentors angrily. Becket never looks down on the King or speaks scornfully of anyone. As a matter of fact, the validity and the beauty of both plays emanate from the delicate balance that Anouilh establishes in the psychology of all the characters. He goes to great lengths to avoid opposing abstract "types" to his protagonists. In *The Lark,* although both Cauchon and Warwick represent the opposition of materialism to Jeanne's spiritualism, Cauchon conveys the devious thirst for power hidden in some prelates, while Warwick displays the callousness of political expediency. In *Becket* the king is a more defined individual than Créon in *Antigone.* He is coarse, but he admires and understands the value of Becket's subtlety. His ruthlessness does not preclude his continued love for his protégé; he lucidly plans the defeat of Becket but gallantly applauds him when he escapes the traps set for him. The King is a sympathetic mixture of roughness and tenderness.

As a result of this careful characterization, we feel that, although the characters do not share the ideals of their opponents, they still belong to the same "race." There is no need for two groups, the elect and the damned, as there was in the *pièces noires.* The protagonists' plight in the *pièces costumées* seems the more pathetic, since there should be a way for at least the men of the same group to live in harmony.

Although the two plays are similar insofar as meaning is concerned, the resemblance stops there. Each does more than conform to the patterned discussion of idealism that Anouilh started in his early plays. *Becket* unfurls the gripping history of a friendship that was meant to bring each partner lifelong comfort; it is the story of a mutual affection that lasts even through enmity. *The Lark* illustrates Anouilh's image of the lark that still sings in the sky while being shot at. It depicts the combination of strength and vulnerability that characterizes mankind. It is proof of the moral indestructibility of the man or the woman who is truly good.

Both excellent plays in which no aspect of dramatization has been neglected, *The Lark* and *Becket* had long runs on Broadway. The dialogue in each is a masterpiece of nuances. In *Becket* the strong, earthy language of the King and the barons is played against the measured, restrained language that Becket uses to seek understanding. In *The Lark,* Jeanne uses a language that seems rudimentary but that translates her acute common sense in such a way that what she says becomes irrefutable. At the same time Cauchon uses expressions filled with double meaning, while the short exclamations of the *promoteur* betray his lewdness in a hilarious manner. The pageantry one expects in a historical play is smoothly fitted into the plot so that one has the impression of witnessing an authentic yet modernized version of the story. In both plays Anouilh pushes the boldness of staging to the point of representing people on horseback. Finally, to stress the victory of the protagonists and to allow the spectator the satisfaction of a happy ending, he uses the flashback in various ways so that the last scene is one of triumph. The spectator leaves the theater not with the image of Jeanne being burned but with the sight of her radiant as she watches the consecration of the king of France. *Becket* ends not with the assassination of the archbishop but, as it had started, with the flogging of the repentant king in the church. Here the body of the play constitutes the flashback.

After the *pièces costumées* Anouilh concentrated on individual plays, including *La grotte* (*The Cavern*), published in book form in 1961. A clever mystery play of Pirandellian inspiration, supposedly written under the spectator's eyes, it introduces a long-awaited character in Anouilh's theater, "the author," who becomes Antoine de Saint-Flour in *Dear Antoine* and in *Les poissons rouges.*

In 1962 a one-act "concert play," *L'Orchestre,* appeared in *L'Avant-scène,* a literary journal. The same year Anouilh unknowingly took a major step in his development when he reproduced *Victor; ou, Les enfants au pouvoir* (Victor; or, The Children in Power),written by a longtime friend, the late Roger Vitrac. In this surrealistic play he found a technique that answered his own yearning to stylize the flow of human consciousness for the theater. Directed for the first time in 1928 by Antonin Artaud at the Théâtre Alfred Jarry, this work had been very poorly received by public and critics alike. When Anouilh saw *Victor* produced by the Michel de Ré Company in 1947, he was so impressed by it that, as he admitted, he slightly plagiarized it in *Ardèle.* His own production of *Victor* fifteen years later won wide acclaim. A subtly poetic "bourgeois drama," this play deals with Anouilh's favorite topic, the family circle; the plot focuses on the cruel fate of a child who suddenly realizes the true nature of the adult world and who accepts, along with this knowledge, his symbolic death. Anouilh was ready to investigate this particular subject; but, more important than its thematic value, *Victor* offered him an example of dialogue that follows the capricious meanderings of the consciousness of some of the characters.

*Le boulanger, la boulangère et le petit mitron* (The Baker, His Wife, and His Little Apprentice, 1969), the first play written by Anouilh in the six years following his production of *Victor,* shows the repercussions of his faithful efforts to vindicate Vitrac. In it a child becomes the central character and the play develops according to all the swirls and eddies of the stream of consciousness.

As far as children are concerned, Anouilh became preoccupied with their condition in the so-called family bosom quite early in his vocation, with *Humulus the Mute* and *Traveler Without Luggage.* Later he concentrated his attentions on adults. But after his exposure to *Victor,* he again gave a larger share of the limelight to children, reserving special treatment for the small boy Toto. In *Ardèle,* Toto is encountered as the child whose presence is overlooked by the family plunged into its petty problems. With Anouilh's delighted approval he unconsciously gets even with his family by mimicking its grotesque behavior at the most crucial moment. In *L'Hurluberlu* (*The Fighting Cock,* 1959), Toto becomes an incarnation of General Saint-Pé's childhood. When the general encourages him to eat a dose of magic "mininistafia," he is addressing not only his little boy but also the alter ego of his own youth, the vestiges of which are still visible in himself. In *Les poissons rouges* Toto attains a more complex status. He brings consolation to his father, the playwright Antoine de Saint-Flour; and to the extent that Anouilh can be identified with Antoine de Saint-Flour, one wonders how much of Toto is still a part of Anouilh.

In *Le boulanger, la boulangère et le petit mitron,* Toto represents all children. Writing this tragicomic bedroom farce in the aftermath of the "May events" (the student revolt in Paris of May 1968), Anouilh doggedly insists on showing the origins of the social troubles involving young people: in his view children are abandoned and lost in the average family, where Papa takes refuge from his wife and his boss in dreams of power and feminine conquests, while Maman either flies into dreams of passionate love or complains because she is not living in the grand style she feels she deserves. If the wife in this play is to be believed, had she married one of the glamorous suitors who lined up at her door before she condescended to marry her husband, she would have lived like a queen.

In a preface written in defense of young people, Anouilh points out that although children are neglected within their families, they must be psychoanalyzed and submitted to bewildering tests when they dare to revolt and ask for their rights in a society hopelessly oblivious to their existence and needs and primarily concerned with the rights of adults. The French public did not take too kindly to Anouilh's position and soon refrained from seeing the play, although it was hailed as a triumphant comeback on Anouilh's part.

The value of *Le boulanger, la boulangère et le petit mitron* lies especially in its surrealistic structure. Anouilh would object to the use of the term "surrealistic," for when he commented on Vitrac's *Victor* he purposely avoided it; he considered surrealism in the theater an evolution of the desire to represent the flow of consciousness, which, as he declared in an interview, was started by Aeschylus and was continued by Corneille, Shakespeare, and Pirandello. It is not surprising that Anouilh tried his hand at surrealism, for he steadily tore down the barriers between illusion and reality. In this play the dialogue exchanged on a conscious level by the protagonists matters little compared with the dialogue they use when they engage in their daydreaming, for it is then that their motives and their foolishness come to the fore, providing an explanation of their unreasonable behavior. Toto's dilemma also draws its emphasis from the impeccably timed intrusions of his daydreams into his parents' flight into fantasy. Peopled with storybook Indians and poetic historical figures, such as Louis XVI, Marie Antoinette, and their children facing danger as a family, Toto's dreams help us to measure the void in which he grows up. Though he should find warmth in the family nest, he must instead seek solace from his parents' bewildering quarrels in his books. And while he needs guidance and encouragement in the arduous process of getting an education, he must study his history lesson in utter loneliness, drawing conclusions as best he can.

Modern society has ceased to produce truly mature adults, and the children's problems stem from that fact, says Anouilh. It is significant that in his portrayal of the infantilism of present-day adults, some of the father's flights into illusion originate in the little boy's questions about American Indians (who still belong to the realm of fiction for the French). The father thus proves he stands just a step removed from the world of make-believe that his child lives in.

Begun as a bedroom farce, the play becomes a voyage into the inextricable mixture of reality and dream in which the characters are immersed, and it ends with Toto's nightmare about his parents being killed by Indians. Such an end is particularly effective, for within the play it serves to explain how Toto finds release from the mental torture caused by his parents' incessant arguments; outside of the play it satisfies somewhat the spectator's need to see the parents punished for their incorrigible thoughtlessness. Nevertheless, when the lieutenant kindly takes Toto under his protection and asks forgiveness for the parents, who have simply behaved like fallible human beings, the play closes on a compassionate note.

It was inevitable that Anouilh, indefatigable observer of men, would reach a point where he could not remain impassive at the sight of the excesses they commit, and would create a sort of spokesman. He did so in *Dear Antoine,* his first play of the 1969–1970 season, in which he introduced the playwright Antoine de Saint-Flour. After obtaining rave reviews for this play, Anouilh daringly presented a second play that season, *Les poissons rouges,* in which the same protagonist, seen at an earlier time, takes stock of himself. As he searches his past and present, he discovers that although he has tried to be a compassionate, fairly honorable human being, he is held responsible for every possible ill by the people around him. At home his wife nags him, his mother-in-law remains unconcerned at his being abused, his fifteen-year-old daughter declares she became pregnant out of wedlock so that she could leave home. In the outside world a childhood friend, who is a worker's son and whom he treats with unusual forbearance, insults him, morning, noon, and night, as if he had caused all the social ills the proletariat suffers from. Even his mistress is afflicted with a suicidal obsession and complicates his life no end. Plagued by all this, Antoine comes to feel at times that he should walk like a hunchback or even limp, in order to placate hunchbacks like his doctor (a frustrated literary critic), who chastises him for being healthy.

Permeated with the good-natured reactions of Antoine, opposed to the sourness and self-righteousness of others, the play greatly amuses by its wealth of impish repartee. In the exchange lies many a truth about the privileged and the not so privileged of our society. "Refreshing" is the epithet critics have used to describe this comedy, both *rose* and *noire.* Actually, Anouilh was never anything else.

## Selected Bibliography


### EDITIONS

#### COLLECTED PLAYS

*Pièces noires.* Paris, 1945, 1958 (*L'Hermine, La sauvage, Le voyageur sans bagage, Eurydice*).

*Nouvelles pièces noires.* Paris, 1946, 1958 (*Jézabel, Antigone, Roméo et Jeannette, Médée*).

*Pièces grinçantes.* Paris, 1956 (*Ardèle ou la marguerite, La valse des toréadors, Ornifle ou le courant d'air, Pauvre Bitos ou le dîner de têtes*).

*Pièces roses.* Paris, 1958 (*Humulus le muet, Le bal des voleurs, Le rendez-vous de Senlis, Léocadia*).

*Pièces brillantes.* Paris, 1960 (*L'Invitation au château, Colombe, La répétition ou l'amour puni, Cécile ou l'école des pères*).

*Pièces costumées.* Paris, 1960 (*L'Alouette, Becket ou l'honneur de Dieu, La foire d'empoigne*).

*Nouvelles pièces grinçantes.* Paris, 1970 (*L'Hurluberlu, La grotte, L'Orchestre, Le boulanger, la boulangère et le petit mitron, Poissons rouges*).

*Pieces baroques.* Paris, 1974 (*Cher Antoine, Ne reveillez pas Madame, Le directeur de l'opera*).

*Pièces farceuses.* Paris, 1984 (*Chers zoiseaux, La culotte, Episode de la vie d'un amateur, Le nombril*).

#### INDIVIDUAL PLAYS

*La petite Molière.* In *L'Avant-scene,* no. 210 (15 December 1959).

*L'Hurluberlu ou le réactionnaire amoureux.* Paris, 1959.

*La grotte.* Paris, 1961.

*Le boulanger, la boulangère et le petit mitron.* Paris, 1969.

*Cher Antoine ou l'amour raté.* Paris, 1969.

*Les poissons rouges ou mon père ce héros.* Paris, 1970.

*L'Orchestre.* In *Monsieur Barnett suivi de L'Orchestre.* Paris, 1975.

## TRANSLATIONS

### COLLECTED PLAYS

*Plays.* 4 vols. New York, 1958–1987. Vol. 1: *Antigone, Eurydice, The Ermine, The Rehearsal, Romeo and Jeannette.* Vol. 2: *Restless Heart, Time Remembered, Ardèle, Mademoiselle Colombe, The Lark.* Vol. 3: *Thieves' Carnival, Medea, Cecile, Traveler Without Luggage, The Orchestra, Episode in the Life of an Author, Catch as Catch Can.* Vol. 4: *Leocadia, Antigone, Waltz of the Toreadors, The Lark, Poor Bitos.*

*Collected Plays.* 2 vols. London, 1966–1967.

### INDIVIDUAL PLAYS

*Becket; or, The Honor of God.* Translated by Lucienne Hill. New York, 1960.

*The Cavern.* Translated by Lucienne Hill. New York, 1966.

*The Fighting Cock.* Adapted by Lucienne Hill. New York, 1960.

*Poor Bitos.* Translated by Lucienne Hill. New York and London, 1964.

*Ring Round the Moon.* Translated by Christopher Fry. New York, 1950; London, 1956.

*Thieves' Carnival.* Translated by Lucienne Hill. London, 1952.

*Traveller Without Luggage.* Translated by John Whiting. London, 1959.

*The Waltz of the Toreadors.* Translated by Lucienne Hill. New York, 1958.

## BIOGRAPHICAL AND CRITICAL STUDIES

An extensive bibliography of books and articles on Anouilh and his work is available in *French VII, Bibliography of Critical and Biographical References for the Study of Contemporary French Literature.* New York, 1949–. In 1969 the title was changed to *French XX, Bibliography: Critical and Biographical References for the Study of French Literature Since 1885.*

Borgal, Clément. *Anouilh: La peine de vivre.* Paris, 1966.

Comminges, Élie de. *Anouilh: Littérature et politique.* Paris, 1977.

Della Fazia, Alba Marie. *Jean Anouilh.* New York, 1969.

Didier, Jean. *À la rencontre de Jean Anouilh.* Liège, 1946.

Falb, Lewis W. *Jean Anouilh.* New York, 1977.

Gignoux, Hubert. *Jean Anouilh.* Paris, 1946.

Kelly, Kathleen White. *Jean Anouilh: An Annotated Bibliography.* Metuchen, N.J., 1973.

Lassale, Jean-Pierre. *Jean Anouilh, ou La vaine revolté.* Rodez, France, 1958.

Lenski, B. A. *Jean Anouilh: Stages in Rebellion.* Atlantic Highlands, N.J., 1975.

McIntyre, H. G. *The Theatre of Jean Anouilh.* Totowa, N.J., 1981.

Marcel, Gabriel. *L'Heure théâtrale de Giraudoux à Jean-Paul Sartre.* Paris, 1959.

Marsh, Edwin O. *Jean Anouilh: Poet of Pierrot and Pantaloon.* London, 1953; repr., New York, 1968.

Pronko, Leonard C. *The World of Jean Anouilh.* Berkeley and Los Angeles, 1961.

## INTERVIEWS

Ambrière, Francis. "Le secret de Jean Anouilh." *Les Annales* 15:45 (January 1952).

Archer, Marguerite. Paris, 25 August 1962, and Arcachon, 3 August 1969. Also present at the second interview was Roland Piétri, Anouilh's longtime codirector.

Delavèze, Jean. "Pour la première fois Jean Anouilh parle. . . . " *Les Nouvelles Littéraires,* 5 February 1959, pp. 1, 9.

Farrell, Isolde. "Anouilh Returns." *New York Times,* 3 January 1954, sec. 2, p. 3.

MARGUERITE ARCHER

# SAINT THOMAS AQUINAS AND SCHOLASTICISM

## (ca. 1224–1274)

THE ELEVENTH AND twelfth centuries in Europe were an age of intellectual reawakening that was reflected above all in the scholastic movement. Scholasticism's chief feature was the stress placed on human reasoning, and more especially on dialectic, in the interpretation of sacred and secular knowledge. Although no orthodox thinker would then or later have challenged the basic assumptions of the Christian faith, upon which rational investigation itself had to be based, rational inquiry into matters of faith was henceforth to become an indispensable element in the elucidation of Christian belief. The study of dialectic was to impose upon the student certain rules of logical inquiry drawn from the works of Aristotle then available (such as the *Categories* and *Posterior Analytics*), the *Isagoge* of Porphyry, and the *Commentaries* of Boethius. The study of dialectic also involved the classification of concepts, and the application of logical and metaphysical criteria to judge whether such concepts were true or false. Thus, while faith was to continue to guide reasoning, reason and dialectic became an integral part of the approach to an understanding of the truths of revelation. The nature of the relationship between faith and reason constituted the heart of the scholastic movement, which was to reach its peak in the thirteenth century. Its greatest exponent, the scholar who was to create a majestic synthesis of faith and reason, was Thomas Aquinas.

The groundwork of the scholastic movement had, however, been laid in earlier centuries. Its theoretical basis had been provided by Saint Augustine (A.D. 354–430) and by Boethius (*ca.* 480–524). Augustine had stressed the need for dialectic in his *De doctrina Christiana* (*On Christian Doctrine*) and in his *De praedestinatione sanctorum (On the Predestination of Saints)*. "Understand," he had written, "so that you may believe. Believe so that you may understand." By his translations of, and commentaries on, Aristotle and Porphyry, Boethius provided the basic material that enabled later medieval thinkers to develop their own views on logic; in his *Opuscula sacra (Sacred Studies)* he indicated that philosophy and theology were interrelated subjects, a notion that Cassiodorus (485–580) followed up in his *Institutiones divinarum et humanarum litterarum (Instruction in Divine and Human Letters)*, in which he described the seven liberal arts as the foundation of all secular and sacred learning. Some such features appeared in the Carolingian Renaissance of the ninth century; one of its outstanding scholars, John Scotus Erigena (810–877), distinguished between *auctoritas* (holy scripture) and *ratio* (reason) in accordance with Saint Augustine's dictum. While Scripture was still the principal fount of human knowledge of God, reason, he argued, could be used to investigate and to expand the truths revealed by scripture.

Scholastic thought had its pioneers in the late tenth and early eleventh centuries, among them the scholar Gerbert of Auxerre (later Pope Sylvester II). It owed much to the setting up of cathedral schools, especially the one established at Chartres by Gerbert's pupil Fulbert in 990. Through such schools a new approach to learning, in which dialectic played an increasingly prominent part, was gradually disseminated. Masters such as Lanfranc of Bec (later archbishop of Canterbury), Alger of Liège, and other scholars agreed that dialectic could be used in theological disputations without peril to revealed truth. But the stress on the use of dialectic as a means of interpreting the truths of theology was resented by more orthodox theologians, who claimed that truths about God and matters of faith lay outside the reckoning of the human mind and were not capable of being effectively subsumed by human reason. The conflict between basic conservatism and incipient radicalism was well demonstrated in the mid-twelfth century by the stormy debate between the mystic and monk Saint Bernard of Clairvaux (1096–1153) and the logician Peter Abélard (1079–1142), one of the most brilliant minds of the period.

In practice, an intellectual middle way that was to condition future academic thinking came into operation. Dialectic was to become more and more an indispensable tool in the interpretation of faith. The scholar and monk Anselm (1033–1109), who became archbishop of Canterbury in 1093, declared that reason could be properly used to inquire into and explain revealed truth, since it was a Christian duty to make sure that we understand what we believe. His guiding principle was summed up in the words *credo ut intelligam*, "I believe that I may understand," a concept that every future schoolman accepted as the basis of his thought. Faith sought understanding *(fides quaerens intellectum)*. Yet while logical inquiry was henceforth to form an essential ingredient in the understanding of faith, it was still of secondary importance to faith. Anselm and his immediate followers were intellectual traditionalists principally indebted to Saint Augustine, whose ideas underlay all their writings.

Like Augustine, Anselm insisted on the primacy of faith; reason was a tool that enabled the believer to understand his faith better. For both Anselm and Augustine, eternal ideas originating in the mind of God (a concept that could be traced back to the writings of the Greek philosopher Plato) were the source from which all knowledge was derived, so testifying to the existence of God himself as the divine source of such ideas. Nonetheless, by applying dialectic to the preconceived ideas of faith, Anselm had broken new ground. Anselm's ideas were to be developed in the twelfth century in the school of Anselm of Laon (*d.* 1117) and of his brother, Ralph. In the *Sentences* (a title given to many manuals of medieval theology) ascribed to the school of Laon, topics were, for instance, arranged under systematic theological headings. So while the authority of Scripture remained predominant, the argument from reason had its integral place.

A further milestone in the development of the methodology of scholasticism was reached in the writings and teaching of Peter Abélard. In the course of a stormy career, this French dialectician greatly extended the use of logic. Although not a great original thinker, he had a crisp, critical mind that he applied to explain the meaning of words and the understanding of concepts. This appeared most forcibly in his book *Sic et non (Yes and No)*, a work in which he sought to reconcile conflicting theological views by the application of dialectic based on questioning *(quaestio)*, inquiry *(interrogatio)*, and the resolution of what was at dispute *(disputatio)*. His aim was thus to reach a satisfactory solution to theological and philosophical problems by a process of rational inquiry. "By doubting," as he wrote in the preface to *Sic et Non*, "we come to inquiry; by inquiring we are led to the truth." In his approach, Abélard certainly claimed more for dialectic than most previous thinkers. He established, though not without bitter criticism from more conservative theologians, some sort of scientific basis for the exposition of theology. His method of approach formed the foundation for the scholastic system of the thirteenth and fourteenth centuries.

This method appeared in one of the most influential books of the Middle Ages, the *Sententiae in IV libris distinctae* (*The Four Books of the Sentences*) by Peter Lombard, who became bishop of Paris in 1159. The four books, which deal with God, Creation, the Incarnation and Redemption, and the sacraments of the church, are in format composed of a systematic collection of questions, drawn in the main from the Bible and the Fathers, most notably Saint Augustine. Each question consists of differing propositions *(pro et contra)* based on different authorities. Dialectic was to be used to help resolve the problem. Whereas most previous books had been monographs that treated of particular subjects, Lombard's *Sentences* is an attempt at a systematic and comprehensive survey of the whole field of Christian doctrine. Lombard declared that his main purpose was to present the faith "in a small volume consisting of patristic views [*Patrum sententiae*] together with their testimony, so that the inquirer will not have to search through numerous tomes, for the synthesized brevity which he seeks is offered here without much labor." Although Lombard's position was philosophically moderate, he was strongly criticized together with the more radical thinkers Abélard, Gilbert of Poitiers (1076–1154), and Peter of Poitiers, especially by Walter of Saint Victor (*d. ca.* 1180). But by the early thirteenth century,the *Sentences* had become an established textbook.

A further important development took place in the late twelfth and early thirteenth centuries that was to be of magisterial significance in the intellectual history of the age: the rediscovery and reexamination of the lost works of the Greek philosopher Aristotle. Apart from a limited number of books, already widely read, Aristotle's works had been long lost to the Western world, but they had been preserved by Jewish and Arabic scholars. In their turn, they had written learned commentaries and in some respects changed or modified the original ideas put forward by Aristotle. The Western intellectual world was therefore to receive not an undiluted Aristotelianism but an Aristotelianism diluted by Islamic and Jewish thought. The leading writers—the Muslims Avicebron (*ca.* 1020–1070), Avicenna (980–1037), and Averroës (1126–1178), and the Jew Moses Maimonides (1135–1204), did more than act as mere vehicles for the transmission of Aristotle's ideas. In their studies they had to relate his concepts to their own religious faiths. Thus, what was received was not a pure Aristotelianism, but an Aristotelianism interlaced with Neoplatonic ideas and taken in the main from Plotinus' *Enneads* and Proclus' *Elements of Theology*, and related to the basic religious teachings of Islam and Judaism. Nor, of course, were such writings in any sense homogeneous.

Of these writers, it was Averroës, a Spanish Muslim, who made the greatest impact on Western thought. Like Aquinas later, he sought to define the limitations of faith and reason, but, unlike him, he did not seek to reconcile or harmonize the two spheres of thought. Averroës also largely deleted from Avicenna's philosophy much of its Neoplatonic content; his philosophy was closer to that of Aristotle than that of his forebears. Like Aquinas, he sought to define existence in terms of being (rather than, as in Avicenna's case, in terms of essence). He posited the individuality of substances, affirming that being could not exist apart from individual things. For him, God was an unmoved mover, the being from whom all existence came, as well as its final cause.

The legacy of Arabic and Arabic-Jewish philosophy was a pertinent ingredient in the development of Western scholastic thought. But it had a negative as well as a positive side. Positively, it underlined the importance of delineating the separate spheres of reason and faith. It strengthened the theistic concept. Through the articulation of metaphysical categories, it differentiated God's existence from that of his creatures. Negatively, it undermined orthodox Christian conceptions, intimating that God was an impersonal rather than a personal being. It stressed doctrines of determination and necessity. It denied the possibility of creation *ex nihilo* (out of nothing) and asserted the eternity of the world. It had little or no place for revelation and tended to deny the immortality of the soul. The reception of neo-Aristotelianism was thus both an illumination and a challenge. If the ideas that it embodied could assist in the understanding and interpretation of Christian theology, in some sense they also imperiled orthodox and traditional teaching. Although there was much that could be assimilated into Christian culture, there was obviously much that challenged the tenets of faith and queried the truths based on revelation.

The reception of these Aristotelian texts was a slow process. The first translations had been made into Latin in the early twelfth century by Constantine the African and Adelard of Bath; the principal location for such transmission was Toledo in Spain, where in about 1150 Archbishop Raymond of Toledo sponsored a school for translations that spread slowly into the West. In the first instance such translation bore the imprint of the teaching of Avicenna with a strong Neoplatonic influence, rather than that of Averroës. The introduction of Averroism owed much to the scholar Michael Scot (1180–1235), who worked in Sicily as well as Spain. Hermann the German also translated the works of Averroës, as well as Aristotle's *Nicomachean Ethics, Rhetoric,* and *Poetics,* between 1240 and 1256. The Englishman Robert Grosseteste, who was bishop of Lincoln from 1235 to 1253, translated, or revised previous translations of, the *Ethics* between 1240 and 1245; Alfred Sareshal translated the *De anima (On the Soul)* and other works. But the most important figure was William of Moerbeke (1215–1286), a Flemish Dominican who was made archbishop of Corinth in 1277. William was a friend and collaborator of Aquinas, supplying him with translations directly taken from the Greek text. He was the first scholar to translate Aristotle's *Politics* (1260) and his *Economics* (1267). He also retranslated and revised most of Aristotle's other works, thus providing Aquinas and other Western scholars with safe and accurate texts.

William of Moerbeke's work was comparatively late; many of Aristotle's works, in addition to the commentaries of the Arabic and Jewish philosophers, had become known to the Western world by the first decades of the thirteenth century. As they were disseminated in centers of learning, the works created an intellectual revolution, the more significant since it coincided with the foundation and growth of universities, of which the one in Paris was far and away the most influential. Conservative scholars regarded the intrusion of ideas drawn from pagan and infidel sources, many of which appeared to conflict with Christian orthodoxy, with suspicion and hostility. In 1210 the provincial synod of Sens forbade the reading of Aristotle's works on natural philosophy, a ban that was incorporated into the statutes for the university at Paris promulgated by the papal legate Robert of Courçon in 1215. The official attitude of the Roman Catholic church was made plain in a further condemnation of Aristotle's scientific works, by Pope Gregory IX in 1231 with reference to the university at Paris, by Pope Innocent IV in 1245 with reference to the university at Toulouse, and again by Pope Urban IV in 1263; the process culminated in the condemnation of Aristotle and his Averroist interpreters in 1277.

But the church's attempt to stem the rising influence of Aristotle proved unavailing, even on its most highly reputed teachers. Scholars were too impressed by the intellectual cogency of the new ideas to discard them willingly. In the curriculum of the universities, logic and dialectic had already taken their nearly exclusive part as the basis of the faculties of arts. It was, however, undeniable that Aristotelianism, especially in its Averroistic guise, contained much that was unacceptable to Christian theologians. The problem of accommodating Aristotelianism to Christian teaching remained. Indeed, the principal intellectual question confronting the thirteenth-century theologian lay precisely in the need to create a synthesis that could accommodate the non-Christian system of Aristotle within the framework of an authentically Christian philosophy.

All theologians and philosophers were by then to a greater or lesser extent influenced by the Aristotelian revolution. The more conservative response was provided by the so-called Augustinians. They studied, and even to some extent accepted, the writings of Aristotle and his commentators, but they were concerned to place them firmly within the traditional framework of Christian theology and to reconcile them with the predominantly Christian teachings of Saint Augustine. Such, for instance, was the teaching put forward by William of Auvergne (1180–1249), bishop of Paris from 1228. William took note of, but reacted unfavorably to, the ideas of Aristotle and Avicenna, reverting to the belief, ultimately Platonic, that the knowledge of forms came from a special illumination planted in the soul by God and known only through the gift of grace implanted by him. Similar was the standpoint of the English scholar Robert Grosseteste, one of the few who knew any Greek, whose influence was more especially prominent in the recently founded university at Oxford, where he had taught. All knowledge, Grosseteste argued, originated as reason in the divine intellect and is known to us by the forms of things.

The Augustinians were not a single school, but they were held together by their belief in the principle of divine illumination and by the fact that, while they utilized dialectic and the new learning, they rejected it where it could not be brought into harmony with traditional theology. Above all, they insisted on the primacy of faith, the inseparability of truth from revelation, and the necessity of grace for its comprehension. They held, unlike most of the Arabic thinkers, that such comprehension was a direct gift of God, dependent more on the inclination of the soul, injected with divine illumination, than on intellectual compulsion. As a corollary, they insisted on the plurality of forms, holding that all things existed by virtue of the forms that subsisted in them, which themselves originated in God.

The clearest expression of Augustinianism was to be found in the teaching of the Franciscan school at Paris, of which the most distinguished exponents were Alexander of Hales (1170–1245) and Saint Bonaventura (1221–1274). Bonaventura, who was appointed by the pope to the Franciscan chair of theology at Paris in 1253, wrote his major work, the *Commentary on the "Sentences,"* at the age of thirty, in 1251. The book shows that he was well acquainted with Aristotelian ideas, but Bonaventura stresses strongly the primacy of faith, arguing that all knowledge depends upon revealed truth, made comprehensible through the divine gift of grace. Bonaventura's teaching, strongly tinged with mysticism, marked the high point of thirteenth-century Augustinianism, welding its various strands into a coherent whole.

If the Augustinians represented, as it were, the right wing of the scholastic movement, the Latin Averroists formed the scholastic left.

The term "Averroist" is itself misleading if it is taken to suggest that these scholars were simply disciples of Averroës. The Averroists owed much to other Arab commentators, but they had a common ground in Aristotelian philosophy, which they accepted far more fully than their critics, especially in respect of its more deterministic tenets. They followed Averroës in supposing that faith and reason formed two separate spheres that could not be reconciled or unified. For the church, the Averroists' teaching, of which Siger of Brabant and Boethius of Dacia were the leading exponents, constituted a challenge, since it could very well generate heterodoxy and heresy. As a result, they were to experience a series of official condemnations of which the first occurred in 1270.

It is against this background that the life and work of Thomas Aquinas has to be set. He was neither an Augustinian nor an Averroist, neither a conservative nor a radical; he was a profound scholar and thinker who sought to reconcile the truths of revealed religion with the faculty of human reason. His philosophy took shape under the influence of the recently rediscovered metaphysical writings of Aristotle. Yet he was never a rigid Aristotelian. While he was criticized in his own day and by later philosophers, no theologian ever created so masterly a synthesis, embodying but distinguishing between faith and reason, nor exerted such immense influence over Christian thought. In the history of scholasticism Aquinas is the preeminent figure.

Aquinas' life was comparatively uneventful. He was born, probably in 1224 or 1225, at the castle of Roccasecca, near Aquino in the Roman Campagna, in the vicinity of Naples in the kingdom of Sicily. His father, Landulf, a knight, was a member of the lower nobility and had married as his second wife a Neapolitan of noble birth, Theodora, originally of Norman stock. There were four sons of this second marriage, of whom Thomas was the youngest, and four or five daughters. Thomas, the seventh child in the family, was educated from the age of five to thirteen at the Benedictine abbey of Monte Cassino; he was brought up there as an oblate, instructed in the spiritual life as well as given an elementary grounding in grammar. In 1239 the abbey, caught up in the strife between the pope and the emperor Frederick II, was occupied for a time by imperial troops. Thomas returned to his father's house, and he was then sent to the *studium generale,* or university college (founded by Frederick II in 1224) at Naples. There he studied philosophy, including the natural philosophy of Aristotle, probably under the direction of Peter of Hibernia, as well as the liberal arts. It was at Naples that he became acquainted with the Dominican friars. Attracted by their life of evangelical poverty and the emphasis they placed on the "assiduous study of divine truth," he decided, in the spring of 1244, to seek membership in the order. "The highest place," he was to write later, "among religious orders is held by those which are ordained to teaching and preaching, which functions belong to and participate in the perfection of bishops."

Aquinas' decision created a crisis in his life. His brothers—his father had died the previous year—were greatly alarmed by the move, for while they were not opposed to a religious vocation, they disapproved of Thomas' becoming a mendicant friar. Thomas left Naples for Rome in May 1244, in the company of the Dominican master general John of Wildershausen, probably with the intention of studying in Paris. In the course of the journey he was abducted by a company of the emperor's soldiers, led by his brother Reginaldo, and was taken to the castle of Montesangiovanni en route to his mother's home at Roccasecca. Kept under some form of surveillance until the summer of 1245, he may well have composed there the short treatise on Aristotle's *De fallaciis (On Fallacies),* though some critics believe it to be much later in date, together with the *De propositionalibus modalibus (On Modal Propositions),* a fragment of 114 lines that is little more than a youthful student exercise. The *De fallaciis,* a work of some eighteen chapters discussing fourteen types of syllogistic error that may occur in a scholastic disputation, is dedicated to "certain nobles in arts," possibly his fellow students at Naples. Eventually, his brothers gave up the attempt to dissuade him from becoming a friar, and in practice his relations with his family (Reginaldo was executed in 1246 for involvement in an unsuccessful plot against the emperor) appear to have remained affectionate.

In the summer of 1245 he returned to Naples, probably in the company of his fellow Dominican John of San Giuliano, but he soon moved to Paris, where he spent three years studying for the novitiate at the priory of Saint Jacques. Whether he then actually studied under the German scholastic Albertus Magnus (1200–1280), who was teaching in Paris, is a moot point. If he did so, Thomas would have heard him lecturing on the Bible and disputing in theology. Albert had just begun to compose his encyclopedic work on Aristotelian learning in an endeavor to make Aristotle's works on the natural sciences "intelligible to the Latins," a project that was to occupy him for the next two decades. There is, however, no doubt that in 1248 Aquinas accompanied Albert to Cologne, where Albert was to organize a new Dominican *studium generale* that the general chapter of the order had commissioned the previous June. He was with Albert in Cologne for the next four years.

Albert was probably the most influential of Aquinas' teachers. A Swabian by birth, he was at Paris from 1240 to 1248, graduating with a degree in theology in 1245 under Guéric of Saint-Quentin and lecturing as the professor holding the Dominican chair for "foreigners" until 1248. The Dominicans had two chairs of theology at the university. One was filled by members from the French province of the Dominican order, the other from all the other Dominican provinces outside France. Above all, Albert was a magisterial compiler and mediator, concerned with communicating Aristotelian thought to the Christian world. In his approach he was eclectic, still retaining many Platonic strands in his thought. He wrote commentaries upon and edited many of Aristotle's works, providing Aquinas as well as others of his pupils with a storehouse of learning. His philosophical gifts were limited. His thought could be confused and unsystematic, but he had an exceptionally wide range of knowledge that earned him the title among his contemporaries of *Doctor universalis* (the universal doctor) and *Doctor expertus* (the skilled doctor). His importance and originality arose in part from his unusual interest in nature and natural phenomena; he was a keen observer and experimentalist. He was also the first Western Christian writer to distinguish clearly between faith and reason, a distinction that Aquinas was to follow. Aquinas was, however, to surpass him not simply in his grasp of philosophy but in the clarity and systematization of his thought. Albert's *Summa,* voluminous as it was, should not be seen as the effective precursor of Aquinas' greater work of the same title.

Nevertheless, Aquinas' stay with Albert in Cologne was of seminal importance. William of Tocco wrote that Aquinas "had no sooner heard [Albert] expound every science with such wondrous depth of wisdom, than he rejoiced exceedingly at having so quickly found that which he had come to seek, one who offered him so unsparingly the fulfillment of his heart's desire." At Cologne he may have written three biblical commentaries, on Jeremiah, the Lamentations of Jeremiah, and some chapters of Isaiah. He was ordained a priest at Cologne sometime between 1250 and 1251. Impressed by his taciturnity and assiduity in study and prayer, his Dominican brethren there nicknamed him "the dumb ox" *(bovem mutum),* a phrase that also indicates his bulky physique. "We call him the dumb ox," Albert is supposed to have said after hearing Aquinas respond in a scholastic disputation, "but the bellowing of that ox will resound throughout the whole world." In 1252, on Albert's recommendation, he was sent to Paris to study for the mastership of theology. He was two years below the required age to lecture on the *Sentences* of Peter Lombard, but a dispensation was procured for him through the good offices of the Dominican cardinal Hugh of Saint Cher, a former master of Paris and then papal legate in Germany.

Aquinas' years at Paris, where he graduated as a master of theology in 1256, proved to be exceptionally prolific ones. When he came to Paris, he had to study under a master, to lecture on the *Sentences* from two to four years, and to respond to objections in certain theological disputations. He relied heavily on the lectures of Albert, but he showed a clarity of thought and a directness of approach that were to become familiar characteristics of his other writings. Bernard Gui wrote:

> God graced his teaching so abundantly, that it began to make a wonderful impression on the students. For it all seemed so novel—new arrangements of subject matter, new methods of proofs, new arguments adduced for the conclusions; in short, no one who heard him could doubt that his mind was full of a new light from God.
>
> *(The Life of Thomas Aquinas,* Kenelm Foster ed., p. 33)

In lecturing, as he did later in writing, Aquinas followed the contemporary procedure: reading a passage from the text aloud, analyzing it through a *divisio textus* (a division of the text), briefly explaining the meaning of each point made, and then analyzing the questions arising from the text. The *quaestio* (question), subdivided into articles and *quaestiunculae* (lesser questions), was at the heart of the scholastic method of teaching.

In his lectures, known as the *Scriptum super Sententias (Commentaries on the Sentences),* his first major work, Aquinas divided Peter Lombard's four books into two groups. He discusses those subjects that deal with the *exitus,* or derivation, of all things from God and their ultimate *reditus,* or return, to God, thus emphasizing the flow of all things from God's creative activity, which was always to form the basic thread in his thought. In his consideration of the first question, he affirms that God is most properly described as the "to be," the *esse*—"He Who is" *(qui est)*—making a distinction between *esse* (being, i.e., God) and his dependent creatures, *quod est* (what is), and their identity in God. This distinction reappears throughout his arguments in the *Summa theologica.* Other typical views also make their appearance in this early work: the rejection of the hylomorphic composition, that is, the relationship of matter and form, in beings termed separated substances or, more familiarly, angels, the pure potentiality of first matter, and the unity or unicity of substantial form in corporeal creatures—though there were also a number of ideas that he was later to modify or abandon.

Before he began lecturing as a master, he had already written two treatises, *De ente et essentia ad fratres et socios meos (On Being and Essence)* and *De principiis naturae ad Fratrem Sylvestrum (On the Principles of Nature),* both by their titles indicating that they were written at the request of his brethren. The first, a short treatise of six chapters surviving in some 180 manuscripts, is an expository work in which he explains the various meanings of metaphysical terms. The second also consists of six chapters, in which he discusses the nature and interrelation of natural principles and causes; the work depends largely on the first and second books of Aristotle's *Physics.*

Ten works in all may be ascribed to his tenure of the mastership at Paris, among them commentaries on Saint Matthew, Saint John, and Saint Paul's Epistles, and possibly, though less certain in date, on certain chapters of Isaiah, all in addition to important extracurricular writing. His scriptural commentaries fall into two categories: *reportationes*—reports of lectures taken down by a scribe or student, such as the lectures on Saint Paul's first Letter to the Corinthians and some others, among them the lectures on Saint Matthew, taken down apparently in the classroom by Friar Peter d'Andria and a secular clerk, Ligier of Besançon; and *ordinationes* (regular lectures)—a finished product written or dictated by Aquinas himself.

He had also to participate in public disputations throughout the academic year, of which the *Quaestiones disputate de veritate (Disputed Questions of Truth)* seem to have occupied him during his first sojourn in Paris. Toward the end of February 1256, Aimeric of Veire, chancellor of the university, informed the prior of Saint Jacques that Aquinas should "receive the *magisterium* in theology, notwithstanding any custom whereby others might be preferred to him, and to prepare himself accordingly without any contradiction." Aquinas accepted his position with reluctance, sometime between 3 March and 17 June 1256; by this ceremony he became a member of the faculty of the university, with the right to lecture and to determine disputed questions in theology. He gave his inaugural address on the text *Rigans montes de superioribus suis; de fructu operum tuorum satisabitur terra* (He watereth the hills from his chambers; the earth is satisfied with the fruit of thy works: Psalm 104:13); its theme was that all higher gifts, spiritual and physical, have been ordained by divine providence to descend from the higher to lower levels, just as rain falls upon the earth to form rivers and to fertilize the soil. Teachers in similar fashion receive spiritual wisdom from God and disperse it, just as waters fall upon the mountains, and streams flow from them. It was probably on the second day of his inception that he introduced a disputation on the question *De opere manuali (On Manual Labor)*: whether manual labor is a matter of moral obligation or whether those who are involved in spiritual works could expect to be justifiably excused from it. He agrees that manual labor was designed to overcome indolence, to control sensuality, and to provide for the necessities of existence. Yet spirituality may also be seen as an equally if not more effective necessity for the good life. No man can be sufficient to himself. Human relationships oblige all men to assist each other. Some men are endowed with a vocation to provide spiritual sustenance to the community and are thus under no obligation to work with their hands, though the community in its turn may have an obligation to help maintain them, as by giving alms.

The arguments could be related to the bitter quarrel that had developed between the friars and the secular masters in the university at Paris, in which Aquinas had become involved. Aquinas had arrived at the priory of Saint Jacques thirty-five years after the Dominicans first arrived in Paris. The priory constituted the leading Dominican *studium,* with one hundred other members, even though it did not become a *studium generale* until 1248. The secular masters greatly resented the intrusion of the Dominicans into the university, disliking particularly their acquisition of a second chair in theology (between March 1229 and April 1231), their growing reputation as teachers and writers, and the papal patronage they received. In 1252 they had tried to limit the Dominican chairs to one, but they had been resisted successfully by the friars, who had the backing of the pope.

The leading spokesman of the secular masters was William of Saint Amour, who had already in his *Liber de Antichristo et eius ministris (On Antichrist and His Ministers)* attacked the teachings expounded in the *Introductorius in evangelium aeternum (Introduction to the Everlasting Gospel)* by Gerard de Borgo San Donnino, a follower of the late-twelfth-century Calabrian abbot Joachim of Flora; Gerard saw in the mendicants' gosepl of evangelical poverty a prelude to the last age of the eternal gospel that Joachim had predicted. William went to Rome as procurator of the university to persuade Pope Innocent IV of the dangers implicit in the friars' preaching. As a result, the pope, on 21 November 1254, issued the bull *Etsi animarum,* limiting the friars' privileges as preachers and confessors. On

Pope Innocent's death two weeks later, his successor, Alexander IV, revoked the bull and restored the friars' privileges in two bulls, *Nec insolitum* and *Quasi lignum vitae.* William of Saint Amour, angered by the papal change of heart, continued to criticize the Dominicans, publishing in March 1256 a devastating attack *(De periculis novissimorum temporum* [*On the Danger of Most Recent Times*]), which he circulated among the French bishops and a copy of which was sent by King Louis IX of France to Rome. Feeling in Paris was so high that the friars sometimes found themselves victims of mob violence. In the autumn, Aquinas published a clearly reasoned reply *(Contra impugnantes Dei cultum et religionem* [*Against the Assailants of God*]) to William of Saint Amour's book. Meanwhile, a papal commission of cardinals reported unfavorably on William of Saint Amour's book, and Pope Alexander IV explicitly told the bishop of Paris to take strong measures to protect the Dominicans from persecution and to give them his protection.

In addition to his public duties as master and the part he was taking in this controversy, Aquinas found time to devote himself to extracurricular writing, of which the *Summa contra Gentiles (A Summary Against the Gentiles)* was the most important work. The book, of which the autograph survives in the Vatican, was apparently started at the request of Raymond de Penaforte, master general of the Dominican order from 1238 to 1240, who was especially interested in missions to the heathen. "Ardently desiring the conversion of infidels," Raymond asked Aquinas "to write a work against the errors of the infidels that would both take away the thick atmosphere of darkness and unfold the doctrine of true light to those willing to believe." From the testimony of Antonio of Brescia at the time of Aquinas' canonization, it appears that he began to work on the *Summa contra Gentiles* in Paris, though it was not completed until he was at Orvieto in 1264.

The *Summa contra Gentiles* consists of four books. Books 1 to 3 deal with truths about God that can be known by human reason; book 4, with truths about God and divine things that can be known only by revelation, such as the Trinity (chs. 1–26), the Incarnation (chs. 27–55), the sacraments as effects of the Incarnation (chs. 56–78), and the resurrection of the body and final judgment (chs. 79–97). The work is much more than a missionary's handbook. Aquinas was concerned with refuting the prevalent naturalistic philosophy drawn from Greco-Islamic writings to show that the Christian faith was itself based on a rational foundation. Since Muslims and Jews had assimilated the ideas of Avicenna and Aristotle, he was especially concerned with refuting errors that had arisen as a consequence, using arguments that were to be repeated more systematically in the *Summa theologica (A Summary of Theology).*

Before he left Paris, he wrote a short exposition of Boethius' *De trinitate (On the Trinity),* dealing with man's knowledge of divine truth and commenting on the division and methodology of the speculative sciences, and *De hebdomadibus (On Axioms),* a phrase from the opening sentence of the work that deals with the question "how substances insofar as they exist are good." The work is a commentary divided into five *lectiones,* or readings. In it, as in others of his works, there appears the significant distinction between *esse* and *quod est,* i.e., being (God) and his dependent creatures, mankind. Although, he concludes, there are many kinds of good, "all things are good insofar as they are derived from the first good." Before the end of his stay in France, he took part at a meeting of the Dominican general chapter, held at Valenciennes in June 1259, with the object of discussing the promotion of studies in the order.

Aquinas left for Italy possibly in June or July 1259. The evidence for the details of his life during the next decade is somewhat sparse and confused. He probably went first to San Domenico in Naples, for in 1260 he was appointed preacher-general for Naples, an office that gave him the right to vote in the provincial chapters. But on 14 September 1261 the provincial chapter meeting appointed Aquinas "lector" at the priory of Orvieto. During his four years at Orvieto, he became very friendly with the new pope, Urban IV, himself a great friend and promoter of philosophical studies. Aquinas' former master, Albertus Magnus, also resided at the papal court at Orvieto. It has often been stated that Aquinas was here in contact with the translator of Aristotle, William of Moerbeke, but it seems likely that Moerbeke was in Greece at this time. Moerbeke was, however, at the court of Urban's successor, Clement IV, between the summer of 1267 and the autumn of 1268. The relationship between the two scholars was very important, for though it seems improbable that Moerbeke undertook the majority of his translations of Aristotle at Aquinas' suggestion, Aquinas quickly made use of them. He was not at this time contemplating a commentary on Aristotle's works. This was to be promoted by his second stay in Paris between 1269 and 1272.

At Orvieto he acted as lector of the Dominican priory; his primary duty was to lecture on Scripture, the principal fruit of which was his *Expositio*, or commentary, on the Book of Job. He also continued to work on and, eventually, to complete the *Summa contra Gentiles*. At the request of Urban IV, who was interested in bringing about a reunion of the Greek and Latin churches, Aquinas composed his commentary on the four Gospels, the *Catena aurea (The Golden Chain)*, and wrote his *Contra errores Graecorum (Against the Errors of the Greeks)*, a critical examination of the *Libellus de processione Spiritus Sancti (Concerning the Procession of the Holy Spirit)* of Nicholas of Durazzo, bishop of Cotrone, expounding the Catholic teaching on the procession of the Holy Spirit in the doctrine of the Trinity. Like Albertus Magnus, Aquinas did not know Greek, except for a few technical words and phrases, but, again like Albert, he was exceptionally skillful at detecting the Greek nuances in the available Latin translations. Between 1260 and 1263 he studied the acts of the first five ecumenical councils of the church, which he was to use profitably for his interpretation of Christology in the *Catena aurea* and in the *Summa theologica*. In 1274 Pope Gregory X was to request Aquinas to bring his treatise to the Council of Lyons.

The *Catena aurea*, a continuous gloss on the four Gospels, was a work of major importance, widely used and demonstrating an astonishing range of well-chosen patristic quotations, characterized, as the nineteenth-century scholar Mark Pattison put it, "by masterly and architectionic skill" and "learning of the highest kind." The commentary on Saint Matthew was completed by the death of Urban IV, to whom it was dedicated, and the other glosses were finished shortly after Urban's death, in October 1264. "My intention in this work," Aquinas wrote in the dedication, "is not only to pursue the literal sense [of the passage] but also to set out the mystical; sometimes to demolish errors, as well as to confirm the Catholic truth." Elsewhere he commented that Scripture had two senses: the literal, the words used to convey the writer's literal meaning; and the spiritual, shown by internal evidence to convey other and deeper interpretations. The literal or historical sense formed the foundation from which the spiritual sense could be drawn. There were three kinds of spiritual interpretation: moral, or tropological, having a bearing on the actions required to achieve beatitude, or man's final end; allegorical, or typical, signifying forward truths, as with Old Testament teaching that anticipated events relating to Christ and his church; and anagogical, the New Testament prefiguring the church. Because of the research into Greek sources that the *Catena aurea* involved (Aquinas quotes twenty-two Latin fathers and fifty-seven Greek fathers), it marked a significant stage in his own theological development. He was especially influenced, as were many of his contemporaries, by the writings of the so-called Pseudo-Dionysius, or Dionysius the Areopagite, the supposed disciple of Saint Paul (Acts 17:34). Aquinas wrote a commentary on Pseudo-Dionysius, *De divinis nominibus (On the divine names)*, sometime before 1268; another work of this period, probably written in 1264, was a long letter, *De rationibus fidei contra Saracenos Graecos et Armenos ad cantorem Antiochiae (The Foundations of Faith Established Against the Saracens, Greeks, and Armenians)*.

It has been generally believed that, at the request of Pope Urban IV, Aquinas composed the liturgy for the eight-day festival of Corpus Christi that Urban had instituted in 1264 as a festival for the universal church, though its exclusion from the original list of his works composed by Reginald of Piperno for the process of his canonization throws some doubt on the attribution. But the sequence *Lauda Sion salvatorem* (Laud, O Sion, O my salvation) in the poetically and theologically compelling mass for Corpus Christi seems reminiscent of Aquinas' eucharistic teaching. Four fine new hymns, "Pange lingua gloriosi" (Of the glorious body telling, O my tongue, its mysteries sing) for the first vespers and "Sacris solemnis" (Let us with hearts renewed, or, At this solemn feast), "Panis angelicus" (Behold, the bread of angels), and "Verbum supernum prodiens" (To Earth descending, Word sublime) for lauds, incorporated in it, may be of his authorship. While the final verdict may be doubtful, the general chapter of the Dominicans meeting at Vienne in 1322 asserted that the office of Corpus Christi "was composed, as it is said [*asseritur*], by the venerable doctor Thomas d'Aquino."

After Urban's death, Aquinas continued to reside at Orvieto for a further year, possibly composing the *De regno*, or *De regimine principum (On the Rule of Princes)*, his only explicit commentary on the relations of church and state, for the king of Cyprus, probably Hugh II (who died in December 1267). This seemingly incomplete tract was later finished by Tolomeo of Lucca, a Dominican, later bishop of Torcello. In 1265 Aquinas was ordered by the provincial chapter meeting at Anagni to go to Rome to establish a *studium* at Santa Sabina on the Aventine Hill; his task was to instruct young friars in the elements of theology. To this period must be dated his disputation *De potentia Dei (On the Power of God)*, which comprises ten questions that are subdivided into eighty-three articles and are concerned with issues relating to divine omnipotence demonstrated in creation and its governance. Theologically, it stands between the *Summa contra Gentiles* and the *Summa theologica*. Another series of questions, *De malo (On Evil)*, dealing as its title suggests with the nature, causes, and character of evil and a discussion of the seven deadly sins, may have been disputed during his stay either in Rome or in Paris; so too with the disputation *De spiritualibus creaturis (On the Spiritual Creatures)*, which, in eleven articles, discusses the human soul united to but separated from the body and angelic substances.

During his time in Rome, he worked on the *Catena aurea*, on Saint Mark, Saint Luke, and Saint John; the commentary on the latter was completed in 1267 and dedicated to his former pupil Cardinal Annibaldo d'Annibaldi. While teaching at Rome, he planned a scheme to instruct those starting to study theology "to present those things that pertain to the Christian religion in a manner befitting the education of beginners." He found existing works unsuitable because they were too verbose, too unsystematic, and too repetitive. The *Summa theologica*, which was to engage his attention for the next seven years, was to prove one of the most influential theological works ever written, without equal in its formal structure.

The first part of the *Summa theologica* is simple in argument, but the remainder is profound and sophisticated in approach. The first part is in the main devoted to a consideration of God and creation, and the "procession of all creatures from him." The second part is divided into two sections, the *prima secundae* and the *secunda secundae*. In it he treats of man's moral life: the first section deals with man's final end and the general moral question of "the movement of rational creatures toward God," and the second section with virtues and vices. The third part considers the sacraments and Christ, "who as a man is the way of our tending toward God." Each part is subdivided into questions, and the questions generally contain several articles. In each article, Aquinas puts forward objections against the doctrines that he wishes to propose. He then expounds his doctrine in the body of the article before replying to the objections raised. The final work consists of 512 questions, 2,669 articles, and approximately 10,000 objections with their solutions. The first part was written at Rome and Viterbo between 1266 and November 1268; the second part occupied his time at Paris; and the third part was written and left incomplete at Naples before December 1273.

In June 1267 the general chapter assigned Aquinas to the Dominican priory at Viterbo, where the French pope Clement IV had been living since April 1266. Clement is said to have offered Aquinas the archbishopric of Naples, together with the revenues from the monastery of Saint Peter ad Aram, but he had no wish for preferment. In addition to working on the *Summa,* he was in close contact with the translator of Aristotle, William of Moerbeke, the pope's "chaplain and penitentiary," and at his instigation William may have revised a number of the older translations of Aristotle's works, among them *De anima* (*On the Soul,* 1268). Then, in November 1268, the Dominican master general, John of Vercelli, recalled Aquinas to Paris. He arrived there early in 1269 to occupy the second Dominican chair in the university.

The principal occasion for Aquinas' recall seems to have been a renewal of the controversy between the secular masters and the friars. William of Saint Amour had dispatched a revised edition of his earlier book, now entitled *Collationes Catholicae et canonicae scripturae (Collations of Catholic and Canonical Scripture),* to Pope Clement IV in 1266; and William's friend and supporter Gérard of Abbeville took up the cudgels in Paris to the same effect. The Dominicans, in need of a champion to defend the mendicant cause, brought back Aquinas. Their opponents initiated a series of disputations in which they argued that begging was sinful for anyone who could work with his hands; declared that preaching and the care of souls, including confession, belonged to bishops and the parish clergy; and challenged the stress laid by the friars on evangelical poverty. Between March 1269 and December 1271 Aquinas disputed in the schools with Gérard of Abbeville in the Lenten and Advent *quodlibets,* debates or discussions on disputed questions *(Questiones quodlibetates).* He published a defense of the religious orders, *De perfectione spiritualis vitae (On the Perfection of the Spiritual Life),* expounding the nature of perfection and the significance of monastic vows as a means to it. It consisted of some twenty-three chapters but was later enlarged and revised. In the summer of 1271 he composed a refutation of Gérard of Abbeville's teachings, *Contra doctrinam retrahentium a religione (Against the Doctrine of Defection from the Religious Life),* in particular a response to the charge that friars were wrongly inducing young boys to embrace the religious life. "If any man," Aquinas concluded, "desires to contradict my words, let him not do so by chattering before boys, but let him write and publish his writings, so that intelligent persons may judge what is true, and may be able to confute what is false by the authority of the truth." In two questions that he disputed at the start of Lent 1271, *De ingressu puerorum in religione (On Entry of Boys into Religous Life),* he defended the entry of boys into religion before the age of puberty, allowing, however, that on attaining puberty they were entitled to make up their own minds as to whether they wished to take permanent vows.

Assisted by his secretaries, of whom Reginald of Piperno was the chief, Aquinas was working with incredible speed, eating and sleeping little. In addition to his writing, he was occupied in the study of ancient and contemporary authors as well as fulfilling his duties as regent master. He continued to lecture and composed commentaries on Saint John, Saint Paul's Epistle to the Romans, and part of the first Epistle to the Corinthians (up to chapter 10). His *lectura* (lecture) or *reportatio* on Saint John, recorded by Reginald and corrected by Aquinas himself, is distinguished by its profound examination of trinitarian doctrine and the exemplification of God's love for man. His two other scriptural commentaries reveal his commitment to Pauline teaching on justification and grace; they also contain an explanation and refutation of early heresies, including Pelagianism.

The questions for disputation that he then discussed were apparently under the headings *De anima (On the Soul); De virtutibus (On the Virtues),* though on this point there is in respect of authorship some degree of doubt; and *De unione verbi incarnati (On Union with the Incarnate Word). De anima* consists of twenty-one articles, or questions, and it was probably disputed in the spring of 1269. The first five objections discuss the views of Avicenna and Averroës, especially questions relating to the individuation of the soul, pluralities of forms, the unity of the intellect, and survival after death. Aquinas' views on the unity of the intellect brought him into collision with the formidable English Franciscan John Pecham, future archibishop of Canterbury and then a master at Paris, who described Aquinas' teaching on this subject as "profane novelty."

The question was much in Aquinas' mind because of his concern with the prevalence at Paris of a small group of intellectuals, headed by Siger of Brabant, known as the Latin Averroists. Their principal teachings—the unity or unicity of the intellect, the denial of free will, the restriction of divine providence, and the eternity of the world—were derived in the main from the commentaries of Averroës on Aristotle. Their views were to be condemned by the bishop of Paris in 1270 and again in 1277. Before the condemnation of 1270, Aquinas wrote a tightly argued refutation of Siger's views on the nature of the human intellect, *De unitate intellectus (On the Unity of the Intellect),* in which he stressed that the possible intellect is not a substance separate in being. Aquinas wrote in *De unitate:* "From this careful examination of almost all the words of Aristotle concerning the human intellect it is clear that he was of the opinion that the human soul is the act of the body (i.e., the substantial form of man), and that the possible intellect is a part of power of the soul." The intellective soul of man, he argued, is the unique substantial form of each man.

His concern about refuting the Averroists, without falling back on the conservative views of their more extreme critics, and about composing the second part of the *Summa* convinced him of the need to supply scholars with commentaries that would correctly interpret Aristotle's teaching, even when it had to be rejected. He began, therefore, a series of studies that would show not merely the text *(litera)* of Aristotle but also his intended meaning *(intentio Aristotelis);* most were written between 1269 and 1273: *Super physicam (On Physics); Peri Hermenaias,* dedicated to the provost of Louvain; *Super posteriora analytica (Posterior Analytics); Sententia libri ethicorum (Commentary on Ethics); Super metaphysicam (On Metaphysics); De caelo (On the Heavenly Bodies); De generatione (On Coming-to-Be); Meteorologica (On Meteorology); Liber de causis (On Causes).* His comparative liberalism evoked the hostility of the more conservative theologians, especially the Franciscans Bonaventura and Pecham, as well as the secular masters patronized by Bishop Tempier of Paris himself.

Sometime after Easter 1272, Aquinas, accompanied by Reginald of Piperno, left Paris for Italy. A subsequent chapter of the Roman province, following a general chapter meeting held in Santa Maria Novella at Florence in June 1272, entrusted Aquinas with the establishment of a new *studium generale,* leaving the location to him. He selected Naples, his home country, where he received the patronage of the king, Charles of Anjou. His energies were now concentrated on finishing the *Summa* and the commentaries on Aristotle. The only fruit of his purely academic work as a regent master was a series of lectures on Psalms 1 to 54, in which he laid stress on the spiritual interpretation. He may also have continued to work on various other works: the *Compendium theologiae (Compendium of Theology)*, a short account of the whole of the Christian life considered under three headings, faith, hope, and charity; and the *De substantiis separatis*, or *De angelis (On Separated Substances*, or *On Angels)*, both dedicated to Reginald of Piperno and both left unfinished. In Lent of 1273, he preached a series of sermons at Naples. "He was held by the people with such reverence," William of Tocco commented, "that it was as if his preaching came forth from God."

Then, on Wednesday morning, 6 December 1273, during the mass, he had what seems to have been a stroke; he was suddently *commotus* or struck, so that he appeared profoundly changed *(mira mutatione)*. Henceforth, his speech was somewhat impaired, and there was a loss of manual dexterity. He had long been overworking and taxing his brain, and there had been recent evidence of even more marked mental abstractedness than before. "After the mass," Bartholomew of Capua said, "he never wrote or dictated anything." When Reginald of Piperno sought the reason—"Father, why have you laid aside such a great work which you began for the praise of God and the enlightenment of the world?"—Aquinas at last replied, "Reginald, I cannot because all that I have written seems like straw to me" (*Life of Aquinas*, p. 109). Later in the winter he visited his sister, the countess Theodora of San Severino, but he appeared abstracted almost to the point of stupefaction. He was ordered to go to the Council of Lyons, summoned by Pope Gregory X, but his health was failing. The winter journey greatly taxed him, and he died on 7 March 1274 at the Cistercian abbey of Fossanuova.

When the authorities of the university at Paris heard the news, they wrote to the Dominican chapter meeting on 2 May 1274, expressing their grief and requesting that he might be buried in Paris: "For news has come to us which floods us with grief and amazement, bewilders our understanding, transfixes our very vitals and well nigh breaks our hearts" (*Life of Aquinas*, p. 153). But Aquinas' body remained at Fossanuova until, on instructions from Pope Urban V, it was transferred to the Dominican priory at Toulouse on 28 January 1369; early in the French Revolution, the body was moved for safety to the church of Saint Sernin there.

Although Aquinas had strong critics in his lifetime and after his death, his reputation as a scholar and holy man stood high in his own day. In Dante's *Divine Comedy*, written half a century after his death, it is Aquinas who quenches the pilgrim's thirst for knowledge as he mounts to the highest heaven. The movement for Aquinas' canonization, given early approval by Pope John XXII, grew in strength; a commission of investigation was set up in 1318, resulting in his official canonization on 18 July 1323. Pope Pius V declared him to be a doctor of the church in 1567. As his first feast day, 7 March, had invariably to be celebrated in Lent, it was transferred to 13 November, and then, in 1970, to 28 January.

Aquinas was a modest and unassuming man. He was given to periods of silence and abstraction. Bernard Gui recorded that when he was dining with the French king, Louis IX (Saint Louis), who greatly admired him, he so far forgot where he was as to bang his fist on the table and declare, to the astonishment of his fellow diners, "That's finished the heresy of the Manicheans!" His powers of concentration were such that when he was writing his commentary on Boethius' *De trinitate*, he was so absorbed that the candle he was holding in one hand melted completely without his noticing the pain of the hot wax (*Life of Aquinas*, pp. 44, 47). He was a man of the most prodigious industry, the author of more than thirty large volumes, who died before he was fifty years old. "Whatever he had once read and grasped, he never forgot." "Still stronger is the testimony of Reginald [of Piperno], his *socius,* and of his pupils and those who wrote to his dictation, who all declared that he used to dictate in his cell to three secretaries, and even occasionally to four, on different subjects at the same time." One secretary, a Breton, Evan of Tréguier, actually affirmed that Aquinas had been known to dictate in his sleep. His writing by and large is singularly impersonal and rarely throws any light on his personality. Yet all testified not merely to his kindly nature but to his spiritual depth and to the rich life of prayer and contemplation in which his intellectual work was rooted. Bernard Gui described him as "tall, erect, large and well-built, with a complexion like ripe wheat and whose head early grew bald" (*Life of Aquinas,* p. 53).

Thomas Aquinas' philosophy was based upon and found its culmination in his concept of a supramundane, personal God. "God," he wrote, "is the object of theology. . . . In this sacred science everything is contemplated from the standpoint of God" *(sub ratione Dei: Summa theologica* 1.1.7). God is a being without limitation within or without. His being is necessary and essential, for in him essence and existence are one and the same, whereas in everything else there is a distinction between the two. Although the proposition "God exists" is objectively self-evident, since the predicate is contained in the subject, finite men cannot realize the truth of God's existence intuitively.

God has therefore to be known not in himself but through his works. The truth of God's existence has to be demonstrated by and acquired through the observation of external reality and by the use of man's natural reason. To those who argued that God is within us and may be apprehended intuitively without argument, Aquinas replied that such experience, however dramatic, has to be accepted by the reason before it can be known to be true. So the discovery of God will depend on man's apprehension of his own finite existence; man will be able to deduce the existence of God from his knowledge of sensible reality.

It was on this foundation that Aquinas rested his famous five proofs for the existence of God. He rejected, though with reluctance, the ontological argument of Saint Anselm, that God is he of whom nothing greater can be thought; if nothing is greater than God, God is not merely a mental concept but must exist. Aquinas wrote:

> The existence of God is not necessarily self-evident as soon as the meaning of the name "God" is known. . . . There will be no necessity of that something than which nothing greater can be conceived, existing otherwise than in the mind; and from this it does not follow that there is anything *in rerum natura* than which nothing greater can be conceived.
>
> (*Summa theologica* 1.2.1)

Yet, as some critics have observed, his argument for a first cause needs to be supplemented by the ontological argument, if only to explain the mind's direct awareness of the relevance of the question under discussion.

The five proofs are all aspects of a similar argument: experience, dependence, completeness, participation in full being. First, since the world is moved, it must be moved by something other than itself:

> Everything that is moved is moved by something else, since nothing is moved unless it is potentially that to which it is moved, whereas that which moves is actual. . . . If, then, that by which it is moved is itself moved, this also must be moved by something else, and this in turn by something else again. But this cannot go on forever, since there would then be no first mover, and consequently no other mover. . . . We are therefore bound to arrive at a first mover which is not moved by anything, and all men understand that this is God.
>
> (*Summa* 1.2.3)

From the argument from motion he proceeds to the argument of the nature of an efficient cause:

> We find that there is a sequence of efficient causes in sensible things. But we do not find that anything is the efficient cause itself. . . . If the regress of efficient causes were infinite, there would be no efficient first cause. . . . But this is plainly false. We are therefore bound to suppose there is a first efficient cause. And all men call this God.
>
> (*Summa* 1.2.3)

The third argument is from the "nature of possibility and necessity":

> Not all existence is merely possible. Something in things must be necessary. . . . We are therefore bound to suppose something necessary in itself, which does not owe its necessity to anything else, but which is the cause of the necessity of other things. And all men call this God.
>
> (*Summa* 1.2.3)

In the fourth case, Aquinas examines the "degrees that occur in things":

> Things are said to be more and less because they approximate in different degrees to that which is greatest. . . . There is therefore something which is the cause of the being of all things that are, as well as of their goodness and their every perfection. This we call God.
>
> (*Summa* 1.2.3)

Finally, from the "governance" or subjection of things to guidance, Aquinas argues that "there is therefore an intelligent being by whom all natural things are directed to their end. This we call God" (*Summa* 1.2.3).

The essence of God consists simply in being, the *ipsum esse;* "in God his being is his essence." Because God is unlimited and absolute being, he must unite in himself all the perfection of being. He is neither contingent nor dependent nor incomplete. He is changeless but the fount of all change, a being necessary and absolute. Yet it is possible to elicit the nature of this changeless, absolute being who is the prime cause, for in the first book of his *Summa contra Gentiles,* Aquinas shows that although God is infinite, "inasmuch as there is no limit to his perfection," his creatures must, if imperfectly (Jesus Christ alone excepted as the perfect Son of God), reflect his infinite essence. As the first active principle and first efficient cause of all things, God not only is perfect in himself but contains within himself the perfection of all things. On this is founded the argument from analogy, *analogia entis,* whereby it is possible to trace the outlines of the divine nature from existing beings. Aquinas argues constantly that every agent acts according to its own likeness. God's creatures must, therefore, in some respects resemble God, at least in the regions where it is possible for an effect to resemble its first cause and insofar as the effects are good. Such understanding is necessarily limited; mysteries such as the doctrine of the Incarnation or the doctrine of the Trinity are not susceptible of proof or even of argument. But though such knowledge may be imperfect, it is sufficient in itself and must be true rather than fallacious.

Since God is absolute good, and goodness must involve love, and love must give itself *(bonum est diffusivum sui),* the outcome is the created universe. It was created not because it was necessary for God to create but because it was natural for him to do so:

> The proper object of [God's] will is good apprehended as such by the understanding. Now the divine understanding apprehends, not only the divine being, or divine goodness, but other good things likewise; and it apprehends them as likenesses of the divine goodness and essence, not as constituent elements of the same. Thus the divine will tends to them as things becoming its goodness, not as things necessary to its goodness.
>
> (*Summa contra Gentiles* 1.82)

The relation between God and the world is naturally determined by the divine act of creation and by its nature. Whatever exists is caused by a principle in which that something exists essentially. Since God alone is pure act and substantial being, without distinction existing between his essence and his existence, all being outside of God must be imparted being. So all things owe their existence to God, for nothing of which we have experience can be described as a self-caused being, an *ens a se*.

Creation as the bringing forth of substance, of being, is an act proper to God, and is indeed his exclusive prerogative. God is the *summum bonum*, possessor and possessed in one act; all that is desirable he has, and to an infinite degree. Being in want of nothing, he has fruition of himself and desires nothing out of selfishness. If he diffuses good, as he must do by the açt of creation, then that good redounds to the credit of finite being and can make for finite excellence. It cannot add anything to what is already personified goodness, but it can partake of it. The world was created by divine free will, though, according to revealed truth, in time. Influenced by the argument of Moses Maimonides, Aquinas admits that it cannot be proved that an eternal creation, *ab aeterno*, is wholly inadmissible. Indeed, on this point Aquinas was strongly criticized as promoting the Aristotelian doctrine of the eternity of matter, a teaching he explicitly refutes in his *De aeternitate contra murmurantes (On Eternity Against the Critics)*.

He sums up the doctrine of creation thus: "We have to think not only of the emanation of some particular being from some other particular being, but also the emanation of the whole of being from a universal cause, which is God, and it is this emanation we call by the name of creation" (*Summa* 1.45.1). God is not only the first cause but also the exemplary cause of all being, in that in his creation he fulfills his divine ideas. The prototypical forms, the ideas of all things, exist in the divine wisdom. God is the cause not only of the becoming in creatures, but of their very being. Since created being is essentially imparted being, created being depends on and needs essential and absolute being as the sufficient ground of its existence throughout its life. Every creature is thus necessarily related to its creator. For though God transcends the world, he is yet immanent within it, coactive in every created activity, whether as the final, efficient, or formal cause of it.

Yet, in spite of the contingent character of man's being, there is no contradiction between God's sovereign and universal causality and the self-determination and free will of men:

> A free will is the cause of its own action, because man by his free will moves himself to action. But it is by no means necessary to the concept of freedom that the free creature be the first cause of its own activity, just as little as a thing, to be the cause of another, must be the first cause of the latter. God is the first cause, moving both the causes that act by nature and without freedom, and those that are freely active. And just as God, in moving causes that act by necessity of their natures, in no way takes away their natural activity, so his moving influence on free causes in no way implies that their actions lose the character of freedom. On the contrary, it is precisely by his causal motion that he effects in them the character of voluntariness.
>
> (*Summa* 1.82.4)

Furthermore, God's providence extends to the totality of existing things, and can therefore permit a deficiency in this or that being by which the perfection of the totality is brought about or performed. In this way Aquinas accounts for the existence of sin and evil. Evil is not created by God but is a sequel to the imperfection of certain types of being. Original sin is the disordered disposition of nature that has resulted from the loss of original justice and that in man appears to have become instinctive as a transmitted habit. Sin is unnatural, not natural, opposition to God, and the natural inclination to virtue is thus never destroyed entirely by sin. Indeed, the most serious feature of sin is that it deprives men of the effects of the providential order whereby they are directed to God as their final end.

Man has a unified nature, consisting of spirit and matter. Having such a nature, he must have a definite end, or good, and what will be good for him is that which accords with the law of his nature and assists in perfecting it. Since he is in part spirit, he will be at least to some extent conscious of the law of his being, and so conscious of objective truth and objective goodness, however they may be barred by sin. The soul is the spiritual core of man. It is the substantial form of the living organism; it is the first principle of the phenomena and activities of life, immanent in all human beings:

> It is clear that the first thing by which the body lives is soul. And as life appears through various operations in different degrees of living things, that whereby we primarily perform each of all these vital actions is the soul. For the soul is the primary principle of our nourishment, feeling, and local movement; and likewise the primary principle whereby we understand. Therefore this principle by which we primarily understand, whether it is called the intellect or the intellectual soul, is the form of the body.
>
> (*Summa* 1.76.1)

The soul is the first actuality *(entelechy)* of the body; it is immaterial but it has substance, existing of and by itself. It is by reason of this that the human soul is distinct from the animal soul. While animals have powers and constitutions similar to those of men, they are not informed by an intellectual or rational soul. From its spirituality and substantiality, man's immortality can be deduced, since it does not cease to exist when the body ceases to exist. Furthermore, by reason of its own nature in and of itself, it is indestructible, since it is impossible for a subsistent form to cease to exist.

But the soul is not the man. Man is a unity composed of body and soul. In seeking to explain the relationship between body and soul, Aquinas was much influenced by the Aristotelian theory of the relationship between matter and form, usually known as hylomorphism. Matter and form are the essential constituents of all physical objects. Matter is undetermined but possesses potential. It is form that makes matter into an actual and differentiated being. Matter is passive; form is active. Both are necessary to the essence of the physical object. But whereas matter has no existence apart from form, form can exist without matter: "Form is the principle of existence." Man is a single being composed of matter and form. There can be only one form in a substance, since it is the form that is the nature of the substance. The soul in man is the form of the body, determining it to be a human body: "The principle of intellectual activity, the rational soul, is the essential form of the human body." It was such teaching that was much criticized by some of Aquinas' contemporaries, notably the Franciscans John Pecham and William de la Mare.

Since for Aquinas the personality is an integral union of body and soul, he had to resolve a difficulty that would be posed by the survival of the soul alone. He does so by arguing that "though the mode of our understanding according to the conditions of the present life is wrecked with the wreck of the body, it will be replaced by another and higher mode of understanding" (*Summa contra Gentiles* 2.81).

Another difficulty was caused by the nature of generation, for if, as he insists, the rational soul comes from without, then the embryo has only what may be described as a vegetative soul. "The body of man," he states, "is formed at once by the power of God, the principal and prime agent, and by the power of the semen, the secondary agent. But the action of God produces the human soul, which the power of the male semen cannot produce, but only disposes thereto" (*Summa* 2.88).

Aquinas was much influenced by Aristotle in his theory of human knowledge. As against the Augustinians, who assumed that the mind acquired knowledge less from the senses than from the divine ideas, Aquinas posited an active intellect, an *intellectus agens.* This is a faculty of the soul that prepares intelligible, that is, intellectually knowable, concepts by means of the abstraction of the universal from the materials presented to the mind by the senses. Mind is not intuitive but discursive reason. It will formulate concepts only through observation: *Nihil est in intellectu nisi prius fuerit in sensu* (There is nothing in the mind that was not first in the senses). The external world impinges on the senses and is perceived by means of the sense impression, the *species sensibilis.* The information is stored up by memory, imagination, and the *vis aestimiva.* It is the *intellectus agens* that makes this intelligible. Consequently, our intellectual knowledge is dependent on sensory experience for its materials.

What is known first by the intellect is being. Intellectual grasp of being is included in every thought of man: "For every nature is essentially a being [*ens*], something that is" (*De veritate* 1.1). Each being has its essence *(essentia)*, and what the essence is is expressed by the word "thing" *(res)*. Hence, we have the first indemonstrable principle, that we cannot at once both affirm and deny a being. Another necessary ingredient is substance, a self-dependent thing that is the subject of actions, motions, activities, and changes that occur in the world. "Substance," Aquinas writes, "is a thing, whose essence it is, not to have its being in another thing, whose nature it is to be in another" (*Quodlibet* 9.5.2). God is the supreme substance, the creator of all other substances. In each man the substantial soul forms the basis of all mental and bodily life.

Knowledge acquired through the senses is not, however, the exclusive and total cause of our intellectual knowledge. "The intelligible species are subjective forms that determine our intellect to a knowledge of the objective reality" (*Summa theologica* 1.85.2). But outside our minds, though capable of being apprehended by them, there is a reality that corresponds to our intellectual concepts. Such a reality forms the essence and core of the things and activities of the world of appearances perceived by the senses. Aquinas was convinced that it is possible to appreciate the reality of the supersensory order that lies beyond the world of appearances. For over and beyond the world, there is the supernatural order in which God lives and reigns and in which are to be found the mysteries revealed by God that man can approach by reason, though he can ultimately realize them only through the light of faith.

In the last analysis, the unseen things of faith are beyond the reach of finite human reason. Human reason can attain to certain truths about God of its own accord, such as the doctrine of monotheism, and it can formulate reasons for God's existence. It can remove obstacles in the way of faith, but it can never do more than provide a preamble to faith. It cannot reveal the inner nature and life of God, a self-limitation that itself suggests the existence of deeper superrational truths of which we are unaware.

Yet there is no ultimate disharmony or contradiction between the truths of faith and the truths of natural knowledge. Reason and faith are fundamentally compatible: *Gratia non tollit naturam sed perfecit* (Grace does not destroy nature; it perfects her: *Summa* 1.8.2). Nor can there be opposition between God and the world that he has made. God is the origin of both series of truths. What we accept on the basis of revelation cannot be in opposition to natural reason. Aquinas thus refuted the current Averroistic doctrine of the double truth. Reason subserves theology by enabling us to establish through philosophy the rational truths that form the necessary presuppositions of faith, clarifying the mysteries of faith and distinguishing the fallacies of arguments brought against it.

Man's final end may be found not in this world but in God, through whom alone he is and lives, and by whose help alone can he attain his true end. That God is the last end of man can be proved by starting either from the existence of God or from a consideration of the nature of man and of his rational desire. In this last end is comprised man's surpassing beatitude, his final happiness.

It was within this framework that Aquinas embedded his ideas on politics, where his debt to Aristotle appears most forcibly. Earlier medieval thinkers had accepted the Augustinian conception of the state as an imperfect institution, marred by sin, with political authority seen chiefly as a remedy for that sin. But Aquinas believed that the state or political community was, as Aristotle had described it in the *Politics,* a natural development:

> It is a demand of man's nature that he inclines to live in society and state [*animal sociale et politicum*], that he lives in social fellowship with many others. . . . If, then, it is natural for man to live in society, there must also be some way in which the many are governed. . . . In the individual man the soul governs the body. . . . Among the members of the body there is likewise one that is the most noble, is guide of the others, namely the heart or the head. In every manifold there must be a governing principle.
> (*De regimine principum* 1.1)

So for Aquinas, unlike Saint Augustine, the state is not simply a consequence of man's first sin, but an essential sequel to his creation. Man is a political animal because he is from the start a social being. Even in the state of innocence, there must have been *dominium politicum,* in part because life in society is unthinkable without a directing authority and in part because men will recognize the right to authority of those who surpass them in knowledge and justice. The *subiectio civilis* (subjection) of man to man, but not his enslavement, is a necessary sequel to man's intrinsic sociability, and essential for the attainment of the common good.

As it was for Aristotle, politics for Aquinas was basically a branch of ethics. It is through the state that man can approach perfection, though he does allow that there may have been exceptional men, such as hermits, who were able to attain perfection outside the fellowship of men. But for most men the pursuit of the good life is intelligible only in terms of the community. "All men being a part of the city, they cannot be truly good unless they adapt themselves to the common good" (*Summa theologica* 1a2ae.92.3). Like Aristotle, he distinguishes between good and bad types of constitutions; but, unlike Aristotle, he selects monarchy as the most perfect practicable type. Monarchy is analogous to the rule of God. It is the most natural constitution, being the most directed toward unity and the most likely to serve the cause of peace. Tyranny is the worst type, and in certain circumstances may justify rebellion (though not, as Jean Petit inferred in 1407 from Aquinas' writings, tyrannicide). Monarchy would seem perfectly to have many of the features of Aristotle's "mixed constitution," with the prince depending on the rule of law as an expression of the community's will.

The mission of the state, and the object of kingship, is to direct the citizens toward a happy and virtuous life through the preservation of peace and justice and the assurance of prosperity. In secular terms the state should make possible the highest achievement of man. It is to be a recipe for virtue rather than a remedy for sin. But there is a higher end still that the state may promote but cannot of itself make possible: the possession of God, the *perfecta beatitudo* (perfect beatitude) that can be effectively realized only in the future life. Indeed, the individual is never completely absorbed by the state, since he is necessarily reserved for a higher end.

It is the office of the church, acting through the pope, the successor of Saint Peter, the vicar of Jesus Christ, the royal priest, to direct men toward that end:

> To him [the pope] all kings of the Christian people are to be subject as to our Lord Jesus Christ himself. For those to whom pertains the care of

> intermediate ends should be subject to him to whom pertains the care of the ultimate end and be directed by his rule. . . . In the new law there is a higher priesthood by which men are guided to the heavenly good. Consequently, in the law of Christ, kings must be subject to priests.
>
> (*De regimine principum* 1.14)

The secular state has to be fitted, therefore, into a hierarchical and divinely graded order supermundane in its character. In the fourteenth chapter of *De regimine principum,* Aquinas underlines the insufficiency of the *humanum regimen* and the need for recognition of the *divinum regimen,* represented by the clergy and headed by the *summus sacerdos,* the pope, in order to guide the *humanum regimen* to its final and heavenly end. Yet he allows the secular state a degree of autonomy within recognized bounds:

> Spiritual as well as secular power comes from the divine power. Hence, secular power is subjected to spiritual power in those matters concerning which the subjection has been specified and ordained by God, that is, in matters belonging to the salvation of the soul. Hence, in these we are to obey spiritual authority more than secular authority. On the other hand, more obedience is due to secular power than to spiritual power in the things that pertain to the civic good.
>
> (*Commentary on the Sentences of Peter Lombard* 2.44)

In the event, however, of a collision between *sacerdotium* and *regnum,* the former, because of its divine character, must have the last word. "The temporal power is subject to the spiritual as the body to the soul."

Aquinas' teaching had been criticized in his lifetime and immediately after his death was regarded by some with grave doubts. In 1277 Bishop Tempier of Paris, acting on instructions from Pope John XXI, condemned a series of two hundred nineteen propositions, heterogeneous in character, mainly of an Averroist nature, but listing non-Averroist articles, including some of Aquinas' theses. While Aquinas was not named, their nature—the individualization of the soul by the body, the determination of the will by the good, the theory of knowledge put forward there—recalled Aquinas' ideas. This condemnation was eventually to be withdrawn in 1325 by Bishop Étienne de Bourret. Archibishop Robert Kilwardby of Canterbury, himself a Dominican, followed Bishop Tempier's example, condemning some thirty propositions, three related to the unity or unicity of the substantial form, at Oxford on 18 March 1277, a condemnation repeated later by Aquinas' old critic, Kilwardby's successor, Archibishop Pecham. In 1279 William de la Mare, a Franciscan professor at Paris, compiled a "correctory" in which he sought to correct what he regarded as dubious teaching, where Aquinas had diverged from the notions of Bonaventura and Saint Augustine. The critics of Aquinas provoked a reply from a number of Dominican scholars, among them the Englishmen William Hothum and Richard Knapwell and the Italian Rambert of Bologna. Another criticism came in Durandus of Saint-Pourçain's commentary on the *Sentences,* which appeared in 1307–1308.

Thus the unitary system of thought, the finely structured synthesis of faith and reason, that Aquinas had compiled was further challenged within less than fifty years of his death by scholastic philosophers who sought to divorce faith from reason rather than to marry them. Duns Scotus, a Scot who had studied at Paris (1293–1296) and Oxford (1290–1293 and 1297–1301), called by his contemporaries the *doctor subtilis,* challenged Thomism in a series of writings, learned, powerful, but obscure, of which two *Commentaries on the Sentences,* known from their place names as the *Opus Oxoniense* and the *Reportata Parisiensia,* were the most important; he was also the author of a series of questions on metaphysics, the *Quodlibeta.* He differed from Aquinas more especially in his views on the question of being. For Aquinas, created being was an analogue of God's being, positive in quality and the only positive entity. Duns, however, declared that being lacked a positive content and was the same wherever it was found. He denied also the differentiation between essence and existence on which Aquinas laid much stress. While Duns's theory of knowledge owed much to Aristotle, it diverged from Aquinas' theory by stating that the mind could be informed intuitively, thus querying the emphasis that Aquinas had placed on sense experience. Where Aquinas had taught that the will was a blind faculty determined by the good once this had been realized by the mind, in Scotist teaching the will qua will played a decisive part. Indeed, for Duns, God's will was probably his most fundamental attribute; goodness must be seen as his command. Duns seemed also to deny the competence of the natural reason to reach beyond finite being. He thus further limited the range of truths accessible to the human mind, making a gulf between God and men that could be bridged only by faith.

The challenge that Duns Scotus offered to Thomism was put more bluntly by an English Franciscan, William of Ockham. His theological views were early thought to be suspect; in 1324 he was ordered to the papal court at Avignon to answer charges, and two years later, in 1326, fifty-one of his propositions were condemned. He sided with the Spiritual Franciscans in their dispute with the pope, and later joined the imperialist cause, championing the emperor against the pope. For the last twenty years of his life he was excommunicate. In spite of Ockham's heterodoxy, he occupied a central position in the development of scholastic philosophy and exerted considerable influence over scholastic teaching during the next two centuries. His principal works are a *Commentary on the Sentences,* the *Quodlibeta,* and treatises on predestination, composed before 1324; he also wrote commentaries on Aristotle's *Physics* and books on logic.

Ockham was the father of a new system of scholastic logic and epistemology, known as nominalism, which earned him the title from his contemporaries of *venerabilis inceptor.* Even more than Duns Scotus, Ockham narrowed the range of truths open to the natural reason. He rejected every kind of intellectual abstraction in the process of knowledge. Cognition was, so Ockham argued, a matter of intuition; what is known is individual and singular: "This I say, that no universal is existent in any way whatsoever outside the mind of the knower." By thus attacking universal and realistic philosophy, Ockham in practice eliminated metaphysics and so made nonsense of Aquinas' assertion that the so-called truths of religion could be demonstrated by the natural reason. By delimiting the mind's ability to comprehend the fundamentals of theology and making them solely the province of faith and revelation, Ockham effectively fragmented the structure of thought so painstakingly erected by Aquinas and the Christian Aristotelians.

Although the late-medieval scholastic tradition was far from being exclusively nominalist, nominalism rather than Thomism was the dominant scholastic teaching in the late Middle Ages. Thomism continued to have its exponents, notably Giles of Rome (*ca.* 1247–1316), Thomas of Strasbourg, John Capreolus (1380–1444)—who in the early fifteenth century wrote a masterly exposition of Aquinas' thought, *Defensiones theologiae divi Thomae Aquinatis*—Thomas Cajetan (1469–1534), Sylvester of Ferrara (1471–1528), and John of Saint Thomas (1589–1644). It was, however, only with the theologians of the Counter Reformation, and even more so with those of the nineteenth-century church, that Aquinas' thought came properly into its own. In 1879 Pope Leo XIII's bull *Aeterni patris* enjoined the study of Aquinas' works on all theological students. In the next year he was made patron of all Catholic universities, and on 29 June 1923, the sixth centenary of his canonization, Pope Pius XI reiterated his status as an authoritative doctor of the church in *Studiorem ducem.* Aquinas' contribution, not merely to scholastic thought but to philosophy, was indeed such that he may be safely regarded as the most outstanding philosophical writer of the medieval world.

## Selected Bibliography


### SAINT THOMAS AQUINAS

#### TEXTS

*Opera omnia. . . .* Edited by S. E. Fretté and Pauli Mare. 34 vols. Paris, 1871–1880. Vives edition.

*Opera omnia iussu impensaque, Leonis XIII. P. M. edita.* Rome, 1882–1948. Leonine edition.

*Sancti Thomas Aquinas . . . opera omni. . . .* 25 vols. Parma, 1852–1873. Reprinted New York, 1948–1950.

#### TRANSLATIONS

*Basic Writings of St. Thomas Aquinas.* Translated by A. C. Pegis. 2 vols. New York, 1945.

*Nature and Grace: Selections from Summa Theologica of Thomas Aquinas.* Translated by A. M. Fairweather. Philadelphia, 1954.

*On Being and Essence.* Translated by A. A. Maurer. Toronto, 1949. Translation of *De Ente.*

*On Kingship.* Translated by I. T. Eschmann. Toronto, 1949. Revision of translation by Gerald B. Phelan under the title *On the Governance of Rulers.* Translation of *De regimine principum.*

*Philosophical Texts.* Translated by Thomas Gilby. New York and London, 1951.

*Selected Political Writings.* Translated by A. P. D'Entrèves and J. G. Dawson. Oxford, 1948.

*Selected Writings.* Translated by M. C. D'Arcy. London, 1934; New York, 1950.

*The "Summa contra Gentiles" of Saint Thomas Aquinas . . .* Translated by the English Dominican Fathers. 5 vols. London, 1924–1929. One of the standard English translations.

*Summa theologica.* Edited by Thomas Gilby and P. K. Meagher. 61 vols. to date. New York, 1963– . Latin text with English translation. The Blackfriars edition.

*The "Summa theologica" of St. Thomas Aquinas.* 20 vols. New York, 1911–1925. One of the standard English translations.

*Truth.* Translated by R. W. Mulligan, J. V. McGlynn, and R. W. Schmidt. 3 vols. Chicago, 1952–1954. Translation of *De veritate.*

#### LEXICON

Deferrari, R. J., M. I. Barry, and I. McGuiness. *A Lexicon of St. Thomas Aquinas.* Washington, D. C., 1948–1949.

#### GENERAL WORKS AND CRITICAL STUDIES

Bourke, V. J. *Aquinas's Search for Wisdom.* Milwaukee, 1965.

Callus, D. A. *The Condemnation of St. Thomas at Oxford.* Oxford, 1946.

Chenu, M. D. *Towards Understanding St. Thomas.* Chicago, 1964.

Chesterton, G. K. *St. Thomas Aquinas.* London, 1933. A popular short account.

Copleston, F. C. *Aquinas.* London, 1955. Authoritative.

D'Arcy, M. C. *St. Thomas Aquinas.* London, 1953. Philosophical in approach.

D'Entrèves, A. P. *The Medieval Contribution to Political Thought.* Oxford, 1936.

Farrell, W. *A Companion to the Summa.* 4 vols. New York, 1945–1949.

Foster, K., ed. *The Life of St. Thomas Aquinas: Biographical Documents.* Baltimore and London, 1959.

Gilson, E. *The Christian Philosophy of St. Thomas Aquinas.* Translated by L. K. Shook. London, 1957. With a catalog of Saint Thomas' works by I. T. Eschmann.

Garrigou-Lagrange, R. *The One God. A Commentary on the First Part of St. Thomas's Theological Summa.* St. Louis, Mo., 1944. Very sound.

Glenn, P. J. *A Tour of the Summa.* St. Louis, Mo., 1960.

Grabmann, M. *Thomas Aquinas, His Personality and Thought.* London, 1928. An excellent introduction.

Kenny, A. J. P., ed. *Aquinas: A Collection of Critical Essays.* Notre Dame, Ind., 1976.

Lonergen, B. *Verbum: Word and Idea in Aquinas.* Notre Dame, Ind., 1967.

Mandonnet, S. *Siger de Brabant et l'Averroisme Latin au XIIIe siècle.* 2nd ed. Louvain, 1911.

Maritain, J. *The Angelic Doctor.* New York, 1931.

Maurer, A. A., ed. *St. Thomas Aquinas, 1274–1974, Commemorative Studies.* 2 vols. Toronto, 1974.

Patterson, R. L. *The Concept of God in the Philosophy of Aquinas.* London, 1933.

Pieper, J. *Guide to Thomas Aquinas.* Translated by R. C. Winston. New York, 1962.

Rousselot, P. *The Intellectualism of St. Thomas.* London, 1935.

Sertillanges, A. *St. Thomas Aquinas and His Work.* Translated by G. Anstruther. London, 1931.

Weisheipl, J. A. *Friar Thomas d'Aquino.* Oxford, 1974. A scholarly biographical study.

## MEDIEVAL SCHOLASTICISM

### GENERAL WORKS AND CRITICAL STUDIES

Carré, M. H. *Realists and Nominalists.* Oxford, 1946.

Copleston, F. C. *History of Philosophy.* Vols. 2 and 3. London, 1952–1953. Very sound.

de Wulf, M. *History of Medieval Philosophy.* 3 vols. London, 1935–1947.

Gilson, E. *History of Christian Philosophy in the Middle Ages.* London, 1955. Good.

————. *The Spirit of Medieval Philosophy.* New York, 1948.

Knowles, D. *The Evolution of Medieval Thought.* London, 1962. Valuable introduction.

Leff, G. *Medieval Thought.* London, 1958.

Vignaux, P. *Philosophy in the Middle Ages.* London, 1959.

## EARLY MEDIEVAL WRITERS

### GENERAL WORKS AND CRITICAL STUDIES

Barth, K. *Anselm's Fides Quaerens Intellectum.* 2nd ed. London, 1958.

Chenu, M. D. *Nature, Man and Society in the Twelfth Century.* Chicago, 1968.

de Ghellinck, J. *L'Essor de la litterature latine au XIIe siècle.* Brussels and Paris, 1946.

————. *Le Mouvement théologique du XIIe siècle.* Bruges, 1948.

Evans, G. R. *Anselm and Talking About God.* Oxford, 1978.

Haskins, C. H. *The Renaissance of the Twelfth Century.* Cambridge, Mass., 1927.

Hopkins, J. *A Companion to the Study of St. Anselm.* Minneapolis, 1972.

Luscombe, D. E. *Peter Abelard's Ethics.* Oxford, 1971.

————. *The School of Peter Abelard.* Cambridge, 1969.

McIntyre, J. *St. Anselm and His Critics.* London, 1954.

Paré, G., A. Brunet, and P. Tremblay. *La Renaissance du XIIe siècle.* Paris, 1933.

Sikes, J. G. *Peter Abailard.* Cambridge, 1932.

Southern, R. W. *Anselm and His Biographer.* Cambridge, 1963.

van Steenberghen, F. *The Philosophical Movement in the Thirteenth Century.* London, 1955.

Weingart, R. E. *The Logic of Divine Love: A Critical Study of the Soteriology of Peter Abailard.* Oxford, 1970.

## LATE MEDIEVAL THOUGHT

### GENERAL WORKS AND CRITICAL STUDIES

Baudry, L. *Guillaume d'Occam.* Paris, 1950.

Boehner, P. *Medieval Logic, c. 1250–1400.* Manchester, 1952.

de Lagarde, G. *La Naissance de l'esprit laique.* 6 vols. 3rd ed. Paris, 1959.

Duns Scotus, John. *God and Creatures.* Translated by F. Alluntie and A. B. Wolter. Princeton, 1975.

Gilson, E. *Jean Duns Scotus.* Paris, 1952.

Leff, G. *Bradwardine and the Pelagians.* Cambridge, 1954.

————. *Gregory of Rimini.* Manchester, 1961.

————. *William of Ockham.* Manchester, 1975.

Oberman, H. A. *The Harvest of Medieval Theology, Gabriel Biel and Late Medieval Nominalism.* Cambridge, Mass., 1963.

Vignaux, P. *Le Nominalisme au XIVe siècle.* Montreal, 1948.

### BIBLIOGRAPHIES

Bourke, V. J. *Thomistic Bibliography, 1920–1940.* St. Louis, Mo., 1945.

Mandonnet, P., and J. Destrez. *Bibliographie Thomiste.* Paris, 1921.

V. H. H. GREEN

# ARTHURIAN LEGEND

LEGEND IS AS unpredictable and fickle in its ways as Fortune herself. The memory of some great men it leaves largely to the care of historians, that of others it enhances and magnifies in the popular mind, while to that of lesser figures it chooses on occasion to impart the illusion of greatness. In the Middle Ages legend showed particular concern for Charlemagne and King Arthur; but if, in the case of the emperor, it increased a luster already there, it may well have favored Arthur far beyond his historical deserts.

A sixth-century chronicler tells, but without naming the victor, how the westward advance of the Anglo-Saxons was halted by their defeat at the hands of the Celtic Britons at a certain Mount Badon around A.D. 500. In a composite chronicle given final shape by Nennius in about 830, the British commander is specified as Arthur, who on the field performed prodigious feats with the aid of Christ and the Virgin Mary. Mention is made of the footprint of his dog, wonderfully preserved in a stone, and the tomb of his son Amr, which varied in length every time it was measured. So by this time we find legend already beginning to weave spells around the name—surprisingly Roman ("Artorius" is earlier attested both in Britain and on the Continent)—of this shadowy British captain.

A scattering of Latin and especially Welsh texts, all difficult to date and ranging from the allusive to the positively cryptic, give tantalizing glimpses of the accretion of tales about an Arthur raised to the dignity of king and gathering around him warriors who, in time, will become household names. Most prominent among them at this early stage is Kay "the fair," who is not yet the fractious seneschal of later tradition. Here too, besides figures less familiar or otherwise quite unknown, we see Guenevere, Mordred, Bedivere, and Gawain, the king's nephew. Other testimony suggests that before the twelfth century was very old, a belief in Arthur's immortality was current on both sides of the Channel and that tales about him may have circulated as far as Italy.

It appears, then, that a British military leader distinguished himself in at least one engagement and possibly a number of others around the year 500 in an attempt to limit the expansion of Anglo-Saxon rule. Seen by his people as a hero, he was credited with divine help in his exploits, which were exaggerated in the common memory as the years and centuries passed. These Celts were great tellers of tales, and the professional class that purveyed them was held in high esteem. The characters in their stories might be real kings and heroes of the past, gods from the decayed ruins of an ancient mythology, gods turned men, or men marked with divinity; all moved easily between this world and another, where the logic of everyday did not necessarily prevail and the new religion of Christianity was little countenanced. From stories such as these was eventually to come much of the supporting cast for that nostalgically remembered leader who, said the chroniclers, had once fought triumphantly for the Britons, bearing the image of the Virgin on his shoulders.

The chief collection of medieval Welsh tales is the *Mabinogion;* and of these the earliest in which Arthur appears is *Culhwch and Olwen,* thought to have been current before 1100. There he already enjoys a kind of imperial status; and this was to be confirmed and reinforced by Geoffrey of Monmouth, to whom must go most of the credit for establishing Arthur's illustrious place in literature. Geoffrey lived and wrote in Oxford, where he may have taught; and in 1135 or 1136 he completed his *Historia Regum Britanniae (The History of the Kings of Britain),* in which he traced the fanciful (though supposedly true) history of the British kings from a certain Brutus, three generations after the Trojan War, to Cadwalader, who died in A.D. 689. He claims as his source an ancient book in the British tongue, but this is commonly regarded as one of the fabrications to which he appears frequently to have resorted. His work is indeed a strange mixture of fact with fictions borrowed from known sources, picked up perhaps by hearsay, or simply invented. In its course he provides Arthur with a biography worthy of Charlemagne. The analogy may be apt, since Geoffrey seems to have been consciously providing the English monarchy with an imposing and more venerable tradition to rival that by which the French kings derived their authority from the great Holy Roman Emperor.

Geoffrey tells of the unusual circumstances in which Arthur was conceived and born, and how at the age of fifteen he succeeded his father, Utherpendragon, as king of Britain. At once he marched against the Saxons and, after a long and ultimately successful campaign, next turned his attention to the Picts and Scots. These he subdued along with the Irish, and then extended his conquests to Iceland having, in the meantime, married the lovely Guenevere. Very soon his fame spread throughout the earth on account not only of his military exploits but also of the fine manners and elegance of his court. Then he conceived the ambition of subjugating all Europe and eventually forced Norway and the whole of Gaul to submit. One Whitsuntide, as he held court at Caerleon-on-Usk, messengers arrived from Rome, summoning him to make reparation for his outrageous conduct. His response was to assemble an army with the aim of humbling Rome itself. Crossing the Channel, he personally slew a giant on Mont-Saint-Michel before defeating the Romans at Saussy. About to carry the fight on to the imperial city, he received news that his nephew Mordred, to whom he had entrusted the government of Britain in his absence, had usurped both crown and queen. Returning posthaste, he engaged and defeated Mordred twice (on the first occasion losing his other nephew, Gawain); then, pursuing him to Cornwall, he fought the great Battle of Camlann, in which Mordred was slain and he himself mortally wounded. Yet we read that Arthur was transported to the Isle of Avalon "ad sananda vulnera sua" (that his wounds might be healed). Geoffrey thus respects the tradition of Arthur's immortality.

His *Historia* immediately took the literate public, both insular and continental, by storm, as is attested by the great number of surviving manuscripts. It was translated into French (on at least two occasions), English, Welsh, and Old Norse, and was frequently put to use by later writers of history and fiction. Wace, who was born on the island of Jersey but spent most of his life in Caen, turned it into French verse as the *Roman de Brut* in 1155, the year of Geoffrey's death. Wace's version is quite free and contains a number of elaborations on the *Historia,* including the first reference we have to the Round Table. It ousted a somewhat earlier translation, presumably on the grounds of literary merit; and it is said that he presented a copy to Eleanor of Aquitaine, the new queen of England and mother of Marie de Champagne, for whom Chrétien de Troyes was to compose at least one of his romances, *Lancelot.*

There is no doubting, then, that Geoffrey,

partly through his translators, did much to make the name of King Arthur ring through the courts of northern Europe by the middle of the twelfth century or soon after. In view of this it may seem strange that Chrétien, composing in the second half of that century and often dubbed "the father of Arthurian romance," used him as little as he did: only for one major episode (in *Cligés*) and a handful of lesser borrowings, all apparently by way of Wace's rendering. Why should this be? An answer is, I think, to be sought in the shifting norms of literary taste.

By the middle of the twelfth century fashions in the more cultured courts of northern France were undergoing a significant change. Until then the staple literary entertainment there had been the *chansons de geste,* epics performed by professional *jongleurs* to some kind of musical accompaniment. These martial poems, developed usually from a grain of historical truth, celebrated great deeds and events of the heroic Frankish past. Most dealt with Carolingian times, many with Charlemagne and his barons. Offering more than mere entertainment, they also served to illustrate the high virtues of the feudal ideal as well as some of its flaws. The job of both poet and performer was to pull their audiences into the turmoil of the action, playing on their emotions, leaving no time or cause for reflection. High though the craftsmanship of many of the *chansons* is, they do not parade their technical subtleties; but, declaimed by the expert *jongleur,* they would have marched along with a strong, hypnotic rhythm, evoking stark yet brilliant scenes through their stylized, formula-packed descriptions and almost ritually measured actions. Bare of authorial analysis and intricate dialogue, they revealed characters through forthright deeds and declarations, and reactions to those of others. They presented individual heroisms, but always in the context of communal endeavor. Questions of right and wrong needed no elucidation by the poet or debate at the song's end: the moral was self-evident and indeed assumed.

The *chansons de geste* did not fall suddenly from grace; but increasing leisure was helping to refine the literary palates of the knightly classes, who, as relief from the epic imperative, came to enjoy stories that allowed time for reflection and a freer play of the imagination. These tastes were admirably served by a class of poets that had passed through the Latin schools and there had come to know the great writers of antiquity and learned the arts of composition as well as debate. It was they who devised the new genre of romance for their courtly patrons; and naturally enough they looked first to the ancient world for their subjects: Alexander, Aeneas, the Theban wars, and, later, Troy, besides shorter tales from Ovid. They composed their works to be read, either aloud to groups or privately by the literate, whose numbers increased as the century wore on. This relieved them of any fear of overtaxing a *jongleur*'s memory and so of the need for the baldness, concision, and formulaic diction of the *chansons de geste.* They could expand their descriptions to cater, for instance, to their public's interest in the exotic and in marvels beyond those associated with their Christian faith. They were free to round out the portraits of their characters by means of comment and, more especially, extended passages of dialogue or monologues, in which doubts might be expressed as well as certainties, the personal as well as the common point of view. Motives could be explored as well as deeds, the psychological roots of behavior and not just its superficial causes and effects.

These poets of romance, then, had both the opportunity and the inclination to dwell more on individual than on collective endeavor, a preference fostered by their patrons' growing acceptance of love between the sexes as a matter worthy of literary development. For them Ovid was a revered master of the subject; but it had also been cultivated as their main lyric theme by the troubadours of Provence from the beginning of the twelfth century; and they had shown how it could be, rather factitiously, reconciled with the feudal ideal by in part patterning the relationship of lover to mistress on that of vassal to lord. They thus elaborated a code of amorous conduct that we know today as courtly love. The term is modern (medieval poets spoke of *fin amor,* or noble love) and is used to cover a wide spectrum of relationships, from the highly formalized, quite often adulterous, Provençal concept to a more natural love affair conducted within the polite conventions of an aristocratic society and finding its appropriate end in marriage. Though the songs of the troubadours must have been known to audiences in the north by the middle of the century (Chrétien de Troyes was familiar with them a little later and composed in their manner), the taste there inclined toward love between equals leading to stable wedlock rather than a passionate wooing of an imperious lady, the *domna* figure, ending most often in frustration. In any case, the northern public of the romances was prepared, indeed eager, to accord a greater place in narrative literature to adventures of the heart than had been allowed in the warrior world of the early epic.

So by the middle of the twelfth century a need was being felt in courtly society for an alternative to, if not a replacement for, the heady but intellectually limited entertainment provided by the *chansons de geste.* The poets were at hand. What of the subject matter? Ideally it would offer a series of exciting, colorful adventures capable of being given some contemporary relevance in contrast to the epic's nostalgic dwelling on past glories and saturation in an ethos that was becoming progressively less fitted to the new conditions of life. It would afford scope too for the presentation of an individual rather than group mentality and for some psychological study, if possible in the context of a love relationship. With all this, it would provide food for thought and discussion once the reading was over. The so-called Matter of Rome, as exploited, for instance, in the *Roman d'Eneas* at about this time, fulfilled some if not all of these conditions. Geoffrey of Monmouth's *Historia,* and particularly his account of Arthur, might seem to have come as a godsend to the practitioners of romance.

The truth is that Geoffrey had produced merely the scenario for a new narrative tradition. Here is the great monarch well equipped, with his conquests and imperial ambitions, to rival the Charlemagne of the epics. He holds splendid court, crowned in state and surrounded by his knights and tributaries. He fully displays the noble quality of largesse and presides over a company whose polished manners are unsurpassed. The ladies wear the colors of their chosen knights, who are admitted to their love only after proving themselves thrice in combat and are seen tourneying for their favors and for the rich prizes Arthur bestows. There was something very up to date in the 1130's about this show of courtly manners; but there was also something very traditional in Geoffrey's account of the king's military activities, which savored of the *chansons de geste.* We should not be surprised at this, or blame him, since he was setting out not to inspire a new genre but rather, surely, to depict an imposing figure who could compete with Charlemagne in epic or quasi-historical tradition. In this he was successful.

Perhaps we can now see why Chrétien drew so little on Geoffrey or on Wace. Although they had provided, with Arthur and his court, a magnificent backcloth or starting point for individual adventures, the exploits they recounted were in the old epic fashion. (Interestingly, Chrétien's one extended borrowing is for an episode in *Cligés* that he stiffens with authentic epic material, as is seen in the essay on Chrétien in this volume.) Where, then, are the new-style adventures to come from, given that medieval writers seldom invent on a large scale? Fortunately another fund of Celtic legend was now becoming available to continental writers.

I have already spoken of the tales of gods and heroes that circulated from time immemorial in the Celtic world and of which little more than the debris has survived for us, recorded for the most part in late manuscripts. The richest store is in Irish and represents the legacy of countless generations of *filid,* a caste of highly trained storytellers whose familiarity with the heroic and arcane traditions of their race earned for them a privileged position in society. Their lore was transmitted by word of mouth; and what we find in the manuscript pages is little more than the shadow of a fragment of their vast repertoire. The Welsh bards *(cyfarwyddiaid)* also traded in legends, but were more popular entertainers of lower status than the Irish storytellers. Our knowledge of their wares comes from the assemblage of partially redacted tales known as the *Mabinogion* and from allusions to others scattered through various early Welsh texts.

Kindred peoples, the Irish and Welsh shared a common cultural heritage; and though the extent and nature of their physical contacts in the early Middle Ages have still to be clarified, there must have been some give and take of legendary material between them. Thus the Welsh *Culhwch and Olwen,* which has the character of a prototypical Arthurian romance, contains certain themes and elements found also in Irish legend. So although Wales is generally agreed to be the principal point of departure for Celtic matter on its way to the Continent, numerous narrative threads in the later romances would appear ultimately to lead back to Ireland, if not always without tangles for scholarly unraveling. A celebrated case is the legend of Tristan and Isolt; for in its development the Picts, Irish, Welsh, and Bretons all seem to have had a hand, to say nothing of the possibility of even more exotic influences from the East.

In the romances the preponderance of Welsh names, as well as the existence of themes that can plausibly be traced back to stories circulating earlier in Wales, argues strongly for that country's being a clearinghouse for much Arthurian material. There has, however, been considerable debate as to how this Matter of Britain came into the hands of Chrétien and his continental contemporaries. The obvious answer, that it was passed by way of the Anglo-Normans, may be overly simple in view of the presence in the French romances of Breton name-forms and certain affinities with tales localized in Brittany, where Arthur was certainly well known quite early in the twelfth century. When these facts are taken into account, there seem to be five main ways in which transmission could have occurred.

First, the tales could have been carried across the Channel by Welshmen: scholars pursuing their studies in the French schools, men in the company of prelates or diplomats, mercenary soldiers, or even professional storytellers versed in French as well as their native tongue. This last alternative is given substance by a handful of references, mainly in romances, to a famed teller of tales by the name of Bleddri, who seemingly had a high reputation in France in the first half of the twelfth century. Of course this in no way lessens the likelihood that the Anglo-Normans often played some intermediary role. Even before the Conquest of 1066, there were Normans established on the Welsh marches; and although during the next century their attempts to achieve hegemony over the whole land had mixed success, their influence was considerable, particularly in the south. There were no sealed frontiers; and if many Normans served or even settled in Wales, some Welshmen we know were hired to fight in England, churchmen moved to and fro between the two territories, and marriage alliances between their peoples were not infrequent. Legend needs no broad highways for its wanderings, and such routes as there were between the Welsh and the Normans were wide open. If the language difference was a potential barrier, there were the Bretons.

William brought large numbers of Bretons with him in 1066; and some enjoyed positions of authority in various parts of England and Wales. At home in both tongues, they would have made ideal translators of Welsh material; but it would not have been surprising to find them giving some of the names involved a characteristic Breton form. This could explain, for instance, why the Welsh Geraint became known to the French as Erec (Breton "Guerec"), or Owein as Yvain (Breton "Ivan"). Easy as it is to justify a Breton link in the chain of transmission, it is less simple to decide how the rest of it was formed. Three possibilities suggest themselves. Stories could have passed from the Welsh to the Bretons, from them to the Anglo-Normans, and so to the continental French; or the Bretons could have carried them directly to France; or they could have taken them to their Armorican homeland (where, as I have said, tales about Arthur did circulate long before the first known romances were composed), and the French could then have obtained them from Brittany. Thus our five alternatives are transmission by the Welsh directly to the French, or by way of the Anglo-Normans, or with the Bretons acting as go-betweens in three possible ways. But of course these are not true alternatives, since all five routes could have carried some of the traffic. I would merely add that strong arguments can be adduced for supposing that the Anglo-Normans did play a leading role in the whole process and that a good number of the Celtic stories were retold and perhaps written down in their language, whether in verse or prose. The disappearance almost without trace of such versions may be due to their lacking the literary polish of the romances that superseded them. But the matter is controversial, and this is not the place to pursue it.

Whatever their routes of transmission, we can be sure that the stories were profitable merchandise and that those who conveyed them from one milieu to the other did their best to adapt them to the tastes of their new public; and this might well have involved bringing originally independent tales into the Arthurian orbit. Before turning to the emergence of Arthurian romance proper, however, let us consider for a moment some features of the native Welsh tradition, as seen in the more primitive of the *Mabinogion* texts, and how the French on both sides of the Channel might have reacted to them.

If I suggest they would have thought some things uncouth, this is not to disparage the work of the Welsh bards, but to recognize on the one hand that much formal excellence does not survive translation and, on the other, that the tales contain various elements that their new public might have found it hard to reconcile with their own view of the world. This view was essentially logical, based on the belief that everything can be explained, even if only on the supernatural plane in accordance with Christian cosmology. Magic and sorcery were accepted by the French, though with the underlying assumption that this was the work of divine, or more often infernal, powers; but it did not pervade their literature with the same regularity and absence of comment as it did that of the Celts. There, characters practice the magic arts at every turn, conjuring up their needs of the moment, turning enemies into beasts, or flowers into the loveliest of maidens. Others have preternatural gifts or peculiarities: in *Culhwch and Olwen,* for example, Kay's heart and hands are eternally cold, yet otherwise he possesses great heat; moreover he could go without sleep and hold his breath under water for nine days and nights; he could make himself as tall as a tree, and any burden he carried would be invisible. Shape-shifting is as common as it can be bewildering. Even time and place are alarmingly flexible: a lady rides past at a leisurely pace, yet galloping pursuers cannot catch up with her; questers see ahead a great fort, but after a day's journey they are no nearer to it than before. This is a world of illusion and uncertainty, and those who enter must leave all notions of logic behind.

It is a complex world in which three spheres of activity interlink: those of the gods, of men, and of animals. The gods are seen walking the earth with common mortals, and the nearest we come to a distinct otherworld is to catch an occasional glimpse of one of those fairy mounds that are its entry points. So the supernatural seems to commingle with the everyday to a degree that might have created a surfeit of ambiguity in French eyes. At the same time one finds a remarkably intimate relationship between the human and animal worlds. Not only do men and women assume animal form or have it inflicted upon them, but the beasts themselves often have human attributes and sometimes more than human wisdom, which they can communicate through an interpreter. These creatures, from grateful ants to a talismanic boar, seem to have strayed from a once more coherent mythology; and they retain a vitality unfamiliar to a public more used to the stuffed, symbolic figures of the bestiaries, the faithful steeds of the epics, or the humans masquerading as animals that people the fables.

These Welsh tales contain, too, elements of gratuitous brutality unlikely to appeal to a courtly audience: a suitor lured into a bag, then kicked and belabored to the point of death; warriors in another bag slain by having their heads squeezed and crushed; horses maimed out of resentment toward their owner; a young lad thrust into a fire; an attempt to roast a giant and his wife in an iron house. Some of this may be *fabliau* material, but is hardly the stuff of romance.

Equally uncourtly is the general attitude to women, who are by no means exempt from harsh or demeaning treatment, as witness the queen compelled to act as cook for the household and receive a daily box on the ear from the court butcher. In love affairs reciprocal passions are found; but more often the man lights on a suitable bride and obtains her without more ado, or at most after negotiating with her parents. Things are no better, and often worse, for women than in the *chansons de geste.* There is no suggestion of the man's having to earn his bride by proving himself worthy of her, and no question on her part of putting him to the test. The general absence of psychological probing extends to the love situation. True, a thwarted Irish or Welsh lover may fall into a wasting sickness as readily as a hero or heroine of romance; but the condition is mentioned only tersely and not described in the clinical detail learned by the romance authors primarily from Ovid.

Students of early French literature know well the poets' practice of adapting to their own social and cultural environment matter that originated outside it. It is therefore easy to imagine them smoothing away some elements that their public might find crude or puzzling in the Celtic tales and generally decking them out in more fashionable attire. Unfortunately it is a process we cannot study closely in the absence of any direct Welsh (or Breton) source for a French romance. In any case, as we saw, it may have occurred in two stages, with some stories being retold in the first instance for the Anglo-Norman market and then further adapted on the Continent. The best evidence for this is, curiously enough, in the shape of two Welsh texts of the *Mabinogion: Gereint* and *Owein* (or *The Lady of the Fountain*). Though in their present form they are likely to date from the thirteenth century, it can be shown that they were most probably translated back into Welsh from Anglo-Norman originals quite close to Chrétien's sources for his *Erec et Enide* and *Yvain.* A third Welsh text, *Peredur,* tells the same basic story as Chrétien's *Conte del Graal;* but its testimony is more suspect in that it appears to stand in part in his debt, though with an admixture of primitive Celtic matter. I must say in fairness that these relationships are widely, but not universally, accepted. But if this was the way of it, then the Anglo-Norman stage shows few of those typical Celtic features I mentioned as being potentially offensive to a French public: a first attempt seems therefore to have been made to restyle the primitive material, and Chrétien takes the process much further in his own romances.

We can now attempt with reasonable assurance to reconstruct the early history of a typical twelfth-century French Arthurian romance. There circulates in Wales a story incorporating age-old motifs, in the course of which a hero has a series of adventures and encounters, some with an air of the supernatural about them, some grotesque in other ways, a little haphazard, but including his acquisition of a bride. A bilingual entertainer, a Breton perhaps, adapts the tale for his Anglo-Norman patrons toward the middle of the twelfth century. If Arthur does not already appear, the adapter has a strong incentive for introducing him, now that Geoffrey of Monmouth has established him as the Charlemagne of British legend. Moreover, by using the Arthurian court at least as the starting point of the adventures, he gives them a quasi-historical context and a scene of operations identifiable with the real world. He thus brings the shadowy and disturbingly fluid Celtic universe into sharper focus, though not so sharp as to abolish all mystery. At the same time he reduces the supernatural elements with their haunting, pagan sense of destiny to what he deems acceptable; and this he does as far as possible by rationalizing rather than eliminating the features in question. Providing plausible motivation where it was lacking in the original, he brings the tale further into the realm of reality and may at the same time develop a little the love theme, making some concessions to the more refined sensibilities of the men and women of the Anglo-Norman aristocracy. These modifications add up to a certain stabilization of the fictional world and a more realistic presentation of the adventures, which now take place not in the unfamiliar and relatively unpolished society of the Celts, but in courts and castles peopled by characters acting out the customs and manners of contemporary chivalry. Our adapter is less a dedicated artist (he may not even have been a poet) than a professional entertainer with thoughts more on his purse and present needs than on immortality. He has done a good job as a middleman and performed the vital service of making this rich vein of legendary material available in the French tongue, leaving those of higher literary gifts to effect the final transformation into the sophisticated verse romances now in demand.

It will be seen in the next essay what the skillful hands of Chrétien were to forge from such rough ingots smelted from the native Celtic ore, but a few general observations can be made here. He developed the concept of Arthur's court as a kind of home base from which characters depart and to which they periodically return. It is seen as the focal point of the civilized, chivalric world, the center of the web of narrative threads, thereby having both an exemplary and a structural function. At its heart sits the king:

> *Artus, li buens rois de Bretaingne,*
> *La cui proesce nos ansaingne,*
> *Que nos soiiens preu et cortois.*
> (*Yvain,* 1–3)

Arthur, the good king of Britain, whose prowess teaches us valor and courtliness.

Nevertheless, Chrétien takes care to make a little less than an ideal realm presided over by a perfect sovereign, and this will have implications for the whole development of the romance genre. Already it seems to carry the telltale signs of its own eventual disintegration. In *Cligés* we see tension between Queen Guenevere and the vengeful Arthur over the fate of captured traitors; in *Lancelot* the king is remarkably acquiescent as Guenevere is abducted, only to cuckold him later; in *Yvain,* despite the lofty note of its opening, his court is the scene of undignified bickering, and more than one character refers to Arthur's folly; in the *Conte du Graal* he sits helplessly by as his own dignity is assaulted and the queen driven to the brink of suicide by an intruder knight.

In Chrétien, then, King Arthur has something of the puppet king *(roi fainéant)* about him, more so than in Welsh tradition or in Geoffrey of Monmouth. This can no doubt be accounted for in part by the fact that these are stories about one or other of his knights, and so he cannot play an overactive role himself. At the same time Chrétien may well have had in mind the example of Charlemagne (a clear reminiscence occurs at the end of the *Conte du Graal*); for the emperor, though a venerated and almost patriarchal figure, shows even in the *Chanson de Roland* moments of ineptitude, lethargy, and almost suicidal despair. Surely too this discreet reduction of Arthur's stature owes something to the fact that Chrétien was essentially a realist, more interested in human beings than in idealized figureheads. It is part of his contribution to the process already begun of reducing the outsize heroes of Celtic legend to human proportions.

In handling the adventures he similarly carries further the move toward rationalization. He is prepared to retain extravagant elements that have a significant function in the plot. Thus in his romances we find a number of outlandish creatures such as giants, demons, and a fire-breathing serpent; the heroes are helped by magic potions and cures as well as a variety of protective rings; we come across wonders like the underwater and sword bridges in *Lancelot,* a hedge of mist in *Erec et Enide,* and in the *Conte du Graal* a lance that oozes blood in a castle that apparently languishes under a spell; and one feature essential to the plot of *Yvain* and that also acts as an important structural element is the magic spring or fountain. It is interesting, though, to find Chrétien giving this latter feature a precise geographical location in the real world: it is in the Forest of Broceliande in Brittany, where it can be visited to this day. Indeed, a particular characteristic of Chrétien's art is the care he usually devotes, with due allowance made for fictional compression, to a realistic detailing of matters of time and place; and when, particularly in *Lancelot,* he appears to revert to the tantalizing vagueness of the Celtic legends, we have a right to suspect him of an ulterior motive.

Not content with extending the rationalization of the story elements and so conveying the illusion of the events happening in a logically organized world, he also took pride in giving them "a very fine structure" (*Erec,* 14), that is to say, an artistically pleasing arrangement of the tale's constituent parts, some of which he was prepared to insert from secondary sources or even, on occasion, to invent by himself. Such structural changes as we can point to with reasonable confidence seem designed to provide a logical progression in the adventures, building up to an imposing climax: the coronation of Erec or, in *Yvain,* the hero's extended duel with Gauvain immediately preceding the resolution of his marital crisis. The typical bipartite structure of his romances Chrétien inherited in part from his sources: the hero achieves initial success, then suffers a reversal of his fortunes and enters on a second train of adventures that lead to his final triumph (in *Cligés* the same pattern is provided by the hero's story being preceded by that of his parents). His structure benefits greatly from a special talent he had for bearing in mind future developments in his narrative as he composed, preparing for them well in advance, and dropping hints we may catch if we can but which, even if we only half-remember them, leave us with the impression when the events actually occur that they have happened quite naturally. In this way he bound his romances together, reinforcing our conviction that the adventures, however full of surprises, really have taken place in a world where causes determine effects. This is not at all the feeling we have about the ambiguous and often dislocated setting of the Welsh tales.

Perhaps Chrétien's greatest achievement was in the area of character development, the investigation of motives as well as actions, of the psychological as well as physical reactions to events. This he did primarily by a generous infusion of skillfully handled and often surprisingly natural, varied, informative dialogue. Committed as he was by his choice of subject to a series of more or less fortuitous happenings, he could not be expected to make the romance's entire action proceed from the psychology of the characters, even had he wished; but by allowing us to see quite deeply into their thoughts and feelings, he ensures that our interest stays more with them than with the events, so that we ask ourselves not what will happen to them in this or that predicament, but how they will deal with it and how it may affect their future conduct. And when all has been said and done, although Chrétien was not in the habit of being explicit in these matters, we suspect that most of the chief actors in the drama learned something from their experiences and so not merely won success but grew as human beings.

For obvious reasons, it is not customary to examine traditional tales like those in the *Mabinogion* for interpretations in the sense of authorial points of view or morals to be drawn. The effort is reserved for more highly organized works like Chrétien's, where it is tempting to suppose that so much intellectual and artistic care implies more than the simple wish to tell a good story in an admirable way. It is the common view that he wishes to tell us there something important about love, or chivalry, or the relationship between them. These are undeniably the leading themes we find; though whether he is proposing solutions or simply investigating problems is a moot question, to which I shall return briefly while leaving a fuller discussion for the essay on Chrétien.

That he was fascinated by the whole question of love between the sexes is apparent from the way in which he dwells on its treatment and elaborates it far beyond what his sources could have contained. In *Erec* he treats an all-absorbing love between two ideally matched partners and the painful process of its accommodation to the responsibilities of marriage and public life. There is something rather archaic and uncourtly about the way in which Erec claims his bride as of right (glad though she is to accept the honor); but for all her meekness, Enide eventually emerges as an equally strong personality, worthy to sit beside her husband at their coronation. Having given short shrift here to the process of falling in love, Chrétien more than remedies his neglect in the first part of *Cligés* by analyzing in abundant detail the tender burgeoning of a passion that is again fulfilled in an ideally happy marriage. In its second part he turns to an illicit affair between the young Cligés and his uncle's wife, seemingly as a riposte to a rival poet's treatment of Tristan's fatal passion for Isolt. From disparaging references to that story and his use of various subterfuges to mitigate the sin of adultery, one senses his disapproval of a love rather less than honest; and although here too the plot is resolved in the partners' marriage, the outcome is very contrived.

The adultery in his next romance is much more flagrant, involving as it does the ardent Lancelot and the queen herself. More than this, it gives Chrétien the chance to transpose into narrative the essentially lyric concept of a courtly love in which the man nurtures a consuming, desperate, and sometimes despairing passion for a lady above him in rank who is apt more often to trifle with his aspirations and stand on her capricious dignity than grant him the ultimate joy of her surrender. Here too Chrétien seems uneasy with his subject, to the point, it can be argued, where he treats the whole business tongue-in-cheek (though if so, his successors failed to appreciate the humor as they made of Lancelot's reciprocated passion one of the main tragic themes of Arthurian literature). In *Yvain* he seems to treat, as he had done in *Erec,* the problem of the conflicting demands within marriage made by the hero's love and his need to pursue active chivalry. But the theme is less simple than that and, as in *Lancelot,* embraces questions connected with the more rigid, if unwritten, code of courtly love. The Perceval adventures in the *Conte du Graal* map the progress of the inexperienced youth from frolics with his mother's chambermaids, then a gauche wayside encounter with a maiden of breeding, to his pledging of heart and service to the young mistress of a castle: this is a full apprenticeship in love. For the remainder of the unfinished text we follow the philandering path of Gauvain from frustration to frustration; but more of that later.

It is as if Chrétien were using the romance form as a kind of laboratory for studying the workings of sexual love in a variety of situations and conditions: how does it begin? how does it mature? how does it become adapted to a permanent partnership in marriage (which he seems to regard as its only legitimate final repository)? We know he had received clerical training in the Latin schools; and it is tempting to think of him viewing the vagaries of human passion from the outside, with the curiosity of the celibate. Be that as it may, by his range of treatments of the subject he showed how the romance could be used as a medium for psychological exploration and, most strikingly, in the sentimental field. He had set the heart of romance beating to the courtly rhythm.

He also went further than any predecessor in attuning the old heroic adventures to contemporary notions of chivalry and *courtoisie*. Chivalry denoted both the institution and formal attributes of knighthood and a code of conduct refined out of the standards of behavior necessary to the preservation of a feudal, warrior society. A knight's duty began with himself: complete integrity of thought and deed, physical and moral courage pushed to the limits. Then came his duty to his fellows: loyalty to kinsmen, companions, and overlord, fair play even toward an enemy, promptness to espouse a just cause, especially on behalf of the weak or oppressed or of women in general. Finally, he had to keep faith with God and the church, a duty, however, not overstressed in many of the romances.

Whereas the chivalric ethic governed the knight's conduct qua knight, the ideal of *courtoisie* ruled his behavior within the social unit of the court. He must show consideration for others and a humility and modesty foreign to the heroes of epic or Welsh legend. He must be open in character, generous both in spirit and in material things. In the everyday life of the court he must show an easy self-assurance and be elegant in dress and conversation, a good listener as well as talker. Toward all ladies he must behave with gallantry and respect, but to the one of his choice he must give proof of a particular devotion. For their part the ladies were as bound as the knights by the conventions of *courtoisie,* which they had after all played a leading part in establishing.

The twin ideals of chivalry and *courtoisie* were the mark of a society gradually freeing itself from the hard practical constraints of embattled feudal communities. The extent of their observance in the northern French courts would have varied greatly; but in one like the seat of the counts of Champagne at Troyes, where we know Chrétien enjoyed some patronage, they were cultivated almost to the point of preciosity and formed the subject of sophisticated debate. Pride of place in these deliberations was given to the ethics and practice of love in the courtly fashion. This was the climate in which Chrétien composed. We may like to imagine him participating personally in the lively exchanges of the debate: he certainly did so indirectly through his romances. Thus the pursuit I mentioned of an authorial viewpoint there is by no means unreasonable. Opinions as to his intentions can be reduced to three basic propositions: either his works are exemplary, showing how the ideals presented there should work in a properly oriented society; or, through an artful presentation of the detail of his stories, he implies criticism of the fictional order of things and, by extension, of his own world; or he is content to let the events and characters pose questions for his public to answer in their own way. The number of defenders to be found for the first two propositions speaks in favor of the third; but in any case Chrétien has shown, perhaps better than any, how the romance can serve the intellect as well as the emotions or satisfy a simple taste for marvelous adventure. With him Arthurian romance in particular became the main showcase for the display of these medieval secular ideals; and it was he who gave it its high polish. For his many imitators, he set its style and provided characteristic themes, which they were to exploit with varying degrees of originality and success.

We have seen a grain of history germinate in the popular imagination so that the exploits of a leader of the Britons in their struggle against the Anglo-Saxons grew to fabulous proportions in the telling, earning him a royal place among the folk heroes of the Welsh. Strands of ancient legend gathered about him; and, independently, an Oxford scholar ranked him among the early kings of Britain and endowed him with a biography to rival that of Charlemagne. His fame spread; and stories in which he figured became a source of revenue for professional entertainers in England and on the Continent. These for the most part dealt with other traditional heroes of the Celts, who were eagerly enrolled in his illustrious company and in later romance earned their places as knights of the Round Table. In France a receptive, aristocratic society awaited these stories, which most probably reached them by way of the Anglo-Normans. In the course of their transmission they were much modified and embellished with matter from many sources, not least from the Latin learning of the composers of verse romance, with Chrétien in their van. He demonstrated the full capabilities of a genre that, superseding the epic as favored court entertainment, exchanged its essentially centripetal movement (the securing of the feudal homelands and the Christian faith against external threats) for an outward-looking pursuit of adventure, albeit from the firm base of the Arthurian court. Whereas the epic warrior is sure of his own identity, his rights, and his obligations in the communal effort, Chrétien's heroes set out to make their own way in the world, armed with chivalry and *courtoisie,* but otherwise discovering their values as they go. With him the inspiriting certainty of the epic has been abandoned for a provocative uncertainty.

Although Chrétien pioneered the Matter of Britain, he enjoyed no monopoly of it. In *Cligés* he mentions that he had once told of King Mark and the fair Isolt; and this must mean that he had treated the story of Tristan or some part of it, despite his curious failure to mention the hero by name. Of his version no other trace remains. However, the legend has come down to us in two full-scale, though incomplete, French verse romances: a "courtly" rendering by Thomas of England seems to date from about 1160 and to have been the target of some sly digs by Chrétien in *Cligés;* then, toward the end of the century (some think earlier), a Norman, Béroul, produced a less polished version. A German *Tristan* by Eilhart von Oberge may have been composed between these two dates, whereas Gottfried von Strassburg's lofty adaptation of Thomas came somewhat later. A study of these texts together with a few short, episodic poems has led scholars to posit the existence of a lost archetype, perhaps Anglo-Norman, around the middle of the century: one more enigmatic pointer to a short-lived intermediate stage in the transition from legend to full-fledged romance. The Tristan story, however, does not lie in the mainstream of Arthurian romance; and although these poems do not ignore the king entirely, he plays no significant role. Only with the prose redactions of the thirteenth century is the hero admitted to the fellowship of the Round Table.

Another significant treatment of the Matter of Britain, but again only tangentially Arthurian, is in the Breton *lais,* short narrative poems so named because of their Armorican features and, indeed, the repeated claim of Breton origins made by their chief exponent, Marie de France. Marie lived in England toward the end of the twelfth century (her name indicating her continental origin); it may have been there that she picked up her tales from Breton entertainers. Only one of her *lais* speaks of Arthur and his court. It is, however, interesting to find much of their charm in her reluctance to rationalize completely her source material, so that she is often more ready than Chrétien to lead us through those enchanted between-worlds typical of Celtic legend.

To attempt a systematic account of the development of Arthurian romance is to be caught at every turn in the tangled thickets of relative chronology. Surviving works are unlikely to predate Chrétien, though they may contain primitive material in a form suggestive once again of an organized "pre-Celtic" phase of transmission. With his Continuators at least we know roughly where we stand. These were the poets who attempted to complete the *Conte du Graal,* which the master had left in suspense. The first of the Continuations must have been composed soon after Chrétien dropped his pen. It deals largely with Gauvain, and in quite engaging fashion, but itself expires after almost ten or twenty thousand lines (there is a short and a long redaction). The Second Continuation is equally verbose and incomplete on the subject of Perceval; but by about 1230 one man, Manessier, managed to bring matters to a conclusion, while another, Gerbert, worked independently to the same end, though in the manuscripts his contribution has been tailored to lead into Manessier's. These poets were not expending so much time, effort, and precious parchment to indulge their artistic fancy or desire to see a job completed: their toil suggests a public craving for more and yet more Arthurian storytelling. It shows too how, without the controlling and unifying imagination of a Chrétien, the romances could be spun out endlessly by the adding of new and only loosely related episodes drawn, at least in some cases, from independent Celtic fictions. The First Continuator, for instance, artificially inserts into Gauvain's adventures a series of exploits by a certain Caradoc.

Other of the verse romances provide good entertainment as well as a more unified structure, and all have interest of one kind or another. Renaut de Beaujeu's *Le Bel Inconnu,* for example, is told in quite polished verse and has the added merit of being the earliest extant version of the venerable legend of the Fair Unknown (a young man who attains knighthood, the discovery of his identity, and ultimate renown), which had considerable fortune in England, Germany, and Italy as well as in France and was also, I believe, at the root of Chrétien's *Conte du Graal.* A certain Guillaume le Clerc composed, probably in the 1220's, the romance of *Fergus,* which is unusual in that its action is located with uncommon precision in the south of Scotland and its hero, like Chrétien's Yvain, wins the hand of a lady of Lothian (the name of Yvain's bride, Laudine, and that of her father, Duke Laudunet, being derived from the name of the region). Two short romances dealing with Gauvain's exploits and probably composed for recital in a single session may also be noted here (I shall return to them later). They are *Le Chevalier à l'épée* and *La Mule sans frein* and have several points of interest. In the first, Chrétien is mentioned in a way that could imply he was the author, although the poet of the second, using the pagan/Christian antithesis, names himself as Paien de Maisières, a play on "Chrétien de Troyes." Despite linguistic difficulties, a possibility exists that one or both are by the master, thrown off perhaps as potboilers while he was working on his full-length romances. In any case they appear to show knowledge of Chrétien's sources as well as his major works and were themselves, it seems, used in a number of early verse and prose romances, as well as by the great English poet of *Sir Gawain and the Green Knight.* Here is an instance of the cannibalistic tendency inherent in the genre, as writers fed their plots with any good stories that came to hand, including the romances of their predecessors. It takes the vision of a Chrétien or a *Gawain* poet to create a masterpiece by this method; but in the crowd of very competent professionals, there were few artists even to approach their caliber.

A number of later poets mention Chrétien's name with reverence and were only too happy to imitate features of his technique, if without his finesse and tact. One thinks of his quiet humor, doubtless much appreciated in his day. There is little to be found in *Erec;* in *Cligés* and the *Conte du Graal* a sympathetic smile plays about the accounts of the young lovers and the fledgling knight; there is humor in Yvain's wooing of Laudine and almost farce in the attempted suicide, in the fashion of Thisbe, of his heartbroken lion; in *Lancelot* and the latter part of the *Conte du Graal* we can fairly speak of burlesque. Nowhere though does Chrétien seem to be ridiculing the romance, or Arthurian, tradition. But some of his successors, as if despairing of matching his mastery of the genre, appear to be doing just that. There are episodes in works such as *La Vengeance Raguidel* and *Hunbaut* that carry a coarse-grained buffoonery worthy of the *fabliau* (which itself parodied the romance on occasion); and I shall mention later other instances of comedy that might be supposed to poke fun at the tradition through one of its most illustrious characters. Perhaps too much should not be laid directly at Chrétien's door, as a spirit of mockery was abroad in the late twelfth and early thirteenth centuries that seemed aimed at literary as well as social norms; but he did at least hint at the possibility of its finding an outlet in Arthurian romance.

Similarly it would be foolish to credit him with the invention of the quest theme, so intimately associated with the genre; but he certainly did much to popularize it not only as a narrative subject but also as a structural device. If one takes a quest to be the dedicated pursuit of a goal difficult of achievement and involving a large element of uncertainty, then one finds several examples in his romances: a quest for knighthood *(Conte du Graal),* to avenge a relative *(Yvain),* for an abducted lover *(Lancelot),* or, less specific, the search for a new and more stable relationship *(Erec).* The theme has two particular advantages: it focuses attention on an individual (for even when the quest later becomes a communal enterprise, the authors usually present its participants as traveling on their own toward the same goal); and it provides a clear narrative line, easy to follow, to interrupt, and to resume, ideal for presentation in a series of readings. So this became the most characteristic of romance structures; and quests are commonplace in the verse texts, ranging from the search for a mysterious object (like the bridle in *La Mule sans frein* or the sword in *Meraugis de Portlesguez*) to the rescue of a lady in distress *(Le Bel Inconnu)* or the amorous pursuit of another on account of her beauty known only by hearsay *(Durmart le Gallois).* But the theme stamped its presence even more indelibly on the prose romances.

The vogue for prose narratives grew quickly in the early thirteenth century, partly in step with the spread of literacy and the accumulation of libraries by the nobles and rich bourgeois, and partly because the medium was felt to give an account greater credibility than did verse. One finds Arthurian poems being turned into prose, although other romances were composed or compiled in that medium from the beginning. There are works devoted to Joseph of Arimathea, the enchanter Merlin, Perceval (or Perlesvaus), Lancelot, Tristan, and to the downfall of the entire Arthurian company. Five texts enjoyed particular success. Copied in vast and ever more lavish manuscripts, they constitute what we know today as the Vulgate cycle. They are the *Estoire del Saint Graal,* the *Merlin,* the imposing and complex *Lancelot,* the *Queste del Saint Graal,* and the *Mort Artu,* which tells in almost apocalyptic terms of the death of the king, Gauvain, and the flower of his knights. (Based on Geoffrey of Monmouth, it shows the queen and Lancelot seeking final solace in religion.) How many authors were involved and how far these five romances reflect a single grand design are still matters for debate; but this was of no concern to their medieval public, who took them to their hearts and cherished them almost as a handbook of courtly and chivalric conduct. It was the prose account Dante had in mind when in his inferno he has Francesca da Rimini tell that it was while reading with Paolo of Lancelot's passion that their own fatal love was kindled. Some hundred manuscripts and later printed versions testify to the immense popularity of these forerunners of the modern novel well past the end of the Middle Ages. They were known and adapted throughout Europe, not least of course by Sir Thomas Malory.

Part of their attraction for the leisured reader must have lain in what Dante termed the "ambages pulcerrimae Arturi regis," the delightful meanderings of these tales of Arthur and his company. For they exploit, sometimes to a bewildering extent, the technique known as interlace: the crisscrossing of themes and the temporary abandonment of one hero for another, until he is recalled perhaps many thousand words and numerous episodes later. Analogies have been drawn with the intricate interwoven designs in medieval art and sculpture or with the development of polyphony in music, it being suggested that here is a feature endemic to the aesthetics of the age. This may be, but I would see a very practical impulse behind it. Concerned to extend their stories, authors might send their hero off on a quest, then multiply the obstacles he had to overcome on his way to his goal. To vary the simple linearity of a long work or perhaps to incorporate an originally independent train of adventures, a second or even a third quest might be initiated by other characters, while knights might set out in search of the original hero, to the point where the reader seems to be watching a game of multiple hide-and-seek. But the author will have caught the reader in what by now is his web of interlace and may hope to hold him fast until the initial quest is completed.

The development of this art is clearly seen in the treatment of the greatest quest of all, that of the Grail, which was the central matter of the Vulgate romances. Theories on the origin and development of the Grail legend are too many and multifarious to review here. So what follows is a summary of my own views, and I refer my readers to the bibliography for those of others. I believe that Chrétien, having come across some version of the Fair Unknown legend, set about converting it into a romance of Perceval, while incorporating a few elements in a Gauvain romance, which he was working on concurrently. On his death, his unfinished texts were run together, perhaps by the First Continuator. Thus the sources of his scene at the Grail Castle are ultimately to be sought in Celtic lore. Some of the old wonder still hangs about it, but there is no hint of any Christian significance attaching to the castle, its inmates, or the marvelous objects that are borne through its hall. Nor is there as yet any quest of the Grail, though Perceval, denounced for not having inquired about the vessel or the bleeding lance he has seen, does vow not to rest until he has learned the truth.

In the First Continuation Gauvain twice visits the Grail Castle; on the second occasion he asks the nature of the lance and is told it is none other than that of Longinus, which had pierced the side of the crucified Christ. In this way a first step was taken in the Christianization of the legend. It fired the imagination of another pious man, who proceeded to add to the text of the Continuation an unsolicited explanation of the Grail itself: it was another Passion relic, namely the vessel in which Christ's blood was caught by Joseph of Arimathea, who later brought it to England for safekeeping. Aware of Chrétien's totally profane description of the Grail, the same man felt obliged to give some hint of its nature at an early stage. This he did by rather clumsily interrupting Chrétien's account of Gauvain's adventures to introduce a new episode, in which Perceval learns from a hermit-uncle that the vessel he had seen was a most holy object and contained a consecrated wafer served to a man in an inner room of the castle. These dramatic developments are likely to have taken place within a few years of Chrétien's death. Sometime later (*ca.* 1200) another poet, Robert de Boron, whose devoutness outran his talent, elaborated the story of the Grail as Joseph's vessel into a full-scale romance. His work enjoyed a success undeserved by its artistic merit and confirmed that the Grail ("un graal," as Chrétien had first introduced it) was now truly the Holy Grail.

Holy it was for the authors of the prose romances, and preeminently for the unknown Cistercian who composed the solemn and magnificent *Queste del Saint Graal.* Here the quest is firmly established as a historical event, predicted and anxiously awaited by the whole of Christendom. From the first, Galahad is recognized as the knight destined to achieve it; about a quarter of the way through the romance, two others, Perceval and Bors, are identified as those who will share in his success. With these revelations, the author has rejected surprise and suspense as the mainspring of his narrative, features that we have seen generally distinguishing romance from epic, in favor of the progressive disclosure of the divine purpose and of man's relation to God. The purpose of the quest is not to find the Grail, which appears to the whole Arthurian court at the beginning of the work and to Lancelot on two other occasions, but to have its mystery fully disclosed. The search is not geographical, but spiritual; and the function of the adventures is to test and refine the natures of those engaged in them and to discriminate between them, not merely to put obstacles in their way. The whole theme has been sublimated into an exemplary spiritual allegory, nothing less than a quest for Christ, who at its climax actually appears from the Grail and ministers to the questers; indeed, on the allegorical level, Galahad, the pure knight, is a figure of Christ, and his achievement is a symbolic enactment of the Savior's coming. So this remarkable work, which represents both an apotheosis of Arthurian romance and the negation of some of its most typical features, attempts to renew the romance ideal by enlisting it in the service of religion as conceived in Cistercian terms. The genre could scarcely aspire higher than this; and it may seem surprising that the church, so indulgent to apocryphal material in its teaching and art, never gave the Grail legend its blessing. Its association with romance cannot have advanced its cause.

Although France was not the birthplace of Arthurian legend, that was where it reached maturity and acquired its polished manners. No stay-at-home, though, it was not slow to cross into other lands. By the 1190's the somewhat humorless and moralistic Hartmann von Aue had produced a German version of Chrétien's *Erec* and soon followed it with a treatment of *Yvain.* A Swiss contemporary, Ulrich von Zatzikhoven, showed a lighter if more haphazard touch in composing his *Lanzelet.* He tells us the material came into his hands by way of a French book supplied by a nobleman from England standing as hostage for King Richard Coeur de Lion. This is interesting in that, though Ulrich seems to have known Chrétien's romances, his main source was a form of the Fair Unknown legend (not a primitive Lancelot story, as some have believed), and might well have been one of those lost "intermediate" Anglo-Norman works. The same basic legend turns up again a few years later in the *Wigalois* of the East Frankish Wirnt von Gravenberg. But towering above all other German contributions to Arthurian romance, if one excludes Gottfried's *Tristan,* is the very personal, imaginative, and at times quizzical *Parzival,* which was completed by Wolfram von Eschenbach between about 1200 and 1212. Having claimed that Chrétien did not do justice to the story, and having mischievously invented a certain Kyot as his authority, Wolfram was himself to be berated for obscurity and eccentricity by Gottfried. Today we are more appreciative and recognize his work as one of the greatest achievements of medieval romance. This is by no means the sum of the German contributions to the tradition, but the rest do not advance it significantly; rather they mirror its progressive deterioration.

Enigmatic references in troubadour poetry to Arthur and some of the heroes associated with him seem to indicate that from as early perhaps as the 1130's Arthurian tales circulated in the Provençal region. One might, then, have expected it to provide a richer legacy than a single romance: *Jaufré,* probably composed in the early years of the thirteenth century and seemingly compounded from a variety of sources, including Chrétien. Beyond the Pyrenees we have to await the fourteenth and fifteenth centuries for confirmation of an Arthurian vogue in the shape of numerous translations from the French and allusions and borrowings in other literature. Italy offers a richer harvest. There as in Provence one finds remarkably early evidence for the penetration of possibly quite primitive material. By the thirteenth century the lyric poets showed easy conversance with the Tristan story as well as sundry Arthurian themes; and toward the end of that century Italians were composing romances in Franco-Italian as well as their own tongue, with the story of Palamedes, drawn from a French prose work, finding particular favor. The major Italian achievement in the genre is the *Tavola Ritonda,* a lengthy new amalgam of different elements of Arthurian tradition, including the Tristan and Grail legends. Short prose narratives and popular verse tales also put the Matter of Britain to use; Dante, Boccaccio, Boiardo, Ariosto all had a much better than nodding acquaintance with it, and the last two continued its spirit as well as some of its techniques in their own chivalric fabrications.

By the 1220's the royal Norwegian court had become the scene of much translation or adaptation from French literature; and prose renderings were made of various Arthurian texts, including Thomas' *Tristan* and Chrétien's *Erec, Yvain,* and *Conte du Graal.* Almost a century later *Yvain* was translated far more faithfully into Swedish verse. In Scandinavia as in Italy knowledge of the heroes and their deeds spread beyond the courts to become common property, as is shown by their presence in popular songs and ballads. It was perhaps in the second half of the thirteenth century that the Arthurian vogue reached its height in the Netherlands, being represented by long compositions in both prose and verse, largely but not always based on identifiable French originals. The concern of their authors seems to have been the stringing together of ever more exotic or implausible adventures to cater to a public demand for excitement rather than moral or social comment.

It is small wonder that the exploits of Arthur and his knights were told as enthusiastically as anywhere in the land that claimed him as its erstwhile ruler. It would be profitless to try here to survey even the most important of the hundred or so romances and tales in prose or, more often, verse that survive in Middle English from the latter part of the thirteenth century to the end of the Middle Ages and beyond: indeed, has the torrent ever run dry? A few remarks may, however, help to situate this impressive English contribution within the whole tradition.

Most striking is its large dependence on continental French romance. Some Celtic matter may have seeped in from other sources; and very possibly it drew on Anglo-Norman works now lost (*Libeaus Desconus,* another Fair Unknown text, probably did so). But in general we may think of King Arthur being called home from France for the entertainment of those who had no French. The latter were not confined to the lower classes: the poet of *Arthour and Merlin,* perhaps the earliest of the surviving works, declared he would use English, since even among the nobility there were many unfamiliar with the French tongue. Doubtless the public for the Middle English productions spanned all the social ranks. Their authors too ranged from the uninspired professional journeyman to the talented minstrel or court poet, and from the worthy burgess to the man of rank. Most are anonymous; but Chaucer turned his hand to an Arthurian subject in his "Wife of Bath's Tale," and to most people Sir Thomas Malory is synonymous with the legends of the Round Table.

The texts reflect this range of talents and publics, and also literary fashions from rough ballads or flat prose to that jewel of the alliterative revival, *Sir Gawain and the Green Knight,* unsurpassed in all Arthurian romance. In some of the works, especially the later ones, scholars have detected political allusions, burlesque, or even parody, features that might be diagnosed as symptoms of an aging genre. In a sense, though, the English tradition, and one might almost say the whole course of Arthurian composition, has led inevitably toward Malory. Drawing to some extent on English material (the alliterative *Morte Arthur*) but principally on French prose sources, he did much to shake the legend free of the forms and characteristic courtly ideology of the romance, unraveling its interlace, couching it in a measured, uncluttered style that set its face toward the new modes of expression that were to carry it forward into modern times. Just as by the end of his work we have watched the darkness settling over the world of the Round Table, so we may feel it now enshrouding the entire landscape of medieval romance.

Malory stands at the end of a line of development that to a considerable extent had already been predetermined by features of the work of Chrétien de Troyes and stemmed from it naturally, even inevitably. For romance was not a stable genre like the *chanson de geste.* The latter's exemplary function inhibited fundamental change, as did its conditions of performance and reception, conditions that were already ceasing to exist by the thirteenth century. Though it suffered some contamination from outside, it lacked the means to evolve from its own resources and was doomed to extinction. Romance was different. It might be called a "questing" genre, in the sense that it was committed less to the fixed, divinely sanctioned feudal ethic than to a search for new norms, ideals, and behavior patterns not ordained by the survival mentality of a warrior society. In this it echoed to some degree the speculative spirit of the new dialectic practiced in the schools. Moreover, its guiding principle, *courtoisie,* was more pliant than that of the epic. Embracing the gentle art of courtly love, *courtoisie* was a code of sensitive and sensible behavior necessitated by a need for people to live in harmony within the claustrophobic confines of the courts. It was a matter of discreet adjustments and accommodations requiring a flexibility of attitude more than strict obedience to peremptory rules of conduct; and this flexibility was transmitted to the genre itself, which showed an adaptability foreign to the epic. *Courtoisie* was an ideal, but an ideal to be explored rather than proclaimed. And inevitably, between the ideal and everyday reality there existed a tension, as appears most notably in the work of Chrétien, who examined with great perception some of its causes and effects. Certain of his successors, more cynical perhaps, were inclined to exploit the discrepancy between what should be and what was as a source of humor; and a burlesquing tendency, already glimpsed here and there in Chrétien, becomes more obtrusive in a number of verse romances. With them one feels the courtly ideology already losing some of its impetus. Unlike the feudal ethic, it did not lean on the authority of religion, for which it often showed scant respect. But certain pious writers, sensing perhaps its vulnerability, sought to woo away the knights of romance from the pursuit of mere *courtoisie* to that of lofty Christian values; and so the course of the genre took another turn. After them I think it is less possible to speak of a single, distinctive ideological core of romance. What exploration there is is found mainly in the formal sphere, in the weaving of intricate narrative tapestries. But more often we see the stringing together of increasingly extravagant adventures in order to satisfy the market for pure entertainment. It is a decline that continues, with one or two notable exceptions, to the end of the Middle Ages and Malory's writing of the *Morte Darthur* (1485), the genre's noble, elegiac epitaph.

As a narrative tradition like this grows, matures, and declines, so may some of the characters who play their parts within it. If they appear in work after work, they become familiar to many generations of writers and their publics; and although their representation may not change radically at any given moment, it is likely to evolve in step with the genre itself. In the case of Arthurian romance it might seem natural to turn to the king for illustration. He, though, is hardly typical, since except in his early exploits and those last agonizing days when he watched the destruction of his world before being borne away to Avalon, he is seldom more than a background figure, buffeted by circumstances perhaps, but taking little active control. In one French prose romance, *Le Chevalier du Papegau,* he does, in company with the talking parrot of the title, indulge like any lesser knight in a train of marvelous, even grotesque, adventures both chivalrous and amatory; but this is a very late and idiosyncratic work. In general he is given a static role, presiding but not participating. His nephew Gawain offers a much better example, since no other character is as omnipresent in romance or shares more intimately in its vicissitudes.

The Welsh Gwalchmei may originally have been a different hero, but he soon became identified with the Gawain we know (I shall use the English form of the name in the following sketch of his literary career). Already in Wales his eloquence had earned him the epithet "golden-tongued"; in *Culhwch and Olwen,* as well as being described as unequaled in walking and riding, he is said never to have returned unsuccessful from a quest. In 1125 the Anglo-Norman chronicler and scholar William of Malmesbury speaks of Arthur's "not degenerate" nephew, a most valiant warrior who had reigned in Galloway, though his tomb had been found in Pembrokeshire, where some say that he had been shipwrecked, others that he was murdered at a banquet. Clearly some of what he elsewhere calls the "nugae Britonum," the trifling tales of the Bretons, had come to William's ears. Ten or eleven years later, Geoffrey of Monmouth composed his *Historia,* in which Gawain plays a prominent role with Arthur and his company. One Whitsuntide the festivities at court are interrupted by Roman messengers bearing threats of war. One of Arthur's counselors makes a fire-breathing speech welcoming this news on the grounds that a long period of peace has made the Britons soft, and fighting would restore their mettle. At this point Wace, Geoffrey's rather free translator, chooses to introduce some words from Gawain, putting the other case:

> *"Bone est la pais emprés la guerre,*
> *Plus bele e mieldre en est la terre;*
> *Mult sunt bones les gaberies*
> *E bones sunt les drueries.*
> *Pur amistié e pur amies*
> *Funt chevaliers chevaleries."*
> (*Roman de Brut,* 10767–10772)

"Peace is good compared with war, the land fairer and better for it; excellent is the gay talk and good are the love affairs. It is for love and the beloved that knights perform deeds of chivalry."

It may well have been these gallant words that launched Gawain on his amatory career. In any case the hero of legend has now taken his bow in courtly literature.

Chrétien begins by accepting him as an exemplary figure, in his first romance ranking him at the head of all Arthur's good knights, before Erec himself. It is a high honor for the young hero of the first part of *Cligés* to have him as companion and win his sister's hand in marriage. In *Lancelot,* however, Chrétien allows Gawain a slight vulnerability. Perhaps it is only with hindsight that we smile to catch him in intimate conversation with a charming chatelaine. "I don't know what about," says the poet slyly. We are surprised, though, when a little later he chooses knowingly to take the easier of two perilous passages, an underwater bridge, which he in fact fails to cross: falling into the torrent, he has to be fished out with branches, poles, and hooks, speechless from the water he has swallowed. As far as his prowess is concerned, he remains in *Yvain* the model or, as Chrétien puts it, the sun of chivalry; and it is by fighting a drawn duel with him that the hero proves his valor. But here the hint dropped in *Lancelot* is developed; and one wonders if it may not have been Gawain's words in Wace that prompted Chrétien to show him flirting with the vivacious Lunete and offering her his service, whether she needed him or not. His chivalric side reasserts itself when he lures Yvain away from his new wife with talk of the danger of too much dalliance; yet he does concede that had he so fair a mistress he would find it hard to leave her. Elsewhere in the romance we hear that he never denied help to a distressed damsel; and the point is illustrated as we are shown him overprompt in championing a maiden without looking into her cause, which happens to be manifestly unjust. In this way we find Chrétien humanizing Gawain just as he added a human dimension to the adventure tales he took as his sources; and as he used his romances to probe the ideals, conventions, and relationships of *courtoisie,* so too he took to scrutinizing the character of its most renowned exponent.

In the Perceval section of the *Conte du Graal* Gawain plays to perfection his exemplary role, being the very soul of tact, silken-tongued, courteous. However, in what remains of the incomplete work (conceived, if I am right, as a separate romance devoted solely to his adventures), his philandering propensities claim our main attention. At Arthur's court, on hearing news of a besieged damsel he at once vows to be her rescuer. He is on the point of leaving when he is summoned to defend his honor in a duel at Escavalon; so that is where he heads, but only to be caught up in a tournament at Tintagel, where he pledges lifelong service to a maiden of tender years. He hardly needs to be told (though he is) that love has such great dominion over those in its power that they would not dare disobey any of its commands. Less than a day later he is at Escavalon flirting with another girl, who turns out to be the sister of his bitter enemy. Extricating himself from the resulting embarrassment, he soon casts covetous eyes on another damsel, only to feel the sharp edge of her tongue and be obliged now to suffer her company, like it or not, though she wishes him only ill. More promising seem a castle that looms in his path and the maidens and ladies gazing down from its many windows. Having been told of its enchantments, he cannot wait:

> *" . . . m'an irai, si m'aït Deus,*
> *Veoir cez dames la amont*
> *Et les mervoilles qui i sont."*
> (7616–7618)

"I shall go, so help me God, to see those ladies up there and the marvels of the place."

We note his priorities. So he braves the perils there and is overjoyed to find yet another radiant beauty pledging him her service along with that of all the other girls in the castle. If his cup of bliss now seems full, it is an illusion, since he discovers not merely that he may not leave this place of which he is now lord, but also that the welcoming damsel is actually his own sister. With the loss of his liberty all his old ebullience departs as he sits pensively with downcast, melancholy face. Having just proved himself yet again the finest knight in the world, he sees life turn sour on him.

Just as Chrétien's handling of the romance material suggested to his successors several possible lines of development, so he left Gawain a more complex character than he had found him, with a number of traits ripe for further investigation. He may even have gone a little further himself, if he was the author of *La Mule sans frein* and *Le Chevalier à l'épée.* In both Arthur's nephew lives up to his reputation as a model of *courtoisie,* loyalty, prowess, honor. Indeed in the *Mule* he performs admirably a quest for which Kay had proved too craven. Yet one is left somewhat skeptical about the value of his mission (which, incidentally, carries some parodic echoes of Perceval's Grail adventure) in view of the apparent triviality of its object: the recovery of the purloined bridle of a maiden, which he eventually finds in the possession of her sister, who gives it up without demur. The story makes systematic use of bathos, and some of its incidents might be thought somewhat demeaning: Gawain's journey astride the mule of the title (which, despite its supernatural air, loses the tip of its tail as it leaps into a spinning castle), the beheading test he suffers at the hand of a churl, his combat with a wounded knight, the sister's offer of herself and her castle coupled with the disclosure that she owns thirty-eight others. Then, on Gawain's return with the bridle, its owner, though she had promised to belong entirely to any knight who should recover it, greets him with joy and kisses in profusion, but then rides off into the unknown. The hero, though acclaimed at one point as a near-divine savior, has been made to look rather foolish—so too, perhaps, have the romance conventions.

In the *Conte du Graal* Chrétien had left Gawain in a somber, pensive mood: in *Le Chevalier à l'épée,* his introspection becomes a leitmotif. His adventures begin when in a forest he falls into a reverie so deep and long that when darkness comes he is lost. He chances upon a knight, who invites him to his castle. There Gawain, having been alerted to its perils, behaves with great circumspection until the host puts him to bed with his daughter. Then, however, despite his ardent endeavors, an automatous sword protects the girl's chastity, causing him much concern for his reputation as a lover. Despite these frustrations, his mere survival proves him the best of all knights, in recognition of which the host formally makes over his daughter to him in the morning. Eventually he leaves with her for Arthur's court; but on the way they encounter a stranger, to whom she precipitately transfers her affections and company, leaving her dogs to give a lesson in fidelity. Gawain is driven to bitter reflections on the perverse nature of women and moodily returns to his companions at court. Again one has the impression of romance itself, through its most brilliant protagonist, turning in on itself and reassessing some of its values. Gawain's escapades, particularly in the verse romances, mirror the genre's growing tendency to sacrifice debating points such as Chrétien provided to a taste for the sensational in adventures, chivalric and sentimental, that often became extravagant to the point of comedy. Along this tide is borne the erstwhile paragon of knights, trying, not always successfully, to keep an even keel, and at times appearing little better than love's buffoon.

In the First Continuation of Chrétien's last work, Gawain has the good fortune to come across a maiden who habitually greets all and sundry with the words:

> *"Cil Sires qui fist soir et main*
> *Saut et gart monseignor Gauvain*
> *Et vos aprés, et beneïe."*
> (MSS ASP, 1639–1641)

"May the Lord who made evening and morning save and keep my lord Gawain and bless him, and you as well."

Gawain promptly reveals his identity and exploits the situation to the full. But the consequences are less favorable, involving his slaying the father of his new beloved and a bitter feud with her brother. Though all ends well, this was never for our hero more than a passing, if exciting, affair. His more ludicrous ups and downs are well illustrated in *Les Merveilles de Rigomer.* Under attack in a castle, he takes his stance on a plank that happens to be part of a mill wheel driven by a torrent beneath the walls. The wheel turns, projecting him toward the depths. But God, we are told, does not want his death: on the river there happens to be a boat, on the boat a richly appointed bed, and on the bed a radiant damsel, at whose side Gawain suddenly lands, to their mutual delight.

By contrast, in the Grail quest his luck runs very thin. The First Continuation shows him falling asleep at the moment of revelation. In the prose *Lancelot,* things go badly wrong. He fails to drag a girl from a tub of boiling water, since only the best knight in the world could deliver her, an unwonted authorial snub for Arthur's nephew. At the appearance of the Grail such is his preoccupation with its lovely bearer that he omits to bow and kneel like the others and is consequently the only one to get none of the succulent food it provides. Worse follows: a dwarf attacks him with a stick, he is the target of flaming lances, fights with a knight to the point of exhaustion, and is finally carried from the castle bound to a cart driven by an old crone and pelted with mud and dung. In *Perlesvaus,* another prose romance, he undertakes the quest in order to bring comfort to two more damsels; yet he does pursue it in a pious spirit, and this time it is the breathtaking sight of the vessel and its marvels that puts all thought of asking an explanation from his mind.

We can understand, then, why the pious author of the *Queste del Saint Graal* made Gawain, as it were, the standard-bearer of the unsuccessful questers. Though he is the first to pledge himself to the enterprise, his commitment to it is far from total; and he seems more desirous of Galahad's company than of learning the secrets of the Grail. A hermit, though, tells him he is too wicked and disloyal to be a fitting comrade for the unblemished knight. Another holy man calls on him to repent his sins, since he has been unshriven for fourteen years; but he has no mind for this and says he could not abide the burden of penitence. After finding no adventures worth the telling, and learning from a vision that he would achieve nothing, he declines with a polite prevarication yet another hermit's bidding to return to God and returns instead to Camelot. The new spirituality of the genre is not for him. Only in the German romance *Diu Krône* by Heinrich von dem Türlin does he achieve this supreme quest; and it is perhaps fitting that there his success brings the disappearance of the Grail and its enchantments.

In the prose *Tristan* our sun of chivalry is presented as an out-and-out villain. This is exceptional, though in other texts too a certain grimness and lack of compassion tarnish his old *courtoisie.* His palmy days, one feels, are now in the past. Late in the fourteenth century the brilliant English poet of *Sir Gawain and the Green Knight,* drawing on *La Mule sans frein* and *Le Chevalier à l'épée* as well as a number of other verse romances, took it upon himself to rehabilitate and even reform him to the best of his ability. His chivalry and *courtoisie* are again beyond reproach. Now, however, when a lady of surpassing beauty visits him in his bed, keenly though he feels the temptation, he uses all his old eloquence to play her off, taking from her no more than a few kisses and the girdle she presses on him. Developing the side of Gawain highlighted in the *Chevalier,* the poet has banished his early carefree exuberance to show him apprehensive and introverted in his present endeavors. When he finally makes his way back to the royal court, he is in a melancholy mood, and even the sympathetic encouragement of his friends fails to cajole him from his scarcely justified gloom: it is as though he is feeling the weight of previous disappointments in his literary career and even in success is conditioned to think he has failed. It is hard to avoid the impression that both he and the genre he had come in many ways to epitomize are now drained of their old spirit and left to face an uncertain future.

The Arthurian legend itself survived the decline of the genre that had long been its chief vehicle. Never totally eclipsed, at least in popular tradition, its flame burned low on the passing of the age of chivalry until, a couple of centuries or so later, the Middle Ages caught the interest of antiquarians, and the old tales, however garbled, attracted a wide reading public. Before long they were feeding the romantic imagination, filling the dreams of the Pre-Raphaelites, and inspiring artists and musicians as well as poets like Tennyson and Swinburne. Today the legend in its many aspects may be more familiar through Wagner's operas or through more popular musical comedies, films, television productions, or novels catering to a variety of tastes: Arthur now, it seems, has as many subjects as ever. People still drop flowers on his supposed grave in Glastonbury, the mythical Avalon, climb the nearby Tor in search of "vibrations" from the past, or visit Cadbury Castle to set their feet where they fancy he once strode. Why has his story this continuing attraction for ordinary folk, and for talents as diverse as those of T. S. Eliot, Apollinaire, and Steinbeck? Perhaps by evoking that somehow purer world of courtly splendors and ideals, now shadowed with mystery, now luminous with spiritual values, it gives brief substance to our utopian visions, allowing us to share for a while the ancient belief in the restoration one day of the golden realm of the once and future king.

## Selected Bibliography

### EDITIONS

*The Continuations of the Old French "Perceval" of Chrétien de Troyes.* Edited by William Roach. 4 vols. Philadelphia, 1949–1971. Continuations 1 and 2.

Geoffrey of Monmouth. *Historia Regum Britanniae.* Edited by A. Griscom. New York, 1929.

———. *Historia Regum Britanniae.* Edited by J. Hammer. Cambridge, Mass., 1951. Variant version.

Gerbert de Montreuil. *Continuation of the "Perceval" of Chrétien de Troyes.* Edited by Mary Williams and Marguerite Oswald. 3 vols. Paris, 1922–1975.

Hartmann von Aue. *Erec.* Edited by A. Leitzmann and L. Wolff. Tübingen, 1963.

———. *Iwein.* Edited by G. F. Benecke, K. Lachmann, and L. Wolff. Berlin, 1968.

*Lancelot do Lac. The Non-Cyclic Old French Prose Romance.* Edited by Elspeth Kennedy. 2 vols. Oxford, 1980.

*Lancelot. Roman en prose du XIIIe siècle.* Edited by Alexandre Micha. Geneva and Paris, 1978–

*The Mabinogion.* Edited by John Rhŷs and J. Gwenogvryn Evans. Oxford, 1887. From the Red Book of Hergest.

*The Mabinogion.* Edited by J. Gwenogvryn Evans. Pwllheli, 1907. From the White Book of Rhydderch.

Malory, Sir Thomas. *Works.* Edited by Eugène Vinaver. Oxford, 1947.

*Les Merveilles de Rigomer.* Edited by W. Foerster and H. Breuer. 2 vols. Dresden, 1908–1915.

*La Queste del Saint Graal: Roman du 13ème siècle.* Edited by A. Pauphilet. Paris, 1923.

*Sir Gawain and the Green Knight.* Edited by J. R. R. Tolkien and E. V. Gordon. 2nd rev. ed. by N. Davis. Oxford, 1967.

*Sir Gawain and the Green Knight.* Edited and translated by W. R. J. Barron. Manchester, 1974.

*Tristan et Yseut: Les Tristan en vers.* Edited by J. C. Payen. Paris, 1974. Old French texts with modern French translation.

*Two Old French Gauvain Romances: "Le Chevalier à l'épée" and "La Mule sans frein."* Edited by R. C. Johnston and D. D. R. Owen. Edinburgh and London, 1972.

Ulrich von Zatzikhoven. *Lanzelet.* Edited by K. A. Hahn. Frankfurt, 1845. Reprinted Berlin, 1965.

*The Vulgate Version of the Arthurian Romances.* Edited by Heinrich Oskar Sommer. 8 vols. Washington, D.C., 1909–1916. Reprinted New York, 1979.

Wace. *Le Roman de Brut.* Edited by I. Arnold. 2 vols. Paris, 1938–1940.

———. *Le Roman de Brut.* Translated by Eugene Mason. In *Wace and Layamon: Arthurian Chronicles.* London, 1912. Everyman's Library.

### TRANSLATIONS

*The History of the Kings of Britain.* Translated by Lewis Thorpe. Harmondsworth, 1966.

*Iwein*. Translated by J. W. Thomas. Lincoln, Nebr., and London, 1979.

*Lanzelet*. Translated by K. G. T. Webster. New York, 1951. With revisions, notes, and introduction by R. S. Loomis.

*The Mabinogion*. Translated by Gwyn Jones and Thomas Jones. London, 1949. Everyman's Library.

*The Mabinogion*. Translated by Jeffrey Gantz. Harmondsworth, 1976.

*Le Roman de Brut*. Translated by Eugene Mason. In *Wace and Layamon: Arthurian Chronicles*. London, 1912. Everyman's Library.

*Tristan et Yseut* (versions by Gottfried and Thomas). Translated by A. T. Hatto. Harmondsworth, 1960.

*Tristan et Yseut*. Reconstructed by Joseph Bédier. Paris, 1946.

*Tristan et Yseut* (version by Béroul). Translated by Alan S. Fredrick. Harmondsworth, 1970.

## CRITICAL AND BACKGROUND STUDIES

Barber, Richard W. *King Arthur in Legend and History*. Ipswich, 1973.

Bruce, J. D. *The Evolution of Arthurian Romance*. 2nd ed. 2 vols. Göttingen, 1928.

Chambers, E. K. *Arthur of Britain*. London, 1927. Reprinted with supplementary bibliography. London, 1964.

Faral, Edmond. *La Légende arthurienne. Études et documents*. 3 vols. Paris, 1929.

Frappier, Jean. *Le Roman breton. Des origines à Chrétien de Troyes*. Paris, 1950.

Gerdner, Edmund G. *The Arthurian Legend in Italian Literature*. New York and London, 1930.

International Arthurian Society. *Bibliographical Bulletin*. Paris, 1949

Köhler, Erich. *Ideal und Wirklichkeit in der höfischen Epik. Studien zur Form der frühen Artus und Graldichtung*. Tübingen, 1956.

Loomis, Roger S. *The Development of Arthurian Romance*. London, 1963.

————. *The Grail: from Celtic Myth to Christian Symbol*. Cardiff and New York, 1963.

————, ed. *Arthurian Literature in the Middle Ages*. Oxford, 1959.

————, and Laura H. Loomis. *Arthurian Legends in Medieval Art*. London and New York, 1938.

Marx, Jean. *La Légende arthurienne et le Graal*. Paris, 1952.

————. *Nouvelles recherches sur la littérature arthurienne*. Paris, 1965.

Owen, D. D. R. *The Evolution of the Grail Legend*. Edinburgh and London, 1968.

————, ed. *Arthurian Romance: Seven Essays*. Edinburgh and London, 1970.

Schmolke-Hasselmann, Beate. *Der arturische Versroman von Chrestien bis Froissart: Zur Geschichte einer Gattung*. Tübingen, 1979.

Schoepperle, Gertrude. *Tristan and Isolt. A Study of the Sources of the Romance*. Frankfurt and London, 1913.

Vinaver, Eugène. *The Rise of Romance*. Oxford, 1971.

D. D. R. OWEN

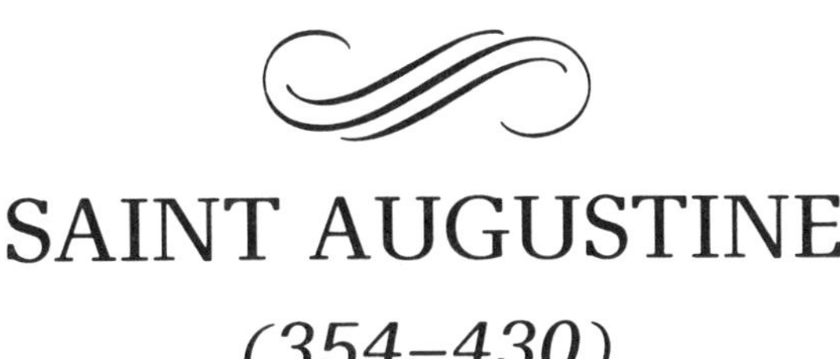

# SAINT AUGUSTINE
## *(354–430)*

BY ANY CRITERIA, Saint Augustine's influence on Western culture, at least until the second half of the seventeenth century, is comparable to that of any of his classical forebears, including Homer, Plato, the Greek tragedians, Aristotle, Cicero, and Vergil, none of whom he resembled. Among Christian writers, only Thomas Aquinas may be said to have exerted an influence approaching that of Augustine, although the content and method of Thomism depend heavily on the writings of Augustine. Nor did Thomism supplant Augustinianism. On the contrary: what was new in Thomism summoned forth creative encounters with Augustinianism among such leading Scholastic philosophers of the later Middle Ages as Duns Scotus and William of Ockham. Moreover, among Christian sources most germane to early humanists, such as Petrarch and Erasmus, Augustine became once again preponderant, side by side with the direct knowledge that the humanists had acquired of classical and Jewish antiquity.

Augustine was born in 354 to a family of Roman citizenship but modest means in Thagaste, a small city of Berber stock some 200 miles inland from the Mediterranean coast of what is now Algeria. He began there a classical Roman education whose essentially rhetorical character determined his cast of mind during his whole intellectual career. However, Augustine was eclectic and was also strongly influenced by Stoic and Neoplatonic philosophy at various moments in his development, even after his conversion to Christianity. After a sojourn of twelve years in Carthage (interrupted by a brief return to Thagaste) Augustine left the African capital to teach rhetoric in Rome, but soon afterward he was appointed to a chair in rhetoric at Milan. There, having lost his interest in the Manichean religion, Augustine became a Christian convert and was baptized in 387. Abruptly renouncing his career as a teacher of rhetoric, he soon returned to his native North Africa. He was ordained a priest in Hippo in 391, was consecrated a bishop in 395, and spent the remainder of his career in Hippo until his death, following a brief illness, in 430, twenty years after the sacking of Rome.

Augustine's writings form a body of colossal dimensions. Near the end of his long life, he undertook a retrospective work entitled the *Retractations (Retractationes),* in which he lists ninety-three treatises by his hand that he reread in order to correct their errors and to evaluate them in the light of his mature wisdom. Many are short, comprising only a "book" or two (a "book" being a formal unit containing an introduction and a conclusion); but some are very long. His *City of God (De civitate dei)* is twenty-three books long. This work takes a robust reader at least a month to read—and years to master. The total number of books in his corpus of treatises is 232, according to modern scholars. The *Retractations* do not, however, mention his letters and hundreds of sermons, many of which have been preserved.

Although Augustine's writings are all centered in his Christian faith, his more immediate goals are multiple and constantly overlap. However, one may identify several broad categories of treatises among his writings. Many are polemically motivated and directed against specific heretical sects and doctrines of his time (among them the Arians and the Priscilianists, and, of course, the Manicheans, whose views Augustine himself had espoused prior to his conversion to Christianity). Many are speculative or theological, dealing with problems of faith and the life of the soul that called for systematic exploration (such as the relationships expressed by the Trinity or the notions of free will and grace). Many are ethical and bear upon such subjects as the institution of marriage, the evils of lying, the virtues of chastity and widowhood, and the expediency of fasting. Many are didactic and deal with aspects of teaching, preaching, interpreting the Bible and other texts, and arguing properly. Many others are exegetical; that is, concerned with explaining passages in the Old and New Testaments that are obscure or in apparent contradiction to other passages. A few are technical or scientific, treating such subjects as dialectics, music, and grammar. One treatise, the *City of God,* is apologetic, at least by pretext.

Although we learn from the *Confessions* (*Confessionum*) how deeply Augustine was affected by his relationships with individual people (especially his relatives and friends), and although he was responsive to the major doctrinal controversies of his age, his thought remains antihistorical (at least in the modern sense of "history"), remote from immediate political and social concerns other than those surrounding heretical movements, and disdainful of the technology of such practical affairs as commerce, agriculture, warfare, navigation, and architecture: "Knowledge of the terrestrial and celestial world is highly esteemed among men; however, the best of these are certainly those who prefer to know themselves" (*On the Trinity* [*De trinitate*] 4.1).[1]

As a rule, Augustine's writings do not fall into the distinct categories of natural, ethical, and speculative philosophy proper to the classical tradition that preceded and followed him. At the same time, as a rhetorician, Augustine is willing to use, in one treatise, a plurality of modes of argument in order to make or reinforce a point. He passes, often without transition, from scriptural exegesis to logical analysis to numerological symbolism and then to claims of illuminated intuition. This mixture of modes whose presuppositions are at least superficially at odds with one another is often startling to the modern reader, and it may be partially explained by the fact that Augustine's turn of mind is more that of a rhetorician than that of a philosopher. He *uses* ideas more often than he analyzes them, and he is rarely exhaustive in his line of reasoning.

Augustine's discourse is governed more by criteria of expediency than of logic, and his thought is more fragmentary, associative, and contrastive than linear and systematic. (*On Free Will* [*De libero arbitrio*] and *On the Trinity,* however, are partial exceptions to this general claim.) Given this trait of mind, we can grasp what Augustine has to say on a specific topic (for instance, "language," "time," or "concupiscence") only by extensive reading and by subsequent synthesis. But even then we discover that Augustine does not always use a given concept in the same way. Since some of Augustine's shrewdest insights into major intellectual problems are scattered in his commentaries on Genesis or the Psalms and in his sermons, one always undertakes to read him with the assurance of being surprised and with a sense of sharing in a process of spontaneous adventure and discovery. Au-

[1]References to Augustine's works use the English titles, with the Latin version given only at the first mention. Numerical references are to book and chapter. Except when indicated, translations are by the author.

gustine often speaks of his writing as a process of discovery. His strategies as a rhetorician are often stunning, complex, and profound, as we shall presently see in our discussion of the *Confessions.*

Given the magnitude of Augustine's body of writings, merely to describe in a few sentences (were this even possible) each of his individual works would exhaust the limits of space available here. Accordingly, bearing in mind the advantage of selecting elements of his thought that are both representative and likely to engage the mind of the general reader of our time, we shall confine the discussion that follows to a handful of his major treatises, while at the same time indicating the importance of various ideas to the literary heritage of modern culture. Since Augustine's *Confessions* is not only his most immediately engaging masterwork but expresses, in germ, many of the intellectual and moral concerns that underlie his other writings, we shall give special prominence to that work.

Written over a period of several years beginning in 397 (that is, just after his ordination as a priest), the *Confessions* is the work of a man entering middle age whose intellectual power was at its height. His spiritual position was by then secure enough to allow him to analyze with lucidity many troublesome events of his youth that were still fresh in his memory.

The *Confessions* is commonly called an autobiography. However, it is important to recognize that this generic term is inappropriate to the character and purpose of the *Confessions* as a whole. The term *autobiography* is a neologism of late-eighteenth-century European culture, when a specifically romantic notion of literature began to emerge, having as its foundation a theory of subjective self-knowledge quite different from that of the Christian Platonic tradition. The structure of romantic autobiography rests on a dialectic of consciousness in which an "I" writing in the present seeks self-knowledge by exploring his or her otherness in the historical past, in order to return to itself more fully in the present. Augustine's *Confessions* certainly does explore with frankness and poignancy the spiritual evolution of an individual self; yet it does so with the purpose of leading its readers not to the presence of Augustine's own subjective consciousness but to the presence of God as he inhabits *every* consciousness. We should recall that the word *confession* signified to Augustine far more than the penitential disclosure of one's sins in order to be free of them: the profession of one's faith in sacrifice (as in martyrdom) is also a confession; so too is the act of praising God. Thus, Augustine's purpose as God's servant is comparable to that of John the Baptist: "He must increase, but I must decrease" (John 3:30). This unliterary (that is, antisubjective) priority of the *Confessions* as a work of Christian piety must be borne in mind by modern readers if they are to understand the relationship of the last three books of the *Confessions* to its structure as a whole.

The goal of Augustine's *Confessions* as a spiritual quest is clearly set forth in the opening chapters, though in the form of ontological questions rather than narrative. How, Augustine asks, can he, a mere fragment of Creation (and a sinning fragment besides), presume to praise his whole and uncreated Creator? For must a mortal not first invoke God—that is, call God inside him—before he can return God's love as praise? But how can he invoke God without already knowing what he is invoking? And how can he know God? The answer to such seemingly unanswerable questions lies in the Scriptures: if he will seek he will find, since God has been forespoken by Christ his Word. Since God's Word now stands accessible to all in the Scriptures, Augustine's dialogue with God, his otherwise silent interlocutor, takes the form of scriptural citations woven into the fabric of Augustine's own discourse, illuminating the events of his life with a meaning that is both immanent and transcendent, both personal and divine. Self-knowledge leads, finally, to the discovery, through recollection, of God's presence within the self. The conclusion of the *Confessions,* which takes the form of a commentary on the opening chapters of Genesis, is the logical fulfillment of Augustine's spiritual evolution, and it is clear that such a conclusion does not correspond to the expectations of the modern reader of autobiography—at least in the romantic sense of that term.

Augustine's conjectures about his earliest infancy have drawn the attention of many who are concerned with developmental psychology and, especially, with the acquisition of language by children. Augustine surmises that if, like all children, he enjoyed a kind of tranquillity as a newborn child, it was possible because he was still close to that natural universal law into which he was born and which was born in him. This inner law is innate and spiritual and is therefore opposed to the law revealed to Moses, which is what Saint Paul calls the law of sin. His proximity to that first law preserves him momentarily from the basic dichotomies that torment ordinary human life (inner/outer, spiritual/corporeal, wisdom/ knowledge, and so on). However, not even infants are free of the effects of original sin: not only did the infant Augustine cry immoderately for the breast and pale at the sight of other infants being suckled at the same breast (covetousness, despising of one's neighbor), but he even tried (as best he could) to strike and hurt those around him who would not obey his childish whims. Clearly, Augustine's selection of details from early childhood is governed by firm theological and psychological doctrines that are their "truth."

The process of acquiring those verbal signs by which the child learns to express himself coincides with Augustine's subjection to the external law of sin imposed by a just God on fallen humans. First, as a nonspeaking baby, Augustine allied his inner thoughts to corporeal signs (kicking, crying). Corporeal signs belong to a broad class of signs that Augustine calls natural signs, by which he means that the relationship between the signifier (kicking) and the signified (anger) is not conventional or arbitrary, but necessary, in the same way that smoke necessarily signifies fire (we shall return to this distinction later).

However, corporeal gestures have only a limited range of expressivity, so the child passes on to the acquisition of verbal signs (which are conventional or arbitrary), thanks to the corporeal gestures of adults who point with their finger to objects while repeating the words that conventionally name those objects. The child gradually acquires the skill to use these signs. However, the character of these "given signs" is that they are purely social institutions, and Augustine says that through his acquisition of language he "entered more deeply into the stormy society of human life" (*Confessions* 1.8, Ryan trans.).

Moreover, human society is based on repression and authority, which relies on brutal punishment—especially the whip—to educate the young. Augustine tells us that he was constantly beaten in his early years at school. However, he explains that the toil and sorrow of school are also the consequence of Adam's sin of disobedience, whose punishment by a vengeful God has been institutionalized in the schoolmaster's just and necessary wrath. In *On Free Will* (3.18), Augustine explains in detail why this wrath is just and necessary. Any child born after the Fall has inherited the consequences of original sin. They are manifested not as deliberate acts of evil, but rather as conditions of ignorance and of "difficulty" in being virtuous: "From ignorance comes the shame of error; from difficulty, the affliction of anguish." A child must be chastized in order to overcome these inherited deficiencies in his soul, though the child ultimately does so by free will. Moreover, God mercifully makes his aid available through Christ to every soul that seeks it in the search for wisdom and repose. As a schoolchild, Augustine encountered ignorance and difficulty most often in the studying of Greek, which he hated, even though he affirms in the *City of God* that Greek is preeminent over all other languages. It is in keeping with Augustine's intellectual priorities that, even though he was born into a rural, agricultural society, he should experience the toil of Adam's punishment as the toil of studying classical Latin and Greek.

In primary school Augustine learned to read and write under a master called a *litterator,* that is, a teacher of letters *(litteras):* literature meant at that time the domain of the written word, not works of the imagination. In secondary school Augustine came under the authority of a grammaticus who introduced the eleven-year-old schoolboy to the more intellectual disciplines of reading and explicating Greek and Latin poets, historians, and orators. It is noteworthy that Augustine's first love in literature (in the modern sense of that word) was Vergil's *Aeneid,* especially the episode of Dido's grieving over the departure of her lover, Aenẻas, from Carthage, and her suicide. By weeping at this story of fornication, Augustine himself "fornicated" against God. Augustine says that he hated Homer (*Confessions* 1.16), but his attitudes toward Latin poetry were clearly more complex. As a youth he loved it and won a prize for writing it. As a Christian convert he continued to love the intrinsic beauty of poetry as a musical art—an art whose metrical proportions and harmonies reflected a divine order that is also expressed in created things—yet he scorned what poetry expressed semantically; that is, its content as opposed to its form.

Despite his calumny of Vergil, Augustine's writings are more heavily indebted to—and burdened by—Vergil's art than that of any other classical author; moreover, in the *City of God* (1.3, Dods trans.) Augustine concedes that Vergil is "the most famous and approved of all poets." Indeed, in his *Confessions* he did not fail to perceive and exploit the similarities between Aeneas' wanderings in his quest to found the earthly city of Rome and his own inner quest to discover the city of God. For instance, the very tragedy of Aeneas' departure from Dido's Carthage that Augustine bewailed as a schoolboy gives special poignance to a moment of intense conflict in Augustine's own life.

Augustine's mother, Monica, as Augustine himself recognized, was driven by a passion for her son that was far from ordinary, and she pursued her son wherever she could, to his occasional hindrance. When Augustine decided to leave Carthage, where he was both student and teacher—where "we were seduced and seduced others" (4.1)—he decided that he also needed to be free from his mother's domination. He therefore lied to Monica in order to mask his departure in the darkness of night, leaving her, afflicted by what Augustine euphemistically called "the remnant of Eve" in her, grieving like Dido at dawn: "The wind blew and filled our sails, and the shore receded from our sight. On that shore in the morning she stood, wild with grief, and with complaints and groans she filled your ears" (5.3). Unlike Vergil in the case of Dido, Augustine would construe the later events of his life as Christian remedies for this potentially tragic relationship with the passionate woman who was his mother. The implicit comparison of Dido, Aeneas' lover, with Monica gives rise to rich psychological overtones in the *Confessions.* In general, however, we should see Augustine's epic of the soul as an anti-*Aeneid,* just as the city of God is to be seen as an anti-Rome.

If Augustine felt compelled to repudiate his love of the classical poets, so too the lessons of Cicero as orator (though not as philosopher) needed to be unlearned, at least to the extent that the Roman master's criteria for eloquence not only made the Scriptures seem unworthy to Augustine but made him blind to their inner, or spiritual, meaning (3.5). The need for a new and explicitly Christian rhetoric became, moreover, the motive for Augustine to begin writing, at the same time as he worked on the *Confessions,* his famous treatise *On Christian Doctrine (De doctrina christiana).* The problems with Ciceronianism would be finally overcome when Augustine met Ambrose, the bishop of Milan; through his preaching Augustine found a new pattern of eloquence based on humility that was a path into the spiritual meaning of the Scriptures. Not only was Augustine's accession to the inner meaning of the Scriptures a turning point in the story of his life, but he concludes the *Confessions* by undertaking to explicate the spiritual meaning of Genesis, thanks to his illumination through the Gospel.

Augustine's famous narration of his theft, at the age of sixteen, of some pears from a garden in Thagaste—fruit that he neither needed nor enjoyed—illustrates his special lucidity in selecting details from his personal life in such a way as to convey what he considered universal patterns of human experience. That the theft actually occurred we have no special reason to doubt; but Augustine himself is aware of the paradox of selecting such a trivial detail to express truths that have many levels and ramifications. Obviously this story of fruit stolen in a garden harks back to the story of the forbidden fruit in Genesis. Against his better judgment and by his own free will, Augustine has actively recapitulated the original transgression of Adam. At Eve's bidding, Adam had broken the law of God's commandment; now, at the bidding of his companions, Augustine has transgressed, by his theft, the eighth commandment of the law of sin revealed to Moses. This event illustrates the moral consequences of Augustine's love for his fellow men: taken as an end in itself, the temporal society of the earthly city is an agency of bondage that alienates the individual both from himself and from God. On a more abstract level, Augustine's act of pride involves choosing the Creation over its Creator, and this sin of pride extends, in the story that follows, to all spheres of his moral and intellectual life. In short, this episode inaugurates a counterpoint of themes in the *Confessions* that is reminiscent (and worthy) of Vergil and would not be matched until Dante's *Divine Comedy* some nine centuries hence.

Augustine's intellectual and spiritual itinerary following the theft is marked by decisive phases. His first real encounter with ideas remote from the realm of the senses and from the world of material goals resulted from his reading of Cicero's philosophical treatise the *Hortensius*. However, Cicero's skepticism could not satisfy a mind of such burning impulses, and Augustine soon espoused the doctrines of Mani, founder of a dualistic religion distinct from Christianity, one that granted to the forces of evil and darkness an autonomy from God that the Judeo-Christian tradition did not accept. His adherence to the sect lasted nine years and ended after he became disillusioned with its leading teacher, Faustus, who, despite his magnetic personality and his seeming humility, lacked the mastery of ideas that Augustine naturally required of a valid intellectual guide. During this period of adherence to Manicheanism, Augustine was appointed to a chair in rhetoric at Milan. Indeed, it was the rhetorician in Augustine that attracted him at first to Ambrose, bishop of Milan. Ambrose's spiritualism both of temperament and of thought freed Augustine from the constraints of a materialistic approach to the Scriptures. Ambrose taught him, instead, to read figuratively, thereby removing certain obstacles to Christian doctrine that Augustine had previously encountered, notably, the problem of the anthropomorphism with which the Scriptures seemed to speak concerning God, the problem of evil in a universe created by a good God, and the problem of the virgin birth of Christ.

Ambrose's personal example also enhanced Augustine's transcendence of his carnal understanding of spiritual things. Not only did Ambrose (unlike Faustus) shun unnecessary contact with his disciples in order to preserve his inner life of the spirit, but he was abstemious in his bodily habits. He even read without moving his lips, a feature that seemed especially remarkable in a culture whose modes of communication and understanding were still so preeminently oral.

The next crucial phase in Augustine's development coincided with his discovery of the Neoplatonists, especially Plotinus, whose writings led him to grasp the potential of the human soul not only to reflect upon its own spiritual nature, but also to transcend, in moments of rapture and ecstasy, all corporeal limits and to be momentarily united with God. However, Augustine also quickly realized that such mystical joys were also vexing for their brevity, and he came to see the necessity of a permanent mediator of God's presence to man. Augustine's subsequent readings of Saint Paul led him beyond Neoplatonist metaphysics into Christianity as a religion based on the principle of a mediator whose dual status as both man and God answered perfectly to the condition of men who were mortal sinners, yet who sought union with a transcendent, immortal, uncorruptible God. Augustine's intellectual life began with an infatuation, as a rhetorician, with the institutions of human speech, and it culminated in an espousal, in a spirit of humility, of Christ as God's Word.

Augustine's linear progression toward his final goal as a servant of God in the Church was deeply marked by a sequence of interpersonal relationships. If his father, Patricius, not yet a Christian, displayed in his violent nature (he beat his slaves savagely) the wrathful authority of a vengeful, Old Testament God, his mother, a Christian, exemplified charity and submissiveness in her conduct toward others.

The theft of the pears coincided with the onslaught of adolescent sexuality, and Augustine speaks of his emotional ties at that time with great frankness and feeling, though in terms that also underscore the metaphysical dimension of his torment. Lust, he says, was a cloud that boiled out of the limy pit of his puberty and obfuscated his soul, hurling it into the abyss of vice: "I was tossed about, I was dispersed, I was dissolved, and I boiled in my fornications, and you were silent" (2.2). If Augustine tells us here that lust carried his soul into the abyss of an inner chaos, that this inner chaos reflects the larger chaos that preceded the Creation by the Word, he is anticipating his explication, at the end of the *Confessions,* of those passages in Genesis that deal with God's creation of the universe. This victory of understanding coincides with his victory over the forces of evil in his soul, evil being understood, of course, as a deprivation of good, that is, as nothingness. Augustine's personal story, then, is a story of re-creation out of "nothing" that reflects God's creation of the universe ex nihilo.

As Augustine moved on to Carthage (where Aeneas had fornicated with Dido), he began to feed both his intellectual and his physical desires: as he mastered rhetoric, he fornicated; as he espoused the false religion of Mani, he took a concubine. In general, an interesting counterpoint runs through the *Confessions* between Augustine's lusts and his life in language.

Augustine discovers the link between mortality and sin not through contemplating his own death, but rather through the death of a friend whom he loved as much as himself—as if, he says, they were a single soul in two bodies (4.6). In contrast with unions between angels, who need only to hold similar affections in order to unite or dissimilar ones to separate (*On Free Will* 3.11), unions between mortals can only lead to change and, ultimately, to loss. So extreme was his grief for his friend that Augustine marveled that other men should live on when his friend was dead. Though his own life became a horror to him, Augustine feared to die lest the part of his friend's soul that lived on in him should perish too. In other words, Augustine experienced in friendship the force of human love in its most absolute form.

Passionate love between human beings has, of course, been a constant force in Western literature, and it remains understandable to us in our time. That such a force should be expressed in a bond of friendship rather than in an erotic relationship between man and woman is a reflection of a distinctly classical ideal of friendship, one that begins in the *Iliad* (Achilles and Patroclus) and runs through Greek and Latin literature (as in works by Plato and Cicero). Even in the Renaissance, the ideal of friendship remained on an equal footing with a more recent resurgence of medieval courtly eroticism; nor were the two ideals in any way mutually exclusive. However, Augustine's attitudes toward friendship and love in later life are not, perhaps, so easy for us to accept in our time. They rest on his conviction that we must never love another person either for his or her sake or for our own sake, but must always love a person (even an enemy) only for and in God. This latter love is charitable; the former is concupiscent. Since God is man's sole proper object of enjoyment in love, all lesser things, including man himself, must only be used, not enjoyed for their own sake. That charity should absolve a strictly human bond between individuals rather than intensify it is a principle that may seem to go against the grain of a certain strain of modern romanticism; however, in high romanticism itself (as in Wordsworth and Shelley) the tension between human and divine love remains real and is a source of much artistic complexity.

Augustine's relationship to his mother, a devout Christian, was more determining in his life than any other single relationship, whether to a man or a woman. Though Augustine felt compelled to leave Monica behind in Carthage, her compulsion to follow him would not be outdone, and so she pursued him to Milan. Just as she succeeded in calming the despairing sailors on the stormy sea during her crossing, so too she brought calm to her son in Milan when she found him in a state of spiritual crisis following his break with the Manicheans. Monica immediately sought and received the spiritual aid of Ambrose in her quest for her son's conversion—that is, for his rebirth as a spiritual son in the mother church of Christianity. As we have said, this is precisely the moment when Augustine began to discover the spiritual rather than the carnal meaning of the Scriptures. Monica subsequently succeeded in breaking up Augustine's relationship with his concubine, to whom he had been faithful for some eighteen years and who had borne him a son, Adeodatus. (Concubinage, in Roman society, was a respectable institution.) When Monica arranged for Augustine's marriage with a very young girl who was still two years from the age of consent, his concubine returned to Africa, vowing never to love another man. The cleavage was immensely painful for Augustine as well: "My heart still clung to her: it was pierced and wounded within me, and the wound drew blood from it" (6.15). Monica not only experienced intense fantasies about the projected marriage in her dreams but even related them to her son. However, her fantasies were never realized, for the marriage did not take place. Augustine took another mistress instead; yet not even this new bond could appease his distress over the destruction of his earlier love. The immediate pain subsided, but his despair hung on.

Indeed, as Augustine progressed in his spiritual indoctrination as a catechumen in the Church, the most persistent obstacle to his conversion was his attachment to women. His will became a battlefield where a violent struggle ensued between his desire for eternal things and for temporal pleasures. Thus, on the one hand he was assaulted with visions of his mistresses pinching him and taunting him with the prospect of an eternity without his being able to do "this and that" with them, and on the other he experienced an allegorical vision of Continence and her disciples, who chided him for his weakness. The torment overwhelmed him until, one day as he wept alone beneath a fig tree in a garden, he heard a strange voice, either that of a boy or a girl, singing: "Take up and read. Take up and read" (8.12). Augustine is careful not to identify this disembodied, consoling voice as a predestined visitation of the Holy Spirit, although he does not rule this out either. In this moment of climax he impulsively took out the Scriptures and cast his eyes at random on a sentence from Paul, which just as suddenly rescued him: "Not in rioting and drunkenness, not in chambering and impurities, not in strife and envying; but put you on the Lord Jesus Christ, and make not provision for the flesh in its concupiscences" (Corinthians 27–35).

Augustine's itinerary from the bondage of evil and of the law of sin to the freedom of grace is framed by two archetypal episodes of crisis set in gardens, the first corresponding to man's alienation from God in Eden, the second to the promise of spiritual reunion with God in the terrestrial paradise, or in the living city of God as it is mediated to man on earth through the Gospel and the Church. This pattern of alienation and return is not only proper to the Judeo-Christian conception of history, but implicit in classical epic as well (as in the *Odyssey* and the *Aeneid*). The special interest of the *Confessions* lies not, then, in its basic plot, but rather in the way in which Augustine relates universal, mythical patterns and literary models both to specifically Christian doctrine and to specifically individual experience.

The final major episode of the narrative portion of the *Confessions* deals with Augustine's final days with his mother, who was shortly to die. Monica had chosen to return to her native Africa, and he decided to accompany her. As they rested in Ostia before the crossing, they experienced together a vision of salvation that surely stands as one of the most exalted moments of mystical spirituality in the Christian West. Their mystical ascent moves upward by a process of negation: what is higher is *not* like what is lower, with God as that principle of Being who is *absolutely* different from all created things. This mode of ascendance to God is called, in theological terms, the "negative path" *(via negativa)* and recurs in spiritual literature in the European tradition (the *Divine Comedy* and *Paradise Lost*) whenever heroes yearn to know God as an immediate presence to the soul. Only by first purging the soul of its knowledge of terrestrial things can man undergo direct illumination by God's grace from within. Since Augustine and his mother now love each other in the purer love of God, they may enjoy this love together in these final moments of Monica's life.

However, such raptures commonly leave those who experience them in a state of despondency and nostalgia when they return to the ordinary world. Monica, for her part, was, in a sense, fortunate: her return to ordinary consciousness was soon alleviated by death. Augustine's situation, however, was more complex, since he was fated to live on, and this complexity determined his artistic strategies in the four remaining books of the *Confessions.* Given that Augustine's spiritual story was complete, although his life story was not, he was apparently faced with the question of how to complete a narrative whose goals had been more or less achieved in this climactic vision at Ostia. But how does one gracefully end the story of one's own life when that story not only is factually incomplete but has become, in one's own eyes, irrelevant? Augustine apparently hesitated for some time over the composition of the remaining books of the *Confessions:* scholars surmise that in all likelihood Augustine composed them later—perhaps even separately—and then appended them to the narrative portions. However, this apparent digression from his original design in the *Confessions* is in reality a brilliant fulfillment of that design in the light of his Christian Neoplatonic priorities.

Book 10 of the *Confessions,* which immediately follows the story of Monica's death, is a philosophical analysis of the faculty of memory, and books 11–13 consist of a commentary on the opening verses of Genesis, which tell of the Creation. It is not difficult to see how such shifts responded to imperatives that had arisen earlier in his text. As a Christian Neoplatonist, Augustine had learned, first, to detach himself from the knowledge of corporeal things in order to compel his soul to contemplate its own spiritual nature, and, secondly, to strive to contemplate God. As he wrote in a soliloquy: "I want to know God and my soul. Nothing else? Nothing at all" (*Soliloquia* 1.2.7). The self-knowledge of the soul precedes, then, the knowledge of God as pure Being that may be apprehended in brief flashes of illumination, and book 10 of the *Confessions* corresponds to that moment when it was appropriate for Augustine to put aside his life story in order to lead the reader to a higher awareness of the spiritual nature of the human soul. Hence, he stopped remembering the details of his historical life in order to remember memory itself.

The exegetical portions of the *Confessions* complete Augustine's intellectual program as a Christian Neoplatonist in a more complicated way. Though a Christian, he obviously could not know Christ as mediator except through the Gospel, which is also God's Word, and through the Spirit, thanks to which that Word is understood. However, for the Christian, the attainment of such understanding must be far more than an occasion for personal exultation: it must be shared. Thus, Augustine's withdrawal from the world immediately after his conversion to "babble forth" his joy in knowing God was not sufficient, for such babbling was only what Saint Paul called "speaking in tongues." By this Saint Paul meant the private, unintelligible language of the inspired, and he believed that it is better for the Christian to "prophesy"—that is, to preach and teach—than merely to speak in tongues. Augustine's purpose in undertaking an allegorical commentary on the opening verses of Genesis conformed, then, with Paul's injunction that Christians should "prophesy"—that is, through ordinary language share their knowledge with their fellow members of the Church, the Church being understood as the mystical body of Christ that lives in the spirit. Such was the strategic reason for Augustine's turning from the revelations of the New Testament back to the Old, to an understanding of God at the origin of the Creation. Augustine's ability to read Genesis figuratively rather than literally was definitive proof that he had finally overcome his previous incapacity, as a concupiscent Ciceronian, to penetrate with charity into the inner meaning of the Scriptures veiled by the Letter.

Thus, if Christ once sacrificed his life for man in a supreme act of charity, and if the goal of the Christian is to imitate Christ, now Augustine sacrificed the life of his mind as he undertook his commentary upon Genesis in a gesture of individual charity: "O Lord my God, be attentive to my prayer, and in your mercy graciously hear my desire, for it burns not for me alone, but desires to be for the use of fraternal charity. . . . I will sacrifice to you the service of my thought and tongue; give me what I offer you" (11.2).

The commentary that follows this prayer is a far-ranging, often philosophical elaboration upon the text of Genesis, and it includes an ingenious attempt to define the notion of time. However, Augustine's meditation must be seen as something more than a gesture of charitable pedagogy: his enlightened retelling *(enarratio)* of the Creation is also a kind of ritual celebration of his own re-creation from the abysss of his sins, thanks to his illumination by the Spirit, through whom God allowed there to "be light" in Augustine's soul. Since evil is nothingness, to understand God's Creation ex nihilo is, for the sinner, to be remade, to be made complete and whole again. Such is the sense of the Latin verb *perfacere,* which is so poorly rendered by the English when Augustine writes, "O Lord, perfect me and reveal to me these things" (11.2.3). Moreover, during his writing, only the constant actions of prayer and confession protected Augustine's mind from the darkness of the abyss: "O may it be the Truth, the light of my heart, not my own darkness that speak to me" (12.10).

If Augustine concludes his so-called autobiography by substituting the story of Genesis for the story of his own genesis, if he becomes a commentator *(enarrator)* rather than a narrator, a reader instead of a writer, he does so with the confidence that one day he too will number among the saved who inhabit a spiritual realm called the "sky of sky." Unlike mortals below, the saved enjoy immediate intellection of God's will. Here, the angelic and the blessed spend their nontime reading, though not reading as mortals who have been enslaved (as Augustine had been) by the liberal arts: instead, they read a language without syllables unfolding in temporal sequence, and they contemplate a text that is unequivocal and eternal because it is nothing less than the Word itself. Thus, in contrast to fallen men, who are in bondage to the law of sin, and for whom the sabbath is a mere day of rest on earth, for the redeemed the seventh and last day of the Creation is a symbol of the eternal rest of salvation for men whose good works please God just as the work of the Creation pleased God on the sixth day, when he "saw that all he had made was very good" (Genesis 1:31). By analogy, assuming that Augustine's exegesis of the letter of Genesis is a "good" work, a work of charity, then he may aspire to an eternal sabbath with God:

> But the seventh day is without an evening, and it does not have a setting, because you have sanctified it to endure for all eternity, so that by the fact that you rested on the seventh day, having fulfilled all your works, which are very good, your book may proclaim to us beforehand that we also, after our works, which are very good because you have given them to us, may rest in you on the sabbath of eternal life.
>
> (*Confessions* 13.36)

If Augustine's *Confessions* manifest a universal pattern of fall and redemption through the drama of an individual consciousness, another of Augustine's most influential works, the *City of God,* adopts the language of classical historiography in order to defend the validity of the Christian faith not only in the perspective of recent calamities in the destiny of Rome, but also in the perspective of the universal history of mankind since the Creation. Thus, the *City of God* is an attempt to construe the basic message of the Bible in such a way as to liberate Christians from the political disappointments of decaying *romanitas* and to reorient their minds toward spiritual rather than terrestrial glory.

Augustine's immediate pretext for undertaking the *City of God* was that of defending his Church against the accusations of certain Romans who blamed the Christians in power for the downfall of their capital city. It was charged, for instance, that the Christians had hastened the fall of Rome by refusing to allow sacrifices to the gods of Roman religion. Augustine began his defense in 412, two years after the sack of Rome, and published sections of it over the next fifteen years as he finished them. The *City of God* is Augustine's most erudite and most historically oriented work, yet its core is solidly mystical and theological, and his purpose is magnificently single-minded. Hence, the *City of God* is minimally a work of historical documentation. Rather, its goal is to interpret the entire history of mankind as a complex dialectic between two principles or entities: the earthly city or city of man, and the heavenly city or city of God. The foundations of these two archetypal cities were laid by God at the beginning of time, and their interaction has been manifested through all epochs of man's history. However, we are not dealing with a clear-cut dualism between good and evil, for, as Augustine says, "In truth, these two cities are entangled together in this world, and intermixed until the last judgment effects their separation" (1.35). Thus, the modes of existence of the city of God are multiple. It can be represented in time and place, as in the case of Jerusalem in opposition to Babylon; it can exist in time as the mystical body of Christ, the Church; it can exist eternally and immaterially as the community of angels and the saved. Multiple, too, are the modes of participation in that city. It is possible for men outwardly to serve the city of God as members of the Church, yet, by their inner actions, to serve the city of man. Such is the case, for instance, with heretics. Inversely, it is possible for pagans serving the city of man to do so spiritually, rather than carnally, and to become, thereby, servants of the city of God. Such is the case with Job.

Although there were many antecedents for the "ideal" city in both classical and biblical antiquity and among certain postclassical thinkers (Christian and non-Christian alike), the final guideline for Augustine's evocation of the city of God is, of course, his understanding of the Scriptures themselves.

Like the *Confessions,* the *City of God* has a definite structure, although once again such a structure is not always apparent; moreover, even where apparent, it displays odd proportions. For instance, after declaring, at the end of book 1, his intention of elaborating upon the concept of the city of God, Augustine embarks instead upon a seemingly interminable attack on pagan culture in all its aspects—moral, artistic, and religious. Thus, books 2–5 are against pagans who worship their gods to serve this world, and books 6–10 are against pagan philosophers who serve their gods for the life beyond. Only after book 10 does Augustine abandon his attack on Roman culture in order to resume his more positive task of evoking an explicitly Christian history of man and his world. The remaining books (11–22) form a whole with subdivisions whose proportions are more harmonious, and Augustine periodically orients his reader (and himself) within this program. Books 11–14 deal with the origin of the city of God from the creation of the world until the Fall of man; books 15–18 trace the progress of the two cities through the course of historical time; books 19–22 are eschatological: they deal with the "ends" (purposes and conclusions) of the two cities at the end of time, that is, at the Last Judgment and the resurrection of the dead. Thus, with the exception of the polemics against the institutions of pagan culture, Augustine's treatise reflects the structure of the Bible itself, since both works begin with the Creation and end with the end of time and the Last Judgment, as announced in the Apocalypse or the Book of Revelation.

Modern readers, including specialists, find themselves considerably exercised by the extravagance of Augustine's apparent digression into polemics against the pagans. Simply to follow Augustine's tracks among the authors and doctrines that he attacks would demand of us nothing less than a late-Roman, classical education. However, it is not difficult to understand why Augustine's assault on pagan institutions and culture should be so exhaustive. Christian letters had not yet achieved anything of the prestige and credibility of the authors *(auctores)* of pagan Greece and Rome, and in Augustine's time the Roman aristocracy still clung to its pagan traditions. Indeed, as we see from the *Confessions* (7.2), Christians still counted with glee the public conversions of highly placed Romans to their cult. Augustine himself had had to overcome his own contempt for Christian letters. In his *Confessions* he had demonstrated that he was capable of constituting a Christian discourse adequate to the microhistory of his own individual experience, which was at once pragmatic and mystical; however, huge obstacles had to be overcome before he could presume to inaugurate a Christian discourse adequate to the macrohistory of the human race, extending from the Creation through the calamities of the present and into the future as well. Clearly, Augustine felt obliged to confront Roman culture on its own terms, displaying, in this tour de force, his credentials as an authoritative interpreter of the past.

It is interesting to modern students of literature that Augustine's first point of reference in Roman letters is neither a historian nor a philosopher, but rather the poet Vergil, whom Augustine holds to be the chief spokesman for the ideology of *romanitas.* Such priorities coincided, of course, with Augustine's essentially rhetorical education, but they testify to the extraordinary prestige of the Latin epic poet. Thus, we may sense high cultural drama in Augustine's pitting of Vergil and the Bible against each other as rival authorities when he juxtaposes the famous injunction by Anchises (Aeneas' father) that future Romans should "spare the conquered and tame [*debellare*] the proud" (*Aeneid* 6.853) with a similar claim made in the Scriptures about the Christian God: "God resisteth the proud, but giveth grace unto the humble" (James 1:6 and Peter 5:5). Augustine then cites Vergil and others to show that the legacy of Rome has been, to the contrary, one of domination and pride, and he argues for the historical uniqueness of the fact that when the barbarian Visigoth Alaric (himself a Christian) invaded Rome, he spared the Christian faithful (and even some pagans) who had taken asylum in churches: God *had* tamed the proud and spared the humble. However, Augustine does not seem to have glimpsed in Vergil a kind of dark irony with regard to Augustan ideology that modern readers of Vergil have clearly detected.

Although Augustine acknowledges the supremacy of Vergil among poets, he remains deeply hostile (as had been Plato) to the institution of poetry within classical culture: the poets lie about the gods. In book 6 of the *City of God,* Augustine reflects about Varro's classification of theology into three kinds: the fabulous or mythic, the civil, and the natural or physical. The fabulous is that of the poets and playwrights, the civic that of the priests in the temples, and the natural that of the philosophers. The first two theologies, Augustine says, are in reality one and the same, and are inadequate to deal with either worldly or eternal life. Both are to be reviled: "the one sows base things concerning the gods by feigning them, the other reaps by cherishing them; the one scatters lies, the other gathers them together . . . the one sounds abroad in human songs impious fictions concerning the gods, the other consecrates these for the festivities of the gods themselves; the one sings the misdeeds and crimes of the gods, the other loves them" (6.6). Augustine's attack on poetry was of enormous consequence during the next thousand years. Not only was it the basis of later condemnations of secular poets by the Church, but it even affected the performance of devoutly Christian poets as well, who tended to include, within their poetry, expressions of concern as to the validity and legitimacy of their art. Not until the rise of humanism did poets, following the initiative of Dante, begin to vindicate their vernacular art with any kind of aggressiveness.

The third theology, that of the philosophers, commands much more respect from Augustine, even though his attempts to address the philosophers are not themselves philosophical. Indeed, despite Augustine's intelligence as a reader of the Scriptures and his skill as a Christian rhetorician, no one with a serious philosophical mind could defend the adequacy of Augustine's attack on the pagan philosophers, at least in this treatise. Although he was capable of disciplined philosophical reasoning (as we see in *On Free Will* and in *On the Trinity*), the heyday of Christian philosophy was not to come for another six centuries, in the generation of Saint Anselm and Peter Abelard.

The second part of the *City of God* (from book 11 on), in which Augustine carries out his project of tracing the history of the two cities through time, is a much more satisfying demonstration of his special genius. According to him, the heavenly city originated at the moment before historical time when God first created light. This was a spiritual light, and angels partook of that light. Angels are the most blessed of the celestial citizens (10.9). The earthly city originated, in turn, with the fall of the angels. Although the Bible does not tell us these things directly, Augustine believes that they may be extrapolated, and it is precisely the shrewdness with which he extrapolates evidence for his theories from the Scriptures that makes the *City of God* so curiously attractive. Indeed, this treatise is one of the great zones of interaction between the historicism of Jewish thought and the drive to elaborate static spiritual systems that was the legacy of Greek Platonism, both of which now needed to be absorbed into a self-consistent, Christian theology centered on Christ's mediation between the temporal and the eternal.

Since the person of Adam contained, in a sense, the whole of the human race, the foundations for the temporal manifestation of the two cities were laid when Adam was created (12.27), and the principle underlying their history is that of two distinct loves, the earthly and the heavenly. Earthly love is above all the love of self, even to the contempt of God; heavenly love is the love of God, even to the contempt of self (14.28). The two cities first manifested themselves in human society with the birth of Cain, who belonged to the city of man, and his brother Abel, who was of the city of God (15.1). However, the latter city was never materially constructed: "it is recorded of Cain that he built a city, but Abel, being a sojourner, built none. For the city of the saints is above, although here below it begets citizens, in whom it sojourns till the time of its reign arrives, when it shall gather together all in the day of the resurrection" (15.1).

The histories of the cities of God and man are thenceforth traced by Augustine through the genealogy of the early Jews to Noah's ark, which is a prefiguration of the Church, and then through the kings and prophets to Christ and the Church. Roman that he was, Augustine also grafts the histories of Greece and Rome (18.19–22) onto biblical history, although hardly to the glory of Rome. A point of convergence of Jewish and classical thought (one that was important to Augustine's own intellectual position) occurred when the Old Testament was translated from Hebrew into Greek. Augustine held that Hebrew was divinely instituted, that it was the first written language, and that it survived the Flood in the tribe of Eber, from whom the name "Hebrew" supposedly derived. According to a legend to which Augustine subscribed, the Old Testament was translated from Hebrew to Greek when Ptolomy Philadelphus invited seventy-two Jewish scholars (six from each of the twelve tribes) to Alexandria to effect the translation. Working separately, the translators miraculously agreed with each other, both in the choice of words and in syntax. The text that resulted, called the "Septuagint," was considered by the early Church to have been inspired by the Holy Spirit, as had been the original Hebrew text; hence, if things are said in the Septuagint that are lacking in the original, it is simply because the Holy Spirit chose to reveal such truths to men only at that later occasion. Although Augustine was aware of the more recent—and more accurate—translation of the Old Testament by Saint Jerome, he believed in the spiritual validity of the earlier translation (28.11), no doubt in part because its inspiration protected Augustine from his own ignorance and also permitted him a certain freedom of interpretation that would not have been possible under more scholarly constraints.

Although Augustine's conceptions of the two cities often give the appearance of a radical dualism between good and evil, between this world and the next, near the end of his treatise he mitigates this tendency in his thought (19.10). To the degree that the city of man loves earthly justice and peace, he says, such love is in harmony with the spiritual love of the city of God, where justice and peace are absolute and eternal. The city of man must relate to the city of God as the body relates to the soul: only then does the city of man truly serve its citizens; however, unless there is love of God, there can be no true virtue in the earthly city.

The *City of God* was of great importance to the course of political history in postclassical culture, and all of the great ideological movements of the Middle Ages and the Renaissance may be seen as attempts on the part of those in power to reconcile the competing claims of the secular and the ideal in the body politic. It was said that Charlemagne considered the

*City of God* his favorite book and had it read aloud to him at meals, though one wonders whether the great warrior found the time to hear the work to the end. In any case, its concerns were certainly pertinent to his dual status as king of the Franks and emperor of the Holy Roman Empire, and they would continue to exert themselves on the political ambitions of Otto the Great and Frederick I Barbarossa, especially in the latter's relationships with Italy. Indeed, Augustinian ideology was pertinent wherever there was a conflict between monarchical and papal authority during the Middle Ages. During the Renaissance, Augustine's method of tracing the lineage of the city of God would be adopted by the apologists of nearly every burgeoning nation of Europe as a way of establishing divine legitimacy for those who ruled.

The *City of God* was also important for having perfected archetypal modes of thought that shaped mystical and visionary literature throughout the Middle Ages and the Renaissance, and in England up to the time of Milton and even Blake. Augustine's theological methods tended to perpetuate themselves in historiography as well, at least until Gibbon, and no doubt beyond.

If the *Confessions* may be seen as an attempt to arrive at a theology of the empirical self, and if the *City of God* is an attempt to arrive at a theology of history, Augustine's treatise *On the Trinity* may be seen as an attempt to elaborate a theology of the human soul. Undertaken in 399, while he was still writing the *Confessions,* and composed while he was working on the *City of God, On the Trinity* was published prematurely in 416 and in its final version in 419. Like the *Confessions* and the *City of God, On the Trinity* is a work in which a drama of intellectual growth and discovery is constantly palpable. Augustine himself says that the mind that concluded this treatise has progressed far beyond the mind that began it (1.8). As in all of his best works, the writing of this treatise was not a mere product of thought, but rather a process, and Augustine frequently invites his readers to share in this special momentum. The modern reader perhaps feels additional excitement, licensed by hindsight, from knowing that, as Augustine wrote, he forged a new matrix for the consciousness of Western Christian culture as a whole.

However, the originality of *On the Trinity* does not derive specifically from Augustine's trinitarian position itself, since this was a development of Alexandrine thought, in particular the tendency to consider the Holy Spirit to have proceeded from the Father and the Son (the "filioque" position) and not merely from the Father through the Son. Augustine's originality lies, rather, in his strategies of mixed modes of argumentation, in his resourcefulness in probing the inner economy of the soul, and in his articulation of the relationship between knowledge and grace. Moreover, since *On the Trinity* complements intuitions already present in the *Confessions,* we may infer that the theological and psychological achievements of *On the Trinity* were extrapolations from intensely personal psychological victories.

Unlike the *City of God,* portions of which are no longer pertinent to concerns of our era, *On the Trinity* deals throughout with problems that still command active reflection. Theology, of course, is a living science in which a constant process of renewal is both possible and necessary, but *On the Trinity* is a book of theology that remains seminal to other modern disciplines as well, among them philosophy, psychology, linguistics, semiology, and literary criticism.

Augustine states his purpose for this treatise in the introduction: it is to justify the claim that the Trinity is a single and true God, and that the Father, the Son, and the Holy Spirit are of one and the same substance and essence. He also specifies his method: first, he says, he will demonstrate the validity of trinitarian doctrine by recourse to the authority of the Scriptures; then he will undertake to speculate further on this doctrine by employing the instruments of human reason, by which he means dialectics or logic. (On this score, Augustine was an important precursor of Scholastic logic, a movement that began with Anselm and Abelard at the end of the eleventh century.) Augustine displays great caution, however, as he undertakes his task. Not only does he question his own ability to understand and communicate the truth of his subject, but he enjoins the reader who has trouble understanding his treatise to put it down right away (1.3). *On the Trinity* is something of an epic of the intellect.

Obviously, it would not be possible to summarize or to simplify Augustine's trinitarian theology here, since we are dealing with one of the supremely irreducible mysteries of Western spirituality as that mystery has been apprehended by a very great mind. We may, however, suggest several reasons as to why this particular subject elicited from Augustine what many feel to be his most profound intellectual achievement.

First, we may point to the fundamentally paradoxical aspect of a Christian doctrine postulating a "triune" God—that is, a God whose essence is unique and indivisible, yet expresses itself as three distinct persons; and we may suggest that there was a deep compatibility between this paradox and Augustine's own cast of mind. Indeed, a constant feature of Augustine's thought is his penchant for paradox; paradox pervades his performance, from the level of wordplay and contrastive syntax to his underlying structure of thought. His awareness of himself as a creature both carnal and spiritual, both bestial and in God's image; his frequent dwelling upon servitude that is freedom, upon babbling that is eloquence, upon humility that is strength, upon stupidity that is intelligence, upon light that is darkness, upon death that is rebirth, punishment that is grace—all these paradoxes emanate from a single habit of mind. Although such a habit was perhaps natural to Augustine as a person, it was surely buttressed by his training in Ciceronian rhetoric, in which the mastery of figures of words and figures of thought (or tropes) was a privileged goal. Moreover, Augustine had inherited from Saint Paul, his chief spiritual mentor, a deep sense of the epistemological primacy of enigma (a trope very similar to paradox) in Christian mysticism. Indeed, the case has been made that the single most important point of departure for Augustine's theology, as well as for his epistemology, is Paul's statement, "We see now through a glass in an obscure manner, but then face to face" (1 Corinthians 13:12). In any case, the goal of *On the Trinity* is to explore both the modes by which God's essence manifests itself through and to the Creation, and the modes by which the soul both apprehends and reflects that essence.

A second feature of trinitarian theology that Augustine no doubt found compelling was the importance of kinship relations—especially the relationship of father to son—as a conceptual model that allows man to speak of the first two persons of the Trinity. Although it should be remembered that there is an important difference between using kinship models analogically and using them anthropomorphically, the fact remains that Augustine's use of a kinship model was far more than a neutral strategy of argumentation, and that such a model was deeply implicated in problems of Augustine's own psychological development. Let us pursue this question briefly.

It is noteworthy that Augustine wrote the first portions of *On the Trinity* as he was concluding the *Confessions,* a text in which we are allowed to see a "family drama" (to use Freud's term) of extraordinary force. In the *Confessions,* the dominant, and most problematical, principle of kinship to be expressed was that of mother and son. From an early age, Augustine tells us, Monica militated to make God his father rather than Patricius, her husband, whom she served in marriage only because God ordered her to do so (1.11). To the extent that Monica's attachment to her son was (at least in his eyes) inordinate, she could be seen as an heiress of Eve; to the extent that Monica procured her son's rebirth in the Church, she was like Mary, mother of the Church as mystical body of Christ. In its broad lines, then, the narrative portion of the *Confessions* depicts a long and difficult passage from an impure and mortal love between mother and son to a pure and immortal love, and we may say that Augustine's rebirth as a Christian corresponds to his transcendence of a fatal taboo.

However, in the *Confessions* Augustine's relationship to his father, Patricius, remains cloudy. Even though we are told that Patricius was finally converted to the religion of his wife, Augustine gives no evidence of a deep personal reconciliation with a father whom he feared and resented in his youth. That Patricius predeceased Monica obviously thwarted such a reconciliation definitively, and to judge by Augustine's conspicuous silence about Patricius' death, a process of grieving never occurred. However, we scarcely need to be reminded by psychologists that a father-son relationship is as determining as that of mother to son, and that the two relationships are inseparable within the deployment of family life. It is plausible to imagine that one important motive, conscious or not, underlying Augustine's speculation about the Trinity as he concluded the *Confessions* was to conceive of a return to the Original Father that in some way might help resolve the persisting dilemma of Augustine's personal alienation from Patricius. This is a return to a father made possible both by the expiation of the son's guilt through the death of the Son and by the dispensation of grace through the Holy Spirit. *On the Trinity* is a speculative scenario of a return and submission to the Father of a sort in which the Son is not effaced: on the contrary, the Son returns to his own plentitude and integrity—his own, and the Father's as well (5.6).

In other words, Augustine could proffer in the discourse of theology a model of metaphysical reunion of father and son that the more personal and historically constrained discourse of autobiography did not allow:

> Our Lord Jesus Christ will thus return the reign to God the Father; nor shall he be excluded, neither he nor the Holy Spirit, when he leads believers to the contemplation of God, which is the end of all good works, and eternal rest, and a joy that will never be diminished.
>
> (*On the Trinity* 1.10)

Moreover, this metaphysical version of a reunion of persons that seems not to have taken place in life entails, as well, a subordination of the mother—a voluntary one on her part, of course. Indeed, Augustine takes considerable care to dissociate the operations of the Holy Trinity from the familial trinity of father, mother, and son: the mother, he specifies, must not be seen as the analogue of the Holy Spirit. Woman, he recalls, was derived from a man who was already created in the image of the Trinity. Woman is therefore not of the same order as man in the hierarchy of the Creation, and it would be shameful, Augustine says, to imagine the spiritual knowledge associated with the Holy Spirit as something comparable to the carnal union of woman to man (12.7). Since woman was created from man, she is not in God's image (12.7), and for a man to "know" a woman sensually is to know an inferior reality. Such knowledge is "passionate" because it is in the nature of the senses to be "passive." Augustine does limit, if not obviate, this apparent misogyny. Women as sexual beings may not be in God's image, but women have souls identical to those of men (12.8); women have coinherited divine grace; and women too may be renewed in God's image, an image that is without sex.

Such conjectures about the relationship of Augustine's theology to his personal disposition are not demeaning. Rich as it is, Augustine's theology can only gain in interest when we glimpse the grounds for its human and psychological necessity in the *Confessions.*

The first half of *On the Trinity* is metaphysical, that is, devoted to speculation about the mode of being and the relations of the Trinity. The second half is devoted more to an analysis of modes of knowing that Trinity within the human soul; its concerns are epistemological. Augustine seems eager to elaborate a more thorough theoretical basis for the process of spiritual discovery that he himself had already undergone more pragmatically in the *Confessions.* Augustine's chief mode of reasoning as he passes from analysis of the Trinity to analysis of the inner life of the soul is basically that of analogy. Analogy, we should remember, is a comparison not of things to each other but of relationships (A is to B as X is to Y). This speculative mode has the double advantage of being both doctrinally rigorous and intellectually flexible.

Indeed, Augustine's attempt to elaborate a trinity of processes within the soul passes through several transformations. Since Augustine himself does not develop his ideas in a linear way (he jumps back and forth), we shall not try to retain his order in what follows here.

The lowest trinity of which Augustine speaks is not really in the soul itself, but involves our perception of objects through the senses. When we direct our vision toward some material object, that object shapes our vision, Augustine says, just as a ring imparts its shape to wax when pressed upon it (11.2). The vision, the object, and the impression are a trinity of the senses.

When we perceive an object through the senses, the impression made by that object may be stored in the soul as an impression on the memory, and we may thenceforth perceive that object from within, even though it is no longer corporeally present. This perception of forms that have been stored in the memory involves an inner vision, and such an act occurs thanks to another trinity involving the *memory,* which is the repository of forms, the *inner vision* by which forms are perceived, and the *will,* which directs the vision toward those forms. This inner process of the soul is called thought or, more precisely, cogitation, because of the union of memory and inner vision effected by the will (11.3). However, when we think of forms that have been imparted to the memory through the senses, such forms, because they derive from exterior things, are not truly engendered by the memory, but are foreign to it. Since they are not engendered like sons from a father in a way analogous to the engendering of Christ by God, the act of cogitation is not yet in the image of the Holy Trinity (11.7).

However, it is possible for the memory to engender things known that derive not from exterior objects but from the memory itself—for instance, numbers, measurements, weights, and time. These things are spiritual in origin, not corporeal, and the knowledge of such spiritual things, which Augustine calls "intelligibles," is, of course, superior to the knowledge of sensible things existing in the Creation. This higher knowledge is called "wisdom," whereas the lower knowledge is called "science." Moreover, it is within the power of the soul to take itself as an object of knowledge and to love such knowledge, and such a trinitarian process occurs without any differentiation between its components. It is in this trinitarian action, in which the soul knows and loves its own spiritual nature, that man comes closest to realizing the image of the divinity that has been in him since the Creation: "Behold, then, how the soul remembers itself, knows itself, and enjoys itself: if we grasp this, we grasp a trinity that is certainly not yet God, but already the image of God" (14.8). However, to love oneself in such a way is also to love God; indeed, unless one loves God, the soul cannot love itself properly. When man loves the God in whose image he is made, he discovers dialectically how superior and how different God's essence is from his own. Yet this is a postive difference, for man thenceforth tries to perfect his own being in anticipation of that moment after death when his knowledge of God will no longer be enigmatic, but face to face (15.24).

Augustine's *On the Trinity* is a major point of departure for a long tradition of speculation about the nature of the soul in the Christian West, a tradition that would be periodically renewed by such figures as Thomas Aquinas, Descartes, Leibniz, Locke, Hume, Kant, Hegel, and Freud; and Augustine is worthy of that tradition in all of its best moments. Moreover, even where attempts to elaborate a model of mind do not originate in an explicitly metaphysical horizon, interesting similarities with the Augustinian model may often be found. Freud's trinity of the mind is an obvious case.

Like Augustine, Freud speculated for many years about three components of the mind that he called the "id," the "ego," and the "superego." The id is constituted by impulses of sensory experience and by biological drives. The superego is constituted when the child is subjected to the moral authority of the parents, which furnishes the child both positive ideals to be fulfilled and a conscience with respect to what is morally bad. The ego mediates between the competing claims of the id and the superego. The terms of the Freudian model do not correspond exactly with those of Augustine. Nevertheless, in Augustine's model, when the will chooses between knowledge of things impressed on the memory by the senses and knowledge of spiritual things deriving from the memory itself, such a choice corresponds to the ego's function of reconciling the impulses of the id with the higher demands of the superego. As in Augustine's model, Freud's processes of the mind do not have sharp boundaries, and they interact with each other throughout life. Both systems emphasize the primacy of memory and the model of the family, and both include a process of deferral and repression; both, finally, set self-knowledge as a privileged goal that must never be abandoned as long as we live.

Although the abstraction and complexity of Augustine's theories of the Trinity and of the soul did not easily lend themselves to direct exploitation by vernacular poets, the quest for spiritual knowledge of the self as an image of the divine has remained in the mainstream of poetic objectives in our literary heritage. It is not difficult to find instances in many epochs in which poets mobilize their symbols and their fictions in such a way as to achieve that quest: one thinks, for example, of the Grail romances, the conclusion of Chaucer's *Troilus and Criseyde,* Dante's *Paradiso,* the religious poetry of Donne, Milton's *Paradise Lost,* and Wordsworth's *Prelude.* Moreover, such a quest frequently invites poets to reflect, as well, upon the powers—and limits—of poetic language itself.

Among those treatises by Augustine that influenced the shapes and modes of Western literature most directly, surely the most important is *On Christian Doctrine.* In this text Augustine's theological and epistemological concerns are brought to bear on methodological problems of grasping the truth of the Scriptures and edifying the faithful. This work is short, easy to read, and easy to apply to the sphere of poetic composition. *On Christian Doctrine* is another of Augustine's works written over a span of several decades: he probably began it in 387, about the same time as he began the *Confessions,* but it remained unfinished until the period when he wrote his *Retractations,* at which time he completed book 3 and added book 4. We may surmise that Augustine undertook this text as a kind of methodological companion piece to the *Confessions,* since many of the concerns expressed in it—especially those pertaining to the theory of signs, biblical exegesis, and rhetorical theory—are discernible in the *Confessions* as well, whether at the level of themes in the narrative of his own life story or at the level of pragmatic experiments in artistic form.

Augustine's main purpose in writing *On Christian Doctrine* was to teach the rules of interpreting the Scriptures properly. Another purpose, closely related to the first, was to teach the art of imparting the truth of the Scriptures to the faithful.

One may easily discover in the *Confessions* why the writing of such a treatise was personally and intellectually important to him. Augustine's early training in grammar—the art of writing properly—and in Ciceronian rhetoric had prevented him, as a youth, from understanding the Scriptures: he could neither penetrate beyond their literal message nor appreciate their eloquence, which seemed unworthy in comparison with Cicero's. Furthermore, Augustine's moral disposition before his conversion, particularly his carnal love of people and things, had preempted the spirit of charity necessary for an understanding of the figurative meaning of the Scriptures. The act of exegesis demands that one first love God and then love one's neighbor with the purpose of making that neighbor love God as well (1.29). Such is the nature of love that is charitable: the inordinate desire for lower things is concupiscent love. True Christian Neoplatonist that he was, Augustine elaborated a hierarchy of seven spiritual degrees that must be ascended by the biblical exegete: (1) fear of God; (2) piety, in which we submit our minds to the wisdom of the Scriptures; (3) knowledge, by which we gain access to the meaning of charity; (4) strength, by which we detach ourselves from the world and turn to God; (5) counsel, by which we properly evaluate worldly things and practice the love of God and of neighbor; (6) purification of the soul by death to the world; (7) wisdom, by which we enjoy the pleasure of divine contemplation. One may easily see the relationship of this hierarchy to Augustine's spiritual progress as it is narrated in the *Confessions.*

Augustine approaches questions of exegetical method by making some important statements about the relationship of signs, especially verbal signs, to things. Although science is the knowledge of material things, such things can be known not directly by the mind, whose nature is not material, but only through signs (1.2). Furthermore, things ought not to be studied for their own sake, but rather for what they signify. The tendency to study things not for themselves but as signs that, like words (which are also things), signify something *else* became a dominant feature of intellectual life until the late Middle Ages, when the empirical sciences at last acquired new legitimacy and material things began to be studied in their own right.

Augustine defines a sign as "a thing which causes us to think of something beyond the impression the thing itself makes upon the senses" (2.1, Robertson trans.). There are two basic classes of signs. First, there are *natural* signs, which signify automatically—that is, without there being any *intention* to signify on the part of someone, as when smoke signifies fire, or when someone cries out in pain. Secondly, there are *conventional* signs, by which living creatures intend to communicate with each other, as when a cock makes noises to signify to a hen that he has found food, or when a dove calls its mate (2.2). Conventional signs can be visual (nods, flags), tactile (the act of anointing), or auditory (music, words). Among conventional signs, words are preeminent, since words can express the meaning of all other signs, but not the inverse (2.3). Since words pronounced are ephemeral, words can be signified by visual signs (letters), and letters can conserve words through intervals of time or space. However, when words are deprived of their context of utterance, their meanings become obscure; such is the case when words are used figuratively rather than literally, and only through a combination of labor and charity may the exegete disperse such obscurities (2.6). The letter kills, the spirit vivifies.

Because languages are unstable and diverse, the exegete must first know languages in order to reduce the ambiguity of terms and to correct errors of translation. He must also know the sciences of nature (geography, botany, astronomy) if he is to understand how material things may be employed as symbols, and he must know arithmetic and music in order to understand the symbolism of numbers and notes. However, the exegete must avoid superstition and denounce the magic of demons.

Once Augustine has described the conditions and instruments of knowledge that are indispensable to proper exegesis, he passes (book 2) to the more specific rules of surmounting the ambiguities of the Scriptures and of resolving their apparent contradictions. These rules rely heavily on principles of dialectical reasoning and on familiarity with rhetoric, in particular with figures of speech and tropes. In all exegetical procedures, however, charity must be the guiding principle, for only the charitable mind is illuminated by God.

Augustine concludes *On Christian Doctrine* by passing from problems of understanding the truth of the Scriptures to problems of communicating that truth to others. His discussion is centered on the art of preaching as a specifically Christian kind of eloquence distinct from (and superior to) the precepts of classical rhetoric that he had both learned and taught before his conversion. In general, in the classical Roman institutions, rhetoric progressively lost its predominantly legal or forensic (from the word *forum*) functions, and Augustine's redefinition of the purpose of oratory became the basis of a formal branch of medieval and Renaissance rhetoric called the "art of preaching."

However, Augustine's theories of Christian oratory were of vast importance to Christian culture as a whole. Because he had dared to attack the institution of Ciceronian rhetoric head on (as only a distinguished rhetorician could presume to do), he gave Christian culture new credentials of its own.

No doubt the most innovative aspect of Augustine's theory of Christian oratory is his demolition of the Ciceronian theory of a hierarchy of styles. Cicero had defined three general levels of style—low, middle, and high—each with its specific function. The low style served to please an audience, the middle style to teach them, and the high style to move them to action. Augustine denies that divine truths either were or should be promulgated in accordance with the norms of classical, pagan eloquence. He illustrates this point by showing how the writings of Saint Paul, which were basically sermons, were composed in a mixture of styles. The positive emphasis that Augustine gave to the mixed style became the point of departure for a tradition that would extend through Christian letters well into the seventeenth century, even though the Ciceronian hierarchy of style began to re-exert influence on literature at the end of the Middle Ages and in the Renaissance (hence, Spenser's *Eclogues* and his *Faerie Queene* are examples of the low and high styles of English, whereas *Hamlet* and Donne's lyrics display the mixed style).

It would be difficult for us to overestimate the importance of *On Christian Doctrine* as a cornerstone of Western culture, whether ecclesiastical or secular. Augustine's theories of interpretation not only dominated the techniques of biblical commentary throughout the Christian Middle Ages and the Renaissance (although the impact of Aristotelian logic also became strong after the twelfth century), but played a determining role in the development of vernacular poetry as well. Vernacular poetry of the Middle Ages and the Renaissance is suffused with explicitly biblical symbolism (the Grail romances, Chaucer's "Nun's Priest's Tale," the *Divine Comedy*, the *Faerie Queene*), and poets accommodated allegorical modes of understanding to nonreligious experiences as well, especially those of erotic love and dreams (as in part 1 of the *Romance of the Rose*). The signifying possibilities of such poetry rested squarely on Augustinian theories of signification and of figurative expression. In the late eighteenth century, an essentially Augustinian science of biblical interpretation received new theoretical attention among the early romantics, and this in turn heavily influenced both the production of poetry throughout the romantic movement and the new discipline of literary criticism that interpreted that literature. In short, Augustine's treatise inaugurated a basic model of reading, writing, and understanding that has played a constitutive role in Western culture as a whole.

Among the most influential treatises that Augustine wrote in the fecund period soon after his baptism is *On Free Will.* Begun in Rome in 387 and finished in Thagaste in 389, just as Augustine was about to write the *Confessions,* it explores the difficult questions of the origin of evil in a divinely ordered universe and of free will in man. A year earlier Augustine had dealt with the problem of the origin of evil in *On Order (De ordine),* but found the subject too difficult for his young interlocutors and decided to defer it until later.

*On Free Will* is both an accomplished philosophical dialogue between Augustine and Evrodius (a mature fellow convert and future bishop) and a transitional piece, many of whose concerns would be explored more exhaustively in Augustine's major treatises of the two decades to follow. In contrast with most of Augustine's major works, the method of this treatise is consistent, and its philosophical discourse is relatively homogeneous. *On Order* is an important mediator of Ciceronian, Stoic, and Neoplatonic thought (especially that of Plotinus) to Christian spirituality of the Middle Ages and the Renaissance. Hence, it exalts the traditional values of classical philosophy (reason, truth, wisdom, repose, goodness, and justice) as primary values of Christian life as well.

Augustine defines sin in man as the submission of reason to passion. The Latin word that we translate as "passion" is *libido,* a term designating human desire in the broadest possible sense. Even acts committed out of fear or anger are done so out of desire for security. Although certain acts of passion are not only licensed by the temporal laws of society but necessary for the well-being of the individual or the group, such acts transgress the eternal law of God. Augustine elaborated upon this notion of the two laws later in the *City of God.* Reason is man's sovereign faculty, and reason becomes subordinated to passion in the sinful soul by man's free will. Since reason enables man to apprehend God's eternal goodness, and since passion is the affliction of temporal forces in the soul, sin may be understood as a turning from eternal to temporal things.

In book 2 of *On Free Will,* Augustine performs what appears to be a logical proof of the existence of God. Such an enterprise recurs in later Christian philosophy; for instance, in the writings of Anselm, Thomas Aquinas, and Descartes. Augustine appeals to logic here as an instrument of faith, not as its substitute. That we exist, he says, is certain, and we cannot err on this question, since unless we exist we cannot err: if I err, I am. Augustine's performance immediately calls to mind Descartes's famous *cogito,* but modern logicians do not consider Augustine's argument as a valid proof of man's existence. Its only achievement is to refute the skeptic's taunt: that I might be mistaken in my apprehension that I exist. Instead of dwelling on such a logical problem, Augustine presses ahead to the inference that if we exist and if our existence is manifested to us, we not only exist but are alive. That we understand we both exist and are alive implies that we are also intelligent. Man exists, he is animate, and he is intelligent, then, and these are three distinct orders of his being. If reason is man's highest faculty, God is not that to which man's reason is inferior, but rather that to which nothing is superior (2.6.14). Wisdom *(sapientia)* is that state of mind where we apprehend the truth of God as supreme goodness *(summum bonum).* This truth, which is the source of man's freedom and security, may be apprehended not in things themselves but in the eternal and universal numerical proportions by which created things exist.

Having established in book 2 that man participates in a hierarchy of being, Augustine in book 3 elaborates upon his notion that sin occurs when man freely chooses to subordinate his reason to passion, thereby subverting within his soul a divinely instituted hierarchy of being. Since this hierarchy of being is good, even a sinning soul is both good in itself and better than an inanimate being. Even though God foresaw man's choice to fall, God did not hinder man's basic freedom to fall. Evil is born in human beings either from spontaneous thoughts arising from within or from suggestions made by some exterior agent (3.20.29). As part of God's divine order, evil is in the service of good. God's Word took on human form as the Son, in order to free man from servitude to the devil, who first tempted man to sin (3.10.31). Because God is supremely just, even God's punishment of man for his sins is praiseworthy: to blame vice is to praise God.

Although children are born to the condition of sin, they first sin through either ignorance or weakness, and not by intention (3.18.52). Weakness and ignorance are consequences of the original sin. Augustine speculates that man's soul may exist before birth; but when the soul is joined to a mortal body, the soul forgets its previous existence and becomes subject, instead, to the ignorance and difficulty of mortal, corporeal existence (3.20.57). However, the question of our origin is less important than our destiny in the future.

*On Free Will* concludes with a brief explanation of the psychology of Adam before and during the Fall, and of the role of free will at that time. Its closing statements remind man of Christ's sacrifice, by which man may be redeemed, and they exhort man to love the beauty of justice, immutable truth, and wisdom.

*On Free Will* is subtle and brilliant, but relatively impersonal, and lacks the rhetorical urgency and sense of intellectual adventure that mark Augustine's later masterpieces. Still, it remained a catalyst for Christian thought, especially during those centuries of medieval and humanist philosophy framed by Anselm and Descartes. Students of literature will notice that many of its central themes also appear in the most sublime works of European poetry, for instance, those of Dante, Petrarch, Chaucer, Spenser, Shakespeare, and Milton.

If there is warrant for saying that the treatises discussed so far are the best known and most influential of Augustine's works, by way of conclusion we shall briefly consider several others that are bound to interest the modern reader for diverse reasons, whether historical or theoretical.

For instance, an early treatise dating from 389, *On the Christian Teacher (De magistro),* is especially valuable for its theories of signification and memory. The treatise opens with the question of whether the purpose of language is to teach or to recall. The question seems simple enough, but it leads promptly into a complex discussion of verbal signs and into a theory of signification that exemplifies Augustine's deep skepticism about the reality of interpersonal communication. Such question are all the more interesting in the context of the essay, a playful dialogue between Augustine, the teacher, and his son, Adeodatus, the pupil, who cheerfully conclude that teachers, when they teach, impart absolutely nothing to their pupils: they only incite the pupils to recall truths that are a priori in the memory.

All words are signs, the speakers agree (2), but what and how do they signify? For instance, how can the word *nothing* signify "something"? (This kind of question anticipates the concerns of Scholastic logicians and of speculative grammarians from the twelfth to the fourteenth centuries.) As in *On Christian Doctrine,* Augustine insists upon the radical difference between the sign and the signification it conveys. *Letters,* which are visual, signify *sounds* that are audible; *sounds,* which are audible, signify *words; words* signify to the mind things or concepts that are *signifiables* (4). In all cases, we normally prefer the knowledge of *what* is signified to the sign itself by which something is signified (9). However, how can a sign signify something unless we already hold in our memory what it signifies (10)? The teacher who employs signs recalls only significations that have already been learned, whether through empirical association of words with things or through the use of other signs (as when we use words to explain words). Since words never present the actual things that they signify, it is only through the prior knowledge of things that words become signs (11).

If words are impotent to teach, but can only recall what we know, how do we know? We know some things through the senses, and we retain images of those things in our memory (12). Words cause us to summon their meanings, which have been stored in our memory. However, other things that can be known are spiritual and eternal rather than sensible and material. But how do we know them? We know spiritual or intelligible things only through contemplation, which leads to illumination of the inner man by the light of God (12). Once again, language itself is not the source of such illumination. The only true teacher is Christ, who teaches us from within how to become enlightened by the truth.

Although it is an early work, *On the Christian Teacher* raises questions about language and epistemology that Augustine would later explore more thoroughly in the *Confessions* and *On the Trinity.* The spirit of play that animates the dialogue does not diminish the seriousness of the subject, as he himself says (8), and we may infer that Augustine's unmagisterial tone and Adeodatus' good cheer as a pupil not only correspond to their conclusion about the very limited role played by teachers in learning, but constitute a model of charitable Christian pedagogy that is the very opposite of Augustine's own boyhood experience in the classroom, where he was savagely beaten by vindictive masters.

Although Augustine felt compelled as a Christian to repudiate both the fabulous content of pagan poetry and the function of poetry in the secular body politic, he nevertheless recognized the irreducible fact that poetic language itself could be truly beautiful and that such beauty could be held to be worthy of love. The beauty of poetic language lies, however, not in its meaning, but in its musicality; and in his dialogue *On Music (De musica)* Augustine elaborates upon this duality in poetic language. For, despite its title, *On Music* is really devoted more to metrics than to what we now consider music. The music of poetry is manifested not in its content, but in the rhythm and proportion that are imparted to the material substance of poetic language through meter.

Music, he tells us, may be defined as the "science of measuring well" (1.2). But the Latin word meaning "to measure" *(modulari)* also means "to move," and "musical" movement is harmonious movement that is accomplished for its own sake, as distinct, for example, from the movements of an artisan that produce an artifact on a lathe (1.2). Although harmonious movement may be produced by many different actions (singing, playing the flute, dancing), the art or science of music is quite distinct from such movement, for such bodily movement is the product of imitation and rote memory: in this sense, musicians and dancers are like parrots or dancing bears (1.4). Nor is the song of the nightingale music, because it is instinctive (1.4). The art of music does not, then, lie in execution, for execution is merely an imitative technique, whereas music as a "semidivine" art is a product of reason, and those who practice music practice reason (*ratio:* 1.4). A parrot or a flute player can produce musical sounds without reason, but the art or science of music must be rational. Such a distinction between execution and art in music, between technique and science, remained a constant feature of the medieval theory of music, understood as a liberal art belonging to the *quadrivium* (arithmetic, music, geometry, and astronomy). Since its basis is mathematical, music is distinct from grammar and cannot be learned from the grammarian (1.1).

Augustine exposes the principles of harmony and proportion in music by discussing poetic meter, which, in Latin, was composed of patterns of long and short syllables called "feet." Since the long syllable is twice the length of the short syllable, or of a ratio of 1:2, the short syllable, he says, is the foundation of rhythm in poetry (and music). Augustine's identification of the poetic dimension of language with mathematical equivalences and proportions has much in common with modern linguistic theories about poetic language, especially those of Roman Jakobson and his followers.

One important feature of Augustine's poetics that is lacking in modern poetics is the presupposition that numerical proportion and ratio in poetic language are the expression of metaphysical relationships as well: Augustine tells us in *On the Trinity* that the ratio of 1:2 that underlies harmony is also an expression of the relationship of the indivisible Creator to the Creation (4.2–3). In *On Music* he follows principles of numerological symbolism inherited from the Greeks to develop a theory of harmony based on the mystical values of 1, 2, 3, 4, and 10. These theories are followed by an extraordinarily meticulous description of all the existing metrical patterns of Latin poetry, as well as by speculation about other patterns that could possibly exist. Vergil and Horace, unsurprisingly, are the principal sources of Augustine's examples. Augustine's metrical analyses are of interest to specialists of Latin meter, but less so to musicologists. Augustine does not deal with principles of stress and unstress (as opposed to metrical quantities), which came to dominate the composition of Latin poetry in the Christian Middle Ages.

Given Augustine's claim that the material substance of language can express proportions that are rational, beautiful, and divine, whereas the meaning or semantic content of poetic language can express mere fables, we may easily understand why, in his treatise *On Order* (2.14), Augustine speaks of poetry as an art of "reasonable lies." However, just as the art of music does not inhere in its execution, so too the art of poetry inheres not in the making of concrete poetic verse itself, but in the knowledge of those rules that make the verse possible. In another treatise, *Of True Religion (De vera religione),* Augustine elaborates on this distinction in a way that can only astonish modern readers of poetry. A poetic line, he says (12.40), may be appreciated only when its multitude of syllables are pronounced one after another, until the line is finished. Such access to the abstract whole through the unfolding of its material parts in time is vexing to the human soul. For this reason, the beauty of a poetic line is a mere "trace" of the more abstract and greater beauty of poetic art itself, whose realm is immutable and outside of time. Hence, that man is perverse who prefers poetry itself to the art by which it is made: such a man has chosen temporal things over Divine Providence, which is the source and principle of order in time (12.43).

In a similar line of reasoning in the final book of *On Music,* Augustine demonstrates once again the obligation of the human soul to ascend a Neoplatonic hierarchy of rhythms, beginning with that manifested in the poetic line itself and ending with the contemplation of God. First, there is the rhythm of material sonorities that occur in a line of poetry itself; then the rhythm that is the apprehension of that first rhythm; then the rhythm that occurs when apprehended rhythm is committed to our memory; then the rhythm that, instead of being apprehended or remembered, is purely by the memory from within; finally, the "rhythm of judgment," by which Augustine means our innate capacity of intellect to know and judge the perfection of all lesser rhythms, and this purely intellectual rhythm of judgment derives from the harmony of divine wisdom itself. Thus, Augustine's treatise on music is nothing other than a calculated strategy for emancipating the soul from the very art (whether poetical or musical) that he pretends to describe.

Augustine's contempt for poetry both as concrete sounds and as fable or fiction (that is, as lies) endured in certain ecclesiastical circles until the end of the Middle Ages, although, in practice, poets and audiences obviously composed and enjoyed their art with the assurance (or at least the hope) that they would not be eternally damned because of it. Not until Dante did poets presume to venture rational arguments for poetry as an art that was both sensual and spiritual. It was only with the rise of humanism, with its vigorous defenses of poetry (exemplified in English by Sir Philip Sidney), that poets established firm moral and philosophical grounds for the validity of poetry as a vehicle of a truth whose inspiration was at once human and divine. As for Augustine, the only exception to his condemnation of poetry was the Psalms, whose beauty was obvious and whose truth was infallible; his voluminous and brilliant commentaries on the Psalms are ample proof of his own genius as an interpreter (not a critic) of poetry.

We shall end with the mention of two of Augustine's lesser-known treatises, on the topic of lying, whose value and importance have not yet been properly appreciated by modern readers. Entitled *On Lying (De mendacio)* and *Against Lying (Contra mendacium),* written in 395 and 420 respectively, they are formal manifestations of a concern for a problem of language that recurs constantly in Augustine's other writings.

The pretext of the first treatise was to defend the Scriptures from allegations (allowed by Saint Jerome) that the patriarchs and the Apostle Paul deceived and lied; the pretext for the second was both to denounce heretics who shunned ostracism by pretending to be orthodox Christians and to admonish Christians not to resort to strategic lies in order to propagate their faith. Augustine raises problems that at first may seem narrowly conceived, but no modern reader can escape seeing their relevance to contemporary political and social affairs.

Augustine's treatises are also relevant to the modern philosophy of language, notably to that branch called "speech act theory," represented in the writings of J. L. Austin and J. P. Searle. Speech act theory is concerned with the empirical definition and description of different classes of speech act that comprise interpersonal and social relationships.

Augustine's treatises are interesting precisely because of the rigor of his attempts both to define the notion of lying and to establish a typology of the different kinds of lies that men commonly commit. However, as is usually the case with Augustine's reflections on language, he situates his theories of lying in a metaphysical as well as social horizon, and by doing so he sustains a framework that is deliberately shunned by modern theoreticians of language, at least in the tradition of Ludwig Wittgenstein.

As we might expect, Augustine's moral and intellectual position on lying is uncompromisingly categorical: quite simply, one must never do it. For Augustine, the act of lying involves the intention to deceive, rather than the utterance of statements that are objectively untrue. The latter statements are falsehoods, rather than lies, for a speaker may very well say something false while believing that it is true. Inversely, a liar may say something objectively true, yet intend to deceive someone by doing so. Moreover, a person may lie even by remaining silent, if his silence is intended to convey a deceptive message.

However, Augustine does exempt from moral condemnation jesting lies and those mixtures of fact and fiction whose intention is to amuse rather than deceive.

In *On Lying* 14, Augustine discerns eight different types of lies and arranges them in a hierarchy of moral gravity. The first and worst kind of lie is one told in the teaching of the Christian faith; second is the lie that harms someone unjustly; third, the lie uttered for the simple pleasure of deceiving; fourth, the lie that renders service to one person yet harms someone else; fifth, the lie that is told to please someone else; sixth, the lie that is useful to one person without harming someone else; seventh, the lie undertaken to save someone's life; eighth, the lie that spares someone an impure assault. Augustine is often concrete and specific in his examples of lies. For instance, if a woman begs a man to lie to a pursuer in order to save her from being raped (type eight), should he do so? No; the innocence of the body is not comparable to the integrity of the soul, and the soul must not be compromised in order to protect someone's body. If the woman is raped, her soul is not corrupted unless she experiences pleasure in the act; but the soul that lies is necessarily corrupted (7). Obviously, Augustine's rigor does not always put him in a favorable light, at least by relative standards of human justice.

The second treatise on lying is more closely bound to problems of scriptural exegesis. If, in the Scriptures, good men appear to lie, we must take as a matter of faith that this is simply not true, and we must be guided by charity as we read in order to discover a figurative or symbolic meaning to their actions that is both good and true (10). As for those who resort to strategic lying in matters of faith, Augustine mentions two classes of lies that are especially reprehensible: perjury and blasphemy. The perjuror invokes God as a witness to his lie; the blasphemer attributes false things to God himself (19).

Augustine's theories about lying were the point of departure for a long tradition of reflection about lying whose repercussions on the poetry of the Middle Ages and Renaissance often involve ethical dilemmas that invite the reader to recognize and discriminate between different kinds of lying. A problematics of lying is central, for instance, to such diverse works as the *Song of Roland;* Dante's *Inferno;* Chaucer's *Canterbury Tales* (especially those of the Pardoner and the Wife of Bath) and *Troilus and Criseyde; Sir Gawain and the Green Knight;* Shakespeare's *Hamlet, Othello,* and *King Lear;* and Milton's *Paradise Lost.* Moreover, such authors tended to bear in mind, as Augustine did, the ultimately theological dangers not only of lying as an act of speech but of fiction itself. These concerns diminished in the Renaissance, however, when artistic allusion, which earlier had been attacked as lying, was now defended, even exalted, as ideal truth.

# Selected Bibliography


EDITIONS

*Confessionum libri tredecim.* Edited by Pius Knöll and Martinus Skutella. Leipzig, 1934.

*Corpus scriptorum ecclesiasticorum latinorum.* Prague, Leipzig, Vienna, 1866–
- Vol. 18: *De vera religione.* Edited by William M. Green. 1961.
- Vol. 36: *Retractationes.* Edited by Pius Knöll. 1902.
- Vol. 40: *De civitate dei.* Edited by Emanuel Hoffmann. 1899–1900.
- Vol. 41: *Contra medacium* and *De mendacio.* Edited by Joseph Zycha. 1900.
- Vol. 77: *De magistro.* Edited by Guenther Weigel. 1961.
- Vol. 80: *De doctrina christiana.* Edited by William M. Green. 1963.

*De civitate dei.* Edited by B. Dombart. Leipzig, 1909.

*De dialecta.* Edited by Jan Pinborg. English translation by B. Darrell Jackson. Dordrecht and Boston, 1975.

*De magistro.* Edited by Sister Thérèse Sullivan. Washington, D. C., 1930.

*Oeuvres de Saint-Augustin.* In *Bibliotèque augustinienne.* Paris and Bruges, 1939–
- Vol. 2: *Contra mendacium* and *De mendacio.* French translation by Gustave Combès. 1948.
- Vol. 4: *De ordine.* French translation by R. Jolivet. 1939.
- Vol. 6: *De magistro* and *De libero arbitrio.* French translation by F. J. Thonnard. 1941.
- Vol. 7: *De musica.* French translation by Guy Finaert and F. J. Thonnard. 1947.
- Vol. 8: *De vera religione.* French translation by J. Pegon. 1951.
- Vol. 11: *De doctrina christiana.* French translation by Gustave Combès and F. Farges. 1949.

Vol. 12: *Retractationes.* French translation by G. Bardy. 1950.

Vols. 13–14: *Confessionum.* French translation by A. Solignac. 1962.

Vols. 15–16: *De trinitate.* French translation by M. Mellet and T. Camelot. 1955.

*Opera.* In *Corpus Christianorum, Series Latina.* Turnholt, 1954–

Vol. 27: *Confessionum.* Edited by Martinus Skutella and Lucas Veheijen, O.S.A. 1981.

Vols. 50 and 50a: *De trinitate.* Edited by W. J. Mountain. 1968.

*Opera omnia.* In *Patrologiae latinae,* edited by J. P. Migne. Paris, 1841–1847. Reproduces the basic edition by the Benedictines of St.-Maur (France), 1681–1700.

Vol. 32: *Confessionum; De magistro; De musica; De ordine; Retractationes.*

Vol. 34: *De doctrina christiana; De vera religione.*

Vol. 40: *Contra mendacium; De mendacio.*

Vol. 41: *De civitate dei.*

Vol. 42: *De trinitate.*

## TRANSLATIONS

*Ancient Christian Writers.* Westminster, Md., and London, 1946–

*The City of God.* Translated by Marcus Dods. New York, 1950.

*The City of God Against the Pagans.* Translated by Henry Bettenson. Harmondsworth, 1976. Penguin edition.

*Concerning the Teacher.* Translated by G. C. Leckie. In *The Basic Writings of Saint Augustine,* edited by Whitney J. Oates. New York, 1938. Pp. 301–308.

*Confessions.* Translated by E. B. Pusey. London, 1953. Everyman's Library.

*Confessions.* Translated by John K. Ryan. Garden City, N. Y., 1960.

*Divine Providence and the Problem of Evil.* Translated by Robert P. Russell. New York, 1942.

*Library of the Fathers of the Holy Catholic Church.* Oxford, 1838–1858.

*Of True Religion.* Translated by J. H. S. Burleigh. Philadelphia, 1953.

*On Christian Doctrine.* Translated by D. W. Robertson, Jr. Indianapolis and New York, 1958.

*On Dialectics.* Translated by B. Darrell Jackson. Dordrecht and Boston, 1975.

*The Works of Aurelius Augustinus.* Edited by the Reverend Marcus Dods. Edinburgh, 1871–1874.

*Writings of Saint Augustine.* In *Fathers of the Church: A New Translation.* New York and Washington, D. C., 1947–

Vol. 2: *On Music,* translated by R. C. Taliaferro. 1947.

Vol. 16: *Against Lying,* translated by Harold B. Jaffe. 1952. Pp. 111–179. *Lying,* translated by Mary S. Muldowney. Pp. 45–110.

Vol. 18: *The Trinity,* translated by Stephen McKenna. 1963.

Vol. 60: *The Retractations,* translated by Mary I. Bogan. 1968.

## BIOGRAPHICAL AND CRITICAL STUDIES

Abrams, M. H. *Natural Supernaturalism.* New York, 1971.

Battenhouse, R. W. *A Companion to the Study of Saint Augustine.* New York, 1955.

Brown, Peter. *Augustine of Hippo: A Biography.* Berkeley, 1967.

Burke, Kenneth. *The Rhetoric of Religion.* Boston, 1961. New edition, Berkeley and Los Angeles, 1970.

Colish, Marcia. *The Mirror of Language: A Study in the Medieval Theory of Knowledge.* New Haven and London, 1968.

Courcelle, Pierre. *Recherches sur les confessions de saint Augustin.* Paris, 1950.

Gilson, Étienne. *The Christian Philosophy of Saint Augustine.* Translated by L. E. M. Lynch. New York, 1960.

Markus, R. A. *Augustine: A Collection of Critical Essays.* Garden City, N. Y., 1972.

Marrou, Henri, I. *Saint Augustin et la fin de la culture antique.* Paris, 1938.

Murphy, James J. *Rhetoric in the Middle Ages.* Berkeley and Los Angeles, 1974.

O'Connell, Robert J. *Art and the Christian Intelligence in Saint Augustine.* Cambridge, Mass., 1978.

O'Donovan, Oliver. *The Problem of Self-Love in Saint Augustine.* New Haven, 1980.

O'Meara, John J. *The Young Augustine: The Growth of Saint Augustine's Mind Up to His Conversion.* London and New York, 1961.

Testard, Maurice. *Saint Augustine et Cicéron.* Paris, 1958.

EUGENE VANCE

# ISAAC BABEL

## *(1894–1941?)*

ISAAC BABEL WAS perhaps the first Soviet prose writer to achieve a truly stellar stature in Russia, to enjoy a wide-ranging international reputation as grand master of the short story, and to continue to influence—through his own work as well as through criticism and scholarship—literature produced in our own day. All this acclaim notwithstanding, Babel, whom contemporaries remember as a man with a penchant for mystification, remains one of the more enigmatic figures of Russian modernism. Even the corpus of his writings is uncertain and may never be firmly established. The works by which he wished to be known, however, indeed his best-known works, have gone through thirty-five editions in the Soviet Union alone and, beginning in 1926, have been translated into all the major European tongues. In contrast to this renown, Babel's "authorized" legacy is quite compact. Begun and finished, for the most part, between 1921 and 1926, it consists of three major story cycles, two plays, and several pieces of short fiction—all fitting comfortably into an average-sized volume. Together they account for approximately half of Babel's extant output: movie scripts, early short fiction, journalistic sketches, one translation, and a few later stories that remained unpublished in Babel's lifetime (they were considered offensive either to the party or to the censor's sense of public delicacy).

His most famous work, the cycle of short stories and vignettes *Konarmiia (Red Cavalry),* was first published in a separate edition in 1926. It dealt with the experiences of the Russo-Polish War of 1920 as seen through the bespectacled eyes of a Russian Jewish intellectual working, as Babel himself had, for the newspaper of the Red Cossack army. This autobiographical aura was critical to the success and popularity of the cycle. The thirty-three jewel-like pieces, strung together to form the first edition of *Red Cavalry,* were composed in a short period of time, between the summer of 1923 and the beginning of 1925, and together constitute Babel's longest work of fiction (two more pieces would be added subsequently). They also represent his most innovative and daring technical accomplishment. For the first time in Russian letters at least, the opulence and subtlety of modernism lent themselves to the expression of the cruelest and basest sensibility. An instant success, *Red Cavalry* met with virtually universal acclaim as the first true masterpiece of Russia's postrevolutionary prose fiction; it had generated a critical response that had exceeded Babel's own output even before the appearance of the separate edition. Clearly he touched the raw nerve of contemporary culture.

Another cycle, *Odesskie rasskazy (Odessa Tales),* contains four novellas: "Korol'" ("The King," 1921), "Kak eto delalos' v Odesse" ("The Way It Used to Be Done in Odessa," 1923), "Otets" ("The Father," 1924), and "Liubka Kozak" ("Liubka the Cossack," 1924). Although completed between 1921 and 1923, for a long time the cycle was believed to have preceded *Red Cavalry.* United, like the stories of *Red Cavalry,* by their protagonists, the setting, and the narrator, *Odessa Tales* presented a larger-than-life, Rabelaisian picture of the city's Jewish underworld, whose members go about their carnivalesque business, meting out poetic justice to the melancholy powers of prudery, capital, and the local police. Inherently theatrical, *Odessa Tales* had an easy time crossing over into film and drama. In 1925 and 1926, Babel wrote a script based on the story cycle, naming it *Benia Krik* after the chief protagonist of the Odessa stories. By contrast with *Odessa Tales,* where the action takes place in the years 1905 to 1907 and the king of the Odessa gangsters reigns unchallenged, the script stretches to include the 1917 revolution and the civil war. It ends with a close-up of the back of Benia Krik's head as it is being shattered—deservedly, we are supposed to think—by a Red executioner's bullet. Perhaps by coincidence, the characters in the script fall without exception into two groups: the traders and the criminals are Jews (like the author of the script and the film director), whereas the proletarian revolutionary activists, who finish off the gangs, are ethnic Russians. Produced in 1926, the film ran into brief trouble with the censors but was released in January 1927 to enjoy considerable popularity.

Also in 1927, Babel completed his first play, *Zakat* (*Sunset,* 1928). Thematically different, it was in other respects closely related to the *Odessa Tales;* from this common milieu derives some of the most comical dialogue known to Russian theater. As the title suggests, *Sunset* offered a melancholy meditation on the passage of time as revealed through a bloody conflict between a brutal father who refuses to act his age and his children, who do not hesitate to use force in order to age him. Although the younger generation prevails and the play ends with the children's triumph, theirs is a Pyrrhic victory, and not only because it anticipates their eventual defeat at the hands of their own children. The small Jewish, bourgeois, and criminal world in which such a victory possessed some relative value would soon be ground up by the revolution and the new Soviet state. Babel's contemporaries understood this without any prompting from the playwright. In print, the play made for good reading; on stage, the response was mixed. In Odessa *Sunset* played to packed audiences in two theaters simultaneously (in Yiddish and in Russian), but the Moscow production of 1928, staged while Babel was in Paris, ended in disaster, largely, it seems, because the director tuned it to a crudely ethnic and anecdotal key.

Babel began work on the book *Istoriia moei golubiatni* (*The Story of My Dovecote*), his other major tetraptych, in 1925, when two of the stories were published, but did not complete the other two until five years later. An episodic fictional chronicle of the author's childhood years, the four stories combine into a portrait of the artist not as a young man, but rather as a studious Jewish boy poised at the edge of adolescence. Less exuberant in their style, the four novellas have more in common with the more traditional autobiographical fiction of Leo Tolstoy and Maxim Gorky than with the more probing explorations of the consciousness of a gifted child found in *The Noise of Time* by Osip Mandelshtam, *The Childhood of Luvers* by Boris Pasternak, and, earlier, *Kotik Letaev* by Andrey Bely. Indeed, the cycle appears to have been aimed at a wider audience, one that possessed only limited patience and little taste for modernism. Nevertheless, crafted as skillfully as anything that Babel ever wrote, *The Story of My Dovecote* must be counted among the minor masterpieces of short fiction.

After *Sunset* came out in February 1928, Babel published very little that had not appeared previously, although editions of his writings, revised and expanded to include a most recent story or two, kept being issued with what was surely an enviable regularity. Close to thirty separate editions, among them a volume of collected works, rolled off the presses during the decade following the publication of *Red Cavalry.* One work not related to the three cycles, the play *Mariia* (*Maria,* 1935), represented a rather uninspired attempt to appease Babel's official "creditors"—the high cultural and, it seems, political establishment that had allowed the "silent" author to continue maintaining a remarkably high profile. With its pathos directed against the remnant of the aristocracy and the unscrupulous Jewish bourgeoisie under the New Economic Policy (NEP, 1921–1928), the play arrived long after the NEP, with all of its remnants, had been obliterated in the Stalinist revolution. Babel worked too slowly, political winds were changing fast, and the play misfired, although it may have earned him a brief respite—just for trying—from the intense official pressure to produce.

In the 1930's Babel devoted much of his energy to film, random journalistic work, and almost compulsive travel, roaming ceaselessly across the Soviet Union, ostensibly in search of new material for his work in progress. Throughout this period he assured his family and friends in correspondence as well as in conversation that he was working on a major project—a novel, perhaps. In 1925 he told Dmitrii Furmanov, a fellow writer, he was considering a novel about the Cheka. Possibly some echoes of this project may be discerned in the rumors, circulating in Russia in the late 1920's and reported in the émigré press, that the Cheka had stopped the publication of a new piece by Babel. According to several memoirists, including Ilya Ehrenburg, in the late 1920's and early 1930's Babel was working on a novel, "Kolia Topuz," in which a con man successfully reforms himself through work in socialist construction. During the period of the first Five-Year Plan (1928–1932), when the prison population engaged in forced labor was rapidly expanding, such topics were in the air. Babel's patron and protector, Gorky, at the time the most important figure in Soviet culture, actively encouraged fellow writers to explore this subject. Whether Babel tried his hand at it or merely wished to appear to is a question that will most likely remain unanswered.

His tendency to subtitle his stories as part of a larger work in progress—a consistent practice beginning with *Odessa Tales*—confuses matters further. "V shchelochku" ("Through the Crack"), an odd piece about a scene observed by the narrator through a peephole in a bordello, was published in 1923 and came, according to its subtitle, "From the Book *Etchings.*" It has no acknowledged companions in the published Babel, although it resembles his two stories published by Gorky in 1916. Some fifteen years later, "Gapa Guzhva" (1931, in *The Lonely Years*), a story about a Ukrainian village whore caught up in the collectivization of agriculture, was published as "The First Chapter of *Velikaia Krinitsa.*" Its companion piece, "Kolyvushka," published posthumously in 1963, also in *The Lonely Years,* and yet to appear in the Soviet Union, bore a slightly different subtitle: "From the Book *Velikaia Staritsa.*" There are no traces of other chapters. In response to the harsh criticism of *Mariia,* Babel declared that he was revising the play as part of a trilogy covering the period 1920 to 1935. But in the words of the Soviet commentator on the play, "No materials testifying to Babel's continued work on the trilogy have been preserved." When Babel was arrested on 15 May 1939, all the papers that were with him at his dacha in Peredelkino were confiscated. Now they are presumed lost, destroyed together with a portion of the NKVD (as the KGB was known in the 1930's) archive in 1941, when the seizure of Moscow by the German armies seemed imminent. For years, Antonina Pirozhkova, the writer's widow, had been pressing the KGB to reveal the fate of Babel's papers only to be informed in 1988 that the KGB possessed no record of Babel's papers. Thus we may never know whether Babel was writing for the drawer or trying to produce literature that could be officially accepted. Nor will we ever know whether any of his efforts, if indeed there were such efforts, led to substantial results.

The only extant manuscript of an unfinished work of fiction, *Evreika* (The Jewess, 1979), lends credence to the claims that Babel had indeed tried his hand at a different genre and a different thematic material. A third-person narrative with an unmarked, "objective" style, it tells the story of a recently widowed woman who leaves her decaying shtetl for Moscow to settle there with her only son. He insists on this move and she follows him, but apprehensively; for as she puts it, the capital already has too many Jews. A civil war hero, a decorated Red Army commander, and a student at a military academy, her son belongs to the new Soviet elite, and yet, he also acknowledges, if only to himself, the unease he feels in his new prestigious surroundings. The manuscript breaks off just as the narrative reaches its first potential conflict: the more cultivated neighbors are beginning to complain about the smell of his mother's Jewish cooking. It is a bitter but fitting irony that the unfinished novella was finally published in the Soviet Union in 1988, not in the original Russian, but in Yiddish, in Yiddish-language journal *Sovietish Heimland.* The fate of the work itself has remained enigmatic. Did Babel abandon this project for reasons of censorship or for fear that its publication might damage his reputation? Or could it be that he simply failed to sustain the narrative style that seems alien to the rest of his known fiction? Or did he complete *Evreika* only to lose it once and for all in the incinerators of the Lubyanka prison?

We do know, however, that with the exception of *Mariia,* the unfinished *Evreika,* and two or three later stories, Babel's major fiction is all of a piece. The three cycles share the same narrator, although they emphasize his different facets, and we continue to encounter him in the later stories, which, accordingly, borrow their settings, or sets, from *Red Cavalry, The Story of My Dovecote,* and *Odessa Tales.* Even the two novellas dealing with the collectivization—both third-person narratives—recall with such pungency and vividness the style of *Red Cavalry* that a knowing reader of Babel would find the absence of that bungling and humane *intelligent*—who failed to acquire the hoped-for "simplest of human skills," the ability to kill—at least conspicuous and at most profoundly telling. It is this narrator who represents the chief protagonist of what has reached us of Babel's fiction. The author's mask, he came with time to be identified with the name of Isaac Babel, blending into one the man, the character, and the persona that straddled the two—the writer.

For an author whose best-known works were composed and published during a six-year period (1921–1928), the spectacular renown enjoyed during the remaining eleven virtually barren years and a remarkable posthumous fame must be considered, on a par with his texts, as part of his literary career. A member of the post–World War I generation of European and American writers, he developed, not unlike Ernest Hemingway and F. Scott Fitzgerald, a charismatic public persona that could appeal, often justifiably, to different facets of the European and American literary taste. To some Babel appeared first and foremost as an artist whose genius, forged in the revolution, transcended the boundaries of ethnicity and class; others, for whom the aesthetic criterion took pride of place, admired him as an avant-gardist who reinvigorated Russian prose and elevated the short story, a humbler genre, to the lofty heights of great art. And those of his readers who felt disillusioned with the Russian Revolution or never accepted its promise could focus their attention on Babel's meager output in the 1930's and, after 1939, his disappearance in the Gulag, citing them as evidence for the incompatibility of true art and Communist totalitarianism.

Babel's posthumous "rehabilitation," the official clearing of his name of all charges in 1954, and the subsequent reissuing of his work in the Soviet Union at the time of de-Stalinization made him an attractive symbolic figure to the less orthodox members of the Soviet cultural elite. They eagerly promoted his name and his writings, eliciting protest from the die-hard Stalinists whose interference made it easier for the champions of Babel to dissociate themselves retrospectively from the worst brutalities of the Soviet state. But in identifying with this "martyred" star of Soviet literature (and by implication with the more tolerant 1920's, when Babel made his spectacular debut), these advocates tended to magnify the author's tragic demise while underplaying his—and by implication, their own—loyalty to the regime during the period of worst terror.

An analogous revision of the writer's legacy, if on a smaller scale, took place among the intellectuals of the Left in the West in the late 1950's and 1960's. With new editions of his writings running off the presses throughout Western Europe and the United States, Babel's name was once again coming into vogue—even as more and more evidence testified to the catastrophic scale of the Stalinist purges. In the United States in particular, where the later, post-McCarthy fashion for Babel had been anticipated at least as early as 1947, according to Raymond Rosenthal, the figure of the writer was recruited to perform a multiple duty by such influential critics as Lionel Trilling and Irving Howe. Presented as a symbolic distillation of beauty and truth (Russian authors victimized by the regime seem to lend themselves naturally to such treatment), Babel served as a powerful indictment of Stalinism and at the same time as a man committed to the promise of Bolshevism. He provided a vindication for the long-standing fascination with the Russian Revolution on the part of the intellectual Left. Moreover, at a time when the exclusively political and Manichaean formulas for political engagement were losing their appeal, Babel turned into an exemplary case of the ambivalences and ambiguities faced by an intellectual—and a Jewish one, too—whose identification with the "people's cause" is tested most rudely by his supposed beneficiaries.

As a Russian Jew who in his writings thematized the advantages and liabilities of this double designation, Babel attracted a substantial Jewish readership both in his own country and abroad, and especially in the United States. For this audience, too, and with special poignancy after World War II, he served not only as a storyteller and playwright, but as a powerful symbolic figure whose life reproduced the recent history of the Jews of Europe, with all their accomplishments and tragic fate. Because there is no more consensus regarding this history than that of modern Europe or Russia, Babel has been alternately called upon to provide evidence for the failure or success, or merely the complexity, of the attempts made by Diaspora Jews to identify with the political or cultural agenda of their native country. More recently, Babel's biography and his writings, in which Jewish characters often assert themselves with vigor and militancy, provided a stimulus for a new sense of collective identity among the Jews of the Soviet Union—an unanticipated consequence of the coming together of de-Stalinization, awareness of the Holocaust, and Israel's 1967 victory in the Six-Day War.

Babel's writings, which made his effectiveness as a symbolic figure possible in the first place, have influenced the course of literary history in a significant and productive way. As in the history of political and aesthetic sensibility, Babel's achievement in this area possesses an exemplary character. He was one of the first major Jewish writers, along with Franz Kafka, to develop and practice a particular literary idiom in the language of the dominant culture, the idiom that has come to be associated with the experience of the assimilated, modern European Jew. Some of his more perceptive compatriots understood this at once. A. Z. Lezhnev, a well-known critic and a member of the editorial board of the influential *Pechat' i revolutsiia* (Press and Revolution), wrote in 1926:

> Babel is the first Jew who entered Russian literature as a Russian writer, at least the first prose writer. Up until now we only had Jewish writers attached to Russian literature. . . . [Their work] was interesting for the reader curious about the ethnographic details rather than art. It is only in Babel's hands that the life of [the Jews of] Odessa has acquired aesthetic value. . . . *Odessa Tales* and "The Story of My Dovecote" prove that he is

capable of transcending the limitations of anecdotal or ethnographic tendencies.

(p. 85)

Judging by his impact on such an accomplished and mature author as Osip Mandelshtam (*The Egyptian Stamp,* 1928), on a score of lesser and younger writers who began in his shadow, and, most remarkable, on Jewish-American writers like Philip Roth and Grace Paley, Babel established the foundation for what might have emerged as a Jewish Russian literature had it not been for the Great Russian chauvinism of the Soviet state.

Equally important, the exemplary character of Babel's achievement goes beyond the properly Jewish theme to encompass other forms of what sociologists call the phenomenon of cultural marginality. A member of the intelligentsia, a Jew, and because of this doubly different from his fictional setting, Babel's author-narrator rejected some aspects of his Jewish heritage and combined others, openly and skillfully, with powerful strands in his adopted milieu. In the process he produced a master script for future writers who, whether Jewish or not, wished to play the role of the other at the very center, and not the margins, of their country's culture.

A protagonist in the drama of his own making (although he had to share the directing with the times), Isaac Babel not only produced some of the best short fiction of this century, he also performed the role of a "marginal" writer with consummate skill. Indeed, he was able to maintain the illusion of authorship during those years when, by his own sardonic admission made from the stage of the First Congress of Soviet Writers, he was practicing "silence—the most difficult of all literary genres." Thus the oeuvre alone, especially its "authoritative" version, cannot account with sufficient fullness for the whole complex of ideas, texts, and events that have come to be associated with Babel's name. His background, the cultural tradition that he entered when he embarked on a career of literary authorship, the expectations of the more powerful segment of the reading public, his fiction, and his strategy for achieving and maintaining a high literary profile—all have contributed to the formation of what constitutes Babel's legacy for us.

Isaac Emmanuilovich Babel or, according to the records of the Odessa rabbinate, Isaac Manievich Bobel, was born to Man' Yitzkhovich and Feiga Bobel in the city of Odessa on 30 June 1894. His only sibling, Meri (after her emigration to Belgium, Madame Marie Chapochnikoff), was born in 1900. Even these two facts, which should be as innocuous as any birth certificate, are hard to disentangle from the two sets of narratives we associate with Isaac Babel. One of them, his own fiction, follows the autobiographical convention and centers on the narrator whose biographical attributes identify him (apparently) with the author himself. The other set is harder to circumscribe: simply put, it consists of what the reading public knows about the history of culture, politics, and society in modern Russia, including the history of Russia's Jews.

The two narratives impart a specific meaning to the fact that Babel's family was Jewish, secular, and, at the time of his birth, well on its way toward joining the middle class. Although lacking in systematic education, the parents identified with the Haskalah, the Jewish Enlightenment movement that had accepted Russian as the language of emancipation. And so it was embraced in the Babel household, functioning as the intergenerational lingua franca, with Yiddish reserved for the parents as their private tongue. Obviously, the culture of the shtetl and the ghetto, inseparable from Yiddish, was still very much their culture. Born and raised in an enclosed, small, homogeneous community which they later fled, Babel's family nevertheless experienced it as an irreducible place of origin, one where they had once wholly belonged, and one whose spiritual and emotional resources were still accessible to them. By contrast, their children, who were expected to make the final break with this culture, would never be part of either that or any other undivided world. With his wife and daughter living in France, his mother and sister in Belgium, another wife and another daughter in Russia, scores of relatives in Odessa and Kiev, and his own career as a Soviet writer now reaching for the stars, now descending into silence, Babel was the mobile (or homeless) man of the twentieth century par excellence.

Mobility had already distinguished his parents' generation. The comfortable financial position his father achieved early in his son's life placed the family in a distinct minority among the subjects of the Russian empire. It belonged to an even more distinct minority among Russia's Jews, who had to contend with the official and informal, but officially sponsored, anti-Semitism as well as severe legal disabilities. The latter included the prohibition to dwell outside the Pale of Settlement, specially designated urban areas in Russia's southwest, and rigid restrictions on access to education. "In Odessa, there is a very poor, populous and suffering Jewish ghetto, a very self-satisfied bourgeoisie, and a very pogromist city council," wrote Babel in 1917 about the city of his birth, fully aware of the misery and humiliation he was spared because his parents belonged to the second, fortunate category.

To be born in Odessa, or rather to have lived there in the years 1905 to 1915, was another stroke of luck Babel frequently acknowledged. The revolution of 1905, although it failed to destroy the old regime, immensely strengthened civil society, creating in the urban centers of Russia a heady atmosphere replete with political debate, strikes and demonstrations, a pluralistic press, and a thriving market for art and literature. Under these conditions, no matter how hostile the official policy, the Jewish community of Odessa was too large (in 1900, a third of Odessa's half a million citizens were Jewish), too well organized, and too varied to be kept in a state of hopeless oppression. On this count alone, Odessa was unique. As Simon Markish tells us in his essay on Babel, the city resembled Jewish communities in turn-of-the-century America more than it did those in Russia. The effect of the government policy regarding Jews was further limited by the heterogeneity of the city population, the rest of which constituted a mélange of ethnic Russians, Ukrainians, Poles, Greeks, and, in addition, small but culturally important enclaves of French, German, and English merchants. The pungent, freewheeling atmosphere of a major port city and industrial center, the remarkable ethnic mix, and a considerable, heavily Jewish bourgeoisie supporting a network of secondary schools, newspapers and journals, several theaters, an opera company, and a university provided an Odessa Jew in search of a worldly fortune with an opportunity to breach the isolation of third-class citizenship and the ghetto milieu. Surmounting the legal and social obstacles would have been much harder in a smaller, less cosmopolitan place and would have involved more painful compromises with the official policies in St. Petersburg or Moscow, the two capitals kept largely free of Jews.

Equally important, in a country that was growing weary of the old regime—symbolized by the aristocratic, decorous, northern St. Petersburg—the thoroughly middle-class, southern Odessa could be seen as one of the sources of the country's social and cultural rebirth. True, a Petersburg snob was likely to turn his nose up at this "very awful city," but the growing contribution to Russian culture by the provincial artists and writers gave substance to Babel's prediction in "Moi listki: Odessa" ("My Notes: Odessa," 1917) that the spirit of Odessa, bright, merry, and bourgeois, would soon be challenging the dominant Petersburg sensibility, its Dostoevskian moodiness, classical splendor, and imperial chill:

> A man from Odessa is the opposite of a Petrogradian. It is becoming an axiom that Odessans do well in Petrograd. They make money. Because they are brunets, plump blondes fall in love with them. . . . This, one might say, begins to sound too much like a joke. No, sir. Something more profound is involved here. The point is simply

> that these brunets are bringing with them a little sun and a little levity.
>
> Apart from the gentlemen who bring with them a little sun and a lot of canned sardines with interesting labels, I think there must arrive—and soon—the fertile, invigorating influence of the Russian South, the Russian Odessa, perhaps *(qui sais?)*, the only city in Russia where our national and so badly needed Maupassant can emerge.
>
> ("Moi listki: Odessa," *Zabytyi Babel',* pp. 48ff.)

Babel's optimism was, in part, borne out by the history of Russian literature and society in the 1920's. As soon as the imperial center ceased to hold, the provincial intelligentsia quickly stepped in to fill the vacancy, with the "men of Odessa" marching stylishly in the forefront. Some of the better-known writers and poets of the postrevolutionary decade, indeed, the "classics" of Soviet literature, including Valentin Kataev, Konstantin Paustovsky, Illia Ilf, Eduard Bagritsky, and, of course, Babel himself, came from Odessa. What was happening in literature paralleled the postrevolutionary reshuffling of the empire's social and demographic deck. Together with the limited free enterprise permitted under the New Economic Policy, these changes may well have imparted to Petrograd or Moscow some of the Levantine commercial atmosphere of Odessa during its most thriving period, inaugurated by the 1905 revolution and brought to a close by World War I.

This was the Odessa Babel knew and liked best, and credit for the city's reputation as the Russian Marseille, which is how some imagined it in its halcyon days, must go to *Odessa Tales.* Conceived in the austere world of 1920 and 1921, these tales paint a picture of the city as Babel remembered or wished to remember it during his school years, 1905 to 1911. But books have their own fate, and in the imagination of Babel's readers, this cycle of four stories has forever transformed Odessa, or, more precisely, its Jewish ghetto, with its underworld, into a romantic *pays de Cocagne,* historically the first Jewish or, for that matter, Russian Jewish or, simply, Russian version of such a place.

Few facts are available on which to base a reconstruction of Babel's childhood or family. His own autobiographical writings have often proved to be misleading sources, as least when compared to the recollections of his sister, to those of two Odessa poets who had some contact with his family, and to his own, only partially published, correspondence. A writer, above all a writer with a cultivated public persona, he was more concerned with following the spirit of the truth than its letter. He admitted as much in a 1931 note to his mother that accompanied his autobiographical fiction: "All the stories are from the childhood years, with lies added, of course, and much that is altered." More important, by modifying the facts of his childhood, Babel was not simply exercising the prerogative of a writer of fiction; he was, it seems, carrying out a deliberate strategy—one with significant consequences for an author with a high public profile. "When the book is finished, then it will become clear why I needed all that," he ended the explanation, suggesting, cryptically, that the four stories were only a part of a larger cycle. Indeed, a 1937 story, "Di Grasso," would have fitted neatly with the earlier four, whereas most of the stories that appeared in the 1930's fill the "autobiographical" gap between childhood years and *Red Cavalry.*

Given Babel's talent for cyclization, it would appear that he had in mind a larger autobiographical frame designed to incorporate his known and future work, enclosing the entire life span of the boy who grew up to be the author-narrator of *Red Cavalry* and, finally, a major Soviet writer. The great success enjoyed by the autobiographical fiction of Gorky and its elevation to the status of a national epic in the 1930's lend support to this conjecture. Furthermore, in the early 1930's, when Babel's output was diminishing, such a master frame would have helped to allay the pressure to produce, permitting him to present his past achievement, perhaps even the writings he had previously suppressed, in a fresh, more contemporary light. Far from being opportunistic, this strategy would make use of the essential attributes of Babel's art, its apparent autobiographical character. The other, no less significant properties of his writings, especially *Red Cavalry*—their modernistic fragmentariness and the delirious mixture of pathos and baseness for which the broad reading public and the cultural bureaucracy were losing tolerance—these "outmoded" properties would have lost their prominence, after they were integrated into a more coherent, epic narrative frame.

How early did Babel decide to pursue this strategy? The pressure to follow the ragged and fragmented vision of the post–civil war literature with the Apollonian gaze of an epic masterpiece was already noticeable in the middle 1920's. An epic, it was felt, was needed to certify the revolution as a fait accompli, to transform it from the event of an overwhelming immediate experience into a holiday that all would happily celebrate. Treated in this way, the revolution would be wrapped in the magical aura of Origin, conferring legitimacy on the status quo and constituting the present as a natural order. Some writers, among them Yevgeny Zamyatin, actively resisted this sort of program, but many, if not most, went along with it out of either conviction, opportunism, or sheer exhaustion with the revolutionary flux. This need for a revolutionary epic intensified as the 1920's progressed and became a key issue in the broader political project of nation- and citizenship-building under the new Stalinist order. Babel, whose friendship was appreciated among the discerning members of the Soviet elite, was sensitive to the literary as well as political trends and eager to stay in the forefront of the emerging Soviet Russian literature. This ambition can be seen clearly in many statements both public and private in which he expressed his desire for a new style and a different genre.

"Istoriya moey golubyatni" ("The Story of My Dovecote"), which bore a meaningful dedication to Gorky and gave its name to the entire childhood cycle, was published in 1925. It was also during this time that Babel was trying to make up his mind on the future of *Red Cavalry*—whether to freeze the cycle in its present form or to expand it until the number of pieces approached fifty (his original plan). That he published it as a separate edition in 1926 shows the project to have been essentially completed. Babel was ready or, better, was compelled to go on to other things if he wished to remain among the key players in Soviet Russian literature. The anxiety of falling behind, indicative of Babel's own ambition, was typical among the Russian literati of the time. The 1920's and early 1930's were a period when neither the reading public nor the cultural establishment, neither the printing nor the distribution of literature, had yet to be stabilized or, rather, Stalinized—that is to say, reach the stage when publishing became strictly regimented and the reading public atomized. True, the inclusion of "Argamak" (1924–1930) in the 1933 and subsequent editions of *Red Cavalry* and the publication in 1937 of "Potselui" ("The Kiss"), a story clearly associated with it, changed the élan of the book, but these were two master strokes meant to ease the incorporation of *Red Cavalry* into the larger autobiographical framework.

The romantic tradition of playing art and life against one another has had a particularly welcome reception in Russia. With the tremendous growth in educated readership and literary commerce by the 1900's, it virtually set the tone for the literary world for the rest of the twentieth century. Indeed, such authors as Alexander Blok, Vladimir Mayakovsky, Mandelshtam, Gorky, Pasternak, Marina Tsvetaeva, not to mention Tolstoy and Dostoevsky, are remembered as much for their gesture as for their art. The phenomenon of literary celebrity did not become an object of systematic study until shortly after the death of Blok in 1921, when the formalist critics attempted to come to terms intellectually with the passing of the foremost figure among the Russian modernists. Using Blok's career as a paradigmatic case, they persuasively demonstrated the tendency of an author's life, whether fictional or real, toward a powerful symbolic transformation in the eyes of his readership. Some of the best writings of Yurii Tynianov (on Blok and Khlebnikov), Boris Eikhenbaum (on Blok and Tolstoy), and Roman Jakobson (on Mayakovsky), and Boris Tomashevskii's work on the typology of authorship, were devoted to charting this aspect of Russian literary culture. According to the formalists a single contingent fact in an author's biography could acquire in the eye of the devoted public the fateful necessity of an event in a fictional narrative and at the same time retain the undeniable materiality of a lived experience. The life of an author therefore had the potential of being at once symbolic and real: a biographical detail could function as a "literary fact" (Tynianov's paradoxical coinage); the biography as a whole could become transformed into what we now call myth and its protagonist-author into an object of veneration among the reading and sometimes even nonreading public.

Needless to say, this complex phenomenon had its own history. Literary expression began to play a pivotal role in the formation of the self-image of the Russian intelligentsia in the middle decades of the nineteenth century, when the educated classes grew progressively alienated from the institutions of the autocratic state. Combined with the primacy of the artist in the ideology of European modernism and its corollary, the crisis of faith, this aspect of Russia's cultural history helps explain the facility with which the figure of a Russian writer could acquire the charismatic aura of a secular saint. Indeed, it was (and to a lesser extent still is) a matter of general belief that a writer had his or her hand on the pulse of the nation, which the reader could feel only by keeping his or her hand on the writer's pulse.

Babel was very much part of this tradition, indeed, one of its more masterful vehicles in this century. As a member of the Russian intelligentsia, he was its product; as a writer, he paid tribute to it all his life. This is why in order to bring his fictional construct into a sharper relief and to gain a better understanding of his literary project as a whole, it is important, where possible, to juxtapose the author's own narrative account with historical testimony, including memoirs, documents, and correspondence. Almost everything written on Babel has been done with the awareness of these two interdependent paths, however often writers may have conflated them, as did Lionel Trilling in his influential 1956 essay, or kept them too far apart, treading softly on one and marching merrily along the other.

Soon after Babel's birth, most likely for business reasons, the family moved to Nikolaev, a small port town about a hundred miles northwest of Odessa, where in the course of ten years his father had established himself as a representative of an overseas manufacturer of agricultural equipment. When in Nikolaev, the boy had a dovecote to keep, a yard to play in, and a garden to pick fruit from, and he witnessed a pogrom that happily did not directly affect the Babel household or diminish its fortune. It was also in Nikolaev that at the age of nine or ten he began to attend the Count Witte Commercial School, an institution that did not discriminate on the basis of religion. We do not know whether Babel ever tried to enroll in the less liberal but far more prestigious gymnasium, but his fictional alter ego in "The Story of My Dovecote" does, and more. That boy nearly loses his mind from the pressure of preparing for the entrance examination, which he, a Jew, has to pass with distinction; and having passed and having been admitted, he finds himself in the middle of a pogrom and nearly loses his life.

In 1905 Babel's family was affluent enough to return to Odessa, where all of the son's childhood distractions, save for the school and, perhaps, an occasional pogrom, were replaced by tutors—in French, English, German, in the "hated" violin, and, until the age of sixteen, in Hebrew, the Bible, and the Talmud. The mix of the subjects is significant, for some have tended to imagine the young Babel as a rather stereotypical Jewish youth immersed in the traditional scriptural studies until the age of fifteen, when he discovered secular learning, sex, and Maupassant. As with many images of Babel, this one can be traced to the author's own self-presentation, which in 1926, when the "Avtobiografiia" ("Autobiography") was published, may have been perceived as a fresh conceptualization of the experience of an assimilated Jew. In fact, it may stand at the origins of what by now has become a cliché:

> I was born in 1894 in Odessa, in the Moldavanka, the son of a tradesman Jew. On father's insistence, I studied Hebrew, the Bible, the Talmud till the age of sixteen. Life at home was hard, because I was forced to study a multitude of subjects. Resting I did at school.

Thus begins Babel's "Autobiography." The items are carefully selected to produce the highest contrast with the author's present position as a famous Russian writer. The oppressive "ghetto" Jewishness is emphasized through detailed enumeration whereas the cosmopolitan nature of Babel's home education is represented as an indiscriminate agglomeration of anonymous disciplines. But emancipation was not long in coming. By the end of this opening paragraph, the typical product of the traditional ghetto milieu was fluent enough in French to produce what would appear as competent French fiction: "At the age of fifteen, I began writing stories in French. I wrote them for two years and then stopped: my *paysans* and all sorts of authorial meditations came out colorless; only the dialogue was a success."

The educational fervor, befitting a middle-class family on its way up, was matched by the residence on the second or third floor of an imposing building that stood at the intersection of Post and Richelieu, two of the city's more fashionable avenues. The new address contrasted sharply with their former home in the Moldavanka, the humble Jewish neighborhood where the author was born. Two decades later, he would headquarter his fictional family there after its move from Nikolaev to Odessa ("V podvale" ["In the Basement," 1931], and "Pervaia liubov'" ["First Love," 1925]). Of course, in fiction, what this "populous and suffering Jewish ghetto" ("Odessa," 1917) lacked in life's comforts—and the script *Benia Krik* paints a horrific picture of Jewish poverty—it made up in the local color that Babel had been applying unsparingly beginning with the first story of the Odessa cycle, "The King," in 1921.

Even a cursory comparison of the biographical details with the autobiographical fiction published between 1925 and 1932 reveals a certain tactic: the author's bourgeois background was an acceptable part of the constructed biography only if it was *bourgeois manqué.* A number of Babel scholars have suggested that the author tried to "proletarianize" his fictional background in order to curry favor with the class-conscious Bolshevik regime. In the 1920's, however, this sort of humbling could yield no more than small change, especially coming from a "fellow traveler" and not a "proletarian" writer. It did, however, make perfect narrative sense: it echoed the tried-and-true "bourgeois" novelistic convention according to which heroes were to be cultivated not in a well-endowed hothouse, but in the open—and preferably on top of a social compost heap. Babel must receive credit for producing a stunningly effective Jewish version of this plot motif, which, after the Soviet climate had turned inhospitable, migrated to New York and Hollywood, where it continued to enjoy a thriving career.

In keeping with this principle, Babel's fictional parents have been completely ruined in a pogrom. In addition to this misfortune, their son has become severely ill, forcing them to move to Odessa in search of a qualified medical cure. Their only child, he has developed a nervous condition in reaction, it seems, to a triple shock caused by the violence, the scene of his father's self-abasement before a cossack officer, and the unexpected proximity of the luscious bosom and hips incautiously paraded by the family's Russian neighbor, Galina. She is the first woman to steal the boy's heart and is kind enough to offer temporary refuge to the Babel family ("First Love"). From the reader's perspective, the story provides a "realistic" (in psychoanalytic terms) motivation for the sensibility Kirill Vasilievich Liutov (meaning literally "the vicious one") displays in *Red Cavalry.* But in the sense of Babel's emerging bildungsroman, it was not the child who, as the saying goes, was father to the man. Rather, it was the man who was fathering his own childhood.

According to family lore, Babel's grandmother played an important role in his upbringing. Babel's sister remembers her as quarrelsome. She was excessively strict with her granddaughter and equally indulgent with her grandson. Babel left a portrait of her in a 1915 unfinished story entitled "U babushki" ("At Grandmother's"), which was to be part of a cycle, *Detstvo* (Childhood). He spent Saturdays at her frightfully overheated home, doing his homework and receiving tutors while she sat and watched. At regular intervals she would interrupt her vigil in order to indulge them both in largely recreational eating. If the story is to be trusted, this formidable woman was rather informal about observing the Sabbath, but worshiped ardently and with complete devotion her grandson's secular education. Illiterate herself, she was in a sense a child of the Enlightenment and believed fervently in knowledge as the sole means of conquering the world. And that, in its turn, was the only end she thought worth pursuing: " 'Study,' she says suddenly with great force; 'you will achieve everything—wealth, fame. You must know everything. Do not trust people. Do not have friends. Do not give them your money. Do not give them your heart.' "

Some of the elements making up Babel's poetics are already present here: hyperbole, in the mountains of food; contrast, in the difference between the grandmother's own illiteracy and the studiousness of her charge; and even sadomasochistic sensuality, in the overwhelming excitement the boy feels as he reads and rereads the famous "whipping scene" in Ivan Turgenev's "First Love" (1859). As in the later stories, a key metaphor here becomes thematized—unfolded to produce its own minor narrative, a mini-myth. Consider the story's physical ambience: the atmosphere of the grandmother's room was literally stifling and that of the household in which the boy grew up was figuratively so. By now a cliché, this figure of speech can still provide fictional motivation for young men in a hurry to take flight from their nests—Jewish young men, and also Southern young men, in North American fiction, and Irish ones in English fiction. However, the air at the grandmother's was not only stifling, it was also intolerably hot. This atmospheric item, placed in a suggestive context, begins to translate into desire, a tightly wound spring of desire typical for a narrative of sexual frustration. Babel would have it uncoil spectacularly in the numerous episodes of sexual violence and abandon in *Red Cavalry, Odessa Tales,* and "First Love"—episodes that powerfully stir the narrator destined only to observe and never (or almost never) to participate. "At Grandmother's" displays parts of this narrative machinery operating still at a relatively low idle:

> I was then reading Turgenev's "First Love." I liked everything about it: clear words, descriptions, the dialogue, but it was that scene when Vladimir's father hits Zinaida on the cheek with his whip that would cause in me an extraordinary turmoil. I would hear the swishing of the whip; its pliant, leather body, sharply, painfully, would light into me. I would be gripped by an ineffable anxiety. At that point I would have to abandon the reading and pace the room. But Grandma sat motionless, and even the air, hot and stupefying, was motionless as though it knew that I was studying and was not to be disturbed.
>
> (*Literaturnoe nasledstvo,* vol. 74 [1965], p. 486)

However much it anticipates the later Babel, "At Grandmother's" would not have fit the master autobiography without major revisions, for it offered no visible escape route nor any palpable future. The material of the story lacked variety, and its virtual uniformity tended to dominate the story unchallenged, depriving the episodes of relative scale. Under such conditions, hyperbole and contrast were prevented from growing into a Babelian grotesque, and the slightly bizarre sensuality was kept from evolving into something more orgiastic. Even the proverbial detachment of Babel's narrator, so unsettling in his later work and already detectable here, might appear quite natural, given the soporific monotony of the milieu. What seems to be entirely absent but what would distinguish the later stories beginning with "The King" is excess—whether in emotional intensity or affectless detachment—excess born of an unclouded Nietzschean admiration for the beauty and power of life that exists, if not beyond, then to the side of the "accursed" worries about good and evil.

"The Story of My Dovecote" provides an instructive contrast. There a Jewish boy who has finally earned his acceptance by the state and become a student at an elite school runs into a pogrom. The rewards for his efforts, four long-coveted pigeons, are taken away from him and are literally smashed against his head, but this is done by a man whose hands are touched by leprosy, a man who has no legs. These details of the grotesque, one might say excessive, deficiency (absence of legs) and overabundant presence (can there be just the right amount of leprosy?), provide an aesthetic escape hatch, which at first is too narrow to notice but soon becomes as wide as the doors of the church:

> I was lying on the ground and the entrails of a smashed bird were dripping down my temple. They were flowing down my cheeks, in small rivulets, dripping and blinding me. The tender intestine of a pigeon was crawling across my forehead and I was closing the other, still unstuck eye in order not to see the world lying about me. This world was small and horrifying.
>
> (*Izbrannoe* [Moscow, 1966], p. 217)

Still, the boy gets up. Walking home, he finds his attention drawn to the sight of a young peasant lad smashing the window frames of the house belonging to a certain Kharitos Efrussi. Mentioned only in passing, the address is significant because it transforms the pogrom into an all-too-visible hand of poetic justice. This hand not only punishes Jewish boys who play successfully by the rules of the hated empire, but also takes revenge on the Jewish merchant Efrussi, who does not, and who used bribes the previous year to place his son in the gymnasium at the expense of the more deserving protagonist. Once the economy of vengeance has been established, the reader can begin to enjoy vicariously—through the eyes of the narrator—the sight of the unrestrained natural beauty and pure strength displayed unabashedly by the pogromist:

> He was bashing at the frame with a wooden mallet, swinging with his whole body and, when he sighed, he smiled all around with an amiable smile of intoxication, sweat and spiritual strength. The entire street was filled with the cracking, snapping, and singing of the breaking wood. The fellow kept on bashing just to bend his body, just to break into sweat, and to shout the words of an unknown, non-Russian language. He was shouting them and singing, and tearing from the inside of his blue eyes.
>
> (p. 218)

A dozen or so years later, this Slavic version of Nietzsche's *blonde Bestie* would be riding with (or against, it does not matter) Budennyi's cavalry, followed by the narrator's admiring gaze.

Like his formidable mother, Man' (or more urbanely, Emmanuel) Babel placed great value on education and the worldly accomplishments it was bound to facilitate. He enforced his convictions with the vigor and excess of a self-made man, creating for his male offspring a studious and extremely tense household. "Resting I did at school," was how Babel qualified his home academic program. Babel's father—moody, sarcastic, and given to memorable fits of anger—was not averse to literary composition and penned satires in Hebrew or Yiddish aimed at the failings of his relatives and friends. In his son's fiction, with its unconcealed oedipal economy, he played the role of a weak man who cared more about property than dignity, as in the following from "First Love":

> Ahead of them, at the corner of Fish Street, the pogromists were smashing our shop, throwing out boxes with nails, tools, and my new portrait in the gymnasium uniform.
>
> "Look," said my father, and did not get up from his knees, "they are taking my sweat and blood, Captain, why . . ."
>
> The officer mumbled something, saluted with his lemon glove and touched the bridle, but the horse did not move. Father was crawling around it on his knees, rubbing himself against its short, kindly, slightly shaggy legs.
>
> "Yes, sir," said the Captain, pulled at the bridle, and was off; the Cossacks followed. . . .
>
> "Lousy kopecks," mother said as father and I were entering the room, "your life, and children, and our unhappy happiness—you have given up everything for them. . . . Lousy kopecks.
>
> (p. 223)

Because such a character was unworthy of being cast as a closet writer (an anticipation of the author's own vocation), Babel pressed the cherished gift into the hands of an exorbitantly colorful maternal grandfather, Levi-Yitzkhok—a ragtag type stitched together from patches of a bohemian fantasy, Dickensian and Rabelaisian characters, and, perhaps, a boyhood wish ("In the Basement"). A different picture emerges from Babel's letters, in which he could treat his father's memory with conciliation and generosity, even if tinged ever so slightly with the feelings that posthumous effusiveness and forgiveness had not completely effaced:

> When I go through moments of despair, I think of Papa. What he expected and wanted from us was success, not complaining. . . . Remembering him I feel a surge of strength, and I urge myself forward. Everything I promised him, *not in words but in thought,* I shall carry out because I have a sacred respect for his memory [emphasis added].
>
> (*Lonely Years,* p. 87)

As far as his public persona was concerned, Babel's father was a well-respected businessman who radiated so much dignity and honesty that his neighbors felt honored to be sharing a building with him.

We know considerably less about Babel's mother, except that she was given to worry, a trait to which her son's correspondence provides repeated testimony. "I think that you and Mama are suffering from an anxiety mania that is becoming pathological," reads one of Babel's letters to his sister, in an oft-repeated epistolary expression of filial exasperation. In another, Babel castigates his mother for a "weakness of character," an especially vexing trait that he believed he had inherited from her. The glimpse afforded by her daughter's reminiscences is less conflicted, if bland: "Mother was kind, had a gentle character, often had to humor father when he was upset; he was quick to anger. Mother ran the household and brought up the children. She taught my brother to read." In his fiction, Babel sketched her as a woman capable of grand emotions, disillusioned in marriage ("our unhappy happiness"), nobly ashamed of her husband's acquisitiveness, and eager to make up for these misfortunes by loving her son much too much ("First Love").

As for Babel's sister, she was denied the role of a protagonist in the family's ambitious script. In her brother's stories she appears not at all except in the plural of the reference in "First Love" to the children that the fictional father had ignored in his capitalist pursuits. It is tempting to think that in acknowledgment of her conspicuous absence, Babel paid her an ironic tribute in naming after her the lead character, who, in turn, gave her name to the play *Mariia.* Like his sister in his fiction, Mariia never steps out onto the stage but, remaining invisible, exerts a crucial influence on all the other dramatis personae.

However complicated Babel's relationship with his parents and sister, the bonds established in his youth remained powerful throughout his life. They were strong enough for him to accept financial responsibility for his mother and sister after they emigrated to Belgium in 1925 (a little over a year after his father's death); and, more remarkable, he corresponded with them regularly throughout the worst years of terror in the 1930's, insisting, from all indications sincerely, that they join him in the Soviet Union. His last letter to them was postmarked 10 May 1939, antedating his arrest by only five days. Perhaps the clearest echo of Babel's attachment to his mother and sister, so evident in his correspondence, can be found in the unfinished *Evreika,* in which his nostalgia for his family and his desire to reunite and share a household with them found fictional fulfillment.

A man of broad and varied education, Babel had bypassed the gymnasium and the university, the two elite, although not exclusive, educational institutions of the Russian empire. In 1906 his parents enrolled him in the second grade of the Nicholas I Odessa Commercial School No. 1. According to their charter, schools of this type prepared young men for careers in business or industry, or if they wished to continue their studies, for admission to specialized colleges and polytechnics. By contrast with the gymnasium's classical curriculum, commercial schools emphasized "practical knowledge," such as sciences and modern languages. The shibboleth of the higher stratum in the empire's educational system, the study of ancient tongues, was excluded from the curriculum of the commercial schools, an exclusion that made it more difficult for their graduates to go on to a university.

Notwithstanding the obvious liability, some schools of this type, among them the famous Tenishev, had a good academic reputation and were popular. They were also less regimented (Jews, for example, were freely admitted), and they tended to have a more varied student body whose members, as in the case of Babel's class, were distinguished by the impurity of their pedigree, "the sons of foreign merchants, Jewish brokers, titled Polish nobility, Old Believers, and a lot of superannuated billiard players." (The order of Babel's listing may give some idea of the social hierarchy at the empire's outer fringe.) Many "progressive" families, including the aristocratic Nabokovs, the academic Struves, and the well-off Mandelshtams, found this sort of schooling preferable to the "conservative" gymnasium education.

Whether Babel's parents enrolled their son in a commercial school as a matter of choice or for reasons of necessity cannot be determined with certainty. What we know, however, is that Babel completed the course of study two years ahead of his contemporaries, earning the highest grades in such subjects as Russian literature, Russian grammar, German, French, English, commercial geography, law, history, and political economy. It may be tempting to see some residue of bitterness in Babel about being sent to the commercial school in "The Story of My Dovecote," in which the boy protagonist succeeds, under his father's relentless pressure, in being admitted to a gymnasium. But Babel had sufficient narrative reasons for giving his plot a different spin: the admission in the story's first movement serves as a perfect counterpoint for the denouement of the second movement, the pogrom.

Three of Babel's lifelong attachments can be traced to his years at the commercial school: the first to Russian literature; the second to France (encouraged by his French teacher, Mr. Vadon); and the third to Odessa. None of these should be taken for granted. The fact that an ambitious young man, a Jew, chose a career in Russian letters indicates that opportunities in this area existed even for a Jew and that pursuit of a writer's career was deemed significant enough to satisfy what surely must have been an intense desire for fame and attainment. Russian literature, the literature of Dostoevsky and Tolstoy, Anton Chekhov and Nikolai Chernyshevsky, Gorky and Blok, served the intelligentsia as a symbol of everything worthy and magnificent in the country's culture, and for an educated Russian Jew it was surely one of the ultimate elective affinities. Nor was there anything self-evident in Babel's identification with Odessa. He lived there continuously for only six out of his forty-five years (while studying at the commercial school) and returned to it only briefly in the years after the revolution. Indeed, few writers raised in the provinces grow up to identify with the city of their birth.

Equally significant, among the three languages he learned well at the commercial school, only French happened to become a point of identification for Babel. Even if he made the selection under the influence of an exceptionally gifted teacher, the choice cannot be regarded as accidental, as it fell on the supremely cosmopolitan language, one associated with a nobility of manner and spirit, literary high culture, and diplomatic intercourse. It was a significant move in Babel's strategy of self-presentation to point out that he began to write Russian fiction only after he had tried his hand at producing stories in French under the tutelage of his French teacher. Mr. Vadon was not merely French, he was a native of Brittany, a provincial man, like Babel himself. Babel displayed this attribute prominently during the years when he was lionized in Petrograd and Moscow. It was also around that time that Vladimir Shklovskii, who pronounced Babel the best contemporary author, praised him for "having seen Russia the way a French writer accompanying Napoleon's army could." Emphatic, cultivated identification with what was outside Russia proper served to give Babel the reputation of being a writer who could penetrate to the very heart of things.

Yet neither Odessa nor France would have played a role in Babel's legacy if he had not developed a style in which the two became mutually reinforcing. The southern port city of Odessa made more palpable the riper aspects of French cultural heritage, while *les lettres françaises* enabled Babel to transform the prosaic "dusty Odessa," as Alexandr Pushkin once referred to it, into a mythic metropolis that he would later on serve up to his readers, exhausted by the years of war and revolution and starved for color and abundance, in a pungent Rabelaisian sauce. In fact, it would not be an exaggeration to say that Odessa became a meaningful entity on the literary map only after Babel had put it there, and Babel thought about putting it there only after he had been able to see in it a city that bore some resemblance to Nikolai Gogol's frivolous Ukraine, but situated to the west of it, halfway between the Mediterranean of romantic fiction (Shklovskii pointed to Gustave Flaubert's *Salammbô* [1863]) and the *Cocagne* of the French popular tradition and François Rabelais. Indeed, no native son of Odessa in Babel's generation has produced a picture of the city that owes a greater debt to the Gallic carnivalesque.

Even more important, although Babel had in his possession all the necessary ingredients as early as 1917 (see "My Notes: Odessa"), the particular style emerged only after the civil war, when he returned to his native city after a stint as a war correspondent in Budennyi's cavalry army. The experience of the revolution combined with the ability to see beauty in the exercise of power unrestrained by the notions of good and evil—this is what enabled Babel to produce a feast for the mind's eye rather than a series of rough and wordy collage portraits of desolate and ravaged Russia à la Boris Pilniak or Vsevolod Ivanov. Both *Red Cavalry* and *Odessa Tales* embodied the simple twentieth-century discovery—it had been prophesied before, most notably by Nietzsche—that power could be justified by form, not by the measure of evil or goodness, but by the criteria that discriminated against the sick, the weak, and the ugly. What made Babel's version of the superman particularly moving and ethically acceptable to people who identified with the oppressed was his success at endowing lowly characters with all the attributes of life's supreme masters. Hitherto they had been depicted as the humiliated and the wronged, whose credo, in Nietzsche's terms, never went beyond the hissing *ressentiment* of the downtrodden. In Babel's work these people acquire a joyful Gargantuan stature. A Jew can "pick a fight in the streets and stammer on paper, be a tiger, a lion, a cat, spend a night with a Russian woman and leave her satisfied" ("The Way It Used to Be Done in Odessa"). A soldier elevated by the revolution to the rank of division commander can make one wonder at the "beauty of his giant body" (a phrase from "My First Goose"):

> He stood up and, with the crimson of his breeches, the tilted red little cap, the medals nailed into his chest, cleaved the hut in two like a battle flag cleaving the heaven. He exuded the smell of perfume and the cloying coolness of soap. His long legs resembled young women sheathed up to the shoulders in the shining riding boots.
>
> (p. 53)

Like his Jewish counterpart, the gangster boss Benia Krik, this cossack general "stammered on paper." His irresistible vitality is unaware of civilization's restraint, as the narrator discovers while watching him finish writing out an order:

> "With the destruction of which" [the enemy], continued the division commander, and messed up the entire sheet, "I charge the above Chesnokov up to and including the capital penalty, whom I will blow away on the spot, which you, Comrade Chesnokov, having worked with me at the front for more than a month, cannot doubt."
>
> The Division Commander signed the order with a curlicue, tossed it to his orderlies, and turned to me, his gray eyes dancing with merriment.
>
> ("Moi pervyi gus" ["My First Goose," 1924], p. 53)

Already Dostoevsky had acknowledged the supreme seductiveness of the combination of power and beauty (as in the handsome Stavrogin in *The Possessed* [1871–1872]), and the idea animated the writings of Babel's immediate predecessors, foremost among them Gorky, Blok, and Nikolai Gumilev. But Babel was the first one to surround with a deceptively ethical aura the cruel truth that even the most brutal power could be made palatable if it was beautifully attired.

After graduating from the commercial school in 1911 and finding himself unable to enter the University of Odessa because of the quota for Jews, Babel was sent to Kiev to enroll in economics at the Kiev Commercial Institute. It was in Kiev that he met his future wife, Evgeniia Gronfein. She came from a much richer and far more cultivated family than his own, and Babel appreciated the intellectual and artistic atmosphere that existed in her household, and especially the ease that came with the family's inherited wealth and well-established social status. Her father, an importer of agricultural equipment, had done business with Babel's father and was happy to receive his partner's son in his house, although not happy enough to favor his daughter's interest in the aspiring economist. From both the testimony of Nathalie Babel, the writer's daughter, and his own correspondence, we know that the future in-laws saw in Babel a provincial upstart, an opinion that Mrs. Gronfein was to change only when he became a famous and well-connected Soviet writer.

An echo, and only an echo, of Babel's experience at the Gronfeins may be heard in "Guy de Maupassant" (1932), a story about an aspiring writer who is hired by the wife of a Jewish banker to help her translate the complete Maupassant. Like the Gronfeins, Raisa Bendersky, the banker's wife, is a native of Kiev; she also happens to bear the first name of Babel's sister-in-law. Mrs. Bendersky possesses the "ravishing body" of a Kievan Jewess, literary pretensions supported by a genuine artistic sensitivity, and a bottle of 1883 Muscadet, her husband's favorite and most intoxicating vintage. Predictably, the writer, by contrast with Mr. Bendersky, is poor as a church mouse but has imagination, energy, talent, and style. While working on "L'Aveu" he finds himself reenacting clumsily, together with the banker's wife and in the banker's absence, the novella's artlessly seductive plot. Another glimpse of Babel's Kievan period (1911–1915) is afforded by his daughter's biographical sketch *(The Lonely Years),* which outlines a complementary picture. Aware of his weakness for the bourgeois opulence and self-indulgence displayed in the Gronfein household, Babel responded by cultivating a heroic stance of life-affirming asceticism. Nathalie Babel writes:

> My mother refused to wear the furs and pretty dresses her parents gave her. My father, to harden himself, would walk bareheaded in the dead of winter without an overcoat, dressed only in jacket. These Spartan efforts ended abruptly one day when my parents were walking, in their usual costume, and a woman stopped, and, apparently mesmerized by what she saw, pointed at my father and shouted, "A madman!" Thirty years later my mother was still mortified when she remembered this incident. Nor had she forgotten her astonishment when her fiancé took her out to tea for the first time and she watched him gobble down cake after cake with dizzying speed. At the Gronfeins, he refused everything but tea. The explanation was simple. "When I start eating cake, I can't stop," he said. "So it's better for me not to start at all."
>
> (p. xvii)

It was also while in Kiev that Babel made his debut in print. "Staryi Shloime" ("Old Shloime," 1913) tells the story of one Jewish family's response to forced resettlement: the younger generation decides to convert rather than be uprooted, but the old man, who discerns the truth through the fog of senility, hangs himself. Written in a sentimental key and in the third person (both uncharacteristic for the later Babel), the three-page story belongs wholly to the genre of bleak "socially aware" Russian prose, including its Jewish variety, in which government oppression and calls for liberation follow one another with the same unimaginative inevitability as night follows day. Nothing about "Old Shloime," not even its violent outcome, is unexpected, and the protest implied by the story is so grimly conventional that instead of challenging the status quo, which was apparently the intention, it tends to do the opposite, implicitly affirming the present as part of the order of things. However, what is significant about "Old Shloime," as well as the far more sophisticated "At Grandmother's," is a lack of hesitation on Babel's part to engage openly the Jewish theme. One would look in vain in the pre-1917 Mandelshtam or Pasternak, roughly Babel's contemporaries, for overt signs of such identification.

In October 1915, the Kiev Commercial Institute was evacuated to Saratov, a town in the provincial heartland of Russia, where Babel remained until graduation in May 1916. Only two years had passed after the publication of "Old Shloime," but "At Grandmother's," completed in Saratov, displayed a different literary sensibility. The protagonist himself narrates the story, and his voice, still hesitant but growing hollow with distance, presents the most intimate milieu, that of his childhood, as a strange world, driven by forces unacknowledged and unmatched by conventional narrative patterns:

> It was quiet, spectrally quiet; not a sound could be heard. At that moment, everything seemed extraordinary, and I wished to flee from it all, and I wanted to stay here forever. The darkening room, Grandma's yellow eyes, her slight frame wrapped in a shawl, hunched over and keeping silent in the corner, the heated air, the closed door, and the stroke of the whip, and that piercing swishing sound—only now I understand how strange it all was and how full of meaning.
>
> (*Literaturnoe nasledstvo,* vol. 74 [1965], p. 487)

At the end of 1915, Babel completed his course work at the commercial institute, but before taking the final examinations, he transferred his credits to the law faculty of the Petrograd Psychoneurological Institute. This was a private establishment with the rank of a university that, among other things, qualified its Jewish students for temporary residence in the capital. Living in Petrograd illegally for months at a time, Babel was finally enrolled as a fourth-year student on 10 October 1916, and received his residence permit a few days later. The permit was to expire on 15 February 1917, timed perfectly, as fate would have it, to coincide with the expiration of the issuing body. Although the "Autobiography" creates the impression that he abandoned all plans for a respectable business or professional career as soon as he moved to Petrograd, the record shows otherwise. A certain amount of hesitation is evident in his decision to proceed with qualifying examinations at the commercial institute in the spring of 1916. He did well, receiving "excellent" in political economy, general accounting, and urban and rural economics with statistical analysis, "good" in commercial law, and "satisfactory" in economic geography. On the basis of this performance, he was informed more than a year later, he had been awarded the degree of candidate of economic sciences of the second rank. Such academic diligence, especially in a nonphilological field, was considered unbecoming by the author, whose loyalty could not be divided between material matters and the essential world of art. From the reader's view the clutter of factual detail might have obscured the bohemian and heroic persona that Babel was cultivating during the publication of *Red Cavalry*.

Whether or not he took seriously his law studies at the Psychoneurological Institute, Babel pursued his literary interests with concentration. In a matter of months after his arrival in Petrograd, a short period for a beginner—even a talented one—without connections, his persistence paid off. At first, he wrote in his "Autobiography," setting up another situation of high contrast, the Petrograd editors gave him the cold shoulder, suggesting that his future was in the retail trade. Then, in 1916, a sudden success: he was discovered by Gorky, who published two of his stories, "Ilia Isaakovich i Margareta Prokofievna" ("Ilia Isaakovich and Margarita Prokofievna") and "Mama, Rimma, i Alla" ("Mother, Rimma, and Alla"), in the November issue of *Letopis'* (The Chronicle), a prominent left-wing journal edited by the grand man of letters himself.

The stories are masterly, vintage Babel in subject matter as well as style. Similar to his later writing, they invite the reader to an unblinking examination of the detritus of existence, rewarding the reader who is not too fastidious to persevere with the pleasurable jolt of discovering a shining, if slightly oversized, human pearl. Written in the third person, they project a consciousness (based on the self-image of the Russian intelligentsia) that incongruously combines detached perspectivalism with a delicately muted appeal to a sentimental heart. In the first story, a plump prostitute with a penchant for squeezing her pimples in view of her clients gives grudging refuge to a Jewish businessman without a residence permit who eats herring for supper and has a habit of airing his toes before climbing into bed. As the story winds to a close, each, it turns out, possesses a heart of gold and is capable of striking up a fleeting and touchingly disinterested friendship. The ending of the second story surprises the reader with a lightning glimpse of the emotional treasure concealed under the grimly incautious romances of two adolescent girls and the insidious pressures of middle-class poverty crushing their aging mother. Pointing to the other shore, where the view of human misery and ugliness was unclouded by conventional compassion, Babel was ready to make the crossing.

Throughout his career Babel emphasized Gorky's recognition of his talent to the exclusion of all others, treating it virtually as a divine sanction to practice his art and later invoking it as a talisman for protection. The publication of the two novellas, however, did not pass unnoticed, which shows that in the literary world of Petrograd, Babel had more than one friend. "The stories are simple, full of observation and a sense of measure," wrote a critic on the staff of *Zhurnal zhurnalov* (Review of Reviews), "qualities that are not as ordinary as one might think. In effect, to learn literary technique means to acquire a sense of measure and an awareness of scale. Here Babel has a gift." This recognition led to an invitation to contribute a regular column to this journal and a productive association with Gorky's postrevolutionary anti-Leninist newspaper *Novaia zhizn'* (New Life). The first carried Babel's name on its masthead in October–February 1916–1917: "Bab-El' [and later, I. Babel]: Moi listki" ("Bab-El: My Notes"). The second published Babel's "Dnevnik" (*Diary*), a series of sketches about revolutionary Petrograd, from February to November 1918. These writings stand halfway between Babel's fiction and ordinary reportage, and although not as distinguished as Babel's stories, they firmly established him as a professional writer.

Like most of his contemporaries among the intelligentsia, indeed, like the entire country, Babel led a peripatetic existence during the years of revolution and civil war. In the spring of 1917, he joined the Russian army at the Rumanian front, resurfacing in Petrograd early in 1918 as a reporter for Gorky's *Novaia zhizn'.* His "Diary," published regularly until the closing of the newspaper by the Bolsheviks at the end of 1918, followed the general direction of Gorky's critical stance, combining pleas for greater humanity with dispassionate observations of the daily cruelties brought about by the revolution and exacerbated by the ruthlessness of the Bolshevik regime. "To hoist a rifle and shoot one another—on occasion, this may not be so stupid, but this is not the whole revolution," Babel wrote in 1918 on the subject of a new maternity hospital. He concluded in a typical *Novaia zhizn'* fashion with a defense of the noble institution of motherhood: "Who knows, maybe this is not the revolution at all? Children must be born under good conditions. And this—I know for certain—is the real revolution."

This early collaboration with Gorky found only a partial acknowledgment in Babel's official self-portrait. A mention of *Novaia zhizn'* (in 1918, Babel also wrote for *Zhizn' iskusstva* [Life of Art]) is nowhere to be found. What must have felt as an honor for a beginning writer turned out to be, in retrospect, a politically imprudent association. In addition (and it is difficult to determine which was a more decisive factor), dwelling on a regular literary employment could dull the luster of Babel's cultivated reputation as an extraordinary author who bore the mark of election visible only to the genius of Gorky and who was, as it were, disgorged complete on the literary scene by the revolution itself. He writes in his "Autobiography":

> To this day, I pronounce the name of Alexei Maximovich [Gorky] with piety. He published my first stories in the November issue of *Letopis',* 1916 . . . , he taught me remarkably important things, and when it turned out that two or three tolerable youthful works of mine were merely an accident, that nothing was coming out of my literary efforts, and that I wrote remarkably badly—Alexei Maximovich told me to go into apprenticeship among the people.
>
> And for seven years—from 1917 to 1924—I have been apprenticing among the people. During this time I served as a soldier at the Rumanian front, in the Cheka, in the People's Commissariat of Enlightenment, in the food requisitioning teams of 1918, in the Northern Army against Iudenich, in the First Cavalry Army, in the Executive Committee of the Odessa Guberniia, in the 7th Soviet Printing House in Odessa, did reporting in Petrograd and Tiflis, etc. And only in 1923 did I learn to express my thoughts clearly and concisely. Then I once again began to compose fiction.
>
> (*Izbrannoe* [Moscow, 1966], p. 23)

There is a certain irony in the fact that this humble "apprenticeship among the people," the phrase serving as title for the second volume of Gorky's autobiographical trilogy, consisted of writing essays and sketches for several newspapers, chief among them Gorky's *Novaia zhizn'.* The chronology of events, too, is intentionally jumbled, with the Petrograd reporting of 1917 and 1918 sandwiched between the items referring to 1920 and 1922. Such stories as "Khodia: Iz knigi *Petersburg 1918,*" ("The Chinaman: From the Book *Petersburg 1918,*" 1923), an anecdote that possibly planted the seed of Yury Olesha's "Envy," and the hilariously anti-Dostoevskian "Iisusov grekh" ("The Sin of Jesus," 1923), were passed over in silence. Some significant events were omitted, among them Babel's marriage to Evgeniia Gronfein in 1919—an absence that, like his failure to mention the hard-earned degree in economics, served to magnify his commitment to the writer's vocation. Otherwise he would not have been able to write, as he did in "Guy de Maupassant":

> When I was only twenty, I said to myself: I'd rather starve, go to jail, have no home of my own than do accounts ten hours a day. There isn't any special valiancy in this vow, but I have not broken it, nor ever will. The wisdom of my ancestors was sitting in my head: we are born in order to enjoy working, fighting, loving—that's what we are born for, and nothing else.
>
> (p. 271)

Still, however distorted factually, the account conveys the spirit of the truth. A one-time employee of the Cheka and a member of the food requisitioning teams, Isaac Babel must have had a hard time subsisting exclusively on a vegetarian diet. It is tempting to imagine that these experiences as well as his participation in the revolution and the civil war had made him a very different writer. His most astute and least sentimental admirer, Victor Shklovskii, appears to have thought as much:

> Russian literature is as gray as a siskin, it needs raspberry-colored riding breeches and leather shoes the color of heavenly azure.
>
> It also needs that which prompted Babel to leave his Chinamen to their own devices and to join *Red Cavalry.*
>
> Literary protagonists, maidens, old men and young lads and all the situations have been worn thin. What literature needs is concreteness and to be cross-fertilized *with the new style of life* [emphasis added].
>
> ("Isaac Babel: A Critical Romance" [1924], in Bloom, p. 14)

In June 1920, soon after Babel had returned to Odessa, he published four short novellas adapted from a popular collection of war anecdotes by Gaston Vidal, *Figures et anecdotes de la grand guerre* (1918). A short step separates the "ridiculous" fare of Vidal from the true sublime of *Red Cavalry,* reminding one of Anna Akhmatova's poetic apostrophe to the pious reader: "If only you knew from what trash poetry emerges, unaware of shame." In the staccato precision and the brevity of the adaptations, Babel easily eclipsed the wordy braggadoccio of the original, but the narrative play with the grotesqueries of life and death lacked sufficient seriousness and was still redolent of the officers' mess and the cheap thrills of the wartime middle-brow periodicals. In retrospect, however, it is apparent that the four pieces represented a crucial exercise in the verbal orientation toward a new consciousness, the source of Babel's future esteem. This was a mind-set steeled by the brutality and misshapen absurdity of life that, in the experience of contemporaries, had no precedent before 1914 or, for the Russian intelligentsia at large, until the beginning of the civil war in 1918. Exotic, alien to the Russian reader (existential curiosities at the western front), Vidal's material, if he still had any, relieved Babel of the compulsion to balance the senseless cruelty of war with sentimental appeals.

A whole new horizon opened up when he decided to interpose between the author and the events the figure of Gaston Vidal, whose voice was borrowed, as it were, for the main narrative. Drawing such a clear distinction between the narrator and the author further obviated the necessity for an explicit judgment. Perhaps the most important discovery was made in "Dezertir" ("The Deserter"), a story about an officer who has just offered a shell-shocked young soldier a choice between the firing squad, with its eternal shame, and suicide with honor. When the deserter proves unable to shoot himself, the officer, who does "not take offense at small things," obligingly pulls the trigger. In a postscript added to the story, the author-narrator removes the mask of the Frenchman and repeats Vidal's characterization of the officer verbatim, demonstrating that the same statement, no matter how trite, can generate a new and profound meaning when uttered by a different speaker:

> Gaston Vidal writes about this incident in his book. The soldier was actually called Bauji. Whether the name Gémier I have given the Captain is the right one, I cannot really say. Vidal's story is dedicated to a certain Firmin Gémier "in token of deep respect." I think this dedication gives the game away. Of course, the Captain was called Gémier. And then Vidal tells us that the Captain was a patriot, a soldier, a good father, and not a man to take offense at small things. That's something if a man doesn't take offense at small things.
>
> (*You Must Know Something,* p. 85)

This "discovery" of the interdependence of the voice and statement, and, therefore, of the relativity of meaning, helps account for Babel's mastery over the overwhelming material in *Red Cavalry*—for his skill in shifting nimbly from one to another voice. The device of narrating in marked voices, which the Russians term *skaz* if the voice happens to be speaking substandard Russian, was used widely in postrevolutionary prose, a literary and linguistic tribute to the post-1917 social leveling and the saturation of the urban bastions of the intelligentsia culture by members of the semiliterate lower classes and provincial milieu. However, it was contemporary poetry that served Babel as the ultimate model for his narrative technique. Many poets, especially Blok, Mandelshtam, Sergei Esenin, and Mayakovsky, were masters at weaving the voice of the other into the fabric of their verse. What distinguished their use of the voice of the other from *skaz* was the dominant presence of the dramatically complete figure of the poet. Even if merely implied, this chief protagonist whom the reader identified with the author functioned as the central referent in much the same way as a star's gravitational pull defines the course of the orbiting planet.

In *Odessa Tales* and *Red Cavalry,* the function of this Poet (with the capital *P*) would be performed by the man from Odessa, a Jew and a Russian *intelligent* who had "autumn in his heart and spectacles on his nose" but wished to look at life as a green promenade for "women and horses" and was possessed by a still greater desire to retain the intellectual's central position in the country's culture, the position from which the revolution had threatened to displace him. This narrator would be the first to walk into the verbal ambush of the changing world. Camouflaged from the reader's unaided eye, the author would be moving behind the narrator, maintaining a safe distance for himself (but not necessarily the reader), yet staying close enough to keep the narrator in full sight. If in "The Deserter" Babel went out of the way to emphasize this distance, in *Red Cavalry,* more sure of his craft, he caused it to emerge imperceptibly and grow from story to story.

Kirill Liutov, the compassionate, humane—all too humane—narrator, cannot grant his mortally wounded comrade the last wish: to be put out of his misery before the attacking Poles take him prisoner ("Smert' Dolgusheva" ["The Death of Dolgushev," 1923). But the author, who remains invisible, can and does—through his emissary, a wild, violent, and only slightly "Red" cossack, Afon'ka Bida. In a sense, Babel reveals the nature of his authorial pathos in the ostensibly autobiographical "Guy de Maupassant," in which the young narrator—more Babel than Liutov—flings down the gauntlet before the venerable ghost of Tolstoy. Drunk on wine bought with his first honorarium, he launches into a monologue:

> "He got scared, your Count [Tolstoy], he lost his nerve . . . . His religion is—fear. . . . Scared by the cold, by old age, the Count made himself a shirt out of faith. . . ."
>
> "And then what?" Kazantsev asked me, his birdlike head swaying from side to side.

The question remained unanswered, because the response—only in part to Tolstoy's *The Cossacks* (1863)—had been provided in *Red Cavalry.* There the narrator would play the role of a latter-day Count Tolstoy, a distant relative of the noble protagonist of *The Cossacks* and a spiritual heir to the vegetarian humanism of the late Tolstoy. But the author, who had learned from Nietzsche, not Dostoevsky, about the tragic sense of life and the beauty of power, and who had experienced both, would know no fear, accepting calmly and with majesty all the gifts from the Pandora's box of life. In the adaptations from Gaston Vidal, Babel's author functions as a Russian voice conveying a Frenchman's witness to the carnage at the western front. In *Odessa Tales* and *Red Cavalry,* Babel constructed a "foreign" author, foreign in his sensibility, watching with cool curiosity a Russian Jewish intellectual as he picks his way through a minefield of daily life in a cossack army fighting for the "world revolution" and—the overused, bland pathos is spiced up with irony—"a pickled cuke" ("Konkin," 1924).

The spectacular acclaim Babel enjoyed during the publication of *Red Cavalry* and *Odessa Tales* helps us to understand why his later writing was dominated by the figure of the autobiographical narrator-protagonist. The intelligentsia, who were sympathetic to the Revolution but shocked and disoriented by the catastrophic events of the preceding decade, embraced his stories as the first true masterpiece of the new era. What they saw in them was above all a new language, a new way of speaking about the world, that made it possible to assimilate revolutionary change without compromising their moral and, even more important, aesthetic sense. "Babel knows about the necessity of cruelty," wrote the influential critic A. Lezhnev in his 1926 essay,

> no less than those who criticize him. In his work, it is justified ("Salt," "The Death of Dolgushev"), justified with the revolutionary pathos. His cavalrymen are no brutes; otherwise *Red Cavalry* would have amounted to a libel of the Cavalry Army. But the justification of cruelty—in a strange and conflicting way—exists side by the side with his rejection of it. This contradiction cannot be resolved.
>
> (p. 85)

Instead of trying to solve this paradox by conceptual manipulation, Babel opted for a mimetic construct, inventing an exemplary, aesthetically convincing model of the self. As Lezhnev's analysis implied, this model, if internalized, would help one become reconciled to the brutal and unsightly way that power was exercised in the good revolution. But not everyone was able to discern in Babel's art a complex truth and a positive spirit.

The most sophisticated among Babel's detractors accused him of the cardinal sin of the intelligentsia: apologizing for the revolution by appealing to abstract moral principles. That Babel's "bourgeois humanism" was no longer moving sluggishly through the veins of a typical "intelligentsia" hero but was pulsating mightily through the hearts of muscular protagonists—that fact made Babel's stance particularly pernicious. The most impressive bill of particulars, entitled "Poeziia banditizma" (The Poetry of Banditry, 1924), was drawn by V. Veshnev (Vl. Przhetslavskii), a critic associated with the Komsomol journal *Molodaia gvardiia* (Young Guard). Trying to dispel Babel's considerable mystique, Veshnev cautioned youthful readers to be wary of what he believed to be Babel's insidious moral economy:

> For the most part, Babel depicts the greatest cruelties of our civil war. But these cruelties are presented in the light of total justification of those who perpetrated them. . . . Babel approached the revolution with a moral yardstick. This is damning enough. Revolution is not subject to morality. On the contrary, morality is subject to the revolution.
>
> (p. 276)

Paying homage to Babel's craft, Veshnev saw the greatest danger precisely in the effectiveness of his fiction, implying that Babel made the acceptance of the revolution a matter of not ideological or even moral choice, but aesthetic judgment: "The bandit stories with their poetry of anarchism are written simply, transparently, and seductively. They can and they will enjoy ideological success. Are we going to be pleased by this?" Apparently Veshnev was not pleased, but his prediction turned out to be correct. The stories were successful and, what is more, they soon achieved the reputation of the foremost masterpieces of Soviet fiction and maintained this status, despite repeated assaults, throughout the 1930's.

Whatever one might say, the cultural sphere of the revolution belonged to the intelligentsia, and Babel fulfilled, in the Marxist critical parlance of the day, the social command of this "pseudo-class"; he endowed, according to N. Stepanov, the experience of the revolution and the civil war with a heroic and romantic aura. Many were called to the task, but Babel alone was chosen, not least because he had managed to continue looking at the world through the traditional perspective of the Russian intelligentsia, that established in the masterpieces of Russia's literary art. Wrote Ia. Benni (Ia. Cherniak) in 1924:

> Writers are compulsively drawn to the plots and events of the revolution that lie about at every corner. They grab at and burn their fingers on the still smoldering logs. There is neither enough strength nor aesthetic stability. And how can there be enough to enable one to clear away the fiery ashes and, burning with memories, to touch the smoldering and bloody years. . . .
>
> [Intentional] propaganda destroys art, depriving it altogether of its true effectiveness as a tool of mobilization. . . . The revolution in the soul of contemporary reader is much more terrifying, more profound, and its voice is softer than the thunderous sighs of the so-called revolutionary art. . . .
>
> What overwhelms in Babel's stories is their truthfulness, a strange echo of the familiar Ukrainian laughter of the "little Gogol," conjoined with the great intensity of the justification of sacrifice.
>
> (p. 136)

Benni comes the heart of the matter when he seeks an explanation for the effectiveness of Babel's art and locates it in the "autobiographical" basis of his writings. Nothing could be more convincing, according to him, than the individual experience of an *intelligent,* mediated though it might be by the invention of fiction:

> Babel's stories are heroic stories. Their biographical, even autobiographical, truthfulness, which at once determines the reader's trust in the artist and his writings, constitutes their sole foundation. Literary mastery, rich and colorful language, even the invention itself, emerge out of this biographical truth as naturally as grass and flowers on a meadow.
>
> (p. 139)

A writer who was able to justify the revolution morally and aesthetically, who made this justification the matter of self-sacrifice, Babel was likewise credited with the invention of the new linguistic culture. "In the art of using live language, Babel is successfully catching up with the classics," wrote a Marxist literary critic, Georgii Gorbachev, offering what counted, perhaps, as the highest praise for a contemporary writer. He continued in an awkward but, for this reason, more telling manner:

> Babel's work with the language serves the cognition of life, development of technique, aesthetic expressiveness, the cause of the creation of a [new] linguistic culture, which is so important for us, for language represents the most important tool of the enlightenment and communication among the masses, which have entered a period of great cultural and social ferment.
>
> (p. 275)

As in an echo chamber, the praise continued to amplify Babel's achievement until *Red Cavalry* was declared by V. Polonskii to "constitute, alone, a factor determining the development of our art" and a "token of the urban, industrial future of Soviet Russia." The editor of *Krasnaia nov',* Alexander Voronskii, a pivotal figure in the literary life of the 1920's, stated clearly and simply that "Babel was strengthening the association of literature with the Soviet republic and the Communist party." Coming from the man whom the party had commissioned to win the intelligentsia to the cause of the Bolshevik Revolution, this was high praise indeed. No wonder Babel dismissed his pre-1917 literary efforts as insignificant, declaring in the "Autobiography" that his career had commenced in 1923 and 1924, when the trend-setting avant-garde *LEF* and *Krasnaia nov'* (Red Virgin Soil), the most prestigious and weighty of contemporary journals, began publishing stories from his two major cycles.

Controversy was an unwelcome part of Babel's celebrity; *Red Cavalry* was centered on events in the immediate past and had a strong documentary flavor. Not only could the places of action be located on the map of the Polish campaign, but many actors in *Red Cavalry* retained their prototypes' names. (These would be altered only in the later editions.) However, perhaps because it was risky, this strategy contributed to Babel's success. Even when the notable verity of his civil war cycle impinged on the self-image of Commander of the First Cavalry Army Semyon Budennyi, it was the author, not the warrior, who came out the winner. Unlike his more urbane comrades-in-arms (Kliment Voroshilov, for one), who patronized the arts and knew the value of being made part of Babel's canvas, this semi-educated warrior could not make sense out of Babel's unconventional expression and failed to appreciate his admiration for the mighty barbarians of the revolutionary war. Affronted by the lurid detail in *Red Cavalry* and exploited by the enemies of Voronskii's journal, he accused Babel in print of vicious libel of the heroes of the First Cavalry Army. The verbal charge, which bore the title "Babizm Babelia iz 'kraznoi novi' " ("Floozy-ism of Babel from *Krasnaia nov'* "), a clumsy pun on the Russian *baba* (a common condescending term for a woman), succeeded only in bestowing on Budennyi himself a reputation as a comical Goliath. When another opportunity arose in 1928, after the fall of Voronskii, Budennyi once again stepped into the fray—only to be snubbed in *Pravda* by Gorky himself. The great man of letters, an undisputed authority on culture at the time, explained to the general with barely concealed exasperation that in a backward country like Russia, it was not the business of undereducated men to meddle in matters concerning enlightenment. Any subsequent attempts to reignite the controversy had little chance of success after Stalin pronounced his laconic verdict: "There is nothing wrong with *Red Cavalry.*"

It is not easy to walk away from a gold mine that has yielded a great treasure, no matter how scant the present return may be. Babel's gold mine was his invention of a new theme and style, and he was either unwilling or unable to surrender them, even at the risk of becoming a prisoner of his uncommonly good fortune. The theme was that of an emancipated Jewish intellectual who was trying to integrate himself into a world that was his by claim of reason but that could offer him only a dangerous and palpably very alien way of life. Like the narrator of *Red Cavalry,* Liutov, this character wishes to learn to accept the vibrant brutality and the baseness of existence (the Dionysian element) and to transfix it in the cool, contemplative beauty that, according to Nietzsche, was the gift of Apollonian art (the theme received a narrative development in "Pan Apolek," 1923). Together with his nonfictional contemporaries, Liutov had seen humanistic values pulverized in World War I, and he found the conventional, ultimately Christian ethic unacceptable. To do otherwise was for him tantamount to the loss of sight—symbolic castration—a motif that runs throughout Babel's fiction, especially *Red Cavalry* ("Perekhod cherez Zbruch" ["Crossing the Zbruch," 1924], "Gedali" [1924], "Liniia i tsvet" ["Line and Color," 1923]).

Indeed, the spirit of the Antichrist is in Liutov's blood. He is described in "Kostel v Novograde" ("The Novograde Cathedral," 1923): "I see you from here, the treasonous monk in lilac habit, the plumpness of your hands, your soul, tender and merciless, like a cat's soul, I see the wounds of your god, oozing semen, the fragrant poison intoxicating virgins."

The more astute among Babel's sympathetic readers recognized in his writings the ethos of Nietzsche, although they avoided pronouncing his name, preferring such code words as "paganism," "nature," and "life." The style was such that it undermined any discourse that could be defined as dominant. "Babel speaks in one voice about the stars and the clap," wrote Shklovskii in 1924 in his essay on Babel, giving what to this day is, perhaps, the sharpest and, certainly, most concise formulation of the Babelian style. That theme and that style, with only slight variations, Babel continued to practice well into the 1930's.

The four novellas of 1937 and 1938, which were his last fiction to appear in Soviet journals in his lifetime, do not suggest that his writing was likely to change. "Sud" ("The Trial," published in *Ogonek,* vol. 23 [1938]) tells the story of a deracinated White officer who is being convicted of petty fraud by an indifferent French court. Written in a staccato style, thematically it belongs to the genre of exposing the ills of the capitalist West that is practiced by Soviet writers wishing to justify their travels beyond the Soviet borders. Babel, who belonged to a handful of well-traveled authors, must have felt a particular sense of obligation. He had three long sojourns in France between 1928 and 1935, the briefest lasting several months. He had a wife and a daughter in France and a mother and a sister in Belgium, and he had to contend with persistent rumors about his alleged intention to emigrate. "The Trial" was also one of the few third-person stories Babel ever wrote; he ordinarily eschewed the objective authority associated with this narrative stance. But the other three return once again, whether ostensibly or by implication, to the narrator of *Red Cavalry.*

"The Kiss," the only story about Liutov's successful seduction, ends in the narrator cruelly betraying the woman that he has won by displays of sentimental humanity. "The Kiss" could easily have been integrated into yet another edition of the civil war cycle (the last one came out in 1932), but the central motif of the story represented, if anything, a sign of the more recent times. "Sulak" (1937), named after a peasant rebel killed in the story, fills a chronological gap in the Liutov "epic," placing the bespectacled narrator in the Ukraine in 1928, at the beginning of the collectivization drive. He is accompanying a Cheka officer ordered to seek out, arrest, and, if need be, destroy Sulak. The story is as grotesquely brutal as anything in *Red Cavalry.* Published, as chance would have it, in the journal *Molodoi kolkhoznik* (Young Collective Farmer), "Sulak" must have been especially appreciated by the young inhabitants of the terrorized countryside.

"Di Grasso," the fourth story, belongs thematically to the childhood cycle. Seen against the background of the Great Terror, and one of the writer's last stories, it begs to be interpreted as Babel's literary testament: a retrospective allegory of his life in art. The story is set in the familiar Rabelaisian Odessa of the early 1910's and told in the first person—in the voice of a man and writer sharing with his readers a formative episode from his bygone youth. A boy of fourteen, he becomes involved with a gang of scalpers who do a lively business, exploiting the Odessans' weakness for the performing arts. Incautiously, he chooses to obtain the start-up capital by pawning his father's watch with the head scalper, an unscrupulous man who thinks nothing of keeping both the watch and the money. The boy, on the contrary, is terrified by the prospect of facing his father's Jehovah-like wrath. What saves him is the sudden popularity of a visiting Sicilian actor, the tragedian Di Grasso, and not only the money he is able to make by scalping tickets to Di Grasso's performances, but quite literally his art. Night after night, in a spirited interpretation of his role, Di Grasso leaps into the air, flies across the stage, kills his wealthy rival with his bare teeth, and proceeds to drink the enemy's blood, growling and shooting fiery glances at the enraptured audience as the curtain slowly descends on the crime of the heart. This extraordinary display of the power of passion so moves the scalper's wife that she forces her husband to return the watch to the boy, who has already arranged to flee Odessa aboard an English steamer. The story ends with the boy—delivered from his misfortune by the orgiastic art of Di Grasso—transfixed by a sudden experience of an Apollonian epiphany:

> Clutching the timepiece, I was left alone and suddenly, with the kind of clarity I had never experienced before, I saw the towering pillars of the City Hall, the illuminated foliage of the boulevard, the bronze head of Pushkin under the pale gleam of the moon—for the first time, I saw what surrounded me as it really was: quiet and ineffably beautiful.
>
> (*Izbrannoe* [Moscow, 1966], p. 301)

Babel's predicament in the 1930's was not unlike that of the boy in "Di Grasso." He, too, was living on borrowed time, hoping for a deliverance through an artistic miracle. Confronted with the choice between the materialist Scylla of the West, with art at the mercy of scalpers, and the revolutionary Charybdis, presided over by the father figure Stalin, he chose not to emigrate (and he had plenty of opportunities to do so) but to remain in Russia, which he continued to see through the eye of his art. By no means blind to the Stalinist repression, he continued to measure the social and political experience of his country, so massively tragic and irreducibly complex, with the aesthetic formula according to which unbridled and violent passion revealed the real world—"quiet and ineffably beautiful." Whether or not Babel ever intended "Di Grasso" to be interpreted in this manner, many of his contemporaries among the intelligentsia, desperate for a rationalization of the Great Terror, could hardly have misread the story's subtle appeal.

It must have seemed for a while that Babel would be spared the fate of millions of his contemporaries who disappeared in the massive waves of arrests in 1937 and 1938. This was not to be. Babel's turn came on 16 May 1939, when he was arrested on unspecified charges at his country home in Peredelkino. Until recently, the circumstances of Babel's arrest and death have been shrouded in mystery. Now we know (Arkady Vaksberg, "Protsessy" [The Trials]) that a warrant for his arrest was issued thirty-five days after he had been taken into custody, that he was charged with belonging to a secret Trotskyist organization since 1927 and, since 1934, serving both French and Austrian intelligence. The litany of fantastic charges contained in the verdict suggests the actual motive for Babel's arrest: his association with Gladun-Khaiutina, a longtime Odessa friend and colleague at the editorial offices of *SSSR na stroike* (USSR in Construction), who also happened to be the wife of the recently deposed head of the secret police, Nikolai Yezhov (he was last seen in public on 31 January 1939). Babel's verdict read in part: "Having been organizationally associated in his anti-Soviet activity with the wife of an enemy of the people Yezhov—Gladun-Khaiutuna—Babel was drawn by the latter into anti-Soviet conspiratorial terrorist activity, shared the goal and tasks of this organization, including terrorist acts . . . against the leaders of the Communist party of the Soviet Union and Soviet government." Even Babel's famous *Red Cavalry* became an item in the writer's indictment as a "description of all the cruelties and inconsistencies of the civil war, emphasizing only the sensational and rough episodes." In the course of seventy-two hours of continuous interrogation (the "conveyor belt," as it is known in the language of the Gulag), Babel, who at first denied all the charges, finally relented and "confessed" to having been recruited into the spy network by Ilya Ehrenburg and to having provided André Malraux with, of all things, secrets of Soviet aviation. The latter charge must have been suggested by the film script that he had just completed: it dealt with uncovering saboteurs among the Soviet dirigible designers (Falen, pp. 231ff.).

The list of Babel's co-conspirators read like a who's who of Soviet culture. In addition to Ehrenburg, it included such writers as Valentin Kataev, Leonid Leonov, Yury Olesha, Lydia Seifullina, and Vsevolod Ivanov; filmmakers S. Eisenstein and G. Alexandrov; actors S. Mikhoels and L. Utesov, and even one polar explorer, the academician Otto Shmit. As Vaksberg suggests, the NKVD must have been planning a large-scale show trial involving the flower of the Soviet intelligentsia. But plans changed and the operation had to be mopped up. On four separate occasions, in October and November 1939, and finally in January 1940, Babel wrote appeals renouncing the testimony he was forced to give under torture, pleaded to have witnesses called, and asked for an attorney. On 26 January these appeals reached the chairman of the Military Collegium of the Supreme Court, V. Ul'rikh, who responded to them by signing the death warrant. A day later, Babel was shot. Fourteen years later, in a posthumous review of his case by the same Military Collegium, Babel was cleared of all charges "for lack of any basis" in the original indictment.

At the time of his arrest, Babel was forty-five —"the middle of life's way" for a prose writer, with a lot more to tell us about what happened to Liutov as he was trying to integrate himself into the new world of Soviet Russia. But whereas Babel, man and writer, could be arrested and executed, the theme and the style he invented found their own separate fate. The Soviet soil may have been increasingly inhospitable, but in a more temperate climate, grafted to the English language, they emerged in the American version of the narrator "with the autumn in his heart, spectacles on his nose," and, as Philip Roth expanded the formula in his *The Ghost Writer* (1979), "an erect penis." Victor Shklovskii, who better than anybody understood the intensely "writerly" *(scriptible)* nature of Babel's art, had anticipated this turn of phrase when he cautioned the readers not to identify the narrator type with the writer himself: "Babel is not like that: he does not stammer. He is brave, I even think that he 'can spend the night with a Russian woman, and a Russian woman would be satisfied.' Because a Russian woman likes a good tale." As do all Russian and non-Russian men and women. They now can satisfy their desire for a good Babelian narrative in Philip Roth and—marvel of marvels, considering the hairy-chested machismo of Babel's characters—in the stories of Grace Paley. Even American television is known to make use of the themes and styles invented by Isaac Babel, as it did in the PBS series *Gustav Mahler,* where the Austrian composer, perhaps in deference to the expectations of the Babel-touting audience, was forced into living the childhood of Babel's narrator in "Probuzhdenie" ("The Awakening," 1931). We have not heard the last of Isaac Babel.

## Selected Bibliography

### EDITIONS

#### INDIVIDUAL WORKS

*Liubka Kozak: Rasskazy.* Moscow, 1925.
*Rasskazy.* Moscow, 1925.
*Benia Krik: Kinopovest'.* Moscow, 1926.
*Bluzhdaiushchie zvezdy: Kinostsenarii.* Moscow, 1926.
*Istoriia moei golubiatni: Rasskazy.* Moscow, Leningrad, 1926.
*Konarmiia.* Moscow, 1926.
*Zakat.* Moscow, 1928.
*Odesskie rasskazy.* Moscow, 1931.
*Mariia.* Moscow, 1935.
*Bezhin lug (vtoroi variant).* In Sergei Eizenstein, *Izbrannye proizvedeniia,* 6 vols. Vol. 6. Moscow, 1971.
*Evreika.* Moscow, 1987.

#### COLLECTED WORKS

*Rasskazy.* Moscow, 1936.
*Izbrannoe.* Introduction by I. G. Erenburg. Moscow, 1957.
*Izbrannoe.* Introduction by L. Poliak. Moscow, 1966.
*Izbrannoe.* Kemerovo, 1966.
*Zabytyi Babel': Sbornik maloizvestnykh proizve-*

*denii I. Babelia.* Compiled and edited by Nikolas Stroud. Ann Arbor, Mich., 1979.

*Evreika, god za godom. Literaturnyi ezhegodnik* 4. Moscow, 1988.

*Izbrannye proizvedeniia.* 2 vols. Introduction by G. Belaia. Moscow, 1988.

## MEMOIRS AND DOCUMENTS

Annenkov, Iurii. *Dnevnik moikh vstrech.* New York, 1966.

Anonymous. "Vyderzhki iz pisem I. E. Babelia k materi i sestre (1925–1939)." *Vozdushnye puti* 3 (1963).

Ehrenburg, Il'ia. *Liudi, gody, zhizn'.* In *Sobranie sochinenii,* vols. 8–9. Moscow, 1966. Translated as *Men, Years, Life* by Tatiana Shebunina and Yvonne Kapp. London, 1962–1963.

"Gor'kii—I. E. Babel' [Correspondence]." *Literaturnoe nasledstvo* 70. Moscow, 1963.

Ivanova, T. "Isaak Emanuilovich Babel'." In *Moi sovremenniki, kakimi ia ikh znala: Ocherki.* Moscow, 1984.

Nikulin, L. "Isaak Babel'." In *Gody nashei zhizni: Vospominaniia i portrety.* Moscow, 1966.

Paustovskii, K. *Povest' o zhizni.* 2 vols. Moscow, 1966. Translated as *Years of Hope (The Story of My Life)* by Manya Harari and Andrew Thompson. New York, 1968.

Pirozhkova, A., and N. Turgeneva, eds. *Babel': Vospominaniia sovremennikov.* Moscow, 1972.

———, and I. Smirin. "I. Babel': Novye materialy." *Literaturnoe nasledstvo* 74. Moscow, 1965.

Sinkó, Ervin. *Roman eines Romans: Moskauer Tagebuch.* Cologne, 1962.

Solajczyk, J. "Polzki epizod w biografii Izaaka E. Babla." *Zeszyty naukowe wyzszej szkoly pedagogicznej im. Powstancow slaskich w Opolu. Filologia rosyjska.* 9 (A). Opole, 1972.

Souvarine, Boris. *Souvenirs sur Isaak Babel, Panait Istrati, Pierre Pascal; suivi de Lettre à Alexandre Soljenitsine.* Paris, 1985.

Vaksberg, A. "Protsessy." *Literaturnaia gazeta* (4 May 1988).

## TRANSLATIONS

*Benya Krik: A Film-Novel.* Translated by Ivor Montagu and S. S. Nalbandov. London, 1935.

*Benya Krik the Gangster and Other Stories.* Edited by Avrahm Yarmolinsky. New York, 1948.

*The Collected Stories.* Introduction by Lionel Trilling. Edited and translated by Walter Morison. New York, 1955.

*The Forgotten Prose.* Edited and translated by Nicholas Stroud. Ann Arbor, Mich., 1978.

*The Lonely Years: 1925–1939.* Edited by Nathalie Babel. Translated by Max Hayward and Andrew R. MacAndrew. New York, 1964. Unpublished stories and private correspondence.

*Red Cavalry.* Translated by John Harland. London, 1929. Translated by Nadia Helstein. London, New York, 1929.

*Sunset.* Translated by Raymond Rosenthal and Mirra Ginsburg. *Noonday* 3. New York, 1960.

*You Must Know Everything: Stories, 1915–1937.* Edited by Nathalie Babel. Translated by Max Hayward. New York, 1966.

## BIOGRAPHICAL AND CRITICAL STUDIES

Baak, J. J. van. *The Place of Space in Narration: A Semiotic Approach to the Problem of Literary Space. With an Analysis of the Role of Space in Isaak Babel's "Konarmija." Studies in Slavic Literature and Poetics* 3. Amsterdam, 1983.

*I. Babel': Vospominaniia sovremennikov.* Moscow, 1972.

Benni, Ia. (Ia. Cherniak). "Isaak Babel'." *Pechat' i revoliutsiia* 3 (1924).

Bloom, Harold, ed. *Isaac Babel.* New York, 1987.

———, ed. *Modern Critical Views: Isaac Babel.* Introduction by Bloom. New York, 1987. This anthology of Babel criticism and scholarship (twenty items) is the most comprehensive collection of its kind in any language.

Bydennyi, S. "Babizm Babelia iz *Krasnoi novi.*" *Oktiabr'* 3 (1924).

———. "Otkrytoe pis'mo Maksimu Gor'komu." *Pravda* (26 October 1928).

Carden, Patricia. *The Art of Isaac Babel.* Ithaca, N.Y., 1972.

Eastman, M. *Writers in Uniform: A Study of Literature and Bureaucratism.* New York, 1934.

Ehre, M. *Isaac Babel.* Boston, 1986.

Falen, James E. *Isaac Babel, Russian Master of the Short Story.* Knoxville, Tenn., 1974. Includes comprehensive bibliography.

Freidin, G. "Fat Tuesday in Odessa: Isaac Babel's 'Di Grasso' as Testament and Manifesto." *The Russian Review* 40/2 (April 1981).

Gorbachev, Georgii. "O tvorchestve Babelia i po povodu nego." *Zvezda* 4 (1925).

Gor'kii, M. "Otvet Budennomu." *Pravda* (27 November 1928).

Hallett, R. W. *Isaac Babel.* New York, 1973.

Howe, Irving. "The Right to Write Badly." *The New Republic* (4 July 1955).

———. "The Genius of Isaac Babel." *New York Review of Books* (20 August 1964).

Hyman, Stanley Edgar. "Identities of Isaac Babel." *Hudson Review* 8/4 (1956).

———. "New Voices of Isaac Babel." *New Leader* (20 July 1964).

Jovanovic, M. *Umetnost Isaka Babelja.* Belgrade, 1975.

Kaun, A. "Babel: Voice of New Russia." *Menorah Journal* 15 (November 1928).

Lelevich, G. "Babel'." *Na postu* 1 (1924).

Levin, F. *Babel'.* Moscow, 1972.

Lezhnev, A. Z. "Babel'." *Pechat i revoliutsiia* 6 (1926).

Luck, C. D. *The Field of Honor: An Analysis of Isaac Babel's Cycle "On the Field of Honor" (Na pole chesti) with Reference to Gaston Vidal's "Figures et anecdotes de la Grand Guerre." Birmingham Slavonic Monographs* No. 18. Birmingham, 1987. The study contains the original text of Babel's cycle *On the Field of Honor.*

Luplow, Carol. *Isaac Babel's "Red Cavalry."* Ann Arbor, Mich. 1982.

Maguire, Robert A. *Red Virgin Soil: Soviet Literature in the 1920's.* Princeton, 1968.

Marcus, Steven. "The Stories of Isaac Babel." *Partisan Review* 22/3 (1955).

Markish, Simon. "The Example of Isaac Babel." *Commentary* 64 (1977).

Mendelson, Danuta. *Metaphor in Babel's Short Stories.* Ann Arbor, Mich., 1982.

Meney, L. *L'Art du recit chez Isaac Babel.* Quebec, 1983.

Mirsky, D. S. "I. Babel: Rasskazy." *Sovremennye zapiski* 26 (1925).

———. "Babel." *Nation* (23 January 1926).

Morsbach, P. *Isaak Babel auf der sowietischen Buhne.* Munich, 1983.

Osinskii, N. "Literaturnyi god." *Pravda* (1 January 1926).

Polonskii, Viach. "Kritičeskie zametki Babele." *Novyi mir* 1 (1927).

Pozner, Vladimir. *Panorama de la littérature russe contemporaine.* Paris, 1929.

Rosenthal, Raymond. "The Fate of Isaac Babel: A Child of the Russian Emancipation." *Commentary* 3 (February 1947).

Shklovskii, Victor. "I. Babel': Kriticheskii roman." *Lef* 2/6 (1924). Translated as "Isaac Babel: A Critical Romance" in Edward J. Brown, ed., *Major Soviet Writers.* London, 1973.

Sicher, E. *Style and Structure in the Prose of Isaac Babel.* Columbus, Ohio, 1986.

Sinyavsky, A. "Isaac Babel." In Edward J. Brown, ed., *Major Soviet Writers.* London, 1973.

Spektor, Iu. "Molodoi Babel'." *Voprosy literatury* 7 (1982).

Stepanov, Nik. "Novella Babelia." In *Mastera sovremennoi literatury II: I. E. Babel',* edited by B. V. Kazanskii and Iu. N. Tyniainov. Leningrad, 1928.

Stora-Sándor, Judith. *Isaac Babel': L'Homme et l'oeuvre.* Paris, 1968.

Strelets (M. Stoliarov). "Dvulikii Ianus." *Rossiia* 5 (1925).

Terras, V. "Line and Color: The Structure of I. Babel's Short Stories in *Red Cavalry.*" *Studies in Short Fiction* 3/2 (1966).

Trilling, Lionel. "The Fate of Isaac Babel." *London Magazine* 7 (1956).

Veshnev, V. (V. Przhetslavskii). "Poeziia banditizma (I. Babel')." *Molodaia gvardiia* 7–8 (1924).

Voronskii, A. "Babel', Seifullina." *Krasnaia nov'* 5 (1924).

GREGORY FREIDIN

# HONORÉ DE BALZAC
## (1799–1850)

*INTRODUCTION*

BALZAC HAS INSPIRED many biographers, each one adding new documentation and often fresh insight into the novelist's life, but the biographer's task is particularly daunting in the case of a writer who has been the subject of so many legends and myths.

Although he was extremely short (about five feet, two inches tall), Balzac's stocky build and enormous head seemed to suggest the amplitude of his art. Often disheveled and untidy (a state reflected in page proofs scrawled over with additions and corrections that were the despair of his publishers), he had an insatiable taste for elegance and fine clothes, despite a body not suited to either. He had a gargantuan appetite for food and wine, but when he worked he lived on the meagerest nourishment. Fortified by potent cups of coffee, writing through the night, he taxed himself with a work pace that ruined his health. Renowned for the hard-edged depiction of reality found in his novels, Balzac also believed in second sight, in magnetic mind control, in the most ethereal spiritualism.

The bare facts of his life read like fiction. Born on 20 May 1799 in Tours, he was sent off to boarding school at the Collège des Oratoriens at Vendôme, where he spent six unhappy years. His mother appears to have been distant and unfeeling. The Balzac family moved to Paris in 1814, and in 1816 young Honoré enrolled as a law student and began clerking in a law office. He received his degree three years later but persuaded his family to grant him one year to pursue his ambition—to become a writer. The result, a tragedy, was deemed dreadful by a professor of literature. Then Balzac began his true literary apprenticeship, writing novels of adventure under various pen names.

The decade of the 1820's was also marked by his liaison with Madame de Berny, a woman more than twenty years his elder, and by his failure as a businessman. At the end of that decade, with his first great successes as a writer, the historical novel *Les Chouans* and the humorous pamphlet *La physiologie du mariage,* he began contributing to the most important literary journals. Soon he was received by Parisian salon society and by the group of young writers who defined French romanticism, the *cénacle* that met at Charles Nodier's apartment in the Bibliothèque de l'Arsenal.

Balzac's fame spread throughout Europe during the 1830's. In 1833 he signed an important contract for the novel cycle that received its ultimate title, *La comédie humaine,* in 1841. It was in 1832 that Balzac received an admiring letter from a Ukrainian reader who identified herself only as "l'étrangère" (the stranger). In 1833 he met this woman, Madame Hańska, in Geneva. The love affair of Balzac and Madame Hanska, beset by many complications, was carried on in a voluminous correspondence and in increasingly frequent meetings all over Europe. Their marriage on 14 March 1850 and the last months of Balzac's life constitute an episode melodramatic enough to have found a place in *La comédie humaine*. Balzac was gravely ill. The couple set out on their arduous wedding trip from the Ukraine to Paris, to the house that Balzac, a fanatic collector of bric-à-brac, had so painstakingly furnished and appointed for his bride. When they arrived, the door was locked, the servant had gone mad, and the place was in total disorder. Balzac died barely three months later, on 18 August 1850.

If the man and his creation ultimately escape definition in prose, something of the spirit of both was caught by the sculptor Auguste Rodin in his gigantic figure of Balzac, with its rough texture and minimally articulated body concealed by a great cloak. The energy is focused in the wild, passionate face, in the head that seems to emerge from matter, to dominate matter, dynamically related to the mass and the wide world around it. The eyes concentrate the density and volume of the figure and transcend the physical in the depth of their gaze.

## *WORK*

The reader of any novel by Balzac is supplied with a superabundance of clues to its meaning. If the novelist's intentions are not made clear by the plot, they emerge in the portraits of the characters, in metaphors, or through other purely narrative devices. Failing that, at crucial moments Balzac often stops the novel in its tracks to state unequivocally what he thinks it means. There is something for every kind of reader. Balzac was determined to communicate to the widest possible audience—those who read because they love stories, those who want to know how stories are written, those who look for edification and for fictional versions of sociology and history, those for whom reading is a comforting escape.

The accessibility of any single novel of Balzac's must be measured, however, against the body of works to which it belongs, *La comédie humaine* (*The Human Comedy*), a set of books daunting to the reader in the density of their interconnections, in the multiplicity of references, in variety of expression, and ultimately in sheer bulk. The final version of *La comédie humaine* contains nearly a hundred works of prose fiction of which approximately forty percent are of average book length. Some of the novels far surpass any common notion of book length. *La comédie humaine* escapes our most strenuous efforts to possess it fully. In its mass, it cannot be reduced to explanation, despite Balzac's repeated efforts to describe its structure and justify its coherence. Whatever meaning is ascribed to the whole, it cannot begin to account for that seemingly endless flux of words that simulates a world as full as the one in which we live. Although we may sense that we have learned as much as the novelist knows about a given character, place, action, or idea, even a given novel, our knowledge is small when measured against the tens of thousands of pages that compose *La comédie humaine*. This play between knowledge and the unknowable, between singularity and multiplicity, between the graspable detail and the colossal construct, is what animates our reading of Balzac. We know enough to continue, but never enough to stop.

The scope of reading experiences that Balzac invites has inspired commensurate critical activity. In addition to providing a variety of pleasures, his works have lent themselves to an array of critical methods, to exegeses of individual texts, and to synthetic guides through the accumulated, labyrinthine mass of novels. In the nineteenth century Balzac was studied by numerous literary historians and critics (Hippolyte Taine, Spoelberch de Louvenjoul) who concerned themselves with the relation between the life of the author and his fiction. Twentieth-century critics have been attracted to the workings of the novelist's imagination, and his place in European literature (Curtius, Béguin, Bardèche, Poulet, Auerbach). The essays of Marcel Proust and of Henry James demonstrate the degree to which the genre of the novel is a function of other novelists' responses to Balzac (see also Gustave Flaubert, Émile Zola, the "New" novelists Michel Butor and Alain Robbe-Grillet). Balzac has proved to be a useful exemplar for Marxist criticism (Lukács) as well as for semiotics and narrative analysis (Barthes). Each year brings new books and scores of articles. Indeed, the Balzac bibliography serves as an ongoing history of literary criticism.

The limited scope of this essay excludes the possibility of adequately examining either Balzac's career and works or the critical discourses they have generated. Even a survey of the major novels (and to define "major" would be a hopeless task) would require a great many omissions. What follows, then, is not an itinerary through *La comédie humaine,* but rather a consideration of the kinds of reading Balzac elicits. The focus will be on those elements in the novels that represent the activity of reading. And it is through that activity that we can begin to perceive the shape of the itinerary, the length of the voyage.

A work of great artistic audacity, *La peau de chagrin (The Wild Ass's Skin)* contains many of the narrative and thematic concerns that inform the rest of *La comédie humaine,* and is therefore a particularly apt point of departure for the examination of how we read Balzac. Published in 1831, *La peau de chagrin* was only the second volume of book-length fiction to bear the author's name, the first being *Les Chouans* (1829). Balzac served his literary apprenticeship by writing a number of potboilers, sometimes in collaboration, but always using a pseudonym. *La peau de chagrin* came at that moment in his career when his fame was growing and his ambition was boundless, as it typically was for the generation of romantic writers so productive in the years just before and after the July Revolution of 1830—Victor Hugo, Alfred de Musset, George Sand, Stendhal, Prosper Mérimée, and Alfred de Vigny. The novel is filled with the enthusiasm of a young writer who believes that fiction will do whatever he bids.

### *Plot*

Storytelling is one of the main features of the novel in the nineteenth century, and the countless stories that make up *La comédie humaine* celebrate narrative inventiveness. Stories are told throughout *La peau de chagrin,* and listeners act and react on the basis of what they hear. The range of the stories, from the fantastic to the plausible, is one of the keys to Balzac's attitude to fiction. The rendition of banal phenomena is juxtaposed with the most unlikely events. These opposing orders of reality qualify each other. The unusual invests the everyday with its high relief and memorability; the everyday lends credibility to the unusual. This alternating rhythm of storytelling satisfies the expectations of those many readers who want their fiction to be fictional yet who want it grounded in a familiar reality. The status of plot is constantly being tested as the reader passes from a story that is brazenly fictional, "made up," to one that hides its fiction beneath a simulation of ordinary life, as it passes from the "fiction effect" to the "reality effect."

The briefest résumé of *La peau de chagrin* suggests the kind of reading the novel sets in motion. Raphaël de Valentin is on the verge of suicide. Momentarily distracted, he enters an antique shop that appears to be a repository for the riches of all past civilizations. The proprietor offers him a talisman, a portion of the skin of a wild ass. Whoever possesses the skin has only to wish, and the wish will be satisfied. But each time the skin is invoked it shrinks, and along with it shrinks the life of the user. Raphaël accepts the talisman and soon discovers that the life he was so anxious to terminate has become precious. That evening, at an orgy, he tells how he was driven to the point of suicide by his failed career and his infatuation with Foedora, a beautiful, ice-cold woman. The last section of the novel recounts his love for the warm-hearted Pauline; his realization that his desire for her is fatal because, as with all desire, it causes the skin to shrink; the futile efforts of men of science and medicine to stop the process; the hero's flight from Paris. An outcast, a misfit, he is rejected by nearly everyone he encounters. In a fit of passion, Raphaël dies in the arms of his beloved Pauline.

Divided into three parts, the novel contains at its center a long flashback, a story told to a within-the-novel audience whose raptness sets a standard of concentration and absorption for us, the readers of *La peau de chagrin.* The flashback is in fact a representation of storytelling itself. By tampering with linear time, it forces the reader to acknowledge the freedom of fiction to organize discourse for effect. When we are attentive to the time of fiction we are relieved of paying attention to the time of life and necessity. We are then able to lend credence to the unusual, the miraculous. Plot is a miracle of coherence, a system that can order such quite disparate elements as the commonplace dilemma of the poor young man in the city; a magic, all-powerful skin; the tedium of existence and the extravagance of an orgy; Paris as it is and an antique shop that represents the whole history of art and culture.

### *Character*

Belief in character, in the integrity of a character's life, is essential to the aesthetics of the novel as the genre was generated in the eighteenth century, both in France and in England. The novel as journal, as memoir, is a guarantee of the authenticity of character, usually that of the protagonist, who records his or her own life. But character in *La peau de chagrin,* indeed throughout most of *La comédie humaine,* is manifestly created by an omniscient narrator, and is subject to the same degree of fictional manipulation as the plot. Raphaël, through the first episodes of the novel, emerges from a complicated set of circumstances. He is introduced as a nameless young man as if the novelist himself were trying to identify him. The reasons for his despair will not be revealed until the second third of the novel, when he himself becomes the narrator, thereby reinforcing his own credibility as a character. In the last section of the novel, he is transformed yet again, by the possession of the talisman, into an allegorical figure for destructive desire, and finally, just before dying, into an image of animal vitality. This transformation of character is effected also in the novel's two-page epilogue, in which the female protagonists are explicitly allegorized, one as a phantom who protects the countryside from the invasion of the modern world, the other as a symbol of high society. So it is for most of the principal characters in *La comédie humaine:* Balzac preserves their status as representations of human beings while reminding us that they are verbal, conceptual, aesthetic constructs. A character in *La comédie humaine* is used with as much freedom and creativity as is an image, a metaphor, any element of expression and style.

### *Prose*

The reader recognizes fictional human beings through meticulously contrived word portraits that foster belief in a resemblance to creatures of flesh and blood. The cause of resemblance is served when characters communicate through conventional spoken language. Time and again, this illusion of speech is challenged by the author's promptness to transform characters into ideas or images, and words into verbal artifacts. The text constantly shifts in its relation to the language we speak or write. It alternately identifies Balzac's insistently authorial voice and plunges the reader into what appears to be the transcription of speech. The conversations at the orgy sequence in *La peau de chagrin* are rendered so as to simulate the helter-skelter of voices. Yet even that illusion of reality is structured in accordance with an artistic model specifically alluded to by the author—the overture to one of Gioacchino Rossini's comic operas. Throughout *La comédie humaine* Balzac pays great attention to human speech, the only "reality" in the novelist's purview. (A description of a table is neither a table nor a picture of a table; even written words are meant to echo utterance, the stuff of speech.) Just as frequently he writes passages whose density, complexity, rhetorical patterns, and lyricism demonstrate to the reader the gulf between the page and life.

### *Reality*

Plot, character, and prose in *La peau de chagrin* call attention to the issue of reality in fiction, a concern often stressed by Balzac in his remarks about the genre of the novel. He conceives of *La comédie humaine* as a sort of historico-sociological record of his time, thereby promoting the genre as a depository of scientific observation and truth. He presumes his portraits to be a zoology of the human race, its types documented, case by case, in novel after novel. The systematic taxonomies of men of science are important models for Balzac:

> I saw that . . . Society was like Nature. Does not Society make of man, according to the environments in which the events of his life unfold, as many different men as there are varieties in zoology? . . . Thus, there have always existed, and there will exist for all time, Social Species, just as there are Zoological Species.
>
> (preface to *La comédie humaine,* Pléiade ed., 1935–1962, 1.4)

If the animal world, its types, properties, behaviors, and the relation between creatures and their environment submit to analysis, systematization, and exposition, why not the human species? The novelist wanted to do for human life in France in the first half of the nineteenth century what Buffon and Geoffroy St. Hilaire (to whom Balzac dedicated *Le père Goriot*) did for the animal species.

Raphaël de Valentin is indeed an element in Balzac's zoology, a prototypical character, the ambitious young man who seeks to conquer Paris with his talent. In this case the talent is Balzac's own. Raphaël is a writer, and part of his story reflects that period in which Balzac himself, living in a squalid garret that overlooked the rooftops of Paris, struggled to write the great work that would make his fame and fortune. *La comédie humaine* contains an array of young men who are engaged in conquering Paris by strength, wit, or even genius. But just as Balzac himself both exemplifies the type and is so exceptional that he defies the very concept of type, the single novels and individual characters defy the systems to which they belong. While calling upon scientific and sociological justifications for his novelistic world in prefaces and articles, with each memorable eccentricity, each extraordinary description, Balzac draws the reader's attention away from a synthetic view to the pleasure and wonder of the particular instance, of the unique. The plot of *La peau de chagrin* juxtaposes a magic skin and the *reality* of Paris. Its modes of characterization shift between an emphasis on type and an emphasis on individuality. In the works that follow, individuals proliferate, the unique is the rule, hyperbole is rampant. Thus, the monolithic ideological coherence of *La comédie humaine* is sometimes compromised, and each separate novel resonates with its own integrity.

### *The World in a Fiction*

Balzac does not let the reader forget scientific and sociological models for long. Raphaël de Valentin may appear to live and die according to the size of the magic skin, but ultimately his life, and those of all the others in *La comédie humaine,* are determined by geography, physical appearance, and social circumstances:

> Every effect has a cause in the world, every cause has a principle, and every principle is derived from a law. The principles that have created extraordinary men can be studied and known. Nothing is unimportant—neither the father nor the mother's condition, neither posture, nor season, nor former diet, nor places, nor images.
>
> (*Pensées, sujets, fragmens,* Jacques Crépet ed., p. 156)

Much of the dramatic and narrative interest of *La comédie humaine* is generated by the way characters understand or fail to understand the determinism to which reality is subject. Those who are attuned to the ways of the world will succeed; the others are destroyed.

The most insistent elements of that determinism come from nature itself. One of its laws, to which Balzac refers obsessively, is that of growth, greatness, and decadence. It is applied to the history of an individual life or of a society. The rhythm of growth is, in fact, incorporated into the structure of many of his novels. It fits the tripartite *La peau de chagrin* as well as the story of Raphaël, reborn when he first acquires the magic skin, then all-powerful, finally wasted and dying. The organic sequence of growth and decay is also incorporated in the brilliant orgy scene to which I have already referred. There, parallel to the conversation that grows in a great crescendo only to die away in a drunken sleep, are women and men who are sumptuous and elegant at the start, hideous the morning after. A second basic law, the survival of the fittest, is a repeated test of reality in *La comédie humaine.* It too is illustrated in *La peau de chagrin,* particularly near the end, when Balzac evokes the world of a spa, yet another microcosm of society at large. Raphaël has left Paris and Pauline in an effort to prolong his life by curbing his desire. The others at the spa are offended by his unusual manner. As is always the case, society rejects the unusual, that which is unfit according to its common standard.

How indeed is one to survive in the world? Success lies only in the individual's ability to focus his or her will on the dominant system of values—power and money. The greatest mind in *La comédie humaine,* Louis Lambert, says it concisely: "Here, in everything, the right way to start is money." And very early in his career, in a satirical piece, "Le code des gens honnêtes" (The Code of Honest People), Balzac writes, "Life can be seen as a perpetual battle between the rich and the poor." The accumulation of money, the story of business, of contracts, of estates to be inherited or lost, of avarice and unscrupulousness—these form the main configurations in *La comédie humaine.* Again, in *La peau de chagrin* Balzac offers a powerful image, an initial motif that establishes the priority of money in the real world as in the world of these novels. Life is money. Even before he is introduced by name, Raphaël is identified by his relation to money. He goes to a gaming house to bet and loses "his last gold coin [napoleon]." Balzac, of course, uses the figure of gambling, of winning and losing, of life and death riding on the turn of the roulette wheel, for the notion of existence itself. The regular gamblers, another representative collection of social types, are stand-ins for the author himself. Living on the edge, their lives being the daily stakes for which they play, they are particularly sensitive to the despair of others; through their eyes we make our first serious acquaintance with the hero.

Balzac, who understands that money makes the world go around, also understands its pertinence to a writer of novels. When money becomes crucial to lives, it shapes and highlights stories about those lives. It is a standard for seeing and then telling the truth. The moneylender of *La comédie humaine,* Gobseck, has access to the novelist's truth: "My gaze is like that of God. I see into hearts. Nothing is hidden from me. People refuse nothing to the man who ties and unties the purse strings" (*Gobseck* 2, p. 636). Balzac, the omniscient novelist, is the god of his fiction, one who reads and rereads the world he has created, more and more convinced that it is the world he is reading and not a fiction. Like Gobseck, he merely tells the stories to which he is privy; he merely ties and unties the plots as well as the purse strings. "The spectacles are always varied: hideous wounds, mortal sorrows, love scenes, miseries for which the waters of the Seine lie in wait, a young man's pleasures that lead him to the scaffold, the laughter of despair and sumptuous parties" (*Gobseck* 2, p. 635). Gobseck's words fit Raphaël de Valentin just as well as they do many other characters in *La comédie humaine,* an oeuvre whose terrible story is that of a rapacious society and its destructive "gold" standard.

Persuaded of the universal application of the laws of reality, Balzac also sees his novels as a universe, a system with its own coherence. Almost from the beginning, the novelist conceived of each of his works as belonging to a larger fiction. In 1830 a series of short novels appeared with the collective title *Scènes de la vie privée (Scenes from Private Life).* That series was augmented in 1832. The ever-lengthening list of titles was called *Études de moeurs au XIX*[me] *siècle* (Studies of Manners in the Nineteenth Century) in 1834. This contained the previous series, and was further subdivided into *Scènes de la vie de province (Scenes from Provincial Life), Scènes de la vie parisienne (Scenes from Parisian Life),* and yet more *scènes,* from *la vie politique* (political life), *la vie militaire* (military life), and *la vie de campagne* (country life). That is not all. The *Études de moeurs* is one section of a tripartite structure, the other two being *Études philosophiques (Philosophical Studies)* and *Études analytiques (Analytical Studies).*

One of the reasons for this proliferation of interconnecting fictional networks was undoubtedly financial. A text, having appeared in a newspaper, a literary magazine, or as a separate title, takes on a new life when it is republished, remarketed, and therefore resold as part of a series. Yet aside from the persistent financial predicament caused by his business failures and the need to promote his own works in order to guarantee an income in the risky profession of writing novels, there was the appeal of the "extra-fictional," the fiction that extends itself through its relation to other fictions. It is one thing to proclaim the truth of a novel by using scientific and sociological analogies; it is quite another to link a single novel to a vast system of other novels. As the stories and characters of *La comédie humaine* accumulate they begin to reflect upon each other. Then the reader's belief in any one novel depends to some degree on remembering a previously read novel. The authority of one's own memory brings a fiction of truth to bear on the individual text.

*La comédie humaine* did not acquire its final title until 1842, retaining the three-part structure outlined in 1834. The form is that of a gigantic pyramid. The base is the *Études de moeurs,* stories of exemplary individuals in a great variety of situations, a fresco of contemporary French society. The next, denser layer is that of the *Études philosophiques,* designed to make explicit the physical, social, psychological, and mystical laws at work in the *Études de moeurs.* At the tip of the pyramid Balzac meant to place the *Études analytiques,* essays that would synthesize all that preceded. But apart from mention of two titles, this part of the project was left unrealized.

The novels Balzac wrote long before 1842 demonstrate the encyclopedic nature of his work. The evocation of the antique shop, for example, in the first pages of *La peau de chagrin* prefigures the world within a text that is the Balzacian novel. And each novel is a microcosm of *La comédie humaine.* In this multiplicity there is coherence, a consistent manner of rendering phenomena in prose. Balzac's patient description of physical reality—objects, persons, places—teaches the reader to observe the connections, to measure the relationships among situation, psychology, and action. One of the fascinating reading activities offered by *La comédie humaine* is the perception of those unchanging laws and patterns in the ever changing fictions, an activity related to the pleasure in hearing theme and variation in music. Balzac's vision is unwavering, his invention inexhaustible.

Balzac was not without models for novel cycles. Sir Walter Scott's Waverley novels were greatly admired by the French romantic writers; James Fenimore Cooper's Leatherstocking Tales enthralled readers with their recurring characters, familiar figures encountered like old friends in novel after novel. Balzac adopted Cooper's technique as early as 1833, and eventually changed the names of characters in novels written previously so as to conform to his personal census of France. This is the case in *La peau de chagrin,* where many of Raphaël's friends and others at the orgy are either named or renamed in the 1845 edition to fit into Balzac's familiar cast of characters. Protagonists of major novels turn up in other novels as minor characters. Rastignac, the hero of *Le père Goriot* (*Old Goriot,* 1835) and *La maison Nucingen* (*The Firm of Nucingen,* 1838), appears in no fewer than fourteen other novels. But it is the secondary characters who are the recurring presences in the unfolding pages of the giant cycle. Bianchon, the medical student in *Le père Goriot,* seems to have tended everyone of importance in the Balzacian gallery, including, in the 1845 edition, the dying Raphaël. (Bianchon also finds his way into the orgy.) The ubiquity of the doctor, Bianchon; the moneylender, Gobseck; the dandy, Henri de Marsay, who is the hero of the novella *La fille aux yeux d'or* (*The Girl with the Golden Eyes,* 1835); and so many others helps us find our way through the myriad relationships and settings. The familiar figures lead us through the unfamiliar terrain of each new novel. The writers, lawyers, courtesans, society ladies and gentlemen constitute a theater of repertory actors. One is brought into focus for a particular episode; another becomes the protagonist of a particular novel. The reappearing characters furnish as much consistency to the overall fiction as do the recurring themes and ideas. It is often precisely through these characters that we are able to apprehend the nuances of theme and variation that make us expert and avid readers of Balzac. Balzac seems to expect that our reading of *La comédie humaine* should match, in knowledge and passion, his own creative enterprise.

### *The Short Story*

Balzac's fiction cannot be characterized in terms of a fixed shape, duration, tone, or mode of narration. While certain patterns emerge and certain techniques are favored, the stylistic and textural variety of *La comédie humaine* makes most categories arbitrary, and therefore misleading. If, for example, we take particular note of the grand dimensions of Balzac's scheme, we are apt to overlook the novelist's liking for the short story and the novella, forms that dominated Balzac's production at the beginning of the 1830's. His bent for the fantastic, the melodramatic, and the philosophical are served by relatively brief texts in which attention to milieu and character type is less insistent than it will be later.

The early works are daring in their subject matter. They reflect the romantic taste for the exceptional and the ambition of a young writer who knows the market value of shocking his readers. In *Sarrasine* (1830), for instance, the hero falls in love with a beautiful being he takes to be a prima donna, but who turns out to be a castrato. In yet another reversal, we learn that the castrato is none other than a horrible old man described at the beginning of the story. The "passion" of *Une passion dans le désert* (*A Passion in the Desert,* 1830) refers to the bizarre attraction between a French soldier, escaped to the desert after having been captured during Napoleon's Egyptian campaign, and a beautiful panther. As we read on in *La comédie humaine* and discover the frequent use of animal imagery to describe human behavior, the premise of *Une passion dans le désert* comes to seem less and less unlikely. (At the end of *La peau de chagrin,* Raphaël is characterized as a bird of prey; his love-death is consummated as he bites Pauline's breast.)

In *Adieu* (1830), both Napoleon and animals are significant motifs. The figure of Napoleon haunted and inspired European artists in the first half of the nineteenth century, and there is certainly something of the sweep of Napoleon's vision of a French Europe in the epic fictional horizons of writers like Hugo and Balzac. (The battle of Eylau is one of the central events in *Le Colonel Chabert* [1832]; the retreat from Moscow and the passage of the Berezina are evoked in *Adieu* and, more extensively, in the novel *Le médecin de campagne* [*The Country Doctor,* 1833]). But Balzac also managed to suggest epic size in the forty densely written pages of *Adieu.* Furthermore, the flashback structure of the story anticipates the form of many of the later novels. The heroine, Stéphanie, has gone mad as a result of terrible experiences in Russia, climaxed by her last-minute escape from the advancing Russian troops and the grisly death of her husband (decapitated by a chunk of ice when he falls into the river). Stéphanie's dementia is manifested by her inability to say anything except "adieu" and by her birdlike movements.

At the end of the story Balzac affirms the power of representation, the power of fiction itself: Stéphanie's lover attempts to restore the woman's sanity by restaging the Russian disaster that caused her madness. This vivid reenactment succeeds in shocking her back into reality and, a moment later, in shocking her to death. For Balzac, the symbolic stuff of art—words, images, fabrications—are matters of life and death.

### *The Philosophical Novels*

The relation between symbol, imagination, intelligence, and the psyche is crucial to the *Études philosophiques,* the series of short novels written, for the most part, in the first years of Balzac's career. They illustrate several of the author's guiding principles: the power of will and thought and the often tragic effect of that power on the individual who exercises it; the incompatibility between the genius figure and a materialistic society. *Louis Lambert* (1832) contains most of the salient features of the series. The hero, Louis, an exceptionally brilliant child, is miserable in boarding school, where he is ridiculed for his "differences" by both classmates and teachers. (This section of the novel describes Balzac's own boyhood at the Collège des Oratoriens in Tours.) Louis has even less liking for life in Paris than he had for the provincial dormitory. His is the realm of pure thought. When he falls in love, the clash between his physical desire and the pure concentration of his intellect causes his mental breakdown. Nearly autistic for the remainder of his short life (recalling the heroine of *Adieu*), he utters cryptic remarks that are meant to suggest conversation with angels. He cannot survive the brutal forces at work in everyday life. (The theme of angelism, evidence of the influence on Balzac of the Swedish mystic Emanuel Swedenborg, is most fully treated in the novella *Séraphita* [1835], the story of an androgynous being, an angel, who teaches that love is the encounter between two pure spirits.)

The destiny of Louis Lambert is that of the host of geniuses in *La comédie humaine,* figures for whose quality of thought conventional discourse, communication, and representational modes are inadequate. In *Le chef-d'oeuvre inconnu* (*The Unknown Masterpiece,* 1831) the painter Frenhofer has poured years of his life into the creation of a portrait; when he finally shows it, the viewers see little more than random splotches of paint. In despair, he burns his canvases and dies. *Gambara* (1837) tells of the composer whose opera has so far surpassed the musical language of the epoch that it seems utterly cacophonic to listeners. This genius ends his days as a street musician. (Remarkably prescient, Balzac suggests something like abstract expressionism and atonality in his evocation of the works of Frenhofer and Gambara.) The most extensive examination of idealism and obsession in *La comédie humaine* is *La recherche de l'absolu* (*The Quest of the Absolute,* 1834). Balthazar Claës, a chemist, is literally seeking the ideal, the essence common to all matter. In the process, he destroys his family and ultimately himself.

This gallery of failed geniuses would lead us to surmise that Balzac was critical of obsessive thought, of exclusive concentration. Indeed, *La comédie humaine* recounts the destructive nature of nearly all fixations—love, passion, virtue. Yet the reader cannot fail to sense an affinity between these single-minded characters and the author himself, doggedly in pursuit of his own impossible absolute, the superfiction that contains nothing less than the whole of contemporary history. Sleeping little (he worked through the night, fortified by ever more strongly brewed coffee), endlessly revising his page proofs, maintaining a pace that taxed his body and mind, Balzac was finally undone by his effort, his health wrecked by "excessive" writing. He died at fifty-two, a victim of his notion of fiction, as were his genius figures to their notions of painting, music, science, and thought itself.

### *Detail and Focus in the Short Fiction*

The novellas *Le Colonel Chabert* and *Le curé de Tours (The Vicar of Tours)*, both published in 1832, exemplify the technique of meticulous description of everyday life that characterizes Balzac in the minds of many readers and critics. While the author never fully lost his taste for the fantastic and the philosophical, so well suited to the short prose forms, after 1831 he concentrated increasingly on fictions about tangible reality: objects, bodies and faces, rooms, buildings, the countryside, village, town, and city, the accessible matter of the quotidian. The tangible is the starting point for the reader's grasp of a vision that finds meaning in a dynamic exchange between the particular and general. The reader is actively engaged in the fiction by having to traverse the distance, back and forth, from a frayed hat to a character's life, from the way a duchess snaps shut her fan to the physiognomy of an entire social class, from the furnishings of a room to the passions of the person who lives there, from face to mind. Balzac's images of reality reach far in two directions—toward the secret workings in an individual and toward those in the world at large.

In the opening pages of *Le Colonel Chabert* the hero is introduced indirectly: he is perceived by the clerks and flunkies of a law office (certainly echoing Balzac's brief apprenticeship to a lawyer years before). It is through the voices and milieu of these secondary characters that the reader quickly penetrates to the center of the fiction, which is the status of the hero according to the civil code. The virtuoso rendering of Chabert creates a reality, in the fiction, as reliable and credible as the one we experience in life. Soon we meet the lawyer Derville, a surrogate for the novelist. He, like Balzac, works through the night exercising phenomenally acute powers of analysis.

The crux of the plot is Chabert's identity in the eyes of the law. Believing him killed in the battle of Eylau, his wife has remarried. Upon his return to Paris, no one believes Chabert to be himself. He has lost his name, his fortune, his right to live as Chabert. The legal activity and the novelistic activity are parallel; they both proceed to the identification of character through evidence. From the initial scene of the bantering clerks, we pass to Napoleon's dream of empire, to a flashback in which Chabert is buried alive in a mound of corpses on the battlefield, and to the explanation of his wife's high position in the restored aristocracy upon her remarriage. The novel poses the question whether one can exist in society, or exist at all, without a name. When Chabert realizes that his beloved wife will resort to the vilest trickery to deprive him of his identity, he becomes totally demoralized and renounces all claim to his name. At the conclusion, the once glorious Colonel Chabert appears as a pathetic figure whose failure in life parallels the failure of Napoleon's dreams of glory. He bears a number and a false name in a home for destitute old people.

The initial focus in *Le curé de Tours* is sharper. Here, the structure of power in the small city of Tours and in all of France is traced from the seemingly banal inconveniences suffered by the simple abbé Birotteau, the title character. At the beginning of the novel, Birotteau is made to wait in the rain for a few minutes before being let into his lodgings in the home of Mademoiselle Gamard. This minor annoyance is followed by three other signs of ill omen—his misplaced bedroom slippers, a missing lamp, and the absence of a fire in his hearth. Thus, the rather slow-witted Birotteau is forced to reflect on what has become a radical deterioration in his once comfortable living situation. He has become the victim of his landlady, a woman he has unknowingly offended by abandoning her modest social circle for the more congenial one of the aristocratic Madame de Listomère. From a foundation of domestic details, Balzac erects a complex set of events in which great power is ironically related to trivia and banality. The pettiness of Mademoiselle Gamard is exploited by another of her boarders, the abbé Troubert, whose obsequious manner serves to mask his ruthless ambition. Troubert's plan to destroy Birotteau is the means by which he exerts his tyranny over the provincial city and extends his influence as far as the highest echelons of ecclesiastical and political life in France—all this from a rainy night, bedroom slippers, a lamp, and a cold fireplace. In fact, the wide-ranging action of *Le curé de Tours* is graspable because of its modest point of departure. Everyday objects and everyday dilemmas mark the course of the story's development. The mock-heroic battle between the supporters of Mademoiselle Gamard and those of Birotteau, waged over the rights of the poor abbé to keep his furniture, modulates into a truly epic campaign. At its end, Mademoiselle Gamard is no longer alive to enjoy her victory over Birotteau, who has been banished to a poor church across the river. The victor is Troubert, who, in the final pages, is compared with two men who exerted enormous power through the concentration of their energy—Pope Innocent III and Peter the Great.

Both *Le Colonel Chabert* and *Le curé de Tours* exhibit the novelist's dual focus on the microscopic and the macroscopic. Although these viewpoints are apparently opposed, Balzac persuades us that they are part of a single coherent vision, one in which minute detail is not merely part of a grander system, but rather defines and governs the grander system. The novelist shows the reader the failure of Napoleon's dream of empire in Chabert's haggard face, shows reflected in the highly polished furniture of a provincial sitting room desires that go far beyond those of a poisonous spinster and a nearly simpleminded, egoistical priest. Balzac allows us to see simultaneously the near and the far as he shifts between physical details such as Birotteau's flannel socks and philosophical reasoning as comprehensive as that of Troubert.

### *The Measure of a Novel*

The absence of a fixed durational form is one of the defining characteristics of the novel. We recognize as novels both the short confession of Chateaubriand's *René* and Proust's multivolume *À la recherche du temps perdu*. Yet we also have an idea of conventional length in a novel: a text of some 300 or so pages with a certain density of episode; a number of principal and secondary characters; and a fairly broad temporal, topographical, or ideological scope. For many, *Le père Goriot* is the prototypical nineteenth-century novel that fulfills these requirements.

Balzac guarantees *Le père Goriot* a privileged position in *La comédie humaine* in its preface; there he explains his system of reappearing characters, major and minor, conceived as a device to order the reader's progressive familiarity with the progressively accumulating fiction. Yet the preface, no matter how important, is irrelevant to the popularity of *Le père Goriot,* probably the most widely read of Balzac's works. The appeal of the novel stems from the way it exploits the conventions of Balzacian fiction, the organization of its ingredients, the efficient and satisfying proportion of vivid characterization to plot structure, the range of its references. I do not wish to suggest that there is some absolute norm of excellence to which *Le père Goriot* adheres or that it is Balzac's "best" novel. Such value judgments do not contribute to an understanding of Balzac's works or of this novel. Nor do they withstand changing cultural and critical standards and the shifts in taste to which all art submits. And finally, the evaluation of a single novel in *La comédie humaine* gives too little weight to the force of coherence that operates throughout the oeuvre. But because its texture, shape, and length are taken to be exemplary, *Le père Goriot* is an apt text in which to examine in some detail how, and perhaps why, its elements have become canonized.

We first encounter the exemplary quality of *Le père Goriot* in its opening, one of the most celebrated pieces of descriptive writing in nineteenth-century prose fiction. This section occupies approximately one-tenth of the span of the work. Before initiating linear action, the novelist painstakingly sets the scene and delineates character. Everything and everyone are interconnected. We are drawn from the facade of the house to its garden, to the interior of the house—its downstairs rooms with their hideous wallpaper and odor of last year's stew—to the disposition of the rooms on the various floors: a miniature geography of society, with the more affluent boarders residing on the lower floors, the poorer ones closer to the roof. Several portraits follow: Mademoiselle Michonneau, an old maid; Monsieur Poiret, a former civil servant; a young woman, Victorine, exiled to the pension by her cruel father. Young Rastignac, eager to make his way in Parisian society, is the novel's main character. Vautrin, jovial, yet a figure of mystery, will emerge as the clearest spokesperson for the novelist's hard-minded vision of life. Balzac brings the boarders together at the dinner table and then introduces Goriot, a strange old man who is the butt of humor. These portraits are animated by a mode of representation that passes freely from physical appearance to clothing, past history, tone of voice, accent, and gesture.

When the action finally begins, the attentive reader has already acquired a wealth of information, a dense body of evidence that serves as a basis for belief in the fiction. The novelist is eager that we know as much as he does, and that we accord him our credence through the course of the novel. One of the ways he achieves this aim is through the patient elaboration of place and character. It is that patience and the meticulousness of the observation that have the effect of defictionalizing the descriptive elements of the text. There is no reason to disbelieve the prose representation of the Pension Vauquer and its inhabitants. The representation of physical reality, given such prominence in the novels of Balzac, takes on the aura of the nonfictional. It is from this quality of documentary reproduction (analogous to the cinematographic capture of reality in narrative film) that the subsequent events take much of their authority. Once we have accepted the texture of Balzac's world, we have been seduced into playing his game. We see through his eyes, first the surfaces that are accessible to any pair of sharp eyes, then the working out of imaginary destinies. The kind of plot that unfolds in *Le père Goriot,* with its theatricality, its excessive coincidences, its hyperbolic tone, and even its burden of meaning, is characteristic of fictional invention.

The degree of invention becomes apparent as soon as we make a résumé of the plot. A résumé is, in fact, a plot of a plot. It brings into relief the properties of the organized events that constitute stories—the links, the relations, the symmetries, the clarity of meaning that allow for storytelling in the first place. In fact, it would be difficult to summarize a plot that does not possess a high degree of invention. Without recourse to the fantastic fabulations of *La peau de chagrin, Le père Goriot* projects the fantastic of the purely fictional in the particular (perhaps arbitrary or mad) logic of its chain of events and characters. What we see as invention in the résumé appears inevitable in the reading.

The Pension Vauquer both generates the fiction and serves as a metaphor for the wide range of fictional invention in the novel. It is the locus that contains all the threads of the plot, the place of meetings and revelations, of mysteries presented and solved. Old Goriot and Rastignac live on the same landing at the Pension Vauquer. At a ball, Rastignac dances with one of Goriot's daughters, Anastasie. The next day he is banished from her salon when he reveals that he knows her father (and therefore the old man's poor circumstances). From his rich cousin, Madame de Beauséant, Rastignac learns how Goriot has sacrified his fortune to provide brilliant marriages for his daughters. Madame de Beauséant teaches Rastignac the politics of high society. His fellow boarder Vautrin suggests that there are quick and violent ways to satisfy ambition. Why not marry Victorine Taillefer? Her brother is the only obstacle to her father's great fortune. (Taillefer is the host of the orgy in *La peau de chagrin.*)

Rastignac eventually wins the gratitude of Goriot by becoming the lover of the old man's other daughter, Delphine, who, unhappily married to the boorish financier Baron Nucingen, has just ended her liaison with the dandy Henri de Marsay. In the meantime Vautrin continues to engineer the marriage of Rastignac to Victorine and the murder of Victorine's brother. But Vautrin has aroused the suspicions of two of the boarders, who inform on him to the police. During his dramatic capture the man of mystery is revealed to be a master criminal.

Goriot falls gravely ill, in torment over his daughters' marriages, their jealousy toward each other, and his inability to give them the money they need to help them out of financial difficulty and satisfy their luxurious tastes. He is tended by Rastignac and the ubiquitous Bianchon, who in this novel is still a medical student. Goriot's daughters fail to appear at his deathbed, and what is more, Rastignac must escort Delphine to a ball given by Madame de Beauséant. The young man discovers that this is his cousin's farewell to Parisian society. Cruel "friends" have come to gloat over the predicament of this noble figure, abandoned by her lover for a young heiress. When Rastignac returns to the Pension Vauquer he finds Goriot in the throes of his death agony. Delphine and Anastasie are absent during both their father's last hour and his funeral. At the end of the novel, Rastignac, disabused of his illusions about love, family, loyalty, and idealism, determines to conquer society.

This series of unlikely events becomes the inexorable working out of a collective destiny. Balzac's view of human nature and the world is made accessible to the reader through the devices of plot and rhetoric, the logical links upon which the invention is sustained. Watching the movement of characters, we learn that avarice and jealousy belong to a rich salon as much as they do to a poor pension. We are at first shocked, and then not so shocked, when we come to realize that Goriot, the all-sacrificing father, this "Christ of paternity," harbors an incestuous passion. This is a father who dotes on his daughter's lover and vicariously enjoys the sexual intimacy of Rastignac and Delphine. Goriot is both the soul of paternal devotion and the sinning father; Goriot's daughters seem to be monsters of ingratitude but also, as we learn here and in other novels of Balzac's, victims of painful marriages and circumstances; Vautrin is Madame Vauquer's most amiable boarder and a criminal force that threatens to shatter society altogether. Each of these characters contains an extraordinarily wide range of human experience; many of them are versions of one another. There is no more graphic evidence of this coherence than our discovery that Goriot and Madame de Beauséant are both symbols for love in a materialistic society. While initially presented as poles of the novel's social universe, the dotty old man and the beautiful aristocrat are linked in the last third of the novel, as Rastignac shuttles between Goriot's deathbed and Madame de Beauséant's final ball.

Rastignac passes from pension to salon, from the Left Bank to the Right Bank, from an old man's agony to the voluntary withdrawal from life of a noble woman. Culminating in Goriot's funeral procession, these scenes animate a novel that is a series of interconnected maps, charts that measure geographical and topographical entities of various dimensions. This project of spatial schematization is announced in the opening of the novel, with its emphatic insistence on place. One of the dominant notes of the text is the juxtaposition of the maps, or rather the creation of an elaborate network that provides communication over the impassable gulfs between mansions and boardinghouses, between rich neighborhoods and poor ones. As characters move about, they establish links in ever greater density, so that by the end of the novel both they and we are able to perceive difference and sameness simultaneously. The maps of the Pension Vauquer and of Paris are distinct and mutually defining. They put into high relief the obvious areas of wealth and poverty, areas that become progressively confused when we learn that other oppositions—crime and law, love and despair, dignity and degradation—are not neatly relegated to either mansions or boardinghouses. This is the lesson in moral relativity learned by Rastignac through the course of the novel. In the last page he climbs a hill and surveys Paris. He has earned this vantage point, having followed the tortuous paths from the lowly Pension Vauquer to a privileged elevation. From there, the character, the novelist, and the reader assess the completed journey (novel) and are able to see it all at once.

If *Le père Goriot* is the model for the novel of standard length, *Illusions perdues (Lost Illusions)* suggests that Balzac has outgrown his model. *Illusions perdues,* in fact, is the collective title for three separate novels published in 1837, 1839, and 1843. The first was called *Illusions perdues,* then *Les deux poètes (The Two Poets);* the second and third were *Un grand homme de province à Paris (A Provincial Celebrity in Paris)* and *David Séchard ou les souffrances d'un inventeur (David Séchard; or, The Sufferings of an Inventor).* Although Balzac's works often appeared in serialized form or went through transformations and other groupings of their parts, the scope of *Illusions perdues* is exceptional. This novel and its sequel, *Splendeurs et misères des courtisanes (Splendors and Miseries of Courtesans,* 1838–1847), constitute a mini-*Comédie humaine,* a novel within a novel. Both of these novels contain other novels; together they form an uninterrupted fiction, four times longer than *Le père Goriot.* Thus Balzac challenges the notion of formal limitations to the novel and helps define that genre in its essential expansiveness. The singleness and plurality of texts, plots, and characters are set in counterpoint, thereby requiring encyclopedic and hyperbolic tasks of composition and reading.

Among the most dominant motifs in *La comédie humaine* is the ambitious young man (the arriviste, the parvenu) and the loss of illusions. In addition to the obvious example of *Le père Goriot,* many of the works already mentioned are versions of the Balzacian novel of education, or bildungsroman. To these must be added *Le lys dans la vallée* (*The Lily of the Valley*, 1836), *Une fille d'Eve* (*A Daughter of Eve*, 1839), *Le cabinet des antiques* (*The Cabinet of Antiquities*, 1839), *La muse du département* (*The Muse of the District*, 1843), and, of course, the emblematic *Illusions perdues*, whose title and dimensions mark it as central to the entire cycle.

The hero, Lucien de Rubempré, gives unity to the sprawling *Illusions/Splendeurs* sequence. He is the most developed version of this Balzacian type—the talented, handsome provincial who is eager to set his mark on Paris. Lucien's weakness and malleability, his ambiguity, both intellectual and physical, make him an apt figure to absorb impressions and reflect the contexts in which he is placed:

> Although destined for the highest inquiries into the natural sciences, Lucien enthusiastically chose the path of literary glory. . . . Lucien struck the gracious pose sculptors have lent to the Indian Bacchus. His face had the distinctive lines of ancient beauty: he had a Greek forehead and nose, the velvety whiteness of a woman, eyes so black that they were blue, eyes full of love, and whose whites rivaled in freshness those of a child.
>
> (4.482, 485)

This admixture of contradictions—misdirected talent, dissipation and innocence, male and female characteristics—also includes provincial and Parisian life; idealism and crassness; heterosexuality and homosexuality; the worlds of high society, politics, theater, finance, and crime.

Journalism and publishing are the professional settings where Lucien's type is most completely brought to life. In his exposé of the corrupt, degrading milieus of the literary business, Balzac refers to his own experience, his own bitterness. Writing is his profession and his sacred calling; he, like Lucien, went to Paris to become a great writer. But while Balzac spent years working as a hack, he had enough talent and stamina to achieve his highest literary ambition. Lucien falls into a professional trap and is never able to extricate himself:

> He will enter one of those places of intellectual prostitution called newspapers. There he will throw away his most beautiful ideas, he will dry out his brain, he will corrupt his soul, he will commit those anonymous acts of cowardice that, in the war of ideas, are like the strategy, pillage, arson, and betrayals in the warfare of *condottieri*.
>
> (4.739–740)

Artistic and intellectual prostitution are Lucien's worst sins. They strike close to a novelist whose own compromises might have led him to a similar fate. And when Balzac vents his rage against opportunistic publishers, he expresses his lifelong struggle to live by his pen; the complicated story of contracts, deadlines, and royalties; the economic history of *La comédie humaine.*

The opening of *Illusions perdues* presents another aspect of Balzac's personal stake in this fiction. Here we meet Lucien's alter ego, David Séchard. A printer, quite literally a man of letters, David is obsessed with developing a revolutionary method for the manufacture of paper. He reflects Balzac's own attempt to become a printer (one of several disastrous business schemes), a venture whose failure haunted the novelist for many years. But more important, the opposition between Lucien and his friend and brother-in-law, David, exemplifies Balzac's method of pairing characters for the purpose of expressing contrast. David's sublimity and self-sacrifice set off Lucien's venality and self-absorption. Lucien will make any compromise to further his career; David will make none. The pairing of contrasting characters is a method favored by many of the romantic writers. The aesthetics of Victor Hugo, for example, are explicitly based on just such tensions between opposites—the beautiful and the grotesque, the lofty and the popular, the tragic and the comic. Lucien's progress through life can be gauged in terms of his relation to characters who demonstrate the qualities he lacks—strength, principle, the single-minded commitment required to succeed in the world.

It is Lucien's passivity, the degree to which he receives the imprint of stronger wills, that determines his purpose in the novel. Lucien is understood through the characters who shape him, the surrogates for Balzac placed in the text. The most powerful of the surrogates is Vautrin, who at the end of *Illusions perdues* saves Lucien from suicide, and who in *Splendeurs et misères des courtisanes* uses the handsome young man as a puppeteer uses a marionette. Lucien is image, surface; Vautrin is thought, will. Vautrin's manipulative power is demonstrated in *Le père Goriot,* where he uses it to govern an underworld of crime, dark dealings, violent passions. In *Goriot* we learn that the escaped convict possesses a power different from that of the financiers, aristocrats, and ambitious young men. Completely outside the law, he cold-bloodedly proposes the murder of Taillefer's son (which is accomplished) so that Victorine can inherit her father's fortune and therefore become a worthy match for Rastignac. Vautrin preaches the amoral pragmatism that is depicted throughout *La comèdie humaine:* "There are no principles, there are only events; there are no laws, there are only circumstances: the superior man espouses events and circumstances in order to control them" (*Le père Goriot,* 2.940). While others live haphazardly according to this credo, Vautrin is the credo incarnate, freed from the manners and laws of any society save that of the underworld.

This shadowy existence holds great fascination for Balzac. In the person of Vautrin, it extends beyond its extralegal aspects into sexuality. The latent expression of the character's homosexuality in *Le père Goriot* is made clear in the *Illusions/Splendeurs,* where Vautrin falls in love with the Rastignac-like hero, Lucien de Rubempré. It is also in *Splendeurs* that we learn of the extent of Vautrin's influence and of his central position in the network that links corrupt policemen and judges with criminals. *Splendeurs* is the most ample version of Balzac's exposé of how the brutal laws of nature govern social and political life. And the crowning irony of this novel, its most telling paradox, is Vautrin's final transformation—from master criminal to master policeman. The master of the underworld becomes master of all Paris.

Correspondences between the hidden city, sexuality, and society at large are the subject of a novella published in 1835, the same year as *Le père Goriot. La fille aux yeux d'or* begins with a lengthy (nearly one-fifth of the text) depiction of life in the capital. Balzac, like so many writers of his generation, makes of Paris an urban myth in which the vital forces of society and self-interest are set in conflict. A wealth of metaphorical renditions of the city are contained in Hugo's *Notre-Dame de Paris* (1830) and later in *Les misérables* (1862), in the popular novels of Eugène Sue (*Les mystères de Paris,* 1842), in Flaubert's *L'Éducation sentimentale* (1869), and in the work of Zola. For Balzac, Paris is the center of *La comèdie humaine* and the center of the world. In *La fille aux yeux d'or* the novelist compares Paris to Dante's *Inferno,* using a hierarchy of circles to convey the ceaseless struggle for money and pleasure at all levels of society. (Balzac also finds inspiration in Dante for the pyramidal structure of *La comédie humaine.*)

Following the opening section, the action descends to one of the most subterranean circles of this hellish city, a nocturnal netherworld of violent and destructive passions. The hero, Henri de Marsay (the omnipresent dandy, the lover of one of Goriot's daughters), is taken with a mysterious beauty and spends nights of sexual delirium in her extraordinary boudoir. The lovemaking perplexes Henri, however, since Paquita's remarks and gestures suggest both experience and naiveté. In a horrific finale, he discovers her dying, her blood covering the walls of their love nest. Paquita has been stabbed in a fit of jealousy by the woman who bought and has been keeping her, none other than Henri's own sister. These unlikely events, heavy with the trappings of melodrama and the Gothic novel, scenes of recognition and gore, appear to be at odds with Balzac's much vaunted realism. Yet they are consistent with his vision of reality's core, that domain where distinctions between brother and sister, man and woman, social conventions and animal instincts are blurred, and then reorganized in a fresh manner. From its opening allegory to its *grand guignol* climax, *La fille aux yeux d'or* concentrates the concerns of the longer novels, where the strains on the reader's belief are less taxing. But the inventions of *La fille aux yeux d'or* remind us that in order to fully grasp the realist intention of *La comédie humaine* we must pay close attention to its status as fiction.

### *Arcadia*

Reflected in the majority of his novels, the realist intention is the familiar mark by which Balzac's place in the history of European literature is identified. The other intention central to *La comédie humaine,* ideal rather than real, the vision that dominates the philosophical novels already discussed, where genius-heroes succumb to the rampant materialism of the infernal city, has its own counterpart. In several utopian works, Balzac projects an idealism with a positive outcome; action and character, detached from necessity, come to signify not what is, but what ought to be. Among the author's models are Oliver Goldsmith's *The Vicar of Wakefield* (1766), Bernardin de St. Pierre's *Paul et Virginie* (1788), René de Chateaubriand's *Atala* (1801), and, of course, Jean Jacques Rousseau's *La nouvelle Héloïse* (1761), all of which evoke rural communities exempt from the corrupting influences of civilization.

*Le médecin de campagne* is a didactic novel designed to express Balzac's profoundly conservative political, social, and religious beliefs. The structure and flow of the narrative are subjected to the author's ideas about strong temporal leadership and a strong church. Most of the novel's considerable length is devoted to leisurely scenes that depict a mountain village, a perfect community presided over by the kindly Dr. Benassis. A selfless benefactor who came to try to alleviate the effects of cretinism, a condition common among the villagers, Benassis accompanies a stranger through his domain, describing the lives that have prospered under his reforms. For hundreds of pages, nothing *happens* in the way things conventionally happen in a novel. The life of the community is, in fact, something like a novel that Benassis has written. He recounts it in digest form to the visitor, not primarily for the latter's enjoyment, but rather for his edification. The writing is superseded by the message: the celebration of a "great man's" positive effect on a docile society. Balzac condemns universal suffrage and the democratic system. For him, only a strictly planned economy and the purest teachings of Christianity can cure the ills of humanity.

Napoleon is the ready analogy for Benassis, ruler of his tiny universe, and indeed for Balzac himself, ruler of a gigantic fictional universe. It was Napoleon who gave France its supreme moment of glory. In a section of *Le médecin de campagne* entitled "Le Napoléon du peuple" (The Napoleon of the People), an old soldier tells of the dramatic crossing of the Berezina, the site of the emperor's ultimate defeat during the Russian campaign. But from this description comes the image of a superman, a Christ-like hero, "le père du peuple et du soldat" (the father of the people and of the soldier). The confession of Benassis follows immediately. In it we again encounter one of the recurring motifs of *La comédie humaine*—the young man corrupted by the city. The high purpose of Benassis is forged by despair and guilt over a dissolute life. At the novel's conclusion, the country doctor serves in death as an ethical paragon for the community, thus reinforcing the lessons of moral imitation he so fervently preached.

*Le curé de village* (*The Village Parson,* 1841), designed by Balzac as a complement to *Le médecin de campagne,* emphasizes more firmly the place of Christianity in the redemption of society. Balzac had the loftiest hopes for this pair of novels. In a letter to Madame Hanska, he wrote: "*Le curé de village* is the application of Catholic repentance to civilization just as *Le médecin de campagne* is the application of philanthropy; the former is much greater and much more poetic. One represents man, the other represents God." Again the story of a sinner, Véronique Graslin, whose penance consists of good works on behalf of an isolated community, the later novel has a conventionally engaging narrative rhythm and consistency. Its plot, replete with murder, execution by guillotine, and adultery, serves an essentially didactic purpose. But that purpose, and the community necessary for its expression, are exceptional in *La comédie humaine.* The benevolence of Dr. Benassis and Véronique Graslin, channeled through the conduit of complex economic–agronomic systems, can operate only in utopias. These never-never lands invalidate the Napoleonic analogy. The myth of Napoleon contains both the grandeur of empire and the raw struggle of battle, the pomp of ceremony and the agony of death in the desert and the snow. It is precisely this mixture of lofty vision and concrete detail that finds its parallel in the main body of *La comédie humaine.* And, as Balzac himself demonstrates in *Les paysans* (*The Peasants,* 1844–1855), country people are not necessarily exemplars of Christian submission or of rustic virtue and wisdom (as they are in the *romans champêtres,* or country novels, of George Sand). The controlled arcadian utopia is as distant from the center of Balzac's imagination as it is from the image of the real world he creates in the majority of his works. Virtue triumphs only in the rarefied atmosphere of mountain retreats, far from cities infested with the desire for money, love, and power—the essence of life for Balzac.

In *Le lys dans la vallée* Balzac's visions of the ideal and the real are held in narrative tension. Written in part as an act of revenge against the critic Charles Augustin Sainte-Beuve (the novel is a recasting of Sainte-Beuve's *Volupté* [*Desire,* 1834]), *Le lys dans la vallée* also expresses many of the author's most urgent preoccupations. The hero's youth closely resembles Balzac's own and reveals his mother's indifference to him; the portrait of the female protagonist owes much to Balzac's first love, Madame de Berny; most of the action takes place in his beloved Touraine; the novel's central conflict pits spiritual against physical love, and echoes, in a nonfantastic register, the angelism of the philosophical novels, and of *Séraphita* in particular.

The novel is cast as an autobiography, written by the hero, Félix de Vandenesse, for the woman he wishes to marry. Following the account of his loveless childhood, Félix tells of seeing, at a ball in Tours, a woman whose beauty so inspired him that he was compelled to kiss her bare shoulders. This is the most purely erotic incident in the love story of Félix and Henriette de Mortsauf, a mother devoted to her sickly children, a wife martyred to her invalid, prematurely old husband. At first worshiped from afar, Henriette comes to represent the valley, nature itself:

> When I sat beneath my nut tree, the noonday sun made glisten the tiles of her roof and the glass of her windows. Her percale dress produced the white spot I saw in the vines, beneath an apricot tree. She was . . . THE LILY OF THIS VALLEY.
>
> (8.788)

Félix attaches himself to the woman and her household, rapt in Henriette's beauty and spiritual qualities. Struggling against his youthful ardor, he accepts her offer of a purely platonic attachment. The expression of their love remains within exquisitely delimited boundaries—glances, half-realized gestures, metaphor, mutual respect. Henriette, in fact, intends that Félix one day marry her daughter. Félix is called to Paris and, following Henriette's extremely practical advice, advances his career in the service of Louis XVIII. During a visit to the idyllic Clochegourde, the estate Henriette manages with a skill that recalls Balzac's utopian economic systems, Félix's desire is rekindled, but again to no avail. However, his affair with an English noblewoman provokes a crisis. Henriette is tormented by both his betrayal and her refusal. She dies, leaving Félix a letter that makes no secret of the physical passion she was unable to express in life. (The extent of that passion is even more apparent in the first version of Henriette's death scene.)

The subject of *Le lys* reminds us that Balzac was a romantic writer. The relationship of Félix and Henriette brings to mind, in addition to Sainte-Beuve's *Volupté,* sections of Musset's *La confession d'un enfant du siècle* (*The Confession of a Child of the Century,* 1836) as well as other narrative fictions that idealize love: impossible love, love at a distance, the love encountered long before the romantic period in chivalric romance and in much medieval and Renaissance poetry. More surprising, though, is the diction of *Le lys dans la vallée.* Balzac turns the novel to poetic purpose, to a register of voice more common to the lyric than to prose. Prohibited from directly expressing his passion to Henriette, Félix gives her elaborate bouquets to convey his passion, exploiting a language of flowers based on visual and olfactory sensations that corresponds to his emotional life. But the indirection does not lessen the degree of his sentiments:

> No declaration, no proof of wild passion could produce a more violent effect than these symphonies of flowers, in which my thwarted desire forced me to the same efforts that for Beethoven were expressed in notes—plunging deeply within himself, stretching up to the sky.
>
> (8.857)

Along with this hyperbole goes Balzac's characteristically dark perspective. Henriette is indeed the ideal romantic heroine, "the lily of the valley"; but her husband, a nervous, morbid presence, has been ruined by his experience of exile from France after the Revolution and by venereal disease. And this virtuous woman, who lives far from society, is the author of a very long letter that becomes the source of Félix's political and worldly knowledge, the pragmatic view of reality that guarantees his success. The valley may offer an arcadian image of beauty, but it contains the failure of the aristocracy and the sexual frustration of a martyr. Despite its defined lack of elevation, the valley takes its place beside those other vantage points from which the reader is granted a comprehensive view of nineteenth-century France—Goriot's cemetery, the law office in *Le Colonel Chabert,* the provincial parish of *Le curé de Tours.*

### *Closure*

Balzac did not live long enough to complete his plan for *La comédie humaine.* Indeed, one wonders if he conceived of the plan in terms of completion and if the cycle could have had an ending. Other cyclical works conclude with a return to the beginning—Dante's *Divine Comedy,* Proust's *À la recherche du temps perdu.* But these fictions tell of an interior journey, a journey toward the self. Balzac's project inexhaustibly stretches forth to an ever changing world. There is always more to write, therefore more to read. Yet readers cannot be denied the pleasure of closure that is part of the experience of art, of grasping a finite object, a statue, a painting, a play, in its entirety. The material presence of a book is a constant reminder of potential completion as its pages are turned one after the other. And if *La comédie humaine* suggests the possibility of an endless fiction, each novel progresses toward closure, emphatic closure, in the dramatic death scene, the recognition, the sharply drawn lesson of its final page.

The last novels completed by Balzac are related to each other under the rubric "Histoire des parents pauvres" ("Story of Poor Relations") and by the word "cousin" in their titles. Their resonant endings announce the privilege of their culminating position in Balzac's career. *La cousine Bette* (*Cousin Bette*, 1846) and *Le cousin Pons* (*Cousin Pons*, 1847) supply a sense of conclusion, of catastrophe in the definition of tragedy, to two of the principal focal points in *La comédie humaine*—the family and material objects.

In *La cousine Bette*, a noble family is destroyed by the sexual insatiability of its patriarch. Baron Hulot admits to Adeline, his adoring wife, that he has squandered their fortune on the mistress he has stolen from his son's father-in-law, Crevel. The latter tries to seduce Adeline by promising to provide a dowry for the Hulot daughter, Hortense. Thus, the complex relations among sex, money, and family are set in a dynamic narrative movement by Hulot and Crevel, two old satyrs. Both men fall under the spell of the beautiful and unscrupulous Valérie Marneffe. Valérie is, in turn, prompted in her greed by the character at the center of a web of deceit, betrayal, and disease (moral and eventually physical)—cousin Bette. This "poor relation" has two prime reasons to visit her revenge on the Hulot family. For years she has been jealous of her cousin, Adeline; and her niece, Hortense, has married Wenceslas, the young artist Bette herself loved. Bette's machinations succeed in heaping scandal on the Hulot family, precipitating its financial ruin, and nearly wrecking the marriage of Hortense and Wenceslas.

Balzac thoroughly exposes the notion of family, uncovering its deep roots in concern for money and in sexual desire. In order to preserve the complex dynamics of individual and familial identity, he mixes melodrama, social history, black humor, bedroom farce, and the pathetic. This creates a variety of fictional strategies, complete with a false happy ending that provides the coup de grâce to the novel's ultimate irony. After the deaths, both violent and natural, of most of the major characters and the utter degradation of the baron, who lives in abject poverty with his fifteen-year-old lover, the Hulots' fortunes are miraculously reversed and the baron is restored to his "proper" place as the head of the family. One night Adeline overhears her incorrigible husband promise his latest lover, a servant girl, that she will be the next Baroness Hulot. Adeline, the paragon of wifely virtue, seems to oblige by dying, and the promise is fulfilled. The family "ends" in money and sex.

The familial history of *Le cousin Pons* is summed up in a last will and testament, a document whose words not only are symbols for objects, but actually convey the value of the objects. Thus, the dramatic action of the novel is specifically focused on the core of Balzac's realism—the representation of objects. So many of the lives in *La comédie humaine* are governed by objects, by possession of the things of this world that have both material and metaphoric weight and density. The fatal skin of Raphaël, the disputed furniture of the curate of Tours, the rooms of the Pension Vauquer, and the flowers of Henriette's love-filled valley never let us forget to what degree the novels are fictions of the tangible.

Old Pons, a "poor relation," has amassed a remarkably rich assortment of objets d'art and paintings. (Balzac was as passionate a collector as Pons, although his own collection was not nearly as precious as the one cataloged by his imagination.) The novel begins when, out of ignorance and insensitivity, Pons's cousin, Madame de Marville, fails to take note of his gift—a fan painted by Watteau. This event establishes the textual importance of material objects in the definition of the various elements of the fiction. A crisis is provoked when Madame de Marville puts Pons out of her house, blaming him for the failed betrothal of her daughter to a wealthy banker. Thoroughly disgraced, excluded by his family and shunned by the society he has always frequented, Pons falls ill. He has willed his collection to his one faithful friend, the old musician Schmucke. The deep attachment of these men is one of the few positive values depicted in a novel that animates, with particular vehemence, the pervasive forces of self-interest at work throughout *La comédie humaine.* As Pons's collection becomes the focus of the narrative, objects become a matter of life and death. Others will stop at nothing to obtain them. For Pons, the collection means beauty, history, the years of his life, his loving friendship for Schmucke. From his landlady, a sinister neighbor, his cousin, a shady lawyer, and another collector, it calls forth unalloyed greed, ambition, cupidity, obsession. For the text, it is the common intersection of significant movement.

In *Le cousin Pons,* as in all of Balzac's novels, where the mass of descriptive discourse is designed primarily to reconstruct a world full of bodies and things, language assumes some of the concrete qualities of what it describes. And in a further effort to "materialize" language, Balzac tampers with its exclusively symbolic function by stressing its phonetic nature. Words become objects; they also become voices. Reading Balzac is an aural experience as well as a function of seeing and touching. These processes are acute in *Le cousin Pons,* with its focus on objects and its challenge to the silence of reading. Balzac has forced us to listen to the sound of voices before in *La comédie humaine,* but never with this degree of insistence. Several characters speak in regional and foreign accents, which are reflected in unconventional spellings that demand careful reading. We are made to hear the words we read through the increased effort to understand them. The text intermittently escapes the status of straightforward narrative writing and partakes of the progressive present of speech and hearing. Thus, it calls attention to prose as presence, as an actual part of the moment in which it is apprehended. And it is here that reading is infused with the vitality of writing. This phenomenon is apparent in many of Balzac's works—in the criminal jargon of *Splendeurs et misères des courtisanes,* in the boardinghouse repartee of *Le père Goriot,* in the pandemoniac verbal orgy of *La peau de chagrin.*

*La peau de chagrin* also emblemizes the life and death of the text as object. The inscription of the fatal skin is equivalent to the life of the hero. When the "page" on which that inscription is written shrinks to nothingness, Raphaël dies and the novel is completed. Balzac's endless cycle has many such definitive endings. This is a writer who exploits the emphatic closure of storytelling to indicate his pessimism. Balzac believes that the forces of nature (and human nature) make impossible "the happy ending," the ending that leads toward the future. The fiction-provoked death of *Adieu,* the departure of Louis Lambert to an angel-filled empyrean, Chabert's renunciation of his own identity, Rastignac's graveyard coming-of-age, the ironic transfiguration of Vautrin, these are only a few of the "last words," the refrains of termination that invite the reader again and again to share Balzac's knowledge of the fatal nature of his genre and his vision.

## Selected Bibliography

### FIRST EDITIONS

#### PSEUDONYMOUS NOVELS

*L'Héritière de Biraque, Jean-Louis ou la fille trouvée, Clotilde de Lusignan, Le centenaire,* and *Le vicaire des Ardennes.* Paris, 1822.

*La dernière fée.* Paris, 1823.

*Annette et le criminel.* Paris, 1824. Republished as *Angou le pirate.* Paris, 1836.

*Wann-Chlore.* Paris, 1825.

#### *LA COMÉDIE HUMAINE*

Note: With the exception of major works, only the final version of text and title are indicated

*Les Chouans* and *Physiologie du mariage.* Paris, 1829.

*Un episode sous la Terreur, El Verdugo, Étude de femme, La maison du chat-qui-pelote, La paix du ménage, Le bal de Sceaux, La vendetta, Gobseck,*

*Une double famille, Les deux rêves, Adieu, L'Élixir de longue vie, Sarrasine,* and *Une passion dans le désert.* Paris, 1830.

*Le réquisitionnaire, Les proscrits, La peau de chagrin, Le chef-d'oeuvre inconnu, Jésus-Christ en Flandre, L'Auberge rouge, and Maître Cornélius.* Paris, 1831.

*Le message, Madame Firmiani, Le Colonel Chabert, La bourse, Le curé de Tours, La femme de trente ans, La grenadière, Louis Lambert, La femme abandonnée,* and *Les Marana.* Paris, 1832.

*Ferragus, Le médecin de campagne, L'Illustre Gaudissart,* and *Eugénie Grandet.* Paris, 1833.

*La duchesse de Langeais* and *La recherche de l'absolu.* Paris, 1834.

*Un drame au bord de la mer, Le père Goriot, La fille aux yeux d'or, Melmoth réconcilié, Le contrat de mariage, and Séraphita.* Paris, 1835.

*La messe de l'athée, L'Interdiction, Facine Cane, Le lys dans la vallée,* and *La vieille fille.* Paris, 1836.

*La confidence des Ruggieri, Illusions perdues* I, *Les employés, L'Enfant maudit,* and *Gambara.* Paris, 1837.

*Histoire de la grandeur et de la décadence de César Birotteau, La maison Nucingen,* and *Splendeurs et misères des courtisanes* I. Paris, 1838.

*Une fille d'Eve, Le cabinet des antiques, Illusions perdues* II, *Les secrets de la princesse de Cadignan, Massimila Doni,* and *Pierre Grassou.* Paris, 1839.

*Pierrette, Z. Marcas,* and *Un prince de la Bohême.* Paris, 1840.

*Une ténébreuse affaire, Le curé de village, Ursule Mirouet,* and *La fausse maîtresse.* Paris, 1841.

*Mémoires de deux jeunes mariées, Albert Savarus, Autre étude de femme, Un début dans la vie, La rabouilleuse,* and *Sur Catherine de Médicis.* Paris, 1842.

*Honorine, La muse du département, Splendeurs et misères des courtisanes* II, and *Illusions perdues* III. Paris, 1843.

*Gaudissart* II, *Modeste Mignon, Les paysans* I, and *Splendeurs et misères des courtisanes* IIa. Paris, 1844.

*Béatrix, Un homme d'affaires,* and *Petites misères de la vie conjugale.* Paris, 1845.

*Les comédiens sans le savoir, Splendeurs et misères des courtisanes* III, and *La cousine Bette.* Paris, 1846.

*Le cousin Pons, Le député d'Arcis,* and *Splendeurs et misères des courtisanes* IV. Paris, 1847.

*L'Envers de l'histoire contemporaine.* Paris, 1848.

*Les petits bourgeois* (uncompleted novel published posthumously). Paris, 1854.

THEATER

*L'École des ménages* and *Vautrin.* Paris, 1839.

*Les ressources de Quinola* and *Pamela Figaud.* Paris, 1842.

*La marâtre.* Paris, 1848.

*Mercadet (Le faiseur).* Paris, 1851.

## MODERN EDITIONS

*Comédie humaine.* Edited by George Saintsbury. New York and London, 1895–1900.

*La comédie humaine.* 11 vols. Paris, 1935–1965. Pléiade edition.

———. 7 vols. Paris, 1965–1966.

*Oeuvres complètes.* 40 vols. Paris, 1912–1940. Revised and annotated by M. Bouteron and H. Longnon.

———. Édition de la Société des Études Balzaciennes. Paris, 1955–1963.

———. 25 vols. Paris, 1965–1973.

## CORRESPONDENCE AND MISCELLANY

*Les contes drolatiques.* Paris, 1832, 1833, 1837.

*Correspondance.* Edited by Roger Pierrot. Paris, 1960–1969.

*Lettres à l'étrangère.* Edited by S. de Louvenjoul and M. Bouteron. Paris, 1899–1950.

*Pensées, sujets, fragmens.* Edited by Jacques Crépet. Paris, 1910.

TRANSLATIONS

Note: All of Balzac's novels have been translated into English, many of them frequently. Those currently in print are listed below.

*The Black Sheep (La rabouilleuse).* Translated by Donald Adamson. Harmondsworth, 1976.

*Cousin Pons.* Translated by Herbert J. Hunt. Harmondsworth, 1978.

*Lost Illusions.* Translated by Herbert J. Hunt. Harmondsworth, 1976.

*Murky Business (Une ténébreuse affaire).* Translated by Herbert J. Hunt. Harmondsworth, 1972.
*Old Goriot.* Translated by Marion A. Crawford. Harmondsworth, 1951.
*Ursule Mirouet.* Translated by Donald Adamson. Harmondsworth, 1976.
*The Wild Ass's Skin.* Translated by Herbert J. Hunt. Harmondsworth, 1977.

## BIOGRAPHICAL AND CRITICAL STUDIES

Abraham, Pierre. *Créatures chez Balzac.* Paris, 1931.
Affron, Charles. *Patterns of Failure in "La comédie humaine."* New Haven, Conn., 1966.
Alain. *En lisant Balzac.* Paris, 1935.
Auerbach, Erich. *Mimesis: The Representation of Reality in Western Literature.* Translated by Willard Trask. Garden City, N.Y., 1957.
Barbéris, Pierre. *Balzac et le mal du siècle.* Paris, 1970.
Bardèche, Maurice. *Balzac romancier.* Paris, 1940.
————. *Une lecture de Balzac.* Paris, 1964.
————. *Balzac.* Paris, 1980.
Barthes, Roland. *S/Z.* Paris, 1970.
Béguin, Albert. *Balzac visionnaire.* Geneva, 1946.
Bersani, Leo. *From Balzac to Beckett.* New York, 1970.
Brooks, Peter. *The Melodramatic Imagination: Balzac, Henry James, Melodrama and the Mode of Excess.* New Haven, Conn., 1976.
Curtius, Ernst-Robert. *Balzac.* Paris, 1933.
Dargan, Preston E., and Bernard Weinberg, eds. *The Evolution of Balzac's "Comédie humaine."* Chicago, 1942.
Guyon, Bernard. *La pensée politique et sociale de Balzac.* Paris, 1947.
James, Henry. *French Poets and Novelists.* London, 1893. New York, 1964.
Kanes, Martin. *Balzac's Comedy of Words.* Princeton, N.J., 1975.
Levin, Harry. *The Gates of Horn.* New York, 1963.
Louvenjoul, Spoelberch de. *Histoire des oeuvres d'Honoré de Balzac.* Paris, 1875.
Lukács, George. *Balzac et le réalisme français.* Translated by Paul Laveau. Paris, 1969.
————. *Studies in European Realism.* New York, 1964.
Maurois, André. *Prometheus: The Life of Balzac.* Translated by Norman Denny. New York, 1965.
Poulet, Georges. *La distance intérieure.* Paris, 1952.
————. *Les métamorphoses du cercle.* Paris, 1961.
Proust, Marcel. *Contre Sainte-Beuve.* Paris, 1965.
Pugh, Anthony. *Balzac's Recurring Characters.* Toronto, 1974.
Taine, Hippolyte. *Balzac: A Critical Study.* Translated by Lorenzo O'Rourke. New York, 1973.
Wurmser, André. *La comédie inhumaine.* Paris, 1964.
Yücel, Tahsin. *Figures et messages dans "La comédie humaine."* Tours, 1972.
Zweig, Stefan. *Balzac.* Translated by William and Dorothy Rose. New York, 1946.

CHARLES AFFRON

# SIMONE DE BEAUVOIR

## *(1908–1986)*

> Man, my friend, you willingly make fun of women's writings because they can't help being autobiographical. On whom then were you relying to paint women for you . . . ? On yourself?
>
> (Colette, *Break of Day*)

## *I*

SIMONE DE BEAUVOIR'S life was by all accounts a scandal. Her writing is doubly scandalous, since it is the stubborn celebration of a singular female life. She was born in Paris on 9 January 1908 into a family safely ensconced in the comforts of the imperial *Belle époque.* At the age of seventeen, after a secret apprenticeship in revolt nurtured by forbidden books, she chose to disobey paternal and class decree by becoming a teacher. At a stroke she reneged on her destiny—the "maternal slumber" of bourgeois wife and mother—and crossed at once into what her father and her class regarded as "the enemy territory of the intellectuals" (*Mémoires d'une jeune fille rangée* [*Memoirs of a Dutiful Daughter*], 1958).

"Dutiful daughter" of the French bourgeoisie, she dedicated her life and art to denouncing passionately the "splendid expectations" that had illuminated her childhood. When World War II burst over her, she inherited history in its most terrible form. From then on, her life and work as a writer, teacher, and intellectual bore witness to virtually every major turbulence of twentieth-century Europe: the Spanish Civil War, the Occupation and Resistance, the rise and defeat of Fascism, the bloody dismantling of French imperialism, the heyday and demise of the French intellectual Left, and the resurgence of French feminism. Her great literary output—five novels, a play, the monumental polemic *Le deuxième sexe* (*The Second Sex,* 1949), her essays, short stories, travel writing and journalism, the radical treatise *La vieillesse* (*Old Age,* 1970), the vast autobiography—would amount to an impassioned and sustained refutation of the alluring promises of bourgeois culture, the delusion of "a happy life in a happy world" for all. In 1963 de Beauvoir gave an intimation of how deep ran her sense of betrayal: "Turning an incredulous gaze towards that young and credulous girl, I realise with stupor how much I was cheated" (*La force des choses* [*Force of Circumstance*]).

It is thus not difficult to fathom the "festival of obscenity" that greeted the publication in 1949 of *The Second Sex.* Flung into the ravaged world of postwar France, it was a hugely erudite, radical, and eloquent rebuttal of the "false certainties" over which the war had raged: the male management of the world, international capitalism, the middle-class family, maternity, and marriage. De Beauvoir was accused, as a result, of every infamy; frigid, priapic, neurotic, she had trampled underfoot everything that was good and beautiful in the world. The Right detested her; the Left lacerated her with contempt. She was blacklisted by Rome. Rumor had it that she danced naked on the rooftops of Rouen. Male friends threw her book across the room. Her open liaison with Jean-Paul Sartre became the subject of public notoriety and vilification.

Yet her revolt also had its paradoxical side. De Beauvoir often denied, in the face of much evidence to the contrary, that her femininity had ever been a hindrance: "No, far from suffering from my femininity, I have . . . accumulated the advantages of both sexes" (*Force of Circumstance*). Certainly, her special position was that she was both an intellectual and a woman. As Mary Evans points out, she thus escaped the two fates of most of the women of the world: poverty and motherhood. De Beauvoir declared with that same "fearless sincerity" she so exalted in life and art: "I have not shared in the common lot of humanity: oppression, exploitation, extreme poverty. I am privileged" (*Toute compte fait* [*All Said and Done,* 1972]). No doubt the paradox of privileged revolt—a paradox that engaged not only the course of her own life, but also the political fate of an entire generation of intellectuals—arose from the conditions of her time. But for her the paradox had a special urgency: it was the paradox of being both a writer and a woman. Understanding this paradox, and thereby the limits of freedom and responsibility drawn within it, became the single preoccupation of her life.

Some time must therefore be spent on the meaning of these special conditions, for she consecrated her life to the search for their meaning. To answer the apparently naive question: "Being a woman, French, a writer . . . what does it mean?" one would, as she herself knew, "first have to know the historical meaning of the moment in which I am actually living" (*All Said and Done*). Finding the uncertain and obscure answer to this question became the "grand project" that enflamed her life and all her writings. One might call this project the scandal of identity.

Why should the identity of a female writer be a scandal? In the false, autumnal calm before the outbreak of World War II, at the age of thirty, de Beauvoir had started her first novel, *L'Invitée* (*She Came to Stay,* 1943). Her literary output until then comprised a slim bundle of short stories. Discussing the fate of this new work, Sartre had suggested with sudden vehemence, "Why don't you put *yourself* into your writing?" (*La force de l'âge* [*The Prime of Life,* 1960]). De Beauvoir recalled receiving the suggestion with the force of a blow to the head: "I'd never dare do that. . . . It seemed to me that from the moment I began to nourish literature with the stuff of my own personality, it would become something as serious as happiness or death." Furthermore, we learn from her autobiography that for some time crime had been featuring insistently in de Beauvoir's dreams and fantasies. In these dreams she found herself standing on trial before a crowded courtroom, perpetrator of an unmentionable deed for which she alone was responsible: "I saw myself in the dock, facing judge, prosecutor, jury, and a crowd of spectators, bearing the consequences of an act which I recognized as my own handiwork, and bearing it alone." The dream played out the obscure and perilous intuition that the crime for which she stood accused was nothing other than female independence:

> Ever since Sartre and I had met, I had shuffled off responsibility for justifying my existence on to him. I felt that this was an immoral attitude, but I could not envisage any practical way of changing it. The only solution would have been to accomplish some deed for which I alone, and no one else, must bear the consequences. . . . Nothing in fact, short of an aggravated crime could bring me true independence.
>
> (*The Prime of Life*)

The dream unveiled the insurrectionary cast of a female identity fashioned apart from the sanction of men. Female autonomy is seen as an unpardonable condition that carries the stigma of a crime and erupts with the force of an insurrection. The discovery that the handiwork of autonomy was itself a deed tantamount to murder subsequently entered *She Came to Stay* as its founding theme and became, in metaphysical clothing, the stuff of much of her early fiction and philosophical thought.

Nevertheless, the fact that de Beauvoir could commit the "aggravated crime" of female independence on paper relieved her for a long time of the necessity of doing so in life. By choosing to be an intellectual she escaped the social fate decreed by class and birth, her mother's "dull, grey kind of existence." The solitary role of intellectual safeguarded her personal autonomy. As she declared, "Writing guaranteed my moral autonomy; in the solitude of risks taken, of decisions to be made, I made my freedom much more real than by accommodating myself to any money-making practice." In so doing she escaped for a long time the imperative of a more arduous and dangerous revolt: "For me, my books were a real fulfilment, and as such they freed me from the necessity to affirm myself in any other way" (*Force of Circumstance*). Nevertheless, de Beauvoir's great power and distinction are that by exploring with the utmost seriousness, integrity, and passion what it meant to be a female writer in her time, she drove the possibilities of her life beyond its limits and left us with an exemplary testimony of the conditions of the female life.

What is at stake, then, in all de Beauvoir's writing is not simply the scandal of female identity—"How does a woman adjust herself to her womanly state"—but also how she represents it. Here one comes directly upon the autobiographical nature of so much of de Beauvoir's writing. One of the first things to notice about her work is that it is a sustained circling around the creation of a female persona: Simone de Beauvoir. Most of her writing is in some form or other a radical project of self-justification: "I wanted to realise myself in books that . . . would be existing objects for others, but objects haunted by a presence—my presence. . . . Above all I wanted my contemporaries to hear and understand me" (*All Said and Done*). "I wanted to be widely read in my lifetime, to be understood, to be loved" (*Force of Circumstance*). This desire to haunt the memory of her contemporaries inspired her fiction with no less urgency. As she said of *Les mandarins* (*The Mandarins,* 1954), "I wanted it to contain all of me—myself in relation to life, to death, to my times, to writing, to love, to friendship, to travel."

Any autobiography, as George Gusdorf has said, is not so much the vivid and truthful portrait of a life as it is a work of "personal justification." This is part of what de Beauvoir meant when she announced that art was "a means of protecting my life." As she herself so well knew, "a man would never get the notion of writing a book on the peculiar situation of the human male. But if I wish to define myself, I must first of all say: 'I am a woman'; on this truth must be based all further discussion" (*The Second Sex*). More than this, a woman who lives a life that flies in the face of convention and authority is already a scandal. To justify that life in public (to publish: *publicare simulacrum*—to erect a statue in a public place) is, as Nancy Miller has remarked, "to *reinscribe* the original violation." The autobiography of an exceptional woman is therefore a double scandal; it is to stand defiant in the dock.

For precisely this reason de Beauvoir wanted to be the one to "rummage through my past. . . . So long as it is I who paints my own portrait, nothing daunts me." As with Colette, the urgency that enflamed her art, "a passion, a madness," came from the knowledge that if she left the painting of her portrait to any other, her life would "trickle into the sand," and nothing would remain of her childhood self except "a pinch of ashes."

Autobiography as a form scarcely exists before the seventeenth century. It is commonly accepted that its rise has something to do with the historical discovery of the self-conscious individual during the Renaissance. Estelle Jelinek has also pointed out that "autobiography must share with the novel the distinction of being one of the first literary genres shaped with the active participation of women." Nevertheless, there are a number of clear differences between autobiographies written by women and those written by men. Women's autobiographies do not flourish at the high points of male history—revolutions and battles and national upheavals and so on. They wax according to the climactic changes of another history. Male autobiographies are also characteristically embellished and gracefully shaped into chronologically elegant wholes. Female autobiographies are typically fragmentary, irregular, anecdotal, and oblique, eloquent of the ingenuity and effort taken in negotiating a female life past the magisterial forms of male selfhood. As a result de Beauvoir always chafed against the elegant restraints and mannered symmetries of fictional form, for these turned art into a collector's item, "a statue dying of boredom in a villa garden." Events in an autobiography, on the other hand, "retain all the gratuitousness, the unpredictability, and the often preposterous complications that marked their original occurrence" (*Force of Circumstance*).

At the same time de Beauvoir was temperamentally and politically averse to the idea of autobiography as the heroics of an inner life, the unfolding saga of a single mind. If she wanted to voice the originality of her own experience, it was only to the extent that it was also illuminated by the incandescence of her epoch. As she insisted, "The background, tragic or serene, against which my experiences are drawn gives them their true meaning and constitutes their unity" (*Force of Circumstance*). She was impatient of the "pointless and in any case impossible undertaking" of building up a single portrait of herself. "What I should like to do above all is provide myself an idea of my place, my locus in the world" (*All Said and Done*). For this reason it is necessary to spend some time on the difficult, unruly, and elusive conditions that gave her life its meaning. To write her autobiography and keep faith with her deep commitment to veracity, de Beauvoir ransacked libraries, newspapers, diaries, letters, and memoirs, and conferred lengthily with friends and with Sartre. Yet she well knew that autobiography involves a "welter of caprice," whimsical omission, and crafted evasions, governed overall by the contrivances of artistic convention. Autobiographies are, as she put it, "fictions of selfhood." It is therefore well to bear in mind that one is dealing not only with the portrait of a real life, but with a fiction of selfhood—what Colette called a fabulation of "rearranged fragments."

## *II*

On her return from China in 1956, at the age of forty-eight, de Beauvoir set out to write the story of her childhood. This story swelled to four fat volumes, some 2,200 pages in all, engaging more than sixty years of her life, and was some sixteen years in the writing. *Memoirs of a Dutiful Daughter,* the evocative first volume of her autobiography, covers the years 1908–1929, from her birth to the death of her beloved friend Zaza.

Daughter of Françoise and George de Beauvoir, a disappointed Catholic woman from a rich Verdun banking family and a well-off Parisian attorney, de Beauvoir faced a predictable future: "It was laid down what this child's state should be—French, bourgeois and Catholic; only its sex was unforeseen" (*All Said and Done*). She was raised in Paris in the "big village" that stretched from the Lion de Belfort to the rue Jacob, and from the boulevard Saint-Germain to the boulevard Raspail. Except for some years as a teacher in Marseilles and Rouen, and despite an insatiable appetite for travel, she always lived in more or less the same district in Paris.

Her childhood was the perfectly commonplace story of a girl born to an upper bourgeois French family of the years before the war. A "madly gay little girl," de Beauvoir had until the age of eleven "virtually no problems." Safely cushioned in the red velvets and silk drapes of her boulevard Raspail apartment, she indulged to her heart's content her fierce yearning for happiness, becoming apprenticed thereby, as was only fitting, to the bourgeois promise of individual happiness that was to enchant her for so long. In the *Memoirs* de Beauvoir discharges a debt: more than anything else it was to the "calm gaze" of the young female maidservant Louise that she owed the sense of "unalterable security" which was her class birthright until the outbreak of war. From the comforting security of this gaze sprang the "vital optimism" and unswerving will to happiness that de Beauvoir felt was her own peculiar gift: "I have never met anyone, in the whole of my life, who was so well equipped for happiness as I was, or who labored so stubbornly to achieve it" (*The Prime of Life*).

To Louise's calm gaze was added another comforting dimension: a whole race of supernatural beings bent over her from a Catholic heaven their "myriad benevolent eyes." A more mundane race of aunts and uncles in ostrich plumes and panamas played "the role of a kindly mirror," their flattering solicitude safeguarding de Beauvoir's illusion of standing in the privileged center of the world. Only the "black looks" of her unswervingly pious mother were capable of troubling these early years. She had difficulty distinguishing her mother's look from the eye of God.

Mirrors, eyes, and glances flash everywhere in de Beauvoir's writing, and the power of the gaze to shape identity figures powerfully in her existentialism and feminism. The crystalline certainties of class, religion, and family that graced her childhood with their special radiance, only to become the dark figures of her betrayal, were unveiled within what can be called the metaphysical tradition of the gaze. As she wrote, "A child receives its image and even its very being from others. . . . It perceives itself as something that is *seen*" (*The Second Sex*). The intellectual tradition of the gaze reaches back to G. W. F. Hegel and has been taken up in recent times by Sartre, the French psychoanalyst Jacques Lacan, and a certain tradition of feminism. But it is de Beauvoir's special distinction in *The Second Sex* to have been the first to flesh out the geometry of the gaze and transform the idealist Hegelian ontology of self and other, frozen in faceless combat, into a politics of seeing and being seen, governed by socially consecrated rituals of dominance and submission and violently scored by history and gender.

By all accounts de Beauvoir inherited something of her early talent for impersonation from her father. Her paternal grandfather had enjoyed a sizable fortune and a 500-acre estate, but had chosen instead to take up an administrative post in the Town Hall in Paris. As a consequence his son, de Beauvoir's father, grew up lodged comfortably, if somewhat ambiguously, "halfway between the aristocracy and the bourgeoisie, between the landed gentry and the office clerk," and came to feel himself "neither completely integrated with society nor burdened with any serious responsibility." Attracted by the stability of the legal profession and eventually joining a law firm, his first passion remained the theater. Possessing the name but not the means to swim with the aristocracy, he contented himself with a theatrical impersonation of their manner of living.

In all other respects de Beauvoir's father was "a true representative of his period and his class." Fiercely patriotic, anti-Dreyfus, and anti-Republican, respecting but not believing in the church, his only religion was nationalism and his only private morality "the cult of the family." Epicurean, pagan, and vital, his neglect of his daughters' spiritual well-being stood in direct contrast to his wife's strict supervision. Françoise de Beauvoir, made bitterly resentful as a child by the whalebone collars and narrow spaces of her female upbringing, was diffident in society but passionately overbearing with her daughters, Simone and Poupette, in private. Her convent morality seeped into every recess of their life. From her de Beauvoir inherited the ethical fervor that infuses her early thought, her hunger for the absolute, her passion for travel, her faith in and enormous capacity for work, her dogmatism, and the lessons in self-abnegation that were to mark her early relation to her body.

As a consequence de Beauvoir lived out in her childhood the cultural contradictions of her period. To her father she was "simply a mind"; it was his duty to give his daughter the education that would be a discreet adornment to her role as wife and mother. Her body and her spiritual education were in the sole charge of her mother. Thus her being fell into two: "I grew accustomed to the idea that my intellectual life—embodied by my father—and my spiritual life—expressed by my mother—were two radically heterogeneous fields of experience which had absolutely nothing in common" (*Memoirs*).

This division had a profound effect on de Beauvoir's future. Her desire to be an intellectual was not a whimsical determination but rather the outcome of the jostling forces of her world. Her cultural inheritance was rife with contradictions: "My father's individual and pagan ethical standards were in complete contrast to the rigidly moral conventionalism of my mother's teaching." Suspended as she was between the aristocratic skepticism of her father and the bourgeois sobriety of her mother, her attempt to make sense of these ambiguities turned de Beauvoir's inner life into "a kind of endless disputation" and became, as she claims, the main reason she became an intellectual.

In 1914 her parents became the victims of calamity. As was the fashion of their class, her family spent their summers in the ancient province of Limousin on her grandfather's estate. Not only did the expansive property of Meyrignac give de Beauvoir material grounds for her mystical yearning for the infinite, but it was there among the water lilies and the peacocks, at the age of six, that she heard the news that war had been declared. The war did little to cloud her small horizon, but by the end of it her father's Russian stocks had plummeted, and the family plunged with them into the newly poor.

Her father's legal career finished, the family in near poverty, they moved to the rue de Varennes. De Beauvoir lost Louise, her plush red and black apartment, space, and solitude: "I didn't even have a desk to put my things in. . . . I found it painful to never be on my own." She had in effect fallen into a different class. It was at this time that books came to play a more and more vital role in her life.

In 1913 de Beauvoir had been sent to a private Catholic school with the beguiling name of Le Cours Desir. There she was fed the "ersatz concoction" that was her allotted fare as a girl, and there she learned to hide her intellect "as though it was a deformity." Crimped and curtailed, hers was the typical inferior training of a caste firmly destined to live in exclusion within its own culture. Her education was in every respect a limitation, differing markedly from that enjoyed by, say, a Sartre or an André Gide.

The act of reading is therefore central to the *Memoirs,* as it is to any autobiography. The autobiographer, in what amounts to a ritual gesture, conjures up the reader, in order that the reader may in turn conjure the autobiographer's self into being: without this collaboration the voluble "I" would fall silent. But above and beyond this, reading played a peculiarly poignant role in de Beauvoir's childhood: she began to feel most urgently the ambiguity and uncertainty of her sexual identity.

Reading was from the outset linked to transgression. In the very first remembered action of the *Memoirs* she had crept under her father's desk in "the awful sanctum" of his black-pearwood study: a willful self-insertion into the seat of cultural and paternal power, and thus a small mimicry of the act of female autobiography itself. For de Beauvoir reading was a solemn rite promising a sorcerer's power and autonomy, and relief from the galling tedium of domesticity; it was also the punishing reminder of an exclusion that she could barely begin to comprehend.

"Impassable barriers," for example, prohibited her entry into the library in the rue Saint-Placide. Her books were carefully disfigured by her mother's censoring hand, and her reading was constantly and strictly circumscribed: "You *must not* . . . *you must not touch* books that are not meant for you" (*Memoirs*). This ban she recalls shuddering through her body with the same punitive and obscure jolt she had received when she had stuck her finger into the black hole of an electric socket. On both occasions she had been sitting in her father's black armchair. Here reading, transgression, and a forbidden eroticism merge in a scene that played itself out again and again in her adolescence. The overdetermined metaphor of forbidden holes, the furtive and secret touchings, the barred entry into places of obscure pleasure and power, disobedience answered by a swift and annihilating punishment—these profoundly colored her view of books as the place of a secret, libidinous insurrection. For this reason she always saw the act of female writing, and therefore the intellectual life, as a sexual and political revolt in itself.

At the same time de Beauvoir had inherited from her parents a "deep reverence for books." This was a cultural value typical of her father's background, but it had become raised to a family fetish by their loss of social face. For M. de Beauvoir the elite of the earth were those who had "intelligence, culture, and a sound education," but this was strictly an upper-middle-class prerogative. As Sartre has pointed out, the generation of writers before the war could not support themselves by literature alone. Gide had property, Proust independent means; Claudel was in the diplomatic service. In short, they had deep loyalties to the state; they were, as Sartre says, "integrated into the bourgeoisie."

Contemptuous of the kind of material wealth and success that took effort, M. de Beauvoir consoled himself for his social dishonor by an exaggerated attachment to culture. Nevertheless, it was indecorous for a woman to have too much of that magical ingredient which distinguished his class from all others. As de Beauvoir grew older and began to make her ungainly entry into puberty, she found it more and more difficult to play the role of "dutiful daughter," particularly with respect to curtailing the precocious mind of which her father was alternately proud and resentful. If, for de Beauvoir, identity is shaped by the male gaze, it did not help matters that her father, like her culture, had double vision. As she entered puberty, with all the reluctance a Catholic upbringing could induce, she came to live in her father's eyes as the vivid emblem of his failure. Without a dowry, she would never marry; she would have to work for a living. His attitude to de Beauvoir became more and more acrimonious, and her sense of his withdrawal plunged her into despair. The recriminating gaze of the "sovereign judge" began to hold all kinds of dangers for her.

If her father's pride had once been her "man's mind," it was a mind now discovered to inhabit a very female body, and she could not help but regard the "silent upheaval" of her importunate body as the culprit and cause of his disgust. Her femininity itself became a blemish and a malady: "I thought of myself in relation to my father as a purely spiritual being: I was horrified at the thought that he suddenly considered me a mere organism. I felt as if I could never hold up my head again" (*Memoirs*).

Her body became an embarrassment. She regarded the delirious and obscure desires that shook her with much the same "sickening curiosity" that forbidden books had formerly elicited. Shamed by the displeasure of the male eye, she directed the full arsenal of her lessons in Catholic self-abnegation to her body's defeat. She began to develop phobias. Clearly the paroxysms of dizziness, nausea, and anemia she began to suffer served as a hysterical protest against the incomprehensible paradoxes of her situation. Her horror at the "tyranny of the flesh" was more than anything else a fierce resistance to the social denigration of the female body. Her later rejection of maternity and marriage—which brought a great deal of fire on her head—was the most extreme revolt she could envisage against the imposed ignominy of her female situation. In an era with no legal contraceptives and no legal abortion, this revolt was the only recourse she had to protecting the autonomy she glimpsed in the vocation of writer.

One may note here an important discrepancy in the *Memoirs.* She often made the brave announcement: "I felt no disappointment at being a girl." Yet she could also recall: "My father's attitude towards the 'fairer sex' wounded me deeply." And again, later: "If he had continued to interest himself in me . . . I should certainly not have felt rejected, thrust out and betrayed." Her peculiarly willful blindness to the hobbling restraints of her femininity constituted a protest of its own and remained a defining feature of her identity until she wrote *The Second Sex.*

Her cousin Jacques, notable otherwise only as her first adolescent love, awakened her fully to the existing plenitude of her cultural heritage and at the same time to the baffling fact that she was exiled from this plenitude:

> He knew a host of poets and writers of whom I knew nothing at all, the distant clamor of a world that was closed to me used to come into the house with him: how I longed to explore that world! Papa would say with pride: "Simone has a man's brain, she thinks like a man; she *is* a man." And yet he treated me like a girl. Jacques and his friends read real books and were abreast of all current politics, they lived out in the open; I was confined to the nursery.
>
> (*Memoirs*)

How far removed from this passionate resentment is Sartre's memory (in *Qu'est-ce que la littérature?* [*What Is Literature?,* 1948]) of his confident childhood accession to the patrimony of books:

> We were used to literature long before beginning our first novel. To us it seemed natural for books to grow in a civilized society, like trees in a garden. It is because we loved Racine and Verlaine too much that when we were fourteen years old, we discovered, during the evening study period or in the great court of the lycée, our vocation as a writer.

For de Beauvoir books became the occasion of a secret revolt and a double life. She began to trespass clandestinely on the "forbidden territory" of male culture; curling up in her father's leather armchair, she dipped "quite freely into all the books in the bookcase."

It was also fitting that her primordial act of disobedience—the unseating of God—should engage the three most tortuously entangled forces in her life: sex, books, and religion. Sitting under a tree devouring forbidden apples and reading "in a book by Balzac—also forbidden—the strange idyll of a young man and a panther," she decided that she was too attached to sensual joys to be able to live any longer under "the eye of God." She summarily emptied heaven of its occupants and inherited at once the "haunting anxiety about death" which never left her, and which she struggled unremittingly to conquer in her fiction. Death as the absence of God, a kind of spectral, ever-present black electric socket, never ceased threatening to suck her being into the void.

I have spent some time on de Beauvoir's relation to books, since her early experience of reading as a libidinous insurrection deeply marked not only her choice of career and her motivation to write, but also much of her fictional and philosophical thought about the nature of desire, freedom, and limitation.

De Beauvoir thus fell between two stools: books, she was constantly reminded, were the only precious things; yet, as a female, she could touch but not possess them. She was faced with two options: either to take blind refuge under the wing of authority and submit, or to rebel.

In 1925, in violation of paternal and class decree, she chose to become a teacher, betraying herself at once, as far as her father and the scandalized matrons at Le Cours Desir were concerned, to be "a traitor to her class." If writers elicited her father's ardent approval, intellectuals were a "dangerous sect" bent on peddling incendiary ideas about socialism, equality, and democracy. Moreover, it was decidedly indecorous for a woman of her station, however reduced, to enter the professions. Thus the first watershed of de Beauvoir's identity was marked by the resolute denial of her femininity as difference. Instead she placed all her hope in riding with the renegade class of the intellectuals. At roughly the same time she began to write. She was seventeen.

## *III*

> I am an intellectual, I take words and the truth to be of value.
>
> (*The Prime of Life*)

In 1925 de Beauvoir took her *baccalauréat* and enrolled at the Institut Saint-Marie at Neuilly, where she studied literature and philosophy under R. Garric. Garric was a spellbinding Catholic socialist and founder of the Équipes Sociales, an experiment to unite students and the working class. He offered de Beauvoir her first glimpse of working-class life, but despite a delirious crush on him, this encounter did little to cure her itch for the metaphysical: she did not identify with the working-class youths she met, and she was still nurturing exalted dreams of the inner life. Nevertheless, her brief exposure to this radical environment had one decisive effect: she made the brutal discovery that the class values she held most precious (progress, eternal peace, universalism) were being betrayed by the very class which exalted them. The bourgeois promise of universal humanity and happiness was a lie: universalism cloaked a niggardly class interest and a narrow materialism that excluded most of humanity, including herself.

These years were marked by a sense of exile that could only be compensated for by dreams of lonely defiance. She took refuge in the solace of a radical individualism, in a rationalistic self-sufficiency that she believed would distinguish her from her hated class but that was, in fact, a direct cultural inheritance: "I existed only through myself and for myself." She decided to "be a soul; a pure, disembodied spirit. . . . I found escape in the clouds." Her solitude bred a dogged pride that flowed directly into her aspirations to write. Her path was marked. The lofty vocation of the genius would assuage her loneliness: "I felt I should already be trying to communicate the experience of solitude. . . . In April I wrote the first pages of a novel" (*Memoirs*).

The main force of her fierce repudiation of family and class, and her turn to writing as a refuge, came from this deeply felt sense of exile, a dark leitmotif coursing through the latter half of the *Memoirs:* "I am alone. One is always alone. I shall always be alone. . . . I'm not like other people. . . . I was 'outside life.' . . . Loneliness continued to lower my spirits. . . . I felt shut out. . . . I shall always be ostracised," and so on. She had interrupted the Catholic hosts in their consoling progress across the heavens and had swept them away; henceforth she would be a pariah, an outcast. Her anxious accession to adolescence had doubly exiled her from her body and from her father. Her secret trespass on forbidden books left her morally alienated from her mother and, indeed, from the entire moral climate of her childhood. The niggardly habits of her society refused her entry into the world of men. There was only one recourse: "I felt myself an exile, whose one remedy against solitude lay in self-expression."

The act of writing became a radical project of self-creation and self-justification. On the other hand, it was also clearly a plea for social legitimacy: "above all I wanted my contemporaries to hear and understand me." Writing was, into the bargain, the sole path that a few women had trodden before her. Literature would be her calling, because there she glimpsed the shimmering promise of autonomy. Already, it is clear, the project was scored with contradictions. The lonely vocation of the genius immured de Beauvoir from the dangers of the world. Yet what she wanted above all was social recognition: "I wanted to be loved." Her desire to write expressed a stubborn will to impress herself on the public memory and insinuate herself into the records of the scribes. But in this way she fell at once into the quandary of seeking recognition, even confirmation, of her very identity in the eyes of the established order she had vowed to despise. She could win authenticity only if she fled the world, but the flight would have meaning only if it was remarked and approved by the world. Driving through these contradictions, de Beauvoir came to represent the fundamental social difficulty of writing in her period, a general difficulty, but one deeply complicated for women.

De Beauvoir's early, steadfast individualism left its unmistakable mark on her thinking for a very long time. But hers was not a singular unease. If the fact that she was female was the first cause of her alienation, she also inherited a particular literary crisis that was part of a more general social crisis deepening at just the time she started to write. The discovery she soon made—that to write about herself meant more than anything else giving "an idea of my place, my locus in the world"—permits one to ask the question Raymond Williams asked of George Orwell: What did it mean, in that particular generation, to be a writer?

De Beauvoir, like Orwell, began to write in a period of literary crisis, at a time when the act of writing, the legitimacy of representation itself, was in serious trouble. Earlier writers of the fin-de-siècle avant-garde, like Charles Baudelaire and Arthur Rimbaud, out of key with the general social and political climate of their period, had run amok among the canons of literary and social authority, flinging the relics of tradition into violent, unholy patterns. The rage for modernity, the "shock of the new," had discredited any appeal to the ancestral shibboleths of order and proportion, harmony, beauty, and perfection. As Williams points out, the antagonistic relation between artist and society had reached its first climax throughout most of Europe in the 1880's and 1890's, and had by the 1920's become more embattled and more polarized. For the stolid middle class, the successful writer was one who made money: in violent reaction to this and to their slow disinheritance from cultural authority, a postwar generation of artists came to define themselves in terms of their distance from society. As Williams describes it, "The 'writer,' the true writer, had no commercial aims, but also at root, no social function and by derivation, no social content. He just 'wrote.' And then as a self-defined recognizable figure, he lived 'outside' society—unconventional, the 'artist.' " Paris became the spiritual home for these artistic exiles and emigrés, the self-styled pariahs and bohemians, the peddlers of decadence, the dilettantes, aesthetes, and voyeurs of derangement who plied their wares in the smoky cafés and bars of the 1920's.

It was to these "disciples of disquiet" that de Beauvoir became drawn in her years at the École Normale and the Sorbonne (1927–1929). She read feverishly, intoxicated by the possibility that her loneliness was not a personal affliction, but the mark of an exalted breed of thinkers, who could, with Gide, shout: "Family, I hate you! Your dead homes and shut doors." These conspirators in cultural unease also wanted to set a bonfire in the family house, to murder their father the landlord, their brother the cardinal, and their cousin the imperial colonel. Her cousin Jacques had already introduced her to "the poetry of the bars," and de Beauvoir began to haunt them with deliberate intent, indulging in drinking bouts, aping the dress and manners of the prostitutes, and from time to time knocking off people's hats or breaking a glass or two. She delighted in the excesses of the avant-garde, "the outrageous jokes of pure negation . . . the systematic derangement of the senses, suicidal despair." At the same time, as she admits in the *Memoirs* with a self-irony colored with nostalgia, "since they had no intention of overturning society, they contented themselves with studying the states of their precious souls in the minutest detail." Nevertheless, the bar, like the café, became emblematic in her fiction of her fixation with the dark, liminal places that lay on the threshold of social respectability and social alienation. Characteristically, her imagination was always pitched at the places of the shadowy commerce between self and other, crime and authority, desire and law.

De Beauvoir was an extravagantly talented academic. She subjected herself to a taxing regimen of reading, and began to grope her way through Descartes, Spinoza, Kant, Bergson, Schopenhauer, and Nietzsche, accepting with exhilaration, as she did for the rest of her life, Gide's challenge "assumer le plus possible d'humanite," to take voracious possession of the immense emporium of created things. During this time her political ideas remained hazy and her sense of history muddled. The "incomprehensible uproar" of world affairs held small attraction for her. All forms of conformity and obscurantism elicited her untempered scorn. Temperament and the happenstances of her life inclined her to the Left: "One thing I knew. I detested the extreme right"; but it was a political Manichaeism that had little form or content and was in many ways a quasi-religious relic of her Catholic morality. Her vehement denunciations of society remained very much a rebellion of the mind, and she continued to exalt metaphysics and morals over the humdrum of social matters.

De Beauvoir was initiated during this period into the elite triumvirate of Sartre and his friends André Herbaud and Paul Nizan, three exceptional philosophy students who had formed a tight coterie. The sheer virtuosity of de Beauvoir's mind attracted their attention, and they gradually opened their ranks to her. This was a momentous event for her. Not only did she quickly form with Sartre the relationship she called the one "unquestioned success of my life," but she had for the first time found a community of intellectuals. The cost was that for a long time she could not admit that her femininity set her apart from them in the world's eyes, for then she would have had to grant that having been "expelled from the paradise of childhood, [she] had not yet been admitted into the world of men."

De Beauvoir called these years before the war her "golden age." By her own account she and Sartre lived like "elves" in the enchanted circle of their own company. Consciously repudiating the "discreet trafficking in betrayal" of middle-class monogamy, they contracted an open relationship in which each was free to have deep and lasting liaisons with others, founded on a scrupulous honesty. Their loathing of bourgeois society was their first premise: they had, they believed, jettisoned every craven evasion of family, class, and tradition. Society, they were confident, "could change only as a result of a sudden cataclysmic upheaval on a global scale," and capitalism was already being "shaken by a crisis of the utmost gravity." They were all for revolution and the overthrow of the ruling class, but they remained resolutely dubious of both Marxism and socialism, which, they felt, demanded the surrender of autonomy and of individual judgment.

In *The Prime of Life,* the second volume of her autobiography, covering the years 1929–1944, de Beauvoir lashes herself and Sartre with characteristically inclement honesty for the airy insouciance with which they prided themselves on their "radical freedom." Their circumstances as young petit-bourgeois intellectuals gave them a great deal of independence, leisure, and license. This specifically privileged social circumstance they confused with an ontological "sovereign freedom," which they identified as the fundamental condition of all human existence; those who genuflected to circumstance were morally complicit with the forces that trammeled them. They believed themselves, on the other hand, to "consist of pure reason and pure will" and raised the idea of freedom to a ghostly fetish that served as a spectral image of their disembodied role as intellectuals.

As de Beauvoir later attested, their notions of radical individual freedom served simply to conceal and protect their interests as members of an intellectual caste: "We fondly supposed that we were representative of mankind as a whole; and thus, all unknown to ourselves, we demonstrated our identity with the very privileged class that we thought to repudiate" (*The Prime of Life*). Bathed in the radiance of their own magic circle, they were deaf and blind to the insistent tramp of history. The fascists were massing, the world was on the move, but they remained spectators.

All the elements that flowed into de Beauvoir's aspirations to write and gave shape to the aesthetic form they would take were now in place. The relics of her Catholicism, her hankering for the infinite, her sense of exclusion as a female, her ambiguous class inheritance, her contact with sympathetic artistic movements—all conspired in a flight into aestheticism. But this was really an aesthetics of escape. De Beauvoir longed for an art of "inhuman purity," a cold, entranced art: faceless statues, landscapes bare of human figures, oceans caught in the immobility of a pure moment, men turned into salt, public squares scorched with the fire of death—the aesthetics of absence she would question and abandon in her second novel, *Le sang des autres* (*The Blood of Others*, 1945). She wanted "literature to get away from common humanity" and was drawn as a result to "hermetic poems, surrealist films, abstract art, illuminated manuscripts and ancient tapestries, African masks." Completed works of great beauty broke free of humanity: "dumb, inscrutable, like huge abandoned totems: in them alone I made contact with some vital, absolute element." Reading Katherine Mansfield, she consoled herself that she, too, was a romantic personification of Mansfield's "solitary woman."

The logic of this asocial stance was, nevertheless, a social logic, and began to reveal itself as just that as the darkening cataclysm of war descended on the world. As Williams put it:

> The "aesthetic attitude towards life" was a displaced consciousness relating to one of many possible artistic decisions, but above all related to a version of society: not an artistic consciousness but a disguised social consciousness in which the real connections and involvements with others could be plausibly overlooked and then in effect ratified: a definition of "being a writer" that excluded social experience and social concerns.

But de Beauvoir's writing moved, in fact, in quite the opposite direction. What happened was the intervention of a historical crisis of such magnitude that it fundamentally discredited an entire way of thinking about literature and became thereby an example of what Orwell, living in Paris at the time, called "the invasion of literature by politics," the dramatic shift from the aestheticism of the 1920's to the socially committed writing of the 1930's.

In 1931 de Beauvoir was appointed to a teaching post in Marseilles, and Sartre received a similar position in Le Havre. In 1932 she moved to Rouen to teach literature at a *lycée* for girls. During these years she began to write in earnest, beginning and abandoning two novels, both of which evoked the memory of a "beloved face." The *Memoirs* were originally composed, we know, in order to lay two ghosts to rest: de Beauvoir's childhood self and the pale yellow face and black, brittle hair of her dead friend Zaza. Zaza—Elizabeth Mabille—was murdered, as far as de Beauvoir was concerned, by a class—the "monstrous alliance" of upper-middle-class families, with their Sunday-afternoon tea parties and croquet, the sham decor of their sobriety, their lethal decorum, and, most unforgivably, their disfiguring of the female life.

De Beauvoir had met Zaza at the age of ten as a fellow student at Le Cours Desir. Zaza's fire and temerity, her talent for cocking a snook at every propriety while playing the cool role of dutiful daughter, her easy mastery of ideas, books, and social graces, plunged de Beauvoir into the ignominy and delirium of an inadmissible passion. It was an (assiduously repressed) homoerotic love that lay outside the city of language as de Beauvoir knew it, a "flood of feeling that had no place in any code." She and Zaza quickly became conspirators in defiance against the suffocating tedium of domesticity, secreting themselves in M. Mabille's study to discuss forbidden ideas and books. The "tribal rites" of arranged marriage, the bartering of female bodies to cement familial prestige and property, elicited their particular loathing and fear, a fear much more pressing in Zaza's case. De Beauvoir planned to work for a living; in Zaza's class "a woman had to get married or become a nun." Zaza's mother, by all accounts a "perfect specimen of a right-minded bourgeois upbringing," hailed from "a dynasty of militant Catholics" and spent most of her waking hours in the commerce of arranging marriages. Her amiability cloaked an unrelenting fealty to Catholic propriety; as time went by and de Beauvoir began her studies, she came to recognize Zaza's friend, not inaccurately, as the enemy within, an ungracious, self-righteous, and stubborn-minded little atheist who planned to be an intellectual and work for a living.

Zaza differed from de Beauvoir in that her background was virtually airtight: it lacked the vivid contradictions that had pushed de Beauvoir's early attempts at understanding to the point of exhaustion and revolt. Zaza had been taught by a Catholic upbringing that brooked no argument to kneel before suffering as her natural female condition. In any event, the forces ranged against her were too strong: her beloved mother, bent on marrying her profitably, refused to countenance Zaza's love for de Beauvoir's friend "Herbaud," who for various family reasons could not immediately propose marriage, and Zaza after months of a deadly struggle to escape, surrendered to the impossibility of her situation, contracted brain fever, and died.

De Beauvoir never forgave the bourgeoisie for Zaza's death or herself for not being able to save her. The unacceptable fact of Zaza's death became the theme in all de Beauvoir's early attempts to write. In her first fictional false starts she stalks restlessly around it, again in *Quand prime le spirituel* (*When Things of the Spirit Come First,* 1979), in *La femme rompue* (*The Woman Destroyed,* 1967), and in *Les belles images* (1966). Her autobiography breaks chronology in the final volume, returning obsessively to begin again the process of understanding. It was, by her own account, only when her political thinking had matured to the point where she could finally root Zaza's death in its full social context that the ghost would return to haunt her no more. This long attempt to account for the death of a friend involved in the process the dismantling of some of the more revered shibboleths of Western culture, the elaboration of an alternative ideology, and the writing of the first classic account of the social meaning of the female condition.

During the 1930's de Beauvoir struggled to find her literary feet. She produced two derivative novels that eventually, by her own account, degenerated into a mere hodgepodge and a bundle of short stories, *When Things of the Spirit Come First,* which borrowed its title, ironically, from Jacques Maritain and much of its tone, "a certain concealed irony," from John Dos Passos. The book, written over the years 1935–1937, though published only in 1979, is neither a novel nor independent stories, but a collection that orbits around the central ambition of unveiling the "multitude of crimes, both petty and great" which hide behind the "spiritual hocus-pocus" of bourgeois Catholicism.

Each story is concerned with a central female protagonist who falls victim in a different way to the intrigues, mortifications, and lethal charades of religion. The protagonist of the fourth story, Anne, is the first of a number of concealed Zazas who make their progress through de Beauvoir's fiction. Her murder in this virtually autobiographical tale serves as a vivid exemplum of all the themes that fascinated de Beauvoir: death, the scandal of otherness, the despised bourgeoisie, the conflict between crime and desire, freedom and responsibility, and the overwhelming question of how a woman comes to lead her life. Zaza's death became an exaggerated symptom of the difficulties besetting de Beauvoir's own life and inaugurated the twin obsessions round which almost all her writing revolved: the "black enlightenment" of death and "the mirage of the Other."

Indeed, it may be said that the nub around which all de Beauvoir's fiction turns, melding her political, metaphysical, and aesthetic concerns, is the paradox of death, the problem that "life contains two main truths that we must face simultaneously, and between which there is no choice—the joy of being, the horror of being no more." Almost all her novels are in some sense a "stratagem against death." Her first novel, *She Came to Stay,* ends with a murder, commited a moment before the collective debauch in death of World War II. Her second novel, *The Blood of Others,* set during the French Resistance, "attempted to show death laying siege in vain to the fullness of life." Her third novel, *Tous les hommes sont mortels* (*All Men Are Mortal,* 1946), was envisaged as a kind of "protracted wandering around the central theme of death," and much the same can be said of her nonfictional requiem to her mother, *Une mort très douce* (*A Very Easy Death,* 1964), and her exploration of old age, *La vieillesse* (*Old Age.*)

Many of of her novels open from an aboriginal darkness: the deathbed of a woman, a concierge's dead baby, a theater full of blackness. All her writing is in some sense a refusal of this void, a defiance in the face of all the evidence of the black electric socket, the metro rail, Louise's dead baby, Zaza's yellow face. Paradoxically, her writing springs in turn from this void; in defiance of the void it finds its meaning, an ambiguity she pursued tenaciously in her existentialism. Death exemplified in this way, more than anything else, the metaphysical ambiguity to which de Beauvoir was disposed.

This metaphysical ambiguity, that "all absences are contradicted by the immutable plenitude of the world," is one of the main themes of *All Men Are Mortal.* Fosca, a fifteenth-century Italian prince, bound by an elixir to immortality and condemned to witness to infinity the farcical repetition of wars, crises, and revolutions across the centuries, discovers that death gives life its savor and its import; without it there would be no stubborn "projects" to surpass it, no will to transcendence, and hence no human value. This is also one of the chief arguments in *Pyrrhus et Cinéas,* her first existentialist tract, written in 1943. Death serves as a kind of metaphysical syntactic structure, a dark invisibility on which depends the living tenses of past and future: without this differentiation time would be an unbroken monotone and would in effect cease to exist. It is in this sense that she asserts: "Our death is inside us, but not like the stone in the fruit, like the meaning of our life . . ." (*Force of Circumstance*).

De Beauvoir was in many respects breathing the tragic sigh of agnosticism of her generation. Having toppled God from the altar of the Absolute, death now designated a void that had all the "splendor of the plenitude of grace." Death was not simply an absence; it was a negative manifestation of God. This was almost necessarily so, considering the epoch, for the historical death of God was still too fresh for it to be felt in any other way. Her fascination with death was in part a historical response to the climate of anguish in a disenchanted world. War had exposed the visceral nakedness and organic vulnerability of the human body. Death, like sexuality, was a reminder of the body's animality, proof against all the immortal urges and lucid ambitions of the mind. A "secret and appalling organic disorder," death had the power to flagrantly flout the ideal of rational individual autonomy that de Beauvoir clung to so tenaciously.

Elaine Marks has, therefore, pointed correctly to a recurrent, almost ritualistic moment in de Beauvoir's fiction: a *divertissement,* an abrupt turning away from the evidence of death into a sunlit garden. The significant image is the old jacket, which occurs first in the unpublished *recit* of the childhood of Françoise Miquel, again in *Memoirs,* and again in *She Came to Stay.* In each variation a child stands alone in her mother's room, hemmed in by furniture that is suddenly felt to have a threatening opacity: "thick and heavy and secret; under the bookcase and under the marble console there lurked an ominous shadow" (*She Came to Stay*). The child's anxious gaze lights on an old jacket flung over a chair, enclosed about an enigmatic stillness. Emblematic of the ancient, black root of the chestnut tree in Sartre's *Nausea* (1938), the jacket remains stubbornly itself and utterly strange. Imprisoned in this mute indifference, the jacket neither emits nor admits any consoling word, rebutting thereby the ancient wisdom that the world is the word made flesh, and, by condemning the child to a radical silence, yields dire intimations of her own extinction. Turning in fright, the child dashes downstairs and out into a sunlit garden.

But the flight into the garden, as Elaine Marks notes, is not a "significant evasion." De Beauvoir brilliantly argued in *Faut-il brûler Sade? (Must We Burn Sade?,* 1953) that death, like sexuality, is not a biological matter. It is a social fact. If death exudes in some sense the vertiginous quality of nothingness, it is more importantly for de Beauvoir a material presence. In her novels and in her nonfiction, death's force is felt as a material and a social force. It is felt tangibly in the body: it is an odor; it is fluid and viscous; it is the blackish stuff vomited up by Uncle Gaston; it is Hélène's red blood on cotton wool. It is an organic fate, "the utter rottenness hidden in the womb of all human destiny," but more than anything else this organic secretion that leaks into the world smelling of the void insinuates itself into human lives in a social form and a social shape.

In *The Blood of Others,* written during the war and hailed as the first Resistance novel, the odor of death is indistinguishable from the odor of social guilt. For Jean Blomart, son of a wealthy industrialist, the smell of guilt seeps up through the floorboards from the dark printing workshops below, sousing the whole house, the blue velvet upholstery, the shining copper, the summer flowers. At the age of eight, like de Beauvoir, he had learned of the death of their servant Louise's baby and had inherited at once the "original curse" of the guilt of being consolable, of surviving another's death, the "sin of being another being." Shunning his class future, Blomart enters a factory and joins the Communist party. Events entrap him in responsibility for the deaths of a friend and of a lover, yet he decides in the end that no one can escape being tainted by social injustice and that the only moral recourse is to act—the same morganatic gift of responsibility bequeathed to de Beauvoir by the war.

In the same way that Michel Foucault challenged the traditional view of sexuality as a spontaneous upwelling within the body, replacing it with the idea of sexuality as *produced* by society, a creation of unstable social institutions and discourses that give it historical shape within practices of confinement, exclusion, and domination, so does de Beauvoir unfold within her fiction the idea that death is not an anonymous scandal, but rather a social and institutional force that polices garrets, workshops, and hospitals, an instrument for managing poverty, social difference, and political power. This is not to deny that death and sexuality are bodily matters, but rather to insist that they are never experienced in naked organic form. They are always social scripts, carved on the body in different ways in different historical times.

Encounters with death in de Beauvoir's novels are therefore always encounters with social reality, and death is made meaningful in collective action, revolt, and resistance—hence the sustained importance in her work of the *fête* as a collective, celebratory defiance. Death in itself is not a scandal. Only when humans deny other humans the right to exist does it become a social outrage. Clarice, in de

Beauvoir's only play, *Les bouches inutiles* (*Useless Mouths*, 1945), vows to kill herself rather than be returned to slavery: "They have not allowed me to live. But they will not steal my death from me."

De Beauvoir's prolonged combat with death finds its double in the theme that recurs in every plot line she sketched out: the "mirage of the other." The phantasmagoric other has haunted philosophy ever since the seventeenth century, when, as Hegel pointed out, Western thought began the long attempt to reinterpret history in terms of the individual subject. In Western philosophy the Cartesian Cogito became a kind of *Kaspar Hauser*, found standing alone in the marketplace, without origin or social history, heir without parents to the reshaping of history. But at the same time as the individual stepped into history as a cultural idea, the other stepped out with it, an unbidden Frankenstein's monster that would shadow the luminous progress of the individual self well into the twentieth century.

As a philosopher trained in the French academy, de Beauvoir was heiress to the powerful legacy of Cartesian dualism. In addition, at much the same time that she discovered Hegel, the problem of the other presented itself to her in personal terms, in the figure of a former student of hers, Olga Kosakiewicz. Chafing with ennui in the provinces, de Beauvoir and Sartre had drawn Olga into their magic circle, both seduced by the iridescent glamour the much younger woman cast over their lives. Capricious, moody, generous, in constant revolt against every social arrangement, Olga thumbed her nose at convention and propriety and became for them the passionate incarnation of the cult of youth and rebellion. She served for them as "Rimbaud, Antigone, every *enfant terrible* that ever lived, a dark angel judging us from her diamond-bright heaven." Passionately attached to both de Beauvoir and Sartre, Olga turned their magic circle into an intolerable triangle, and de Beauvoir, "led [in] a terrible dance by this quietly infernal machine we had set in motion," discovered for herself the "curse of the other." She readily interpreted her dilemma within the ideology of the other that she had inherited. "The curse of the other" entered *She Came to Stay* as its founding theme.

In 1936 de Beauvoir was appointed, as was Sartre, to a *lycée*—he to Lyons, she to Paris. There, in the autumn before the war, she began *She Came to Stay.* Though she claims she discovered Hegel when she was well into the novel, it opens with the Hegelian epigraph "Each consciousness seeks the death of the other." For Hegel consciousness emerges only in opposition to another self. The self comes to consciousness only when it sees itself reflected in the eyes of another self-consciousness. The paradox of consciousness is that this alien being is immediately experienced as being outside the self, unknowable and malign. The primal relation between self and other is thus one of inescapable hostility and estrangement. As each self sees the alien other standing before it, it struggles to manifest the sovereignty of its own will by the subjection of the other. So the tragic paradox of consciousness is that it is founded on a life-and-death struggle between two beings, each trying to escape the sorrowful state of self-estrangement by the subjugation of the other, the very being on whom its own consciousness depends.

*She Came to Stay* opens at night with Françoise, a writer, cupped in the rosy light of her theater office. Enfolding this luminous center is the darkened theater, inhuman and black. As Françoise steps out into the office, objects spring to life, materializing before the conjuring glance of her eye: "when she was not there, the smell of dust, the half-light, the forlorn solitude, all this did not exist for anyone; it did not exist at all." This scene captures in miniature the grandiose illusion of individual autonomy—Françoise's fantasy of being her own cause and her own end, and philosophy's long dream that the rational, individual mind might illuminate at a glance the entire world. When Xaviere Pages intrudes into Françoise's longstanding relationship with her lover, Pierre, this crystal illusion shivers into pieces. Passionate, elusive, and unfathomable, Xaviere occasions for Françoise the shattering and unacceptable discovery of the other, the opacity of another being spellbound in the solitude of its own self. Xaviere becomes a "living question mark," an intolerable affront to Françoise's fierce will to autonomy: "Other people could not only steal the world from her, but also invade her personality and bewitch it." Expelled from her sovereign position at the center of the world, Françoise's answer to the ethical problem of coexistence is to defend herself against the invasion of the other in the most violently decisive way. At the end of the novel she turns on the gas in Xaviere's room, murdering her while she sleeps. Released at the same time from her bondage to Pierre, Françoise becomes the triumphant possessor of her own autonomy: "It was her own will which was being fulfilled. Now nothing separated her from herself. At last she had chosen. She had chosen herself."

Through Françoise, de Beauvoir was exploring the virtually demonic urge to devour the world that had bewitched her from her childhood, the will to imperialism of the human consciousness that she explores in social terms in *The Second Sex.* With the murder of Xaviere, de Beauvoir unfolds, though at this stage uncritically, the murderous and fatal logic of radical individualism. The barbaric simplicity of the metaphysics of individual freedom, as de Beauvoir later attests, reveals as its dark underbelly a vision of primordial conflict.

With the outbreak of war in 1939, de Beauvoir's life was invaded by a much more brutal and tragic intruder: "Suddenly History burst over me, and I dissolved into fragments. I woke to find myself scattered over the four corners of the globe." She made the radical discovery of solidarity and dependence on others. If until then her thought had been "riddled with bourgeois idealism and aestheticism," the spring of 1939 "marked a watershed. . . . I renounced my individualistic, anti-humanist way of life. I learned the value of solidarity. . . . I now came to know that in the very marrow of my being I was bound up with my contemporaries."

Sartre had been mobilized in 1939 and taken prisoner of war in Lorraine in 1940. With Sartre snatched away from her, her life in turmoil, she learned for the first time what it was to live "under the domination of events." She now embarked on what she called "the moral period of my literary career." Her immediate postwar writings were thus more than anything a response to one inescapable lesson of the war: "the ghastly uncertainty of our moral state." Nevertheless, she could not jettison her individualism overnight; first she had to pass through existentialism, which can in many respects be seen as a last-ditch attempt to save the individual in a historical context.

Existentialism is a philosophy of crisis. Violently born into the political cradle of the French Resistance, it rapidly became, in Mark Poster's phrase, the "continental sensation" of the postwar 1940's and 1950's. Although de Beauvoir and Sartre originally protested the use of Gabriel Marcel's label to describe their work, existentialism was fully inaugurated in 1943 with the publication of Sartre's *L'Être et le néant* (*Being and Nothingness*). This huge, often impenetrably difficult work was at first reluctantly received but came to enjoy a phenomenal success, traveling rapidly from the corridors of philosophy into every nook and cranny of the cafés and nightclubs of Saint-Germain-des-Prés, where a mélange of discontented and iconoclastic artists and *poets maudits* flirted with fashionable versions of nausea, futility, and disenchantment.

The austerity and discipline of existential atheism, its combatant refusal of every traditional solace, and its loyalty to freedom and authenticity caught the mood of a bereft world. Fascism had triumphed and stalled, France had felt the German boot on its soil, and western civilization had been ransacked by its own fascist offspring and was in disarray. French culture cast about for a faith that could help it make sense of its world.

The existentialist climate for consciousness was as a result anxiety and introspection, negativity and frustration. Nevertheless, both de Beauvoir and Sartre always denied, against their critics, that existentialism was a doctrine of despair. They protested that it offered instead a sturdy and vital anxiety which did, indeed, snatch away every traditional strut, but replaced these with the challenge to accept full responsibility for living in a world without appeal. Still, between the years 1945 and 1950 existentialism faced a barrage of Marxist denunciation. Henri Le Febvre condemned it as a "neurosis of interiority," a pathological narcissism that arose from the morbid symptoms of petit-bourgeois anxiety. Existentialism was accused of fostering as a result a morose decadence and an infantile regression to anxious abandonment. The Right, in turn, viewed Sartre as the *poet maudit* of the sewers, peddling a godless credo of nothingness and futility.

Existentialism had, in fact, begun for Sartre during the war as an attempt to reconcile the German idealist tradition—and his freedom of intellectual judgment—with the political lessons of solidarity and commitment he had learned as a prisoner of war. The central tenor of all his writing in the 1950's and 1960's is the attempt to fuse into a livable doctrine a system that would unite the intelligentsia and the working class in an alliance against the old ruling classes of the world. His appointed role was that of mediator: "Coming from the middle-class, we tried to bridge the gap between the intellectual petite-bourgeoisie and the Communist intellectuals." Later he defined the writer's role in much the same way: "The writer is, par excellence, a mediator and his commitment is to mediation."

The original tenet of existentialism is freedom. Over the years de Beauvoir and Sartre both constantly revised their formulations of freedom and eventually abandoned altogether the notion of absolute freedom—in 1977 Sartre confessed the absurdity of such an illusion and wondered how he could ever have entertained it. But freedom nevertheless remains the founding principle of their thought. For both of them God had been emptied from the world. The roar of meaning the Greeks had heard in a torrential sky was a nostalgia for unity without foundation. Humanity no longer lived in a place in which stones and blossoms spoke of God. For de Beauvoir and Sartre the appetite for religious transcendence became an illusion as remote as a lost paradise; and having faded, it exposed the unending task of creating meaning from the ordinary heroics of human effort. In the early formulation of existentialism, humans are flung at birth into the paradox of an inescapable freedom; or as the famous slogan has it, "Man is condemned to be free." For de Beauvoir, as for Sartre, humans are nothing other than what they make of themselves. As Blomart chides Hélène in *The Blood of Others,* "I think that where you go wrong is that you imagine that your reasons for being ought to fall on you, ready-made from heaven, whereas you have to find them."

From this radical assertion of freedom sprang the ethics of authenticity through action: "From the point of view of freedom, all situations could be salvaged if one assumed them as a project" (*Force of Circumstance*). As Blomart says: "We only exist if we act." Any evasion of authenticity—the lucid defiance of things as they are—smells of the sin of *mauvais foi,* of bad faith against the *réalité humaine* of freedom. Hélène's attempt in *The Blood of Others* to use "the infinity of the future as an alibi" to escape from the intolerable present is just such an evasion.

Existentialism thus contains within it a political agenda and an ethics of action. As de Beauvoir puts it in *Force of Circumstance,* the third volume of her autobiography, "Existentialism was a definition of humanity through action; if it condemned one to anxiety it did so only in so far as it obliged one to accept responsibility. The hope it denied one was the idle reliance on anything other than oneself; it was an appeal to the human will." The ethics of authenticity entails in turn the politics of *engagement,* the moral obligation to intervene directly in changing the world. Moreover, the refusal to act politically is itself a political action. Freedom is authentic only if it is *engagé,* pitted against the unacceptable conditions of the present.

The abiding dilemma of existentialism now begins to make itself felt. Sartre defines existentialism as a philosophy according to which "existence precedes and perpetually creates the essence." But this apparently radical rejection of "natural humanity" still cloaks a faith in human essences. In existentialism the absurd adventure of freedom plays itself out more as a state of mind than anything to do with prisons, armies, asylums, or factories. The human being is willy-nilly identified with freedom and the politics of *engagement,* but this is strictly an affair of the individual and of individual will. For Sartre responsibility is "total responsibility in total solitude." As he defines it, "The basic idea of existentialism is that even in the most crushing situations, the most difficult circumstances, man is free. Man is never powerless except when he is persuaded that he is, and the responsibility of man is immense because he becomes what he decides to be." Existentialism was still haunted by its idealistic origins.

The plantation slave, the harem chattel, and the tyrant possess in these terms an identical potential for freedom, and hence the same moral culpability for resignation. Into the bargain, each choice is random and without prior foundation, a hazardous leap into the future. At the same time, the radical severance from history cripples any attempt to explain the tenacity of certain systems of power and authority; why, for example, some groups rather than others control the pathways of freedom. As a result, despite its radical promise and its exhilarating appeal to action, early Sartrean morality remains what Mary Evans calls "the morality of the free market."

De Beauvoir shed the ethic of absolute freedom more rapidly than Sartre; yet Sartre's actual political involvement was much in advance of hers. She admitted much earlier that Sartrean freedom is the abstract fantasy of intellectuals privileged to be able to intervene only sporadically in history. It might be said that the great arc of de Beauvoir's thinking describes a veering away from this Sartrean vision to a much more somber recognition of the dense historical limits to freedom. Out of this recognition evolved a persistently more radical view of social relations, perhaps best articulated in the words of her friend Colette Audry: "Relations with the Other . . . are transcended; they become relations with others."

There is no doubt that de Beauvoir's vision was initially more optimistic than Sartre's. *Pour une morale de l'ambiguité* (*The Ethics of Ambiguity*), first published in 1947 in *Les temps modernes,* a journal that Sartre and de Beauvoir founded, was undertaken to defend existentialism against the charges that it was a "sterile anguish." Sartre had insisted on the "abortive aspect of the human adventure"; as Anne Whitmarsh points out, it is "the positive, optimistic side of his philosophy, well hidden and often ignored, which she attempts to explore" (*Simone de Beauvoir*). For de Beauvoir existentialism defined itself as "a philosophy of ambiguity." The fundamental condition of being is lack-of-being, the frustration of potential: humanity is *manqué* from the start. But each person can "deny the lack as lack and confirm itself as a positive existence."

The example de Beauvoir gives is suggestive, for it captures her old affliction of loneliness, identified here as a metaphysical frustration before the "otherness" of a landscape: "I should like this sky, this quiet water to think themselves within me, that it might be I whom they express in flesh and bone, and I remain at a distance." The stubborn will to appropriate the landscape unfolds the lust for transcendence that sets humans apart, even in opposition, to nature: "I cannot appropriate the snowfield where I slide. It remains foreign, forbidden, but I take delight in this very effort toward an impossible possession. I experience it as a triumph, not as a defeat" (*The Ethics of Ambiguity*).

De Beauvoir sets herself deliberately at odds with Hegel, who sought to reconcile all ambiguity in a final flowering of reason, but here she acquiesces at the same time in a specifically Hegelian tradition of defining the very ground of identity in terms of violence, appropriation, conflict, and possession, a metaphysics of violence she does not fully abandon even in *The Second Sex.* She later repudiated *The Ethics of Ambiguity* as her least satisfying book: "Of all my books, it is the one that irritates me the most today. . . . I was in error when I thought I could define a morality independent of a social context." As she puts it in a different context, at the very moment she was rejecting the language of her class, she was still using their language to do so: "The fact remains that on the whole I went to a great deal of trouble to present inaccurately a problem to which I then offered a solution quite as hollow as the Kantian maxims." "Why," she asks, "did I write *concrete liberty* instead of *bread*?" (*Force of Circumstance*).

In May 1946 de Beauvoir had finished *The Ethics of Ambiguity* and was casting about for a new subject. *The Blood of Others* had been very well received, *All Men Are Mortal* less so. Her play *Les bouches inutiles* strode rather baldly around the existential problem of whether the male council of a besieged town, Vauxcelles, should expell all the "useless mouths"—the women, the elderly, children, and the infirm—to die in the gullies beyond the town. It had a brief and disappointing season, and she never again tried her hand at drama. Now what she wanted above all was to write about herself. But this meant first of all answering the question that had been plaguing her for so long and to which she had turned a stolidly deaf ear: "What has it meant to me to be a woman?"

For nearly forty years de Beauvoir had pretended that being female made no difference: she was an intellectual and that was that. One might say therefore that the first forging of her adult identity was a negative one: a refusal of family, class, and the specifically female fate that had dragged Zaza down. She had fashioned her adult identity in deliberate opposition by becoming an intellectual. As an intellectual she could staunch her acutely feminine sense of exile by taking refuge, not as a woman, but as an individual within the tradition of radical individualism: "Just as previously I had refused to be labelled 'a child,' now I did not think of myself as a 'woman.' I was *me.*" For quite a while, it worked: "Since I was twenty-one, I have never been lonely."

Yet through all her novels and writings there courses a very deep problem: that other identity, that other self, which *was* her, whether she liked it or not, and which remained an obscure and nagging obsession until she herself wrote about it, for the simple reason that her culture was not going to do it for her. So that the very choice she had made to be an intellectual ("writing would reconcile everything") inexorably returned her to the riddle of feminine identity from which it had originally promised a refuge.

One of the reasons she balked so long at the obvious was that it meant abandoning the morality of individualism which embued her entire life and bound her to Sartre. It meant accepting the intolerable and tragic fact that in the world's eyes being a woman was not the same as being an individual. Her position in the collective "we" of her relation to Sartre had in any case been presenting her for some time with a dilemma that arose out of the very individualism which buoyed her up. How could she define herself in relation to others within a philosophy that defined the other as the thief and enemy of selfhood and that, moreover, excluded her as a woman from its privileges? Specifically, how could she express fealty to a man without entering into vassalage: "Is there any possible reconciliation between fidelity and freedom? And if so, at what price. . . . To accept a secondary status in life, that of a mere ancillary being, would have been to degrade my own humanity"—a puzzle that is one of the founding themes of *The Mandarins.* For years she had shrugged off the discomfiting fact that "the only reason for the problem presenting itself to me in these terms was because I happened to be a woman. But it was qua individual that I attempted to resolve it. The idea of feminism and the sex war made no sense whatsoever to me."

Now, in May 1946, with an itch to write a personal confession, she followed Sartre's suggestion to explore what difference growing up female had in fact made: "I looked, and it was a revelation: this was a masculine world, my childhood had been nourished by myths forged by men, and I hadn't reacted to them in at all the same way I should have done if I had been a boy." This revolution in personal identity was summed up in one simple sentence: "Wanting to talk about myself, I became aware that to do so I should first have to describe the condition of women in general" (*Force of Circumstance*). The shock of identity was a genuine breakthrough, and with it de Beauvoir's life and thought moved into a new dimension. She was forty years old.

## *IV*

> Today I know that the first thing I have to say if I want to describe myself, is that I am a woman.
> (*All Said and Done*)

*The Second Sex* was written out of its time. Published in 1949, it stood on an empty horizon, years after the suffrage movement at the turn of the century, years before the feminism of the 1970's. But it could not conceivably have been written at any other time. Its very untimeliness bears witness, in fact, to its paradoxical origins. Written by a woman who was also an existentialist intellectual, *The Second Sex* is scored through and through with the eddies and crosscurrents that arose from this special position. Quickened into life by the founding tenets of existentialism, the book came to reveal their phantasmic nature and delivered the *coup de grâce* to the alluring vision of individual autonomy and will that had enchanted de Beauvoir for so long.

*The Second Sex* is a remarkable document not only because many of its denunciations of the male management of the world remain tragically valid, but also because it records the fascinating record of the demise of an old way of thinking and the turbulent upheaval of a new—the emergence of a radical feminism that was in turn deeply colored, some would say blemished, by the very existentialist climate which had nourished it. In this respect it is what de Beauvoir would call an "epochal" book.

It has become easy to dismiss *The Second Sex* as an "unread classic." There is no doubt that it is a demanding book, an exhaustive thousand-page raid on biology, history, mythology, cosmology, politics, medicine, and literature to answer the single question of women's subjection. In its form it is turbulent, cataclysmic, and self-contradictory, virtually buckling under the stress of its innovatory brilliance and erudition. So it is important to remember how extraordinary a book it was in its time. The first volume, published in *Les temps modernes,* was read politely. The second met a storm of abuse and outrage, which did not abate. De Beauvoir had trampled publicly on very hallowed ground: the cult of the family, the mystique of maternity, the economy of domestic production, the cultural denigration of the female, the plundering and policing of female sexuality, lesbianism, and abortion. Ultimately, the revolution she was calling for would mean the most extensive redistribution of property and privilege in the history of the world.

The enabling idea of *The Second Sex* is existentialist freedom. For de Beauvoir, as for Sartre, there is no human nature, since there is no God to see it. Since there is no human nature, there is no fountain of the "eternal feminine," no feminine essence, no female fate. Women's subjection has nothing to do with the moon's drag or the flow of the tides. In the now famous terms that open Book II of *The Second Sex,* "One is not born, but rather becomes a woman." If everywhere women are subdued, beset, and distressed, the blame lies at the door of culture, which can be broken down. For de Beauvoir, dismantling the cities of custom erected by men to barricade their privilege will be an incendiary, revolutionary development. Moreover, this liberation "must be collective, and it requires first of all that the economic evolution of women's development first be accomplished."

At the same time feminists themselves have been dismayed by some of the arguments in *The Second Sex*. De Beauvoir was deeply indebted to existentialism, which nevertheless dragged in its train certain consequences that cast their ambiguous influence over the book. In *Being and Nothingness,* Sartre defines the origin of consciousness as the consequence of being seen by another: "On principle, the Other is he who looks at me." The glance of the other becomes the fundamental category of human consciousness and is, therefore, also the foundation of human relations. For Sartre the gaze of the other steals the world from me and turns me into an object: the other is the death of my possibilities and my "original sin." Here the gaze is a social idea, since it binds people and shapes identity, but it remains barren of social content, dramatizing social relations as a hostile clashing of equal and fleshless selves. In *The Second Sex* de Beauvoir discovers that the Sartrean idea of conflict as the crucible of consciousness becomes radically unstable when applied to women: by tradition and decree it is the man who gazes, it is the woman who is other. On her "journey into history," de Beauvoir was everywhere returned to a stark revelation: "What peculiarly signals the subjection of woman is that she—a free and autonomous being like all human creatures—nevertheless finds herself living in a world where men compel her to assume the status of the Other."

Rifling through anthropology, history, mythology, and culture, de Beauvoir finds that "Otherness is a fundamental category of human thought." In other words, self and other is a primordial division in all consciousness. It was therefore "not originally attached to the division of the sexes." De Beauvoir retains in this way the idea of consciousness as conflict, but makes the radical discovery that everywhere in history "man put himself forward as the Subject and considered the woman as an object, as the Other" (*Force of Circumstance*). At once the formal Sartrean categories of freedom, the autonomous individual, and the other are flooded with history and capsize, and the existentialism that quickens *The Second Sex* slowly begins to subvert itself.

The fundamental question of *The Second Sex* is historical. What is the origin of woman as the other? Jews, blacks, foreigners, proletarians are also periodically condemned to the ghetto of otherness. Yet de Beauvoir finds a crucial difference: "Proletarians say 'we'; Negroes also. Regarding themselves as subjects, they transform the bourgeois, the whites, into 'others.' But women do not say 'we.' " (Neither in fact does de Beauvoir; women in *The Second Sex* are "they.") For de Beauvoir, women are alone among the oppressed in that we have never risen up to dispute men's thrall; there is something in the condition of otherness that seduces us, and we become complicit in our own enchainment. This position has been fiercely disputed, and we will return to it shortly, but for the moment it is enough to say that de Beauvoir begins to answer the question of the origin of women's submission by importing into *The Second Sex* the existentialist distinction between immanence and transcendence.

For de Beauvoir, all humans, women and men, harbor within themselves a primitive conflict between immanence and transcendence. Immanence is a condition of blind submission to existence, torpid, submerged, and organic. Transcendence, on the other hand, expresses the insatiable will to "imperialism of the human consciousness, seeking always to exercise its sovereignty in objective fashion." Transcendence leaps up out of immanence into the realm of aggression, revolt, art, culture, and the risking of life: "Every time transcendence falls back into immanence, stagnation, there is a degradation of existence into the *en-soi*—the brutish life of subjection to given conditions."

As de Beauvoir sees it, there are powerful inducements to surrender to immanence. The ethical urge to liberty is challenging and fearful; alongside this there is a deep-seated temptation to "forgo liberty and become a thing," to acquiesce in the ruinous inertia of immanence. The anxiety of liberty is so tormenting and fundamental that "immediately after weaning, when the infant is separated from the whole, it is compelled to lay hold upon its alienated existence in mirrors and the gaze of its parents" to escape the heaviness of its own selfhood. Women, in particular, have been tempted to enshrine themselves in immanence, beguiled by the promise of security. This is their "original treason." Woman, for de Beauvoir, is "often well pleased with her role as the Other."

Certainly feminists have been most alarmed by those parts in *The Second Sex* where de Beauvoir treats the female body. At certain moments in the text the female body appears to serve as the incarnation of immanence itself: "Woman is doomed to the continuation of the species and the care of the home—that is to say, to immanence." The pregnant female is "victim of the species," which gnaws at her vitals. Her maternal fate is to be "prey to a stubborn and foreign life that each month constructs and tears down a cradle within her body . . . aborted in the crimson flow." Pregnant, she is "tenanted by another, who battens upon her substance."

Sexually, woman exists for man as inwardness, enclosure, a resistance to be broken through; in penetrating her the male bursts forth into transcendence and manifests the power of life. Her sexuality, on the other hand, conveys the essence of a mysterious, threatening passivity: female sexuality is "the soft throbbing of a mollusc," mucous, humid, and secretive. De Beauvoir consistently reaches for an array of what might be seen as perverse, neurotic metaphors that identify female eroticism as an organic degeneration to primitive life forms: "Woman lies in wait like the carnivorous plant, the bog in which insects and children are swallowed up." This metaphoric consistency reaches beyond *The Second Sex* into her fiction. In *The Blood of Others* Hélène abandons herself voluptuously in a sensual delirium that takes on all the appearance of an evolutionary metamorphosis to a primordial organic state: enveloped in sticky vapors, her flesh turns to plant, then to "a humid and spongy moss . . . forever enclosed in that viscid darkness," then to "an obscure and flabby jellyfish lying on a bed of magic sea-anemones."

It is not surprising that feminists have reacted with dismay to this depiction of female sexuality as submerged in a viscid, erotic night. It has, however, been pointed out that de Beauvoir inherited the nightmarish metaphors of "slimes and holes" from none other than Sartre, who devoted a portion of *Being and Nothingness* to an analysis of the "slimy": "The slimy is docile. . . . Slime is the revenge of the In-itself. A sickly-sweet, feminine revenge." The slimy reveals the threat of the "envenomed possession" of the male by the female. So does the "hole," which serves for Sartre as a fundamental, existential quality expressive of the "obscenity of the feminine, . . . that of everything which gapes open." For Sartre the tendency to fill, to plug holes, is a fundamental tendency of the human psyche: "The experience of the hole envelops the ontological presentiment of sexual experience in general; it is with his flesh that the child stops up the hole." It is important to note here, as Michèle Le Doeuff does, that this fundamental "human" tendency is suddenly revealed to be male: "The female child will no doubt have to trade in her . . . fundamental human tendency," which is to fill, in order to be filled. The subject is suddenly and forever male; the female is banished beyond the frontiers of subjectivity.

Sartre needed the metaphors of knowledge as penetration, of the female as a slimy, gaping immanence, in order to give closure to his system. The Sartrean transcendental self needs the sticky, threatening female to guarantee (male) identity through conflict and conquest. In *The Second Sex* de Beauvoir unfolds this timeless scenario as an epochal point of view, a cultural attitude so fashioned as to perpetuate the intolerable condition of women. There in fact runs alongside the troubling nightmare of the female as organic regression another quite different vision, often overlooked or ignored, a lyrical panegyric to the silky beauty and magnificence of the female body.

It is therefore important at this stage to read de Beauvoir's text very carefully. For accompanying, and in opposition to, her account of immanence and transcendence, runs a far more radical explanation of women's subjection. One of the reasons for the widely contradictory interpretations of *The Second Sex* is the intricacies of its tone. It is deeply ironic, an often satirical, dramatic tissue of many voices. De Beauvoir has, as a consequence, been hauled over the coals for pronouncements that, if read carefully in context, are experiments in ventriloquism, the ironic voicing of a view which she rapidly proceeds to demolish.

Her notions of immanence and transcendence appear to signal a fall back into "human nature," as does her account of the female body helpless in the iron grip of the species. There is little doubt that de Beauvoir's sense of "the primitive misery of being a body" was in part a relic of the Catholic denigration of the flesh, compounded by her fear that her own flesh would eventually plunge her into extinction. The body threatened in every way the lucid rationality she so treasured. As she saw it, women in orgasm, for example, literally "lost their minds." Yet while she insists on biological differences between men and women, she states clearly: "I deny that they establish for her a fixed and inevitable destiny. They are insufficient for setting up a hierarchy of the sexes; they fail to explain why woman is the Other; they do not condemn her to remain in this subordinate role forever. . . . I categorically reject the notion of psychophysiological parallelism."

Indeed, *The Second Sex* appears to describe a sporadic zigzag course: affirmation of a primordial conflict between transcendence and immanence as the origin of all action, and a categorical insistence on the primacy of the "situation." This is one of the reasons why the book is so variously interpreted. In fact, for her it is neither one nor the other, which is why it is so important to read her dialectically, in the full sense of the word. Part of what is happening in the book is the settling of a long debate with Sartre. We learn from her autobiography that for some time she had been disagreeing with him on the nature of freedom: "I maintained that from the angle of freedom as Sartre defined it—that is, an active transcendence of some given context rather than mere stoic resignation—not every situation was equally valid: what sort of transcendence could a woman shut up in a harem achieve?" (*The Prime of Life*). In the end, she says, she made a "token submission" to Sartre's point of view, even though she remained sure: "Basically I was right." Why this token submission? To defend her position would have meant abandoning the entire intellectual basis of all their work, "the plane of the individual, and therefore idealistic, morality on which we set ourselves." *The Second Sex* amounts to a tremendous, contorted, incendiary effort to wrest from this precious heritage of the individual an alternative, fully social history of the female condition.

What is the "situation" of women? It is not biology. Muscular force cannot be the basis for domination, since violence itself is a social category. Human privilege rests on anatomical privilege only by virtue of the total social situation. It is not psychology. De Beauvoir respects the fertile insights of psychoanalysis but rejects its portrayal of humans as the playthings of subterranean drives. Psychoanalysis robs humans of the responsibility for choice, and, far more damagingly, it fails to explain why woman is the other: "The phallus assumes the value it does because it symbolizes a sovereignty realized in other domains." Yet psychoanalysis is bankrupt when it comes to explaining the social sovereignty of the male.

Finally, it is not economy that ensures men their thrall over women. Despite the fact that *The Second Sex* owes so much to Marxism, de Beauvoir remained skeptical of its easy promises to women. For Friedrich Engels the arrival of private property ushered in the "world-historical defeat of the female sex." Maternal right yielded to patriarchy as property was handed down from father to son and no longer from mother to clan. Women became subsumed in property, passing from father to husband. Yet although de Beauvoir is deeply sympathetic and indebted to Engels, what she found missing was, firstly, an account of how the institution of private property came about, secondly, how this entailed the enslavement of women, and, thirdly, where the *interest* lay in the passing of inheritance from father to son, rather than from father to daughter, or to the clan. In the last analysis de Beauvoir faults Engels for his neglect of the original imperialism of the human will: "If the human consciousness had not included the original category of the Other and an original aspiration to dominate the Other, the invention of the bronze tool could not have caused the oppression of women."

There is, ultimately, only one reason why woman remains enchained: "Woman does not assert her demands as a subject because she lacks the concrete means." These concrete means have been stolen from her and are scrupulously denied her during her passage from infancy, to adolescence, to womanhood. It is to woman's "situation," the key word of *The Second Sex,* that de Beauvoir returns again and again: "It is said that woman is sensual, she wallows in immanence; but she has first been shut up in it." This, then, is the project of the book: "We shall study woman in an existentialist perspective with due regard to her total situation."

Since there is no founding, aboriginal cause of women's abjection, de Beauvoir employs her expansive intelligence to expose the "forest of props" that men have erected to barricade their privileges. As Le Doeuff puts it, "Daily life is all the more narrowly policed because the subjection of women has at each moment to be reinvented." The cultural invention of woman's lot begins at infancy, which is embattled by the capricious magic of the adult gaze. The arduous and dangerous accession to female adolescence is shaped by a host of damaging conventions: our crimped education, our enshrinement in the family, the theft of our sexuality, our economic servitude. Everything conspires against the young girl, but, for de Beauvoir, our vassalage is ultimately secured by two major institutions: marriage and maternity.

Marriage inspires nothing but de Beauvoir's unrestrained animosity. Following Claude Lévi-Strauss, she views matrimony as an institution whereby women become a fleshly coinage exchanged from man to man: "Woman, as slave or vassal, is integrated within families dominated by fathers and brothers, and she has always been given in marriage by certain males to other males." Marriage is an organized plundering of women's labor and sexuality. Women perform two-thirds of the world's work, yet own only one percent of the world's property. This situation is perpetuated by restricting a woman's aspirations to a career that reduces her to virtually total financial dependency and all her ambitions to the Sisyphian torture of housework.

Even granting, as de Beauvoir does, the different historical shapes that marriage has taken, much of her criticism remains valid. But her bleak portrayal of motherhood has drawn particularly hostile fire. For de Beauvoir the mother is "confined in a limbo of immanence and contingence"; doomed to repetition and futility, "she is occupied without ever *doing* anything." Moreover, for de Beauvoir, woman in the early history of the world was "nourishing, never creative. In no domain whatever did she create." Her picture of women as victims of their own seething, organic fecundity collapses the rich and historically diverse sphere of women's activities into the single "natural function" of maternity.

In fact, women were for the most part the gatherers and horticulturists in early societies and were thus in all likelihood responsible for the major cultural and technological advances in horticulture, medicine and healing, pottery, weaving, and so on. By way of dealing with the early history of the world de Beauvoir echoes Lévi-Strauss in claiming that "this has always been a man's world." But a rich body of knowledge has now been made available by anthropology and history that testifies to the paramount political and cultural authority women held in the myriad egalitarian, or matrilineal-matrilocal societies that have been documented (Eleanor Leacock, *Myths of Male Dominance*). Moreover, de Beauvoir's notion that women have never risen up to resist men's thrall is refuted by much historical evidence to the contrary. Throughout history, women have revolted individually or in groups, sporadically or for sustained periods, successfully or futilely, in different ways in different periods, but yielding overall a long and intricate history of stubborn refusal to genuflect before their fate.

It is hard to escape the fact that de Beauvoir's denunciation of maternity, if perfectly legitimate as a personal though privileged choice, is unrealistic as a general exhortation and connives ultimately with the male denigration of domestic life that produces precisely the crippling dependence of women she was combating. Her nausea of the flesh can, however, also be seen as a fierce protest against the socially conspired denial of female reproductive rights in an era with no legal abortion and no legal contraceptives. As she says: "There are many aspects of feminine behavior that should be interpreted as forms of protest."

What matters, therefore, is not to judge de Beauvoir from an absolute point of view, but rather to understand her in her time. The current renaissance in the industrial West of freely chosen motherhood is in fact a privileged heritage of the fight for abortion rights that de Beauvoir herself ignited, and remains, sadly, the privilege of a small number of the world's women. In her time de Beauvoir's unveiling of the glamorous cult of the family, the hypocrisy of middle-class monogamy and its historical alliance with prostitution, the grueling monotony of domestic labor and the economic servitude of the housewife, her assault on marriage as a "surviving relic of dead ways of life," and her call for full control by women over their bodies—all this was extraordinarily radical, and still is, to which the fury of public response is sufficient testimony.

De Beauvoir maintained that she was never hostile to motherhood as such, only to the suffocating cultural myths in which it has been swaddled and the social circumstances that make it a special burden to women. She also said that if she were to write *The Second Sex* today, she would root the oppression of women not in a primitive and Manichaean struggle between consciousness, but in a materialist analysis of the economic vicissitudes of scarcity and a struggle over vital resources. Nevertheless, she called *The Second Sex* "possibly the book that has brought me the deepest satisfaction of all that I have written."

One personal outcome of *The Second Sex* for de Beauvoir was that it loosed a flood of autobiographical creativity that did not abate until she ceased writing altogether. In October 1950 she began writing *The Mandarins,* for which she won the Prix Goncourt (1954) and the admiration of France. In her autobiography she has this to say of the novel: "I started a vast novel, the heroine was to live through all my own experiences. . . . I wanted it to contain all of me—myself in relation to life, to death, to my times, to writing, to love, to friendship, to travel." That is to say, in it would finally flower the autobiographical stirrings so long denied and now quickened into bud by *The Second Sex.* Like almost all of her writing after *The Second Sex, The Mandarins* amounts to the creation of a persona, Simone de Beauvoir: the bold assertion of a female figure stubbornly determined to haunt her epoch, in person and in public. For *The Mandarins* unites the three impulses—the autobiographical, the social, and the political—that had always dominated her life but that had been held apart until now: "I also wanted to depict other people, and above all to tell the feverish and disappointing story of what happened after the war" (*Force of Circumstance*).

*The Mandarins* explores de Beauvoir's own very special, paradoxical milieu: the heady, conflicted world of the French intellectual Left after the war. France has often been called the paradise of the intellectuals, and great weight is traditionally given intellectuals' writings. (Charles de Gaulle, for example, stung by Sartre's fierce public opposition to the attempts to crush the Algerian war of independence, nevertheless declined to arrest him: "One does not arrest Voltaire.") But the aftermath of World War II found the French intelligentsia standing unsteadily in a new and difficult world. The political system had capsized in 1940; the Third Republic, after defeat, occupation, and collaboration, had proved itself bankrupt of all credibility and became a political fatality. The nineteenth-century capitalist order had entered its dog days in the 1930's. The aftermath of war inspired as a result a great flaming of intellectual activity in politics. As de Beauvoir put it, "Politics had become a family affair, and we expected to have a hand in it."

In 1945 de Beauvoir had helped found *Les temps modernes,* which was consistently anticolonialist, independently socialist, and anti-Gaullist, with a largely intellectual rather than populist readership. In 1948 a group of intellectuals, activists, trade unionists, and journalists formed the Rassemblement Democratique Revolution, which "wanted to unite all the socialist forces in Europe behind a definite policy of neutralism." The Communists had consistently spurned Sartre's overtures of friendship, so he joined the RDR, which reflected his own unsteady class position "astride two classes, the bourgeoisie and the proletariat." Sartre resigned from the RDR in 1949 to protest its listing toward the Right; the RDR soon collapsed and with it hope in a middle way. Sartre left the RDR convinced that the individual was powerless to effect change; the individual can be defended as an end in itself, but an effective political organization cannot be founded on the principle of radical individualism, which by definition cripples all collective action and renders political organizations inoperable. De Beauvoir voiced the bleak sense of disillusionment this occasioned: "History was no longer on my side. There was no place for those who refused to become part of either of the two blocs" (*Force of Circumstance*).

According to de Beauvoir, "Before the war few intellectuals had tried to understand their epoch." One notable and celebrated exception was Julien Benda, whose *La trahison des clercs* (*The Treason of the Intellectuals,* 1928) was a passionate defense of the intellectual vocation as a tradition of detachment. For Benda the intellectual life was a monkish calling, inspired only by "a pure passion of the intelligence, implying no terrestrial love," a position not at all remote from De Beauvoir and Sartre's early vision of themselves as ordained to be celestial "hunters of truth." Benda fulminated against the sight of intellectuals tramping in the marketplace and raising their voices in the political hubbub. But postwar France had moved irrevocably into a world in which cultural clout was passing from the hands of the traditional intellectuals into those of a new breed of media technocrats.

Regis Debray discerns three stages in French intellectual history: the academic (1880–1930), the publishing (1920–1960), and the reign of the media, on the ascendant since 1968. (In *Les belles images* de Beauvoir evokes the atmosphere of commercial peddling, the counterfeit images, the trafficking in banalities, and particularly the deleterious effect on how women are seen and see themselves in the impact of the media on the lives of two women: Laurence, who works in advertising, and her mother, Dominique, a powerful radio figure.) *The Mandarins,* written soon after Sartre resigned from the RDR, stands on the brink of the changing of the guard from the publishing era to that of the media.

De Beauvoir, standing on a "ground littered with smashed illusions," once more decided to turn failure to good purpose by redeeming it in words. Set in Paris between 1944 and 1947, *The Mandarins* follows the fate of an intimate group of Left intellectuals, loosely based on de Beauvoir's friends and associates, Sartre, Maurice Merleau-Ponty, Raymond Aron, Albert Camus, and others. The book opens into the jubilant "orgy of brotherhood" of the Liberation and travels a darkening trajectory from solidarity through a slow splintering into factions, internal dissent, and disillusionment, and then out into a glimmering of optimism.

The novel circles round the central intellectual debate at the time of how to act and write politically in a world that had been cloven into two imperialist blocs: the Soviet Union and the United States. Much of *The Mandarins'* momentum springs from a quarrel between two close friends, Henri Perron, a writer and editor of a paper called *L'Espoir,* and Robert Dubreuillh, a writer and founder of an independent, leftist political group, the SRL. At issue is whether to publish the news of the Soviet labor camps and thereby keep faith with the intellectual vocation of truth-telling, as Henri would, while at the same time knowing full well that doing so would be politically and strategically disastrous, fanning the dangerous fires of the Right and alienating the SRL from the French Left. The personal undertow of the novel is chiefly fed by the love affair between Anne, a psychoanalyst and Debreuillh's wife, and an American, Lewis Brogan. Brogan takes most of his life and veracity from de Beauvoir's own four-year affair with the American writer Nelson Algren, and occasions thereby the full fictional attempt to come to terms with the simultaneously tormenting and exhilarating consequences of her open relationship with Sartre.

The great distinction and power of the book stem from de Beauvoir's fiercely honest efforts to answer the political and aesthetic question that had begun to plague her and that can perhaps best be summed up in Franz Fanon's question to Sartre during the Algerian war: "We [that is, the Algerians, the Third World, the dispossessed] have claims on you. How can you continue to live normally, to write?" Sartre spoke of de Beauvoir's "staggering" reluctance to become fully embroiled in the "sordid manoeuvres of politics." She herself openly admitted that despite her lifelong hatred of her class and of the Right (which deepened to loathing as France waged brutal and futile wars in Indochina, Algeria, and at home), despite her "furious solidarity with the poverty of France," and despite her extensive and passionate political involvement, "I am not a woman of action; my reason for living is writing."

Podium politics waged in the glare of publicity was constitutionally abhorrent to de Beauvoir. She was temperamentally impatient with the tedium and bureaucratic squabbles of endless rounds of committee meetings, but at the same time, as she was well aware, her choice to avoid them was a privileged one. As Anne Whitmarsh has pointed out, her political activity was characteristically pitched behind the scenes in small, intimate groups. During the Algerian war she became more active, at demonstrations, speaking, and writing articles, campaigning in particular on behalf of Djamila Boupacha, an Algerian woman tortured by the French.

In 1971 the Mouvement de liberation des femmes (MLF) was founded, emerging from the clandestine *gauchiste* groups of 1968. The MLF soon appealed to de Beauvoir to intercede against the new and inadequate abortion bill. She joined the MLF soon afterward and was a signatory to the famous Manifeste des 343, a public declaration by 343 women, many of them prominent, that they had undergone abortions. The MLF subsequently split into two factions, the Groupes de quartier (community groups) and Psychoanalyse et politique (Psych et Po), a non-Marxist, largely semiotic and psychoanalytic group that rapidly became a flourishing publishing business. It alienated itself from the other French feminist groups by appropriating the name "mouvement de liberation des femmes" for itself, by its hierarchical structure, and by its divisive legal battles with the other groups. De Beauvoir publicly disassociated herself from Psych et Po, as well as from the privileging of *gynesis,* an essentially feminine form of writing, defined without reference to history.

In June 1972 de Beauvoir and the lawyer Gisèle Halimi founded Choisir to fight for abortion rights at the judicial level. In 1974 de Beauvoir was elected president of the Ligue du droits des femmes, which wages legal battles for women and publishes a monthly journal, *Questions Feministes.* For de Beauvoir the politics of reproduction, rape, and violence to women were the fundamental concerns of feminism. If in *The Second Sex* she left the feminist revolution to follow willy-nilly from the socialist revolution, from the 1960's she lost faith in Marxist promises to take care of the feminist cause: "Now when I speak of feminism I mean the fact of struggling for specifically feminine claims at the same time as carrying on the class war." In other words, Marxism is necessary but not sufficient. In the final analysis she summed herself up as an activist, Marxist feminist, committed to dismantling the present management of society by a vigilant, sustained, and cataclysmic disruption. But she was resolutely skeptical of all existing political parties and vehemently insistent that feminism remain unhierarchical and flexible, generously open to anomaly and indecision, contradiction, unpredictability, and change.

De Beauvoir's life described in this way a great arc from her first allegiance to the solitary vocation of intellectual to a passionate solidarity with the collective, incendiary progress of feminism. But, finally, it was writing that inspired her deepest commitment and melded the two great tendencies in her life: "Writing has remained the great concern of my life." De Beauvoir remained as wary in her fiction as in her politics of easy solutions. Often scathingly impatient with the didactic strains in her early work, she saw the ultimate task of art as conveying the "perpetual dance" of nuance and ambiguity, anomaly and an often preposterous unpredictability in human lives. Irritated by well-proportioned plots (in fiction as in politics), she wanted above all to imitate "the disorder, the indecision, the contingency of life." The elusive ambiguity of language, "the black sorcery" of words that had bewitched her as a child, spilled out from her fiction to include her ambiguous relation to her public. Often misread, praised when she wanted to give offense, condemned when she thought she would please, she was acutely aware of the uncertain fate of a book once it left her hands. She always saw writing as a collaboration; for this reason, and motivated perhaps by a deep-seated sense of incompletion, she ended her autobiography with an open hand: "This time I shall not write a conclusion to my book. I leave the readers to draw any they may choose" (*All Said and Done*). She died in Paris on 14 April 1986 at the age of seventy-eight.

## Selected Bibliography

### EDITIONS

*L'Invitée.* Paris, 1943.
*Pyrrhus et Cinéas.* Paris, 1944.
*Le sang des autres.* Paris, 1945.
*Les bouches inutiles.* Paris, 1945.
*Tous les hommes sont mortels.* Paris, 1946.
*Pour une morale de l'ambiguité.* Paris, 1947.
*L'Amerique au jour le jour.* Paris, 1948.
*L'Existentialisme et la sagesse des nations.* Paris, 1948.
*Le deuxième sexe.* Paris, 1949.
*Faut-il brûler Sade?* Paris, 1953.
*Les mandarins.* Paris, 1954.
*Privilèges.* Paris, 1955.
*La longue marche.* Paris, 1957.
*Mémoires d'une jeune fille rangée.* Paris, 1958.
*La force de l'âge.* Paris, 1960.

*Brigitte Bardot and the Lolita Syndrome.* London, 1960.
*La force des choses.* Paris, 1963.
*Une mort très douce.* Paris, 1964.
*Les belles images.* Paris, 1966.
*La femme rompue.* Paris, 1967.
*La vieillesse.* Paris, 1970.
*Tout compte fait.* Paris, 1972.
*Quand prime le spirituel.* Paris, 1979.
*La cérémonie des adieux.* Paris, 1981.
*Simone de Beauvoir heute.* West Germany, 1983.

## TRANSLATIONS

*Adieux.* Translated by Patrick O'Brian. 1984.
*After "The Second Sex": Conversations with Simone de Beauvoir.* Interviewed by Alice Schwarzer. Translated by Marianne Howarth. London, 1984.
*All Men Are Mortal.* Translated by Leonard M. Friedman. Cleveland, 1955.
*All Said and Done.* Translated by Patrick O'Brian. New York, 1974.
*America Day by Day.* Translated by Patrick Dudley. London, 1952.
*Les belles images.* Translated by Patrick O'Brian. New York, 1968.
*The Blood of Others.* Translated by Yvonne Moyse and Roger Senhouse. New York, 1948.
*The Ethics of Ambiguity.* Translated by Bernard Frechtman. New York, 1948.
*Force of Circumstance.* Translated by Richard Howard. London, 1964.
*The Long March.* Translated by Austryn Wainhouse. New York, 1958.
*The Mandarins.* Translated by M. Friedman. London, 1960.
*Memoirs of a Dutiful Daughter.* Translated by James Kirkup. New York, 1959.
*Must We Burn Sade?* Translated by Annette Michelson. London, 1953.
*Old Age.* Translated by Patrick O'Brian. London, 1972.
*The Prime of Life.* Translated by Peter Green. New York, 1962.
*The Second Sex.* Translated by H. M. Parshley. New York, 1953.
*She Came to Stay.* Translated by Yvonne Moyse and Roger Senhouse. London, 1966.
*A Very Easy Death.* Translated by Patrick O'Brian. New York, 1966.
*When Things of the Spirit Come First.* Translated by Patrick O'Brian. London, 1982.
*The Woman Destroyed.* Translated by Patrick O'Brian. London, 1968.

## BIOGRAPHICAL AND CRITICAL STUDIES

*L'Arc* 61 (1975). Special issue on Simone de Beauvoir and the Women's Movement.
Armogathe, Daniel. *Le deuxième sexe: Beauvoir.* Paris, 1977.
Benda, Julien. *The Treason of the Intellectuals.* Translated by Richard Aldington. London, 1928.
Bieber, Konrad. *Simone de Beauvoir.* Boston, 1979.
Blair, Deirdre. *Simone de Beauvoir.* New York, 1990.
Brée, Germaine. *Women Writers in France.* New Brunswick, N.J., 1973.
———. "The Fictions of Autobiography." *Nineteenth-Century French Studies* 4 (1976):446.
Brombert, Victor. *The Intellectual Hero.* London, 1960.
Cayron, Claire. *La nature chez Simone de Beauvoir.* Paris, 1973.
Cottrell, Robert D. *Simone de Beauvoir.* New York, 1975.
Collins, Margery, and Pierce Christine. "Holes and Slime: Sexism in Sartre's Psychoanalysis." In *Women and Philosophy,* edited by Carol C. Gould and Marx W. Wartofsky. New York, 1976.
Debray, Regis. *Teachers, Writers, Celebrities.* London, 1981.
Dijkstra, Sandra. "Simone de Beauvoir and Betty Friedan: The Politics of Omission." *Feminist Studies* 6 (2):291–303 (1980).
Epstein, Cynthia Fuchs. "Guineas and Locks." *Dissent* 4:581–586 (1974).
Evans, Mary. *Simone de Beauvoir.* London, 1985.
Felstiner, Mary Lowenthal. "Seeing *The Second Sex* Through the Second Wave." *Feminist Studies* 6 (2):247–275 (1980).
Fuchs, Jo-Ann P. "Female Eroticism in *The Second Sex.*" *Feminist Studies* 6 (2):305–313 (1980).
Gagnebin, Laurent. *Simone de Beauvoir; ou, Le refus de l'indifférence.* Paris, 1968.
Gusdorf, George. "Conditions et limites de l'autobiography." In *Formen der Selbstdarstellung.* Berlin, 1956.
Harth, Erica. "The Creative Alienation of the Writer: Sartre, Camus, and Simone de Beauvoir." *Mosaic* 8:177–186 (1975).

Hourdin, Georges. *Simone de Beauvoir et la liberté.* Paris, 1962.

Jardine, Alice. "Interview with Simone de Beauvoir." *Signs* 5 (2):224–236 (1979).

Jelinek, Estelle C., ed. *Women's Autobiography.* Bloomington, Ind., 1980.

Leacock, Eleanor. *Myths of Male Dominance.* New York, 1981.

Le Doeuff, Michèle. "Simone de Beauvoir and Existentialism." *Feminist Studies* 6, 2:277–289 (1980).

Marks, Elaine. *Simone de Beauvoir: Encounters with Death.* New Brunswick, N.J., 1973.

McCall, Dorothy Kaufmann. "Simone de Beauvoir, *The Second Sex,* and Jean-Paul Sartre." *Signs* 2:209–223 (1979).

Miller, Nancy. "Women's Autobiography in France: For a Dialectics of Identification." In *Woman and Language in Literature and Society,* edited by Sally McConnell-Ginet, Ruth Borker, and Nelly Furman. New York, 1980.

Poster, Mark. *Existential Marxism in Postwar France.* Princeton, 1975.

*The Second Sex—Thirty Years Later.* A Commemorative Conference on Feminist Theory. New York Institute for the Humanities. New York University, 1979.

Whitmarsh, Anne. *Simone de Beauvoir.* Cambridge, 1981.

ANNE MCCLINTOCK

# *BEOWULF* and ANGLO-SAXON POETRY

## *INTRODUCTION*

THE EARLIEST EXTANT epic and the first great poem in the English language is *Beowulf.* Although its availability and influence within its era (*ca.* 600–1066) seem to have been minimal, and although its scope (3,182 lines in the only extant manuscript, *Brit. Lib. Cotton Vitellius A. XV, ca.* A.D. 1000) is constricted compared with later, more self-consciously literary and derivative epics like Spenser's *Faerie Queene* and Milton's *Paradise Lost,* it has stimulated ever-increasing study and admiration during the last hundred years because of the excellence of its artistry, the nobility of its heroic vision, and its uniqueness as a primary epic within early medieval Germanic literature.

Despite the substantial attention paid to *Beowulf* by philologists, folklorists, anthropologists, and social and literary historians, we can still only guess at the circumstances of its composition and offer tentative judgments about its unity, significance, and essentially Christian or pagan outlook. Given the traditional (that is, inherited rather than created) materials, of Germanic or even Indo-European origin, from which it is largely constructed, *Beowulf* resists many types of analysis easily applied to an original narrative fiction composed by a self-conscious verbal artist for a literate audience. To begin to understand its values and perspective, we must first attempt, as much as our literacy-conditioned processes of thought and imagination will allow us, to reconstruct those processes as they might function in a preliterate, traditional culture. Then we must use all available information about the transitional (partly Germanic and traditional, partly Christian and literate) culture of Anglo-Saxon England, and other analogous civilizations, to try to place *Beowulf* within it in time and place, and to form plausible opinions about the poem's poetics, historical consciousness, and commitment (or lack of commitment) to Christianity. Finally, we must be attentive to *Beowulf*'s presentation of the heroic ideal—an ideal it shares with primary, or traditional, epics from several cultures—in order to evaluate the protagonist and his battles with monstrous adversaries.

The following discussion of *Beowulf* will focus successively on its pre-insular cultural heritage; its Anglo-Saxon context; its physical state as a manuscript; and its unity, structure, significance, and art as a poem.

## *SUMMARY*

The poem opens by recalling Scyld Scefing, founder of the Scylding dynasty of the Danish nation. God sends Scyld to the lordless Danes; he comes as a child in a boat and grows up to be a great war-king. When he dies, his followers send his body back out to sea in a treasure-laden boat. Scyld's son, Beowulf (not the hero of the poem), continues his father's reign, and the Danes prosper through generations. Hrothgar, in his kingship, builds Heorot—a great mead hall—and plans to dispense treasure within it to his war band. The joyful songs of the celebrating Danes attract and infuriate Grendel, a border-dwelling semihuman monster descended from Cain, whose lineage was banished by God from the haunts of humanity after the first murder. When the Danes are asleep, Grendel bursts into Heorot and kills and eats thirty warriors. So begins a twelve-year reign of terror: Grendel invades Heorot each night, effectively disrupting Danish social existence, and the Danes have no warrior strong enough to oust him. In their misery, they make offerings to idols; Hrothgar endures helpless, terrible grief.

In Geatland, the young hero Beowulf, strongest of men, hears of the Danes' plight and sets out across the sea with a small troop of companions. They arrive in Denmark and are received with courtesy by Hrothgar. Unferth, the *þyle* (orator? jester? official challenger?) of the Danish court, expresses doubt that Beowulf, who lost a swimming (or rowing) match to a famous warrior called Breca some time before, can now conquer Grendel. Beowulf denies the allegation of defeat and tells the true story, including how he killed nine sea monsters. He then impugns the Danes' courage, and says that he is ready to destroy Grendel or die trying. Hrothgar is pleased by the visitor's reply and leaves the Geats alone in Heorot as night falls. Grendel arrives, expecting to feast on more sleeping warriors. He devours one Geat, but Beowulf, who has disavowed the use of weapons against Grendel, takes the monster in a handgrip. A terrific battle ensues, which nearly wrecks Heorot. The terrified Grendel tries to escape; Beowulf tears his arm off, and the monster flees to his swampland home to die.

The next morning the Danes rejoice at Grendel's fate and celebrate Beowulf's deed in songs. Celebrations begin in Heorot; a *scop* (court poet) recites the story of the battle at Finnsburh between the Half-Danes under Hnaef and the Frisians under Finn. The fight was a standoff, but Hnaef was killed, and Hildeburh, his sister and Finn's wife, mourned him and her son, also a victim. Hengest, Hnaef's henchman, entered into a treaty to serve Finn with the other Half-Danes, but ultimately broke the agreement and avenged Hnaef by killing Finn. The story over, gifts are given and Wealhtheow, Hrothgar's queen, asks for support for her young sons from Beowulf and Hrothulf, Hrothgar's nephew.

After the Danes and Geats go to sleep, Grendel's mother enters Heorot seeking vengeance for her dead offspring. She seizes one Danish warrior and flees to her swamp. The Danes and Hrothgar are desolate at this new attack, but Beowulf promises to avenge the dead man and is escorted to the dreadful, fiery pool beneath which the monsters live. Armed and bearing Unferth's sword, Hrunting, Beowulf dives to the bottom, finds the monsters' hall, and does battle with Grendel's mother. The fight is difficult; Hrunting fails its user, but Beowulf sees a great old sword, too big for anyone but himself, and uses it to kill the mother and behead the body of the son, whose blood destroys the blade. The hero returns to the surface of the purged pond, finds the Danes gone and his own men despairing, and returns to Heorot with Grendel's head and the sword hilt, which he gives to Hrothgar. The old king stares at the hilt and instructs the young warrior on the shortness of life and the necessity of sharing out treasure. After an exchange of gifts and protestations of friendship between Geats and Danes (who had been feuding), Beowulf returns home and tells his king, Hygelac, of his exploits; he also indicates that the political marriage between Hrothgar's daughter, Freawaru, and Ingeld, prince of the Heathobards, will only briefly quiet the feud between the two peoples. Beowulf passes on to Hygelac the gifts he has received from Hrothgar, and Hygelac gives him a large tract of land and a hall.

Many years later, when Beowulf has been king of the Geats for fifty years, a dragon begins a feud against him because an unknown slave (or thane—the manuscript is unclear) has robbed a cup from the hoard that the dragon has guarded for 300 years. The dragon burns down Beowulf's hall with his fiery breath, and the old king sets out to fight him unaided, except for specially constructed fireproof armor. Before the fight, Beowulf recalls the deaths of Hygelac and Hygelac's son Heardred in feuds with other nations, and recapitulates some of the battles between Geats and Swedes in earlier years. Having established an elegaic mood, Beowulf challenges the dragon, who emerges from his barrow to begin the fight. Beowulf's sword breaks (we are told that he has always been too strong for swords), and the dragon gives him a lethally poisonous wound.

All his retainers run away, terrified by the dragon, except young Wiglaf, who recalls Beowulf's munificence and vows to fight with him to the death. The two men succeed in killing the dragon, striking him in his soft belly, but Beowulf is also dying. Wiglaf brings him some of the treasure that he has fought to win for his people; placed in the dragon's barrow by the last survivor of an ancient race, it has a curse upon it, unknown to the Geats' king. Beowulf looks on the treasure and dies. Wiglaf chastises the cowardly retainers and sends a messenger to tell the Geats of their lord's demise; the messenger warns that, with Beowulf gone, the Geats can expect renewed hostility from the Swedes, Franks, and Frisians, and a bleak future. (Beowulf has no son, and Wiglaf, his apparent successor, is young and untested.) Beowulf's body is ritually burned, and the remains are placed with the gold (as useless as before, the poem says) in a barrow that the dying king instructed to be built by the sea, where passing ships can see it. The poem ends with the Geatish warriors riding around the barrow, sadly uttering the praises of the dead Beowulf.

## *HERITAGE*

*Beowulf*'s obvious debt to traditional culture takes four main forms: (1) its depiction of a German warrior aristocracy (in the main plot and in numerous digressions and allusions) and of the poetic practices of this society; (2) its quasi-formulaic diction, reminiscent of preliterate poetic composition; (3) the form and narrative method of its three main stories; (4) its preoccupation with a hero—a warrior whose strength and courage distinguish him from other mortals and whose dedication to glory at all costs makes him at once a savior of, and threat to, society. This section will examine each of these four aspects of the poem.

### Beowulf *and Germanic Society*

Scholars who deal with material relating to pre–Anglo-Saxon Germanic history (classical sources of varying reliability, the most famous being Tacitus' *Germania,* and Germanic texts from the Christian era) find evidence of a society organized around a sacral kingship that functioned as the link between the tribal group and its gods. Attached to the sacral king was a tribal poet whose primary task, it would seem, was to utter the praises of the king and his ancestors in improvised, non-narrative eulogistic poetry with strong religious, even shamanistic, overtones. The purpose of such eulogies was to preserve the fame of its subjects after their deaths and thus to keep them alive in order that they might protect their royal descendants and the tribe as a whole. In addition to this "official" poetry, Germanic society would have fostered poems and songs of all kinds, improvised and memorized, recited by warriors and their womenfolk before battle to increase valor and win the favor of the gods, by peasants as they farmed their lands or watched their cattle, and by families in order to bring the living into close and fruitful contact with the tutelary spirits of their ancestors. At this stage of society, it has been argued, there would be no narrative poetry; the deeds of the great kings and warriors of the past recalled in eulogies would live on as a body of traditional stories, unfixed in form and passed on from generation to generation as the property of the entire tribe.

The causes and nature of evolution beyond the phase just described are subject to dispute. H. M. Chadwick long ago noted that many references to the past in postclassical Germanic texts are international in character—that is, kings and heroes from one nation appear in the literature of another, as in *Beowulf,* an Anglo-Saxon poem about Danes, Geats, and Swedes—and look back to a period between the fourth and sixth centuries of our era, which Chadwick calls the "heroic age" of the Germanic peoples and which coincides with their triumph over the Roman Empire in the West. Drawing on analogies between Germanic material and the Homeric poems, Chadwick posited the heroic age as a stage through which many physically mobile societies pass, perhaps as a response to the challenge of a new, superior power with which they come into contact. A warrior aristocracy comes into being, one that places comitatus, or lord-retainer, relationships above kindred ties and subordinates a primarily religious view of life to a code of heroic values centered on loyalty to ruler, bravery, and willingness to die in the pursuit of fame and glory. During this period, among the Germanic nations, a new class of bards, held in high esteem as preservers in narrative song of the deeds of heroes, moved about from nation to nation, cross-fertilizing the traditions in which the warrior aristocracy found its inspiration, ideals, and even identity as a group.

Jeff Opland, who has done pioneering work among the Xhosa and Zulu nations of southern Africa and finds among them many analogies to Germanic society in its pre- and postconversion phases, takes a different view of the extant evidence. He contends that non-narrative eulogy remained the dominant, official form of poetry among the Germanic nations until the coming of Christianity, which, by redefining and Christianizing the office of the cultic king, deprived the tribal poet of his traditional function as eulogizer of the ruler and, through language, controller of people and gods. In Opland's view, wandering singers who lacked the special rank and privileges of the eulogizing tribal poets began to circulate among some Germanic nations, carrying with them an international fund of memorized heroic songs, the result of coming into contact with Roman traditions of public entertainment by professional performers. The fact that narrative is embryonically present in eulogy facilitated the shift in poetic genre. Later, after the Anglo-Saxons received Christianity, in good part through missionary activity originating in Rome, narrative "heroic" poetry—with *Beowulf* as an extreme example—sprang up in England as a type of nostalgic entertainment for small monastic or aristocratic communities, under the influence of classical literature, biblical stories, and militant early-medieval hagiography.

We may infer from Opland's interpretation of the evidence that Germanic heroic narrative poetry tells us little or nothing about a separate "heroic age" of Germanic society, since it reflects the conditions of a later, postconversion period and the impact of ecclesiastically fostered literacy rather than the domination of a secularized warrior aristocracy in the period between the sacral king and the Christian God.

It seems unlikely that we will ever know the development of Germanic society thoroughly enough to perceive within it the precise sequence of, or relationships among, eulogistic verse, narrative lays sung to a mixed audience by peripatetic entertainers who presumably accompanied themselves on the harp, and heroic narrative poetry intended for a secular or religious elite. We can, however, distinguish between a religious, God-centered view of the world (or cosmos) and a heroic one, in which the struggles of mortals are central and the finality of death magnifies the glory won by defying it in battle. *Beowulf* is obviously a narrative poem, and its most overt, consistently proposed values are earthbound and "heroic": loyalty to lord and, subsidiarily, kindred; bravery; generosity; and the hero's search for glory through the acceptance of challenges to combat. The presentation of the poem's kings—Hrothgar of the Danes, Hygelac and Beowulf of the Geats—has little of the overtly sacral about it, although Hrothgar does offer moral warnings and guidance to Beowulf in a passage often characterized by modern critics as a sermon (1700–1784). But, as Opland indicates, *Beowulf* contains clear elements of eulogy amid its narrative. The opening eleven lines of the poem constitute a "praise poem" of Scyld Scefing, founder of the Danish Scylding dynasty, culminating in the celebratory exclamation "þæt wæs god cyning!" (he was a good king: 11). A little later, after the construction of Heorot, while the Danes feast in the hall, a court poet sings a song that sounds much like a eulogy of God the creator (90–98; compare *Caedmon's Hymn,* discussed later in this essay). When Beowulf has mortally wounded Grendel, the Danes follow the tracks of the dying monster to his lair and then return rejoicing; along the way a wise old thane who knows many stories sings or recites the praises of Beowulf, then of the Germanic hero Sigemund, whose legendary feats provide a sympathetic context for the young Geatish warrior (853–900).

In other parts of the poem, the consistent linking of poetic utterance—including references to Germanic heroic stories such as the Finnsburh episode—to moments of communal joy in Heorot (after the hall is built; after Beowulf has cleansed it of Grendel and then of Grendel's mother) seems clearly to reflect an established tradition of songs or recited poetic entertainment, probably narrative in nature, within an aristocratic, warrior society.

Whatever conclusions one may draw about the precise stage of Germanic society that saw the nascence of *Beowulf,* the fact remains that characteristics of several evolutionary phases coexist in our text. Furthermore, the various functions of poetry during these phases—eulogy, inspirational heroic narrative, social entertainment—all seem present as well.

## Beowulf *and Oral Culture*

The various kinds of poetry mentioned in the preceding section would not have been conceived or preserved in writing in pre-Christian Germanic culture, since it was an oral rather than a literate culture. (Literacy, as already noted, came to the Germanic nations with their evangelization by Christian missionaries.) The differences between an oral and a written culture are numerous and profound; inhabitants of a literate culture can never fully appreciate the implications of nonliteracy for a society and its members, but much can be deduced from texts rooted in an oral culture and subsequently preserved (in however modified a form) by literates, and from observations of the world's remaining nonliterate or partially literate societies.

In an oral culture certain distinctions that we take for granted do not exist: distinctions, for example, between hearsay and fact, between history and tradition or legend. Furthermore, the division of knowledge into areas such as law, history, philosophy, and literature, each of which constitutes a separate (written) body of information, is also foreign to an oral culture. Replacing (or rather, preexistent to) all these categories is the collective memory of the group, which determines both its identity and its sense of right and wrong by keeping alive exemplary stories of great deeds and heroes of the past. The ultimate purpose of an oral culture's recollections is to link past and present, living and dead, humanity and its gods in an ongoing relationship, in order to maintain the group and inspire its individual members. The past, in other words, remains a vivid presence to be called up and shared by members of a tribal group whenever they gather together and one of them begins to recite or sing of the tribal past as it has been preserved in genealogy, eulogy, or narrative.

By contrast, writing objectifies the past so that, although it is always available (in the form of records) and not contingent upon strength or weakness of memory, it also becomes discontinuous with, and therefore remote from, the world of experience. The absence of written records to freeze information in a final, limiting form means that in an oral culture the past is fluid and constantly evolving, not because of new research or discoveries—as in a literate culture when unknown or forgotten documents are discovered that change our understanding of the past—but because, as events recede further into the past, they conform more and more to certain basic story patterns; and in the crucible of memory the deeds of one hero are confused with those of another, while people from different eras are recalled as contemporaries or vice versa.

The contemporary scholar Walter Ong has characterized the main features of an oral culture as *dynamism, polemicism,* and *traditionalism.* All relate to the function of memory in a culture without literacy and records.

Dynamism, an epistemological category, refers to the centrality of unpredictable, dynamic events, not static theories or systems, in apprehending the world. When knowledge is a function of recollection rather than abstraction, things most easily recalled—unexpected actions that have brought about change, confrontation, crisis—define the contours of what is known.

Polemicism, an evaluative and structural category, reflects the fact that the most remarkable actions, and therefore the most influential across generations, are battles between good and evil or between exemplary figures and groups in similarly definitive opposition. From this fact follows the intertwining of action and judgment in an oral culture: for any generation, the past is not a neutral record, but a challenge to identify with some characters and events and to reprobate others. Another result of polemicism is that material we might, from our literate perspective, consider extraneous—catalogs, historical allusions, gnomic or sententious utterances—tends to become attached to, and encrusted upon, memorable stories to facilitate its preservation. (Hence, for example, the ship catalogs in the *Iliad.*)

Traditionalism, a methodological category, refers to techniques of preserving and transmitting the recollections that define knowledge, values, and identity. These include fixed or highly conservative verse forms, diction, and narrative patterns. The object of traditionalism, to *preserve* rather than to innovate or to define with precision, has two important consequences. The first is the very slow evolution of poetic art, since originality would run counter to poetry's mnemonic function. The second is that, instead of narrative structure and language conforming to events as they happen, new events are made to conform to preexisting structures and diction so that they can be more easily understood and transmitted from age to age. Traditional poetry takes two distinct, though never absolutely separate, forms: improvisation and memorization. An improvising poet/singer articulates his material in a traditional, formulaic diction. The act of articulation differs somewhat from performance to performance: each retelling of a story will be a fresh act of improvisation and therefore to some extent creative. By contrast, performances of deliberately memorized poems or songs are re-creative, literal repetitions, and the singer/poet is but the passive medium through whom are transmitted the verbal patterns previously composed by another. In most traditional cultures, improvisation is the more appreciated skill.

Since an oral culture lacks the larger political systems made possible by abstractions and recordkeeping—both products of literacy—its experience tends to consist of repeated, tradition-based conflicts (or feuds) among small sociopolitical units, each held together by links of kindred and common recollection. The end of constant local warring between such fragmentary polities must await the (literate) articulation of constitutions, treaties, and theories of strong central authority and the res publica; lacking these instruments, neighboring villages or tribes in an oral culture can seek to resolve feuds only by concrete gestures: money payments to injured kin groups, intermarriage between ruling families, or de jure kinship between leaders.

Although few students of *Beowulf* would now classify the poem as in any direct way the product of an oral culture, it abounds in techniques and characteristics denoting its ultimate kinship with such a culture. In fact, *Beowulf* seems in some respects quite self-conscious about the nature and limits of an oral culture, a phenomenon suggesting its attainment of literate detachment.

The characteristic movement of *Beowulf* stresses the instability and unpredictability of life, summed up most strikingly in the sudden appearances of monsters who transform a social situation of peace, joy, and harmony into one of misery and strife. The poem's term for this depiction of the dynamism inherent in oral culture's recollective way of knowing reality is *edwenden,* a sudden, unexpected change. Hrothgar tells Beowulf of his career as victorious king, "Hwæt, me þæs on eþle edwenden cwom, / gyrn æfter gomene, seoþðan Grendel wearð,/ ealdgewinna, ingenga min" (See how a great turnabout came to me in my homeland: grief after joy, once Grendel, the old adversary, became my invader: 1774–1776). Interestingly, the poem's insistence on the Danes' ignorance of the biblical origin of Grendel's lineage (discussed later) and of providence in general as it concerns their own history seems to be a self-conscious critique of the epistemological limitations of an oral culture. The Danes lack crucial knowledge because they lack the book that would tell them the truth—the book on which Christianity depends and which determines its literate impulse.

The polemicism of *Beowulf* is one of its most obvious features: its core comprises the three battles between Beowulf, an exemplary protagonist, and his equally exemplary monstrous antagonists. The quasi-symbolic absoluteness of the adversarial relationships—attained by identifying Grendel and his mother with Cain, the first murderer, and the dragon with devouring time—suggests the poem's self-consciousness about the polemical nature of preliterate civilization. Also, the sharp contrast between the poem's two main subdivisions, Beowulf's youth and age, constitutes a kind of displaced polemicism transferred from the hero's main battles to his life, and from characters in the poem to the poem itself. Finally, the assimilation into the poem of gnomic sayings ("Gæð a wyrd swa hio scel" [Fate always goes as it must: 455]), sententious maxims ("Sinc eaðe mæg,/gold on grunde gumcynnes gehwone / oferhigian, hyde se ðe wylle" [Treasure, gold in the earth, can easily outdo any of humankind, whoever hides it: 2764–2766]), and historical allusions (Hama stealing the necklace of Eormenric: 1198–1201) illustrates the process of encrustation whereby such material is preserved by association with memorable conflicts such as Beowulf's heroic combats.

The traditionalism of *Beowulf* manifests itself not only in quasi-formulaic diction (see below) but in its use of traditional themes such as the presence at battles of the eagle, raven, and wolf as creatures of prey (3024–3027). The traditional folktale-like structure of the battles will be examined in the next section.

The political fragmentation and instability that mark preliterate society underlie the feuds in *Beowulf,* which are so omnipresent as to constitute a basic theme of the poem (see below). Beowulf's statement that political marriages rarely succeed in permanently settling a feud ("Oft seldan hwær/æfter leodhryre lytle hwile/bongar bugeð, þeah seo bryd duge" [Only seldom after the fall of a prince does the war spear remain at rest for any length of time, however excellent the bride: 2029–2031]) reflects wisdom that clearly derives from recollection. In fact, the processes and consequences of recollection hold a great self-conscious fascination for the poet, as two examples will demonstrate: an ancient weapon or piece of jewelry (usually called a *laf* [a relic, inheritance, survivor: 1688, 2036]), passed on from hand to hand, stimulates recollection of past events (the necklace Wealhtheow gives to Beowulf: 1195–1214), maxims whereby one generation teaches the next (the hilt Beowulf gives Hrothgar: 1677–1698; 1724–1768), or actions that reopen an old feud (the Heathobard sword worn by a Danish warrior: 2036–2069); the *laf* also stands as a metaphor for the nature and function of an oral culture's legacy of recollection. And the old man who recalls everything ("se ðe eall gemon": 1700–1701; 2042; 2427) represents with equal force the ideal of total recall, and therefore complete wisdom, toward which an oral culture must always strive.

## Beowulf *and the Traditional Story*

As noted above, basic narrative patterns are one of the oral culture's methods for preserving and transmitting its recollected past. A traditional story is one that cannot be assigned to a particular author and that circulates widely in a variety of versions, none of which can be considered original or definitive. While many traditional stories originate in an oral culture, they have enormous longevity and can continue to exist for centuries in multiple oral and written (or transcribed) versions having the same basic plot but many variants of character and motivation.

Common forms of the traditional story include the joke, or short humorous tale; the folk or fairy tale (which looks inward, to fears and desires, for its inspiration); and the heroic tale (which looks outward, to deeds and experiences). Patterns assumed by the traditional story for purposes of recollection and clarification show remarkable persistence and invariability: in 1928 the Russian formalist critic Vladimir Propp demonstrated by studying a body of Russian folktales that the plot of a traditional story can be separated into thirty-one parts or functions that always appear in the same order, though not every tale has all the functions. These functions are the building blocks of the story; they recount the occurrence of a crisis and the stages of its eventual resolution.

The constant patterns of the traditional story take its hero through peril to final triumph or satisfaction. The many versions of a particular story will share the same pattern of events, all of which revolve around the central character(s). Other characters exist *not* independently and with their own psychological complexities, but rather only to test and define the protagonist. Hence these other characters—companions adversaries, fairy godmothers—often appear to behave inconsistently or without motivation. Indeed, even the protagonist's actions will sometimes appear arbitrary or unmotivated and his (or her) character to lack consistency. Everything is subordinated to the working out of the plot; character and motivation constitute rationalizations of the plot and vary from teller to teller. (In the mimetic tradition of the novel, by contrast, plot often seems to evolve organically from character.)

Propp's study shows that many folktales have a multiple, paratactic structure: the hero, having seen one adventure through to a happy conclusion, must face another version of the same adventure with a different antagonist.

The additive principle at work here also appears in other, less structurally coherent guises in traditional stories based on historical deeds or characters. As written down, often hundreds of years after the event, such stories can be highly composite (like the Middle High German *Nibelungenlied,* for example), combining material from several versions with results that seem to us contradictory and ineffective. We see here that the impulse behind this type of traditional story is synthetic—it retains all available material about the past, adding and combining stories because all are part of its culture's memory-defined identity—rather than analytic, as is the case in a literate culture where students of the past, attempting to determine which account of an event tells "what really happened," make choices among available versions and discard the "inauthentic" ones.

A notable feature of history-based traditional stories is their lack of the surprise that depends on the audience's ignorance of the outcome. Instead, the audience is constantly reminded of the denouement in narrational asides or prophetic dreams and utterances of characters, all of which recognize and capitalize on the audience's familiarity with the obligatory traditional events recounted. The story absorbs into itself its audience's foreknowledge, translating it into an often overwhelming sense of inescapable destiny; the story's inability to avoid the denouement established for it by tradition becomes the characters' inability to avoid the denouement established for them by fate.

*Beowulf* conforms to the norms of the traditional story in many ways. Daniel Barnes has submitted the poem to Proppian analysis and demonstrated the considerable extent to which the hero's three battles are three repeated adventures, or "moves," comprising the same order of functions. Comparison between the *Beowulf* episodes of Grendel and his mother and two adventures involving the hero of the fourteenth-century Icelandic *Grettissaga* shows that the two works are utilizing versions of the same two-move traditional story: a double struggle between a brave, strong hero and his monstrous opponents. In the first move, the evil antagonist invades a place that should be tranquil and safe (in *Beowulf,* Heorot; in *Grettissaga,* the farmhouse of Þorhallr), dominating and terrorizing it until defeated and expelled by the hero. (The persistence even today of this plot, in "alien invasion" science-fiction films, for example, should be obvious.) In the second move, the momentum is reversed, and the hero enters an alien environment (the fiery, blood-stained swamp in *Beowulf;* a cave behind a waterfall in *Grettissaga*), risking his life to confront and extirpate the evil at its source. (Science-fiction and other types of action-adventure films fall into this category.)

The basic story shared by *Beowulf* and *Grettissaga* is rationalized in each work according to its artistic intent and the expectations of its audience. The saga writer has domesticated the struggle between good and evil by placing it in the agrarian society and known geography of Iceland. *Beowulf,* by contrast, exalts the struggle by investing it with a setting in the Germanic heroic past, by linking it to the antagonism between God and Cain's kin, and by endowing the monsters' swamp home with trappings of Gothic horror closely paralleled in an Anglo-Saxon homily describing St. Paul's vision of hell.

The third move in *Beowulf* is equally traditional; fights between heroes and dragons occupy a central place in the folklore and mythology of northern Europe—Saint George and Siegfried, for example. Here again we find in *Beowulf* elements of rationalization to explain the story of the hero's death: the curse on the gold guarded by the dragon (3051–3057); the failure of Beowulf's sword because his strength has always been too great for weapons (2680–2687); the cowardice of his retainers, except for Wiglaf (2596–2601).

The inconsistencies of traditional stories grounded in history find ample representation in *Beowulf.* Perhaps the most famous instance occurs in Beowulf's recapitulation of his Danish adventures to Hygelac. Here the previously unnamed Geatish victim of Grendel is called Hondscio, and Grendel is retrospectively equipped with a *glof* (glove-shaped sack) into which he attempts to thrust Beowulf before the latter engages him in the fatal grip. Another possible inconsistency of a traditional nature comes at this point—in the reference to Beowulf's unpromising youth (2183–2189), hitherto unmentioned—relating his career to the "young slacker" folklore motif familiar from the much later tale of *Jack and the Beanstalk.*

The prediction of the outcome of battles, a characteristic of stories known to their audience, occurs before the fights with Grendel (696–700, 716–719) and with the dragon (2309–2311, 2419–2424).

As with its relation to oral culture, *Beowulf* appears to manifest, on at least two occasions, an intriguing self-consciousness about its own treatment of the traditional stories it utilizes. Both occur shortly after Beowulf arrives in Denmark. First, Hrothgar employs the technique of rationalization in interpreting Beowulf's journey to his court to fight Grendel and win glory as the result of a desire to repay Hrothgar for having settled, some years earlier, a feud involving Ecgtheow, Beowulf's father (456–472). Then, when Unferth questions Beowulf's heroic credentials by alluding to the latter's contest with Breca, he bases his challenge on a version of the adventure significantly different from the one Beowulf himself proceeds to tell. The multiple forms of the same story that mark traditional narrative here rise up to confront the hero; he can control the contest with Breca as a deed, but not its subsequent recounting as a story.

## BEOWULF *AND THE HEROIC IDEAL*

As a poem about a hero and his heroism, *Beowulf* reflects the fascination of Indo-European civilization with the figure of the warrior who performs prodigies of strength and courage in pursuit of glory—the man who, in the words of an Icelandic saga hero, would rather die than yield. The ultimate mystery of the hero is that, fully cognizant of his mortality, he chooses to behave as though he were immortal, deliberately exposing himself to danger when the normal human response would be to opt for safety and survival. To put it another way, the hero pushes to the limits the possibilities of the human will by choosing to take risks that all the instincts of self-preservation resist. The reward of this triumph of will over the knowledge of mortality and the instinct for survival is glory: the recognition by others that there is something of the divine about the hero—hence the phrase "hero worship"—when the frenzy of action seizes him. (The unforgettable image in the *Iliad* [book 21] of Achilles, in all his fiery energy, battling the river Simois perhaps best conveys our culture's response to heroic glory.)

The hero's energy and unwavering commitment to glory, his unwillingness ever to recognize the arguments of diplomacy or prudence against heroic action, also make him a problem to those who depend on his strength—whether, like Achilles, he chooses to withdraw from the Trojan war rather than seem to lose face to Agamemnon, or, like Roland, he dooms 20,000 Frankish warriors to Charlemagne's rear guard by refusing to summon the main army with his horn, lest he seem cowardly. The hero's dread of appearing unheroic—the key to his problematic status—leads him always to choose the option in any situation that cannot possibly be interpreted as motivated by fear. Sooner or later, that choice brings his world to disaster and himself to death, since it rules out the possibility of compromise, restraint, and prudent withdrawal, which are sometimes required in every sphere of life, domestic or political.

The great medieval primary epics—*Beowulf,* the *Chanson de Roland,* the *Nibelungenlied*—celebrate the life and mourn the death of their heroes. In the climactic battles of the epic, the hero's antagonist must in some way be a match for him if he is to win glory from the encounter and the epic is to hold the interest of its audience. A subtler conflict involves the hero's relationship to the king he serves, often as a visitor from another land. The king finds his authority implicitly or explicitly threatened by the outsider hero; as a result, the epic may focus on the rituals and strategies whereby a king and a society receive a visiting hero and domesticate him.

The hero's death marks the end of an era or seals the fate of a civilization; it is accordingly an occasion for sadness and gloomy prophecies. The story of the hero's fall serves a social function as an explanation of *our* fallen, postheroic state, an etiological myth to account for our unwillingness to be heroes, as well as our continued allegiance to the heroic ideal of self-sacrifice in the interest of glory. One might also argue that the fall of the hero is a symbolic account of growing up, of coming to the realization that we are mortal and cannot, therefore, afford to behave as heroes do if we are to survive. Heroes, in their absolutism, self-absorption, and refusal to compromise, are wondrous children who haven't grown up enough to appreciate the complexities of life that render their pursuit of glory an unaffordable luxury. Yet even as we outgrow a heroic outlook, we mourn its loss within us, just as we mourn all of childhood's passing. Such an analysis may explain the continued hold on us of tales about quasi-mythical mortals who lived (if at all) eons ago; it may also provide an insight into the deep ambivalence we feel about the descendants of those heroes in our own society: much-decorated generals who charge when they should retreat, outrageously self-centered sports stars who thrive on confrontation. Magnificent self-destruction continues to attract and disturb us as few other phenomena in our experience of life.

When Beowulf first appears in his poem, his exceptional ability in the heroic mode takes precedence over his name by almost 150 lines: "se wæs moncynnes mægenes strengest/on þæm dæge þysses lifes" (he was the strongest of mankind at that time: 196–197). His words after his arrival at Hrothgar's court convey quintessentially heroic sentiments: he will fight Grendel alone (424–426) and without weapons (677–687) to maximize his chance for glory; if he fails, he is fully aware that it will mean death: "Ic gefremman sceal/eorlic ellen, oþðe endedæg/on þisse meoduhealle minne gebidan!" (I shall perform noble deeds or come to the end of my days in this mead hall: 636–638). Throughout the poem, Beowulf's rhetoric remains constant. When Hrothgar tells him that Grendel's mother has carried off Aeschere, Beowulf replies that it is better to avenge a friend than to be immobilized by mourning (1384–1385); his speech continues paradigmatically:

> Ure æghwylc sceal ende gebidan
> worolde lifes; wyrce se þe mote
> domes ærdeaþe; þæt bið drihtguman
> unlifgendum æfter selest.
> (1386–1389)

Each of us must come to the end of life in the world; let each who can, obtain glory before death; that will be best afterward for the departed warrior.

The dragon episode finds the old Beowulf proclaiming to his retainers that he would rather fight the dragon without armor and weapons, if the beast's fiery breath would allow. He will not retreat, but will engage the creature singlehandedly, for it is no one's task but his:

> Ic mid elne sceall
> gold gegangan, oððe guð nimeð,
> feorhbealu frecne frean eowerne!
> (2535–2537)

I shall bravely win the gold, or battle—terrible, deadly evil—will take away your lord.

It is Beowulf's singlemindedness about fighting the dragon alone—Wiglaf calls him *anhydig,* consistent in resolution (2667)—and his unwillingness, as is proper for heroes, to forfeit *dom,* or glory (2666), that wins him the final judgment he seeks from those who judge correctly (*soðfaestra dom:* 2820), but also brings his death and the danger of destruction to the Geats. This problematic side of Beowulf, shared by all heroes who seem too big for their worlds and their mortality, finds metaphoric expression in the fact that his strength has always been too great to allow him to use weapons well. Only his grip, the full expression of his energy and frenzy, fully represents the hero's *mana* (power)— when used not only on Grendel, but on the Huga (Frankish) champion, Dæghrefn, as well (2501–2508).

Beowulf's superhuman (and isolated from human) heroic essence underlies the verbal and imagistic equivalency between him and the monsters he fights. He and Grendel meet, equally unarmed and dependent upon a handgrip. They share feelings and status: "Yrre wæron begen, / reþe renweardas" (They were both furious, the fierce hall-guardians: 769–770). He and the dragon appear like two old kings fighting (or bargaining) over a single treasure (2413–2419), or two warring monsters (*aglæcean:* 2592). Indeed, when Beowulf dies in battle, he has a barrow built to his orders, and the treasure that the dragon has guarded is buried with him; he has become the dragon in death.

Beowulf's departure leaves a terrible sense of loss as well as danger hanging over the Geats—and the poem. The eulogistic lament uttered by the twelve warriors who ride around Beowulf's barrow not only puts the final testimony to the hero into place at the end of the poem—its last word, describing Beowulf, is *lofgeornost* (most eager for renown: 3182)—but summon up a last image of his centrality in his world, and of the emptiness now at the circle's midpoint.

## *THE ANGLO-SAXON CONTEXT*

Anglo-Saxon England, the immediate cultural context of *Beowulf,* came into existence sometime around 550 with the Germanic settlement of the heartland of Britain and ceased with the Norman Conquest of 1066. Its civilization demonstrates with particular clarity the uneven, sometimes traumatic process of assimilation whereby three cultural traditions—classical, Christian, and Germanic—were fused into the unique indigenous culture of medieval Europe. In fact, the picture is even more crowded in England, where a fourth strand, the idiosyncratic, ascetic religious culture of Celtic Ireland, had to be woven into the tapestry. A brief consideration of some aspects of the evolution of Anglo-Saxon England will help to illuminate *Beowulf's* combination of Christian and Germanic elements. In addition, an equally abbreviated survey of the contents and techniques of Anglo-Saxon poetry will help us to understand the artistic context of *Beowulf* as a necessary preliminary to grappling with its artistic achievement.

### *The Cultural Synthesis*

In 596 Pope Gregory the Great sent a mission, headed by Augustine, to convert the Germanic peoples then occupying much of Britain—Angles, Saxons, Jutes, and others, organized in small kingdoms isolated from, and often at war with, each other. The missionaries landed in Kent (whose king had a Frankish Christian wife) and set out from there. Throughout the first half of the seventh century, Christianity made uneven progress in England through the uncoordinated efforts of evangelists dispatched from Rome and Ireland; not until the Synod of Whitby in 663 did the Roman party succeed in imposing its loyalty to the pope and liturgical discipline (including the dating of Easter) on the entire English church.

Thanks to Bede's *Historia ecclesiastica gen-*

*tis Anglorum* (*Ecclesiastical History of the English Nation,* 731), we have a richly documented, ideologically committed, and brilliant depiction of the conversion of the English. From Bede we learn that the conversion of an Anglo-Saxon kingdom usually depended upon the conversion of the prince, often the result of a confluence of factors. These included the prior conversion of his wife, the eloquent preaching of a missionary, and a calculation on his part (rooted in Germanic sacral kingship) that the new God offered him and his nation a greater chance of success in battle and overall prosperity than did the older Germanic pantheon. Conversion, in short, was a political and self-interested process, not a spiritual and self-sacrificial one.

In the famous account of the conversion of King Edwin of Northumbria, Bede shows many factors at work on the king, including letters from the pope and quasi-visionary experiences while Edwin was in exile and great danger. Bede's vivid dramatization of the council meeting at which Edwin makes his momentous decision is the masterpiece of the *Historia* (2.13): Coifi, the pagan priest, argues that the old gods have not repaid the king's efforts on their behalf, so Coifi is ready to see if the new God will show greater munificence. An unnamed counselor, also urging conversion, compares human life, surrounded by the mysteries of human origins and destiny, to a sparrow who flies into, then out of, a brightly lit hall on a dark winter night; while the bird is in the hall, it is known, but not before or after. He argues that the new religion, offering knowledge about life beyond life, should be embraced. Edwin acquiesces and is rewarded by God with victory at war until he is martyred in 632 and his kingdom is divided.

Given the political basis of many of the conversions of Anglo-Saxon rulers, frequent backsliding into paganism or syncretism was inevitable. Bede tells of several cases of reversion by sons of Christian kings or by apostatizing kings themselves. Redwald, king of the East Angles, had both pagan and Christian altars in his chapel (*Historia* 2.15) during the first quarter of the seventh century. Such combining of new and old religions could stem from an understandable desire to receive "luck" from as many divine sources as possible; in addition, it may have been inadvertently encouraged by missionaries if they followed Pope Gregory's advice to Mellitus (*Historia* 1.30) not to destroy pagan shrines but only the idols in them, substituting Christian altars and relics and thus luring the people to new worship in familiar settings.

We can see the continued attraction of traditional customs, and their partial integration with Christianity, in the magnificent seventh-century ship buried at Sutton Hoo in East Anglia and unearthed in 1939. The artifacts in the tomb (or cenotaph; there is disagreement over whether there was a body) come from Sweden and other places on the Continent as well as England; among them is a pair of baptismal spoons. In the latter part of the seventh century and thereafter, Christian monastic culture flourished in England as practically nowhere else in western Europe under the influence of Rome and (through Theodore, archbishop of Canterbury from 668) of Greek culture. Manuscripts were brought from Rome to be copied; scriptural commentaries (especially Bede's), hagiography, and scientific treatises were written in the thriving monasteries of Northumbria. There, too, the Hiberno-Saxon style of manuscript illumination evolved, combining Mediterranean representational traditions with the Germanic and Celtic love of abstract patterns and fanciful zoomorphic forms.

While integration of the various traditions vitalizing English life proceeded apace, tensions remained. Bede relates (*Historia* 3.22) that Sigeberht, king of the East Saxons, was murdered (*ca.* 660) by his two brothers; "when they were asked why they did it, they could make no reply except that they were angry with the king and hated him because he was too ready to pardon his enemies, calmly forgiving them for the wrongs they had done him, as soon as they asked his pardon." Presumably, the brothers saw Sigeberht as undermining the Germanic imperative of vengeance, against which the church set itself, but without complete success, as is shown in the famous entry in the *Anglo-Saxon Chronicle* about the slaying of King Cyneheard of Wessex as an act of vengeance in 786.

During the eighth century the English church sent missionaries to the Germanic nations on the Continent, and English monks such as Alcuin aided Charlemagne in his ecclesiastical and educational reforms. Then in 793 began the period of Scandinavian raids on Britain; though halted by King Alfred of Wessex in the late ninth century, they began again in the tenth and culminated in the rule over a joint kingdom of England and Denmark by the Dane Cnut and his sons from 1016 to 1042. The Danish invasions disrupted monastic life and Christian intellectual and educational activity. Alfred attempted to turn the tide of cultural decline by having the leaders of the Danes baptized and by translating or having translated a number of important works from Latin into English. Later in the tenth century a monastic revival, under the reforming influence of Benedictine monasticism from the Continent, led to renewed cultural achievement, especially at Eynsham Abbey under its abbot, Aelfric.

We see, then, a pattern of advance and decline in Christian culture in Anglo-Saxon England; concurrently, there were sure to be numerous survivals (if not revivals) of Germanic pagan religion and superstitions (some of which surfaced in the collections of charms from the period preserved in a manuscript). And the heroic traditions of continental Germany remained alive and were frequently rehearsed, even in monasteries; Alcuin's famous letter to the monks of Lindisfarne in 797 scolds them for their attachment to Germanic heroes and asks rhetorically, "Quid Hinieldus cum Christo?" (What has Ingeld to do with Christ?) On the other hand, Alcuin also praised a *thegn* of the murdered King Etheldred of Northumbria, who avenged his lord's blood.

We may safely conclude that the interaction of Christian and pagan-Germanic elements continued in dynamic and unsettled fashion, at least at intervals, throughout most of the Anglo-Saxon period. At almost any time, the situation depicted in *Beowulf*—a heroic civilization embracing the values of loyalty and vengeance, intermittently aware of divine providence and, with one exception, monotheistic in religious expression—could be presented and understood as an evocation of a past era denied the fullness of Christian truth yet possessed of attractive nobility and quasi-Old Testament patriarchal attitudes. Scyld Scefing's ship burial, full of parallels to Sutton Hoo (the poem was used in the 1939 inquest as evidence of who owned the hoard), is mysterious to the Danes, who do not know Scyld's destination, but not to the reader, who has been told (in line 27) that the king goes to the Lord's protection.

## *The Poetic Corpus*

The greater part of extant Anglo-Saxon poetry has been preserved in four codices datable on paleographic grounds around the year 1000 (one, containing *Beowulf,* is perhaps of later compilation). Two, the Exeter and Vercelli books, are miscellanies containing religious, secular, and mixed texts of various lengths and functions. The Junius manuscript contains only religious pieces, and the *Beowulf* manuscript also contains *Judith,* based on the apocryphal Old Testament story. The late date of the codices suggests either a major revival of interest in the poetic heritage or a continuing tradition happily saved for posterity by the labors of monks in the reformed Benedictine monasteries. Several poems included in tenth- and eleventh-century entries of the *Anglo-Saxon Chronicle,* and the traditional eleventh-century heroic poem commemorating the defeat of an English force under Bryhtnoth by the Danes at Maldon in Essex, testify to the continued or renewed attraction of the Germanic poetic form and outlook well after the age of conversion in England.

The intermingling or antagonism of Christian and Germanic elements in Anglo-Saxon poetry continues to stimulate scholarly debate. As mentioned before, Jeff Opland believes that Christianity ruptured the nexus between eulogizing *scop* and sacral king in the early stages of conversion; bishop or priest replaced tribal poet as the interpreter of past to present, and the new touchstone (as we see in Bede's record of letters written to kings by churchmen) was biblical, not recollective and traditional. On the other hand, England's Rome-based Christianity opened the culture to Roman traditions of entertainment, which resulted in the popularity of the *gleoman,* the peripatetic entertainer who sang songs about the deeds of the past. The church may have frowned on such doings, in and out of the monasteries, or tried to capitalize on the popularity of traditional songs by adapting them to Christianity—as when Bishop Aldhelm of Sherborne (*d.* 709) supposedly disguised himself as a minstrel and lured his congregation to consider the Christian mysteries with the bait of Germanic song—but the continued attraction of the poetic legacy of the pre-Christian past can be taken for granted throughout our period.

Meanwhile, as monastic culture flourished in the seventh and eighth centuries, it attracted not only children given to monasteries by their parents early in life (as Bede was), but also warriors and rulers who sought peace and salvation within the cloister after a life of instability and violence. The resulting society would presumably take equal pleasure from Germanic heroic song and the rich deposit of native and continental hagiography in Latin that vividly portrayed the battles of ascetic saints and hermits against diabolical temptations and assaults.

Such appears to be the context within which Bede's story of Caedmon must be placed (*Historia* 4.24). Caedmon was a lay brother at the monastery of Whitby, an unlettered man who performed duties necessary to the operation of the institution. He could not sing and fled when the harp was passed around the evening table, until one night an angelic stranger appeared who instructed him to sing about creation, which the surprised Caedmon proceeded to do. Abbess Hild learned of the miraculous occurrence, and thereafter Caedmon was instructed in scriptural story, which he turned into English narrative verse.

Of Caedmon's poetry only his first song, the nine-line *Hymn,* is extant, preserved in copies of Bede's *Historia* when the latter was translated in the late ninth century. Opland points out that the *Hymn* is a praise-poem to God the creator and argues that Caedmon's first achievement was the Christian domestication of the Germanic eulogistic tradition. Thereafter, given the adumbrations of narrative present in eulogy, it was quite simple to apply traditional poetic diction and techniques to biblical narrative subjects.

Several biblical poems in Old English survive; they are marked by the more or less adroit application of Germanic concepts and diction to the sacred story. *Exodus* (early eighth century?) treats the escaping Israelites as a war band following their leader, Moses; the superb, visionary *Dream of the Rood* (late eighth century?) imagines Christ as a young hero leaping up onto the cross. Other religious poetry attributed to Cynewulf, of whom nothing is known except that his name is worked in runes into the text of four poems, has been translated more closely from Latin hagiographical material. And a poem like *Seafarer* (eighth or ninth century?), which fits no modern generic category, appears to reconceive Germanic ideas of exile and endurance as metaphors for the Christian life, letting their true meaning emerge ever more clearly as the poem moves from a description of life at sea to meditations on the afterlife.

## *BEOWULF* AND ANGLO-SAXON POETRY

The continuing appeal of Germanic traditions explains the preservation in the Exeter Book (copied *ca.* 1000 in Exeter, where it has remained in the cathedral library) of *Widsith* (seventh century?) and *Deor* (date unknown), poems cataloging allusively many recollections of preconversion and pre-insular nations, heroes, and events. The obscure *Wulf and Eadwacer* (date unknown) may also hide nostalgic evocations of the Germanic past, while collections of gnomes and charms are clearly rooted there.

The Danish invaders of England from the ninth century onward brought with them intact traditions of eulogy and poetic improvisation centered on the *skald,* or Scandinavian court poet. Opland perceives skaldic influence in a revived eulogistic tradition underlying some of the chronicle poems of the tenth century, most especially the *Battle of Brunanburh,* which celebrates but does not describe King Athelstan's victory over a Scandinavian army in 937, using heavily conventional diction and evoking (as does the later *Battle of Maldon* [*ca.* 1025]) the traditional values of Germanic heroism.

We see then that uses of traditional poetic form and content varied widely in Anglo-Saxon England. Nothing in the corpus, however, can directly "explain" *Beowulf,* the longest extant poem in Old English and the only complete narrative based on Germanic traditions (there are fragments of an Anglo-Saxon poem on the Waltharius legend).

### *Poetic Technique*

The same techniques govern Anglo-Saxon poetry from Caedmon's *Hymn* to *The Battle of Maldon,* and the presence of these techniques in continental Germanic texts testifies to their preliterate origin. Although there is substantial agreement about the major technical norms of Anglo-Saxon versification, several questions remain unanswered and subject to debate. The problem is that we lack any handbook of poetics from Anglo-Saxon times, and the poems themselves do not discuss their techniques. (Lines 870b–871a of *Beowulf*—"word oþer fand, / soðe gebunden"—have sometimes been read as a reference to alliterative technique, but a more probable translation would be: "he found a new subject [*word oþer*], one guaranteed to be true.") Accordingly, the rules given here have been deduced, not always without controversy, from the poetry we possess. One result is that we risk oversimplifying or overgeneralizing because our statistical sample is too small. We have but a small fraction of the poetry composed during this era; the cost of parchment and the animosity of the church would have doomed much to oblivion. Or our deductions are too restrictive, and we emend texts to remove the evidence of this fault by making them conform to our patterns.

Anglo-Saxon poetry is strongly rhythmic, in keeping with the marked tonic-vowel stress of Germanic languages. The basic unit is the half-line, comprising two stressed syllables and a varying number of unstressed syllables. Two half-lines joined by alliteration across a caesura make up the standard Anglo-Saxon poetic line. The first accented syllable of the second half-line determines alliteration; it can alliterate with either or both of the stressed syllables in the first half-line, but normally not with the other stressed syllable of the second half-line. (Double alliteration—*ab, ab*—seems exceptional, but may serve a not yet understood affective or technical function.) A consonantal sound normally alliterates only with itself (although palatalized and nonpalatalized *g* alliterate); all vowels, by contrast, form an alliterating group, and initial *h* seems not to impede vocalic alliteration. (The name printed in editions of *Beowulf* as Unferth, and alliterating with vowels, always appears in the manuscript as *Hunferth.*)

The metrical patterns into which Anglo-Saxon half-lines fall seem basically five in number, as determined by the placement of the two syllables of primary stress (and in some cases a syllable of secondary stress) in relation to the unfixed number of unstressed syllables that may precede, follow, or intervene between them. Primary stress falls on long syllables (that is, with a long vowel or blocked by a double consonant) or, as a "resolved" stress, on two consecutive short syllables; and there is a hierarchy of parts of speech that may receive stress, with nouns and adjectives generally preceding verbs and adverbs.

Anglo-Saxon poetic diction derives its characteristic effect from the fact that the half-line, rather than the word, is its basic unit. Many half-lines appear in exactly, or almost exactly, the same form more than once in the extant poetic corpus. This fact led F. P. Magoun in 1953 to apply to Anglo-Saxon poetry the oral-formulaic theories developed by Albert Lord and Milman Parry to explain the poetic techniques and origin of the Homeric epics and tested by them during the 1930's on the improvisatory oral poetry of Yugoslavian *guslars* (bards who recite poetic narratives accompanied by the *gusla,* a stringed instrument). Magoun's argument is that (1) the repeating half-lines of Anglo-Saxon verse are formulas; (2) in an oral culture, poetic diction is formulaic for mnemonic purposes; (3) only oral (that is, unlettered) poets compose in formulas; literacy and formulaic composition are mutually exclusive; therefore (4) Anglo-Saxon poetry was orally composed by illiterate improvisational poets; and (5) it follows that our extant texts are transcriptions of individual performances improvised from an extremely conservative stock of formulas, within which context the creation of new, original diction is practically impossible. If we had other texts of these works, they would manifest differences in formula consistent with the fact that different performances by the same poet will be different acts of composition, albeit drawing on the same formulaic stock.

Magoun's premises have been widely challenged. Larry Benson has shown that even Anglo-Saxon texts closely translated from Latin originals share the same formulaic diction as more obviously traditional texts. It is clear that literates can easily learn to write formulaically: Magoun's own pupil, Robert Creed, arguing for the oral-formulaic composition of *Beowulf,* "recomposed" part of it using half-lines from other texts, thereby proving that a literate, twentieth-century scholar can write Anglo-Saxon poetry. Furthermore, as Parry and Lord themselves discovered, an oral poet who knows his work is being transcribed for posterity will produce a longer, more carefully structured version of a poem showing the effects of his awareness. Thus one cannot speak of transcription as a neutral process not affecting the material transcribed.

Perhaps the most important obstacle to the Magoun-Parry-Lord thesis, as applied to Anglo-Saxon poetry, lies in its assumptions about formulas. Parry and Lord demonstrated that Homeric texts practice "formulaic economy": each fixed formula has a metric pattern that makes it fit into a certain part of the Greek hexameter line; when the concept or fact embodied in it is needed at the place in the line where it fits, *that formula only* is used, and its form never varies, no matter how frequently it appears. By contrast, in Anglo-Saxon verse, the "formula" corresponds to an entire half-line, the looser structure and alliterative requirements of which result in a wide variety of related but distinct utterances. Compare, for example, these phrases from *Beowulf*: *weox under wolcnum* (he grew up under the skies [i.e., on earth]: 8), *wan under wolcnum* (dark under the skies: 651), *Wod under wolcnum* (He advanced under the skies: 714), *wæter under wolcnum* (water under the skies: 1631), *weold under wolcnum* ([I] ruled under the skies: 1770); the kinship of these half-lines is clear, but the variant word is sometimes a verb, sometimes a noun or adjective. And how does one characterize the relationship between this system and *hæleþ under heofenum* (hero under the heavens: 52) or *gehedde under heofenum* ([anyone should] care for under the heavens: 505)? One system would clearly suggest the other to a poet wanting to make the kind of general statement involving "on earth" as an intensifier, and the choice would depend on alliteration, an element lacking in the Greek poetic system.

In short, the basic characteristics of the Anglo-Saxon poetic line promote dictional variety within limits imposed by the same characteristics (number of stressed syllables, alliterative patterns). Greek practice encourages the fixity and economy underlying Parry and Lord's definition of a formula—a definition that is of little use in attempting to understand the traditional norms underlying even the most indisputably literate poetry in Old English. This conclusion is doubly important for the study of *Beowulf:* we need deny its ultimate poet neither literacy nor originality in his manipulation of the flexible style and inherited content at his disposal; nor must we assume that the particular form in which we have it is the result of a chance preservation of one performance as opposed to many others, all somewhat different (and some presumably much better than ours, as dictated by the law of averages).

Two other elements of poetic style, common to Anglo-Saxon poetry but uncommonly well handled in *Beowulf,* deserve brief note. One is the technique of *variation*—the use of successive half-lines to vary the content of a preceding one, adding nuances or new information or merely saying the same thing in a different way for aesthetic effect. At its simplest, such variation substitutes a title for a proper name: "*Hroðgar* maþelode, *helm Scyldinga*" (Hrothgar spoke, protector of the Scyldings: 456); or expands and specifies a verb: "Beowulf *maðelode, beotwordum spræc*" (Beowulf spoke, uttered boasting words: 2510). Piling up variations slows down the forward movement of the narrative, an effect useful for giving an impression of particular solidity to a character or for conveying the sense of almost pompous solemnity appropriate for ceremonial discourse. We see both intentions in the variation technique of lines 340–346:

> Him þa *ellenrof* andswarode,
> *wlanc Wedera leod,* word æfter spræc
> *heard under helme:* We synt Higelaces
> beodgeneatas; Beowulf is min nama.
> Wille ic asecgan *sunu Healfdenes,*
> *mærum þeodne* min ærende,
> *aldre þinum*. . . .
>
> The man famed for courage answered him,
> The bold prince of the Geats, the brave,
> helmeted one,
> spoke these words: We are Hygelac's
> table companions; Beowulf is my name.
> I wish to give my message
> to Healfdene's son, the famous king,
> your lord. . . .

The first three italicized lines are varied epithets for Beowulf, the warrior-leader; the last three for Hrothgar, the king whom Beowulf must approach respectfully if he is to be allowed to fight Grendel. Separating the two groups of variations and heightening our awareness of them by its stark simplicity is the poet's first mention of his hero's name. There are many more subtle and complex uses of variation in *Beowulf,* contributing to our sense of poetic mastery.

The other noteworthy stylistic feature that *Beowulf* shares with Germanic poetry—and language as a whole—is the propensity for word compounding with metaphorical effect. Old English has many compounds meaning "sea," including *swanrade* (swan's road), *ganotes bæð* (gannet's bath); "ship," including *famigheals* (foamy-necked [one]), *hringedstefn* (ring-prowed [one], referring to ornaments on the ship's prow); "warrior," including *lind-hæbbende* (linden[-wood shield] bearer), *hildedeor* (battle-brave [one]); and, more imaginatively, for "sword," *homera laf* (relic of hammers, or what is left when the weaponsmith has finished beating the hot iron). Studies by Arthur G. Brodeur and others have shown *Beowulf* to be rich in compounds not elsewhere recorded in Old English. Even allowing for much verse irrevocably lost, we must conclude that ingenious and inveterate compounding distinguishes *Beowulf* among Anglo-Saxon poems.

The poetic language in which most Anglo-Saxon poetry is preserved constitutes a special speech, rich in words (presumably archaic) that do not appear in Old English prose (a later development, dependent upon literacy) or that are used there with different meanings. In addition, the poetry seems to have incorporated features from various Old English dialects, so that placing a poem geographically merely from its language, as opposed to its content or external evidence, is usually impossible. The effect of this special, nonconsuetudinary language, combined with the diction and techniques just surveyed, must have been to endow Anglo-Saxon poetry with considerable affective force, quite apart from the impact made by the subject of a given poem.

## *MANUSCRIPT*

A long-standing scholarly consensus has held that *Brit. Lib. Cotton Vitellius A. XV* comprises two separate codices joined in the seventeenth century, probably after they came into the possession of Sir Robert Cotton (1571–1631), the English antiquarian. Cotton's manuscript collection was housed in bookcases atop each of which stood the bust of a Roman emperor; "Vitellius" in the manuscript's title refers to the bust atop its case. A fire destroyed part of the Cottonian collection in 1731, but only scorched the edges of *Vitellius A. XV.* Some words were lost as the damaged pages crumbled, and this process continued until the manuscript was rebound and the pages protected in 1845. (Two late-eighteenth-century transcripts of *Beowulf,* one made by the Icelandic diplomat Grímur Jónsson Thorkelin and another commissioned by him, preserve some words subsequently lost due to crumbling.)

*Beowulf*'s segment of *Vitellius A. XV,* called the Nowell codex because the inscription "Laurence Nouell, 1563" appears on its first page, contains five works—three in Old English prose, followed by *Beowulf* and the fragmentary poem *Judith*—written down by two scribes, the second taking over at line 1939b of *Beowulf.* As in the other three manuscripts preserving most of the extant Anglo-Saxon poetry, *Beowulf* is written out as prose.

The integrity of the Nowell codex has been universally assumed, but so has its lack of authority as a witness to the text of *Beowulf.* Proposed dates for the poem are many, but until recently all have antedated the manuscript by at least a century; in addition, the mixture of dialectal forms in the text has supported the thesis that several copyings in different parts of England stand between the composition and the extant version of *Beowulf,* a situation conducive to error and loss by scribal ineptitude. (Such a hypothesis justifies frequent editorial intervention to eliminate textual corruption.).

The earliest date proposed by modern scholars for composition of the poem is the seventh century, based on its Germanic outlook, apparently incomplete Christian overlay, and archaic linguistic forms. Parallels between the seventh-century Sutton Hoo ship burial and the sea burial of Scyld Scefing buttress the argument that some form of *Beowulf* existed as early as the era, and perhaps in the kingdom, of Redwald, the East Anglian syncretist whose sponsorship of both Christian and pagan worship might well find reflection in *Beowulf*'s ambiguous presentation of the Danes' religious culture.

The next claimant as the setting for *Beowulf*'s composition is Northumbria in the age of Bede (*ca.* 700–750). Support for this attribution comes again from linguistic forms, primarily from the fact that the level of culture in Northumbrian monasteries was sufficiently high to make possible the composition of the poem (in this view, a highly literate work perhaps indebted to Vergil's *Aeneid* as well as to the Bible).

Dorothy Whitelock, in *The Audience of Beowulf,* argues that certain locutions in *Beowulf* (*non dæges* [the ninth hour of the day: 1600]; *helle hæfton* [captive of hell, translating Latin *captivus inferni:* 788]) suggest a full assimilation into the English language and culture of ecclesiastical institutions and ideas by the time the poem was composed. Citing the apparent compliment to King Offa of Mercia intended in the story of Offa the Angle (1944–1962), she suggests that the poem may have originated in late-eighth-century Mercia, then the dominant Anglo-Saxon kingdom.

Eric John suggests a similar conclusion on different grounds: he interprets Hygelac's gift of land to Beowulf (2195–2196) as *folcland,* a fief belonging to Beowulf's father that reverted to the king on Ecgtheow's death until such time as Beowulf could reclaim it by honorable deeds and the payment of a fee *(heriot)*—in this case the gifts that Hrothgar had given him. Since the custom of *folcland* seems to have disappeared during the eighth century, the poem's genesis must antedate the disappearance. John also places the poem on the margins of Anglo-Saxon society where Christian and Germanic views overlap; he sees the concern with swords, feuds, and treasure throughout *Beowulf* as evidence that it was composed for an audience of retainers—men in search of honor and security—who would have especially appreciated Beowulf's Danish expedition as the great successful gamble of a young mercenary soldier who had until that point done nothing to earn back his father's land.

The positive view of the Danes offered by *Beowulf* has struck many as an argument against composition after 793, when the Danes began their incursions into the north of England. Nonetheless, a few scholars prior to 1980 had found evidence in the poem to support a ninth- or tenth-century date. One argument, by Levin Schücking, even proposed to read the poem as a "mirror for princes" composed to educate young Danish princes living in the recently captured north. Such a view would place the composition of *Beowulf* in the first half of the tenth century.

A thorough review of received opinions on *Beowulf's* date is now underway, thanks largely to a conference held in Toronto in 1980. (The proceedings were edited by Colin Chase and published in 1981.) Several scholars have pronounced in favor of a ninth- or tenth-century date of composition, basing their arguments on the poem's meter and language, its use of tribal names and royal genealogies, or its reflection of Anglo-Danish political and cultural interactions. The most striking challenge to all previous theories appears in Kevin Kiernan's 1981 study, *Beowulf and the Beowulf Manuscript.* Kiernan's examination of *Vitellius A. XV* has convinced him that the "Beowulf codex" is a separate manuscript, written very soon after the poem took its final shape during the reign of King Cnut, shortly after 1016. Originally, he argues, two separate *Beowulf* poems, one about his youthful deeds (and a tribute to Cnut's heritage) and the other about his last battle and death (a nostalgic tribute to the House of Alfred, now extirpated), were being copied by two scribes in the same Mercian monastery when Scribe B had the idea of combining them by means of the newly composed transitional section (Beowulf's return to Geatland and report to Hygelac). Differences in the construction and lineation of manuscript gatherings convince Kiernan that the original *Beowulf* projects were conceived as quite distinct from one another; the linking section offers clues that the revision of the ending of the first story ran longer than planned and had to be crowded into too little space because the rest of the newly unified poem had already been copied.

Kiernan's revisionism extends to a new explanation for the partly unreadable condition of folio 179r: it is a palimpsest (one text erased, another written over it). Scribe B returned to the manuscript some twenty years after copying the new transition with new material to make it smoother. He scraped off the apposite page and recopied the beginning of the dragon episode in its new form, but some of the ink did not take well, so he erased several places and never filled them in, which would account for the gaps on this folio. At this time, he also erased the first three lines of folio 180r, a fact hitherto unnoticed.

This summary omits much of Kiernan's argument and all of his supporting evidence. His hypothesis transforms the "Beowulf codex" (now seen as an independent manuscript) from a late, nonauthoritative copy into something very close to an autograph, one containing much more important evidence of the process of combinative composition of a traditional epic than can be found in any other manuscript. Further examination of the manuscript, his logic, and the poem's text will be necessary to corroborate or combat Kiernan's argument.

Meanwhile, some general judgments about *Beowulf* dating theories can be made. The main problem in attempting to date tradition-based texts is that early or archaic elements may be preserved for atmospheric or mnemonic effect long after they have ceased to have direct relevance to the poem's audience. Furthermore, episodes of varying derivation can be added to the main narrative stock at any time, out of nostalgia or a desire to preserve a record of the past. It is impossible to determine what completed material the last poet of *Beowulf* (who may or may not have been the first literate poet to assemble the poem's components in their present shape) had at his disposal, or what his compositional task may have been. We must live with this uncertainty and not press the text for genetic information that its links to traditional Germanic culture in form and content prevent it from supplying.

## *CRITICAL APPROACHES*

The evolution and variety of this century's critical responses to *Beowulf* as the earliest English epic provide guidance—and in some cases cautionary examples—to the modern student attempting to deal with the poem.

For a long period it was customary to judge the poem by standards of decorum derived from, and appropriate to, later literature. In his edition of *Beowulf,* Frederick Klaeber speaks of the disproportion between "the main plot, three fabulous exploits redolent of folk-tale fancy" and "a number of apparently historical elements which are introduced as a setting for the former and by way of more or less irrelevant digressions." He adds, "We may well regret that those subjects of intensely absorbing interest play only a minor part in our epic, having to serve as a foil to a story which is in itself of decidedly inferior weight." Other objections to the poem included lack of suspense and the intrusion of "Christian coloring" into an essentially pagan-heroic vision. Behind such censure of *Beowulf* we can detect a class bias against (lower-class, peasant) folktale and in favor of (aristocratic) heroic digression, as well as a professional bias in favor of historical study and against the symbolic imagination.

The era of patronizing *Beowulf* ended, and the era of serious, sympathetic literary criticism began, with the publication of J. R. R. Tolkien's 1936 British Academy lecture, "*Beowulf,* the Monsters and the Critics." Tolkien defends the unity of the poem and the seriousness of its concern with monsters: the hero's three nonhuman opponents are symbolic embodiments of evil, and Beowulf himself of quintessential heroism in combating them fearlessly, even to the death. Nothing could be more timelessly noble. Tolkien argues that the poem possesses a highly self-conscious, unified two-part structure embodying a principle of balance analogous to the balanced tension of the two-part Anglo-Saxon poetic line, and illuminating the dynamic of youth and age in the life of a hero. The young Beowulf rescues old King Hrothgar; as an old king himself, Beowulf receives crucial assistance from the young hero Wiglaf in his last fight. The ultimate balance is between the triumphant life and unflinching but immeasurably sad death of the hero. With Beowulf's death, an era ends and the future darkens.

Tolkien's rehabilitation of *Beowulf* revitalized study of the poem in many ways. Successors studied the monsters for clues to their significance and for distinctions between the clearly evil Grendel lineage and the (perhaps) less theologically tinctured dragon; or they attempted to refine and support Tolkien's argument about the poem's unity. Many critics have concerned themselves with the nature of the judgment being passed on the heroic world by the poem's Christian author. Tolkien's view of the poem as noble, nostalgic, and concerned with timeless symbols of human greatness and the evil that attacks it can safely be called romantic (or romanticizing), and he falls at times into overly enthusiastic hyperbole, largely in response to the legacy of patronization that he was combating. For example: "[Beowulf's] final foe should not be some Swedish prince, or treacherous friend, but a dragon: a thing made by imagination for just such a purpose. Nowhere does a dragon come in so precisely where he should." Attempting to defend *Beowulf* against the charge of being inferior history, Tolkien lyrically (and anachronistically) evokes the ahistorical imagination as its driving force.

Several critical positions since Tolkien, and directly or indirectly influenced by him, have been less nuanced and more prescriptive or anachronistic. Adrien Bonjour, seeking the poem's unity, has submitted the many historical allusions and digressions in the work to often ingenious analysis, attempting to show their appositeness to the main plot. For other scholars, the unifying factor is thematic (the feud), modal (ironic reversals and parallels), or structural (the interweaving of motifs in a manner analogous to the interlaced patterns in the decoration of Anglo-Saxon manuscripts). Some readers have sought to explain events and characters by applying to them psychological and motivational analysis inappropriate to a traditional story that, as we have seen, presents subsidiary characters and events as reflections of or subordinate to the needs of the basic plot and the protagonist. To take one example, Unferth, the Danish court figure who challenges Beowulf, has been explained by some in terms of his earlier career, moral defects, and personality traits. Elaborate lives have been constructed for him outside the poem in a manner all too similar to the "how many children had Lady Macbeth" methodology. However unified *Beowulf* may be at its core, it cannot be criticized as if it were a carefully plotted Victorian novel.

Such rationalizing criticism coexists with a Christianizing approach to the poem that may take one of two forms: despite the relatively few Christian references in the poem and the absence of any references to Christ, the poem's pervasive Christianity shows itself in the assimilation of Beowulf to Christ *or* in the poem's condemnation of Beowulf as a sinner in his old age and its disapproving view of the world of Danes and Geats. Obviously, these two views are mutually exclusive. The first establishes parallels between the hero's career and the gospel or apocryphal accounts of Christ's passion and resurrection: the journey to the bottom of the swamp and subsequent return after defeating the she-monster qualify as a version of the harrowing of hell, while the Danes' departure from beside the fiery lake, when they see it welling with what they take to be Beowulf's blood, recalls the disloyalty of the disciples at Jesus' moment of betrayal. Beowulf's self-sacrifice in the final part of the poem, as he attempts to protect his people and secure treasure for them, offers final proof of his Christlike status.

The negative Christian judgment of *Beowulf* draws its support primarily from the dragon episode, where Beowulf, in this view, stands convicted of pride in attempting to fight the dragon alone, or of avarice in seeking the dragon's hoard and succumbing to its curse. The passage early in the poem that condemns the Danes for placing their trust in idols when harassed by Grendel (175–188)—a passage that Tolkien, with his more favorable view of the Danes, wished to see as a late interpolation—places the whole poem under the cloud of paganism, and a Christian author, however sympathetic to the plight of his preconversion ancestors, would have no choice but to consign the Danes to everlasting punishment.

The difficulty with the Beowulf-Christ hypothesis is that it relies on forced or imagined parallels for too much of its support; for the rest, it relies on universal narrative patterns displaced from myth into less cosmic literary genres in many cultures throughout the world. The judgmental approach stems from a misunderstanding of the accretive nature of the traditional story (Christian maxims about the joys of heaven and pains of hell [183–188] mixed with reflections on the Danes' ignorance of God [175–183] are making two different points, although they have been drawn together by a similar subject in the poem's traditional economy). It also stems from too univocal a view of Anglo-Saxon society, in which, as Benson and others have shown, Christian missionary zeal could coexist with—indeed, be inspired by—favorable attitudes toward still-heathen continental Germanic nations that shared the same heroic heritage. (The constant "marginal" overlap of Christian and Germanic values noted by John and Whitelock in areas such as loyalty and revenge also renders categorical judgments in *Beowulf* less likely, though by no means impossible.)

Finally, one should point to what might be called a demythologizing tendency in some recent assessments of the poem, attempts to strip it of some of the resonances found by previous critics and used to support, on slender evidence, one or another interpretation. One instance of this tendency has already been noted: Eric John's submission of the poem to historical scrutiny and his explanation of Beowulf's trip to Denmark not as the expression of heroic nobility but as an Anglo-Saxon retainer's search for booty and honor sufficient to claim the *folcland* that had reverted on his father's death to the lord. (Oddly, John seems to overlook the passage in *Beowulf* that most supports his argument: Wiglaf undertakes to aid Beowulf in battle because he remembers that the latter had given him "wicstede weligne Wægmundinga,/folcrihta gehwylc, swa his fæder ahte" [the rich dwelling place of the Wægmundings, every right to the *folcland* that his father had held: 2607–2608].) Similarly, John believes that an audience of retainers would condemn Beowulf as a foolhardy king for attempting to fight the dragon alone. John implicitly rejects Tolkien's lyrical symbolism in favor of hard-headed historicism.

Kenneth Sisam had earlier proposed an analogous debunking of some interpretations that stress the unity and artistic complexity of the poem, as well as its affective impact and symbolic force. In the scene of rejoicing after Beowulf has killed Grendel, the Danes carouse in Heorot; Hrothgar and his nephew Hrothulf sit together with Unferth at their feet. The text says, "Heorot innan wæs/freondum afylled; nalles facenstafas/Þeod-Scyldingas þenden fremedon" (Heorot was filled with friends within; not at all did the Þeod-Scyldings then engage in treachery: 1017–1019). Later, when Wealhtheow approaches Hrothgar and Hrothulf, we are told of them, "þa gyt wæs hiera sib ætgædere,/æghwylc oðrum trywe" (their peace [or kinship] still joined them, each was true to the other: 1165–1166). Wealhtheow then expresses confidence that Hrothulf will be kind to her children if he should outlive Hrothgar, as long as he remembers her and Hrothgar's kindnesses to him when he was young (1180–1187). From these three moments and some stories in later Scandinavian chronicles, many readers have deduced that the poem here alerts its audience to the coming feud between Hrothgar and Hrothulf, in which the former's children will be victims. Sisam argues that a straightforward reading of the text, without circular arguments from distant and unconvincing analogues, shows no such future treachery being forecast. His position, if accepted, renders unacceptable the eloquent analysis of Edward Irving and others that the scene in Heorot balances present joy with future sorrow, and that the Finnsburh episode, by asserting a proleptic parallel between Hildeburh and Wealhtheow as queens tragically victimized by an intrafamilial feud, has thematic relevance at this point in the poem.

Recent years have seen a philological demythologizing of Beowulf himself in the work of Fred C. Robinson ("Elements of the Marvelous in the Characterization of Beowulf") and others. This initiative involves scrutinizing Beowulf's exploits, especially their more fantastic components, with a view to discovering their basis in the words of the text instead of the imaginations of critics. For example, Beowulf's swimming exploits against Breca and in the Geats' retreat from Friesland after Hygelac's last raid have been reinterpreted as feats of rowing or sailing, based on lexicographical evidence that words for "swim" and "swimming" had wide, metaphorical applications to all seagoing activities in Old English. Basically, this type of demythologizing has two aims: to expose and combat the tendency to derive special meanings for words from an interpretation of their context in the poem (a subjective act) and then to give these meanings objective force by enshrining them in dictionaries; and, incidentally, to make Beowulf less a superhuman or monstrous figure and more a strong but normal human being. Of these aims the first is laudable and unassailable, but the second seems at times to fly in the face of the entire Indo-European presentation of the hero as a quasi-divine figure and the consistent representation of Beowulf as peculiarly like his monstrous opponents in many ways.

Surveying these major approaches to the poem—patronizing, romanticizing, rationalizing, Christianizing, and demythologizing—we are again struck by their common unease with the techniques and cultural function of a traditional, or tradition-based, narrative. Each in its own way wants the poem to be simpler, more accessible than it is to our thoroughly literate, post-Renaissance culture, which finds *Beowulf*'s outlook and method as profoundly alien as it is profoundly attractive. This is not, however, to deny the need and pleasure of coming to critical grips with the poem, nor to gainsay the contributions of each of the perspectives just rehearsed. Keeping before us the need to respect at all times the complexities inherent in dealing with a poem that is in one sense the product of a literate Christian culture and in another the legacy of a preliterate Germanic traditional culture, we offer some suggestions toward a tentative, open-ended, but useful interpretation of *Beowulf.*

## *INTERPRETATION*

### *Unity and Structure*

Kiernan's hypothesis that the "*Beowulf* codex" reveals the creation of our poem from two antecedent ones by the ex post facto composition of a hinge or transitional section recalls the waggish suggestion of many years ago that all Anglo-Saxon poetry had three authors: Germanic poets A and B and the monkish redactor who cobbled their work together and added Christian references. The lack of unity by modern standards of traditional literature has, over the years, prompted theories that *Beowulf* was constructed by stringing together three heroic lays about the same hero, each with its separate prehistory. More recently, the oral-formulaists sought proof for their theories by maintaining that *Beowulf*'s inner inconsistencies could be traced to separate performances of the same work later synthesized by a literate scribe.

Most readers of the poem, however, though fully aware of its digressiveness and impulse toward inclusiveness, its penchant for explanation by accretion rather than analysis, still experience it as a profound unity. Various explanations of *Beowulf's* coherence have been offered. Barnes, following Propp, has argued that it has the paratactic unity of a folktale in three moves, each with the same structure. Other scholars in recent years have sought what may be called mechanical unity, three types of which are ring composition, envelope structure, and tectonic (numerical) structure.

Ring composition means the symmetry of subsections of the poem placed within each other, like boxes within boxes. *Beowulf* begins and ends with a funeral (Scyld's, Beowulf's), with a lordless nation (Danes before Scyld, Geats after Beowulf), and with contrasting statements about retainers (Beowulf the Dane gives treasure to his retainers so that they will support him in battle later; Beowulf the Geat, having given treasure to his retainers, finds that they flee instead of supporting him in battle). These sections will in turn enclose other, briefer segments, and so on. Cedric Whitman has performed this sort of analysis on the *Iliad,* pairing books 1 and 24, 2 and 23, etc. Although *Beowulf* is divided into forty-three *fitts* (sections) in the manuscript, they lack the autonomy of books or chapters; and two section numbers are missing, creating ambiguity in the sequence.

Envelope structure seeks to find subunits, often overlapping, within the poem by the occurrence of key words and phrases in widely separated groups. One might point here to the same phrase in 100b and 2210—"oð ðæt an ongan" (until someone began)—at the beginning of the Grendel and dragon fights, as an indication of rhetorical envelopes.

Tectonic analysis seeks to demonstrate the unity of a poem by showing the numerical proportions, organized around a few key numbers, multiples of which control the placement of all the key incidents, as revealed by repeated words that call attention to the underlying numerical structure. Impressive as some of the results obtained by T. E. Hart may be, his analysis of *Beowulf* depends completely upon our having in the extant manuscript exactly the same number of lines, in the same sequence, written by the final author—a situation that would be argued only by Kiernan, who, however, also argues definitively against tectonic composition by his insistence that the manuscript reveals two originally separate poems joined only after composition and copying.

Given the conflict inherent in all schemes of mechanical unity between their ostensible objectivity and actual subjectivity, it seems more satisfying to seek *Beowulf's* unity through frankly subjective literary analysis, however sophisticated. The subsequent discussion proposes that *Beowulf* embodies a complex unity of contrasting narrative *contents* and *methods* held together, not without tension, by the grip (to use a central image of the poem) of the hero's life. We can begin to understand this statement by comparing *Beowulf* to the other two great tradition-based medieval epics, the *Nibelungenlied* and the *Chanson de Roland.* All three are composed of linked, separate adventures, a structural scheme that has led modern critics to try to dissect them in search of "original" shorter poems. *Beowulf* is unique in ending with its hero's death, while the other two place this traumatic event in the middle and devote their final sections to recounting its consequences. The latter narrative strategy raises the theme of vengeance for the hero's death to a position of importance equal to the hero's character and achievement; by so doing, it creates a duality of focus: the hero himself while he lives, and the fate of his world after his death. In *Beowulf,* by contrast, the hero is always on hand to provide a unifying focus. But the binary structure of the poem profoundly modifies and complicates the cohesive force of the omnipresent hero by dividing his life into two segments clearly separated in time and strongly in contrast with each other. Tolkien has characterized this structure as a balance of youth and age, but this analysis, although accurate, is insufficient. In the two contrasting parts of *Beowulf,* youth versus age functions as a clarifying metaphor, along with several others, subordinate to the larger opposition between a vision of the possibilities of heroism in part 1 and the limits of heroism in part 2.

There is a strong tension at the heart of *Beowulf* between the centripetal force of the hero's life—as a testimony to human possibilities of will, bravery, and accomplishment—and the centrifugal force of its two main parts, embodying testimony to the tragic divergence in impact and result of the resolute heroic will operating amid life's multiplicity. This tension finds reflection and amplification in two other structural features of the poem: first, the alternation and opposition in each main part between an impulse toward intensity—focusing on the isolated hero and his titanic struggles with quasi-equal but monstrous antagonists—and another toward expansiveness, a movement beyond concern for the hero to a full picture of a society, the continuities and burden of history, the action of memory, and even the designs of providence; second, the construction of part 1 in two "movements," clearly related but further diverting the broad stream of narrative unity into subsidiary channels of comparison and contrast between the two monster fights.

We see, then, how precarious and contingent the concept of unity is in *Beowulf* and at how many levels it sustains pressure from strong centrifugal, diversifying forces. A brief examination of the poem's two main parts will heighten an appreciation of its parallel impulses toward the one and the many.

Part 1 comprises a two-movement structure bracketed by an introductory section taking place before the hero's arrival on the scene (1–193) and a postlude recounting Beowulf's return to Geatland and the report of his adventures to Hygelac (1888–2199). The bracketing sections contextualize the hero and his deeds in several ways, as well as provide an aesthetically satisfying beginning and end for them.

Structurally, the introduction establishes the need for the hero in the story; thematically, it demonstrates that his exploits have their ultimate origin in occurrences before his birth and establishes a broad historical and even providential level of significance for heroism. Its basic purpose is to supply the antagonist (Grendel) and the setting (Heorot) for Beowulf's first great fight, but it also provides them—and therefore the hero's deed—with far-reaching significance. Heorot's is dynastic because the hall represents the zenith of the Scyldings' power, as well as of Hrothgar's career as king, and social because it represents the ideal functioning of a heroic society. The founding of the Scylding dynasty with which the poem begins clarifies Heorot's historical importance, while Hrothgar's announced intention to share out within it all that he has won in battle (71–73, 80–81) embodies the proper use by a king of his power and possessions to ensure social harmony and cohesion.

Heorot is no sooner built than the joy within its walls—the joy of a triumphant, harmonious war band—attracts Grendel, who invades the hall, kills its occupants, disrupts its function, and possesses it nightly for twelve years while Hrothgar mourns and the helpless Danes pray to idols. Grendel opposes Heorot's social joy as an eternal, angry outsider, the lonely border walker (*mearcstapa:* 103). The elemental nature of this feud, which can never be peacefully settled (154–158), is corroborated by the information that Grendel's alienation, as a descendant of Cain, is the result of God's perpetual banishment of the first murderer and his offspring from human society. In other words, the opposition between sharing and feuding in human life is absolute; the two cannot coexist. God opposes the sowers of discord, but the legacy of discord embodied in Grendel is so strong that it can overpower even the most harmonious society. So Beowulf's resolve in undertaking to cleanse (*faelsian:* 432) Heorot is, according to the introduction, no mere youthful exploit or folktale giant killing, but the intercession of heroism, however unknowingly, into a struggle of divine intention and social aspirations against ancient forces seeking to thwart them.

The two moves of part 1 have three-part structures; the outer sections are expansive, the middle one intensive. The first section of the first move (194–661) integrates the hero into Hrothgar's court, giving in the process a sense of the court's etiquette and rituals, through Beowulf's successive encounters with the coast guard, door guard, Hrothgar, and Unferth. The narrative also expands, through Beowulf's recollection, to include his youthful contest with Breca and first monster fight. But opposing this leisurely, inclusive current is the intention to define Beowulf's heroism through his voice, his sentiments, and his response to Unferth's challenge. The modulation from diplomatic, circumlocutory rhetoric (267–285), through direct request (426–432) and the recognition of possible consequences (442–445), to the account of his lonely sea battle (559–573) makes Beowulf a more and more vivid presence in the poem. His final dismissal of Unferth's (and the Danes') courage (581–601) and his promise that Grendel is about to discover Geatish *eafoð ond ellen* (might and courage: 602) announces unmistakably that a hero has arrived in Heorot, full of the confidence and bellicosity that set him apart from other men.

In the first fight (662–836), the expansive, public, daylight world contracts to the closeup spectacle of two great hostile forces wrestling in the dark, joined together by an irresistible handgrip and, as if by a collision of matter and antimatter, nearly tearing Heorot apart as they battle (767–782). The focus of the episode shrinks at the moment of greatest intensity to the even smaller field of the grip itself: its first moment, when the two antagonists tangle in a syntactically undecipherable mingling of hands and arms (745–749), and its last, as we watch in horror, with Grendel, the violent separation of his arm from his body (815–818). (The instant of greatest collapse inward thus far in the poem comes in 761b: *fingras burston* [fingers burst].) The monster's frantic flight from the hall leaves Beowulf in possession (820–827), his boast fulfilled: "Hæfde East-Denum/Geatmecga leod gilp gelæsted" (The prince of the Geats fulfilled his heroic promise to the East-Danes: 828–829). The flight also marks a change of direction away from maximum centripetality and back toward expansiveness.

The last section of the first move portrays a tremendous release of tension and a strong impulse toward inclusiveness to compensate for the extreme isolation of Beowulf in the fight scene. The release takes many forms: Danish warriors race their horses (864–867), songs are sung, gifts given; there is joy again in the hall. Beowulf's deed begins to pass into history (871–874) and to be placed in the context of other exemplary, memorable events—Sigemund's dragon fight, Heremod's crimes (874–915). It provokes, or at least provides the occasion for, other acts of recollection: the Finnsburh episode, the stories prompted by the necklace that Wealhtheow gives Beowulf. This last artifact especially galvanizes the poem's centrifugal energies, driving them backward but also forward to recount Hygelac's last raid, and thus to darken, if only momentarily, the joyful mood, perhaps in preparation for the second move shortly to begin.

The attack by Grendel's mother on Heorot begins the second move and returns us momentarily to the mood of ignorance and helplessness that surrounds her son's attack in the introduction. Beowulf's earlier journey into the poem from Geatland finds a parallel in the journey to the hideous, seething, monster-infested swamp. The expansiveness here is geographical rather than social; it brings into the poem glimpses not of Beowulf's heroic past but of the hunted stag who chooses death rather than enter the poisonous waves beneath which Beowulf must now dive (1368–1372). Again, events isolate Beowulf from his fellows and provide the occasion for the cry of the hero defying mortality in quest of glory:

"ic me mid Hruntinge/dom gewyrce, oþðe mec deað nimeð!" (I shall win glory with Hrunting [Unferth's sword, which in fact fails him], or death will take me: 1490–1491).

The hero enters the lair of evil for his second fight, following the pattern of reversal we have noted in this traditional story. There are elements of contrast, even deterioration, vis-à-vis the first battle: Beowulf has armor and a (useless) sword; he comes closer to death (1541–1553) than before as he once again wrestles with a monster (1533–1534; 1541–1542, recalling 745–749). But Beowulf thinks of fame rather than survival (1534–1536) and endures the moment of supreme constriction in the fight, when Grendel's mother holds him on the floor and hacks at his armor with her knife (1545–1549). Now begins the outward movement: the hero finds the *ealdsweord eotenisc* (old sword of giants: 1558), too big for any man but him. In short order he kills the she-monster; beheads the body of her dead son, cleansing the swamp as he did Heorot (1620; compare 825: the same verb, *fælsian,* is used); and returns to the surface, thence to Heorot for the last part of the move. The poem flows outward into expansiveness, from the claustrophobic intensity of the underwater hall, by means of its only extended simile (comparing the melting of the sword blade in Grendel's blood to the flowing of spring waters when God sets them free from their winter ice-fetters: 1607–1611).

The return to Heorot has less of the expansiveness of exaltation (as in the equivalent part of the first move) than of meditation. Hrothgar, staring at Grendel's head and the now bladeless sword hilt brought back by the hero, sets his recollections free of their fetters in order to praise Beowulf and to warn him by once again invoking Heremod (1709–1722) and urging him to learn from the wicked and stingy king's example: "ðu þe lær be þon,/ gumcyste ongit!" (You learn from him; understand [the importance of] generosity: 1722–1723). Memory shades into moralizing as the old king paints the picture of a ruler who hoards his wealth, forgetful of his mortality until he is swept away by it and his successor disperses what he has so carefully gathered (another image of inflow giving way to outflow: 1748–1757). As the section ends, Beowulf and Hrothgar exchange pledges of friendship and future assistance (a beneficent version of the hostile grip that bound Beowulf and the monsters) that expand their own personal bond outward to include their two nations, and forward in time to include future generations, when Beowulf may also be a king (1822–1865).

The part 1 postlude returns Beowulf to Geatish society and shows us his deeds beginning their passage through future ages as recollected stories. (The fact that we see him beginning the transmission constitutes an implicit claim of authenticity on the part of the poem.) Two concessions to expansiveness balance each other: Beowulf's account (or prediction) of renewed feuding between Danes and Heathobards, despite Freawaru's marriage to the Heathobard prince, Ingeld (2020–2069), shows peace becoming war; the exemplary career of Offa's wife (1931–1962) reaches farther into time to show violence becoming tamed.

Part 2 offers every possible contrast with part 1. It opens with a brief prologue (2200–2210) putting Beowulf in place as an old king, paralleling Hrothgar in part 1; but while the Scylding dynasty moves from Scyld to Hrothgar in an ascending curve, imparting to the poem's opening a sense of forward movement, Beowulf gains his throne by the deaths of Hygelac and Heardred in battle, a sad, descending process. The dragon then assumes the central role (2210–2311) in a section that seems a deformed parody of the analogous introductory segment of part 1. The dragon, as scholars have suggested, is a "stingy king" who hoards his gold instead of sharing it like Hrothgar. His "Heorot," an old cave he finds rather than a new hall he builds, contains a treasure left there by the last survivor of a vanished race—the opposite of Scyld, who founds a dynasty and leaves as his treasure for posterity a son who distributes, rather than hoards, wealth (20–21). The anti-Hrothgar in his anti-Heorot is now violated by an *ingenga* (invader, trespasser)—no Grendel seeking the lives of men, but a pathetic slave who takes one cup from the hoard to use as a bribe in ending a feud with his master. (Grendel's feud with his lord, and his unwillingness to settle his feud with the Danes by payment, here find parodic echo and reversal.) The elemental attack in part 1 on the center of a living society has been transformed into a pathetic, sneaky raid on the inert remains of a dead one.

Hrothgar responds to Grendel's depredations by sitting, sad and helpless (129–134); the dragon launches into an almost comic flurry of activity (2293–2302), whirling around inside and outside the barrow looking for the trespasser. The preliminary section ends when the energy of the narrative moves out from the barrow with the dragon as he flies off at night in search of vengeance. The centripetal, inertial force of part 2 (embodied in the heavy hoard in the ground around which the dragon lies coiled), by now established, contrasts strongly with the images of intense energy—mighty handgrips and tremendous struggles—compressed at the center of the two fights in part 1 and, as it were, fighting against the act of compression.

The next section (2312–2537) parallels the hero's arrival in Denmark. It begins when the dragon burns down Beowulf's hall, an action that brings the old king into the work as a homeless exile. The dragon's deed in effect establishes his inhospitable barrow as the setting of this part of the poem, and Beowulf will succeed not in cleansing the barrow, but in getting one of his own (2802–2808) into which he transfers the still inert, still cursed, still useless hoard—an action programmatically opposed to cleansing. (We are repeatedly told that the treasure has no one to polish it: 2253, 2256, 2761.) Beowulf responds to the dragon's aggression not with a boasting speech, but with anxious, Hrothgar-like introspection (2327–2332), which the poem rightly characterizes as unusual for him, since heroes should not meditate, but act: "breost innan weoll/þeostrum geþoncum, swa him geþywe ne wæs" (within, his breast swelled with dark thoughts, as was not usual for him: 2331–2332). This inward movement, so unlike the Beowulf of part 1, gives way to a movement outward in space to the barrow, where Beowulf utters an expansive speech recalling his past battles. But recollection has gone bad in part 2: the words, even as they goad the old warrior to action against the dragon, recount moments when action and vengeance are impossible (Hæþcyn's accidental slaying of his brother; a man hanged as a criminal) and focus on would-be avengers condemned to impotent grief and decline (2435–2472). The effect of Beowulf's expansive speech is oppressive rather than liberating.

Beowulf now undertakes to fight the dragon (2538–2709) not, as in the Grendel encounter without weapons, but with a special set of armor to protect against the dragon's poisonous flames. (The hand-to-hand combat of part 1 becomes a battle in which the hero can only with difficulty approach his foe: 2546–2549.) By the end of his speech, his voice is that of the hero of old (2535–2537), promising to obtain the dragon's gold or die trying; his battle cry (2550–2552) marks, in effect, the full recovery of heroic energy and the readiness to discharge it. The battle itself, however, mocks the intensity of the encounters in part 1: the dragon puffs fire and retreats, while Beowulf strikes ineffectual blows with his sword until it finally breaks. Beowulf's mortal wound is a bite on the neck; the dragon is punctured in his soft underbelly. Only Wiglaf's intervention, prompted by the recollection of favors from Beowulf and expressed as a willingness to die with his lord (2606–2608; 2646–2660), brings the spirit of Beowulf's youth into the poem. (Even his sword, with its inheritance of attached stories, partakes of the expansive, heroic recollections of part 1 more than the doom-laden retrospection of part 2.)

The dragon's death (2697–2709) ends the central section of part 2. The next section (2710–2845) ironically pairs Beowulf's death and the violation of the treasure, some of which Wiglaf brings into the open air so that his lord can see it before dying. Wiglaf's penetration to the heart of the barrow, with its bizarre scene of rusting treasure strewn about in disarray, expands the circle of desolation, recalling and reversing the joyful trip to the swamp after Grendel's demise. The old, ravaged hoard, like a reified recollection, glosses the old king who has won it: time is the enemy. The treasure now brought to Beowulf by Wiglaf parallels the hilt brought to Hrothgar by Beowulf, but this time the recipient's vision expands only as far as his funeral barrow. The hero's last words to Wiglaf in effect rename him, in a grisly, eschatological pun, as the *endelaf* (last survivor: 2813) of the Wægmunding line; the speech constitutes a melancholy expansion of the moment's significance, for it reminds us of the treasure's own status as *endelaf* of the nation whose human *endelaf* placed it in the ground to await the dragon and Beowulf (2247–2270).

Meanwhile, the dragon's body lies coiled nearby, fallen to earth for the last time (2834). Each warrior has killed the other (2844–2845), bringing to completion the bargain (*ceap:* 2415, 2482) that the two old merchants entered into over the gold they both wanted, one to brood over, the other to pass on to his people (2413–2419). The relationship between Beowulf and his last opponent is, in effect, trivialized by the language in which it is presented—yet another contrast to the language of part 1, which elevates Beowulf's monster fights almost to the status of providential encounters (696–702; compare the description of God's battles with the giants on the hilt of the sword that Beowulf uses to kill Grendel's mother: 1688–1693).

The poem's final centrifugal movement begins inauspiciously with the return of Beowulf's cowardly retainers from the woods to which they fled when the dragon appeared (2596–2599). Wiglaf sends a messenger to tell the Geats of their lord's death; his message forms the last great expansion of the poem's vision, and what it beholds is not the promise of future allegiance, as Beowulf and Hrothgar pledged for their respective nations at the end of part 1, but the grim foreboding of unremitting hostility from the neighboring nations that Beowulf had long kept at bay. Beowulf's funeral, balancing Scyld's, ends the work; while part 1 concluded with Beowulf receiving land and honor from Hygelac, part 2 sees a dead hero buried with useless treasure "given" him by the king who also killed him. Beowulf's seaside barrow will remind his people, as well as passing shipmen, of him (2804–2808); the hero who told his own story to Hygelac in part 1 now becomes a story to be recalled by others when they see his *laf* (remains).

The pervasiveness of the contrasts between parts 1 and 2, focused by structural parallels, cannot be denied. It remains to formulate their significance for the poem as a whole.

### *Thematic Contrasts and Unity*

Beowulf's life derives its form from, and imparts unity to, the clash of contrasts between the two main sections of the poem and the complex rhythms of alternating expansion and intensification within each section. This relationship between hero and structure is paralleled by another between the thematic continuities and the different forms taken by key concepts and images in the two parts. Thematic constancy and transformation hold the key to the overall meaning that we derive from our experience of *Beowulf.*

The poem's central concern is clearly the

nature and uses of heroism or, in other words, the interaction of the heroic will with the social and temporal world in which it functions. Part 1 of *Beowulf* presents a positive model of this interaction, part 2 a negative one. Each model revolves around the presentation and treatment of several main themes—time or history, treasure, feuds, reversals, and recollection—which attract other subsidiary themes to them. Part 1 also has a theme of providence—the action of God in history—crucially lacking in part 2.

All the main themes appear at once, tightly interwoven, in the poem's introduction, which, as we have seen, prepares for Beowulf's arrival by establishing a feud between Grendel and the Danes, set in Heorot. Heorot represents the confluence of power and generosity in Hrothgar—power that protects the Danes from external feuds (as Hrothgar says he has done: 1769–1773), generosity that protects them from the internal misery caused by a stingy, vicious king such as Heremod (1718–1720). Heremod's banishment in fact created the lordlessness that the Danes endured until Scyld established the dynasty of which the building of Heorot stands as the crowning achievement (12–16). But God sent Scyld a son to succor the Danes, so the great reversal *(edwenden)* that begins the poem (and is paralleled by Scyld's own reversal from destitute foundling to powerful king: 4–11) has providence at its root.

The presence of Heorot attracts Grendel, who creates by his malice and violence the next reversal—sorrow in the hall after joy: "þa wæs æfter wiste   wop up ahafen" (then weeping arose after prosperity: 128). Grendel presents himself as a perverse hall-thane (142) who wants—and takes—as his share of the hall's treasures one of the two things Hrothgar cannot give out: the lives of men (73). Grendel can never be part of Heorot's system of sharing, which binds the nation together—we are told he cannot approach the *gifstol* ("giftstool," or throne) from which Hrothgar dispenses treasure, even though he controls the hall at night (168–169)—because he will not come to terms with the Danes, will not settle his implacable feud (154–156). He is the perpetual outsider, banished with the rest of Cain's kin after Cain began the human feud by murdering his brother. Providence has, in effect, set the Danes and Grendel on a collision course. His advent establishes the primacy of the feud over the peaceful sharing of treasure, sours the triumph of the Scylding dynasty, and reverses the providentially guided flow of events from Scyld to Hrothgar. Grendel's effect is division (the negative version of sharing out) and deprivation among the Danes, who must abandon their hall, the symbol of their national identity, each night and sleep dispersed in the outbuildings. The poem relates the Danes' helplessness to their ignorance, another key theme of part 1, sounded at the time of Scyld's death (the Danes do not know who receives his body: 50–52) and repeated with respect to Grendel (they do not know where he lives: 162–163) and God (180–182). The cumulative force of the ignorance formulas that dot this part of the text is to induce not condemnation of the Danes but pity for them, and recognition that they will need crucial help from outside their own knowledge-deprived world to break Grendel's hold on their society and history.

The complex thematic preparation for Beowulf's arrival elevates his two battles in Denmark far above the level of folktale exploits. As he says to Hrothgar, he has come not just to kill a monster, but to cleanse Heorot (*Heorot fælsian:* 432) by fighting Grendel singlehandedly, an activity that the hero describes as if it were a judicial meeting: "ond nu wið Grendel sceal,/wið þam aglæcan ana gehegan/ðing wið þyrse" (and now I shall with Grendel, alone hold a meeting with the monster: 424–426). In fact, the poem suggests that the fight will be almost a judicial combat, with God on the side of the hero, whose strength the text equates with God's grace (670). Although Beowulf is as ignorant as the Danes of God's purposes and Grendel's lineage, he makes choices here and in the later battle with Grendel's mother that suggest a profound harmony between his heroism and providence: he refuses to fight Grendel with weapons, lest he seem to be afraid of, or have an advantage over, the unarmed creature (432–440; 677–687); but, as it turns out (798–805), Grendel is immune to swords, so Beowulf's choice is the necessary one. Later, in the underwater hall, he will find the old sword, too big for any other mortal to use, just in time to kill Grendel's mother with it; when the hilt is described, we learn that it portrays God's battle against antediluvian giants, and we understand that God's protection of Beowulf against the she-monster (1553–1556) is the result of the hero's usefulness in continuing the old feud against new enemies.

Beowulf's destruction of Grendel has several salutary consequences for the Danes. The grip in which he traps the monster symbolizes another great *edwenden,* the reversal of the disruption that has driven the Danes apart by denying them Heorot as a place for socially cohesive gift-giving. The poem uses forms of the word *dæl* ("part," "portion") and its verbal derivatives to express the paradoxes and significance of Beowulf's function as reuniter of Hrothgar's nation. Hrothgar builds Heorot to share (*gedælan:* 71) all his God-given treasure, thereby bringing the Danes together in harmony. Grendel, taking the forbidden share, men's lives, enters Heorot on his last visit, rejoicing in the prospect of dividing the sleeping warriors' souls from their bodies by eating them: "mynte þæt he *gedælde,* ær þon dæg cwome,/atol aglæca anra gehwylces/lif wið lice" (the terrible monster intended, before daylight came, to divide [take away] the life from each of the [sleeping] bodies: 731–733; emphasis added). The verb is the same in both cases. Furthermore, Grendel arrives at Heorot deprived of joy (*dreamum bedæled:* 721), and there he experiences departure (or division) from life (*lifgedal*: 841). His death takes the ironic form of a literal dividing-up of his body and a sharing of some of it with the Danes when he leaves his arm behind as a grisly trophy in Heorot (984–990). Against this rich verbal background, the metaphoric as well as the literal force of Beowulf's grip becomes clear: he has brought the Danes together again to experience the joy that they have lacked for twelve years and that resounds in Heorot again the following night.

The *edwenden* accomplished by Beowulf redeems time and sharing; treasure can flow again, and it does as a sign of Hrothgar's gratitude and desire to integrate Beowulf's heroism into the Danes' world. The result of the king's generous response to the hero's liberating and consolidating feat of strength is that an old feud between the Geats and Danes is settled (1855–1864), and Beowulf can now obtain his share of land from his own lord. Hrothgar's vision of a future in which boats will bring booty and tokens of friendship back and forth across the sea between the two nations (1862–1863) suggests that the cleansing power of Beowulf's heroism extends well beyond Heorot in time and space. The hero has set his strength and will against a feud between Grendel and the Danes; played an important part in prosecuting God's feud with Cain's kin; and brought about the resolution of feuds between neighboring nations. When we are told that he never killed his hearth companions (2179–2180), we can almost believe that Beowulf has singlehandedly reversed the legacy of Cain.

The main themes find in the Beowulf of part 1 a most favorable interpreter who emphasizes their positive and diminishes their negative dimensions. The connection between the efficacy of heroism and divine providence is never clarified, but it is clearly suggested, while the salutary effect of heroic endeavor on the social processes of humanity and the relations between nations cannot be doubted. In part 2, everything changes as heroism itself must endure a catastrophic reversal.

Part 2 forces Beowulf—and us—to confront the limitations, rather than the possibilities, of heroism. The hero's will has not changed, except for his one moment of doubt, but everything else in his world has, and the changes have rendered heroism either irrelevant, useless, or counterproductive. Now treasure does not lubricate the operation of society; it lies in the earth, rusting and inert, seeming to pull down with it, like some great magnet, the dragon and Beowulf. Time has become, in the absence of providence, a negative medium, bringing old age, the ending of civilizations, the rusting of treasure. History becomes a ticking time bomb, full of unsettled old scores: the messenger who enumerates them relentlessly to the Geats offers the prospect of a future completely opposed to the golden vision imagined by Hrothgar when Beowulf leaves Denmark. What has darkened history in part 2 is the feud—a legacy of strife, especially between Geats and Swedes, passed on from generations and turning kinsmen against each other. (Onela must overlook the fact that Weohstan has killed his nephew Eanmund, and reward him for the deed, because Eanmund had rebelled against his uncle: "no ymbe ða fæhðe spræc,/þeah ðe he his broðor bearn abredwade" [he didn't speak of the hostile act, even though he (Weohstan) had killed his brother's son: 2618–2619]. The word *fæhð* also means feud; Onela can't speak of one feud because another takes precedence.) Everyone in this part of the poem seems caught in the inescapable coil of feuds, or old age, or ill fortune that prevents fathers from avenging their sons—Hrethel because one son has accidentally killed another; the nameless old *ceorl* (2444–2462) whose son has been hanged—or ancient, unknown curses laid on treasure hoards. The dragon's coiled shape (and other shapes curving back on themselves), kept before us by forms of the verb *bugan* (or *gebugan*) and nominal derivatives, takes on symbolic significance for this sense of futility and entrapment hanging over part 2. The curse on the gold (whether or not we read the obscure lines 3074–3075 as saying that Beowulf has been felled, even damned, by it) expresses the motif of victimization, but the curse also serves as a metaphor for the poisoned well of time and history, the compressed equivalent of the "curse" laid on history by feuds, which will sooner or later so pile up as to come tumbling down on a nation (here the Geats) and bring it to its knees.

Amid this world gone bad, Beowulf's (and Wiglaf's) heroism gleams and goes out. Given time's negative function as a bringer of age, the hero's will must eventually outlive his strength and seal his fate. Given the omnipresence of feuds, even the most heroic death of a king leaves his people vulnerable to catastrophe. Given the curse on treasure, and its inertia as well, to win it is to win something useless (*unnyt*: 3168). While Beowulf's ignorance in part 1 did not prevent him from serving providence, his ignorance of the curse on the gold may have cost him his life. Part 2's pessimism—its conviction that all activity is ultimately fated and futile—finds perhaps its purest expression in almost identical pronouncements about the dragon's hoard-guarding (recognized as involuntary in Germanic folklore) and Beowulf's use of a sword in battle: of the dragon, *ne byð him wihte ðy sel* (he is not at all the better for it: 2277); of Beowulf, *næs him wihte ðe sel* (he wasn't any the better for it: 2687).

What are we to make of the heroic diptych that glorifies Beowulf in part 1 and surrounds him with gloom, impotence, and pessimism in part 2? Perhaps, if the poem is indeed a meditation on the Germanic past and its ideals by a Christian poet, the message is that heroism, like any other human activity, is subject to God's will. Perhaps it is a "best case–worst case" analysis of heroism, suggesting its absolute as well as its pragmatic value within the range of human behavioral options. It may even be that the poem is an attempt to recapture and preserve the full range of a traditional culture's experiences, good and bad, as gathered, in the best traditional manner, around the polemic core of the hero's supreme moments of combat. We can, in any case, enjoy and learn from this great poem even while freely admitting that much of its consciousness and social institutions have become so alien as to be beyond the reach of all but the most creative recollection.

## Selected Bibliography


### EDITIONS

*The Anglo-Saxon Poetic Records.* Edited by G. P. Krapp and E. V. K. Doobie. 6 vols. New York, 1931–1953. The standard collection of texts.

*Beowulf.* Edited by G. J. Thorkelin. Copenhagen, 1815.

*Beowulf.* Edited by J. M. Kemble. London, 1833. With other poems.

*Beowulf.* Edited by B. Thorpe. Oxford, 1855. With other poems.

*Beowulf.* Edited by F. Klaeber. 3rd ed. with 1st and 2nd supplements. Boston, 1950. The standard text.

*Beowulf.* Edited by E. V. K. Dobbie. New York, 1953. With *Judith* in *The Anglo-Saxon Poetic Records,* vol. 6.

*Beowulf.* Edited by C. L. Wrenn. 3rd ed. revised by W. F. Bolton. New York, 1973.

*Beowulf.* Edited with translation by Howell D. Chickering. Garden City, N.Y., 1977.

*Beowulf.* Edited with translation by Michael Swanton. Manchester, 1978.

*Finnsburh: Fragment and Episode.* Edited by D. R. Fry. London, 1974.

### FACSIMILES

Malone, K., ed. *The Nowell Codex (British Museum Cotton Vitellius A. XV, 2nd ms.).* Copenhagen, 1963.

————. *The Thorkelin Transcripts of Beowulf.* Copenhagen, 1951.

Zupitza, J., ed. *Beowulf: Facsimile with Transliteration.* London, 1882. 2nd. ed. with new reproductions of the manuscripts and an introductory note by N. Davis. London, 1959.

### TRANSLATIONS

Donaldson, E. T. *Beowulf.* New York, 1966. The best translation.

Gordon, R. K. *Anglo-Saxon Poetry Selected and Translated.* London, 1926.

Greenfield, S. B. *A Readable "Beowulf."* Carbondale, Ill., 1982.

Hamer, R. *A Choice of Anglo-Saxon Verse.* London, 1970.

Hieatt, C. B. *"Beowulf" and Other Old English Poems.* New York, 1967.

Kemble, J. M. *Beowulf.* London, 1837.

Kennedy, C. W. *An Anthology of Old English Poetry.* New York, 1960.

### CONCORDANCES AND BIBLIOGRAPHIES

Bessinger, J. B., and P. H. Smith. *A Concordance to the Anglo-Saxon Poetic Records.* Ithaca, 1978.

————. *A Concordance to Beowulf.* Ithaca, 1969.

Fry, D. R. *Beowulf and the Fight at Finnsburh: A Bibliography.* Charlottesville, N.C., 1969.

Garmonsway, G. N., and J. Simpson, trans. *Beowulf and Its Analogues.* London, 1968. A collection of translations from Old English, Latin, Old Norse, and other languages.

Greenfield, S. B., and F. C. Robinson. *A Bibliography of Publications on Old English Literature to the End of 1972.* Toronto, 1980.

Short, D. D. *Beowulf Scholarship: An Annotated Bibliography to 1978.* New York, 1980.

### RELATED TEXTS

Albertson, C., trans. *Anglo-Saxon Saints and Heroes.* New York, 1967. Studies of several Anglo-Saxon saints' lives.

Bede. *Ecclesiastical History of the English People.* Edited and translated by B. Colgrave and R. A. B. Mynors. Oxford, 1969.

Goldin, F., trans. *The Song of Roland.* New York, 1978.

Hatto, A. T., trans. *The Nibelungenlied.* Harmondsworth, 1965.

Homer. *The Iliad.* Translated by R. Lattimore. Chicago, 1951.

Sandars, N. K., trans. *The Epic of Gilgamesh.* Harmondsworth, 1960. Rev. ed., 1964.

Whitelock, D., D. C. Douglas, and S. Tucker, eds.

and trans. *The Anglo-Saxon Chronicle.* London, 1961.

## BACKGROUND STUDIES

Amos, A. C. *Linguistic Means of Determining the Dates of Old English Literary Texts.* Cambridge, Mass., 1981.

Barnes, D. "Folktale Morphology and the Structure of *Beowulf.*" *Speculum* 45: 416–434 (1970).

Benson, L. "The Literary Character of Anglo-Saxon Formulaic Poetry." *PMLA* 81: 334–341 (1966).

————. "The Originality of *Beowulf.*" *Harvard English Studies* 1: 1–43 (1970).

————. "The Pagan Coloring of *Beowulf.*" In *Old English Poetry: Fifteen Essays.* Edited by R. Creed. Providence, R.I., 1967. Pp. 193–213.

Blair, P. Hunter. *Introduction to Anglo-Saxon England.* 2nd ed. Cambridge, 1977.

————. *The World of Bede.* London, 1970.

Bliss, A. J. "*Beowulf,* Lines 3074–75." In *J. R. R. Tolkien, Scholar and Storyteller.* Edited by M. Salu and T. Farrell. Ithaca, N.Y., 1979. Pp. 41–63. Argues that Beowulf is damned at the end of the epic.

Bonjour, A. *The Digressions in "Beowulf."* Oxford, 1950.

Bowra, C. M. *Heroic Poetry.* London, 1952.

Brewer, D. S. *Symbolic Stories.* Cambridge and Ottawa, 1980.

Brodeur, A. G. *The Art of "Beowulf."* Berkeley and Los Angeles, 1959. Especially the first two chapters on compounding and variation.

Campbell, A. "The Old English Epic Style." In *English and Medieval Studies Presented to J. R. R. Tolkien on the Occasion of His Seventieth Birthday.* Edited by N. Davis and C. L. Wrenn. London, 1962. Pp. 13–26.

Campbell, J. *The Hero with a Thousand Faces.* 2nd ed. Princeton, N. J., 1960.

Chadwick, H. M. *The Heroic Age.* Cambridge, 1912. Reprinted 1967.

Chambers, R. W. *"Beowulf": An Introduction to the Study of the Poem.* 3rd ed. Cambridge, 1959.

Chaney, W. A. *The Cult of Kingship in Anglo-Saxon England.* Berkeley and Los Angeles, 1970.

Chase, C., ed. *The Dating of "Beowulf."* Toronto, 1981.

Creed, R. P. "The Making of an Anglo-Saxon Poem." *Journal of English Literary History* 26: 445–454 (1959).

De Vries, J. *Heroic Song and Heroic Legend.* Translated by B. J. Timmer. London, 1963.

Donahue, C. "*Beowulf* and Christian Tradition: A Reconsideration from a Celtic Stance." *Traditio* 21: 55–116 (1965).

Frye, N. *Anatomy of Criticism.* Princeton, N.J., 1957.

Girvan, R. *"Beowulf" and the Seventh Century.* London, 1971. This reissued edition includes a chapter on Sutton Hoo.

Godfrey, C. J. *The Church in Anglo-Saxon England.* Cambridge, 1962.

Goldsmith, M. E. *The Mode and Meaning of "Beowulf."* London, 1970.

Greenfield, S. E. *A Critical History of Old English Literature.* New York, 1965.

————. *The Interpretation of Old English Poems.* London, 1972.

Haarder, A. *"Beowulf": The Appeal of a Poem.* Aarhus, 1975. History of *Beowulf* criticism.

Hamilton, M. P. "The Religious Principle in *Beowulf.*" *PMLA* 61: 309–331 (1946).

Hanning, R. W. "*Beowulf* as Heroic History." *Medievalia et Humanistica* 5: 77–102 (1974).

————. "Sharing, Dividing, Depriving: The Verbal Ironies of Grendel's Last Visit to Heorot." *Texas Studies in Literature and Language* 15: 203–214 (1973).

Hart, T. E. "*Ellen:* Some Tectonic Relationships in *Beowulf* and Their Formal Resemblance to Anglo-Saxon Art." *Papers on Language and Literature* 6: 263–290 (1970).

Hieatt, C. B. "Envelope Patterns and the Structure of *Beowulf.*" *English Studies in Canada* 1: 250–265 (1975).

Hume, K. "The Concept of the Hall in Old English Poetry." *Anglo-Saxon England* 3: 63–74 (1974).

Irving, E. B. *A Reading of "Beowulf."* New Haven, Conn., 1968.

Jabbour, A. "Memorial Transmission in Old English Poetry." *Chaucer Review* 3: 174–190 (1969).

Jackson, W. T. H. *The Hero and the King, An Epic Theme.* New York, 1982.

John, E. "*Beowulf* and the Margins of Literacy." *Bulletin of the John Rylands University Library of Manchester* 56: 388–422 (1974).

Kiernan, K. *Beowulf and the Beowulf Manuscript.* New Brunswick, N.J., 1981.

Lee, A. A. *The Guest-Hall of Eden: Four Essays on the Design of Old English Poetry.* New Haven, Conn., 1972. Especially pp. 171–223.

Levy, G. R. *The Sword from the Rock: An Investigation into the Origins of Epic Literature and the Development of the Hero.* London, 1953.

Leyerle, J. "Beowulf the Hero and the King." *Medium Aevum* 34: 89–102 (1965).

———. "The Interlace Structure of *Beowulf.*" *University of Toronto Quarterly* 37: 1–17 (1967).

Lord, A. B. *The Singer of Tales.* Cambridge, Mass., 1960. Sets forth Parry and Lord's work in Yugoslavia.

Magoun, F. P., Jr. "*Beowulf* A: A Folk Variant." *Arv* (Journal of Scandinavian Folklore) 14: 95–101 (1958).

———. "*Beowulf* B: A Folk Poem on Beowulf's Death." In *Early English and Norse Studies: Presented to Hugh Smith in Honour of His Sixtieth Birthday.* Edited by A. Brown and P. Foote. London, 1963. Pp. 127–140.

———. "Oral-Formulaic Character of Anglo-Saxon Poetry." *Speculum* 28: 446–467 (1953).

Niles, J. D. "Ring Composition and the Structure of *Beowulf.*" *PMLA* 94: 924–935 (1979).

O'Loughlin, J. L. N. "*Beowulf:* Its Unity and Purpose." *Medium Aevum* 21: 1–13 (1952). Discussion of the feud.

Ong, W. J. "World as View and World as Event." *American Anthropologist* 71: 634–647 (1969).

Opland, J. *Anglo-Saxon Oral Poetry.* New Haven, Conn., 1980.

Osborn, M. "The Great Feud: Scriptural History and Strife in *Beowulf.*" *PMLA* 93: 973–981 (1978).

Pearsall, D. *Old English and Middle English Poetry.* London, 1977. *Routledge History of English Poetry,* vol. 1.

Pope, J. C. "Beowulf's Old Age." In *Philological Essays: Studies in Old and Middle English Language and Literature in Honour of Herbert Dean Meritt.* Edited by J. Rosier. The Hague, 1970. Pp. 55–64.

———. *The Rhythm of "Beowulf."* Rev. ed. New Haven, Conn., 1966. Argues that the poem was sung to the accompaniment of the harp.

Propp, V. *Morphology of the Folk Tale.* Translated by L. Scott. Bloomington, Ind., 1958.

Raw, B. *The Art and Background of Old English Poetry.* London, 1978.

Robinson, F. C. "Elements of the Marvelous in the Characterization of Beowulf: A Reconsideration of the Textual Evidence." In *Old England Studies in Honor of John C. Pope.* Edited by R. B. Burlin and E. B. Irving. Toronto, 1974. Pp. 119–138.

———. "Two Aspects of Variation in Old English Poetry." In *Old English Poetry: Essays in Style.* Edited by D. G. Calder. Berkeley and Los Angeles, 1979. Pp. 127–146.

Rogers, H. L. "Beowulf's Three Great Fights." *Review of English Studies* 6: 339–355 (1955).

Schücking, L. "Wann Entstand der *Beowulf?* Glossen, Zweifel und Fragen." *Beiträge zur Geschichte der deutsches Sprache und Literatur* 42: 347–410 (1917). Suggests that the poem was composed in the Danelaw during the tenth century.

Shippey, T. A. *Beowulf. Studies in English Literature, 70.* London, 1978.

Sisam, K. *The Structure of "Beowulf."* Oxford, 1965.

———. *Studies in the History of Old English Literature.* Oxford, 1953. Especially pp. 29–44 on the "authority" of Old English poetical manuscripts.

Stanley, E. G. "*Beowulf.*" In *Continuations and Beginnings: Studies in Old English Literature.* Edited by Stanley. London, 1941. Pp. 104–141.

———. "Hæþenra hyht in *Beowulf.*" *In Studies in Old English Literature in Honor of Arthur G. Brodeur.* Edited by S. B. Greenfield. Eugene, Ore., 1963. Pp. 136–151.

Stevens, M. "The Structure of *Beowulf:* From Gold-Hoard to Word-Hoard." *Modern Language Quarterly* 39: 219–238 (1978).

Tolkien, J. R. R. "*Beowulf,* the Monsters and the Critics." *Proceedings of the British Academy* 22: 245–295 (1936). The widely anthologized Gollancz Memorial Lecture.

Wallace-Hadrill, J. M. *Early Germanic Kingship in England and on the Continent.* Oxford, 1971.

Watts, A. C. *The Lyre and the Harp: A Comparative Reconsideration of Oral Tradition in Homer and Old English Epic Poetry.* New Haven, Conn., 1969.

Whitelock, D. *The Audience of "Beowulf."* Oxford, 1951.

————. *The Beginnings of English Society*. Harmondsworth, 1952. *Pelican History of England*, vol. 2.

Whitman, C. H. *Homer and the Heroic Tradition*. Cambridge, Mass., 1958. Reprinted New York, 1965.

Williams, D. *Cain and Beowulf: A Study in Secular Allegory*. Toronto, 1982.

Wrenn, C. L. *A Study of Old English Literature*. London, 1967.

COLLECTIONS OF ESSAYS

Burlin, R. B., and E. B. Irving, eds. *Old English Studies in Honor of John C. Pope*. Toronto, 1974.

Fry, D. R., ed. *The "Beowulf" Poet*. Englewood Cliffs, N. J., 1968. Twentieth Century Views series.

Greenfield, S. B., ed. *Studies in Old English Literature in Honor of Arthur G. Brodeur*. Eugene, Ore., 1963.

Nicholson, L. E., ed. *An Anthology of "Beowulf" Criticism*. Notre Dame, Ind., 1963.

ROBERT W. HANNING

# GIOVANNI BOCCACCIO
## *(1313–1375)*

### *THE EARLY YEARS: 1313–1348*

THE FATHER OF European narrative, as he has been called, or Giovanni Boccaccio of Certaldo, as he called himself, was born in 1313, most likely in Florence. Certaldo, a small Tuscan city, was the original seat of his agricultural-turned-mercantile family, as well as the home of the author's last years. The son of one Boccaccio or Boccaccino—who with his brother Vanni comprised the first generation of the family to be lured from Certaldo by the financial rewards of Florence, the Tuscan capital—and of an unknown mother, Giovanni was legitimized by his father, who planned a merchant's career for his son and educated him accordingly. But Boccaccio had other ideas, for, as he explains in a famous autobiographical passage of the *Genealogia deorum gentilium* (Genealogy of the Gentile Gods), he came from the womb with his literary vocation already fixed and incontestable:

> Whatever the vocation of others, mine, as experience from my mother's womb has shown, is clearly the study of poetry. For this, I believe, I was born. . . . I remember perfectly that before I reached my seventh year, or had ever seen a story, or heard a teacher speak, or scarce knew my letters, a natural impulse to composition seized me. I produced some little inventions, slight as they may have been. Of course, at that tender age genius was as yet too weak for so great a function. But I had scarce reached my majority when my mind, by its own impulse, seized and assimilated the little I had already learned of poetry, and I pursued the art with the utmost zeal, and delighted myself above all things in reading, studying, and trying with all my might to understand poetry. This took place without a word of advice or instruction from anyone, while my father continually resisted and condemned such a pursuit. Strangely enough, before I knew the proper kinds and number of feet in a verse, my acquaintances, in spite of my most urgent protest, were all calling me a poet, a name I have never really deserved to this day. If my father had only been favorable to such a course at a time of life when I was more adaptable, I do not doubt that I should have taken my place among poets of fame. But while he tried to bend my mind first into business and next into a lucrative profession, it came to pass that I turned out neither a business man, nor a canon-lawyer, and missed being a good poet besides.
>
> (Charles G. Osgood trans., pp. 131–132)

This passage is worth quoting at length, since it presents so lucidly Boccaccio's most distinguishing psychological traits, both as man and as artist; in it are delineated not only his total identification with and commitment to "poetry," but also—counterbalancing this—the humble posture so atypical of the great creative artist and yet so typical of Boccaccio. This attitude, by no means hypocritical or a simple rhetorical topos, had repercussions on all aspects of Boccaccio's life and work. For instance, it informed his friendship with Petrarch, which in turn affected Boccaccio's choice of subject matter and language. Thus, issues that at first glance seem exclusively literary, such as his abandoning of the Italian vernacular for Latin, are in fact intimately connected to matters beyond the text. Although this is in a broad sense true of all writers, Boccaccio's oeuvre is remarkable for features that bring the intertwined literary and psychological components exceptionally close to the surface: one thinks of the pseudoautobiographical content, of the moments of self-deprecation on the one hand and self-defense on the other, of the sudden shifts in genre, and of the issue of the author's so-called conversion. The best emblem for this fundamental Boccaccian problematic is its literary correlative, the *novella* itself—the form that Boccaccio perfected in the work for which he is famous, the *Decameron,* but a form that has always been considered inferior, indeed an "outlaw on Parnassus."

Boccaccio's own sense of inferiority may doubtless be traced to his illegitimate birth, a topic he addresses frequently—if revisionistically—in his early works. This is the negative pole of Boccaccio's early life. On the positive side is his father's removal to Naples, for business reasons, when the boy was approximately fourteen years old. Both events leave their imprint on the idealized autobiography Boccaccio invented in these years and inscribed into his works: one (his birth) being the event he had to overcome; the other (Naples) being the ideal environment, the newly discovered *locus amoenus* with which to replace the less appealing reality. In fact, the kingdom of Naples, known for its aristocratic elegance, gaiety, and culture, was much more suited to the dreams of the young poet than was dour and bourgeois Florence. Much later, in a letter to a friend, Francesco Nelli, Boccaccio remembered with pride that he was accepted by the best Neapolitan society (*Epistola* 12).

But if this life-style fulfilled certain aspirations, it also presented dilemmas, which were resolved by the creation of a romantic fable that had the merit not only of correcting the past but also of improving the present. Its main lines are as follows. The author's father, on one of his business trips to Paris, courted and seduced a French lady of high degree, perhaps even a daughter of the king of France. From this liaison the author was born. After the death of his mother, the child was brought to Italy and educated in Florence until he moved to Naples, where the great event of his life took place.

According to the fable, on Holy Saturday, 30 March 1336, Boccaccio attended the church of San Lorenzo in Naples, where he espied and fell in love with "Fiammetta" (little flame), the code name for one Maria d'Aquino, an illegitimate daughter of King Robert of Naples, the wife of an aristocrat, and a lady of consequence. The author pursued her to a convent where she was passing the time with her companions; here he distinguished himself by responding to her request that someone retell in Italian the French romance of Floire and Blanchefleur. Their love proceeded apace; he won her and enjoyed supreme bliss. But soon his troubles began. He grew jealous, suspecting her of taking other lovers. Finally his suspicions were confirmed, and all was over.

This fanciful story was pieced together by critics from scattered, presumed indications in Boccaccio's early works. In the nineteenth and early twentieth centuries, biographers were particularly adept at this game, becoming veritable cryptographers intent on deciphering the "clues" in the various proems and authorial dedications to Fiammetta. The French scholar Henri Hauvette dedicated his *Boccace* (1914) "à la mémoire de la parisienne inconnue qui donna le jour à l'auteur du *Décaméron* en 1313" (to the memory of the unknown Parisian lady who gave birth to the author of the *Decameron* in 1313). He was, in fact, merely revitalizing a long tradition: Filippo Villani (1325?–1405?) writes in his life of Boccaccio that the poet's father "fell in love with a young Parisian girl whose social status was between noble and bourgeois." One of the tasks of more recent criticism has been to recognize this pastiche for the fable that it is, a fable that draws on both psychological and literary motivations. Thus, the love story is complete with the traditional meeting in the church, a topos of love literature exploited by Petrarch as well. Vittore Branca, today's leading Boccaccio specialist, points out in his biography of Boccaccio that not only is there no discernible trace of Maria d'Aquino in genealogical and dynastic records but that there are glaring inconsistencies in Boccaccio's accounts. In particular, the year of her birth changes from book to book, in order to keep her forever young.

Naples, then, was the first catalyst of Boccaccio's inspiration, a place that allowed him to change his image of himself and that remained the idealized center of his desire for the rest of his life. Despite his father's attempts to direct his son first into business and then into canon law, Boccaccio in fact spent these years tuning his rhetorical skills (witness the early Latin exercises, the *Elegia constantiae* and the *Allegoria mitologica,* a retelling of the first two books of the *Metamorphoses*) and reading voraciously in King Robert's well-stocked library. He was fortunate enough to have as one of his law professors Cino da Pistoia, a lyric poet and friend of Dante. Dante was Boccaccio's first literary inspiration—years later Petrarch in a letter referred to Dante as Boccaccio's "primus studiorum dux et prima fax" (first guide and first light of your studies: *Familiari* [Letters on Familiar Matters] 21.15)—and we may presume that the young writer took this opportunity to learn more about his idol. Another figure of importance whom Boccaccio was to meet in this period was the Augustinian father Dionigi of Borgo San Sepolcro, who was responsible for directing Boccaccio to the works of Seneca and Saint Augustine. Dionigi was also the first to introduce Boccaccio to the works of another young protegé of his, Petrarch (in fact, it was Dionigi who gave Petrarch the famous volume of Augustine's *Confessions* that he carried to the top of Mount Ventoux). Thus began the other fundamental literary attachment of Boccaccio's life.

A number of Boccaccio's minor works date from these years in Naples. The dates of composition for most of them are uncertain, but a rough chronology has been established. The first of these works is the *Caccia di Diana (Diana's Hunt),* a slight poem from about 1334. Formally, the poem is modeled on Boccaccio's "first guide," Dante, in that it consists of eighteen brief cantos of terza rima. In a peculiar mixture of mythological fantasy and social realism, Boccaccio tells how, in the form of a stag, he witnesses a hunt led by Diana, whose nymphs are the best of Neapolitan society, named by Boccaccio in a catalog that takes up most of the poem. At the end of the hunt, as the ladies gather around their slaughtered prey, Diana suggests that they sacrifice their booty to Jupiter and that they honor her, the virgin goddess. Suddenly there is a rebellion, led by the author's unidentified lady, who announces that their allegiance shall be not to Diana, but to Venus. Venus triumphantly descends, and transforms all the animals, including the narrator, into young men. The poem ends with the poet's stock tributes to this lady, source of all virtue and destroyer of all vice.

The *Caccia di Diana* has the merit not only of presenting *in nuce* some of Boccaccio's typical topoi (*locus amoenus,* nymphs) and themes (the Diana/Venus dialectic, the effect of the women on the men) but also of having prompted some of the standard critical reactions to his work. The chief problem of Boccaccio criticism, a problem that has plagued interpretations of the *Decameron* as well as of the minor works, has been whether or not to take Boccaccio seriously. Is the *Decameron* merely a collection of stories, or is it more? Is the *Caccia di Diana* a social paean to the ladies of the Angevin court, or is it more? This question is doubtless more important when addressed to the greater work. Nonetheless, it is worth noting that the issue of how to deal with Boccaccio criticially becomes an issue at the very beginning of his oeuvre. The positivists' acceptance of the romantic version of the author's life allowed them to eschew questions of interpretation in dealing with the minor works and, instead, to plumb them as sources of biographical information. This prelapsarian world of Boccaccio criticism is now behind us, with the result that we must distinguish between the author and the narrator of a given work. Whether the *Caccia* is a celebration of Venus or, conversely, an ironic attack upon the religion of love (both have been suggested), no interpretation any longer assumes that from the statements or actions of the narrator we may learn about the life of the author.

Boccaccio's characteristic verse form, and one of his great contributions to literature, is the octave. Already present in the popular *cantari,* or street romances, ottava rima (the eight-line stanza with six lines of alternating rhyme and a final rhyming couplet) was raised to the level of art by Boccaccio, who thus initiated its illustrious career in Italy and abroad. First used by Boccaccio in the *Filostrato* (1335?), the octave was particularly suited to his gifts, since it generates a more narrative than lyrical flow.

The *Filostrato* presents a number of new developments: the use of ottava rima, the title coined on Greek words ("Filostrato" is intended to signify "vanquished by love"), and the plot borrowed from a French romance. The setting is ancient Troy; the protagonists are the lovers Troiolo and Criseida, and their go-between Pandaro. Benoît de Sainte-Maure's *Roman de Troie (Romance of Troy)* is Boccaccio's chief source for the *Filostrato.* It is as a brief episode in the voluminous *Roman de Troie* that the story of Troiolo and Criseida—destined for fame in the full-fledged accounts of Boccaccio, Geoffrey Chaucer, and William Shakespeare—makes its first appearance on the literary scene. As told by Boccaccio, the story revolves around the love of Troiolo, a son of Priam, for Criseida, the widowed daughter of the seer Calchas. After the passionate consummation of their love, engineered by Pandaro (a figure Boccaccio introduces into the tradition, from whose name we derive our "pander"), Criseida is sent to her father in the Greek camp. Instead of keeping faith with Troiolo, she deserts him for Diomede: "cotal fine ebbe la speranza vana / di Troiolo in Criseida villana" (such end has the vain hope of Troilus in base Criseida: 8.28). Troiolo-Filostrato dies at the hands of Achilles, a victim of his own reckless love and despair.

The *Filostrato* shares some features with the *Caccia di Diana* that are trademarks of the works of the Neapolitan period: the subject is love and its effects (this is true despite the martial background); the boundaries between lyric and narrative are loose (one of Filostrato's laments is an interpolated *canzone,* or lyric poem, by Cino da Pistoia); the poem is framed by a narrator's proem and conclusion (much more obviously than in the *Caccia,* where there is a narrator but no separate narrative segments mark his entrances and exits). The narrator of the *Filostrato* explicitly identifies with Troiolo, saying that he has chosen this story because it corresponds to his own unhappy love for Filomena, the lady to whom he dedicates the poem. (Interestingly, this lady is not yet Fiammetta, a fact that has influenced critics in assigning the *Filostrato* so early a date.) The persona of the unhappy lover is a narrative technique of great importance to Boccaccio, culminating in the far more complex proemial personas and framing strategies of the *Decameron.*

The *Filocolo* (1336–1338?) continues and develops the use of a lover persona who opens and closes the book. In the first chapter Boccaccio describes the scene in which he first sees and falls in love with Fiammetta, as well as his subsequent undertaking to write the story of Florio and Biancifiore for her. It is interesting, because of Boccaccio's decisive role in the transformation of the ottava from a popular rhyme scheme into a literary one, that here too he explicitly voices his concern lest a story be left in the hands of the ignorant that should be "exalted by the verses of a poet" (1.1.25). Boccaccio's role is frequently that of a mediator between popular and high culture. Indeed, his greatest work is also his most daring act of such mediation. At the end of the *Filocolo,* in addressing his "little book" (hardly that at 615 pages), Boccaccio makes clear to what tradition he intends it to belong. Emulating Statius' humility at the end of the *Thebaid,* he instructs his book to follow in the wake of the *Aeneid;* he adds that it should also keep well behind Lucan, Statius, Ovid, and Dante (this tribute to his Florentine predecessor is noteworthy in comparison with the fastidious attitudes toward Dante prevailing among the humanists, beginning with Petrarch). The story sung in the piazze is thus inserted—through Boccaccio's mediation—into the highest of cultural canons.

Although a romance, the *Filocolo* attempts to imitate the classical masters by affecting an epic/historic garb, complete with prolonged displays of mythological erudition and digressions on the foundings of cities (Certaldo, in fact). The rhetorically elaborate prose and the lengthy periods brimming with subordinate clauses and participial phrases point the way forward to the *Decameron,* although in the latter work the baroque Latin models of Apuleius and Valerius Maximus have ceded to the influence of the more sober and classical Livy (whose *Decades* Boccaccio had in part translated). Both the first sight of Fiammetta in San Lorenzo and the second meeting at Sant'Archangelo a Baiano are marked by that typically Decameronian storyteller's introduction: "Avvenne che un giorno . . ." (and so it happened, one day: 1.1.17, 23). But the *Filocolo* anticipates structurally its prose successor in more concrete ways as well.

In the midst of his quest for his love, Biancifiore, Floriò (whose parents, the king and queen of Spain, have sold Biancifiore to oriental merchants to prevent their son from marrying her; he will, of course, find her, rescue her, marry her, and even convert to Christianity with her) is forced by a tempest (like Aeneas) to land in Naples, still called Parthenope in this pre-Christian era. Florio, who has by now taken the pseudonym Filocolo ("labor of love"), is entertained by a group of noble young men and women, of whom the most beautiful is Fiammetta, daughter of the king. (This is a deliberate anachronism on Boccaccio's part, since he is also dedicating the book to her.)

Fiammetta proposes that, to while away the afternoon, they all repair to a meadow where they may "with sundry discourses try to forget the heat of the day" (H. G. trans., p. 12). They begin to talk, but "because at times, unthinking, one did interrupt another's tale," Fiammetta suggests a framework for their discussions. They should ordain one member of the group to be king and then each in turn propound a question of love, which the king must resolve. Eventually the others prevail upon Fiammetta herself to accept this office, and so she becomes the queen of a circle of speakers very similar to the one we shall encounter in the *Decameron.* In the *Filocolo,* however, they beguile each other not with the spicy stories of the later work, but with "quistioni d'amore," along the lines of "Who is it better that a young man should love: a maiden, a married woman, or a widow?" The theoretical nature of these questions notwithstanding, in a number of cases the speaker begins to tell a bona fide story; in two instances (questions 4 and 13) the stories they tell surface later as *novellas* in the *Decameron* (10.5 and 10.4, respectively).

The *Teseida,* or *Book of Theseus* (the title is modeled on classical epic, as in the *Aeneid* or the *Thebaid*), is a poem with serious pretensions to epic status. Like Vergil's *Aeneid,* it is written in twelve books. Boccaccio sets this work, written about 1339–1341, apart from his more youthful endeavors by providing his own glosses to mythological figures and obscure textual allusions. Some of Boccaccio's annotations are full-scale essays, as for instance his remarks on the temples of Mars and Venus in book 7, which explain the temples and their gods in allegorical terms and offer important clues to Boccaccio's mythography. The most explicit statement regarding the author's intentions can be found at the poem's conclusion, where, in an address to his book analogous to the one in the *Filocolo,* Boccaccio writes: "But you, O book, undertake first to sing to them of the struggles endured for Mars, struggles never before seen in the Italian vernacular" (12.84). Referring to the three categories for vernacular poetry established in the *De vulgari eloquentia* by Dante—war poetry, love poetry, and moral poetry—Boccaccio here claims to fill a major lacuna in Italian literature: the *Teseida* is the poem of war that Italy needs, its epic answer to Bertran de Born.

The *Teseida* is really much less, or much more, than a conventional epic. The difference is indicated by Boccaccio in his dedicatory epistle to Fiammetta, where he is once more, as in the *Filostrato*'s proem, the unhappy lover. Here he writes that the matter treated in the *Teseida* is love—for the true subject of the poem is not Theseus, or his return from battling the Amazons with their queen, Hippolyta, as his bride, but rather the love of two young Thebans, Arcita and Palemone, for Emilia, Hippolyta's sister. Written in the same ottava rima as the *Filostrato,* the *Teseida* succeeds in being less lyrical a narrative than its predecessor. The best emblem of the poem's literary synchretism is the composite title the Muses coin for the work in a closing sonnet: "Teseida delle nozze d'Emilia" (Theseid of the nuptials of Emilia). Boccaccio's fusion of the background atmosphere and the machinery of epic (the two lover-kinsmen finally battle for Emilia in a grand pan-Hellenic tournament sponsored by Theseus) with a plot whose basic motivation is determined by a love theme (who will marry Emilia?) will be fortunate indeed. Besides being the principal source of Chaucer's "The Knight's Tale," the *Teseida* is the predecessor of such Italian chivalric epics as Boiardo's *Orlando innamorato* and Ariosto's *Orlando furioso.*

There is in the *Teseida* an uneasy coexistence that points to the changes occurring at the time in Boccaccio's life and affecting his work. On the one hand there are scenes such as the one in which Arcita and Palemone first view Emilia—the archetypal lyric/romance lady—who is singing and gathering flowers, dressed only in her shift; on the other hand there are passages like the moralizing glosses that accompany the description of the temple of Venus in book 7 ("This Venus is twofold, since one can and must be understood as every honest and licit desire, as to desire to have a wife in order to have children. . . . The second Venus is the one through which all sensuality is desired, commonly called the goddess of love": 7.50). Toward the end of 1340, Boccaccio's Neapolitan sojourn—a period marked from a literary standpoint by his prolific and varied output as well as by his autobiographical inventiveness and one he was later to look back on as the happiest in his life—came to an end. Because of financial reverses he was called back to Florence by his father. His choice of the allegorical/didactic mode for his next works, the *Comedia delle ninfe fiorentine* (*Comedy of the Florentine Nymphs,* 1341–1342) and the *Amorosa visione* (*Amorous Vision,* 1342), was doubtless connected to his return to Florence. The allegorical/didactic tradition was particularly strong in Tuscany, and Boccaccio's works in this vein can be seen as an act of cultural acclimatization.

The *Comedia delle ninfe fiorentine,* popularized by the fifteenth-century copyists as the *Ninfale d'Ameto* after its protagonist, is a pastoral allegory in fifty chapters of not quite alternating prose and verse (terza rima). It tells the story of the rough hunter Ameto, who chances on the nymph Lia and falls in love with her; he later rediscovers her at a celebration of Venus with six other nymphs, her companions. In the central portion of the work, chapters 17–38, the nymphs recount their lives and loves to Ameto. Their stories turn out to be highly edifying when the allegory is unveiled in the last section of the *Comedia ninfe,* for we learn then that the nymphs are the seven virtues (Mopsa is wisdom; Emilia, justice; Adiona, temperance; Acrimonia, courage; Agapes, charity; Fiammetta, hope; and Lia, faith). Moreover, the lovers for whom they forsake their husbands represent a corresponding human flaw that they as the virtues will correct. Thus, the striptease, described in sensuous detail, to which Mopsa resorts in order to attract her lover, Affron, is retrospectively revealed as the lengths to which wisdom will go to prevail over human folly. Fiammetta's story (25) has, predictably, received the most attention; Boccaccio intended it to be a major installment in his ongoing literary myth. Her lover is Caleone (he is desperation to her hope), a repetition of the *Filocolo,* in which the youth in love with Fiammetta is also named Caleone. Following a recapitulation of her family history up to the founding of the ancestral seat of Aquino, Fiammetta tells how her chaste mother was seduced by the king of Naples. Then, moving to her own amorous situation, she recounts how she woke up to find Caleone in her bed, and how—in what has traditionally been accepted as a description of Boccaccio's own prowess as a lover—he succeeds in remaining there.

If Ameto learns something from his experience with the nymphs (by the end of the *Comedia ninfe* he is ashamed that he ever harbored "concupiscible thoughts" toward them: 46.3), it is more than we can say for the protagonist of the *Amorosa visione.* This singular character reminds one of the pilgrim protagonist of the *Divine Comedy*—if he had refused to follow Vergil out of the dark wood and had instead insisted that Vergil follow him into it. Indeed, the *Amorosa visione,* a rather laborious imitation of the *Comedy* on the one hand (it is an allegorical dream vision in fifty cantos of terza rima), can be seen as a subversion of the sacred poem on the other. The narrator meets an unidentified female guide (although critics have debated her identity, the celestial Venus would seem to be the most likely choice) who leads him to a small narrow door; he refuses to pass through it, insisting on turning to the left (a direction with iconographically negative associations: in paintings of the Last Judgment the damned are always to God's left) toward a wide and open door from which sounds of festivity emerge. On learning that through this door lies all worldly pleasure, the narrator reverses the arguments of conventional morality (and, interestingly, anticipates Franciscus, who succumbs to the same logical fallacy in Petrarch's *Secretum*) by arguing that they must first experience the world's vanities and only then proceed to the graver things in life (3.37–39). In brief, the narrator prevails; in allegorical terms, he guides the guide onto the wrong path. Here they witness the "triumphs" of the great forces that dominate humanity: Wisdom, Glory, Riches, Love, and Fortune. These narrative tableaux, in which each abstraction, personified as a beautiful woman, is surrounded by the human beings she has subjugated throughout history and literature, are an important feature of the *Amorosa visione.* As a literary device, the triumph was to gain great popularity; it was imitated almost immediately by Petrarch in his *Trionfi.*

All Boccaccio's works from the *Filocolo* on are dedicated to Fiammetta. Indeed, as part of his "amorous vision" the poet even has the good fortune to find the elusive Maria d'Aquino (43.37–63). It is, however, in the *Elegia di madonna Fiammetta* (*Elegy of Madonna Fiammetta,* 1343–1344?), his next work, that Boccaccio's Fiammetta story reaches its culmination, as the title itself, containing her name, bears witness. The *Elegia,* which has been called the first modern psychological novel, is a penetrating study of the deranging effects of love. The heroine writes in the first person of her passion for the fickle Panfilo; the originality of the *Elegia* is apparent if one considers the rarity, despite the profusion of medieval analyses of love, of texts from the woman's point of view. Fiammetta, highly literate, addresses herself to other literate ladies, so that they will feel compassion for her and learn from her mistakes. This implied epistolary form is an interesting anticipation not only of the literate ladies to whom the *Decameron* is dedicated but also of later lovelorn heroines who like to read and write, like the heroine of Samuel Richardson's *Clarissa Harlowe* (1747–1748).

Fiammetta's story is simple: she falls in love with a young man she sees in church; for a while they are supremely happy; he leaves to pay a visit to his native city, and although he has promised to return, he does not. The nine chapters of this prose elegy do not contain much action. At one point after Panfilo's departure, Fiammetta hears that he has married. Later she hears that he is not married but has taken a mistress. Still later she hears that he has returned, only to find that it was someone else. Such nonevents carry the reader along, not through the twists of a quickly moving plot, but rather through the labyrinth of Fiammetta's mind.

The hold of the *Elegia* lies in its stunningly acute depiction of a love that has become a pathology. The plot is really nothing more than a series of ups and downs. Every time Fiammetta finds a new pretext for hope—for instance that Panfilo was not married after all—she "waxeth fair again," in the Elizabethan translator's apt rendition, only to wane at Fortune's next blow. But she never gives up. Fiammetta's last words are a prayer for Panfilo's return. Her refusal to face reality is the sign of her sickness, brought on essentially by confusing life with art. She not only attempts to mold her affair to the books she has read but believes that her words will alter events. This, after all, is why she writes her book.

The *Elegia* takes the form of an inversion of the dominant myth whereby "Boccaccio" is enamored of "Fiammetta," who briefly satisfies him but soon rejects him. Specifically, it is a reversal of the *Filostrato,* in many ways the most mythologically straightforward of the early works. Fiammetta falls for Panfilo in a church, as Troiolo succumbed to Criseida in a temple; Fiammetta, like Troiolo, is abandoned by a lover who leaves for ostensibly good reasons, promising to return; Fiammetta, like Troiolo, falls into greater and greater depression as she awaits Panfilo's arrival. Even the minor characters have corresponding roles: Fiammetta's confidante, the Nurse, takes the place of Pandaro. But where the early work ends in a resolution of sorts—Troiolo realizes that Criseida has betrayed him and hastens to his death—Fiammetta remains suspended, buoyed by her eternizing rhetoric; a neat romance ending has thus given way to the psychologically more suggestive nonending of the *Elegia*. One could say that Boccaccio has grown up; he is telling us that he has taken his literary fable as far as it can go.

The major inversion of the *Elegia* is, of course, the substitution of a woman for a man. Here, Fiammetta is the one betrayed; before, she was the betrayer. Far from taking this, as did the positivist critics, as Boccaccio's bid for revenge, his vindication through literature, I would see this inversion as precisely his sign that the whole story is nothing but literature. By turning the tables, reversing the terms as it were, Boccaccio makes clear that these characters, including Fiammetta, are not tied to the dull grid of quotidian reality; indeed, they are even free to exchange roles. The Fiammetta myth here peaks, inverts, and ends all at once: with the *Elegia,* Boccaccio brings this chapter of his artistic life to a close.

The extent to which the *Elegia* constitutes an ending can best be measured by looking at the poem that follows it in Boccaccio's canon, the *Ninfale fiesolano* (*Nymphs of Fiesole,* 1344–1346?). Despite the use of ottava rima, which could seem to indicate a throwback to the earlier "epics," the *Ninfale* is in fact the herald of the *Decameron*. Its distance from the works that precede it is immediately underscored by a significant lacuna: there is no dedication to Fiammetta, nor is that obligatory name (in Provençal poetry such a name, or "senhal," was used to address a lady in order to conceal her identity) ever mentioned. The work takes the form of a pastoral etiological fable on the founding of Fiesole. The shepherd Africo falls in love with the nymph Mensola, seduces her despite his father's warning, and later kills himself because she fails to meet him again. Mensola gives birth to a son, Pruneo, but her transgression is discovered by Diana, who transforms her into a stream. Pruneo is raised by Africo's grieving parents and later becomes governor of Fiesole under its founder, Atalante.

What this summary of the plot, similar to so many others, fails to suggest about the *Ninfale fiesolano* is its artistic maturity, Boccaccio's achievement of a simultaneously light and profound touch. Like the *Elegia di madonna Fiammetta,* the *Ninfale* controls one stylistic register throughout; whereas in the earlier work this was a prolix, rhetorical, and courtly style suitable to its subject, in the *Ninfale* Boccaccio uses the popular style of the wandering storytellers. The important point is Boccaccio's new consistency. He suppresses the learned digressions and mythological excursions that so retarded the unfolding amours of Florio and Biancifiore. Nor does he vacillate between lyric, epic, and romance as he did in the *Filostrato* and even the *Teseida.* At the same time he is free to tell a story, unencumbered by the heavy-handed allegorical trappings of the *Comedia ninfe* and the *Amorosa visione.* Indeed, the *Ninfale* is in many respects a verse *novella.* Boccaccio's ability to impose an artistic unity on his material, already manifested in the *Elegia,* is a great step toward the variegated tapestry of the *Decameron,* in which so many registers can be blended harmoniously because they are held so firmly in hand.

Another key feature of the Boccaccian narrative that stands out in the *Ninfale* is the peculiar authorial blend of balance and distance, calculated to create a sense of multiple perspectives, that will be the mark of the *Decameron.* Two opposing forces dominate the world of the *Ninfale,* Venus and Diana; although critics have long maintained that the poem is a celebration of the former goddess, recently Robert Hollander has argued to the contrary, that the story is a "cautionary moral tale" vindicating Diana. In fact, the poem cannot be cast into either mold. Boccaccio describes the lovers with irony and with affection, and most of all with an uncanny realism that admits no "sides" but simply tells what is:

*Sentì Africo allora gran letizia,*
*veggendo che a ciò era contenta,*
*e donandole baci a gran dovizia,*
*a quel che bisognava s'argomenta;*
*più da natura che da lor malizia*
*atati, s'alzâr su le vestimenta,*
*faccendo che lor due parevan uno,*
*tanto natura insegnò a ciascheduno.*

*Quivi l'un l'altro baciava e mordeva,*
*e strignean forte, e chi le labbra prende:*
*—Anima mia!—ciaschedun diceva,*
*—All'acqua all'acqua, chè il foco s'accende!—*
*Il mulin macina quanto poteva,*
*e ciaschedun si dilunga e distende:*
*—Attienti bene! Omè, omè, omè,*
*aiuta aiuta, ch'i' moio 'n buona fè!—*
(st. 309–310)

Africo then was filled with joy, seeing she was prepared to grant his wish. Bestowing a swarm of kisses, he set about to do as he desired. Assisted more by nature than by cunning, they raised their garments; and indeed nature was so instructive that soon the two lovers seemed but one.

Exchanging feverish kisses, they clasp each other with abandon. "Oh, my sweet soul," they cry, "to the water, the water, for the fire burns!" The mill grinds with all the haste it can, and the two tighten their embrace. "Oh hold, hold me," they cry, "for indeed I'm dying."

(D. J. Donno trans.)

Neither Venus nor Diana "wins" in the *Ninfale fiesolano.* If anything, the love championed by the author lies between the two extremes—either the love of Africo's parents or of Pruneo and his bride. If, on the one hand, Africo and Mensola do not survive, neither are Diana's nymphs allowed to roam the woods perpetually. One of Atalante's first acts is to chase away the nymphs or force them to marry, thus ridding society of an unnatural source of tension and tragedy. As for the unhappy protagonists, it is difficult to say if they are "wrong" or "right," whether Boccaccio would have us view them as justly punished or unjustly destroyed by forces larger than they. The author's manifest respect for the complexities of the human psyche generates too much resistance to such moral pigeonholes.

## *THE* DECAMERON: *1349–1351*

Resistance and multivalence are the decisive features of the *Decameron* as well, where they go hand in hand with realism and psychological verisimilitude. Although present even in Boccaccio's earliest and most courtly works (for instance, in the delineation of Criseida's motives in the *Filostrato* or in the meeting of the lovers in the *Filocolo*), as well as in the later allegorical ones (as in the humor with which the narrator is shown to undercut the guide in the *Amorosa visione*), these traits are first coherently realized and sustained in the *Elegia di madonna Fiammetta* and the *Ninfale fiesolano.* The two stanzas cited above are evidence for the *Ninfale.* It is interesting to note that the metaphor for lovemaking taken from everyday life—in this case the grinding of the mill—which does so much to embed the event within a casually realistic context, is typical of the *Decameron.* The *Decameron* represents the zenith of Boccaccio's development in this mode.

Boccaccio is able to accomplish what he does in the *Decameron* because of two key elements: first, the use of the *novella* (a short tale, rather than a long story or short novel, as in the modern sense), of all genres traditionally the one that permits greatest accuracy and objectivity in the representation of all levels of society; second, the use of a framing structure in which the *novelle* are situated. Boccaccio's handling of the *novella* is masterly; he raises the genre from a simple mechanism based on a crude plot (as in the French *fabliaux* or the Italian *novellino*) to a polished synthesis in which plot is integrated to character and the form perfectly reflects both.

But the most brilliant stroke of the *Decameron* is its frame. The realism of the individual stories is mirrored by the ultimate realism of a rhetorical structure that always keeps the author at a distance from his characters and therefore prevents him from ever taking an explicit stand regarding their actions—as in "real life" we are all finally distanced from and unable to judge one another. Resistance to an absolute morality is thus programmatically structured into the *Decameron.*

The *Decameron* begins, like all Boccaccio's fictions, with a narrator's proem. In this one the author informs us that he has recently been freed from the pains of love by the comfort and succor of his friends, and that, since gratitude is the most commendable of virtues, he would like to repay the favor. This he proposes to do by offering comfort to those who most need it, the ladies who suffer from love. Lovesick ladies require more assistance than their male counterparts, since they not only must "conceal the flames of passion within their fragile breasts" but are also forced to "spend most of their time cooped up within the narrow confines of their rooms" (G. H. McWilliam trans., p. 46).

Following this dedication of his book to its ideal audience, the author moves on to an introduction in which he explains how the stories of the *Decameron* came to be told. In the first part of the introduction, Boccaccio depicts the effects of the great plague of 1348 on Florentine society; in the second part, we witness the chance meeting of seven young women and three young men in the church of

Santa Maria Novella. Forming a *brigata* (the word Boccaccio uses for his band of storytellers), they flee the city and head for the private estate of one of the group's members. Upon arrival the eldest woman, Pampinea, suggests that they organize themselves by electing a king or queen to rule over each day, chosen on a rotating basis, whose job will be to preside over their activities and generally see to the orderly arrangement of their lives. The others reward her sagacity by electing her their first ruler. Pampinea then further suggests that they pass the hottest part of the afternoon telling tales, like their predecessors in the *Filocolo;* the situating of stories within a narrative frame is of course already a topos of the Boccaccian narrative. Her idea is applauded, with the result that each of the ten characters tells a story on each of ten days; consequently, Boccaccio calls his book *Decameron,* literally "ten days," continuing his habit of borrowing titles from the Greek and also imitating Saint Ambrose's *Hexameron.*

The proem offers us our first clues to the author's intentions. It begins with an explanation of his motives for writing: "To take pity on people in distress is a human quality which every man and woman should possess, but it is especially requisite in those who have once needed comfort and found it in others" (p. 45). In Italian, this sentence begins with the words here translated as "human quality"; thus, the *Decameron*'s first words are "Umana cosa è aver compassione degli afflitti" (Human is it to have compassion for the afflicted). The choice of the first word in the book is by no means arbitrary; it signals simply and explicitly that the world depicted is the human world and that the values embraced are human values.

As the proem continues, Boccaccio's allegiance to a sphere of values that is human and secular, rather than divine and transcendent, is brought increasingly to the fore: "Gratitude, of all the virtues, is most to be commended and its opposite censured" (p. 45), says the author. Yet, far from being one of the three theological virtues (faith, hope, and charity), gratitude is not even one of the four cardinal virtues known to the ancients (temperance, fortitude, justice, and wisdom). Gratitude is technically not a virtue at all, but a social grace, belonging more to the sphere of manners than to that of religion. In other words, this chief of Boccaccian virtues is a human virtue, a virtue that belongs entirely to a social context, a virtue only in that it makes life more livable.

And, because he wants to make their lives more livable, Boccaccio writes for the ladies. His denunciation of their sequestered existence is implicitly a condemnation of the *vita contemplativa,* at least a condemnation of an enforced contemplation (as later in the *De mulieribus claris* [*On Famous Woman*] Boccaccio condemns the practice of sending women who have no religious vocation to nunneries). Men can relieve the suffering of unrequited love by living: "for if they wish, they can always walk abroad, see and hear many things, go fowling, hunting, fishing, riding, and gambling, or attend to their business affairs" (p. 47). In offering his book to the ladies, who are not free to do any of the above, Boccaccio is in fact offering them a surrogate for life; the stories will take the place of life for those who cannot live it. And, like life itself, the stories instruct: "For they [the ladies] will learn to recognize what should be avoided and likewise what should be pursued, and these things can only lead, in my opinion, to the removal of their affliction" (p. 47).

If the *Decameron* is a surrogate for life, specifically it depicts man as he is battered by fortune, subject to his passions, and redeemed by his intellect. *Fortuna, Amore,* and *Ingegno* (Fortune, Love, and Wit) emerge as the forces dominating the Decameronian universe. This domination is confirmed not only by their unifying presence in the otherwise heterogeneous stories but also by the topics that, with the exceptions of Days 1 and 9, are assigned to the various days. After Filomena becomes queen of Day 2, she improves on Pampinea's plan by suggesting a particular topic to which the stories of her day must conform: "Ever since the world began," she says, "men have been subject to various tricks of Fortune, and it will ever be thus until the end" (p. 112). Armed with this general principle, she proposes to discuss lucky resolutions to unlucky situations: "those who after suffering a series of misfortunes are brought to a state of unexpected happiness" (p. 112). Neifile, in Day 3, further defines the role of Fortune in our lives ("it will be all the more interesting if we restrict the subject matter of our stories to a single aspect of the many facets of Fortune" [p. 229]). She alters the equation by adding man's efforts—his *industria*—to the balance, proposing for discussion "people who by dint of their own efforts have achieved an object greatly desired, or recovered a thing previously lost" (p. 229). From Fortune, we pass in Days 4 and 5 to Love, seen in both its sorrowful and joyful garbs: in Day 4 the topic is "those whose love ended unhappily" (p. 320), and in Day 5 it is "the adventures of lovers who survived calamities or misfortunes and attained a state of happiness" (p. 402).

*Ingegno* predominates in Days 6, 7, and 8: first, in Day 6, in the form of the verbal repartee, the *pronta risposta* so prized by Boccaccio. The topic is "those who, on being provoked by some verbal pleasantry, have returned like for like, or who, by a prompt retort or shrewd manoeuvre, have avoided danger, discomfiture or ridicule" (p. 479). In Days 7 and 8 the prevailing *ingegno* takes a less intellectual form. From survival through the clever use of words, we move to survival through deeds, specifically through the use of the *beffa*, or practical joke. Thus, the topic of Day 7 is "the tricks that, either in the cause of love or for motives of self-preservation, women have played upon their husbands, irrespective of whether or not they were found out" (p. 515). The theme of Day 8 is simply an enlargement of the seventh day's: "the tricks that people in general, men and women alike, are forever playing upon one another" (p. 583).

Day 9, like Day 1, is an open day, in which the storytellers are free to discourse on any subject they choose. In fact, however, Day 9 tends to perpetuate the earthy, ribald humor of Days 7 and 8, whereas Day 1, as has frequently been pointed out, anticipates Day 6 in portraying men and women who use their wits to overcome difficulty. On the last day Panfilo submits for discussion "those who have performed liberal or munificent deeds, whether in the cause of love or otherwise" (p. 731). This day differs from the others in thus narrowing the field of human endeavor to one significant form of activity.

It will be noted that the *Decameron* has come full circle, for it is precisely liberality or generosity that engenders gratitude. As the book began with the author's gratitude for the generosity of his friends, which encourages him in turn to show generosity to the ladies, so it ends with the generosity of the characters of Day 10. Generosity, like gratitude, is a social virtue, one that palliates and civilizes the experience of living, and in fact, the stories of the last day are the final step in a process that has made the *brigata* fit to reenter society, to embark once more upon the business of life. Generosity is generated by compassion, the same compassion that Boccaccio signaled as his guiding motive in the *Decameron*'s first sentence: "Umana cosa è aver compassione degli afflitti. . . ." This *compassione,* motivating the author in his proem at one end of the book and the characters of Day 10 at the other end, is lost to Florentine society during the onslaught of the great plague. The loss is systematically depicted in the introduction, which is much more than a pitiable story or a particularly vivid account. The introduction is integral to the coherence and significance of the *Decameron* as a whole, for it is here that Boccaccio motivates the departure of the *brigata* from the city. They leave because their society is dissolving around them. This dissolution is described in two rhetorically well-defined sections, the first concentrating on the loss of *ingegno* and the second on the loss of *compas-*

*sione.* The last will turn out to be the critical failure; it is only with the breakdown in *compassione* that the dikes give way and the city is engulfed. In this way Boccaccio insists that *compassione* is the glue of life, the stuff that holds the fabric of human society together.

After locating us in Florence in the year 1348, Boccaccio begins his story thus: "In the face of its onrush, all the wisdom and ingenuity of man were unavailing" (p. 50). The intellect is incapable of coping with the enormity of the plague: "it seemed that all the advice of physicians and all the power of medicine were profitless and unavailing" (p. 51). The failure of that first quintessentially human quality, *ingegno,* results in the undermining of the other, even more basic, human characteristic, *compassione;* the breakdown in one leads to the breakdown in the other. Boccaccio indicates this chain effect by passing from the symptoms of the plague, which the doctors could not cure, to its contagion. The fact that the plague is contagious causes people to behave in a cruel fashion (*crudele* is the word that Boccaccio contrasts with *compassione* throughout the introduction), for they decide to "avoid or stay away from the sick and their belongings, by which means they thought their own health would be preserved" (p. 52).

The reactions to the plague take various forms: the first group of citizens could be labeled the purists (they lock themselves in their houses and live in isolation); the second group, the voluptuaries (who pursue the policy "eat, drink, and be merry"); then the moderates; and finally those whom Boccaccio labels "di più crudel sentimento" (of a crueler persuasion). These are the ones who, "sparing no thought for anyone but themselves . . . abandoned their city, their homes, their relatives, their estates and their belongings . . ." (p. 53). This total deterioration of all the most sacrosanct bonds of human life is emphasized further:

> this scourge had implanted so great a terror in the hearts of men and women that brothers abandoned brothers, uncles their nephews, sisters their brothers, and in many cases wives deserted their husbands. But even worse, and almost incredible, was the fact that fathers and mothers refused to assist their own children, as though they did not belong to them.
>
> (p. 54)

This, then, is the final collapse of society, when parents abandon their children. It is in the wake of this analysis that Boccaccio proceeds to outline the moral degeneracy of the city: the women who allow themselves to be tended by male servants, the forming of a class of profiteers who for a sum will take bodies to burial, and so forth. Running like a leitmotif throughout is the callous indifference to the suffering of others, the lack of *compassione*—a moral flaw that has relentlessly practical consequences. As Boccaccio emphasizes, many were left to die unaided because they had previously set just this example, having refused to tend the sick while they themselves were healthy. It is no surprise, therefore, when we meet the *brigata* and listen to Pampinea's discourse on their inalienable right to live ("Every person born into this world has a natural right to sustain, preserve, and defend his own life to the best of his ability": p. 59); to hear her stress also that, in leaving the city, they will be abandoning no one, since all their kin are dead.

It is paramount to establish that the *brigata* is not behaving like any of the groups enumerated above. Although their program will share features with some (like the purists, they isolate themselves and refuse to entertain any news from outside; like the cruel ones, they leave the city), the crucial difference is that they are doing these things only now, when there is nothing else left to do. By postponing this action until the last possible moment, Boccaccio makes it clear that, in a healthy society, self-preservation is important, but not at the cost of *compassione,* because without *compassione,* the *umana cosa* (the human quality), we become inhuman, like animals (the motif of the transformation of men into beasts runs throughout the plague description). Therefore, if the *brigata* is going to lay the foundation of a new society, it must first observe the law of *compassione,* because only on such a base will a viable structure be built.

The construction of a new society is the first task undertaken by the *brigata* upon their arrival in an idealized Tuscan countryside. There is no doubt that in leaving Florence the *brigata* leaves reality. They travel only two miles from the city, but although a long section in the previous description of the plague's effects deals specifically with the damage done to the surrounding countryside, they encounter no signs of it. They never see a sick person or animal; their life-style is completely unaffected by the sickness raging around them. They are permitted to do what only gods can do—to reject reality. This rejection is stated programmatically by Dioneo, when they arrive at their first asylum:

> "I know not what you intend to do with your troubles; my own I left inside the city gates when I departed thence a short while ago in your company. Hence you may either prepare to join with me in as much laughter, song and merriment as your sense of decorum will allow, or else you may give me leave to go back for my troubles and live in the afflicted city."
>
> (p. 64)

Dioneo's ultimatum is cheerfully accepted by Pampinea, who proceeds to translate into practical reality his concern with maintaining their isolated ideal existence: "Nothing," she says, "will last for very long unless it possesses a definite form" (p. 65). Hence she suggests a minigovernment to regulate their lives and goes so far as to assign specific tasks to the seven servants who have come along. Her final instruction to them is to "bring us no tidings of the world outside these walls unless they are tidings of happiness" (p. 66). So reality is excluded, and the realism of the details that Boccaccio provides on the *brigata*'s life-style (the beds are made, the house is strewn with rushes, the tables are set with white tablecloths, and so on) only serves to heighten our sense of unreality; reality, after all, would involve at the very least the presence of some unhealthy peasants on this prosperous estate.

Their society as reconstructed by Pampinea is not only orderly; it is also moral. The narrator tells us that in the evening "the young men went away to their rooms, which were separated from those of the ladies" (p. 67); this despite the affection that each of the men is said to harbor for one of his seven female companions. Dioneo, for all his insistence on a good time, carefully specifies that it will be within the bounds "your sense of decorum will allow." The adjective with which Boccaccio modifies the word *brigata,* from the first time that it makes its appearance in the proem, is *onestà* (honorable); he uses it continually as a point of reference for their behavior. They do not stray beyond the limits of *onestà* (probity). Although Neifile had worried about the propriety of their taking the men along, Filomena had assured her thus: "If I live honestly and my conscience is clear, then people may say whatever they like" (p. 63). The *brigata* continues to live honestly. At the end of the *Decameron* the king of the last day, Panfilo, prepares them for the return to Florence by reminding them that *continua onestà, continua concordia* (continual probity, continual harmony) have characterized their communal experiment. The ideal society formed by the *brigata* is (1) based on compassion; (2) structured in an orderly and, vis-à-vis the servants, hierarchical fashion; and (3) characterized by moral probity.

The frame characters have only vaguely defined personalities that on the whole have frustrated attempts at consistent interpretation. In setting up the frame, Boccaccio gives us just enough information to tantalize critics eternally and not enough to arrive at definite solutions. In this spirit, he assigns his ten characters pseudonyms (to protect their reputations, he says, thus teasing us with the notion that they are real people). These pseudonyms are deliberately calculated to send shock waves of intertextuality throughout Boccaccio's own oeuvre and beyond. Pampinea, Emilia, Filomena, and Fiammetta all belong to the early works. The men also have past lives: Panfilo is Fiammetta's fickle lover; Filostrato is the hero of the work bearing his name; and Dioneo makes his first appearance in the *Comedia ninfe.* The other three ladies are tributes to the poets Boccaccio most admired: Vergil, since Elissa is Dido's other name; Petrarch, whose lady is Laura, like Lauretta; and Dante, since Neifile signifies "new love," like Dante's love for Beatrice. The web grows more complex if we consider that Boccaccio goes out of his way to tell us that the men love certain of the ladies, thus awakening speculation that goes resolutely unresolved. Therefore, besides trying to establish relations between the characters themselves, between the characters and the days they govern, and between the characters and the stories they tell, critics have also attempted to grapple with the problem of these characters' relations to their original existences in the minor works.

By and large, patterns in the *Decameron* are established in order to be undermined (for instance, there are a hundred stories, to which one more is added by Boccaccio in his prologue to Day 4). This strategy is part of Boccaccio's programmatic reduction of reality to a level at which allegory is impossible, at which attempts to posit a deeper meaning are always doomed to failure. Three of the characters do have traits that are immediately apparent. Pampinea (whose name means the "vigorous one") is bossy and managerial; she is the force of order. Dioneo, etymologically related to Venus, the daughter of Dione, is the sensual one, who asks for and receives the privilege of being exempted from the daily topics, a privilege he invokes to tell stories that are amusing and lascivious. Like the author in the proem, he defends the rights of women and urges them to seek greater self-expression. This self-expression is, however, primarily sexual; if Dioneo is a feminist, feminism must be defined as the right of women to have as many extramarital affairs as their husbands. Filostrato, as we would expect, is the sorrowing lover; he requires the others to tell stories of sad love so that the day he governs will faithfully reflect his own feelings. These three are the most clearly defined. We could say that Panfilo ("all love") is associated with virtue; he never makes even verbal assaults on the decorum of the ladies, and he governs the last, most moral, day.

These characters can best be seen as various facets of the author and of all of us: our rational side, which tries to order existence; our sensual side, basically life-affirming; and the despairing, defeatist side of human nature, incapable of coping with reality. The *Decameron* depicts human beings in a moment of crisis. The *brigata*'s handling of this crisis—although based on a flight from reality that is not always practicable—can serve as a model for human comportment and for the sage deployment of the three key aspects of our natures. First, Pampinea takes over, and there is an attempt to reimpose structure onto the chaos of life. Under her governance, *ingegno,* lost during the plague, begins to be restored; in Day 1 they tell stories in which human wit prevails. In Days 2 and 3 the restoration of *ingegno* continues: man's wit is matched with Fortune, at first (Day 2) with less success, and then (Day 3) with more. In Days 4 and 5, Love is pitted against Fortune, also with varying results: in Day 4 Love is defeated, whereas in Day 5 it conquers all. Love is, of course, akin to compassion. The storytellers emphasize that telling the tragic tales imposed by Filostrato will move them to pity. In the first story of Day 4, Fiammetta says that these tales "cannot fail to arouse compassion in speaker and listener alike" (p. 332), and this idea is repeated throughout the day. Day 4, then, is the vehicle by which Boccaccio effects the restoration of *compassione.*

Renewed, the *brigata* must be tempered, prepared more specifically for the ultimate return to reality. Day 6, thematically similar to Day 1, marks a new beginning: the theme stresses recovery and reversal. Ready now for immersion in life at its most real, the *brigata* tells the coarse and at times brutal stories of Days 7, 8, and 9. Although their own behavior is always circumspect, a gradual relaxation overcomes them; the stories of these days, heavily influenced by the fabliaux with their eternal love triangle, mark the high point of the *brigata*'s verbal indecency. The last story of Day 9 is perhaps not coincidentally the most sexually explicit story of the *Decameron.* All of this comes to an abrupt halt when Panfilo announces his theme for Day 10.

The *Decameron* frame could be pictured as a large wheel—Fortune's wheel, the wheel of life—on which the *brigata* turn, coming back transformed to the point of departure. In Days 1 through 5 they move steadily away from the city as their *ingegno* and *compassione* are restored; the outward turn of the wheel is completed with their arrival at the *Valle delle donne* (Valley of the Ladies) in the conclusion to Day 6. Geographically, they are now at their farthest remove from the city. Here, where the ladies relax to the point of taking off their clothes for a swim, they stay to tell the stories of Day 7. However, at this juncture, two things occur simultaneously: just as they locate the epitome of the ideal, the place most distanced from reality, the wheel reaches its zenith and begins its inevitable descent, back toward Florence and back toward reality. Thus, it is in the *Valle delle donne,* the *Decameron*'s most perfected *locus amoenus,* that some of the work's most "real" stories will be told. The reality principle enters the *brigata*'s staid world in the form of a squabble among the servants—a unique occurrence—that takes place in the prologue to Day 6. Licisca, a maid, maintains that women do not go to their wedding beds virgins; Dioneo not only supports her contention but decides to base his day (Day 7: the tricks women play on their husbands) on Licisca's observation. It is on this day that the floodgates of sensuality are opened.

Licisca, as reality principle of the *Decameron,* should make her effect felt immediately, even before her theme is adapted for the next day's stories. And, in fact, after wandering all over the world in the previous days, Boccaccio signifies the shift by situating the stories of Day 6 preponderantly in Florence and peopling them with characters known to the *brigata.* Moreover, in the third story of Day 6, Dioneo's rule is broken, and the plague is allowed to intrude on the world of the stories for the first time. In giving the name of her story's protagonist, Lauretta inserts a subordinate clause in which she says that the lady is someone who died in the present epidemic: "questa pestilenzia presente." If the plague can be named without any reaction on the part of Dioneo, the life-affirmer, it must be that by now the *brigata* is able to cope with it, revitalized as they are in *ingegno* and *compassione.*

For all that the stories of Days 7, 8, and 9 are remembered mainly as amusing jokes, there is a serious theme as well, stated explicitly in the subject for Day 7: the *beffe* are frequently motivated by self-preservation, "salvamento di loro." Only when the *brigata* is fully coached in the basic lesson of survival does the wheel complete its turn toward Florence, with Day 10, which shows men and women practicing generosity and renunciation, the very social virtues required for the *brigata*'s reintegration into society. Thus, they return to the city refreshed by their journey into the amoral vagaries of existence and buttressed by the social virtues practiced on the last day. For, although on the one hand the *brigata* represents Boccaccio's ideal for an honest and moral existence, on the other hand the stories they tell are often immoral; and the whole is made deliberately amoral by the play of frames. Neither the *brigata* nor the author can be pinpointed in their reactions to the stories. As a result, no consistent judgment is offered vis-à-vis the manifold complexities of

# GIOVANNI BOCCACCIO

## THE WHEEL OF THE *DECAMERON*

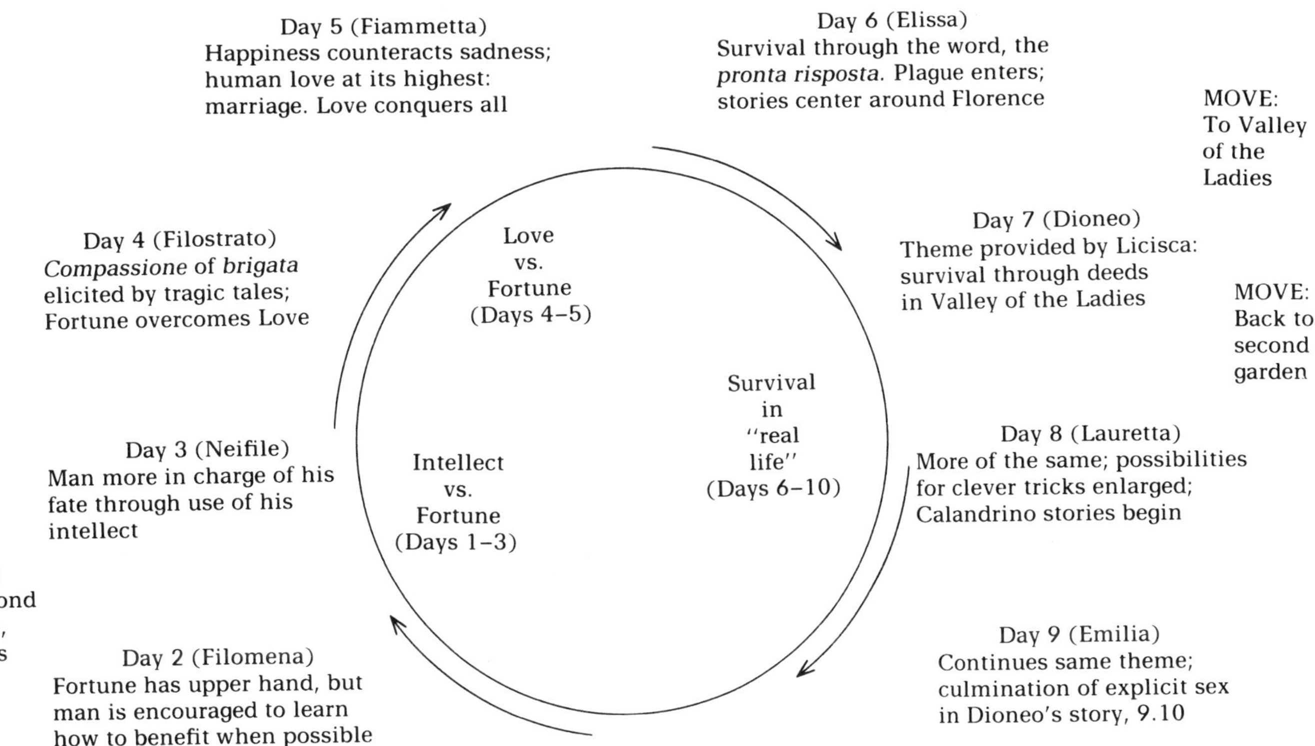

Introduction to Day 6
Licisca and Tindaro argue
Reality enters the frame
The wheel turns back
Day 5 (Fiammetta)
Happiness counteracts sadness; human love at its highest: marriage. Love conquers all
Day 6 (Elissa)
Survival through the word, the *pronta risposta.* Plague enters; stories center around Florence
MOVE: To Valley of the Ladies
Day 7 (Dioneo)
Theme provided by Licisca: survival through deeds in Valley of the Ladies
MOVE: Back to second garden
Day 4 (Filostrato)
*Compassione* of *brigata* elicited by tragic tales; Fortune overcomes Love
Love vs. Fortune (Days 4–5)
Survival in "real life" (Days 6–10)
Intellect vs. Fortune (Days 1–3)
Day 3 (Neifile)
Man more in charge of his fate through use of his intellect
Day 8 (Lauretta)
More of the same; possibilities for clever tricks enlarged; Calandrino stories begin
MOVE: To second garden, 4 miles from city
Day 2 (Filomena)
Fortune has upper hand, but man is encouraged to learn how to benefit when possible
Day 9 (Emilia)
Continues same theme; culmination of explicit sex in Dioneo's story, 9.10
Day 1 (Pampinea)
Uses of *ingegno;* man's intellect affirmed
Day 10 (Panfilo)
Generosity and renunciation: moral/social virtues to prepare for return
MOVE: 2 miles away from city
Introduction to Day 1
Florence during the great plague
Failure of *ingegno*
Loss of *compassione*

The restoration of *ingegno* occurs in Days 1–3; the restoration of *compassione* begins in Day 4.

human life encountered in the world of the stories.

The tension Boccaccio creates between the frame and the stories, far from rendering the frame an artificial device imposed for purely rhetorical reasons, is central to his message. Life itself is amoral; it is up to us to impart whatever structure and form it is going to have. Thus the *brigata,* although vicariously drinking life to the lees in the stories, preserves a sense of morality regarding themselves that is entirely artificial on the one hand, but essential to the preservation of society on the other. We remember that the *brigata*'s key rule for their new life was that no news ("niuna novella"), if not happy, may penetrate to them from outside ("di fuori)". But although they take refuge in an ideal world, they spend their time telling stories that are for the most part drawn from the real world, that are in fact famed for their frank acceptance of the laws of nature. In other words, the *novelle,* news from the real world of Florence, are replaced by the *novelle,* stories of the *Decameron;* it would seem, therefore, that life is the only antidote for life.

The *Decameron* ends on a moral note in Day 10. But it should be noted that the achievements Panfilo would have the *brigata* emulate are rigorously secular and nontranscendent: "And thus our lives," says Panfilo, "which cannot be other than brief in these our mortal bodies, will be preservd by the fame of our achievements—a goal which every man who does not simply attend to his belly, like an animal, should not only desire but zealously pursue and strive to attain" (p. 731). In this great humanistic pronouncement, the *brigata* is instructed not to strive for the life to come but to tend to the fame of their earthly endeavors, because only such fame can preserve them from death. If the *brigata*'s world is a moral one, especially in contrast with that of the stories, theirs is nonetheless a secular morality, concerned exclusively with the living of life on earth.

As we said earlier, Boccaccio's prevailing characteristic is his refusal to be pinpointed. Therefore, this scheme, ending with the morality of Day 10, cannot be allowed to go unchallenged. In the same way that clues regarding the *brigata* are offered to raise expectations that are then dashed, so Boccaccio deliberately frustrates attempts to make too neat a package of his book. The *Decameron* is certainly concerned with proposing a social morality that alone can ensure the perpetuation of human society as we know it. Nonetheless, the fact that nothing can ever be known with certainty remains the book's chief message.

Boccaccio's ultimate vehicle for his message is the controversial last story, the story of patient Griselda's submission to the barbaric trials of her husband, Gualtieri. This is the story that moved Petrarch to tears and to translation and that Vittore Branca, who reads the heroine as a figure of the Virgin, calls the apex of the book's moral itinerary. Attilio Momigliano, on the other hand, considers it a story of stupidity and brutality, thus agreeing with Dioneo, who prefaces it by defining the husband's behavior as "non cosa magnifica ma una matta bestialità" (not a magnificent action but a mad bestiality). Boccaccio only comments that the *brigata*—like the critics—argues about the story, discussing the various pros and cons at length. But—and this is the crucial point—there is no one to give us the answer, the solution, that we crave. Is Griselda a saint, or is she a fool? We shall never know, for in the *Decameron* Boccaccio has critically altered the format of the *Filocolo.* There is no longer an absolute authority, a single ruler, as Fiammetta was in the earlier work, to settle all disputes with the certainty of an imposed resolution. In the *Decameron* there are ten points of view, which is like saying that there is no single right point of view. All questions, therefore, must finally be addressed to the self.

If we look back, we see that this point was first made at the book's beginning, in the second paragraph of the introduction. Here, in a major break from tradition, Boccaccio tells us that the plague was sent either by the workings of the stars (that is, fate) or as a result of God's just wrath (Providence). "Either . . . or" is *the* rhetorical strategy of the *Decameron,* translating the work's fundamental opacity. This is a world without answers. We are—in matters of adultery as in matters of fate and Providence—on our own. It is this programmatic and deliberate openness of the *Decameron* that makes it such a revolutionary text, such a harbinger of things to come.

## *THE LATER YEARS: 1352–1375*

Within the context of Boccaccio's overall artistic development, the *Decameron* marks the apex of his literary career. The success of the *novella* collection was immediate, a success that was most palpable among the class of literate bourgeois merchants from which Boccaccio came and that the *Decameron* celebrates. The work's enormous popularity is attested by contemporary documents, like Francesco Buondelmonte's letter of 1360 in which he anxiously requests a friend to return the copy he had lent him. But Boccaccio's own feelings toward his masterpiece appear to have been ambivalent. In his letter to Mainardo Cavalcanti of 1372 (*Epistola* 21), he refers to the *Decameron* as "domesticas nugas" (domestic trifles) that he composed while young and under duress. He writes of himself in the third person and offers an excuse for his work that he hopes readers will bear in mind: "Iuvenis scripsit et maioris coactus imperio" (He wrote as a young man and impelled by the command of a superior). We find it difficult to understand, since for us Boccaccio's name is synonymous with the *Decameron,* how he could say "iuvenis scripsit" of his masterpiece. Nonetheless, from the perspective of 1372, and considering all he had accomplished since 1351, the statement may be seen as partially true, insofar as the *Decameron* is the culmination and ending of his literary youth, that is, of the first phrase of his artistic development.

Boccaccio himself certainly saw it as such. The turning point marked by the early 1350's was a profound one, involving a shift not only from apparently light tales to learned encyclopedias but also from Italian to Latin. The humanists, scholars, and professional men of letters with whom Boccaccio associated in the latter half of his life, and with whom he more and more identified, did not comprise an ideal audience for the *Decameron,* a fact that helps to explain his own official indifference toward it. The warm reception accorded the *Decameron* by its bourgeois readers was matched only by the coolness that the work met in higher literary circles. As scholars have noted, the *Decameron* was usually absent from the aristocratic libraries of the day. By the same token, it was invariably copied not by professional scribes, but by enthusiastic amateurs.

The evolution in Boccaccio's career occurred under the sign of Petrarch, who was without a doubt the greatest influence on him in his later life. Nor could Petrarch be said to approve of the *Decameron.* He wrote to Boccaccio in 1373, in the last letter of the *Senili* (*Letters of Riper Years*):

> Your book, written in our mother tongue and published, I presume, during your early years, has fallen into my hand, I know not whence or how. If I told you that I had read it, I should deceive you. It is a very big volume, written in prose and for the multitude. I have been, moreover, occupied with more serious business, and much pressed for time. . . . My hasty perusal afforded me much pleasure. If the humor is a little too free at times, this may be excused in view of the age at which you wrote, the style and language which you employ, and the frivolity of the subjects, and of the persons who are likely to read such tales. . . . As usual, when one looks hastily through a book, I read somewhat more carefully at the beginning and at the end. At the beginning you have, it seems to me, accurately described and eloquently lamented the condition of our country during that siege of pesti-

> lence that forms so dark and melancholy a period in our century. At the close you have placed a story that differs entirely from most that precede it, and that so delighted and fascinated me that, in spite of cares that made me almost oblivious of myself, I was seized with a desire to learn it by heart. . . .
>
> (J. H. Robinson and H. W. Rolfe, *Petrarch: The First Modern Scholar and Man of Letters,* letter 17.3)

He goes on about the Griselda story, explaining that he was so struck by it and by Griselda's virtue that he had translated it into Latin under the title "De obedentia ac fide uxoria mythologia" ("Story About Wifely Obedience and Fidelity").

There is much to be learned from this letter, both about Petrarch's attitude toward the *Decameron* and about this most fascinating of literary friendships. For Boccaccio, Petrarch was always the *magister* and he was always the disciple (although there were only nine years between them). The fact that as late as 1373 (a year before his death) Petrarch speaks of having for the first time seen the *Decameron,* which he affects not to have read, tells us a great deal. In other words, in the more than twenty years of their friendship Boccaccio had never proudly presented the *Decameron* to his fellow author. One can see why: Petrarch is not for nothing called the first full-fledged Renaissance humanist. From his point of view the *Decameron* was written for the multitude, on frivolous subjects, in the vernacular. Petrarch's purism regarding the use of Latin allowed him to extend his criticism to a poem of the manifest gravity of Dante's *Divine Comedy* (it also forced him into a posture at least as schizophrenic as Boccaccio's, whereby he insisted on the worthlessness of his own Italian lyrics, although he worked on them continuously until his death). Clearly, where the *Comedy* could not pass muster, there would be little hope for the *Decameron.* The reversal at the end of Petrarch's letter is therefore all the more striking. It seems that one of these vernacular stories has been judged worth saving after all: "I have of my own free will undertaken to translate your work, something I should certainly never think of doing for anyone else. . . ." Petrarch's appropriation—and correction—of Boccaccio's story is a powerfully double-edged compliment.

Boccaccio first met his *magister* in 1350, when Petrarch stopped in Florence on his way to the papal jubilee. From Rome, Petrarch sent Boccaccio a letter, addressed to Johanni Bocchaccii de Certaldo discipulo suo (to Giovanni Boccaccio of Certaldo his disciple: *Familiari* 11), the first of many. In March of 1351, Boccaccio visited Petrarch in Padua, carrying a proposal the poet did not accept. Florence had revoked the 1302 condemnation of Petrarch's father, with its confiscation of goods, and further offered him a chair in the new Florentine university, founded in 1349. This was one of many embassies for his city undertaken by Boccaccio in the politically active years of 1350–1355. By now his initial unhappiness with Florence had passed; he no longer wrote in despair to old friends in Naples. In the winter of 1351–1352 Boccaccio went as ambassador to Ludovico di Baviera, count of the Tirol. In the following year he received his most important commission to date: he went to Avignon as Florentine ambassador to Pope Innocent VI. The man who had circled the globe in his *novelle* thus left Italy for the first time.

The nature of Boccaccio's literary production underwent a radical change in these years. Up to 1350 the bulk of his work is written in the vernacular; after 1350 the bulk of his work is in Latin. Boccaccio now began to compose the erudite works that earned him a reputation as a humanist, works that for centuries were consulted as we consult *Bulfinch's Mythology* or the *Encyclopaedia Britannica.* Although it is possible to say roughly when they were begun and when first redactions were completed, these are books that Boccaccio continued to expand, elaborate, and polish until the end of his life.

The *Genealogia deorum gentilium,* the most famous of the Latin treatises, was begun as early as 1350; the first copy was probably finished about 1360. This is Boccaccio's great mythological compendium, offering information on classical mythology and antiquity. Written in fifteen books, it was used as a reference work until the nineteenth century and was translated into all the major European languages. Boccaccio states his encyclopedic purpose in the preface to the king of Cyprus:

> I will find and gather, like fragments of a mighty wreck strewn on some vast shore, the relics of the Gentile gods. These relics, scattered through almost infinite volumes, shrunk with age, half consumed, well-nigh a blank, I will bring into such single genealogical order as I can, to gratify your wish.
>
> (C. G. Osgood trans., p. 11)

He attempts not only to bring order to his material but to interpret it as well. This he does euhemeristically, by showing that the legend in question was once based in historical fact, or allegorically. He uses allegory to show that ancient legends often foreshadowed Christian truths, thus anticipating a major pursuit of the humanists:

> I must proceed to tear the hidden significations from their tough sheathing, and I promise to do so, though not to the last detail of the authors' original intentions. Who in our day can penetrate the hearts of the Ancients? Who can bring to light and life again minds long since removed in death?
>
> (p. 11)

Boccaccio further intends the last two books (14 and 15) of the *Genealogia* to serve as an apologia for poetry and poets. In his insistence on the moral values of poetry, Boccaccio is indebted to the writings of Petrarch on this subject. In one area, however, Boccaccio was more prescient than his *magister.* He grasped more fully than Petrarch the importance of Greek thought and letters within the Western tradition. Both authors, equipped with only the most rudimentary Greek, collaborated on a project to have Leontius Pilatus translate Homer into Latin. But whereas Petrarch always sustained the superiority of Latin letters, Boccaccio comes to the defense of Hellenic culture: "Though Latin literature may be sufficient unto itself, and enjoys the exclusive attention of the whole Western world, yet without question it would gain much light through an alliance with Greek" (119).

The *De casibus virorum illustrium (On the Fates of Illustrious Men),* begun about 1355 and completed in a first draft about 1360, is a good example of the later Boccaccio's moralistic tendencies. This work proposes to show, through a selective treatment of the famous figures of history, that pride goes before a fall: "From among the mighty I shall select the most famous, so when our princes see these rulers, old and spent, prostrated by the judgment of God, they will recognize God's power, the shiftiness of Fortune and their own insecurity" (L. B. Hall trans., p. 2). Boccaccio imagines that as he sits in his study, these figures present themselves to him, describing their misfortunes. Divided into nine books, the *De casibus* begins with Adam and Eve and arrives eventually at Boccaccio's own times, both legendary (with Arthur, king of the Britons) and all too real (with Walter, duke of Athens, a recent tyrant of Florence). Another of Boccaccio's Latin compendia, the *De mulieribus claris,* consists of 106 biographies of women from Eve to Johanna I, queen of Sicily. Even in his erudite works, Boccaccio exhibits his fascination with the opposite sex.

Petrarch seems to have encouraged his disciple to espouse a more rigorously moral position in his later writings than is evident in the early works. Indeed, by 1360 at the latest, Boccaccio had taken minor orders. This fact, and other events from this period (including the alleged posthumous letter in which the Blessed Pietro Petroni is presumed to have threatened Boccaccio with damnation if he did not give up literature for more worthy pursuits), led critics to the so-called conversion theory, which held that Boccaccio, pressed by the church and by his own conscience, repudiated the licentious writings of his youth, chief among them the *Decameron.* The recent discovery that the Berlin Hamilton 90 codex of the *Decameron* is an autograph manuscript has laid this theory to rest. Studies have shown that the Hamilton 90 was penned about 1370. In other words, Boccaccio painstakingly transcribed his masterpiece long after his imagined conversion, as an old man.

The work that has been cited most frequently as evidence of a change of heart is the *Corbaccio,* the only vernacular work of fiction he wrote after the *Decameron.* The *Corbaccio*'s date is uncertain. Although the traditional date of 1354–1355 has been challenged by a later date of about 1365, the matter remains unresolved. The strange title seems to derive from *corvo* (crow), a bird of ill omen, to which the negative intensifier *accio* would give the sense of "ugly" and "evil." Presumably this appellation is intended for the widow who is the book's antiheroine, in that she is the inspiration of the misogynistic diatribes that make up a good portion of the text.

The narrative is replete with the typical Boccaccian strategies. Briefly, the narrator, suffering from his unrequited love for a widow, has a dream in which he is walking down a beautiful path that becomes thorny and arduous. He is lost until a figure appears who turns out to be the dead shade of the widow's husband. This peculiar guide informs the narrator that he is in a place called variously "Labyrinth of Love," "Enchanted Valley," "Pigsty of Venus," and so forth (A. K. Cassell trans., p. 10). Moreover, he undertakes, for the narrator's salvation, to lecture him on the mistakes that have brought him hither. He dwells particularly on the unseemliness of passion in a man of the narrator's age and occupation. Here he touches on the narrator's love for poetry and hatred for commerce, the paternal difficulties he encountered—all features one associates with Boccaccio's own life. Since the spirit goes on to denounce women in general, and his former wife in particular, the *Corbaccio* has long been read as Boccaccio's autobiographical confession and recantation of sexual love.

Of late, however, scholarly attitudes toward the *Corbaccio* have been undergoing revision, with the result that the work's first-person narration is viewed in a more critical light, as a convention of medieval didactic literature. Similarly, the antifeminist polemic has been reevaluated and placed in the context of the misogynistic tradition. Particularly interesting is the position of the *Corbaccio* with respect to the rest of Boccaccio's vernacular fictions. Like the *Elegia di madonna Fiammetta,* it constitutes an inversion of the prevailing code. As in the *Elegia* his tragic love for her becomes her tragic love for him, so in the *Corbaccio* the ennobling effects of love and the praise of women—two constants of the early works—are transformed into the debilitating effects of love and a disgust for women. Only in the *Decameron* do both codes operate simultaneously. In the plurivalent world of the masterpiece all attitudes and life-styles coexist, from the most rarefied and courtly to the most down-to-earth and frankly sexual.

Within the complete arc of Boccaccio's vernacular production, then, the *Corbaccio* can be seen as one extreme in a literary career that typically functions through dialectic (the Venus/Diana dialetic, for instance) and that achieves a moment of balance only once, in the *Decameron.* For an author who delights in mirror games and shifts of perspective as Boccaccio does (we have only to remember that not one of these works is without a narrator's frame), it seems as inevitable that he should write the *Corbaccio* as it is that he write the *Elegia*—inevitable, moreover, not from an autobiographical but from a literary point of view.

By 1361 Boccaccio had retired to Certaldo, initially perhaps because of the political climate; he had some friends among the conspirators of the failed coup of 1360. His period of public service consequently came to an end. He lived a solitary and rather difficult existence in Certaldo, plagued in his last years by economic hardships as well as by physical ailments like dropsy. His retirement was punctuated by visits to Naples in 1362 and 1370, and by a last visit to Petrarch in 1368. This was the period in which Boccaccio labored over his vast Latin tomes. But, as usual, his life and works bear the mark of his characteristic ambivalence. Not only was he transcribing the *Decameron* in the years around 1370 but he was also summoned in 1373 to Florence again—this time to lecture publicly on the *Divine Comedy* for one year.

Thus the vernacular, in the form of its greatest poet, called to Boccaccio once more, and his earlier *Trattatello in laude di Dante (Treatise in Praise of Dante),* written originally in 1351 but revised in 1360 and again after 1372, finds its ideal counterpart in the *Esposizioni sopra il Dante (Discourses on Dante),* a commentary based on the notes devised for the lessons. Boccaccio's lectures were interrupted at *Inferno* 17 by his failing health, which was doubtless aggravated by the criticism his *lectura Dantis* generated in humanistic circles. Again, the controversy centered around the merits of expounding a vernacular text to a mass audience; the terms of the argument echo Petrarch's remarks on the *Decameron.* That Boccaccio was not immune to these attacks we know from some sonnets written during this period in reply to an unidentified critic:

*Se Dante piange, dove ch'el si sia,*
*Che li concetti del suo alto ingegno*
*Aperti sieno stati al vulgo indegno,*
*Come tu di', della Lettura mia,*
*Ciò mi dispiace molto, nè mai fia*
*Ch'io non ne porti verso me disdegno....*
(*Le rime,* 123)

If Dante cries, wherever he may be,
Because the thoughts of his high genius
Have been laid open to the unworthy crowd,
As you say, by my reading,
This saddens me greatly,
Nor will I ever cease to condemn myself for it....

The pathos of these verses lies in their self-destructive quality, in Boccaccio's inability to maintain his own identity and ideals. In this sense, the *lectura Dantis* controversy and his reaction to it illustrate in microcosm the contradictions he felt throughout his career, contradictions that not even this apparently final capitulation could truly resolve.

Boccaccio died in Certaldo on 21 December 1375, a year and a half after the death of his *magister.* He was buried there, in the Church of Saints Michael and James. The man who in fantasy was the son of a French princess thus died in the home of his Tuscan ancestors. And if in his early works he invokes a far-off mythical birthplace and a unknown fairy-tale mother, in his epitaph Boccaccio knows very well where he comes from and who he is:

Hac sub mole iacent cineres ac ossa Iohannis:
Mens sedet ante Deum meritis ornata
laborum
Mortalis.vite. Genitor Bocchaccius illi,
Patria Certaldum, studium fuit alma poesis.

Beneath this stone lie the ashes and bones of
Giovanni:
His spirit sits before God, adorned with the
rewards of the toils
Of his mortal life. His father was Boccaccio;
His country, Certaldo; his passion, sweet poetry.
(McCoy, *The Book of Theseus,* p. 343)

# Selected Bibliography

## EDITIONS

### COMPLETE WORKS

*Tutte le opere di Giovanni Boccaccio.* Edited by V. Branca. Milan, 1964– . The definitive edition of Boccaccio's complete works. Twelve volumes are projected; the following have been published:

Vol. 1: *Profilo biografico;* edited by V. Branca; *Caccia di Diana,* edited by V. Branca; *Filocolo,* edited by A. E. Quaglio. 1967.

Vol. 2: *Filostrato,* edited by V. Branca; *Teseida delle nozze d'Emilia,* edited by A. Limentani; *Comedia delle ninfe fiorentine,* edited by A. E. Quaglio. 1964.

Vol. 3: *Amorosa visione,* edited by V. Branca; *Ninfale fiesolano,* edited by A. Balduino; *Trattatello in laude di Dante,* edited by P. G. Ricci. 1974.

Vol. 4: *Decameron,* edited by V. Branca. 1976.

Vol. 6: *Esposizioni sopra la Comedia di Dante,* edited by G. Padoan. 1965.

Vol. 10: *De mulieribus claris,* edited by V. Zaccaria. 1970.

INDIVIDUAL WORKS

*Amorosa visione.* Milan, 1521. Editio princeps.

————. Edited by V. Branca. Florence, 1944.

*Buccolicum Carmen.* Florence, 1504. Editio princeps. Collection of pastoral ecologues. See *Opere latine minori* below.

*Caccia di Diana.* Florence, 1832. Editio princeps. See *Le rime,* 1958, below.

*Comedia delle ninfe fiorentine (Ameto).* Rome, 1478.

————. Edited by A. E. Quaglio. Florence, 1963.

*Corbaccio.* Florence, 1487. Editio princeps.

————. Edited by Tauno Nurmela. Helsinki, 1968.

*Decameron.* N. p., *ca.* 1470. The editio princeps is the so-called Deo Gratias edition, based on the manuscript of Francesco Mannelli. For modern editions the manuscripts that have been most used are the Mannelli, Laurenziano 42, 1 (1384) and the Berlin, Hamilton 90 (*ca.* 1370). Twentieth-century editions vacillated between the two until the autography of the Hamilton 90 was firmly established (see V. Branca and P. G. Ricci, *Un autografo del Decameron* [Codice Hamiltoniano 90], Padova, 1962). Having recourse to the Mannelli for the portions of the text missing from the autograph, Branca followed the Hamilton 90 in his authoritative edition for the Accademia della Crusca (1976). The edition is reproduced by Branca as *Tutte le opere di Giovanni Boccaccio,* vol. 4 (see "Complete Works" above). Besides the Deo Gratias, there are fourteen other *incunabola* of the Decameron. Selected modern editions are:

V. Branca, ed. Florence, 1951–1952. New edition 1965.

P. Fanfani, ed. Florence, 1888.

A. F. Massèra, ed. Bari, 1927.

C. Segre, ed. Milan, 1966.

C. S. Singleton, ed. Bari, 1955.

————, ed. Baltimore, 1974. Edizione diplomatico-interpretativa dell'autografo Hamilton 90.

*De casibus virorum illustrium.* [Strassburg], *ca.* 1475.

————. Gainesville, Fla., 1962. Facsimile reproduction of the Paris edition of 1520. Introduction by Louis Brewer Hall.

*De Montibus, Silvis, Fontibus, Lacubus, Fluminibus, Stagnis seu Paludibus et de Nominibus Maris Liber.* Venice, 1473. First dated edition.

*Elegia di madonna Fiammetta.* Padua, 1472. First dated edition.

————. Edited by V. Pernicone. Bari, 1939.

*Filocolo.* Florence, 1472.

————. Edited by S. Battaglia. Bari, 1938.

*Filostrato.* Venice, 1480–1483. Editio princeps.

*Filostrato e il Ninfale fiesolano.* Edited by V. Pernicone. Bari, 1937.

*Genealogia deorum gentilium.* Venice, 1472. First dated edition.

————. Edited by V. Romano. Bari, 1951.

*Le rime, Caccia di Diana.* Edited by V. Branca. Padova, 1958. See *Caccia de Diana* above. The collected lyrics, *Rime,* were first published integrally in 1802.

*Ninfale fiesolano.* Venice, 1477. First dated edition. See *Filostrato* above.

*Opere latine minori.* Edited by A. F. Massèra. Bari, 1928. Contains *Buccolicum carmen,* remaining Latin poems, *Epistolae,* shorter writings.

*Teseida.* Ferrara, 1475.

————. Edited by S. Battaglia. Florence, 1938.

*Vita di Dante.* N. p., 1477. Detailed descriptions of early editions through 1874 can be found in A. Bacchi della Lega, *Serie delle edizioni delle opere di Giovanni Boccaccio: Latine, volgari, tradotte e trasformate.* Bologna, 1875. Reprinted Bologna, 1967. Later editions, as well as any missed by Bacchi della Lega, are listed in V. Branca, *Linee di una storia della critica del Decameron, con bibliografia boccaccesca completamente aggiornata*. Milan, 1939.

## TRANSLATIONS

*Amorous Fiammetta*. Translated by Bartholomew Young. London, 1587. Revised by Edward Hutton, London, 1926. Reprinted Westport, Conn., 1970.

*Boccaccio on Poetry, Being the Preface and Fourteenth and Fifteenth Books of Boccaccio's Genealogia Deorum Gentilium*. Translated by Charles G. Osgood. Princeton, N. J., 1930. Reprinted Indianapolis, 1956.

*The Book of Theseus*. Translated by Bernadette Marie McCoy. New York, 1974. Includes Boccaccio's epitaph.

*Concerning Famous Women*. Translated by Guido Guarino. New Brunswick, N. J., 1963.

*Corbaccio*. Translated by Anthony K. Cassell. Urbana, Ill., 1975.

*Decameron*. Translated by John Payne. London, 1886.

————. Translated by J. M. Rigg. London, 1903.

————. Translated by Richard Aldington. New York, 1930.

————. Translated by G. H. McWilliam. Harmondsworth, 1972. McWilliam's introduction provides an excellent survey of English translations of the *Decameron*.

————. Translated by Mark Musa and Peter E. Bondanella. New York, 1982.

*The Fates of Illustrious Men*. Translated by Louis Brewer Hall. New York, 1965.

*The Filostrato*. Translated by N. E. Griffin and A. B. Myrick. London, 1929. Reprinted New York, 1970.

*The Life of Dante*. Translated by James Robinson Smith. In *The Earliest Lives of Dante*. New York, 1963.

*The Nymph of Fiesole*. Translated by Daniel J. Donno. New York, 1960.

*Nymphs of Fiesole*. Translated by Joseph Tusiani. Rutherford, N. J., 1971.

*The Story of Troilus*. Translated by R. K. Gordon. London, 1934. Contains *Filostrato*. Reprinted Toronto, 1978.

*Thirteen Most Pleasant and Delectable Questions of Love*. Translated by H. G. London, 1566. From the *Filocolo*. Revised by Harry Carter, New York, 1974.

## BIOGRAPHICAL AND CRITICAL STUDIES

Almansi, Guido. *The Writer as Liar: Narrative Technique in the Decameron*. London, 1975.

Baratto, Mario. *Realtà e stile nel Decameron*. Vicenza, 1970.

Bergin, Thomas G. *Boccaccio*. New York, 1981.

Billanovich, Giuseppe. *Restauri boccacceschi*. Rome, 1947.

Bosco, Umberto. *Il Decameron: Saggio*. Rieti, 1929.

Branca, Vittore. *Boccaccio medievale*. Florence, 1956. Reprinted, revised, and enlarged, Florence, 1970.

————. *Boccaccio: The Man and His Works*. Translated by Richard Monges. New York, 1976.

————. *Giovanni Boccaccio: Profilo biografico*. Florence, 1977.

Clements, Robert J., and Joseph Gibaldi. *Anatomy of the Novella: The European Tale Collection from Boccaccio and Chaucer to Cervantes*. New York, 1977.

Cottino-Jones, Marga. *An Anatomy of Boccaccio's Style*. Naples, 1968.

Deligorgis, Stavros. *Narrative Intellection in the Decameron*. Iowa City, 1975.

Di Pino, Guido. *La polemica del Boccaccio*. Florence, 1953.

Dombroski, Robert S., ed. *Critical Perspectives on the Decameron*. New York, 1976. Reprinted 1977.

Getto, Giovanni. *Vita di forme e forme di vita nel Decameron*. Turin, 1966.

Hastings, R. *Nature and Reason in the Decameron*. Manchester, 1975.

Hauvette, Henri. *Boccace: Étude biographique et littéraire*. Paris, 1914.

Hollander, Robert. *Boccaccio's Two Venuses*. New York, 1977.

Lee, A. C. *The Decameron: Its Sources and Analogues*. London, 1909.

Marcus, Millicent. *An Allegory of Form: Literary Self-Consciousness in the Decameron*. Saratoga, Calif., 1979.

Marino, Lucia. *The Decameron "Cornice": Allusion, Allegory, and Iconology*. Ravenna, 1979.

Momigliano, Attilio. *Il Decameron, 49 novelle commentate*. 2nd ed., revised. Milan, 1936.

Musa, Mark, and Peter E. Bondanella. *The Decameron: Twenty-one Novelle, Contemporary Re-*

*actions, Modern Criticism.* New York, 1977. Norton Critical Editions series.

Muscetta, Carlo. *Giovanni Boccaccio.* Rome and Bari, 1972.

Padoan, Giorgio. *Il Boccaccio le muse il Parnaso e l'Arno.* Florence, 1978.

Potter, Joy Hambuechen. *Five Frames for the Decameron: Communication and Social Systems in the Cornice.* Princeton, N. J., 1982.

Robinson, James Harvey, and Henry Winchester Rolfe, eds. *Petrarch: The First Modern Scholar and Man of Letters.* 2nd ed. New York, 1914. Translation of Petrarach's letter to Boccaccio, *Senili* 17.3.

Scaglione, Aldo D. *Nature and Love in the Late Middle Ages.* Berkeley, Calif., 1963.

Šklovskij, Viktor. *Lettura del Decameron: Dal romanzo d'avventura al romanzo di carattere.* Bologna, 1969.

Todorov, Tzevtan. *Grammaire du Décaméron.* The Hague, 1969.

## BIBLIOGRAPHIES

Branca, V. *Linee di una storia della critica del Decameron, con bibliografia boccaccesca completamente aggiornata.* Milan, 1939.

———. *Studi sul Boccaccio.* Florence, 1963.

Esposito, E. *Boccacciana. Bibliografia delle edizioni e degli scritti critici.* With the collaboration of Christopher Kleinhenz. Ravenna, 1976.

Traversari, G. *Bibliografia boccaccesca. Scritti intorno al Boccaccio e alla fortuna delle sue opere.* Città di Castello, 1907.

TEODOLINDA BAROLINI

# BERTOLT BRECHT

## *(1898–1956)*

IN THE EDITION of Bertolt Brecht's works which his West German publishers issued to commemorate the seventieth anniversary of his birth (1968)—and which, for all its omissions and editorial imperfections, is likely to remain the fullest and most nearly complete corpus of Brecht's oeuvre for a very long time to come—just over three thousand pages are occupied by his dramatic output; over a thousand by his poetry; fifteen hundred by his novels and stories; and well over two thousand by his theoretical essays on aesthetics and politics. It is an impressive body of work, and one must always keep in mind that a very large proportion of it remains untranslated into English. The fact that the bulk of the translations are of plays and that only relatively few poems, essays, and stories are accessible to the English-speaking public has a distorting effect on Brecht's image in the English-speaking world. It may indeed sound heretical today, but may well be true nevertheless, that posterity might attribute greater importance to Brecht's poems and some of his short stories than to his work as a dramatist; or that of his twenty-one full-length and sixteen shorter plays, and six major adaptations, perhaps no more than half a dozen might stand the test of time. As to his theoretical writings, they have played an important part in creating Brecht's worldwide fame, for they have stimulated discussion about his plays among actors, directors, and critics and have made the study of his work particularly attractive in academic circles. They might, however, also prove the most vulnerable element in Brecht's posthumous reputation, resting, as they do, on the fairly shaky foundations of Brecht's own peculiar view of Marxism, a very questionable conception of the psychological basis of the audience's experience in the theater, and on many passing fashions of the political and aesthetic climate of his times.

Much of Brecht's future reputation will also depend on another vital element in his artistic personality: his work as a practical man of the theater, as a teacher of actors and directors. Brecht's sudden rise to world fame in the last years of his life was, in fact, primarily due to the success of his theater, the Berliner Ensemble, which he founded after his return from exile in 1949, and which took Paris by storm on the occasion of the international festival of 1954. The Berliner Ensemble was created to test Brecht's theory of drama in performance. It is still an important theatrical company, but fears that it might deteriorate into a mere museum, exhibiting fossilized productions of Brecht's plays, have proved at least partially well grounded.

In the English-speaking world and in France Brecht's reputation has, as it were, been standing on its head: his work as a director (largely in the spheres unaffected by ignorance of the text—design, lighting, music) came first and has exercised the deepest influence; then, because it stimulated fruitful and endlessly interesting discussion, came his work as a theorist of left-wing aesthetics; and only in the third place followed his output as a dramatist, with far less convincing success. Whether in France, Britain, or America, relatively few of Brecht's plays have really achieved a decisive breakthrough and many have been signal failures. And Brecht the great poet and prose writer is virtually unknown.

Yet it is this aspect of Brecht that should come first. That many of his plays remain failures in translation is often directly attributable to the fact that in German they succeed mainly by the force of their language, their poetry, far less so as drama.

No wonder, therefore, that meaningful discussion of Brecht is very difficult in English, that a great deal of the vast literature which has grown around him and continues to proliferate has an air of irreality and is bedeviled by fierce controversy directly attributable to the widely differing basic assumptions from which different commentators start their arguments. And this situation, already complex enough, is further complicated by the highly inflammable political content of Brecht's work.

Brecht was converted to communism before he was thirty and remained a communist to the end of his life; yet much depends on the nature of his communism. It would be equally naive to regard Brecht as a mere follower of the party line at any given period or to label him a consistent deviationist; to assume that his ostensible support of, say, the Stalinist show trials also implied support for Stalinist aesthetics—or, conversely, that having been accused of being a formalist by the supporters of orthodox Stalinist aesthetics, he must also have disapproved of Stalinist policies in other fields. In fact the much-delayed publication in 1982 of his hitherto suppressed poetry showed that he had written some short poems and epigrams highly critical of Stalin, whom he dubbed "the meritorious murderer of the people."

What all this ultimately amounts to is the need to reiterate again and again the obvious, yet frequently ignored, truism that to understand Brecht one must see him against his background: the background of his language and its culture and literature, the background of the history of his times, the background of the theater against which he rebelled, the background of Marxist theory and Marxist politics.

Brecht was born at Augsburg, the chief town of the Bavarian part of Swabia, on 10 February 1898. He thus belongs to the generation that reached maturity in World War I. When the war ended in 1918 Brecht was almost twenty-one and ready to take the plunge into the whirlpool of experimentation—in life as well as in art—which was the inevitable consequence of the collapse of the hallowed—now seen to be hollow—values of respectable Wilhelmian society that, only a few years earlier, had seemed immovable and eternally stable. The feeling of liberation which the breakup and sudden disappearance of that social order produced was exhilarating, but at the same time it must also have been very frightening to be propelled directly from the straitjacket of small-town petty-bourgeois gentility into the void of almost total permissiveness. Brecht's later decision to subject himself to the new straitjacket of party discipline—and, indeed, the whole German nation's equally morbid drive to do likewise in the acceptance of the iron rule of Hitler—must be seen in the light of this experience.

The first phase of Brecht's career as a writer represents the period of that liberation into nothingness (ca. 1918–ca. 1927); it produced the plays *Baal* (1918), *Trommeln in der Nacht* (*Drums in the Night,* 1918), *Im Dickicht der Städte* (*In the Jungle of Cities,* 1923), *Leben Eduards des Zweiten von England* (Edward II, 1924), *Mann ist Mann* (*A Man's a Man*, 1926), and culminated in *Die Dreigroschenoper* (*The Threepenny Opera,* 1928) and *Aufstieg und Fall der Stadt Mahagonny* (*The Rise and Fall of the State of Mahagonny,* 1929) (the last two written after 1927 but still imbued with an afterglow of that period) and the volume of poems *Hauspostille* (*Manual of Piety,* 1927). This phase of anarchic nihilism was followed by a period of austere didacticism, a frantic search for discipline (ca. 1927–ca. 1934) which resulted in the most severely controlled, the seemingly—but only seemingly—most arid portion of Brecht's oeuvre, the *Lehrstücke* and *Schulopern* (teaching plays and school operas), *Das Badener Lehrstück vom Einverständnis* (*The Didactic Play of Baden: On Consent,* 1929), *Der Flug der Lindberghs* (*The Flight of the Lindberghs,* 1929), *Der Jasager/Der Neinsager* (*He Who Says Yes/He Who Says No,* 1930), *Die Massnahme* (*The Measures Taken,* 1930), *Die Ausnahme und die Regel* (*The Exception and the Rule,* 1930), *Die Horatier und die Kuriatier* (*The Horatians and the Curiatians,* 1934), as well as the more "conventional" but nonetheless highly austere political plays *Die heilige Johanna der Schlachthöfe* (*Saint Joan of the Stockyards,* 1929–1930), *Die Mutter* (*The Mother,* 1932), and *Die Rundköpfe und die Spitzköpfe* (*The Roundheads and the Peakheads,* 1932). The volume of poems which represents this phase is *Lieder, Gedichte, Chöre* (Songs, Poems, Choruses, 1934), a compendium of strictly propagandist poems and songs which forms a complete contrast to the wild exuberance and parodistic anarchism of *Manual of Piety.*

In the first years of exile, particularly in the period of the Popular Front, when the Communist party sought the cooperation of all liberal and left-wing forces against the Nazi danger, the uncompromising all-or-nothing attitude of this didactic phase was clearly out of place, and it gave way to a brief period (1934–1938) of openly propagandistic writing in more conventional styles. *Dreigroschenroman* (*Threepenny Novel,* 1934) and the plays *Furcht und Elend des Dritten Reiches* (*The Private Life of the Master Race; Fear and Misery in the Third Reich,* 1935–1936) and *Die Gewehre der Frau Carrar* (*Señora Carrar's Rifles,* 1937) were the products of this period in Brecht's life as a writer.

After the threat of world war became only too obvious following the Nazi occupation of Vienna and the Munich crisis (1938), the chances of influencing the course of events by writing propaganda were clearly reduced to zero. This freed Brecht and enabled him to turn his creative energies back to more personal poetry and the composition of his most mature and greatest series of plays. In this period (ca. 1938–ca. 1947) he wrote *Leben des Galilei* (*Galileo,* 1938), *Mutter Courage und ihre Kinder* (*Mother Courage and Her Children,* 1939), *Der gute Mensch von Sezuan* (*The Good Woman of Setzuan,* 1938–1940), *Herr Puntila und sein Knecht Matti* (*Puntila and Matti, His Hired Man,* 1940–1941), *Der authaltsame Aufstieg des Arturo Ui* (*The Resistible Rise of Arturo Ui,* 1941), *Die Gesichte der Simone Machard* (*The Visions of Simone Machard,* 1943), and *Der kaukasische Kreidekreis* (*The Caucasian Chalk Circle,* 1944–1945) as well as some of his most deeply felt poetry (contained, together with some propaganda verse from the preceding phase, in the volume *Svendborger Gedichte*).

Following his return to Europe from the United States (where he lived from the summer of 1941 to the fall of 1947), Brecht concentrated on his theoretical writings and his work as artistic director of his own theater. His output as a playwright in this period (1947 to his death on 14 August 1956) is disappointing both in quantity and in quality. Apart from minor original plays (*Die Tage der Kommune* [*The Days of the Commune,* 1949], *Turandot oder Der Kongress der Weisswäscher* [*Turandot, or The Congress of Whitewashers,* 1950–1954]) his work for the theater consists largely of adaptations: *Die Antigone des Sophokles* (*The Antigone of Sophocles,* 1948), after Hölderlin's translation; *Der Hofmeister* (*The Tutor,* 1950), after J. M. R. Lenz; *Don Juan* (1952), after Molière; *Der Prozess der Jeanne d'Arc zu Rouen 1431* (*The Trial of Joan of Arc at Rouen, 1431*), after a radio play by Anna Seghers based on the record of Joan's actual trial; *Coriolan* (*Coriolanus,* 1953); and *Pauken und Trompeten* (*Trumpets and Drums,* 1956), after Farquhar's *The Recruiting Officer.* On the other hand, in this phase of relatively low creativity as a playwright, Brecht found an outlet for his emotions (of resignation at the coming of old age, of disillusionment with the philistine East German regime) in what must be regarded as his finest achievement as a lyrical poet: a body of elegantly elegiac, sadly ironical, highly economical free verse.

Brecht's career thus shows a clear pattern of development and its own dialectic: anarchic exuberance (1918–ca. 1927) abruptly turning to the opposite extreme, austere self-discipline (ca. 1927–1934); a brief interlude of openly propagandist, almost journalistic, work, undertaken to help the good cause of antifascism (1934–1938); then, as a synthesis of emotional exuberance, severe Marxist rationalism, and some elements of political special pleading, the great works of the mature phase (1938–1947); and, finally, to crown the whole, the period from Brecht's return to Europe to his death (1947–1956), when in the theater he fulfilled his theories by his practice as a great director, while, as a lyrical poet, he reached sublime heights of detached self-knowledge and melancholic self-irony. It is a pattern which bears the marks of the great career of a great man.

The anarchic exuberance of the youth and the severe rationalism of the Marxist find their common denominator, however, in the concept of rebellion: the adolescent rebelled against the narrowness of small-town life, of desiccated stiff-collared bourgeois teachers, the musty smell of respectability and sexual repression; the Marxist clung to self-discipline and Spartan abnegation of self (including its anarchic longings for freedom) only in order to accomplish effective rebellion against the social order which had produced two wars and National Socialism. The recognition that rebellion to accomplish freedom can only succeed if the rebel's own freedom is ruthlessly suppressed in the discipline of the party forms the ironical, yet tragic, leitmotiv of Brecht's oeuvre. This ambivalence—which must also be seen as a highly characteristic German quality—explains the fascination which the Hegelian dialectic held for Brecht; it is also the basis of his genius as a dramatist.

For what is a playwright if he is not an individual who can experience and express a multitude of contradictory impulses and passions with equal comprehension and empathy for each of them? Just as Shakespeare could momentarily assume the personality of Iago as well as Othello, of Shylock as well as Antonio, Brecht also was able to be at the same time Garga and Shlink, Joan Dark and Mauler, Galilei and the Grand Inquisitor, Edward II and Mortimer, MacHeath and Peachum, dumb Katrin and Mother Courage. But he went further: the tensions and contradictions often actually split Brecht's characters wide open. Anna I and Anna II in the ballet *Die sieben Todsünden der Kleinbürger* (*The Seven Deadly Sins,* 1933) express the emotional and rational components of the same girl and are the forerunners of a line of dialectical characters: Shen Te/Shui Ta in *The Good Woman of Setzuan;* Puntila, who is good when drunk and evil when sober; Azdak, who can be a good judge only because he is a rascal; Mother Courage, who is destructive in her professional capacity as a businesswoman profiting from war and a positive character in being a mother intent on keeping her children alive and well; Galilei, whose sensuality and cowardice are balanced by his heroic greatness as a scientist. At the base of this deeply ambivalent attitude toward the world there is a sense of deep disillusionment. World War I was the end not only of an epoch but of a whole system of values in Germany. And Brecht belonged to the generation which had to grow up into this moon landscape of collapse and bankruptcy. Brecht's early poetry is full of images of despair. "The blind," he says in one passage, "talk about a way out. But *I* can see." And elsewhere he speaks about an epoch when the tables of the law itself have crumbled and not even sleeping with one's own sister gives pleasure any more. There is a persistent feeling of guilt in these early poems, disgust with sex and life, and a wild strain of accusation against God, who, it is said, does not exist, but "how can *that* not exist, which can betray man so deeply?" Thus the existence of God, an evil, malevolent force, is postulated to explain the measure of suffering and corruption in the world. As to the Devil—he too has become inefficient and lazy. It is no longer worthwhile to lie; from sheer despair men speak the truth, unaware of the danger of speaking the truth. "And the Devil no longer takes his best customers."

Passages like these, which Brecht wrote in his early twenties, for all their adolescent pose of cynical world-weariness, show the background of horror which must always be kept in mind in trying to understand Brecht's later political commitment. Only the experience of the desolation caused by so total a collapse of values can explain the frantic search for a new set of values to replace those which have been discredited; only the emptiness of total isolation in a world deprived of all social ties can account for the frantic craving for a new collective consciousness, for the discipline and fellow-feeling engendered by merging into a dedicated fellowship of fighters like the Communist party. When even murder had become too strenuous for the disillusioned, then even the will to violence could appear as a positive value:

> Terrible is it to kill.
> But not only others, ourselves too, we must kill, if
> necessary
> For this world, this killing world, can only
> Be changed by violence, as
> All living beings know.
> As yet, we said, it is not granted to us
> To be able not to kill. Only with our
> Unbending will to alter the world we justified
> The measure we took.

Thus do the four agitators (i.e., party activists) in Brecht's starkest tragedy, *The Measures Taken,* justify the liquidation of their young comrade who had broken the iron rules of discipline. It is the horror of the world which justifies the horror of the measures which have to be taken to alter the world. If man's meanness to his fellowmen, his greed and brutality, are merely the product of irrational and fossilized property relations, then a rational organization of society would enable the inherent goodness of man's nature to assert itself; greed and selfishness, meanness and brutality, would disappear from the earth. This essentially Rousseauist rejection of the concept of original sin (which is indeed one of the basic assumptions of Marxism) plays an immense part in Brecht's political and also in his aesthetic thought. For Brecht's theory of drama—the epic or, later, the dialectical theater with its *Verfremdungseffekt* (wrongly translated as "alienation effect," more correctly as "strange-making effect")—ultimately stems from his conviction that Aristotle's definition of the dramatic as distinct from the epic form of poetry implied the notion of an unchanging and unchangeable human nature.

In their famous essay *Uber epische und dramatische Dichtung* (*On Epic and Dramatic* Poetry, 1797), Goethe and Schiller asserted that the "great, essential difference" between the two kinds of literature "lies in the fact that the epic poet presents the event as totally past, while the dramatic poet presents it as totally present." If the foundation of Marxism, Brecht argued, is the notion that the world can only be apprehended rationally as a dialectical, historical process, in the course of which all human values are in constant flux, ever changing, then this conception of drama was not only un-Marxist but, if accepted, a complete denial of everything that Marxism stood for. After all, if audiences could not only be brought face to face with the world of Shakespeare, Sophocles, or Goethe, but could be made to experience the events in these plays as totally present, if they could suffer with Oedipus, rage with Othello, weep with Iphigenia, then the eternally unchanging sameness of human nature would be a proven fact and Marxism would have been refuted! Had not Goethe and Schiller expressly stated in their essay that the actor, in their definition of drama,

> wants the spectators to participate exclusively in his actions and in his immediate surroundings so that they should feel the sufferings of his soul and body with him, share his embarrassments and forget their own personalities for the sake of his. . . . The listener and spectator . . . must not be allowed to rise to thoughtful contemplation; he must passionately follow the action; his imagination is completely silenced and must not be taxed; and even things that are being narrated must, as it were, be brought before the audience's eyes by the actor.

If a contemporary spectator could be made to identify himself with Oedipus or Othello to the point of actually forgetting his own personality and becoming Oedipus and Othello, how could he ever, argued Brecht, be brought to realize that Othello and Oedipus had been men determined by the social systems of their times and therefore by definition inaccessible to any such identification on the part of twentieth-century man, determined as he is by totally different social and economic conditions?

There can be little doubt that Brecht's entire theory of a truly Marxist theater springs from his angry reaction against the very essay by Goethe and Schiller we have just quoted. In Brecht's theater the action must not take place in a total present, but in a strictly defined historical past—hence the streamers with precise dates for each scene in plays like *Mother Courage;* in Brecht's theater the spectators must not be allowed to identify with the actors on stage to the extent of forgetting their own personalities—hence Brecht's striving for a multitude of *Verfremdungseffekte,* that is, devices which would prevent identification to the point of annihilating the suspension of disbelief (that is, the actors stepping out of their parts, or grotesque masks that clearly reveal them to be puppets). And, finally, the spectator in Brecht's theater must be made to rise to thoughtful contemplation, must be led to detached critical reflection on the play and its meaning. For only a detached spectator could appreciate the distance between the historical characters, determined by the social relations of their time on the one hand and contemporary man on the other. Even the familiar, argued Brecht, would yield its message only when seen with new eyes, as though it were something never before noticed. It was because Newton was capable of perceiving a falling apple as a strange and wonderful phenomenon that he had discovered the laws of gravitation. Hence Brecht asked his audience, at the end of *The Exception and the Rule:*

> You have seen the familiar, which always happens.
> But we beg you:
> What is not strange, find it disquieting!
> What is ordinary, find it inexplicable!
> What is usual, let it astonish you!
> What seems the rule, recognize it as an abuse.
> And where you have recognized abuse,
> Put things right!

Brecht's theory of "epic—i.e., nondramatic—drama" can thus be seen both as an earnest endeavor to find a Marxist aesthetic of the theater and as an angry rejection of the official, classical aesthetic codified by those twin deities of the German cultural establishment, Goethe and Schiller.

The rise of German nationhood, belatedly achieved in 1871, was intimately linked with the search for a national literature (as, indeed, the search for the great American novel sprang from the need to reassert American nationhood and the emancipation of American letters from being a mere provincial variant of British culture!). To buttress the German claim to be a great nation rather than a motley collection of barbarous tribes (whose rulers refused to use the crude vernacular and insisted on speaking French right into the middle of the eighteenth century) the need was urgent for writers of unquestioned international stature, men who could equal a Dante, a Shakespeare, a Racine, a Calderón. The two demigods of Weimar triumphantly met that need; they dominated German nineteenth-century drama by engendering a large number of feeble and insipid imitators of their style. When Germany finally achieved the status of a great power under Prussian leadership, the "classics," their immediate predecessors, and their progeny were made the pivot of the new establishment's ideal of education and became the pinnacle of *Bildung;* indeed the ability to quote Goethe's *Faust* and Schiller's *Wallenstein* was—and still is—the badge of social status in German culture.

As a result the curriculum of schools and universities effectively distorted the true situation. By the very nature of their objective, "the classics" were literary, academic, and highly respectable. Because they had been rude, uncouth, and irregular, on the other hand, the very considerable poets and dramatists of the baroque period, for example, were almost totally neglected; the immense achievement of genuine folk drama, particularly in Austria and Bavaria (a brilliant South German version of the commedia dell'arte; great writers like Nestroy or Raimund), was almost entirely ignored; and a number of dramatists who did not fit the pattern created by the classics were disregarded as freaks and eccentrics (great figures of the Sturm und Drang period like J. M. R. Lenz; drunken geniuses like C. D. Grabbe; revolutionaries like Georg Büchner).

It is against this background that Brecht's revolt must be seen. To him the ugliness and stupidity, the complacency and smugness, of the German bourgeoisie were personified by the pompous teachers at his *Gymnasium,* by the tired, routine performances of the "classics" at the Augsburg *Stadttheater.* He not only rejected the "classics" and their reactionary aesthetics, he ridiculed them by making them the target of a stream of overt and covert parody. And he went for inspiration and example to the alternative sources of a German dramatic tradition: to baroque dramatists like Andreas Gryphius (Greif); the Austro-Bavarian folk theater, whose last living exponent, the great beerhall comedian Karl Valentin, became Brecht's mentor and friend; and above all to Büchner, a dramatist today generally acknowledged to have been at least equal, if not superior, to Goethe or Schiller.

In Büchner's *Danton's Death* (1835) the disillusioned revolutionaries muse, before their execution, upon the futility and glory of the human condition:

> We should take off our masks, and then we would see, as in a room surrounded by mirrors, everywhere but the one age-old, innumerable, indestructible dunderhead, no more, no less. The differences aren't that big, we all are rascals and angels, idiots and geniuses, all at once: these four things find room enough in the same body, they are not as voluminous as is usually assumed. To sleep, to digest, to procreate—that's what we all do; all else is mere variation on the same theme.

In Brecht's first play, *Baal,* the same note is struck by the hero, the drunken, antisocial poet Baal, and his friend the composer Ekart:

> *Ekart:* Sleep's gone to the devil and the wind again plays the organ in the willow-stumps. Thus we are left to lean against the white breasts of philosophy; the dark and the damp until the day of our blessed demise; even to the old hags no more is left than their second sight.
>
> *Baal:* In this wind you need no gin, and you are still drunk. I see the world in a mild light: it is God's excrement.
>
> *Ekart:* God's who has sufficiently revealed his true character once and for all by combining the genital organ with the urinary tract.
>
> *Baal:* It is all *so* beautiful.

Büchner was not yet twenty-four years old when he died in February 1837; Brecht wrote *Baal* in 1918 when he was just twenty. Like Büchner's Danton, Brecht's Baal is a sensualist, who drifts through life, letting himself be carried by its currents, whirlpools, and eddies. There is an element of parody in Brecht's character, however: he wrote the play as an answer to a dramatized biography of the drunken playwright Grabbe by Hanns Johst, a minor expressionist who later became one of the leading Nazi poets. So Baal can also be seen as a caricature of the ridiculous worship of the overflowing vitality of genius in a certain type of German nationalist literature (which later became the worship of Hitler's "genius"). And yet, the lyrical passages Brecht gives to his antisocial giant of vitality have such force and beauty that we cannot but feel that there is a great deal of Brecht's own attitude in them. Thus Brecht's very first completed play already contains that characteristic tension that will dominate his entire oeuvre: the tension between a desire to drift in the glorious, passive stream of life, on the one hand, and, on the other, a yearning for rationality which rejects that oceanic feeling with its passivity and amoral yielding to sensual impulse.

In the first, anarchic phase of Brecht's career, it is the sensuous, emotional, uncontrolled, passive attitude, the yielding to impulse, which dominates, while the rational, disciplined, activist attitude merely appears in the undertone of satire, mockery, and ridicule with which the impulsive demeanor of the main character is portrayed. Kragler, the antihero of *Drums in the Night,* refuses to join the Spartacist rising because he has become totally disillusioned with fighting of any kind, having risked his hide in the war. He decides to take his bride, who is pregnant by another man, in spite of her blemish.

Irrational selfishness is driven to its utmost limit in Brecht's most enigmatic play, *In the Jungle of the Cities.* Two men are locked in a totally unmotivated fight to the death in a mythical Chicago largely derived from Upton Sinclair: Shlink, a middle-aged Malayan timber trader, and young Garga, whose family has come into the big city from the "Savannahs." They do not know why they are fighting; only at the end do they realize that their struggle was a desperate attempt to establish contact, human communication. "The infinite isolation of man makes enmity an unattainable goal," says Shlink. "Love, warmth from the contact of bodies, is our only mercy in the darkness. But the conjunction of bodies is the only possible one, it cannot bridge the division of language. . . . Yes, so great is our isolation that there cannot even be a struggle." Here then, in the blind working out of irrational impulse, society itself appears as a place of icy desolation. When Schlink is dead, Garga, left alone, decides to go on living, in society. His last words—and those of the play—are: "The chaos has been used up. It was the best time."

Emotion/Reason—Selfishness/Discipline—Chaos/Order, these three polarities sum up the dialectic of Brecht's life and work. In *A Man's a Man* the emphasis has shifted away from passivity: a mild little workman, Galy Gay, is here transformed into a highly disciplined and ferocious soldier. From a self-contained individualist who wallowed in chaos he is turned into a paragon of order, a cog in a vast collective entity—a mythical, Kiplingesque British-Indian army. In *A Man's a Man* this process is shown satirically, as a grotesque and monstrous act. But in *The Measures Taken* almost the same process, the acceptance of iron, soldierly discipline by an emotional individualist, has become a heroic act of self-abnegation cast in the great tragic mold. For here it is not the discipline of an imperialist army but that of the Communist party itself which is accepted. *Das grosse Einverständnis*—the great act of consent—has been made the leitmotiv of Brecht's thinking.

The change from the anarchic to the didactic phase of Brecht's development is clearly marked in the evolution of his language. The Büchneresque exuberance of daring metaphors strung together in chains of image-laden main clauses yields to laconic severity and sparseness of expression:

> One man has two eyes
> The Party has a thousand eyes.
> The Party sees seven nations.
> One man sees one city.
> One man has his hour
> But the Party has many hours.
> One man can be destroyed
> But the Party cannot be destroyed.
> ("Praise of the Party," from
> *The Measures Taken*)

The antimilitarist and dedicated pacifist Brecht does not seem to have noticed that he was in fact expressing the philosophy of the samurai, of the Prussian officer, in these stark lines, the harsh creed of soldiers who do and die without asking the reason why. The school opera *He Who Says Yes,* which also deals with the concept of the great act of consent, is, indeed, derived from a Japanese No play (which Brecht had come to know in Arthur Waley's translation). Here a young boy whose illness impedes the progress of a party of travelers crossing a dangerous mountain range asks to be killed in the general interest. When it was pointed out to Brecht that the moral of this self-sacrificing action was questionable, he rewrote the piece with a different ending: with the boy refusing to die and declining to abide by old, inhuman customs. This new play, *He Who Says No,* was to be performed together with the first play, which it does not replace, but complements, as an example of a dialectical tension between two attitudes.

In the great plays of his years of exile Brecht's style has lost the austerity of his didactic phase; and his characters, who had been reduced to the bare essentials (reminiscent of the highly stylized characters of French classical tragedy, who also lack all individual little human touches), again acquired a rich texture of personal idiosyncrasies. Nevertheless, these plays remain didactic in the sense that they are conceived as parables, models of human situations, cited, like the parables in the New Testament, not for their own intrinsic interest, but because of their general applicability to other human situations and problems. Galilei stands for all scientists who have submitted to the dictates of political authority (and for the atomic scientists of our time in particular); Mother Courage, for all little people who do not realize that, deriving their small profit from war or the preparation of war, they are themselves guilty of causing the death of their children and the destruction of their country (as the little people of Hitler's Germany did); Puntila—evil when sober, human when drunk—is an emblem and exemplar of the irreconcilability between capitalistic attitudes and genuine humanity; while Shen Te, the good woman of Setzuan, demonstrates the impossibility of goodness in a world where survival depends on commercial success. The greatest of these plays, *The Caucasian Chalk Circle,* quite openly uses the parable form. It illustrates the solution of a problem which is posed in the prologue: who has the better right to a tract of land in a socialist country (a fairly mythically drawn Soviet Union), the legal owners or those who cultivate the land to the best purpose? The ancient legend of the child claimed by its natural and its foster mother is retold with a new variant to provide the answer. Solomon's judgment elicited a loving response from the natural mother and showed that it is the real mother who must also be the one who wants to spare her child pain and therefore is the one who loves it truly. In Brecht's parable it is the foster mother who really loves the child and refuses to hurt it, while the natural mother merely wants to use her abandoned child to reestablish her legal title to some property of which her son is heir. In other words, rather than to its legal proprietors, the land should belong to those who till it to the best effect and thereby show that they truly love it.

Brecht's use of the parable form expresses another aspect of his revolt against the state of German culture and the German theater in his youth. As much as he rejected the grandiloquent classicism of the followers of Goethe and Schiller (and, to a lesser extent, of the masters themselves), he also detested the naturalistic theater which had become dominant in Germany at the turn of the century. All of Brecht's dramatic work can be seen as a refutation of naturalism, the use of the stage to reproduce photographically accurate slices of life. The only plays he wrote in a realistic convention (*Señora Carrar's Rifles, Fear and Misery in the Third Reich*) were propagandist potboilers. *Drums in the Night,* which takes place in a real contemporary historical and political situation (the Spartacist uprising in Berlin in 1919), transcends any suspicion of realism by the exuberance of its language and Brecht's insistence on a nonrealistic set. At the end the romantically ominous blood-red moon that dominates the action is brought down and revealed to have been no more than a Chinese lantern.

As an anti-illusionist in the theater Brecht was logically driven toward the parable form; in the austere experimental situation of a *Lehrstück,* in the fairy-tale world of distant Setzuan or the Caucasus, it is possible to deal with real problems without having to put a realistic image of the world onto the stage. For naturalism, and indeed any attempt at a realistic convention, Brecht argued, had the drawback of overindividualization. If one showed *one* family of starving, unemployed workers in loving detail, how could one convince the audience that this was not just one individual and exceptional case and was, therefore, without general validity? To do social good the theater, Brecht felt, must be able to convince its audience that its examples were typical and of wide applicability. Hence he never shrank from openly drawing the moral from his examples, largely by the use of songs which stand outside the action, interrupt it, and underline its general conclusions, but also by pointed epilogues (*Puntila, The Good Woman of Setzuan*), projected slogans, and so forth. In the dramatic parable, distanced through the remoteness of its setting in time or space, the need for realism is greatly reduced. An audience in contemporary Germany will demand convincing realism for a play set in contemporary Germany, but will accept a highly stylized Renaissance Florence, or a picture of Germany in the Thirty Years' War, or even contemporary Finland or China. It is in these settings that the familiar can be made to appear strange so that it can be critically appraised and evaluated by an uninvolved audience.

The irony was that this doctrine of a politically efficacious left-wing theater fell afoul of the official Communist doctrine in the Soviet Union where, after 1934, socialist realism had become the orthodox doctrine. In the theater this manifested itself in a rigid insistence on the Moscow Art Theater style of meticulous naturalism as the only permissible form of "Marxist" theater. Great directors like Meyerhold and Tairov fell victim to this doctrine. Brecht wisely avoided settling in the Soviet Union after his exile from Germany; he even acted as coeditor of the German émigré literary magazine published in Moscow, *Das Wort,* from his home in Denmark. He attempted to conduct a mild polemic against the official doctrine: pointing to examples of progressive literature like Shelley's *Masque of Anarchy* or Swift's *Gulliver's Travels,* he argued that, after all, it was the political intention that mattered, not the form. But the essay on "The Range and Variety of the Realistic Style," which he wrote in 1938 for publication in *Das Wort,* did not see the light of day until almost twenty years later. Cautious as always, Brecht thought better of publishing it, which would have incurred the open wrath of the Stalinists.

Brecht, brought up on the grandiloquent cardboard heroism of the bombastic nationalist ideology of the Wilhelmian *Reich,* detested all manifestations of heroism: as Mother Courage points out, only a bad general needs brave soldiers. Mother Courage is of the same tribe as that great archetype of unheroic irony and subservient resistance, the Good Soldier Schweik as depicted in Jaroslav Hašek's immortal picaresque novel. Brecht knew and loved the book; in 1928 he had collaborated on a stage adaptation for Piscator in Berlin and during World War II he wrote a sequel to Hašek's story, the play *Schweyk im zweiten Weltkrieg* (*Schweyk in the Second World War,* 1944). But there are Schweikian characters in many of his plays and prose writings; indeed, they are among Brecht's most personal creations. The character of Mr. Keuner in the stories about Mr. Keuner, who quite clearly embodies Brecht's model of himself, the man he wanted to be, is also a close relative of Schweik. The "stories" are mostly very short, ranging from one or two sentences to about a page and a half.

And they attempt to portray an attitude of mind to life, or as Brecht himself said in a note preceding the first published batch of Keuner stories, "they constitute an experiment in making gestures quotable." The quotability of gestures is a key concept in Brecht's aesthetics. For him the essence of art, of poetry, is indeed the fact that through its perfection of form, through its concentration of thought, poetry enables truth to become transmittable, accessible to the mass of people. But a merely verbal quotation merely transmits an abstract version of the truth. The importance of drama lies precisely in its concreteness, in its ability to embody actual models of human behavior. Instead of merely hearing people quote the noble words from some play by Shakespeare or Schiller, Brecht wanted them to repeat wholesome, rational, and noble actions they might have seen on the stage. Hence his desire to create quotable gestures, in his narrative prose as well as in his plays.

Each Keuner story embodies one *gestus.* This term, which plays an important part in Brecht's theory and practice of play writing and play production, is not quite the same as a mere gesture. It denotes a basic human behavior model, an archetypal attitude. "A man who had not seen Mr. K. for a long time greeted him with the words: 'You have not changed at all.' 'Oh!' said Mr. K. and went pale." This Keuner story—quoted here in its entirety—does not embody a gesture (going pale could hardly be called that) but it does demonstrate a *gestus*—namely, Brecht's basic attitude that man, a rational, dialectical creature, must fear nothing more than lack of change. The more elegantly, the more thoroughly, such human behavior models could be encapsulated in words and stage performance, the more readily quotable, useful, and practical they would become as tools of learning for mankind.

One of the fundamental structural principles of Brecht's epic theater derives from this concept: each scene, Brecht postulated, should embody just one *Grundgestus* (basic *gestus*), no more and no less, and should be constructed in such a way that that basic *gestus* can be seen most clearly and to best advantage—in other words, most quotably. "The only thing Mr. Keuner had to say about style is: 'it must be quotable.' A quotation is impersonal. Who are the best sons? Those who make you forget their father." The insistence on quotability is thus a deeply anti-individualistic, antiromantic attitude. According to Brecht it is not originality which is the hallmark of the best art but, on the contrary, typicality, that is, the widest possible application and most general validity.

The writing of a play, in Brecht's view, as well as its production, would consist in evolving a sequence of scene-titles indicating the basic *gestus* of each scene (for instance, "Hamlet confronts his father's ghost" or "Three Witches foretell Macbeth's rise to the throne"), so that by simply putting these title captions together the whole story of the play (*Fabel,* or "narrative essence") emerges.

As a follower of J. B. Watson's behaviorist school, Brecht despised all psychologies based on introspection. If Stanislavsky and his followers in the techniques of "method acting" want to derive the gesture from the characters' inner life, Brecht was convinced that what comes first is the attitude which will trigger the appropriate subjective feelings.

These views had important consequences not only for the production techniques of Brecht's drama, but also for the writing of his plays, stories, and poems. Truly dramatic language is, in the last analysis, to be considered not merely in its aspect as a structure of words, form, and content, but as an action. This is the difference between ordinary and genuinely dramatic writing. Of each sentence spoken in a play it must be possible to say what function it performs as an action. For Brecht, therefore, the problem of dramatic writing came down to the development of linguistic forms which already contain the action that inevitably must accompany them. When Othello in his final speech refers to the Turk he once met in Aleppo in order to divert the attention of the bystanders from his intention to kill himself, the words "and smote him thus" cannot be spoken without the sudden suicidal stab toward which they are aimed. This, to Brecht, was ideally gestural language, words which already contain, and which compellingly impose, the *gestus,* the attitude they embody. In this Brecht was immensely successful: the gestural quality lies in the variation of pace of the writing—the alternation of quick short words and long polysyllabic ones—in the clever use of pause and caesura, which often causes the word after the caesura to come as a shock, a surprise, and many subtle devices of rhythm, contrast, and tonal color. These are the subtleties most difficult to transfer into other languages, provided the translator is even aware of them (and that often does not seem to have been the case). Basically, a text by Brecht acts itself.

Quotability of attitude is also the principal factor in Brecht's stress on the use of songs in his plays. Here the music reinforces the gestural character of the language; for the use of music doubles the possibilities for strict control of rhythm, pace, repetition of vital phrases (refrains), and the like. And music, with the added factor of melody, increases the quotability both of the words (a hit tune often cannot be got out of one's consciousness, even if one wanted to get rid of it) and of the *gestus,* the attitude embodied in it.

The actor whom Brecht admired more than any other of his time, Charlie Chaplin, also exemplifies what Brecht meant by quotable *gestus* and gestural acting. So quotable was Chaplin's characteristic grotesque walk, the way he flicked his cane, that in his heyday there was a Chaplin imitator (Brecht would have said a Chaplin quoter) at every party in the land. And these gestures which were so immensely quotable also, in a truly Brechtian sense, embodied an attitude to life—the indomitable little man's defiance of the inhuman pressures of an overly mechanized industrial society. One might formulate it in this way: as a great poet Brecht wanted to use his utmost mastery of language to force the actors appearing in his plays to act in the style of, and as brilliantly as, Chaplin.

Brecht's theory of drama, as well as his theory and practice of poetic, gestural language, ultimately amounts to a striving for simplicity and directness of structure and expression. The concentration on the clear story line (*Fabel*) in the plays and the insistence on language becoming an embodiment of simple human attitudes tend in this direction. The Truth Is Concrete was the slogan Brecht put up over his desk wherever he came to a halt in his travels of exile.

This pursuit of directness and concreteness also can be seen as a reaction against a German tradition. Much of German poetry—and therefore also of the poetic language of drama—revels in grand philosophical abstractions and flowery, nebulous concepts. Brecht not only rejected these bombastic abstractions, he also set himself against the subjectivity, the sentimental self-involvement, of the lyrical tradition. As early as 1927 Brecht rejected any purely lyrical poetry with the argument that such poems "are simply too far removed from the original *gesture* [my italics] of the communication of a thought or emotion which would also be of use to strangers." In his first published collection of poems, *Manual of Piety,* the poems are prefaced by "Directions for Use," which open with the words: "This Domestic Breviary is destined for the use of readers. It must not be senselessly gulped down." Clothing his scandalously free poetry in the outward guise of a prayer book was, for Brecht, an act of blasphemous irony, yet, at the same time, the analogy was also meant very seriously: a book of hymns or prayers is, after all, a genuine article of daily use, an instrument of mental and spiritual hygiene which has its clearly defined part to play in the life of pious folk. And this comes very close to Brecht's idea about the function of literature—and drama—in his ideal society.

Brecht's *Manual of Piety* is typical of his first exuberant, anarchic phase. The ballads it contains celebrate a kind of wild acceptance of nature and its processes of growth and decay. The great rivers that carry the corpses of the drowned down to the sea, the jungle which engulfs the conquistadors in the wilds of Central America, the pirates who roam the seas knowing full well that one day they will be swallowed up—these are typical, ever recurring images of Brecht's early poetry. There is no introspection in these poems; even the few which deal with Brecht's personal life treat him objectively, in the third person almost. There are no elaborate similes; the images are put before the reader directly, starkly, and stand by and for themselves. Formally there is still a good deal of artifice and elaboration: ballad meters, even sonnets, abound. The Bible, Rimbaud, Kipling (who may have been an imperialist but was also a pioneer in the use of vernacular speech, even broad dialect in poetry), and Wedekind—in his bitter, satirical cabaret songs—were the chief models of Brecht's early poetry; Goethe, Schiller, and the masters of the German Protestant hymn, the chief targets for his parody.

Brecht's later poetry is more cerebral, severe, and economical. Arthur Waley's translations from the Chinese became a decisive influence. Rhyme and regular rhythms were sloughed off, free verse in irregular rhythms became the norm, although for special purposes Brecht still could occasionally fall back on classical meters: he was a great believer in the hexameter as a vehicle for didactic poetry. Modeling himself on Vergil's *Georgics* and Lucretius' *De rerum natura,* he undertook, during his Hollywood exile, the gigantic task of putting the essence of Marxism into a great didactic poem in hexameters. He never finished the attempt, yet the remaining fragments are impressively powerful. But Brecht's best late poems are short, almost epigrammatic: they speak of the tribulations of exile, the sorrows of the poet's return to his ravaged homeland, aging, and death. They are among the finest poems in the German language. They reveal the real Brecht behind the facade of cheerful support for the East German regime: a wistful, disillusioned man, dreaming of the landscape of his childhood in Augsburg, praising the humble pleasures of homely food, cheese, bread, and cool beer. There even creeps into this private, late poetry a note of wry rejection of the hollow claims of the totalitarian state to which he had committed his fortunes. After the rising of 17 June 1953, when the regime reproached the people for their rebellion, Brecht, in one famous poem, simply asked why, in that case, the government did not dissolve the people and elect itself another.

At the height of his commitment to Marxism (1940) Brecht's view of the function and nature of poetry was a severely committed one: "Lyrical poetry is never mere expression. . . . The making of poetry must be regarded as a human activity, as a social practice; with all its self-contradiction, changeability, must be seen as historically conditioned and history making. The distinction lies between 'reflecting nature' and 'holding the mirror up' to it." On another, much earlier occasion—in 1927—Brecht had given a slightly wider definition of the function of poetry: "All great poems have the value of documents. They contain the manner of speaking of their author, an important human being." In other words, poetry is the memorable utterance of a memorable man.

Poetry thus holds a central position in any consideration of Brecht as a dramatist as well as a prose writer. "The poet Kin [i.e., Brecht] recognized language as a tool of action." The quotation comes from another collection of pithy short aphorisms, stories, and anecdotes, *Me-ti, Buch der Wendungen* (Me-ti, the Book of Twists and Turns, 1965), in which Brecht continued the method he adopted in the Keuner stories with the further alienation effect of a Chinese classical garb. In another passage the poet Kin (i.e., Keuner/Brecht) confesses: "How am I to write immortal works, when I am not famous? How am I to give answers, when I am not asked? Why should I lose time over writing poems, if time loses them? I write my suggestions in an enduring language, because I fear it will take a long time until they are carried out."

It is to make his suggestions for social change memorable, durable enough to remain long in currency, that Brecht had to turn to poetry. It is through the power of his language to evoke the moods of action that he becomes a great playwright; through the quality of his language as a tool for the expression of thought that he becomes a great prose writer.

In his days as a struggling young playwright—until his breakthrough into financial success with *The Threepenny Opera* in 1928—Brecht wrote numerous short stories for magazines, with the avowed aim of producing a readily salable product. He even won a short story competition run by one of Berlin's most popular illustrated papers. Nevertheless, a good many of these stories are little masterpieces of observation, irony, and, above all, style.

Some of these stories contain the germs of ideas which later blossomed into plays, some cast light on Brecht's psychology and the imagery of his mind. As in his early plays, Brecht loved to situate his action in an Anglo-American world, somewhere between a Kiplingesque India, the "savannahs" of the American West, Jack London's arctic Alaska, Upton Sinclair's Chicago of the stockyards, and a Dickensian London teeming with quaint and sinister characters. For a young German brought up in a small town of Central Europe, but avidly reading stories of adventure, this indeed was the exotic world of romance, the wide-open spaces which beckoned those who had the courage to escape from the stuffy drawing rooms of the respectable German petty bourgeoisie.

It is in the plays *A Man's a Man* (set in Anglo-India on the borders of China and Tibet), *The Threepenny Opera* (a Dickensian Victorian London with some Americanisms—the police chief is called the Sheriff), and *Mahagonny* (the brothel camp for the gold miners returning from Alaska) that the world sketched out in the short stories came to its first full fruition. Out of *The Threepenny Opera* grew Brecht's most ambitious novel, the *Threepenny Novel* (1934), a vast panorama of a pseudo-Dickensian London, brilliantly written, but marred by the extremely naive idea of capitalism which forms the basis of its argument.

A second novel, *Die Geschäftedes Herrn Julius Caesar* (*The Business Deals of Mr. Julius Caesar,* 1957), written between 1938 and 1939 in Denmark, remained unfinished. Here too Brecht attempted to show the sordid business reality behind the facade of glory of a great military hero and dictator, as an indictment of Hitler, whom he regarded, wrongly, as no more than the puppet of rich industrialists and businessmen. Here too there is much fine writing, but Brecht's decision to abandon it shows that he himself did not regard the work as a success.

Another somewhat fragmentary work, the series of dialogues entitled *Flüchtlingsgespräche* (*Refugee Conversations*), largely written between 1940 and 1941 in Finland, must be counted, however, among Brecht's masterpieces. Two men stranded in Finland, Ziffel, an intellectual (who bears many features of Brecht himself), and Kalle, a worker, try to while away the time which hangs heavily on their hands by discussing the world, the war, exile, and all the countries through which they have passed. All the bitterness of exile is in these sardonic, Schweikian dialogues: "The passport is a man's noblest part. Nor does it come into being as easily as a human being. A human being can come into being in the most thoughtless manner and without good reason, but a passport—never. That is why a passport is recognized when it is a good one, while a man can be as good as he pleases and will yet not find recognition. One can say that a man is no more than a stand on which to place a passport." The *Refugee Conversations* is probably Brecht's most openly autobiographical work, even more so than the Keuner stories, in which he deals with an ideal image rather than with a realistic assessment of his personality.

After his return from America to Europe, Brecht compiled a slim volume of stories and narrative poems which he published in 1948 under the title *Kalendergeschichten* (*Tales *from the Calendar*). Clearly designed as reading matter for the common people—German peasants in rural areas in Brecht's youth probably never read anything but the moral tales inserted between the calendar pages in their almanacs—this slim volume contains some of Brecht's finest narrative prose. The eight longer stories are in the mainstream of the tradition of the German *Novelle:* they relate significant incidents from history in a sparse, objective language, eschewing all introspection or attempts at psychological subtlety, but concentrating on the actual events. Yet these stories give deep psychological insights and somehow succeed in making history come alive. In "Der Mantel des Ketzers" ("The Heretic's Coat"), for example, we see the tragedy of Giordano Bruno, the natural philosopher burned at the stake as a heretic, through the eyes of a poor tailor who had made him a coat just before he was arrested and tries to get his money for it, while the philosopher is tried and convicted.

Another story, in a quite different vein, tells of an old woman, the narrator's (and clearly Brecht's) grandmother, who, when widowed at an advanced age, shocked her village by throwing all conventions of bourgeois respectability to the winds. "Thus she might rise in summer at three in the morning and take walks in the deserted streets of the little town, which she had entirely for herself. And, it was alleged, when the priest called on her to keep the old woman company in her loneliness, she invited him to the cinema."

After two years of the joys of freedom, the old woman dies: "I have seen a photograph of her which was taken for the children and shows her laid out. What you see is a tiny little face, and a thin-lipped, wide mouth. Much that is small, but no smallness. She has savored to the full the long years of servitude and the short years of freedom and consumed the bread of life to the last crumb." Only the terse stories of Heinrich von Kleist—another great German dramatist—can rival the economy and power of these short narratives and their mastery of German prose style.

Another large-scale project for a major novel also remained a fragment—the so-called *Tui-Novel* (1965), a satire, also set in a mythical China, on the corruption of the intellectuals (*T*ellekt-*U*ell-*I*ns abbreviated into *Tuis*) in the Weimar Republic. The Tuis are people who live by selling opinions. Brecht devoted a great deal of thought to this project in the thirties; it later led to the far more successful collection of brief anecdotes and sketches, *Me-Ti,* and was finally remodeled, after Brecht's return to East Berlin in the late forties, into the material for his last play, *Turandot, or The Congress of Whitewashers.* As in the case of the *Threepenny Novel,* the partial failure of the Tui project is due to Brecht's difficulty in finding a valid satirical analogy for the vices of capitalist society. That intellectuals sell their opinions is true enough, but after half a century of Communist rule in Russia, it is difficult to maintain, as Brecht certainly wanted to, that this phenomenon is the direct result of a capitalist organization of society.

Apart from his fiction Brecht left a vast and impressive corpus of other prose writings: political articles and essays, theoretical writings on the theater, and diaries and letters. His *Arbeitsjournal* (Working Diary), covering the years of his American exile and return to East Germany until his death in 1956, was published in 1973. This tends to avoid his personal life and concentrates on his problems as a working writer. Fragments of his early diaries and autobiographical jottings, which are far more personal and revealing, were made available in 1975. An extremely selective and incomplete edition of Brecht's letters appeared in 1982. It is difficult to judge how much still remains suppressed for political reasons.

Brecht's endeavors to create a truly Marxist aesthetic of theater are brilliant and stimulating and have given rise to endless misunderstandings. Above all, it must be kept in mind that these writings do not present a unitary, finished theory, but are, themselves, the documentation of a constant process of changing and developing thought. It is very significant that many of the actual practices of Brecht's play writing and direction antedate his commitment to Marxism, so that the Marxist terminology of later writings can be seen as an attempt to find a theoretical backing for intuitions and tastes which are part of Brecht's very personal artistic approach. The same is true of much in Brecht's later theorizing: it can frequently be regarded as an ex post facto rationalization of stage inventions which emerged in rehearsal.

Indeed, in the theater Brecht was the most empirical and undoctrinaire of directors. He conducted rehearsals at the Berliner Ensemble in the most leisurely of fashions, and entirely on a trial and error basis: every actor was given the opportunity to try out as many ways of playing a scene as he could suggest; and in the end the most effective version was chosen, after ample discussion.

The most valuable part of Brecht's theoretical work therefore appears to be that part which is the most concrete—the actual descriptions he gives of the way in which his plays were acted or ought to be directed. Much of this material is contained in the model books (for *Galileo, Mother Courage, Antigone,* and *Señora Carrar's Rifles*) and in the copious notes which Brecht provided for editions of his plays.

Brecht's most ambitious theoretical—and practical—discussion of the theater is contained in the voluminous fragment entitled *Dialoge aus dem Messingkauf* (*The Messingkauf Dialogues,* 1964), which Brecht began to write in 1939 and to which he added material for the rest of his life. It was to take the form of a series of dialogues interspersed with didactic poems. The title refers to the desire of one of the participants in the dialogues (The Philosopher) to find out about the true nature of theater, and above all its usefulness for the purpose to which he wants to put it: "I feel the special nature of my interest so strongly that I see myself like a trader in brass who comes to a brass band to buy not a trumpet but merely brass." In other words, he poses the question whether the theater, in spite of its traditional shape, could ever become the raw material for a new art, "an instrument for the imitation of certain events among people to certain purposes." The four dialogues, involving, apart from the philosopher, an actor, an actress, a dramaturge (literary adviser to a theater), and an electrician, are highly stimulating and amusing; yet it is the poems, which distill the practical side of Brecht's ideas into memorable gnomic language, which prove to be the most valuable part of the unfinished edifice.

The little *Kleines Organon das Theater* (*Organon for the Theater*), a compression of the theory of epic drama into seventy-seven terse paragraphs, written in 1948, is far more dogmatic and apodictic than *The Messingkauf Dialogues,* and it has given rise to far more misunderstandings.

That Brecht evolved a body of extremely fertile ideas for the writing and staging of his type of drama is beyond doubt. What is far more questionable is the basic conception that Marxism, as a philosophy, simply must produce its own, Marxist, aesthetics. Having been brought up in a German philosophical tradition, according to which each philosopher had to produce a unitary system of thought which would provide a complete worldview comprising an epistemology, cosmology, logic, ethics, and aesthetics, Brecht thought that Marxism also should be able to provide all the answers to all the problems of the universe. Yet Marxism, in claiming to be a scientific system, also necessarily must be an open system, relying on a constant testing of its findings by experiment. Moreover, basically, Marxism is a system of political economy. Nobody ever attempted to construct aesthetics to fit Adam Smith's or John Maynard Keynes's ideas of political economy. Why, then, should it be necessary to complement Marxism with such a body of doctrine? Only at the point where Marxism ceases to be a scientific hypothesis and is turned into the pseudo-religion of a totalitarian state does it in fact acquire the need to have an aesthetic doctrine. As it happened, the "aesthetics" developed by Stalinism in the Soviet Union were diametrically opposed to Brecht's ideas about art and drama and corresponded, in fact, very closely to those of Hitler's Germany (rejection of all abstract and experimental art as degenerate). In other words, the aesthetics actually developed by Soviet Communism were not Marxist but totalitarian aesthetics, and derived not from any philosophy but from the needs of thought control in a dictatorship. Indeed, Brecht's insistence that the theater should shock its audience into critical thought made his aesthetics highly suspect in the eyes of the Stalinists and their successors.

There remains the problem about the philosophical implications of the theory of genres enunciated by Goethe and Schiller: that drama, by its insistence that what the audience sees is something which happens here and now and with which they can totally identify, presupposes that human nature is constant and unchangeable. It was this which led Brecht to reject the idea of a dramatic theater altogether and to opt for an epic theater. Yet the implications of the "Aristotelian" conception of drama as understood by Goethe and Schiller need not be quite so drastic. The declared purpose of this conception of drama might be that, human nature being always the same, the spectators ought to be made to identify with the actions of the characters on the stage. Yet, as social conditions change, in fact, the vast bulk of past drama fails to bring about any identification and becomes, indeed, unperformable. Most of the emotions portrayed in eighteenth-century larmoyant comedy, in Victorian melodrama, are incapable of arousing any echo in the minds of contemporary audiences, except perhaps ribald laughter. Only a very small proportion of the drama of past epochs still has the power of making contemporary spectators identify with the experience of characters like Oedipus, Lear, Juliet, or Othello. Yet, it could be argued, it is not with the slave-owning ancient king that audiences identify while watching Oedipus but with the man who feels guilty for having desired his own mother; not with the Moorish general but with the jealous husband; not with the Veronese aristocratic girl but with a girl kept from marrying the man she loves; not with the mythical ruler of a barbaric Britain but with an old man ousted by his daughters. In these cases the social framework behind the characters may have changed decisively, yet in their basic emotional aspects there has been little or no change. In his effort to make his actors see such characters critically, Brecht wrote "practice scenes" to be performed during rehearsals. One of these shows Romeo and Juliet being extremely heartless in their relations to their servants, to whom they deny the freedom of having high-flown emotions like their own love. Thus Brecht wanted his actors—and the audience—to be made aware that in feudal Verona only the masters could indulge in romantic love. That is a valid point, but not the point that Shakespeare wanted to make; why then should Shakespeare's play be used to yield this message rather than the one about young love, which is still valid? Likewise, husbands still tend to be as jealous as Othello. Yet, Brecht argued, they should not be made to feel that they agree with Othello. By inhibiting their tendency to identify with him, the husbands in the audience should be made to see how foolish such jealousy, based as it is on a medieval concept of ownership, must be. Yet the strong tendency toward identification in contemporary audiences exists precisely because these medieval concepts still hold sway, in spite of totally different social conditions. Once a more enlightened age has dawned, when the emancipation of women is complete and love is freed from concepts of ownership, *Othello* will automatically carry its "alienation effect," without any effort on the part of directors or theoreticians.

Conversely, in Brecht's own plays the alienation effect invariably fails in performance whenever the emotions portrayed are of such a nature that they correspond to those of the audience. Brecht wanted the audience to criticize Mother Courage for her involvement with war as a business, to condemn her for causing the death of her children. But in spite of songs, anti-illusionist staging, posters with the exact time and date, the distancing effect does not take place; the mothers in the audience—and not only they—still identify with the predicament of a loving mother who loses her children. Brecht scolded critics and audiences alike for seeing Mother Courage as a Niobe. But they did, and thereby showed clearly that the world of Oedipus and the other archetypes of Greek myth retains its power, that not only might modern audiences identify with Oedipus, but that even the most consciously Marxist conception of a character could ultimately not escape identification with a human type dating back to antiquity. And what is true of Mother Courage also applies to Puntila (whom audiences find lovable because they cannot but identify with his drunkenness); to Galilei (whose sensuousness and cowardice produce similar effects of sympathetic empathy); to Azdak and many other "alienated" Brechtian characters.

This is not to say that Brecht's technique of alienation does not produce results of supreme artistic quality. Precisely because the human tendency toward identification is so strong, the continued efforts to inhibit it produce a tension, a tug-of-war, between opposing tendencies which ultimately creates a kind of double vision, an equal stimulation of intellect and emotion, and an effect of depth, of a multitude of levels of meaning.

Hence—and this is a characteristically Brechtian paradox—those of his works which are most openly political, and therefore unidimensional, invariably turn out to be the weakest. When a play lacks human, or indeed political, truth, it invariably fails to produce identification among the spectators. They notice the author's intention and resent being manipulated.

Brecht's case is a most illuminating illustration of the problems of politically committed art. Where a ready-made political concept is dominant in his mind, even a writer of genius like Brecht cannot make it the basis of a wholly convincing work of art. The political stereotype inhibits the free play of the artist's imagination and forces him to create oversimplified characters and situations. Where, on the other hand, the political motivation is an indirect one, where it springs from the poet's experience of the injustice and suffering caused by the state of the world, and where therefore he is able to give his imagination free rein, so that the characters can develop in the three-dimensional roundness of natural growth, the result is not only a greater human impact but also, ultimately, a greater social and political effectiveness, even though that political effect may not always be the one which had been in the poet's mind.

The history of Brecht's impact on the world and the spread of his fame clearly illustrates the validity of this analysis. In vain do the followers of the totalitarian party line accuse those who make this point of trying to turn Brecht into a harmless article of aesthetic consumption and of denying him his own claim to be more, namely a revolutionary force that effectively will and can change society itself. Yet the fact remains that Brecht is as frequently and successfully performed in the Western world as in East Germany and that, indeed, his message of critical detachment has a more explosive effect in the East, where it appears antitotalitarian, than in the West, where it can easily be taken for granted. *The Threepenny Opera* ran in New York for many years, yet it will be hard to find anyone who was converted by it to a Marxist view of politics.

That this is so makes Brecht a failure only in the eyes of those who measure the values of aesthetics according to political standards. Nobody wants to deny the enormous benefits Brecht derived artistically from his commitment to Marxism, but these benefits were of a personal nature and affected his work as a poet and playwright only indirectly. Of course a dramatist derives great advantages from having a firm philosophy of life, a clear allegiance and purpose. If one considers the wild exuberance of Brecht's early work and its undertone of despair, one realizes how dangerous it would have been for him, as an artist and as a human being, had he failed to find such a firm allegiance. The short-term political objectives of any work of art, however, are bound to be those most likely to be overtaken by events, to become obsolete and even incomprehensible. Who, today, pays any attention to the fact that a play like Shakespeare's *Richard II* was brimful of political implications to an audience who had lived through the Essex rebellion? That does not diminish the human and aesthetic values contained in the play. In the long view, therefore, the only thing that remains relevant in a work of art is its artistic value. A seventeenth-century musket may have become obsolete as a weapon, while it still remains beautiful as a work of craftsmanship. Brecht's plays might have been fashioned by him as weapons, but their aesthetic values will remain long after the conflicts to which they were relevant have been forgotten.

What does matter in a major artist, apart from his talent, is the depth and quality of his human experience: Brecht is unique among the great artists of his time in that he was more deeply involved in the experience of his epoch than almost any other poet of comparative stature. He was directly affected by World War I as well as World War II. He had firsthand experience of what will probably be the archetypal predicament of the twentieth century: political exile. He experienced vicious persecution by the Nazis, was deeply involved with the Soviet Union, lived in the United States, and became a victim of the anti-Communist witchhunt of the forties. At the end of his life, in Communist East Berlin, he took a stand against totalitarian Stalinism, which foreshadowed the renewal of Marxist thought in the Poland of the fifties and the Czechoslovakia of the late sixties. He was equally at home in the turbulent Berlin of the dying Weimar Republic, in the Moscow of the Stalinist purges, and in the torrid climate of postwar Hollywood and New York. He saw Soviet friends, like Tretyakov, hounded to their deaths by Stalin, and Hollywood friends, like Chaplin, persecuted as subversive elements in America. He witnessed the rise and fall of Hitler, had his books burned by the Nazis, and fifteen years later stood on the ruins of Hitler's *Reichskanzlei.*

It is this experience which shines through Brecht's poetry and the best of his prose work and dramatic output. What is remarkable is that his reaction, though frequently violent and impatient, basically amounts to a grim determination to survive and to transcend all the brutality and fanaticism by an ideal of friendliness. This is a concept that owes much to a classical Chinese Confucian view of an ideal society based on mutual politeness and respect. Brecht's poetry in the last years of his life was deeply imbued with these almost quietist, Stoic values, which combine the attitudes of the Good Soldier Schweik and the serenity of Horace with the Confucian ideal.

All this is a far cry from the wild rebellion of Brecht's youth and yet is strangely consistent with the dialectics of his development from a feeling of emotional passivity and the helplessness in the face of the uncontrollable, cataclysmic forces of history, society, and man's own instincts, to a yearning for discipline, rationality, and conscious control over nature and man through science, to an ultimate synthesis of a humble recognition of man's ability to master his environment, tempered by a resolve to do his best within his modest capacity.

Brecht's oeuvre, therefore, must always be judged as a whole; the more deeply committed of his disciples have, in the past, made considerable efforts to minimize, and even to suppress, the more chaotic outpourings of the early Brecht. He himself rewrote his first play to reach the stage, *Drums in the Night,* before he included it in the collected edition of his plays in 1954. Yet gradually pressure from Western critics—and Brecht's West German publisher—induced much of the hitherto suppressed material to be published: an edition of Brecht's letters, by no means complete; his so-called *Arbeitsjournal* that covered the last twenty years of his life; some early diaries from the 1920's; some of his poems on Stalin and his early pornographic verse.

But it was only with the advent of *glasnost* that a decisive break occurred. Publication of a new, much fuller, if by no means a "variorum," edition of Brecht's works started in 1988. But what is even more surprising, this new, thirty-volume *Werke, Grosse kommentierte Berliner und Frankfurter Ausgabe* (Great Berlin and Frankfurt Edition with Commentary) is published jointly by Brecht's West German publisher, Suhrkamp, and the East German Aufbau Verlag in East Berlin, and edited by scholars from East as well as West Germany. The first six volumes that had appeared by the spring of 1989 scrupulously adhere to the first published texts and also include later versions of the plays in full if they differ substantially from the first editions. And much hitherto unpublished material is also being made available in this unprecedented all-German publishing venture, the first of its kind since Germany was divided in 1945.

The title of the new edition, with its reference to Berlin and Frankfurt, contains an obvious allusion to the great Weimar edition of Goethe. It thus finally consecrates Brecht's status as a major German "classic."

He himself would have seen the irony of this development. He always deplored the fact that once a writer had become a classic he lost his bite, his ability to disturb and shock; that he had in fact been rendered harmless as part of the cultural furniture of established power.

His publisher has revealed that, when the first attempt was made at issuing a collected edition of the plays, Brecht insisted on fairly large print and small format so that his output might be made to look more substantial on the bookshelves. He thus had a modest idea of his own oeuvre, and probably did not feel that a good deal of material posthumously published really belonged to the enduring body of his work. In the early thirties he had issued his work in progress in modest gray brochures entitled *Versuche* (experiments) and in these he had always cited a number of names beside his own, as *Mitarbeiter* (collaborators). Brecht looked at the poet's work as a craft comparable to that of medieval architects or painters who either remained anonymous or worked collectively, with a number of disciples taking part in painting one picture. He rejected the romantic ideal of the unique original genius and ridiculed the myth of divinely inspired creativity.

And yet—with the characteristic dialectical tension between opposites within his personality—he was, at the same time, aware of his importance as an artist. When, during his American period, a friend pointed out to him that he had used an Anglicism in something he had written, and that the expression concerned did not exist in German, he retorted: "Well, then, it exists from now on."

Similarly, having ridiculed the worship accorded to the "classics" of German literature in schools and universities and among the educated classes, he himself occasionally referred to himself as a classic.

And that is what, inevitably, he has become. It is Brecht's unique achievement that he has reconciled two traditions in German literature which had been kept in different compartments before him, a state of affairs which had had most unfortunate effects on the cultural life of Germany. In Brecht the rough, plebeian, popular tradition and the sophisticated, academic, refined, respectable tradition have come together. Thanks to Brecht's achievement the work of the Austro-Bavarian folk comedians and the plays of the *poètes maudits* of the eighteenth and early nineteenth centuries appear in a new light and have assumed a new importance. And, what is more, by introducing his new, rough, popular, almost dialect tone,

Brecht succeeded in forging a new German stage idiom, which is neither the highly refined, but unnatural *Bühnendeutsch* (stage German) of the one nor the broad vernacular regional speech of the other tradition. This is an achievement which has greatly eased the difficulties of the generation of young postwar dramatists and poets in Germany.

Moreover, with his preference for exotic foreign locations in his youth, with his experience of Scandinavia, the Soviet Union, and the United States in his years of exile, Brecht had done much to break down the provincialism of much of German dramatic literature. And at the same time, having achieved international success, he put Germany on the map of international drama once again. So Brecht, the outsider and rebel, has a solid claim to enduring fame.

Not that Brecht hankered after posthumous recognition. Indeed, at times he insisted that he dreaded nothing more than elevation to the status of a classic, which to him meant condemnation to ultimate innocuousness as safe reading matter for schoolchildren. He wanted his work to become an active agent for genuine change in the social and cultural condition of man. But for the fact that he had lived, the tyrants might have sat a little more securely on their thrones. That was his hope. It is, however, more than doubtful whether Hitler's fall was speeded even by a second through the exertions of Brecht and other anti-Nazi intellectuals. On the other hand, Brecht's support hardly strengthened the position of that other tyrant, Stalin, by as much as one whit. Can the exertions of writers like Brecht change the social condition of man at all? Only indirectly: by changing man's sensibility, the atmosphere, the moral climate that surrounds him. But whether Brecht's view was correct or not, his striving in its tragic irony raises the matter of the artist's importance with the impact of a major test case. And for that, as well as for the beauty and depth of his poetry, Brecht merits a place among the great writers of his time.

# Selected Bibliography

## EDITIONS

### INDIVIDUAL WORKS

*Materialien zu Brechts "Leben des Galilei."* Edited by W. Hecht. Frankfurt am Main, 1963.

*Materialien zu Brechts "Mutter Courage und ihre Kinder."* Edited by W. Hecht. Frankfurt am Main, 1964.

*Der Jasager und Der Neinsager. Vorlagen, Fassungen und Materialien.* Edited by Peter Szondi. Frankfurt am Main, 1966.

*Baal. Der böse Baal, der Asoziale.* Edited by Dieter Schmidt. Frankfurt am Main, 1968.

*Im Dickicht der Städte. Erstfassung und Materialien.* Edited by Gisela E. Bahr. Frankfurt am Main, 1968.

*Leben Eduards des Zweiten von England. Vorlage, Texte und Materialien.* Edited by Reinhold Grimm. Frankfurt am Main, 1968.

*Materialien zu Brechts "Der gute Mensch von Sezuan."* Edited by W. Hecht. Frankfurt am Main, 1968.

*Der Brotladen: Ein Stückfragment. Bühnenfassung und Texte aus dem Fragment.* Frankfurt am Main, 1969.

*Kuhle Wampe. Protokoll des Films und Materialien.* Edited by W. Gersch and W. Hecht. Frankfurt am Main, 1969.

*Materialien zu Bertolt Brechts "Die Mutter."* Edited by W. Hecht. Frankfurt am Main, 1969.

*Texte für Filme.* Frankfurt am Main, 1969.

*Baal. Drei Fassungen.* Edited by Dieter Schmidt. Frankfurt am Main, 1970.

*Die heilige Johanna der Schlachthöfe. Bühnenfassung, Fragmente, Varianten.* Edited by Gisela E. Bahr. Frankfurt am Main, 1971.

*Die Massnahme. Kritische Ausgabe mit einer Spielanleitung.* Edited by Reiner Steinweg. Frankfurt am Main, 1972.

*Arbeitsjournal.* Frankfurt am Main, 1973.

*Materialien zu Brechts "Schweyk im Zweiten Weltkrieg."* Edited by Herbert Knust. Frankfurt am Main, 1974.

*Tagebücher 1920–1922. Autobiographische Aufzeichnungen 1920–1954.* Frankfurt am Main, 1975.

*Brechts Modell der Lehrstücke. Zeugnisse, Diskus-*

*sion, Erfahrungen.* Edited by Reiner Steinweg. Frankfurt am Main, 1976.

*Briefe.* Edited by Günter Glaeser. Frankfurt am Main, 1981.

*Gedichte aus dem Nachlass.* Frankfurt am Main, 1982.

COLLECTED WORKS

*Gesammelte Werke.* 20 vols. Frankfurt am Main, 1967.

*Werke, Grosse kommnetierte Berliner und Frankfurter Ausgabe.* 30 vols. Berlin and Weimar, 1988– .

## TRANSLATIONS

*Baal, A Man's a Man, The Elephant Calf.* New York, 1964.

*Brecht on Theatre.* Edited and translated by John Willett. New York, 1964.

*Collected Plays.* Edited by John Willett and Ralph Manheim. New York. Vol. 1 (1971): *Baal; Drums in the Night; In the Jungle of Cities; The Life of Edward II of England; The Wedding; The Beggar, or the Dead Dog; He Drives Out a Devil; Lux in Tenebris; The Catch.* Vol. 2 (1977): *A Man's a Man; Rise and Fall of the State of Mahagonny; The Threepenny Opera.* Vol. 5 (1972): *Life of Galileo; The Trial of Lucullus; Mother Courage and Her Children.* Vol. 6 (1976): *The Good Person of Szechwan; Puntila and Matti, His Hired Man; The Resistible Rise of Arturo Ui; Dansen; How Much Is Your Iron?; Practice Pieces for Actors.* Vol. 7 (1974): *The Visions of Simone Machard; Schweyk in the Second World War; The Caucasian Chalk Circle; The Duchess of Malfi.* Vol. 9 (1972): *The Tutor; Coriolanus; The Trial of Joan of Arc at Rouen, 1431; Don Juan; Trumpets and Drums.*

*Diaries 1920–1922.* Translated by John Willett. New York, 1979.

*Edward II.* New York, 1966.

*Galileo.* New York, 1966.

*Happy End.* New York, 1982.

*The Jewish Wife and Other Short Plays.* New York, 1965.

*Jungle of Cities and Other Plays.* New York, 1966.

*Manual of Piety (Die Hauspostille).* Translated by Eric Bentley. New York, 1966.

*The Messingkauf Dialogues.* Translated by John Willett. London, 1965.

*The Mother.* New York, 1965.

*Mother Courage and Her Children.* New York, 1966.

*Parables for the Theatre (The Good Woman of Setzuan, The Caucasian Chalk Circle).* New York, 1961.

*Poems, 1913–1956.* Edited by John Willett and Ralph Manheim. New York, 1987.

*Selected Poems.* Edited by H. R. Hays. New York, 1947.

*Seven Plays.* Edited by Eric Bentley. New York, 1961.

*Short Stories, 1921–1946.* Edited by John Willett and Ralph Manheim. New York, 1983.

*Tales from the Calendar.* Translated by Yvonne Kapp and Michael Hamburger. London, 1961.

*Threepenny Novel.* Translated by Desmond I. Vesey and Christopher Isherwood. New York, 1956.

*The Threepenny Opera.* New York, 1964.

*The Visions of Simone Machard.* New York, 1965.

## BIOGRAPHICAL AND CRITICAL STUDIES

Benjamin, Walter. *Understanding Brecht.* Translated by Anna Bostock. London, 1973.

Bentley, Eric. *The Brecht Commentaries.* New York, 1981.

Chiarini, P. *Bertolt Brecht.* Bari, Italy, 1959.

———. *Brecht e la dialettica del paradosso.* Milan, 1969.

Demetz, P., ed. *Brecht: A Collection of Critical Essays.* Englewood Cliffs, N.J., 1962.

Esslin, Martin. *Bertolt Brecht.* New York, 1969.

———. *Brecht: A Choice of Evils.* 4th rev. ed. London and New York, 1980.

———. *Meditations: Essays on Brecht, Beckett, and the Media.* Baton Rouge, La., 1980.

Ewen, Frederic. *Bertolt Brecht: His Life, His Art, and His Times.* New York, 1967.

Fassmann, Kurt. *Brecht: Eine Bildbiographie.* Munich, 1958.

Fuegi, John. *The Essential Brecht.* Los Angeles, 1972.

Gersch, Wolfgang. *Film bei Brecht.* Berlin, 1975.

Gray, Ronald. *Brecht the Dramatist.* Cambridge, England, 1976.

Grimm, Reinhold. *Bertolt Brecht, die Struktur seines Werks.* Nuremberg, 1959.

———. *Bertolt Brecht und die Weltliteratur.* Nuremberg, 1961.

———. *Brecht und Nietzsche.* Frankfurt am Main, 1979.

Hayman, Ronald. *Brecht: A Biography.* New York, 1983.

Hecht, W., ed. *Brecht im Gespräch. Diskussionen. Dialoge. Interviews.* Frankfurt am Main, 1975.

———, ed. *Bertolt Brecht. Sein Leben in Bildern und Texten.* Frankfurt am Main, 1978.

Hecht, W., H. Bunge, and K. Rülicke-Weiler. *Bertolt Brecht. Sein Leben und Werk.* Berlin, 1969.

Hinck, Walter. *Die Dramaturgie des späten Brecht.* Göttingen, 1959.

Hultberg, Helge. *Die ästhetischen Anschauungen Bertolt Brechts.* Copenhagen, 1962.

Ihering, Herbert. *Bertolt Brecht und das Theater.* Berlin, 1959.

Jendreiek, H. *Bertolt Brecht. Drama der Veränderung.* Düsseldorf, 1969.

Kesting, Marianne. *Bertolt Brecht in Selbstzeugnissen und Bilddokumenten.* Hamburg, 1959.

Klotz, Volker. *Bertolt Brecht, Versuch über das Werk.* Darmstadt, 1957.

Knopf, Jan. *Bertolt Brecht. Ein kritischer Forschungsbericht.* Frankfurt am Main, 1974.

Lyon, James K. *Bertolt Brecht and Rudyard Kipling.* The Hague, 1975.

———. *Bertolt Brecht in America.* Princeton, 1980.

Lyons, Charles R. *Bertolt Brecht: The Despair and the Polemic.* Carbondale, Ill., 1968.

Mann, Otto. *Mass oder Mythos: Ein kritischer Beitrag über die Schaustücke Bertolt Brechts.* Heidelberg, 1958.

Mayer, Hans. *Bertolt Brecht und die Tradition.* Pfullingen, 1961.

———. *Anmerkungen zu Brecht.* Frankfurt am Main, 1965.

———. *Brecht in der Geschichte.* Frankfurt am Main, 1971.

Mittenzwei, Werner. *Bertolt Brecht. Von der "Massnahme" zu "Leben des Galilei."* Berlin, 1962.

Müller, Klaus-Detlef. *Die Funktion der Geschichte im Werk Bertolt Brechts.* Tübingen, 1967.

Munk, Erika, ed. *Brecht.* New York, 1972.

Niessen, Carl. *Brecht auf der Bühme.* Cologne, 1959.

Pietzcker, Carl. *Die Lyrik des jungen Brecht.* Frankfurt am Main, 1974.

Reich, B. *Brecht.* Moscow, 1960.

Rischbieter, Henning. *Bertolt Brecht.* 2 vols. Velber bei Hannover, 1966.

Rosenbauer, H. *Brecht und der Behaviorismus.* Bad Homburg, 1970.

Rülicke-Weiler, Käthe. *Die Dramaturgie Brechts.* Berlin, 1966.

Schmidt, Dieter. *"Baal" und der junge Brecht.* Stuttgart, 1966.

Schuhmann, Klaus. *Der Lyriker Bertolt Brecht, 1913–1933.* Berlin, 1964.

Schumacher, Ernst. *Die dramatischen Versuche Bertolt Brechts 1918–1933.* Berlin, 1955.

———. *Der Fall Galilei. Das Drama der Wissenschaft.* Berlin, 1964.

———. *Drama und Geschichte. Bertolt Brechts "Leben des Galilei" und andere Stücke.* Berlin, 1965.

Schumacher, Ernst, and Renate Schumacher. *Leben Brechts.* Berlin, 1979.

Serreau, Genevieve. *Bertolt Brecht, dramaturge.* Paris, 1955.

Spalter, Max. *Brecht's Tradition.* Baltimore, Md., 1967.

Steinweg, Reiner. *Das Lehrstück.* Stuttgart, 1972.

Subiotto, A. *Bertolt Brecht's Adaptations for the Berliner Ensemble.* London, 1975.

Tatlow, Antony. *The Mask of Evil.* Bern, 1977.

Völker, Klaus. *Brecht Chronicle.* Translated by Fred Wieck. New York, 1975.

———. *Brecht: A Biography.* Translated by John Nowell. New York, 1978.

Wekwerth, Manfred. *Notate. Über die Arbeit des Berliner Ensembles 1956 bis 1966.* Frankfurt am Main, 1967.

———. *Schriften. Arbeit mit Brecht.* Berlin, 1973.

Willett, John. *The Theatre of Bertolt Brecht.* 4th rev. ed. London, 1977.

## BIBLIOGRAPHIES

Ramthun, Herta, ed. *Bertolt Brecht Archiv/ Bestandsverzeichnis des literarischen Nachlasses.* 4 vols. Berlin and Weimar, 1969–1973.

Seidal, Gerhard, ed. *Bibliographie Bertolt Brecht.* Vol. 1. Berlin and Weimar, 1975.

MARTIN ESSLIN

# ALBERT CAMUS

## *(1913–1960)*

"ABOUT CAMUS, THE writer, what can I say that has not been said, and said so aptly, so beautifully, that it debars one from adding any further cliché?" A little over a quarter of a century after Camus's death on 4 January 1960, the flow of critical studies, of books, articles, and colloquia confirms and challenges this statement, so modestly proffered by A. Noureddine. After a brief decline, since the late 1970's interest in Camus has again been on the rise. The span of years that distance us from Camus is brief. But in that interim the intellectual climate, notably in France, has shifted more than once. And so too has the map of the world and its areas of conflict. For Camus's contemporaries, his work punctuated a brief and momentous period between 1942, when *L'Étranger* (*The Stranger*), a short novel by an unknown young Algerian, was published in Paris under German occupation, bringing its author quasi-instant celebrity, and 1957, when *L'Exil et le royaume* (*Exile and the Kingdom,* 1957), a collection of short stories, came out as France and Algeria were about to plunge into the worst phase of a war that would end only in 1962, two years after Camus's death. Today, thanks to the work of many dedicated scholars, we know more about Camus than did his contemporaries—in fact, in some instances, more than he knew about himself. We can also better grasp the sociopolitical forces that transformed the Algeria of his youth from a colonial French territory, administered as a group of three French departments, to the independent Republic of Algeria.

### *A MANY-FACETED LIFE*

Actually, Camus's three-pronged career as journalist, man of the theater, and writer began not in 1942 with his first published work, but ten years earlier, far from Paris, when he was a student in Algiers. In 1960, when he died in an automobile accident in France, he was carrying the first draft of a new novel *Le premier homme* (The First Man). "I have turned down all engagements for 1960," he had written a friend. "It will be the year of my novel. It will require a lot of time, but I'll get it done." He was on his way to Paris to start on another venture, the direction of an experimental theater. Camus at forty-six still felt he could draw on what he once described humorously as a "consternating vitality." It was his death that cut short his writing, not as Patrick McCarthy has suggested, his death that saved him from the anguish of a "burnt-out" creativity. His whole career, to be sure, developed in times of war, revolutions, conflicting ideologies, and concentration camps. Passions ran high—passions that have not yet subsided. But where Camus is concerned we can by now disentangle his personality and accomplishments from the masks and distortions, the legends, misinformation, and gossip of the hour.

"At various times and in various countries," wrote Alexander Solzhenitsyn, the anti-Stalinist Russian writer who had corresponded with Camus, "there have arisen heated, angry and exquisite debates as to whether art and the artist should be free to live for themselves or whether they should be forever mindful of their duty toward society, albeit in an unprejudiced way." For himself, he added in his Nobel Prize acceptance speech (1970), there was "no dilemma." For Camus there was one, however. That dilemma underlies much of his writing. "As artists," he wrote at the time of his own Nobel Prize award in "Création et liberté" (Creation and Liberty),

> perhaps we do not need to intervene in the affairs of our time, but as men, yes. . . . From the time of my first articles to my latest book, I wrote a lot, perhaps too much, but because I cannot help being drawn to everyday concerns, on the side of those, whoever they may be, who are humiliated and downtrodden."
>
> (*Actuelles II: Chroniques 1948–1953,* in *Essais,* pp. 802–803)

Camus placed himself within a tradition that saw art as serving the needs of human beings, not human beings as serving the needs of art. He took no answers comfortably for granted but rather sought to reframe basic questions concerning human existence and commitments in the world, as truthfully as possible, in terms of the situation in the contemporary world as he knew it. What were the possible human answers to these questions? It is characteristic of Camus's work that in an age given to absolutes he, from the outset, thought in terms of diverse possibilities. The writer, he felt, could project such possibilities, leaving it up to readers to select among them and reach their own conclusions. The question of the artist's role was hotly debated by the European intelligentsia between the 1920's and the 1970's, fueled by the doctrinaire tenets of Marxist-Leninist thought. Camus's basic positions did not change over the years; what touched him deeply, rather than ideologies or aesthetic theories, was what he called "the human face," certainly not the allegedly inevitable "march of history."

Of all European writers of his generation, Sartre among them, Camus was, during his lifetime, the writer who commanded the widest international attention. A journalist by profession, he had started his career in uneven combat against the inequities suffered by the Muslim population under French colonial rule in Algeria. Later, during the years of clandestine warfare in Nazi-occupied France, he found himself at the hub of the ideological warfare that sharply divided that country through the climactic mid century years into the early 1970's. He could hardly have avoided becoming enmeshed in what seems to us today the obsessive, often specious, political argumentation of intellectual infighting. The Algerian war of independence was not calculated to ease the tensions and hostilities that his meteoric fame inspired among those rivals he had outdistanced, or those who disagreed with his stance. Yet his critics, momentarily disarmed by his death, registered dismay in the face of the double loss: of the man himself and the anticipated work he would have produced. "Whatever he did or decided in the future," wrote Sartre, "he could never have ceased to be one of the major forces in our cultural field, nor in his way could he have ceased to represent the history of France and our century."

Admirers of Camus tended to represent an idealized, often sentimentalized, image of the man; opponents tended to distort and to diminish the character, scope, and accomplishments of the complex human being he was. His contemporaries tended to cast Camus in the role of "representative man," often reproaching him, then, with the image. Camus did not cherish the role. His ambition had never been to "represent the history of France" or that of the century, but only to produce a literary work of intrinsic worth that would truthfully reflect his own experience. Such works, he often repeated, alone allowed him to integrate, reconcile, and discipline the violent feelings and contradictions that characterized his own passionate and basically unruly personality. His writing expressed his feelings, struggles, perplexities, and development—transmuted into objective literary works by the severe discipline he imposed upon himself. That is perhaps why Camus's work elicited so wide and immediate a response from far beyond the boundaries of France. Already in 1968 a complete bibliography, prepared by Robert Roeming, of articles dealing with Camus listed some three thousand items from almost every part of the world, including, in addition to the countries of Western Europe, Scandinavia, Poland, Hungary, Turkey, Israel; the United States, Puerto Rico, Mexico; the nations of South America and of Africa; Japan, Formosa, and India. According to a UNESCO survey made in the 1960's, Camus's work had been translated by then into thirty-two foreign languages.

### *Origins*

Albert Camus was born on 7 November 1913 in the small town of Mondovi (now called Drean), south of Bone (now Annaba) in what was then French Algeria, which the French considered not a colony, but a "department" of France. Camus did not live to see the change that in 1962, with the end of the Algerian war for independence, made Algeria a fully autonomous republic. There, as noted above, French place-names were soon replaced by Arabic or Berber ones. Camus's forebears, according to a legend in the family, had supposedly come to Algeria from Alsace after the Franco-Prussian War. Actually, as Camus's biographer Herbert Lottman has proved, they had come to Algeria much earlier, probably soon after the 1830 conquest by the French. They came from the Bordeaux region and the Massif Central, the very heart of France. Camus on his father's side was thus a fourth-generation French Algerian. His maternal ancestors came from the island of Minorca, a Spanish possession with an ancient culture and character of its own. In a sense, then, Camus was indeed justified when he claimed a "Mediterranean" rather than a French inheritance. His was a family of poor, illiterate, hardworking people. Lucien Camus, the father, was employed in a wine-making enterprise and had learned to read and write; his wife, Catherine Camus, like the rest of the family, had not. Drafted in 1914, Lucien was badly wounded at the battle of the Marne and died in France of his wounds.

Shortly before Albert's first birthday, Catherine moved into her mother's two-room apartment in the working-class section of Algiers with her two sons. She worked first in a munitions factory, then, after the war, as a cleaning woman. Camus was brought up in stringent circumstances. Five people were crowded into the apartment: a harsh grandmother, an infirm uncle, Camus's almost deaf, silent, and strangely undemonstrative mother, and the two boys. The younger boy, Albert, was deeply though mutely attached to his mother, whose presence haunts many of his books. His childhood world laid the foundation for his lifelong commitment to the nonprivileged and the manner in which he related to them; he always saw them as individuals, with their human idiosyncrasies, foibles, and needs, never under collective categorizations such as "the proletariat" or "the masses." This is the human world that marks his first books.

Of a family that "lacked almost everything and envied almost nothing," Camus spoke retrospectively with gratitude: "Merely by its silence, its reserve, its natural and restrained pride, these people, who could not even read, gave me the highest teaching." He enjoyed, besides, the freedom of the working-class boy, in a world devoid of television and, for him at first, empty of books. He roamed the beaches and the busy port and silently absorbed the sensuous beauty of the Mediterranean coast. It was shaping his vision of the world, his sense of his physical bond with his environment long before it became a concept and a personal myth. "Poverty was never a misfortune for me," he wrote of those childhood years, "for it was flooded with light." Many years later he linked together in a single sentence the "two or three great and simple images" that defined his sensitivity—the silent, uncomplaining mother, the light, the beauty of the world. Unlike the childhood of many of France's prominent writers, his predecessors or contemporaries—notably Proust, Gide, and Sartre—his was not a childhood turned in on itself. He was an active, outgoing child who participated in the physical pleasures of his peers—swimming, football, and later, as a spectator, boxing.

Camus was ten years old when an intervention from outside gave a new impetus to his life. His grade-school teacher, Louis Germain, noticed his unusual potentialities, tutored the child, and persuaded his somewhat recalcitrant family to let him pursue his education, first as a scholarship student at the lycée, to which he was admitted in 1924, and then, with the help of another great master, the writer-philosopher Jean Grenier, at the University of Algiers (1933). Louis Germain was a stern disciplinarian who shaped Camus's meticulous attention to the rigors of "classical" French as codified in the rules and examples taught in the French academic system. Camus, who was a born mimic, could use and enjoy the popular Algerian street idiom, the "Cagayous," as it was called. But as a writer he remained faithful to the established literary patterns of the French language; this at a time when in France, under the impetus of Dada and surrealism, writers like Raymond Queneau, Louis-Ferdinand Céline, and (to a lesser degree) Sartre were attempting to bridge the gap between spoken and literary French. In part it may have been the combination of Camus's fresh lyrical sense, his vision of a world steeped in light, and a literary style stripped of all irrelevancies that contributed to his initial success.

### *Beginnings*

At twenty, Camus had come a long way from the austere world of his childhood, yet not without some setbacks. At seventeen he had suffered the first virulent attack (very nearly fatal) of the pulmonary tuberculosis that was to plague him all his life. After a period of despair he reacted with typical energy. He left home, worked at various jobs, and began his studies in philosophy at the University of Algiers.

The University of Algiers was a good place for a talented young man to be and it had a decisive influence on his career. There he was soon one of a group of friends, some of them lifelong, who shared his enthusiasms and with whom he came to know a freedom and range of thought and speech new to him. The group, in the liberal context of the university, voiced its disagreements with the sociopolitical attitudes and institutions of colonial society and with the optimism of youth set out to challenge them. Its members were not popular with the local colonial authorities. They were eager too to keep abreast of Paris, proud of their "Mediterranean" heritage, and determined to put North Africa on the literary map. They were of varying origins: French, Italian, Spanish, and in the case of a few—very few—Muslim. In the early 1930's there was a feeling of excitement and hope abroad before the upsurge of fascism, the hope that a new world was in the making, the utopian world of official Marxism. Far from the European scene, in the happier, more relaxed atmosphere of prewar Algiers, Camus and his group shared this optimism. These were happy days for the young man who, off and on, shared the communal life of student friends living in what he called "the house facing the world," a starkly furnished villa overlooking the bay of Algiers. These friendships certainly softened the emotional disaster of his marriage at age 21 to a brilliant, much sought-after young woman who had charmed him by her fanciful turn of mind, which was in large part due to her addiction to drugs. Two years later they separated, when Camus discovered she was not given to marital fidelity.

In 1935, Camus joined the Communist party, though rather unenthusiastically. He soon became restive under the constraints imposed on him and was excluded from the party, or—according to his version—resigned. This brief association had positive consequences. Under the aegis of the Communist party leadership, anxious to develop a sense of cultural solidarity with the working class, cultural centers were being organized. For a while Camus directed the cultural center in Algiers and realized one of his dreams: the creation of a theater group. His "workers' theater," launched in 1935, outlived his commitment to the party. It became a "group theater," was renamed Le Théâtre de l'Équipe, and ran successfully until the outbreak of World War II. It presented an eclectic program ranging from an adaptation of Aeschylus' *Prometheus Bound* to the adaptation of a recent André Malraux novel, *Le temps du mépris* (*Days of Wrath,* 1935) and included works by Synge, Gide, Gorky, Pushkin, and Rojas. Camus, director, adaptor, actor, and publicity manager, was at the center of all the activity. A collectively written play of immediate sociopolitical relevance, *Révolte dans les Asturies* (Revolt in the Asturias), based on a 1934 miner's strike in Spain, was scheduled for production in 1936 but was banned by the administrative authorities: the outbreak of the Spanish Civil War had served to reinforce the reactionary tendencies of the local colonial authorities. Camus was by now skirmishing on two fronts: against the PCA (the Communist Party of Algeria) on the Left, and against the local colonial authorities on the Right. He had begun to write around 1932, and from 1935 on—as shown by the notebooks he kept until his death (published as *Carnets* in 1962 and 1964)—he was determined to become a writer. In those early years he was working simultaneously on a novel, on a play already entitled *Caligula,* and on an essay. Two slim books of essays came out in Algiers—*L'Envers et l'endroit* (*The Wrong Side and the Right Side,* 1937) and *Noces* (*Nuptials at Tipasa,* 1939).

The year 1938 was a crucial one. Camus had intended to become a professor, but he could not pass the medical examination required by the government. He then turned to journalism, writing for a liberal left-wing paper, *Alger Républicain.* Reporting on scandalous instances of the miscarriage of justice, then on the desperate plight of the Berber peasants in Kabylia, Camus began to show unsuspected strengths.

### *The Years in Europe*

Literature, philosophy, theater, journalism, a deep concern with social justice—by 1938 the main lines of Camus's activity and interests were established. With the outbreak of World War II, events beyond his control were to project him out of Algeria and onto the European scene. Although Camus was released from the obligation to serve in the military for reasons of health, his paper was suppressed by the Algerian authorities because of its openly pro-peace and pro-Arab sentiments, and he himself was requested to leave; Camus consequently moved to Paris in March 1940 to work on the staff of the daily *Paris-Soir.* He married again in Lyons in December 1940 and returned to Oran in January 1941. From that time until the end of 1943 or early 1944, the date to which his activity in the clandestine underground network Combat can be traced, Camus led a somewhat disjointed life. Without a job, he first taught in a private institution for Jewish children who had been crassly expelled from the Oran lycée. His health deteriorated, however, and in 1942 he returned to France, moving to the Cévennes mountains for therapeutic treatment. The Allied landing in Casablanca cut him off from his wife and Algerian friends; he would be able to return only in 1945. Meanwhile in Paris, *The Stranger* and *Le mythe de Sisyphe* (*The Myth of Sisyphus,* 1942) brought him immediate recognition. He left for Paris in the spring of 1943 to work as a reader for the publishing firm of Gallimard. In the fall of that year, under the name of Beauchard, he assumed the responsibility for the publication and diffusion of the news sheet *Combat* (organ of the network of the same name)—a dangerous task. Camus also wrote under the name of Albert Mahé. He narrowly escaped from the

Gestapo when arrested while carrying a layout for an issue of *Combat.* When, with the liberation of Paris on 24 August 1944, *Combat* came out in the open, Camus, at thirty-one, enjoyed a double fame. He was awarded the Medal of the Liberation, a rare honor.

From 1944 on, Camus's public life reflects the agitations and the almost unbearable disappointments that followed the Liberation. After 1954 the savage Algerian conflict that he had predicted tore at his heart. Of the many editorials and articles he wrote during that decade, only a few are available in English—unfortunately, for they present a chronicle of the swiftly changing atmosphere and the startling events of those years. They show the evolution of a thought that was to lead, in 1951, to the publication of *L'Homme révolté* (*The Rebel*), an essay that sparked a bitter controversy and consecrated the rift that had been growing between Sartre and Camus. Four plays, produced with varying success—*Le malentendu* (*The Misunderstanding,* 1944), *Caligula* (1944), *L'État de siège* (*State of Siege,* 1948), and *Les justes* (*The Just Assassins,* 1949)—had been accompanied by a long novel, *La peste* (*The Plague,* 1947). *The Rebel* marked a new point of departure, which *La chute* (*The Fall,* 1956) emphasized. New themes and new techniques characterized his volume of short stories *Exile and the Kingdom* (1957). Once again Camus became involved with the stage, adapting and directing a half dozen plays, two with success—Faulkner's *Requiem for a Nun* (1956) and Dostoevsky's *The Possessed* (1959).

A merely factual account of Camus's life leaves out the essential. Camus belonged to a generation deeply affected by historical circumstances. He recalled in his Nobel Prize acceptance speech in Stockholm the "more than twenty years of absolutely insane history," when he had felt "lost hopelessly like all of [his] age in the convulsions of the epoch." He had been twenty when Hitler came to power in the politically agitated 1930's. He had seen the rise of several great totalitarian states, the collapse of the socialist and liberal movements in Europe, the purges in Russia, police terrorism and torture spreading over Europe, total war, and concentration camps. The Algerian conflict was at its height when he died. It was an era not calculated to inspire serenity. Besides the toll taken in time, energy, and health, Camus felt that the times had also imposed on his work an orientation it might not otherwise have had.

Like many young intellectuals—even more than most, perhaps, because he came from an inarticulate proletarian group—he felt the need to rethink the world, to make sense of what he, along with millions of others, was witnessing and experiencing. The ideas he developed in his essays, the themes that patterned his work, were not abstract exercises in theoretical logic or literary games. He was accustomed to harsh realities, and with these he grappled intellectually, convinced that thought must be welded to action, that there are more fundamental elements involved in human conduct than the niceties of theoretical verbal argumentation.

Brutal as they were, the years between the two world wars in France were rich in artistic achievement and intellectual ferment. There were undoubtedly two sides to the coin: a sense of doom, but also a restless, exciting sense of a new world in the making. Both were reflected in the arts and the violence of the ideological conflicts that kept the French outside totalitarianism but took them instead to the brink of civil war. Algeria as Camus knew it was, at first, the coastal city of Algiers on the periphery of all the European agitation, more stable in appearance, gayer, more confident in the future. In his first essays, with a keen eye for the shortcomings of his compatriots and a sense of humor all the freer because it was directed at himself as well, Camus described the typical North African attitudes—the elementary ethics, the reliance on immediate, uncomplicated physical satisfactions in a land that lavishly proffered them, the religious and metaphysical void, a mute accord with the natural elements and the beauty of the Mediterranean homeland, and an equally mute horror of death—attitudes of a people he described as gay and resigned, without traditions, "without questions." Camus's illness seemed to have awakened his mind to questions he might otherwise have ignored, questions that dominated post–World War I philosophical debate. He explored the many avenues of secular philosophy, the Greeks, the philosophers of history—G. W. F. Hegel, Karl Marx, and Oswald Spengler—and the existential and phenomenological thinkers who were rapidly replacing Kant in the minds of the young: Søren Kierkegaard, Friedrich Nietzsche, Edmund Husserl, Karl Jaspers, Martin Heidegger.

But unlike his brilliant French predecessors and contemporaries Gabriel Marcel, Maurice Merleau-Ponty, Jean-Paul Sartre, and Simone de Beauvoir, Camus did not think of himself as a professional philosopher. He was not interested in building a coherent, systematic, philosophical explanation of man's situation in the world. In fact, he had a rational aversion toward all such systems. He never wished to speak as a specialist. Perhaps because of his background he was much more interested in becoming, in a Socratic sense, a man with an ethic. On ethical grounds he had rejected an ideology that in the Stalin-dominated 1930's was, he had come to feel, merely a facade cynically masking political opportunism and the repressive mechanisms of a police state. What he diagnosed as the dominant mood of his time was the widespread existence of a fundamental nihilism, whether latent or carefully reasoned. The intellectual skepticism born of political experience and philosophical eclecticism; the onslaught against the various forms of rationalism inherited from the Enlightenment; Nietzsche's attacks on Western values; Spengler's prophecies of doom, grafted on prevalent notions concerning the predetermined course of history—these merely gave that nihilism its arguments.

With literature, Camus was thoroughly at home. His early book reviews in *Alger Républicain,* two of them of Sartre's first fictional works; the critical essays he wrote throughout his career, the two earliest of which (on Dostoevsky and Kafka) he later included in *The Myth of Sisyphus;* the notes he jotted down and the prefaces he wrote—all give a fair account of his tastes. He shared the predilection of his generation for Dostoevsky, Kafka, Faulkner, and Hemingway. But he also made his own choice among the "greats" in literature, a classical choice—the Greeks, Shakespeare, and the French classics, along with Herman Melville (according to Camus, one of those truly great writers). Of the brilliant group of French writers during the 1920's and 1930's, three gained his sympathetic attention: Henry de Montherlant, whose haughty isolation and aristocratic ethic he admired; Jean Giono, whose love of the elemental beauty of the world he shared; and André Malraux, whose tense and dramatic investigation of modern man's "fate," as it was being molded in the great revolutionary movements of the Far East, raised questions that echoed in Camus's own mind. But to no one of the moderns did he give his full allegiance.

In these prewar years, still bathed for him in Mediterranean light and vibrant with energy, Camus wrote his first series of works. A novel, *The Stranger,* a play, *Caligula;* and an essay, *The Myth of Sisyphus,* developed almost simultaneously. In his *Notebooks* he later grouped them together under a single label—"Sisyphus: Cycle of the Absurd." A fourth work, belonging to the same group, *The Misunderstanding,* was in an embryonic state in 1939. It serves as a kind of transition to the second group of Camus's works, the Promethean cycle.

Although, toward the end of his career, the lyrical essays collected in *L'Été* (*Summer,* 1954) and the short stories of *Exile and the Kingdom* seem unrelated to any preconceived design, the pattern of this first series of works was maintained by Camus. In the postwar years he produced a novel, *The Plague;* two plays, *The Just Assassins* and *State of Siege;* and an essay, *The Rebel.* He grouped these under the label—"Prometheus: Cycle of Revolt." His *Notebooks* show that he had projected further developments: a cycle of Nemesis, or measure; a cycle dealing with love or compassion. In each case he projected a novel, plays, an essay. To a question that concerned the relationship of his essays to his novels and plays, Camus answered:

> I write on different levels precisely to avoid mixing genres. So I wrote plays in the language of action, essays in the rational form, novels about the heart's obscurity. True, these different kinds of books say the same thing. But, after all, they were written by the same author and, together, form a single work.
>
> ("A Final Interview" [with Robert Spector], *Venture* 3–4:35–38 [1960])

A single work, a single author, but the "cycles" of Camus's work reflect in turn different atmospheres: prewar Algiers, with its predictable routines and enjoyments; the tense dreary days of occupation, with their regimentation and dull horror; the intellectual confusion and frustrated political idealism of the fifties; the slow return to the rhythm and concerns of private living. Camus seems to have been exceptionally sensitive to the complex emotional, political, and intellectual currents of his time.

## *THE WRITING*

### *Early Work: The Writer as Reporter*

Readers of *The Stranger,* the first of Camus's works to reach a wide audience, were tempted to identify the narrator's point of view with Camus's own, so persuasive was the author's use of first-person narration. The facts belie any such simple identification. During the years when he was working on the novel Camus was at work on other projects, including his writing as a journalist—one of a small team of men, French, French-Algerian, and Muslim—who labored to keep afloat an "independent" local paper, dedicated to the defense of the working class and to "the political and social emancipation of the Algerian people," while maintaining high standards of accuracy in reporting. The wave of reaction against the social reforms of the Socialist "popular government" was running strong in Algeria. The intent of the paper was to counteract that reaction by informing its readers as to the implications of both local and metropolitan policies. *Alger Républicain,* a daily morning paper, under ever-closer surveillance by police forces as international tensions increased, became *Soir Républicain,* an afternoon sheet reduced in format, until it was suspended early in 1940. Both papers were judged locally as highly subversive.

Camus's contributions to the paper, largely unknown in France, were later collected and published in toto under the apt title *Fragments d'un combat* (Fragments of a Combat, 1978), though perhaps "skirmish" would be a better term; they are "fragments" because taken together they furnish a kind of running commentary on the local Algerian situation as it developed from day to day in those years. "Algeria" at the time designated a vast territory, comprising a variety of regions, from the rich coastal Sahel to arid stretches of desert. Tribes and villages, widely scattered as one moved south, offered different modes of social organization, the single bond betweeen them being Islam. Algerian nationalism was to grow and define itself only in the coming years. Young Camus's Algeria was essentially the coastal Algiers in which he lived. It was his work as a reporter that took him farther afield and broadened his Algiers-centered point of view, one that the disastrous French situation between 1940 and 1945 was temporarily to eclipse. In the following years Camus joined forces in another combat. World War II had strengthened his aversion to the use of violence for resolving power conflicts in the world. One of his major concerns in the next years would be the battle for peace. But in the prewar years Camus's commitment was simpler, within a complex and sometimes contradictory situation. For him the inequities suffered by the Muslim population under the colonial regime were intolerable and in contradiction with the principles of a democratic regime. This position never changed; rather, as the political climate degenerated, the proposals he put forward as a political solution to the problem were changed.

Camus's reports and investigations are concerned with specific events in clearly defined conditions, and they aim at achieving practical results. He had been active for a couple of years in the local Communist party cell and was familiar with the infighting among the Muslim factions dissatisfied with the colonial regime. However, his articles are aimed not at them, but at his European-Algerian readers: his targets were the arrogant, high-handed local administrators, more particularly the notoriously reactionary mayor of Algiers.

A reporter is, in essence, an observer. As narrator of what he was observing, Camus often wrote in the first person singular. The "I" brought into play the rhetoric of a detached "cool" witness. But Camus also used pseudonyms: Zaks, Demos, Vincent Capable, Irenaeus, Jean Meursault. Camus devolved functions to these "I's" and to each an elementary personality defined by a style: tongue-in-cheek candor, deadly irony, earnest puzzlement, and bland self-righteousness. These stylistic games open the text to laughter and allow a distancing of the reader from the text that encourages critical readings: satire, irony, parody, caricature enter into play, creating complicity between readers and writer; "everyday" modes of behavior and opinion take on the aura of patent absurdity. An example in the realm of parody is "The Manifesto of Integral Conformism," presented as a solemn declaration of unconditional support for administrative policies by a group of "conscious and determined conformists." Their earnest endorsements of current slogans, regardless of consistency, builds up to a deadpan phantasmagoria of absurdity. Behind the masquerades of language, Camus was tilting at the masquerades of power. More serious are his attacks against the "regrettable" mayor of Algiers and the "puppet show" of city council meetings at which the mayor is described as making a mockery of the rules of democratic representation by blatantly manipulating the procedure in order to reduce the legally elected Muslim delegates to a humiliating silence. Masks and masquerades, "voices" rising in dialogue or confrontation within a common situation, are inherent to Camus's literary creations. Consciously used, they illustrate Camus's refusal to deal in verbal absolutes or the dialectics so popular with intellectuals at the time.

When, in contrast, Camus comes face to face with the reality of human degradation within the system, masks are discarded, and the "I" speaks in the voice of Camus himself, as in his reportage on the plight of the Berbers in the famine-stricken mountain community of Kabylia. The report is accompanied by photographs. Shame, pity, horror, outrage, and revolt accompany Camus's "itinerary" through the lands of famine, where the degradation of individual human beings is inseparable from the disintegration of a community. Famine is a plague. The famine in Africa in the mid 1980's recorded on our television screens, has made those images of extreme deprivation familiar to us. The young reporter's reaction is not far removed from the popular upsurge of emotion that triggered the flow of help to aid the victims of famine in Ethiopia in 1984. Camus's urgent appeal for immediate practical forms of help, beyond all political or ideological concerns, came up short against that other reality—a European war and then, a world war, which for a short while made of North Africa an adjunct to France. But ideological conflicts had definitely given way in Camus's vision of reality to a concern for the devastations wrought by political powers under whatever language they were officially justified.

The Kabylian episode seems to have been an important stage on Camus's way in search of his own "voice," a voice that would account for his experience in the world. Camus had left behind for good the temptation to accept doctrinaire systems of meaning such as Marxism offered. He was an agnostic, but also a philosophy student. The unexamined life of the working-class men and women among whom he lived as a child could not satisfy him. He shared the human need to make sense of the world and alongside his craft as journalist had turned to other forms of writing.

### *The Cycle of the Absurd*

In 1937 and 1939 two small, very different, autobiographical volumes of essays by Camus, *The Wrong Side and the Right Side* and *Nuptials at Típasa,* were printed locally in Algiers. Meanwhile he was working on a more ambitious project, a three-pronged group of connected works: novel, play, essay. All three dealt with a single theme, a theme that had become familiar to the post–World War I generation of intellectuals attuned to the "anti-Kantian–anti-Hegelian" philosophical trend represented by Kierkegaard and Nietzsche: the confrontation between the human need to make sense of the world and the human perception of the world's silence and opacity. This was the experience of what he called "the absurd." Camus's trilogy deals with alternative ways of confronting it, of construing a lived experience in an attempt to give it significance, if not meaning. The *Notebooks* indicate that he worked on the trilogy for many years; preliminary versions were completed while he was living in Algeria and were later revised considerably, no doubt under the impact of the historical conjuncture.

The five essays in *The Wrong Side and the Right Side*—"Irony," "Between Yes and No," "Death in the Soul," "Love of Life," and the title essay—combined brief vignettes of the Algerian working-class milieu with an orchestration of two fundamental and contradictory themes: the "nothingness" that lies at the heart of human life and the glory of life itself. *Nuptials at Típasa* develops with lyrical eloquence the two themes of life and death against the background of the Mediterranean landscape: the glory of life in "the morning sun" of Típasa and the "great joy" filling the vast space of sky and sea; the certainty of death voiced by the "arid splendor" of the dead city of Djémila; life, savored on the burning Algerian beaches in the heart of the summer; the reconciliation with death glimpsed among the gentle hills of Italy. In no immediate sense was young Camus a stranger among men or to this earth. "I am happy, on this earth," he wrote in his *Notebooks,* "for my kingdom is of this earth." And Patrice, his first fictional hero, reiterates: "I shall speak of nothing but my love of life."

It has become customary, when discussing *The Stranger,* to see the story not as fiction but as the fictionalization of an abstract philosophy of the "absurd." Camus perhaps is partly responsible for the misunderstanding, having himself launched the term. But the preface to the *Myth of Sisyphus* expressly states that a philosophy of the absurd is precisely what we lack, and it was not Camus's intent to furnish that philosophy. Through the *Notebooks* we can follow the adventures the novel underwent between 1935 and May 1940, when it was finished. Publication was delayed until 1942 amid the chaos of the French defeat.

Camus had envisaged a quite different book, *La vie heureuse* (A Happy Life), as a semiautobiographical novel to be presented through a third-person hero, a would-be writer, Patrice Mersault. Camus wrote a first and then a second version, in the course of which the title shifted to *La mort heureuse* (*A Happy Death,* 1971). As he worked, certain themes of *The Stranger* appeared, sometimes separately, sometimes connected with the story but lost in a maze of other themes. *The Stranger* took shape slowly, through trial and error, the result of a long circuitous search. The book that emerged was strikingly different from the one Camus had planned.

*The Stranger.* The story of *The Stranger* is uncomplicated, on the surface at least. Meursault, an office clerk in Algiers, receives a telegram announcing the death of his mother in an old people's home. He asks for a two-day leave, attends the funeral, and then comes back to Algiers. He goes to the beach, picks up a girlfriend, Marie, and takes her to the movies. They then go to his apartment and make love. By chance, he becomes involved in the unsavory affairs of a neighbor, Raymond, a pimp who starts a dangerous feud with some Arabs. One Sunday, Raymond, Meursault, and Marie go off together for an outing. The Arabs follow them. Raymond gets into a fight. Later, Meursault, who prudently had taken Raymond's revolver, encounters one of the Arabs. A knife flashes in the sun, Meursault pulls the trigger. . . . He is arrested, tried, and condemned to death.

Although *A Happy Death* had little in common with *The Stranger,* two of its themes point to the two centers of tension in the later novel: a mother-son estrangement and a man sentenced to death. It is only little by little that the estranged son became the man sentenced to death and that Camus provided him with an act—a murder—justifying the sentence. Whatever interpretations *The Stranger* may suggest, and they are many, one should not forget that his novels, as Camus said, speak of the "obscurity" of the human heart. It was the voice of the man sentenced to death that had spoken first, though not alone, in the heart of the young Camus, who as an adolescent had almost died in complete solitude, faced with the surprising indifference of the world, an indifference which seems to have long echoed in his own empty heart. Meursault's fundamental trait, his indifference, seems to be—in part at least—a reflection of that initial experience: hence the power this singular hero derived over his creator's imagination.

"Today Mother died, or perhaps yesterday. . . ." So begins the novel. Camus, after much experimentation, adopted for *The Stranger* a form of the widely used first-person narrative technique. Meursault tells his own story as it evolves. Attempts have been made to discover a definite point in time from which Meursault views the events he recalls, but they have all been unsuccessful. Questionable if discussed on realistic grounds, the device was obviously chosen for aesthetic reasons and proved to be remarkably persuasive. Because of the shifting perspective of his story, the controlling point of view is not entirely Meursault's. He is unaware of the future ramifications of his acts, himself advancing blindly toward a trap carefully laid for him by the circumstances he notes. His position is curiously analogous to what happens in a dream, where the dreamer both evolves the dream and lives in it; yet, unlike the nightmarish world of Kafka, the world of Meursault is a brilliantly lighted, clearly delineated, everyday world—that of Algiers.

The narrative device chosen by Camus has advantages: the persuasive immediacy of the situations described, the creation of a climate of chance, suspense, and yet inevitability, and for Camus the freedom to create sharp fluctuations in the reader's emotional reaction to Meursault. The first pages are told in a low-keyed, matter-of-fact tone, and the reader views the funeral and the old people's home and its inhabitants through Meursault's eyes. But as Meursault proceeds, telling of his return, his involvement with Marie and then with Raymond, the reader becomes alarmed. He finds himself obliged to view and judge from the outside, even though he is entirely dependent upon Meursault for the facts and atmosphere of the story itself. A first distancing is created, but strictly within the confines of Meursault's self-contained world. The novel ends in uncertainty, so far as Meursault's immediate fate is concerned. The appeal on his behalf submitted by his lawyer has not been acted upon, a loophole is left. The voice of Meursault therefore is the voice of a living man, a man sentenced to death to be sure, but one who, within the limits of the novel, unlike us, will never die. Begun as the most ordinary of anecdotes concerning the most indistinguishable of men, the novel thus moves toward myth. Set apart from all men because he killed a man, judged and condemned to the guillotine, Meursault, speaking to us as a "man sentenced to death" exemplifies the most universally shared human situation that exists. Thence, no doubt, the enigmatic quality of the character.

The story falls into two parts: the account of the events that lead Meursault from his mother's funeral to the murder on the beach and the events that concern Meursault's imprisonment and trial. They stop just short of his execution. Factual in appearance, the first part describes a routine life, lived among ordinary people, carrying with it a flavor of sun and sea, the sense of a direct semiconscious, nonverbalized enjoyment of simple physical things—swimming, sunshine, the softness and charm of a young girl's presence. The second part of the story brings no new events, only a judgment. It takes place indoors—whether prison or courthouse—and in solitude or, as during the trial, moral solitude. But the young man who in the opening pages of the book had asked his boss for leave to attend his mother's funeral has traveled a long way by the time he reaches the end of his tale.

Behind Meursault there is, of course, Camus the novelist, who controls both Meursault's changing experience and the reader's reactions, invisibly manipulating a situation that seems to move inexorably of its own momentum. He can thus charge it indirectly with a dramatic irony that is not always apparent at the first reading. It underlies the focal situation—murder, however unintentional—and the focal problem: the relation of Meursault to his act. The events that lead to Meursault's fatal encounter with the Arab on the beach are set up with great care. At first they do not concern Meursault at all. The Arabs' anger is directed at Raymond, Meursault's neighbor, for his blatantly brutal treatment of his Arab mistress. Meursault is involved only indirectly, by association. Even the revolver he holds at the time of the shooting is not his. He had taken it from Raymond as a precaution against violence. When he pulls the trigger, in the heat of the midday sun, his gesture is irrational, unforeseen, unmotivated.

Implicated in a quarrel not his own, driven by the violent pressure of outer elemental circumstances—the pitiless glare and heat of the sun—a man has killed another man. There is no going back on the act. Excluding all ordinary "psychological" motivations for the crime, Camus carefully designed Meursault's situation so that the mechanisms of chance and outer pressure would lead to this brief loss of control.

Meursault is obviously not a "criminal" type. There is little to distinguish him except his tendency to say nothing and a kind of passive gentleness: he is friendly, sympathetic to others, apparently content with a life he sees no reason to change. He is scrupulous in the expression of his feelings, but apparently far more indifferent with regard to his acts. He likes to make love to Marie, but he will not say he loves her. Yet he acquiesces when she suggests marriage. He acquiesces too soon when Raymond involves him in his plan of vengeance, and thereby supports Raymond's primitive ethical code. Behind the character's seemingly disconnected acts one begins to see a constant: Meursault is a man who acquiesces in what is. His inertia leads to the irrevocable last acquiescence, the finger on the trigger, and the forcible transformation of his life.

At no time does Meursault plead innocence, nor does Camus at any time suggest that he is innocent. That with the shooting something has gone irrevocably wrong, Meursault knows immediately, though he understands neither what nor why. After the murder is committed, we move away from the deceptively realistic tone of the narrative toward a far more stylized treatment of Meursault's situation.

The second part of the novel is concerned with the enigmatic problem of Meursault's act, a problem as puzzling to Meursault as to the reader. Camus makes short shrift of the usual interpretations, presenting them ironically in Meursault's semiburlesque interviews with the prosecutor, magistrate, and lawyer, and in his account of his trial. The first-person narrative now establishes a strange dissociation between the facts and feelings Meursault had previously described and the attempts made by others to interpret these coherently. A definite shift in perspective is introduced: the reader finds himself in the position of judge, jury, and privileged witness. He and Meursault alone know the facts. Camus has thereby put upon the reader the burden of providing an explanation Meursault is unable to furnish. Self-critical and self-correcting, the novel rapidly moves toward its end.

The official characters Meursault encounters during his imprisonment and trial are little more than subtly wrought masks, incarnating and deliberately satirizing interpretations that Camus rejects as irrelevant—guilt, remorse, atonement, conversion. The trial itself, seen from the outside, is little more than a grotesque preview of the many possible arguments for or against Meursault, his character and motivations. They leave Meursault intact and the problem of his act unsolved.

Meanwhile, in his prison Meursault awakens to a new dimension of life, an inner awareness that he had totally lacked. The death sentence, after an initial shock, finally sets him on the path of an epiphany that reaches back to the beginning of the novel, wrenches Meursault out of his passive state, and prepares him to counter the terror of death with the concentration of all the forces of life. His apparent indifference to his mother's death, to Marie's love, drops from him like a cloak as he confronts the chaplain who comes to speak to him of compensation in an afterlife. In the solitude of his prison, what Meursault reaches for goes deeper than guilt and remorse. He had acquiesced to the "natural death" of his mother and was indifferent to the rituals with which society surrounded it; he had himself participated in the death of another human being, indifferent to the interpretations society put upon his act.

The awakening that follows his death sentence alone can bring into focus those two moments unifying the pattern of his experience. Meursault sees, at last, that to exist is happiness. His indifference to the sights and smells of the world turns into a conscious love; his passive acquiescence to the violence done to human beings turns into a passionate revolt against death and a sense of human fraternity. He can now understand the small joys that filled the last days of his mother's humble life. The revolver shot that precipitated him from his semiconscious existence into the closed universe of his mind has, as its counterpoint, the violent act of consciousness whereby Meursault emerges from his isolation to assume his identity as a human being, the full responsibility for his life in its beauty and incomprehensible strangeness. Camus leaves Meursault on the threshold of a new awareness and a new passion, suspended between life and death. But this change does not account for the two most dramatic passages in the book—the murder itself and Meursault's last imaginary bid for the hatred of the crowd, should his execution take place.

Twelve years after the publication of *The Stranger,* Camus wrote a semi-ironic and typically paradoxical preface that has been widely quoted, often without a glint of humor and out of context. "From my point of view," he remarked,

> Meursault is not a human wreck, but a poor and naked man, in love with the sun that leaves no shadows. Far from lacking sensitivity, he is animated by an intense, because stubborn, passion, a passion for the absolute and for truth. It is still negative truth, the truth of being and feeling, but without it there can be no conquest of oneself or of the world.
>
> (*L'Étranger,* p. vi)

This, then, would be the unexpressed inner compulsion that drives Meursault: the refusal to conclude without evidence, to rely on words, to go beyond what he thinks is true, to strike attitudes, to "plead innocent" or "plead guilty." In Camus's eyes this makes of him a man who, in a sense, accepts death for the sake of truth. "I have sometimes said, albeit paradoxically," Camus concludes, "that in the person of my character I have tried to create the only Christ we deserve." It is a challenging statement, obviously sarcastic.

However we wish to interpret *The Stranger,* it is clear that we cannot be satisfied to read it merely as a story. Camus obviously intended to create an autonomous, exemplary figure. At one time in his *Notebooks* he had envisaged a novel centering on a character conceived as "L'Indifférent" ("The indifferent man"). Meursault's shattering adventure has its source in characteristic indifference, and its significance seems to lie in the revelation of the basic and dangerous inadequacy of this attitude. It leads him into a trap where his initially imperceptible inadequacies are fully revealed and then, in a reverse moment, transcended. This method of creation is typical of Camus's writing, and reminiscent of André Gide, but in Camus's case it would seem more obviously connected with Plato.

*Caligula.* When a revised version of *Caligula* was produced on the Paris stage in 1945, it was an indubitable success, the greatest that Camus was ever to enjoy as a playwright. For each new production of the play—in 1950, 1957, and 1958—he reworked his text, modifying it quite considerably. But by and large it remained the play Camus had written in his twenty-fifth year, Caligula's age in the first version of the play.

If, of the twelve ferocious emperors described by Suetonius, it was Caligula who caught Camus's fancy, this was no doubt because of that emperor's youth and of the peculiar forms his madness took. Camus provided a motivation that transformed the emperor from a historical into a contemporary, though imaginary, figure. In those years Camus was preoccupied with death. The "man sentenced to death"—his double, in a sense—had appeared in the *Notebooks* approximately a year before. At the root of Caligula's adventure is an emotional and intellectual confrontation with the finality and inevitability of death.

The first act of the play sets the stage for the developments that take place in the subsequent acts, three years later. Its purpose is to establish the inner climate of distress that gives coherence to Caligula's fantastic external acts and to set up the outer circumstances that give these acts their dramatic plausibility. Caligula, a "relatively attractive prince," has been absent for three days, since the death of Drusilla, his beloved sister and mistress. The curtain rises, just before his return, on a group of more or less anxious patricians. Four people in the emperor's entourage stand out: Caesonia, his mistress; Cherea, an older, thoughtful, and reserved man; Scipio, a young poet; and Helicon, a former slave freed by Caligula, now his henchman. They sound the note of concern that prepares Caligula's intensely dramatic entry. Distraught, and like Hamlet, proffering strange and incongruous words, Caligula spreads consternation around him. Camus attempts to reveal the emperor's state of mind through gestures and acts and by words that emanate from it but do not explicate it. Violently striking a gong to alert the palace, Caligula effaces from a mirror the image of the "relatively attractive prince," thus announcing the advent of a new Caligula. It is clear to the audience that Caligula's "descent into hell" has sent him back transformed.

When the curtain rises on the second act, three years have gone by and Caligula has become an "impossible" character, a monster, a ferocious tyrant, isolated in his court, attended only by Caesonia and Helicon. Reluctantly, his former friends Scipio and Cherea have been forced to abandon him. As a revolt gains momentum, Caligula accumulates grimly burlesque masquerades that mock, humiliate, kill, and devastate. In a last powerful scene, completely isolated now, Caligula breaks the mirror, confronts his assassins in whose plot he had deliberately acquiesced, and dies with a wild last cry: "I am still alive."

Brilliant in conception, and richly executed in a vibrant lyrical language that moves with ease from irony through pathos to tragic intensity, the play has, nevertheless, certain weaknesses. The first act raises the question of the connection between Caligula's confrontation with death and the crisis heralded by the strokes on the gong. The suspense it creates should be slowly resolved in the successive acts. But the young dramatist has eluded the problem. The three-year lapse between acts 1 and 2 does not bring about a transformation in depth of character or situation. In the next stage, the inner coherence of the play is somewhat sacrificed to the spectacular masquerades that seem to have tempted the stage director in Camus; their arbitrariness detracts from their plausibility. The significance of the main character is overshadowed by the horrifying stage business that accompanies Caligula's ferocious appearances. The primary theme of the play, Caligula's self-destruction, is obscured.

Caligula's inner development, suggested in the first act, has its source in his discovery of a simple yet startling truism: "Men die, and they are not happy." Hence his violent revolt, his intolerable sense that all life is a futile masquerade, his need, as a compensation, to achieve something "impossible"—change the world, possess the moon, reverse the seasons, conquer death itself, assert his absolute freedom. Concomitantly he wants to spread his gospel and communicate his own stark revelation. All-powerful, he decides to impersonate cold fate. Logical to an extreme, he consistently identifies himself with the arbitrary, derisive, or cruel forces that destroy human security. But in the course of this identification, of necessity he destroys his human self. His murder, accepted by him, is a "superior suicide," brought about by the tragic realization that he has miserably failed. *Caligula,* as Camus conceived it, "is the story of the most human and tragic of errors," an error whose nature Caligula recognizes just before he dies. "My freedom was not of the right kind."

*The Misunderstanding.* A tragic human error, implacably carried to its logical limit, is also at the dynamic core of *The Misunderstanding,* a three-act play produced a year before *Caligula* but written some years later. The play reaches back in setting and mood to 1936, to a dismal night of solitude Camus had spent in Prague. Written in the atmosphere of occupation, "in the middle of a country encircled and occupied," it is heavily charged with a gloom and "claustrophobia" that are entirely new in Camus's work. The story of *The Misunderstanding* is a variant of an old folkloric tale whose components are simple: an isolated inn run by an innkeeper who assassinates travelers in order to rob them. The variations on the pattern are innumerable, and its symbolic potentialities are evident. Camus tightened the plot so as to create, he said, an "impossible situation." In his play the inn, situated in the heart of Czechoslovakia, is run by two women, an old mother and her daughter, Martha. When the curtain rises, they are discussing the arrival of a traveler, whom they are to drug and drown in the weir that night, like others before him, but with a difference: he is to be the last, for their ultimate purpose will now be achieved. They will have the money that will bring them freedom and allow Martha at last to reach the sunny beaches of the south. The traveler appears, and the trap closes. He reveals—but only to the audience—both his purpose and his identity. A prodigal son who had left home twenty years before, now a wealthy man living in the warm southern land to which Martha aspires, he has come to help his mother and sister. But he plans to remain incognito until he is recognized. The play moves grimly to its end in a kind of nightmarish tug-of-war between the inflexible mechanism of murder set off by the traveler's arrival and the repressed emotions and hesitations of mother, daughter, and son fumbling unsuccessfully toward its arrest. Jan, the son, will be recognized, but only after he has been killed. His mother will join him in the weir. His sister commits suicide, but only after she sees and denounces the horror of the trap into which she has fallen. Maria, Jan's wife, is left in moral torture to face the bitter uselessness of it all. Her anguished cry for help elicits from the old, enigmatic, and seemingly mute waiter who haunts the inn, only a single syllable: "No." "A son who expects to be recognized without having to declare his name and who is killed by his mother and sister as a result of the misunderstanding—this is the subject of the play"; yet the whole design of the plot points to an underlying, hidden meaning.

Camus admittedly was interested in only one form of drama—tragedy. In this he was not alone. Eugene O'Neill in America; T. S. Eliot in England; Jean Giraudoux, Jean Anouilh, and Henry de Montherlant in France, to mention only a few contemporary names, all experimented in that form. One of the more tempting paths Camus's predecessors had explored was the reinterpretation in modern times of well-known Greek themes. In his own experiments as a dramatist, Camus seems to have deliberately attempted to free his plays from dependency on the ready-made tragic characters and conflicts so often reinterpreted by his contemporaries. He wanted to find a "modern" design that could disclose the particular forms the tragic conflict assumes at the present time.

In its structure, *The Misunderstanding* harks back to the Greeks: the rigid masklike quality of the two women, the fatal chain of crime engendering crime, the murder within the family group, the inflexible working out of an initial purpose, and the recognition theme. *Caligula* is more closely related to the Molière technique of unleashing a Tartuffe or Don Juan to wreak havoc within a relatively "normal" world; but here the nature of the havoc wrought is different and at first eludes the mind. Camus outlined his idea of the "tragic conflict" (partly derived from Nietzsche) as the coexistence of two equally necessary, equally valid but irreconcilable principles or orders that place individuals in "impossible," hence incomprehensible, situations where the irrational prevails. He thus conceived his theater as a "theater of the impossible," presenting in *Caligula* an "impossible character" and in *The Misunderstanding* an "impossible situation." The restless, impatient surge of human beings to transcend their limitations seemed to him the very essence of the modern tragic situation. The "impossible" figuration on stage therefore has a significance beyond itself, not explicated by the characters. The spectator or reader must make his way back to the initial feeling and thought that animates the play. Camus's purpose is to awaken the consciousness—rather than, like Hamlet's, to "catch the conscience"—of his audience.

For *Caligula* the pattern, though somewhat obscured, is clear: Caligula's initial revolt is thoroughly human, involving a sense of the poignancy of living. He cannot accept the haphazard game that nature plays with human life. Since he cannot attach the metaphysical, social, political ordering of human existence to a universal frame of reference, he sees it as a derisory sham. He embodies thereby a tragic conflict: his revolt negates his logical conclusions. This "impossible" position is mirrored in his passionate desire to impose his vision on all about him, while using a method that makes communication impossible. It is mirrored, too, in a sense of moral freedom that leads him only to the dead end of despair. If Caligula embodies one of the latent tendencies of our thinking, it is from Caligula that the play wants to free us.

*The Misunderstanding* is more obscure. Martha and her brother are committed to the same very human project: to transform the bleak situation at the inn, to achieve happiness. Jan, secure in his own happiness and love, vaguely takes for granted a situation where things "work out," a natural order in which a mother will always recognize her son; he walks confidently into the mechanical, abstract pattern of crime set up in the inn by Martha, whose "right" to achieve happiness justifies the means automatically employed. The two approaches, inflexibly pursued by brother and sister, each with the same goal in view, blind them to the recognition of their real situation: the brother and son is not recognized; he does not even glimpse the nature of the situation he came to remedy. It was Camus's contention that, grim though it was, *The Misunderstanding* suggested a perspective beyond itself.

> If a man wants to be recognized, he must simply say who he is. If he is silent or lies, he will die alone, and everything around him will be condemned to disaster. But if he speaks the truth, he will die undoubtedly, but after having helped others and himself to live.
>
> (preface to *Le Malentendu*)

Like *Caligula, The Misunderstanding* is concerned with the passion for an absolute, with human happiness as an absolute in a human world that engenders crime upon crime. The question raised takes us full circle back to *The Stranger* and the enigma of Meursault's relation to an act that he seems not to be troubled about, though he is ready to accept its consequences. In the plays no fatality is involved. The burden of the disaster rests squarely on the decisions of the protagonists. All that outer circumstances offer is blind chance, and it was also blind chance, symbolized by the chain of incidents that led him to the beach, that triggered Meursault's gun. Camus, in his short novel, seems to have wanted to describe "a man," to say "who he is." His hero experiences the full range of a man's possibilities, stopping at none until, face to face with death, he grasps them in their totality: violence and compassion; beauty and death; solidarity and solitude. He is a man, that is, a "stranger"—unique, impossible, and real. Caligula discovers the violence and rejects the beauty and compassion; Martha knows the infinite nostalgia and rejects the present possibilities; Jan believes in innocence and ignores the horror. The hero in each play has only one fragment of the total awareness to which Meursault eventually accedes. Hence the conflict, the mutilation, and the self-destruction that make these people tragic figures in Camus's eyes.

*The Myth of Sisyphus.* Underlying all three works is the same pervasive feeling of moral distress engendered by a human society that can no longer reach outside itself for a coherent system of ethical values. The hubris that sets off the infernal machine of fate is thus bred in the stubborn decisions of distraught human minds. Camus insisted, with some measure of reason, that although they expressed mental conflicts or attitudes, his plays did not involve an abstract philosophy. *The Myth of Sisyphus,* an essay which developed in the same years, and which he defines as a personal testimony, intellectualizes the mood that gave substance to his first fictional works.

The "absurd"—a word that was to hypnotize Camus's readers and critics, somewhat to his distress—seems to have begun to fascinate Camus in the summer of 1938, when both *Caligula* and *The Stranger* were being written. He was not the first to use it. The word was in the air, a part of the restless, anxious mood of the time. It was used in a wide variety of contexts to designate the incomprehensible, the unpredictable, the purposeless, incongruous, "impossible" aspects of life. For Camus as for Sartre, although not to the same extent, the basic mood had been conceptualized through contact with existential and phenomenological approaches to philosophy. Analysis of the failure of the intellect to encompass the complex reality of human existence was common to Pascal, Kierkegaard, and Nietzsche as well as to Husserl, Jaspers, and Heidegger. Unlike Sartre, though, Camus, when he wrote the *Myth of Sisyphus,* was not concerned with a "philosophy of the absurd" but rather, given a "sense" of the absurd, with how profitably to live with it, transforming it into a positive incentive "to live lucidly and to create." The heavy abstract superstructure that has been imposed by critics on his short essay has tended to obscure its essential feature, its lyrical emphasis on the exhilarating reality of a life that transcends the intellect. Life is incomprehensible, to be sure, but in young Camus's eyes its existence is not open to question.

The *Myth of Sisyphus* is a clarification of the problem of "the absurd," valid only within a given mental framework of reference and experience, Camus's own. It is addressed to those who have no religious, metaphysical, or philosophical system of belief to which they can relate their acts, and whose acts thereby lose their relevance. Intellectual indifference and moral irresponsibility, Camus observed, are the price they tend to pay for a freedom that takes the form of an infinite array of equally irrelevant decisions; living tends, then, to become a senseless mechanism pervaded by a paralyzing sense of its nothingness. Without reaching outside his nihilism, one of the essential elements in the problem he had set himself, Camus proposed in his essay to "find a means to go beyond it."

"The fundamental subject of *The Myth of Sisyphus* is this: it is legitimate and necessary to wonder whether life has a meaning; therefore it is legitimate to meet the problem of suicide face to face." From this classical problem, Camus rapidly moved to the equally classical situation in which, in an apparently stable social world, the question of meaning arises, and with it metaphysical anxiety with regard to the whole of existence. Camus briefly enumerated the "walls" that bring rational answers to a halt, then turned to the existential philosophers, only to reject them all for the same reason. Having faced the fundamental relativity of all rational systems of explanation in a nonrational world, these philosophers, Camus charges, "make a leap"; they arbitrarily and irrationally derive from the nonrational a principle of explanation.

Camus's purpose was different—different, too, from that of Sartre, who from the same vision of man's moral freedom and consequent responsibility in a purposeless universe drew his terrifying ethic of a perpetual and anguished creation of the self. According to Camus, the basic limitations of human living cannot be changed, nor the contradictions resolved. If once the mechanism of routine living is stopped, if the shot rings out on the beach and awareness starts, we shall always find the same human creature in the same role: judge, accuser, witness, advocate, accused, a "stranger," whose being must remain forever incomprehensible.

In the first section of *The Myth of Sisyphus* the age-old paradoxes are briefly summarized: the love of life, the inevitable death; the need for coherence, the basic incomprehensibility; the surge toward happiness, the evidence of pain. Camus proposes a lucid acceptance of the situation: to love life, and to live with the knowledge that life is incomprehensible; to multiply all the chances for happiness, knowing its impossibility; to explore the infinite possibilities of life within the narrow limits of a life. That the full reality of experience transcends the intellect was, he felt, an insufficient statement; he defined man's metaphysical existence by the refusal of human reason to accept definition in terms of the irrational.

*The Myth of Sisyphus* proposes to seek in this paradoxical and inescapable situation the source of man's unique and peculiar value, his creativity. To the destructive transgressors—Caligula, Jan, and Maria—it opposes a gallery of truly "absurd" heroes: the actor, the Don Juan, the conqueror, the creative artist, and finally, subsuming them all, Sisyphus. Camus's Sisyphus is a man wedded to his limitations, living out a role assigned to him, each conflicting part of which is integral and must be lucidly confronted.

With *Sisyphus,* the cycle of the absurd can be seen as a whole. Meursault, Caligula, Jan, Martha, and Sisyphus are all objectified, intensely personal projections of certain inner moods. The four works are related by the resurgence of recognizable images, concrete and at the same time symbolic: light (the light that suffuses Meursault's Algiers), but also an inner light, whether the cruel light of evidence, the burning light of violence, the quiet light of beauty, or the soft light of acquiescence; sea, stone, and desert; human faces that appear, merge, and become autonomous, observable by others—judge, jury, or horrified witnesses. It is not by chance that the "creator" is one of the four "absurd men." It is clear that for

Camus in the 1930's, artistic creation was not a solution to a situation that he had diagnosed as insoluble, but rather a confrontation with himself, a way of existing in harmony with himself. The aesthetic urge was already so strong in him that it freed him from the Marxist dogma of "social realism," although in *The Stranger* and *Caligula,* young Camus's antagonism to established society, its institutions and representatives—so clear in his first journalistic writings—comes through in a grotesque satirical lampooning: in the novel, of the court of justice and its clownlike functionaries; and in the plays, of the patricians. In comparison, the murderous actions of a Caligula or a Martha are so violent an expression of revolt against the limitations of reality that one cannot but see in them a deeper anguish and protest whose only check is the creative act itself.

Between the years when Camus conceived the first set of works and the years when they were published, momentous events had transformed the climate of France. The 1930's had been years of social problems, political discussions, ideological battles. Camus had taken a stand on all these; yet his creative works rose as a block, beyond them. His heroes, conscious of the contingency of their existence, all invent an "impossible" existence, based on the full expansion of one part only of the self. At the time they were created they stood outside the mainstream of literary preoccupations. In the 1940's, they reached a disconcerted audience living in a Caligula-like world of insecurity. It was the "absurd" view of man's situation, inherent in the structure, character, and action of Camus's fictional works, that struck his readers. The underlying protest, the ambivalence of the whole, the upsurge of vital force, and the imaginative power that defined the aesthetic unity of the work tended to pass unnoticed. Artist though he was, Camus was disguised as a philosopher. But the foundations of his work were laid. Its basic language, forms, conflicts, and themes were not to vary greatly in the coming years.

### *The Mid-Century Years*

One of Camus's preoccupations, clearly evidenced in his first essays, was a tragic sense of human suffering—as seen, for example, in Caligula's downfall. His first works, concentrating on the discovery and creation of the self, sidestep the theme. The war was to bring Camus face to face with the problem. He had not eluded the question in his personal life, but it had not been an essential source of inner tension and hence of creativity. A Marxist first, then a non-Marxist socialist, he had, it seems, settled the question of human suffering in his own mind. War and occupation, liberation, and the political no-man's-land of postwar Europe imposed on Camus new concepts involving the relation of the artist to the human community. The basic theme underlying the second, "Promethean," cycle of Camus's work is the conflict between an obsessive, collective situation involving large-scale injustice, mass murder, enslavement, and torture, and a no less obsessive longing for the freedom to breathe and to create a harmonious work of art. In his articles and speeches throughout this period, Camus dwells on the inroads that political action makes on an artist's creative powers.

Opposed to Sartre's theory of political commitment, as well as to the Marxist view of the artist, he defined solidarity with the oppressed as one of the sources of the artist's integrity. The artist could not, in certain circumstances, avoid being militant. In the political arena for better or worse, he could not, however, change his language in the interests of a party. He could not let his writing serve in dubious ways, for this would betray his art, corrupting his use of the language itself.

Camus's speeches and works illustrate how deeply he felt the disruptive pull of these two factors in his life during the 1950's. To be free from the harrowing obsession with horror and the petty disputes of politics—to write as he wished—was the nostalgic aspiration of these years. *The Plague, The Just Assassins,* and *The*

*Rebel* constitute a statement and a working out of his conflict. The countermyths that Camus created, incarnating the force of his reaction to the concrete, oppressive world around him, express his claim to something other.

*The Plague.* A first version of *The Plague* was finished in 1943. The plague had appeared early in Camus's personal imagery as a symbol, perhaps first striking his attention in a strange essay, "The Theater and the Plague," written by a former surrealist, Antonin Artaud. The symbol is already at work in *Caligula*—Caligula is the plague—and up to its last appearance, in *State of Siege,* is was to prowl in the background of Camus's imagination as the most representative image of the calamities that can befall a human society. In 1941 he jotted down a title for a novel: "The Plague or Adventure." It was no longer a question of describing a subjective Caligula-like adventure. The plague, by then, had taken on a specific form, so eloquent that retrospectively it was to give *Caligula* and *The Misunderstanding* levels of meaning that Camus had not anticipated. With these topical meanings the new novel originated. "*The Plague,*" Camus wrote a friend, "which I wanted to have read at several levels, has nonetheless as its evident content the struggle of the European resistance against Nazism."

For several years Camus read extensively, plunging into the vast literature extant on the scourge—memoirs, chronicles, treatises, biblical descriptions, and works of fiction—Boccaccio, Kleist, Pushkin, Manzoni, and Defoe. In the course of the writing the novel changed. The fragments of a first draft are charged with savage irony. But by 1943, irony had given way to a bleak and desperate seriousness. Camus was in France, ill and ever more deeply involved in the struggle against the German occupation. He could measure the ruthlessness of the machinery of oppression grinding millions of human beings to death. The plague, which he had first cast in the guise of a grotesque, outrageous bureaucrat, now became a killer, invisible but all pervasive, regulating, tabulating, insulating, dehumanizing, and silencing.

For quite a while Camus searched for a mode and tone for his narrative that would transmit the atmosphere he wanted. A first-person narrative, centering interest in one individual, would not give a sense of the collective nature of the "adventure." Camus did not want the narrator to become an epic hero, but a completely objective recording would lack the immediacy of testimony—the narrator had to be "one of us." The solution was suggested to him by the opening chapter of Dostoevsky's *The Possessed* (1871–1872). The chronicle of the plague is written by Bernard Rieux, a citizen of Oran who in the last pages gives his reasons for undertaking the task and so reveals his identity. His social position is functional: he is a doctor. He writes for several reasons: first, "so that he should not be one of those who hold their peace, but should bear witness in favor of those plague-stricken people"; second, "to state quite simply what we learn in a time of pestilence: that there are more things to admire in men than despise"; and third, because

> he knew that the tale he had to tell could not be one of final victory. It could only be the record of what had to be done, and what assuredly would have to be done again in the never ending fight against terror and its onslaughts, despite their personal afflictions, by all who, while unable to be saints but refusing to bow down to pestilences, strive their utmost to be healers.
>
> (Gilbert trans., p.287)

Rieux knows that the plague bacillus never dies and that the day could come when "it would raise up its rats again and send them to die in a happy city."

Critics have objected both to the symbol Camus chose and the mode of narration, more on realistic or even political grounds than on aesthetic ones. For the socially "committed," the plague as an invisible evil abstracted from human beings—that is, from the Nazis—smacked of "bourgeois idealism," of a conscience "situated outside history," of the refusal politically to accept the "dirty hands" involved in the action. For others, the symbol itself—its appearance and development, the closing-off of the quarantined city—seemed too far removed from the actual medical process, too obsolete to be credible. The deceptiveness of the third-person chronicle, and the carefully controlled factual, "descriptive-diagnostic" tone, seemed to others to circumscribe too rigorously the effectiveness of the book, while the combination of symbol and testimony in the eyes of some turned the novel too obviously into an allegory. Nonetheless, it has remained one of the most widely read novels of our time.

Camus had answered these objections for himself. He had carefully chosen his terrain: the atmosphere of collective suffering, the inner tensions, the gradual snuffing out of individual aspirations, the sense of impotence and frustration. He was dealing with a struggle in which he had proved his own capacity for action, recording rather the price paid in the process. It was not the black and white, the right and wrong of world war, political parties, and their ethics that he wanted to describe and endorse; heroic postures seemed to him irrelevant and inappropriate in the impersonal atmosphere of modern warfare.

Against the terrifying description of the rise, rule, and decline of the plague, what he threw into the balance may seem flimsy: the stubborn, weary, unglamorous struggle of a few men; the deep joy of a night swim outside a pestilence-ridden city. It was a confession, Camus said, but also the creation of a counterimage to liberate him from the grip of his experience—perhaps, too, the book worked to tunnel a way out for others as deeply oppressed as himself. In response to the great plumes of smoke rising from the collective funeral pyres, the inner flame of comradeship rises in the service of human survival, marking the limits of the plague's dehumanizing power.

*The Plague* develops at an even tempo, relentlessly, in five parts, each concerned with a certain phase in an overall movement. The narrator first evokes an everyday existence that the plague, remorseless and compelling, transforms into a fantastic, visionary hell. Each phase in the siege of the city has a countertheme: the muffled orchestration of human voices exchanging views, attempting to elucidate a position with regard to the unthinkable reality. Rieux, Tarrou, Rambert, Grand, Paneloux, and Cottard propose variations of the human answer to the plague, their voices as persistent as the whistling of the scourge over the sun-baked city. What perhaps explains the impact of this most widely read of Camus's works, despite the critics, is the eerie blend of stark realism and poetic vision that characterizes it. A gloomy but courageous book, *The Plague* was an effort in detachment from the tangle of historical and sociological interpretation, so that the reader could be made aware of the affective impact of the experience on the behavior of a social group and of the appalling power of the revelation of the scourge itself.

*State of Siege,* a play Camus wrote in collaboration with Jean-Louis Barrault (who staged it), is a kind of exuberant final exorcism. Camus attempted to give it an epic quality, using a medley of music, mime, and dance. Unsuccessful, so far, at least in performance, the play expresses the great burst of joy and hope that came with the Liberation. Simone de Beauvoir's *La force des choses* (*Force of Circumstance,* 1963) shows how widely this hope and exaltation were shared by other intellectuals. *The Just Assassins* and *The Rebel* now completed an itinerary that had led Camus gradually to counterbalance the constricting demands for public commitments by a new affirmation of *joie de vivre* as the source that he could no longer deny of hope and creativity.

*The Rebel.* In much the same way as *The Myth of Sisyphus* had posed the problem of suicide in order to conclude with a "lucid invitation to live and create," *The Rebel* posed the question of "logical," "legalized," ideologically justified murder in order to conclude with a leap of faith, expressing belief in the value of free, affirmative, individual creativity in the present-day world as it is, "beyond nihilism." But in the politically charged atmosphere of literary Paris in the early 1950's, the book had unforeseen and, viewed from the outside, inexplicable repercussions. The violence of the militant Communist press is hard to take seriously. *The Rebel* was denounced as an "ignoble" book whose purpose was to "justify anti-Communist repression, anti-Soviet war, and the assassination of the leaders of the proletariat." In the ever more "committed" *Les temps modernes,* Sartre's periodical, Camus was soundly taken to task by one of Sartre's then-close friends, Francis Jeanson, sparking a bitter dispute such as periodically shakes the French literary world.

Clearly Camus had touched on a burning issue. Yet he claimed that his essay was a personal exploration in impersonal form of the implications of tendencies apparent in an intellectual climate that was carefully situated in postwar Europe. He presented it as an attempt to clarify his own position in order, "the world being what it is, to know how to live in it." It would be idle to summarize the movement of the essay, entirely directed toward the exposure of the paradox whereby revolt in the name of freedom and justice, a generous, creative, and Promethean impulse, flounders and collapses in police states, Prometheus ending inevitably as Caesar. Whatever the alleged shortcomings of Camus's documentation and point of view, the fact remains that all of his opponents saw his essay as a direct attack on Stalinist Russia and the reduction of the Marxist credo to, in Camus's own words, "a gigantic myth." This no doubt was the case, but only within the framework of one of Camus's persistent themes, the equivocal dynamism whereby, in the human mind, aspirations are rationalized into logical imperatives and then used as justifications for a machinery of action that brooks no opposition: a catastrophic dialectic. With *The Rebel,* Camus was merely carrying this view into the realm of political ideology and action. The more specific criticism of the Marxist "leap," its consequent justification of the means by a hypothetical end, disguised as inevitable, predictable, and concrete—though it could hardly be missed—was a secondary, not a primary, objective. Recently the question of Camus's significance as a thinker, long downplayed by his critics, has begun to be reconsidered. In relation to a general investigation of the function and formal characteristics of the essay in the movement of literature, Édouard Morot-Sir, in *Lettres modernes,* vol. 12 (1985), has detected in *The Rebel* an innovative and modern epistemology.

*The Just Assassins.* Produced in 1949, *The Just Assassins* had created no such stir, yet the themes and conflicts of the play are organically linked to the essay. In those years, justice in relation to politics was a live issue. For Camus it was a disturbing issue that the Liberation and the Stalinist repression in Russia had posed in all its ambiguity. Once again he used the theater to explore the problem—to illuminate it from within, as a problem that by now permeates our society. The play is a dramatization of the tragic human dilemma lived by terrorists, whose actions are motivated by a deep revulsion to blatant social injustice as well as by a hopelessness in regard to the power structure's ability to deal with it.

An austere play, *The Just Assassins* borrows its cast and external design from the history of a small terrorist group who in 1905 had assassinated the Grand Duke Sergei, Russian Minister of Justice. Camus unified the action by dramatizing the internal conflicts and tragic repercussions the assassination itself seems to have created in the tightly knit group of terrorists. The play concentrates on the tragic awareness of the two idealistic central figures, Kalayiev, the thrower of the bomb, and Dora, in love with him. The play, begun in a climate of eager heroism, ends in a disturbing atmosphere of ambiguity and doubt. It has no thesis; it merely shows the irreconcilable disparity between the generous initial impulse, its ideological justification, and the suffering endured by the flesh-and-blood people involved in an act like Kalayiev's. Kalayiev and Dora confront the tragic paradox of their action in its unforeseen personal consequence, the mutilation of their lives. "Scrupulous murderers" in Camus's eyes, they reach the extreme limit of the permissible. The play, again, is a counterimage set up in protest against the vicious cycle of violence whereby complacent "bureaucratic" murderers engaged in mass repression set off the deadly mechanisms of terrorism.

*Camus as journalist.* In the four years between the Nazi victory over France and the liberation of Paris, Camus's activity as journalist was of necessity minimal. From 1944 on, as communications were reestablished and his reputation grew, articles, interviews, and lectures followed one another in quick succession; transient and scattered as such "occasional" texts are bound to be, they were eventually collected in three volumes entitled *Actuelles: Chroniques* (1950, 1953, 1958). These volumes cover, with some overlap, the period between 1944 and 1958. Only a few of these texts have been translated into English. "Actuelles," "Chronicles"—the title designates their function: they are records of contemporary historical events as lived, day by day, by the chronicler-witness Albert Camus.

Like his early articles, these pieces might be described as "fragments of a combat" fought against the fast-changing historical events of the day. But the freewheeling irony and verbal play of the brash young reporter of the prewar days have all but disappeared here. Events were not reassuring: the concentration camps, the atomic bomb, the Berlin Wall; the spread of Soviet power in Eastern Europe, the Korean war, the Algerian war, and the bitter polemics those conflicts generated.

These articles and a number of occasional speeches highlight the writer's basic concerns and are closely linked to his creative work. The texts most often discussed are the Algerian chronicles that punctuate the rapidly deteriorating Algerian situation from 1945 to 1958. They give us many insights into the genesis of Camus's more specific literary work. Camus's detractors have criticized what they call his moralism, and it is true that from article to broader reportage, to lecture or debate, Camus raises the same basic question, the relation of collective to individual morality, a question that—almost a half century later—is one of the crucial issues of the times. In disagreement with critics such as Conor Cruise O'Brien and Simone de Beauvoir, who see in these pieces (the Algerian group more particularly) little more than the hollow rhetoric of abstract moralism, Michael Walzer writes in "Commitment and Social Criticism: Camus's Algerian War":

> Rereading *Actuelles III* . . . it is hard to see the bad faith. Moral anxiety lies right on the surface of the reprinted articles and speeches; universalism and particularism, justice and love, are equally in evidence; nothing is concealed. These are essays in negotiation, the work of a social critic continually aware of the on-the-ground obstacles that the map of right and wrong only inadequately represents.
>
> (*Dissent* 31:425 [Fall 1984])

Camus was antidogmatic and opposed to a rhetoric that defined political solutions only in terms of confrontation, of right versus wrong. He sought other alternatives: conciliation via some form of negotiation. He had hoped that France and Algeria might have avoided the appalling seven and a half years of war with its escalating cycle of vicious terrorism and repression. "By the end of the war," writes David Caute in his *Frantz Fanon,* "the FLN [Algerian Liberation Front] estimated Algerian deaths, including victims of starvation, at over one million out of a population of nine million." The majority of Europeans fled, and by the end of 1962 Algerian industry was at a standstill: two million were unemployed, and four million others were declared "without means of subsistence"; the Algerian government had no alternative but to remain dependent upon French financial and technical aid. And, in fact, peace was brought about in 1962 not by a military victory but by careful negotiations and mutual concessions. As Camus had foreseen, France and Algeria would remain closely bound by economic and cultural ties. Perhaps, as Walzer notes, even though Camus described his reports as "the record of a failure," "that is not to say that he was wrong to try."

### *New Thresholds*

"There are writers, it seems to me," Camus once remarked, "whose works form a whole, each throwing light on the others, and which all look toward one another." Critics accustomed to viewing a writer's work chronologically and seeking to draw simple connections between the writer's "real" world and his imaginary world have often failed to take into account Camus's experiments with simultaneous but separate modes of elaboration of coexistent contradictory moods or drives. The recognition of these contradictory impulses and their inclusion within configurations transcending the previously sacrosanct concepts of unity and noncontradiction define, in Édouard Morot-Sir's analysis of the rhetoric of *The Rebel,* Camus's break with obsolete rules of unilinear discourse. When, in 1952, Camus spoke of the correlation between all his works, he was drawing attention to a pattern clearly present from the start within any one work and from work to work. Indeed, the workaday world of *The Right and the Wrong Side,* the lyrical celebration of the Mediterranean earth in *Nuptials,* and Mersault's itinerary and human relationships in *A Happy Death* are textual projections of a complex experience of reality, no aspect of which excludes the others. Their juxtaposition signals to the reader how resistant experience can be to the exigencies of language, which can never circumscribe it in its entirety. That in the 1950's Camus's life was overshadowed by personal and political events has been underscored. But little attention has been given to the essays collected in *Summer.* "La mer au plus près" ("The Sea Close By"), with its intimations of new departures and vast horizons, counters the darker shades of Camus's writing in the 1950's, with its powerful interweaving of dream and desire:

> At midnight alone on the shore. A moment more, and I shall set sail. The sky itself has weighed anchor, with all its stars like the ships covered with lights which at this very hour throughout the world illuminate dark harbours. Space and silence weigh equally upon the heart. . . . I have always felt I lived on the high seas, threatened, at the heart of a royal happiness.
>
> (*Lyrical and Critical Essays,* p.181)

In the last years of his life, Camus was, it seems, feeling his way toward a work that would encompass more fully in a single structure the contradictory, conflicting "intimations" concerning human life with which human beings live.

More deeply than *The Rebel, The Just Assassins* had underscored the basic theme of the Promethean cycle: the extreme predicament of the artist faced with extreme injustice. What Kalayiev and Dora eventually lose is their flesh-and-blood vitality, the richness of their sensuous relation to the world, to one another. It is the poet who dies, and with him Dora's power to love. With the creation of Kalayiev, Camus was laying aside the heroic romanticism of the war, freeing himself from the obsession with political responsibility that had been characteristic of the Resistance years. The secret inner itinerary he had been following can be traced in those eight lyrical essays, written between 1939 and 1953, that he collected in *Summer.* They revolve around a few central images woven into the fabric of his language: the sea, the desert, the "immense African nights," the "black, buried sun" burning at the heart of the artist's work. Thematically, the essays show an ever more persistent emphasis on beauty, happiness, art; on light as opposed to darkness, night as opposed to black despair; on the great sweep and freedom of the sea as opposed to the closed prisons of men. These themes express an increasingly confident joy in life and serve to qualify the somber atmosphere of the Promethean cycle. That the artist cannot serve the political designs of those who "make" history was by now Camus's firm conviction. He had come to terms with the problem of Sartrean sociopolitical "commitment"; now he was definitely committed to the difficult path of individual integrity, free from doctrinaire imperatives. But before he moved to more personal concerns, Camus fired a parting shot. With *The Fall* he unleashed that most histrionic, equivocal, and sardonic of creatures, Jean-Baptiste Clamence, self-appointed "judge-penitent," "hero of our time," and any conscious man's double.

*The Fall.* Jean-Baptiste Clamence is not an individual but a voice, reminiscent of the demon who spoke with Ivan Karamazov and the one who reveled in Job's torment. *The Fall* is a short novel in the form of an impassioned monologue or "implied dialogue," such as that used by Feodor Dostoevsky in his *Notes from the Underground* (1864) and James Hogg in *Private Memoirs and Confessions of a Justified Sinner* (1824). The speaker is a seedy lawyer who encounters his silent interlocutor in a bar in Holland. Clamence's inspired rhetoric, disguised as a confession, spirals around his interlocutor, apparently at random. But it has design and derives its momentum from a secret, fixed, inner purpose. The patterning of the disconnected facts revealed by Clamence in his specious confession gives *The Fall* the appearance of an irrefutable demonstration, but one whose conclusion is always elided. Clamence's "fall," or so he insinuates, is linked to a leap that he failed to make, a leap over a bridge to save a slim girl in black.

A perfect individual according to the generally accepted nineteenth-century bourgeois ideal, Clamence, one night hearing laughter that rings sardonically behind him, discovers the delights of self-questioning, anxiety, and then guilt. So he runs the full gamut of twentieth-century consciousness, eagerly examining his most ordinary gestures, carrying even further the disintegration of his formerly "noble image" of himself. Vanity, insincerity, and eroticism finally lead through a variety of sins to sacrilege. And all lead back to one reiterated proposition: self-knowledge leads to the contempt of self, and of all men. Carefully selecting his data, Clamence repeatedly follows through to the brink of his indictment and stops, leaving it to the interlocutor to leap, to admit that there is only one remedy to personal perversity—the abdication of freedom. Clamence, fully enjoying his shame, will never leap; he is the Saint John the Baptist of an anti-Enlightment.

The diversity of interpretations proposed for *The Fall* underscores its ambiguity. It has been read as an admission of guilt on Camus's part, as a retraction of his former statements, more particularly in *The Stranger.* Yet the satiric, diabolical figure of Clamence hardly seems to warrant so flat a reading. As we leave the judge-pentitent shivering with fever on his bed, in solitary tête-à-tête with a stolen painting, *The Just Judges* (a panel of van Eyck's *Adoration of the Lamb*), we would be hard put to think of him as a "straight" character. A virtuoso with words, a consummate actor, aggressive, fawning, sure of his ultimate mastery, Jean-Baptiste Clamence is in truth the inspired perpetrator of a colossal fraud; and he is also a man frustrated, shut in upon himself, who cannot break the charmed circle of his isolation. The caricature of the artist as Camus conceived him, a caricature and a perversion, Clamence reveals at last his basic impulse toward self-destruction. Clamence, as Camus indicated, is an "aggregate of the vices of our time," and Camus has fused them all into his hero's fraudulently disguised project.

Perhaps, as it has been suggested, Camus was expulsing Clamence from himself, or attempting to counter the image of himself as a "good man." But these seem banal and very partial explanations. There is something gleefully Swiftian about *The Fall* that savors of vengeance. The battle of *The Rebel* was not far distant, nor were the bitter polemics with Sartre. Even the writing and method of exposition in *The Fall* take on the semblance of the Sartrean dialectic. And there are closer connections. In 1952, Sartre had published his extensive psychoanalytical work on Jean Genet, *Saint Genet, comédien et martyr* (*Saint Genet, Actor and Martyr*)—a characterization that fit Jean-Baptiste Clamence perfectly. A thief and jailbird, and a writer to boot, Genet, Sartre suggested, is a kind of scapegoat, virtually thrown out of the city walls with the secret evils of society magically heaped upon him; it is a thoroughly Sartrean interpretation. Genet became thereby, in Sartre's eye, "one of the heroes of our time," in fact an image and symbol of what we are fated to be, denizens of an impotent society, incapable of "the leap" that would put us on the "right side" of history. Clamence's hollow voice seems curiously to echo Sartre's as Camus leaves him in his rhetorically built "cell of little ease," on the brink of a leap he will never take, free to accumulate the sterile guilt with which he inoculates others.

Whatever the "figure in the carpet," *The Fall* revealed new potentialities, perhaps even to Camus himself. A short novel like *The Stranger*, it had originally been designed as one of a series of short stories that Camus had begun to work on.

*Exile and the Kingdom and The Possessed.* The six short stories of *Exile and the Kingdom* present considerable variety in theme and form, from the quasi naturalism of "L'Hôte" ("The Host") to the elusive symbolism of "La pierre qui pousse" ("The Growing Stone") and the allegorical suggestiveness of "Le renégat" ("The Renegade"). In each story a situation is carefully delineated in concrete terms and presented with apparently complete objectivity and great attention to plausibility. The situations are potentially dramatic and build up to a crucial moment of decision, free and open in its possibility. An insight is reached, experienced, and acted upon—though not verbalized. The resolution turns on a simple impulse, a movement toward greater understanding that casts an aura of nobility on the quite ordinary protagonists. The impulse that "goes wrong" and eventually ends in disaster—so fundamental a theme of Camus's previous work—is fashioned only in "The Renegade," a monologue and lament closely related to *The Fall.* "Jonas; ou, L'Artiste au travail" ("Jonas, or, The Artist at Work"), in contrast, is an ironic variation on the theme of the artist as scapegoat. The painter Jonas, a public figure besieged on all sides by obligations, finally takes refuge in a hideout, where one day he collapses, leaving a single unfinished word scrawled across his empty canvas. Whether the word is "solitude" or "solidarity," who can tell? Somewhere between these two conflicting exigencies, the modern artist has to find his equilibrium. The story is an ironic commentary on one of the most crucial problems of Camus's own existence, one that was operative even in his death; but yet it touches on a fundamental theme: life as a perpetual act of equilibrium between extremes.

It would be impossible to read Camus without noting the prominent place of Algeria in his work. After *The Stranger,* a number of works—*The Plague,* the lyrical essays, and four of the five other short stories of *Exile and the Kingdom*—are set in Algeria, and it is from the use Camus makes of the Algerian landscapes, its coast, its high plateaus, its oases, that they draw their power. The characters are humble people: Janine, a middle-aged woman, travelling with her husband Marcel from the coast to the oases of the south, to seek new opportunities in their small dry-goods business, now suffering from the post–World War II economic slump; the "renegade," originally a peasant from the harsh Massif Central in France; Yvars, an employee in a small cooper's shop in Algiers; Daru, a schoolmaster in an isolated school on the high plateaus. It would be idle to try to analyze these stories or point to their "meaning." Numerous, varied, and often contradictory decodings have been suggested in each case, particularly for the last story, that of d'Arrast, a French engineer in Brazil who is commissioned to build a barrage against the seasonal flooding of estuary lands. The title of each story, like the diversity of the narrative techniques, situations, and *décors,* points to underlying meanings that are never proffered. But it is clear that each adventure is lived from within an initial "climate," a closed world of feeling, which breaks down under the impact of unexpected circumstances. The individual then once again faces life in all its ambiguity. "Symbolic," some critics have suggested; "allegorical," others have said; yet others have spoken of "parables." The metaphors of the overall title *Exile and the Kingdom* are familiar ones, suggesting a close interweaving of joy and suffering in human experience, neither excluding the other. What perspective this title opens on each story and finally onto the volume considered as a unity are questions that are still being widely discussed. *Exile and the Kingdom* is proving to be one of the most resilient of Camus's works.

After *Exile and the Kingdom* only one more work is crucial—*Les possédés* (1959), the stage adaptation of Dostoevsky's *The Possessed,* a novel that had deeply impressed itself on Camus's imagination when he read it as a youth. Dostoevsky's restless cast of men driven by a passion for destruction—"possessed"—are the very embodiment of the enemy Camus had been fighting. This enemy Dostoevsky had defined as "the spirit of negation and death" in all its forms and varieties, from the most frivolous to the most insidious, compounded in the mysterious figure of Stavrogin, on whose secret crime, evolution, and fate Camus centered his play. Moving from "satirical comedy, to drama, to tragedy," Camus's adaptation sets up as a counterimage to the "dead souls" of the nihilists, the poignancy of human love, manifest in Chatov, the victim of a senseless murder. *The Possessed* is a synthesis, a grand orchestration of Camus's previous work, a kind of catharsis before Camus's move to a projected new cycle with *Le premier homme,* a cycle dealing with "a certain kind of love" that the car accident on the road to Paris was to cut short.

Camus's work shows a marked inner coherence and unity. He is not a wide-ranging writer, drawing his power rather from deliberate self-limitation. Like most of his contemporaries, he gave much thought to the relationship between art and the specific circumstances, social and historical, in which he found himself, and to what might truly characterize the modern consciousness. He thereby touched upon some of the crucial issues of the period—in politics, philosophy, and religion.

In his own daily living, in the decisions he made and the actions he carried out, he attempted to achieve and maintain some kind of balance between thought and act, a difficult enterprise that he considered with a rather wry and ironic stoicism. In public affairs he was heir to the reasoned though qualified optimism of the Enlightenment and was opposed to any fanatical cult, whether of the rational or the irrational. He was an advocate of "dialogue," of the open mind and the scrupulous act. He shared with the existentialist philosophers a sense of the contingency of human life and the gratuitous nature of human aspirations and values. But he accepted the situation as fundamental, man as present with his characteristics and limitations. "The absurd" and "revolt" are the two terms he chose for expressing the insoluble paradox of the human situation as he saw it. It was not his purpose to conclude, expound, or dictate, but to live and to write. He was not, he claimed, a philosopher, but an artist. His essays merely define the self-chosen limits of his art. In his 1954 preface to the reissue of his first book of essays, *The Wrong Side and the Right Side,* he compared the artist's career to a tightrope walker's performance—a traditional image that illustrates the aesthetic urge to achieve an apparently harmonious equilibrium by a hard-won control over conflicting forces. Some of the disruptive forces at work at mid century were ostensibly social; but there were, too, personal disruptive impulses in Camus's own personality that furnished the more fundamental substance for his art: the Meursault-like urge to give free rein to a sensuous enjoyment of life, indifferent to the rest; and the equally strong urge to achieve a Caligula-like nihilism in lucidity. To keep both impulses in check, without plunging into one extreme or the other, Camus needed his art. His often-repeated statement that he could not live without it is not merely rhetorical. It also explains each work's ambiguity. Camus is never absent from his work, nor is he on one side or the other in conflicts he describes; he is affiliated with all his characters, examining and recognizing them all. But only with *Exile and the Kingdom* does he seem to have replaced the ultimate criticism and rejection of his "impossible" characters by the creation of "possible" and acceptable ones. Camus's rejection of extremes, in an age given to excesses, is a powerful factor of originality.

His work clearly belongs to one of the main currents of modern Western literature, which he himself has designated by his references to Melville, Dostoevsky, Proust, and Kafka. For these writers, the external patterns of the narrative, concrete and specific, lead to a central inner meaning, which initially organized them. Camus's narratives and plays combine a surface simplicity and apparent realism with a consistent design. The titles he gives his works, some of which have biblical echoes, all have a concealed relation to the theme developed therein. Camus's intent, like those of the writers to whom he refers, is carefully delineated through fiction and by means of situations and characters to illuminate an aspect of experience, an illumination that is *experienced* within the narrative and not demonstrated. The integrity of the work and its force of conviction depended, Camus felt, on the artist's effort to "sacrifice" nothing. Hence Camus's power to reach his readers, even if such concepts as "the absurd" and "revolt" seem to some unpersuasive.

What characterizes his own techniques as a writer is formal control, a natural consequence of his preference for the Greek ideal of beauty, an effect, too, of his fierce drive for coherence. The clarity of outline, the sharpness and precision of the details observed, the overall effect of detached objectivity transmit a sense of formality, even of constraint, that runs counter to the more powerful trends in contemporary art. The human content and significance run counter to others in that they are more abstract.

The recurrence of images, figures, themes, and patterns within each work and from one work to another; the rhetorical texture of the language, its range of tempo and rhythm—these give Camus's writing an enigmatic intensity, in direct relation to the restraint he imposed on his expression. The limitations inherent in this combination of clarity and controlled design very much concerned Camus. He wanted to overcome them, envisaging for the future a greater freedom of expression. But he belongs to the tradition of conscious thinking and hard discipline in art. His control of his medium, coupled with his conception of art as the illumination of an individual experience that has been communicated and universalized, sometimes pushed the work to the border of parable. Wherever the tension in the quality of Camus's writing slackens and rigor of thought shades off into truism, or emotion into pathos, a certain moralism tends to overshadow the deeper underlying theme. This occurs more particularly in the works of the Promethean cycle, which deals with conflicts that were less deeply rooted in Camus's own complex personality and in fact were hostile to what he felt impelled to say. Camus defined his own realm quite early and explored it with sustained intellectual and artistic integrity, thus achieving a difficult balance between the erotic and the critical, between the solitude of the self and the claims of society. There are, of course, other works, other expressions just as valid as his, but his writing seems to have the decisive resonance that we associate with durable works of literature.

## Selected Bibliography


EDITIONS

INDIVIDUAL WORKS

FICTION

*L'Étranger.* Paris, 1942.
*La peste.* Paris, 1947.
*La chute.* Paris, 1956.
*L'Exil et le royaume.* Paris, 1957.
*La mort heureuse.* Paris, 1971.

PLAYS

*Caligula.* Paris, 1944.
*Le malentendu.* Paris, 1944.
*L'État de siège.* Paris, 1948.
*Les justes.* Paris, 1949.
*Les possédés.* Paris, 1959.
*Caligula.* (1941 version.) Paris, 1984.

ESSAYS

*L'Envers et l'endroit.* Paris, 1937.
*Noces.* Paris, 1939.
*Le mythe de Sisyphe.* Paris, 1943.
*Actuelles I: Chroniques, 1944–1948.* Paris, 1950.
*L'Homme révolté.* Paris, 1951.
*Actuelles II; Chroniques, 1948–1953.* Paris, 1953.
*L'Été.* Paris, 1954.
*Actuelles III: Chronique algérienne.* Paris, 1958.
*Écrits de jeunesse.* Paris, 1973.
*Fragments d'un combat.* Paris, 1978.
*Journaux de voyage.* Paris, 1978.

COLLECTED WORKS

*Carnets, 1939–1958.* 2 vols. Paris, 1962, 1964.
*Théâtre, récits, nouvelles.* Edited by Roger Quillot. Paris, 1962.
*Essais.* Edited by Roger Quillot and Louis Faucon. Paris, 1965.

TRANSLATIONS

*Albert Camus: The Essential Writings.* Edited with interpretive essays by Robert E. Meagher. New York, 1979.
*Caligula and Three Other Plays: The Misunderstanding, The Just Assassins, State of Siege.* Translated by Stuart Gilbert. New York, 1958.
*Exile and the Kingdom.* Translated by Justin O'Brien. New York, 1958.
*The Fall.* Translated by Justin O'Brien. New York, 1957.
*A Happy Death.* Translated by Richard Howard. New York, 1972.
*Lyrical and Critical Essays.* Translated by Ellen Conroy Kennedy. New York, 1968.
*The Myth of Sisyphus and Other Essays.* Translated by Justin O'Brien. New York, 1955.
*Neither Victims nor Executioners.* Translated by Dwight Macdonald. Berkeley, Calif., 1968.
*Notebooks 1935–1942.* Translated by Philip Thody. New York, 1963.
*Notebooks 1942–1951.* Translated by Justin O'Brien. New York, 1965.
*The Plague.* Translated by Stuart Gilbert. New York, 1948.
*The Possessed.* Translated by Justin O'Brien. New York, 1960.
*The Rebel.* Translated by Anthony Bower. New York, 1954.
*Resistance, Rebellion, and Death.* Translated by Justin O'Brien. New York, 1961.
*The Stranger.* Translated by Stuart Gilbert. New York, 1946.
*Youthful Writings.* Translated by Ellen Conroy Kennedy. New York, 1976.

BIOGRAPHICAL AND CRITICAL STUDIES

*À Albert Camus, ses amis du livre.* Paris, 1962.
Brée, Germaine. *Camus.* Rutgers, N.J., 1959.
———. *Camus and Sartre: Crisis and Commitment.* New York, 1972.
Brisville, Jean-Claude. *Camus.* Paris, 1950.
Coombs, Ilone. *Camus, homme de théâtre.* Paris, 1968.
Costes, Alain. *Albert Camus et la parole manquante.* Paris, 1973.
Cruikshank, John. *Albert Camus and the Literature of Revolt.* New York, 1959.
Gay-Crosier, Raymond. *Les envers d'un échec: Étude sur le théâtre d'Albert Camus.* Paris, 1967.
———. ed. *Camus 1980.* Gainesville, Fla., 1980.
Grenier, Jean. *Albert Camus: Souvenirs.* Paris, 1968.
Lazere, Donald. *The Unique Creation of Albert Camus.* New Haven, Conn., 1973.

Lottman, Herbert R. *Albert Camus: A Biography.* Garden City, N.Y., 1979.

McCarthy, Patrick. *Camus.* New York, 1982.

Onimus, Jean. *Camus.* Bruges, 1965.

Parker, Emmett. *Albert Camus: The Artist in the Arena.* Madison, Wis., 1965.

Quillot, Roger. *The Sea and Prisons: A Commentary on the Life and Thought of Albert Camus.* Translated by Emmett Parker. University, Ala., 1970.

Rizzuto, Anthony. *Camus' Imperial Vision.* Carbondale, Ill., 1981.

Sarocchi, Jean. *Camus.* Paris, 1968.

Sprintzen, David. *Camus: A Critical Examination.* Philadelphia, 1988.

Sutter, Judith D., ed. *Essays on Camus's Exile and the Kingdom.* University, Miss., 1981.

Tarrow, Susan. *Exile from the Kingdom: A Political Rereading of Albert Camus.* University, Ala., 1985.

Thody, Philip. *Albert Camus.* New York, 1962.

Treil, Claude. *L'Indifférence dans l'oeuvre d'Albert Camus.* Montreal, 1971.

Weis, Marcia. *The Lyrical Essays of Albert Camus.* Ottawa, 1976.

Willhoite, Fred H. *Beyond Nihilism: Albert Camus' Contribution to Political Thought.* Baton Rouge, La., 1968.

## BIBLIOGRAPHY

A bibliography of writings on Camus would fill a volume. For a bibliography of Camus criticism, see *Albert Camus,* edited by Brian T. Fitch and Peter C. Hoy (Paris, 1972). This list has been updated periodically in Peter C. Hoy's *Carnet bibliographique* in the Albert Camus series of the *Revue des lettres modernes,* nos. 2–12 (Paris, 1968–).

Germaine Brée

# MIGUEL DE CERVANTES
## *(1547–1616)*

MIGUEL DE CERVANTES SAAVEDRA was born in 1547 in Alcalá de Henares, a university town near Madrid, probably on Saint Michael's day, 29 September; he died on 23 April 1616. Like William Shakespeare's life, his is imperfectly documented, so that his biographers must have recourse to speculation and untrustworthy inferences drawn from his fictional writing. What can be said with certainty about his life is that he was several times in jail, although not a criminal, and that he turned to professional writing as a second-best career only after he found himself incapacitated for soldiering.

Cervantes' father, Rodrigo, was a poorly trained, peripatetic, and impoverished surgeon. With or without his wife and some of their seven children, he was constantly on the move throughout Castile and Andalusia. Of Miguel, the fourth child, we know nothing between his birth and 1567, when he wrote in Madrid a sonnet praising Elizabeth of Valois, third wife of Philip II. The next year he wrote two more sonnets, two poems in traditional Spanish meters, and an elegy in tercets lamenting the queen's death. These works were included in an obituary volume in her homage, which Miguel's teacher edited and published in 1569. The editor's identification of the poet as his well-beloved disciple tempts one to think that the poems were school exercises.

At this time Cervantes was twenty, considerably older than the average pre-university student. We have no knowledge of any previous education he may have received, and in any case he spent only half a year at the Estudio de la Villa de Madrid, a preparatory liberal arts school. Presumably he had some education before this, perhaps from relatives or paid tutors, but there is no record of it. Allusions in his works to actual schools in Seville and Cordoba hardly justify the general assumption that Cervantes attended them. His brief formal education in Madrid seems, however, to have contributed much to his intellectual maturity.

The master of the Estudio, Juan López de Hoyos, was an unusual man. At a time when nearly all the works of the humanist Erasmus were banned in Spain, he occasionally cited them in a public address, without of course identifying his source. Few scholars today doubt that Cervantes too was familiar with certain works by Erasmus, particularly his *Praise of Folly*. Whether or not Cervantes first studied these works in clandestine lessons with López de Hoyos, the imprint of them is clearly present in his writing.

Erasmus and the other humanists of the Renaissance cultivated and advocated a critical attitude to everything: customs, classical literary texts, but also the traditions of the Catholic church, the Vulgate version of the

Bible, and monasticism. Erasmus criticized the church from within it, urging internal reform. Nevertheless, to some prelates this kind of reform movement seemed almost as perilous as Luther's schismatic Reformation. The Council of Trent (1545–1563) confirmed with conservative zeal most of the ancient traditions and dogmas, thus putting a serious constraint on humanistic criticism of the church. After the publication of the council's decrees in 1563, the age of Renaissance criticism gave way to an age of conformism, known to historians as the Counter-Reformation. In no country more than in Spain did the spirit of Trent reign; its decrees, incorporated into the legal code, became the law of the land.

The change in the cultural climate surely contributed to the intellectual formation of Cervantes. Raised, however tentatively, in the humanistic spirit of criticism, he lived his adult life under the societal imperative to be a conformist. It is not suggested that he rebelled in any way against the monolithic theocracy of the Philips, but he did tend to view most issues ambivalently. At a time when most writers were dogmatic, he was tolerant; in his works he scrupulously presents both sides of every question on which the church claimed no privilege for the truth.

One such question that is often discussed in Cervantes' works is whether the life of action is superior to that of reading and writing books. Is soldiering better than clerking? Is it preferable to fight or to pray for victory? In this famous debate between arms and letters, Cervantes, as always, marshals all the arguments, pro and contra, that he can think of. But on this particular issue he leaves no doubt where his sympathies lie: the defenders of the truth, by risking their lives for it, prove their supremacy over the seekers and disseminators of truth. Since he clearly believed this, it is not surprising to find him in the army.

After a brief stint in 1569 as a steward in the household of Cardinal Acquaviva in Rome, he embarked on a decade of truly heroic action. For the period between 1571 and 1580 there is fairly abundant documentation. At the battle of Lepanto (1571), when Turkish naval power in the Mediterranean was decisively defeated by the Spanish fleet, Cervantes fought bravely and was twice wounded, losing the use of his left arm and hand. Undaunted, he continued his military service, chiefly in the eastern Mediterranean. In 1575, with his brother Rodrigo, Miguel embarked at Naples in the galley *Sol* with the intention of returning to Spain to petition for a promotion. His luck had run out. Shortly after the vessel passed from French to Spanish waters, the two brothers and a few other passengers were captured in a skirmish with Algerian pirates. For five long years Cervantes languished in captivity in Algiers, where he was treated brutally. His repeated and unsuccessful attempts to escape merely added to his tortures, which eyewitnesses declare he bore with extreme fortitude. After protracted negotiations, some Trinitarian friars who were engaged in the mission of ransoming prisoners of Islam finally secured his release. Toward the end of October 1580 Cervantes returned to Spain for the first time in twelve years, now aged thirty-three.

For the next few years Cervantes tried in vain to persuade the crown that his distinguished military service deserved recognition, preferably in the form of a civil-service appointment in the New World. Apparently convinced that his career as a soldier was over, he turned to letters. He began writing his first major work, the pastoral romance *La Galatea,* which was published in 1585. In December of that same year, he married Doña Catalina Palacios Salazar, daughter of a country squire. It was an unhappy marriage, ending in separation. Always harassed by the lack of money, Cervantes secured a commission to acquire the grains, oil, and other foodstuffs needed to provision the great fleet that Philip II was assembling for the invasion of England. It was an unpleasant job: he had to travel about Andalusia commandeering supplies from farmers who suspected, with reason, that they would never receive proper compensation. The bankruptcy of others and his own slipshod accounting periodically landed Cervantes in jail. It may well have been—as tradition has it—that in one of these prisons *Don Quixote* was, as Cervantes puts it in his first prologue, begotten. For Cervantes, the great days of Lepanto, the battle he calls "the most memorable and noble occasion that past centuries ever saw or future ones expect to see," had been replaced by the grim irony of a defeated Armada, dubbed Invincible. The courageous soldier had become a pen pusher on the home front. His disillusionment with the national will for heroism shines forth in his poetry of this period; this disillusionment is surely a major source of his imaginative creation of *Don Quixote*.

Reduced to surviving the humdrum perils of a bureaucrat but still hoping for a more prestigious post in the Indies, Cervantes turned at last to what was to be a full-time career as a writer. Toward the end of the century he moved from Andalusia to Castile, eventually establishing residence in the temporary capital, Valladolid. When the court returned to Madrid in 1606 he went with it, and he stayed in that city for the rest of his life. Even then, he cannot be said to have settled down, for he moved four times within the capital. His success as a writer did not lift him out of his poverty: having received no university education, he could not call on an old-boys' network to introduce him to the monied and the privileged, whose financial support normally supplemented the meager royalties paid by publishers. Eventually, somehow, he obtained the favor of the duke of Béjar for *Don Quixote*, part 1; and the count of Lemos graciously consented to allow Cervantes to dedicate to him most of his other works. With these aristocratic connections, publication, if not wealth, was feasible. After the first part of *Don Quixote* (1605), the books followed one another in quick succession: the *Novelas ejemplares* (*Exemplary Tales*, 1613); the *Viaje del Parnaso* (*Journey to Parnassus*, 1614); *Ocho comedias y ocho entremeses* (*Eight Plays and Eight Interludes*, 1615); *Don Quixote*, part 2 (1615); *Los trabajos de Persiles y Sigismunda* (*The Trials of Persiles and Sigismunda*, 1617).

Although it is important to realize that Cervantes' literary production is that of an aging man, the publication dates, crowded into the last years of his life, can be misleading. Much of that final burst of literary energy can be accounted for by the fact that Cervantes was taking advantage of the demand for his works that followed the success of *Don Quixote*, part 1. His plays, he tells us, had been gathering dust in a drawer. There is reason to believe that at least one of those published in 1615 had been written at the end of the previous century. Similarly, the *Exemplary Tales* had been written over a period of several years. There is a reference to one of them, "Rinconete and Cortadillo," in *Don Quixote*, part 1. A manuscript of this tale and another, "El celoso extremeño" ("The Jealous Hidalgo"), is dated 1606. Nevertheless, the bulk of Cervantes' published work is that of a sexagenarian. It springs from the experience, the reading, and the meditation of an older man who had not in his youth expected to end up as a professional writer. It is hardly surprising, then, that Cervantes found himself out of tune with others, like the playwright Lope de Vega (1562–1635) and the poet Luis de Góngora (1561–1627), who were writing around 1610. To them he seemed a latecomer ill at ease with the literary innovations that they were sponsoring. There was indeed some animosity between them; and it must be admitted that in the literary world of seventeenth-century Madrid, Cervantes was a marginal author.

In a letter dated August 1604, Lope wrote that "no poet is as bad as Cervantes or so foolish as to praise *Don Quixote*." From this and other supporting evidence it appears probable that *Don Quixote*, part 1, was published in 1604, since it is unlikely that Cervantes' presumably bulky manuscript circulated far before it went to the printers. If this edition existed, no trace of it and no bibliographical reference to it have been found. On the other hand, its existence cannot be authoritatively denied, for we possess the titles of many Spanish books of the period that have not survived. In spite of Lope's adverse judgment, *Don Quixote* proved an instant success; on the strength of this one novel Cervantes became a famous writer overnight. It did not go so well with some of his other works, such as his poetry. With his customary irony, Cervantes tells us that "much may be expected of my prose, but nothing of my verse," joking, in the words of one of his characters, that he was "more versed in misadventures than in verses." He confesses also that he had such a conspicuous lack of success in persuading producers to stage his plays that, in order to derive some profit from his exertions in writing them, he decided to publish them. Everything in his literary career points to the inability of an older man to fall into step with a dominant younger generation. But in prose fiction Cervantes' debt to a humanistic past brought fresh values to a homogenized Spain. The part of the masses that was literate devoured *Don Quixote* avidly, and most of the literary establishment conceded its merit. Admiring references to the novel abound in the writing of the seventeenth century. So great was its success that, in dedicating part 2 to the count of Lemos, Cervantes claims—fictionally, of course—that the emperor of China had written to ask his permission to adopt part 1 as a textbook in a Spanish-language college he planned to found in his empire. Yet even in prose fiction success sometimes seemed to elude Cervantes. His early pastoral romance, *La Galatea,* had made little impression on the public. Only half of his *Exemplary Tales* seem to have been admired. The posthumous *Persiles and Sigismunda* has not been appreciated until recent times, and at that by only a select group of Cervantine scholars. Posterity tends to regard Cervantes as a one-book author. This narrow vision of his work is manifestly unjust. It is time for general readers, not just specialists, to read with open minds not only *Don Quixote* but also some of Cervantes' marvelous sonnets, his intricate plays and dense interludes, and the final masterpiece on which he expended so much imaginative and artistic energy.

The best starting point for a survey of Cervantes' writing is his poetry. We have seen that it was generally despised and was apparently disparaged by Cervantes himself. The curious thing is, then, that throughout his life Cervantes wrote poetry. By interpolating poems in his prose works, he actually published more poetry than did most of the recognized poets of that time. Unlike the poets Góngora and Francisco de Quevedo (1580–1645), Cervantes was not content to allow his verse to circulate among friends in manuscript, leaving it to some editor to anthologize it posthumously. Except for the last great romance, *Persiles and Sigismunda,* all Cervantes' fiction is liberally adorned with the various forms of his poetry. His full-length plays are in verse, as are two of the eight farcical interludes. The *Journey to Parnassus* consists of some 3,000 poetic lines. In the light of such complete dedication to poetry, is it reasonable to see Cervantes as nothing but a poet manqué?

In assessing Cervantes' poetic achievement, we must not fail to take into account two facts: the rivalry and personal animosity among the poets of his day, and his own ironic stance in all that he discusses, not excluding his own work.

Lope de Vega, as we have seen, declared that there was no worse poet than Cervantes. Such a trenchant judgment reflects a persistent rivalry between the two men. In his forties, Lope was becoming the major literary figure of his time as a dramatist, writer of romances, and poet. When *Don Quixote,* part 1, was published, Cervantes must have seemed to him a superannuated upstart. Be that as it may, for the last ten years of Cervantes' life the two authors were neighbors in Madrid, attending the same literary academies and functions. When in 1621, at his mistress' behest, Lope wrote his first short story, "Las fortunas de Diana" ("The Fortunes of Diana"), he found it possible at long last to express a grudging admiration for the stories of his late rival. "Miguel de Cervantes' tales," he wrote, "did not lack grace and style." For his part Cervantes was also grudging in his praise of Lope, calling him "a monstrosity of Nature who had made off with the realm of comedy." Without their being outright enemies, there was no love lost between the two. When such jealous competition exists, literary verdicts are suspect. The same can be said of the poet Esteban Manual de Villegas, who, addressing a fictitious muleteer, writes: "Sooner than that bad poet Cervantes, / you'll go and conquer Helicon, / where it won't avail him to be a Quixotist." This venom is almost certainly an expression of Villegas' resentment at being spurned when Cervantes omitted him from the lists of both good and bad poets in his *Journey to Parnassus.*

Cervantes' own evaluation of his poetry is less readily understood. In the two passages already cited he seems to deprecate his verse, but it is important to realize that the comments are made in a fictional context. It is an imagined stage producer in the prologue to the *Eight Plays* who supposedly tells Cervantes that his verse is hopeless; and it is the village priest in *Don Quixote* (pt. 1, ch. 6) who utters the conceit that Cervantes is more versed in misadventures than in verses. When an ironist speaks of himself through the lips of one of his characters, we must be cautious about attributing such opinions to the author. A surer, but still not entirely reliable, guide to Cervantes' estimate of his poetic ability is his *Journey to Parnassus,* which contains among other things his soul-searching inquiry into his status as a poet. He represents himself as a starving poet, somewhat neglected by the deities and muses who dwell on Mount Parnassus. Even so, Apollo expresses his joy at seeing him in that eminent place. Cervantes' elation at the cordial greeting is, however, quickly dashed when Apollo praises him not for his poetry but for his virtue. At the end of the long poem, criticized by his friends for his literary judgment, Cervantes is seen to be despondent over the poor results of his encounter with the muses: it is with rancor that he returns to his dismal and squalid house. But a cheerful appendix in prose ("Adjunta al Parnaso") belies Cervantes' sadness in the poem: Apollo has just sent him a letter in which he declares his particular affection for this mortal. It would seem that on this issue, as on so many others, Cervantes was of two minds. His standing as a poet he leaves to the judgment of the individual reader.

What the reader familiar with Spanish poetry notices in Cervantes' earliest poems, those written under the aegis of his schoolmaster, is their dependence on the work of Garcilaso de la Vega (1503–1536). Garcilaso was the first poet to successfully naturalize Italian meters and themes in Castilian verse. An elegantly classical imitator of Horace, he founded Renaissance poetry in Spain and was never surpassed by his successors. Cervantes pays tribute to him by imitating and quoting him in his own poetry. The fame of Garcilaso was such that no one could criticize Cervantes for his choice of a model. But Spanish poetry had changed, if not actually progressed, during the sixteenth century. Some of these developments exerted a modest influence on Cervantes' poetry. In his patriotic odes, Fernando de Herrera (1534–1597) had shown that the epic tone could be made to sound in shorter poems than epics. At the time when Cervantes was publishing his major works, Góngora was writing in a complex Latinate style, and Quevedo was burlesquing ancient myths in verse. Cervantes unreservedly expressed his admiration for this so-called new poetry, but in his practice he remained loyal to Garcilaso; and so to many he appeared to be out of date.

Cervantes' poem that he himself most admired was a sonnet with an *estrambote,* or extra tercet. It is an occasional piece. When Philip II died in 1598, an elaborate but empty catafalque was constructed in Seville cathedral. For two months famous architects, sculptors, and painters worked to create this useless work of art, which they knew was destined to be promptly destroyed. When the requiem mass for the king was supposed to be celebrated, however, a petty political quarrel broke out and deferred it for a month. During this time the catafalque became a sort of tourist attraction; thousands came to gape at its ephemeral splendor. When the political dispute was finally patched up, Cervantes went into the cathedral and gave a dramatic reading of his sonnet, acting out the part of each of the two characters. He drew a lot of attention to himself, and his sonnet, "To the Catafalque of Philip II in Seville," became very popular. A translation of it will give some sense of its effect:

> "By God, that grandeur scares me. / I'd give a doubloon to be able to describe it. / Who wouldn't be struck and amazed / by that noble engine and such a display of wealth? / By the living Christ, each piece / is worth more than a million, and it's a shame / that this thing won't last a century, O great Seville, / a Rome victorious in spirit and nobility! / I'll bet the dead man's soul, / to enjoy this place, has today left / heaven, where it lives for all eternity."/
>
> This was heard by a braggart, who said: "It's true, / everything you say, sir soldier, is true, / and whoever says the opposite is a liar." / And then straightway / he fixed his hat, felt his sword, / looked sidewise, went away, and nothing happened.

The sonnet shows Cervantes at his best as a poet and a dramatist. The naiveté and profanity of the soldier, the arrogance and posturing of the thug betray an emptiness in the actors that corresponds to that of the catafalque. Even the monarchy itself, the Spanish state, is upheld by no one but a pair of unthinking nonentities. The author of this sonnet clearly views the national life differently from the soldier who fought so valiantly at Lepanto.

In another famous sonnet, written in 1596 after the earl of Essex had sacked Cadiz with impunity for twenty-four days, Cervantes presents a grotesquely ironic picture of Spanish troops drilling in Seville in preparation for recapturing the city. It ends with another superb evocation of emptiness: "At long last into Cadiz, with measured pace, / now that the earl had left without concern, / triumphantly marched the great duke of Medina Sidonia." The victor over the absent Essex is none other than the admiral who once commanded the Invincible Armada. The veteran Cervantes is learning to live in a Spain from which heroism has departed, to be revived only fictionally and ironically in his character Don Quixote.

It would be wrong to think that the failure of heroism was an obsession with Cervantes. It was, rather, one of the sources of his poetic inspiration. In addition, he wrote elegies, love poems, religious verse, and much else. Above all, he wrote dramatic poems.

When, despairing of ever seeing them staged, Cervantes gave to a printer the manuscripts of those eight plays and eight interludes that had been lying unread in a drawer for years, the Spanish theater was dominated by Lope de Vega. Single-handedly, Lope had imposed a dramatic model, that of the new comedy, on all Spanish playwrights. He had thoroughly tested it in both public and private theaters. Its main virtue was that it pleased the public and thus was a financial success. Lope called his plays "comedies," without regard to their subject matter, the nobility or baseness of their characters, or the happy or tragic nature of their endings. They were written in three acts and about 3,000 lines of verse. Aristocrats and peasants, gallants and ladies jostled one another in them. They might be historical or imagined, set in contemporary Madrid or far-off Hungary. Lope had little respect for the classical unities of time, place, and plot. His only basic rule, he freely admitted, was to please the masses. And please them he did: the expression "It's by

Lope" entered the language to signify anything highly regarded. It must not be thought, however, that Lope's dramatic art was artless. It only pretended to be. His drama and that of his contemporaries and successors constitute the Golden Age of the Spanish theater.

As a dramatist, Cervantes had the misfortune to be a precursor of Lope. His first plays, *El trato de Argel (The Commerce of Algiers)* and *El cerco de Numancia (The Siege of Numantia),* were probably written in the 1580's, after his return to Spain from captivity in North Africa. The first draws heavily on his experience as a prisoner. The second, which has enjoyed more popularity than Cervantes' other plays, reflects his early hopes for a heroic Spain. In 133 B.C. the Celtiberian city of Numantia was besieged by Roman legions under the command of Scipio Africanus. Rather than surrender, the starving inhabitants committed collective suicide, thus depriving Scipio of even a single captive to exhibit in a victory parade in Rome. Cervantes dramatizes these events through the lives of his invented characters. The climax comes when, after occupying the city of the dead, Scipio finds a small boy still alive at the top of a tower to which he has fled; the triumph of a captive for the parade still eludes Scipio's grasp, for, resisting his blandishments, the boy hurls himself to his death. Cervantes employs allegorical personifications—of Spain, the river Duero, Opportunity, Necessity, and Fame—to expound the meaning of Numantia's heroic self-sacrifice for his Spain: out of the ashes of the city will rise the future greatness of the Hapsburg empire, which will be sustained by a similar heroism. The message conveyed by the allegory is unambiguous. But the plot adumbrates the ambiguity that Cervantes later perceived in the concepts of victory and defeat.

These two plays were not published until the eighteenth century. Some other plays that Cervantes claimed to have written were never published and have been lost. All that remains of his dramatic output are the two plays preserved in manuscript and the eight plays and eight interludes published in 1615. The eight plays were probably written over a period of years stretching from the late sixteenth century to the date of publication. Three of them are concerned with relations between Spanish Christians and their Moslem foes. One is based on Carolingian matter, another on romance. There is a play about a pimp who became a saint. Another seems to be either a parody or an imitation of Lope de Vega's new comedy. The best is probably *Pedro de Urdemalas,* whose eponymous protagonist is a protean figure from Spanish folklore; here Cervantes plays with illusion and apparent reality, much as he does in *Don Quixote.*

The great student of Cervantes' drama Jean Canavaggio has concluded that it was above all experimental. Rather than submit to the ready-made formula proffered by Lope de Vega, Cervantes constantly reconsidered the problem of how to write a good play. His theater is thus innovative but tentative. He could not, like Lope, present stereotyped characters who are entirely in the control of their creator. His characters are always in search of themselves. They are, therefore, more like characters in a novel. Pedro de Urdemalas and the saintly pander find their identities, much as Don Quixote and Sancho Panza do, only after journeying through many experiences. One may doubt that this fictional base can properly serve the ends of drama. But one must be grateful to Cervantes for the fact that, by means of his experimentation, he clearly defined the opportunities and the limitations of drama.

Later ages have been more favorably impressed with Cervantes' experimentation with short interludes. Even though they were not performed in his lifetime, they have been since; they are first-rate theater. Here Cervantes was building on a well-established tradition. Lope de Rueda, who died in 1565, was an actor-writer whose chief claim to fame rests on his early interludes, playlets performed between the acts of a full-fledged play. He is the inventor of the interlude, called by Spaniards the *género chico* (tiny genre). Reminiscing in the prologue to the edition of his plays, Cervantes tells us that he "remembered having seen performances by the great Lope de Rueda, a fine man notable both for his acting and for his mind." He goes on to describe the primitive conditions under which Rueda worked successfully. But the most interesting detail in this part of the prologue is Cervantes' boast that he could still recall from his boyhood a number of Rueda's poetic lines. Clearly this first Spanish professional man of the theater had made a great impression on him. In writing his own interludes, Cervantes felt comfortable in accepting the genre as Rueda had forged it, limiting his own invention to working within the received framework—an act of homage he was not able to pay Lope de Vega in writing three-act plays. Within Rueda's constraints, however, Cervantes carried the humble interlude to new heights. It is one of the more successful of the literary genres that he cultivated.

Like his long *Pedro de Urdemalas,* Cervantes' eight interludes owe much to folklore. One major theme is that of conjugal dissatisfaction. In *El juez de los divorcios (The Divorce Judge),* wives and husbands declare each other insufferable. The antihero of *El viejo celoso (The Old Jealous Husband)* is inevitably cuckolded by the young, attractive wife whom he has, in effect, bought from her poor parents. A wry twist on marital relations is found in *El rufián viudo (The Widowed Pimp):* now that the whore he has protected for many years has died, the procurer makes a brave effort to behave as a faithful widowed husband might. The other major theme of folk origin is the successful swindle or cheat. A gullible husband, in *La cueva de Salamanca (The Cave of Salamanca),* is easily persuaded that his wife's incipient adultery, upon which he has stumbled, classically, by returning home before he is expected, is merely an apparition produced by a university student who claims to have studied necromancy. *El retablo de las maravillas (The Wonder Show)* offers us two swindlers whose nonexistent puppet show can be seen only by spectators whose blood is untainted by Jewish or Moorish stock and who were born in wedlock. Swift-moving and hilarious, these farces tend to end with blows or dancing, the dupes discomfited and the beguilers triumphant. They are sheer entertainment.

The unsettling thing about these entertainments is that we sense in them a challenging of institutions, a social criticism that reminds us of the then proscribed Erasmus. We cannot forget that the absurdity of *The Wonder Show* was played out against the historical reality of statutory racism. In the notable year of 1492, the Iberian peninsula was finally rid of seven centuries of partial domination by Islam when the kingdom of Granada fell to the forces of Ferdinand and Isabella; and Spanish Jews were required either to leave the now united kingdom of Castile and Aragon or to embrace Christianity. What began as religious intolerance ended in the sixteenth century as official racism. To qualify for many honors and positions, a petitioner had to prove that he had no trace of Jewish blood in his genealogy, that he was—as the formula put it—an Old Christian. In *The Wonder Show,* the midget who plays the rebec to accompany the invisible performance is said by the confidence man to be "a very good Christian, and a gentleman of known lineage." To this the town's governor, the king's appointee, retorts: "And necessary qualities these are to be a good musician!" This casual disrespect for the law on the part of a law officer prepares us for the savage ending. When a stranger who is not privy to the mystery of the wonder show intrudes on the scene of mass hysteria and calls them all mad, those who have pretended to see—or who have deluded themselves into seeing—the nonexistent puppets turn on him jubilantly with the very Latin words, "Ex illis es" ("Thou art also of them": Luke 22.58), that caused Peter to deny his Christ. A sober and somber chill thus pervades this merry farce. But the overall levity is not dampened by this suggestion that even the law may exemplify credulity rather than genuine belief.

Not all of Cervantes' interludes question the Spanish way of life as clearly as *The Wonder Show.* But none fails to disturb as it entertains. As the great Spanish scholar Eugenio Asensio puts it judiciously: "Without forcing things too much, we detect [in the interludes] gusts of hostility toward some customs and institutions. Can it be that we are taking jokes too seriously?" This is always a good question to ask about our reaction to comedy, for academics are too prone to be serious. But in the case of Cervantes there is corroborating evidence from other works that his critical spirit could not be stifled by post-Tridentine conformism. This ever ambiguous writer invariably sees the serious base of levity. As a result the interludes of Cervantes cannot be dismissed as pure farce; they are generally recognized as among the most artistic of his works.

It is, nevertheless, as a writer of prose fiction that Cervantes is famous. It is in this realm that his greatness lies. In an age much given to imitation, especially of the classics of antiquity, Cervantes innovated in all his writing. Such a pioneering writer did well to cultivate prose fiction, because its virtual absence from ancient Greece and Rome absolved him of the pressure to model his works on classical authors. This is not to say that Cervantes did not build on previous prose fiction. It means rather that he could pick and choose from among it and treat earlier fiction either with deference or with disrespect as his purpose required. It is important, then, to understand the legacy of the kind of writing that Cervantes inherited.

The reason the novel hardly existed in antiquity is that on the whole verse was used for fiction, whereas prose was reserved for such empirical writing as histories, treatises on medicine or astronomy, and cookbooks. It is as though a work in prose signals to the reader that this is an effort to convey the truth, whereas a poetic work tells him at once that it is based not so much on recognized facts as on the writer's imagination. So Ovid's *Metamorphoses,* in verse, is an imaginative re-creation of old myths; on the other hand, Caesar's *Gallic War,* in prose, recounts what really happened—or what Caesar says really happened—during his military campaigns. The use of poetry and prose thus embodied a universally accepted code, which precluded the reader's misinterpretation of the author's intention. This code was obviously valuable, if we suppose that mutual understanding between author and reader is always desirable.

There have always been some lighthearted writers who delight in leading readers astray. In late antiquity one such was Lucian (A.D. 115–*ca.* 200). He is best known for dialogues in which he makes fun of the pagan gods and exposes the follies of all sorts of people. These dialogues were very popular among the humanist scholars of the Renaissance. One of Lucian's works, *Vera historia (True History),* is particularly relevant to Cervantes, for this is the term repeatedly applied in his major novel to refer to *Don Quixote,* a work neither true nor historical. Lucian's *True History* parodies the farfetched adventures and sightings of monsters that some of the less scrupulous historians admitted into their histories. In his preface Lucian tells his reader frankly: "I shall be a more honest liar than my predecessors, for I am telling you frankly, here and now, that I have no intention whatever of telling the truth. . . . So mind you do not believe a word I say." Lucian then launches into a fantastic adventure story, which includes a voyage to the moon. If he had failed to warn the reader that his true history was not true, the reader would have had a rare early experience of reading a short story: he would have received one message (prose-truth) and been duped by the author's perversion of the message (prose-falsehood)—until he came perhaps to realize that the author was manipulating both him and the code. It is from this kind of manipulation that prose fiction arises.

The greatest flourishing of antique prose fiction occurred in the third century A.D. in the form of the Greek romances. These are very long stories about separated lovers who remain faithful while undergoing incredible adventures and trials. The plots are intricate, containing many subordinate stories within the main one. The best known of these romances in Cervantes' time was the *Historia Aethiopica (Ethiopian History),* by a Syrian called Heliodorus. This story and others like it had survived in the eastern Roman Empire, Byzantium, after the fall of Rome to the Goths. Rediscovered in Western Europe during the Renaissance, they delighted not only their new readers but also those literary theorists who had previously been unable to find a justification for the novel in the literary treatises of antiquity. Prose fiction now had classical models to imitate. We will see that Cervantes based *Don Quixote* and, even more, *Persiles and Sigismunda* on Heliodorus' narrative art.

At this point it becomes necessary to distinguish between the kinds of prose fiction known as romance and novel. The romance makes no pretense of representing the everyday world of the reader; it describes events unlikely to happen; it is a product of an imagination little trammeled by the reality of the human experience. The novel, on the other hand, is rooted in a world we recognize as resembling our own; its characters and events have therefore an air of familiarity, and we are easily deceived into believing that they could be real; we tend to feel in ourselves the joys, sorrows, triumphs, and defeats of the fictional characters. Many have said that in *Don Quixote* Cervantes created the novel. It is certainly true that we come to believe in the existence of Don Quixote and Sancho Panza, and even to love them. We also come to sense the inns and villages through which they pass, and even (as Gustave Flaubert pointed out) those dusty roads that are not in fact described in this work. It cannot be doubted that in *Don Quixote* Cervantes wrote a novel. But it is not necessarily true that he wrote the first one; and it is certainly not true that in it he parted company with romance.

*Don Quixote* is, among other things, a parody of a certain kind of romance, that which recounted deeds of derring-do performed by fictional knights-errant. In the Middle Ages there were of course knights and orders of knighthood. But the romances of chivalry pay little attention to this historical reality. They are set in unverifiable circumstances, imaginary kingdoms and times. The knight is accompanied only by his squire, although he may at times volunteer to lead an army. He performs superhuman feats, such as splitting a giant in two with a single stroke of the sword. Besides being a warrior, he is a lover, constant to his lady even though the distressed damsels he rescues are nearly always exquisitely beautiful and tempting. In pursuit of battle or love, the knight may be whisked thousands of miles through the air by some miraculous horse. Even though there is probably no direct relationship, a kind of family resemblance with the Greek romances may be seen in the romances of chivalry. They existed in manuscript form before the invention of printing. In the sixteenth century modernized versions of them appeared in print, as did sequels and imitations. These romances were the most popular reading of the century. It was—as Cervantes seems to say, though always through the mouth of invented characters—to put an end to such pernicious romances that *Don Quixote* was written.

Another kind of romance, the pastoral, arose in Spain in the second half of the sixteenth century. In this fiction shepherds and shepherdesses are found, in a pleasant landscape of eternal springtime, discoursing and singing about their normally unhappy loves. These shepherds are often described by the authors of the romances as disguised. They are, then, in no sense real shepherds but courtiers and nobles masquerading fictionally as shepherds. A perhaps oversimple explanation of the pastoral convention is that in it the aristocratic shepherds live on close terms with a nature conceived of as beneficent, without having to work hard as farmers do. The fictional shepherds are thus free—free of social obligations and free to concentrate on the life of the psyche, especially on the feelings that accompany the state of being in love. Love at court or in the city is anything but pure. It is directed to marriage, which, besides being a religious sacrament, is also a social pact, involving family and financial interests. True love appears submerged in a sea of obligations. In pastoral literature the lover is imagined divested of such responsibilities. Alone, or in the company of like-minded lovers, he can indulge himself in the luxury of doing nothing but thinking and talking about his love, which here is of concern to no one but himself, his beloved, and a few sympathetic friends. In his distress, if the beloved has repudiated him, he may derive consolation and strength to go on living from Mother Nature, in whose bosom he reclines. The pastoral convention thus abstracts human love from its social and material circumstances so that it can be seen in its pure form. Whereas the Greek romance and the romance of chivalry are full of action, there is very little in the pastoral. What replaces action are soul-searching and the exploration of motives and behavior. The pastoral romance, although it still lacks verisimilitude, makes possible the intimate understanding of human beings without which the novel, and particularly *Don Quixote,* could hardly have arisen. Cervantes' apprenticeship as a writer of prose fiction was served as he trained himself in the writing of his pastoral romance, *La Galatea.* As we shall see, the idea of pastoral was an inspiration to him and to his fiction until his dying day.

One last kind of fiction remains to be discussed before we turn to Cervantes' own. In 1554, in three widely separated cities of Spain and the Low Countries, *Lazarillo de Tormes* appeared in print. The book purports to be the autobiography of a very poor boy who can survive only by serving a series of poor masters, among them a blind beggar, a miserly priest, and a bankrupt squire. Performing this meanest of service, the boy wanders with his masters from Salamanca to Toledo, through a number of small towns, all of which in fact exist. The plot unfurls in a geographic reality that many readers could recognize from their own experience. By his own account the boy is treated cruelly; but gradually he learns from the school of hard knocks how to defend himself, and eventually to better himself economically. At the end he describes himself as at the peak of his good fortune: he has cynically consented to be the faithful husband of an archpriest's mistress in exchange for favors of value, while he plies the demeaning trade of town crier (which involves participation in public whippings and executions). This fiction focuses on the lowest class of society; it seems to reflect what readers consider the real world; it contains none of the heroics or ideal love that we associate with the romance. An argument could be, and has been, made for regarding the anonymous *Lazarillo de Tormes,* published half a century before *Don Quixote,* as the first novel. However that may be, it was not imitated until 1599, when Mateo Alemán published the first part of *Guzmán de Alfarache.* Thereafter several similar works were written, constituting the genre we have come to call the picaresque novel. Cervantes was fascinated by this genre. He never wrote a picaresque novel; but he flirted with its potentiality.

When Cervantes began his career as a writer of fiction, he had before him, then, various modes upon which to draw. The Greek romance offered him a classical—and so respectable—model of fiction, and the romance of chivalry offered him a similar, though popular, model: episodic plot, interpolated short stories, adventure, true love, the whole bound together by nothing less than the unbridled imagination of the author. Pastoral romance showed him techniques for delving into the inner life of mankind. The picaresque novel demonstrated the credibility a tale acquires by being located in a recognizable social and topographical setting.

It was surely no accident that Cervantes first turned his hand to writing a pastoral romance. Recently returned from an agonizing captivity in Algiers, in which his everyday thoughts were of survival, he may well have found this first exercise in literary composition a solace, a means of restoring to himself the spiritual life of Spain. As pastoral offers an escape from the chaos of loving in society to the orderliness of a love disciplined by art alone, so the writing of a pastoral romance may have brought the order of art to this soldier, aware that the military career he had so assiduously sought had been ended.

Cervantes' pastoral romance is divided into six sections called "books." This kind of division he inherited from his predecessors in the genre. Like the first of its kind, Jorge de Montemayor's *La Diana* (1558 or 1559), *La Galatea* is left incomplete, the author promising to provide a sequel. This promise was regularly repeated during the rest of Cervantes' life. In 1616, sensing that he was to die within a few days, he dedicated his *Persiles and Sigismunda* to the count of Lemos, assuring him that he would yet see the "ending of *La Galatea* . . . , if perchance, to my good fortune (yet it would not be fortune but a miracle), heaven should grant it to me to go on living." The second part of *La Galatea,* of course, never appeared.

In the romance, Galatea is a shepherdess of incomparable beauty who lives with her father, Aurelio the Venerable, on the banks of the river Tagus. She is loved by two shepherds, Elicio and Erastro, who are good friends. Galatea neither favors nor disdains either one for most of the romance. But Erastro, suspecting that she is more fond of his friend than of him, lets it be understood that he supports Elicio's suit; he is content to bask in the reflected glory of Galatea's beauty. Many other shepherds and shepherdesses crowd in on this amicable rivalry with their tales of love, most of which occurred away from the idyllic Tagus valley. The romance is a mosaic of the life stories of those who have gravitated toward this natural setting for Galatea's radiance. It is not until the middle of the fifth book that anything happens to disturb the settled relationship between Galatea and her two suitors. Then Elicio learns that Aurelio plans to marry Galatea to a rich foreign shepherd who lives on the river Lima in northern Portugal. The Portuguese intruder is the only character who is not named. As a dutiful daughter, Galatea cannot imagine disobeying her father's will. Elicio is dismayed to think that he will be deprived forever of the sight of his beloved. The other shepherds, his friends, are equally distressed, for they too find it unthinkable that their valley should be denied the presence of Galatea's loveliness. In the last pages of the romance, they decide to call on the venerable Aurelio to beg him "not to banish from those meadows Galatea's unequaled beauty; and if that did not suffice, Elicio planned to impose such obstacles and fears on the Lusitanian shepherd that he would declare himself unhappy with the arranged marriage; and if pleading and trickery got him nowhere, he determined to use force to restore her freedom." The romance ends as this threefold plan of action is about to be set in motion: the shepherds begin their attempt to prevail upon Aurelio. The author "promises" to let us know the outcome of this central story (and other subordinate ones) in his second part; but, as noted above, for all his good intentions throughout his life, Cervantes never kept this promise.

We have seen that the love affair of Elicio and Galatea is static until near the end of the romance. Intertwined with the sketchy main plot are the numerous tales of the shepherds who live in or visit the Tagus valley. These may be seen by a modern reader as extraneous or distracting, however interesting each story may be. The Renaissance reader would, however, have seen them as variations on the pastoral theme or as variegated samples of narrative fiction. *La Galatea* is a showcase, too, for a wide selection of poetry.

It would be a mistake to conclude from this description that *La Galatea* is a miscellany book. Its structure is much too complex. Cervantes is here experimenting with forms of narrative, including the overall problem of narrating a story at length. He is schooling himself in the art of writing fiction. Each of the stories responds to the character who tells it. Each therefore reflects a different human reality; and each is told from a different point of view. There is here an attempt to enlarge the scope of pastoral romance so that it may include more than a limited convention for investigating the complex nature of love. There is violence, and not just from dehumanized evil forces, as in Montemayor's *La Diana.* Soon after *La Galatea* begins, a murder is committed; and we have seen that as a last resort Elicio is prepared to use force to prevent Galatea's exile to Portugal. Here Cervantes has expanded the possibilities of the genre he has inherited. The placid eclogue—the term Cervantes used to designate his romance—has been made active by the introduction into it of ingredients more proper to Greek romance. Cervantes' last publication, *Persiles and Sigismunda,* frankly announces itself as a revival in modern times of Heliodorus' *Ethiopian History.* His fascination with this action-packed kind of romance never dwindled. In *La Galatea* he experimented with grafting it onto the pastoral. In *Don Quixote* he would force it into the mold of the chivalric romance.

Before we turn to Cervantes' acknowledged masterpiece, let us consider his *Exemplary Tales,* since, though not published until 1613, they were written at various times before that date and so can give us a further insight into the progress of his career as a writer. There are twelve tales, although the last one, "El coloquio de los perros" ("The Dialogue of the Dogs"), is an appendage of the one preceding, "El casamiento engañoso" ("The Deceitful Marriage"), so that the two together form a single diptych.

Cervantes calls his tales *novelas* (Hispanicizing the Italian word *novelle*), thus indicating their affiliation with the Italian short story of the Renaissance. He claims to have been the first to write *novelle* in Spanish. This claim is true in the sense that other Spanish writers had only translated or closely imitated the Italians; original short stories in Spanish tended to be yarns of a folksy kind rather than the carefully contrived art form developed by the Italians. "I have entitled my stories *Exemplary,*" writes Cervantes in his prologue to them, "and if you consider it well, there is not one from which one cannot extract a salutary moral example." He has in mind the *exempla,* moralizing or illustrative anecdotes used by medieval preachers to enliven their sermons. Cervantes continues: "If it wouldn't make this prologue too long, perhaps I would show you the delightful and proper lesson that could be deduced both from the tales as a whole and from each one separately." Withdrawn before it is made, this offer to provide a key to the exemplariness of the *Exemplary Tales* has tantalized readers across the centuries. Not only is there no general agreement as to their moral sense, but many find it hard to believe that there is one. Nevertheless, Cervantes occasionally points one out. At the end of "El celoso extremeño" ("The Jealous Hidalgo"), the narrator tells us that the event just related is "an example and mirror of how little trust can be put in keys, turnstiles, and walls when the will is left free; and how much less can be put in innocent tender years if there are duennas in their nun-black attire and long white coifs to whisper things in guileless ears." This "example" is so obvious to one who has just read the tale that Cervantes has not really helped him to understand its subtle meaning. He is forever teasing. It is best perhaps to leave each individual reader to determine for himself in what way the tales illustrate or inculcate moral truths.

The next words in Cervantes' prologue purport to define the author's intention in writing them: "My purpose has been to set up in the central square of our commonwealth a billiard table, to which each person may repair to entertain himself without harm to body or soul, since entertainment taken in moderation benefits rather than harms." He adds that we can't spend all our time performing religious duties or attending to business; there is a proper time for recreation, when the weary spirit may legitimately rest. Cervantes is here expounding the doctrine—enunciated by Aristotle and confirmed by Saint Thomas Aquinas—that there is a virtue in relaxation because it enables us to return with better purpose to the activities that give our life its meaning. It may well be that this forgotten virtue, technically called "eutrapelia," is what the *Exemplary Tales* as a whole exemplify.

The tales have been thought of traditionally as falling into two main groups, the idealistic and the realistic. These inaccurate terms are intended to designate, respectively, those stories that seem to partake of the improbabilities of romance and those that produce in the reader the recognition of everyday reality characteristic of the novel. The division is not, in fact, useful, for Cervantes' short stories defy such categorization. How are we to classify, for instance, the "Dialogue of the Dogs," in which two dogs improbably confer with each other about the evident daily reality of human life in seventeenth-century Spain? It is nevertheless clear that most modern readers, more attuned to the novel than to the romance, vastly prefer some stories to others. "El amante liberal" ("The Generous Lover") is a miniature Greek romance about two lovers who undergo singly the most horrible misadventures at the hands of Turks, Moslem pirates, and Christian renegades, only to be miraculously restored safe and sound to each other's company at the end, and it has no more appeal to today's average reader than Heliodorus. On the other hand, despite its inconclusive ending, "Rinconete and Cortadillo" has all the attractions of a picaresque novel: two poor boys who survive by cheating and stealing discover that their freedom as petty criminals is restrained when they are obliged to enter the minisociety of an organized and grotesque underworld. "The Generous Lover" belongs to the realm of the wondrous, and "Rinconete" belongs to that of the probable. We believe in one story's claim to reflect the human experience while strongly denying that of the other.

Because Cervantes has been generally credited with inventing the novel in *Don Quixote,* most scholars have thought that his writing program consisted of working toward this goal. Therefore, it was felt, his earliest stories must be those that least resemble novels. The less readable ones must be early efforts in the form of the short story, imitations of Italian *novelle;* the readable ones, then, must be the result of his gradual realization that, to engage a reader's interest, prose fiction must seem to him like a slice of life as it is really lived. The difficulty with this hypothesis is that, as we have seen, "Rinconete and Cortadillo," the tale I have chosen to exemplify the novel in short-story form, had been written several years before its publication. By comparing the texts of "Rinconete" and its companion piece, "The Jealous Hidalgo," that appeared in the manuscript of 1606 with the texts in the printed edition of 1613, it is evident that Cervantes revised and polished these tales before publishing them. As was the case with the *Eight Plays,* some of his short stories had long awaited an opportunity to be printed. And these are of the novelistic type that attracts the modern reader. From a consideration of the fact that in his longer fiction Cervantes progressed from *Don Quixote* to *Persiles and Sigismunda,* from novel to romance, Ruth El Saffar has recently concluded that the composition of the *Exemplary Tales* proceeded along a like course. She argues that today's favorites were the first ones written, while the unpopular ones, like "The Generous Lover," were written specially for the 1613 volume. Her ingenious thesis reverses the usual way of regarding the chronology of the tales. If it had taken greater account of the varieties of romance contained in *La Galatea,* it might have been wholly persuasive. In any event, it must be treated with the utmost respect. It is beyond all doubt that in his later years Cervantes felt himself increasingly drawn to the fiction of the miraculous.

In spite of this evidence of the direction taken by Cervantes' prose, it is the traditionally approved tales that continue to appeal to the modern reader, just as *Don Quixote* does, for in them he detects the nascent art of the novel and of the modern short story. "El licenciado Vidriera" ("Master Glass") may serve to illustrate this important phase of Cervantes' writing. A poor peasant boy, aged about eleven, who gives his name as Thomas Rodaja, is picked up by some well-to-do and gentlemanly students at the famous University of Salamanca. Thomas tells them that he plans to be a servant to a university student in exchange for the opportunity to be a student himself. He will not reveal the names of his parents or of his native village until he can bring honor to them by becoming a distinguished scholar. The gentlemen hire him; he becomes not so much the servant as the companion of his employers. For eight years Thomas studies hard to become a lawyer, though his preference is for the humanities. When his masters graduate, they give Thomas enough money to see him through the remaining three years needed to obtain a master's degree in law. At this time he falls in with Diego de Valdivia, a dashing army captain who tries to persuade him to enlist. Without mentioning the boredom and the risks of military service, the officer describes the excitement of army life in Italy in such glowing colors that Thomas' curiosity is piqued. Refusing to join the army, he nevertheless accepts Valdivia's invitation to accompany his unit to Italy. Once there, Thomas sets off on his own to see the great cities, their art objects, and their historical monuments. With his analytical mind, "he contemplated, reflected on, and put everything in its rightful place." After a side trip to the Low Countries, Thomas decides to return to Salamanca to finish his studies. He graduates brilliantly as a Master of Jurisprudence.

Soon thereafter he meets a crafty lady whose amorous advances he spurns. Surreptitiously she administers to him a drug that she is confident will cause him to love her. Instead, it drives him insane. He conceives the delusion that he is made of glass, and thus is extremely fragile. More than that, he is transparent: he sees and speaks the truth about his fellow men without the social hypocrisy that common life requires. The central section of the tale, in which Thomas, now Master Glass, makes witty, satirical judgments about various social types and individuals to groups of curious bystanders, is the longest. His point is that all people pretend to be other than they are in an obvious attempt to deceive their neighbors. The story of Thomas Rodaja seems designed to display this wide range of social criticism made by a clear-sighted madman.

At long last, Master Glass is cured by a monk. Dressed as a lawyer, and calling himself now Master Rueda (not Rodaja), he prepares to embark on a successful legal career. But the crowd of those who had listened to his aphorisms about his fellow men continue to follow him about, giving him no peace. No clients want his professional services. In disgust Rueda returns to Flanders, "where the immortal fame he had begun to win in the field of letters he finally achieved on the field of battle, in the company of his good friend Captain Valdivia, leaving behind him at his death the name of a wise and brave soldier."

When we stand back to contemplate the events in this story, we note that it is chiefly concerned with Thomas' quest for fame. He begins his quest as Rodaja (a "little wheel") and ends it as Rueda (a "wheel" of proper size). He hopes to bring glory to his obscure family by being a success in a learned profession. His plan miscarries, but whether as a result of an accident or of providential design we cannot be sure. There is a similar ambiguity in the long series of social criticisms. Is his perception of the all-pervasiveness of hypocrisy a true one because he is "made of glass?" Or is it false because he is mad? Thomas becomes famous not as a lawyer but as a soldier. In this last detail, which caps the story of his life, there is a reflection of Cervantes' long-standing concern with the relative value of arms and letters. This is a story that raises more questions than it answers. Its problematic structure inversely parallels that of the story of Don Quixote, the madman who wants to win fame by force of arms, but whose immortality ultimately rests on Cervantes' second-best career as a man of letters.

Some of the other popular stories in this collection also reflect themes in *Don Quixote.* "The Deceitful Marriage," for example, is similarly based on the debate between arms and letters. An army ensign has just been discharged from a hospital where he has taken the sweat cure for syphilis. He meets an old friend, a man of letters called Master Peralta. He tells him how he contracted the venereal disease. Attracted by his ostentatious jewelry, a handsome lady who owned her own house married him, to their mutual advantage, they hoped. As it turned out, the lady did not own the house in which they lived together for a few days; she fled with the ensign's jewels and her lover, leaving him with nothing but her disease. His paltry consolation is that his jewelry was fake and valueless. A different solace stems from the fact that, as he lay sweating in the hospital, he heard two dogs talking. He has written down one of their conversations, which he would like Master Peralta to read. He will write the second only if Peralta believes, or at least does not despise, the first. After demurring on the grounds that dogs cannot talk, Peralta consents, and we the readers join him as he reads "The Dialogue of the Dogs." After this short story in dialogue form, we return to the officer and the man of letters. Peralta observes: "Although this colloquy may be imagined and never have happened, it seems to me that it is well composed, and that you, Sir Ensign, may proceed with the second." Another literary promise goes unfulfilled, since, as far as we know, the second "Dialogue of the Dogs" was never written. What happens in this pair of related stories is that Cervantes fictionalizes the author-reader relationship as he explores in his fiction the creative process and the way a fiction becomes credible. An art of the novel and a theory of the novel are incorporated into the tales. This story about how a story is written and how it affects the reader repeats a fundamental thread running through *Don Quixote.*

Besides the ones mentioned so far, other *Exemplary Tales* that have succeeded in pleasing twentieth-century readers are "La gitanilla" ("The Gypsy Maid") and "La ilustre fregona" ("The Illustrious Kitchen Maid"). Both have as heroines girls found in humble circumstances who were born into the nobility. Because of their beauty, Preciosa, the gypsy, and Costanza, the servant in an inn, are courted by noble suitors who reduce themselves to the girls' social level in order to win their hands. The resolution is a happy one: the girls resume the aristocratic station from which they have been toppled by circumstance, and the men resume the station from which they have removed themselves. The resultant happy marriages indicate that a beneficent Providence has been watching over these predestined couples. What is important to note is that among the outcast gypsies Preciosa preserves her aristocratic scale of moral values, as does Costanza in the rough-and-tumble of a hostelry. Blood confers on them a moral superiority to those with whom they must consort. They exemplify the title of a less read tale in the collection, "La fuerza de la sangre" ("The Force of Blood"). Accordingly El Saffar regards these stories as the final transition in Cervantes' move to the romance mode in the short story. If "Master Glass" and

"The Deceitful Marriage" tend toward the manner of *Don Quixote,* the stories of the two virtuous maids tend toward that of *Persiles and Sigismunda.* It is that first stage, when the novel predominates over the romance, on which Cervantes' claim to posterity rests.

Strictly speaking, there are two *Don Quixotes,* that of 1605 and that of 1615. Cervantes developed as a writer so late in life and with such rapidity that we would hardly expect the sequel, published at a time when Cervantes was again fascinated with romance, to resemble the original. That it does to a large extent is the result of its having the same cast of main characters. The very success of the 1605 book also constrained Cervantes not to depart too markedly from its formula. We must, then, treat the two books as one, while taking care to note the major differences between them.

Even though Cervantes' interest in writing romances revived between the publication dates of the two *Don Quixotes,* the novel seems to have been conceived, or begotten, as an antidote to romance. In his prologue to part 1, which is an autobiographical fiction, Cervantes has a friend say to him that "this book of yours aims at no more than destroying the authority and influence that books of chivalry have in the world and among the common people." Cervantes neither endorses nor contradicts this assertion of his friend's: "I listened in complete silence to my friend's words." The last sentence of *Don Quixote,* part 2, expresses the same purpose: "my sole object has been to arouse men's contempt for all fabulous and absurd stories of knight-errantry, whose credit this tale of my genuine Don Quixote has already shaken, and which will, without a doubt, soon tumble to the ground." The first person ("my") in this case is Cervantes' imagined narrator of most of his novel, the Moor Cide Hamete Benengeli, who is alternately represented as a scrupulously honest historian and as a lying, infidel dog. The consistent statement of intention is founded on a fictional base, and thus is worthy of no more of the reader's belief than he is willing to repose in the historical foundation of the whole novel. An uncritical reader may—temporarily, as he reads—believe in the existence of Don Quixote and Sancho Panza; a critical reader is at all times aware that he is confronted with a work of fiction, an imagined, only tentatively credible, falsehood. For the novelist, however, the uncritical reader is the ideal reader of novels, since the art of the novel is to manipulate the reader into believing the story. Generations of readers, some of them mistakenly believing themselves to be critical, have been cajoled into believing on the basis of fictitious statements that *Don Quixote* was written for no other reason than to destroy the popularity of the romances of chivalry. The fact is that it may or may not have been.

The novel is the ultimate consequence of the undermining of the ancient, universally accepted convention whereby one recognized factual material because it was written in prose and fiction because it was written in verse. It is Cervantes' recognition of this erstwhile generic reality that makes *Don Quixote* the novel it is. To believe, however provisionally, in the truth of a fiction is to be out of one's mind. The gentleman in that unnamed village of La Mancha who is to become Don Quixote is, like the reader of his adventures, a reader of adventure stories. He is perhaps more seriously addicted to fiction than most, since he has sold his real estate in order to buy books of romances. But the effect on the reader and on the protagonist is similar. Don Quixote "used to say that the Cid Ruy Díaz must have been a very good knight, but that he could not be compared to the Knight of the Burning Sword, who with a single backstroke had cleft a pair of fierce and monstrous giants in two." Indeed, Spain's national hero, the Cid, cannot be compared to the Knight of the Burning Sword because the historical figure dwells in a different dimension from that of the fictional hero. It is Don Quixote's inability to distinguish between reality and fiction that drives him mad. His madness, with its lucid intervals, is essentially that of the ideal reader of fiction, who, as long as he is reading, believes in the reality of Don Quixote. From the very first chapter, Cervantes raises the question of the nature of the fictional experience.

It is clear from the many early references to the novel that most of Cervantes' readers were—as he must have wanted them to be—uncritical. For them *Don Quixote* was a funny book, an uproarious source of merriment. In this judgment they were of course right. There is something wrong with readers who do not laugh, or at least smile, at the pseudoknight's antics. A few scholars do well to remind us that, since the romantic revolution of the nineteenth century, we have taken *Don Quixote* too seriously and have found in the novel depths of which Cervantes could not have been aware and which he could not possibly have intended. It is absurd that readers should ever have considered the mad gentleman to be a figure of Christ or even a Christlike figure. And yet we have seen that Cervantes' hero has undergone the experience the reader is now undergoing. There are undeniable complexities underlying the fun. And there is no denying that Cervantes plays skillfully with his readers for the purpose of making his fiction credible. The only question is whether he fully understood the implications of what he was doing as he wrote his complex modern novel.

One of the devices he uses to disorient and so to gain control of his reader is the multiplication of narrators. We all know that the "I" of fiction is not necessarily the author or even a spokesman for the author. When we come across that pronoun in the first sentence of *Don Quixote* ("In a certain village in La Mancha which I do not wish to name . . ."), we are too sophisticated to believe that Cervantes has a reason for not identifying Don Quixote's place of residence. Who, then, is this narrator? We are not told. We are told, however, that the narrator is recounting historical events that he has exhumed from the archives of La Mancha. Until we realize that a district that has a geographical but not a political identity cannot have official archives, we are momentarily tempted to believe this cock-and-bull story. But soon Cervantes strains our credulity still further. At the end of chapter 8, Don Quixote is engaged in single combat with a comic Basque, who is using a cushion as a shield: each man's sword is raised over the other's head ready to deal a mortal blow. "But the unfortunate thing is that the author of this history left the battle in suspense at this critical point, with the excuse that he could find no more records of Don Quixote's exploits than those related here." That "I" of the novel's first sentence—is he "the author of this history" or only its transcriber? The text continues: "It is true that the second author of this work would not believe that such a curious history could have been consigned to oblivion." We now worry about "the second author." In chapter 9 a certain "I"—the same as the first, or another?—appears: "I really could not bring myself to believe that such a gallant history could have been left maimed and mutilated." At that time this "I" finds a parchment book written in Arabic being sold on the streets of Toledo by a lad. Finding a Spanish-speaking Moor, the current narrator asks for an instant interpretation of the newly found text. It turns out to be a continuation of the history of Don Quixote as written by the Arabic historian Cide Hamete Benengeli. Here is yet another narrator; and if the interpreter diverges from the original in his translation, he must be thought of as yet one more. Some Cervantine scholars think that they can identify and number the narrators of *Don Quixote*. They may be too self-confident. Cervantes controls us better than we control his narrative.

This is not to say that at all times Cervantes was in full command of his novel. He made a mistake when he sent Don Quixote on his first sortie without a companion and so without an interlocutor. With hindsight we can see that Don Quixote could not be viable unless he had a Sancho Panza. Cervantes quickly recognized his error, recalled his hero, and invented for him a constant squire and companion. One wonders why the author did not simply rewrite the first few chapters to include Sancho in them.

There has been some speculation that when Cervantes sat down to write *Don Quixote* he had it in mind to write just another short story, another treatment of madness like "Master Glass." Perhaps the first sortie is this tale. One thing certain is that some of the inspiration for *Don Quixote* came from an anonymous *Entremés de los romances (Interlude of the Ballads),* in which a peasant named Bartolo goes mad from hearing too many ballads. Don Quixote's first adventure, his encounter with the Toledan merchants (ch. 4), is modeled on an episode in the playlet. And as he is being taken home, battered and bruised, by his neighbor Pedro Alonso, Don Quixote thinks that he is not a knight-errant but the marquis of Mantua, a ballad hero. He recites some of the same ballad lines as Bartolo. It is certainly more conceivable that a short play would inspire a short story than a full-length novel. After the first sortie Don Quixote never again identifies himself with characters from ballads; he bases his conduct firmly on that of Amadís de Gaula, the most famous hero in the romances of chivalry. Cervantes has rectified what he must have seen as an error in his initial characterization of Don Quixote. From these blunders in the false start one can see that writing part 1 was to some extent a process of trial and error.

A very important study by Geoffrey Stagg has proved conclusively that the first chapters were written as continuous prose, without division into chapters. The fact that there are textual references to certain "chapters" from chapters 18 through 22 is evidence that at about this point in the composition of the novel Cervantes became preoccupied with the problem of chapter division, and began to break his unfinished work into units. The decision to use chapters necessitated a reconsideration of all his material. Stagg has shown that the pastoral episode of Marcela and Chrysostom (chapters 11–14) was originally set in the Sierra Morena, after the first segment of chapter 25. Clearly Cervantes was doing some major surgery on what he had already written. He was seeking a better balance in his episodic material; but he did this with a most unfortunate result: the unexplained and inexplicable loss and reappearance of Sancho's ass. In chapter 25, at the point at which the Marcela episode was excised, the reader is faced with mysterious allusions to the loss of the animal, which thereafter is treated as absent until chapter 43, where its return is implied. Cervantes did not notice his blunder, but his readers did. In part 2, chapter 3, the student Sampson Carrasco is reviewing the reception of part 1; he tells Don Quixote and Sancho that "'there are some who have found fault, and taxed the author's memory for forgetting who it was that robbed Sancho of his Dapple.'" In the next chapter Sancho explains how he lost his donkey, but even he has no idea how it turned up again: "'All I can say is that perhaps the history-writer was wrong, or it may have been an error of the printer's.'" This is hardly a brilliant recovery on Cervantes' part; but at least he has turned the awkward defect in his narrative to his advantage by making it a part of the ongoing discussion in the novel of the art of writing novels. What is evident from Stagg's study of Cervantes' revisions and their consequences is that they betray considerable haste in composition. Cervantes was in fact racing to get *Don Quixote,* part 1, to the press before the eagerly awaited sequel of the popular picaresque novel *Guzmán de Alfarache* was published. *Don Quixote* did come out first, and it was an instant success. If it had been written more carefully and thus more slowly, it might have been overlooked in the publicity attendant on *Guzmán,* part 2. In that case it is probable that Cervantes would not now be world-famous as Spain's most important writer.

Cervantes took greater pains over the composition of part 2. He was undoubtedly writing other works as well during the ten-year interval between the two *Don Quixotes*. But this time he was himself scooped by another author, who pirated his literary property and published in 1614 a different sequel from the one Cervantes was working on. The title page of the apocryphal *Don Quixote* gives the author's name as Alonso F. de Avellaneda, a pseudonym. It has not proved possible to identify the writer. Evidently he wrote his *Don Quixote* not only to cash in on some of Cervantes' potential profits but also to express his hostility to the creator of *Don Quixote*. In his prologue Avellaneda proffers some gratuitous personal insults to Cervantes, going so far as to mock his war wounds. His novel is essentially a protest against Cervantes' fiction. The author seems to have been a leader of the intellectual and spiritual world of his time, convinced that it was necessary to support the belief that a man (or a fictional character representing man) cannot be thought of as forging his life in accordance with his own needs and his own values. So, following the program laid down for Don Quixote at the end of Cervantes' first part, Avellaneda has the knight set out for the jousts in Saragossa. Unlike Cervantes' Don Quixote, who dies in sanity and with dignity in his own bed, Avellaneda's is cast into a lunatic asylum to finish his days on earth. Avellaneda obviously despised his hero, who, no longer in love with Dulcinea, is little more than a clown. Avellaneda's publication of this anti-*Quixote* was naturally offensive to Cervantes. The latter learned of the existence of the spurious *Don Quixote* while he was writing chapter 59 of the second part. In this chapter the knight and his squire overhear at an inn two men discussing "the second part of *Don Quixote de la Mancha*." When one of these men observes that what he likes least about it is that Don Quixote has ceased to love Dulcinea, the real Don Quixote is indignant, and cries out: "The peerless Dulcinea can never be forgotten, nor is Don Quixote capable of forgetting." Don Quixote then looks quickly through the book, pointing out several errors it contains that cast grave suspicion on its authenticity. He decides to give the lie to Avellaneda's clumsy imitation of his "true history" by changing his itinerary and going not to Saragossa but to Barcelona. Thereby Don Quixote declares not only his independence of Avellaneda but also his autonomy vis-à-vis Cervantes, endorsing the very understanding of human life that had so distressed Avellaneda and his like. After turning this setback to his advantage, Cervantes hastens to complete his own second part with a perceptible rhythmic acceleration.

The evidence of casual revision, hasty composition, and improvisation in response to external pressures should not suggest that *Don Quixote* is loosely structured. The first narrator's feigned ignorance of the surname of the man who was to become Don Quixote—Quijada, Quesada, or Quejana (1.1); Quijana (1.5)—leads to the knight's own adoption of various names—Don Quixote de la Mancha, the Knight of the Sorrowful Countenance (1.19), the Knight of the Lions (2.17)—and finally to the reader's discovery of his real name, Alonso Quijano the Good (2.74). Don Quixote's search for an identity parallels the reader's search for it. This is surely a deep structure of the novel. The master-man relationship of the knight and the squire is another: the literate man and the illiterate rub shoulders, exchanging with each other the experience of each one's culture—book lore and folklore—so that the gulf between them is progressively diminished.

There are carefully constructed bridges from one point to another of the novel. The poor boy Andrew, who is "rescued" by Don Quixote from the beating given him by his master, the rich farmer Juan Haldudo (1.4), reappears much later (1.31) to humiliate the knight in the presence of his elegant friends by telling him that, thanks to his intervention, the beating had continued more mercilessly. The rascally galley slave–novelist Ginés de Pasamonte (1.22) links the two parts when he shows up in part 2, chapters 25–27, as Master Peter the puppeteer. There is even some echoing of incidents in the *Don Quixotes* of 1605 and 1615. The hero's disastrous defeat by windmills (1.8) is repeated in a different tonality in part 2, chapter 29, when he receives a drubbing from the race of a watermill. Don Quixote's act of penance for Dulcinea on the heights of the Sierra Morena, the critical episode of part 1 (ch. 26), is matched by his grotesque vision of her, surrounded by motheaten heroic figures from the Carolingian ballads, in the depths of the Cave of Montesinos, the critical moment of part 2 (ch. 23). From these and many other connections within each part and between the two, it is clear that Cervantes constructed his novel with a fine sense of form.

For both early and modern readers a thorny structural problem is raised by the tales that Cervantes intercalated into the *Don Quixote* of 1605. The stories of the lovers—Dorothea and Ferdinand, Cardenio and Luscinda, Luis and Clara—are told by them at the inn in the presence of a company that includes Don Quixote, and Dorothea volunteers to play the part of Princess Micomicona to entice him back to his village; but the actual love affairs have nothing to do with the main story about Don Quixote's anachronistic knight-errantry. The Marcela-Chrysostom episode is equally extraneous. Even more glaring is the autonomy of "The Tale of Foolish Curiosity" (1.33–35), which is simply read from a manuscript at the inn by the parish priest of Don Quixote's village. Scholars have sought, not very successfully, for thematic relationships between these tales and the main story about Don Quixote. The first readers of the novel, as Sampson Carrasco reports to Don Quixote and Sancho, found "The Tale of Foolish Curiosity" not "bad or badly told" but "out of place" and irrelevant to the story of Don Quixote (2.3). It is a little strange that people found fault with the intercalated tales. As we have noted, their use was common in pastoral romances and indeed in all longer prose fiction. But no previous fiction had succeeded in creating such an entrancing character as Don Quixote. As those characters in part 2 who have read part 1 (and there are many of them) make plain, the Spanish nation, or at least the literate part of it, had fallen in love with Don Quixote. All were greedy for more of his adventures and were unwilling to be deflected from them by extrinsic stories. Cervantes, who had hoped by means of these tales to bring a variety of generic experience to his novel, bowed to the criticism and made sure that the fewer tales of the second part (for example, Camacho's wedding, 19–21) were more closely integrated with Don Quixote's adventures.

*Don Quixote* is a complex novel that defies simple interpretation. No formula on the lines of "This novel is about . . ." suffices. When he has finished, each reader must reflect on the whole novel, or on such parts as he can recall, and reach his own understanding of it. What follows is a suggestion of some points that have to be pieced together in any such personal critical enterprise.

At the beginning of the novel, the man whose name is eventually disclosed to be Alonso Quijano is leading a routine life, eating the same uninteresting meals week after week. He is living with two females, his niece and his housekeeper. He has never married, but he has looked lustfully on a strapping farm wench, Aldonza Lorenzo, who is his social inferior. By an act of the will he creates a new, though false, identity for himself, that of an anachronistic knight; and out of that frustrated lust he creates the most Platonic of loves for the most beautiful lady his imagination can fashion, Dulcinea del Toboso. By these acts of will Alonso Quijano makes himself free. For the first time in his fifty years of boredom he is free to travel, free to consort with all sorts of men and women, and free to act. He has created himself and his world just as surely as Cervantes created them. He has brought art to his life: the fictional character has transformed himself into a different fictional character, and his dull environment into a richly varied one. But because life belongs to the realm of nature, it cannot be art. The fictional life in what purports to be a real world necessarily conflicts with reality. When the dust has settled, the hostile armies turn out to be a harmless flock of sheep (1.18). The only way Don Quixote can react to the imposition of reality on his art is to refashion reality, by seeing it as it is not. A barber's basin is transformed by the magic of his creative imagination into the helmet of Mambrino (1.21). The clashes with reality can be uncomfortable, as, when Don Quixote puts on this helmet (which Sancho has been using as a container), curds and whey stream mysteriously and unpleasantly down his face.

Well-meaning characters in the novel who originally had no artistic streak in them are disturbed by Don Quixote's bouts with reality. They think—rightly, but without recognizing the poetic furor of which it is composed—that he is afflicted with madness. He must be brought back to his monotonous life and his humdrum home to be cured. In part 1, it is the priest who accepts this mission. Without realizing it, to achieve this end the priest must awaken in himself the same artistic impulse that stirred in Alonso Quijano. The priest creates for himself, however temporarily, a new identity as a damsel in distress. He discovers that he too enjoys fictionalizing his dreary existence. In *Don Quixote* of 1615, the priest's counterpart is the university student Sampson Carrasco. Playing the part of the Knight of the Woods or the Knight of the Mirrors (2.12–15) or the Knight of the White Moon (chs. 64–65), he aspires to defeat Don Quixote in battle so as to order him to return to his village. In comparison with Carrasco's conscious fictionalizing of life, the priest's seems innocent indeed. But Sampson's conversion of life into art is in the nature of part 2. As a rule, it is no longer reality itself that thwarts Don Quixote's attempt to lead life as if it were art; it is others making the same attempt. Sampson is but one character who creates his own fictional world. More impressively, the duke and the duchess have transformed their country house of pleasure and the surrounding estate with its many inhabitants into an artificial theater of the world. If in part 1 Don Quixote could deal with reality by changing it in his imagination into something more manageable, in part 2 it is others who change reality for him, making it impossible for him to cope with it. The reader must reflect on the ethics of the uses to which art is put in the novel.

The most significant adaptation of life to art is the one performed by Sancho Panza, the illiterate to whom the world of bookish fiction is closed. In part 1, chapters 30 and 31, sent on an impossible mission to Dulcinea, Sancho is told by the priest to tell his master the lie that he has seen her; his lie is very badly executed. In part 2, chapter 10, on a similar mission to El Toboso but this time accompanied by Don Quixote, he lies on his own initiative, telling the knight that an ugly, ungainly peasant girl is the glorious Dulcinea of his dreams. This lie has transgressed the border between falsehood and fiction; indeed it launches the basic fiction that binds together the various episodes of the *Don Quixote* of 1615. The knight, trusting Sancho to be truthful, has no choice but to believe Dulcinea enchanted. Sancho reveals the secret of his lie to the duchess (ch. 33), who has a servant masquerade as Merlin the Magician and prophesy that Dulcinea will be disenchanted only when Sancho has administered 3,300 lashes to his own buttocks. The remainder of the novel witnesses the continual tussle between master and man over the disenchantment of the knight's lady. Sancho's artistic lie has unleashed a veritable flood of fictional art that—very intimately—affects the lives of both master and man.

In the long run, art is ineffectual against the final force of life, which is death. Don Quixote is restored from his fiction to the drab reality of his home, finding his true identity as a country gentleman. But he is no longer the nobody he was—someone called Quijada, Quesada, somebody or other. He is somebody in a different sense, Alonso Quijano the Good—somebody who because of his fictionalized life has acquired immortality. Whatever the fate of his immortal soul, his earthly fame is guaranteed by the fictional life he has led and by the masterpiece that has recorded it. Perhaps, after all, the metamorphosis of life into art is a legitimate undertaking and has a lasting value. That is why the art of creating fictions is such a constant preoccupation in this novel. It is a novel about the importance of novels.

Cervantes' last work of fiction, *Persiles and Sigismunda,* is even more than this: "It is a novel, it is an idea of the novel, and it is the sum of all points of view possible in its time about the novel," writes Juan Bautista Avalle-Arce ("Introducción biográfica y crítica" to his edition, p. 27). Probably Cervantes wrote the first two of its four books between 1599 and 1605, while he was still working on *Don Quixote,* part 1. At the end of chapter 47 of the latter, a canon of Toledo explains in detail to Don Quixote's priest how an intelligent author might reform the genre of the chivalric romance so as to produce a worthwhile work of epic proportions. "The epic," the canon concludes, "may be written as well in prose as in verse." The canon, before this conclusion, has just given us a synoptic description or stencil of the first two books of *Persiles and Sigismunda.* What the Renaissance intellectuals saw—and admired—in the Greek romance was a prose epic. And Cervantes, in the prologue to his *Exemplary Tales,* proudly calls the unpublished *Persiles* a superlative Greek romance, "a book that dares to compete with Heliodorus." He regarded this work, and not *Don Quixote,* as his masterpiece. He surely devoted a huge amount of his time and energy to writing it. Having finished books 1 and 2 by 1605, he then wrote his exemplary tale "La española inglesa" ("The English Spanish Girl") as a trial run in which he experimented with the direction to be taken in books 3 and 4 of *Persiles and Sigismunda.* It is clear that he was still writing these last books when death overtook him in 1616, for he had little time to make a final revision: most of the chapter headings of all four books are missing; the last chapters are hastily written. Part 1 of *Don Quixote* involves a winning race against the sequel to *Guzmán de Alfarache;* part 2, a losing race against Avellaneda's spurious *Don Quixote; Persiles and Sigismunda,* a tied race against death.

The hero and the heroine of this last romance are initially presented to us as brother and sister, under the names Periandro and Auristela. They are really not siblings but Persiles, prince of Thule, and Sigismunda, princess of Friesland. They travel from the Barbarous Isle, through the vast frozen wastes and empty seas of northern Europe, on to better-defined countries like Portugal, France, and Italy, until they reach their proper destination, Rome, "the earth's heaven." There the pope blesses their love, which has remained constant and chaste in the face of horrendous assaults on it and the forcible, repeated separation of the lovers. Cervantes has given us a Christian version of that "prose epic," the Greek romance.

The simple plot line, complicated by systematic interruptions, is based on the Great Chain of Being, the assumption (of many intellectuals from Plato to those of the nineteenth century) that an unbroken connection links all natural and supernatural forms, from the mineral world, through the vegetable, animal, human, and angelic, to the feet of God. Cervantes' romance progresses along this chain, from the dungeons of the Barbarous Isle to the hills of the Eternal City. For the protagonists the progress is a pilgrimage of human life, and a pilgrimage of love, from lust to charity.

The author has been writing an "idea of the novel," a universalization of a particular novel, that is, an abstraction. His characters are therefore not representations of individuals but personifications of ideas. Alban K. Forcione is close to the mark when he baptizes the work "Cervantes' Christian Romance." Cervantes has sacrificed the novel on the altar of an ideological and a theological intention. It is his right. His pride in his accomplishment is justified. But it is not surprising that posterity prefers a novel to this "idea of a novel."

When Cervantes was dedicating his "idea of a novel" to the count of Lemos, he was but a day or two away from his death. To Lemos he wrote: "Yesterday they gave me Extreme Unction, and today I write this." In spite of its intimate association with Cervantes' life and death, we tend to overlook his Christian romance. Like the younger Cervantes who wrote *Don Quixote,* we set our minds on life, and not on a possible afterlife. Perhaps we are shortsighted. Unlike Cervantes, most of us are prouder of *Don Quixote* than of *Persiles and Sigismunda.* Our orientation is not to death and its uncertainties but to life and its known quantities.

## Selected Bibliography


### EDITIONS

#### COLLECTED WORKS

*Obras completas.* Edited by Rodolfo Schevill and Adolfo Bonilla. 18 vols. Madrid, 1914–1941.

———. Edited by Angel Valbuena Prat. Madrid, 1943. Frequently reprinted.

#### INDIVIDUAL WORKS

*Entremeses.* Edited by Eugenio Asensio. Madrid, 1970. Clásicos Castalia.

*La Galatea.* Edited by Juan Bautista Avalle-Arce. Madrid, 1961. Clásicos Castellanos. Frequently reprinted.

*El ingenioso hidalgo don Quixote de la Mancha.* Madrid, 1605.

———. Edited by Luis A. Murillo. 3 vols. Madrid, 1978. Clásicos Castalia. Vol. 3 contains a bibliography that lists the other early editions.

*Novelas exemplares.* Madrid, 1613.

———. Edited by Francisco Rodríguez Marín. 2 vols. Madrid, 1914–1917. Clásicos Castellanos. Contains only seven tales. Frequently reprinted.

*Ocho comedias y ocho entremeses nuevos nunca representados. . . .* Madrid, 1615.

*Primera parte de la Galatea, dividida en seys libros. . . .* Alcalá, 1585.

*Segunda parte del ingenioso cavallero don Quixote de la Mancha. . . .* Madrid, 1615.

*Los trabaios de Persiles y Sigismunda, historia setentrional. . . .* Madrid, 1617.

*Los trabajos de Persiles y Sigismunda.* Edited by Juan Bautista Avalle-Arce. Madrid, 1969. Clásicos Castalia.

*Viaje del Parnaso.* Madrid, 1614.

### TRANSLATIONS

*The Adventures of Don Quixote.* Translated by J. M. Cohen. Harmondsworth, 1952. Penguin Classics.

*Don Quixote.* Translated and edited by Joseph R. Jones and Kenneth Douglas. New York, 1981. Norton Critical Editions. Includes background materials and critical essays.

*Exemplary Novels.* Translated by Norman MacColl. Glasgow, 1902.

*Six Exemplary Novels.* Translated by Harriet de Onís. Great Neck, N.Y., 1961.

*The Ingenious Gentleman Don Quixote de la Mancha.* Translated by Samuel Putnam. 2 vols. New York, 1949.

*The "Interludes" of Cervantes.* Translated by S. Griswold Morley. Princeton, 1948. Spanish text on facing pages.

### BIOGRAPHICAL AND CRITICAL STUDIES

Allen, John J. *Don Quixote: Hero or Fool?* Gainesville, Fla., 1963.

———. *Don Quixote: Hero or Fool? Part 2.* Gainesville, Fla., 1979.

Avalle-Arce, Juan B. *"Don Quijote" como forma de vida.* Madrid, 1976.

———, and E. C. Riley, eds. *Suma cervantina.* London, 1973. Surveys of Cervantine scholarship by various scholars.

Bell, Aubrey F. G. *Cervantes.* Norman, Okla., 1947.

Canavaggio, Jean. *Cervantès dramaturge: Un théâtre à naître.* Paris, 1977.

Castro, Americo. *El pensamiento de Cervantes.* Madrid, 1925. Revised ed., Barcelona, 1972.

Close, A. *The Romantic Approach to "Don Quixote."* New York and Cambridge, 1977.

Duran, Manuel. *Cervantes.* New York, 1974.

El Saffar, Ruth. *Distance and Control in "Don Quixote": A Study in Narrative Technique.* Chapel Hill, N.C., 1975.

————. *Novel to Romance: A Study of Cervantes's "Novelas ejemplares."* Baltimore, 1974.

Entwistle, William J. *Cervantes.* Oxford, 1940.

Flores, Angel, and M. J. Bernardete, eds. *Cervantes Across the Centuries.* New York, 1947.

Forcione, Alban K. *Cervantes, Aristotle, and the "Persiles."* Princeton, 1970.

————. *Cervantes' Christian Romance: A Study of "Persiles y Sigismunda."* Princeton, 1972.

McGaha, Michael D., ed. *Cervantes and the Renaissance.* Easton, Pa., 1980.

Murillo, Louis A. *The Golden Dial: Temporal Configuration in "Don Quijote."* Oxford, 1975.

Nelson, Lowry, Jr., ed. *Cervantes: A Collection of Critical Essays.* Englewood Cliffs, N.J., 1969.

Predmore, Richard L. *The World of Don Quixote.* Cambridge, Mass., 1967.

————. *Cervantes.* New York, 1973. An authoritative biography.

Riley, Edward C. *Cervantes's Theory of the Novel.* Oxford, 1962.

Stagg, Geoffrey. "Revision in *Don Quixote, Part 1.*" In *Hispanic Studies in Honour of I. González-Llubera.* Edited by Frank Pierce. Oxford, 1959. Pp. 347–366.

Van Doren, Mark. *Don Quixote's Profession.* New York, 1958.

Wardropper, Bruce W. "La eutrapelia en las *Novelas ejemplares* de Cervantes." In *Actas del Séptimo Congreso de la Asociación Internacional de Hispanistas.* Edited by Giuseppe Bellini. Rome, 1982. Pp. 153–169.

Willis, Raymond S., Jr. *The Phantom Chapters of the "Quijote."* New York, 1953.

BRUCE W. WARDROPPER

# ANTON CHEKHOV

## *(1860–1904)*

ANTON PAVLOVICH CHEKHOV is recognized today as perhaps the most important short-story writer of all time. His formal and thematic innovations in the art of narration have altered literary conventions. Although the bulk of his work is in the form of prose narrative, he was also a master of the art of the drama. His plays, first produced by Constantine Stanislavsky at his Moscow Art Theater, have had an equally radical influence; together with the plays of August Strindberg, they have laid the basis of modern dramaturgy, and the development of the Western version of Stanislavsky's dramatic method, called in America simply the "Method," owes a good deal to the acting techniques realized in their production.

### *LIFE*

Chekhov was born on 17 January 1860[1] in the town of Taganrog in southern Russia, on the Sea of Azov. His paternal grandfather was a serf on the estate of Count A. D. Chertkov (the father of one of Leo Tolstoy's most ardent disciples) who had been able to buy his freedom. Chekhov's father, Pavel Egorovich, ran a grocery store in Taganrog, but he was more interested in music than in business, to the detriment of his fortunes. He was a severe and intensely religious man who forced his children to attend interminable church services and sing in the choir he had organized, as well as to work long hours in the small family store, which was freezing cold in winter. Chekhov said later that in his childhood he had had no childhood at all. He recalled that his father was as "hard as flint . . . you could not make him budge an inch" (letter to his brother Alexander, February 1883).

Chekhov's studies began at the Greek school in Taganrog, a town that had a large and prosperous Greek population, and only when he was eight years old did he enroll in the local Russian secondary school. Here he showed a marked interest in literature and wrote for the school newspaper. At this time his passion for the theater revealed itself: he organized amateur theater performances and acted out little sketches of his own invention at home.

In 1876, the family store failed, and Chekhov's parents were forced to move to Moscow in order to escape debtors' prison. Anton remained in Taganrog for two more years to complete his secondary schooling. He then enrolled in the medical school of the University of Moscow, from which he received his degree of Doctor of Medicine in 1884. Al-

[1]All dates are marked according to the Julian calendar (Old Style), used in Russia until 1917. In Chekhov's lifetime, the Julian calendar was twelve days behind the Gregorian (New Style) calendar used in the West and used in Russia since 1917. Thus January 17 (OS) would be January 29 (NS).

though he never seriously pursued a medical career, he did practice intermittently, and his scientific training and interest are noticeable in his writings. He used to say of his two fields of activity that medicine was his wife, whereas literature was his mistress.

Soon after arriving in Moscow, Chekhov began his professional literary career in earnest, contributing brief sketches to popular humor magazines under the name Antosha Chekhonte. His quick mind and gift for words enabled him to turn out quantities of jokes, anecdotes, and potboilers of all kinds, thus providing much-needed income for his impoverished family, who were living in a wretched basement apartment in a Moscow slum. At the same time, he also composed more complex anecdotes, several literary parodies, and his first serious prose works.

In 1884, the first collection of Chekhov's short stories appeared in book form, under the title *Skazki Mel'pomene* (Tales of Melpomene). Two years later, he contributed his first piece to a serious journal, the conservative Moscow daily *Novoe vremya* (New Times), whose editor, the writer Aleksey S. Suvorin, was to become one of Chekhov's closest friends. The friendship continued, in spite of their political differences (Chekhov was becoming increasingly liberal, while Suvorin was ultraconservative), until 1897, when Chekhov's open defense of Captain Alfred Dreyfus and support of Émile Zola's contribution to the case brought him into sharp conflict with Suvorin, who took part in the anti-Semitic wave that accompanied the Dreyfus affair not only in France but also in Russia. Chekhov's letters to Suvorin are of great interest; they contain some of his most penetrating remarks on literature and politics. The break with Suvorin marked the beginning of Chekhov's friendship with several writers of the radical left, including Maxim Gorky. When, in 1902, the Russian Academy of Sciences, ceding to government pressure, canceled Gorky's membership, Chekhov resigned in protest.

We can divide Chekhov's career, somewhat arbitrarily, into three main periods. During the first period, 1880 to 1887, Chekhov wrote primarily for humor magazines and produced a great number of short prose pieces at a rapid pace. During the second period (1888–1893), Chekhov no longer contributed to the humor journals and paced his writings in a more leisurely fashion. In 1888, there appeared the long prose narrative "Step" ("The Steppe"), which introduced his experimentation with a lyrical prose style. From this period on, much of his work is dominated by the theme of contrast between, on the one hand, beauty, sensitivity, and life, and, on the other, ugliness, banality, and death. As in later stories and plays, isolation also becomes a dominant theme. Other stories from these years reveal Chekhov's search for a coherent world view, a concern that led him to a sympathetic study of Tolstoy's philosophy of nonresistance. Dependence on Tolstoy's ethics came to a halt in 1889, after Chekhov—already ill with the pulmonary tuberculosis that caused his death—traveled to the penal colony of Sakhalin in the northern Pacific, the Russian Devil's Island. The injustice and cruelty Chekhov observed during this expedition, set down in his long sociological monograph *Ostrov Sakhalin* (*The Island: A Journey to Sakhalin,* 1891–1894), changed Chekhov's attitude to Tolstoyanism fundamentally. In several stories of this period, such as "Ward No. 6" (1892), the Tolstoyan doctrine of nonresistance to evil is satirized.

In general, this second creative period is marked by increased concern with social and psychological problems: the oppressed position of the peasants ("Peasant Wives," 1891), the hypocrisy of the upper classes ("The Wife," 1892), the life of missed opportunities ("The Teacher of Literature," 1889–1894), and narcissism ("The Princess," 1889, as well as "The Grasshopper," 1892).

The last period of Chekhov's creative life, from 1894 to his death in 1904, is marked by the appearance of his most complex stories;

they have little external action, and lyrical-musical elements predominate. It is during these years that Chekhov became active in the theater and wrote his four great plays, *The Seagull* (1896), *Uncle Vanya* (1899), *The Three Sisters* (1901), and *The Cherry Orchard* (1904). This burst of dramatic writing was related to an important event, Chekhov's association with Stanislavsky's Moscow Art Theater, which began in 1898 with a production of *The Seagull* and continued until Chekhov's death. The stylized image of a seagull adorns the curtain of the Moscow Art Theater even now to commemorate the theater's production of Chekhov's first great play, which catapulted both the play and the theater to fame.

In May 1901, Chekhov married Olga Knipper, a leading actress in Stanislavsky's company. It was a happy marriage, but it came at a time when both knew that he was marked by death. Chekhov's life was marred by persistent ill health. Even in the late 1880's, when he was not yet thirty, there were the first warnings of the disease that was to blight his remaining years. From 1887 until his death, illness forced him to live either in the mild climate of the Crimea or at German and French spas; and, except for few and rare intervals, he was no longer able to live in Moscow or Saint Petersburg, cities he loved. He died on the night of 2 July 1904 at the German spa of Badenweiler, with Olga Knipper at his side. His body was transferred to Moscow and was buried in the cemetery of the Novo-Devichy monastery, in the section reserved for artists, writers, and musicians.

Chekhov's career comes at the end of the last generation of writers contributing to the great age of Russian literature, the generation of Tolstoy and Feodor Dostoevsky. When Chekhov began working for the humor journals, Tolstoy had already rejected his own major novels as frivolous and was turning to religious-didactic writing. Dostoevsky died in 1881, shortly after Chekhov had begun writing his short humorous sketches; and Ivan Turgenev died in 1883. Chekhov's artistic life thus spans the end of the so-called Golden Age of Russian letters, the age of the great novelists, and the threshold of its Silver Age, associated with the Russian symbolist movement. Clearly, Chekhov's prose evolved from the "realistic" prose tradition, and was influenced by the lyrical and somewhat melancholy work of Turgenev. But Chekhov went on to create fundamentally new forms; for example, the plotless short story. In the western European tradition, Chekhov's closest kinship is with the short stories of Guy de Maupassant, from whom he learned the art of brevity and of the surprise ending. But the poetry and symbolic weight of his stories are Chekhov's own creation, and the new literary forms he created anticipate in many ways the contemporary short story. Many Russian writers of the turn of the century, including such diverse figures as Ivan Bunin, Alexander Kuprin, and even Gorky, can be looked on as his disciples. Today, there is hardly a more popular prose writer and dramatist in Russia than Chekhov; his plays are constantly in the repertory of the Moscow Art Theater and other Soviet theaters. A definitive and fully annotated edition of his complete works and letters in thirty volumes has been published by the Soviet Academy of Sciences (1974–1982), and a somewhat smaller edition, in twenty volumes, appeared between 1944 and 1951; individual works and collections are continually being republished. Some of his stories and plays have been made into films in the Soviet Union.

In Western literature, Chekhov's influence has never abated. Of writers in the English language, Katherine Mansfield is probably the most strikingly indebted to Chekhov's prose. In both theme and form, Chekhov also influenced Franz Kafka, Albert Camus, and the creation of the French *nouveau roman* (new novel). Themes that are taken up by later writers include the fate of the little man, the phenomena of absurdly wasted lives and social isolation, and the failure of communication, together with ineffectuality. Chekhov's plays find echoes in the actionless dramas of such writers as Samuel Beckett.

Thus Chekhov has clearly influenced much of modern prose and dramaturgy, and indirectly modern theater production. At the same time, Chekhov's art resists classification and cannot be fitted neatly into any traditional school or movement; for it was revolutionary in ways that still demand analysis. For example, a frequently discussed problem is the nature of Chekhov's relation to impressionist art. No historical data yet found support the view that Chekhov was directly acquainted with the works of the Western impressionist painters. Furthermore, impressionism never existed as an organized school in Russia; only Chekhov's friend the painter Isaac Levitan exhibited some of the qualities of impressionist painting, but he did not take part in the theoretical development of the French school. While some characteristics of Chekhov's prose and dramaturgy suggest the impressionist movement, these resemblances remain diffuse and difficult to pinpoint. There was a general current in the air by the end of the century: the fresh and immediate approach to color and situations and the depiction of the everyday mediocre rather than the ideal or dramatically poignant marked both the visual and verbal arts.

We shall now turn directly to Chekhov's works, examining first the boisterous humor stories of his youth and then his increasingly mature prose and his plays.

## *EARLY PROSE*

### *Humor Stories*

From 1883 to 1886, most of Chekhov's stories were published in the important Saint Petersburg popular humor magazine *Oskolki* (Fragments). During this period, Chekhov wrote great quantities of stories at prodigious speed. In 1883 alone, he published more than one hundred stories. In 1886, the novelist Dmitry V. Grigorovich, who had read and praised Chekhov's tale "Eger" ("The Huntsman," 1885), wrote to implore him to write in a more serious and leisurely fashion. It was only then that Chekhov abandoned the breakneck speed of his writing and resolved to go more slowly, in order to escape the limitations of the humor magazines. In fact, 1884 was the last year in which Chekhov wrote stories that are predominately humorous.

Even in his earliest anecdotal pieces, we find Chekhov testing the limits of literary norms and conventions. It is particularly with Turgenev, from whom Chekhov learned so much, that Chekhov took issue in his works. The formal structure of the Turgenev short story, with its lengthy introduction, elaborate prologue, digressions elucidating the past of the characters, apostrophes to the reader, and epilogues, is not found even in Chekhov's earliest works. Rather, Chekhov favored terse introductions, impressionistic characterization by significant details, internal rather than external action, and unexpected endings.

Two techniques for endings are characteristic of Chekhov's early stories. The first, closing by means of a surprise, was well known from the prose of Maupassant; but the second, closing by means of what the Russian critic Viktor Shklovsky has called a "zero ending," is a Chekhovian innovation. In the first, the story line anticipates a certain denouement but veers off from it in an unexpected direction. Thus in Chekhov's "Orden" ("The Decoration," 1884), the teacher Pustyakov wears a borrowed government decoration to cut a better figure at a dinner, only to find himself seated opposite a colleague who knows that he does not have the right to wear this decoration. Throughout the dinner, the terrified teacher eats and drinks using only one hand, so he can hide the decoration on his chest with the other. The story builds up to a dramatic climax when Pustyakov, who is standing with a glass in his hand waiting for a toast, is asked to pass another glass. Now he must remove his shielding hand and reveal his fraud. But the expected catastrophe is replaced by a farcical outcome: the other teacher is equally guilty—he also wears a borrowed decoration. Two more surprises follow: the other teacher's borrowed decoration is a higher one than Pustyakov's; and Pustyakov, far from being chastened by this experience, only regrets that he was not clever enough to borrow an even higher order to outshine his colleague.

In the zero ending, the conflict of the story leads us to expect a dramatic denouement, but the story ends instead in a seemingly unmotivated relaxation of tension, without a climax. The most interesting early story of this type is "Mstitel" ("The Avenger," 1887). A man who has surprised his wife with a lover enters a gunsmith shop to buy a pistol for his revenge. However, as the salesman describes the murderous capacities of the various models, the husband's fury begins to give way to an uneasy embarrassment. Finally, instead of a pistol, he buys a net for bird catching and retreats sheepishly from the shop. Not only does the dramatic denouement for which the story prepares the reader not occur, but the story line is inverted. The thoughts of the cuckolded husband are played in diminuendo against the crescendo fervor in the salesman's talk. Both the surprise and the zero ending play on the tension between the expected and the actual. It is, of course, the zero ending, which relies less directly on external action, that is of particular importance in Chekhov's mature prose and in his plays as well. In the early stories, the relation of the conclusion to the body of the story is sometimes contrived. In the later stories, conclusions become an organic part of the story's inner action and frequently contribute to the lyrical inner rhythms and equivalences of the work.

Other characteristics of the early anecdotes that suggest some of the innovations important in Chekhov's later style include terse introductions, contrasting, for example, with Turgenev's leisurely openings. Thus the story "Ekzamen na chin" ("Examination for Advancement," 1884) opens abruptly with a terse internal monologue: "The geography teacher Galkin does not like me and I shall fail his part of the examination today." The speaker is identified only by the ensuing dialogue and action.

Chekhov's compact style also affects his characterizations: the traditional leisurely revelations familiar from Turgenev's writings are replaced by a few significant details of external description. Such details in the later stories often connote general moods and atmosphere, whereas in the early stories the use of such elements is more specific and frequently serves as a means of caricature.

Thematically, the early stories assault social traditions and values, just as in their formal innovations they run counter to prevailing literary conventions. Many of the early narratives are social satires, assailing consciousness of rank, the Russian police state, the vulgarity of the press, and the mistrust of education. It is not surprising that the young Chekhov, who delighted in taking issue with existing social and artistic conventions, would find parody appealing. His early parodies are not often attacks on serious belles-lettres, but rather attack the periphery of literature, such as the comic sketches of the humor magazines, the Gothic tale, the crime thriller, and the like. Examples are "Tysyacha i odna strast, ili strashnaya noch, roman v odnoy chasti s epilogom (Posvyashchaetsya Viktoru Gyugo)" ("One Thousand and One Passions; or, A Terrible Night [A Novel in One Part with an Epilogue, Dedicated to Victor Hugo]," 1880). Gothic horror stories are parodied in "Krivoe zerkalo" ("The Crooked Mirror," 1883), "Strashnaya noch'" ("A Terrible Night," 1884), and "Bespokoyny" ("The Restless Guest," 1886).

In two of Chekhov's best-known parodies, "Svedskaya spichka" ("The Swedish Match," 1883) and "Drama na okhote" ("The Shooting Party," 1884), the object of ridicule is the popular whodunit. Elaborate complications and misleading clues caricature the traditional devices of this genre and are followed by a surprise ending: in "The Swedish Match," the victim turns out to be alive and well; in "The Shooting Party," the murderer turns out to be the narrator.

### *Serious Stories*

The early Chekhov was not only a humorist, however; some of his early works are serious in tone and begin to suggest the transition to be effected by the end of the 1880's, when Chekhov dropped Antosha Chekhonte to become Anton Chekhov, the creator of the significant stories and plays on which his fame rests today. The first serious stories, "Barynya" ("The Lady of the Manor") and "Tsvety zapozdalye" ("Late-Blooming Flowers"), appeared in 1882, just two years after Chekhov had begun his career as a professional writer. Both these pieces, while still conventional in many ways, anticipate some of the themes and story-telling devices of the later works. "The Lady of the Manor" initiated a series of stories about peasant life that was to culminate in "Muzhiki" ("The Peasants," 1897). It is a rather traditional treatment of the conflict between peasant values and those of the aristocracy, and the resulting disintegration of a peasant family. "Late-Blooming Flowers," while traditional in form, anticipates Chekhov's later theme of the life of missed opportunities and presents a foretaste of the many characters in the stories and plays who fail to act to attain their goals.

An important group of serious early stories are told from the point of view of a child, a technique that Tolstoy had used earlier in his *Childhood* (1852). Many of these "children stories" are satires of the adult world, as seen through the distorting prism of the child's perspective. The most significant of these is "Spat khochetsya" ("Sleepy," 1888), the protagonist of which is an exploited child forced to watch nightly over her employers' baby; in her exhaustion she strangles the infant and then falls asleep, relieved of her burden. The story contains a masterly treatment of a child's dreams.

One of the few early stories that Chekhov later included in his first collected works, and perhaps the most significant of the early serious narrations, is "The Huntsman." In a brief dramatic sketch two contrasting characters are presented: a freedom-loving huntsman and his placid peasant wife, whom the huntsman married while he was drunk. The focus of the story is the tragedy of two individuals who cannot communicate with each other. It is limited to a brief description of their meeting in an open field, and of their parting, with their differences unresolved. (This lack of resolution becomes ever more frequently the conclusion of Chekhov's stories.) "The Huntsman" is distinguished by a marked syncretism, as nature is depicted almost in painterly fashion with a few blotches of color. But, unlike the works of Turgenev, in which nature is simply presented as an accompaniment to the action, in "The Huntsman" it is part of the total instrumentation of the story: nature themes, much like musical motifs, are woven through the action and characterization. Nature is a part of the conversation of the two protagonists, not only as a topic, but also as its background, and it is depicted both in colors and in sounds ("Again, silence. From the harvested fields a quiet song rises, only to be broken off at the very beginning. It is too hot to sing . . . "). As we shall see, this intermingling of elements of color and of music with the verbal material will become ever more pronounced in Chekhov's mature years.

## *1888–1893*

### *"The Steppe"*

In 1888, Chekhov's "The Steppe" was accepted by *Severnye vestnik* (The Northern Messenger), then one of Russia's principal intellectual journals. It is one of Chekhov's longest works and his first truly important story. We shall therefore analyze it in some detail.

Superficially, "The Steppe" is modeled on the traditional tale of the adventures and observations of a traveling hero. Unlike the traditional model, however, it is almost completely devoid of external action. Rather, it presents an inner symbolic action expressed through the interplay of themes and counterthemes, motifs and countermotifs.

"The Steppe" recounts the journey of a young boy, Egor, through the steppe country of southern Russia. But unlike the hero of the usual travel tale, Egor is not an active participant in the adventure. His role is passive; he travels across the steppe in spiritual and psychological isolation from his environment. Even his arrival at his destination, where he is to remain in boarding school, does not alter his condition; he remains as lonely as he was when the carriage set out on the long journey. The multiple meanings of "The Steppe," as well as its construction, give a foretaste of Chekhov's later prose and plays. A recurring motif is the contrast between art, beauty, and sensitivity and the vulgarity, ugliness, and banality that Russians sum up in the word *poshlost,* a fundamental conflict in Chekhov's mature work. On a philosophical level, this opposition is expressed as the struggle between the forces of life and death in the steppe, the latter always gaining on the former. There is the melancholy song heard during the travelers' noonday rest, in which nature appears to brood over the realization that nature soon will have to die unsung and unnoticed because of the dry heat. In another passage, nature utters one last desperate shout: "A singer, a singer!"; but no one hears nature's forlorn cry of death. The stifling heat, a graveyard, distant funeral mounds function as images of death against which the hope of the morning's freshness, the pleasantly warming sunlight, the shimmering of a distant hill struggle in vain as forces of life. As the carriage rumbles through the monotonous landscape, impressionistic pictures continue to play upon the theme of futility and death: a kite flies aimlessly overhead "and suddenly stops in mid-air, as though reflecting on the dullness of life"; a young girl lies on top of a passing wagon laden with grain, "sleepy and exhausted by the heat"; a lonely poplar appears on the horizon, "but who planted it there and why it is there, no one knows"; the carriage passes a group of reapers whom the heat seems to be suffocating; wild dogs hurl themselves against the carriage and Egor fears that he will be torn apart by their teeth; a sad song sounds; a birdlike child appears from nowhere, its belly swollen from hunger; animals kill animals, human beings kill animals. Against these images of death, there is one detail that stands throughout the narrative as a symbol of vitality: Egor's bright red shirt, which is blown about by the steppe winds and fascinates those whom the boy meets.

"The Steppe" is still marked by signs of artistic immaturity, such as the frequent interpolation of authorial comment, but it suggests major concerns of the mature Chekhov. A technique that becomes increasingly important is the use of recurrent sound motifs, which symbolically signify the song echoing through the steppe, doors creaking, drivers shouting to the horses, and many instances of onomatopoeia.

With the completion of "The Steppe," Chekhov reached a turning point: he never again returned to the short, hurriedly written, humorous story. "The Steppe" is distinguished from the later works, however, not only by its length (there is only one other story quite as long, "The Duel," 1891) but also by its marked allegorical character.

### *Chekhov and Tolstoy*

It was during this period that Chekhov briefly came under the influence of Tolstoyanism. Examples of the influence of Tolstoy's "postconversion" views can be found in some stories of the 1880's; for example, "Pripadok" ("The Nervous Breakdown," 1888), which depicts the debasing nature of prostitution. For a brief time, Chekhov seems to have been swayed by Tolstoy's doctrine of nonresistance to evil, as evidenced by such stories as "Khoroshie lyudi" ("Good People," 1886), which contains an extended discussion of Tolstoy's doctrine. This moralizing story praises, in Tolstoy's terms, nonresistance to evil and the moral beauty of humble labor; it differs markedly in tone from Chekhov's later work. Fifteen years after its publication, Chekhov revised "Good People" for his collected works of 1901 by eliminating part of the debate and by weakening the Tolstoyan emphasis. Other works, notably "Nepriyatnost" ("An Unpleasantness," 1888) and "Vragi" ("Enemies," 1887), are sympathetic to Tolstoy's injunction against giving vent to anger. In the latter story, a doctor whose child has just died answers an emergency call to the house of a rich neighbor; there he discovers that the neighbor's wife, whose life-threatening illness was given as the reason for the call, has only pretended illness in order to facilitate her elopement with a lover. There ensues an angry verbal duel between the cuckolded husband and the enraged doctor, but the story ends on a Tolstoyan note: the immorality and futility of violent thoughts and actions.

After 1890, Chekhov wrote no further stories influenced by Tolstoy's religious and ethical views. As he explained in a letter to his editor, Suvorin, with typical facetiousness:

> Maybe it is because I no longer smoke that Tolstoy's teachings have ceased to move me. In the depths of my soul, I feel hostile to them and that is plainly unjust. In my veins courses peasant blood, and no one can impress me with examples of peasant virtues. . . . Yet, Tolstoy's philosophy touched me strongly . . . for some six to seven years. I was influenced not so much by Tolstoy's basic positions . . . as by the Tolstoyan manner of expressing himself, by his wisdom and probably by some kind of hypnotism. Now something in me protests; prudence and justice tell me that there is more love for humanity in electricity and steam than in chastity and vegetarianism. War is an evil; law courts are evil; but this does not mean that I must walk around in bast shoes and sleep on the stove with the workmen. But the question is not whether I am "for" or "against" Tolstoy, but that somehow Tolstoy has become remote from me, that he is no longer in my soul.
>
> (27 March 1894)

But Chekhov never stopped admiring Tolstoy's art. It is clear from the diaries of Tolstoy and Chekhov that the two men exerted a magnetic influence on each other. Chekhov's own letters express this admiration: "In my entire life I have never respected a single man so profoundly, I might even say so extremely, as [Tolstoy]" (9 November 1889). And on 28 January 1900, apropos of Tolstoy's illness: "I am afraid of Tolstoy's death. If he should die, there would be a huge void in my life. . . . Without him, [the world of literature] would be a flock without a shepherd."

Tolstoy's mysticism and rejection of science and medicine never attracted Chekhov, even in his brief period of discipleship. Many of Chekhov's most positive characters are scientists. Science, to him, was an indispensable adjunct to art, although he was later to take issue with those who worshiped science uncritically. His medical training undoubtedly affected his artistic outlook. His almost anatomical dissection of character and his conciseness clearly are part and parcel of a scientific method that he acquired through his professional schooling. Nor could Chekhov ever agree with Tolstoy's renunciation of art as sinful. Concerning Tolstoy's *What Is Art?,* which contains the essence of his attack on art, Chekhov wrote that it

> represents nothing of interest. All this is old hat. To say of art that it has become enfeebled and has entered a cul-de-sac, that it is not what it should be, is like saying that the desire to eat and drink has become old-fashioned and that it is no longer what it should be. Of course, hunger is an old phenomenon, and in our desire to eat we

> have come to a cul-de-sac; yet to eat is necessary, and we shall continue to eat no matter what the gentlemen philosophers tell us.
>
> (letter to Suvorin, 4 January 1898)

In the 1890's, Chekhov began to take direct issue with Tolstoy's philosophy. Certain of his protagonists, for example Gromov in "Palata No. 6" ("Ward No. 6," 1892), strongly attack the doctrine of nonresistance to evil. Chekhov's attitude toward the old master was tempered by his own scientific and artistic skepticism, yet remained complex, so that even after 1890 certain characters continue to be presented in something like the Tolstoyan spirit.

### *Hypocrisy and Narcissism*

A persistent Chekhovian theme—self-admiration to the point of self-deception—has a significant beginning in the period under discussion. Two stories stand out here, "Knyaginya" ("The Princess," 1889) and "Poprygunya" ("The Grasshopper," 1892).

In "The Princess," the picture of a hypocritical and sentimental woman is achieved by a skillful manipulation of the point of view. While the voice of the story is that of the omniscient author, the work develops a many-faceted picture by presenting her as others see her and as she sees herself.

The most significant among the stories that develop the theme of the narcissistic woman is "The Grasshopper," which makes further use of the multiple point of view. This novella contrasts an idealized physician, Osip Ivanovich Dymov, with his shallow and pretentious wife, Olga, who imagines herself to possess great artistic talent. When Dymov discovers that his wife is having an affair with a mediocre painter, he allows himself to become infected by one of his patients in an act of self-sacrifice that causes his death.

The story opens at the wedding of Dymov and Olga, presented initially from Olga's point of view:

> "Look at him: it is true, isn't it, that there is something in him?" she said to her friends, nodding toward her husband as though wishing to explain why she had married such a simple, very ordinary, in no way distinguished man.

This description of Dymov is clearly Olga's disdainful view of her husband; what follows is an authorial objective view, contrasting with the negative estimate just expressed:

> Her husband, Osip Ivanovich Dymov, was a physician with the rank of Titular Councillor. He worked in two hospitals: in one, as a visiting physician, in the other, as a pathologist. Daily, from nine in the morning until noon, he saw patients and made rounds in the wards; and in the afternoon, he took a horse tram to the other hospital, where he dissected bodies. His private practice was small and earned him only some five hundred rubles a year. That was all. What else could be said about him?

Here, again, the objective authorial tone is modified by a phrase of reported speech, representing Olga's point of view ("That was all"). And so it continues, with one perspective qualified or contradicted by its opposite. As the Soviet critic Alexander Chudakov has pointed out, the insincere value words and attitudes of the heroine are continually juxtaposed with the neutral tone of the objective observer. So are the details that characterize her: the fake artiness that mixes a Renaissance lamp with a pair of peasant bast shoes, a medieval halberd with a sickle; the clichés in which she speaks. All these are given side by side with the authorial voice that describes Olga and her actions in objective tones.

Olga Ivanovna in her narcissism is a prototype of Chekhov's many men and women who, like Madame Ranevskaya in *The Cherry Orchard* and Professor Serebryakov in *Uncle Vanya,* have a falsely exalted view of themselves.

### *Early Social Stories*

As a result of his sociological research trip to Sakhalin Chekhov not only rejected Tolstoy's religious doctrine, but also experienced an increase in social awareness that aligned him with the liberal camp in Russia. The only stories of 1890, "Vory" ("Thieves") and "Gusev," both completed after his return from Sakhalin, as well as "Baby" ("Peasant Wives," 1891), "Zhena" ("The Wife," 1892), and "V ssylke" ("In Exile," 1892), reflect this strengthened social awareness.

"Thieves" depicts a group of horse thieves. Suvorin, for whose journal the story was written, criticized it for failing to distinguish clearly between good and evil. Chekhov's letter of reply is a manifesto of method that is as close to the ideology of Zola's naturalism as Chekhov was ever to come:

> You criticize me for objectivity, calling it indifference to good and evil, absence of ideals and ideas and so on. You wish that when I depict horse thieves, I should say that horse stealing is bad. But this has been known for a long time, even without me. Let the jurors pass judgment on this; my task is only to show what horse thieves are like. I write: you are dealing with horse thieves, so you should know that they are not beggars, but well-fed people, that they are people of conviction, and that horse stealing is not only thievery, but a passion. Certainly, it would be nice to combine art with preaching, but for myself personally this is extremely difficult, and almost impossible because of problems of technique. In order to show horse thieves in seven hundred lines, I always have to speak and think in their tone, and feel in their spirit, otherwise—if I added subjectivity—my images would become diluted and the tale would not be as compact as a short tale must be. When I write, I put all my faith in the reader, presuming that the subjective elements lacking in my tale will be supplied by him.
>
> (March 1889)

"Peasant Wives" is a study of hypocrisy and oppression; its chief protagonist is a trader, one of whose victims is a peasant woman. With its treatment of the oppression of women in patriarchal peasant society, "Peasant Wives" anticipates many of Chekhov's later stories that depict the cruel treatment of women, such as "The Peasants" and "V ovrage" ("In the Ravine," 1900).

In 1889, Chekhov took an active part in famine relief. He worked in a program organized to buy up the horses that peasants were forced to sell for lack of food and fodder, so as to return the animals to the peasants in time for spring ploughing. He collected money for this project and helped to publish a volume of articles and belles-lettres in aid of the famine victims. "The Wife," published in January 1891, deals with the famine. It depicts the indifference of the landowners to the lot of the peasants and satirizes the ineffectiveness of aristocratic philanthropy. This is contrasted with the harsh realities of peasant life, naturalistically conveyed through the tone and mood characteristic of Chekhov's later peasant stories. But "The Wife" is marred by heavy-handed didacticism and a black-and-white presentation.

A work also concerned with broad social problems but more subtly drawn is "In Exile," inspired by Chekhov's observations in Sakhalin. It treats the exiles in Siberia, to whom human dignity is denied. The protagonists are two men of different social background, a young Tatar who is ill and yearns for his warm land and his wife, and an old aristocrat, deserted by his wife, who desperately searches for a doctor to cure his hopelessly ill daughter.

### *The Quest for a World View: 1889–1894*

Simultaneous with Chekhov's concern with social problems and his estrangement from Tolstoy's ideology is his search for a coherent world view of his own. One cannot say that Chekhov ever evolved a unified philosophy. He was, after all, an artist and not a philosopher. But search he did, and this quest is expressed in a series of stories that deal more directly than his other works with specific philosophical questions. These stories are: "Skuchnaya istoriya" ("A Dreary Story," 1889) "Duel'" ("The Duel," 1891), "Gusev," "Ward No. 6," "Chorny monakh" ("The Black Monk," written in 1893 and published in 1894). After "The Black Monk" Chekhov never again showed so intense an interest in philosophical ideas. Subsequent to this story questions of moral philosophy are never posed directly; rather, they are suggested obliquely by the inner movement of the work.

One of the most important themes in the "philosophical stories" is man's dedication to intellect and science; as Chekhov was himself a man of science, this is not surprising. It has become almost a cliché to depict Chekhov as a man dedicated to the scientific point of view. His clinical probing of character, his lack of moralizing (with a few exceptions), and his objective approach to the problems his heroes face frequently bring Chekhov close to the method of Zola, whom he greatly admired, although this influence must not be exaggerated. Chekhov was intimately acquainted with Zola's *Le roman expérimental* (The Experimental Novel, 1880), as well as with Claude Bernard's *Introduction à l'étude de la médecine expérimentale* (Introduction to the Study of Experimental Medicine, 1865), which strongly influenced Zola's literary theories. The sympathetic portraits of medical men, who in Chekhov frequently represent the humane point of view in the conflict between beauty and vulgarity, have struck many readers. Yet it would be oversimplifying to say that Chekhov's identification with the scientific outlook was unqualified. While he was clearly inclined toward the spirit of empiricism, positivism, and scientific optimism that reigned at the end of the century, he was skeptical about the *scientistic* attitude, also very strong in his day, which tended to place science above man. This conflict between science and traditional humanistic values is reflected in the stories we have labeled "searching."

In "A Dreary Story," an exaggerated dedication to scientism by a capable scientist is one of the causes of his isolation and unhappiness; in "Gusev," the superiority of intellect is satirized; in "The Duel," belief in a scientific superman is voiced by a cold Nietzschean scientist; in "Ward No. 6," the idea of the overpowering importance of the intellect serves to justify submission to evil; and in "The Black Monk," a scientist hallucinates the phantasmal figure of a monk who persuades the former that he is a superman, made all-powerful by the strength of his scientifically trained mind.

"A Dreary Story" portrays a noted professor of medicine who realizes in his old age that, in spite of his scientific accomplishments, his life has been a failure. His search for a unifying world view has proved unsuccessful; his fame has brought him moral and philosophical isolation. Perhaps the underlying error is the professor's total commitment to the scientism of the age. Although realized at the highest level, this dedication proves in the end to be inadequate. The professor vaguely feels the imperfection of his science and faintly yearns for beauty and art; he cannot experience life as an integrated whole. In "A Dreary Story," as in all the "searching" stories, the philosophical perspective is tied to the psychological one, as the narratives examine man's search for life as wholeness, the elusiveness of this unity, and the individual's consequent isolation.

"Gusev" combines elements of social protest with some of the same philosophical considerations. It is set in the squalid ward of a military hospital ship and unfolds through the conversation of two moribund patients: the simple peasant Gusev, who accepts his illness and impending death stoically, and the intellectual Pavel Ivanych, who opposes Gusev's humility and its Tolstoyan implications with a powerful assertion of intellectual protest.

"The Duel" is Chekhov's longest prose work, longer even than "The Steppe," from which it is distinguished by its greater dependence on action and dramatic conflict. It pursues the theme of overcommitment to science in the character of a young natural scientist, von Koren, who is contrasted with an uncommitted, drifting intellectual, Laevsky. The conflict of the story lies in the philosophical and personal antagonism of these two. In opposition to the lackadaisical but sensitive Laevsky, cursed by indecisiveness, is the young scientist, a puritanical fanatic who believes that Charles Darwin's theory of the survival of the fittest justifies the destruction, in the name of humanity, of all those who do not make a material contribution to mankind, including Laevsky. Von Koren speaks of his desire to destroy Laevsky, and his opportunity arises when the latter challenges him to a duel. This duel, presented as a parody of all the duels in Russian romantic literature, leads to a quite unmotivated reconciliation between the two: Laevsky can now set to work and von Koren is chastened. "The Duel" is the only one of the "searching" stories in which Chekhov attempted to resolve the philosophical conflict within the context of the story; and this attempt, as well as the story's uncharacteristically wordy conclusion, constitute its weakness.

The clinical naturalism of "Ward No. 6" extends the mood of "Gusev," and a treatment of Tolstoyan issues relates it to "The Duel." "Ward No. 6" also continues the search for a unifying idea and studies the consequences of a heightened intellectualism. But the main issue is the doctrine of nonresistance to evil. We are shown two individuals of differing, though not quite opposite, temperaments: Ivan Gromov, a patient in the psychiatric ward of a provincial hospital, and Dr. Andrey Ragin, a physician in the same hospital. Gromov, an intelligent and sensitive man, will not acquiesce in the brutality and injustice he sees around him, and he continues to yearn for the fullness of life that escapes him. In contrast to Gromov's sincere, though sterile, idealism is the hypocrisy of the satirically drawn administrator of the disorderly hospital, Dr. Ragin. He too is repelled by conditions in the hospital, but he withdraws from all conflict. His attitude leads him into an isolation even more profound than that of the protesting Gromov. Ragin meekly accepts evil; but unlike the submissive Tolstoyan type whom he emulates, he makes of his humility an intellectual justification for moral impotence and sterility. He loves "deep" books, but his manner of reading them betrays his dilettantism.

> He does not read as rapidly and passionately as Gromov. He reads slowly, frequently stopping over a passage which seems to him particularly pleasing or incomprehensible. He always has a decanter of vodka next to his book, and a salted pickle or a pickled apple always lies before him, directly on the tablecloth, without a plate. Every half hour, without taking his eyes from the book, he pours himself a glass of vodka and drinks it. Then, without looking, he gropes for the pickle and bites off a little piece.

Ragin's idealism, at odds with his untidy pickle-eating reading habits, emerges in his discussions with Gromov, to whom he attempts to justify his passivity by preaching his version of the stoic philosophy of Marcus Aurelius: we only imagine pain, he tells Gromov; the pain will disappear if we do not complain. Again, if you can find inner happiness, it does not matter if you are not physically free. Gromov rejects the doctor's defense of submissiveness with an appeal to the overwhelming importance of sensation. He who does not react to pain with protest no longer lives, Gromov asserts. Christ himself "reacted to reality by smiling, by sadness, by anger, and even by melancholy. He did not meet his suffering with a smile on his lips; on the contrary, he prayed in the garden of Gethsemane that this cup might pass him by." In a final ironic twist, Ragin's close association with Gromov leads to his also being considered insane by the society that has passed judgment on Gromov. He too is locked in the cruel Sixth Ward, and in the face of his own suffering he protests and, implicitly, renounces his Tolstoyan submission.

In 1894, Chekhov completed the last of the philosophical stories begun in 1889, "The Black Monk," which he had worked on during the summer of 1893. While in his later works philosophical questions are no longer treated as directly as they are in the stories we have called "searching," they continue to be posed and are increasingly integrated into the psychological and dramatic action. This trend is already evident in "The Black Monk."

The protagonist of "The Black Monk" is a mediocre and ineffective scientist, Kovrin, who begins to have visions in which a black-robed monk tells him that he is an intellectual superman. The belief in a scientific and intellectual superman, already posed in "The Duel," is now explored through the hallucinations of a most ordinary man. The monk talks beguilingly of Kovrin's mission to lead mankind to immortality and eternal truth; but the charm the monk casts by his eloquence is broken when he fails to answer Kovrin's question about the nature of that "eternal truth." At this point, the monk falters and disappears.

"The Black Monk" is probably the least successfully analyzed of all of Chekhov's stories, for it is often read in an oversimplified manner. Some critics have attempted to find a single key to the story, or have tried to find Chekhov's "answer" to the problems posed in the work. But Chekhov never meant to "solve" the problems he posed; rather, he followed the method he had explained to Suvorin, "to pose a question correctly, as a judge should," and to leave it to the readers, as the jury, "to make up their own minds, each according to his taste."

As to the phantom monk himself, one cannot agree with those critics who have claimed that the monk's views are rejected by the story. While it destroys the monk's premise, belief in the intellectual superman, one cannot say that all the monk's beliefs are shown as delusions. When the monk speaks of "the great and brilliant future" of mankind in the wake of science humanely conceived, he echos the hopes of Chekhov's most positive heroes, although these hopes are never presented without some irony.

In Chekhov's mature work, the conflict between the exceptional person and a venal and vulgar environment recurs frequently; but in "The Black Monk," this theme acquires a new and bitter twist. Kovrin's wish to recapture his hallucination is both pathetic and ironic. The pathos of a life without illusions, be they even delusions, which must be Kovrin's as he is treated with sedatives, leads to an almost tragic conclusion; he has lost both his illusions and his sanity. But Chekhov's Kovrin is not a tragic hero; he is only a little man, the victim of a sensitivity that does not allow him to accept his mediocrity. Interesting parallels to the theme of "The Black Monk" can be found in Henry James, another writer whose characters perpetually search for the elusive meaning of life. Thus in James's early story "The Madonna of the Future" (1873), a mediocre artist believes himself to be an especially sensitive and intelligent interpreter of art and philosophy, and the creator of a great masterpiece. He dies when he is made aware of his illusion. In "The Beast in the Jungle" (1903), the mediocre Marcher, who lives in total isolation and uncertainty, is sustained only by his obsession that his life is reserved for some strange, momentous, and perhaps terrible purpose. Only after the death of Mary Bartram, who personifies his ideal vision, does he realize that his fate was to have no passion at all; he is the man to whom nothing was ever to happen.

## *MATURE STORIES (1894–1904)*

### *The Bourgeoisie and the Village*

In the 1890's, Chekhov's notebooks and letters begin to express his growing interest in the various strata of society in Russia. This interest is reflected in several stories of the

1890's in which a realistic depiction of the Russian social scene is of the first importance. These stories bear on the growth of Russian industry, the new bourgeoisie, industrial labor, and life in the villages, where the emancipation of the serfs in 1861 had not served to relieve the peasants' misery. In these stories, the sources of human frustration are related to flaws in a social order that forced a majority of Russians to live in deprivation while, as Chekhov indicated, giving no satisfaction to the ruling group either. It is in these stories that we find Chekhov's closest approach to Zola's naturalism. Written between 1894 and 1900, they form a cohesive series; Edmund Wilson, struck by their unity, was reminded of Balzac when he referred to them as a miniature *Comédie humaine,* but this claim seems excessive. Social facts, although fundamental to these stories, are subordinate to Chekhov's main preoccupation—the isolation of people because of their inability to communicate.

Three of these stories depict the new bourgeoisie: "Babe tsarstvo" ("A Woman's Kingdom," 1894), "Tri goda" ("Three Years," 1895), and "Sluchay iz praktiki" ("A Doctor's Visit," 1898). Stories dealing with the social order and the village are "Dom s mezoninom" ("The House with a Mezzanine," 1896; also translated as "An Artist's Story"), "Moya zhizn'" ("My Life," 1896), "The Peasants," "Na podvode" ("A Journey by Cart," 1897; in Constance Garnett's translation, "The School Mistress"), "Novaya dacha" ("The New Villa," 1899), and "In the Ravine."

"A Woman's Kingdom" tells of the frustrated life of a factory owner, Anna Akimovna, who lives in a provincial industrial town. Here, the familiar Chekhovian theme of human isolation is played out against a social background that contributes to the heroine's unhappiness.

Chekhov was not to return to the problem of the industrial proletariat or the new bourgeoisie until 1898, when he published "A Doctor's Visit," a story set in a provincial town that examines the baneful influence of the local factory owners. But in 1895, the story "Three Years" appeared. A long work set in Moscow's milieu of rich merchants, it evokes the atmosphere of emptiness and cruelty associated with this new class. The merchant milieu had already been forcefully depicted in the plays of Alexander Ostrovsky. We are often reminded in Chekhov's story of Ostrovsky's tyrannical patriarchs *(samodury),* as well as the playwright's recurrent theme of the impossibility of love and happiness in these merchant households. But whereas Ekaterina, the heroine of Ostrovksy's tragedy *Groza* (*The Storm,* 1860), is driven to suicide by the cruelty of her relatives, there is no such dramatically stated consequence in Chekhov's more oblique depiction of the degeneration of this class. On the contrary, all external conditions appear to be positive and business prospers.

The publication of "The House with a Mezzanine" and "My Life" in 1896 marks the beginning of the group of stories focusing on the Russian peasant. It is clear from his earlier works that Chekhov knew and understood the peasant milieu better than he did the world of factory and trade. The rural characters in these early stories—"The Huntsman," "Agafya," "At the Mill," "The Steppe," "Gusev," "Peasant Wives"—are excellently drawn. In the first two stories of the later cycle, Chekhov examines certain intellectual attitudes. In "The House with a Mezzanine," he explores the view of the Russian populists *(narodniki)* that the peasants could be saved by education and hygiene, and in "My Life," the Tolstoyan tenet of "simplification." Both solutions to social evils are found wanting. In the peasant cycle's subsequent stories, naturalistic pictures of village life overshadow social issues.

The April 1897 issue of the journal *Russkaya mysl* (Russian Thought) contained Chekhov's story "The Peasants." Though a few passages were deleted by the censor, Chekhov was able to reinstate them in the first edition in book form, published in the same year. Books were not subject to the same stringent censorship laws as periodicals. The story concentrates on the members of one peasant family, the Chikildeevs. Each member of this family has his own tragic fate, caused by poverty and the resulting degradation, drunkenness, and brutality. It is through the eyes of Nikolay Chikildeev, a Moscow waiter who falls ill and decides to return to his native village, that we see the life of these peasants who drink and beg, the men beating their wives and children. Through Chikildeev's wife and children we also see how and why these creatures live like animals—crowded in a filthy hut, tortured by lice, cold, and stench. These peasants, just like those of Zola in *La bête humaine* and *La terre,* are stripped of the slightest trace of idealization. Only the sexual violence of Zola's peasants is lacking. The naturalistic approach is also evident in the objectivity and lack of sympathy for the characters, which is carried here to an extreme unusual for Chekhov.

In sharp contrast to "The Peasants" is Chekhov's longest story of the cycle, "In the Ravine," published in 1900 in the Marxist journal *Zhizn* (Life). Chekhov had written it at the urging of Gorky, and he himself called it "a strange story" (letter to Olga Knipper, 2 January 1900). We may agree with this estimate, for in the characterization of its protagonists Chekhov has sacrificed realism and produced figures in the spirit of Dostoevsky's philosophical heroes and of the late works of Tolstoy—symbols of ideas. The creation of an atmosphere of power and cruelty is the most striking effect of the story, whose conflict, rather simplified and exaggerated for Chekhov, is essentially that between natural labor and materialistic greed.

"In the Ravine" describes a family of rich peasants, the Tsybukins, who live in a village that has been reached by industrialization. They have abandoned farming and keep a store in which they secretly sell vodka. The picture of commercial greed connects this work to "Three Years," but the Tsybukins, who have remained peasants, are not only hypocritical and greedy, they are also very cruel, and recall the peasants in Tolstoy's play *The Power of Darkness* (1889).

As the story opens, we are introduced to the Tsybukin world. The patriarch of the family hates the other peasants. He rides through the streets on an expensive horse to show that he is better than them. His oldest son is a police informer, as well as a counterfeiter.

The stark juxtaposition of two sets of characters—like those of the medieval mystery play—can be seen to epitomize the conflict between the kingdom of darkness and the kingdom of light. The world of darkness is composed of the Tsybukins and various factory owners. To the world of light belong all those who live by the labor of their hands, not by exploiting others. "In the Ravine" expresses more clearly than any other of Chekhov's peasant stories his theme of beauty and sensitivity stifled by vulgarity, banality, and a "purely businesslike relation among people," to use a phrase from "The Steppe." Beauty belongs to those who perform useful labor. This idea, treated satirically by Chekhov in the early peasant stories, where it is related to the hypocritical adoption of Tolstoyan simplification, is treated sympathetically in many of his later works. Its spokesman in this work is the laborer Kostyl (The Crutch), whose remarks function as a kind of chorus to the main action. His saying "He who works and suffers is better" could be taken as an epigraph for this late work. Vanya in the play *Uncle Vanya* and Tuzenbakh in *The Three Sisters* make similar statements. "In the Ravine" concludes Chekhov's peasant cycle. Its moralism and romanticism set it apart; it is not surprising that Tolstoy, who had criticized "The Peasants" for its objectivity, was enthusiastic about "In the Ravine."

### *"Rothschild's Fiddle"*

In "Skripka Rotshilda" ("Rothschild's Fiddle," 1894), a story of premature death, we find the opposition of life and death expressed in the contrast between music and what Chekhov had called earlier "a purely businesslike attitude." This conflict is embodied in Yakov the coffin maker, who plays the violin beautifully but sees everything as an aspect of his business—and the business is death at that. He accepts orders for children's coffins only grudgingly, since they are smaller and cheaper; he grumbles that people die out of town, thus depriving him of business; he takes his wife's measure for her coffin while she is still alive, builds it in the room where she lies dying, and then enters it in his account book in the debit column.

This story, like "The Steppe," is based on a musiclike interplay of several motifs and images. In the opening of the story, the theme of Yakov's greed is introduced in a passage the neutral tone of which is modified by a subtext that points to the narrow outlook of the coffin maker: "The little town was small, worse than a village and inhabited almost only by old people who died so rarely that it was even annoying. In the hospital and the prison few coffins were ordered. In a word, business was miserable."

Many details convey Yakov's narrowness and materialism, and the omnipresence of death. He is surrounded by coffins and hates Jews. He is cold to his wife and subservient to the medical assistant who examines her when she is dying. The metonymic detail that indicates Yakov's crassness becomes a leitmotif; it is the word "deficit" *(ubytok);* he views life as a persistent struggle against "deficits," and this view leads him to a final absurdity, for when he is himself dying, he finds death to be the most rational and economical state: "Since man lies in his little grave not one year, but hundreds, thousands of years, one must figure that there really is a tremendous profit." Yakov concludes with logical consistency: "Life brings only deficit, but death brings profit."

Played against the motifs of ugliness and death are the notes of life, beauty, and art, represented by music. When Yakov lies sleeplessly in bed, thinking of deficits, he is comforted by touching the strings of his violin. When his wife is dying, she reminds Yakov of the willow tree under which they used to sing when they were young; and Yakov's violin playing moves those around him.

The opposing themes have their complexities and contradictions. Motifs of banality, greed, and death may deform those of beauty and life. Even music may be so deformed; it is first stated in terms of the profit it brings Yakov. The stifling atmosphere of the Jewish orchestra in which Yakov plays occasionally, at weddings, to earn extra money, is seen from Yakov's point of view, in a picture that points only to his hate: "When Bronza [Yakov's nickname] sat in the orchestra, his face was sweaty and red. It was hot, there was a choking smell of garlic. The fiddle was screaming, the double bass sounded hoarsely in his right ear; in his left ear, the flute was weeping."

Here, synesthetic images transform the scene of harmony into one of dissonance and ugliness; and these images are strengthened by the sound orchestration of the verbal material, which, in the Russian original, through assonance and alliteration, achieves a pejorative onomatopoeia. "Rothschild's Fiddle" is the first major story of the last period in which the technique of zero ending is extended from the formal to the ideological. Chekhov's hero has posed a question: "Shall one live a life in which the struggle against 'deficit' predominates? Can a life in which beauty and art prevail extinguish the battle for profit and the struggle of man against man?" The story does not provide an answer; the problem persists even after Yakov's death—in the life of Rothschild, the Jewish fiddler to whom Yakov bequeathes his instrument. The story contains, albeit in a somewhat simple fashion, many of the elements that characterize Chekhov's mature prose and also his plays: the thematic indeterminacy, the syncretic character, and the "musical" construction that replace external action, in which nothing really happens and nothing is resolved.

### *"The Teacher of Literature"*

"Uchitel slovesnosti" ("The Teacher of Literature," 1889–1894) suggests parallels to "Rothschild's Fiddle" in the treatment of the conflict between beauty and vulgarity. It is the story of the love of the young teacher Nikitin for Masha Shelestova, the daughter of a prominent member of the society of a provincial town, and depicts the gradual disillusionment of Nikitin. The central theme is the contrast between Nikitin's idealized vision of Masha and her family and the stagnation and pretense of their lives. In each of the story's two chapters motifs of banality and vulgarity on the one hand, and of beauty on the other, are interwoven; the center of emphasis gradually shifts from expressions of beauty and happiness to manifestations of materialistic crassness.

The first chapter opens on an idyllic note, though subtly infused with ugliness. Nikitin and Masha are on a romantic horseback ride; Nikitin dreams of his love for an idealized Masha. A beautiful atmosphere is described:

> Here the acacias and the lilac no longer smelled, music was no longer heard; instead, the smell was of fields; young rye and wheat stood green, marmots were whistling, crows were crowing. Wherever your eyes fell, there was green.

But it is tempered by an antistrophe immediately following:

> . . . only somewhere there could be seen the blackness of melon fields, and far on the left, at the graveyard, one could see the white of apple trees whose blossoms were beginning to wilt.
>
> They passed the slaughterhouse and then the beer brewery.

And so the story continues, always playing images of life and death against each other. The balance gradually shifts toward the death motifs when Nikitin and Masha marry and Nikitin's disillusionment grows. At the end Nikitin has lost all his dreams, and the motifs of banality and vulgarity are all-pervasive.

### *The Little Trilogy*

In 1898, *Russkaya mysl* published three stories by Chekhov that, because of their close formal and romantic relationship, can be considered a trilogy. They are all part of a frame story. These stories are "Chelovek v futlyare" ("The Man in a Shell"), "Kryzhovnik" ("Gooseberries"), and "O lyubvi" ("About Love"). All three are exemplary tales, each illustrating a particular kind of constricted life in which a person "encases" himself, as it were, in a shell to avoid contact and communication with others. This, of course, is one of the central problems of Chekhov's protagonists. The characters of these stories suffer from isolation and the inability to participate in life. The theme of dedication to an excessively narrow segment of life, one of the unifying themes of the "searching" stories, can now be seen as only one aspect of the general problem of man's inescapable limitation of spirit. Perhaps a phrase from "Gooseberries"—in turn a reference to Tolstoy's moral tale "How Much Land Does a Man Need?"—states the theme of the trilogy most succinctly: "Man needs not six feet of soil, not a farm, but the whole earth, all of nature, where, unhindered, he can display all his abilities and the properties of his free spirit." The protagonists of all three stories are constrained by a shell, a mental-psychological-moral "six feet of soil" that prevents them from living full or satisfying lives.

The frame that unites the three stories is a familiar one. After a day's hunting, three huntsmen pass the time in the barn where they have settled for the night by telling each other stories. The theme of the trilogy is presented in the introductory frame story: two of the huntsmen, the teacher Burkin and the veterinary surgeon Ivan Ivanych Chimsha-Gimalaysky, the narrators of the first two stories, are talking about Mavra, the wife of the village elder who owns the barn. She has never been beyond the confines of her village and for ten years has left her house only at night. Burkin remarks that he does not find that surprising; after all, there are many people "who try to withdraw into a shell like a hermit crab," a thought that launches him on the story of his colleague, the secondary-school teacher Belikov, who is the "man in a shell" of the story of that title. The story elaborates the theme of withdrawal suggested by Mavra's behavior, investing it with the broadest symbolic import, in which a man so fears life beyond its outward forms that he goes to excessive lengths to protect himself with various types of "shells." This story leads to the next, "Gooseberries," in which a different kind of narrowness is exemplified in the yearning of the hero for his own plot of land (his "six feet of soil"). When he gets his wish, its achievement makes him even smaller and more selfish. Finally, in "About Love," deadening conventionalism and emotional paralysis prevent the realization of a love affair.

In "The Man in a Shell" the teacher Belikov tyrannizes an entire town in his self-appointed role as the guardian of the "proper" forms of life. When he becomes engaged to Varenka, a pretty, vivacious girl, the results are disastrous, for his outlook on life clashes with that of his fun-loving fiancée. After a violent argument, Varenka's brother throws Belikov down the stairs. Belikov's fragile self is shattered; he locks himself in his room and dies.

Belikov is insulated from life's content by form, the shell: "Any infringement of the rules, any deviation from them, plunges him into gloom." Belikov's estrangement from life, his inability to live, are expressed by the trivialities behind which he hides his soul and by the external barriers with which he shields himself. He speaks only in clichés; he is never without dark glasses; he wears galoshes and a quilted coat even when the weather is fine; his face is always hidden by a high collar; his ears are stuffed with cotton plugs. At home, he wraps himself in a dressing gown and covers his head with a nightcap; the curtains and shutters of his room are always kept closed, the doors and windows securely bolted; he will not ride in an open carriage; his umbrella, his pocket knife, and his watch are protected by cloth covers; and his thoughts are of the past rather than of the present:

> Actuality irritated and frightened him, kept him in constant anxiety; and perhaps to justify his timidity, his aversion for reality, he would always praise the past and things that had never existed. And the ancient languages he taught were actually for him the same galoshes and umbrella behind which he sought protection from the realities of life.

Belikov's compulsive attachment to forms of behavior destroys his marriage plans and leads to his death. He withdraws to his bed behind curtains, covered by a heavy quilt, hiding himself beneath several protective layers as he prepares to die. Only when he lies in his coffin, shielded forever from the perils of contact with life, does he appear happy: "His expression was meek, pleasant, even happy, as though he were glad at last to have been placed in a shell which he would never leave again. Yes, he had achieved his ideal."

"Gooseberries" is the story of the narrator's brother, who, obsessed with the desire to own his own "estate," scrimps and saves, denying himself all the pleasures of life, even food. The idyllic life of retirement on the land is symbolized for him by a gooseberry bush from which he can eat "his own" berries. When he finally realizes his dream, the narrator visits him and finds that he has grown old and fat, and that the homegrown gooseberries are hard and sour. The narrator realizes the futility of the achievement, and is appalled at the price in humanity with which it was bought.

In "About Love," the third narrator, Alekhin, tells of his love for Anna, the beautiful wife of a judge; he feels himself unworthy of her. While Belikov is destroyed by fear and the owner of the gooseberry bush by the pettiness of his aims, Alekhin's limitations are more elusive. Unlike the earlier protagonists, he is vaguely aware of a failing; but he is prevented from taking action by inertia. Only when it is too late does he realize that inertia has ruined his chances for happiness.

### *A New Mood*

During the last six years of Chekhov's life, a change in his point of view can be noted. After the trilogy and "Ionich," which represent the fullest expression of Chekhov's concern with man's destruction by venality and vulgarity, we find a somewhat less pessimistic tone; some stories written after 1898, as well as the major plays (all written after 1896), express a slight hope, albeit strongly qualified, that perhaps man can find a measure of happiness. The three stories that express most clearly the mood of Chekhov's later years are "Dushechka" ("The Darling," 1898), "Dama s sobachkoy" ("The Lady with a Dog," 1899), and "Nevesta" ("The Betrothed," 1903).

"The Darling" is the story of Olenka, a young woman who can exist only in total submission to a love object. She cannot live without love and remarries every time she is widowed. Her husband's world becomes totally hers; she speaks in his clichés and is interested only in his work. When she is married to the manager of an open-air theater, she can talk only of the lack of culture of the audience. When, after her first husband's death, she marries the manager of a lumberyard, she talks only about the price of lumber and the taxes that threaten to ruin her husband. After the death of the lumber dealer, she becomes friends with an army veterinarian. Although they are not married, everybody knows what the situation is when Olenka suddenly begins to complain about the danger of animal epidemics. When her lover is transferred, she is left alone:

> And above all, and worst of all, she no longer had any opinions whatever. She saw objects around her and understood what was going on, but she could not form an opinion about anything and did not know what to talk about. And how terrible it is not to have any opinions! You see, for instance, a bottle, or the rain, or a peasant driving a cart, but what the bottle is for, or the rain, or the peasant, what is their meaning, you cannot tell, and you could not, even if they paid you a thousand rubles. When Kukin was around, or Pustovalov, or, later, the veterinarian, Olenka could explain it all and give her opinion about anything you liked, but now there was the same emptiness in her head and in her heart as in her courtyard.

In the end, Olenka finds a new love in the veterinarian's schoolboy son, whom she mothers. Now she can have opinions again—about teachers, school textbooks, the burdensome character of homework.

The picture of Olenka, devoid of a personality of her own, is of course partly satirical. But "The Darling" is not just the story of an empty woman. Tolstoy liked "The Darling" better than any other work by Chekhov, and he called Olenka a "wonderfully holy being"; whether one agrees or disagrees with Tolstoy's view, his interpretation cannot be ignored. While it appears at first that Olenka may become one of Chekhov's typical figures of emptiness and hypocrisy, that she is capable of love, albeit so submissive and possessive a love, distinguishes her from the many of Chekhov's lonely protagonists. Yet Tolstoy's view that in elevating the submissive Olenka Chekhov had—at least subconsciously—rejected his earlier ideas on women's emancipation is not justified, for Olenka's absurdity cannot be overlooked. The satire in the depiction of Olenka is strengthened if we consider, as did Renato Poggioli, the relation of Chekhov's story to the myth of Eros and Psyche. Poggioli saw "The Darling" as a modern version of the ancient myth. He noted that Chekhov's heroine is called by the Russian nickname *dushechka,* an endearing expression close to the English "darling," which is also the title of the story. *Dushechka* is also the affectionate diminutive form of the Russian word *dusha,* "soul," which also has the meaning of the Greek *psychē.* Poggioli saw the similarity of Olenka and Psyche as Chekhov's "furtive hint that even in the profane prose of life, there may lie hidden poetry's sacred spark." But he did not note the ironic implication of the parallel with the myth. Psyche breaks Eros' command not to look at him during their lovemaking. When she disobeys, the god vanishes. Like Psyche, Olenka loves blindly; but she is satisfied to love unseeingly and never attempts to "inspect" the object of her love. And those whom Olenka loves successively are but absurd shadows of the god of love; it is their prosaic qualities and their insignificance, not their godlike characteristics, that cannot stand up to inspection. Thus Olenka and her lovers are lower versions of the personages in the myth; and its echo, rather than indicating a romantic interpretation of Olenka's unquestioning love, implies that Chekhov's heroine, who retains her illusions, is too naive and weak to see or bear the ensuing doubt.

In "The Lady with a Dog," written one year after "The Darling," the note of gentle sympathy becomes more pronounced and the story ends on a note of qualified—though highly muted—hope. The plot can be summarized as follows: In a Black Sea resort town, Gurov, a married, cynical ladies' man, meets Anna, a young married woman, and lightly enters into an affair with her. But he is transformed by a love that transcends the casual summer affair. Many of the stories we have discussed depict the ruin of love by banality and vulgarity. "The Lady with a Dog" suggests that banality and vulgarity can be conquered by love.

This story has some points in common with Tolstoy's novel *Anna Karenina* (1875–1877). But while much in the story—the first name of the heroine, the opening situation, the initial behavior of Gurov—parallels the details of Tolstoy's novel, Chekhov's story reverses the traditional romantic-realistic adultery theme of which *Anna Karenina* is the classic example; it contains none of Tolstoy's dramatic turns of action, nor is there a tragic denouement.

"The Lady with a Dog" evolves along parallel lines. There is the simple linear story that evolves in a manner typical of traditional plot development: Gurov meets Anna, they start an affair; the lovers suppose the affair is over when they leave the resort to return to their respective spouses. But they discover that they are attached to each other with a new and profound kind of love. Behind this linear plot, where event follows event, there evolves another text, with other meanings that cast light on the conflict between two ways of living and loving: the conventional way, which permits superficial affairs but strictly circumscribes them; and a life and love free from artifice and falsehood. These two story lines intertwine, forming a network of harmonies and contrasts; and it is these parallelisms that determine the story's lyricism and govern its poetic rhythms.

In December 1903, only seven months before Chekhov's death, there appeared in *Zhurnal dlya vsekh* (Journal for All) his last story, "Nevesta" ("The Betrothed"), a work pervaded by the tone of melancholy optimism that we have noted in this late group. In many respects, "The Betrothed" represents the apotheosis of the innovation Chekhov brought to the art of the short story. And it is the work that best demonstrates the revolutionary character of his narrative art. In its treatment of time and space, in its inner lyricism, in its high degree of syncretism, "The Betrothed" is the culmination of Chekhov's striking out in new directions. We have already noted the frequently nonlinear character of time in Chekhov's work. The usual relation of forward movement *in* space *through* time—in short, directionality— is in fact suspended, and a heightened artistic tension results from the interplay between the temporal and the atemporal, the directional and the nondirectional. Thus, for example, in "Arkhierey" ("The Bishop," 1902), the action is based on the motif of the coming and going of the bishop from home to church, to home, to church, repeatedly, until he returns home to die. Similarly, in "The Darling," the movement of the heroine from one dependent love relationship to another remains in the end directionless. She has moved in a circle, and her apparent cause-and-effect relations are all without consequence.

"The Betrothed" concerns Nadya, a young girl who lives in a provincial town with her widowed mother and her loud and coarse grandmother. She is engaged to the handsome but dull Andrey, the son of the local priest. The artist Sasha, a protégé of the grandmother, awakens in Nadya a sense of futility about her life. Responding to his plea, she leaves her home to study in Saint Petersburg, thus breaking off her engagement. On her way back home for a visit, she stops briefly at Sasha's quarters in Moscow, realizes that he is not a liberator, and sees that he lives poorly and is ill. Once home, she sees her environment with new eyes, and leaves again. The story ends with the phrase: " . . . she left the town—as she supposed, forever."

The underlying meaning of the story concerns Nadya's attempt to free herself from what is first depicted as the stifling environment of her grandmother's household, her shallow mother, and her fiancé. Nadya's soul is torn between the banality of her home and a vague idea of freedom, the most extreme form of which is the utopia preached by Sasha. Psychological space is molded by actual dimensions, ranging from the most circumscribed (Nadya's bedroom; the house) to the most unbounded (Russia; all of nature). But the ambiguity of this opposition is realized later, when the bedroom becomes an infantile haven, nature becomes hostile, and Nadya can no longer see them in their pristine opposition. While there is a value relation, the outside being marked as positive and the inside as negative, this relation is fluid and never fixed; it is not always as fluid as this in Chekhov's work. The theme of opposition between ugliness and beauty, banality and art, epitomized in Nadya's revolt, is played out through her changing perceptions.

The story has evoked considerable debate over the question of its optimism. Does Chekhov imply Nadya's liberation as she is awakened to a new life and rejects the old one? This is the common interpretation of the story, and clearly, there is in the ending a melancholy optimism, also characteristic of Chekhov's later plays: Nadya has returned to her home, which she sees with a new maturity: "And it seemed to her that . . . everything was merely waiting—waiting not so much for the end as for the beginning of something young and fresh."

But the wistful remarks that follow—"Oh, if only this new clear life would arrive more quickly" and "Such a life would come sooner or later"—disturb the hopeful tone, as does the modifier in the phrase that ends the story: "The next morning, lively and gay, she left the town—*as she supposed,* forever" (emphasis added). Thus while the story ends on a positive note (there is a new life), it is contradicted by a multitude of signs implying that nothing has really changed. The question raised in the critical debate as to the optimism or pessimism of the story therefore seems misplaced, since the very essence of the artistic form of "The Betrothed" is that it consists of two interpenetrating, contrapuntal voices. Chekhov has not only asked a question; he has also shown that in life there are no simple answers.

## *CHEKHOV THE DRAMATIST*

The bulk of Chekhov's literary output was narrative prose, and one might well argue that he was first and foremost a writer of short stories who revolutionized this genre. But his dramaturgy was equally revolutionary, and in many ways similar in development and artistic innovation. Chekhov's dramatic production is usually divided into two categories: (1)

traditional-action plays, in which the action takes place onstage in full view of the audience; and (2) indirect-action plays, with little external action onstage: Only the results of action, which takes place elsewhere, are shown. To the latter category belong Chekhov's four major plays, *Chayka* (*The Seagull*, 1896), *Dyadya Vanya* (*Uncle Vanya*, 1899), *Tri sestry* (*The Three Sisters*, 1900–1901), and *Vishnevy sad* (*The Cherry Orchard*, 1904).

Chekhov began writing plays later than stories. His first play, *Ivanov*, was written in 1887, during the time when he was writing "The Steppe." Most of his early works are one-act comedies, very similar to his early anecdotes—some, in fact, are adaptations of these sketches. Others are serious, even tragic. Ronald Hingley called two of them, *On the High Road* (1885) and *Swan Song* (1887–1888), "tearjerkers." But Chekhov's early farces have significance because they anticipate some of the revolutionary techniques of his later plays. These farces, *Medved* (*The Bear*, 1888), *Predlozhenie* (*The Marriage Proposal*, 1888–1889), *Tragik po nevole* (*A Tragic Role*, 1889–1890), *Svadba* (*The Wedding*, 1889–1890), *Yubeley* (*The Anniversary*, 1891), and *O vrede tabaka* (*The Evils of Tobacco*, worked on for sixteen years and finally published in 1902), are not so much situation comedies as comedies of character, each character individualized through idiosyncratic speech patterns and gestures. The farces have little intrigue: the dramatic tension is determined by the characters and their interrelations.

Chekhov's first full-length play, *Ivanov* (1887–1889), contains elements of traditional dramatic action, with situations strongly reminiscent of the one-act farces. Many characters show the influence of the traditional "humors," that is, they are characterized by a single predominant trait: stinginess, ignorance, and so forth. Of the more complex characterization, much also is traditional: the characters "introduce" themselves in soliloquies in which they reveal their essence. But the use of subtext, often evoked by nonverbal sounds (for example, the repeated hooting of the owl) and running counter to the text; the use of silences; the idiosyncratic language of the characters; the importance given to intonation, for which stage directions are provided ("through tears," "happily," "calmly," "jokingly")—all presage the masterpieces to come.

It is with *The Seagull* that Chekhov begins his search for new dramatic forms. The play revolves around the question of the nature of art and love, and the relations of the characters are expressed in terms of both love and art. The action reflects the debate of Chekhov's day about art—especially the so-called decadent art of the symbolists—and about the role of the artist in society. The dramatic construction is innovative. There is practically no overt action onstage. What is important takes place outside the play and is merely talked about onstage. Even the suicide of Treplev, the young playwright, which might have been a dramatic climax, takes place offstage and is reported with remarkable understatement by another character. Indeed, the play is devoid of the traditional kind of conflict between characters; all conflicts are primarily inner conflicts. This means that dramatic tension is created by new means, no longer by opposition but by the unresolved difficulties within each character and secondarily in their mutual relations. Therefore there are no dramatic climaxes expressed in action or dialogue. The most important events are referred to only in passing.

Chekhov's next play, *Uncle Vanya*, carries forward the style and technique of *The Seagull*. Again, the play lacks a single "hero" and a dynamic action plot; the external action is minimal; and there are no real positive heroes or any real villains. And again, Chekhov's method does not rest on the action on the stage, for that is trivial and ineffective (even a shot fired does not kill and remains without result). Rather, the play is informed by a general mood that cannot be verbalized and might perhaps best be compared to the manner in which music touches our sensibilities. The definition of character, the qualities of the dialogue, the lyrical composition of the endings of the acts—all develop directly out of the lyrical conception of *The Seagull.*

The success of *The Seagull* and *Uncle Vanya* on the stage of the Moscow Art Theater impelled Chekhov to write his next two (and last) plays with an orientation derived from the principles of stagecraft of Stanislavsky's theater—his subtle and profound psychological realism and his fanatical attention to the minutiae of stage business and stage effects. This effort first produced his masterpiece, *The Three Sisters.* Again the movement of the acts is lyrical, the onstage action derived from emotional developments occurring offstage and presented to the audience usually in moments of crisis. The expressive speech of the characters is frequently commented on by a choruslike second "action" on the stage, and consists of pauses and literary allusions. Thus, for example, *The Three Sisters* opens with a lyrical conversation among the sisters, Olga, Irina, and Masha, reminiscing on the occasion of Irina's name day, their lyrical mood brought on by the beautiful spring morning and their dreams of Moscow. But the lyrical, somewhat sentimental, tone of the sisters' conversation is abruptly disturbed by the remarks and laughter of Chebutykin, Tuzenbakh, and Solyony, who have been standing at the back of the stage and acting out a kind of pantomime. Thus:

> CHEBUTYKIN: The hell you say!
> TUZENBAKH: Of course, it's all nonsense.

Tuzenbakh's and Chebutykin's remarks are, we are given to understand, a part of their private conversation and overtly have no connection with the conversation of the three sisters stage front. But the import is clear to the audience; they comment indirectly, in choruslike fashion, on the sisters' words. And later in the same act, Solyony suddenly quotes two lines from Krylov's fable *The Peasant and the Farm Laborer:*

> Before he had time to let out a yell,
> The Bear was squeezing him to hell.

This is also a multifaceted chorus statement. It comments not only on the energetic way Masha has counterattacked against Solyony, but also on Protopopov, who has just been mentioned and is to be responsible for evicting the three sisters from their home. Chekhov makes this connection even clearer by having Masha flounder for Protopopov's name and patronymic, at one point calling him Mikhail Potapych, the humorous name given to bears by Russian peasants. Plays on this name and on the Krylov quotation are woven, together with other literary quotations, throughout the dramatic action, where they act as subtle subtexts. Again, the play ends not in a tragic denouement (although we learn that one of the characters has been shot in a duel and one of the sisters must part from her lover), but in a lyrical ebbing away, similar to the zero ending of the mature stories. Perhaps a subdued optimism sounds the last note.

*The Cherry Orchard* has probably been Chekhov's most consistently misunderstood play, both in Russia and abroad. From the very beginning, Chekhov insisted that the play was a comedy, not a tragedy, and that it should be played as a comedy. In fact, the play is subtitled "A Comedy in Four Acts." The insistence of Stanislavsky and Vladimir Nemirovich-Danchenko, the literary director of the theater, on producing the play as a symbolic tragedy almost led to a serious rift between Chekhov and the Moscow Art Theater.

The subject of *The Cherry Orchard* is the forced sale of an estate. Again, what occurs onstage is ancillary action derived from events that take place offstage and are not dramatized. The result is a patchwork of almost static pictures, the cause of Chekhov's reputation as the author of actionless plays. The characters are conceived in absurdly comical poses, many of them broad caricatures. Sometimes the action is reminiscent of the early farces, as, for instance, when Lopakhin, who is later to buy the estate, suddenly sticks his head in a room where a serious conversation is taking place and imitates the lowing of a cow. But here the absurd interruption does not just serve the cause of farce; it also acts as a choruslike commentary, admonishing the audience not to take the earnest talk too seriously. At times, the speeches are of less importance than the nonverbal means the characters use to communicate with each other: pauses, silences, guitar-strumming, and the sound of an ax chopping down trees. All these are of great semantic import, as are intonations, for which there are detailed instructions in the text, more so in *The Cherry Orchard* than in the preceding plays—it contains about 175 directions for delivering lines. Speeches often have no clear denotative meaning; the meaning must be sought in the connotations that hide behind the spoken words. Thus in the final act Varya and Lopakhin meet when others are not present. The preceding speeches have hinted that Lopakhin entertains romantic feelings for Varya, and Madame Ranevskaya, who has just sold the estate, hopes for an understanding and a proposal. But the dialogue that ensues is disconcerting. Lopakhin is alone onstage, having been left by Madame Ranevskaya, who has suggested that he propose to her ward; Varya enters, also at Madame Ranevskaya's insistence:

> VARYA: *(Examines the luggage for a long time)* It's strange, I just can't seem to find . . .
> LOPAKHIN: What are you looking for?
> VARYA: I packed it all myself, and I can't remember. *(Pause)*
> LOPAKHIN: Where are you going now, Varvara Mikhaylovna?
> VARYA: Me? To the Ragulins. . . . I've agreed to look after their place . . . as the housekeeper. At least, that's the impression I get.
> LOPAKHIN: That's at Yashnevo, isn't it? About twenty versts from here. *(Pause)* And so life is over and done with in this house. . . .
> VARYA: *(Examining the luggage)* Where on earth could it . . . Or maybe I packed it in the trunk. . . . Yes, life in this house is over and done with. . . . It will never come back here anymore. . . .
> LOPAKHIN: And I am just now on my way to Kharkov . . . on the next train, you see. I've got plenty to do. I am leaving Yepikhodov here to look after the work outside. I've hired him.
> VARYA: Well, hmm!
> LOPAKHIN: Last year at this time we already had snow on the ground, if you recall, but now it is pretty quiet with plenty of sunshine. It's just cold, that's all. . . . About three degrees of frost.
> VARYA: I haven't looked. *(Pause)* Besides, our thermometer is broken. . . . *(Pause)*
> *A voice from outside is heard calling through the door: "Yermolay Alekseich!"*
> LOPAKHIN: *(As if he had been waiting a long time for this summons)* Coming! *(Quickly goes out)*
> *Varya sits on the floor, lays her head on a bundle of clothing, and quietly sobs.*

Clearly, what is important here is *how* the words are spoken; nothing else will tell the audience the meaning behind them.

Another example is the nonverbal "dialogue" in the third act of *The Three Sisters* between Masha and Vershinin, who have become lovers:

> MASHA: Tram-tam-tam . . .
> VERSHININ: Tram-tam . . .
> MASHA: Tra-ra-ta . . .
> VERSHININ: Tra-ra-ta . . .

This conversation is repeated a second time:

> VERSHININ: Tram-tam-tam . . .
> MASHA: Tram-tam . . .

The conversation takes place a third time, as Vershinin's voice is heard offstage:

> VERSHININ: Tram-tam-tam . . .
> MASHA: *(Getting up, in a loud voice)* Tra-ta-ta . . .

It is clear, as was pointed out by Nils Åke Nilsson, that these nonsense words form a love dialogue of mutual understanding between the two—in fact, as Nilsson called it, a love duet.

There is no climactic ending in *The Cherry Orchard.* The estate is sold; the buyer is the former serf Lopakhin; the owners of the estate must now leave. Thus the material of a great tragic climax is provided, but it never occurs; it is avoided by understatement and by the inappropriate reactions of the owners, who go off to new, totally unsuited occupations. Instead of the tragic denouement we are led to expect, we are given a zero ending: not words, but sounds. The last words of the play do not belong to any character; they are stage directions:

> *A distant sound is heard. It seems to come from the sky, the sound of a breaking string mournfully dying away. Then, all is silent once again, and nothing is heard but the sound of the ax on a tree far away in the orchard.*

All four plays end on a symbolic, nonverbal note. In *The Seagull,* it is the noise of the suicide shot of Treplev, sounding offstage and perhaps coming closest to a true dramatic climax. *Uncle Vanya* ends with this scene:

> SONYA: . . . *(Through tears)* You have never known happiness in your life, but wait, Uncle Vanya, wait a little while. . . . We shall rest. . . . *(Embraces him)* We shall rest! *(The watchman taps. Telegin quietly plays the guitar. Maria Vasilevna writes on the margin of her pamphlet. Marina knits a stocking.)* We shall rest!

And *The Three Sisters* ends as follows:

> OLGA: *(Embraces both her sisters)* Listen, listen to the band play so joyfully, so happily, you want to live! Oh, dear God in Heaven! Time will pass, and we shall be gone forever. We won't be remembered, they will forget what we looked like, forget our voices and how many of us there were. But our sufferings can turn to joy for those who live after us. In time, happiness and peace will come to this earth, and people will remember and speak kindly and bless those of us who live now. Oh, my dear sisters, our life is not over yet. We shall live, we shall! The band plays so joyfully, so happily, and it seems that in a little while we shall know the reason we live, the reason we suffer. . . . If only we knew, if only we knew!
>
> *(The band plays more and more softly; Kulygin, happily, smiling, brings the hat and the cape; Andrey pushes the baby carriage, in which Bobik is sitting.)*
>
> CHEBUTYKIN: *(Hums quietly)* "Ta-ra-ra boom-di-yay, sitting on a curb today . . . " *(Reads newspaper)* It doesn't matter! It doesn't matter!
>
> OLGA: If only we knew, if only we knew!

## Selected Bibliography


EDITIONS

*Polnoe sobranie sochinenii.* 23 vols. Edited by A. F. Marks. Saint Petersburg, 1903–1918.

*Polnoe sobranie sochinenii i pisem.* 20 vols. Edited by S. D. Balukhatii. Moscow, 1944–1955.

*Sobranie sochinenii.* Edited by V. V. Ermilov. Moscow, 1960–1964.

*Polnoe sobranie sochinenii i pisem.* 30 vols. Edited by N. F. Belchikov. Moscow, 1974–1982.

TRANSLATIONS

*Anton Chekhov: Peasants and Other Stories.* Translated by Edmund Wilson. New York, 1956.

*Anton Chekhov's Plays.* Translated by Eugene K. Bristow. New York, 1977.

*Chekhov: The Major Plays.* Translated by Ann Dunnigan. New York, 1964.

*Chekhov: Plays.* Translated by Elisaveta Fen. Harmondsworth, 1951.

*Chekhov: Selected Stories.* Translated by Ann Dunnigan. New York, 1965.

*The Island: A Journey to Sakhalin.* Translated by Luba and Michael Terpau. New York, 1967.

*Lady with a Lapdog and Other Stories.* Translated by David Magarshack. Harmondsworth, 1964.

*Letters of Anton Chekhov.* Translated by Michael Henry Heim in collaboration with Simon Karlinsky. London, 1973.

*Letters of Anton Chekhov.* Selected and edited by Avrahm Yarmolinsky. New York, 1973.

*Letters on the Short Story, the Drama and Other Literary Topics by Anton Chekhov.* Selected and edited by Louis Friedland. New York, 1964.

*Notebook of Anton Chekhov.* Translated by S. S. Koteliansky and Leonard Woolf. New York, 1921.

*The Oxford Chekhov.* Translated by Ronald Hingley. Oxford, 1961–.

*Plays of Tchehov.* Translated by Constance Garnett. London, 1923–1924.

*The Portable Chekhov.* Translated by Avrahm Yarmolinsky. New York, 1965.

*Six Plays of Chekhov.* Translated by Robert W. Corrigan. New York, 1962.

*The Tales of Tchehov.* Translated by Constance Garnett. London, 1916–1922.

*Tchekov's Plays and Stories.* Translated by S. S. Koteliansky. London, 1937.

BIOGRAPHICAL AND CRITICAL STUDIES

ENGLISH

Bruford, W. H. *Anton Chekhov.* New Haven, 1957.

———. *Chekhov and His Russia.* Hamden, Conn., 1971.

Chudakov, A. P. *Chekhov's Poetics.* Translated by E. J. Cruise and D. Dragt. Ann Arbor, Mich., 1983.

Eekman, T., ed. *Anton Čexov, 1860–1960.* Leiden, 1960. Essays by N. A. Nillson, T. A. Eekman, V. Markov, Z. Papernyj, Gleb Struve, D. Tschižewski, T. G. Winner, and others.

Elton, Oliver. *Chekhov.* Oxford, 1929.

Garnett, Edward. *Chekhov and His Art.* London, 1929.

Gerhardi, William. *Anton Chekhov: A Critical Study.* New York, 1923.

Gilles, Daniel. *Chekhov: Observer Without Illusion.* New York, 1968.

Gorky, Maxim. *Literary Portraits.* Translated by Ivy Litvinov. Moscow, n.d. Pp. 134–168.

Hahn, Beverly. *Chekhov: A Study of the Major Stories and Plays.* New York, 1977.

Hingley, Ronald. *Chekhov: A Biographical and Critical Study.* London, 1966.

———. *A New Life of Anton Chekhov.* New York, 1976.

Jackson, Robert Louis, ed. *Chekhov: A Collection of Critical Essays.* Englewood Cliffs, N.J., 1967.

Kirk, Irina, *Chekhov.* Boston, 1981.

Kramer, Karl. *The Chameleon and the Dream.* The Hague, 1970.

Llewellyn-Smith, Virginia. *Anton Chekhov and the Lady with the Little Dog.* Oxford, 1978.

Magarshack, David. *Chekhov: A Life.* New York, 1955.

———. *Chekhov the Dramatist.* London, 1952.

———. *The Real Chekhov.* London, 1972.

Pitcher, Harvey. *The Chekhov Play: A New Interpretation.* New York, 1973.

Poggioli, Renato. *The Phoenix and the Spider.* Cambridge, Mass., 1957.

Rayfield, Donald. *Chekhov: The Evolution of His Art.* London, 1975.

Simmons, Ernest J. *Chekhov: A Biography.* Chicago, 1970.

Styan, J. L. *Chekhov in Performance.* Cambridge, 1971.

Toumanova, Nina Andronikova. *Anton Chekhov: The Voice of Twilight in Russia.* New York, 1937.

Valency, Maurice. *The Breaking String.* New York, 1966.

Winner, Thomas G. *Chekhov and His Prose.* New York, 1966.

RUSSIAN

Belichikov, M. P. *Chekhov i ego sreda.* Leningrad, 1930.

Berdnikov, G. *A. P. Chekhov.* Moscow and Leningrad, 1961.

Bicilli, P. *Tvorchestvo Chekhova: Opyt stilisticheskovo analiza.* Sofia, 1942.

Bunin, I. *O Chekhove.* New York, 1955.

Chudakov, A. P. *Poetika Chekhova.* Moscow, 1971.

Derman, A. *Anton Pavlovich Chekhov: Kritiko-biograficheskii ocherk.* Moscow, 1939.

———. *O masterstve Chekhova.* Moscow, 1959.

———. *Tvorcheskii portret Chekhova.* Moscow, 1929.

Ehrenburg, Ilya. *Perechityvaya Chekhova.* Moscow, 1960.

Ermilov, V. *Anton Pavlovich Chekhov: 1860–1904.* Moscow, 1953.

Gushchin, M. *Tvorchestvo A. P. Chekhova.* Kharkov, 1954.

Grossman, Leonid. "Naturalizm u Chekhova." *Vestnik Evropu* 7:218–247 (1914).

Papernyi, Z. *A. P. Chekhov: Ocherk tvorchestva.* Moscow, 1960.

Roskin, A. *A. P. Chekhov.* Moscow, 1959.

Shklovsky, Viktor. *Khod konya.* Moscow and Berlin, 1923.

Sobolev, Yu. *Chekhov.* Moscow, 1930.

Trofimov, I. I. *Tvorchestvo Chekhova: Sbornik statey.* Moscow, 1956.

Vinogradov, V. V. *Literaturnoe nasledstvo: Chekhov.* Moscow, 1960.

Zaytsev, B. *Chekhov: Literaturnaya biografiya.* New York, 1954.

BIBLIOGRAPHIES

Magarshack, David. "Biographical Index of the Complete Works of Anton Chekhov." In his *Chekhov: A Life,* New York, 1955. Pp. 393–423. Gives Russian titles and titles of English translations.

THOMAS G. WINNER

# COLETTE

## *(1873–1954)*

COLETTE IS ONE of the most prolific literary geniuses of the modern era, the author of a phenomenal number of works: novels, short stories, plays, libretti, dialogues, translations, film scripts, essays, dramatic criticism, fashion articles, book reviews, and a voluminous correspondence. She is a genius who, if we are to believe her, was not so much born as made. Recognized as one of the great stylists of the French language, she liked to insist that she did not have a true writer's vocation and that writing never came easily to her. To the contrary, she says that as a child she neither made excellent grades in composition nor felt any particular impulse to confide her thoughts, hopes, or ambitions to paper; her enchanted adolescence was free from writerly anxiety. She wrote her first book more or less accidentally and the next few practically under duress; necessity, she tells us, one day put a pen in her hand, and the pact was sealed when she received a little money in return for the pages she produced. It was Willy who started it all, just as it was Willy who initially took to calling her by her last name, the name by which posterity knows her.

Willy was her first husband, born Henry Gauthier-Villars, but better known to turn-of-the-century Paris by his pseudonym. He was thirteen years older than Colette, a man-about-town, a music critic, and a ruthless entrepreneur, somewhat sinister and pot-bellied, but unaccountably sexy and genial. He signed his name to dozens of publications produced by a stable of ghostwriters he called his "secretaries." Willy was nothing if not resourceful, spending more time orchestrating the composition of a book to which he would sign his name than he might have spent writing it himself; enamored of publicity of all kinds, he put great quantities of energy into launching his countless publications.

According to Colette, he was also parsimonious and chronically short of money, or he pretended to be. They had been married for a couple of years and she was recovering from a long illness when Willy suggested that she jot down recollections of her school days, specifying that she was not to spare the spicy parts. Perhaps he could make something of her scribblings, for as usual (it was Willy's characteristic lament) there was no money in the house. Obediently, she complied. She bought a supply of exercise books like the ones she had used at school; the ruled pages, the watermark, the red line of the margin, and the black cover with its medallion took her back in spirit to an earlier day and gave her fingers the itch to complete her assignment. Over the next few months she filled the pages with her careful writing (taking care to respect the margins). Then she handed them over to Willy. He took a look, decided they were of no use, and tossed them aside. But one September a few years later, while Willy was cleaning out his monstrous desk, he came across the forgotten notebooks. He understood then that he had been a fool to dismiss them: here was a gold mine. Willy grabbed the notebooks and his flat-brimmed hat and raced to his publisher. In March of 1900 they appeared as *Claudine à l'école* (*Claudine at School*), signed Willy. "And that," explains Colette, "is how I became a writer."

Forty thousand copies were sold in the first couple of months. Naturally, Willy wanted more, so he locked Colette in her room for several hours daily and instructed her to produce a sequel. Thus it was that the next three years saw the appearance of *Claudine à Paris* (*Claudine in Paris,* 1901), *Claudine en ménage* (*Claudine Married,* 1902), and *Claudine s'en va* (Claudine Goes Away, translated as *Claudine and Annie,* 1903), all of them signed by Willy. In 1903, when the last of the series appeared, Colette herself was thirty years old. She separated from Willy a few years later.

This is the story as Colette told it when in her sixties she published *Mes apprentissages* (*My Apprenticeships,* 1936), her account of life in the formidable shadow of Willy. It is without a doubt one of the crucial events of her life, a story that can be interpreted for what it tells us about her first experience of love, a certain kind of victimization, her initial separation from the fruits of her work, and the creation of her first literary persona and alter ego.

But like most of the stories Colette tells, there are problems with this one. She was apparently not nearly so mediocre a student as she would have us believe: according to her teacher, she was in fact always first in composition. And subsequent investigation of Willy's correspondence and those manuscripts of the Claudine series that have been preserved in the Bibliothèque Nationale has revealed evidence that is not completely consistent with Colette's account in *My Apprenticeships:* Willy's role in the creation of Claudine was more extensive than Colette chose to acknowledge. If she was Willy's victim, she was, as has been pointed out, a willing one. She spoke harshly of Willy in her later years, and indeed it is easy to judge him severely for his unscrupulousness, his questionable values and acts—he sold the Claudine manuscripts, for example, without apparently so much as consulting his former wife—and his exploitation of her talent. But it was nonetheless Willy who intuited and nurtured that talent in the first place and whose brilliant guidance and editing helped give birth to the skilled writer she came to be. It was under his tutelage that she acquired her mastery of the craft, and for this she does not seem to have given him credit. Willy did, in any event, become part of her legend. Colette's third husband, Maurice Goudeket, tells how in 1942 he made a nostalgic visit to the house in Saint-Tropez where he and Colette had once lived. "I am Colette's husband," he told the proprietors. "Come in, Monsieur Willy," they said.

Writing about Colette's life is not easy, precisely because she herself never stopped writing about it, and her own accounts embroider on history. Her characteristic narrative is a subtle, innovative, and virtually unclassifiable mixture of autobiographical fact and fiction. The historical record of her life, then, and the uses to which she put her autobiography stand in fruitful tension. Because Colette herself made constant artistic use of the material of her own life, reviewing its patterns is essential. But it is likewise essential not to allow a profusion of biographical color, excitement, and scandal to eclipse consideration of her work as literature.

She led a life of drama, movement, audacity, intense activity, bizarre symmetries, and stunning contradictions. Mentioning a few of the latter is as good an introduction as any to her work. She dreamed of becoming a dancer and an actress, and as a young adult made good on those dreams. Nevertheless, despite her repudiation of the idea of a literary vocation, she wrote obsessively for over fifty years, while complaining that work was unhealthy for her. Her publications appeared during the entire first half of the twentieth century, the period of dada, surrealism, and existentialism, yet she kept her own literary counsel and affiliated with none of these movements. One of the great writers of what is perhaps the most philosophical of national literatures, she never had more than a rudimentary formal education, and she was fond of pointing out that she herself was no intellectual, that she had no *pensées.* Her books deal with neither politics, philosophy, history, nor religion, and indeed she always seemed uninterested in the Parisian literary and political milieu.

She was vitally attached to home, yet she lived, as one of her secretaries described it, the life of a nomad. If there is an uncanny equilibrium between her first seventeen years spent in the house where she was born and her last sixteen in the apartment where she died, between these extremes she changed Paris apartments and country residences almost as one might change winter coats. In the years of her marriage to Willy she was interested in physical culture and had a gymnasium installed in her flat, complete with parallel bars, ladder, rings, and trapeze; but a decade and a half later, she began to allow herself to become obese. The elderly Colette seems to have impressed visitors both for her genius and, like Léa in *La fin de Chéri* (*The Last of Chéri,* 1926), for her bulk. She died a stout old woman.

Colette had an exuberant love of life, a keen interest in everything human, and enormous curiosity about the vegetable and animal worlds. She loved flowers, food, butterflies, and tapestry, yet as a young woman she nearly died of an illness caused by depression. All her life she was sexually attracted to women, but she married three times for a total of some forty-eight years. With her second marriage, to Henry de Jouvenel, this woman who had danced almost nude on the stage and lived the déclassée life of a bohemian became a baroness. Her greatest attachment was to her mother, Sido, and she wrote compellingly of the maternal bond; but to her only child, Colette de Jouvenel (nicknamed, like Colette herself when she was young, "Bel Gazou"), she was a mediocre mother. Despite the fact that she adored Sido, she did not attend her funeral, nor that of her brother Léo, nor for that matter her daughter's wedding. In 1932, at the age of nearly sixty, when she was one of France's most renowned writers, already *chevalier* of the Légion d'Honneur and something of a national monument, she scandalized observers by opening a beauty institute, manufacturing perfumes, and applying cosmetics to her clients. After her death she was accorded a state funeral, but on the grounds of her divorces and failure to take the last sacraments the Catholic church refused her a religious burial.

Born Sidonie-Gabrielle Colette, she was called "Bel Gazou" by her father and "Gabri" by other members of the family, while all her life her mother called her "Minet-Chéri." After her first marriage she was known as Colette Willy and after her second as Baroness de Jouvenel (a title that Jouvenel's former wife was also still using); by her third marriage she legally became Madame Maurice Goudeket. But from 1923 on, she signed her publications by a single name, and like many of the most consecrated authors—Molière, Voltaire, Balzac—she is known by that name alone.

## *LIFE*

Colette began life as a robust country girl, born on 28 January 1873 in her mother's house in Saint-Sauveur-en-Puisaye, a village in the countryside of Burgundy—a house and village that her writings immortalized. In two of her autobiographical books, *La maison de Claudine* (*My Mother's House,* 1922) and *Sido* (1929), she speaks at length of her family, her birthplace, and her youth. Her father, Captain Jules Colette, was a one-legged war veteran and her mother Sidonie's second husband; he was passionately jealous of his wife. Sido was irreligious and unconventional; she took her dog to mass, and he barked during the sermon while she read Corneille behind the cover of her missal. There were four children in the household: Achille and Juliette Robineau-Duclos, by Sido's first husband, and two more by the captain, Léopold and Colette, the youngest. She grew up in a house and garden where Sido reigned, and, under her watchful, tender, and disabused eye, learned love and respect for nature. But when she was seventeen, the paradise of her youth vanished. Her elder sister Juliette had married, and her husband, Dr. Roché, demanded their share of the Robineau-Duclos inheritance. The captain, who was not a notably efficient manager, could not comply. There was a break with Juliette, and the Colette family was eventually forced to sell the house at auction and to move in with Achille, who was by then a country doctor in nearby Châtillon-Coligny.

In *My Mother's House* Colette relates Sido's fondness for books and her discriminating taste in literature, and she also tells the bizarre story of her father's literary ambitions. On the top shelf of his study was an impressive display of carefully bound and lettered volumes, bearing titles like "My Military Campaigns" and "From Village to Parliament." After his death in 1905 the family removed them from their shelf and found that only a single page was written upon, the dedication page of the first volume: "To my dearest soul, her faithful husband: Jules-Joseph Colette." The rest of his opus was no more than a hope. Colette recounts the difficulty of disposing of all the paper—sign and legacy of her father's failure; Sido gave it to her granddaughters for drawing and used it to decorate the Sunday leg of lamb. It was up to his daughter to become the writer he never was.

In fact it was her father's literary connections that determined Colette's odd fate. Relegated to the provinces as a tax collector, he had nonetheless kept in touch with a former classmate, Albert Gauthier-Villars, a Parisian publisher of scientific volumes. Gauthier-Villars's son Henry had an illegitimate son of his own, Jacques, who had been put to nurse near Châtillon-Coligny. When Henry came to visit the baby, he visited the Colette family as well—and fell in love with Colette. They married in 1893. She wrote discerningly of her wedding and of the abyss of carnal knowledge that afterward separated her from the simple village girl she had been.

Neither Colette's feelings for Willy nor her relations with him were simple. In *My Apprenticeships* she describes the simultaneous fascination and repulsion she felt for everything he represented: sophistication, experience, celebrity, corruption, Paris. It was to the Paris of the gay nineties that he took her to live, the Paris of André Gide, Marcel Proust, Émile Zola, Henri de Toulouse-Lautrec, Paul Valéry, the music hall, and the café-concert. Willy had entrée into the most important artistic, literary, and musical circles of the era, and Colette soon became intimate with members of his coterie: the actress Marguerite Moreno, who became her dearest friend and with whom she kept up a regular correspondence for decades; the poet Catulle Mendès; the writers Marcel Schwob and Paul Masson. She settled with Willy in his bachelor apartment on the Left Bank, upstairs from the offices of Gauthier-Villars. Kitchenless, gloomy, dank, and drafty, it was painted bottle green and chocolate brown and strewn with old newspapers and Willy's collection of erotic German postcards. A little later, they moved to an apartment on the rue Jacob that was scarcely more reassuring, and it was there that Colette fell ill of resentment and boredom. Sido came and nursed her back to health, and during her convalescence Colette wrote *Claudine at School.*

With its 1900 publication, things changed. Suddenly, Willy's picture was everywhere; the names Willy and Claudine became household words in Paris, and "Claudine" collars, lotions, cigarettes, perfume, and ice cream became everyday items. When a stage version of the Claudine story was created a couple of years later, the title role was given to a wasp-waisted young actress named Polaire. Willy had her and Colette dress alike, and Colette sacrificed her long tresses to match Polaire's short hair. In Paris restaurants, nightclubs, and parks Willy paternally exhibited his two "Claudines," his "twins," one on each arm, encouraging gossip about the provocative trio.

But something else was happening to Colette as well. She had begun to acquire the taste for and, as she later put it in an interview, the honor of writing. If she never had what she called an "irresistible" vocation, she was nonetheless unable to stop once she had begun. She had learned to savor, as her heroine puts it in *La vagabonde* (The Vagabond, 1911), "the voluptuousness of writing, the patient struggle with the sentence as it becomes more supple and coils itself up like a tamed animal, the motionless waiting and stalking of a word which is at last captured." For half a century more she wrote laboriously; she wrote while she danced and acted and sold cosmetics, wrote while her third husband was under arrest by the Nazis, wrote when she was sick, desolate, on vacation, or in love.

In 1904 she signed the book *Dialogues de bêtes* (*Creature Conversations*) with the name Colette Willy. With its appealing cat and dog protagonists—Kiki-la-Doucette and Toby-Chien—the volume was a success, and the following year a second edition (titled *Sept dialogues de bêtes*) was enthusiastically prefaced by the poet Francis Jammes. He called Colette "a true poet" who "sings with the voice of a pure French stream." She was, at last, a writer with a separate identity—or almost. She continued to sign her work Colette Willy until the 1923 publication of her novel *Le blé en herbe* (*The Ripening Seed*), which she signed Colette.

Her domestic life was unhappy. Colette maintains that Willy's miserliness, his infidelities, the whole sordid side of his life, eventually filled her with disgust, and she dreamed of escape. But it was Willy, in the end, who asked her to leave, precipitating their separation in 1906, when Colette moved to a ground-floor apartment on the rue de Villejust. That year marks the beginning of one of the most active periods of her life; its events are refracted in hundreds of letters written to Colette by Sido between 1905 and her death in 1912. (Colette's own letters to her mother were destroyed by Achille shortly after Sido died.)

During the years of marriage to Willy, Colette frequented Parisian lesbian milieus, and Willy himself encouraged her to write about lesbianism in the Claudine series. After the separation she became the lover and occasionally the housemate of the marquise de Belbeuf, née Mathilde de Morny, or "Missy," as she was called. Intelligent, refined, and rich, the marquise was the great-niece of Napoleon III and a transvestite. Photographs show her dressed in contemporary men's clothing—mechanic's overalls or a coat and trousers—or as a Roman emperor, a monk, or an Arab rider. Missy took lessons in mime so that she could appear onstage with Colette, and she even wrote the scenario for a pantomime entitled "Rêve d'Egypte" (Dream of Egypt). When they exchanged a passionate kiss in the 1907 Moulin Rouge production, in which Missy was cast in the male lead, it caused a tumult, and the police closed the show.

But Colette was still not emotionally free of Willy either, and she maintained contact for a while at least. After her departure Willy had set up housekeeping with a young performer who took the stage name Meg Villars (whom he also set to writing). As late as 1907, Willy, Meg, Colette, and Missy vacationed more or less together, occupying adjoining villas. Colette's choice of Missy as a successor to Willy seems to have pleased him, for Willy always liked notoriety. He was reputed to travel in train compartments reserved for "ladies only," and on one occasion when the conductor reprimanded him, he is said to have declared, "But I am the marquise de Belbeuf." Colette stayed with the marquise for almost half a dozen years, and Missy not only nursed her younger friend through hard times but also bought her a house in Brittany, which they called "Rozven." In *Le pur et l'impur* (*The Pure and the Impure,* 1941; originally published in 1932 as *Ces plaisirs* [Those Pleasures]), a long meditation on forms of love and sexuality,

Colette describes Missy as "Le Chevalière," a discreet and unhappy woman whose appearance belied her timid and sensitive nature. Later in life Missy took to calling herself the marquis de Mora; she commited suicide at the age of eighty-one.

Around the time when she moved in with Missy Colette also began her grueling stage career, going on tour throughout France as a dancer and a mime. All the while she continued publishing; and as though her dancing, acting, and novel-writing were not enough, in 1910 she started working as a journalist for a Paris newspaper, *Le matin.* Henry de Jouvenel was its editor, and he and Colette soon fell in love. Three years younger than she, Jouvenel was exceedingly handsome and enjoyed the prestige of an aristocratic heritage and the accomplishments of a talented man. In short order he had turned *Le matin* into one of the most important newspapers in Paris; in later life he became a diplomat, a senator, representative to the League of Nations, and ambassador to Rome. He had already fathered two children by two different mothers, Bertrand in 1903 and Renaud, illegitimately, in 1907. Numerous letters document the upheavals of Colette's relations with Jouvenel, structured by paroxysms of passion, quarrels, and reconciliations. In her correspondence she describes an incident in which Jouvenel's former lover (Renaud's mother, nicknamed "The Panther") in a jealous fury threatened to kill Colette—a menace that Jouvenel took seriously enough to provide protection for her. In 1912 Colette found herself pregnant by him, and they married at the end of the year, not quite three months after the death of Sido. Colette de Jouvenel was born in July 1913, when Colette was thirty-nine years old.

This marriage too was difficult. There were financial problems; Jouvenel was attractive to women and was unfaithful, as Willy had been; and Colette, who was working as a reporter and a film critic, seems to have resisted the considerable demands of her husband's political and journalistic career. Nor was the relation enhanced by Colette's seducing her husband's shy, intellectual elder son one summer at Rozven when Bertrand was not quite seventeen years old and Colette was forty-seven. The liaison endured for several years—a situation not unlike that of Chéri and Léa in her best-known novel, although the composition of *Chéri* (1920) actually came earlier. Bertrand eventually became a distinguished conservative political theoretician of the right. He has always written and spoken tenderly of Colette (just as Willy's son Jacques has recalled fondly the woman he described as "my very seductive stepmother"), but the recollections of Bertrand's half-brother Renaud are not nearly so flattering: Renaud's interpretations of events during the years she lived with Henry de Jouvenel conflict with Bertrand's on many points. In any event, the marriage to Jouvenel lasted eleven years, a period during which Colette published much of her best work: in addition to *Chéri,* there was *L'Entrave* (*The Shackle,* 1913), *Mitsou, ou comment l'esprit vient aux filles* (*Mitsou, or How Girls Get Wise,* 1919), *The Ripening Seed,* and *My Mother's House,* a collection of exquisite sketches largely focused on Saint-Sauveur.

In 1925 she met the man with whom she spent the last three decades of her life. A businessman who dabbled in literature, he was Maurice Goudeket, born of a French mother and a Dutch father in 1889, sixteen years later than Colette. By Goudeket's account, as well as Colette's letters, they lived an idyll for the next few years, part of which were spent at her house in Saint-Tropez. With Goudeket she embarked in 1932 on her career as owner of a Paris beauty salon. The enterprise lasted long enough for them to inaugurate a branch in Saint-Tropez, but it was nonetheless short-lived; if we are to believe a few of their friends, Colette had more enthusiasm than talent for this sort of thing. She also tried to increase her income by writing subtitles for foreign films. In 1935 she and Goudeket married and sailed to New York on the maiden voyage of the *Normandie,* and a few years later, as reporters for the newspaper

*Paris-soir,* they traveled to Fez, where they covered the murder trial of a Moroccan prostitute. With the 1944 publication of her last work of fiction, Colette's career had come full circle: *Gigi,* a novella, is the story of an adolescent like Claudine and of her awakening to love.

Colette was elected to the Académie Goncourt in 1945, and 1948 saw the publication of the first volume of her complete works, a project on which she and Goudeket had been collaborating for some time. She was gradually immobilized by arthritis, and starting in 1950 she sought medical treatment annually in Monte Carlo. There she discovered a young British actress who she decided would be perfect in the American adaptation of *Gigi,* and in 1951 Audrey Hepburn created the role on Broadway. In her last years she received national and even worldwide homage, and her mail daily brought letters from admirers and suppliants. She enjoyed the friendship of her Palais-Royal neighbor Jean Cocteau, and in her bedroom she watched actor Jean Marais rehearse for the revival of a stage version of *Chéri.* Meanwhile her best novels, *Chéri* and *The Ripening Seed,* were turned into films. Disabled, insomniac, and in pain, she was confined to her bed, where, in the blue light of a bulb she had fitted with colored paper, she wrote for as long as she could.

On 3 August 1954, in her Palais Royal apartment on the rue de Beaujolais, she died quietly of cardiac arrest, surrounded by her husband Goudeket, Pauline Tissandier, who had been her servant for thirty years, and her daughter Colette de Jouvenel. Her state funeral—she was the first Frenchwoman ever to be honored in this way—attracted thousands to the courtyard of the Palais Royal. It was followed by a private secular burial in Père Lachaise cemetery.

## *WORKS*

Although Colette was reticent about any explicit discussion of her feelings, her friends, or her family, she was, paradoxically, an exhibitionist—charming, genial, and often sad, but an extrovert all the same. In an era when the camera was not quite the household article it has become, she was photographed a great number of times, frequently semi-clad or in intimate settings. She loved to show herself on stage, sometimes topless or nearly nude, and to write scarcely disguised stories about her life and loves, sketches in which the names Sido, Willy, Bel Gazou, Achille, and Colette appear routinely. The uses to which she put her persona in her works are the most vital aspect of the discipline she acquired, of the profession she so perfectly understood. She seems to have recorded almost every event of her long life, and she never ran out of material: an encounter with a cat, a few days' residence in a provincial hotel, the recollection of her adolescent appetite for the paraphernalia of writing, a visit with a masseuse or a hat saleswoman, her feelings about passersby, an imperfection in a pane of glass—all these inspired stories. And in life she saw herself as "Colette," the greatest character in her books and one she spent all her adult years creating. Goudeket has written about his first meeting with her: she was over fifty years old, stretched out like a big cat on a sofa, lustily eating a piece of fruit. At first, he thought she was playing the part of Colette. She was an uncommonly seductive woman.

Throughout her opus traditional genres tend to metamorphose into each other so that many of her works, varied and ambiguous, fall between recognizable literary categories. Just as her autobiography takes considerable license in dealing with historical fact, so it is almost impossible to draw the line between her essays and short fiction. Colette herself is both the narrator of and a character in "Le képi" ("The Kepi," 1943), the melancholy "La dame du photographe" ("The Photographer's Missus," 1944), and the strangely haunting "La lune de pluie" ("The Rainy Moon," 1940). The anchoring of stories like these to periods of Colette's own life and the confusion of the authorial and narrative voices that distinguishes them seem to suggest that they are more autobiographical than they in fact are. At the same time works like the Claudine series and *La naissance du jour* (*Break of Day,* 1928) shade into autobiography, and *The Vagabond* and *Julie de Carneilhan* (1941), her last full-length novel, are also coded versions of her own experiences. But the relation between fiction and life was not unidirectional: just as *Chéri* anticipates Colette's affair with Bertrand de Jouvenel, *Claudine and Annie,* in which the author eliminates Claudine's "daddy-husband" Renaud, preceded by three years Colette's 1906 separation from Willy. And Claudine cut her hair before Colette. "Everything one writes happens," Colette said.

Since it is impossible to discuss her vast and varied oeuvre at length here, or even to deal properly with all her important pieces, it seems reasonable to concentrate on a few of the major novels. The best of them can be read in one or two sittings, their length typically falling somewhere between that of a novella and that of a short novel.

It all began, of course, with *Claudine at School,* a fictionalized account of some of Colette's experiences as a schoolgirl in Saint-Sauveur. The volume takes the form of the journal that Claudine, the fifteen-year-old narrator, keeps during her last year in a village school. With its eroticism, lesbianism, and cuteness it capitalized on the vogue for stories of nubile schoolgirls and schoolish pranks, although Claudine's diary is distinguished by the fact that the heroine is simultaneously sexually alert and clinically innocent, a curious combination of sensuousness, irreverence, and analytical power. In a way the originality of all of Colette's work can be found in this combination. After the first novel her books began to appear in rapid succession. The next four novels—including *La retraite sentimentale* (*The Retreat from Love,* 1907), which, despite the absence of the name from the title, continues Claudine's story—take Claudine from the village school to Paris, marriage, sophistication, disillusionment, and widowhood. In their use of Colette's and Willy's contemporaries as models of dissolution, jealousy, and homosexuality, these novels are sometimes very indiscreet, although they are doubtless less titillating now than they were in the first decade of the twentieth century. All her life, moreover, she remained faithful to the loosely autobiographical conception of literature that worked so well with *Claudine at School:* she continually exploited her own sensual experience in ways that are unusually direct, and she tirelessly memorialized the landscapes she loved.

Colette's next important work of fiction is *The Vagabond,* a transposition of the career she began in 1906 as a music-hall dancer. It examines, also in journal form, female work and independence, and, speaking more urgently than her later works to concerns of women of the late twentieth century, it anticipates what has come to be considered the feminist novel. This is a lucid portrayal of a woman alone—"une dame seule," as the heroine labels herself with bemused sarcasm, borrowing the phase that the proprietors of her apartment house use to describe the building's clientele—and the novel gives just measure to questions of female loneliness, health, money, friendship, and aging.

It is based loosely on Colette's affair with Auguste Hériot, the department store magnate who vigorously courted her, encouraged by Missy after the separation from Willy. The main characters are only barely camouflaged. Like Colette, the heroine, Renée Néré, is an ex-writer who has been divorced for several years from a man whom she initially adored, a man older than she, the portraitist Adolphe Taillandy, a "seductive and unscrupulous ruffian" and inveterate Don Juan like Willy. The recollections in Renée's journal of her marriage to Taillandy are never sustained descriptions, but the choice of details is piquant and suggestive. In conversation with her friend she attempts to explain what marriage meant to her:

> No, it's not a question of betrayals, you're mistaken. It's a question of conjugal domesticity,

> which turns so many wives into a kind of wet nurse for adults. To be married means—how shall I put it?—to tremble for fear that Monsieur's cutlet is overdone, his mineral water insufficiently chilled, his shirt badly starched, his detachable collar limp, or his bath too hot.
>
> (4:150)[1]

Renée nurses the wounds inflicted during eight years of marriage while earning a meager living as a music-hall dancer and mime, working in partnership with her teacher, Brague (Colette herself took lessons from and performed with the celebrated mime Georges Wague). She is disillusioned about love, which has a tendency, she says, to throw itself unexpectedly across one's path, either obstructing the way or leaving the path in ruins. She confides regularly in her old friend Hamond (in the early 1900's Léon Hamel, a kind and wise dilettante, became Colette's confidential friend) and occasionally in Margot, her former sister-in-law, who resembles the marquise de Belbeuf in her generosity and who, like Missy, has divorced and sworn off men. Maurice Chevalier recognized himself in the portrait of a singer named Cavaillon.

This volume, along with *Mitsou,* another work about a dancer's love affair, and *L'Envers du music-hall* (*Music-Hall Sidelights,* 1913), a series of vignettes that unfold against a theatrical backdrop, is a behind-the-scenes portrait of the cabaret and the life of the artiste in all its shabby splendor. Renée's journal conveys the texture, the peculiarities, and the satisfactions of that existence. Poor, tubercular, or suffering from enteritis, her colleagues are an uncomplaining lot, nimble, resourceful, thrifty, and seclusive despite their apparent promiscuity. She feels a wistful pride in her association with them.

A man erupts into Renée's life and disturbs the fragile balance of edifying hard work and weekend lunches with Hamond. Maxime Dufferein-Chautel is rich and leisured and is as tender and direct as Taillandy was shameless. He has fallen in love while watching her night after night onstage. Renée is at first exasperated by his persistent attentions, then bored, then aroused and even jealous, but she inevitably compares him to her first husband and is continually reminded of that disastrous experience. Max's admiration makes her understand that she would relish a friend, a lover, a spectator of her life and person, but that she is afraid of once more acquiring a master. Does a new love, she asks Hamond rhetorically, destroy the memory of a first love or revive it? Gradually she gives herself over to the pleasure of loving again, but she must soon leave Max to go on a forty-day tour of music halls in the south of France. She decides that they will not become lovers until her return, and she writes to him daily. Her letters describe the theaters, hotels, and trains that punctuate her exhausting and exhilarating trip, as well as the enchanted countryside and cities through which she passes; but they gradually become letters of dissimulation, for absence, meditation, and the very act of writing modify her perspective. When Max writes that on her return she will no longer be Renée Néré but "Madame ma femme," Renée senses the threat of entrapment and alienation implied in the suppression of her name, and in the end she decides to foresake the lover who trustfully waits and whom her body craves. To a settled life in the shadow of a man, even a man as devoted as Dufferein-Chautel, she prefers the solitary life of a professional and a vagabond.

The novel describes the manifestations of masculine lust and the contours and contradictions of feminine desire. Colette excels at conveying everything undefinable, inevitable, and inexplicable about love: the surface feelings, the almost invisible reflexes, the subtlety and force of unexpected arousal. Renée understands from the moment that Max first enters her dressing room what he ultimately wants. Of her attempts to rebuff him in a lighthearted way, she notes: "He does not laugh because he desires me. He does not

[1]All quotations are from *Oeuvres complètes de Colette,* 15 vols. (Paris, 1948–1950).

want what is best for me, that man, he simply wants me. . . . The ardent desire he feels for me gets in his way like a clumsy weapon. He has no interest in jokes, even dirty jokes." As she grows to like him, she still cannot forget his desire for her, which is palpable and menacing: "My admirer's slightest glance, his most proper handshake, remind me of why he is there, and what it is he hopes for." Her astute sense of detail translates her hesitation, the incompatibility of her sensual needs and intellectual doubts, her simultaneous attraction and repulsion:

> I cannot touch the fabric of his vest without a nervous little shudder, and when he speaks I instinctively turn away from his breath, even though it is healthy. I would never consent to tie his tie, and I would rather drink from Hamond's glass than from his. Why? Because . . . this fellow is *a man*. In spite of myself, I keep remembering that he is *a man*.
>
> (4:84)

But even as Renée disdains his conversation and avoids his breath and touch, she is sufficiently flattered to allow him to court her with flowers and fruit and automobile excursions and his adoring gaze, all the while feeling uncomfortably that his presence in her home is "as out of place as a piano in a kitchen."

Colette frequently uses animal imagery to convey the beast in humanity, to throw into relief qualities at once beautiful and threatening. Renée speaks of her feline feelings, while in Max's uncomplicated, obstinate adoration she identifies a canine quality. He watches her from the first row of the orchestra "like my dog Fossette when I am dressing to go out" and then follows her with "a dog's obstinacy" or turns to her with "the cumbersome friendliness of a big dog" or again looks at her with the eyes of a sheepdog. One of his first gifts is, appropriately enough, a collar for her dog, a gesture whose symbolism Renée is subtle enough to grasp. When a doe crosses their path on a walk through the woods, Renée asks whether Max, a hunter, would ever kill such a beautiful creature. One might as well kill a woman, he responds.

During the weeks when she tries to resist him, she understands the nature of her response to him: "He makes me remember, too often, that desire exists, imperious demigod, unbridled faun who cavorts around love and does not obey love; and that I am alone, healthy, still young, and rejuvenated after my long moral convalescence." With desire and all it represents, she contrasts her laboriously won peace of mind and body; but when she closes her door behind her with a sigh, she wonders whether it is "a sigh of fatigue, of relaxation, of solace, or the anguish of solitude."

Margot, Renée's former sister-in-law, is cynical like Taillandy, but benevolent, and the pension she gives Renée helps her to survive. Scornful of the institution of marriage, which she labels monstrous, Margot warns Renée away from men even as she dismally predicts the unlikelihood of her advice being followed. She raises dogs, on whom she bestows all her severe affection, and she preaches the importance of good health in animals and humans. She has taught Renée to take scrupulous care of her throat, her skin, her intestines:

> Margot and I know the price of health and the anguish of losing it. A woman can get by living alone, we get used to it; but to languish alone and feverish, to cough all through the endless night, to struggle on tottering legs as far as the rain-beaten windowpane, only to return to a crumpled, rumpled bed—alone, alone, alone!
>
> (4:63–64)

Colette writes pressingly of the nature of desire and of questions that she understands to be equally female: not just health but also money (Renée speaks of her "very female appetite for money") and aging, work, and writing. She is thirty-three-and-a-half years old—counting not just the years but also the months. At every opportunity she instinctively looks to her mirror for reassurance of her beauty, and as she becomes progressively more attached to Max, her glances toward the mirror become almost compulsive. How fast everything changes, she laments—especially women. She is frightened at the thought of growing older and losing her looks, and is fearful of the effect this would have on her handsome lover: he is, after all, "only a man." And if she declines to take him with her on her tour, it is because, despite her physical and emotional craving for him, she is persuaded that it would be folly to expose herself, overworked, tired, traveling, unkempt, and bad-humored, to his gaze.

When she refuses him in the end, it is partly because of her fear of ultimate rejection but partly too for a more positive cause: Renée realizes the value of having her own work and a life of her own; from the start she has written almost lyrically of her pride in earning her living. (Combining marriage and a career is not an option that occurs to the heroine of a 1911 novel.) She is vaguely scandalized each time she recollects that Max has no occupation, no function, but lives a life of idle comfort, enjoying the revenues of his family's holdings in forestland. She decides that she must act, after all, "as if there were nothing more urgent in the world than my desire to possess with my own eyes the marvels of the earth"; she must see the world for herself, not through the reducing lens of a man's eyes. In her "poor woman's pride" she must remain as she was, "frightfully alone and free."

In 1913 there appeared a sequel to *The Vagabond* entitled *The Shackle.* By the time of its publication Colette had married Jouvenel and had given birth to their daughter. In fact, she commented humorously on the race between the manuscript and the baby trying to be born. She was about to begin a more stationary, more bourgeois existence, and in the novel, too, the heroine has given up her career for a life of travel and relative ease, made possible by an inheritance from Margot. When she meets a man who desires and arouses her, after some hesitation and an anguished affair Renée chooses to settle down with him, compromising her sense of identity and independence and turning from a life of wandering to one of bondage, firmly moored to a man who is himself something of a roamer. This work is less compelling, less tightly woven, than *The Vagabond,* and the ending is more conventional and disappointing. Colette tried to rewrite it but could not.

Like much of Colette's fiction, *Chéri,* her next major novel and the one for which she is best known, appeared in serial form before its publication as a book. It was published in 1920 but is set around 1912 against a background of luxury and moral laxity, in a decor of silks, laces, pearls, and fabulous beds, where middle-aged courtesans try to preserve elusive charms and console themselves for amorous contretemps by drinking creamy hot chocolate and eating amber grapes in bed. In this atmosphere the protagonists have little to do but make love.

At forty-nine Léonie Vallon—known as Léa de Lonval—is sumptuously beautiful—blue-eyed and long-legged—and leads a life of ordered elegance. She dresses, with the help of a maid named Rose, in tender shades of pink and judges her fruits and wines with the eye of a connoisseur and the palate of an epicure. She manages her servants with benevolent firmness and is quick to point out to her *maître d'hôtel* any spot of dust or sign of negligence. After a long (and, dare we say, distinguished) career as a kept woman, Léa is keeping a lover of her own. Half her age, Chéri (a character inspired, like Max in *The Vagabond,* by Auguste Hériot) is gorgeous and is as vain and spoiled as Léa is gracious and giving. Only his wife will call him by his real name, Fred Peloux, while his nickname, Chéri, suggests the sexual ambiguity surrounding this slightly too handsome young man. His mother, another ex-courtesan named Charlotte Peloux, is Léa's friendly enemy, and they engage periodically in verbal sparring matches. Charlotte has arranged his marriage of convenience to nineteen-year-old Edmée, rich and timid daughter of still another courtesan, and neither Chéri nor Léa imagines the event as having much consequence. In the novel's opening pages the lovers discuss wedding arrangements with detachment and mockery. At the end of the first chapter Chéri leaves Léa's bedroom to meet Edmée, and Léa watches from the window as shopgirls in the street pay homage to his good looks. His departure from Paris for an extended honeymoon involves a revelation for both.

After his wedding Léa is beset by vague anxiety and chills and realizes at last the folly of having kept the same lover for six years—an "adoption," she sarcastically labels it. Practical-minded and decisive, she resolves to take a trip of her own; six months in the south, she hopes, will cure her of Chéri. When he returns to Paris to find her gone, Chéri in turn slumps into lassitude, forsaking the bedroom of his young wife and moving into a hotel with Desmond, a down-and-out friend, and frequenting bars and opium dens. He stalks Léa's street for signs of her return. When at last he sees the "electric globe of the courtyard shining like a mauve-colored moon above the lawn," the service door wide open, and light filtering through the blinds on the second floor, he is overwhelmed: " 'Ah!' he said very low, 'Is this happiness? . . . I didn't know. . . .' " It is not so much that he needs to see her right away as that he needs to know that she is there. "Exorcised," he can return to his wife.

Léa has come home, fifty years old and full of good resolutions about creating a new life without Chéri, but she is a little thinner, under stress, and a trifle fretful about what the future holds. "How good you smell!" Charlotte tells her, cattily adding, "Have you noticed that as skin becomes flabbier, perfume goes on better?" The lovers' ultimate reunion one night after a separation of more than six months is spectacular. Chéri arrives unannounced, and, hearing his footsteps on the stairs, Léa runs to powder her nose in an instinctive gesture of self-preservation. He bursts into her bedroom and throws himself at her with a kind of brutality: "I've come home!" At first she tries to keep a cool distance, but when she realizes how much he wants her, she can hardly suppress a burst of laughter, which warns her that her rational self is about to be submerged and "that she is about to give herself up to the most terrifying joy of her life."

But the passion reborn that midnight is undone in the light of day. Léa has aged not altogether imperceptibly in the previous half year, and Chéri, with a young and beautiful wife at home, has grown up a little. In the small morning hours, after making love, he looks with a new eye at a thoroughly infatuated Léa, contemplating her "with the frightening force and fixity of a confused child or an incredulous dog. An illegible thought was being born in the depths of his eyes." But he falls asleep in her arms, and she rises early, elated, planning an elopement and in her mind drafting a letter of explanation to Edmée, calculated to cause the least pain possible. Chéri watches her surreptitiously from the bed, dissembling his wakefulness as he has never before done. Inattentive for once to her appearance, she has imprudently stood in the light of the window, and her sagging chin and wrinkled neck are clear to his critical gaze. But Léa is still blissfully unaware of this. "You came back," she tells him. "It was our destiny." And then:

> "Ah!" she added in a lower voice, "when I think of all I haven't given you, of all I haven't told you. . . . When I think that I took you for a passerby like the others, only a little more precious than the others. . . . How stupid I was, not to understand that you were my love, love itself, the love that comes only once."
>
> (4:145–146)

Half numbed and incapable of making any response, Chéri returns a dazed stare. In the devastating conversation that follows, Léa finally understands that the young man's vision of his old lover has inevitably changed: describing her role in his life, Chéri instinctively uses the past tense. Distraught, she reproaches herself for allowing "perverted mother love" to dominate her, but even in her disarray she finds the strength to comfort him and to send him back to Edmée. He leaves at the very end, and Léa's eyes move from the reflection in her long bedroom mirror—where "a panting old woman" repeats her gestures—to the window: "Chéri lifted his head toward the spring sky and the flowering chestnut trees, and . . . as he walked, filled his lungs with air, like an escapee."

*Chéri* covers just under a year, from June 1912 to April 1913. The main action occurs entirely in Paris and its suburbs, although the novel includes several flashbacks that allow us to grasp the characters' past: the childhood of Chéri, alternately neglected and pampered as the son of an egotistical and frivolous ex-dancer; and the beginnings of his liaison with Léa in Normandy, where she puts weight and muscle on her "naughty nursling" of nineteen, feeding him farm-grown chicken and strawberries and cream and arranging boxing lessons with an ex-lover of hers. There are also allusions to several trips, especially Chéri's honeymoon and Léa's escape to the Pyrenees. The ending returns the action to its point of departure, and the cyclical and symmetrical structure is reflected in the multiple symbolic details that expand the implications of the drama.

The most important of these include Léa's bed, mirrors, and pearls, symbols of luxury with lustrous surfaces and dreamy depths in which the play of reflections fascinates and menaces. The enormous wrought-iron and ornamental brass bed, shining "like a suit of armor," dominates Léa's bedroom; in and around it occur the novel's first and last scenes. Arena of Léa's triumphs, it is also the setting of her final defeat. Strategically located mirrors decorate the house: not only the mirror in the bedroom where she catches the glimpse of a mad old woman at the novel's end, but even a large dining-room mirror in which she can complacently watch her reflection at table. Chéri looks at mirrors, at home and in the street, at least as frequently as Léa. They silently emphasize invisible change, distortion, vanity, futility, and the fragility of beauty.

Léa's pearl necklace appears in the first sentence of the novel, its forty-nine pearls representing the forty-nine years of her life. She no longer sleeps with it because the exquisite pearls fascinate Chéri, whose morning gaze she prefers not to fix on a neck that is less white and firm than it once was. "You're straining the thread," she explains as Chéri, garbed in silk pajamas and doeskin slippers, fondles the necklace. "The pearls are heavy." Léa's magnificent necklace of pearls contrasts with those of other characters: Edmée wears a "milk-white" necklace of "little pearls, very beautiful, very round, all equal," suggesting her youthful, innocent, bland, and tentative beauty. La Copine, on the other hand, an aged, opium-smoking ex-courtesan with whom Chéri attempts to forget for a while his misery during Léa's absence, wears a necklace of "big, hollow, light pearls" on which Chéri fixates. As a wedding gift, Léa proposes to buy Chéri a pearl to wear on his shirt. "A rosy one," he exclaims, but Léa retorts: "Not on your life, a white one, something masculine, if you please!"

Homes are symbolically important throughout Colette's fiction, reflecting and explaining the characters. According to Renée Néré of *The Vagabond,* her tiny apartment, which appears cosy and intimate to her admirer and in which she is almost seduced by him, in fact reeks of indifference, abandonment, impending departure, and a sense of uselessness: casually fitted with the cast-off furnishings of her marriage to Taillandy, the flat is the very image of her vagabond existence. And later, on tour, she realizes that she feels more at home and freer in a shabby hotel room than among her haunted furniture. In another paired set of novels, *Duo* (1934) and *Le toutounier* (1939), virtually all the action occurs either in and around the country residence of the heroine, Alice, in the first of the two novels, or in her sisters' Paris flat in the second; the uses the author makes of these intensely concentrated spaces, dilapidated or claustrophobic, elucidate the jealousy, antagonism, eroticism, and violence on which the stories turn.

In *Chéri* the interior scenes are set chiefly in two homes, Léa's and Charlotte's. While Léa's is a place of luxury and refinement, good taste and good cooking (she prides herself on her recipes for lobsters and dessert creams), where visual and auditory sensations, such as rose-colored curtains and clothes, the blue of her eyes, and the silky sound of her voice, all suggest comfort and warmth, Charlotte's is a house of turbulence and false economy. "Peloux's Palace," Chéri calls it sarcastically, and Léa labels it a "bazaar." It is painted hospital green and is filled with the "successive errors of [Charlotte's] preposterous taste and greed." "The house of a mad ant," one of her friends calls it. Throughout it reverberate the piercing, "trumpeting" accents of undersized Charlotte Peloux and the cackling, obsequious tones of the desiccated cronies who live off her. When Léa visits Charlotte after the wedding, the sight, sound, and touch of these "mummies" precipitate a terrible crisis for her, both moral and physical: is her attachment to Chéri as absurd as the liaison between seventy-year-old Lili, who looks like a "corseted eunuch" in sailor dress, and her mute, adolescent Italian lover? Léa stares aghast as Lili's pearl necklace plays a grotesque game of hide-and-seek, now visible, now buried in the "deep ravine" of her neck. Is all this a cruel caricature of Léa and Chéri in a few more years? Léa races home and takes to her bed shivering; she rises to pack and leave for the south, determined to give up her lover gracefully.

The novel demonstrates that despite its links with money, one-upmanship, and infidelities—the dubious values governing the marginal class to which Chéri and Léa belong—love is finally a question of something more than all of these. *Chéri* is a story that might have been vulgar but that is redeemed by the power of Colette's art, for the intelligence of her writing rivals its sensuousness. There is dignity in her portrayal of Léa, whose complicated love for her protégé, part maternal, part romantic, seems neither sordid nor indecent. Colette shows us the depths of Léa's wit, humor, and loss, just as she shows us the opaqueness of Chéri's character, alternately comparing him to a hunting dog, a ram, or a jungle dweller.

*La fin de Chéri* (*The Last of Chéri*) was published in 1926 and modulates the sense of the conclusion of the earlier novel. If Chéri left Léa's house that spring morning surrounded by signs of renaissance while his lover interrogated the mirror image of an aged fool, in the sequel we find Léa happily installed in comfortable old age whereas Chéri founders in despair. Colette said of the two novels that they show that a love affair between a young man and an older woman is potentially more dangerous for him than for her.

Some six years separate the plots of the two novels (the chronology is imprecise), and Chéri has returned from the war. From the frightened innocent she appeared to be in *Chéri,* Edmée has turned into a self-assured woman, a little impudent and rather plebeian but with a certain poise and even a bit of social conscience. She efficiently manages their stocks, works as a hospital administrator, and has taken an American doctor as a lover. Even Charlotte Peloux has found a useful niche for herself in postwar society, and Chéri, mirthless and mopish, drifts aimlessly in a world whose values he does not recognize. In the central scene he pays a visit to his old lover, who appears in the novel only this once, and as he crosses from the dark hall into the daylight of her apartment, he expects this apparent dawn to signal the rebirth of his world. Once inside, however, he discovers not the slim and seductive being he left years earlier but an immensely stout woman in nondescript dress with cushions of flesh below her armpits, whose very bulk is the visual sign of her repudiation of sexuality. She is asexual in her size and shape, masculine in her tone of voice, and virile in her gestures, but intensely human; her startling blue eyes and rich womanly laughter link her to his former mistress.

She calls him "child" and lectures him benevolently about the "disease of his generation," the pitfalls for soldiers like him returning from war; he must resist nostalgia, disillusion, and lethargy. He finally kisses the puffy hand she extends and dizzily retreats. After the visit Chéri becomes progressively more despondent and haunts the smoky flat of La Copine, who reminisces about Léa's exploits as a beautiful young woman and entertains him in a room papered with pictures of the earlier Léa. One day he stretches himself out on the couch in La Copine's absence and, staring at all the Léas on the wall, whose downward gaze returns his own, he thinks about the war and about Léa, how, together, they have dispossessed him, expelled him from the very times in which he lives. Murmuring over and over "Nounoune," his pet name for her, he puts a revolver to his head and pulls the trigger.

The acceleration of the aging process that afflicts Léa during the war years adds to the novel's symbolic and mythical weight. This is an allegory of love and aging, a demonstration of melancholy truths. The sequel is slower, wordier than the original novel, and almost oppressive in its atmosphere of sullen despair—a volume for aficionados of Colette. But as with the first novel, this scrutiny of a single character and the tawdry trappings of his mind and existence is paradoxically a work of impressive scope, a review of the ambiguity of masculinity and femininity. Together the two novels comprise a classic study of the irresistible enticements of an old love, an astute analysis of an affair between a young man and an older woman, and a sensitive portrait of torturous middle age and cheerful old age.

Before its 1923 appearance in book form, *The Ripening Seed* was serialized in *Le matin,* but its publication in the newspaper was abruptly suspended when readers expressed outrage at the plot. Like *Chéri* it portrays a love affair between a woman and a young man half her age, but it is also a story about the sexual awakening of two adolescents, set against the sun-drenched coast of Brittany in late summer. Colette knew the area well, for she had spent the summers of 1921 and 1922 there with the three Jouvenel children. In her observations and interactions with them (including the beginning of her liaison with Bertrand) she found some of her inspiration.

The novel evokes the peculiar mingling of the carnal and the sentimental that characterizes adolescent love. The young heroine and hero, Vinca Ferret and Philippe Audebert, symbolize the purity and intransigence of youth, the joys of summer, and the mysteries of desire. They have known each other since birth, having shared each summer the villa their families rent. At sixteen and a half and fifteen and a half, respectively, "an invisible thread joins them"; their love is tender and anguished, full of awkwardness, impatience, and contradictions. But this summer a more mature lodger, a woman of about thirty named Camille Dalleray, arrives on the coast and rents a neighboring villa. Sophisticated, beautiful, acerbic, and even virile, "the lady in white," as he calls her, seduces the boy in a setting of fire and ice. On a sultry late-summer day, she invites him into the unnatural coolness of her villa, with its red and black living room full of the odor of burning incense, and startles him as she plunges her diamond-studded hand into his drink to remove the ice cube. Overwhelmed and overwrought after their first tentative encounter, he tosses her a bouquet of sea thistle—and bloodies her cheek with it. When they make love shortly thereafter, he feels as though she speaks to him "from depths where life is a terrible convulsion," and his sexual initiation seems to him a seismic event. In the hours and days that follow he trembles, faints, and cries, for the world appears a harsher place and less comprehensible. Strolling with Vinca on the day after he has first made love with Camille, he nervously winces when she nonchalantly steps on a little crab, making it crack like a hazelnut, and he becomes weak and pale when she stabs a conger eel:

> He tried his best to hide a pain he did not understand. What then had he conquered the night before, in the perfumed shadows, in arms intent on making of him a victorious man? The right to suffer? The right to swoon with weakness before a child both innocent and hard? The right to tremble inexplicably, before the delicate life of the animals?
>
> (7:316)

But his adolescent pride is strong enough for him sullenly to refuse Camille Dalleray the homage she wants: that he should act as a suppliant, grateful for her favors and eager to articulate his attachment to her. It is sex he has shared with her and not love, for Philippe remains aware that the woman who has revealed to him some perplexing truth and in whose arms he has tasted the thrills of pleasure is in fact only a stranger, a passerby. How to reconcile this with his love for Vinca? For her part, the girl intuitively grasps what has happened and simply wants to know why Philippe did not ask *her* rather than Madame Dalleray. After the latter's departure, in the last few days of summer, she gently forces Philippe to initiate her just as Madame Dalleray initiated him.

Vinca, whose name means periwinkle, has eyes whose blue rivals the sea, the sky, and spring rain: her purity imitates nature too, as do likewise her strength and endurance. On the morning after they make uneasy love for the first time, Philippe waits outside her window, trembling for the girl whom, despite all the evidence to the contrary, he persists in regarding as delicate. He imagines her inconsolable, tearful, convulsive as he was a few days earlier, and he plans to reassure her, to explain that love is of course more than a botched encounter in the grass. But when she appears at her balcony window, she has roses in her cheeks; her first act is to remove a twig from her lovely, unkempt hair, her second to water the fuchsia. And then she begins to sing. Philippe is stunned, almost devastated. Is it possible that she reacts so casually, as though nothing had happened, as though today were just like yesterday? His bitter meditation is the novel's last line: "Neither a hero nor an executioner. A little pain, a little pleasure. That's all I will have given her, that's all."

*The Ripening Seed* (which Colette originally intended to be a play entitled *La seuil* [*The Threshold*]) is a trenchant study of adolescence as the threshold to adulthood and of the agonizing conflicts between adolescent sexual awareness and emotional immaturity. It is also a stunning description of the sand coves, the sea, the shore wind, the thistle, the eels, the shrimp, and the peaches and melons of late August, all of which are portrayed with a conviction that makes Colette's melodic prose vibrate in primary hues of white, red, and blue. Philippe and Vinca are individualized, memorable in their beauty, their love, and their suffering, yet Colette takes pains to emphasize that they are not really special. The narrator pokes gentle fun at the predictability of their ambitions and the likely future of these thoroughly enculturated members of the bourgeoisie, who have assimilated not just the gestures but also the values of their class. Vinca's mother, well-intentioned and boring like the other adult members of the family (the narrator calls them "phantoms"), has decreed that her daughter will help out at home until her inevitable marriage. No career for her. Vinca acquiesces, obediently dresses as instructed for dinner, and dutifully mends hand-me-downs for her little sister, a carbon copy of Vinca herself. If her docility in this regard annoys Philippe, he is in fact no more original than she, for he is destined to do his military service and to go to law school or into business with his father. In fact, neither Vinca nor Philippe inspires in the reader the desire to know them ten years hence, and this is precisely how Colette must have wanted it. But that fact in no way renders the story of their adolescence less engaging or their youthful experience less affecting.

The novel demonstrates as well as any the peculiar mixtures that characterize Colette's craft: susceptibility to the sensual as well as the sentimental and an understanding of the perverse connections between them. There is a simultaneous disdain for both these areas, the conviction that they should never be allowed to interfere with a good meal or a night's sleep. Typically in Colette's fiction, the female characters understand these things far better than the silly males.

Twenty years later, in 1943, Colette published a short story called "The Kepi," which returns to the subject of the love affair between a middle-aged woman and a young man. Here Marco, a mild and mousy woman of forty-five who earns her living as a ghostwriter, answers an ad in the personals and becomes the mistress of a handsome young lieutenant of twenty-five. The experience transforms her, and in her "belated puberty" she discovers the range of sensual pleasures. She discovers too the intensely feminine concerns of dress and make-up, which she discusses with the narrator (named Colette), and she grows plump on sex. But in her gratification she forgets, like Léa, that an aging woman must always think of her appearance. One rainy day, gamboling with her lover on the divan bed, unkempt and in a crumpled chemise, she jauntily slaps the young officer's cap on her head and begins to hum a military tune for his and her own amusement. He is not amused. The playful gesture exaggerates the evidence of Marco's age, and her lieutenant stares at her with a look that she cannot understand and that she finds almost "hideous." It is, for all intents and purposes, the end of the affair.

In fact, a favorite theme of Colette is the irreconcilability, the incompatibility of men and women, the vague and persistent hostility that animates them even in moments of union—just as Philippe and Madame Dalleray or he and Vinca are worlds apart as they make love, just as Léa still wonders until the end what makes Chéri tick, and just as Marco never quite grasps the meaning of the lieutenant's "incomprehensible" look. Colette describes love and friendship between the sexes, and yet, beneath the surface, there is a nagging lack of understanding, a strange and subtle enmity: even her good friend Hamond does not really understand Renée Néré's qualms about marriage. A collection of very short stories called *La femme cachée* (*The Other Woman*) appeared in 1924, the year of Colette's separation from Jouvenel. In the title story a young wife goes to a fancy dress ball at the Paris Opéra without telling her husband, who winds up there in disguise himself. He recognizes her in her Pierrot costume and follows her obsessively throughout the evening, determined to learn whom she has come to meet. He finds out, contrary to his expectation that her pleasure is both more innocent and more guilty. She is meeting no one; she has simply given in to the temptation of enjoying for a time "the monstrous pleasure of being alone, free, honest in her natural brutality, of being the unknown woman, forever solitary and shameless." Her disguise has paradoxically liberated her for a few hours from the necessity of role-playing.

Colette excels at showing woman's "irremediable" solitude and healthy knack for dissembling, often in stories of female rivalry. *La seconde* (*The Other One,* 1929) is the account of a wife's discovery that her playwright husband has been having an affair with his live-in secretary, Jane. That the brash and dashing Farou is unfaithful comes as no surprise to Fanny, who has tolerated with good grace his previous affairs. But this time his lover is Fanny's friend, and she is devastated at Jane's betrayal. When the wife insists that the secretary leave, Jane explains that Farou really means nothing to her; her deepest attachment to the household has always been to Fanny. The two women acknowledge then that although Farou is indispensable, the essential bond for both is the female bond. In a sobering and bittersweet conclusion they admit that men are as fundamentally contemptible as they are necessary, and they recognize the need for alliance between women. Jane will stay. How could Fanny do without her?

In other volumes Colette has written in a similar vein about the ravages of jealousy and about the resolution of rivalries. In the last pages of *The Pure and the Impure* she gives a wonderful account of the former jealousy between the narrator and a "Madame X." They hated each other, but as long as they expended an equal amount of energy on it, everything was kept in equilibrium and no harm done. Once, though, Colette got caught up in her writing and forgot her maledictions. Her antagonist, meanwhile, devoted all her leisure to wishing Colette ill, and this imbalance resulted in Colette's bronchitis, the loss of a manuscript of which she had not kept a copy, and the death of three angora cats. But in the end they became friends and regaled each other with stories of how each had once wished the other dead, or worse. This story recalls an experience Colette recounts in *My Apprenticeships,* her first discovery of Willy's infidelity a few months after her wedding. On the basis of information contained in an anonymous letter, she rushed off to the flat of a dwarflike woman named Charlotte Kinceler, and there the young wife did indeed find her husband—not in Charlotte's bed but bent with her over an account book: how like that calculating scoundrel to mix his love affairs and his business! But Colette became friends with Charlotte and visited her in her herbalist's shop until Charlotte committed suicide a few years later.

In another triangular story that appeared in 1933, the rival is a cat. The short novel called *La chatte (The Cat)* is one of Colette's most elegant and original. Twenty-four-year-old Alain and nineteen-year-old Camille marry. He comes from an old family whose fortune was made in the silk trade; hers, more prosperous but with shorter roots, owes its wealth to the washing-machine business. They are young, leisured, and gorgeous. Never was a couple so well matched and so ill suited to each other. Alain characteristically retreats from life, while Camille meets it head on. Red-blooded, high-spirited, and good-humored (if initially flat-chested until, like Marco in "The Kepi," sex puts a little weight on her), she is a fitting scion of a family whose money comes from the manufacture of electrical appliances, for she loves everything new and modern, and she drives their roadster fast and well. Alain, on the contrary, is dreamily attached to his past, represented by his white-haired mother, their elderly servants, and their stately old house and ample garden in Neuilly, outside of Paris. His home is one focus of Camille's mental energies. She wants eventually to rearrange the kitchen and the servants' quarters: what a lot of wasted space in the old place! Already the building is in renovation and lodgings are being prepared for the young couple. Meanwhile they set up housekeeping in a small borrowed flat in the city, located on the ninth floor of a triangular edifice of glass and chrome. If Alain feels alienated and insecure there, Camille is at ease, and within weeks it is clear to Alain that he must at all costs prevent this modern young woman from violating his ancestral home.

The symbols surrounding Alain are his bedroom, his bed, his dreams, and the sleepiness to which he continually abandons himself. Camille, on the other hand, like Léa and Vinca and so many Colette heroines, astonishes by her eyes—exorbitant, constantly alert eyes that Alain finds by turns menacing and ugly. Before the wedding he takes a pencil to his fiancée's photograph and tries to make them look smaller. Camille's sensuality follows the course of the season: it is sleepy in May, blossoms in June, grows intense in July, and becomes fatal in August. "You are like the smell of roses," her new husband rebukes her, "You take away one's appetite." Her nonchalant nudity as she walks about the bedroom on the morning after their marriage stuns and offends him, and, like Chéri after his last night of love with Léa, he watches her secretly and disapprovingly from the bed.

Between the two protagonists is Alain's beautiful and intelligent cat, Saha; while Alain is fair and Camille dark, the cat is gray. As the difficulties between the honeymooners become accentuated, Alain turns more and more to his cat. On hot July nights he leaves the nuptial bed to sleep with Saha on a sofa. One afternoon Camille and the cat are alone on the terrace of the ninth-floor apartment. The young wife succumbs to an impulse for revenge on her rival, for a chance at survival in her marriage. After a tense encounter in which she silently pursues the cat from one end of the narrow terrace to the other, she pushes her off the parapet. The cat survives, and Alain is almost glad for this excuse to divest himself of the young woman whose uninhibited appetite for food, drink, sex, and laughter intimidates him. He packs his suitcase and Saha's basket and retreats to his mother and garden.

The story is told with such subtlety that it is credible; Alain's love for his cat, his apprehensions, his anger at Camille, and the choice he makes between his two females do not really surprise. Colette cannily analyses the animal side of human nature and the quasi-humanness of animals—areas that, from *Creature Conversations* through her last writings, interested her deeply. Her women are, like Camille, healthy and practical, strong and sensual. Her men are, like Alain, a little indolent and unreasoning, a little caught up in their chimeras, a little out of tune with reality; or, like Chéri, they are weak and opaque, flaccid and indecisive, lacking the vigor, the sureness of women. Even after her attempt to get rid of the cat, Camille is eager to try to save the marriage. She comments to Alain that she should not have admitted what she did. He is shocked: "That idea does you honor," he says ironically. And Camille responds: "Oh, honor, honor. . . . It wouldn't be the first time the happiness of a couple depended on something shameful or unconfessed."

## *CONCLUSION*

Like Camille in *The Cat,* Colette understood the uneasy alliances that exist among shame, dissimulation, and happiness; she knew that honor is a relative term, like everything else. Like Renée Néré, she understood the grace, the inconvenience, and the "clumsiness" of desire. She was not unusually pessimistic, but she was no fervent romanticist either. Her writing interests us precisely because it shades the differences between traditional opposites: the pure and the impure, heterosexuality and homosexuality, maternal and romantic love, friendship and infatuation, femininity and masculinity, sensuality and intellect. Just as she blurred literary distinctions, she refused to abide by easy classifications such as "natural" and "unnatural" and recognized instead the complexity of the human animal, which she studied with as much curiosity as respect. Hers is a sensuous, rhythmic style, rich or austere, variegated or blanched, with carefully constructed and balanced sentences and selective details. For her, preoccupations with dress, cooking, sewing, and gardening go hand in hand. Nothing human seemed to her discordant. Her endings tend to be neither happy nor unhappy.

In her essays the subject may initially seem imprecise, elusive, or nonexistent; and in her fiction neither narrator nor characters announce their concerns in clear speeches. They avoid directly addressing the larger moral or philosophic issue at hand and concentrate instead on its manifestations at the level of the quotidian. Even though they leave many things unsaid, their conversations about plants, cats, brassieres, or remedies for various ills reveal their compassion and even their identity. Their gestures, offhand remarks, questions—all these translate the depths of their feelings as well as the humanness and impurity of their motives. We discover that Colette's exquisite adolescents and middle-aged women may well be hedonistic, fierce in the determination to survive, and sagacious in their view of human nature, all at the same time. In memoirs like *L'Étoile vesper* (*The Evening Star,* 1946) and *Le fanal bleu* (*The Blue Lantern,* 1949), rich and digressive meditations that she wrote in her last years, the subject, in all its apparent diffuseness, turns out to be life itself, an effort to elucidate her own existence and her life's work.

Colette was especially interested in women's experience of love, the female element in life, and the feminine in writing. She wrote not only of love and sex but also of home and cooking, of flowers and sewing—subjects with strong feminine associations—and of words and writing. And she wrote about the female nature itself. In *The Vagabond,* Renée Néré warns:

> "She is dying of grief. . . . She died of grief. . . ." When you hear these words, shake your head with more skepticism than pity: a woman hardly ever dies of grief. She's such a solid animal, so hard to kill! You think grief gnaws at her? Not at all. Far more often, even though she was born weak and sickly, in grief she acquires hard-wearing nerves, an unbending pride, the ability to wait, to dissimulate, which makes her greater, and the disdain for those who are happy. In sufferance and dissimulation, she exercises herself and grows supple, as though from a daily routine of risky gymnastics.
>
> (4:34–35)

Colette's opus is in some ways a gloss on these lines. In the gymnastics of life her women are heroic, even if their heroism is confined, as in the case of "The Photographer's Missus," to facing the daily routine of cooking her husband's supper: "I did breast of veal with peas just last Saturday," she says; "One must not overdo it." It is the heroism of tolerance and unarticulated loyalty to some all-embracing notion of creation that distinguishes women from men, who tend to be of a frailer nature, fixated on a single idea, or incapable of functioning outside a specific sphere. The women demonstrate the capacity for healthy adjustment to life's changes, whereas Alain (*The Cat*), Chéri (*The Last of Chéri*) and Michel (*Duo*) cannot quite disentangle themselves from their past. While Philippe struggles to reconcile sex with family and nature, Vinca spontaneously perceives the links among emotional and sensual needs, family loyalties, bourgeois values, and the world of crabs and shrimps—and she assimilates them all.

Colette's favorite writers were Honoré de Balzac, whom she admired all her life, and her contemporary Marcel Proust, born two years before she was. Her books have affinities with both. Like Proust she was an assiduous worker who grappled doggedly through revision after revision to find *le mot juste.* Her correspondence alludes continually to the effort writing cost her, even to the trouble she had in creating protagonists who were not herself. Like Balzac's her characters can be forcefully allegorical and larger than life, and like Balzac she used reappearing characters; not only do we meet the same protagonists in pairs of novels like *The Vagabond* and *The Shackle* or *Duo* and *Le toutounier* and in series like the Claudine books, but Sido, Willy, the narrator Colette, and other characters—Valentine, Clouk, Chéri—recur in a variety of fictional and essay forms. Like Balzac's *La comédie humaine* (*The Human Comedy,* 1842–1848) Colette's work investigates, almost as though it were a kind of natural history, representatives of a certain class, a certain time, and a certain mentality.

Her books are concerned, in the last analysis, with vision; nothing was too trivial, too dubious, or too unpleasant to merit her patient gaze. Sido, she recounts, used to whisper in almost religious accents: "Regarde!" (Look!) And Goudeket reports that this was Colette's own dying imperative. It is no accident that eyes play a central role in her writing, that they are the most visible signs of humanity and of erotic interest. Colette herself seems to have seen and known just about everything. Her astonishing accumulated wisdom characterizes her multi-volume work, including details on everything from how to dress (pink flatters aging skin), how to wear makeup, and how to choose jewels, to how to catch shrimp and eat lobsters. She understands how the acacia sheds its leaves, how dogs and cats communicate, and that raw beans make the breath smell bad. In short, she knows recipes for truffles and for life. She inventories not only flowers and vegetables but also forms of love-making, and she sharpens the focus on sizes and shapes of women's breasts.

Her work is firmly anchored in a time and place—a provincial school of the late nineteenth century, the Parisian demimonde of 1912, the music hall, café-concert, or boudoir at the turn of the century—yet it is in some senses universal in scope. Its effect may be compared to a play of mirrors—one of her chief literary metaphors—with their smooth, shiny, meretricious surfaces, their apparent distortions, and their alluring depths. The milieus she expended the energy of a lifetime describing may appear trivial and vulgar, and it is true that her characters may be either marginals or middle-class bunglers. But she forcefully associates her gigolos, courtesans, young wives, or adolescents with the spaces in which they live, and at the same time her portrayal of them transcends the conditions of their immediate existence. As restricted as individual pieces on, say, a corset maker or a playboy or a sick child may appear, they are in fact perceptive psychological studies. *L'Ingénue libertine* (*The Innocent Libertine,* 1909), an early novel that has dismayed critics who find little to redeem its explicit preoccupation with sexual fulfillment, nevertheless contains a stunning description of female orgasm, as graphic as it could possibly be without becoming pornographic, and ending with the designation "miracle" for this carnal encounter—which reconciles a sensual young woman and her pimply-faced husband. Colette knew, as Cocteau said, how to make soap bubbles out of mud. She was alive to the ephemeral, the unexpected, the intuitive—in vegetables, animals, and humans alike—and she worked miracles on men, women, and words. She was fascinated by shifting sexual differences, which unite and estrange, liberate and shackle her fictional couples, and in portraits of Claudine and Renaud, Chéri and Léa, Phil and Vinca, Farou and Fanny, Michel and Alice, or Alain and Camille, these kaleidoscopic allegiances and couplings create a dazzling play of meaning. She understood eroticism and jealousy, the anxieties of youth, the melancholy pleasures of love, and the repose and vexations of old age, and she conveyed these subtle truths in a style alternately lush and pungent.

# Bibliography

## EDITIONS

### INDIVIDUAL WORKS

*Claudine à l'école.* Paris, 1900.
*Claudine à Paris.* Paris, 1901.
*Claudine en ménage.* Paris, 1902.
*Claudine s'en va.* Paris, 1903.
*Sept dialogues de bêtes.* Preface by Francis James. Paris, 1905.
*La retraite sentimentale.* Paris, 1907.
*L'Ingénue libertine.* Paris, 1909.
*La vagabonde.* Paris, 1911.
*L'Envers du music-hall.* Paris, 1913.
*L'Entrave.* Paris, 1913.
*Mitsou, ou comment l'esprit vient aux filles.* Paris, 1919.
*Chéri.* Paris, 1920.
*La maison du Claudine.* Paris, 1922.
*Le blé en herbe.* Paris, 1923.
*La femme cachée.* Paris, 1924.
*La fin de Chéri.* Paris, 1926.
*La naissance du jour.* Paris, 1928.
*La seconde.* Paris, 1929.
*Sido.* Paris, 1929.
*Ces plaisirs.* Paris, 1932. Reissued in 1941 as *Le pur et l'impur.*
*La chatte.* Paris, 1933.
*Duo.* Paris, 1934.
*Mes apprentissages.* Paris, 1936.
*Le toutounier.* Paris, 1939.
*Chambre d'hôtel.* Paris, 1940. Includes "La lune de pluie."
*Julie de Carneilhan.* Paris, 1941.
*Le képi.* Paris, 1943. Includes "Le képi."
*Gigi et autres nouvelles.* Lausanne, 1944. Includes "La dame du photographe."

*L'Étoile vesper.* Geneva, 1946.
*Le fanal bleu.* Paris, 1949.

COLLECTED WORKS

*Oeuvres complètes de Colette.* 15 vols. Paris, 1948–1950. Reissued in 16 illustrated vols., including some posthumous pieces, 1973–1976.

## TRANSLATIONS

*The Blue Lantern.* Translated by Roger Senhouse. New York, 1963.

*Break of Day.* Translated by Enid McLeod. New York, 1979.

*The Cat.* Translated by Antonia White. In *Seven by Colette.* New York, 1955.

*Chéri and The Last of Chéri.* Translated by Roger Senhouse. Baltimore, 1974.

*The Complete Claudine.* Translated by Antonia White. New York, 1976. Includes *Claudine at School, Claudine in Paris, Claudine Married,* and *Claudine and Annie.*

*Creatures Great and Small: Creature Conversations, Other Conversations, Creature Comforts.* Translated by Enid McLeod. New York, 1978.

*Duo and Le Toutounier.* Translated by Margaret Crosland. New York, 1974.

*The Evening Star.* Translated by David Le Vay. London, 1973.

*The Innocent Libertine.* Translated by Antonia White. New York, 1978.

*Julie de Carneilhan and Chance Acquaintances.* Translated by Patrick Leigh Fermor. London, 1952.

*Letters from Colette.* Translated by Robert Phelps. New York, 1980.

*Mitsou and Music-Hall Sidelights.* Translated by Anne-Marie Callimachi. New York, 1957.

*My Apprenticeships.* Translated by Helen Beauclerk. New York, 1978.

*My Mother's House and Sido.* Translated by Una Vicenzo Troubridge and Enid McLeod. New York, 1979.

*The Other One.* Translated by Elizabeth Tait and Roger Senhouse. New York, 1960.

*The Other Woman.* Translated by Margaret Crosland. New York, 1975.

*The Pure and the Impure.* Translated by Herma Briffault. New York, 1979.

*The Retreat from Love.* Translated by Margaret Crosland. New York, 1980.

*The Ripening Seed.* Translated by Roger Senhouse and Herma Briffault. New York, 1978.

*The Shackle.* Translated by Antonia White. New York, 1976.

*The Tender Shoot and Other Stories.* Translated by Antonia White. New York, 1958. Includes "The Kepi," "The Photographer's Missus," and "The Rainy Moon."

*The Vagabond.* Translated by Enid McLeod. New York, 1955.

## BIOGRAPHICAL AND CRITICAL STUDIES

Cottrell, Robert D. *Colette.* New York, 1974.

Crosland, Margaret. *Colette: The Difficulty of Loving.* New York, 1973.

Dormann, Geneviéve. *Amoureuse Colette.* Paris, 1984. Translated as *Colette: A Passion for Life* by David Macey and Jane Brenton. New York and London, 1985.

Eisinger, Erica, and Mari McCarty, eds. "Charting Colette." Special issue of *Women's Studies.* Vol. 8, no. 3 (1981).

———. *Colette: The Woman, the Writer.* University Park, Pa., and London, 1981.

Goudeket, Maurice. *Près de Colette.* Paris, 1956. Translated as *Close to Colette* by Enid McLeod. London, 1957.

Marks, Elaine. *Colette.* New Brunswick, N.J., 1960.

Phelps, Robert. *Belles saisons: A Colette Scrapbook.* New York, 1978.

———, ed. *Earthly Paradise: An Autobiography of Colette Drawn from Her Lifetime Writings.* New York, 1966.

Richardson, Joanna. *Colette.* New York, 1984.

Rosasco, Joan Teresa, "*Chéri,* ou le collier de Léa." *Teaching Language Through Literature* 19: 3–21 (1979).

Sarde, Michèle. *Colette, libre et entravée.* Paris, 1978. Translated by Richard Miller as *Colette Free and Fettered.* New York, 1980.

Stewart, Joan Hinde. *Colette.* Boston, 1982.

JOAN HINDE STEWART

# DANTE ALIGHIERI
## *(1265–1321)*

### *LIFE*

DANTE ALIGHIERI was born in Florence in May 1265 in the district of San Martino, the son of Alighiero di Bellincione d'Alighiero. His mother died when he was young; his father, whom he seems to avoid mentioning as much as possible, remarried and produced two more children. The Alighieri family may be considered noble by reason of the titles and dignities bestowed upon its members, although by Dante's time it seems to have been reduced to modest economic and social circumstances. According to Dante himself, the family descended from "the noble seed of the Roman founders of the city" (*Inferno* 15.73–78). This claim remains largely unsubstantiated, as nothing is known of Dante's ancestors before his great-great-grandfather, Cacciaguida, who was knighted by Emperor Conrad III and died, as Dante tells us, during the Second Crusade, about 1147 (*Paradiso* 15.139–148).

Like most of the city's lesser nobility and artisans, Dante's family was affiliated with the Guelf party, as opposed to the Ghibellines, whose adherents tended to belong to the feudal aristocracy. These two parties came into Italy from Germany, and their names represent italianized forms of those attached to the two quarreling houses of Germany, Welf and Waiblingen. In Italy the parties were at first identified with broad allegiances: to papal authority for the Guelfs, and to imperial authority in the case of the Ghibellines. Eventually, however, this church-empire distinction disappeared, and the two parties became less clearly defined in outlook and purpose. The local connotations of the parties became much more important as their issues and activities became tied to geographical situation, rivalries of neighborhoods in the same city, family feuds, and private interests. Thus, the Guelfs and Ghibellines of Florence were factions peculiar to that region alone.

As far as one can tell from his writings, Dante's recollections of family life were pleasant ones. It is fairly certain that he received a careful education, although little of it is known precisely. He may have attended the Franciscan lower schools and, later, their schools of philosophy. The family's modest social standing did not prevent him from pursuing his studies, nor was he hindered in his effort to lead the life of a gentleman. His writings indicate that he was familiar with the ways of the country as well as with city life. Dante probably studied rhetoric with the scholar and statesman Brunetto Latini (*ca.* 1220–1294), from whom he says that he learned "how a man becomes eternal" (*Inferno* 15.85), during a period when he was driven by a desire to master the techniques of style. It seems that Brunetto fed his keenness for study and learning, and this may account for a trip in about 1287 to Bologna, where

Dante elected to pursue his study of rhetoric in the highly renowned school there.

Dante tells us that as a young man he taught himself the art of writing verse (*Vita nuova* 3.9). In time he became acquainted with the best-known troubadours of Florence, corresponding with them and circulating his own love lyrics. For the youthful Dante, writing poetry gradually became an important occupation, nourished by his sincere love for art and learning, and his interest in the nature of genuine love. Equally significant at this time was his friendship with the wealthy, aristocratic poet Guido Cavalcanti (*ca.* 1255–1300). Guido exerted a strong influence on his early poetic endeavors. This period was also marked by the death of Dante's father (*ca.* 1283), and by his marriage to Gemma, a gentlewoman of the Donati family. The marriage had been arranged by Dante's father in 1277, well before his death. Gemma and Dante had two sons, Pietro and Jacopo, and at least one daughter. (There exist the names of two daughters, Antonia and Beatrice, but they could refer to the same person, the second, Beatrice, being a monastic name.) Dante's marriage and children seem to have had little influence on him as a poet; nowhere in his works does he make direct reference to his wife.

Besides his associations with Guido Cavalcanti and Brunetto Latini, Dante knew well the notary Lapo Gianni and became acquainted later on with the youthful Cino da Pistoia. Both of these men were poets. Dante was also on friendly terms with the musician Casella (*Purgatorio* 2.76–114), about whom there exists little information. The artists Oderisi da Gubbio and Giotto may also have been among his acquaintances. A comrade chosen with far less discrimination, perhaps, was Forese Donati (*Purgatorio* 23), a kinsman of Dante's wife and a regular rogue, with whom Dante had an exchange of reproaches and coarse insults in sonnet form. The exchange may have begun only as a joke in a moment of good humor.

Along with Guido, Dante refined and developed his poetic skill in Latin and began to distinguish himself in his art from the other writers of the time. In their poetry Dante and Guido presented their ideas on the nature of love and its ability to contribute to the inner perfection of man. Guido, however, was more interested in natural philosophy than was Dante, who, because of his more artistic orientation, favored the study and emulation of the Latin poets. He particularly admired Vergil, from whom he learned so much about matters of style. Though Dante was deeply influenced in his writing by the example of his friend Guido, he eventually responded to his own artistic temperament, to his study of Vergil, and to the example provided by a more recent poetic master, Guido Guinizzelli (*ca.* 1230–1276). The result was a shift to composition in the vernacular, a poetic innovation that is praised by Bongiunta Orbicianni in the *Purgatorio* (24.49–62).

Dante's life and writings were also influenced by his acquaintance with a noble Florentine woman of outstanding grace and beauty. He had named her among the sixty fairest women of Florence, but it was not until later that the poet truly "discovered" her. This revelation proved to be an extremely powerful force in his artistic development. According to the testimony of Boccaccio and others, the woman, called Bice, was the daughter of Folco Portinari of Florence. She later became the wife of the banker Simone de' Bardi. Dante called her Beatrice, the bringer of blessings, the one who brought bliss to all who looked upon her.

Dante is said to have met Beatrice for the first time when he was nine. Theirs was not an easy relationship, for Beatrice took offense at the attention he paid other women. The resulting rebuff caused Dante great sorrow. His emotional attachment to Beatrice brought him to idealize her more and more as the guide of his thoughts and feelings, as the one who would lead him toward the inner perfection that is the ideal of every noble mind. In his poems Dante praises his lady as a model of virtue and courtesy, a miraculous gift given to earth by God to ennoble and enrich all those who appreciated her qualities. Such an exalted view of this woman was bound to carry with it the fear that she would not remain long in this life; in fact, premature death did befall her. Beatrice's father died first, and then she died on 8 June 1290. Dante was overcome with grief at his loss. There followed a period of contemplating Beatrice's significance after her death. After the first anniversary of her death, another woman, who is never mentioned by name, succeeded in winning Dante's affection for a brief time. However, Beatrice soon came vividly to mind again, and while feeling guilt and remorse for having neglected the memory of her, Dante reaffirmed his fidelity to her. This experience prompted him to gather together all the poems he had written in her honor, in an attempt to celebrate her virtue. This collection, to which Dante added a commentary on the meaning and occasion of each poem, became the little volume that he called the *Vita nuova (New Life)*, about which I shall have more to say later on in this essay.

During all of this time Dante's passion for study had continued unabated. His vision had been broadened by the reading of Boethius and Cicero. The dissemination of Aristotle's works on physical and metaphysical subjects brought recognition of the need to harmonize the ideas of the great guide of human reason with the truths and teachings of the faith. Dante, by now a grown man, was attracted to many of the new schools and universities that were operating under the tutelage of the new religious orders. Among the Franciscans, Dominicans, and Augustinians were many eminent teachers and scholars. In this brisk intellectual environment of around 1290 Dante applied his energies to philosophy with such fervor that "in a short time, perhaps thirty months," he began "to be so keenly aware of her sweetness that the love of her drove away and destroyed every other thought" (*Convivio* 2.2.7). Dante read so much, it seems, that his eyes were weakened considerably because of it. Among Christian scholars and theologians, he certainly read Saint Thomas Aquinas, Albertus Magnus, Saint Augustine, Hugh and Richard of Saint Victor, Saint Bonaventura, Saint Bernard, and Peter Lombard. In the area of history he took up Livy and Paulus Orosius, among others. Evidence of this extensive course of study found its way into his poetry as he became interested in the glorification of philosophy as mistress of the mind. Dante also treated questions of moral philosophy, such as nobility and courtship, in a number of beautifully composed *canzoni,* or odes. Nevertheless, in spite of this ardent pursuit of philosophical matter he retained his view of love as the most important force behind noble actions and lofty endeavors. To his appreciation of the Latin poets he added an admiration for the Provençal troubadours, and this encouraged him to attempt new poetic techniques that would serve him well in his later writings.

Along with his spiritual and intellectual activities Dante engaged in civic enterprises as well. In 1289 he had fought on the Guelf side at the battle of Campaldino. In 1295 he began an active public life, and within a few years he became an important figure in Florentine politics. He had joined the Guild of Physicians and Apothecaries in order to participate in government (except for certain offices, government was closed to those without guild affiliation), and there is evidence that he served as a member of the People's Council of the Commune of Florence (1295), on the Council for Election of the Priors of the City (1295), and on the Council of the Hundred (1296), a body that dealt with finance and other important civic matters.

This was a time of political ferment and instability. Between 1215 and 1278 the Guelfs and Ghibellines of Florence had engaged in a bitter struggle for power, with numerous reversals of fortune for both sides, countless plots and conspiracies, and frequent expulsion orders issued against whoever was on the losing side. The Guelfs finally prevailed. Around 1300, however, there occurred a split in the Guelf party into two very hostile factions: the Blacks and the Whites. The Blacks, staunch Guelfs, remained in control of the commune. The Whites eventually associated themselves with the Ghibellines. Dante, meanwhile, fought to preserve the independence of Florence, and repeatedly opposed the schemes of Pope Boniface VIII, who wanted to place Florence and all of Tuscany under the control of the church. Boniface attempted to take advantage of the unrest in the city and undermine his opponents by promising protection to those who displayed some sympathy with his cause. He met with firm opposition from the six priors (magistrates) of Florence, of whom Dante was one in the summer of 1300. To show his displeasure Boniface moved to excommunicate the members of the priorate. Dante was spared this fate only because his term of office was soon due to expire. Obviously, none of this served to improve Dante's opinion of the pontiff. He made no secret of his opposition to the pope's ambitious policy; he regarded Boniface as an enemy of peace.

In 1301 Boniface summoned Charles of Valois and his army to Italy in an attempt to neutralize antichurch forces in Florence. It was at this time, as Charles approached the city, that Dante was sent as one of three envoys on behalf of the commune to the pope, in order to request a change in papal policy toward the city and to protest the intrigues of the Blacks. After the initial talks the other envoys were dismissed, but Dante was retained. During his absence Charles of Valois entered Florence, and the Blacks staged a revolution and gained complete control of the commune. Dante found himself sentenced to exile on trumped-up charges of graft, embezzlement, opposition to the pope and his forces, disturbance of the peace of Florence, and a number of other transgressions. Dante always felt that his difficulties had been brought on by the trickery of Boniface, and this only aggravated his already pronounced hatred for the pontiff and his methods. When Dante failed to appear to answer the charges against him, and when he did not pay the fine levied against him for his "crimes," a second sentence was imposed: should he ever return to the commune, he would be seized and burned alive. There is no evidence that Dante saw his beloved Florence again.

In 1302, shortly after his banishment, Dante conspired with his fellow exiles, most of them Whites, to regain admission to Florence. However, disapproving of their machinations and possibly in danger of his life because of their violence, he abandoned them and set off on his own to lead the life of an exiled courtier. It appears that he first took refuge with the Scala family at Verona. He is believed to have visited the university at Bologna, where he had been known since 1287. This visit probably occurred after the death in 1304 of his generous patron, Bartolommeo della Scala. It is generally thought that Dante traveled extensively in Italy, particularly in the north. He may have been in Padua in 1306. During that same year he appeared in Lunigiana with the Malaspina family, and it was probably then that he went to the mountains of Casentino, on the upper Arno. It is also thought that he went to Paris sometime between 1307 and 1309.

In 1310 Henry VII of Luxembourg, Holy Roman emperor from 1312 to 1313, entered Italy in an effort to reunite church and state, restore order, and force various rebellious cities to submit to his authority. His coming caused a great deal of excitement and conflict. Florence generally opposed him, but Dante, who attributed the woes of Florence and all of Italy to the absence of imperial guidance, welcomed Henry as a savior. Dante's state of great exaltation is documented in three letters that he wrote in 1310 and 1311. However, Henry's invasion proved fruitless; he met opposition from all sides, including Pope Clement V, who had sent for him in the first place. Just as the situation for Henry and his supporters began to improve, the emperor died near Siena in 1313. With him went Dante's every hope of restoring himself to an honorable position in his city. Thus in 1314 he took shelter with the Ghibelline captain Can Grande della Scala in Verona.

Dante did not totally abandon his quest to return to his native city. He wrote letters to individual members of the government, attempting to appease those who ruled. He even sent a *canzone* to the city of Florence, praising her love for justice and asking that she work with her citizens on his behalf. Dante strove to be acceptable to the Florentines, but for many reasons the public associated him with the Ghibellines; no matter how Dante tried to free himself of suspicion, he did not succeed. He also tried to appeal to them on the grounds of his poetic ability, and sought to show that if he had cultivated poetry in the vernacular it was not for lack of skill or study. He was compelled to display his love for learning and his great respect for philosophy and matters having to do with civic education. He therefore composed two treatises (both left incomplete), the *De vulgari eloquentia* (*On Eloquence in the Vernacular*) and the *Convivio* (*Banquet*), sometime between 1304 and 1307. In them can be seen his longing to reestablish himself in the good graces of his city and to find consolation for his wretchedness in the study of matters useful to man's well-being and his art. Thus, in the ten years or so between the *Vita nuova* and the *Commedia* (*Divine Comedy*), Dante's studies were essentially of a philosophical and artistic nature. The *Convivio* is often acknowledged as the key to his philosophical researches, while the *De vulgari eloquentia* is viewed as the key to his artistic inquiries.

Though he desperately hoped to restore his reputation as a Florentine and resume his life in the city that had turned against him, Dante refused to compromise his principles and turned down more than one opportunity to return to Florence, because such opportunities involved answering the false charges made against him. Such unwillingness to dishonor himself brought him yet another sentence of death, this one extending to his sons as well.

The last years of the poet's life were spent at Ravenna, where he was offered asylum by Guido Nevella da Polenta, the nephew of the famous Francesca da Rimini, the only woman sinner who actually speaks in the *Inferno*. These years seem to have been serene ones. In Ravenna he was greatly esteemed, and he enjoyed a very pleasant social life and an eager following of pupils, for he was already well known for his lyrics, especially the *Convivio, Inferno,* and *Purgatorio*. Shortly before his death he was sent by Guido on a mission to Venice. Although Florence still rejected him, other cities very much valued his presence. Dante's friendship with Can Grande della Scala remained intact, and Dante placed great store in him; it is to him that he dedicated the *Paradiso*. Ravenna was Dante's home until his death on 13 or 14 September 1321.

## *WORKS*

The *Vita nuova,* one of Dante's earliest works, is a combination of prose and poetry (thirty-one poems inserted into the prose text). It is one of the first important examples of Italian literary prose and probably the first work of fiction that has come down to us in which the prose serves the purpose not only of offering a continuous narrative but also of explaining the occasion for the composition of each of the poems included. The originality of the *Vita nuova* consists of the functional relationship between the poetry and the prose.

In recent years the critics of the *Divine Comedy* have come to see more clearly the necessity of distinguishing between Dante the poet, the historical figure who wrote the poem in his own voice, and Dante the pilgrim, who is the poet's creation and who moves in a world of the poet's invention. In the case of the *Vita nuova* it is more difficult to distinguish between Dante the poet and Dante the lover, because in this book the lover, the protagonist, is himself a poet. More important, however, is the fact that the events of the *Vita nuova,* unlike those of the *Divine Comedy,* are surely not to be taken as pure fiction, and the protagonist himself is no fictional character: he is the historical character Dante at an earlier age. But we must attempt, just as we must in the case of any first-person novel, to distinguish between the point of view of the one who has already lived through the experiences recorded and has had time to reflect upon them in retrospect, and the point of view of the one undergoing the experiences at the time. What we have in the *Vita nuova* is a more mature Dante, reevoking his youthful experiences in a way that points up the folly of his younger self.

Also significant is the chronological relationship between the composition of the poems and that of the prose narrative, which reflects the way in which the author has adapted to a new purpose some of his earlier writings. In general scholars agree that when Dante, sometime between 1292 (that is, two years after the death of Beatrice) and 1300, composed the *Vita nuova*, most, if not all, of the poems that were to appear in the text had already been written. The architecture of the work, as has been said, consists of selected poems arranged in a certain order, with bridges of prose that serve primarily a narrative function: to describe those events in the life of the protagonist that supposedly inspired the poems included in the text. By giving the poems a narrative background, Dante was able to make their meaning clearer or even to change their original meaning or purpose.

For example, though the beauty of the first *canzone* in the book, "Donne ch'avete intelletto d'amore" ("Ladies who have intelligence of love"), is independent of its position in the work, the poem owes entirely to the preceding narrative its dramatic significance as the proclamation of a totally new attitude adopted by the young poet-lover at this time in the story. This is also true, though from a different point of view, of the most famous poem in the *Vita nuova* (and probably one of the most exquisite sonnets in all of world literature), which is quoted below in the original (as well as in my own translation):

*Tanto gentile e tanto onesta pare*
*la donna mia quand'ella altrui saluta,*
*ch'ogne lingua deven tremando muta,*
*e li occhi no l'ardiscon di guardare.*
*Ella si va, sentendosi laudare,*
*benignamente d'umiltà vestuta,*
*e par che sia una cosa venuta*
*da cielo in terra a miracol mostrare.*

*Mostrarsi si piacente a chi la mira,*
*che dà per li occhi una dolcezza al core,*
*che 'ntender no la può chi no la prova;*
*e par che de la sua labbia si mova*
*un spirito soave, pien d'amore,*
*che va dicendo a l'anima: "Sospira!"*

*Such sweet decorum and such gentle grace*
*attend my lady's greeting as she moves*
*that lips can only tremble into silence,*
*and eyes dare not attempt to gaze at her.*
*Moving, benignly clothed in humility,*
*untouched by all the praise along her way,*
*she seems to be a creature come from heaven*
*to earth, to manifest a miracle.*

*Miraculously gracious to behold,*
*her sweetness reaches, through the eyes, the heart*
*(who has not felt this cannot understand),*
*and from her lips it seems there moves a gracious*
*spirit, so deeply loving that it glides*
*into the souls of men, whispering: "Sigh!"*

Just how much of the narrative prose is fiction we shall never know. We can never be sure that a given poem actually arose from the circumstances related in the prose preceding it. A few critics believe that all of the events of the narrative reflect biographical truth; most, fortunately, are more skeptical. But it goes without saying that to enjoy reading the

*Vita nuova* we must suspend our skepticism and accept as "true" the events of the narrative. For only by doing so can we perceive the significance that Dante attributed to his poems by placing them where he did. And most critics of the *Vita nuova* seem to be agreed that in interpreting this work as a piece of literature, in seeking to find its message, the reader must try to forget the biographical fact that any given poem may have been written before Dante could know the use he would make of it later on.

In the opening chapter or preface (for it is so short) of his little book the author states that his purpose is to copy from his "book of memory" only those past experiences that belong to the period beginning his "new life"—a life made new by the poet's first meeting with Beatrice and the God of Love, who together with the poet-protagonist are the three main characters in the story. And by the end of chapter 2 all of the motifs that are important for the story that is about to unfold step by step have been introduced.

The first word of the opening sentence is "Nine": "Nine times already since my birth the heaven of light had circled back to almost the same point, when there appeared before my eyes the now glorious lady of my mind, who was called Beatrice even by those who did not know what her name was." The number nine will be repeated twice more in the next sentence (and it will appear another twenty times before the book comes to an end). In this opening sentence the reader not only finds a reference to the number nine of symbolic significance, but he also sees the emphasis on mathematical precision that will appear at frequent intervals throughout the *Vita nuova.*

In the opening sentence also the child Beatrice is presented as already enjoying the veneration of the people of her city, including strangers who did not know her name. With the words "the now glorious lady of my mind" (the first of two time shifts, in which the figure of the living Beatrice at a given moment is described in such a way as to remind us of Beatrice dead) the theme of death is delicately foreshadowed at the beginning of the story. As for the figure of Beatrice, when she appears for the first time in this chapter she wears a garment of blood-red color—the same color as her shroud will be in the next chapter.

In the next three sentences the three main spirits are introduced: the "vital" (in the heart), the "animal" (in the brain), and the "natural" (in the liver). They rule the body of the nine-year-old protagonist, and they speak in Latin, as will the God of Love in the chapter that follows (and once again later on). The words of the first spirit describing Beatrice anticipate the first coming of Love in the next chapter and suggest something of the same mood of terror. The words of the second spirit suggest rapturous bliss to come (that bliss rhapsodically described in chapter 11), while in the words of the third spirit there is the first of the many references to tears to be found in the *Vita nuova.* It is the spirit of the liver that weeps. It is only after this reference to the organ of digestion that Love is mentioned. He is mentioned first of all as a ruler, but we learn immediately that much of his power is derived from the protagonist's imagination—this faculty of which there will be so many reminders in the form of visions throughout the book.

We are also told that Love's power was restricted by reason, and later in the book the relation between Love and reason becomes an important problem. Two more themes are posited in this beginning chapter, to be woven into the narrative: the godlike nature of Beatrice and the strong "praise of the lady" motif. Both sound throughout the chapter as the protagonist's admiration for Beatrice keeps growing during the nine years after her first appearance.

Thus the opening chapter prepares for the rest of the book not only in the obvious way of presenting a background situation, an established continuity out of which single events will emerge in time, but also by setting in motion certain forces that will propel the *Vita nuova* forward—forces with which Dante's reader will gradually become more and more familiar.

In chapter 42, the final chapter of the *Vita nuova,* the poet expresses his dissatisfaction with his work: "After this sonnet there appeared to me a miraculous vision in which I saw things that made me resolve to say no more about this blessed one until I should be capable of writing about her in a more worthy fashion." As the result of a final vision, which is not revealed to the reader, he decides to stop writing about Beatrice until he can do so more worthily. The preceding vision he had in the course of the story had made him decide to keep on writing; this one made him decide to stop. If the main action of the book is to be seen, as some critics believe, as the development of Dante's love from his preoccupation with his own feelings to his enjoyment of Beatrice's excellence and, finally, to his exclusive concern with her heavenly attributes and with spiritual matters, then this action, and the *Vita nuova* itself, ends in an important sense in failure.

To understand the message of the book, to understand how it succeeds through failure, we must go back in time and imagine the poet Dante, somewhere between the ages of twenty-seven and thirty-five, having already glimpsed the possibility of what was to be his terrible and grandiose masterpiece, the *Divine Comedy.* We must imagine him rereading the love poems of his earlier years and feeling shame for a number of them. He would have come to view Beatrice as she was destined to appear in the *Divine Comedy,* and indeed as she does appear briefly in the *Vita nuova,* specifically in that essay (chapter 29) on the miraculous quality of the number nine (the square of the number three, the symbol of the Blessed Trinity)—that is, as an agent of divine salvation.

Having arrived at this point, he would have chosen from among his earlier love poems many that exhibit his younger self at his worst, in order to offer a warning example to other young lovers and especially to other love poets. This would imply on Dante's part, as he is approaching the midmost part of life (the "mezzo del cammin di nostra vita" of the *Divine Comedy*), a criticism of most of the love poetry in Italian literature, for which his century was famous, and also that for which Provençal poetry was famous in the preceding century.

One might even say that the *Vita nuova* is a cruel book; cruel, that is, in the treatment of the human type represented by the protagonist. In the picture of the lover there is offered a condemnation of the vice of emotional self-indulgence and an exposure of its destructive effects on a man's integrity. The "tender feelings" that move the lover to hope or despair, to rejoice or to grieve (and perhaps even to enjoy his grief), spring from his vulnerability and instability and self-love; however idealistically inspired, these feelings cannot, except spasmodically, lead him ahead and above as long as he continues to be at their mercy. In short, he must always fall back into the helplessness of his self-centeredness. The man who would realize a man's destiny must ruthlessly cut out of his heart the canker at its center, the canker that the heart instinctively tends to cultivate. This is, I am convinced, the main message of the *Vita nuova.* And the consistent, uncompromising indictment it levels has no parallel in the literature of Dante's time. But of course the *Vita nuova* offers more than a picture of the misguided lover: there is also the glory of Beatrice and the slowly increasing ability of the lover to understand it, although he must nevertheless confess at the end that he has not truly succeeded.

Both in the treatment of the lover and in that of Beatrice, Dante has gone far beyond what he found at hand in the love poetry of the troubadours and their followers. He has taken up two of their preoccupations (one might almost say obsessions) and developed each of them in a most original way: the lover's glorification of his own feelings, and his glorification of the beloved. Of the first he has made a caricature. Unlike his friend Guido Cavalcanti, also highly critical of the havoc wrought by the emotions within a man's soul, who makes of the distraught lover a macabre portrait of doom, Dante has presented his protagonist mainly as an object of derision.

As to the glorification of the lady, all critics of the *Vita nuova* admit that Dante has carried this idealization to a degree never before reached by any poet, and one that no poet after him will ever quite attempt to reach. However blurred may be the lover's vision of the gracious, pure, feminine Beatrice, Dante the poet, in chapter 29, probes to the essence of her being and presents the coldness of her sublimity. Thus the tender foolishness of the lover is intensified by contrast with the icy perfection of the beloved.

With a few exceptions, Dante's lyrical poems (and not only those contained in the *Vita nuova*) are inferior as works of art to those of Cavalcanti and Guinizelli, or, for that matter, to those of Bernart de Ventadorn and Arnaut Daniel. The greatness of the *Vita nuova* lies not in the poems but in the purpose that Dante made them serve. Certainly the book is the most original form of recantation in medieval literature—a recantation that takes the form of a reenactment, seen from a new perspective, of the sin recanted.

The *Convivio,* or *Banquet,* which Dante wrote in Italian sometime between 1304 and 1308, is an unfinished piece of work (it would be difficult to call it a work of art). His purpose in writing it is explained in the opening sentence, which is a quotation from Aristotle's *Metaphysics:* "All men by nature desire to know." Dante invites his reader to a feast consisting of fourteen courses (only three were completed), of which the "meat" of each is a *canzone* concerning love and virtue, while the "bread" is the exposition of it. Dante invites to his *Banquet* all those worthy people who, because of public duties, family responsibilities, and the like, have not been introduced to the science of philosophy. It is the laymen whom Dante invites to his feast, for it is through philosophy, he believes, that they can attain the temporal goal of happiness.

While the *Vita nuova* is Dante's monument to his first love, the lady Beatrice, the *Convivio* is a monument to his "second love," the lady Philosophy. That the lady who offers to console Dante a year after the death of Beatrice in the *Vita nuova* is that same lady Philosophy of the *Convivio* is revealed in book 2, chapter 2:

> To begin with, then, let me say that the star of Venus had already revolved twice in that circle of hers that makes her appear at evening or in the morning, according to the two different periods, since the passing away of that blessed Beatrice who dwells in heaven with the angels and on earth with my soul, when that gentle lady, of whom I made mention at the end of the *Vita nuova,* first appeared to my eyes, accompanied by love, and occupied a place in my mind.

What attracted the poet-protagonist to this lady was her offer of consolation. In the *Vita nuova* his love for the lady at the window lasts for a short time, and he refers to this love as "the adversary of reason" and "most base," but in the *Convivio* he calls this love "most noble." It should be remembered, however, that Philosophy in the *Vita nuova* tries to make the young protagonist forget the fact that he has lost Beatrice—something of this earth (such as Philosophy) cannot replace the love of Beatrice. After the vision in chapter 39 of the *Vita nuova,* after grasping the true significance of his lady, he returns to Beatrice and vows to never again stray. In doing this he is to be thought of not as rejecting Philosophy, but rather as rejecting the ideal of replacing Beatrice with Philosophy. Never in the *Convivio* does he consider such a replacement.

Here Dante exalts learning and the use of reason to the highest, for only through knowledge can man hope to attain virtue and God. The *Convivio* seems to be the connecting link between the *Vita nuova* and the *Divine Comedy,* since a love that at first has earthly associations turns out to have religious significance. Furthermore, just as Dante praises reason in this work, we know that in the *Divine Comedy*, reason in the pursuit of knowledge and wisdom is man's sole guide on earth, except for the intervention of divine grace.

One might say that the *Convivio* is the philosophical counterpart of the *Vita nuova*. Even from a quick reading of the *canzone* that opens book 2, "Voi che 'ntendendo" ("You who by understanding"), the reader easily sees that, given the appropriate prose background, it might well have fitted into the *Vita nuova*. But when Dante begins the exposition of this ode it is "the sail of reason" that bears him on.

In the preamble to the *Convivio* Dante suggests reform in his declaring the vernacular suitable for ethical subjects as well as amorous ones. He was a leader in considering the vernacular a potential medium for all forms of expression, and his impassioned defense and praise of it manifest his awareness of its value in scientific interpretation as he comments at length on its uses.

He tells his reader that writings should be expounded in four senses. The first is the literal level. The second is the allegorical; for example, when Ovid tells his reader that Orpheus moved both animals and stones with his music he is signifying the power of eloquence over what is not rational. In this case the literal level of the story or poem need not be true. If it is not true, it is known as the allegory of poets; if the literal level is taken to be the truth, it is known as the allegory of theologians, because the literal level of the Scriptures was considered to be true. The third is the moral level, and this has a didactic purpose: when Christ took only three of his disciples with him on the occasion of the Transfiguration, it was another way of saying that for those things that are most secret we should have little company. The fourth sense is the anagogical, as when Scripture signifies certain spiritual or mystical truths. When we read, for example, that the people of Israel came out of Egypt and that Judea was made free, we must take this to be literally true, but the statement also signifies the spiritual truth that when a soul turns away from sin it becomes holy and free.

The literal level of a writing must always be exposed first, for it is impossible to delve into the "form" of anything without first preparing the "subject" upon which the form is to be stamped—you must prepare the wood before you build the table. Dante, in book 2, chapter 1 of the *Convivio*, proposes to expound the literal level of his *canzone* first and then the allegorical, bringing into play the other levels or senses when it seems appropriate. There are very few passages in Dante's work where all four senses are at work; in fact, of the three *canzoni* expounded in the *Convivio* he manages to treat only the first two poems on two levels, while the third he discusses only on the literal level. And when Dante talks about the literal sense he means, of course, not the words but what the words mean. We must bear in mind that the literal sense contains all the other meanings.

In the third book Dante expounds the *canzone* "Amor che ne la mente mi ragiona" ("Love that converses with me in my mind"), which Cosella in the *Divine Comedy* will sing to the newly arrived souls on the shores of Purgatory. In discussing the literal level of this ode he gives most of his attention to the meaning of *amor* (love).

Dante begins the fourth book, which treats the third and final *canzone*, "Le dolci rime d'amor ch'i'solìa" ("Those sweet rhymes of love that I was wont"), by stressing the fact that his love of philosophy has led him to love all those who pursue the truth and despise those who follow error. He also tells us in chapter 1 of this book that in order to have the utmost clarity he will discuss the poem only on the literal level. The lady involved, however, is still Philosophy.

Critics have proposed a number of theories on why Dante completed only four of the projected fourteen books of the *Convivio*. Thomas Bergin goes as far as to suggest that the *Convivio* might be thought of as the *selva oscura* (dark wood) of the *Divine Comedy,* from which the poet's lady, Beatrice, in a more graceful and harmonious work of art, felt obliged to rescue her poet-lover. I tend to agree with Rocco Montano, who suspects that it was some kind of personal crisis or "conversion" that made Dante stop working on this project. Montano assigns such a conversion and the writing of the *Divine Comedy* to the insight that resulted from Dante the poet's great disappointment at the failure of Henry VII's expedition into Italy. In any case, whatever Dante's reason for cutting short his work on the *Convivio,* whether it was personal or political, if this meant he could get on with the *Divine Comedy* and complete his masterpiece, we should be grateful that he did.

In all his works Dante shows his concern for words and the structure of language. In chapter 25 of the *Vita nuova* he takes time to explain and illustrate the use of personification, as he does in the early chapters of the *Convivio,* where he defends the use of Italian rather than Latin. But this concern is most evident in his Latin treatise *De vulgari eloquentia.* Before it there was no such scholarly treatment of a language. Dante completed only the first and second books, but he refers to a fourth; it is not known if that one was to be the last.

In book 1 Dante deals with the origin and history of the Italian language. The first five chapters cover the basic definitions of human speech while a good deal of the rest is given over to a discussion of dialects and the principles of poetic composition in the vulgar tongue, which he calls the "illustrious" vulgar tongue—the language of Guido Guinizelli and, most perfectly, of Guido Cavalcanti, Cino da Pistoia, and Dante himself.

The second book of the *De vulgari eloquentia* is devoted to a more thorough discussion of Italian, which, Dante asserts, is just as appropriate for works of prose as for poetry. Early in this book (chapter 2) he discusses what kind of subject is worthy of this vernacular and concludes that it is suited for only the most elevated subjects. And they are three: war (or prowess of arms), love, and virtue (or direction of the will). He states that the greatest writers using a vulgar tongue wrote only on these three subjects. Among Provençal poets, Dante cites Bertran de Born, who wrote about war, Arnaut Daniel on love, and Guiraut de Bornelh on virtue; he also mentions that in Italian Cino da Pistoia wrote about love and "his friend" (Dante), about virtue, citing an example of verse from each poet and including one of his own. Then he admits that he can find no Italian poet who has written on the topic of war. In chapter 3 of this book we learn that while poets have used a variety of forms (*canzoni, ballate,* sonnets, and other irregular types), the most excellent form remains the *canzone,* and it is this form that is most suited to lofty subjects. In the remaining chapters of book 2 the author goes on to discuss style and the rules and form of the *canzone;* the work ends abruptly with the incomplete chapter 14, in which he intended to treat the number of lines and syllables in the stanza.

Most scholars agree that the *De vulgari eloquentia* is not a finished work, but is rather an unfinished first draft. There are three basic reasons for this belief: the paucity of manuscripts (there are only three), the way the work breaks off in chapter 14, and the fact that references to points the author promises to discuss in coming chapters are never followed up. Perhaps Dante stopped writing the work, as Aristide Marigo suggests, because he was not certain of the direction he was taking. There is an obvious difference between the wide, humanistic scope of book 1 and the dry, manual-like approach of book 2. Or could Dante simply have become bored with it?

The date of composition of the *De vulgari eloquentia* has not been definitively resolved. Boccaccio claims that it was written in Dante's old age. Marigo, who has done the standard edition of the work (Florence, 1938), dates it between the spring of 1303 and the end of 1304. And because in the *Convivio* Dante makes an allusion to this work in progress we must assume, at least, that he had the project in mind during this time.

It is also difficult to assign a date of composition to Dante's *De monarchia (On Monarchy),* primarily because it contains no references to the author's contemporaries or to events taking place at the time. Some say that it was written before Dante's exile because the work contains no mention of it; others tend to think that it was written even later than the *Convivio,* because a number of ideas appearing in an embryonic stage in that work are fully developed in the *De monarchia.* Nevertheless, it was most likely written between 1312 and 1313 (sometime before or after the coronation of Henry VII) to commemorate Henry's advent into Italy.

The treatise is divided into three books. In the first book Dante attempts to prove that temporal monarchy is necessary for the welfare of the world. Temporal monarchy, or the empire, means a single command exercised over all persons; that is, in those things that are subject to time as opposed to eternal matters. In the opening sentence of the *De monarchia* the author pays tribute to both God and Aristotle while he establishes the reason for undertaking the present work: "All men whom the higher nature has imbued with a love of truth should feel impelled to work for the benefit of future generations, whom they will thereby enrich, just as they themselves have been enriched by the labors of their ancestors." According to Dante (and we find the idea throughout his writings) the man who does not contribute to the common good fails sadly in his duty.

Clearly Dante is convinced that he is doing something new in his treatise. There is nothing new, however, in his ideas of justice, freedom, and law—they are very much in line with the medieval philosophy of his day. The idea so elaborately set forth in book 1, that a higher jurisdiction is necessary whenever there is a possibility of discord or strife, was an argument that had already been used by Pope Boniface VIII and his followers. The originality of the *De monarchia,* the new element that Dante brings to the old idea of empire, rests precisely in its main premise, upon which and around which the treatise is constructed: Dante's justification from a philosophical point of view of a single ruler for all the human race. It is in his concern with founding a "universal community of the human race" ("universalis civilitas humani generis") that he is new and even daring—daring because in Dante's day this idea of a universal community existed only as a religious one, in the form of the church. His new idea, then, took its shape from universal Christendom; it is, in a sense, an imitation of it elaborated from a philosophical point of view. Working from the Averroistic concept of the "possible intellect," Dante affirms that the particular goal of mankind as a whole is to realize to the fullest all the potentialities of this intellect (to have all the intellectual knowledge it is capable of having); this can happen only under the direction of a single ruler, under one world government. And the most important essential, if we are to secure our happiness and if the human race is to fulfill its proper role, is universal peace.

Dante considers the monarch to be the purest incarnation of justice, for there is nothing for him to desire, nothing more to be greedy about. He is a man who has everything, having authority over all territories. Dante also tells us that the human race is at its best when it is most free—meaning self-dependent. Under the monarch the citizens do not exist for his sake; on the contrary, it is the monarch who exists for his citizens.

In the closing paragraph of the first book we hear the desperate voice of Dante the poet warning all humanity. Rarely do we hear this voice in the poet's Italian or Latin prose works, where his intention is to remain as objective as possible. It is a preview of what is to come, for Dante makes frequent and effective use of this device of authorial intervention in the *Divine Comedy.* After presenting his case for the necessity of a monarch in a logical and scholastic fashion, as Saint Thomas Aquinas or Aristotle might have done, Dante the poet bursts forth:

> O humanity, in how many storms must you be tossed, how many shipwrecks must you endure, so long as you turn yourself into a many-headed beast lusting after a multiplicity of things! You are ailing in both your intellectual powers and heart. You pay no heed to the unshakable principles of your higher intellect, nor tune your heart to the sweetness of divine counsel when it is breathed into you through the trumpet of the Holy Spirit: "Behold how good and pleasant it is for brethren to dwell together in unity."

In book 2 Dante is primarily concerned with showing that the Romans were justified in assuming imperial power. He attempts to prove his thesis first by a number of arguments based on rational principles, then by the principles of the Christian faith.

In book 3 the poet proposes the question he has from the start wanted to ask and can ask only now that he has prepared the way in books 1 and 2: whether the authority of the Holy Roman emperor is directly dependent on God or whether his authority comes indirectly from another, a vicar or minister of God, meaning the pope. Dante ignores the vast historical distance between the Roman Empire and the Holy Roman Empire, preferring to see the two governments joined by historical and political continuity. First Dante must refute those scriptural arguments (based on Genesis 1:16: "And God made two great lights: the greater light to rule the day and the lesser light to rule the night") used by his opponents to show the dependence of the emperor on the pope. Having done this, he turns to those historical arguments that must be refuted. The main one he must deal with is the very one that up to this point in his treatise he has been able to cope with only in a rather subjective, emotional, and even poetic way: the painful reality of the Donation of Constantine, a document that purported to prove that the emperor Constantine had invested Pope Sylvester with temporal authority. Dante proceeds by means of his two preferred sources: Scripture and philosophy (from Matthew and, on this occasion, Aristotle).

Man, who participates in two natures—one corrupt (the body), the other incorruptible (the soul)—has a twofold goal, and since he is the only being who participates in both corruptibility and incorruptibility, he has a goal for his body and a goal for his soul. God, who never errs, has, then, given man two goals: happiness in this life and happiness in the eternal life. The pope leads mankind to eternal life in accordance with revelation, while the emperor leads mankind to temporal happiness in accordance with philosophical teaching. The temporal monarch, who must devote his energies to providing freedom and peace for men as they pass through the "testing time" of this world, receives his authority directly from God.

Intellectual perfection, the happiness of this world, can therefore be attained without the church. With proper guidance from the universal monarch, man can regain the happiness of the earthly paradise—this is a dangerous conclusion that can easily follow from Dante's arguments in his treatise, and one that Dante himself does not draw. Not surprisingly, the book was placed on the *Index of Forbidden Books*. Unfortunately for Dante, what he wished and wrote for in the *De monarchia* did not come about. It is for this reason that the poet's main political focus shifted from the empire to the church when he wrote the *Divine Comedy*. With the death of Henry VII, Dante's hopes for the empire and the universal monarch began to fade; he was forced to put aside his ideal and face facts: a monarch and an empire would not overcome the power of the pope and the church.

While Dante divides temporal and spiritual authority in the *De monarchia* by means of ingenious logic and scholastic arguments (and in the *Divine Comedy* by its larger allegorical structure), his masterpiece reveals the sad truth that temporal and spiritual authority are often in the same hands. There are many passages that lament this fact. In the *Purgatorio* (canto 16), to cite one of the more famous passages, Marco Lombardo tells the pilgrim why the world has gone bad ("la cagion che 'l mondo ha fatto reo": 106–112):

> On Rome, which brought the world to know the good,
> once shone two suns that lighted up two ways:
> the road of this world and the road of God.
>
> The one sun has put out the other's light,
> the sword is now one with the crook—and
> fused together thus, must bring about misrule,
>
> since joined, now neither fears the other one.

No one is quite sure if Dante is the author of a pedantic little essay written in Latin with the title *Questio de aqua et terra (Discourse on the Nature of Water and Earth)*. According to a statement attached to the original manuscript, the essay is in essence a lecture delivered at Verona in 1320. It consists of twenty-four brief chapters that debate in detail the question of whether or not the water of the sea anywhere rises higher than land emerging from it. The document was first published in 1508 by G. B. Moncetti, who claimed that he had copied it from an autograph manuscript of Dante's; the manuscript, however, was never found.

Among Dante's other minor works we find his two pastoral odes in Latin, addressed to Giovanni del Virgilio, who was a professor of Latin at the University of Bologna, where Dante at one time had probably studied. The exchange of Latin hexameters between the two men took place when Dante was staying in Ravenna some two years before his death. In his verses Giovanni del Virgilio reprimands Dante for writing his great poem in Italian rather than Latin. The eclogues are interesting insofar as they reveal Dante's mood toward the end of his life: he seems to be playful, happy, and at peace with himself. Also evident in these verses is the poet's pathetic wish to return to his fair city to receive the laurel crown, as well as his feelings and hopes for the *Divine Comedy*.

A brief mention should be made of *Il fiore (The Flower)*, the authenticity of which has been questioned by many scholars. It is a sequence of 232 sonnets based on the French *Roman de la Rose*. Those few who are sure that this allegorical story of a successful seduction was written by Dante give two reasons: first, the author is referred to as Durante, which is a form of Dante; second, it is much too well composed to have been written by anyone else but Dante. *Il fiore*, which is worth reading in its own right, is to be found in one manuscript of the late thirteenth century (first published in 1881 in Paris by Ferdinand Castets).

There are approximately fifty-four (and a possible twenty-six more) short poems (not included in the *Vita nuova* or *Convivio*) that Dante did not group together or organize in any way, but that modern editors have collected and called the *Canzoniere* or *Rime* (Songbook or Rhymes). They consist of scattered lyrics written over a long period of the poet's life, many of which he probably tried to, but could not, fit into the structure of the *Vita nuova* or *Convivio*. Many, of course, were inspired by Beatrice, but there are some written for other women; some done as exercises, as part of his correspondence with other poets; and some composed simply to please ladies and gentlemen who were fond of poetry.

Dante undoubtedly wrote many letters. Unfortunately, only ten letters considered authentic have come down to us; all ten are written in Latin, and none is of a personal or intimate nature. There are also three other letters that Dante may have written on behalf of the countess of Battifolle, but they do not reflect his own thoughts.

To the student of the *Divine Comedy* the most interesting of Dante's letters is the one addressed to Can Grande della Scala in which the author sets forth his purpose and method in writing his poem. The letter is extant in six manuscripts, three of which (all sixteenth-century) contain the letter in its entirety. He talks about the different meanings contained in the *Divine Comedy:* the first is called literal, the second allegorical or mystical. We learn that on the literal level the poem is about the state of souls after death; on the allegorical level, "The subject is man, liable to the reward or punishment of Justice, according to the use he has made of his free will."

In his letter he also discusses why he has called his poem a "comedy." The word, he says, is derived from *comus* and *oda* and means a "rustic song." Unlike tragedy, which begins in tranquillity but comes to a sad end, comedy may begin under adverse circumstances, but it always comes to a happy end. The style or language of comedy is humble while that of tragedy is lofty. Therefore, because his poem begins in Hell and has a happy ending in Paradise, and because it is written in a most humble language, which is the Italian vernacular, it is called the *Commedia.* The letter goes on with a meticulous, almost word-by-word examination of the beginning verses of the opening canto of the *Paradiso* up to the invocation to Apollo. The letter is thought by many to be an important piece of literary criticism seen in the framework of Dante's time and tradition, and as such it certainly is worth reading in its own right.

## The Divine Comedy

Dante's masterpiece is, of course, the *Divine Comedy* (the word *divina* was added to *commedia* by posterity). It is to some degree a result of his determination to fulfill the promise he made at the close of the *Vita nuova:* "If it be the wish of Him in whom all things flourish that my life continue for a few years, I hope to write of her that which has never been written of any lady."

No one knows when Dante began composing his great poem; some say perhaps as early as 1307. In any case the *Inferno* was completed in 1314, and it is probable that the final touches to the *Paradiso* were, as Boccaccio states, not made until 1321, the year of Dante's death. The purpose of the poem, which has moved readers through the centuries, is, as Dante reveals in his epistle to Can Grande, "to remove those living in this life from the state of misery and lead them to the state of felicity."

The poem is divided into three major sections: *Inferno* (Hell), *Purgatorio* (Purgatory), and *Paradiso* (Heaven). Each section contains thirty-three cantos, with the exception of Hell, which has thirty-four—the opening canto serving as an introduction to the work as a whole. For the *Commedia* Dante invented a rhyme scheme known as terza rima (tertiary rhyme: *aba bcb cdc*), thus continuing to display his fascination with the number three, which was so much on his mind when he was composing the *Vita nuova* many years earlier. And each canto is divided into three-line stanzas called *terzine,* or tercets, in which the first and third lines rhyme, while the middle or second lines rhyme with the first and third of the next *terzina.* The basic metrical unit of the verse is the hendecasyllabic line, quite common in Italian poetry: it is an eleven-syllable line in which the accent falls on the tenth syllable.

The drama or main action of the poem centers on one man's journey to God. It tells how God through the agency of Beatrice drew the poet to salvation; and the moral that Dante wishes his reader to keep in mind is that what God has done for one man he will do for every man, if every man is willing to make this journey. The reader of the poem would do well to distinguish from the very beginning of the *Commedia* between the two uses of the first-person singular: one designates Dante the pilgrim, the other Dante the poet. The first is a character in a story invented by the second. The events in the narrative are represented as having taken place in the past; the writing of the poem and the memory of these events, however, are represented as taking place in the present. For example, we find references to both past and present, and to both pilgrim and poet, in verse 10 of the introductory canto of the *Inferno:* "How *I entered* there *I cannot* truly say."

There are times in the poem when the fictional pilgrim (Dante the pilgrim) embodies many of the characteristics of his inventor (Dante the poet); for the *Commedia,* though it is above all the journey of Everyman to God, is in many ways a personal, autobiographical journey. It is often difficult, most times impossible, to say whether what is happening in the poem belongs to the real-life biography of the poet or the fictional biography of the pilgrim. For instance, at the beginning of canto 19 of the *Inferno* the pilgrim alludes to having broken a baptismal font in the church of his "lovely San Giovanni" (verse 17). Now Dante the poet may well have broken the font to save someone who was drowning within, but it is highly unlikely (and most inartistic) that he would mention the incident for the sole purpose of clearing his name in connection with an act that some of his contemporaries would have thought sinful. The breaking of the font is an event that took place in the life of the pilgrim, and the pilgrim is not trying to "clear his name," as critics have suggested. Rather the poet is giving an example to the reader of the true nature of the sin of simony (the sin punished in canto 19), which "breaks" the holy purposes of the church by perverting them.

The poet is the poet, but he is not the pilgrim, and the story traced in the *Commedia* is the story of Dante the pilgrim, who is at once himself and Everyman. We must keep in mind the allegory of the opening verse of the poem: "Nel mezzo del cammin di nostra vita / mi ritrovai . . ." ("Midway along the journey of our life / I found myself . . ."). Dante begins to construct his allegory of the double journey; that is, his personal experience in the world beyond ("I found myself"), open to Everyman in his own journey through this life ("of our life"). The poet finds himself wandering in a dark wood (the worldly life). He tries to escape by climbing a mountain that is lit from behind by the rays of the sun (God). His journey upward is impeded by the sudden appearance of three beasts: a leopard, a lion, and a she-wolf (the three major divisions of sin, signifying the three major divisions of Hell: fraud, violence, and concupiscence). The poet is about to be driven back when, just as suddenly, Vergil (reason or human understanding) appears. He has been sent by Beatrice (divine revelation) to aid Dante, to guide him on this journey that cannot fail. The only way to escape from the dark wood is to descend into Hell (man must first descend into humility before he can raise himself to salvation or God). The way up the mountain, then, is to go down: before man can hope to climb the mountain of salvation, he must first know what sin is. The purpose of Dante's journey through Hell is precisely this: to learn all there is to know about sin as a necessary preparation for the ascent to God. In fact, from the opening canto of the *Inferno* to the closing one of the *Paradiso,* Dante the poet presents his pilgrim as continuously learning, his spiritual development being the main theme of the entire poem. His progress is slow, and there are even occasional backslidings.

In *Inferno* 4 the pilgrim and his guide, Vergil, who are now in Limbo, see a hemisphere of light glowing in the distance, and as they move toward it they are met by four great pagan poets. Vergil explains to his ward:

> "Observe the one who comes with sword in
> hand,
> leading the three as if he were their master.
>
> It is the shade of Homer, sovereign poet,
> and coming second, Horace, the satirist;
> Ovid is the third, and last comes Lucan.
> (86–90)

Together with Vergil these four non-Christians form the group of those classical poets whom Dante most admired and from whom he drew much of the material for his poem. It must be said, however, that while Homer was known in the Middle Ages as the first of the great epic poets, the author of the *Iliad* and *Odyssey,* few people, including Dante, could read Greek; thus Homer's great epics were known almost entirely second-hand through the revised version of Dares and Dictys, who told the tale of the Trojan war in a way that exalted the Trojans and often disparaged the Greeks. Dante admired Homer more for his reputation than for any intimate knowledge that he had of his works. The second of the four is Horace, whom Dante calls the "satirist" but whom he must have thought of mainly as a moralist since Dante was familiar only with the *Ars poetica.* Ovid, who comes next, was the most widely read Roman poet in the Middle Ages, and he was Dante's main source of mythology in the *Commedia.* Dante, however, seems to have been acquainted with only the *Metamorphoses.* Coming last is Lucan, author of the *Pharsalia,* which deals with the Roman civil war between the legions of Pompey and those of Caesar. The book was one of Dante's important historical sources.

When the pilgrim and his guide have seen all there is to see of sin (canto 34) they find they must exit from Hell by climbing down Lucifer's monstrous, hairy body. Only by grappling with sin itself, by knowing the foundation of all sin, which is pride, personified in the hideous figure of Lucifer frozen in the ice at the very center of the universe, can they hope to make their way out "to see again the stars."

The island-mountain of Purgatory, invented by Dante, is divided into three parts. At the very top is the Earthly Paradise; the upper part of the mountain is sealed off from the lower by a gate that a resplendent angel guards, equipped with St. Peter's keys. This upper half, with its seven cornices corresponding to the seven deadly sins, is reserved for those who have been permitted to enter the gate from below in order to begin the self-willed torments of their purgation; after its accomplishment they pass to the Earthly Paradise, from which they ascend to Heaven. In the lower half, the "Antepurgatory," dwell those souls who are not yet ready to begin their purgation. As for the reason why certain souls are forced to put off the experience they all desire, the pilgrim is told by a number of individuals he meets that, while alive, they had put off repentance until the end (thus their delay is in the nature of a *contrapasso,* or retribution); it is generally accepted that all of the inhabitants of the Antepurgatory are to be considered as "late repentants." (The Antepurgatory is dealt with in the first nine cantos.) This mountain (whose creation was the miraculous result of Lucifer's fall) keeps not only those assigned to Purgatory but also those destined for immediate passage to Heaven.

The middle portion of the mountain of Purgatory is surrounded by seven concentric ledges, each separated from the other by a steep cliff. On each ledge, or terrace, one of the seven capital sins is purged: Pride, Envy, Wrath, Sloth, Avarice (and Prodigality), Gluttony, Lust. The setup of the First Terrace (cantos 9–12), where souls are being punished for the sin of Pride, establishes the pattern of purgation that is followed throughout Purgatory proper.

Each group of souls on its particular terrace is assigned a prayer. When a soul has finished purging his sin on one level, he climbs to the next via a stairway, where there is an angel-sentry who performs a final cleansing gesture. A beatitude appropriate to the sin that has been cleansed is assigned to each ledge. In addition, on each terrace of Purgatory, representations of the sin being purged there are found, as well as examples of the virtue which is opposed to that sin. The representation of the sin is intended to incite disdain for the sin, while that of the virtue is designed to inspire souls to the emulation of virtuous behavior. These representations take on various forms—on the First Terrace they appear as carvings in the stone of the mountain—and both "disdain for the sin" and "inspiration for virtuous behavior" are drawn from examples of Christian and pagan love. But the first example of every virtue is always taken from the life of the Blessed Virgin Mary.

In the first canto of the *Purgatorio* Dante and Vergil are at the foot of a mountain again, and the reader is naturally reminded of the first canto of the *Inferno:* it is the same mountain, the one they could not climb then, because Dante was not spiritually prepared. But now, having investigated all sin, having shaken off pride during his perilous descent into humility, Dante will be able to climb the mountain.

Purgatory is a place of repentence, regeneration, conversion. Though the punishments inflicted on the penitents here are often more severe than in Hell, the atmosphere is totally different: it is one of sweet encounters, culminating in Dante's reunion with Beatrice in the Earthly Paradise and Vergil's elegant disappearance. Brotherly love and humility reign here, necessary qualities for the successful journey of man's mind to God. Everyone here is destined to see God eventually; the predominant image is one of homesickness (especially in the Antepurgatory), a yearning to return to man's real home in Heaven. Toward the close of the *Purgatorio* the time comes for Beatrice (divine revelation) to take charge of the pilgrim; human reason (Vergil) can take man only so far; it cannot show him God or explain his many mysteries.

The *Paradiso* is an attempt to describe the religious life, one in which man centers his attention wholly on God, divine truth, and ultimate happiness. Only in perfect knowledge of the true God can man have perfect happiness.

Unlike Hell and Purgatory, Heaven in Dante's poem does not exist in a physical sense. The celestial spheres through which the pilgrim and his guide, Beatrice, ascend and in which the souls of the blessed appear to the wayfarer are not part of the real Paradise. That place is beyond the spheres and beyond space and time; it is the Empyrean, and Beatrice takes pains to explain this early in the *Paradiso*, while they are in the first sphere of the moon:

> Not the most godlike of the seraphim,
> not Moses, Samuel, whichever John
> you choose—I tell you—not Mary herself
>
> has been assigned to any other heaven
> than that of these shades you have just seen here,
> and each one's bliss is equally eternal;
>
> all lend their beauty to the highest sphere,
> sharing one sweet life to the degree
> that they can feel the eternal breath of God.
> (4.28–36)

The dominant image in this realm is light. God is light, and the pilgrim's goal from the very start was to reach the light (we are reminded of the casual mention of the rays of the sun behind the mountain in the opening canto).

The formal beauty of the *Commedia* should not be dissociated from its spiritual message. The universal appeal of the poem comes precisely from a combination of the two: poetry and philosophy. For Dante, though not for the majority of poets of the Renaissance, ultimate truth was known—in principle it was contained in the *Summa* of Saint Thomas Aquinas, and the doctrine of the *Commedia* comes largely from the writings of Aquinas and the other church fathers.

Dante was in accord with Hugh of Saint Victor, who, in his *Didascalia* (6.5), says: "Contemplating what God has done, we learn what is for us to do. All nature speaks God. All nature teaches man." Dante, then, with his special kind of allegory, tries to imitate God: the symbolic world he creates in his poem is in principle a mirror of the actual world created by God himself.

## DANTE ALIGHIERI

# Selected Bibliography


EDITIONS

*Commedia* [*Divine Comedy*]. Foligno: Johannes Numeister, 1472. Reprinted with the texts of Jesi, Mantua, and Naples by Lord Vernon as *Le prime quattro edizione della "Divina commedia."* London, 1878. A copy is in the Fiske Collection of the Cornell University Library.

*Convivio.* Florence: Francesco Bonaccorsi, 1490. Copies are in the Fiske Collection of the Cornell University Library and in the Yale University Library.

*De monarchia.* Basel: Joannes Operinus, 1559. Reprinted, edited by Enrico Rostagno, in the *Opere* of the Società Dantesca, 2nd ed. (Florence, 1960).

*Vita nuova.* Florence: Bartolomeo Sermatelli, 1576. There are forty manuscripts, many of which are not complete.

*De vulgari eloquentia.* Paris: Jacopo Corbinelli, 1577. A translation into Italian by G. G. Trissino appeared before this (Vicenza, 1529).

*Prose antiche di Dante, Petrarcha, et Boccaccio, etc.* Edited by Anton Francesco Doni. Florence, 1547. The first printed edition of Dante's letters. The first edition of all of the letters is by Alessandro Torri (Livorno, 1842).

TRANSLATIONS

Ciardi, John. *The Paradiso.* New York, 1970.

Foster, K., and P. Boyde. *Dante's Lyric Poetry.* 2 vols. Oxford, 1967.

Haller, Robert S. *Literary Criticism of Dante Alighieri.* Lincoln, Neb., 1973.

Longfellow, Henry Wadsworth. *The Divine Comedy.* Boston and New York, 1895.

Musa, Mark. *Dante's "Inferno."* Bloomington, Ind., 1971.

———. *Dante's "Purgatory."* Bloomington, Ind., 1981.

———. *Dante's "Vita nuova": A Translation and an Essay.* Bloomington, Ind., 1973.

Sayers, Dorothy L. *Purgatory.* New York, 1955.

Schneider, E. W. *On World Government.* Indianapolis, 1957.

Sinclair, John D. *The Divine Comedy.* New York, 1948.

Temple Classics edition. London, 1899. Reprinted New York, 1904. Contains all of Dante's works in six volumes: *Vita nuova and Canzoniere* (Italian and English); *Convivio* (English only); Latin works (English only: includes *De vulgari eloquentia, De monarchia, Epistles and Eclogues, Questio de aqua et terra*); *Inferno* (Italian and English); *Purgatorio* (Italian and English); *Paradiso* (Italian and English).

COMMENTARIES

Brewer, Wilmon. *Eclogues.* Boston, 1927.

Burbi, Michele. *Vita nuova.* Florence, 1932.

Busnelli, G., and G. Vandelli. *Convivio.* Florence, 1934.

Chimenz, Siro A. *La "Divina commedia" di Dante Alighieri.* Turin, 1968.

Contini, Gianfranco. *Rime di Dante.* Turin, 1946.

Grandgent, Charles H. *La "Divina commedia."* Revised by Charles S. Singleton. Cambridge, 1972.

Marigo, A. *De vulgari eloquentia.* Florence, 1938.

Momigliano, Attilio. *La "Divina commedia" di Dante Alighieri.* Florence, 1956.

Petrocchi, Giorgio. *La "Commedia" secondo l'antica vulgata.* 4 vols. Milan, 1966–1967.

Porena, Manfredi. *La "Divina commedia" di Dante Alighieri.* Bologna, 1964.

Sapegno, Natalio. *La "Divina commedia" di Dante Alighieri.* Florence, 1955–1957.

Toynbee, Paget. *Dante's Letters.* Oxford, 1920.

Vandelli, Giuseppe. *La "Divina commedia."* Milan, 1952.

Vinay, Gustavo. *De monarchia.* Florence, 1950.

REFERENCE WORKS AND BIBLIOGRAPHICAL SOURCES

Barbi, Michele. *Life of Dante.* Edited and translated by Paul Ruggiers. Gloucester, Mass., 1962.

Bosco, Umberto, ed. *Enciclopedia dantesca.* 5 vols. Rome, 1970.

Cosmos, Umberto. *Handbook to Dante Studies.* Oxford, 1950.

Dante Society of America, Inc. *Dante Studies: With the Annual Report of the Dante Society.* Edited by Anthony L. Pellegrini. Albany, N.Y., 1966. First published as the *Annual Report of the Dante Society.* Cambridge, Mass., 1882–1954.

Dinsmore, Charles Allen. *Aids to the Study of Dante.* Boston and New York, 1903.

Esposito, Enzo. *Gli studi danteschi dal 1950 al 1964.* Rome, 1965.

Gardner, Edmund G. *Dante.* London, 1905.

Toynbee, Paget. *Dante in English Literature from Chaucer to Cary.* 2 vols. London, 1909.

———. *A Dictionary of Proper Names and Notable Matters in Works of Dante.* Revised by Charles S. Singleton. Oxford, 1968.

## CRITICAL STUDIES

Auerbach, Erich. *Dante: Poet of the Secular World.* Translated by Ralph Manheim. Chicago, 1961.

Bergin, Thomas. *Dante.* Boston, 1965.

———. *A Diversity of Dante.* New Brunswick, N.J., 1969.

Brandeis, Irma. *The Ladder of Vision: A Study of Dante's Comedy.* New York, 1961.

Carroll, John S. *Prisoners of Hope.* Port Washington, N.Y., 1971.

Davis, Charles Till. *Dante and the Idea of Rome.* Oxford, 1957.

Demaray, John I. *The Invention of Dante's "Commedia."* New Haven, Conn., 1979.

D'Entrèves, Passerin. *Dante as a Political Thinker.* Oxford, 1952.

Dunbar, H. Flanders. *Symbolism in Medieval Thought and Its Culmination in the "Divine Comedy."* New York, 1961.

Fergusson, Francis. *Dante's Drama of the Mind: A Modern Reading of the "Purgatorio."* Princeton, 1952.

Fletcher, Jefferson Butler. *Dante.* Notre Dame, Ind., 1965.

Gardner, Edmund G. *Dante and the Mystics.* London, 1913.

Gilson, Étienne. *Dante the Philosopher.* New York, 1949.

Lansing, Richard H. *From Image to Idea: A Study of the Simile in Dante's "Commedia."* Ravenna, 1977.

Mazzeo, Joseph Anthony. *Structure and Thought in the "Paradiso."* Ithaca, N.Y., 1958.

Montanari, Fausto. *L'Esperienza poetica di Dante.* Florence, 1959.

Montano, Rocco. *Storia della poesia di Dante.* Naples, 1962.

Musa, Mark. *Advent at the Gates: Dante's "Comedy."* Bloomington, Ind., 1974.

———. *Essays on Dante.* Bloomington, Ind., 1964.

Nardi, Bruno. *Nel mondo di Dante.* Rome, 1944.

Nolan, David, ed. *Dante Commentaries.* Totowa, N.J., 1977.

Orr, M. A. *Dante and the Early Astronomers.* Rev. ed., London, 1956.

Sayers, Dorothy L. *Further Papers on Dante.* New York, 1957.

———. *Introductory Papers on Dante.* New York, 1959.

Singleton, Charles S. *Dante Studies (I).* Cambridge, 1954.

Thompson, David. *Dante's Epic Journeys.* Baltimore, 1974.

MARK MUSA

# RENÉ DESCARTES
## *(1596–1650)*

RENÉ DESCARTES, "the father of modern philosophy," was one of the pivotal characters in the intellectual transition from the Middle Ages to the Renaissance. His revolutionary picture of the sciences as constituting a unified whole liberated the scientist from medieval dogma and was the single most significant contribution to the sciences until the publication of Sir Isaac Newton's *Principia* more than half a century later. Equally important as the scientific doctrines are their underpinnings in the metaphysical view of the universe that Descartes propounded. With the publication of the *Meditations* in 1641, Descartes changed man's conception of the world.

This essay will attempt to provide a three-dimensional picture of Descartes. Interspersed throughout a sketch of his life are discussions of the major historical and philosophical trends that Descartes challenged. Most important, the reader will be introduced to Descartes's monumental work, the *Meditations,* and will have the opportunity to explore this treatise with a certain degree of philosophical rigor. The motivations for Descartes's views will also be discussed in order to help the reader appreciate him not only as a great philosopher and scientist but also as a man—one of those rare men whose thoughts and speculations have come to shape our vision of the world.

René du Perron Descartes was born at La Haye, Touraine, on 30 March 1596, the third son of Joachim Descartes. His father had chosen the profession of law, and had obtained the independent judicial appointment of counsellor to the Parlement of Britanny. His mother died of a lung infection a few days after his birth. He tells us, "I inherited from her a dry cough and a pale complexion, which I retained to the age of more than twenty, and which caused all the doctors who saw me before that time to condemn me to die young" (*Oeuvres de Descartes* 1:300–301).

At the age of eight, Descartes was sent to the Jesuit school of La Flèche in Anjou. La Flèche had recently been founded by Henry IV to offer a superior education to the sons of the nobility. The king was so committed to the school that he directed in his will that his heart be buried there—a directive that was carried out six years after the young Descartes arrived, in a ceremony that found him one of twenty-four young gentlemen who walked in the funeral procession.

Descartes was apparently quite happy at La Flèche; he speaks highly of his life there. Indeed there was one event that seems to have made a lasting mark on him. On the anniversary of the death of Henry IV, the *Henriade* sonnets (as they were called) were read by the students celebrating various advances in the sciences. One sonnet, "On the Death of King Henry the Great and on the Discovery of Some New Planets or Stars Moving Around Jupiter, Made This Year by Galileo, Celebrated Mathematician of the Grand Duke of Florence," seems to have caught the attention of the young Descartes. For not only was the discovery of the moons of Jupiter important, but the use of the telescope was enlarging man's view of the universe. Descartes was wholly in favor of this expansion of man's horizons, and it is not unusual that a young man's curiosity might be piqued by such discoveries. Descartes remained interested in the heavens throughout his life, his interest culminating in such works as *Le monde,* the *Meteors,* and the *Dioptrics.* From this celebration at the *Henriade* Descartes grew to respect Galileo as he did few other men, and as we shall see, Galileo's condemnation would have a profound effect on Descartes's published works.

While at La Flèche, Descartes was considered an extraordinary student; teachers and fellow classmates acknowledged his remarkable talents. Yet after eight and a half years, he left the school resolved to forsake the study of books forever because he thought they were a waste of time. In his own words:

> I have been nourished on letters since my childhood, and since I was given to believe that by their means a clear and certain knowledge could be obtained of all that is useful in life, I had an extreme desire to acquire instruction. But so soon as I had achieved the entire course of study at the close of which one is usually received into the ranks of the learned, I entirely changed my opinion. For I found myself embarrassed with so many doubts and errors that it seemed to me that the effort to instruct myself had no effect other than the increasing discovery of my own ignorance. And yet I was studying at one of the most celebrated Schools in Europe, where I thought that there must be men of learning if they were to be found anywhere in the world. I learned there all that others learned; and not being satisfied with the sciences that we were taught, I even read through all the books which fell into my hands, treating of what is considered most curious and rare. Along with this I knew the judgments that others had formed of me, and I did not feel that I was esteemed inferior to my fellow-students, although there were amongst them some destined to fill the places of our masters. And finally our century seemed to me as flourishing, and as fertile in great minds, as any which had preceded. And this made me take the liberty of judging all others by myself and of coming to the conclusion that there was no learning in the world such as I was formerly led to believe it to be.
>
> (*The Philosophical Works of Descartes* 1:83–84)

It was for these reasons that Descartes "abandoned the study of letters, and resolved to seek no other science than I could find within myself or in the great book of the world."

At the age of sixteen and a half Descartes returned to his family in Rennes. He was now obliged to decide on a career. He pondered the possibilities, apparently at great length, but was unable to convince himself of the suitability of any of the traditional occupations for a person of his standing. He spent two years at home and finally settled on joining the army. His father sent him to Paris, a necessary preliminary to his service.

In Paris he became reacquainted with an older schoolmate, Père Mersenne, who was at the time a Franciscan monk in a Minorite convent. His conversations with Mersenne caused Descartes to return to those matters that had preoccupied him at La Flèche. He began to wrestle with the two conflicting parts of his mind—the one part with its aversion to book learning and the other with its craving for "intellectual occupation." Descartes's need to effect a fusion of these two divided parts prompted a search that eventually led to the formation of his famous method. It was only a year after Descartes's renewed friendship with Mersenne that the latter left Paris to take up a professorship in philosophy at Nevers. Descartes disappeared from Paris after Mersenne left and turned up in the army several months later.

It is fair to say that Descartes's military career was not a particularly distinguished one. He first took service under the banners of

Maurice of Nassau (May 1617); two years later he passed into temporary service with the Catholic emperor Ferdinand. If Descartes ever fought in battle, was wounded, or indeed drew a sword, it is not recorded. There is but one surviving anecdote concerning his military career. One day, as Descartes was walking down a street in Breda, a placard on a wall caught his eye. The placard contained a mathematical problem with an invitation to solve it. Descartes was familiar with the diagram, but the terms were in Flemish. He asked a bystander for translation. The bystander happened to be the famous mathematician Isaac Beeckman, who answered that he would provide one only if Descartes would provide a solution. The next day Descartes called on Beeckman with the problem solved.

Beeckman was eight years older than Descartes, and he assumed the role of teacher in their relationship. He was fond of comparing Descartes to a top that remains upright while spinning. "René," he wrote, "makes me think that a man could hold himself upright in space." The first result of Beeckman's influence was Descartes's treatise on music, the *Compendium musicae* (completed 1618). Descartes dedicated the work to his friend with the stipulation that it would be kept secret, as he felt it was unsuitable for publication. The work was not published until 1650, after Descartes's death. Because of Beeckman, Descartes was once more drawn toward the intellectual life. He wrote:

> To speak truthfully, you alone have drawn me from my idleness and made me remember what I had learned and almost forgotten; when my mind was wandering from serious occupations, you brought it back to the right path. If I produce anything of merit, you will be entitled to claim it entirely for yourself.
>
> (*Oeuvres* 1.14)

But by 1630 Descartes would regret having made such a statement of indebtedness. Beeckman bragged to Mersenne and others that it was he who was the source of Descartes's ideas. In an uncommon fit of temper, Descartes requested that Beeckman return the manuscripts in his possession and wrote to him:

> When you boast of such things in front of people who know me, it injures your reputation. . . . And you have shown my letters as testimony for naught because one knows that I am accustomed to instructing myself even with ants and worms, and one will think that this is how I used you.
>
> (1.144–145)

The quarrel soon passed, and they were friends again a year later.

Beeckman left Breda for Middleberg on 2 January 1619, leaving behind a Descartes who was full of creative energy. For several months Descartes stayed in or around Breda, consumed in his work. Finally, at the end of April he set off for Germany, where he spent almost six months touring the country. By winter he had settled at Neuberg on the Danube. There he rented a heated room, his *poêle,* and spent long hours locked inside in contemplation. He became more and more convinced that there was something important to come of his studies, a conviction that caused him to push himself even harder.

On 10 November 1619, Descartes found what he had been looking for. Having worked himself into an almost delirious state, he was struck with a "blinding flash" of insight and he realized his discovery—that all of the sciences should be studied as a unified whole. He described the significance of this idea twenty years later in *Discours de la méthode* (*Discourse on Method*, 1637):

> Those long chains of reasoning, simple and easy as they are, of which geometricians make use in order to arrive at the most difficult demonstrations, had caused me to imagine that all those things which fall under the cognizance of man might very likely be mutually related in the same fashion; and that, provided only that we

> abstain from receiving anything as true which is not so, and always retain the order which is necessary in order to deduce the one conclusion from the other, there can be nothing so remote that we cannot reach to it, nor so recondite that we cannot discover it.
>
> (*Philosophical Works* 1.92)

The significance of Descartes's discovery should not be underestimated. The discovery of the unity of human knowledge was a major (if not *the* major) breakthrough of the modern era.

The evening of 10 November was one of the most important in Descartes's life. The *Discourse on Method* refers to the three dreams in which his "vocation" was revealed. Descartes wrote out in minute detail a description of these dreams, which is now unfortunately lost to us. We have, however, an account (paraphrased below) of them by Descartes's earliest biographer, Adrien Baillet.

In the first dream Descartes struggles against a strong wind that constantly whirls him about as he tries to reach the church of the college (presumably La Flèche) in order to say his prayers. At one point, as he is turning to bow to someone he has neglected to greet, the wind blows him violently against the church. Someone yells to him from the middle of the courtyard, telling him that an acquaintance of his has a gift for him—a melon. At this point Descartes awakened and rolled over on his right side. He prayed to God for protection from the effects of the dream.

He then had a second dream—of a burst of noise like a crack of thunder—and awakened from it to see thousands of sparks in his room.

His third dream, unlike the first two, contains nothing frightening, but is much more complicated. In this dream, Descartes notices a book on a table. He goes over to it, opens it, and is delighted to find that it is a dictionary. He then finds a second book, a collection of poems entitled *Corpus poetarum.* Out of curiosity he opens the book and the line "Quod vitae sectabor iter?" (What path shall I follow in life?) catches his eye. As Descartes is reading, an unknown man hands him some verses beginning with the words "Est et non." Descartes tells the man that he knows the poem well, that it comes from the *Idylls* of Ausonius, one of the authors in the bulky dictionary on the table. As Descartes goes to the table to fetch the book, the man asks him where he got it. Descartes is unable to answer and notices that the book has disappeared. No sooner does he say so than it reappears on the other end of the table. But this book is slightly different from the dictionary he saw before. He searches for the passage from Ausonius beginning "Est et non," but he cannot find it. At this point both the book and the man disappear, yet Descartes does not awaken. While still asleep, he proceeds to interpret the significance of the dream. He judges that the dictionary signifies all the sciences, and that the *Corpus poetarum* signifies the unity of philosophy with wisdom. The words "Est et non," which are the "Yes and No of Pythagoras," represent truth and falsity in human achievement in the secular sciences; the section beginning "Quod vitae sectabor iter?" marks the good advice of a wise person, or even moral theology.

Descartes believed that the first two dreams were admonitions touching his past life. The melon offered in the first dream symbolized solitude. The wind that whirled him around toward the church was an evil genius who, according to Baillet, "was to throw him by force into a place where it was his design to go voluntarily." Finally, the lightning of the second dream was nothing less than the spirit of truth descending on him (*Oeuvres* 6.9).

It is interesting that many of those whom Descartes told of his dreams counseled him to keep them a secret, lest he be thought a madman. Yet these very dreams told Descartes what path to follow. He had found the synthesis that he had sought for so long. With the sciences now unified in his thinking, he was able to fuse his own divided thoughts. Not only had he found what he saw as the correct way of interpreting the sciences, but his method—always proceeding from the most simple to the most complex, and never assuming the truth of anything that has not been proven to be true—assured his concept a validity that was not present before this point in the history of ideas. His method supplied a degree of certainty to our metaphysical picture of the world, and it was this certainty that Descartes saw as all important.

During the following years Descartes spent much of his time traveling. By 1628 he had settled in Paris and prepared to reveal his discovery. Monsieur de Baigne, the papal nuncio, had invited a group of scholars to listen to a lecture by Chandoux—"an extremely capable professor of chemistry"—who was to speak against the Aristotelian system of scientific inquiry. His lecture was eloquently delivered and urged opposition to what he called the "yoke of scholasticism." He went on to propose another system to replace the one currently taught in the schools. The lecture was received enthusiastically by everyone in the hall except Descartes. His coolness was noticed by Cardinal de Bérulle, who requested that Descartes explain his dissatisfaction with the lecture. Descartes responded that the cardinal was surely a more capable judge than he concerning matters such as these, and asked to be excused. The cardinal, seconded by the nuncio, urged him to voice his opinion, making it clear that Descartes could not refuse.

Descartes began by praising Chandoux for his attempt to pull philosophy away from scholasticism. He then pointed out that unless any system, including the one propounded by Chandoux, had some foundation in certainty, it could be only a plausible system, not one that could be considered metaphysically true. At this point the audience began to voice its dissent. Descartes urged the audience to bear with him. He proceeded to take a statement that was widely considered to be true, and by "twelve evident reasons" showed that it was false. He did likewise with a proposition that everyone considered false. Just what these "twelve evident reasons" were is lost to us now, but they apparently had quite an impact on the audience. Descartes went on to argue that any system not grounded in certainty would be caught in paradoxes, and hence could be called only a plausible system. Entreated to tell the audience what his method was, Descartes gave only several hints and apologized because his theory was incomplete. His performance at this public lecture had a profound effect on everyone in the room. Chandoux, who felt he had been humiliated by Descartes, gave up the study of philosophy altogether. He was hanged a few years later for passing counterfeit money. Cardinal de Bérulle took Descartes aside after the lecture and convinced him that he must go forth and complete his method, telling him that it was God's will for him to do so.

At the end of 1628 Descartes left Paris for Holland to begin what he called a self-imposed exile, which lasted almost twenty years. The immediate cause of his move was the difficulty of maintaining in Paris the anonymity he thought was essential to his work. Descartes found Holland an almost ideal place to study. He wrote to his friend Balzac:

> Here I sleep ten hours every night without being disturbed by any care. After my mind has wandered in sleep through woods, gardens, and enchanted palaces where I experience every pleasure imaginable, I awake to mingle the reveries of the night with those of the day.
>
> (*Oeuvres* 1.86)

In another letter to Balzac, Descartes praised city life because it ensured his all-important anonymity. And in 1639 he wrote Mersenne:

> I work very slowly, because I take much more pleasure in instructing myself than in putting into writing the little that I know. . . . I pass my time so pleasantly in instructing myself that I never set myself to writing my Treatise except by constraint, and in order to acquit myself of the resolution I have taken, which is, if I live, to put

> myself in a condition to send it to you in the beginning of the year 1633.
>
> (1.190)

While Descartes was in Holland he went to great lengths to protect his privacy. Only Mersenne knew of his whereabouts for long periods of time. His life was a shuttle back and forth between the anonymity of the city and the quiet of the country. But whenever he felt that someone was looking for him, or that he was in danger of being found, Descartes would move. He didn't want to waste time explaining or justifying his thoughts to others and, above all, he needed the time to refine them.

In July 1633 Descartes wrote Mersenne that his treatise was almost finished and that he would send a completed copy to him by the end of the year. Just as all was ready, Descartes learned of the fate of Galileo. The church had just condemned Galileo's *Dialogue Concerning the Two Chief World Systems.* It forced the author to sign a formal abjuration of his belief in the Copernican system and imprisoned him for an indefinite term. It also ordered copies of the work to be publicly burned. So distressed was Descartes, a devout Catholic, that he wrote Mersenne:

> I was so astounded that I have half a mind to burn all my papers or at least not to show them to anyone. I cannot imagine that an Italian, and especially one well thought of by the Pope from what I have heard, could have been labeled a criminal for nothing other than wanting to establish the movement of the earth. I know that this had been censured formally by a few Cardinals, but I thought that since that time one was allowed to teach it publicly even in Rome. I confess that if this is false then all the principles of my philosophy are false also. . . . And because I would not want for anything in the world to be the author of a book where there was the slightest word of which the Church might disapprove, I would rather suppress it altogether than to have it appear incomplete—"crippled" as it were.
>
> (1.241–242)

Mersenne was never to see a copy of the work referred to in the letter. *Le monde* would not be published until after Descartes's death. One might imagine that the shock over Galileo would have caused Descartes to cease his work altogether, but fortunately he did not. Descartes embarked on another project. In March 1636 he wrote Mersenne to ask him to arrange for the printing of a volume that would contain four treatises, entitled *Project of a Universal Science, Which Can Raise Our Nature to Its Highest Degree of Perfection; also Dioptrics, Meteors, and Geometry, Wherein the Most Curious Matters Which the Author Could Select, In Order To Give Proofs of the Universal Science He Sets Forth, Are Explained in Such a Manner That Even Those Who Have Not Studied May Understand Them.* The book was published in 1637, although not in Paris; and it bore the more modest title *Discourse on the Method of Rightly Conducting the Reason and Seeking Truth in the Sciences. Next to the Dioptric, the Meteors, and the Geometry, Essays in This Method.*

This first published work by Descartes astounded many of those who read it. A work of far-reaching genius, it was accessible to many nonscholars because it was written in French, almost unheard of at a time when all "serious" books were written in Latin. Concerning this, Descartes wrote:

> If I write in French, which is the language of my country, rather than in Latin, which is that of my preceptors, it is because I hope that those who use only their natural reason will be better judges of my ideas than those who only believe in ancient texts; and as for those who join good sense with study, those alone whom I desire as judges, they will not be so partial toward Latin that they will refuse to understand my reasoning just because I explain things in the vulgar tongue.
>
> (6.77–78)

The cornerstone of the *Discourse* is Descartes's formulation of the four rules of method. An examination of these rules should lead the reader more closely to modern scientific method than any other single work, for it is these rules that in fact define scientific method. Descartes writes:

> The first of these was to accept nothing as true which I did not clearly recognize to be so: that is to say, carefully to avoid precipitation and prejudice in judgments, and to accept in them nothing more than what was presented to my mind so clearly and distinctly that I could have no occasion to doubt it.
>
> The second was to divide up each of the difficulties which I examined into as many parts as possible, and as seemed requisite in order that it might be resolved in the best manner possible.
>
> The third was to carry on my reflections in due order, commencing with objects that were the most simple and easy to understand, in order to rise little by little, or by degrees, to knowledge of the most complex, assuming an order, even if a fictitious one, among those which do not follow a natural sequence relatively to one another.
>
> The last was in all cases to make enumerations so complete and reviews so general that I should be certain of having omitted nothing.
>
> (*Philosophical Works* 1.92)

Descartes goes on from this point to describe how following these simple rules leads to the establishment of a system whose foundation is certainty.

The *Discourse* is a most interesting work. It is organized into six chapters, each of which treats a completely different subject. These chapters are followed by three separate works—*La dioptrique* (the *Dioptrics*), *Météores* (the *Meteors*), and *La géométrie* (the *Geometry*)—each of which is an attempt by the author to extend the method to matters of current scientific interest. The first six chapters of the *Discourse* comprise a work that is part biography, part philosophy, part science. Chapter 1 is concerned almost exclusively with Descartes's life at La Flèche and explains his rejection of the "schools" and academic life. Chapter 2 concerns the three dreams of 10 November 1619 and contains the four rules given above. Chapter 3 concerns the best way to conduct one's life. Chapter 4 is given over to more purely metaphysical speculation and contains the "I think, therefore I am," which may be the most famous adage in the history of philosophy. In chapter 5 we find a discussion of physics and biology, and chapter 6 serves as a conclusion.

Concerning the *Discourse,* Descartes wrote to a friend: "My only purpose in printing at this time is to prepare the way for another work which I hope to bring out in case the public should desire it, and I think that they will. I am testing the waters" (*Oeuvres* 1.300–301). The publication was most certainly successful in "testing the waters." It plunged Descartes into a controversy with all manner of learned men. It seemed that the public would want another work.

In November 1639 Descartes wrote Mersenne:

> I am now working on a discourse in which I try to clarify what I have hitherto written on this topic. It will be only five or six printed sheets but I hope it will contain a great part of Metaphysics. To make it as good as possible, I plan to have only twenty or thirty copies printed, and send them to the twenty or thirty most learned theologians I can find, so as to have their criticisms and learn what should be changed, corrected or added before publication.
>
> (*Descartes: Philosophical Letters* 68)

This letter marked the first announcement of what was to become one of the most influential works in the history of philosophy. Descartes did in fact distribute copies to some of the learned men of the time. Among them were Mersenne, Pierre Gassendi, Thomas Hobbes, Antoine Arnauld, Pierre Bourdin, and the Jesuit fathers of the Sorbonne. Descartes explained to them that their objections to the work, *Meditations on First Philosophy,* would be published together with his replies. In August 1641 the text of the *Meditations* and the

"Objections and Replies" (which constitutes the largest portion of the book) was published in Paris. The *Meditations* is Descartes's most representative work. It provides a nearly complete expression of his epistemological and metaphysical doctrines.

In order to understand the motivations behind the *Meditations,* and before examining it in detail, it is useful to look at the social and intellectual context in which it was produced. The sixteenth century was a period of considerable intellectual upheaval for a number of reasons. Chief among these were the effects of the recent explorations by European seamen who returned with stories of strange cultures and foreign lands where beliefs, values, and ways of living were at wide variance with established customs at home. The overturn of Ptolemaic astronomy following the publication in 1543 of Copernicus' heliocentric theory of planetary motion and the Protestant Reformation brought about by Martin Luther's challenge to the authority of the Catholic church also had an unsettling effect on the confidence with which people held the philosophical and religious beliefs they had grown up with.

The overthrow of the geocentric theory in astronomy tended to undermine the confidence of intellectuals in the security of scientific theory. If a belief that had existed for a thousand years and seemed obviously true could be subverted in such a short period of time, it was not clear whether any of the other accepted opinions regarding the nature of the physical world could still be held with confidence. Even more disturbing was the confusion engendered by the Protestant Reformation regarding the question of religious truth. Prior to Luther's time there was no question about the methodology for settling disputes in matters of religion. In the Catholic church the pope was the final authority on religious questions, and when he spoke ex cathedra on the interpretation of Scripture, he spoke as God's representative on earth. However, Luther's challenge cut at the very heart of religious dogma. Whereas the Catholic church held the pronouncements of papal authority to be the sole criteria of religious truth, Luther claimed that what was true in religion was what one's conscience compelled one to believe after thorough and careful reading of Scripture. That Luther's judgment of religious truth was accepted by many would have been sufficient in itself to cause a general intellectual upheaval. The real damage done by Luther was much more severe: he had raised the question of the adequacy of any putative criterion of truth.

The problem posed by Luther's challenge was this: How can we adjudicate disputes between competing criteria of truth? In attempting to answer the question, one quickly sees that what is needed is some criterion to enable us to select among competing criteria. The possibility of selection raises the further question, however, of how one would defend challenges to the criterion in question. If Luther were asked "How do you know that your conscience is what is right to believe in religious matters?" he would respond that he was convinced of this because his conscience compelled him to believe it. Similarly, a spokesman for the Catholic church would argue that the pope is the final authority on matters of religion because that is what the pope says, and he speaks for God. Appeal to advocates will not help solve the problem, but neither does it appear that the answer lies in the search for some independent standard of adjudication. Any criterion that we select for objective determination of the matter will itself be open to challenge, and additional criteria will be needed to defend it. The task is obviously a hopeless one. Recognition of this fact led naturally to the skeptical conclusion that one person's opinion is as good as another's and that no rational means can be found for proving any one opinion correct over another.

In accounting for the general intellectual upheaval of the time, something else is as important as the revolutions in astronomy and religion: the discovery in the middle of the sixteenth century of the manuscript of Sextus Empiricus, a third-century skeptic. Sextus distinguished two varieties of skepticism: academic skepticism and Pyrrhonian skepticism. Academic skepticism maintains that no one knows anything, but that some opinions are probably more true than others, and it is prudent to act on those opinions that have probability in their favor. Pyrrhonian skepticism denies that some opinions are more probable than others. It does this in virtue of a problem like Luther's: the impossibility of defending criteria of the adequacy of criteria themselves. The problem, according to Pyrrhonian skeptics, is that one who maintains that some opinions are more probable than others must have some means of assessing relative probability. The difficulty is that there is no way to be sure that any criterion of probability is correct. Again we need a criterion to validate a criterion of probability, and no such criterion is available. Were a candidate offered, we would have the additional problem of validating it, and so on. The problem, as before, seems unsolvable. The effect of recognizing as much is often intellectual despair.

Sextus' catalog of skeptical arguments was made known to sixteenth-century Parisians through the works of Michel de Montaigne, particularly his *Apology for Raymond Sebond* (1576). Montaigne's arguments for skepticism gained popularity, and it became quite widely held that any intellectual doctrine could be defended or defeated by one possessed of sufficient intellectual tools. Reason came to be seen as inducive to an attitude of skepticism.

It was probably in response to the popularity of skepticism and the apparent hopelessness of any attempt to acquire concrete human knowledge that Descartes believed any attempt to construct a philosophical system was doomed to failure without indubitable and certain foundations. At any rate there is no doubt that in the First Meditation he is at pains to discover a proposition that he can know with certainty and that can form the basis of his philosophical system.

The subtitle that Descartes gives his First Meditation is "What Can Be Called into Question," and is, as one might guess, a direct result of his first rule of method from the *Discourse.* He begins by telling the reader that it will be necessary to take a fresh look at all accepted opinions:

> But inasmuch as reason already persuades me that I ought no less carefully to withhold my assent from matters that are not entirely certain and indubitable than from those which appear to me manifestly to be false, if I am able to find in each one some reason to doubt, this will suffice to justify my rejecting the whole. And for that end it will not be requisite that I should examine each in particular, which would be an endless undertaking; for owing to the fact that the destruction of the foundations of necessity brings with it the downfall of the rest of the edifice. I shall only in the first place attack those principles upon which all my former opinions rested.
>
> (*Philosophical Works* 1.145)

That "reason already persuades me" demonstrates Descartes's acceptance of and reliance on the conclusions reached in the *Discourse.* He now begins a survey of his opinions: "All that up to the present time I have accepted as most true and certain I have learned either from the senses or through the senses . . ." (1.145). But, he then reminds himself, we have at times caught our senses deceiving us (such things as optical illusions "deceive" the senses), and a wise man never trusts what has once deceived him. But it is not only such things as distant objects (if you look at a coil of rope from a distance, you might mistake it for a snake) and optical illusions that give us reason to doubt the senses; there is something even more misleading. It is possible to be asleep and dream that one is having sensory impressions when in fact one is not: "How often has it happened to me that in the night I dreamt that I found myself in this particular place, that I was dressed and seated near the fire, whilst in reality I was lying undressed in bed!" (1.145–146).

The importance of this realization should not be underestimated; it is the first step in the "radical" Cartesian program of hyperbolic doubt (doubting everything that can be doubted), which is mandated by the first rule of method. The extension of this argument, or realization, proves to be equally interesting. The question that Descartes raises is this: How can we be sure of what is real and what is not real if we cannot distinguish dream life from nondream life? What mark is there that distinguishes the dream world from the real world? What criterion can we use to adjudicate the distinction? A brief survey of the possible criteria will serve to demonstrate the problem. One might respond that one knows one has been dreaming because at the end of a dream one awakens. But surely it is possible to dream that one is waking up. Another answer is the familiar pinching test. If you pinch yourself, you can be sure you're awake. But surely this won't work either. It is entirely possible to dream that you are pinching yourself. Many philosophers have considered the question about dreaming. It seems that there is no test, no criterion, that one can rely on to distinguish dream life from the real world.

The dream argument against the certainty of knowledge should appear very potent at this point, but Descartes noticed there were some truths, not dependent on the senses, that seemed to be outside its scope:

> That is possibly why our reasoning is not unjust when we conclude from this that Physics, Astronomy, Medicine and all other sciences which have as their end the consideration of composite things, are very dubious and uncertain; but that Arithmetic, Geometry and other sciences of that kind which only treat of things that are very simple and very general, without taking great trouble to ascertain whether they are actually existent or not, contain some measure of certainty and an element of the indubitable. For whether I am awake or asleep, two and three together always form five, and the square can never have more than four sides, and it does not seem possible that truths so clear and apparent can be suspected of any falsity [or uncertainty].
>
> (1.147)

Had Descartes found his core of certain truths? He would have, had he been armed with only the dream argument, but he advanced an even more powerful argument at this point: the second "radical" step in the program of hyperbolic doubt, which we will call the move to the evil demon.

Descartes argues in the second "radical" step that there is "implanted in my mind" an idea that there is an all-powerful God, one who can bring about any state of affairs. What would prevent such a God from bringing it about that one is always deceived?

> But how do I know that He has not brought it to pass that there is no earth, no heaven, no extended body, no magnitude, no place, and that nevertheless [I possess the perceptions of all these things and that] they seem to me to exist just exactly as I now see them? And, besides, as I sometimes imagine that others deceive themselves in the things which they think they know best, how do I know that I am not deceived every time that I add two and three, or count the sides of a square, or judge of things yet simpler, if anything simpler can be imagined?
>
> (1.147)

Descartes admits that God probably wouldn't do such things, but then asserts that the postulation of such an evil demon provides grounds for the doubt of all opinions, and that these opinions cannot be trusted if one's quest is certainty. His conclusion of the First Meditation includes the following:

> I shall then suppose, not that God, who is supremely good and the fountain of truth, but some

> evil genius not less powerful than deceitful, has employed his whole energies in deceiving me; . . . I shall remain obstinately attached to this idea, and if by this means it is not in my power to arrive at the knowledge of any truth, I may at least do what is in my power [i.e., suspend judgment], and with firm purpose avoid giving credence to any false thing, or being imposed upon by this arch deceiver, however powerful and deceptive he may be.
>
> (1.148)

As if to reinforce the conclusion of his First Meditation, Descartes begins the second, "The Nature of the Human Mind: It Is Better Known Than the Body," with the following:

> The Meditation of yesterday filled my mind with so many doubts that it is no longer in my power to forget them. And yet I do not see in what manner I can resolve them; and, just as if I had all of a sudden fallen into very deep water, I am so disconcerted that I can neither make certain of setting my feet on the bottom, nor can I swim and so support myself on the surface. I shall nevertheless make an effort and follow anew the same path as that on which I yesterday entered, i.e. I shall proceed by setting aside all that in which the least doubt could be supposed to exist, just as if I had discovered that it was absolutely false; and I shall ever follow in this road until I have met with something which is certain, or at least, if I can do nothing else, until I have learned for certain that there is nothing in the world that is certain. Archimedes, in order that he might draw the terrestrial globe out of its place, and transport it elsewhere, demanded only that one point should be fixed and immoveable; in the same way I shall have the right to conceive high hopes if I am happy enough to discover one thing only which is certain and indubitable.
>
> (1.148)

Descartes then begins a survey of the possible truths. He again rejects all sensory data and all mathematical truths, but fixes upon the one thing that constantly reappears in his doubts about the world, the "I" that refers to himself:

> But how can I know there is not something different from those things that I have just considered, of which one cannot have the slightest doubt? Is there not some God, or some other being by whatever name we call it, who puts these reflections into my mind? That is not necessary, for is it not possible that I am capable of producing them myself? I myself, am I not at least something? But I have already denied that I had senses and body. Yet I hesitate, for what follows from that? Am I so dependent on body and senses that I cannot exist without these? But I was persuaded that there was nothing in all the world, that there was no heaven, no earth, that there were no minds, nor any bodies: was I not then likewise persuaded that I did not exist? Not at all; of a surety I myself did exist since I persuaded myself of something [or merely because I thought of something]. But there is some deceiver or other, very powerful and very cunning, who ever employs his ingenuity in deceiving me. Then without doubt I exist also if he deceives me, and let him deceive me as much as he will, he can never cause me to be nothing so long as I think that I am something. So that after having reflected well and carefully examined all things, we must come to the definite conclusion that this proposition: I am, I exist, is necessarily true each time that I pronounce it, or that I mentally conceive it.
>
> (1.149–150)

What is certain for Descartes is that as long as the I thinks, the I exists. This is the famous *cogito ergo sum* (I think, therefore I am). The argument he presents can be looked at in the following way: in the First Meditation Descartes examines several doubt-makers within his method of hyperbolic doubt, each of which is designed to strip away those opinions that are not certain. They are: (1) my senses are deceiving me, (2) I am dreaming, (3) God is deceiving me, and (4) an evil demon is deceiving me.

What Descartes notices about the doubt-makers is that each assumes the proposition "I exist." None of the reasons that Descartes can adduce for doubting what he previously believed provides any reason for doubting the truth of his own existence. In fact, "I doubt that I exist" embodies "I exist," because doubting requires some agent. Doubting cannot be carried out without something to do the doubting. Therefore, Descartes concludes, no unclouded mind could rationally hold that the proposition "I doubt that I exist" is true.

The question that Descartes has to settle is just what sort of being this I is. He begins with an assessment of the corporeal side of his existence and quickly rejects it as part of his *essence.* This term is introduced in a technical sense in Cartesian philosophy: the essence of an object is that property or set of properties without which the object would cease to continue as that object. For example, we might say that the essence of a nail is that it exists in the universe, and that it is made of matter; clearly, if the nail didn't exist in the universe, we would be hard pressed to identify it as a nail.

There are two reasons for Descartes's rejection of body as a part of his essence. The first is the familiar evil demon argument: the "malign spirit" could be deceiving him into believing that he has a body when in fact he doesn't. The second reason is that Descartes can imagine himself without a body; therefore the body cannot be a part of his essence. If you couple the first reason with Descartes's insistence that we accept only the certain, his rejection of body as the essence of the I is an obvious move. He then continues the search for the elusive essence of the I:

> I find here that thought is an attribute that belongs to me; it alone cannot be separated from me. I am, I exist, that is certain. But how often? Just when I think; for it might possibly be the case if I ceased entirely to think, that I should likewise cease altogether to exist. I do not now admit anything which is not necessarily true: to speak accurately I am not more than a thing which thinks, that is to say a mind or a soul, or an understanding, or a reason, which are terms whose significance was formerly unknown to me. I am, however, a real thing and really exist; but what thing? I have answered: a thing which thinks.
>
> (1.151–152)

Descartes thereby identifies himself as thinking substance, distinct from nonthinking or corporeal substance. The answer to the question What sort of thing is the I? is *sum res cogitans* (I am a thing that thinks).

At this point Descartes goes on to consider the nature of corporeal objects, taking as his example a piece of wax. He notes that the wax possesses many properties, including smell, color, texture, shape, and temperature, but he also notices that it is possible for the wax to lose its color, change its shape, lose its smell, and so on, and still lay claim to being the same piece of wax. But what then is the wax—what is its essence? "Let us attentively consider this, and, abstracting from all that does not belong to the wax, let us see what remains. Certainly nothing remains excepting a certain extended thing which is flexible and movable" (1.154). But what are these properties? Descartes tells us that they are accessible only through the intellect, for there are too many possibilities encompassed by extension, flexibility, and changeability. And he concludes:

> It is now manifest to me that even bodies are not properly speaking known by the senses or by the faculty of imagination, but by the understanding only, and since they are not known from the fact that they are seen or touched, but only because they are understood. . . .
>
> (1.157)

Descartes therefore feels comfortable asserting that as a *res cogitans* his mind is more "easily or manifestly perceptible" than are bodies. Another conclusion that the reader is to absorb sub rosa is that there are two distinct sorts of substance in the world: minds, whose essence is thinking; and bodies, whose essence is extension. This last point is treated much more fully in the Sixth Meditation.

Descartes begins his Third Meditation, "Concerning God: That He Exists," by establishing a general rule: "that all things which I perceive very clearly and very distinctly are true" (1.158). Perhaps the best account of what Descartes means here by "clear" and "distinct" can be found in a later work of his, the *Principia philosophiae* (*The Principles of Philosophy*, 1644), where he writes:

> For the knowledge upon which a certain and incontrovertible judgment can be formed, should not alone be clear but also distinct. I term that clear which is present and apparent to an attentive mind, in the same way as we assert that we see objects clearly when, being present to the regarding eye, they operate upon it with sufficient strength. But the distinct is that which is so precise and different from all other objects that it contains within itself nothing but what is clear.
> (*Philosophical Works* 1.237)

In other places Descartes tells us that the "clear and distinct" are perceived by the "natural light of reason." At any rate it is important to understand the Cartesian move to clear and distinct knowledge. Descartes wanted to claim any knowledge that he perceived clearly and distinctly as true knowledge—an application of the general rule that was presented earlier. His reliance on clear and distinct knowledge caused a serious problem for him—a problem known as the Cartesian Circle—which we will examine later.

At this point in the Third Meditation, Descartes begins examining the ideas that he had on his mind. He observes that he had an idea of God. But from whence comes this idea? He notes that ideas are only representations:

> For just as this mode of objective existence pertains to ideas by their proper nature, so does the mode of formal existence pertain to the causes of those ideas (this is at least true of the first and principal) by the nature peculiar to them. And although it may be the case that one idea gives birth to another idea, that cannot continue to be so indefinitely; for in the end we must reach an idea whose cause shall be so to speak an archetype, in which the whole reality [or perfection] which is so to speak objectively [or by representation] in these ideas is contained formally [and really]. Thus the light of nature causes me to know clearly that the ideas in me are like [pictures or] images which can, in truth, easily fall short of the perfection of the objects from which they have been derived, but which can never contain anything greater or more perfect.
> (1.163)

Descartes's proof of God's existence follows directly from these conclusions. The steps are:

1. I have an idea of God, an infinitely perfect being.
2. This idea of God has formal existence.
3. Whatever has formal existence must have a formally existing cause.
4. There must be as much total perfection in the cause of an idea as there is in the idea itself.
5. My idea of God has infinite total perfection.

Therefore:

6. God has formal existence.

An intuitive way to understand this proof is as follows: Descartes had an idea of God. This idea had to have come from somewhere. The cause of an idea must be at least as perfect as the idea itself; as the idea is of a supremely perfect being (God), the cause of the idea must be at least as supremely perfect. Therefore, for Descartes to have had an idea of God (a supremely perfect being), God must exist.

Descartes saw himself as proving the existence of God. It is important to note here that Descartes remained faithful to his method up to this point in the *Meditations*. Following his dictum to accept nothing as true that one could find the least reason to doubt, he searched his opinions and established the certainty of "I exist." He then established that this I must be a thinking thing essentially, and that it has in it *ideas*. Now, these ideas must come from somewhere, especially the idea of God. Where do they come from? Well, at least in the case of God, the only way to explain the existence of the idea is to allow for the existence of the source of the idea, since ideas can be nothing more than imperfect representations of their subjects. Descartes built his universe up from the most simple (the *sum* of the Second Meditation) to the point at which he established the existence of God.

Descartes concludes the Third Meditation:

> —a God, I say, whose idea is in me, i.e. who possesses all those supreme perfections of which our mind may indeed have some idea but without understanding them all, who is liable to no errors or defect [and who has none of all those marks which denote imperfection]. From this it is manifest that He cannot be a deceiver, since the light of nature teaches us that fraud and deception necessarily proceed from some defect.
> (1.171)

Descartes enters into the Fourth Meditation, "Truth and Falsehood," with the assertion that God can be no deceiver. The burden of the meditation is to prove the assertion. Up to now in the *Meditations,* Descartes has proven the existence of God, but he has yet to dismiss the evil demon argument, or the deceiving God argument. It is at least possible at this point in the evolution of the Cartesian system that there be both a good God and an evil one, or that there exists a God who is a deceiver. Descartes needed to establish that there is but one God, and that he is supremely perfect, which would in one stroke rule out the possibility of the existence of both the evil demon and the deceiving God.

The problem, quite simply put, is that Descartes noticed there was evil and error in the world, and this was manifestly incompatible with an all-powerful veracious God. Why is the existence of error and evil in the world incompatible with a veracious God? Descartes begins by noting that any faculty he possesses must have come from God:

> In the next place I experienced in myself a certain capacity for judging which I have doubtless received from God, like all the other things that I possess; and as He could not desire to deceive me, it is clear that He has not given me a faculty that will lead me to err if I use it aright.
> (1.172)

As Descartes rightly notes, it seems to follow that it is impossible to go wrong. But this is obviously a ludicrous conclusion. People do go wrong; they are susceptible to error. The question is: Why would an all-powerful veracious God have given us an imperfect faculty (imperfect in that we can be deceived through its use); and isn't the fact that we are deceived reason enough to conclude that God in fact condones such deception and is therefore a deceiver? The argument for God as a deceiver seems quite powerful.

Descartes begins the refutation of this argument by noting that so long as he thinks only of God, he can discern no cause of error or falsehood. The problem begins when he contemplates himself and matters concerning himself. God, Descartes reminds us, is the supremely perfect being; and just as we have an idea of God, we also have an idea of nothingness or nonbeing. The first attempt to resolve the problem of error goes like this:

> I am in a sense something intermediate between God and nought, i.e. placed in such a manner between the supreme Being and non-being, that there is in truth nothing in me that can lead to error in so far as a sovereign Being has formed me; but that, as I in some degree participate likewise in nought or in non-being, i.e. in so far as I am not myself the supreme Being, and as I find myself subject to an infinitude of imperfections, I ought not to be astonished if I should fall into error. Thus do I recognize that error, in so far as it is such, is not a real thing depending on God, but simply a defect; and therefore, in order to fall into it, that I have no need to possess a special faculty given me by God for this very purpose, but that I fall into error from the fact that the

> power given me by God for the purpose of distinguishing truth from error is not infinite.
>
> (1.172)

The answer to the question "How is error possible?" seems to come down to the answer "Because I am not God." That is, man is susceptible to error because he is not infinitely capable of applying the faculty of right judgment to all decisions that he must make. Only God is capable of doing so.

The next phase of the meditation is to examine the nature of error in man more closely. Descartes tells us that it depends on two concurrent causes: the faculty of cognition and the faculty of choice, or free will. God has given humankind an infinite faculty of choice, but we do not have infinite understanding, as this is reserved for God alone. We are therefore prone to error, not because God has restricted our choice or determined that we should err—indeed we are always free to choose rightly—but rather because we choose on the basis of insufficient information. Choices that we make are prone to error because our will extends much further than our understanding. When we do perceive something clearly and distinctly, there is no doubt that we understand it; God guarantees this. But what happens is that we are constantly making decisions, exercising our faculty of choice, on the grounds of nonunderstanding:

> Whence then come my errors? They come from the sole fact that since the will is much wider in its range and compass than the understanding, I do not restrain it within the same bounds, but extend it also to things which I do not understand: and as the will is of itself indifferent to these, it easily falls into error and sin, and chooses the evil for the good, or the false for the true.
>
> (1.175)

Descartes's conclusion then is that God is no deceiver. He provides an analysis of error that at once allows error to exist in men and preserves the veracity of God. What of those who complain that by giving us such a widely ranging faculty of choice, God in fact placed error in the world and hence could be seen as a deceiver? Descartes replies:

> I have further no reason to complain that He has given me a will more ample than my understanding, for since the will consists only of one single element, and is so to speak indivisible, it appears that its nature is such that nothing can be abstracted from it [without destroying it]; and certainly the more comprehensive it is found to be, the more reason I have to render gratitude to the giver.
>
> (1.177)

Descartes concludes the Fourth Meditation:

> . . . it seems to me that I have not gained little by this day's Meditation, since I have discovered the source of falsity and error. And certainly there can be no other source than that which I have explained; for as often as I so restrain my will within the limits of my knowledge that it forms no judgment except on matters which are clearly and distinctly represented to it by the understanding, I can never be deceived; for every clear and distinct conception is without doubt something, and hence cannot derive its origin from what is nought, but must of necessity have God as its author—God, I say, who being supremely perfect, cannot be the cause of any error; and consequently we must conclude that such a conception [or such a judgment] is true. Nor have I only learned to-day what I should avoid in order that I may not err, but also how I should act in order to arrive at a knowledge of the truth; for without doubt I shall arrive at this end if I devote my attention sufficiently to those things which I perfectly understand; and if I separate from these that which I only understand confusedly and with obscurity. To these I shall henceforth diligently give heed.
>
> (1.178–179)

In the Fifth Meditation, "The Nature of Material Things: God's Existence Again Considered," Descartes revives a theme from the First Meditation in considering the question of the certain existence of material objects. But, he tells us, before we can entertain the question, we must consider the ideas possessed in the mind about these objects. In our examination of these ideas we must determine which are distinct and which are confused.

Descartes notes that there are some ideas of objects which are such that even if they have no existence, they cannot be called non-entities. As an example he cites the triangle:

> . . . when I imagine a triangle, although there may nowhere in the world be such a figure outside my thought, or ever have been, there is nevertheless in this figure a certain determinate nature, form, or essence, which is immutable and eternal, which I have not invented, and which in no wise depends on my mind, as appears from the fact that diverse properties of that triangle can be demonstrated, viz. that its three angles are equal to two right angles, that the greatest side is subtended by the greatest angle, and the like, which now, whether I wish it or do not wish it, I recognize very clearly as pertaining to it, although I never thought of the matter at all when I imagined a triangle for the first time, and which therefore cannot be said to have been invented by me.
>
> (1.180)

What he concludes is: That which we clearly and distinctly understand to belong to the true and immutable nature of anything, essence or form, can be truly affirmed of that thing.

This principle is a very close relative of the general rule discussed earlier. Although we will not consider the ramifications of the principle (it has a long and rich philosophical tradition), we should note that it is the foundation of Descartes's ontological proof of God's existence, and will enable him to prove the existence of material objects. Descartes states:

> But now, if just because I can draw the idea of something from my thought, it follows that all which I know clearly and distinctly as pertaining to this object does really belong to it, may I not derive from this an argument demonstrating the existence of God?
>
> (1.180)

Descartes continues with his famous ontological proof of God's existence:

1. God is a total of all perfections.
2. Existence is a perfection.

Therefore:

3. God exists.

He then writes:

> I clearly see that existence can no more be separated from the essence of God than can its having its three angles equal to two right angles be separated from the essence of a [rectilinear] triangle, or the idea of a mountain from the idea of a valley; and so there is not any less repugnance to our conceiving a God (that is, a Being supremely perfect) to whom existence is lacking (that is to say, to whom a certain perfection is lacking), than to conceive of a mountain which has no valley.
>
> (1.181)

By "a mountain which has no valley," Descartes means an uphill slope without a downhill slope.

Descartes thus holds that God exists precisely because it is inconceivable that he does not exist, if we ponder his essence. Yet how did we discover his essence? We perceived it clearly and distinctly:

> But after I have recognised that there is a God—because at the same time I have also recognised that all things depend upon Him, and that He is not a deceiver, and from that have inferred that what I perceive clearly and distinctly cannot fail to be true.
>
> (1.184)

Descartes holds that God exists because he clearly and distinctly perceives that God's existence is necessary, as it is a part of his essence. But recall that Descartes's reason that clear and distinct ideas are necessarily true is God's veracity. It is hard to see how Descartes can have it both ways. Either he should use clear and distinct ideas to validate God's existence, or he should use God's existence to validate clear and distinct ideas.

As it stands the reasoning is circular. One cannot say that the reason for A's being true is B, while at the same time holding that the reason for B's being true is A. This is the famous Cartesian Circle, which is complex and has no easy solution.

Descartes concludes his Fifth Meditation:

> And so I very clearly recognise that the certainty and truth of all knowledge depends alone on the knowledge of the true God, in so much that, before I knew Him, I could not have a perfect knowledge of any other thing. And now that I know Him I have the means of acquiring a perfect knowledge of an infinitude of things, not only of those which relate to God Himself and other intellectual matters, but also of those which pertain to corporeal nature in so far as it is the object of pure mathematics [which have no concern with whether it exists or not].
>
> (1.185)

In the Sixth Meditation, "The Existence of Material Things: The Real Distinction of Mind and Body," Descartes proves the existence of the material world, thus fulfilling his promise to explain the most complex problems only in terms of the most simple truths. He moves from the simple truth of *cogito ergo sum* to a reconstruction of the rational world. Thus the Cartesian universe will satisfy the quest for certainty that Descartes mandates in his *Discourse.*

Briefly, Descartes's proof of the external world is: There is an inclination to believe in an external world because there must be objects of sensations; and since a veracious God would not allow him to be deceived in a matter such as this, the external world must necessarily exist. At the end of the Fifth Meditation, Descartes argues that the existence of the external world is at least possible, and by the Sixth he argues that this possibility is an actuality, the appeal to God's veracity being the step of the argument that validates its legitimacy. If God is truly veracious, then the material world must exist, as Descartes clearly and distinctly perceives it must.

Descartes also argues for the "radical" distinction between the mind and the body—between the two sorts of substance in the Cartesian universe. He argues that they are distinct precisely because he can imagine the two as separate:

> Because I know that all things which I apprehend clearly and distinctly can be created by God as I apprehend them, it suffices that I am able to apprehend one thing apart from another clearly and distinctly in order to be certain that the one is different from the other, since they may be made to exist in separation at least by the omnipotence of God.
>
> (1.190)

Descartes goes on to argue that because his essence is thinking, it cannot also be extension, and therefore the two must be distinct:

> . . . and, therefore, just because I know certainly that I exist, and that meanwhile I do not remark that any other thing necessarily pertains to my nature or essence, excepting that I am a thinking thing, I rightly conclude that my essence consists solely in the fact that I am a thinking thing [or a substance whose whole essence or nature is to think]. And although possibly (or rather certainly, as I shall say in a moment) I possess a body with which I am very intimately conjoined, yet because, on the one side, I have a clear and distinct idea of myself inasmuch as I am only a thinking and unextended thing, and as, on the other, I possess a distinct idea of body, inasmuch as it is only an extended and unthinking thing, it is certain that this I [that is to say, my soul by which I am what I am], is entirely and absolutely distinct from my body, and can exist without it.
>
> (1.190)

The mind and the body are distinct but closely bound. He explains:

> I am not only lodged in my body as a pilot in a vessel, but . . . I am very closely united to it, and so to speak so intermingled with it that I seem to compose with it one whole. For if that were not the case, when my body is hurt, I, who am merely a thinking thing, should not feel pain, for I should perceive this wound by the understanding only, just as the sailor perceives by sight when something is damaged in his vessel.
>
> (1.192)

The entire analysis of the mind/body distinction is perhaps best summarized in this way:

> In order to begin this examination, then, I here say, in the first place, that there is a great difference between mind and body, inasmuch as body is by nature always divisible, and the mind is entirely indivisible. For, as a matter of fact, when I consider the mind, that is to say, myself inasmuch as I am only a thinking thing, I cannot distinguish in myself any parts, but apprehend myself to be clearly one and entire; and although the whole mind seems to be united to the whole body, yet if a foot, or an arm, or some other part, is separated from my body, I am aware that nothing has been taken away from my mind. And the faculties of willing, feeling, conceiving, etc. cannot be properly speaking said to be its parts, for it is one and the same mind which employs itself in willing and in feeling and understanding. But it is quite otherwise with corporeal or extended objects, for there is not one of these imaginable by me which my mind cannot easily divide into parts, and which consequently I do not recognise as being divisible; this would be sufficient to teach me that the mind or soul of man is entirely different from the body, if I had not already learned it from other sources.
>
> (1.196)

The *Meditations* are the rules of method worked out. They are an attempt to provide a bedrock of certainty for opinions about the world. Descartes was challenging scholastic doctrines by establishing the validity of the rational universe, both physical and spiritual. His method of hyperbolic doubt was largely successful in clearing away most of the usual stumbling blocks. But even the great Descartes was himself guilty of dogmatic positions. His rejection of the certainty of sensory data forced him to reject the empirical scientific method and brought him in direct conflict with a group of philosophers organized around Pierre Gassendi.

The publication of Sextus Empiricus' texts in 1621 had a profound impact on the intellectual world of the time. One of the philosophers most deeply affected was Gassendi, a young faculty member at the University of Aix. It was Gassendi's aim to use the wisdom of the ancients as a weapon against the scholastics. In 1624 he published his *Arguments Against the Aristotelians,* a work that challenged the foundations of scholastic teachings and cemented his reputation in the French intellectual community. In the 1630's he began a project reviving the philosophy of Epicurus, most notably his atomism.

Gassendi and Descartes were quite famous combatants. Gassendi's "Objections" to the *Meditations* were well received in the intellectual circles that also served as the forums of philosophic debate. He was the first to point out the Cartesian Circle, as well as one other famous Cartesian problem. Gassendi noticed that Descartes's proof of the existence of the self, the *cogito ergo sum,* could apply not only to thinking but to any other active verb as well. Using Descartes's argument, one could prove the *sum,* the "I am," not only by thought (as in the *cogito*) but also by activities such as walking, talking, or any other that requires an implied subject. Consequently, "I walk, therefore I am" is every bit as valid a proof of the "I am" as is "I think, therefore I am." Descartes never found a way out of this problem; his answers in the "Replies to the Objections" are disappointing.

Gassendi was a philosopher committed to the rise of empirical science. He was one of the first modern philosopher-scientists to insist that the confirmation of scientific theories was dependent on their conformity with observed phenomena. Gassendi held that the philosopher-scientist had an obligation to examine various hypotheses by subjecting them to experiments and tests. It was Descartes's belief, however, that the answers to questions of science could be arrived at without such experiments—that the "true" answers would be obtained not by checking their conformity with the "real" world, but by checking their conformity with certain metaphysical principles that the theorist held. As one might guess, this sort of rationalistic science at times formed hypotheses about the world that observation did not bear out.

There is one surviving anecdote concerning Descartes and Gassendi that demonstrates the inevitable clash between two such radically different approaches to science. In attempting to work out a complete theory of the physical world, Descartes formulated several theories of motion, to which he was committed because of his background in metaphysics. His fourth "law" of motion held that in any collision, the larger of the two bodies colliding would always win out. Gassendi noted that if the larger of the two bodies was at rest, Descartes was committed to holding that this body would continue at rest, no matter how fast the smaller body was moving. Gassendi set up the following test of Descartes's fourth law of motion: he placed a cannonball at rest in the middle of a floor and aimed a musket at it. When the musket ball, which was much smaller than the cannonball, struck the cannonball, the cannonball began to move. This result was clearly opposed to the hypothesis of the Cartesian theory, and Gassendi concluded that Descartes's fourth law was inaccurate. Descartes, of course, responded that Gassendi's test proved nothing, for all it showed was that the cannonball "appeared" to move, not that it really moved at all—Gassendi merely saw it incorrectly. At this point Descartes reiterated his proof of the fourth law and denied the validity of Gassendi's conclusion.

As one can see from the above, the differences between the two conceptions of the role of science are irreconcilable. Gassendi saw the purpose of science as explaining the observed phenomena of the world around us, while Descartes saw it as a reflection of his theories about the material world—"the way that it should be." That these two conceptions would clash—and clash in a grand way—should not be surprising; indeed, these differences actually helped to further the cause of science in the seventeenth century.

With the publication of the *Meditations,* Descartes had gone a long way toward establishing a substantial reputation for himself. The Cartesian school of thought soon became the rage in intellectual circles across the Continent. As Descartes's popularity grew, so did his circle of acquaintances. Among his friends was Heinrich Reneri, a professor of philosophy at the University of Utrecht. Reneri considered himself a close friend and disciple of Descartes's, and he said as much to both colleagues and students. Reneri died suddenly at an early age, and at his funeral, Amelius, a professor of history and rhetoric, delivered the eulogy. He took the occasion to praise Descartes above all else, thinking that this would have pleased Reneri, and called Descartes "the only Atlas and Archimedes of our age." This was praise that offended several in the audience, particularly Gysbertus Voetius, pastor of the Reformed Church of Utrecht.

Voetius possessed neither remarkable intellectual gifts nor personal charm. But he did possess a fanatical resentment of the Cartesian school and a personal hatred for Descartes himself. His first salvo against Descartes was to publish a pamphlet under the title *Theses on Atheism* in which he attacked the "new philosophy," the Cartesian philosophy, as being committed to atheism. He reasoned that Cartesian doubt led to skepticism; people who propounded skepticism were of course skeptics, and skeptics were but atheists in disguise. In order to gain more support for his crusade, Voetius attempted to enlist the aid of some prominent theologian. He settled on Mersenne, not knowing that he was Descartes's most trusted friend, and wrote a letter requesting the good father's assistance. Mersenne promptly delivered the letter to Descartes, who read it and sent it back to its author.

In 1641 Voetius was appointed (by rotation) to the rectorship of the University of Utrecht. By 1642 he managed to get the University Senate to reject the new philosophy, and reaffirm its commitment to scholasticism. It was at this point that Descartes entered into the controversy directly. In a letter to the Reverend Father Dinet, provincial of the Jesuits, he wrote:

> A man who passes in the world as a theologian, having, by vigorous abuse of all who differ from him, in a style of broad humor, which takes the ear of the vulgar, gained credit for an ardent zeal for religion; and who likewise, by continually putting out little pamphlets—though not worth reading—and citing many authors—though these so often are against his position that it is likely that he knows them only from the table of contents; and by speaking with great confidence, though very much at random, concerning every branch of knowledge, passes for learned among the ignorant.
>
> (*Oeuvres* 7.584)

Voetius responded by citing Descartes and calling him up before the courts of Utrecht. Descartes, claiming to be a French citizen and viewing the whole matter as ridiculous, responded that the courts had no jurisdiction in this case, and did not attend the trial. The decision of course went against him. Descartes was found guilty of libel (because of the letter to Father Dinet) and was sentenced to be burned at the stake. Voetius went so far as to request that the pyre be large enough to be seen several miles away.

At this point Descartes fled to the Hague and placed himself under the protection of the French ambassador. The dispute was resolved on 11 June 1645 in a decree imposing silence on both Descartes and Voetius, which of course neither party heeded. The battle raged on for several more years, although not much more came of it.

While Descartes was having his problems with Voetius, he met Princess Elizabeth of the Hague. Elizabeth was a young woman of twenty-two who reportedly spoke six languages and was quite adept in mathematics. She wanted to meet Descartes after having read and been favorably impressed by his *Meditations.* Descartes and Elizabeth soon formed a warm friendship that generated a good deal of correspondence. He demonstrated his respect and admiration by the effusive dedicatory letter to her, which praises her intelligence and charm, in his *Principles of Philosophy,* his third published work.

Descartes's *Principles* is a masterly work; therein he explicates more fully the philosophical system that he set forth in the *Meditations.* The work is organized into four parts: part 1 concerns the principles of human knowledge; part 2, the principles of material things; part 3, the visible world; and part 4, the earth. In a letter to the abbé Claude Picot, the French translator of the *Principles* (which were written in Latin), Descartes wrote:

> I would like to explain here what seems to me to be the order which should be followed in our self-instruction. To begin with, a man who as yet has merely the common and imperfect knowledge which may be acquired by the four methods before mentioned, should above all try to form for himself a code of morals sufficient to regulate the actions of his life, because this does not brook any delay, and we ought above all other things to endeavor to live well. After that he

> should likewise study logic—not that of the Schools, because it properly speaking is only a dialectic which teaches how to make the things that we know understood by others, or even to repeat, without forming any judgment on them, many words respecting those that we do not know, thus corrupting rather than increasing good sense—but the logic that teaches us how best to direct our reason in order to discover those truths of which we are ignorant. And since this is very dependent on custom, it is good for him to practise the rules for a long time on easy and simple questions such as those of mathematics. Then when he has acquired a certain skill in discovering the truth in these questions he should begin seriously to apply himself to the true philosophy, the first part of which is metaphysics, which contains the principles of knowledge, amongst which is the explanation of the principal attributes of God, of the immateriality of our souls, and of all the clear and simple notions which are in us. The second is physics in which, after having found the true principles of material things, we examine generally how the whole universe is composed, and then in particular what is the nature of this earth and of all the bodies which are most commonly found in connection with it, like air, water and fire, the loadstone, and other minerals. It is thereafter necessary to inquire individually into the nature of plants, animals, and above all of man, so that we may afterward be able to discover the other sciences which are useful to man.
>
> (*Philosophical Works* 1.210–211)

Perhaps the best statement of the organization of Cartesian philosophy is given in the same letter to Picot, where Descartes writes: "Thus philosophy as a whole is like a tree whose roots are metaphysics, whose trunk is physics, and whose branches, which issue from this trunk, are all the other sciences" (1.211). Descartes saw his *Meditations* as establishing the "roots" of this tree, and the *Principles* were the "trunk." In the same letter to Picot, Descartes advises that no one read his *Principles* without first having read his previous works.

The explication of the physics in the *Principles* drew fire from many quarters. The most severe criticisms focused on part 2 of the work, and were aimed by none other than Gassendi. In part 2 Descartes sets forth his controversial laws of motion, one of which (the fourth) we have already discussed. But Descartes seems to have had another goal besides stabilizing the "trunk" of his philosophical tree. He seems to be counterattacking the school that was establishing itself around Gassendi. As previously noted, Gassendi revived the notion of Epicurean atomism in the seventeenth century. In part 2 Descartes challenges the notion of atoms, and provides a proof of their nonexistence. He insists that whatever is material is necessarily divisible, and hence the idea of an indivisible material atom is nonsensical. The controversy raged on for years, with neither Descartes nor Gassendi willing to admit defeat.

Descartes and Elizabeth's correspondence grew more and more technically philosophical following the publication of the *Principles,* eventually resulting in the last work that Descartes was to publish in his lifetime, the *Passions de l'âme* (*The Passions of the Soul,* 1649). There he seeks to explain how all psychological manifestations can be reduced to mechanical causes. One should read Descartes's *Passions* as his attempt to complete the picture of philosophy set forth in the *Principles.* In 1647 circumstances required that Elizabeth leave the Hague. She became the abbess of the Lutheran abbey of Hervorden, in Westphalia. Her correspondence with Descartes continued until his death.

In the summer of 1647 Descartes left the Netherlands for Paris, where he met Blaise Pascal. The two apparently became close friends, although little is known about their relationship. While in Paris, Descartes also made a number of close friends at the royal court and secured the promise of a pension from the crown.

After returning to Holland in May 1648,

Descartes was persuaded to go back to Paris by the crown's promise of a handsome pension. Once there he realized that there would be no pension, since the rebellion of the Fronde had broken out. Dejected and unsure of what to do, he again returned to Holland.

In Sweden, Queen Christina took an interest in the new philosophy. She had never met Descartes, but one of her advisers, Pierre Chanut, was a friend and correspondent of his. Christina began by reading the *Meditations,* asking Chanut to help her through them. By 1647 Descartes and Christina were corresponding and were cultivating a friendship. In 1649 Christina invited Descartes to visit her in Sweden, and at the beginning of October he arrived in Stockholm.

Descartes tutored Christina in philosophy and found her an eager student—so eager, in fact, that she resolved to keep him in Stockholm by offering him a pension, a title, or whatever else he desired. But before any arrangements were made, the Swedish winter began and Chanut was taken ill with an inflammatory disease of the lungs. Descartes nursed him to the point of recovery until on 2 February 1650 he himself was struck by the same illness. Descartes, who had a history of weak lungs, died holding the hands of his two friends, Chanut and Christina, on 11 February 1650.

Descartes not only unlocked the door of scientific progress by releasing the seventeenth-century scientist from medieval dogma, he completely revised the metaphysical view of the universe. He originated a method of inquiry, a systematic program that, if correctly followed, would validate progress in any number of fields—science, epistemology, or metaphysics. The *Meditations* stand as one of the great masterworks in the history of philosophy; and Descartes stands as one of the greatest intellectuals in the history of thought.

## Selected Bibliography


### EDITION

*Oeuvres de Descartes.* 12 vols. Edited by Charles Adam and Paul Tannery. Paris, 1897–1913. Reprinted 1964.

### TRANSLATIONS

*Descartes: Discourse on Method, Optics, Geometry, and Meteorology.* Translated by Paul J. Olscamp. Indianapolis, 1965.

*Descartes: Philosophical Letters.* Translated and edited by Anthony Kenny. Oxford, 1970.

*Descartes: Philosophical Writings.* Translated by G. E. M. Anscombe and Peter Geach. Edinburgh, 1954.

*The Essential Descartes.* Edited by Margaret Wilson. New York, 1969.

*The Philosophical Works of Descartes.* 2 vols. Translated by Elizabeth Haldane and G. R. T. Ross. Cambridge, 1911–1912. Reprinted New York, 1955.

### BIOGRAPHICAL AND CRITICAL STUDIES

Beck, L. J. *The Metaphysics of Descartes: A Study of the "Meditations."* Oxford, 1965.

Curley, E. M. *Descartes Against the Sceptics.* Cambridge, Mass., 1978.

Doney, Willis, ed. *Descartes: A Collection of Critical Essays.* New York, 1967.

Frankfurt, Harry. *Demons, Dreamers, and Madmen: The Defense of Reason in Descartes' "Meditations."* Indianapolis, 1970.

Hooker, Michael, ed. *Descartes: Critical and Interpretive Essays.* Baltimore, 1978.

Kenny, Anthony. *Descartes: A Study of His Philosophy.* New York, 1968.

Lowndes, Richard. *Descartes: Life and "Meditations."* London, 1878.

Vrooman, Jack. *René Descartes: A Biography.* New York, 1970.

Williams, Bernard. *Descartes: The Project of Pure Enquiry.* London, 1978.

Wilson, Margaret. *Descartes.* Boston, 1978.


MICHAEL HOOKER

# ISAK DINESEN

## *(1885–1962)*

ISAK DINESEN WAS the name under which the Danish baroness Karen Blixen made her unique, and uniquely international, contribution to the literature of the twentieth century. She wrote all her major works first in English and then in Danish, producing—as it were—two originals; and, though her subjects were, on the one hand, twentieth-century Africa and, on the other, Europe of a hundred and more years ago, her first literary success was in the United States, with the publication of *Seven Gothic Tales* in 1934.

It is necessary to appreciate that Isak Dinesen is not so much a pseudonym for Karen Blixen as a symbolic definition of her persona as a storyteller. Dinesen, her father's family name, defines her roots; Isak, Hebrew for "laughter," points to her aims as a kind of divine joker. For Isaac was the son whom the Lord made Sarah conceive and bear to Abraham when she was ninety and he a hundred; a victory of the imagination over impossibility. Not only was Isaac late-born, as were Isak Dinesen's tales—she was forty-nine when *Seven Gothic Tales* appeared—but he was also the token of a divine comic plan, for "Sarah said, God hath made me to laugh, so that all that hear will laugh with me" (Genesis 21:6). Sarah's laughter is at that end of the range where the comic meets the marvelous, as in Shakespeare's late romances. Similarly Isak Dinesen, who felt a deep affinity with the creator of those plays and even borrowed from one of them the title for her second collection of stories, *Winter's Tales* (1942), wanted her readers to laugh with her at the human condition—a laughter similarly provoked by a compound of wit, irony, and awe.

Nor, therefore, was the original intention behind her half-pseudonym (the anonymity of which was in any case soon exploded) to hide her feminine identity as much as to create imaginative space for herself. Toward the end of her life she could claim that she had never concerned herself with feminism, that "competition between man and woman is a sterile and disagreeable phenomenon," and that woman's function is "to expand her own being" ("En baaltale," 1953; English translation, "Oration at a Bonfire," in *Daguerrotypes and Other Essays* [1979]). Unlike Currer Bell (pseudonym of Charlotte Brontë) or George Eliot (pseudonym of Mary Ann Evans) in the nineteenth century, she was not aiming for a male author's freedom but rather for a detached, godlike freedom from her ordinary self. She had chosen to write under a pen name, she told an interviewer in 1934, for the same reason that her father had done so: in order to "express himself freely, give his imagination free rein" (*Politiken,* 1 May 1934).

There are, then, at least three classes of reasons why Isak Dinesen is important to the student of literature, and those three will structure this essay. She is important as a brave and gallant person who wrung serene and elegant art out of an often harrowed life. She is important as a Danish talent, yet also as an utterly individual one, in a European literary tradition of which she was always conscious. And above all, she is important as a supreme teller of stories. Like Scheherazade in the *Thousand and One Nights,* to whom she so often compares herself, and like the other storytellers who appear within her own stories, she exercises her imaginative powers to hold the reader spellbound. She was defiantly aware that such powers might well be out of tune with modern society and modern literature. Interviewed by Daniel Gillès for Belgian television shortly before her death, in the summer of 1962, she voiced this defiance:

> I am periodically accused of being "decadent." That is no doubt true, as I am not interested in social questions, nor in Freudian psychology. But the narrator of the *Thousand and One Nights* also neglected social questions. . . . As for me I have one ambition only: to invent stories, very beautiful stories.
>
> (Svendsen, ed., pp. 177–178)

The very fact that the Baroness Blixen is here obviously playing up to the interviewer's expectations of her persona helps to make these statements characteristic of Isak Dinesen. Her life and her art have merged, and for the moment she has become a character out of one of her own stories—like the ancient aristocratic Miss Malin Nat-og-Dag in "The Deluge at Norderney" (in *Seven Gothic Tales*), who scorns the idea that "the Lord wants the truth from us." "Why," she says, "he knows it already, and may even have found it a little bit dull. Truth is for tailors and shoemakers, my lord. I, on the contrary, have always held that the Lord has a penchant for masquerades." The same old lady, as the ineluctably rising floodwaters spell imminent death, transforms that dull factual truth into the vicarious fiction of the closing lines of the story: " 'À ce moment de sa narration,' she said, 'Scheherazade vit paraître le matin, et, discrète, se tut' " ("At this moment in her story," she said, "Scheherazade saw the morning dawn and fell discreetly silent").

## *LIFE INTO ART*

The French word *discrète* can be translated by several English adjectives, all hovering around the notion of the effortlessly decorous, the consciously simple, the art which—in the words of Shakespeare's *A Winter's Tale*—"itself is nature." Isak Dinesen, with the feeling for the exactly right word that characterizes all her writing, does *not* translate it—handing us thereby a word that denotes not only the decorousness of Scheherazade and the self-consciousness of Miss Malin Nat-og-Dag, but also the manner in which, in her published work, Dinesen transmutes her own life into art. Two of her works are ostensibly autobiographical: *Out of Africa* (1937) and its after-vibration nearly twenty-five years later, *Shadows on the Grass* (1961). But the relation between these accounts of African experience and the facts of her life in Africa—marriage, syphilis, divorce, love affair, business failure, death of her lover—is nothing if not *discrète.* She left it for the "tailors and shoemakers" to deliver the "dull" truth. Not that it *is* dull, nor that biographers as sensitive and scholarly as Clara Svendsen and Frank Lasson in Denmark or Judith Thurman in the United States could ever be called shoemakers. Thanks to them, and to others who knew Dinesen well, not least her own brother, Thomas Dinesen, her life history has been very fully documented.

But the voice that opens *Out of Africa*—"I had a farm in Africa, at the foot of the Ngong Hills"—is that of a storyteller rather than that of a personal historian. It is the voice of Scheherazade as much as of Karen Blixen. Of course there is a factual background to the book, but what matters is not whether the events she relates *really* happened. For example, toward the end, in the section entitled "Farewell to the

Farm," she tells us about trying to find "some central principle" in the series of disasters that were befalling her: the loss of the farm, the death in an airplane crash of her beloved Denys Finch-Hatton, and so on. She goes out looking for a "sign" that will make clear to her "the coherence of things," and what she sees is a big white cock confronting a small gray chameleon:

> He was frightened, but he was at the same time very brave, he planted his feet in the ground, opened his mouth as wide as he possibly could, and, to scare his enemy, in a flash he shot out his club-shaped tongue at the cock. The cock stood for a second as if taken aback, then swiftly and determinately he struck down his beak like a hammer and plucked out the Chameleon's tongue.
>
> (p. 369)

She kills the chameleon, as he could not live without his tongue, and then she sits there, unable to move; "such a dangerous place did the world seem to me." But gradually, over the next few days, it dawns on her that she has been "in a strange manner honoured and distinguished" by this answer to her call for a sign:

> The powers to which I had cried had stood on my dignity more than I had done myself, and what other answer could they then give? . . . Great powers had laughed to me, with an echo from the hills to follow the laughter, they had said among the trumpets, among the cocks and the Chameleons, Ha ha!
>
> (pp. 369–370)

The question whether this really happened is irrelevant. The pressure of the writing and the significance given to the event show that, if the chameleon had not existed, it would have been necessary—as Voltaire says of God—to invent him. For this little tale of two African animals makes the point so often reiterated in Dinesen's more obviously fictive stories: tragedy, pity, and self-pity are for human beings, but the vision of the gods is comic. To be granted that vision is the gift of the artist, and of the aristocrat. As the old lord says in what is probably the most Danish of all Dinesen's tales, "Sorrow-Acre" (in *Winter's Tales*): "The very same fatality which, in striking the burgher or peasant will become tragedy, with the aristocrat is exalted to the comic. By the grace and wit of our acceptance hereof our aristocracy is known."

Another example of the unimportance of fact in Dinesen's accounts of African life is the story of the king's letter that forms the second part of *Shadows on the Grass,* "Barua a Soldani" (Letter from a King). She tells how she had presented the King of Denmark with the skin of a lion she had shot; and how, coming across a native with a broken leg and having no morphine to relieve his pain, she placed the king's letter of thanks on his chest, telling him that, as a "barua a soldani," it would be efficacious. It was, and thenceforth the letter became a kind of talisman on the farm, asked for by the natives as a magic cure of very serious illness. Now, the letter exists in the Dinesen archives, well-preserved and spotless, to contradict the "truth" of the story; it cannot possibly have passed from hand to hand, as the story has it. But the story exists, to assert a different kind of truth: the bond between two races, or cultures, which consists of a common belief in the magic of kingship. The letter of the story is, in her own words, a sign of "a covenant . . . between the Europeans and the Africans."

This, then, is how autobiography turns into art in Dinesen's two books about Africa. She writes, not about her life and surroundings as such, but about the patterns and meanings she sees in them. No doubt similar processes of transmutation lie behind the more obviously invented stories of *Seven Gothic Tales, Winter's Tales,* and her later collections of tales. Readers of Judith Thurman's fascinating biography *Isak Dinesen: The Life of a Storyteller* will be guided to see the author as an adolescent in "Peter and Rosa" and her childhood sense of otherness in "Alkmene" (both in *Winter's Tales*); and they will see the figures of her aunts in "Supper at Elsinore" (in *Seven Gothic Tales*) and "The Pearls" (in *Winter's Tales*), to mention only a few convincing echoes of her life in her tales. What links all these—her African works and her fiction, her life and her art—is that sense of pattern and meaning that she articulated in a letter to her sister, written to convey the experience of flying "over the African plains and the Ngong Hills with Denys." It is the happiness of seeing not only Africa, but also all life from above: "Here I must say with Father Daniel (?) in 'Jacques,' that God has far more imagination than we have, something I don't consider he shows a great deal of in everyday life. Because by myself I could have discovered neither Africa nor Denys" (Anne Born, trans.). (At this distance in time, she obviously could not be sure of the name of the father confessor, who articulates the moral of the story.) This letter was written in October 1930; and the story she refers to as "Jacques" is one which she had written before leaving for Africa in 1913. (It was published only posthumously, as "Uncle Théodore," in *Carnival: Entertainments and Posthumous Tales,* 1977.) But the idea that "God has far more imagination than we have" is one that, early and late, informs both her life and her work.

She herself certainly felt that God had exercised his imagination in making her the product of a meeting of two opposed traditions in Danish social and cultural life. Born on 17 April 1885, Karen Christentze Dinesen ("Tanne" to her family) was the daughter of Wilhelm Dinesen and his wife, Ingeborg, née Westenholz. The Dinesens were a family of landed gentry, not titled but related to one of the leading families of the nobility, the Frijses. The Westenholzes were wealthy businessmen with their own kind of prominence in Danish affairs: Ingeborg Westenholz' father, Regnar, had been minister of finance and her maternal grandfather a councillor of state. Dinesen undoubtedly exaggerated the polarity in her ancestry, which she defined as aristocracy versus bourgeoisie. But there is no doubt that the two families embodied different, if not antithetical, life-styles. The Dinesens' was basically feudal, self-confident, hedonistic—a latter-day (and, as the twentieth century wore on, somewhat anachronistic) version of the life-style caught so wonderfully in Dinesen's story "Copenhagen Season," published in *Last Tales* (1957). The Westenholzes were self-made, hard-working, and earnest; they had strongly developed consciences, were nonconformists —Unitarians—by confession, and espoused liberal causes—such as feminism—by conviction. Dinesen always claimed that she was like her father's family and that her mother's family disliked her. She seems to have had a particular bond with her father, whose life story could well have come out of one of her own tales. Indeed, biographers suggest that he was the model for Ib Angel in "Copenhagen Season."

True to the military traditions of the family, Wilhelm Dinesen had fought as an officer on the losing side in two wars, the Dano-Prussian War of 1864 and the Franco-Prussian War of 1870–1871. His experience of the Paris Commune left him disillusioned and sick at heart, and he left Europe for America, where he lived for some time as a hunter among the Indians in Wisconsin. He admired their intuitive wisdom and their sense of honor and integrity; they responded with affection and named him "Boganis" (hazelnut)—a name under which he was later to publish several books. Recalled to Denmark in 1874, he spent a few unsettled years in touring Europe, vainly attempting to join the Russo-Turkish War (1877–1878) on the Turkish side. By 1879 he was back in Denmark to settle down for the rest of his life as a landowner and, from 1892, a member of Parliament. As a younger son, he was not to inherit the family estate of Katholm in Jutland; he bought instead a tract of land on the Sealand coast, between Copenhagen and Elsinore. On it were several major houses: one, Folehave, was to become the home of the Westenholz matriarchy, Isak Dinesen's grandmother, known as "Mama," and Aunt Bess, who dominated much of her early life. Another, Rungstedlund, became the home of Wilhelm Dinesen's family: the home in which Isak Dinesen grew up and to which she returned from Africa, in 1931, to spend the rest of her days. It was a romantically historical building, established as a village inn in the sixteenth century and famous for having housed the great Danish poet Johannes Ewald for a couple of years in the 1770's. In 1958 Dinesen was instrumental in establishing the Rungstedlund Foundation which now owns the historic building, keeps the garden and surrounding woodland as a bird reserve, and has the rights of her literary works.

The decisive event of Dinesen's childhood was the death of her father by suicide in 1895, shortly before her tenth birthday. It left her bereaved of not just a father figure but her closest mental and temperamental ally; she felt an alien and a rebel in the household at Rungstedlund where Ingeborg Dinesen was left to bring up five young children with the vigorous support—not to say supervision—of the Westenholz ladies at Folehave. There followed years of being taught by a governess and of attempting to develop a definite but undirected artistic talent. Dinesen went to art school and later (1903–1906) attended the Royal Academy of Fine Art in Copenhagen; in 1907 she made her debut as an author with an uncanny story, "Eneboerne" (The Hermits, reprinted in *Osceola,* 1962). It was published in the Copenhagen monthly *Tilskueren* under the pseudonym of Osceola, the name of a half-caste Indian who had led the Seminoles against American troops in the 1830's and whom her father—significantly—had admired. Under the same pseudonym in the same year but in a different magazine, *Gads danske Magasin,* she published a wildly romantic story, "Pløjeren" (The Ploughman, reprinted in *Osceola*), and in 1909, again in *Tilskueren,* appeared the first story to suggest her mature control and her powers of satire, "Familien de Cats," reprinted in *Osceola* and included as "The de Cats Family" in *Carnival.* If she had hoped to follow in her father's footsteps as an author—his *Jagtbreve* (Letters from the Hunt) in 1889 had been very successful, though a second volume, *Nye Jagtbreve* (New Letters from the Hunt), in 1892 proved less so—she was disappointed. Little note was taken of her tales, and the impulse to write was lost. These last few years before World War I were lacking in aim; a brief period at an art college in Paris in 1910 came to nothing, and her main stimulus seems to have been in the social life of the young aristocratic set centered on the Frijs family.

It was, however, this circle that Dinesen's God decided to step into to exercise his imagination. Among the Frijs relatives there were two young Swedish noblemen, the barons Hans and Bror von Blixen-Finecke, second cousins of Karen Dinesen and twin sons of Baron Frederik of Näsbyholm in the southernmost province of Sweden. Karen fell in love with Hans, who did not return her feelings. At Christmas 1912 she announced her engagement to Bror, and just over a year later, on 14 January 1914, she was married to him, on the very same day that she first set foot on African soil. To ordinary mortals this may seem a strange pattern of events; to Isak Dinesen it had, in retrospect, the self-evidence of an imaginative pattern. In a letter which she wrote to her brother Thomas in April 1931, a few months before leaving Africa for good, a letter that crystallizes all her fears of returning to Rungstedlund and her feelings that "death is preferable to a bourgeois existence," she stated clearly and simply "the fact that the atmosphere at home has never suited me and that I got married and put all my efforts into emigrating in order to get away" (Anne Born, trans.).

Bror Blixen was, as the horrified Westenholzes did not hesitate to point out, an extraordinarily unsuitable marriage partner: pleasure loving, promiscuous, amoral, unintellectual. His main distinction seems to have been an incredible physical stamina; allegedly he is the original of the great white hunter Robert Wilson in Ernest Hemingway's story "The

Short, Happy Life of Francis Macomber" (1938). By the time he died in a car crash in 1946, he had hunted on three continents—Africa, North America, and Europe—and been three times married and divorced, but his greatest glory had been in taking European royalty on safaris in the African highlands. In marrying the wrong twin—insofar as he was not the one she loved—Dinesen married the right man to take her away from "a bourgeois existence" to a world that was, much like the one sought by her father, at once more primitive and more aristocratic.

British East Africa—from 1920 the Crown Colony of Kenya—was in the early decades of the twentieth century not only a hunters' paradise but also a land of peculiar opportunity. The English historian A. J. P. Taylor identifies its settlers as "Englishmen [who] escaped democracy and high taxation by establishing themselves in Kenya as territorial aristocrats on the old model." Other nationalities were attracted, too; and, after toying with the idea of a rubber plantation in Malaya (which might have made of Dinesen a female Joseph Conrad), the engaged couple turned their thoughts to a farm in East Africa. The impetus was in a sense aristocratic; their mutual uncle, Count Mogens Frijs, came back to Denmark from a Kenyan safari and extolled the beauties of the country and its economic potential. The finance, on the other hand, was bourgeois: a family-limited company was set up, its capital almost entirely Westenholz money, its chairman Dinesen's maternal uncle Aage Westenholz, and its purpose to acquire arable land in East Africa to be managed by Bror Blixen. Bror went out to Africa in 1913 and, with a typically highhanded gesture, promptly sold the seven hundred acres that he had come to farm and instead bought the Swedo-African Coffee Company, 4,500 acres, waiting to be turned into a coffee plantation, near Nairobi. This was to be the Ngong Farm of *Out of Africa*. In real life it was also the Karen Coffee Company, whose fortunes were to become part of Karen Blixen's life—as, indeed, of the destiny of Isak Dinesen. It was an ill-fated venture from the start; the land was too high and the soil too acid for securely profitable coffee-growing, and Bror had neither the experience nor the application to be a successful manager. The true story of Karen Coffee is one of continual struggle against droughts, failed or too small crops, falling coffee prices, and pressure from dissatisfied shareholders at home in Denmark. In 1921 the Westenholz family insisted on the dismissal of Bror as manager; thereafter Karen Blixen ran the farm. By the late 1920's it was clear to everyone but herself, stumbling from one financial crisis to another, that the end was inevitable. In December 1930 the company forced the sale of the farm to a property developer who turned the land into residential lots and, ironically, gave this new bourgeois suburb of Nairobi the name Karen. The Baroness Blixen herself stayed on the farm to see the last coffee harvest and the resettlement of her black workers; this done, she returned to Denmark, knowing—as she was later to put it in a letter—that "half of me was lying in the Ngong Hills."

That half is a qualitative rather than quantitative measure; it refers to the quality of life left behind rather than the quantity of experience contained between her landing in Mombasa in January 1914 and her sailing from there at the end of July 1931. The quality of her life in Africa was to be distilled into *Out of Africa* where, because no dates are given and because the material has been so carefully selected, the reader is presented with a timeless and homogeneous past. From that book no reader could guess that, of the seventeen years between her first arrival in Africa and her last departure, three and a half were spent in visits to Europe. These were mainly to see her family in Denmark and to receive painful and often prolonged treatment of the syphilis she had contracted from her husband soon after marriage. Bror Blixen does not figure in *Out of Africa,* nor therefore does the gradual collapse of the marriage, that, despite Karen Blixen's illness, had known a few happy years of shared excitement about African life. It had weathered the problems of the early years of World War I when the Swedes in East Africa were suspected of German sympathies and hence ostracized—a suspicion finally allayed, in the case of the Blixens, when Thomas Dinesen was awarded the Victoria Cross for heroism while fighting with the British army on the French front. Against odds, Karen Blixen retained affection for her husband, just as he in his way remained fond of her; but his promiscuity and general irresponsibility drove their life from crisis to crisis. In 1921 she had reluctantly to agree to a separation, and in 1925 the divorce was made absolute—enabling Bror to marry again and leaving Karen to wonder whether she could still be called Baroness Blixen.

The importance to her of this question must seem strange from a contemporary democratic point of view. But it must be understood in order to appreciate how Isak Dinesen grew out of Karen Dinesen via Karen Blixen. "If it did not sound so beastly," she wrote to her brother Thomas in September 1926, "I might say that, the world being as it is, it was worth having syphilis in order to become a 'Baroness'; but I certainly do not think this is applicable to everyone" (Anne Born, trans.). To most of us, her bargain must seem as unacceptable as that of Faust selling his soul to the devil. But writers—Christopher Marlowe, Johann Wolfgang von Goethe, Thomas Mann—have made great art out of the Faust story, not, obviously, by *being* latter-day Fausts but by exploring the myth. Similarly, what we see in this letter is the writer in the process of turning her own life into myth. To be a baroness was not a simple status question, much as Karen Blixen enjoyed the social position that her title conferred in the colony's hierarchy. The real significance of the title was symbolic, an embodiment of the European aristocratic and heroic past and of the African feudal and heroic present. Her pride in the title is of a different dimension from social snobbishness; it is a proud acceptance of the bargain—however unrecognized as such at the time—by which she had acquired the title. Pride in this sense is defined in the section of *Out of Africa* called "From an Immigrant's Notebook":

> Pride is faith in the idea that God had, when he made us. A proud man is conscious of the idea, and aspires to realize it. He does not strive towards a happiness, or comfort, which may be irrelevant to God's idea of him. His success is the idea of God successfully carried through, and he is in love with his destiny. As the good citizen finds his happiness in the fulfilment of his duty to the community, so does the proud man find his happiness in the fulfilment of his fate.
>
> (p. 261)

To find it worth having syphilis in order to become a baroness is, in the words of this paragraph, to be in love with one's destiny. This idea—of salvation through proud fulfillment of one's own nature or "faith in the idea that God had when he made us"—is fundamental tc Dinesen's life *and* art. That is, Karen Blixen evolved the idea in her life as an "immigrant," and Isak Dinesen informed the characters in her stories with it.

In *Out of Africa* such faith informs not only a few selected European aristocrats but also the natives themselves. "The Negro," she writes, "is on friendly terms with destiny, having been in her hands all this time." Destiny informs the animal creation, too: the gazelle, Lulu, who is the subject of part of the first section of the book, "Kamante and Lulu," and the lions against which the white hunters match themselves. On a euphoric New Year's morning, she tells us in the section called "Visitors to the Farm," Denys Finch-Hatton and she came upon and shot first a lioness and then her mate; and as they sat there drinking their breakfast claret and looking at the magnificent bodies of the dead lions, "they were, all through, what they ought to be."

Of all creatures in *Out of Africa,* Denys Finch-Hatton is, all through, what he ought to be. To make him so, Dinesen was particularly *discrète,* writing as a storyteller and not as a biographer. In the book he seems to appear from nowhere; he listens to her stories; he shares some epiphanic moments, like the vision of the lions just mentioned; he takes her up in his airplane, thus enabling her to get an overview of Africa that is more metaphysical than geographical: " 'I see,' I have thought, 'This was the idea. And now I understand everything.' " His death, when that same airplane crashes, and his burial in the Ngong Hills—in a grave that later becomes a haunt for lions at sunrise and sunset—are part of the extraordinary movement through disaster toward "understanding everything" that forms the last section of *Out of Africa,* "Farewell to the Farm." In real life Finch-Hatton first met Karen Blixen in 1918 and soon became the great love of her life. Their relationship lasted until a rupture that occurred within the last year or so before she left Africa when, it would appear, her distraught state caused her to place too great demands on him. For making no demands, in the worldly sense, had been the keynote of this relationship (so unauthentically romanticized in the Meryl Streep and Robert Redford affair in Sydney Pollack's film of *Out of Africa* [1985]). An aristocratic nomad with a military and adventurous career reminiscent of her father's, Finch-Hatton would turn up at Karen Blixen's farm, bringing wine and books and records, and would vanish again when the next safari called. At various times he owned a great deal of land and property in Africa, but for a period the farm was his only home between safaris. Twice she mistakenly thought herself pregnant by him; at no time was there any question of his standing by her, in the sense of offering marriage or financial security. But none of this comes through in *Out of Africa,* where what matters is not what the "real" Denys has done or not done, but what he *was.*

In many ways the "biographical" Finch-Hatton relates to his namesake in *Out of Africa* as myth does to reality. The younger son of the thirteenth Earl of Winchilsea, educated at Eton and Oxford, he becomes in the book the quintessential, timeless aristocrat:

> He could have walked arm in arm . . . with Sir Philip [Sidney], or Francis Drake. And the people of Elizabeth's time might have held him dear because to them he would have suggested that Antiquity, the Athens, of which they dreamed and wrote. Denys could indeed have been placed harmoniously in any period of our civilization, *tout comme chez soi,* all up till the opening of the nineteenth century. He would have cut a figure in any age, for he was an athlete, a musician, a lover of art and a fine sportsman. He did cut a figure in his own age, but it did not quite fit in anywhere.
> (p. 215)

Sociologically Finch-Hatton was one of these "territorial aristocrats on the old model" referred to by A. J. P. Taylor. In the myth of the book he is the romantic wanderer who does not "fit in" with industrialized and bourgeois Europe and so is drawn to the both more primitive and more aristocratic world of Africa. "Africa was keeping him," she wrote when first introducing him in the chapter "Visitors to the Farm," and so there is a peculiar rightness—a completion of a pattern, a destiny—in his death and burial: "It was fit and decorous that the lions should come to Denys's grave and make him an African monument. 'And renowned be thy grave.' Lord Nelson himself, I have reflected, in Trafalgar Square, has his lions made only out of stone." The life and death of Denys thus fit into the heroic and tragicomic pattern of the book, as no ordinary extramarital love story would have done. Her love for him is diffused throughout *Out of Africa* but is most movingly transmuted into art in the passage in which she both celebrates his being wholly what he ought to be and describes the way this quality brings out the rightness of everything around him. In this exquisite simplicity of its language, it becomes a twentieth-century Song of Songs:

> When he came back to the farm, it gave out what was in it; it spoke,—as the coffee-plantations speak, when with the first showers of the rainy season they flower, dripping wet, a cloud of chalk. When I was expecting Denys back, and

> heard his car coming up the drive, I heard, at the same time, the things of the farm all telling what they really were. He was happy on the farm; he came there only when he wanted to come, and it knew, in him, a quality of which the world besides was not aware, a humility. He never did but what he wanted to do, neither was guile found in his mouth.
>
> (p. 225)

If, then, *Out of Africa* shows Dinesen transmuting her life into art, we are fortunate to have a gloss on that process in the letters she wrote to members of her family in Denmark between 1914 and 1931. These were edited by Frans Lasson and published as *Breve fra Afrika: 1914–1931* in 1978. (An English translation by Anne Born, *Letters from Africa,* was published in 1981.) They provide, on the one hand, documentary evidence of her life in this period, and they are in a very literal sense a source of *Out of Africa;* for, as Frans Lasson points out in his introduction to the *Letters,* Dinesen used her letters to her mother as memoranda while writing her work on Africa. On the other hand, they also provide a portrait of the artist in that they show, in Lasson's words, "a ceaselessly unresting struggle to reach clarification and understanding of herself." In that respect they are as important to an understanding of her artistic nature as are John Keats's letters to students of his poetic genius. They show her feeling her way toward a style as well as toward a philosophy of life.

Not all of the letters are of the same nature. Those to her maternal aunt, Mary Bess Westenholz of Folehave, tend to be part of a continuing debate between the two of them on issues such as religion, the liberation of women, and sexual morality. Here we see the Isak Dinesen who in 1923–1924 labored on a long essay on love and marriage in the modern world. (The essay was published posthumously as "Moderne Ægteskab og andre Betragtninger" in *Blixeniana 1977;* an English translation, *On Modern Marriage,* was published in 1986.) This is the socially conscious woman who wrote to Aunt Bess in 1926 that "feminism should probably be regarded as the most significant movement of the nineteenth century" and whose essay explores what she sees as the basic nineteenth-century error of confusing love—which is an experience between free individuals—and marriage—which is a public, dynastic commitment. (Clearly there is also much autobiography behind this essay.) The letters to her mother are full of domestic details and accounts of social life in the colony and safaris on the plains. They also reveal her deep affection for her family, her plain bourgeois interest in their affairs. But through all this, and rising to a crescendo as the agony of leaving Africa and returning to a bourgeois existence approaches, runs a note of self-analysis and self-assertion. Thus, in one of the last letters she wrote to her mother, in March 1931, she felt prompted to sum up her life, which at this moment meant her African life:

> Of all the idiots I have met in my life—and the Lord knows that they have not been few or little—I think that I have been the biggest. But a certain love of greatness, which could not be quelled, has kept a hold on me, has been "my daimon". . . . A great world of poetry has revealed itself to me and taken me to itself here, and I have loved it. I have looked into the eyes of lions and slept under the Southern Cross, I have seen the grass of the great plains ablaze and covered with delicate green after the rains. I have been the friend of Somali, Kikuyu, and Masai, I have flown over the Ngong Hills,—"I plucked the best rose of life, and Freja be praised."
>
> (*Letters from Africa: 1914–1931,* Anne Born, trans., p. 416)

We hardly need that last self-conscious quotation, from the skald's song in Act IV of the Danish poet-dramatist Adam Gottlob Oehlenschläger's tragedy *Hagbarth and Signe* (1814), to see that here personal misery is translating itself into literature—into the images, patterns, and rhythms of a kind of prose poetry. The step from here to *Out of Africa* is a short one.

It is in her letters to her brother, Thomas

Dinesen, that she is most openly self-revealing. He was her confidant, both before and after his stay on her African farm between 1920 and 1923. Thomas Dinesen's position involved considerable demands on emotional (and sometimes also financial) capital, never more so than when receiving the letter of 10 April 1931 in which his sister, for all her assertion that she is *not* saying "help me and sustain me, or I will die" (Anne Born, trans.), is in fact saying exactly that. (The circumstances surrounding a probable suicide attempt by her at about this time are not clear.) Yet this same letter also mentions her having started to write a book in English and having been told by an English publisher, to whom she had sent a section for comment on her command of the language, that "the leisurely style and language are exceedingly attractive." The seesaw movement between despair and resolution that the letter communicates is no doubt genuinely felt, but it is felt with the partial detachment of the artist who, even as she feels, watches herself feel. Dinesen was aware of this quality in herself, and it is again in a letter to Thomas that she identifies it most clearly. It is a very long letter, written on 5 September 1926, containing among other things her insight that "loving one's destiny unconditionally" is "the condition for real happiness"; from this follows her defiant statement that "it was worth having syphilis in order to become a 'Baroness' "; and then, to show why that statement is not "applicable to everyone," she proceeds to define her own uniqueness:

> I myself feel that a certain kind of shape and color in my surroundings, a certain amount of "showing off" . . . is the expression of my personality, is what is called a natural necessity for me; without these things I am . . . an actor without a stage, a violinist without hands or at least without a violin.
>
> (*Letters from Africa: 1914–1931,* Anne Born, trans., p. 284)

In the letter to her mother quoted earlier we saw how the person named Karen Blixen wrote herself into a persona, soon to be called Isak Dinesen. In this letter to Thomas she insists upon the "natural necessity" to her of such a process with a fierce honesty that refuses to compromise with objections—call them moral or puritanical or bourgeois—to "showing off." Life to her must be an act, a performance. When she wrote the letter, her stage was Africa; some years later it was to be the printed word. That this, too, was a "natural necessity" is foreshadowed in the closing paragraphs of the letter, where she explains to Thomas that writing to him has been a necessity before settling to write fiction: "I was feeling so uncertain and could not do anything about it until I had heard my own voice, seen myself in that mirror that is the person to whom one is speaking,—taken stock of myself." Dinesen's life after Africa can be briefly told, for even though it was only then that she became officially an author, all that really made her the author she is happened before. She did, of course, survive the return to Denmark, where she took up residence with her mother at Rungstedlund. She was ruined, financially, physically, and emotionally, but willpower—the sense that to realize her destiny now was to become a writer—saw her through to the publication of *Seven Gothic Tales,* the manuscript of which was ready by the spring of 1933, not much more than eighteen months after her return. An American publisher, Robert Haas (whose firm subsequently merged with Random House), recognized the merit of her stories, and when he published them in January 1934, the reading public did so too. Chosen as Book of the Month in February, the book was a commercial success as well as a critical one.

Willpower, fed by public acclaim, also saw Dinesen through the rest of her life to her death at Rungstedlund, at the age of seventy-seven, on 7 September 1962. It made her persist through long spells of illness: her syphilis, though brought under control to the point of not being infectious by her early medical treatment, had not been arrested; symptoms of tabes dorsalis—degeneration of the spine—

had begun to appear as early as 1921, and in the last three decades of her life she was to suffer long periods of excruciating pain, despite operations performed to sever spinal nerves. In the end her body literally wasted away, but her spirit remained strong and gallant. "A certain amount of 'showing off,' " as she had put it to her brother, was more than ever "a natural necessity" for her. Its superficial signs were heavy eye makeup (long before such cosmetics were in common use), spectacular clothes, and a penchant for a diet of champagne, oysters, and asparagus. Its fundamental drive was to remain a Scheherazade despite personal suffering and national crisis. (Denmark was under German occupation from 1940 to 1945, and Dinesen was sympathetic to the gathering resistance movement, the position of Rungstedlund enabling her to assist, in the autumn of 1943, the action to help Danish Jews to escape to neutral Sweden.) Again in the words of her 1926 letter to her brother, she remained an actor *with* a stage, refusing to play the part of the invalid.

This was never more true than on her one and only visit to the United States, from January to April 1959, when, emaciated and living largely on stamina and amphetamines, she carried out an amazingly heavy program of talks and readings and kept up a hectic pace of social engagements—including a luncheon party given by Carson McCullers, where the other two guests were Arthur Miller and Marilyn Monroe. For Isak Dinesen those three months in New York, even though she had to spend a few weeks of them in the hospital recharging her energy, were truly a period of being lionized—a term particularly appropriate in her case, as she always prided herself on having been known as "the Lioness" in the Kenya colony. Her American biographer Thurman speaks of the extraordinary rapport that Dinesen established with her New York audiences; the contrast, she notes, between, on the one hand, the physical frailty of the seventy-four-year-old woman, who seemed to them "incalculably old," and, on the other, her sheer presence and personality, whether she delivered an address or retold one of her stories verbatim from memory, made them feel that "this was the wise, noble and heroic survivor of the past—the master—they had been expecting." The talk she gave to the American Academy of Arts and Letters, "On Mottoes of My Life" (reprinted in *Daguerrotypes and Other Essays*), forms the best brief introduction to the life and art of Isak Dinesen, if only because what she describes as "the first real motto of my youth"—the paradoxical order given by Pompey to his crew of timid sailors, "Navigare necesse est, vivere non necesse" (It is necessary to sail; it is not necessary to live)—is so clearly the fundamental principle of her whole life.

In Denmark, where after her mother's death in 1939 she was mistress of Rungstedlund, her audience had more ambivalent feelings. *Seven Gothic Tales,* which she did not so much translate as rewrite into Danish (having been dismayed by the attempts of professional translators), was published as *Syv fantastiske Fortaellinger* (1935) in the middle of the depression in a Europe torn by social and political unrest. True to the Scandinavian tradition of looking for contemporary relevance in works of literature, her countrymen were less able than her American and British readers to see her tales as works of art; to them she seemed at best escapist, at worst reactionary and even perverse. (This last judgment was made in a review by Frederick Schyberg in the leading newspaper *Berlingske Tidende,* 25 September 1935, which Dinesen kept and begrudged till the end of her days.) *Den afrikanske Farm* (1937), the Danish version of *Out of Africa,* did much to reassure her Danish readers of her humanity and sense of reality, and when *Vinter Eventyr* (1942), the Danish edition of *Winter's Tales,* was published in the middle of the Nazi occupation, the Danishness of this book—its feeling for the landscape, the life, and the history of Denmark—had a very special appeal. So, in the 1940's Dinesen began to be recognized as a major author in her own country and as a patriot. Oppressed and bored by the Occupation, she wrote as a light relief her only novel, *Gengaeldelsens Veje* (*The Angelic Avengers,* originally written in Danish and published in 1944 under the pseudonym of Pierre Andrézel and with the smoke screen of "translated into Danish by Clara Svendsen"; English and American editions published in, respectively, 1946 and 1947). The critics, having dismantled the pseudonym, were ready to credit this Victorian Gothic crime story with being an anti-Nazi political allegory. By the early 1950's she was something of a cult figure for a group of young literati, but she was also reaching a wide Danish audience through a series of popular radio talks. Now nationally and internationally famous, she joined the distinguished band of writers *not* to be awarded the Nobel Prize for Literature; in his speech when accepting the prize in 1954, Hemingway referred to her as a writer more deserving of it than himself, and in 1957 she was widely—and, as it turned out, wrongly—regarded as the leading candidate.

The same year—1957—saw the publication of her *Last Tales* (Danish version, *Sidste Fortaellinger,* also 1957), followed the next year by *Anecdotes of Destiny* (Danish version, *Skaebne Anekdoter,* also 1958). Of the five *Anecdotes,* four had already appeared as magazine stories, three of them in the *Ladies' Home Journal,* which published a number of her stories between 1950 and 1962. The table of contents of *Last Tales* is a compendium of her literary plans in the last decade of her life. There are three groups of stories, "New Gothic Tales," "New Winter's Tales," and—the first and largest group—"Tales from *Albondocani.*" Dinesen did not live to complete any of the volumes for which the stories in *Last Tales* had been ultimately intended. The most ambitious of these was *Albondocani,* which she had been planning since 1950. It was to be her own *Thousand and One Nights,* an immense novel of interlocking stories, each self-contained and yet also connected through shared characters with the others, and all set in the kingdom of Naples in the 1830's. She wrote as long as there was any strength left, aided by her faithful secretary, amanuensis, and companion (and, in the end, literary executor) Clara Svendsen. As late as 1961 she was revising old stories and working on new ones. But much of her strength went, at the end of the 1950's, into a final evocation of the Africa that she had left nearly thirty years earlier, *Shadows on the Grass,* which was written in English but first appeared in Danish as *Skygger paa Graesset* in 1960 before being published in English in 1961.

Isak Dinesen never did return to the real Africa, as against that world of memory where "half of me was lying in the Ngong Hills." Twice she had planned to—in 1935 she tried to be appointed war correspondent in the Italo-Ethiopian war, and just before World War II she hoped to make a pilgrimage to Mecca with her old Somali servant Farah—but each time the plans fell through. In 1960 *Life* wanted to send her to report on the struggle for independence in Kenya—an offer that points to the ironic gap between the perceived image of the writer and the actual condition of the woman, who (as she had to accept) would not have survived the journey, and who in any case (as she realized) would not have wanted that kind of a homecoming.

Nor did she ever set any of her tales on African soil. Africa was autobiography, though—as we have seen—when she wrote about her life in Africa, it translated itself into art. Africa made her as an artist, not merely because her *Gothic Tales* was conceived and partly written there, but also because there she learned to see the pattern of things, to recognize aristocracy, whether in animals or men, white or black. Above all, there she learned to treasure the quality that produces such insights: the imagination. It was, according to *Out of Africa,* the natives on her farm that were her best teachers:

> The Negro is on friendly terms with destiny, . . . Amongst the qualities that he will be looking for in a master or a doctor or in God,

> imagination, I believe, comes high up in the list. . . . When the Africans speak of the personality of God they speak like the Arabian Nights or like the last chapters of the book of Job; it is the same quality, the infinite power of imagination, with which they are impressed.
>
> (p. 23)

So of course she puts her own life into her tales, insofar as, whatever their setting and ostensible subject, they trace the patterns of extraordinary destinies and extraordinary greatness of mind. Above all, they both celebrate and exercise "the infinite power of imagination." Rarely do the *facts* of her life enter in even as surreptitious a form as they do in "The Cardinal's Third Tale," one of the *Albondocani* stories included in *Last Tales*. Lady Flora Gordon, a Scottish noblewoman of immense size, beauty, wit, and wealth, whose spiritual arrogance involves both a denial of the love of God and a Swiftian disgust with mankind, is transformed, mysteriously, into someone who experiences "a mirthful forbearance with and benevolence towards the frailty of humanity." The agency of the mystery is partly an old friar and partly the glorious immensity of St. Peter's in Rome, where she spends hours in contemplation of the bronze statue of the apostle. But the crucial part of the pattern is autobiography transmuted into a demonstration of God's imagination. Lady Flora kisses the foot of the statue, still moist and warm from the lips of a young Roman workman; four weeks later she discovers a syphilitic sore on her own lip—and welcomes it as a symbol, a covenant with humanity.

More often autobiography enters the tales as artistic self-reflectiveness. Two of the stories in *Winter's Tales* are about an English writer, Charles Despard, whose experiences mirror her own. In the first, "The Young Man with the Carnation," he is in despair, having written one great book and feeling that he could never write another, until the tragicomic coincidences of one night prove to him the infinite potential of God's, and hence the artist's, imagination. In the second, "A Consolatory Tale," he is older, successful, and bitterly aware of the professional writer's commandments:

> Thou shalt love thy art with all thy heart and with all thy soul, and with all thy mind. And thou shalt love thy public as thyself. . . . All human relationships have in them something monstrous and cruel. But the relation of the artist to the public is amongst the most monstrous. Yes, it is as terrible as marriage.
>
> (p. 291)

Even more radically, Dinesen explores in some tales the wonder of the artist's gift *and* the sacrifice of ordinary human happiness that it demands. Perhaps this is done most poignantly in "Tempests" (in *Anecdotes of Destiny*), which is also one of the very few stories she wrote originally in Danish.

The plot weaves a traveling production of Shakespeare's *The Tempest* together with a real shipwreck off the Norwegian coast, so as to lead the heroine, a wonderfully inspired actress in the part of Ariel, to realize the danger of confusing life and art and the necessity of giving up the idea of marrying the man she loves. The artist's lot is sacrifice, and she is told by her director/Prospero: "In return we get the world's distrust—and our dire loneliness. And nothing else." Yet, for the many storytellers within Dinesen's often Chinese-box–like stories there *is* something else: the story itself. Thus in "The Dreamers" (in *Seven Gothic Tales*) there is "the much-renowned storyteller Mira Jama himself, the inventions of whose mind have been loved by a hundred tribes." Mira has outlived his own talent. He is bored with life; the world no longer cares for him; nor does he much care whether he lives or dies. "But," he says, "the tales which I made—they shall last."

## *TRADITION AND THE INDIVIDUAL TALENT*

That Isak Dinesen's tales have lasted, and are likely to last, is partly because she speaks with a voice that her finest critic, Robert Langbaum, has called "the voice of European civilization." Her readers are bound to sense that she writes with a keen awareness of European literary traditions. She herself, though she was an avid reader, liked to disclaim any erudition; she would refer to the erratic education she had received, and above all she would stress that she belonged, like her own Mira Jama, to the oral tradition of storytelling:

> Denys, who lived much by the ear, preferred hearing a story told, to reading it; when he came to the farm he would ask: "Have you got a story?" I had been making up many while he had been away. In the evenings he made himself comfortable, spreading cushions like a couch in front of the fire, and with me sitting on the floor, cross-legged like Scheherazade herself, he would listen, clear-eyed, to a long tale, from when it began until it ended.
>
> (*Out of Africa,* p. 226)

But she also admitted that the stories she thus told Finch-Hatton were never the entire tales that she eventually published, only the shorter stories-within-stories of which her fiction is so full. She liked to have each story completely worked out in her head—to have told it at least to herself—before she wrote it down; but in writing she would take infinite pains, rewriting a whole page to change a single word. Her written stories are not only rich in incident and detail and polished in style, they are also highly complex literary organizations which demand the reader's attention to allusions and symbols, to echoes and parallels. From "The Roads Round Pisa," which (in the Danish and British—but not the American—editions) opens *Seven Gothic Tales,* to *Ehrengard,* which was the last story she completed (it appeared posthumously in 1963 in both Danish and English), the reader has to be prepared to find himself in a labyrinth, requiring him to retrace his steps and reassess events and characters as new turns in the story change the meaning of what has gone before. If we trust the tale rather than the teller, then her storytelling combines a primitive appeal to everyone's love of hearing a story told with a highly sophisticated literary art.

An obvious aspect of that sophistication is an undertow of reference to major European writers. At the climax of "The Roads Round Pisa" Giovanni and Agnese speak to each other in quotation (in Italian) from Dante's *Divine Comedy*. These two young, noble, and beautiful people have met just once before, a year earlier when, in a tragicomic version of the substitute bride story, he deflowered her, thinking she was someone else. There is no language for them now except Dante's poetry of repentance and forgiveness, but unless the reader recognizes the lines, he will miss the meaning of a crucial episode in the story. This is an extreme example, but less extreme ones abound.

The plays of Shakespeare are so much present beneath many of the stories that they form a kind of background mythology. The use of the Ariel figure and of *The Tempest* as a whole in "Tempests" is only the most outstanding example. The character of Lady Flora in "The Cardinal's Third Tale" needs to be understood in relation to Jonathan Swift's work, as does Councillor Mathiesen in "The Poet" (in *Seven Gothic Tales*) in relation to Goethe's. Indeed, as the Councillor's most treasured and formative memory is of two years spent in Weimar, "in the atmosphere of the great Geheimrat Goethe," the German poet figures both as a theme and as an actual person in the story. So does Lord Byron in the late and not fully revised "Second Meeting" (in *Carnival*), while Henrik Ibsen makes an appearance as a collector of folktales and songs—"our old national treasures,—pearls, if you like"—in "The Pearls." Other Scandinavian writers appear, too, notably the great Danish poet Johannes Ewald, whose connection with Rungstedlund made him particularly alive to Dinesen. He and the wayward young king Christian VII are the principal characters of "Converse at Night in Copenhagen" (in *Last Tales*). These historical figures can appear in person because nearly all

Dinesen's stories are set in the past. But, significantly, in one of her two stories that take place in the modern age, "Carnival" (in *Carnival*)—the story she wrote in 1926 after her therapeutic letter to her brother—one of the young ladies at the masquerade party is dressed as "the young Soren Kierkegaard—that brilliant, deep, and desperate Danish philosopher of the forties."

This does not mean that, to enjoy Dinesen's tales, one must be fully versed in European literary history, but it does mean that part of that enjoyment is a sense of listening to a dialogue between the storyteller and the poets and thinkers of the past. And this in turn is part of a wider experience of being in touch, through the narrator's voice, with the past. In *Seven Gothic Tales* several of the stories open as pieces of cultural history, though without appearing to strain for historical effect. Take, for example, "The Deluge at Norderney":

> During the first quarter of the last century, seaside resorts became the fashion, even in those countries of northern Europe within the minds of whose people the sea had hitherto held the role of the devil, the cold and voracious hereditary foe of humanity. The romantic spirit of the age, which delighted in ruins, ghosts, and lunatics, and counted a stormy night on the heath and a deep conflict of the passions a finer treat for the connoisseur than the ease of the salon and the harmony of a philosophic system, reconciled even the most refined individuals to the eternal wildness of the coast scenery and the open seas.
>
> (p. 121)

By the time of her last completed story, *Ehrengard,* the sense of long ago has entered into the tone of the voice itself, and the story opens with exquisite simplicity:

> An old lady told this story.
>
> A hundred and twenty years ago, she began, my story told itself, at greater length of time than you or I can give to it, and with a throng of details and particulars which we can never hope to know. The men and women who then gradually built it up, and to whom it was a matter of life and death, are all long gone.
>
> (pp. 3–4)

And yet even here, the past is not a general long ago but a specific stage in European history:

> The very country in which it began, developed and came to an end, may be said to have faded out of existence. For it was, in those good days, a fair, free and flourishing small principality of old Germany, and its sovereign was responsible to no one but God in Heaven. But later on, when times and men grew harder, it was silently and sadly swallowed up into the great new German Empire.
>
> (p. 4)

Here we have a key to the settings of Dinesen's stories. Whatever European (and very occasionally Asian) country and whatever decade of the nineteenth century (excepting the tale set in the Danish thirteenth century, "The Fish," in *Winter's Tales*) she chooses for each tale, the choice is of a place and time *before* "times and men grew harder." That is, place and time in her fiction matter less as geography and history as such, and more as conditions for a quality of life, an attitude of mind. The virginal Ehrengard von Schreckenstein in an idyllic German principality in the 1840's, the old Prince Potenziani who fights a duel but dies from love on the roads around Pisa in 1823, the von Galens and Angels of the 1870 Copenhagen winter season—all share, and share with the culture that has produced them, that "faith in the idea that God had, when he made us" that Dinesen found in the natives on her African farm. But to the reader—though not to the characters—these separate worlds also share that sense that is so strong in the last section of *Shadows on the Grass,* "Echoes from the Hills," of a world nearing its end and having, as the narrator in "Copenhagen Season" puts it, "one foot in the grave." They are aristocratic, heroic, and doomed worlds.

From Dinesen's biographers we learn that, when asked about the meaning of "gothic" in the title of her first collection of tales, she explained it as referring to the gothic revival in art and literature and defined her period as beginning with the death of the poet Ewald in 1781 and ending with the fall of the Second Empire in France in 1871, "the last great phase of aristocratic culture." More specifically she would point to her kinship with the English Gothic tradition and the age of Byron. There is no horror in her tales, and little of the supernatural. "The Supper at Elsinore" with its ghost is exceptional, and "The Sailor-boy's Tale" (in *Winter's Tales*) could be seen as a happy inversion of Samuel Taylor Coleridge's "The Rime of the Ancient Mariner" (1798, 1817), in that the sailor boy saves the life of a peregrine falcon that then becomes an old Lapp woman who in turn saves his life. But "The Monkey" (in *Seven Gothic Tales*) is more truly representative of Dinesen's version of the gothic; the way that the Virgin Prioress of Cloister Seven and her pet monkey metamorphose in and out of each other is not seen as supernatural but rather as a natural manifestation of the closeness of the very refined and the brutal or barbaric. What Dinesen most fundamentally shares with the early English Romantics, notably Coleridge, is the ability to make the most fantastic events seem most natural. In her Danish translation of the title of her first book, "gothic" indeed becomes "fantastisk." She also shares with the Gothic movement in late- eighteenth- and early- nineteenth-century English literature the fundamental impulse to provide her readers with an emotional outlet in a rational and mechanistic age. Hence the appeal of, and the sometimes half-guilty response to, her extravagant fiction in the realistic and socially conscious 1930's.

If Dinesen's admiration of aristocratic culture and her regret at its disappearance determined her choice of settings for her tales, there are also clearly more purely aesthetic reasons for her devotion to the past. In an interview in the Danish newspaper *Politiken* on 1 May 1934, when the author of *Seven Gothic Tales* had been revealed as Karen Blixen, she explained that she had set her tales in the past "because . . . only in that way did I become perfectly free." Freedom in this sense is also what her pseudonym aimed at, freedom to create her own fictive world, freedom from the expectations of real life. In the interview with Daniel Gilles for Belgian television shortly before her death she developed the formal implications of such freedom: "With the past I find myself before a finished world, complete in all its elements, and I can thus more easily recompound it in my imagination. Here, no temptation for me to fall back into realism, nor for my readers to look for it." The ultimate attraction of the past, then, is not so much its pastness, or romantic evocativeness, as its completeness. Seeing at once the beginning and the end of a period or a phase in culture is like seeing Africa from Denys' airplane over the Ngong Hills; it gives the artist that godlike detachment which Dinesen saw as so essential to the storyteller. "Recompounding" the past, so that beginnings and ends are seen to be woven together into astounding patterns, is the essence of her narrative art. For a single, compact illustration of this, the reader might turn to her late, never finally revised story "Second Meeting." Within it, the owner of a marionette theater—himself Byron's alter ego, waiting on this "second meeting" to turn the life of the poet into a story—tells Byron of "a very great story" that he has not yet had the courage to make into a play. It is the story of the day of Pentecost, but its focus is not on the apostles, tumbling to the floor as the Holy Spirit descends on them and makes them speak in tongues, but on "one slim and graceful figure only, Milord, [who] in this hour of the hurricane remains serene":

> The Virgin stands unmoving, her face turned upwards, her hands crossed upon her breast. As you will know from the paintings, upon Good Friday all blood had sunk from her face. Now once more it mounts to her cheeks in one sweet roseate wave, and she again looks like a maiden of fifteen. In a low voice—and for this I shall have to use my loveliest soprano—she cries out: "Oh, is it

> you, sir? After these thirty-four years, is it you?" Between the distant first meeting of those two and the present meeting lies the story.
>
> (*Carnival*, pp. 336–337)

Turning the Pentecost into a love story between Mary and the Holy Ghost is bound to seem, to many, in poor taste, at best bizarre, at worst decadently iconoclastic. All those adjectives can be applied to Dinesen's art, but they all need to be tempered by an awareness of how, as here, an extraordinary aesthetic detachment controls the impact of her narration. Through the statuelike beauty of the Virgin as the still center of a tumultuous scene—reminiscent of the miraculous ending of Shakespeare's *The Winter's Tale*—the main impulse communicated is not erotic; it is an aesthetic satisfaction at a destiny fulfilled, a pattern completed. Between the Annunciation thirty-four years ago and the descent of the Holy Spirit in the present "lies the story"; and it lies in the minds of the narrator and the reader rather than on the page.

The "perfect freedom" which Dinesen spoke of as a precondition for her art also meant a freedom both to draw on and to detach herself from the various movements and "-isms" of European literature. Her relationship with the gothic strain in the Romantic movement has already been touched on. Her sense of landscape and of its interaction with man—be it in Africa or Europe—has much in common with the nature romanticism of William Wordsworth. At the same time, in her almost obsessive use of the image of the mask, and of life as a marionette play, she owes something to the more complex, ironic romanticism of the Germans—to Ludwig Tieck and Heinrich Heine—even as she also shares this obsession with more modern poets, such as William Butler Yeats. As early as 1904 she had written a marionette comedy, "Sandhedens Haevn" ("The Revenge of Truth"), for the family; she revised it in Africa, and its publication in *Tilskueren* in May 1926 gave her the stimulus to draft her first gothic tales. (An English translation of "The Revenge of Truth" is included in Donald Hannah's critical study.) But perhaps the most timeless aspect of Romanticism in her work is its central myth: that of a paradise lost.

*Out of Africa,* as Robert Langbaum was the first to show, is one of the great pastorals in European literature; in writing about the feudal society on her farm, the natural aristocracy of the natives, and the wild grace of the animals, she is, Langbaum writes, "reconstructing that organic life of the European past projected by the romantic mythology." And when she loses the farm, he continues, "we see reenacted in miniature the crisis of modern Europe, the breakup of social organization based on love and mutual obligation."

These are large terms, but no larger than those used by Dinesen herself. As late as her American Academy talk, "On Mottoes of My Life," she could describe her meeting with the animals of Africa as "a return to those happy days when Adam gave names to the beasts of Eden" and speak of the understanding and love she felt for the natives as "as strong a passion as I have ever known." In *Out of Africa* she voices the fear that the industrial revolution has cut European civilization off from its roots in nature:

> Perhaps the white men of the past, indeed of any past, would have been in better understanding and sympathy with the coloured races than we, of our Industrial Age, shall ever be. When the first steam engine was constructed, the roads of the races of the world parted, and we have never found one another since.
>
> (pp. 215–216)

She is not writing here about race relations as such, but about what the modern world has lost. In pointing to "the particular, instinctive attachment which all Natives of Africa felt" toward Denys Finch-Hatton and a few other people of his kind, she is both lamenting the state of modern technological and bourgeois civilization and celebrating the few heroic survivors from an older civilization. Primitive instinct and aristocratic refinement meet and merge in all her heroes, whether they come from life, like her father and Denys; from history, like Lord Byron; from folktales, like the old lord in "Sorrow-Acre"; or purely from her own invention, like Prince Potenziani in "The Roads Round Pisa." They are unfit for "real" life; they dream, wander, hunt, and pursue sexual adventures; their love affairs with their own destinies tend to lead to death. In celebrating the beauty and wholeness of their lives, as against the dreariness and fragmentation of modern civilization, Dinesen had much in common with the French symbolist poets whom she and Denys had read and admired together.

Indeed the story in *Winter's Tales* called "The Invincible Slave-Owners," which is about two young German girls' absurdly heroic attempt to keep up their aristocratic life-style though they are penniless, ends with a couple of lines from Charles Baudelaire's poem "Le beau navire" ("The Beautiful Ship")—thus summing up the apparently pathetic life of the heroine, Mizzi, as *triomphant* (triumphant) and *majestueux* (majestic or magnificent). In her admiration of style above morality, of the heroically destructive and self-destructive life above a sympathetic concern for fellow lives, Dinesen could well be seen—and often has been seen—as a decadent in the sense that some French and English writers of the 1890's are termed decadent. The moribund syphilitic baroness who in 1961 wrote of the Virgin's blush when she reencountered the Holy Ghost at Pentecost would seem a classic example of latter-day decadence. But if we use this term, we must also realize that her version of decadence is a peculiarly robust one, as preoccupied with the glorious processes of life as with degeneration and death. In a letter to her mother in 1923 she wrote of having reread Oscar Wilde and found that he had not worn well: "It is all so thin and feeble that one feels like spitting it out again" (Anne Born, trans.). Instead, she writes, she has turned to the great Danish Romantic writers, notably Oehlenschläger, in whom she finds "profundity and nobility." Her own art of storytelling may represent "art for art's sake" in that it disclaims any social and moral purpose and often glorifies the amoral or even immoral. But it is saved from being "thin and feeble" by its profound exploration of how life itself becomes art.

It is perhaps not coincidental that the robustness and the profundity are both most evident in her Danish stories. Take "Peter and Rosa," which is set in the neighborhood of Rungstedlund and in an unsurpassed way renders the arrival of spring after a long Scandinavian winter. The sky over the "dead" landscape "dissolved into streaming life"; the snow melts, and the ice that has covered the sound from the Danish to the Swedish coast begins to break up. The eponymous hero and heroine, who are cousins and both fifteen, have been brought up in a pious and otherworldly parsonage: "Death was zealously kept in view and lectured upon." Peter, held to his books by his uncle who wants him too to become a parson, dreams of becoming a sailor. Rosa, a Cinderella in an old frock and botched shoes, has her own dream, in which she is "the loveliest, mightiest and most dangerous person on earth," but she also believes that "some time, something horrible would happen to her." Both young people are full of contradictions and of potentials; the pattern of the story resolves all these in one glorious catastrophe. The coming of spring stirs Peter to the decision to run away to sea, even as it also stirs both of them into a still unrecognized erotic love for each other. He confides his plan to Rosa, who gives it away to her father, the parson, and then immediately feels like a Judas and so agrees to go with Peter down to the sound to watch the ice breaking up. Caught up in the ecstasy of the "infinite, swaying wet world" of the melting ice, they realize too late that the floe on which they stand has separated from the land ice and is drifting out to sea. Calmly accepting death as their destiny, they are swept down by the current, clasped in each other's arms. Among much that is remarkable in this story, on both the naturalistic and the symbolic levels, there is the fact that as readers we do not in the end focus on the death by drowning, nor on the grief of those left behind. The *Liebestod* becomes a fulfillment, a freezing of two young lives at the moment of their greatest perfection into the kind of immortality that Keats celebrates in his "Ode on a Grecian Urn" (1820). It is not so much art for art's sake as a dialogue between life and art.

The Danishness of this story, like that of "Sorrow-Acre," is partly a matter of the feel of a place and a season; in "Sorrow-Acre" it is the brief high summer, "that week wherein the lime-trees flower" that "seems to unite the fields of Denmark with those of Elysium." Partly it is a matter of style and thought. The Danish literature that she read and absorbed from childhood on has left traces throughout Dinesen's work. Two of its most famous names should be mentioned. Hans Christian Andersen, the nineteenth-century storyteller, is her forerunner in terms of narrative tone, the combination of the deadpan and the fantastic, as in the tale of the figurehead which Peter tells Rosa within the story. Søren Kierkegaard, the writer and philosopher whose influence outside Scandinavia has probably been greater in the twentieth century than it was in the nineteenth, helped to shape the intellectual and moral climate into which Karen Dinesen was born. The writer Isak Dinesen had an ambivalent relationship with him; it is as the author of "A Seducer's Diary" (the famous last section of volume 1 of *Enten-Eller* [translated as *Either/Or,* 1843]) that he is impersonated in "Carnival," and she would associate his insistence on ethical choice—the imperative either/or—with the Westenholz seriousness from which she had to escape. But in the intensity with which her characters embrace their destiny as a calling—Peter thinks "the sight of me will make God sad" because in not becoming a sailor, "I have crossed his plans"—there is a commitment to self-realization that is as strenuous in its way as any Kierkegaardian imperative, or as any Ibsenite hero's or heroine's urge to follow his or her vocation.

Dinesen can write both from inside and from outside a Scandinavian consciousness. In "The Roads Round Pisa," the central intelligence, "a young Danish nobleman of a melancholy disposition," voices the Northerner's customary inferiority complex before southern European civilization. He thinks

> how plainly one must realize, in meeting the people of this country, that they had been living in marble palaces and writing about philosophy while his own ancestors in the large forests had been making themselves weapons of stone and had dressed in the furs of the bears whose warm blood they drank. To form a hand and wrist like these must surely take a thousand years, he reflected. In Denmark everybody has thick ankles and wrists, and the higher up you go, the thicker they are.
>
> (p. 20)

But Count August von Schimmelmann, as the whole story shows, is limited by excessive self-doubt and is not a reliable judge of the two cultures. When the judge is the story itself, the verdict can be more subtle. It is most beautifully so in "Babette's Feast," first published in the *Ladies' Home Journal* in 1950 and later included in *Anecdotes of Destiny*. In a yellow wooden house in a small Norwegian fjord town live two elderly sisters, daughters of a dean who had christened them Martine and Philippa, "after Martin Luther and his friend Philip Melanchthon." He had also founded a particularly pious and pleasure-renouncing sect. Into this home and community comes Babette, a wild-eyed refugee from the fighting on the Paris barricades in 1871, and also (we learn at the end) a superb cook at the Café Anglais. Pity and faith in "the example of a good Lutheran life" persuade the sisters to keep this Papist under their roof; fearing her ability to cook—"in France, they knew, people ate frogs"—they show her how to prepare a split cod and an ale-and-bread soup. Babette watches the demonstration with a face "absolutely expressionless" and proceeds to become a model cook and maid-of-all-work in the puritanical household. After some years she wins ten thousand francs in a French lottery and, as a favor, asks to be allowed to prepare "a real French dinner" for the celebration of the hundredth anniversary of the dean's birth. Mysterious ingredients arrive from Paris, and on the birthday the brothers and sisters sit down to turtle soup, *blinis demidoff,* and *cailles en sarcophage,* which they serenely consume "as if they had been doing so every day for thirty years." They drink the Veuve Cliquot, 1860, which they know cannot be wine, as it sparkles, and this "lemonade," they find, "lift[s] them off the ground, into a higher and purer sphere." When the feast is over, and the brothers and sisters have tumbled home through the snow in a state of bliss, Martine and Philippe seek out Babette, exhausted in a kitchen full of greasy pots and pans, to thank her for "quite a nice dinner." To their amazement they find, first, that she has spent all of her ten thousand francs on this dinner worthy of the Café Anglais and, second, that she insists she has done it for her own sake, or rather for the sake of her art: " 'I am a great artist!' she said."

No thumbnail sketch of this story can do justice to the genial irony with which Dinesen has rendered the meeting of the northern, puritanical and the southern, sensuous consciousness. In the innocent bliss of the brothers and sisters, which they perceive as an exalted spiritual state, lies a tongue-in-cheek answer to a good deal of morally strenuous northern literature. But this is not all. The genuine goodness of the two sisters, their physical as well as spiritual purity and sweetness, is as fully realized and as attractive as the more sophisticated, more "European," attitude of Babette. Hence, there is more than irony in Philippa's speech that ends the story. Holding Babette in an unpuritanical embrace, she finds words of consolation for the artist faced with a future of "second best"; her words bridge the gap between the two cultures: " 'Yet this is not the end! I feel, Babette, that this is not the end. In Paradise you will be the great artist that God meant you to be! Ah!' she added, the tears streaming down her cheeks. 'Ah, how you will enchant the angels!' "

It would be wrong to overemphasize the national aspect of Dinesen's themes; even here the dichotomy is not so much French versus Norwegian as one Kierkegaardian "stage"—the "aesthetic"—versus another—the "ethical." (Possibly Philippa, in her last words, rises to the third, the "religious.") Her characters are on the whole not much determined by their nationalities; they are simply larger than life—sometimes quite literally so, as in the case of the huge Lady Flora Gordon or the Amazonian Athena in "The Monkey." Even then they are, like nearly all the women in the stories, incredibly beautiful. Defying Count August von Schimmelman's notion of thick Danish ankles, the body of one of the masqueraders in "Carnival" is of such perfection that "at whatever place—throat, arm, waist, or knee—you cut her slim body through with a sharp knife, you would have got a perfectly circular transverse incision." In "The Roads Round Pisa" we hear of a girl so lovely that the statue of St. Joseph at the basilica turns his head to look at her, "remembering the appearance of the Virgin at the time they were betrothed"; her daughter in turn "was so fair that it was said in Pisa that when she drank red wine you could follow its course as it ran down her throat and chest." Nationality, in her men and women, is mainly important as giving local habitation and a name to typical qualities, as with the young Danish sailor in "The Immortal Story" (in *Anecdotes of Destiny*) who comes to represent all innocent, virginal youth. He is the Paul of Bernardin de Saint-Pierre's *Paul et Virginie* (1788).

It is in this area—her characterizations—that we most clearly see Dinesen as belonging with her own generation of European writers: the post-Freudians who, in Langbaum's words, "effect a transition from the individual to the archetypal character." Langbaum places her with the "more massive" writers of that generation—Rainer Maria Rilke, Franz Kafka, Thomas

Mann, James Joyce, and T. S. Eliot—and finds a particular kinship between Dinesen and Mann, whose fiction moved from the psychological and naturalistic (as in *Buddenbrooks,* 1901) to the mythical (as in the Joseph novels, 1933–1943, or *Doctor Faustus,* 1947). Clearly this is not a question of following fashion; we have seen in an earlier section how naturally, in writing of Africa, she translates life into myth. Yet part of the excitement of reading her is being, naturally and effortlessly, in contact with European literary history from romanticism to modernism.

The European quality of her writing, finally, is also a matter of language. Dinesen is one of the few remarkable writers—Conrad and Vladimir Nabokov are two others—who, though their mother tongue was not English, have written great literature in English. She is all the more remarkable for being one of those who—like Samuel Beckett—seem to work in two languages with equal ease. As we have seen, for all but some of her late works she did her own "translations" into Danish. She is virtually unique for having continued to write in English while living in Denmark, and while the African experience of using English as a daily language receded further and further into the past.

Initially, she told her brother Thomas in a letter of 10 April 1931, she decided to write in English "because I thought it would be more profitable" (Anne Born, trans.). But the desire for a larger audience and higher sales cannot have been, then or later, the main motive. English would have had a particular emotive connotation in that—though her letters home were written, of course, in Danish—much of her African life was lived within that language. Above all, it was her lover's language, and the language in which, Scheherazade-like, she told him stories. But in the end, what probably matters most is the very fact that it was *not* the language of Karen Dinesen; like her pseudonym and like her preference for the past, the foreign language gave her the freedom to manipulate her material. Anyone operating in a language not his or her own does so with an amount of self-consciousness. In reading Dinesen one is aware of this self-consciousness as a profound aesthetic pleasure, an enjoyment of the sheer craft of handling English and making it—like the lions she shot in Africa—"all through what [it] ought to be." As the many passages quoted will have shown, the English she wrote was in the deepest sense her own, a clear, uncluttered, precise style, able to range from the ecstatic to the wryly comic and to achieve intricate effects by pellucid understatements. By her unerring choice of words and cadences she made her language seem the exact tool for the "very beautiful stories" that she declared it was her ambition to invent.

## *"VERY BEAUTIFUL STORIES"*

We must conclude by asking what Isak Dinesen meant when, in the interview for Belgian television, she spoke of her only ambition as being "to invent stories, very beautiful stories." This can be done briefly, for several reasons. One is that most of the answer should already have emerged in the previous section of this essay. Another is that each reader will obtain the whole answer only by going and reading Isak Dinesen for him- or herself. Yet another is that, in doing so, the reader will find that many of her stories—and especially the stories within her stories, for her characters are forever explaining things to each other by means of telling a story—expound the philosophy and aesthetics (and the two are to her the same) of her storytelling. Thus, in a story such as "The Cardinal's First Tale," one of the *Albondocani* stories in *Last Tales,* we have what is virtually Dinesen's poetics. "The divine art," says the Cardinal, "is the story. In the beginning was the story. At the end we shall be privileged to view, and review, it—and that is what is named the day of judgment." He is lamenting the rise of the novel, a new art form (for this story is set in the 1820's) that is "ready to sacrifice the story itself" for the sake of "individual characters," and that aims to bring the reader into such close sympathy with its characters that, as a consequence, the story "evaporates, like the bouquet of a noble wine, the bottle of which has been left uncorked." In his mannered fashion he reminds us that, while Dinesen's art feeds on many European traditions, it does *not* want to be seen in the tradition of the great English and American nineteenth-century novel. It does *not* direct itself to creating sympathy, "a wide fellow-feeling with all that is human," as George Eliot puts it in *The Mill on the Floss* (1860), nor does it ask for pity for those caught in the web of fate, as do the novels of Thomas Hardy. Dinesen glories in tracing that web and, as we have seen, the divinely *comic* vision it reveals. Nor do her characters struggle with a sense of sin, as do Nathaniel Hawthorne's—one could imagine her rewriting *The Scarlet Letter* (1850) to a very different purpose—or with the problem of making fine moral discriminations, as do Henry James's. From the depths of this tradition it would be natural to exclaim, as Dinesen—cleverly spiking our critical guns—makes the lady listening to the cardinal exclaim: " 'O God,' said the lady. 'What you call the divine art to me seems a hard and cruel game, which maltreats and mocks its human beings.' " For it is clear that in her pursuit of "the divine art," in which the artist imitates God the creator because God has the greatest imagination, Dinesen sees the key to that art in plot and pattern, not in character. And the God of this conception is not one of mercy and love but one who has, above all, what the valet in "The Deluge at Norderney" defines as "the tremendous courage of the Creator of this world." Hence, to appreciate the beauty of her stories, we may need to divest ourselves of some of our Anglo-Saxon preconceptions about fiction and be open to the sheer courage of her plots and the balanced intricacies of her patterns.

By now it will be obvious that to give an account of an Isak Dinesen story is a long-winded business; you cannot simply describe a mood or outline a situation. You have to tell the plot because, in its arabesques, it is the essence of the story; it reveals the presence of the divine storyteller. Of all the stories, none shows this more clearly than "The Roads Round Pisa"—indeed the title itself suggests that the truth lies in the patterns made by the characters' movements *round* Pisa. To slice right through those patterns, the story shows all the characters, in various ways, as schemers and plotters. What they do not understand until the end is what the Witch says at the end of the marionette comedy that two of the characters go to see in the course of the story (the comedy is Dinesen's own "The Revenge of Truth" mentioned above): "The truth, my children, is that we are, all of us, acting in a marionette comedy. What is more important than anything else in a marionette comedy, is keeping the ideas of the author clear." In the end, old Prince Potenziani dies in (if not of) the insight that he has been "too small for the ways of God"; and the old countess in a key speech sums up both the philosophy and the narrative technique (for, again, the two are one) of the story:

> Life is a mosaic work of the Lord's, which he keeps filling in bit by bit. If I had seen this little bit of bright colour [a baby born to Prince Potenziani's ex-wife and the man for whom she abandoned the prince] as the centerpiece, I would have understood the pattern, and would not have shaken it all to pieces so many times, and given the good Lord so much trouble in putting it together again.
>
> (p. 49)

As it happens, even the old countess does not see the whole pattern; and herein lies another aspect of the beauty of Dinesen's stories, that which keeps them from merely being stories about stories, patterns about patterns. "It is not a bad thing in a tale that you understand only half of it," says Lincoln in "The Dreamers."

In the best tales, there is a mystery at the heart of the story. It may be one of identity: even the cardinal in his first story cannot answer the universal question "Who am I?" as he cannot know which of two identical twins (only one of whom was rescued from a fire) he really is: the one destined for the priesthood or the one meant to be an artist. It may be human psychology—despite the cardinal's and Dinesen's tenets—breaking through the pattern; the study of adolescence in "Peter and Rosa" fascinates quite apart from any divine plan. Or it may be a symbol that hints wordlessly at the unspeakable and the unpatternable, like the seashell left by the sailor boy in "The Immortal Story" for his love of one night, or the unstained wedding sheet in "The Blank Page" (in *Last Tales*).

For in the end, while Dinesen's art is immensely self-conscious and self-reflective and draws much of its strength and polish from being so, what humanizes it and leaves the poetics of the Cardinal behind is the awareness that life will forever refuse to be fitted into stories. Four stories, at least, deal directly with the danger of trying to play God with human beings. In "Echoes," one of the "New Gothic Tales" in *Last Tales,* the story of the great singer Pellegrina Leoni, who has lost her voice, is taken up from "The Dreamers." In the earlier story we saw her die; here she is living in a remote Italian village and is trying to write a young boy into her own story by teaching him to sing with the voice she used to have. Ultimately he rejects her, and she realizes that she has been "too bold, venturing to play with human hands on an Aeolian harp." She also understands that "one can take many liberties with God which one cannot take with men." "The Poet," in an ambitious context of historical and cultural reference that has made Langbaum call it "a miniature history of Europe," centers on the old councillor's godlike scheme to turn a young man, Anders, into the kind of poet he, the councillor, thinks he should be. It involves writing a plot for him: an unhappy love story, using the lovely young dancer, Fransine, whom the councillor is about to marry. But the plot misfires; he is shot by Anders and, mortally wounded, given his deathblow by Fransine. "You!" she cries at him, as she lifts and flings a heavy stone at him, "You poet!" And the symbolism, as he crawls at her feet, suggests that, instead of being the creator in an earthly paradise, he has been the serpent. There is something diabolical about trying to usurp God's role, and the same suggestion hovers around Herr Cazotte, the great painter, seducer, and arch plotter of *Ehrengard,* who with wonderfully comic irony is defeated in his elaborate scheme to seduce the eponymous heroine. Life, in the form of the young womanhood and fierce integrity of Ehrengard, defies the artist.

Perhaps the most remarkable of these four stories, at once most bizarre, moving, and haunting in its implications, is "The Immortal Story" (in *Anecdotes of Destiny*). Mr. Clay, an immensely rich tea-trader in Canton—"a tall, dry and close old man"—is unable and unwilling to accept that there is such a thing as fiction, and so, when he hears of a story that "never has happened, and . . . never will happen, and that is why it is told," he insists on making it happen. The story is that of a sailor who is paid five guineas to spend the night with the wife of a rich old gentleman, so as to beget an heir for him. With the aid of his clerk, Elishama—a Wandering Jew figure—Mr. Clay stages this story, using the once beautiful but now blowsy daughter of his onetime trading partner (for whose bankruptcy and suicide he is responsible) as the wife and a fresh young Danish sailor, "little more than a boy," as the stud. But the story refuses to come true. The young man falls deeply in love with the woman, whom he perceives as unutterably young and beautiful, and when, after a night of love, he is told by the clerk of the role he is supposed to have played in the story, he can only say: "But that story is not in the least like what happened to me." He goes off to his ship, leaving behind his greatest treasure, a big shining pink shell, for his beloved Virginie, and leaving Elishama with the shell at his ear:

> There was a deep, low surge in it, like the distant roar of great breakers. Elishama's face took on exactly the same expression as the sailor's face a few moments ago. He had a strange, gentle, profound shock, from the sound of a new voice in the house, and in the story. "I have heard it before," he thought, "long ago. Long, long ago. But where?"
>
> (p. 231)

Here, in one configuration, we may see and hear the answer to the question why Isak Dinesen is a beautiful storyteller. With forms as labyrinthine, as polished, and as beautiful as the seashell, she will please us and tease us until, perhaps, we feel we have had enough of pattern and wish for more of rough, real humanity. And just then she will haunt us with "a new voice," with unanswerable questions and a hint of things heard "long ago. . . . But where?" Only a great writer can do that.

## Selected Bibliography

### EDITIONS

ENGLISH EDITIONS

*Seven Gothic Tales*. New York and London, 1934.
*Out of Africa*. London, 1937; New York, 1938.
*Winter's Tales*. New York and London, 1942.
*The Angelic Avengers* [by Pierre Andrézel, pseud.]. London, 1946; New York, 1947.
*Last Tales*. New York and London, 1957.
*Anecdotes of Destiny*. New York and London, 1958.
*Shadows on the Grass*. New York and London, 1961.

POSTHUMOUS ENGLISH EDITIONS

*Ehrengard*. New York and London, 1963.
*Essays*. Copenhagen, 1965.
*Carnival: Entertainments and Posthumous Tales*. Chicago, 1977.

POSTHUMOUS EDITIONS IN ENGLISH TRANSLATION

"The Revenge of Truth." In Donald Hannah, *Isak Dinesen and Karen Blixen: The Mask and the Reality*. London, 1971.
*Daguerrotypes and Other Essays*. Translated by P. M. Mitchell and W. D. Paden. Chicago, 1979.
*Letters from Africa: 1914–1931*. Edited by Frans Lasson, translated by Anne Born. Chicago, 1981.
*On Modern Marriage, and Other Observations*. Translated by Anne Born. New York, 1986.

DANISH EDITIONS

*Syv fantastiske Fortaellinger*. Copenhagen, 1935.
*Den afrikanske Farm*. Copenhagen, 1937.
*Vinter Eventyr*. Copenhagen, 1942.
*Gengaeldelsens Veje* [by Pierre Andrézel]. Copenhagen, 1944.
*Daguerrotypier*. Copenhagen, 1951. Two radio talks.
*Sidste Fortaellinger*. Copenhagen, 1957.
*Skaebne Anekdoter*. Copenhagen, 1958.
*Skygger paa Graesset*. Copenhagen, 1960.
*Sandhedens Haevn: En Marionetkomedie*. Copenhagen, 1960. First published in *Tilskueren* (May 1926).

POSTHUMOUS DANISH EDITIONS

*Osceola*. Edited by Clara Svendsen. Copenhagen, 1962. Collection of her early Danish stories and poems.
*Karen Blixens Tegninger: Med to Essays af Karen Blixen*. Edited by Frans Lasson. Copenhagen, 1969. Drawings and two essays.
*Efterladte Fortaellinger*. Edited by Frans Lasson. Copenhagen, 1975. Posthumous tales.
"Moderne Ægteskab og andre Betragtninger." In *Blixeniana 1977* (the yearbook of the Karen Blixen Society, edited by Hans Andersen and Frans Lasson). Copenhagen, 1977.
*Breve fra Afrika: 1914–1931*. 2 vols. Edited by Frans Lasson. Copenhagen, 1978. Letters.
*Blixeniana 1983*. Copenhagen, 1983. A selection of juvenilia.

POSTHUMOUS EDITIONS IN DANISH TRANSLATION

*Ehrengard*. Translated into Danish by Clara Svendsen. Copenhagen, 1963.

# ISAK DINESEN

## BIOGRAPHICAL AND CRITICAL STUDIES

Arendt, Hannah. "Isak Dinesen, 1885–1962." In *Men in Dark Times*. New York, 1968.

Bjørnvig, Thorkild. *The Pact: My Friendship with Isak Dinesen*. Baton Rouge, La., 1983.

Blixen-Finecke, Bror von. *The African Hunter*. Translated from the Swedish by F. H. Lyon. London, 1937; New York, 1938.

Bogan, Louise. "Isak Dinesen." In *Selected Criticism*. New York, 1955.

Brandes, Georg. "Wilhelm Dinesen." In *Samlede Skrifter* 3:189–196 (119)

Cate, Curtis. "Isak Dinesen: The Scheherazade of Our Times." *Cornhill Magazine* 171:120–137 (Winter 1959–1960).

———. "Isak Dinesen." *Atlantic Monthly* 204: 151–155 (December 1959).

Claudi, Jørgen. *Contemporary Danish Authors*. Translated by Jörgen Andersen and Aubrey Rush. Copenhagen, 1952.

Davenport, John. "A Noble Pride: The Art of Karen Blixen." *The Twentieth Century* 159: 261–274 (March 1956).

Dinesen, Thomas. *My Sister, Isak Dinesen*. Translated by Joan Tate. London, 1975.

Gillés, Daniel. "La pharoanne de Rungstedlund." *Isak Dinesen: A Memorial*. Edited by Clara Svendsen. New York, 1965.

Hannah, Donald. *Isak Dinesen and Karen Blixen: The Mask and the Reality*. New York, 1971. Includes a translation of "The Revenge of Truth."

Henriksen, Aage. *Det Guddomelige Barn og Andre Essays om Karen Blixen*. Copenhagen, 1965.

Henriksen, Liselotte. *Isak Dinesen: A Bibliography*. Chicago, 1977.

Johannesson, Eric O. *The World of Isak Dinesen*. Seattle, Wash., 1961.

Langbaum, Robert. *The Gayety of Vision: A Study of Isak Dinesen's Art*. London, 1964; New York, 1965.

Lasson, Frans and Clara Svendsen, eds. *The Life and Destiny of Isak Dinesen*. London, 1970.

Migel, Parmenia. *Titania: The Biography of Isak Dinesen*. New York, 1967.

Stafford, Jean. "Isak Dinesen: Master Teller of Tales." *Horizon* 111–112 (September, 1959). Interview.

Svendsen, Clara, ed. *Isak Dinesen: A Memorial*. New York, 1965. Memorial anthology of essays on Isak Dinesen.

Thurman, Judith. *Isak Dinesen: The Life of a Storyteller*. New York, 1982.

Trzebenski, Errol. *Silence Will Speak*. London, 1977. Biography of Denys Finch-Hatton.

Vowles, Richard B. "Boganis, Father of Osceola; or Wilhelm Dinesen in America, 1872–1874." *Scandinavian Studies* 48:369–383 (1976).

Walter, Eugene. "The Art of Fiction: Isak Dinesen." *Paris Review* 43–59 (Autumn 1956). Interview.

Wescott, Glenway. "Isak Dinesen, the Storyteller." In *Images of Truth*. New York, 1962.

Whissen, Thomas R. *Isak Dinesen's Aesthetics*. Port Washington, N.Y., 1973.

INGA-STINA EWBANK

# FEODOR DOSTOEVSKY

## *(1821–1881)*

ONE IS NOW surprised when a Soviet literary critic writes: "A great advance in our knowledge of thinking and creativity is needed to understand why, for example, Albert Einstein believed that he had obtained more from Dostoevsky than from Carl Friedrich Gauss, one of the greatest physicists, astronomers, and mathematicians." For, years ago, Lenin, when asked what he thought about Dostoevsky's novels, is reported to have replied: "I have no time for such trash." And though Maxim Gorky extolled Dostoevsky's genius and compared him to Shakespeare, he also condemned him as "petit-bourgeois and defeatist," guilty of the unpardonable sin in Soviet morality of selfish individualism, which is as certain, Gorky concluded, "as there are no goats without a smell." And the anti-Soviet Vladimir Nabokov, who is partial to the dissidence of dissent in things literary, not unexpectedly lines up on Lenin's side of the barricades when he asserts that Dostoevsky is "a much overrated sentimental and Gothic novelist of the time . . . one of those megaphones of elephantine platitudes."

Nevertheless, there has never been any question of Dostoevsky's position as a novelist and thinker among his countrymen. A staggering bibliography about every phase of his life and work has accumulated. Even Soviet critics, though they disapprove of him as a political reactionary, an admirer of czars, and a professed believer in Russian Orthodoxy, are not disposed to leave him safe and undisturbed in his prerevolutionary immortality, for he is one of the most widely read of the great nineteenth-century Russian novelists and has exercised a profound influence on some of the best Soviet writers. The wealth of Soviet critical and scholarly literature on Dostoevsky is of primary importance for our understanding of him.

Some evidence supports the notion that the upsurge of Dostoevsky's popularity in the Soviet Union since Stalin's death is simply another manifestation—in reverse so to speak—of a renewal of the historical trend of Russian "Westernization" in cultural as well as in social and economic endeavors. For between the two world wars and afterward no nineteenth-century novelist has received as much attention in western Europe and the United States as Dostoevsky, although critical appraisal has tended to concentrate on his significance as a prophet, philosopher, and psychologist, and as a political, social, and religious thinker, rather than as a literary artist. All this is perhaps understandable in our own day of hard choices in intellectual loyalties, for many political, moral, and religious problems that have disturbed generations during these years were most effectively dramatized in Dostoevsky's celebrated works.

The doctrine of Friedrich Nietzsche, who admitted indebtedness to Dostoevsky's psychology, that the creator of good or evil must first destroy all values, closely resembles that of Shigalev in *The Possessed* (1873). And by the time Thomas Masaryk's *Spirit of Russia,* which singled out Dostoevsky as the key figure in the development of Russian nineteenth-century thought, appeared in 1913, a veritable cult of Dostoevsky had begun to sweep over the intellectual world of western Europe. Before the advent of Adolf Hitler, one German critic went so far as to say that since Martin Luther's time there had been no greater spiritual influence on Germany than Dostoevsky. Later André Malraux testified that Dostoevsky had profoundly affected the whole intellectual history of his generation in France. Indeed, Jean-Paul Sartre paid tribute to Dostoevsky, whose condemnation of the tyranny of reason provided inspiration for the existentialist belief that human action becomes simply the expression of a biological urge to self-assertion. And Albert Camus also, in *L'Homme révolté* (*The Rebel,* 1951), drew heavi on the agonizing questions propounded in *The Brothers Karamazov* (1879–1880) in elaborating his thesis that the mistaken belief in reason in modern times has led to a loss of all sense of values and the cynical seizure of power by dictators.

By the time it reached the United States this European cult had dwindled somewhat, but more recently American interest in Dostoevsky has been rising. If the test of a great writer is not so much what he says but what he does to us—the extent to which he imposes his vision and transforms our own experience—in these terms Dostoevsky seems to make a special appeal today to American readers. Though the focus of our interest does not exclude aesthetic considerations, it is mainly concerned with social, political, and religious problems involved in the throbbing human dramas of his characters and with his extraordinary psychological probing of their tormented lives. It is also possible that we feel a special kinship with the "sick consciousness" of these troubled men and women as they struggle to realize their identity in a world from which they are alienated. For Dostoevsky's anti-heroes, like those in so much contemporary American fiction, are overwhelmed with the infirmity of doubt, caught on the treadmill of endless reflection, and doomed to inertia because of a lack of will.

Unlike his great contemporaries Ivan Turgenev and Leo Tolstoy, members of wealthy, cultured families of the landed gentry, Dostoevsky belonged to a family perched insecurely on the lower rung of the Moscow middle-class ladder—he called himself an "intellectual proletarian." The family had no pretensions to culture, and his father, an ex-army surgeon, harsh and rigid in domestic matters, was subsequently murdered by serfs on the small property he owned in the country. This disparity in social position and educational training influenced Dostoevsky's literary interests and the subjects of his novels, so different from those of Turgenev and Tolstoy.

At the age of seventeen Dostoevsky entered the Saint Petersburg Military Engineering School, and during five years there he devoted all the spare time he could steal from dull drill and the science of fortifications to reading belles lettres. A high degree of intellectual curiosity was part of his intense nature. Besides Russian authors, of whom his favorites were Pushkin and Gogol, he read a variety of foreign writers: Homer, Shakespeare, Corneille, Racine, Rousseau, Goethe, Byron, and Schiller, the last with an enthusiasm he never lost (Schiller and the Schlegels contributed much to his later aesthetic theorizing). His youthful delight in stories of adventure was fed by the Gothic romances of Ann Radcliffe, M. G. Lewis, Charles Maturin, and E. T. A. Hoffmann, translations of which had a vogue in Russia at that time. Their lurid trappings and scenes no doubt encouraged his taste for the melodramatic and for the plots of violence and crime that later entered into the structure of his own fiction. Nor did he neglect novelists who could lay claims to realism, such as Sir

Walter Scott, Honoré de Balzac, Victor Hugo, George Sand, and Eugène Sue.

Not much information exists about Dostoevsky's developing personality during these formative years, but there is evidence enough to suggest that the shy, secretive, lonely persona portrayed in biographies is somewhat at variance with the facts. He could be all these things when thrust into contact with official bureaucrats or social superiors, but he also enjoyed nights out with fellow cadets, good food and drink, interesting conversation, music, theater, and the company of young women. There was a plunging, all-or-nothing quality in his nature that manifested itself early in gambling bouts and grandiose plans for achieving quick financial successes, although he was nearly always improvident in money matters. It was a time for dreaming, and he was a passionate dreamer about fame, self-sacrificing deeds, and idealistic friendships.

By 1843, when Dostoevsky had finished his professional training, the career of army engineer had given way to the determination to write. He felt that he had something to say in literature and had already begun his apprenticeship by translating Balzac's *Eugénie Grandet* (1833). In the fall of the next year he wrote his brother Mikhail: "Here is my hope. I am finishing a novel of the size of *Eugénie Grandet.* The novel is rather original." At the age of twenty-three he resigned his commission in the service, revised and recopied his novel again and again, and in the spring of 1845, with many misgivings and entirely unsure of his talent, allowed a young friend to take the finished manuscript of *Poor Folk* to the leading literary critic Vissarion Belinsky for his judgment. Many years later, in *The Diary of a Writer* (1873–1881), Dostoevsky recalled with deep feeling Belinsky's ecstatic reactions. He extolled the infallible artistic instinct with which Dostoevsky had revealed the hidden nature of his hero. "That is the secret of high artistic value," Belinsky declared, "That is truth in art! That is the artist's service to truth! The truth has been revealed and announced to you as an artist, it has been brought as a gift; value this gift and remain faithful to it, and you will be a great writer!"

Though the short novel *Poor Folk* (1846) has some of the usual faults of the beginner, Belinsky's lofty praise was prophetically correct, for he realized that Dostoevsky had created something quite new in Russian fiction. This story of an impoverished, elderly copying clerk who struggles hopelessly for respectability and conceals his real love for a poor orphaned girl beneath a sentimentally expressed paternal affection was the first Russian social novel. This fact and the story's implied condemnation of society's unconcern for the underprivileged delighted the liberal reformer Belinsky and won enthusiastic response from readers. Pushkin's rather exceptional short story of lowly people, "The Station Master" (1830), and Gogol's famous "The Overcoat" (1842)—one of Gogol's works that had persuaded Belinsky to acclaim him as the founder of the "natural school"—certainly helped to inspire *Poor Folk* and led the critic to regard Dostoevsky as a disciple of the "natural school." Dostoevsky had discovered the fantastic reality of the city's humiliated and injured, and he became their poet. In part he introduced to Russia the emphasis of the humanitarian literature of the West, which at this time was supplanting socially privileged heroes and heroines with the poor and rejected, as in the novels of George Sand, Sue, and Charles Dickens. And the epistolary form of his first novel was prompted not so much by Samuel Richardson's *Clarissa* (1747–1748) or Rousseau's *Nouvelle Héloïse* (1761) as by Sand's *Jacques* (1834), whose hero has been compared with Devushkin in *Poor Folk.*

But unlike Gogol or any possible predecessors in this vein of writing, Dostoevsky added a new dimension—an intense psychological interest in which the conflict of his hero is not observed from the outside but is profoundly analyzed from within. Belinsky and others, he wrote his brother about *Poor Folk,* "find in me a new and original spirit in that I proceed by analysis and not by synthesis, that is, I plunge into the depths, and, while analyzing every atom, I search out the whole." The result was a piercing insight into the tragic futility of poor people in love, people victimized by the cruel circumstances of contemporary society. Dostoevsky's handling of the ensuing psychological drama established the fact that with *Poor Folk* he had begun his own school of Russian realistic fiction.

With literary success came social success, and both went to the head of the youthful Dostoevsky. Bumptiously he wrote his brother of endless invitations to salons and dinners by well-bred nobles and literary celebrities. But this short, fair-haired man, with small gray eyes, a sickly complexion, and nervously twitching lips, cut a sorry figure in polished society. He was awkward in his movements, ill at ease, and in conversation alternated between prolonged silences and fiery monologues. Extremely sensitive, he soon realized that he was out of place in such a milieu.

Fortunately Dostoevsky's mind was on writing and he quickly followed up his first effort with another short novel, *The Double* (1846). More confident now of his powers, he announced to his brother that the new tale was "ten times superior to *Poor Folk*. Our crowd says that since *Dead Souls* there has never been anything like it in Russia, that the work is one of genius, and what do they not say!" Despite the laughable comparison to a full-length novel and a great masterpiece, Dostoevsky, like Gogol, had striven for originality but in a much more limited sphere of narrative art. *The Double* is an amazing study (for its time) in abnormal psychology. The hero, Golyadkin, a minor civil servant afflicted by a growing persecution mania, encounters a man who looks exactly like him and bears the same name. At first Golyadkin befriends him and secures a position for him in his office. The remainder of the story relates in meticulous detail the hero's adventures with his Double. With mounting indignation Golyadkin observes him winning the praise and favor of his superiors and fellow workers that he himself had tried so vainly to achieve. In his deranged mind the Double becomes the leader of a conspiracy against him, and he makes futile efforts to denounce the insolent fellow. After a final series of events in which his rival humiliates him, the tale ends with the Double helping Golyadkin into a carriage on his way to an insane asylum.

The ability with which Dostoevsky sustains the illusion of the Double and the subtlety of his psychological insight into Golyadkin's warped mind reveal the young author's impressive artistic skill. The hero's mental disorder is not unrelated to him. This first attempt at analyzing a split personality seems to be connected with Dostoevsky's later preoccupation with various aspects of dualism in the creation of some of his most memorable characters. Though he never again pushes the pathological aspects quite so far as in the case of Golyadkin, he comes close in the famous scene in *The Brothers Karamazov* in which Ivan is confronted by his Double, who so effectively exposes his ambivalence.

Belinsky praised *The Double* when he first heard parts of it in manuscript, but his enthusiasm waned after he read it in print—he found the story incompatible with the social significance he demanded in literature. Worse still, the public pronounced it boring. In a spirit of self-criticism that contrasts admirably with his previous self-praise, Dostoevsky wrote his brother of the failure of *The Double* and then added: "I have a terrible vice: unlimited pride and ambition. The idea that I deceived expectations and spoiled something that could have been a great story has crushed me." Many years later he admitted in *The Diary of a Writer* that the form of the tale had been entirely unsuccessful, but, he insisted, "I never projected a more serious idea in literature."

Between the remainder of 1846 and 1849, when Dostoevsky's early literary period was brought to an abrupt end by his arrest, he wrote more short stories and sketches, such as "Mr. Prokharchin," "The Landlady," "A Faint Heart," and "The Honest Thief." And shortly after *Poor Folk* appeared he had also embarked on his first full-length novel. He obviously intended it to be a major work and an answer to Belinsky and his followers, who by now had dismissed him as a failure. Planned as a psychological novel in depth, *Netochka Nezvanova* began to appear in *Fatherland Notes* in 1849. But only three episodes, the third unfinished, had been published when Dostoevsky's arrest put an end to the work. He never resumed it, perhaps because he recognized its lack of compositional and stylistic unity.

Each of the episodes is in the form of a separate tale connected by the continuing presence of the narrator, Netochka, a pattern that may have been inspired by Lermontov's *Hero of Our Time* (1840). In the first Netochka tells of her childhood with her mother and stepfather, Yefimov, whose talent as a violinist is frustrated by his self-contempt, a confession of defeat that seems to reflect Dostoevsky's own artistic self-disparagement at this time. The little girl is brilliantly drawn. One is impressed by Dostoevsky's technique in the difficult matter of child psychology, employed so effectively in the later novels, especially in his treatment of Netochka's morbid love for her wayward stepfather and her guilt over her dislike for her mother. The second episode is concerned with Netochka's adoption, after the death of her parents, into a wealthy family and her passionate attachment there to Katya, the young daughter of the household. The marked contrast between the meek Netochka and the proud Katya in their love-hate relationship anticipates similar contrasts in characterizations in the great novels. In the unfinished third episode the only notable creation is the sinister, vengeful husband of Netochka's benefactress, who gives evidence of developing into a towering figure of wickedness. This unfinished novel, which Dostoevsky reprinted in his collected works in revised form, is noteworthy as an indication of rapidly maturing art and for anticipating ideas, images, characterizations, and devices, such as the philosophical dialogue or monologue, that would repeatedly appear in novels to come.

To a limited degree one may perceive the main direction of Dostoevsky's future creative development in the writing of this first literary period. Some characters are preliminary studies of later, more famous ones. They are dreamy, unpractical people or wretched clerks and poor students who live in unsavory corners of Saint Petersburg. Though they are not entirely creatures born of literary influences, neither are they in every respect the result of a young man's limited observations of life around him. His intense analysis of their feelings, however, reflects his own emotional, spiritual, and psychological self-examination. But an experience was awaiting him that would deepen his perception of human nature and develop his genius for revealing the inner struggle that goes on in the souls of suffering men and women.

Opposing views on art were the real reason for Dostoevsky's break with Belinsky. The famous critic's social and political beliefs led him to reject "pure art." His approach was a utilitarian one: literature must reveal the life of the masses and in analyzing the contemporary human condition must pass judgment on it. Dostoevsky's position at this time contained elements of an idealistic Kantian aesthetic; it stressed "pure form," the free play of the mind, art without a purpose. He emphasized the autonomy of art and the irrationality of the creative act, in which ideas, problems, questions, theories, dreams, and hypotheses lead to mental struggle and intellectual drama out of which emerges an artistically realistic vision of life. On the other hand, Dostoevsky, although a firm believer in autocracy and the Russian Orthodox faith, was powerfully affected by Belinsky's advocacy of socialism and atheism, which was aimed against a reactionary church and the oppressive rule of Nicholas I.

It is not surprising, then, that Dostoevsky, seeking new friends after his rupture with Belinsky and his disciples, should have found them among the Friday gatherings at the home of the idealistic Mikhail Petrashevsky, where discussions were held on writings of the French utopian socialists Fourier, Saint-Simon, and Proudhon, and on the need for social reforms in Russia. But he also associated himself with a smaller group of more venturesome souls in these gatherings, the so-called Durov Circle, whose members, convinced that reforms could not be achieved by peaceful methods, secretly conspired to promote revolutionary action to free the serfs. They planned to propagandize their views by printing their own writings on a clandestinely procured hand press. It is also known that Dostoevsky repeatedly and enthusiastically read to members of both circles Belinsky's famous contraband letter to Gogol, in which, among other things, he excoriated the church and praised atheism.

The czar's government, aware of these developments through police informers, and fearful of contagion from the revolutionary turmoil in the West at this time, arrested members of the Petrashevsky Circle in April 1849. After a long investigation, twenty-one prisoners, including Dostoevsky, were condemned to be shot. The memory of the horrible experience he and his comrades underwent during the grisly preparations for execution that cold December morning in Semyonev Square before the czar's commutation was announced haunts the pages of Dostoevsky's fiction. His sentence was changed to four years at hard labor in a prison at Omsk, Siberia, and thereafter four years as a soldier in the ranks.

It is important to realize, in the light of Dostoevsky's reaction to this catastrophe, that he had been involved in an illegal activity, and he drew on the experience in writing *The Possessed* in the 1870's, a novel inspired by a political murder committed by the revolutionary S. G. Nechaev and his fellow conspirators. "Probably I could never have become a *Nechaev,*" he wrote in *The Diary of a Writer,* "but a follower of Nechaev, I am not certain; it may be I could have . . . in the days of my youth." In short, he believed his severe penalty justified, and like the sinning characters in his future novels who achieve salvation by suffering, he willingly accepted punishment as an atonement for his crime.

Dostoevsky served his sentence like any of the common murderers and thieves among whom he lived in chains, stench, and hard labor. He endured profound spiritual agony during the ordeal, and he dates his first epileptic seizures from this time. Eventually he got to know well many of his rough fellow convicts and to admire them—"in one way or another, the most gifted of our people," he remarked. Though he was forbidden to write, his imagination actively worked on literary plans. "How many native types, characters, did I take with me from prison!" he later told his brother. "How many tales of vagabonds, robbers, and, in general, of the whole gloomy, wretched existence. There is enough for entire volumes. What a wonderful people! On the whole, I did not lose my time. If not Russia, then I have come to know the Russian people well, as well as only few knew them."

The New Testament was the only book allowed him in prison, and as though repenting for having embraced Belinsky's atheistic belief, he read it at every opportunity. He rediscovered Christ and found spiritual sustenance in the Gospels. Only Christ could raise up the sinner, comfort the fallen, and promise the humble of heart new life on earth. This faith brought him serenity and assuaged the bitterness of prison existence. Not long after his release he wrote a woman who had befriended him during this period of his religious change:

> Here it is: to believe that there is nothing more beautiful, more profound, more sympathetic, more reasonable, more manly, and more perfect than Christ, and not only is there nothing, but, I tell myself with jealous love, there can be noth-

> ing. Besides, if anyone proved to me that Christ was outside the truth, and it *really* was so that the truth was outside Christ, then I would prefer to remain with Christ than with the truth.

The statement is important, for unbelief is implicit in his very assertion of belief. The remainder of his life was to be a holy pilgrimage, an endless search for God, but he combined in his heart the most ardent faith with the greatest disbelief. Perhaps the search itself was the end, the spiritual bread of his existence and, one may add, of his artistic powers.

Dostoevsky entered prison a young radical and unbeliever, and he left it with a heightened respect for the authority of the crown and a new faith in the teachings of Christ. His experience had taught him the doctrine of salvation by suffering, and the New Testament had fortified his belief in it. Finally, he had discovered the virtues of the Russian common people and had become convinced of their special significance in the fate of his country. In the growth of his creative art prison played not a negative but a positive role. It did not change his creative process; there was no essential break with the past in this respect. Prison defined and deepened his creative powers and provided him with rich material for the further study of the suffering individuals in whom he had been interested from the beginning. In his early works he had been concerned with the souls of the "insulted and injured"; in prison he learned to understand and to analyze them more profoundly.

The chains were struck off Dostoevsky's ankles on 23 January 1854; on release from prison he was ordered to Semipalatinsk, a Siberian garrison town, to serve as a common soldier. In keeping with the attitude of patient acceptance he had practiced in prison, he wrote his brother, "I do not complain; this is my cross and I have deserved it." He worked hard as a soldier and strove to win the approbation of his superiors. Starved for reading matter after four years of deprivation, he eagerly absorbed in his spare time quantities of books and magazines he requested from his brother. And once again he began to get the feel of the pen.

This uneventful existence was suddenly complicated by his passionate love for frail, sickly, blonde Marya Isaeva. She was married to a hopeless drunkard whose opportune death hardly improved Dostoevsky's situation—a young schoolteacher promptly claimed her favors. Life seemed to imitate art, for there is nothing more fantastic in Dostoevsky's fiction than this triangular love affair in which he went to unbelievable extremes to promote the cause of his rival while protesting his undying love for this rather pretty, flighty, and somewhat hysterical woman. (The deceased drunkard of a husband and Marya reappear as Marmeladov and his spouse in *Crime and Punishment* [1867].) She married Dostoevsky in 1857, an alliance that turned out to be anything but happy.

Marriage increased his ever-present financial needs, which now intensified the desire to write. As an ex-convict he required permission to publish, but he felt it would soon come, for he had been promoted to a junior officer's rating. Various literary designs crowded his brain, ideas he had thought out in prison. Yet he feared to spoil the major work he had in mind by beginning it prematurely; the conception of the central character, he decided, would take several years to mature in his imagination. Accordingly, the first two pieces he finished after release from prison have no connection with his experience there.

The long short story "Uncle's Dream" (1859) is one of Dostoevsky's best-wrought tales, a Gogolian satire on the sniveling society of a small provincial town for which Semipalatinsk must have been the model. At times situational humor leavens the exposure of cynical human foibles. The ancient prince, whom the town's dowager schemes to marry off to her daughter Zina, is a delightful caricature. The brilliant concluding scene, where the mother's deception is revealed to assembled townsfolk when the befuddled prince insists that his engagement to Zina is simply a beautiful dream, bears comparison with the famous concluding scene in Gogol's play *The Government Inspector* (1836).

The humorous and tragic combine in the short novel *The Village of Stepanchikovo and Its Inhabitants* (1859), better known in English by the title *The Friend of the Family.* Dostoevsky thought this longer work "incomparably above" "Uncle's Dream," and at first he was most enthusiastic over its two main characters, Colonel Rostanev and Foma Opiskin, whom he described as "tremendously typical" and "faultlessly fashioned." Though the work continued the line of his early artistic development, it also opened up new perspectives of greater things to come. Rostanev's mother, a general's widow, arrives to settle on her son's estate, and with her appears Opiskin, a companion of her husband who had been degraded by him to the position of a family buffoon. Now, in altered circumstances, this vain, scheming, Russian Tartuffe, who once aspired to be an author, gains an extraordinary ascendancy over the whole household, and especially over its meek master, Rostanev. Opiskin's ambitious effort is a palpable compensation for his former degradation. Dostoevsky concentrates on the psychological portrayal of this complex, dualistic creature, and the strength of the characterization saves the novel from being a mediocre work. The analytical treatment of Opiskin goes beyond that of the ambivalent creations of the early tales. For in the conflict between self-esteem and self-abasement, Dostoevsky now suggests a kind of reciprocity that is almost psychic; the two states of mind aid and abet each other. The dominant aspect of Opiskin's dualism—the desire to suffer and make others suffer—Dostoevsky developed more cogently in later characters. Critics have pointed out, and with some justification, that the frustrated author Opiskin is a parody of Gogol in that writer's more lamentable guise as a misdirected preacher of asceticism, moral nonsense, and futile religiosity.

Dostoevsky's hope that these two works, particularly *The Friend of the Family,* would help to revive the literary reputation he had enjoyed before prison turned out to be disappointed—they went entirely unnoticed. More than ever he felt it necessary to get back to Saint Petersburg, among remembered scenes and friends who might encourage his writing. He obtained the aid of highly placed officials and wrote pleading letters and laudatory poems to members of the royal family. These expressions of patriotic sentiment and contrition for past offenses, however seemingly sycophantic, represented changed values resulting from his prison experience. He was finally permitted to resign from the army and to settle in Tver. After he had languished there for some months, a plea to the emperor that he required medical aid succeeded. Ten years after he set out for Siberia in chains, he returned, in December 1859, to his beloved Saint Petersburg, a free man.

Life took on exquisite meaning again. Revolutionary elements in the capital wanted to glorify him as a former political prisoner. Dostoevsky would have none of it. He sympathized with the reforms of the new czar, Alexander II, and the pending emancipation of the serfs in 1861, but he distrusted extremes of radicalism, especially its ridiculing of religion. What he really wanted was to start a magazine—a regular source of income if successful and an assured outlet for his own writing. With his brother Mikhail as ostensible owner and business manager (as an ex-convict he could not publicly control the magazine) and himself as editor, the first issue of *Time* appeared in 1861. It was an immediate success, not only because of Dostoevsky's editorial skills, but also because *Time's* announced ideological position—a compromise between contending Slavophiles and Westernizers among the intelligentsia—urged both factions to join with the common people and recognize in these children of the soil the national spirit and salvation of the nation. This conviction, which had dawned on Dostoevsky in prison, now proved to be a popular approach, and he introduced various elements of it into his journalistic writings and fiction.

Old and new like-minded friends rallied around Dostoevsky and his magazine, some of whom were to have considerable influence on his political, social, and artistic views, such as the poet Apollon Maikov and the critics Apollon Grigoriev and N. N. Strakhov. They supported his renewed defense of the autonomy of art, a continuation of his old battle with the deceased Belinsky, whose utilitarian view of literature was now more rigidly advocated by the radical-democratic critics N. G. Chernyshevsky and N. A. Dobrolyubov. "Art is always contemporary and real," Dostoevsky argued, but one cannot impose various designs on it because it has "its own integral, organic life."

During these first years after his return to Saint Petersburg, Dostoevsky wrote *The House of the Dead,* an amazing work that regained for him something of the popularity he had enjoyed on the publication of *Poor Folk.* He had originally planned it as a novel based on a horrific episode he had heard about at Omsk, and he had jotted down notes for it during stays in the prison hospital. But it ultimately took the form of memoirs of a man condemned to ten years of hard labor for killing his wife. The book is really a faithful record of Dostoevsky's own experiences in prison; part of it first appeared in a newspaper, but then this and the remainder were printed in the 1861–1862 issues of *Time.* Turgenev and Alexander Herzen acclaimed it, and Tolstoy valued it as Dostoevsky's best work.

He strove for impersonality and objectivity, for he realized that these qualities would contribute artistically to the authenticity of the account. The plan of the work is carefully thought out: first a general description of prison life; then a consideration of social types among the inmates, with deeper psychological studies of the more striking convicts; and finally a kind of history of this form of penal existence illustrated by detailed realistic descriptions of certain episodes, such as the highly diverting Christmas theatricals of the convicts and the wonderful scene of the prisoners' communal bath, a pandemonium that is "simply Dantean," Turgenev declared. However, running through the whole book is the unifying motif of liberty, which these convicts had lost. It is effectively symbolized by their unconscious efforts to imitate the behavior of free men, and by the wounded eagle the prisoners catch and then happily set free. In the acute psychological studies of such unusual convicts as Gazin and Orlov, indomitable criminal types for whom ordinary morality is childish and reason completely subordinated to the unrelenting will to evil, Dostoevsky gained fresh insights that served him well in handling criminal aspects of such creations as Valkovsky, Raskolnikov, Svidrigailov, and Stavrogin. Yet there emerges from the book Dostoevsky's new conviction that among these rough and lowly convicts were many of Russia's most "extraordinary people."

While writing *The House of the Dead* Dostoevsky was also working on his novel *The Insulted and the Injured,* which likewise appeared in the pages of *Time* in 1861. It was to be "a novel with an idea," he remarked, "and it will bring me into fashion." Though critics roasted the work, the reading public applauded it. Three years later he rather lamely apologized: since the magazine urgently needed a novel, he had obliged, and hence there were in it "walking texts and not characters"; if "a crude work had emerged," there were "two most serious characters portrayed very faithfully and artistically" and "a half hundred pages of which I am proud."

Readers today would agree and perhaps add that in *The Insulted and the Injured* one can detect the authentic feel and atmosphere of the great novels. The idea he mentioned—and ideas were to become a fixed feature of later masterpieces—concerns a woman's right to offer her love to the man of her choice in defiance of convention and family control. The idea is not well sustained; it is lost in the maze of plot and sentimental melodrama inspired by Hoffmann, Sue, Hugo, and even Dickens. Vanya loves Natasha, but he does everything in his power to aid her love for Alyosha; Alyosha in turn loves both Natasha and Katya, and each woman is eager to further the suit of the other. Then this love in triplicate is confounded by little Nellie's love for Vanya.

It is not difficult to guess that Natasha is one of the "two most serious characters." Though aspects of emotional dualism in women in love had been touched on in Dostoevsky's previous writings, Natasha is the first fully portrayed representative of the type that reappears repeatedly in later novels. Dostoevsky writes of her: "She anticipated with pleasure the happiness of loving endlessly and torturing the man she loved simply because she loved him and that was why perhaps she hastened to give herself to him as a sacrifice."

Nor can there be any doubt that little Nellie is the second character, an absorbing psychological study of a child of thirteen in her initial experience with real love. She is the first of those Dostoevskian females who, as he remarks in the novel, "smothered her own impulses; sympathetic but locked up in pride and inaccessibility."

Vanya, the narrator, qualifies as one of the "walking texts" that Dostoevsky mentioned—choosing a method of narration was always a major problem for him; Dostoevsky employed, singly or in combination, the omniscient author, confession, diary, memoirs, and notes. Yet Vanya takes on a special interest, for he is a writer, and up to a point his career is a faithful transcript of Dostoevsky's before his arrest.

If the novel can be said to have a hero, it is the anti-hero Prince Valkovsky; his wickedness dominates all plot lines of the work. In unmotivated villainy he is a direct descendant of those fearsome convicts Gazin and Orlov in *The House of the Dead.* But unlike them, he is not instinctively amoral. Dostoevsky even attempts, unconvincingly, to provide motives for his evildoing. In the defeat of natural goodness by evil, the burden of the novel, the spiritual experience of penal servitude had not yet taught Dostoevsky how to transmute typical villains of melodrama into the artistic criminal types of his masterpieces.

"My name is worth a million," Dostoevsky told a friend after his recent popular literary successes. Leaving the magazine and his ailing wife in his brother's care, he set out in the summer of 1862 to realize an old dream—a trip to Europe. At the end of ten weeks, after visits to various European capitals, he was back in Russia, and in the fall of 1863 there appeared in *Time* his essay "Winter Notes on Summer Impressions." His observations only served to strengthen his faith in the future lofty destiny of Russia if it could be kept free from the poison of the West. The evils of bourgeois civilization he saw in Berlin, Paris, and London distressed him, and the socialist remedy advocated was worse.

In 1863 the government suppressed *Time* because of a seemingly unpatriotic article on the Polish rebellion. At this critical juncture Dostoevsky again left for Europe, to seek a cure, he said, for his epilepsy. But it is known that he hoped to repair his precarious finances at gambling resorts abroad and keep a rendezvous with a beautiful Saint Petersburg woman, Polina Suslova, with whom he was in love. His luck with both was execrable—he lost at roulette and Polina jilted him. He returned to find his wife dying of tuberculosis and his financial affairs in a desperate state. However, an opportune legacy enabled him to revive the magazine, but only if he altered its name.

*Epoch* began to appear early in 1864. It got off to a bad start by identifying itself with Dostoevsky's now sharply conservative position. In fact his first major contribution, *Notes from the Underground* (1864), is in part a satire of the radicals, especially Chernyshevsky. The underground man inveighs against the egoism of socialists, who believe that human beings can be governed by rational self-interest.

But this remarkable work is infinitely more than a polemic, for it reveals, among other achievements, a capacity for psychological analysis unique in literature. "I place strong hopes in it," Dostoevsky wrote his brother. "It will be a powerful and frank thing; it will be truth." If one were to separate his total production into two creative periods, the dividing date would be 1864, for *Notes from the Underground* marks a new emphasis in the more or less uniform pattern of his writings up to this point.

Previous heroes lack a deep moral consciousness of their own personalities. They seem incapable of analyzing their thoughts and feelings in relation to the world in which they live. In this respect the hero of *Notes from the Underground* represents an altered approach to characterization. The underground man is a profound analyst of himself and others. He is deeply, morbidly conscious of his personality and an astute logician in explaining its complex nature. The work highlights what had only been suggested earlier—Dostoevsky's searching dialectic, his extraordinary ability to dramatize conflicts of the human mind. And this feature distinguishes the remaining masterpieces.

*Notes from the Underground* is cast in the form of a "confession," but Dostoevsky adroitly suggests the presence of an unseen interlocutor whose reactions and implied gestures to what the hero says convey to his monologue the heightened impression of overhearing a telephone conversation. When the Soviet scholar M. M. Bakhtin observed that all Dostoevsky's heroes are characterized by their language, he might have added that the verbal portrait of the underground man is the most expressive of them.

In the first part the underground man, an unhappy individual of about forty, engages in a microscopic analysis of himself. It is soon apparent that he is one of those dualistic creatures of the early tales, with the important difference that he is fully aware of his dualism. In fact an irresistible urge to discuss the contradictions of his nature is the entire substance of his self-analysis. He is the supreme alienated man for whom no truth is absolute and every good is relative. His dissection leads him to the conclusion that his ambivalence is based on one fundamental opposition—a conflict between will and reason. For him the whole meaning of human existence lies in self-assertion of the irrational will.

In the second part the underground man relates experiences that illustrate his dualism, and its possible resolution is suggested in the episode with the prostitute who possesses Christian pity and love and therefore can be saved, whereas he has only reason to fall back on and is cut off from life. A more explicit resolution, deleted by the censor, indicated that his salvation was to be found in the realization of a need for faith in Christ.

At the end, however, the struggle between will and reason in the underground man is still unresolved, and Dostoevsky left it so in future editions. It is little wonder that Nietzsche's joy was "extraordinary" when he first read the work, in which he discovered "music, very strange, very un-Germanic music." Indeed, on a purely metaphysical level the first part may be regarded as an overture to existentialism. The hero would fit very well into the tragic and absurd condition of life that Sartre allots to man.

Dostoevsky's emphasis, however, is on the spiritual life of dislocated man in a real and acceptable world, and in this sense *Notes from the Underground* is the philosophical introduction to the forthcoming cycle of great novels. Their basic motifs appear in this introduction. Dostoevsky had taken a long step forward in crystallizing a favorite type character and in involving it with religious, political, and social ideas of immeasurable importance in his later fiction.

In the course of fifteen months (April 1864–June 1865) misfortunes overwhelmed Dostoevsky: his wife died, as did his brother Mikhail, the mainstay of *Epoch;* and finally the magazine expired. Burdened with debts (the magazine's and those of his brother's family, which he assumed), he accepted a trifling advance from a shyster bookdealer for a novel, with the stipulation that if the manuscript were not delivered by 1 November 1866, all rights to his published and future writings would belong to this exploiter. To escape debtors' prison he fled abroad in July 1865, and repeated the debacle of his second trip to Europe—he lost at gambling the little money he had and endured another frustrating episode in his pursuit of Polina Suslova.

While in Wiesbaden frantically trying to raise funds to pay hotel bills and return home, Dostoevsky wrote M. N. Katkov, editor of the *Russian Messenger,* to plead for an advance on a novel. The letter contains a rather detailed outline of *Crime and Punishment:* "the psychological account of a crime" of an expelled university student sunk in utter poverty. "Under the influence of strange, 'incomplete' ideas that go floating about" he decides to kill and rob a useless old woman, a moneylender, save his poor mother and sister, then finish his education and expiate his crime by good deeds. After the murder, "insoluble questions confront" him. He feels "cut off from mankind" and confesses because *"he himself experiences a moral need"* for punishment. Katkov sent the advance, and Dostoevsky went back to Russia to write the novel. It was published in the *Russian Messenger* during 1866 and aroused great popular interest.

Actually, Dostoevsky had conceived *Crime and Punishment* years before—he thought of it then as the confession of a convict. And before he left for Europe in 1865 he had vainly sought an advance for still another story he was writing, "The Drunkards," which, he told the editor, would concern not only the question of drunkenness but "all its ramifications, especially the picture of a family and the rearing of children in these circumstances." Clearly this had to do with the remarkable character Marmeladov and his equally remarkable family, which Dostoevsky now worked into the design of *Crime and Punishment.*

The tremendous effort he expended on the work is revealed in Dostoevsky's notebooks. They take us into his laboratory, as it were, and these rough drafts, preliminary sketches of characters and scenes, and above all his corrections and observations, extending to the minutest details of the material, provide a deep insight into the creative process of a literary genius and the infinite pains he took with everything that made for artistic perfection.

*Crime and Punishment* is closely involved with contemporary events. Dostoevsky's own poverty at the time and the financial crisis in Russia in the 1860's provide background for Raskolnikov's situation and exacerbated state of mind. Money is at the root of his difficulties and in one way or another determines the thoughts and actions also of the Marmeladovs, Sonya, Luzhin, Lebezyatnikov, and Svidrigailov. Raskolnikov's theory of the right to kill on the premise that a noble end justifies illicit means was no doubt suggested by Rastignac's theorizing in Balzac's *Père Goriot* (1835). This proposition, an outgrowth of the "incomplete ideas" of the time mentioned by Dostoevsky, amounts to a continuation of his attacks on the materialist philosophy of the radicals. The hero is one of them, a profoundly human, suffering nihilist in whose soul life and theory conflict. On one level, in fact, the work is a social novel, a satirical debunking of radical youth preaching Chernyshevsky's doctrine of revolutionary democracy.

But the novel's focus is on Raskolnikov's tormented struggle with good and evil. Dostoevsky goes well beyond the "idea of Rastignac" in dissecting the impulses that lead his dualistic hero to kill and then to repent. In these respects the complex motivation is absorbingly reflected in conflicting trial flights in the notebooks. At one point in the notes Dostoevsky warns himself: "The main anatomy of the novel: it is of crucial importance to bring the matter to a real climax and do away with this vagueness, that is, *explain the murder in one manner or another* and establish his character and attitudes clearly." Although motivation for the murder is ambiguous, the novel's central idea is unmistakable: reason cannot take the place of the living process of life. For Raskolnikov, dialectics had taken the place of life. In prison his satanic pride, which had led him to violate the moral law, gives way to the realization that happiness cannot be achieved by a reasoned plan of existence but must be earned by suffering.

Though Raskolnikov dominates the novel, in none of Dostoevsky's previous fiction had the secondary characters been so well individualized, especially the Marmeladov family, and the meek, ineffable Sonya, who is the hero's good angel as the mysterious Svidrigailov is his evil angel. In these and others, all reality, as in the case of Raskolnikov, becomes an element in their self-knowledge. Dostoevsky had given entirely new dimensions to the detective story by infusing into it compelling philosophical, psychological, and social elements. The unity and concentration of the action, with each episode advancing the development of the central theme, and all of this cast against a background of vividly described Saint Petersburg life that adds meaning and tone to the behavior of the characters, made *Crime and Punishment,* compositionally speaking, the most achieved of Dostoevsky's masterpieces.

As sheer story, however, the novel does not rest on dialectics, morality, or the central idea, although these features contribute to its total impression. It is the high seriousness of this drama of crime that attracts the reader. The intensity of the step-by-step revelation of Raskolnikov's plan, the dramatic account of the murder, and then the equally intense psychological analysis of the disintegration of all the forces that had goaded him on to kill—this is the vital story that never loses its grip on the reader's imagination and emotions. And over all radiates a spiritual glow that illumines the darkest recesses of the criminal and the morally debased, and inspires them to seek a deeper meaning in life through suffering to ultimate salvation.

While working on the last part of *Crime and Punishment,* Dostoevsky remembered his contract with the bookseller to deliver the manuscript of a novel. The date was fast approaching and postponement was denied. Fortunately three years earlier he had outlined a novel about a rebel against society who abandons Russia for Europe to devote himself entirely to gambling. He now took up this subject, hired a young stenographer, Anna Snitkina, and in twenty-six days dictated a short novel, *The Gambler* (1866). The work is plainly based on his own passion for gambling and his equally passionate love affair with Polina Suslova. The story centers on the love-hate relationship of Polina Alexandrovna, an imperious beauty, and the gambler Alexei Ivanovich. This masochistic-sadistic emotional duel is an intensified and exaggerated reflection of the relations of Dostoevsky and Polina Suslova. Created in such haste, *The Gambler* was bound to be a minor effort, but it has several powerful scenes that develop further the psychological manifestations of the love-hate syndrome that dominates the relationships of a number of Dostoevsky's men and women.

The stenographer, who was twenty-five years younger than Dostoevsky, soon married him (February 1867). She resented his in-laws' continued demands on his meager funds and wisely suggested going abroad when creditors once more threatened prosecution. They remained in Europe for four years, traveling from country to country. Anna endured long periods of abject poverty when Dostoevsky lost previous advances and money from everything he could pawn in his craze for gambling. There were also epileptic fits, a revival of his love for Polina Suslova, the tragic death of their firstborn, and attacks of sick, nervous irritability. But her devotion to him and his genius never faltered. Dostoevsky's second marriage was one of real love and the most fortunate event in his life.

Abroad he tried to keep informed of happenings in Russia and Europe by avidly reading newspapers and magazines, and by correspondence with literary friends at home. At Geneva he attended meetings of the International League for Peace and Freedom, where diatribes against Christianity, and clarion calls to bloody revolution by fiery orators such as M. A. Bakunin, horrified him. He worried over their influence on like-minded people in Russia, and it was in this disturbed state that he began, in 1867, to think about his next work.

Of all Dostoevsky's novels, *The Idiot* was the most difficult to write. The starting point is a court trial he read about in the Russian press concerning gentry parents who had tortured their children, particularly a daughter of fifteen. He not infrequently drew on newspaper accounts of domestic tragedies and criminal cases for his fiction, and he defended the practice because of its importance to his conception of realism. "I have my own special view of reality in art," he wrote to a correspondent:

> What the majority call almost fantastic and exceptional sometimes signifies for me the very essence of reality. . . . In every issue of a newspaper you meet accounts of the most real facts and amazing happenings. For our writers they are fantastic; they are not concerned with them; yet they are reality because they are facts.

Here Dostoevsky has in mind his great rivals Turgenev and Tolstoy, whose depictions of the gentry class, he believed, dealt with typical, surface features of reality. "I have an understanding of reality and realism entirely different from that of our realists and critics," he wrote another correspondent:

> My idealism is more real than theirs. Lord! To relate sensibly all that we Russians have experienced in our last ten years of spiritual growth—indeed, do not our realists cry out that this is fantasy! Nevertheless, this is primordial, real realism!

In one of his finest short stories, "A Gentle Creature" (1876), we observe him in the process of transmuting "the fantastic facts of reality" into art—a brief press release about a young wife who jumped to her death with an icon clasped to her breast is filtered through the alembic of his analytical mind as he imagines a frame of action consistent with psychological realism and the truth of tragedy.

But Dostoevsky added an important dimension to his notion of "fantastic realism." He preferred to shift the emphasis from the external world to that of the minds and hearts of his characters, for he was primarily interested in the realities of their spiritual existence. Art he regarded as a medium for conveying the wisdom of life, the emotions of the soul. Though convinced that he was fundamentally concerned with social, intellectual, and spiritual problems of average Russians, he insisted that he elevated them to universal significance in his search—as he put it—"with complete realism to find man in man." He defined his innovation as an attempt to represent in fiction spiritual phenomena above and beyond social practices, to resolve the psychological contradictions of man in terms of true and eternal "humanness." "They call me a psychologist," he wrote in his notebook. "It is not true. I'm only a realist in the higher sense; that is, I portray all the depths of the human soul."

A study of the copious notebook material on *The Idiot* shows how the "fantastic realism" of the newspaper report of the trial was eventually transformed into what can only be described as a form of "mystical realism." In the notes Dostoevsky piles up plan after plan, at least eight of them, in an effort to grasp clearly the novel's plot and characters. Family groups appear and disappear, heroes and heroines shove each other off the front stage, lineaments of one possible protagonist are transferred to another, and incidents of murder, suicide, rape, theft, and arson compete for attention. In the early plans the principal character is a typical Dostoevskian Double with traits utterly unlike those of the finished novel's meek hero.

In this bewildering mélange of plot, counterplot, and unresolved characters, what obviously frustrated Dostoevsky was an inability to hit upon a central idea and a hero who fully embodied it. Not until the sixth plan does he suddenly formulate the idea and the image of the character to represent it—the idiot, Prince Myshkin. "The chief idea of the novel," he wrote his niece at this point, "is to portray the positively beautiful man [in a moral sense]. . . . The good is an ideal, but the ideal, both ours and that of civilized Europe, is still far from having been worked out. There is only one positively beautiful man in the world—Christ." But Dostoevsky pulls away from this cul de sac, for in the novel the "divine character" of Myshkin vanishes as the radiance of his pure moral nature is stained by human weaknesses. However, there is nothing humorous in Myshkin, as some critics have maintained. "If Don Quixote and Pickwick as philanthropists are charming," Dostoevsky jotted down in his notes, "it is because they are comical. The hero of this novel, the prince, is not comical but does have another charming quality—he is *innocent!*"

In the fantastic world of the Epanchins, the Ivolgins, and their hangers-on, the main action concerns the love affairs of Rogozhin, Ganya, Nastasya, and Aglaya. From the ensuing complications emerge most of the superb scenes. But Dostoevsky carefully avoids emphasizing Myshkin's spirituality solely in relation to these love intrigues by providing a field of action for him. It is described as the "dark forces" of the new generation given to sensuality, to the accumulation of wealth, and even to crime. All characters are drawn into this crisis of moral decline, and Myshkin alone stands opposed to the "dark forces," preaching his ineffectual doctrine of service, compassion, brotherly love, and man's salvation through the image of Christ. He tells all that the world is beautiful and life is happiness. Despite his faith, he fails. Nearly everyone looks down on him, and his experiences are symbolic of Christ's among the Pharisees. In the end the sinning people he comes in contact with or influences are rendered unhappy, and he himself lapses into idiocy.

The story of Myshkin has sometimes been regarded as Dostoevsky's own spiritual biography. But the image of the "positively beautiful" hero does not wholly succeed. Dostoevsky himself seems to have had misgivings on this score, for he wrote Strakhov: "In the novel much was composed in haste, much is prolix and has not succeeded. I do not stand behind the novel. I stand behind my idea." Nevertheless, he had written one of the great novels of world literature.

In attempting to create a morally perfect hero, Dostoevsky had gambled with popular interest. Readers were baffled by *The Idiot*, and critics regarded it as a falling-off after the tremendously successful *Crime and Punishment*. Further, publishers were not eager to buy up the book rights, and long before the last installment appeared (February 1869), Dostoevsky was in Katkov's debt for another novel. Expenses attendant upon the birth of his second child at this time took every available penny, and he eagerly accepted a small advance from Strakhov for a short story that turned into a short novel, *The Eternal Husband* (1870). Its smooth narrative style and well-constructed plot about a husband, Pavel Pavlovich, born to be cuckolded—in this case by his friend Velchaninov—contribute to a singularly fine achievement. The tale seems like a deliberate exercise piece in Dostoevsky's now finished psychological technique; concentration is mostly on analysis, whereas characters and scenes echo those in previous works. In the careful dissection of Pavel Pavlovich's ambivalent thoughts and actions after he has discovered his friend's betrayal of him, one is reminded of how much Dostoevsky's writing is identified with the history of the human consciousness in its tragic duality.

Meanwhile Dostoevsky had been contemplating a large novel, entitled "Atheism," about a Russian who loses his faith in God and through experiences with people of various intellectual, philosophical, and religious persuasions falls into an abyss of his own creation. Finally he rediscovers a stronger faith in the Russian Christ and the Russian soil.

Some months later this project merged into a still vaster one designed as five separate but connected novels, to be called "The Life of a Great Sinner." The extant notes indicate that Dostoevsky intended to portray his hero from childhood to manhood. He is involved in numerous adventures, including a blasphemous crime that compels a stay in a monastery. Having rejected God, he wanders over Russia, indulges in debauchery, and encounters real figures of a past epoch of vigorous Orthodoxy and well-known representatives among Slavophiles and Westernizers. Christ and anti-Christ, Russia and Europe are debated, and the battlefield of this Dostoevskian conflict is the hearts of the men and women of the novel. In the end the hero achieves sincere love, confesses his sins, and establishes a new life of faith in God and pious good deeds. To portray a great sinner's spiritual pilgrimage through an evil world of little faith to the distant goal of salvation, which he gains through suffering and glorifies by saintliness, was the end of Dostoevsky's creative scheme of things. "This novel is my entire hope," he wrote his niece, "and the whole expectation of my life."

Although "The Life of a Great Sinner" was to remain another of Dostoevsky's unwritten novels, it cast its shadow over nearly everything else he did write, and he pilfered scenes, incidents, and characters from its outline to piece out the imperfections of what he considered lesser works. This is true of his next novel, *The Devils* (better known in English as *The Possessed*), which he began at the end of 1869, putting aside his projected magnum opus in order to send Katkov a work long since promised. For subject he once again seized upon a "fantastic" event in the press—members of a Moscow student revolutionary cell, headed by S. G. Nechaev, a disciple of Bakunin, murdered a comrade who, they suspected, intended to betray them. Initially Dostoevsky thought of it as a short "pamphlet-novel," a frankly tendentious fictionalized treatment of the murder that would give him an opportunity to speak out more directly against radicals, who, he believed, were threatening to undermine Russia. But the work soon took on the proportions of a full-length novel and is one of his indubitable masterpieces. As in the case of *The Idiot,* notebooks for *The Possessed* provide valuable information on the labor he expended in formulating his central idea and the hero who would embody it, in defining numerous other characters in a story packed with action and drama, and in working out the intricacies of an involved plot. Various complications resulted from efforts to regard the young radicals of the newspaper accounts as direct descendants of idealistic revolutionaries of his own generation of the 1840's. The notes indicate that several characters are based upon real figures he knew about; others are composites of people in his own life.

After almost a year of work, he destroyed much of what he had written, for only facts of living reality served to inspire his imagination. Features and figures in the plan of "The Life of a Great Sinner" had begun to fuse in his mind with the Nechaev affair. For the initial hero, Pyotr Verkhovensky (Nechaev), he substituted Stavrogin, suggested by the unnamed hero of "The Life of a Great Sinner," and the novel's field of action was extended to involve, besides revolutionary conspiracy, some of those profound questions of religion and morality implicit in the design of his unwritten magnum opus. He had finally hit upon his central idea. He wrote Maikov that the malady afflicting youth in the 1840's had not ended; the devils had gone out of the Russians and entered into a herd of swine, into the Nechaevs, had drowned, and the healed man, from whom the devils had gone out, was seated at the feet of Jesus. "The whole vocation of Russia," Dostoevsky continued, "is contained in Orthodoxy, in the *light from the East,* which will stream to mankind blinded in the West because it has lost Christ. . . . Well, if you want to know, this is precisely the theme of my novel. It is called 'The Devils'!"

*The Possessed*'s first chapters appeared in Katkov's *Russian Messenger* in January 1871. At this point Dostoevsky faltered. He was ill, was out of funds again, and had become convinced that he could complete the novel only in Russia. Katkov sent him the fare and Dostoevsky returned to Saint Petersburg in July in time to attend the trial of Nechaev and his co-conspirators. His enthusiasm for the novel revived, and by the end of 1872 the last parts were published.

Stavrogin, who dominates the work, was intended by Dostoevsky to integrate its two thematic divisions, the romantic element suggested in part by the plan for "The Life of a Great Sinner," and the revolutionary conspiracy inspired by the Nechaev affair. In Stavrogin, Dostoevsky underlines in his notes, *"in the whole pathos of the novel . . . he is the hero."* His personal magnetism draws all to him, and he exerts a powerful influence, especially on Pyotr Verkhovensky, Shatov, and Kirilov. If we may judge from notebooks and novel, however, Dostoevsky never freed himself from a degree of uncertainty about Stavrogin's image. The ambiguities of his spiritual and political contacts with various conspirators are matched by those reflected in his relations with the principal women: Liza, Darya, and crippled Marya Timofeevna, whom he marries to make a martyr of himself and to outrage people's feelings. Though this obscurity has convinced some critics that Dostoevsky wished to convey a profound symbolic truth in Stavrogin, the notebooks reveal that he deliberately made him mysterious, a tacit admission perhaps of artistic defeat in portraying a character who originally had so much potential significance for him. But the function Stavrogin ultimately fulfills is skillfully maintained and highly effective. In his inner struggle he reaches a stage of psychological amorality in which he is unable to distinguish between good and evil. "At Tiknon," the famous chapter concerning Stavrogin's violation of the little girl that Katkov refused to print, is of primary importance for an understanding of the characterization. There it becomes plain that the forces of evil have taken full possession of Stavrogin; he has lost faith in God and as a consequence the innate goodness of his nature has utterly atrophied. Only one way out remains—suicide.

The reformed radical Shatov, not Stavrogin, is the principal bearer of ideas that amount to Dostoevsky's ideological answer to the would-be revolutionists. Their amazing meeting is a travesty of the movement, and their leader, Pyotr Verkhovensky, is a half-comic, melodramatic villain. The other conspirators, among them Virginsky and Shigalev, emerge as dolts, eccentrics, and rascals who lack their leader's courage. In his treatment of the revolutionists and their activities, Dostoevsky's powerful dialectical method is sacrificed to a polemical purpose.

The old liberal, Stepan Trofimovich Verkhovensky, father of the bloodthirsty Pyotr, is brilliantly depicted as a kind of Russian Don Quixote, in whose image Dostoevsky pokes fun at the political and social beliefs of his own youth. When this lovable old man is offstage, interest in the narrative noticeably wanes. At the novel's conclusion, the last vestige of Stepan's liberalism vanishes before the new faith he has acquired in the religion of the common people whom he had formerly scorned.

*The Possessed* revived Dostoevsky's popularity, which was further enhanced, after his return from Europe, by impressive public readings from his works. He now began to frequent conservative social gatherings, where he made friends with prominent people, some of whom were close to the throne, such as the powerful senator K. P. Pobedonostsev. Such connections helped to secure Dostoevsky's appointment as editor of the conservative weekly the *Citizen,* in January 1873. But its reactionary emphasis proved too much for even him, and he resigned after a little more than a year, in April 1874. Fortunately his financial condition had improved, for his wife had undertaken the publication of his works, from which a substantial income was obtained.

During his editorship of the *Citizen,* Dostoevsky contributed to it the column "Diary of a Writer," and after his resignation he revived it, in January 1876, as a separate monthly publication. He continued it for more than a year and also published additional numbers in 1880 and 1881. The "Diary" contains reporting on current events, such as court trials, suicides, spiritualism, and conditions of children working in factories, but he also used it as a medium for expressing ideas on broad social, political, and religious questions. In its pages may also be found literary reminiscences and criticism, autobiographical matter, and short stories and sketches: "Vlas," "Bobok," "The Peasant Marei," "The Heavenly Christmas Tree," "A Gentle Creature," and "The Dream of a Ridiculous Man," which contains Dostoevsky's best presentation of "The Golden Age"—a vision of earth before the Fall—that captivates several of his heroes. Behind the "Diary," however, is a larger purpose. Journalism and literature were closely allied in his mind, for he firmly believed that the interrelation of art and reality must center in the observation of daily existence, and he draws on such material in this publication for his fiction. The "Diary" attracted numerous readers and is of major importance in any study of Dostoevsky's views as well as his remaining novels.

In the "Diary" Dostoevsky tells of the origin of his next novel, *A Raw Youth* (1875): the confession of the illegitimate, unfledged Arkady Dolgoruky about his adventures in the social world of Saint Petersburg, where he seeks the father he hates for neglecting him so long but whose affection he yearns for. There is an appealing freshness in Dolgoruky, whose thoughts, confusion, bravado, sensitiveness, and youthful idealism are portrayed with keen awareness. In the characterization, as well as in much else connected with the work, Dostoevsky once again borrowed from his plan for the unwritten "Life of a Great Sinner."

When Dolgoruky finally discovers his father, Versilov, interest shifts, and the latter virtually supplants his son as hero. There is some truth in the observation that Dostoevsky despairingly made to his wife: "There are four novels in *A Raw Youth.*" For at the end of the first part, the plot is all but submerged by the excessive motivation forced on him by the introduction of a profusion of new characters. Besides the initial theme, three others are developed, and a fifth barely adumbrated. The ensuing intrigue involves several love stories, the struggle between father and son for possession of the beautiful Katerina Akhmakova, and a mysterious letter compromising her, sewn in the lining of Dolgoruky's clothes, which all the chief characters desperately strive to obtain for their own nefarious purposes. The incomplete fifth theme, only tenuously connected with the whole, concerns a group of revolutionary conspirators, again based on a newspaper account of their activities. On this occasion the surprising fact is that Dostoevsky portrays the radicals almost as heroes, at least compared with the "devils" in *The Possessed.*

Versilov is the novel's most fascinating character, and his puzzling personality recalls that of the enigmatic Stavrogin. He is developed in much the same manner—by flashbacks, hearsay, and the effect he has on other people. As with Stavrogin, the final portrait leaves an incomplete but powerful impression. As a Russian nobleman Versilov is cynical in matters political, believes that no class is so fond of idleness as the toiling masses, and maintains that the delights of labor have been invented by the idle from virtuous motives. His attachment to God is purely sentimental, but he tells his son that the idea of virtue without Christ is the idea of all modern civilization—a Dostoevskian conviction. He also echoes Dostoevsky's favorite belief that Europe stands on the brink of destruction because of its revolutionary materialism and denial of Christ, and that Russia, which lives not for itself but for the whole world, will in the end lead Europe to the kingdom of God and salvation.

In connection with the ambivalent Versilov, Dostoevsky for the first time is emphatically explicit about the underlying principles that inspired his preoccupation with dualism in the portrayal of some of his greatest characters. Its psychological manifestation as the determinant of thought, feeling, and action is demonstrably a reflection of the part that dualism played in his own nature.

*A Raw Youth* is usually ranked beneath the other great novels of Dostoevsky's last period. The notebooks, more nearly complete than those for any of his other novels, indicate that his intentions are unrealized in the finished work. For one thing, the notes call for an expansive attack on contemporary social evils that is lacking in *A Raw Youth.* He seems somehow to have gotten lost in the complexity of plot. The Dostoevskian quality of inwardness is noticeably absent, and the customary concern of his characters with profound moral and religious problems, while occasionally evident on the surface, never penetrates to the core of their relation to life. Action does not develop into thought but often becomes an end in itself. This failure no doubt arises from lack of a convincing central idea, which in the masterpieces provides the dynamics of thought and contributes so much to artistic integration of the total work. Dostoevsky explained that the first stage of his creative process was that of the "poet"—an effort of imaginative inspiration that resulted in the formulation of the central idea of a novel. The next stage he described as "the activity of the artist"—concretizing from his drafts and notes the finished work itself. The notebooks for *A Raw Youth* indicate that to a considerable extent he had been less than successful in both stages.

In the last "Diary of a Writer," for December 1877, Dostoevsky tells his readers that he is discontinuing it in order to devote himself to an artistic work that had been "imperceptibly and involuntarily composing itself" in his mind during the past two years. *The Brothers Karamazov* began to appear in the *Russian Messenger* in January 1879, and the last chapter was completed in November 1880.

In a sense Dostoevsky had been preparing for this supreme effort throughout most of his creative life. The major theme—the charge of parricide against the innocent Dmitri and the judicial error that results in his conviction—was based on a convict's account that Dostoevsky had heard in his Siberian prison. The section on the boys' club, involving Kolya Krasotkin and little Ilyusha, derives from a discarded episode in notes for *The Idiot.* The "Diary of a Writer" contains much material that has a direct bearing on the subject matter and ideas of the novel. The plan of "The Life of a Great Sinner" contributes its increment, especially in the characterizations of Alyosha and Zosima. And several character types he had been developing since he began to write fiction achieve their fullest expression in this last work.

Although *The Brothers Karamazov* is Dostoevsky's longest novel, the plot's bare outline may be summarized in a few sentences: the story of a crime in which Dmitri Karamazov and his father are rivals for Grushenka's love. Prompted by the second son, Ivan, an illegitimate son, Smerdyakov, murders the father, and Dmitri is accused and convicted on circumstantial evidence.

But into this sordid tale Dostoevsky introduces a titanic struggle of love and hate with all its psychological and spiritual implications, cast against a background of the life of a town and its monastery. Throughout the work there persists a search for faith, for God—the central idea of the novel. In no other masterpiece does the white-hot intensity of his ideological world glow so brightly or does he spiritualize ideas so arrestingly and profoundly. In it are concentrated all his mature art, wisdom, and doubts. All that life meant for him—its experiences and symbols, and his vision of them—is reflected in these extraordinary characters.

Although nothing in human experience may satisfactorily explain the extreme motives and actions of old Karamazov, his sons, Zosima, Grushenka, and Katerina Ivanovna, nevertheless these characters, like symbols or personifications of ideas in a modern allegory of life, are treated so realistically that we effect a willing suspension of disbelief and accept them as living human beings. In such creations artistic reality tends to approximate spiritual reality or ideas of spiritual reality.

The father has left his mark on each son. This Karamazov taint is carnal sensuality, which, in its less vicious manifestations, Dostoevsky describes as "a zest for life." It is the father's dominating trait, ruins Dmitri, is just below the surface in Ivan, and even rears its ugly head in the saintlike Alyosha. All the Karamazovs are philosophers, Dmitri remarks, and the animal instinct in them constantly struggles with the moral and spiritual side of their natures.

Alyosha, as the notes indicate, took shape earliest in Dostoevsky's mind, and his description in the novel as "the future hero of my story" suggests that the author hoped to continue his development in one or more sequels. Alyosha was destined to undergo the hero's holy pilgrimage in the plan of "The Life of a Great Sinner." The only brother who loves life more than the meaning of life, Alyosha is identified with the Christian ideal. Though in the sequel Dostoevsky obviously intended him to sin in making his way through the purgatory of modern life, he carries in his heart the secret of renewal that will enable him to wrestle with the devil without losing his soul.

Dmitri loves life, but its meaning continually puzzles him. Simplicity and deep feeling are the essence of his being. "To hell with all who pry into the human heart!" he exclaims. What troubles him most is that a man of lofty mind begins with the ideal of the Madonna and ends with the ideal of Sodom. Out of a feeling of moral guilt for his father's murder—he had wished for his death—he accepts his conviction. "I want to suffer," he declares, "and by suffering I shall purify myself."

Ivan, who is more concerned with life's meaning than with life itself, is the most absorbing character and in many respects the mental image of his creator. He is the last of Dostoevsky's remarkable series of Doubles, and his ambivalence is centered in a cosmic struggle with God. Ivan begins with an act of rebellion and ends in utter metaphysical insurrection against God's world. The Karamazov taint in him takes the form of intellectual pride. In his pride he dreams of becoming a man-god, but when the submissive side of his nature predominates, he accepts the world-god, for he cannot understand the higher harmony between man and the world of God. In this inner struggle Ivan is concerned really with those factors that were at the bottom of Dostoevsky's own search for faith—the problem of sin and suffering and their relation to the existence of God.

The resolution of Ivan's struggle is concentrated in the section "Pro and Contra," one of Dostoevsky's finest artistic achievements. After recounting to Alyosha true stories about the torture of children, Ivan demands justice for these victims, and justice not in heaven or hell but on earth. If eternal harmony is to be obtained at the expense of these persecuted innocent children, he declares, then he must renounce the harmony of God's world. And when Alyosha insists that Christ, who suffered for the sake of all humankind, had the right to forgive those responsible for the suffering of the innocent, Ivan counters with the famous "Legend of the Grand Inquisitor," in which the Inquisitor condemns Christ for preaching man's freedom of choice in the knowledge of good and evil. In both the notes and a letter to the novel's editor, Dostoevsky asserts that Ivan's argument rejecting the meaning of God's world is unanswerable and that Ivan also approves the Inquisitor's reason for denying Christ.

In the next section, however, Dostoevsky attempts an answer, which he puts in the mouth of the old monk Zosima. It had already appeared in Dostoevsky's own words in the "Diary of a Writer": that equality is to be found only in the spiritual dignity of human beings; that suffering does not destroy the harmony of life but is a fulfillment, an act of Godly justice that corrects transgressions for the sake of the whole; that the secret of universal harmony is achieved not by the mind but by the heart, by feeling and faith; that if one loves all living things, this love will justify suffering, all will share in each other's guilt, and suffering for the sins of others will then become the moral duty of every true Christian. This inconclusive debate between Ivan and Zosima reflects the anguished dialogue that went on in Dostoevsky's doubting, dualistic mind in his own search for faith.

Perhaps Dostoevsky intended to elaborate on the answer in the sequel to the novel, but after his celebrated speech at the unveiling of Pushkin's statue, which electrified a distinguished audience with its ringing prophecy of Russia's world mission, he had only a few more months to live. He died on 28 January 1881, and with him died the continuation of his great work. More so than any of his other novels, *The Brothers Karamazov* faithfully mirrors the inner struggle that was the source of his art—his mind was with the reasoning of Ivan, his heart with the precepts of Zosima. This mighty conflict of mind and heart adds an element to the novel that transcends mortal experience. There is a sense of infinity in the book that reaches out beyond the earthy passions of its story to a region where the ultimate, universalized reasons for all human behavior exist. It somehow seems to justify Dostoevsky's belief that the higher realism he took as his province was like that of Shakespeare—not restricted to mere imitations of life, but concerned with the mystery of humankind and the human soul.

## Selected Bibliography


### EDITIONS

*Poor Folk.* Saint Petersburg, 1846.

*The Double.* Saint Petersburg, 1846.

*The Friend of the Family.* Saint Petersburg, 1859.

*The Insulted and the Injured.* Saint Petersburg, 1861.

*The House of the Dead.* Saint Petersburg, 1861.

*Winter Notes on Summer Impressions.* Saint Petersburg, 1863.

*Notes from the Underground.* Saint Petersburg, 1864.

*The Gambler.* Saint Petersburg, 1866.

*Crime and Punishment.* Saint Petersburg, 1867.

*The Idiot.* Saint Petersburg, 1869.

*The Eternal Husband.* Saint Petersburg, 1870.

*The Diary of a Writer.* Saint Petersburg, 1873–1881.

*The Possessed.* Saint Petersburg, 1873.

*A Raw Youth.* Saint Petersburg, 1875.

*The Brothers Karamazov.* Saint Petersburg, 1879–1880.

### TRANSLATIONS

#### INDIVIDUAL WORKS

*The Brothers Karamazov.* Translated by Constance Garnett. New York, 1945.

*Crime and Punishment.* Translated by Jessie Coulson. New York, 1952.

*The Diary of a Writer.* Translated by Boris Brasol. New York, 1949.

*A Disgraceful Affair.* Translated by Nora Gottlieb. Philadelphia, 1963.

*The Friend of the Family.* Translated by Constance Garnett. New York, 1949.

*The House of the Dead.* Translated by Constance Garnett. New York, 1915.

*The Idiot.* Translated by David Magarshack. Baltimore, 1955.

*The Insulted and the Injured.* Translated by Constance Garnett. New York, 1955.

*Letters from the Underground.* Translated by C. J. Hogarth. New York, 1957.

*Poor Folk.* Translated by Robert Dessaix. Ann Arbor, Mich., 1982.

*The Possessed.* Translated by Constance Garnett. New York, 1948.

*Winter Notes on Summer Impressions.* Translated by Robert Lee Renfield. New York, 1955.

COLLECTED WORKS

*Great Short Stories of Fyodor Dostoevsky.* New York, 1968.

*Occasional Writings.* Edited by David Magarshack. New York, 1969.

*The Short Stories of Dostoevsky.* Edited by William Phillips. New York, 1957.

*Works.* Translated by Constance Garnett. 12 vols. New York, 1951.

CORRESPONDENCE, NOTEBOOKS

*Dostoevsky: Letters and Reminiscences.* Edited by S. S. Koteliansky and J. Middleton Murry. New York, 1923.

*Letters.* Edited by Ethel C. Mayne. New York, 1984.

*Letters of Dostoevsky to His Wife.* Edited by Elizabeth Hill and D. Mudie Hill. New York, 1930.

*Letters of Fyodor M. Dostoevsky.* Edited by Ethel C. Mayne. London, 1914.

*The Notebooks for the Five Major Novels.* Edited by Edward Wasiolek. Chicago, 1967–1971.

*The Unpublished Dostoevsky: Diaries and Notebooks (1860–1881).* Ann Arbor, Mich., 1975–1976.

## BIOGRAPHICAL AND CRITICAL STUDIES

Abraham, G. *Dostoevsky.* New York, 1974.

Bakhtin, Mikhail. *Problems of Dostoevsky's Poetics.* Translated by R. W. Rotsei. Ann Arbor, Mich., 1973.

Belknap, R. L. *The Structure of* The Brothers Karamazov. The Hague, 1976.

Berdyaev, Nicholas. *The Spirit of Dostoevsky.* Translated by Donald Attwater. New York, 1957.

Camus, Albert. *The Rebel: An Essay on Man in Revolt.* Translated by Anthony Bower. New York, 1954.

Carr, Edward Hallett. *Dostoevsky, 1821–1881.* New York, 1981.

Cerny, V. *Dostoevsky and His Devils.* Ann Arbor, Mich., 1975.

Coulson, Jessie. *Dostoevsky: A Self-Portrait.* London, 1962.

Curle, Richard. *Characters of Dostoevsky: Studies from Four Novels.* London, 1950.

Dostoevskaia, A. *Fyodor Dostoevsky: A Study.* New York, 1972. (By his daughter.)

Dostoevsky, Anna. *Reminiscences.* Translated and edited by Beatrice Stillman. New York, 1975. (By his second wife.)

Fanger, Donald. *Dostoevsky and Romantic Realism.* Cambridge, Mass., 1965.

Frank, Joseph. *Dostoevsky: The Seeds of Revolt, 1821–1849.* Princeton, N.J., 1976.

———. *Dostoevsky: The Years of Ordeal, 1850-1859.* Princeton, N.J., 1983.

Gide, André. *Dostoevsky.* Translated and with an introduction by Arnold Bennett. New York, 1925.

Grossman, L. *Dostoevsky: A Biography.* Indianapolis, Ind., 1975.

Ivanov, Vyacheslav. *Freedom and the Tragic Life: A Study in Dostoevsky.* Translated by Norman Cameron. New York, 1952.

Jackson, Robert Louis. *Dostoevsky's Quest for Form: A Study of His Philosophy of Art.* New Haven, Conn., 1966.

Jones, M. *Dostoevsky: The Novel of Discord.* London, 1976.

Labrin, Janko. *Dostoevsky: A Study.* New York, 1947.

Linnér, Sven. *Dostoevskij on Realism.* Stockholm, 1967.

Lord, R. *Dostoevsky: Essays and Perspectives.* Berkeley, Calif., 1970.

Magarshack, David. *Dostoevsky.* Westport, Conn., 1976.

Matlaw, R. E. *"The Brothers Karamazov": Novelistic Technique.* The Hague, 1957.

Meier-Graefe, Julius. *Dostoevsky: The Man and His Work.* Translated by Herbert H. Marks. New York, 1928.

Merezhkovsky, D. S. *Tolstoi as Man and Artist, with an Essay on Dostoevsky.* New York, 1902.

Mochulsky, Konstantin. *Dostoevsky: His Life and Works.* Translated by Michael A. Minihan. Princeton, N.J., 1967.

Murry, John Middleton. *Fyodor Dostoevsky: A Critical Study.* New York, 1966.

Passage, Charles E. *Dostoevsky the Adapter: A Study in Dostoevsky's Use of the Tales of Hoffmann.* University of North Carolina Studies in Comparative Literature, no. 10. Chapel Hill, N.C., 1954.

Payne, Robert. *Dostoevsky: A Human Portrait.* New York, 1961.

Peace, R. *Dostoevsky.* Cambridge, Mass., 1975.

Powys, John Cowper. *Dostoevsky: A Study.* London, 1946.

Reeve, F. D. *The Russian Novel.* New York, 1966.

Roe, Ivan. *The Breath of Corruption: An Interpretation of Dostoevsky.* London, 1946.

Simmons, Ernest J. *Dostoevsky: The Making of a Novelist.* New York, 1940.

Steiner, George. *Tolstoy or Dostoevsky: An Essay in the Old Criticism.* New York, 1971.

Troyat, Henri. *Firebrand: The Life of Dostoevsky.* Translated by Norbert Guterman. New York, 1946.

Wasiolek, Edward. *Dostoevsky: The Major Fiction.* Cambridge, Mass., 1964.

Woodhouse, C. *Dostoevsky.* New York, 1974.

Yarmolinsky, Avrahm. *Dostoevsky: His Life and Art.* New York, 1957.

ERNEST J. SIMMONS

# ALEXANDRE DUMAS PÈRE
## *(1802–1870)*

*PLAYWRIGHT*

EARLY IN FEBRUARY 1829 the posters placarded in front of the Théâtre Français, the building in the rue Richelieu that housed the Comédie Française, invited patrons to the production of a new play, *Henri III et sa cour* (Henry III and His Court), by Alexandre Dumas. The author, not yet twenty-seven years old, had an obscure and low-paying job as copy clerk in the secretariat of the duc d'Orléans. He had arrived in Paris seven years previously, determined to make a name for himself by writing for the stage, and had indeed collaborated in the confection of two short vaudevilles (sketches interlarded with songs) that had been produced at different boulevard theaters as makeweights for the evening's entertainment. But one night when he was a boy in his teens he had been introduced to François Joseph Talma in the great actor's dressing room in the Théâtre Français. On that memorable occasion Talma had solemnly laid his hand on Dumas's head, declaiming: "Alexandre Dumas, I baptize you poet in the name of Shakespeare, Corneille, and Schiller." Ever since then Dumas had been fired with the ambition to write a play for Talma's theater that would cause him, if possible, to be acclaimed the French Shakespeare, or at least the French Schiller.

In the intervening years, Talma, the last of the great tragic actors, had died, leaving the first national theater of France in disarray. Its audiences were thin, composed chiefly of the dwindling remnant of those who retained a taste for the neoclassical tragedies that had held the stage during the First Empire (1804–1815). The Parisians by and large greatly preferred as entertainment the spectacular melodramas, gay vaudevilles, and amusing farces they could see at the Gymnase, the Variétés, the Porte-Saint-Martin, and other commercial theaters. But in 1825 there had been a hopeful development: the Brussels-born Baron Isidore Taylor was appointed to the directorship of the Comédie Française. He had had a checkered career: he had served in the army, having been commissioned in 1815, the year of Waterloo, had written and produced five plays, had been stage manager at the Panorama-Dramatique, and was known to be keenly interested in archaeology. For Taylor it was clear that the Comédie Française could only recover its former status and popularity if it were prepared to venture beyond the tradition of the five-act tragedy set in ancient Rome and played by actors in sandals and togas before conventionally drab sets; paying audiences needed something more exciting and appealing to the eye. He scented romanticism in the air, and he felt that unless the senior actors of the Comédie Française were cajoled into risking a new type of drama, their theater would continue its slide into obsolescence.

Alexandre Dumas's father, Thomas-Alexandre Davy or Dumas, was born in Haiti in 1762. His own father (Alexandre's grandfather) was a nobleman of ancient lineage, Alexandre-Antoine Davy de la Pailleterie, and his mother (Alexandre's grandmother) was a black slave called Marie-Cessette Dumas. When he returned to France to claim his inheritance, Alexandre-Antoine arranged for his son to accompany him; the boy, though illegitimate, had every expectation of being made his heir. This never happened: as a result of a violent quarrel with his father, Thomas joined the army as a ranker, assuming the name Dumas out of loyalty to his mother whom the old man had abandoned in Haiti. Only three years later, in 1789, the French Revolution broke out; in 1792 France declared war on Austria and in the succeeding campaigns the young Dumas rose rapidly through the ranks and was ultimately promoted to general. Although fighting with distinction in Italy and Egypt under Napoleon, he eventually became a prisoner of war, and as the result of ill treatment emerged broken in health and was retired from the army, dying eventually in 1806. His widow, whom he had married in 1792, brought up their son, Alexandre, as best she could, for she was left in very straitened circumstances. By the time Alexandre came to Paris, a fresh turn of events had swept Napoleon from power, which explains why the young man, who had been educated in the provinces, had so few contacts of any importance in the capital, either in the political or in the literary world. He had no means of introducing himself to the young romantics, though his literary allegiance lay with them. But he did succeed in interesting Taylor in his first full-length play, based on the life of Queen Christina of Sweden. In spite of Taylor's backing, Dumas's *Christine,* though accepted and put into rehearsal, was never actually produced by the Comédie Française; it was eventually seen, however, at the Odéon, where it had its first night on 30 March 1830.

This disappointment, far from discouraging the young author, seems to have spurred him on to fresh efforts, and in the summer of 1828 he set to work on *Henri III et sa cour.* The theme had occurred to him in the course of a chance reading of certain court memoirs of the sixteenth century; he learned how the duc de Guise, the notorious "Scarface," having got wind of an intrigue between his wife and the comte de Saint-Mégrin, one of the king's favorites, gave her the choice of dying by either cold steel or poison. She chose poison, whereupon the duke, who had merely wanted to frighten her, made her drink a harmless bowl of soup. Elsewhere, in Pierre de l'Estoile's memoirs, he read of the assassination of Saint-Mégrin outside the Louvre by a band of armed men in the pay of the duc de Guise. Finally, the dramatic link between these two stories was provided by an incident that did not concern Saint-Mégrin at all, but that many years later Dumas was to incorporate in his novel *La dame de Monsoreau* (1846; translated as *Chicot the Jester*): another jealous husband forces his wife to send her lover, Bussy d'Amboise, a note asking for an assignation, and then stations a gang of cutthroats to dispatch him outside her window.

Dumas's previous dealings with members of the Comédie Française over *Christine* had taught him a few useful lessons. They were professionals with years of experience of the stage behind them; also they were for the most part middle-aged and did not take kindly to direction from striplings in their twenties, however gifted the young men might be. For, in accordance with regulations drawn up in the seventeenth century, the company was a self-regulating body, and Taylor's functions were little more than advisory. When it came to putting on a new play, there was no direction in the modern sense, though it was understood that the author could attend rehearsals and make comments. Dumas took these duties very lightly; according to one of the actors, Joseph-Isidore Samson, when a particular point caused dissension during a rehearsal, Dumas refused to intervene, saying that they understood such matters better than he and that whatever they decided was, he was sure, the best. In any case he had written the play with parts deliberately fashioned to suit particular members of the cast: Mademoiselle Mars, the leading actress of the period, was to take the part of the duchesse de Guise, and Firmin, the one friend Dumas had in the company, that of Saint-Mégrin. A considerable sum of money—over eight thousand francs—was set aside by Taylor for the production. Four sets were specially designed, and the costumes made for the lead parts were considered remarkable for their historical accuracy. This policy paid off, for the costumes worn by Mademoiselle Mars, Firmin, and Michelot (who played the part of Henri III) provoked a ripple of applause on the opening night.

This first night was in the end a great success. The curtain went up at the start on a scene that might have come straight from a novel by Sir Walter Scott: the laboratory of the astrologer Ruggieri. This first act, and the succeeding one, set in the king's court, were received with polite applause, but the third act drew shrieks of pleasurable terror from the audience. In France at that period overt violence on the stage was a rarity, even in the melodrama. In 1827 Parisian audiences had been overwhelmed when a British company had crossed the Channel to present a season of Shakespeare at the Odéon Theater; for the first time they had been able to witness from their seats the spectacle of Hamlet dueling with Laertes, Othello smothering Desdemona, and Lady Macbeth snatching the dagger still dripping with Duncan's blood from her husband's nerveless grasp. All this was regarded as utterly barbaric by the traditionalists but by the majority of spectators as an exciting innovation. So when the duc de Guise, in Dumas's play, ordered his wife to write to Saint-Mégrin giving him an appointment for that night, and on her indignant refusal squeezed her arm with his mail gauntlet until she cried out in agony, the habitués of the Comédie Française were divided between those who wanted to hiss and those who insisted on clapping—but the latter, mostly the young, were in the majority.

If the first performance of Hugo's *Hernani,* a year later, has come to be regarded as the true turning point by which romanticism replaced classicism, this is because classical tragedy had always been written in verse; *Hernani* was a verse play and therefore, according to the conventions of the time, deserved more serious consideration than *Henri III et sa cour,* which was written in prose. In addition, Hugo was a well-known figure, the acknowledged leader of the romantic school, while *Henri III,* by an unknown author, an outsider claimed by no particular literary movement, took the critics by surprise. Before they could formulate any reservations, the loud applause from the auditorium had decided the issue. By the time Hugo's play was ready for production at the same theater, the forces of reaction had regrouped, and battle was joined.

Dumas's next important play, *Antony* (1831), was written after the "battle of *Hernani.*" It was intended again for the Comédie Française, which accepted it, though without enthusiasm. In his *Souvenirs dramatiques* (1868) Dumas suggests that there were three reasons the theater did not turn the play down flat: first, the earlier success of *Henri III,* which meant that a new play by the same author would be bound to arouse interest; second, the fact that this production, unlike that of *Henri III,* would not involve the Comédie in any major expense, since it was not a costume drama; and finally, Dumas hints that the actors were secretly counting on the censors to refuse the play a license. In this last respect they were disappointed, and Dumas was served, by the historical accident of the July Revolution of 1830. After every revolution in France, from that of 1789 on, the machinery of dramatic censorship came to a halt. It was invariably brought into operation again a little later, but *Antony* benefited from the temporary intermission; Dumas himself admitted, with hindsight, that it was unlikely the play would have been permitted on the stage under normal circumstances.

At any event, the Comédie Française was slow in putting it into rehearsal, and during rehearsal insisted on one modification after another, until finally Dumas lost patience altogether and took the play to the Porte-Saint-Martin, a theater that specialized in melodrama. That company included one brilliant actress, Marie Dorval, who proved far better suited to the part of the heroine than the more coldhearted Mademoiselle Mars could ever have been, while the actor Bocage made a lasting reputation as Antony, the misanthropic lover in revolt against all social conventions, whose name became a byword for a certain type of romantic hero.

*Antony* was set in contemporary Paris and based in certain recognizable particulars on an affair Dumas was currently engaged in with Mélanie Waldor, the wife of an army officer. But there is little resemblance between Antony, brooding over his bastardy, and Dumas, whose birth was legitimate and who was of all the romantics perhaps the least given to melancholy and unsatisfied ambition. The situation at the outset of the play is that Adèle has contracted a loveless marriage with an army colonel stationed away from Paris, and has one daughter—exactly Mélanie's situation. After a long absence Antony, who had known Adèle before her marriage, returns from his travels; in order to escape his importunate lovemaking she sets off to join her husband in Strasbourg. Antony, however, overtakes her on the way and seduces her in the inn where she is spending the night. Back in Paris, at a fashionable gathering, the two lovers realize their secret is now public property, and also learn that the husband is returning to settle accounts. In the fifth act Antony and Adèle are shown wrestling with a moral dilemma that would have been quite understandable to audiences in 1831, however farfetched it might seem today: should the lovers flee together or should they die together? In either case Adèle's honor would still be lost; her little daughter would bear all her life the stigma of her mother's unchastity. The one escape from this situation is that Adèle should die at Antony's hands and that he should pretend to have killed her in exasperation at her rejection of his love. The last line of the play, "the most celebrated curtain-line in France," as Robert Baldick has called it, was spoken by Antony to the irate husband who bursts into the room and stands aghast at the sight of his wife's corpse: "She was resisting me, and so I murdered her."

Why this totally improbable denouement should have stirred audiences of the time to such a pitch of frenzied excitement—Dumas was mobbed in the theater at the end of the first performance by a crowd of young fans who tore his coat to pieces so as to be able to carry off some fragment of it as a relic—remains something of a mystery. But there was a certain primitive male brutality about Dumas's theater that may have had a special appeal for the generation of 1830: his heroes, Richard Darlington in the play of that name (1831), Alfred d'Alvimar in *Angèle* (1833), are young men who use women as the means to the achievement of their social ambitions and then abandon them or get rid of them by some violently criminal act. Dumas in private life never went to this extreme, but his dealings with Catherine Labay, the mother of his first child, with Mélanie Waldor, and with her successor, Belle Krelsamer, who bore him a second child, were all marked by a certain swashbuckling ruthlessness that he needed to exaggerate only slightly to create the villainous but irresistible protagonists of his dramas.

In addition Dumas possessed to a far greater degree than any other of the French romantics a sense of the theater, which meant that he intuitively felt what the audience wanted and gave it to them, occasionally anticipating their longings and forcing their tastes. Arsène Houssaye, who was in charge of the fortunes of the Comédie Française from 1849 to 1856, called him "l'homme-théâtre," meaning that he incarnated as none other did the spirit of the theater; but it was the theater of his time, not of all time. With one exception—*La tour de Nesle* (1832), a melodrama that has proved suitable for film and for television—his plays, some of them enormously successful when first produced, have proved impossible to revive. They incarnate brilliantly certain stereotypes of the romantic age: the tortured, antisocial Antony; later the ruthless, power-hungry Richard Darlington; and especially Edmund Kean, a faithful representation of the notorious Shakespearean actor of the Regency period in England. Dumas clearly enjoyed depicting the last, a violent, eminently theatrical man, a Don Juan riddled with debt, taunting the critics and the aristocrats, a man of the people who chanced to be a genius. *Kean* was written in 1836 for the actor Frédérick Lemaître, who had such an affinity with Kean that he hardly needed to act the part. This is perhaps one other reason why Dumas's plays, even when highly successful in their day, have not survived: they were written for certain actors and actresses, *Richard Darlington* for Lemaître, *Angèle* for Bocage, *Mademoiselle de Belle-Isle* (1839) for Mademoiselle Mars. For this last play, a comedy with tragic overtones, Dumas returned at last to the Comédie Française, giving its senior actress the chance to show how, even at the age of sixty, no one could better play the part of an eighteen-year-old ingenue.

*La tour de Nesle* is of all Dumas's plays the one that comes nearest, both in subject matter and in characterization, to the historical novels that he had not at the time even thought of. Set in Paris at the beginning of the fourteenth century, the novel concerns the lascivious orgies in which Marguerite of Burgundy, queen of France, and her two sisters indulge night after night in a gloomy tower overlooking the Seine. The young men who are decoyed there to pleasure the ladies are never permitted to talk of their adventures subsequently; their usual fate is to have their throats cut by hired ruffians who then fling their bodies into the river. One young man, Buridan, escapes. He then blackmails the queen into having him appointed minister. They pursue their criminal careers together for some time, until in the end they fall out, denouncing each other. André Maurois has called *La tour de Nesle* "a classic of theatrical excess," and other critics have speculated on the play's appeal. What has perhaps not been properly noticed is that this appeal must be the same as that of the novels, for Buridan is a less developed forerunner of all Dumas's impetuous young heroes whose fate it is to love great queens: from La Mole who loves Marguerite de Navarre, to Charny who loves Marie Antoinette. Such attachments are bound to end tragically, for if love implies mastery, as Dumas undoubtedly believed, how can a queen submit to being mastered by a vassal?

## *HISTORY AND FICTION*

Although Dumas built his reputation on his plays, by themselves they could not have given him the wide appeal he still enjoys today. Stage fashions changed rapidly in the first half of the nineteenth century, and before that century was midway through, the romantic drama that Hugo and he had spearheaded no longer drew the eagerly attentive audiences it had in the 1830's. Dumas's son, Alexandre *fils*, in his first play, *La dame aux camélias* (The Lady of the Camellias, 1852; later translated as *Camille*), lit the way to a different kind of theater, one that dealt with difficult questions of domestic morality confronting the smug and self-satisfied bourgeois society of the Second Empire (1852–1870). A new generation demanded a new type of play, essentially modern, serious, sermonizing, calling into question all the by now old-fashioned romantic shibboleths.

Dumas *père* could afford to yield the stage to this new wave of dramatists, for by 1852, as the result of a bare eight years of prodigious and unremitting labor, he had firmly established himself as master in a totally new field.

The period between the publication of *Les trois mousquetaires* (*The Three Musketeers*, 1844) and *Ange Pitou* (1851) saw the appearance of perhaps a dozen full-length historical novels, together with what is usually regarded as his masterpiece, *Le comte de Monte-Cristo* (*The Count of Monte Cristo*, 1844–1845), which is set in contemporary times. Some of these works are dauntingly long: *Joseph Balsamo* (1846–1848) runs into five volumes in the standard edition, *Le vicomte de Bragelonne* (1848–1850; part of which was translated as *The Man in the Iron Mask*) into six. Even taking into account Dumas's amazing constitution and his ability to work eighteen hours out of the twenty-four, and after making due allowance for whatever help he may have received from his collaborators, Auguste Maquet in particular, the feat is still astounding.

The historical novel had been popularized in France by Sir Walter Scott, whose entire works were translated in the 1820's almost as soon as they came out. Thinking to cash in on the current "Scottomania," some of the leading French romantics had brought out imitations, using incidents from the history of their own country as the framework of their romances: Alfred de Vigny in *Cinq-Mars* (1826) had dealt with a conspiracy against Cardinal Richelieu; Prosper Mérimée had written his *Chronique du règne de Charles IX* (Chronicles of the Reign of Charles IX, 1829) around the massacre of Saint Bartholomew's Day (a bloody episode also figuring at the beginning of Dumas's *La reine Margot* [1845; translated as *Marguerite de Valois*]); and Hugo had produced, in 1831, his *Notre-Dame de Paris* (*Hunchback of Notre-Dame*), set in fifteenth-century Paris. These early examples of the genre were appreciated more for their historical content than for their merits as novels, though, in spite of its pedantic displays of erudition, Hugo's first venture into the field still finds plenty of admirers for the vividness of imagination shown in certain outstanding episodes. But it is significant that at the time each of these works was for the author an isolated venture (though Hugo did write a novel about the French Revolution toward the end of his life). Clearly the reception had not been such as to encourage any of these authors to follow Scott's example and write a series of novels about a particular period.

How was it that, a dozen years later, Dumas was able to revive this formula with such outstanding success? The starting point was his friendship with Auguste Maquet, already mentioned. Maquet was a teacher of history at one of the great Paris schools. He had literary ambitions and had written *Le bonhomme Buvat* (Bumbling Old Buvat), a short story about the Cellamare conspiracy against the regent of France in 1718; it was based on the memoirs of the bibliophile Jean Buvat. Unable to find a publisher, Maquet took the manuscript to Dumas, who read it and offered to buy it from him if Maquet granted him the right to rework it. This was the origin of *Le chevalier d'Harmental*, which was published in installments in the newspaper *Le siècle* before appearing in volume form in 1842.

The serialization of popular fiction in the daily press was a fairly new development in France, though it had started some time earlier in England. In 1836 the newspaper proprietor Émile de Girardin, with his eye on the English precedent, launched *La presse* as a cut-price daily. He hoped that he would gain a wide circulation by publishing *feuilletons*, novels that appeared chapter by chapter, in each issue. The fashion caught on, and by the 1840's most newspaper editors had several fiction writers on their payroll and were prepared to pay very highly for the products of their pens if these seemed likely to attract new readers and keep old ones. Dumas's talents were precisely suited to this form of fiction, which depended heavily on the ability to tantalize the public with a plot involving frequent and exciting twists and turns. His fluency helped, as did even the historical pretensions of the fiction, which seemed to engage the readers' attention, giving them the illusion that they were not merely following an enthralling story but also learning something about their country's past at the same time. The sudden flowering of the *roman-feuilleton,* the serial novel, explains why most of Dumas's historical fiction was written over a relatively short period of time. With the advent of the Second Empire and the more rigorous control of the press that the new administration decided was necessary, the *roman-feuilleton,* particularly in the form of the historical novel, was dealt its deathblow, for although it was not an overtly political form of art, it was vulnerable to the new controls. Any fiction that dealt with the crimes, conspiracies, and revolutions of the past could be regarded as having certain political implications for the present that the censors preferred not to risk.

Dumas had no illusions about the historical value of his novels. "We lay no claim to being a historian," he remarked in an aside in *Les quarante-cinq* (*The Forty-Five,* 1848); "if occasionally we become one, it is when by chance history sinks to the level of the novel, or better still, when the novel rises to the height of history" (2.31). This somewhat cryptic utterance is akin to what he once said to Lamartine, when the poet-statesman professed himself astonished at the immense popular acclaim he had achieved with his *Histoire des Girondins* (1847): "The reason, my dear Lamartine," he explained, "is that you have raised yourself to the level of fiction" (*Causeries,* 1860). Dumas was not, of course, implying that fiction was simply a higher form of history, but that a good historian should be able to interest his reader as much by the historical account as by first-rate imaginative writing. For there is nothing dry as dust in history as such; only the dullness of pedantry makes it seem lifeless. Dumas was highly responsive to the fascination of the past. He even tried his hand at writing works of "straight" history: *Gaule et France* (1833), *Isabelle de Bavière* (1836), *Les Stuarts* (1840). History formed the backcloth to many of his plays and intruded to a marked degree in his travel books; there was nothing he loved more than to visit spots "steeped in history."

But there is one marked difference between the historian and the historical novelist. The former deals with all events that he reckons, with hindsight, were important; the latter introduces into his fiction only such historical events as he wishes to, and is governed in his decision to do so by broadly aesthetic considerations. Thus Dumas gives the massacre of the Huguenots on Saint Bartholomew's Day pride of place in *La reine Margot,* mainly because it is illustrative of certain tendencies in his characters: brutality, cowardice, and the readiness to change one's religious allegiances if political ends require it. In *Vingt ans après* (*Twenty Years After,* 1845) he recounts the return of Charles I as a prisoner from Newcastle to London, his trial, and his execution, not for what these events signified in the broadest sense but in order to emphasize certain traits of character in his heroes: D'Artagnan's daring plotting, Athos's devotion to lost causes. But he is just as content to skirt such major issues and concentrate instead on the nine days' wonders, a flood in Paris, a fireworks display that went wrong and caused the waiting crowd to stampede with much loss of life and limb. As for the big events of history, they are for the novelist, as he remarked in *Joseph Balsamo* (ch. 64), "what huge mountains are for the traveller. He observes them, travels round them, salutes them in passing, but he does not cross over them."

History, as Dumas understood it, was far more circumscribed than we would regard it today, being still largely a matter of recording the doings of kings and queens and their ministers. Who will succeed Charles IX when he lies ill and likely to die? Will it be his brother, who already sits on the throne of Poland, or will Henri de Navarre make good his claim? The Valois give way to the Bourbons, but to the men of the sixteenth century it was scarcely conceivable that any country in Europe should not have a monarch at its head. This is Athos's viewpoint in *Vingt ans après*: the king dies, but not the monarchy. "The king is but a man, royalty is the spirit of God" (ch. 24). But Athos was a gentleman of the old school; even before Louis XIV reached his majority, the historical process was whittling away the old feudalism and the monarchy no longer seemed so sacred. Dumas shows Anne, queen and regent, faced with a popular rising because she has ordered the arrest of Broussel, a councillor beloved of the people. Can the rabble tell her what she may or may not do? "Good God," she reflects, "what has become of the monarchy?" What indeed? "The commoners had not spoken up for the princes, but they rose up in arms for Broussel; this was because Broussel was a plebeian, and in defending Broussel they instinctively felt they were defending themselves" (ch. 60).

The history of France of the three centuries preceding the French Revolution, as Dumas covers it in his historical novels, debouches on to that revolution; this is the cataract to which all the currents flow, faster and faster as the brink is approached. Afterward there will be no more kings and queens, or they will be shadows of themselves, mere puppets seated on fragile thrones. "France resembles a centuries-old hourglass," Dumas wrote in *Le collier de la reine* (*The Queen's Necklace*, 1849–1850), "for nine hundred years it marked the hour of the monarchy; then the powerful right hand of the Lord God grasped it and turned it over; for centuries to come it will mark the era of the common people" (ch. 16). And in the new era, as Honoré de Balzac saw, true royalty is to be found incarnated not in any king but in the silver coin that bears the royal effigy, the *pièce de cent sous*, the five-franc piece; autocracy has been succeeded by plutocracy, and the most powerful man in France is neither Charles X nor Louis Philippe, but the mysterious count of Monte-Cristo, whose fabulous wealth sets him higher than the king and gives him more power than any of the king's ministers.

The royal figures that strut through the pages of the historical romances belong to history, and Dumas portrays them much as chroniclers of their own period described them: weak, covetous, lecherous, dilatory, but not entirely cowardly; with flashes of nobility, capable of arousing strong affection and a loyalty too seldom rewarded. We see Charles IX living in terror of his mother, keeping in check her fierce hatred of Henri de Navarre, dying finally of the poison she had destined for the future King Henri IV of France but keeping the secret of her guilt locked in his breast till the end so that no stain should be cast on the honor of the royal house. Then we are shown his successor, Henri III, a sybarite, superstitious, passionately attached to the young men who form his band of "minions," and mourning their deaths with genuine affection at the end of *La dame de Monsoreau.* The queens too are portrayed with their strengths and weaknesses: Louise, the pallid, neglected wife of Henri III; Anne, consort of Louis XIII, proud, petulant, ungrateful, yet inspiring the love of two cardinals and of the duke of Buckingham; the luckless Henrietta of England, living in penurious exile, cheated and swindled by Cardinal Mazarin, but full of dignity, a fond mother and a devoted wife; and above all Marie Antoinette, a tragic figure somewhat idealized by Dumas, who traces her career through five novels (*Joseph Balsamo, Le collier de la reine, Ange Pitou, La comtesse de Charny* [1852–1855], and *Le chevalier de Maison-Rouge* [1845]). Imprudent and capricious at the start, she is shown her final fate—death on the scaffold—in Balsamo's crystal glass, and in the end meets it transfigured by her sufferings, no longer arrogant yet not crushed, bearing herself with a quiet dignity. "Madame Veto," "Veuve Capet," to use the insulting names bestowed on her by the revolutionaries, she is still queen of France, and signs herself so in the prison register.

The historical characters in Dumas's novels

are not invariably kings, queens, princes of the blood royal, powerful ministers. Many of those who play the most important roles, including D'Artagnan himself, Bussy d'Amboise, Chicot the jester, and Cagliostro, are based on real people mentioned in the memoirs he consulted, but in such cases he permitted himself considerable liberties, giving the soldier of fortune greater chivalry, the charlatan greater dignity, all of them much more complexity than the historical record showed. No one would have it otherwise, for this is where the creative writer must be allowed his head. But occasionally he introduces others whose names history has preserved not because they were men of power, but because they were men of influence. In the twenty-third chapter of *Vingt ans après,* Raoul is taken by his father to visit Paul Scarron, a noted wit of the period and the author of a novel on the adventures of a group of strolling players. All the literary lions are in Scarron's chambers: Gilles Ménage, the philologist, whom Molière is supposed to have caricatured as Vadius in his comedy on the bluestockings; Georges de Scudéry, whom Raoul salutes as the author of *Clélie* (1654–1660) and *Artamène, ou le grand Cyrus* (1649–1653)—showing great prescience, for they were not written at the time (Dumas can make mistakes); and Françoise d'Aubigné, the future Madame de Maintenon, whom Scarron was to marry in 1652. The purpose of this catalog of beaux esprits is clear: in that age of battles, conspiracies, and sudden deaths, the arts of society are beginning to be cultivated. "Do gentlemen write verses?" asks Raoul naively; "I thought they would scorn to." Athos laughs. "Only when they are bad verses; when they are good, it is an additional luster."

This chapter in *Vingt ans après* is not an isolated tour de force. Molière and the poet Jean de La Fontaine appear episodically in *Le vicomte de Bragelonne,* while in *Joseph Balsamo* the quirky figure of Jean Jacques Rousseau is given a fairly important part to play, though one still marginal to the main action. Gilbert, the young hero of this long and intricate novel, is introduced at the start of the book reading *The Social Contract;* Rousseau is his god. Later Gilbert meets the great man. At first he does not realize who he is; Rousseau is engaged in his harmless hobby, botanizing, and Gilbert, who is starving, is glad to share the older man's frugal meal when the offer is made to him. After that the philosopher takes the boy home, introduces him to his companion Thérèse, and in spite of querulous protests on her part, insists on letting him sleep in the attic. The following day, he shows him how he earns his living: not by writing immortal works, but by copying music, a task at which Gilbert shows himself unexpectedly apt.

All these details are based on well-attested fact, and the portrait of Rousseau, with his self-pity, his suspicion of his fellow philosophers, his misanthropy, his vanity, is excellently drawn in the teasing scene in which Gilbert talks in glowing terms about the author of the *Discourse on the Origin of Inequality* without realizing that the stranger he is addressing actually wrote the treatise. In a later episode Rousseau is invited to the Trianon to superintend a rehearsal of his early work, the light opera *Le devin de village.* He refuses the offer of a private carriage to take him to Versailles and arrives instead in a public conveyance, dressed in his usual clothes, to be received by the master of ceremonies with ill-concealed astonishment. But he passes unnoticed at the court; only the dauphine, Marie Antoinette, asks to see him, and when he is eventually presented to Louis XV he stands tongue-tied and abashed, while the monarch converses with him politely about trivialities. Apart from the fact that Dumas seems not to have realized that both the *Confessions* (1781) and the *Rêveries d'un promeneur solitaire* (Meditations of a Solitary Wayfarer, 1782) were published posthumously, he does not appear to have done any great violence to the historical record; but there is an obvious risk in mixing real characters with fictitious ones. Rousseau and his cross-grained housekeeper Thérèse actually lived; Gilbert lived only in Dumas's imagination. Goethe could associate *Dichtung* with *Wahrheit*, but in Dumas, too often the truth sits uneasily with the poetry.

## *ORESTES AND PYLADES*

Among the books that Dumas mentions in his memoirs as having impressed him deeply in his childhood is Charles-Albert Demoustier's *Lettres à Émilie sur la mythologie* (Letters to Emily on Mythology, 1786–1798), and it was probably here that he first came across the story of Orestes and Pylades. After the murder of Agamemnon by his wife's lover Aegisthus, the child Orestes, Agamemnon's son, was taken away by his uncle Strophius and brought up in the same household as Strophius' son, Pylades. The two cousins became fast friends, and when they had grown to manhood it was Pylades who helped Orestes in his plan to kill both his stepfather Aegisthus and his mother Clytemnestra. The union between them was finally sealed when Pylades married Orestes' sister Electra.

This legend provides the basis for a persistent motif that recurs in one after another of the historical novels, although often with an odd variant: two young men, predestined to be inseparable friends, may start by being sworn enemies. Thus in *La reine Margot*, on the evening of 24 August 1572 two young cavaliers arrive in Paris, the one from Piedmont, the other from Provence. They both stop in front of an inn bearing the sign La Belle Étoile, and after a few words of conversation, they tell each other who they are: Annibal de Coconnas, Boniface de La Mole. Coconnas is well built and jovial, La Mole slender and melancholic. What is more to the point, this being the eve of Saint Bartholomew, Coconnas is a Catholic, La Mole a Protestant; the one has business with the duc de Guise, leader of the Catholic league, the other with Henri de Navarre, the head of the Huguenot faction. So, having first booked rooms in the inn, they both make their way to the Louvre to report to their respective patrons.

They meet again at supper that night and afterward fall to playing cards. La Mole then goes to bed, and the innkeeper has a private word with Coconnas. Every Protestant is to be put to death that night; this includes La Mole. Coconnas objects: "'M. de La Mole is my companion, M. de La Mole has supped with me, M. de La Mole has played a game of cards with me.' 'Yes, but M. de La Mole is a heretic, M. de La Mole is condemned, and if we do not kill him, others will.'" Coconnas yields reluctantly to these arguments, but La Mole, forewarned, makes his escape over the rooftops.

In the subsequent fighting, the two young men encounter and wound one another, are nursed back to health, fight a duel and again wound one another, this time more seriously. Conconnas is the slower to recover, but La Mole nurses him devotedly, and when they are both on their feet again they are blood brothers for life; or as Dumas puts it:

> The friendship of the two gentlemen, which began in the inn of La Belle Étoile and was violently interrupted by the events of the night of Saint Bartholomew, was resumed henceforth with a new impetus, and soon outstripped that of Orestes and Pylades to the tune of five sword-thrusts and one pistol-shot distributed about their persons.
>
> (ch. 17)

The one falls in love with Marguerite de Navarre, the other with the duchesse de Nevers, but these highborn ladies cannot save them from a cruel and shameful end: both are arrested, tortured, and finally beheaded in public, Coconnas supporting his friend, whose bones have been broken by the executioner.

The formula that served Dumas so well in *La reine Margot* was used, whether consciously or unconsciously, fairly regularly in his historical fiction and can be said to constitute a key myth, one he found strangely irresistible. Essentially the myth requires an encounter between two young men from opposite camps who start by quarreling and then come to appreciate one another's qualities, after which they become bosom friends and sworn allies. In *La dame de Monsoreau,* in some respects a sequel to *La reine Margot,* the two are called Saint-Luc and Bussy d'Amboise. The fact that they serve different masters does not prevent them from espousing each other's interests throughout the book, and at the end, in the fatal ambush that is laid for Bussy, Saint-Luc is by his side to rescue Bussy's mistress Diane, though he cannot save his friend. In *Le collier de la reine* it is Philippe de Taverney and Olivier de Charny who represent the derivatives of this myth: both are young, both are aristocrats, both are new to the court—and both are passionately devoted to Marie Antoinette. Their rivalry is the source of the quarrel between them, finally resolved when the queen, to extricate herself from a compromising situation, arranges a marriage between Charny and Philippe's sister Andrée de Taverney. This union corresponds, of course, to one of the vicissitudes of the original legend, when Pylades marries Orestes' sister Electra.

But it is in *Le chevalier de Maison-Rouge* that the Orestes and Pylades legend is most obviously employed, in the story of the friendship between Maurice Lindey, the republican officer, and Lorin, the Anacreontic poet. It seems that Dumas took deliberate precautions lest it should ever cross his reader's mind that the strong affection that binds the young men together might be due to some more passionate tenderness that in his day was regarded as depraved. He could not altogether conceal the fact of Henri III's homosexuality, but he was careful to provide both La Mole and Coconnas with mistresses who exchange confidences about the prowess of their lovers. In *Le chevalier de Maison-Rouge* Maurice is jealously devoted to Geneviève Dixmer, and Lorin has his own mistress, Artémise, a girl shapely enough to compete for the honor of representing the Goddess of Reason in a kind of revolutionary forerunner of the Miss World competitions of our day.

Both the young men are dedicated republicans, though Maurice's love for the royalist Geneviève puts this friendship to a severe test. As Lorin complains, before matters have gone very far: "You are forcing me to sacrifice my duty to my friendship, or my friend to my duty. And I am very much afraid, Maurice, that it is my duty I shall sacrifice." Later, Lorin remonstrates with him more seriously, warning him he is on a slippery slope: "I am not blaming you, I am arguing with you. Remember the altercations Pylades and Orestes used to have every day, proving beyond question that friendship is a mere paradox, since these model friends were forever quarrelling" (ch. 32). In the end both Lorin and Maurice are arrested, together with Geneviève, and all three are guillotined.

*Les trois mousquetaires,* Dumas's most famous historical novel, shows not two friends, but four; we may regard this situation as a simple reduplication of the original pattern. The opening chapters show the same initial hostility of the characters, springing this time from trivial causes: D'Artagnan, in his impetuous chase after Rochefort, succeeds in provoking the anger of each of the musketeers in turn and agrees to meet them on the dueling ground at half-hourly intervals to settle the quarrel. D'Artagnan is about to cross swords with Athos—Porthos and Aramis are waiting their turn—when a detachment of the cardinal's guardsmen arrives on the scene to arrest them, dueling, under a recent edict, having been prohibited by law. The musketeers refuse to yield their swords and prepare to resist. D'Artagnan, seeing they are three against five, does not hesitate to join the minority. The result of this battle, which Dumas, himself a practiced swordsman, describes in great detail, is the defeat and rout of the cardinal's men. Later, in chapter 9, having buried their quarrel, the musketeers swear their celebrated oath at D'Artagnan's invitation: "All for one, and one for all!"

Of the three musketeers, Porthos may well be the one for whom D'Artagnan feels most affection: Porthos, the gentle, stupid giant, the Obélix to D'Artagnan's Astérix, always astonished at his friend's perspicacity and foresight. Porthos represents brute strength and vanity, two qualities that should hardly commend him to the reader; but in addition he has a certain childlike innocence that one cannot but find endearing; when Dumas eventually killed him off in *Le vicomte de Bragelonne,* his son saw him wipe a tear from his eye. Athos has a nobility of soul that in *Les trois mousquetaires* is obscured by his strange taciturnity and his occasional bouts of heavy drinking; but in *Vingt ans après,* the immediate sequel, this addiction to wine has been conquered, thanks to the need to set an example for his son Raoul. And Athos has at all times *moral* courage (physical courage, needless to say, is something all four possess in equal measure); Athos is the only one who is not overawed by Richelieu. Aramis is, as Dumas calls him, a hieroglyph: he yearns to enter the church when a soldier, but hankers after a life of soldierly activity when in his monastery; and at all times he is a man of mysteries and secrets jealously guarded. But D'Artagnan is the man of good counsel, the planner, and the others realize this and let him organize every strategy. Although the youngest of them all, D'Artagnan is judged by Athos to be the soundest reasoner, "la plus forte tête," of the quartet.

It has been said that *Les trois mousquetaires* is a novel imbued with the spirit of the early morning. It has a juvenile charm and brio, which in *Vingt ans après* has been lost, to be replaced by the lengthening shadows of the afternoon. It is in *Vingt ans après* that the Orestes and Pylades myth can be seen reasserting itself, with the musketeers split into two groups, at first hostile to each other and later joining forces.

*Les trois mousquetaires* had ended on a melancholy note. After all the adventure of the road, after "all quality, pride, pomp, and circumstance of glorious wars," the four friends disperse, and D'Artagnan is left mourning his lost youth. Over the next twenty years, nothing happens to him but to grow into middle age. *Vingt ans après* shows him still awaiting promotion, serving Cardinal Mazarin instead of Cardinal Richelieu and aware of the sad difference. Mazarin has few supporters on whom he can rely, and he has heard of the exploits of the four musketeers in former times. He would feel safer with them as a bodyguard. So he asks D'Artagnan to trace his old friends and bring them together once more, a task that takes him all over France and is only half successful. Porthos alone is willing to join him, on promise of a barony. But Athos and Aramis are not prepared to serve Mazarin, being members of the Fronde, the party of disaffected gentlemen pledged to the overthrow of the cardinal. The discovery that they are on different sides is made when the four clash in a midnight encounter. D'Artagnan and Porthos are outnumbered and forced to retire, but they agree to meet the other two in the Place Royale the following day. Talking over the situation with Porthos beforehand, D'Artagnan makes the point that none of them is so wedded to the cause they serve that they should think their new loyalties outweigh the old one: "No, it is not the civil wars that separate us, it is the fact that none of us is twenty any longer, that the generous impulses of youth have given way to the murmurings of self-interest, the whisper of ambition and the counsels of egoism" (ch. 29). Nevertheless, at the actual meeting there is distrust on both sides until Athos symbolically breaks his sword across his knee and urges Aramis to do the same, swearing he will never again turn his weapon against either Porthos or D'Artagnan. The others are carried away by this effusion of manly sentiment and repeat after him, on Aramis's crucifix, the oath "to be united in spite of all and forever."

And so the "band of brothers" is reconstituted, free to follow the call of adventure. Shortly afterward they all find themselves in England, D'Artagnan and Porthos as Mazarin's ambassadors to Oliver Cromwell, Athos and Aramis obedient to the request of the unfortunate Queen Henrietta, who wants at least two intrepid friends near her husband, Charles I, in his hour of need. It is D'Artagnan, subsequently, who devises successive plans to deliver the king, with as much ingenuity and as little success as the chevalier de Maison-Rouge has trying to save Marie Antoinette from the ferocious Jacobins. Then the musketeers return to France and this time join forces against Mazarin, whose treachery releases D'Artagnan from his duty to him. Everyone is satisfied in the end—the villains all dead, and Louis XIV in the wings, ready to take over when he reaches his majority in a year's time. *Vingt ans après* concludes much as does *Les trois mousquetaires:* Porthos returns to his estate to enjoy his new dignity, Aramis to his monastery; and D'Artagnan agrees to keep an eye on Raoul for Athos: "The four friends embraced with tears in their eyes. Then they separated without knowing whether they would ever meet again." But at least, more fortunate than Coconnas or La Mole, than Lorin and Lindey, they do not meet on the scaffold.

## *PRISONERS AND ESCAPEES*

In *The Romantic Prison* (1978) Victor Brombert establishes the theme of imprisonment as both fundamental and widespread in all romantic literatures in Europe. No author was so preoccupied with the subject as Dumas, and there is scarcely one of his novels in which it is not introduced somewhere or other. In his first successful attempt at a work of fiction, *Le chevalier d'Harmental,* the hero is sent to the Bastille by the prince regent for his part in a conspiracy that miscarried; the book ends with his release, his captor unexpectedly relenting. *La tulipe noire* (*The Black Tulip,* 1850), a historical novel set exceptionally in Holland, opens with a description of the mob bursting into the Buytenhoff prison, in order to drag Cornelius de Witt from his cell and lynch him. Later in the same book the harmless tulip grower Cornelius van Baerle is imprisoned at Dordrecht on a trumped-up charge and is released only with the help of the jailer's daughter.

In France there was one prison above all whose destruction was still regarded as symbolizing the beginning of a new era; this was the Bastille. In *Ange Pitou* Dumas describes at length and in detail its storming and the butchery of its garrison. At the start of the account, he reminds us that "there was not just one bastille in France; there were a score of bastilles, called Fort-l'Évêque, Saint-Lazare, le Châtelet, la Conciergerie, Vincennes, le château de la Roche, le château d'If . . ." (ch. 13). For readers of *Le comte de Monte-Cristo,* a novel set in Dumas's own time, the château d'If is the most celebrated of all, the island prison in the Mediterranean that lies no more than a short boat ride from Marseilles.

On the point of marrying his chosen bride, Mercédès, Dantès falls victim to the machinations of Fernand, his rival in love, and Danglars, a fellow seaman who bears him a grudge. They denounce Dantès to the authorities as a Bonapartist agent, and it falls to a certain Villefort to investigate the case. Unluckily Villefort, a magistrate loyal to the monarchy, happens to be the son of an ardent Bonapartist, and Dantès was the bearer of a highly compromising letter addressed to Villefort's father. Villefort has Dantès brought before him, convinces himself that the young man knows nothing of the contents of the letter, and destroys it in front of his eyes; but to make assurance doubly sure, he signs the order for Dantès's indefinite imprisonment in the château d'If. The lettres de cachet of the ancien régime have been legally abolished, but administrative action can achieve the same ends, sending a man to prison without trial, without his ever knowing the reasons, and with no hope of any revision of the sentence; for he has not been formally sentenced.

Dantès remains in prison for fourteen

years. After the first seventeen months he is visited by a prison inspector, whom he implores to bring him to trial. He waits patiently for a fortnight, three months, ten months, until he begins to wonder whether the inspector's visit has not been a dream. He asks for a glimpse of the sun, the chance to take exercise, books to occupy his mind; all these are refused him, and he is denied even conversation, for the warders have orders not to speak to him. It would be an inhuman punishment for one guilty of the worst crime, and for a man who knows himself guiltless of any crime it is a pointless torture. Dantès realizes he has had the misfortune to cross the path of unscrupulous enemies. He does not know who they are, but he condemns them in imagination to the worst of torments and finds even the worst is too good for them. Then he makes up his mind to die by refusing food; he is near to achieving his purpose when he hears a scratching at the wall near his bed.

It is his neighbor, the abbé Faria, who has been in prison four years longer than he has. Faria has occupied his time tunneling, but in the wrong direction, since he ended in Dantès's cell when he thought he was working his way to the sea. Faria is his salvation; he teaches Dantès everything, for Dantès, a poor sailor, knows nothing but his trade. But Faria gives him little hope of escape:

> I have but rarely seen escapes succeed. Lucky escapes, escapes crowned with complete success, are escapes that have been carefully planned, prepared step by step. That is how the duc de Beaufort escaped from the château de Vincennes, the abbé Dubuquoi from Fort-l'Évêque, and Latude from the Bastille. There are also those that chance may offer; these are the best; let us wait our opportunity, and if it presents itself, let us profit from it.
>
> (ch. 16)

The opportunity arises, not for Faria but for Dantès. Faria dies and is sewn into a sack; Dantès has the courage to reenter the dead man's cell, remove the corpse and put it in his own bed, then hide inside Faria's sack. He expects to be buried somewhere on the island, but the prison officers toss him into the sea, for "the sea is the cemetery of the château d'If." And so at last Dantès, having cut himself out of his sack, swims to freedom.

The escape of the duc de Beaufort, to which Faria made reference, forms a substantial part of Dumas's narrative in *Vingt ans après*. The episode is related in the comic vein as much as Dantès's imprisonment is presented in the tragic. In the social scale the two prisoners are a world apart: Beaufort, a prince of the blood, one of the grandsons of Henri IV; Dantès, an insignificant member of the French merchant navy. The duke is allowed all the amusements, exercise, and delicate fare of which Dantès is cruelly deprived. Beaufort, who is brave, popular, but rather stupid, spends his time breathing fire and slaughter against Mazarin, to whom he owes his imprisonment. One of his pastimes is to draw caricatures of the cardinal, using charcoal from the fire, until Monsieur de Chavigny, governor of the château de Vincennes, forbids the fire to be lit and lets Beaufort shiver. He then spends months training a dog to carry out various tricks highly disrespectful of the cardinal; the dog is poisoned. And so the petty war goes on, the prisoner being treated with all the respect due to his rank, but in fact thwarted at every turn.

Eventually the duke's escape is organized by his friends outside, among whom is Athos, who contrives that his own servant, Grimaud, should be given employment in the prison; Grimaud smuggles in a silk cord under the crust of a venison pasty. The cord allows Beaufort to climb down the outside walls to where three friends wait with horses:

> "Gentlemen," said the prince, "I will thank you all later; but at this moment, there is no time to be lost, we must be on our way. Let him who loves me, follow me!" And he leapt on to his horse and sped off at a gallop, filling his lungs

> with air and shouting out with an expression of joy impossible to convey: "Free! . . . free! . . . free!"
>
> (ch. 15)

One other unforgettable escape, which has catastrophic consequences, is that of Milady in *Les trois mousquetaires* after she has been decoyed by De Winter to his castle near Portsmouth. She has only a few days to break out if she is to fulfill Richelieu's order and prevent the departure of Buckingham with his fleet to the relief of the embattled Huguenots at La Rochelle. Felton, the warder De Winter has found for her, appears incorruptible, until she discovers him to be a religious enthusiast, which gives her a hold over him. She pretends to be a co-religionary and, further, invents such convincing tales about Buckingham's wickedness that Felton not only agrees to arrange her escape, but having done so seeks audience with the admiral and stabs him. The assassination is historical fact, though what the real Felton's motives may have been is a matter for conjecture; Dumas's explanation, if farfetched, is at least dramatically effective as well as psychologically plausible.

Not all imprisonments end with the escape of the prisoner. The Man in the Iron Mask, whose story dominates the last part of *Le vicomte de Bragelonne,* is never released, and La Mole and Coconnas only leave their prison cells for the torture chamber and, some weeks later, for the place of execution. We have seen how, in spite of the efforts of the musketeers, nothing can be done to save Charles I from the ax. Seen from the vantage point of posterity, the fate of Marie Antoinette has a similar inevitability. The imprisonment of the royal family in the Tour du Temple, part of the medieval fortress that used to belong to the Knights Templars in Paris, took place on 13 August 1792. On 5 December the trial of Louis XVI opened before the Convention and on 21 January 1793 he was executed. So much belongs to the history of France; Dumas's *Le chevalier de Maison-Rouge,* the action of which starts on 10 March 1793, follows the developing story quite closely, down to the queen's trial and execution on 16 October. The royal family, or what was left of it—the queen, her fourteen-year-old daughter, and her young son—are at first shown sharing a room in the Temple. But on the refusal of all three to answer questions concerning an attempt the previous night to spirit them away, the boy, the uncrowned heir to the throne, who was always known to royalists as Louis XVII or the Orphan of the Temple, is removed from his mother's care and given into the custody of the brutal shoemaker Simon. After a further attempt by her would-be deliverers that again unluckily fails, the queen is removed to the Conciergerie, the most ancient prison in Paris, destined to hold many other victims of the Terror, including in the last batch Maximilien Robespierre, hoist with his own petard, since he was the man principally responsible for the use of the guillotine as an instrument of policy. Dumas's portrayal of Marie Antoinette at this stage shows her to be no longer the same haughty queen we see in *Le collier de la reine* and in *Ange Pitou;* she is humble, eager to notice signs of compassion in the tone of voice of her warders, however rudely they may address her. One final plot is hatched to set her free, which she refuses to allow since it involves killing two guards, whose deaths she does not want on her conscience. An alternative scheme is devised, in which she is asked to saw through one of the bars of her cell. But there are by now two agents working to rescue the queen, each in ignorance of the other's plans, and their efforts in effect cancel one another out. History, or destiny, did not intend that Marie Antoinette should escape the guillotine.

## *PROVIDENCE: THE GRAND DESIGN*

We have noted how Marie Antoinette had been shown the manner of her death when she first crossed the frontier into France, arriving as the dauphin's bride in 1770. At the start of the long novel cycle that bears his name, the mysterious Joseph Balsamo, an unwelcome guest at the château de Taverney, mentions that the future queen of France will be arriving the following day and will honor the old baron de Taverney by visiting his tumbledown house. The prediction is duly fulfilled and Balsamo's reputation as a sorcerer confirmed. The princess thereupon asks him to tell her fortune, which at first he declines to do, saying it is better she should remain in ignorance of the future. But she insists, and taking a glass of clear water, he places it in a dark corner and tells the princess to look at it kneeling, "so that you will be in the posture needed to pray God to spare you the terrible end that you are about to see" (ch. 15).

Balsamo's injunction raises by implication the whole question of human freedom and predestination, for if the end that is already determined for Marie Antoinette can be averted by her prayers, then it is clearly not immutably fixed; and if it cannot be averted, then why does Balsamo invite her to pray?

Curiously, although the breath of freedom is part of the very atmosphere of Dumas's world, so that no worse fate can befall any of his characters than to be trapped in a prison, in a larger sense his characters often give the impression of being the helpless prisoners of a chain of circumstance variously called Providence, destiny, chance, or God: "chance, or rather God, whom we see at the bottom of everything," he writes in *La tulipe noire* (ch. 14), using the authorial *we*. In an unusual passage of metaphysical argument almost apologetically introduced into *Les quarante-cinq* as one of Chicot's "ingenious theories" (3.19), Dumas develops the idea that chance events are God's "reserve forces," using the term in the military sense. When it seems that men have everything under control and are guiding events in the direction that suits them best, then God "brings up his reserve" and casts in front of the wheels the chance pebble that alters the course of events, causing them to run as he wishes, not as men have calculated they should run. Dumas is saying a little more here than that "the best laid schemes of mice an' men/Gang aft a-gley"; for the best laid schemes ought not to go astray, Dumas reasons, and there is no accounting for the fact that they do unless one allows for the intervention of an intelligent power beyond men's reckoning.

A striking illustration of the working of this power is to be found in the Musketeers saga. In *Les trois mousquetaires* we learn how Athos in his youth met and fell in love with the talented, beautiful, but perversely wicked woman spoken of in the book simply as Milady. He married her, then discovered she had been branded by the hangman on the shoulder, proof that she had been found guilty of some unspeakable crime, sacrilege at the least. He ordered his servants to hang her on the nearest tree, but, as so often is the case in Dumas, the dead have a habit of coming back to life again. Much of *Les trois mousquetaires* is concerned with the attempt by Athos, seconded by his friends, to complete this piece of unfinished business; eventually Milady is captured and, in full view of the four musketeers and of De Winter, her head is struck off by the public executioner. It is a private act of justice. But Athos is never entirely satisfied that he had the right to take the law into his own hands; when he learns that Milady had a son, and that the son, known as Mordaunt, has come of age and is seeking revenge on his mother's murderers, he is thrown into turmoil, seeing the young man as nemesis made flesh, sacred, inviolable. When Aramis aims a musket at Mordaunt, Athos strikes it down, murmuring, "It was quite enough to have killed the mother. . . . The son has done us no harm." Even when Athos learns that Mordaunt had been Charles Stuart's executioner and later came within an ace of blowing up all the musketeers in the ship that was to take them back to France, Athos is still unwilling to let Mordaunt die. In one of the most memorable scenes of *Vingt ans après* Mordaunt is swimming in the open sea, begging them to have pity on him and take him aboard, pleading that a son is always bound to try and avenge his mother's death. Athos, in agony of spirit, stretches out a rescuing hand. But Mordaunt will be avenged even at the cost of his own life and drags Athos off the boat and down into the depths of the sea with him. The others watch in horror, but after an interval the lifeless body of Mordaunt, with a dagger in his chest, floats to the surface, and a little later Athos, exhausted, rises to the surface and clutches the side of the boat. "It was not I who killed him," he whispers, "it was destiny" (ch. 77). Was it destiny that allowed Mordaunt to escape Aramis's musket and D'Artagnan's sword only to die at the hand of the man who least wanted to kill him?

For the novelist, who predetermines the novel's denouement, what can pass as the work of Providence or of destiny is simply the slow achievement of the denouement, and his art consists in persuading the reader that what appears fortuitous is actually foreordained and can take on the semblance of a pattern working itself out. But it is different when the novelist is dealing with large movements of history, where the eventual outcome is known to all. For Dumas, as we have seen, history was largely transacted in the courts and palaces of kings. He deals with the decline of two dynasties, that of the Valois and that of the Bourbons. He seems to have subscribed to the theory that all dynasties degenerate in time. In the case of the Bourbons, he was provided with a majestic instance, stretching over two centuries, of this slow but irreversible decadence. The Bourbons were brought to the throne in the person of the "good" king Henri IV and achieved unparalleled greatness under his grandson Louis XIV. They declined in the person of the voluptuary Louis XV, during whose long reign the storms gathered, and finally collapsed with Louis XVI, a worthy man but a weak monarch, incapable of controlling or combating the revolutionary march of events. The portrait Dumas draws of Louis XVI in *Ange Pitou* testifies amply to the final abjection:

> This short, stout body, with no spring and no majesty, these blurred features devoid of expression, this pallid juvenility wrestling with premature senescence, this unequal struggle of a powerful physique and a mediocre intelligence, to which the pride of rank alone gave intermittent flashes of value . . . all that signified degeneration, debasement, impotence, ruin.
>
> (ch. 22)

Yet Louis XVI was the direct descendant, five generations removed, of Henri IV, the intelligent, ambitious, farsighted king who seems, in the Valois novels, to have no chance at all of succeeding to the throne but who works steadily toward that end. He is secretive, watchful, ready to change his religion back and forth as occasion demands, forcing himself to face dangers boldly when he cannot face them fearlessly, constantly opposed by that most redoubtable of adversaries, the all-powerful queen mother Catherine de Médicis, who is totally unscrupulous, who threatens his life time and again, but who confesses herself in the end beaten: "The hand of God is stretched over this man. He will reign, he will reign!" (*La reine Margot,* ch. 34).

Catherine has her own soothsayer, the perfumer René, whose shop on the Pont Saint-Michel is shunned by the superstitious townsfolk, particularly at night. The scene in the nineteenth chapter of *La reine Margot* is to all intents and purposes a repeat of the first act of *Henri III et sa cour,* written sixteen years before. Catherine is visiting René to watch him read the future in the entrails of chickens that she herself kills and disembowels. The omens are always the same: the chicken squawks three times and its liver is seen hanging on the left; this betokens three deaths followed by the extinction of the line. The deaths are those of her three sons: first Charles, the present king; then François, who will never reign; and finally Henri III, the last of the line, who will be assassinated by Jacques Clément. Inspection of the chicken's brain shows the letter *h* repeated four times; so Henri de Navarre will reign over France as Henri IV.

Given that Catherine clearly believes her interpretation of the omens, it seems illogical that she should strive to prove them false by making a series of attempts on her son-in-law's life: "This hateful Henri, forever eluding her ambushes which would be fatal to others, seemed to walk under the protection of some invincible power that Catherine insisted on calling chance, though at the bottom of her heart a voice told her the true name of this power was destiny" (ch. 37); and destiny controls and provokes the chance event. Her last plot miscarries disastrously. Catherine borrows a rare book on falconry belonging to René and treats each page with a poison she has used before; it is slightly sticky and causes the leaves to adhere. She tells François d'Alençon, her youngest son, to leave the book in Henri's chamber, but it is Charles IX who finds it there and who starts reading it, licking his fingers to turn the pages. François, watching him helplessly and knowing that his brother has already absorbed a mortal dose of the poison, "bethought himself that there was a God in heaven who was perhaps not chance" (ch. 40). Catherine's efforts to defeat destiny are thus turned to her own confusion, for she has no control over chance, the chance that took the king to Henri's chamber in his absence, the chance that always works to turn to predestined ends even the most ingenious of her plans.

Chance, fate, the will of God: to Dumas these bring about the fall of the Valois, in part because the last kings of this dynasty are particularly weak, in part because their ultimate successor is particularly cunning. But it is chance that works as the instrument of destiny: the chance that Charles IX read the work on falconry, the chance that Henri III is a homosexual and has no heir, and the chance that his natural heir, his younger brother François, has incurred the deadly hatred of Diane de Monsoreau and that her faithful follower, Rémy le Haudouin, has discovered the secret of the *aqua tofana,* the poison the Médicis perfected. It is the Valois's own sins and follies that bring destruction on them; in this way Dumas succeeds in equating chance with fate and fate with the will of God without ever wearying the reader with a triumphant demonstration of these equivalences; events are allowed to speak for themselves.

The omens are a different matter, and it is possible that divination by the inspection of animals' entrails (haruspication) was introduced into *La reine Margot* simply to provide the local color of an age when superstition and barbarous cruelty were still rife and men's lives were held almost as cheap as hens'. There is some evidence that Dumas did believe events could be foretold by guesswork based on intelligent interpretation of current trends; but forecasting of this kind is very different from René's precise predictions of the manner in which the line of the Valois will become extinct and very different again from Balsamo's accurate and detailed prophecies, notably in the prologue to *Le collier de la reine.* Here Cagliostro (Balsamo under an adopted name) is attending a dinner party hosted by Cardinal Richelieu in April 1784. Using once more his glass of clear water, Cagliostro is able to predict the violent ends of most of the other guests, beginning with La Pérouse, the explorer. La Pérouse is about to leave on his last, ill-fated expedition, in the course of which he will be killed by the natives of one of the South Pacific islands. This disastrous outcome is predicted by the seer after La Pérouse has left the house. Why did Cagliostro not warn him? ask the others in alarm. "Any warning would be useless," he replies; "the man who sees where destiny is leading cannot change that destiny" (ch. 2). This observation confirms what Dumas wrote in *La tulipe noire:*

> When fate starts ordering some disaster, it seldom happens that it fails to warn its victim in

> charity, just as a swordsman warns his adversary, so as to give him time to put up his guard. Almost always, these warnings come from the instinct of self-preservation in man or from the complicity of inanimate objects, often less inanimate than is generally supposed; almost always these warnings are ignored. The blow whistles through the air and falls on the head of the man whom the noise should have warned and who, on receiving the warning, should have taken cover.
>
> (ch. 17)

This is the law by which Dumas meets the objection that a knowledge of the future that should enable men to avoid disaster seldom does; the god speaks through Cassandra, but her prophecies are always mocked.

A historical figure, today Cagliostro is usually accounted a clever charlatan. The question historians have never resolved is how he managed to win the following he did in such a skeptical age as his, when doubt was thrown on all oracles, portents, and soothsaying. Dumas chose to regard him as a man with occult powers, not just a prophet of the future but a man who had virtually conquered death and discovered the secret of seeing what was happening at great distances by sending a suitable medium into a trance and instructing her spirit where to go and what to look for. Two such mediums figure in *Joseph Balsamo:* the first is Balsamo's own wife, Lorenza, with whom he abstains from sexual relations for fear she should lose her powers; and the second is Andrée de Taverney, the future comtesse de Charny.

The belief, prevalent in the romantic age, that certain mystic powers were vested in virginity, may account for the fact that both Lorenza and Andrée need to remain undefiled if they are to be of any use to Balsamo. But he is eventually unable to resist the temptation to make love to Lorenza, and Andrée, inadvertently left by him in a mesmeric trance, is found by Gilbert, who rapes her. Knowing nothing of what has happened, she is horrified to find herself pregnant, until Balsamo reveals the true facts to her brother Philippe. Gilbert offers to marry Andrée, who contemptuously refuses, so he arranges to steal the child shortly after his birth and have him brought up by a foster mother in a remote village.

It is hard to be certain what Dumas meant us to think of Gilbert. His behavior toward Andrée is atrocious. She is presented as innocent, a dutiful daughter and an affectionate sister, and if she refuses to encourage or even countenance the love of the lowborn Gilbert, she surely has the right to give her heart to which man she chooses. In fact she later falls in love with Olivier de Charny and marries him. In killing Gilbert at the end of *Joseph Balsamo,* Philippe is doing no more than any brother should according to the prevailing convention, especially since he had offered Gilbert fair combat beforehand. Yet Gilbert is not entirely unworthy: he is proud though poor, he is not lacking in courage (there is an occasion when he risks his own life to save Andrée's), and he thinks for himself. He has absorbed the basic philosophy of the Enlightenment: "that all men are brothers, that societies are ill-organized where some are serfs and slaves, that one day all individuals will be equal" (ch. 4). If he is on occasion cruel, if he takes advantage of helpless innocence, he can be said in such instances to foreshadow the cruelties and injustices of the French Revolution. When Dumas resurrects Gilbert in *Ange Pitou,* he gives his previous conduct a certain symbolic value and thereby to some extent excuses it. As Marie Antoinette reflects:

> This under-gardener, this Gilbert, was he not a living symbol of what is happening at this time, a man of the people who can rise above the baseness of his birth to concern himself with the politics of a great kingdom, a strange actor who seems to personify in himself, thanks to the evil genius that is hovering over France, both the insult offered to the aristocracy and the attack made on the monarchy by the plebs?
>
> (ch. 31)

Having violated a daughter of the aristocracy in times past, Gilbert has returned to flout the royal authority by helping to sack the Bastille; it is all of a piece.

The problems of personal power, free will, and the workings of Providence are nowhere dealt with so fully as in *Le comte de Monte-Cristo.* After he has regained his freedom, Dantès remembers how Faria had led him to discover the identity of the secret enemies who had condemned him to perpetual imprisonment. Faria had asked him who could have profited from the crime. Three names were mentioned: Danglars, in whose interest it was that Dantès should not become captain of his ship; Fernand, who envied Dantès his bride, Mercédès, whom he himself wished to marry; and Villefort, to whose father Dantès was carrying the incriminating letter. Once Dantès secures the fabulous treasure that Faria had bequeathed him, he devotes himself single-mindedly to exacting terrible retribution from these three men. He soon discovers that they are still alive and prosperous, never thinking for one moment of the poor sailor they left moldering in the underground dungeons of the château d'If.

A modern Monte-Cristo, in possession of great wealth and desiring vengeance, might have hired an assassin and disposed of the three in short order. But Dantès has noticed that this is not how God works; He moves slowly, along tortuous paths, and Dantès/Monte-Cristo wants to imitate him. He has an important conversation at an early stage with Villefort (who of course has no idea who this multimillionaire really is) in which the count explains his intentions by means of a parable. He relates how Satan once tempted him, as he had tempted the Savior before, offering to give him whatever he wanted if he agreed to bow down and worship him. After long reflection, Monte-Cristo had said to Satan: "Listen, I have always heard tell of Providence, and yet I have never seen it, nor anything that resembles it, which makes me think it does not exist; I wish to be that Providence, for I know nothing finer, more splendid, more sublime in the world than to dispense rewards and punishments." Satan sighed. "You are mistaken," he said. "Providence exists; only you cannot see her, because as a daughter of God, she is invisible as he is. You have seen nothing that resembles her, since she works by hidden devices and walks along obscure ways. All I can do for you is to make you one of the agents of Providence" (ch. 48). So Monte-Cristo accepted the bargain, and declares now that even if it meant consigning his soul to perdition, he would if required strike the same bargain a second time.

As the agent of Providence Monte-Cristo has simply to observe the working of cause and effect and occasionally to intervene actively to smooth its path. But on the whole the criminals bring about their own downfall. What is curious is that they are never brought to book for callously causing an innocent man to spend fourteen years cut off from the light of day, but for other crimes they have committed since, which they had thought so well hidden as to be undiscoverable. The count needs merely to bring these to light for the criminals to suffer their due punishment. It is thus no personal vendetta that he is pursuing; he is the servant of a higher justice. Mercédès tells him that her son blames him for the misfortunes that have befallen his father, but Monte-Cristo replies that they are not misfortunes but the chastisement of the Almighty: "It is not I who strike down M. de Morcerf [Fernand], it is Providence that is punishing him." "And who are you to substitute yourself for Providence?" she asks, and he shows her the letter of denunciation that Fernand wrote those many years ago. It was thanks to this act of treachery that Fernand was able to marry her; but another act, just as treacherous, won him his vast fortune, and Monte-Cristo, who has brought this last one to public knowledge, is having him punished for it: "Betrayed, assassinated, cast into a tomb, I have emerged from this tomb by God's grace, and I owe it to God to avenge myself. He has sent me to accomplish this vengeance, and this I will do" (ch. 39).

Monte-Cristo remains implacable almost to the very end, until he realizes that he had taken on himself more than a man should. When Villefort shows him the dead bodies of his wife and son, "he realized he had overstepped the rightful bounds of revenge; he realized he could no longer say: God is with me and for me" (ch. 111). For the first time he doubts whether he is justified in doing what he has done. For "the gods commit no evil, the gods can stay their hands when they wish; chance is not their master, they on the contrary are the lords of chance" (ch. 112). Monte-Cristo, superman though he is, cannot foresee every consequence of his actions, and so he cannot avoid staining the integrity of his purpose by committing incidental evil. Is he not being punished for blasphemy when he thought to substitute himself for Providence? This uncertainty, this ambiguity, hangs like a dark cloud over the concluding pages of *Le comte de Monte-Cristo.*

## *REMEMBRANCE OF THINGS PAST*

Although it was widely accepted in the nineteenth century that playwrights were free to enlist collaborators (and well over half the plays staged in Paris during this period were the work of two or three writers), it was just as generally understood that a novel could only have one author. The exceptions to this rule—the Goncourt brothers, Erckmann and Chatrian—were regarded as allowable since they signed their works together; there was therefore no deception. Dumas was a different case. It was known that he had several collaborators, among them Auguste Maquet, whose name he never allowed to appear on the cover of any of his novels. As far as is known, Maquet never wished to have credit and was quite content to let Dumas use the discoveries he made in his reading without expecting anything more than the handsome fee the great man paid him. But the arrangement that worked so well for many years broke down around 1851. Dumas, as we have seen, relied on the appetite of the newspapers for serial stories to provide him with the large income he needed for foreign travel, for building himself a palatial house outside Paris, for financing his own theater, and of course for paying Maquet for his research work. Once that source of income dried up, Dumas, always generous to a fault and recklessly improvident, suddenly found himself insolvent; he broke abruptly with Maquet and left Paris for Brussels in full flight from his creditors.

The long succession of historical novels came to an end, the last being *La comtesse de Charny,* in which, as Craig Bell has said, "instead of history being embedded in romance, romance is embedded in history." Much of it reads like raw Maquet, without the leaven that Dumas's imagination and style normally gave to his friend's scenarios. Dumas busied himself instead with his memoirs, a project he had conceived around 1874. Even though he recounts the story of his life only to 1832, the point at which he left France for a tour of Switzerland, they turned out to be the longest single work he ever wrote. In fact the enormously popular *Impressions de voyage en Suisse* (*Travels in Switzerland,* 1833–1837), though written and published long before *Mes mémoires* (*My Memoirs,* 1852–1855) were even started, can be regarded as a kind of continuation of them.

If personal preferences go for anything, the first part of *Mes mémoires* can be recommended as the best; it covers Dumas's boyhood in Villers-Cotterêts and in the surrounding forests, before he left for Paris. At the age of fifty, Dumas could still recall with evident relish and total accuracy the household as it existed before his father's death. In particular he depicts such delightful characters as the black servant Hippolyte, who—with disastrous results—tended to take too literally the orders he was given, and the gardener Pierre, whom Dumas recalls cutting open a live snake before his eyes to free the frog it had swallowed. Dumas remembers his father taking him to see Marie Pauline Borghese, Napoleon's younger sister; on another occasion the child was frightened out of his wits at the sight of what he took to be a witch—it was Madame de Genlis, the illustrious author. After his father's death the family fell on hard times, but the little boy did not experience this change of circumstance as a change for the worse. The forest of Compiègne became a limitless playground; the birds and beasts that were its denizens became his companions and at times his victims; the poachers became his friends, and the gamekeepers his natural enemies. He writes with especial affection of a certain ill-favored, pockmarked villain called Boudoux, whose great talent was his ability to imitate the calls of birds and attract them onto limed twigs; on one occasion the boy spent three days and nights in the woods with him and reappeared only when his mother had given him up for lost. Dumas remembered Boudoux's talent later and attributed it to Ange Pitou, a composite of all the clever poachers he had known in his boyhood.

Compelled to dwell on the distant past to write these opening chapters of his autobiography, in middle age Dumas found the memories returning to him with a sort of magic vividness. Between 1827 and 1847, as he says in the prologue to *Le meneur de loups* (The Wolf Man, 1857), he had scarcely ever thought of the little villages lost in the forest where his boyhood was spent; he was always eagerly pressing on into the future, which seemed to hold so much promise. But once all his literary and worldly ambitions were achieved, he found himself dwelling with nostalgia on the past.

> On the verge of entering the sandy deserts, one is quite astonished to see gradually emerge beside the path one has already trodden, marvellous oases of shadow and greenery, alongside which one had passed not only without stopping, but almost without seeing them. One was in such a hurry those days, pressing on to reach the goal that is never reached—happiness! It is at that moment that one realizes how blind and ungrateful one has been; it is then that one resolves that if ever again one should encounter on one's path one of those leafy groves, one will stop there for the rest of one's life, and plant one's tent to end one's days in that spot.

But, as he goes on to say, these oases never reappear, except in memory.

> Memory, that brilliant will-o-the-wisp, dances above the receding track; memory alone is sure not to lose her way. Then, every time she revisits an oasis, every time she recaptures some past incident, memory returns to the tired traveller and, like a humming of bees, like the song of a bird, like a murmur of spring water, she tells him what she has seen.

So, while Dumas was still writing his memoirs, he also began writing a series of short novels set in the countryside around Villers-Cotterêts, much as George Sand, who counted as one of his most ardent admirers, had written in her forties the stories set in her native Berry that today remain the most widely read part of her oeuvre: *La mare au diable* (*The Devil's Pool,* 1846), *La petite Fadette* (*Little Fadette,* 1848), *François le champi* (*François the Foundling,* 1850). The stories that draw on Dumas's past are set in a different part of France but have the same strongly marked regional flavor, the same tinge of folklore and legend. *Conscience l'innocent* (*Conscience the Innocent,* 1852), *Catherine Blum* (1854), and *Le meneur de loups* are three very different works; the first the tale of a simpleminded village boy, regarded nonetheless with affection and even admiration by the countryfolk; the second an idyll between the son and the niece of an honest gamekeeper in which the course of true love is threatened by rivals and by a villainous vagrant called Mathieu; and the third a weird legend of a wolf man, with overtones of the Faust myth.

From 1853, when he returned to Paris, until 1857, Dumas was busy running his own newspaper, *Le mousquetaire.* In 1858 he set off on a long trip through czarist Russia, starting in St. Petersburg and going as far south as the Caspian Sea and the Caucasus mountains. Then came his celebrated adventure with Garibaldi in Sicily and Naples. When he finally returned to Paris, in 1864, the decline was beginning to set in; he had put on weight, he was no longer as active as before, nor as adventurous, and when an invitation came to visit the United States, he wriggled out of it. He was still writing until the very end: *Les blancs et les bleus* (*The Whites and the Blues,* 1867–1868), a historical novel of the revolutionary wars; two collections of retrospective essays, the *Souvenirs dramatiques* (*Memoirs of the Stage,* 1868) and *Histoire de mes bêtes* (*The Story of My Pet Animals,* 1868), and yet another novel, *Création et rédemption* (*Creation and Redemption,* 1872), not published until after his death. The title is possibly more suggestive than the plot, which concerns the long efforts, ultimately successful, of a doctor to instill intelligence into the mind of an idiot girl.

It is almost an axiom of nineteenth-century French literary history that those writers who were idolized during their lifetime—Dumas, Hugo—should suffer neglect after their death and never totally recover the status they enjoyed, while those who were neglected and misprized while they were alive—Stendhal, Baudelaire—should benefit from rehabilitation and even apotheosis in the twentieth century. Dumas was a highly popular writer among his contemporaries and for perhaps fifty years after his death, but popularity is a somewhat suspect quality in the eyes of posterity. He had infinite powers of invention, both of plot and of character, but this counts for little in an age that looks more for depth of analysis than for fertility of imagination: one Emma Bovary counts for more than any number of Margots, Dianes, or Andrées. He had too little to say, at least in his novels, about his own age (this was almost the exclusive concern of Balzac), and what he had to say about earlier centuries cannot be taken very seriously today when historians are more interested in such questions as the growth of industrialism and the economic causes and consequences of wars than in the struggles of monarchs to keep their thrones. Even when Dumas deals with ideological issues—the wars of religion or the pressure of the Enlightenment on the rigidities of the ancien régime—his treatment is bound to seem superficial. But he was after all a novelist who merely found his subjects in history, and as a novelist he still casts his spell, for he had that supreme politeness of the professional writer, he never forgot his reader, he never treated the reader's demands as unimportant or unworthy. He had the gift of juggling with half a dozen subplots without ever losing the thread, of building slowly up to a dramatic climax so that the excitement rises steadily by carefully graduated steps, of inventing passages of dialogue that can amuse or enthrall but are never tedious. Admittedly the sophisticated will dismiss these gifts as minor ones. Dumas was no intellectual, but he provides a healthy relief from intellectuality. It cannot be said that we ever learn any deep lessons from Dumas, for he offers little to reflect on and few insights. But, as Robert Louis Stevenson asks about *Vingt ans après:*

> What other novel has such epic variety and nobility of incident? often, if you will, impossible; often of the order of an Arabian story; and yet all based in human nature. For if you come to that, what novel has more human nature? not studied with the microscope, but seen largely, in plain daylight, with the natural eye? What novel has more good sense, and gaiety, and wit, and unflagging, admirable literary skill?
>
> (*Memories and Portraits,* pp. 145–146)

## Selected Bibliography

### EDITIONS

The complete works of Alexandre Dumas, excluding the plays, run to 286 volumes in the Collection Michel Lévy (Paris, 1848–1900). Which works should really form part of the canon—that is, those written wholly or largely by Dumas—is a complicated question. F. W. Reed's *Bibliography of Alexandre Dumas Père* (London, 1933) is an attempt to guide the reader through the thickets; other useful bibliographical tools are Douglas Munro's *Alexandre Dumas Père: A Bibliography of Works Translated into English to 1910* (New York, 1970) and his *Alexandre Dumas Père: A Bibliography of Works Published in French, 1825–1900* (New York, 1981).

#### PLAYS

Fifteen volumes were published in the Michel Lévy edition (Paris, 1863–1874). None of Dumas's plays has been translated into English. A start has been made in producing an excellent annotated edition of the plays in French: *Théâtre complet,* edited by Fernande Bassan (Paris, 1974– ). The following are the best-known plays, listed with the dates of first performance, which are also the dates of first publication, unless indicated otherwise. For all plays Paris is the city of publication.

*Henri III et sa cour.* 1829.
*Christine.* 1830.
*Antony.* 1831.
*Richard Darlington.* 1831 (published 1832).
*La tour de Nesle.* 1832.
*Angèle.* 1833 (published 1834).
*Kena.* 1836.
*Mademoiselle de Belle-Isle.* 1839.
*Les demoiselles de Saint-Cyr.* 1843.

#### FICTION

Time has made its own selection in the enormous output under this head. The following list includes all those novels that have deserved to survive. They were published in Paris, and those titles with asterisks are the ones included in the handsome Swiss edition, with prefaces by Gilbert Sigaux on the historical sources of each work (Lausanne, 1962–1967). Scholarly reeditions of these works include *Le comte de Monte-Cristo,* edited by J.-H. Bornecque (Paris, 1962), and *Les trois mousquetaires* and *Vingt ans après* in one volume, edited by G. Sigaux (Paris, 1966).

*Le chevalier d'Harmental.* 1842.
*Georges.* 1843.
* *Les trois mousquetaires.* 1844.
* *Le comte de Monte-Cristo.* 1844–1846.
* *La reine Margot.* 1845.
* *Vingt ans après.* 1845.
* *Le chevalier de Maison-Rouge,* 1845.
* *La dame de Monsoreau.* 1846.
* *Joseph Balsamo (Mémoires d'un médecin).* 1846–1848.
* *Les quarante-cinq.* 1848.
* *Le vicomte de Bragelonne.* 1848–1850.
* *Le collier de la reine.* 1849–1850.
*La tulipe noire.* 1850.
* *Ange Pitou.* 1851.
*Olympe de Clèves.* 1851–1852.
*Conscience l'innocent.* 1852.
* *La comtesse de Charny.* 1852–1858.
*Catherine Blum.* 1854.
*Les Mohicans de Paris.* 1854–1859.
*Le meneur de loups.* 1857.
* *Les compagnons de Jéhu.* 1857.
* *Les blancs et les bleus.* 1867–1868.
*Création et rédemption* (posthumous). 1872.

#### NONFICTION

##### AUTOBIOGRAPHICAL

*Mes mémoires,* 1852–1855. Best consulted in the edition by P. Josserand. 5 vols. Paris, 1954–1968.
*Causeries.* Paris, 1860.
*Histoires de mes bêtes.* Paris, 1868.
*Souvenirs dramatiques.* Paris, 1868.

##### TRAVEL BOOKS

*Impressions de voyage en Suisse.* 1833–1837. Modern reprint in two volumes. Paris, 1982.
*De Paris à Cadiz.* 1848. *Le véloce.* 1851. These two volumes contain an account of his travels in Spain and North Africa in 1846–1847.
*De Paris à Astrakhan.* 1859. *Le Caucase.* 1860. An account of his travels through Russia. The first volume has been edited by Jacques Suffel under the title *Voyage en Russie.* Paris, 1960.

### TRANSLATIONS

The early translations listed in Douglas Munro's bibliographies are not particularly reliable, and the later ones are too often mere abridgments. Those currently available, including some abridgments, are:

*Adventures in Caucasia.* Translated by A. E. Murch. Philadelphia, 1962. Abridged.

*Adventures in Czarist Russia.* Translated by A. E. Murch. London, 1960. Abridged.

*The Black Tulip.* New York, 1951.

*Chicot the Jester.* New York, 1968. Translation of *La dame de Monsoreau.*

*The Companions of Jehu.* New York, 1903.

*The Count of Monte Cristo.* New York, 1941.

*The Forty-Five.* Boston, 1900.

*From Paris to Cadiz.* Translated by A. E. Murch. London, 1958. Abridged.

*The Man in the Iron Mask.* New York, 1965. Translation of part of *Le vicomte de Bragelonne.*

*Marguerite de Valois.* New York, 1969. Translation of *La reine Margot.*

*My Memoirs.* Abridged by A. Craig Bell. London, 1961. Limited to events in which Dumas himself engaged.

*On Board the "Emma": Adventures with Garibaldi's "Thousand" in Sicily.* Edited by R. S. Garnett. New York, 1929. Contains considerably more material than is to be found in the book Dumas published in 1861, *Les Garibaldiens.*

*The Queen's Necklace.* London, 1957.

*The Road to Monte-Cristo.* Abridged edition of *Mes mémoires* by Jules Eckert Goodman. New York, 1956.

*Tangier to Tunis.* Translated by A. E. Murch. London, 1959. Abridged.

*The Three Musketeers.* New York, 1960.

*Travels in Switzerland.* Translated by R. W. Plummer and A. Craig Bell. London, 1958. Abridged.

*Twenty Years After.* New York, 1960.

## CORRESPONDENCE

*Lettres d'Alexandre Dumas à Mélanie Waldor.* Edited by Claude Schopp. Paris, 1982. Apart from this volume, no serious attempt has been made to collect and publish Dumas's extant letters, of which there must be hundreds in libraries and private collections.

## CRITICAL STUDIES

Adler, Alfred. *Dumas und die böse Mutter: Über zehn historische Romane von Alexandre Dumas d.Ä.* Berlin, 1979.

Almeras, Henri d'. *Alexandre Dumas et les trois mousquetaires.* Paris, 1929.

Audebrande, Philibert. *Alexandre Dumas à la maison d'or: Souvenirs de la vie littéraire.* Paris, 1888.

Baldick, Robert. *The Life and Times of Frédérick Lemaître.* London, 1959.

Bassan, Fernande. *Alexandre Dumas père et la Comédie-Française.* Paris, 1972.

Bell, A. Craig. *Alexandre Dumas: A Biography and Study.* Folcroft, Pa., 1979.

Blaze de Bury, Henri. *Mes études et mes souvenirs: Alexandre Dumas, sa vie, son temps, son oeuvre.* Paris, 1885.

Bouvier-Ajam, Maurice. *Alexandre Dumas ou cent ans après.* Paris, 1973.

Charpentier, John. *Alexandre Dumas.* Paris, 1947.

Chincholle, Charles. *Alexandre Dumas aujourd'hui.* Paris, 1867.

Clouard, Henri. *Alexandre Dumas.* Paris, 1955.

Ferry, Gabriel. *Les dernières années d'Alexandre Dumas, 1864–1870.* Paris, 1883.

Gaillard, Robert. *Alexandre Dumas.* Paris, 1953.

Glinel, Charles. *Alexandre Dumas et son oeuvre: Notes biographiques et bibliographiques.* Reims, 1884.

Hemmings, F. W. J. *Alexandre Dumas: The King of Romance.* New York, 1979.

Jan, Isabelle. *Alexandre Dumas, romancier.* Paris, 1973.

Janin, Jules, *Alexandre Dumas, mars 1871.* Paris, 1871.

LeComte, L. Henry. *Alexandre Dumas (1802–1870): Sa vie intime, ses oeuvres.* Paris, 1902.

Maurois, André. *Les trois Dumas.* Paris, 1957. Translated by Gerard Hopkins as *The Titans: A Three-Generation Biography of the Dumas.* New York, 1957.

Neuschaefer, Hans Jörg. *Populärromane im 19. Jahrhundert.* Munich, 1976.

Parigot, Hippolyte. *Alexandre Dumas père.* Paris, 1901.

Pifteau, Benjamin. *Alexandre Dumas en manches de chemises.* Paris, 1884.

Ross, David. *Alexandre Dumas.* Newton Abbot, 1981.

Stowe, Richard S. *Dumas.* Boston, 1976.

Tadie, Jean-Yves. *Le roman d'aventures.* Paris, 1982.

F. W. J. HEMMINGS

# ERASMUS

## *(ca. 1466–1536)*

"HE WAS BORN in Rotterdam on the vigil of Simon and Jude." So begins the short sketch of his life that Desiderius Erasmus once composed. He then tells a sad romantic story about his parents. His mother had been left with child by a young man named Gerard, who had fled to Italy when his family blocked their marriage. After his birth, Erasmus continues, Gerard was sent word that the girl he had sought to marry was dead; and out of grief he became a priest. The deception was soon discovered when he returned home, but he remained a faithful priest and at the same time was solicitous for the education and welfare of his son.

It is a very touching tale, the precision of which, however, is open to doubt. Erasmus was deeply sensitive to the illegitimacy of his birth and may have depicted the circumstances of his origin and background in slightly fanciful terms. The memoir itself is not a fabrication. Although the liaison between his mother and Gerard may have been more commonplace (Erasmus had an older brother, Peter), the basic facts are true enough. He entered life under the bar sinister in a small country town in Holland, then an outlying and watery part of the territories of the dukes of Burgundy and soon after his birth to become part of the vast Hapsburg domain. His birthday, the vigil of the Apostles Simon and Jude, was October 27, but the exact year is uncertain. Erasmus was always vague on chronology. The year 1466 is most probable, although 1467 and 1469 are strong contenders. He was christened Erasmus, which he later expanded into the more elegant Desiderius Erasmus Roterodamus, or Desiderius Erasmus of Rotterdam. The brief autobiography speaks of large families on his mother's and especially his father's side, yet no relatives or their descendants ever appear in Erasmus' story. In view of his later renown, that feature is surprising.

The education that helped form a famous author or scholar or thinker is always important to a biographer, and in Erasmus' case much is made of an influence that soon bore upon him. After Erasmus attended elementary school at Gouda, his father sent him in his ninth year to a well-known school attached to the church of Saint Lebuin in Deventer. His mother accompanied him. There he remained for several years—from about 1475 to 1484—until his mother, and a short time later his father, died of the plague. The influence, or rather influences, to which he was exposed in these formative years were the *devotio moderna* (modern devotion) and the new humanism or classical learning that was making its way out of Renaissance Italy. Erasmus' mature thought is sometimes viewed as a fusion, an amalgam, of these two dissimilar currents. However one may interpret the evidence pertaining to this early time and place, certain facts stand firm. Deventer was the original center of that movement of simple and practical piety that we call the *devotio moderna* and that expressed itself in the work and spirit of the Brethren of the Common Life and the Augustinian monks of the Windesheim congregation. Thomas à Kempis' *Imitation of Christ* (*ca.* 1425) is the great masterpiece of the spiritual life that emerged from the movement. The Brethren engaged in various activities: tending the sick, copying manuscripts—their *scriptoria* are celebrated—teaching school. Some of their members staffed Saint Lebuin's. Erasmus was critical of the instruction there, but two masters, he tells us, began to introduce some better literature. One was Alexander Hegius, a disciple of the first great German humanist, Rudolph Agricola, who became headmaster toward the end of Erasmus' stay; the other was Brother John Syntheim, who was much taken by Erasmus' talent and promise. The better literature they imparted was the Latin classics in their purer form. On one occasion the famous Agricola himself gave a lecture at the school, which deeply impressed Erasmus.

After his father's death, Erasmus came under the care of three guardians whom his father had designated. According to the autobiography, they abused their trust. They poorly managed the legacy his father had left, sent him to a dismal school run by the Brethren at 's Hertogenbosch where he wasted nearly three years, and then pressured him (and his brother) to enter the monastic life. This last step came to be the cause of much bitterness and regret on Erasmus' part, though at the time the attractions of a particular monastery of Augustinians at Steyn overcame his resistance. He was deceived, so he claims, but he remained at Steyn, professed his vows, and was ordained a priest by the bishop of Utrecht in 1492. Meanwhile, he continued to cultivate his now lively interest in the Latin classics and the new humanism. His letters from this period reveal a wide range of reading, a marked literary sensitivity, and warm friendships with several of his fellow monks. Erasmus may never have had a genuine vocation to the religious life, but he seems to have adapted himself without great difficulty at this time and to have profited from the opportunities for study and companionship that the monastery afforded. The lineaments of the future author and scholar now began to appear, and the humanist ideal of *bonae literae* (good literature), which ever remained his guiding light, now first found expression.

Two very disparate works have their origin in this early monastic period of his life: an essay, *De contemptu mundi* (On Contempt of the World), praising the monastic life, and the *Antibarbari* (The Antibarbarians), a defense of classical learning for Christians against its ignorant and narrow-minded opponents. These works were not published until many years later (*De contemptu mundi* in 1522, the *Antibarbari* in 1520, when there were five editions), and by then major changes and additions had occurred. A final chapter, for instance, was attached to *De contemptu mundi* that took a very critical view of contemporary monasticism and nullified many of the arguments advanced in the earlier part of the essay. The whole work is somewhat puzzling. The *Antibarbari,* on the other hand, develops an issue and a theme ever present and foremost in the mind of Erasmus. The early version was recast into dialogue form around 1494 and later expanded still further, but the polemical purpose remained the same; from the start, the work was an affirmation of humanism, which Erasmus came more and more ardently to represent, and a defense of *bonai literae* against its enemies.

Erasmus left the monastery in 1493. He was then about twenty-seven years old, and the wider world now beckoned to his sensitive and eager spirit. He had been offered the post of secretary to Henry of Bergen, bishop of Cambrai, who wanted a good Latinist for his journey to Rome to obtain a cardinal's hat. It was a splendid opportunity for the extremely talented young monk, and Erasmus received the necessary permissions from his superiors and the bishop of Utrecht to join the entourage of this new patron. The journey to Rome unfortunately did not take place, but Erasmus was retained nevertheless, and his service with Henry of Bergen was not without its rewards. He found a new and valued friend in Jacob Batt, town clerk at Bergen and later tutor in the household of Anne of Veere, and he discovered and devoured the works of Saint Augustine. This latter event should be stressed, for the patristic character of Erasmus' thought was strong and is more keenly appreciated now than it was formerly. He already knew and treasured the letters of the other great Latin Father, Saint Jerome, and now the powerful Augustine came more fully within his ken. The influence of these two scholars and theologians of the early church must be added to the fascination and force of the classical humanism that so engaged him, if we would fully appreciate his intellectual growth. His familiarity with Saint Augustine's *De doctrina Christiana (On Christian Doctrine),* for example, is evident in the revision of the *Antibarbari* he undertook at this time.

Erasmus did not go to Rome, but in the late summer of 1495 he did go to Paris. At the urging of Batt, the bishop of Cambrai approved and promised support for Erasmus' theological studies at the University of Paris. "He thus became a Scotist in the college of Montaigu," wrote his first biographer and a close friend and colleague, Beatus Rhenanus; but it was not for long. Erasmus found living at Montaigu, whose principal, John Standonck, was an austere reformer, too hard to bear. The bad eggs and squalid quarters, he felt, permanently injured his health. As for the arid and disputatious theology he confronted—it was the dialectical theology of the medieval schools, or scholasticism, as it is generically called—he shrank from its study with aversion and disgust. It had little in common with the learning and eloquence of the ancients, and he saw nothing of value or virtue in it. He tells us that he would have soon been branded a heretic if he had continued on that path. This antipathy to scholastic theology found constant expression in the writings of Erasmus and is one of the keys to understanding his life's work. His chief aim, very simply put, was to replace that brand of theology with what he deemed the genuine theology of the early Christian church. This goal became the most integral part of the revival of letters and learning Erasmus sought to achieve.

But meanwhile more immediate concerns prevailed during these early days in Paris. Because of illness or the plague he returned several times to the Low Countries. When funds from his bishop failed to arrive, he supported himself by tutoring private students in Latin literature and style. We know that he had two German students from Lübeck and three well-to-do Englishmen, including William Blount, Lord Mountjoy, who in 1499 invited Erasmus to visit England. From these teaching labors eventually derived some of his most popular writings. His famous *Colloquies* has its origin in conversational Latin exercises he composed at this time, and the prototype of other educational materials and manuals dates from this period: *De copia verborum ac rerum* (On Abundance of Words and Ideas) and *De ratione studii* (On the Method of Study), both first published in 1512, and *De conscribendis epistolis* (On Writing Letters), first published in 1522. Education based on the humanities, that is, on the literature and liberal arts of antiquity, is the very essence, indeed the meaning, of Renaissance humanism. (The classical term *humanitas* is the root of our words "humanities" and "humanism"; the term implies the education and training most in keeping with our full human nature and most advantageous to our intellectual and moral growth.) Thus in his early occupation as a teacher, modest though it was, Erasmus was in his proper sphere, and the texts that came out of this experience are among his most important contributions. They were to serve schoolmasters and educators for generations.

Erasmus also entered the threshold of the Paris humanist circle during these years and, in a sense, began his career as a man of letters. He made the acquaintance of the distinguished French scholar and general of the Trinitarians, Robert Gaguin, and by a stroke of good fortune was asked to contribute a commendatory letter to Gaguin's history of France, *De origine et gestis Francorum compendium* (A Brief Account of the Origin and Deeds of the French), which was published in the fall of 1495. The printer required such a piece to fill the blank pages at the end of his edition. It was Erasmus' first published writing and his first association with the new art of printing. The appearance of his name and handiwork in the company of Gaguin's brought him suddenly to the attention of a wider public.

In May 1499 Erasmus went to England. The visit was an important event, perhaps a decisive one, in his life. The biographer Johan Huizinga calls it "a period of inward ripening" and stresses the influence of friends he met there, John Colet in particular, in sharpening his resolve and helping him set his life's goal. Others have emphasized the influence of Renaissance Neoplatonism on him at this time through the mediation of his English friends; many of them had been to Italy and had absorbed elements of the Platonic revival. Be that as it may, Erasmus loved England, was charmed by the pretty girls and their custom of bestowing kisses at every turn (as he jokingly wrote to a friend in Paris), and was even more impressed by the flowering of learning and the zealous scholars he found there. He stayed about eight months, until the beginning of the next year. He visited Mountjoy's estate at Greenwich, where it appears he first met the young and brilliant Thomas More, then but twenty-one or twenty-two, who would become his dearest friend. On that occasion he and More walked to nearby Eltham Palace, where the children of the royal family were residing, and Erasmus was introduced to the boy who ten years later would become Henry VIII. He also spent time in London, where he met the Greek scholars William Grocyn and Thomas Linacre, and in the fall he was at Oxford, where his close friendship with Colet began.

John Colet, the son of a former lord mayor of London, was the same age as Erasmus but his senior in point of view of serious purpose and settled aim. He had traveled and studied widely, and when Erasmus met him he was lecturing on the Epistles of Saint Paul at Oxford, where he had gone in 1496, soon after his return from Italy. These were memorable lectures, and Erasmus was inspired. When he listened to Colet, so he said, he seemed to hear Plato himself. In expounding Saint Paul, Colet used the method of the humanists as well as the insight of the Platonists, and he gave his presentation a moral and theological relevance that struck Erasmus deeply. He commended Colet for doing battle with the "squalid mob" of modern theologians and attempting to restore the true theology of the ancient church—the *vetus ac vera theologia* (the old and true theology), as he called it. Colet wanted him to assist in the task and lecture on the Old Testament at Oxford, but Erasmus, conscious of his present inadequacy, declined the invitation. "As soon as I feel myself to possess the necessary stamina and strength," he declared, "I shall come personally to join your party and will give devoted, if not distinguished, service in the defense of theology" (letter to John Colet, October 1499). And so he did.

He also had an interesting discussion with Colet regarding the nature of Christ's agony in the garden of Gethsemane, which can be followed in letters they exchanged at this time. Erasmus defended the traditional view that Christ's fear of suffering and death proceeded from his human nature, whereas Colet claimed that Christ drew back at that awesome hour out of concern about the crime that would be committed. Not long after, Erasmus published the exchange in the form of a scholarly debate. It is his first theological writing. It may also be worth noting that Thomas More's last work, written in the Tower of London shortly before his execution in 1535, was on this selfsame theme of Christ's passion, though it is a profounder meditation than the Colet–Erasmus debate.

As Erasmus was leaving England on his way back to Paris in early 1500, an unfortunate incident occurred—one that he was long in forgetting because of the personal distress it caused. A customs official at the port of Dover confiscated a modest sum in gold coin he had accumulated to support himself in his studies in the immediate future. Both More and Mountjoy had assured him that he could take the money out, but his young friends were wrong in their understanding of what was permissible under the law (More was not yet a lawyer). The loss was a blow and left him in poverty. It had a bright side, however. It forced him rather hastily to bring out his first book, the *Adagiorum collectanea (Adages)*, a collection of over 800 Latin proverbs drawn from the classics, which he hoped would be of interest and use to students. Greatly expanded in subsequent years, it had many editions during his lifetime and afterward.

Erasmus' return to the Continent following his English visit and the first publication of the *Adages* in 1500 is a convenient point at which to pause and signal a division in our narrative. The early and more formative phase of his life was over, and a highly active and very prolific phase now began. A period of uncertainty had ended, and a time of achievement and renown lay ahead. His books and editions started to appear in increasing numbers; his reputation and his influence grew; his fame reached a pinnacle attained by few other writers or scholars in European history.

This is not to say that suddenly all was smooth sailing and halcyon days. Far from it. The years immediately after Erasmus' return to Paris were very difficult. He was poor, unsettled, fearful of the plague, obsessed with the need to master Greek. He moved about considerably. He was in Orléans for part of 1500, and in the following spring he left Paris for the Low Countries. He again visited his native Holland and then stayed for a while at the castle of Tournehem in Artois, which belonged to Anne of Veere, a temporary patroness; at nearby Saint Omer; and finally at Louvain. But though his movements were somewhat erratic, his scholarly aims were fixed. He was determined to learn Greek, and he had set himself the ambitious task of emending the corrupt text of Saint Jerome and of restoring true theology. The three goals were closely connected in his mind, for a knowledge of Greek was essential in correcting Jerome and studying Scripture, and the one was the representative par excellence and the other the very fountainhead of the true theology Erasmus hoped to restore. His efforts were now directed untiringly toward this end.

"The revival of a genuine science of theology," as Erasmus phrased it in one of his letters, was certainly his basic aim as a humanist scholar. It was not, however, his only concern, nor did scholarly pursuits blind him to the more practical questions of the Christian life and the problems of personal and social reform. Scholarship for Erasmus was never an end in itself but was intended to conduct men to a better life. Learning was to lead to virtue, scholarship to God; and thus the restoration of theology was to be the means toward the revival of a more vital Christianity. Erasmus, in short, was a moralist and reformer, and a treatise he began to write in the fall of 1501 clearly sets forth the essential elements of this aspect of his thought.

When he was at Tournehem, he was asked to write something that might have a salutary effect on a man of unruly temperament and dissolute conduct (who is said to have been a German armament maker by the name of Johann Poppenruyter), and with this incentive he composed a work that eventually became one of his most celebrated—the *Enchiridion militis Christiani.* The title means the handbook—or dagger—of the Christian soldier, the Greek word *enchiridion* having been used as a title by Saint Augustine for one of his treatises. Erasmus' work was first published in

Antwerp in 1503 and had numerous editions as well as translations from the original Latin thereafter. (Erasmus, it must be remembered, wrote in Latin, but translations of many of his works were made into the vernaculars. William Tyndale made an early English translation of the *Enchiridion* that was published in 1533, and Saint Ignatius Loyola read a Spanish version at Alcalá in 1526. Even the Aztecs had it available in their tongue.)

The work is a guide to Christian attitudes and behavior as Erasmus perceived them. It embodies what we may call his spirituality as well as his reformist thought, for, as Huizinga points out, he "had for the first time said the things which he had most at heart." Developing the theme that life is a constant warfare against sin, he explains the weapons that the Christian must employ and the rules and precepts that must govern his unending struggle. Two fundamental and related ideas run throughout the book: one is that the great weapon of the Christian is the knowledge of Holy Scripture (the first weapon is prayer); the other is that religion is not primarily a matter of outward signs and devotions but rather of interior disposition and the inward love of God and neighbor. These views became Erasmus' master thoughts, and we shall see them reflected in all his work. The second concept, which has been interpreted as excessively spiritualizing and even Platonizing the Christian religion to the detriment of more formal observances, is especially prominent. Its implications as well as its source are the subject of some debate. Erasmus derives it from Scripture—"It is the spirit that gives life"—and he urges the Christian soldier to the zealous study of the word of God. As preliminary training, he suggests that reading the ancient pagan authors may be helpful. He views the Platonists as very close to the Gospel pattern, but "any truth you come upon at any place is Christ's," he says, reiterating a not uncommon patristic maxim that Étienne Gilson has called "the perpetual charter of Christian humanism." And in interpreting Scripture, he commends Saint Paul and the ancient Fathers, not the modern theologians who stick to the letter and miss the deeper meaning of the sacred text.

When Erasmus was composing or about to compose the *Enchiridion,* he met at Saint Omer a Franciscan friar, Jean Vitrier, who greatly influenced the work. In fact, Vitrier ranks with Colet in the impact he had on Erasmus, and many years later Erasmus gave impressive testimony to this in a letter he wrote to one of Martin Luther's disciples. He sent him a sketch of both men's lives—"two men of our era whom I consider to have been true and sincere Christians"—as examples to consider and imitate. Vitrier loved Scripture and the early Fathers. He knew the letters of Saint Paul by heart, and he admired above all the ancient Greek Father Origen. Though in a monastery, he was very critical of a religion consisting of rites and ordinances of human invention. He stood, in short, for much of what we read in the *Enchiridion,* and Erasmus tells us how thoroughly he approved of the little book. The imprint of Origen, who became one of Erasmus' great favorites, is likewise very marked in the *Enchiridion.*

During these years of residence in the Low Countries, Erasmus made an important discovery. In the summer of 1504, while browsing in the library of a Premonstratensian monastery near Louvain, he found the manuscript of Lorenzo Valla's *Annotationes* on the New Testament, a collection of grammatical and philological notes wherein the Latin Vulgate text is collated with and corrected by the Greek. Valla was a famous Italian humanist with whose work Erasmus had long been acquainted, though not with this specific one. When he was a young monk at Steyn he had read and been inspired by Valla's *Elegantiae linguae Latinae,* a treatise on the pure Latin tongue and a work that perhaps more than any other helped spread the classical humanism of the Renaissance outside Italy. The discovery of this new manuscript led Erasmus to turn his attention to the task of emending the New Testament itself—a task that became a major part of his program to restore theology. As a first step, so to speak, he arranged for the printing of the *Annotationes* by Josse Badius in Paris in March 1505. It foreshadowed the great edition of the New Testament he brought out in 1516.

In the autumn of 1505, Erasmus made his second trip to England. He was drawn by the promise or hope of a benefice, and, of course, he had many friends there—Mountjoy; Colet, who was now dean of Saint Paul's in London; Grocyn; More. He visited them all, and he made several new friends in the course of his travels—John Fisher, bishop of Rochester; and, most impressively, William Warham, archbishop of Canterbury and lord chancellor of the realm. Erasmus presented the latter with his Latin translations of two of Euripides' plays, *Hecuba* and *Iphigenia in Aulis* (they were published the following year by Badius in Paris). He had attained his command of Greek. He saw a good deal of More, who was now an active young lawyer in London and very recently married. More delighted in the Greek satirist Lucian, Erasmus tells us, and together he and More translated into Latin several of Lucian's dialogues (which Badius also published in 1506). Erasmus himself was enamored of Lucian. "How he mixes the serious with banter, how laughingly he speaks the truth," he exclaimed. "No comedy, no satire can be compared with his." Erasmus' own *Praise of Folly* was to become its peer.

His stay in England was suddenly interrupted in June 1506 when an opportunity to go to Italy was offered. The Italian court physician of Henry VII was looking for someone to accompany his two sons there and supervise their university studies. Erasmus took the post, and he soon found himself back in Paris and, a while later, on the road through the pass at Mt. Cenis to the land he had long desired to see. He was then nearly forty. His years weighed heavily upon him, and as he crossed the Alps, he composed a very touching poem on the passage of time and his approaching old age.

At Turin, where he arrived in early September, he received the degree of doctor of theology. "Thus he carried into Italy dignity and erudition," writes Beatus Rhenanus, "which others have been accustomed to bring back from that country." He then proceeded to Bologna with his wards, but they all withdrew to Florence temporarily because of fighting in the area. He was back in November to witness the triumphal entry of Pope Julius II, who had wrested the city from the Bentivogli tyrant. Bologna was part of the papal state, and Julius was restoring papal control, but Erasmus was aghast at the sight of a warrior pope. He spent most of 1507 in Bologna, and in December he moved to Venice, where he had already made contact with the great Venetian printer Aldus Manutius. Aldus headed the most prestigious press of his day. His aim was to make good texts of the Latin and Greek classics available in small, attractive volumes, and Erasmus was greatly impressed with his scholarly undertaking as well as his technical skill. He stayed in Venice about a year working closely with Aldus and living in the home of his father-in-law, Andrea Asolani, who housed a lively community of scholars, many of them Greek, known as the Aldine Academy. Erasmus shared a room there with the young Jerome Aleander, a future cardinal and papal official of considerable prominence. Their paths crossed again many years later when the Lutheran controversy was dividing Europe, and hostile suspicions disrupted their friendship.

The chief fruit of this year in Venice was a new and enlarged edition of the *Adages*, which Aldus published in his beautiful type and format in September. Called the *Adagiorum chiliades*— literally, "Thousands of adages"—the book now contained over 3,000 proverbs culled from Greek as well as Latin authors. Erasmus learnedly indicated their origin and use and added his own interesting comments and digressions. With the proverb *Festina lente* ("Make haste slowly") for example, which described the trademark of the Aldine press—an anchor with a dolphin entwined about its shaft—he gives a glowing account of Aldus' "tireless efforts" to restore good literature. "Aldus is building up a library which has no other limits than the world itself," he declares. The new edition of the *Adages* was a huge success, and Erasmus' claim to scholarship and brilliant erudition was now firmly established.

At the end of 1508 he went to Padua, where, as a tutor, he joined the household of Alexander Stuart, the illegitimate son of James IV of Scotland. He traveled to Siena and later to Rome with the young nobleman, for whom he had high hopes and warm affection. When the youth was summoned home to Scotland by his father, he gave Erasmus as a souvenir an antique ring with the Roman god Terminus—a god whose stone statue marked boundaries—engraved on it. Erasmus thereafter used this ring, with its motto, *Concedo nulli*—"I yield to no one"—as his seal and device, interpreting it, as he once explained, not in an arrogant sense but as a reminder of mortality, death being the ultimate boundary. The young Stuart was tragically slain a few years later, together with his father, when the Scots invading England were defeated at Flodden Field. It was a dreadful loss in Erasmus' eyes and further evidence for him of the stupidity and waste of war.

In early 1509 Erasmus was in Rome, where, as he himself reports in the brief autobiography, "a distinguished and favorable reputation preceded him." He was cordially received by the most eminent cardinals and prelates—Giovanni de' Medici, who would soon succeed Julius II as Pope Leo X; Raffaele Riario; Domenico Grimani; and Egidio da Viterbo, then general of the Augustinians and a distinguished scholar himself. He was pressed to remain in the Eternal City, and it was tempting, but in June a letter from Mountjoy arrived urging his return to England. The old king had died, and his son, whom Erasmus had met at Eltham back in 1499, had succeeded as Henry VIII. A new day had dawned; an enlightened prince had come to power. Erasmus was bidden to enjoy these blessings. Without great delay he left Rome and headed north. He decided to spend the rest of his days in that favored isle.

As he rode back across the Alps, this time by the Splügen pass into Switzerland at Chur, meditating on the world that he had seen and its vanity and folly, and anticipating his reunion with the wise and witty Thomas More, the idea for his most famous book arose in his mind. This became the masterpiece of humor, irony, and biting satire that he entitled *Moriae encomium (The Praise of Folly).* He dashed it off soon after he arrived at More's house in London, as he recuperated from the long journey back from Italy and from an attack of kidney stone, and he dedicated it to More, punning on his family name in the title and the theme, the Greek word for folly being *moria.* It was not published until two years later, when Erasmus saw it through the press of Gilles Gourmont in Paris. It was then quickly reprinted and republished in many other cities and became what we can truly call a best seller. About forty editions appeared in Erasmus' lifetime. "It delighted the whole of Europe," so it has been said with a degree of exaggeration perhaps, for its banter and its critical thrust were viewed amiss at least by some. It is nevertheless Erasmus' most popular and enduring work. Huizinga calls it his best. In this little book, he says, "Erasmus gave something that no one else could have given to the world."

The form of the work is a declamation, a discourse in praise of folly delivered by a garrulous woman—actually a goddess—who is the personification of folly itself. The imagery is whimsical and paradoxical. Folly praises herself, yet her encomium is not altogether foolish. It is often ironic and in places straightforwardly and severely critical of the self-deceptions and harmful stupidities of this life. The tone and meaning of Folly's address thus frequently vary, and one of the problems in reading the essay, one of its challenges, is interpreting correctly what Folly has to say. Is she speaking foolishly and amusing us—or is she telling us the truth and instructing us? The ambiguity is not always resolved.

Aside from this ambiguity and the book's playful quality, and aside from the final section, where Erasmus eulogizes Christian folly—"the folly of the cross"—as Saint Paul did in his First Letter to the Corinthians, the most striking and best-remembered parts of *The Praise of Folly* are its criticism of religious superstition and its indictment of theologians, monks, and prelates who disfigure religion with their conceits and un-Christian lives. (These parts were greatly expanded in the 1514 and 1515 editions.) The scholastic theologians wrapped up in their syllogisms and irrelevant speculations are given rough treatment, as we might expect. Nor are the popes with their pomp and their wealth and their triumphs spared. It is clear that Erasmus at this point had in mind Julius II, whom he had seen in action in strife-torn Italy, and there follows a ringing condemnation of war as "something so monstrous that it befits wild beasts rather than men" and as completely alien to Christ and his teaching. These critical and satirical parts occupy a fair portion of the book and give it its cutting edge. Its impact on its times should be measured here; and in evaluating it, the historical context of the work as well as Erasmus' deeper purpose should be kept in mind. It was written and published in a Europe still Catholic though urgently in need of religious renewal and reform. This Erasmus grasped and devoted his energies to achieve. He is not playing the mocker or cynic or skeptic in this book, as some have mistakenly believed, but the sincere reformer. In a response to the critic Martin Dorp, he said that his intentions in *The Praise of Folly* were the same as in his other works though his method differed. "The same thing was done there under the semblance of a jest," he wrote, "as was done in the *Enchiridion.*"

From the summer of 1509, when Erasmus wrote *The Praise of Folly* in More's house in London, to the summer of 1511, when he published the work in Paris, we know practically nothing of his life. (The lack of extant correspondence from this period is an enigma.) Most probably these two "lost years" were spent congenially with his English friends and in productive scholarly work. Finally, we find him at Cambridge, where he had gone in August 1511 to teach Greek. Bishop Fisher of Rochester was also chancellor of the university and extended the invitation that led to Erasmus' tenure as a professor. He stayed at Cambridge nearly two and a half years, residing in Queens' College, occasionally riding his horse for exercise and recreation, and working very hard on projects for new books and editions. One of these was a recension of Saint Jerome's letters (he also lectured on Jerome). Another was a fresh Latin translation of the New Testament directly from the Greek. Still another was the preparation of two educational works, *De copia verborum ac rerum* and *De ratione studii,* for publication by Josse Badius in Paris in July 1512. He dedicated the *De copia* to John Colet, and it was intended as a text on Latin composition and style (the word *copia* signifies "richness" or "fullness" of expression) for use in Saint Paul's school in London, which Colet had recently founded. He also worked on a new revision of the *Adages* and on several classical texts and translations, and during this time very probably he wrote a short satiric dialogue entitled *Julius exclusus* (Julius Excluded). The latter is a lampoon in the Lucianic vein of Julius II, who had died in February 1513. In it the warrior pope has a long wrangle with Saint Peter at the gate of heaven and is refused entrance. The contrast between the haughty papal prince and a true Christian pastor is sharply drawn. Erasmus denied authorship of this invective (which was very likely never meant for publication), but there are indications that the work is his, and we know that Julius was a particular scandal to him.

He left Cambridge in early 1514, went to London, and in the summer departed for the Continent. The high hopes that had brought him to England in 1509 had not been realized (he had many complaints about life at Cambridge), and he decided now to try his fortune elsewhere. Back in the Low Countries he soon made his way up the Rhine to Basel, which for the time being was the object of his travels. In that bustling city in the heart of Europe, Johann Froben, partner and successor of the late Johann Amerbach, had his printing office, and it was Erasmus' intention to join forces with him and see some of the projects he had long been working on through the press. He had heard too that the Basel firm was preparing an edition of Saint Jerome, and this in particular was strong motivation for him to go there. He was generally impressed with Froben's work and not entirely satisfied with Badius' labors in Paris. Also, a not too trustworthy printer's agent, Franz Birckmann, had diverted certain manuscripts, including the revised *Adages,* which had been promised to Badius, to the Basel enterprise. Erasmus may not have connived in this transaction, but it probably did not distress him. The switch inaugurated his contact with Froben and marked the beginning of a long and famous association.

We come now to the climactic point in Erasmus' career—a period of culmination when he made many of his most important contributions, when his full program of reform found its most effective expression, and when his fame too reached its peak. Margaret Mann Phillips, in her excellent biography of Erasmus, epitomizes the great humanist's state of mind as well as his actual status in the world of his time during this period:

> Erasmus was attempting the complete reorganization of his world, partly through comparison with the ideas of the maturer minds of the past, and partly through the inspired common sense of his own mind, having before him the ideals of the Gospel. This immense vision had grown upon him slowly, and was coming to fruition now in the years 1514–18 at Basel. Those years placed him in the central and supreme position at the very heart of the Renaissance.
>
> (*Erasmus and the Northern Renaissance,* p. 72)

This busy and vital period of his life opened with an amusing scene—a circumstance not entirely out of character for the author of *The Praise of Folly.* The trip up the Rhine in the midsummer of 1514 had been a triumphal one, and Erasmus was exhilarated by the enthusiastic reception given him at Strasbourg by the German humanists. He was in high good spirits when he reached Froben in Basel. The two men had never met, and Erasmus seized the opportunity to play a joke. He introduced himself as a friend of Erasmus with whom Froben could talk and negotiate as with Erasmus himself. "We are so alike," he said, "that if you have seen one, you have seen the other." Froben soon caught on, however, and welcomed the renowned scholar warmly. Erasmus promptly moved into Froben's household, and their close collaboration began.

The situation repeated to a certain extent Erasmus' experience in Venice in 1508, save that his ties with Froben were more intimate and enduring than his affiliation with the Aldine press. Froben had a coterie of scholarly associates and friends, and Erasmus joined their number. Beatus Rhenanus, his future biographer, was an editor there, and active too were the sons of Johann Amerbach, who was recently deceased. The youngest son, Boniface, became a very close friend of Erasmus. New editions of *The Praise of Folly, De copia,* and the *Enchiridion* were brought out in 1515, as were an edition of Seneca and a still further expanded edition of the *Adages.* This latter work, which had originally been intended for Badius, is a notable revision of the popular anthology. It contains two celebrated essays: a forceful antiwar tract entitled *Dulce bellum inexpertis*—"War is sweet to those who have not tried it"—and an incisive statement aimed at the reform of the church entitled *Sileni Alcibiadis.* ("The Sileni of Alcibiades" are statuettes that are ugly in appearance but can be opened to reveal a beautiful carved figure inside. The image or reference comes from Plato's *Symposium,* and its use was proverbial. Erasmus was very fond of it, and we find it in the *Enchiridion* and *The Praise of Folly.* In this instance he compares Christ and the Apostles to Sileni, and he compares prelates of his own day with their fraudulent outward show to Sileni in reverse.) More important than any of these works, however, were two larger projects that Froben published in 1516 and that Erasmus had been occupied with since his arrival in Basel: a huge edition of the works of Saint Jerome and an annotated Greek and Latin New Testament. The appearance of these together with other circumstances in that year, which we shall consider, make 1516 the annus mirabilis in the story of Erasmus and Erasmian humanism.

The Jerome edition had been in preparation both by Erasmus and quite independently by the Amerbach–Froben press. Erasmus knew Jerome's works from his earliest years and had undertaken to emend and comment on his letters as early as 1500. Johann Amerbach, whose ambition it was to publish good editions of the major Western Fathers (he had brought out an edition of Saint Ambrose in 1492 and of Saint Augustine in 1506), had long planned an edition of Jerome and had gathered manuscripts and employed some excellent scholars in collating and restoring his writings. Froben and Amerbach's sons continued the effort after his death, and it was at this point that Erasmus entered the scene. He now worked assiduously to bring the project to completion. "I have thrown myself into this task so zealously," he wrote to Cardinal Riario, "that one could almost say that I had worked myself to death that Jerome might live again." Finally, the editing and printing were completed in nine folio volumes in the summer of 1516, and the book was on the market in September.

Erasmus' part in this enormous undertaking was confined chiefly to the letters and treatises in the first four volumes, though he assisted in the whole work. He contributed extensive notes, or *scholia,* to the letters, and he composed a long dedication to Archbishop Warham of Canterbury, to serve as a general preface, and a remarkable life of Saint Jerome that has been called his biographical masterpiece. It is the first critical life of the saint, and one of Erasmus' modern editors, Wallace K. Ferguson, has described it as "a labor of love, an act of filial piety by one who considered himself Jerome's spiritual descendant."

The importance of Saint Jerome for Erasmus cannot be overestimated. He identified with this most literary and erudite of the Latin Fathers. His very style resembles the saint's. And he saw Jerome as the model Christian scholar and the embodiment of true theology. From the start, as we have seen, the restoration of Jerome's works was closely linked to Erasmus' program of theological reform. This linkage is crystal clear from the life Erasmus wrote. Jerome's status as a theologian is staunchly defended against those scholastics who follow an entirely different tack: "Who had a more thorough knowledge of the philosophy of Christ? Who expressed it more vigorously either in literature or in life? Are not these the qualities of the theologian?" *(Erasmi opuscula,* p. 179). They were indeed in the purview of Erasmus, who saw theology not as a speculative or academic science but as the living and transforming "philosophy of Christ"—an understanding rooted in Scripture and expressing itself in the moral life.

"The philosophy of Christ" is a famous Erasmian term, actually patristic in origin, which gained currency in 1516. It is first used and defined in the *Paraclesis,* or introduction to the New Testament, that Erasmus published earlier that year. The expression simply means "what Christ taught," and it includes the notion of a doctrine that easily penetrates our minds and transforms our lives. "What else is the philosophy of Christ which He himself calls a rebirth," Erasmus asks in a striking passage in the *Paraclesis* (he uses the Latin *renascentia* for "rebirth"), "than the restortion of human nature originally well formed?" The source of that philosophy of course is the New Testament, and thus the publication of Erasmus' New Testament in March 1516 is an extremely important event.

This edition is unique because it marks the first publication in print of the Greek New Testament, the original language of the Gospels and Epistles. Erasmus accompanied it with an emended Latin version in a parallel column, and he annotated the entire work extensively. The edition is prefaced by a dedication to the reigning pope, Leo X, wherein Erasmus calls a return to Scripture "our chiefest hope for the restoration and rebuilding of the Christian religion," and by the aforementioned *Paraclesis,* as well as by a short essay on theological method. The latter was expanded and published separately as the *Ratio verae theologiae (The Method of True Theology)* in 1518. The New Testament edition, like practically all of Erasmus' works and editions, was revised and republished several times—in 1519, 1522, 1527, and 1535.

It is by no means a modern critical edition of Holy Scripture (it has been often faulted on this score), and it was hastily printed in 1516, but it is nevertheless a landmark book, and it was widely acclaimed. Colet expressed the view of many when, receiving and examining his copy, he exclaimed: "The name of Erasmus shall never perish." The Greek was now readily available to scholars for the first time. (Cardinal Ximenes' even more scholarly polyglot New Testament, which also had the Greek text with an interlinear translation, had already been printed at Alcalá in Spain, but its publication was held up until 1522.) Above all, it focused renewed attention on the sacred writings—the source of Christian faith. The book "struck its perfect hour," in the words of Margaret Mann Phillips, and "stood for the New Learning."

Despite Leo X's full approval (his commendatory letter was published in the second edition), there were many who were shocked at Erasmus' temerity in correcting the Vulgate text and giving priority to the Greek, and who criticized specific changes or comments that he made. Several controversial exchanges took place on these various points. One was with Martin Dorp, a Louvain theologian, who launched his criticism of Erasmus' audacity in altering the Vulgate together with his disapproval of *The Praise of Folly* even before the publication of the New Testament. Erasmus replied in an important apologia, which was published by Froben in 1515 in the first collection of Erasmus' letters to appear. Thomas More also wrote to Dorp in 1515 in Erasmus' defense and is said to have won over the critic, or won him back (for Dorp had been a friend and fellow humanist), to the humanist cause. Another very lengthy and very sharp exchange occurred with the French humanist Jacques Lefèvre over a disagreement about the translation of a Hebrew word in the eighth Psalm that was quoted in Hebrews 2:7. The most interesting criticism of all, perhaps—and one fraught with historical consequence and meaning—came from an obscure Augustinian monk in the Saxon town of Wittenberg, who was lecturing on Scripture at the university there. He had obtained the new publication and found that he disagreed with Erasmus' interpretation of Saint Paul on the matter of justification by works. He conveyed that information to a friend, George Spalatin, secretary to the elector Frederick of Saxony, and the latter relayed the criticism to Erasmus in a letter of December 11, 1516. "His view," wrote Spalatin, "is that we do not become just by performing just actions . . . but that we become just first and then act justly." The Augustinian monk was Martin Luther, and his criticism of Erasmus is one of the early expressions of his basic notion of justification by faith alone.

Spalatin's letter marks Luther's first contact, albeit indirect, with the famous humanist and foretokens the radical divergence between them that later emerged. (Shortly after this Luther wrote to another friend the following: "My opinion of Erasmus decreases from day to day. . . . I fear that he does not promote the cause of Christ and God's grace sufficiently. For him human considerations have an absolute preponderance over divine" [quoted in M. Boehmer, *Martin Luther: Road to Reformation,* p. 160]). The controversy that was to rend the church and overshadow the reforms of Erasmus was near at hand.

Erasmus published another noteworthy book in 1516—a moralistic political treatise entitled *Institutio principis Christiani (The Education of a Christian Prince).* Addressed to and dedicated to young Prince Charles of Burgundy, who became king of Spain in 1516 and was soon to become Holy Roman Emperor Charles V, it is a book of devout maxims in which he who is destined for the highest office may, to quote Beatus Rhenanus, "learn the conduct worthy of a Christian as in a mirror." Erasmus had been named a councillor to Prince Charles in 1516, and the work was an act of homage as well as instruction for him. In his same capacity as councillor to Charles and at the behest of Jean le Sauvage, the chancellor of Burgundy, he also wrote another significant condemnation of war and plea for peace—an essay in the form of a declamation entitled *Querela pacis (The Complaint of Peace).* We must emphasize that Erasmus was a pacifist and that his pacifism was an essential aspect of his Christian humanism and his reform program; we must also stress that his pacifism was not simply the dream of a scholar in an ivory tower. It was conceived and developed as relevant advice and advanced as practical counsel to the rulers and other important figures of his day. And Erasmus indeed was influential. In 1516–1517, with a new and more promising group of princes at the helm—the Medici pope and the kings of England, France, and Spain—all of whom he knew and corresponded with, he was especially hopeful that Europe would have peace and that a better day was dawning.

It will not be amiss to recall at this point that 1516 was also the year of Thomas More's *Utopia.* That fascinating book, a true Renaissance masterpiece, might almost be called the joint work of More and Erasmus. They shared the attitudes and ideas it expressed. In fact, the dialogue between Raphael Hythloday and More that constitutes book 1 of *Utopia* seems in many ways a discussion between Erasmus and More, with Hythloday voicing characteristic views of Erasmus, particularly with respect to war. Erasmus was actually in England in the summer of 1516, when More was working on this portion of the book. And book 2 of *Utopia,* which consists of the description of the ideal commonwealth, where all goods and wealth are held in common and private property does not exist, is actually a highly imaginative rendition of the first proverb in all the editions of the *Adages—Amicorum omnia communia;* that is, "Among friends all things are shared in common." More sent Erasmus the manuscript of the book in September, and Erasmus arranged for its initial printing that fall by Dirck Maertensz in Louvain. It was an immediate success. It too reflected the buoyant and confident spirit of the humanists at this period.

From the late summer of 1516 to November 1521, Erasmus lived in the Low Countries, chiefly at Antwerp and Louvain and finally, for several months, at Anderlecht. At the end of 1521 he returned to Basel, where he took up residence once again at Froben's. Meanwhile, other travels interrupted his sojourn in Brabant. He visited England briefly in April 1517 to receive the full dispensations he had sought from Rome that would permit him to forgo wearing his religious habit, allow him to remain outside his monastery, and, most importantly, enable him to hold church benefices despite the illegitimacy of his birth. These had come through the good offices of a close friend, Andrea Ammonio, a papal representative in London. The summer of 1518 found him once more back in Basel, where he published a new edition of the *Enchiridion* and worked on a revision of his New Testament, replacing, in general, the Vulgate text with his own Latin translation. In the summer and fall of 1520, he was for a time in the entourage of the new emperor, Charles V, and attended his coronation at Aachen in October. His travels would have been even more extensive had he answered the many invitations and appeals that came to him from all sides. He tended nevertheless to be restless wherever he was, like Petrarch "a pilgrim everywhere," truly Erasmus of Christendom, as Roland Bainton appropriately entitled his study of the great humanist.

Shortly after Erasmus' return from his visit to England in 1517—it was his last voyage there—the Antwerp painter Quentin Metsys did an imposing portrait of him as a scholar of serious mien in a black habit and cap writing in a large book. It was Erasmus' first portrait. Others by Albrecht Dürer and Hans Holbein followed. Two years before the Metsys portrait, the youthful Holbein, who had just come to Basel, had done two small ink drawings of Erasmus in the margin of a copy of the 1515 Froben edition of *The Praise of Folly*. One of these depicts Erasmus as a handsome young man seated at a small desk and writing in a book. When Erasmus saw this miniature sketch he is reported to have exclaimed: "Ah! If Erasmus still looked like that, he would quickly find himself a wife!" The Metsys painting was accompanied by a similar portrait of Peter Gilles, town clerk of Antwerp and a good friend of Erasmus as well as of Thomas More. The two portraits formed a diptych and were sent that year as a gift to More from the sitters. (Two copies of each portrait survive today. One Erasmus portrait is in the Galleria Nazionale in Rome; the other is at Hampton Court Palace in England ) In the Metsys painting of Erasmus, the book he is working on is his Paraphrase of Saint Paul's Epistle to the Romans, the first of a series of Paraphrases of the Gospels and Epistles, which he was actually writing at this time. (In the Hampton Court portrait, but not in the one in Rome, the opening lines of the Paraphrase in a hand very similar to Erasmus' are clearly legible.) In Holbein's famous portrait of Erasmus (today in the Louvre), which was painted in Basel several years later, Erasmus is also pictured writing in a book. This time the opening lines of his Paraphrase of Saint Mark's Gospel, which he dedicated to Francis I of France and published in 1523, are represented. The depiction of Erasmus busily writing at a desk recalls Renaissance representations of his great favorite, Saint Jerome, and the similarity, for example, between the Metsys portrait and Antonio da Fabriano's *Saint Jerome in His Study* (dated 1451), even to facial expression, is striking. Saint Jerome is usually shown with a cardinal's hat hanging on the wall behind him. Erasmus had not yet been offered that high dignity.

In 1517 a wealthy friend, Jerome Busleiden, died. At Erasmus' urging he had left a bequest in his will for the establishment of a college at Louvain where the three learned languages—Latin, Greek, and Hebrew—would be taught. Beatus Rhenanus, in his life of Erasmus, lays great emphasis on the importance of this trilingual college and on Erasmus' role in its acceptance. Its example, he tells us, influenced the king of France to set up a similar college in Paris and to invite Erasmus to preside over it. The latter declined, but the steps taken at this time led to the later Collège de France. "And so," Beatus comments, "it is generally acknowledged that the growth of learning in these countries is due most of all to Erasmus."

At the same time that Busleiden's trilingual college was being organized, Erasmus published at Louvain (at Maertensz' press in November 1518) his extended treatise on theological method, the *Ratio verae theologiae*, wherein he stressed the necessity for the theologian of the knowledge of ancient languages in comprehending and expounding Scripture. This publication increased tension between Erasmus and the more academic or conservative theologians at Louvain. The dispute actually was between two very different conceptions of theology—the humanist and the scholastic—the roots of which go back to Erasmus' early days and the reality of which was ever present in his program and writings. In early 1519, it found significant expression in an exchange between Erasmus and the most eminent of the Louvain theologians, Jacob Latomus. Latomus wrote a *Dialogue* defending theology as a dialectical science and taking issue with the whole literary or humanist approach of Erasmus' *Ratio.* Erasmus replied in an *Apologia* focusing on the importance for the theologian of studying the learned languages and the literature of antiquity. It was a high-level debate, but Erasmus was very upset by the opposition he now confronted. The "barbarians" were unrelenting, so it seemed to him, in their efforts to suppress good learning.

It is at this point that Martin Luther and the Reformation impinge on our story, and they do so, it must be noted, in the context of the dispute we have just described. Luther, to be sure, had entered the scene before this. On 31 October 1517 he had posted his famous Ninety-five Theses concerning indulgences on the door of the castle church in Wittenberg, and these, widely circulated, gave rise to the controversy that began the Protestant Reformation. The theses criticized the traffic in papal indulgences, a practice that was a scandal to many, including Erasmus; but there was more to Luther and the controversy that developed than the criticism of this abuse alone. Out of his personal experience as a monk and his exegetical probing as a professor of Holy Scripture, Luther had come to the conviction that it was faith in Christ's merits alone that justified and saved Christians and not works or efforts on the part of sinful man. The implications of this belief as Luther elaborated them were to be very radical in terms of many traditional doctrines and devotions. Luther arrived at this realization, he tells us, as he pondered the message in Romans 1:16–17 that "the just shall live by faith." It was what had inspired his disagreement with Erasmus' interpretation of Saint Paul and his reservations about the humanist, and it came more and more to the foreground in his preaching and polemics as the religious controversy expanded after 1517. Differences of scriptural interpretation, then, separated Erasmus and Luther from the beginning, though superficially at first it appeared that Luther was engaging in the same reform efforts as Erasmus and was contending with the same opposition. Young Luther had broken with scholasticism and seemed to be in the humanist camp of good literature and biblical theology. Indeed, as professor at Wittenberg he was using Jacques Lefèvre's new editions of the Psalms and Saint Paul's Epistles, and he had obtained Erasmus' New Testament.

In March 1519, Luther, the center now of great contention, addressed his first letter to Erasmus. He wrote deferentially, seeking the acknowledgment and, implicitly, the support of Christendom's most renowned scholar. Erasmus answered somewhat reservedly in May, reporting chiefly on the agitation among the theologians at Louvain. They thought that he had helped write Luther's tracts, he said, and was the standard-bearer of his party. The view is the forerunner of the notion that "Erasmus laid the egg Luther hatched." He told Luther, however, that important people there as well as in England thought highly of his writings, and he added: "As for me I keep myself as far as possible neutral, the better to assist the new flowering of good learning; and it seems to me that more can be done by unassuming courtesy than by violence." He concluded on this note: "We must everywhere take care never to speak or act arrogantly or in a party spirit." Not that Luther needed this advice, Erasmus politely assumed, but he gave it clearly—and farsightedly—nevertheless.

Later that year, in October, Erasmus wrote

a longer and more incisive letter regarding the controversy over Luther to Albert of Brandenburg, archbishop of Mainz, the man whose appointment to that see in 1514 had occasioned the papal indulgence Luther had attacked. There is an unusual fitness in Erasmus' forthright remarks to this prelate. The gist of what he has to say is that Luther is being defamed and abused by shameless men who are troublemakers and enemies of learning, and that he deserves a fair hearing: "If he is innocent I do not want him crushed by a faction of rogues, and if he is in error I wish him to be corrected not destroyed." Though he dissociates himself from the actual case of Luther, there is no mistaking his sympathies. And in the midst of his appeal for fairness and moderation in dealing with Luther, he gives a remarkably outspoken analysis of where the real trouble lies:

> The world is weighed down with human ordinances, burdened with scholastic opinions and dogmas, oppressed by the tyranny of the mendicant friars. . . . They preached indulgences in such a way that even the ignorant could not bear it. Due to this and many other similar causes the vigor of the Gospel teaching was gradually disappearing. And it looked as if, with things ever heading for the worse, the spark of Christian piety, whence an extinct charity could be rekindled, would at last be totally put out. The sum of religion was tending towards a more than Jewish ceremonial. . . . Pious minds were troubled when they heard in the universities scarcely any discussion of evangelical doctrine and observed that the sacred writers approved of old by the Church were now regarded as obsolete. . . . This must be blamed, in my opinion, even if Luther has written somewhat intemperately.
>
> (quoted in J. C. Olin, *Christian Humanism and the Reformation,* pp. 137–138)

The causes of the Reformation crisis are not simply explained, and different perspectives on the event can give quite different appraisals. Erasmus' analysis, given in the fall of 1519, however, touches on some key issues and in terms of his reform goals is highly consistent.

We do not have the space here to trace in detail the evolution of Erasmus' attitude toward Luther and the Reformation or describe his reaction to all its developments. We will confine our account to a more general description of his involvement and role. As the controversy became more vehement and widespread, as it certainly did after 1520, he became alarmed about its eventual outcome. It took on for him the proportions of a "tragedy," a great disaster. He sought to moderate the quarrel and prevent a serious breach within the church. This was the natural bent of his mind and the natural direction of his efforts. He stood for renewal and reform but also for unity and peace. "What else is our religion than peace in the Holy Spirit?" he wrote to Jodocus Jonas, one of Luther's followers, in May 1521. It was a profound sentiment on Erasmus' part and one he often repeated. He thus occupied a middle ground in the controversy that raged, and he maintained this position as the schism deepened. But his mediatory efforts were of no avail. The church was seriously rent, and the changes and reforms that were introduced were not exactly those Erasmus had in mind. He ran afoul too of both extremes—of both factions, as he viewed the warring parties—for neither side could see him as their own, and both came to regard him as faithless and disloyal. He became more and more an anomaly in an age of increasing Protestant–Catholic polarization. Even in recent times there has been puzzlement and suspicion among some biographers over the "ambiguity" of his position, though few scholars today question either the sincerity of his Catholic faith or the quality and firmness of his convictions.

At the end of 1521, Erasmus left the Low Countries and his hostile critics at Louvain for Basel. Restless and unsettled though he was, he never again journeyed far from that busy city. Luther, meanwhile, had been excommunicated by Rome in 1521 and placed under the ban of the empire following his defiant stand at the Diet of Worms, and Erasmus was now being pressed to write authoritatively against him. This was probably part of the reason he withdrew to Basel, where the atmosphere was less charged and more congenial. He also wanted closer contact with Froben, and an extremely productive period now followed. Whatever else it did, "the Lutheran tragedy" did not sap Erasmus' energies or becloud his own reform purpose. A further revision of his New Testament appeared in 1522, and Froben that year brought out two major editions of his *Colloquies,* the work that after *The Praise of Folly* remained his most famous and enduring. In September, Erasmus also published an edition of Arnobius' *Commentaries on the Psalms* that he dedicated to the new pope, Adrian VI, a Hollander like himself and a former Louvain professor whom he knew well. Adrian responded by asking Erasmus to write against the heresies of Luther and by inviting him to come to Rome. Others also urged that he take up his pen against the rebellious Wittenberg monk, and finally, one might say reluctantly, he did so in 1524 in a treatise entitled *De libero arbitrio* (*On Free Will*).

In this essay Erasmus took issue with Luther's basic teaching that man is totally corrupt and therefore unable and unfree to do anything that might aid in his own salvation, and he upbraided Luther for being so intemperate and for disputing so dogmatically against the consensus of the church. He argued strictly from Scripture against Luther's point of view, affirming man's obligation to lead a moral life and defending his ability to respond to God's grace and do so. Erasmus' theology was essentially that of Saint Thomas Aquinas; it rested on the principle that grace restores man's fallen nature and liberates and strengthens his will. It was the view that we might expect from a humanist conscious of the need to uphold the dignity and freedom of man. Luther was enraged and after some delay responded in a lengthy diatribe entitled *De servo arbitrio* (*On the Bondage of Will*). He attacked Erasmus mercilessly as a godless skeptic "oozing Lucian from every pore," and he asserted in the most extreme terms his theological determinism and his view of man's helplessness and enslavement to sin. Erasmus subsequently replied to the attack in his twofold *Hyperaspistes*—the word is Greek and means "one who protects with a shield"—of 1526 and 1527, defending himself against Luther's vituperation and further explaining his theology of man's freedom and grace.

Although Erasmus went to the heart of the matter in his dispute with Luther, not all his Catholic critics were satisfied or reassured. For some *De libero arbitrio* was too moderate in tone and too circumspect, and other writings of his continued to rankle and upset. This was particularly true of the *Colloquies,* which came under the formal censure of the Sorbonne, the theological faculty at Paris, in May 1526, a few months after Luther's angry onslaught in *De servo arbitrio.* Erasmus was truly a man caught in the middle. He was now near sixty, and these later years were far from offering that tranquillity and leisure he undoubtedly desired.

The *Colloquies,* as we have already noted, is one of Erasmus' most celebrated works. Its origin goes back to his early days in Paris, when he composed short exercises in Latin conversation for pupils he was tutoring. Some of these *formulae* were first printed in 1518 and 1519, but it was not until Froben's editions in 1522 that the work was greatly expanded and took on the character we recognize today. After that, like the *Adages,* it was enlarged, republished, and reprinted many times. Over a hundred such editions and reprintings appeared in Erasmus' lifetime. By the final edition of 1533, it came to contain more than fifty of the lively sketches or dramatic dialogues called colloquies.

In the Erasmian corpus—in fact, in the literature of the Renaissance—the *Colloquies* occupies a very special place. It harks back to the dialogues of Lucian and in some instances to the dialogues of Plato. It has much of the wit and satire we find in *The Praise of Folly,* and it sets forth those characteristic themes of Erasmus expressed as early as 1501 in the *Enchiridion.* At the same time, it is full of lively scenes and stories and is replete with pungent comment and personal observation. Not the least of its features are the satiric jabs at the abuses of religion that Erasmus had so long criticized—at ignorance and superstition and at the monks and friars whose practices he abhorred. The book is comparable to *The Praise of Folly* in this regard. And it was this aspect that raised the hackles of the Sorbonne and other Catholic opponents. (We might note that Luther also denounced the *Colloquies* and its Lucianic author, albeit for different reasons.) Whatever else may be said about the work, it clearly shows that Erasmus had no intention of softening his criticism of abuses or curtailing his efforts toward reform because of his theological disagreement with Luther or because of the schism that had come.

There is a great variety of scenes and topics in the *Colloquies.* The following will give some idea of their character and scope. In an edition of 1522, one of the greatest appeared—the "Convivium religiosum" (Godly Feast). The setting is a garden where a group of friends are idyllically conversing. Their conversation is very elevated, and one important theme touched on is how Christians can learn and profit from many of the works of the ancient pagans. "Perhaps the spirit of Christ is more widespread than we understand," remarks one of the speakers. Another, a little later, moved by the attitude of Socrates in the face of death, and his resignation and hope, so proper to the Christian, says that he could hardly help exclaiming, "Saint Socrates, pray for us!"—memorable words that go to the heart of Erasmian humanism. The next year the colloquy "The Shipwreck" made its debut. It tells the story of a ship caught and destroyed in a terrible storm. All on board, panic-stricken, scream to the saints for help and make extravagant vows. A young mother with a child in her arms alone retains her calm and dignity and prays in silence. When the ship breaks up, she is the first to reach shore and one of the very few who is saved. The dialogue-narrative is humorous and fast-paced, and the description of the storm at sea is masterly.

Early in 1524, a few months prior to *De libero arbitrio,* Erasmus published a colloquy bearing on the religious controversy—the "Inquisitio de fide" (Inquiry Concerning Faith). It stands in rather sharp contrast to the tone and argument of the later treatise on free will. In it two speakers, one a Lutheran (or Luther), the other a Catholic (or Erasmus), review the articles of the Creed and discover that they agree on all these fundamental beliefs. The point seems to be that their disagreement involves not the basic articles of the Christian faith but rather other matters that are of lesser importance, and that they should keep talking and work out their differences. It seems a plea for continuing dialogue, the idea of which is unquestionably an Erasmian motif, but the fruitfulness of which was belied by the actual Erasmus–Luther exchange that soon took place. The differences that then emerged seemed fundamental.

A surprising number of colloquies feature women, who are depicted with sympathy and affection and who present views on their education and on courtship and marriage that are refreshing and enlightened. The More family, and particularly More's eldest daughter, Margaret, who married William Roper, come to mind in this connection. Erasmus dedicated to her a commentary on two hymns of Prudentius in 1524, and she in turn translated into English Erasmus' meditation on the Lord's Prayer—the first of his works to be published in English. She was also very likely the model for the intelligent young lady in the delightful colloquy "The Abbot and the Learned Lady." The lady in this work, with her love of books and good learning, offers quite a contrast to the witless and unconscionable abbot, who attempts to lure her from her scholarly pursuits.

In the *Colloquies* and other writings, too, Erasmus frequently praised marriage and family life, often upholding the ideal as preferable to celibacy—a view that did not sit well at all with his clerical opponents. He wrote a devotional treatise on Christian marriage in 1526 that he dedicated to Catherine of Aragon, wife of Henry VIII of England—whose husband, ironically, was soon to seek a divorce. Again one thinks of Thomas More and his family, whom Erasmus knew so well and whom he once so fondly described in a famous letter to the German knight Ulrich von Hutten. He had not seen them for a number of years, but the painter Hans Holbein did a marvelous pen sketch of the entire More family in their house in Chelsea in 1527 and brought it back to Erasmus in Basel as a memento from his dearest friend. "I should scarcely be able to see you better if I were with you," Erasmus wrote to More in reply.

Comparable to the *Colloquies* and also related to the controversies that engaged Erasmus in the 1520's is a satiric dialogue entitled *Ciceronianus* (*The Ciceronian*), which he first published in 1528. In it Erasmus responds to certain Italian humanists who pedantically measured everything by the structure and vocabulary of Cicero and in turn were critical of his Latin style and literary abilities. Erasmus, like all the humanists, held Cicero in high regard and indeed viewed him as the great exemplar of Latin prose. Erasmus' humanism, however, far transcended a narrow classicism or Ciceronianism; language or style for him was not the servile imitation of any author but the product of an assimilation more living and more personal. "He himself always loved an open, extemporaneous, pure, fluent and lively style," Beatus Rhenanus tells us in his biography of Erasmus, "and he made certain terms serve the Christian subjects which he treated." The language of Cicero, who lived before Christ, was limited in that last regard, and Erasmus objected to the neopaganism as well as the pedantry of the Ciceronians. In his life of Saint Jerome, defending the Father against criticisms of his eloquence and style, he had launched an attack on Ciceronianism, and now in the *Ciceronianus* he used the same arguments in his own defense, though the satiric mode and the witty banter of the dialogue are different. Erasmus had entered the lists against a new band of foes with banners flying. To his old critics among the scholastic theologians and the friars and to Luther and his militant adherents were added a third contingent—the more purely or puristically classical Italian humanists. Julius Caesar Scaliger was the most vehement respondent. "Indeed I war on three fronts," Erasmus had written as early as 1524 to his friend John Fisher in England.

Erasmus had ridiculed an excessive classicism in the *Ciceronianus*, but it must be remembered that he was one of the great classical scholars of his day and that no one did more in fostering the New Learning, as it is called, than he. In the service of this cultural renewal such works as the *Adages* and the *De copia* were of prime importance, and he also produced many editions of the classical authors. These range from an edition of Cicero's *De officiis* in 1500 to an important edition of Seneca that Froben published in 1515, editions of Pliny's *Natural History* in 1525, and Livy's *History* in 1531, and they include many others, Greek and Latin, as well as translations from the Greek authors into Latin. Here the Greek satirist Lucian must again be mentioned. It is, however, Erasmus' editions of the early church Fathers that should be given pride of place in any account of his textual scholarship and editorial achievements. These form the largest and one of the most important segments of his life's work, and they contribute directly to the chief aim of Erasmus as a humanist scholar—the reform of theology through a return to the earliest theological tradition; that is, to the old and true theology of the first Christian centuries.

The first and foremost of these editions is that of Saint Jerome, which appeared in 1516. (Jerome and Lucian, as we have noted, were

Erasmus' favorite authors—an interesting combination revealing among other things the creatively synthetic quality of Erasmus' mind.) Next came an edition of Saint Cyprian in 1520, and then the Arnobius *Commentaries* in 1522 along with an edition of Saint Augustine's *City of God,* which Erasmus had persuaded the Spanish humanist Juan Luis Vives to edit and annotate. Erasmus wrote a preface to the latter work in which he tells of the preparation of a multivolume edition of the works of Saint Augustine—a project that was finally completed in 1529 and published by the Froben press in ten folio volumes. Erasmus dedicated this massive set to Archbishop Alfonso Fonseca of Toledo, the primate of Spain and a friend sympathetic to humanist studies and reform. It was in part at least a gesture of gratitude for Fonseca's support at a time when Erasmus was under severe attack in Spain. Meanwhile, other patristic editions appeared: an edition of Saint Hilary of Poitiers in 1523 with a memorable and controversial dedicatory preface addressed to Jean de Carondelet, a high official at the Hapsburg court in the Low Countries; a revised edition of Jerome's letters in 1524; various works of Saint John Chrysostom, the first Greek Father Erasmus would edit, publish, and in part translate during the next few years, climaxed by a five-volume *opera omnia* in Latin translation in 1530; a first edition of Saint Irenaeus' *Adversus haereses (Against Heresies)* in 1526; and a four-volume edition of Saint Ambrose in early 1529.

What is the significance of Erasmus' achievement here? He produced more accurate and more complete editions of the Fathers than had hitherto been available. Theologians must know the ancient Christian writers, Beatus Rhenanus stressed, and "it is to this knowledge that Erasmus has so greatly encouraged students." In most cases the prefaces to these editions are notable essays containing incisive comments on each Father as well as observations relevant to Erasmus' own aims and times. Outstanding in this regard is the Saint Hilary preface of 1523. Erasmus used the example of Hilary confronting the Arians of the fourth century to clarify his point of view in the Lutheran controversy, and the preface contains some of his most pungent comments on the nature of theology and the baleful consequences of theological argument and contention. His recurrent theme is that excessive theologizing and dogmatic pronouncement destroy the peace and unanimity that should exist among Christians, for Christianity is a matter more of how we live than of the articles we profess. The preface gave rise to further accusations against him. Several passages were condemned by the Sorbonne in 1526, and still other passages were vehemently assailed at a conference of theologians in 1527 at Valladolid in Spain, where Erasmus was charged with denying the Trinity. He had powerful friends in Spain, however, including the grand inquisitor, Alfonso Manrique, and Archbishop Fonseca, and he was spared formal condemnation.

Erasmus replied vigorously to his Spanish critics in 1528, but difficulties close to home were now causing even greater discomfort. In the course of the 1520's, Basel began to feel the impact of radical reform preaching, and the winds of change began to blow there. The leader of the movement was a scholarly priest, "learned in the three languages," Joannes Oecolampadius, who had assisted with the publication of Erasmus' New Testament in 1516 and had also made an extensive index for the Jerome edition that had been published separately by Froben in 1520. By 1523 Oecolampadius had become a professor of Scripture at the University of Basel and a staunch follower of Ulrich Zwingli, the reformer in nearby Zurich. These reformers preached a cleaner break with tradition than Luther and were particularly opposed to the Mass, the cult of the saints, and the doctrine of the Real Presence of Christ in the Eucharist. They were called Sacramentarians, and from them stems a more Puritanical version of Protestant reform. By early 1529 they had gained ascendancy in the city. In January and February there was much agitation and disorder capped by raids on the churches and the smashing and removal of all images. On the heels of these iconoclastic riots the Catholic members of the town council were expelled, the university was closed, the Mass was suppressed, and the reformers came into full control. Erasmus observed all of this with sadness and dismay and determined at once to leave the city. He departed by boat on 13 April and traveled a short way down the Rhine to the not too distant German city of Freiburg-im-Breisgau. A close friend, Ludwig Baer, once the rector of the University of Basel, moved to Freiburg with him. Another intimate friend of these later years, Boniface Amerbach, accompanied him on the journey. Freiburg was a pleasant town, strongly Catholic and firmly in the orbit of the Hapsburgs. It was a logical refuge, and Erasmus was given a cordial reception there.

He remained in Freiburg for the next six years. Age was now beginning to exact its toll, and Erasmus was ill with kidney stone, arthritis, gout, and other maladies a good deal of the time. He was increasingly weary and disheartened too at the loss of friends and the sad deterioration of the world about him. Nevertheless, he kept at work pursuing his scholarly interests and his publishing projects. He brought out revised editions of many earlier works and produced some important new ones. The huge Chrysostom edition appeared in 1530, and in 1532 he published—with Froben in Basel as usual—an edition of Saint Basil in Greek, the first to be printed in that language. He followed this with his own Latin translations of two treatises of Saint Basil. During these years, he also wrote and published commentaries on several Psalms, the most important being an essay on Psalm 84 (83 in the Vulgate and Erasmus' enumeration) entitled *De sarcienda ecclesiae concordia* (*On Restoring Concord in the Church*). True to his convictions, he pleaded for religious reform in what under the circumstances can be called the moderate spirit of the *Enchiridion* and for tolerance and accommodation in the face of extremism and deep division. Psalm 84 itself was an appropriate prayer for the unity of the church.

The major work that Erasmus completed in these final years was his *Ecclesiastes*, a lengthy, comprehensive treatise on the art of preaching. It had been long in preparation, and it is the most voluminous of all of Erasmus' writings. The mold of his thought was essentially rhetorical; that is, he was ever concerned with the effective communication of virtue and truth, and he viewed rhetoric or eloquence—the true *ars humanitatis*—as basic to everything else. Indeed, this is a characteristic of humanism in general. *Ecclesiastes* is not simply a specialized treatise on sacred oratory but a summing up of all his thought and work—an extended colophon, so to speak, to a long and very productive life. He intended the work for John Fisher, but that saintly man was beheaded on 22 June 1535 just as Erasmus was finishing the treatise, and he dedicated it to the bishop of Augsburg. Fisher, like Thomas More, had run afoul of Henry VIII, who had declared himself supreme head of the church in England, and both were executed as traitors for refusing to acknowledge that title; More followed Fisher to the block two weeks later. England would never see their like again, said Erasmus.

A month prior to Fisher's execution, Erasmus had returned to Basel. Boniface Amerbach had urged him to come back, and besides he wanted to see his *Ecclesiastes* through the press. He hoped also that the change of scene might improve his health, but that was not to be. Crippling arthritis now beset him, and he remained bedridden most of the time in Jerome Froben's home, Zum Luft, where he stayed. (The house still stands in the Baumleingasse, no. 18. Jerome, together with his brother-in-law Nicholas Episcopius, continued the famous press after the death of his father, Johann, in 1527.) In failing health, Erasmus still managed to work; his last undertaking was an edition of the works of the early Greek Father Origen in Latin translation. Erasmus considered him one of the greatest scriptural exegetes. The end came before the edition was complete, and it was finished by his old colleague Beatus Rhenanus and published posthumously.

Erasmus died at Zum Luft on 12 July 1536, in his seventieth year. In the preface to the Origen edition, Beatus gives a moving account of his final hours. Worn and exhausted but at peace, he implored Christ's mercy with his dying breath. "Jesu misericordia! Domine miserere mei!" he prayed, and then at last in his native Dutch, "Lieve God!" He was buried in the old cathedral of Basel, where his red marble gravestone remains.

What appraisal can we make of Erasmus' message, of Erasmus' career? I am inclined to say that his writings and his work, prolific as they are, speak for themselves. Over and over again he declared his intentions and his ideals. There really does not seem to be any mystery about them. In a letter of October 1527, he gave this description of his endeavors:

> I have vigorously raised my voice against the wars which we see for so many years now agitating all of Christendom. I have attempted to call back theology, sunk too far in sophistical quibbling, to the sources and to ancient simplicity. I have sought to restore to their own splendor the sacred doctors of the Church. . . . I have taught good literature, previously nearly pagan, to celebrate Christ. I have supported to the best of my ability the blossoming of languages once again.
> (*Opus epistolarum Erasmi* 7.208)

He tirelessly pursued these goals, and he flooded literate Europe in his day with his own works and with his editions of the ancient authors. No one before him had used the new medium of print so fully and so effectively. His learning was prodigious; his style, albeit Latin, was most fluent and engaging; his purpose was lofty and true. From the humblest beginnings he won world renown. His influence penetrated everywhere.

He had, as we have also seen, his critics on every side. "The Lutheran tragedy," he himself tells us, "had burdened him with unbearable ill will." Both extremes attacked him, and by virtue of what he stood for as well as of the schisms that rent Europe he became highly controversial. And he has, unfortunately, continued to be seen in partisan and prejudicial terms ever since. "That great injur'd Name,/the glory of the Priesthood and the shame," wrote the poet Alexander Pope, and Roland Bainton in his study has reminded us that "Erasmus has never had his due."

Have we succeeded in giving an objective account, an authentic portrait? It is our hope, of course, that in some measure at least we have done so. But Erasmus is a complex and many-faceted individual. His true face is difficult to delineate. And there is also the tendency to picture him in one's own mold or to interpret him in the light of one's own convictions and preconceptions. A study of the studies about him and of the various judgments that have been passed reveals this quite clearly. However, we strive for the historical truth, and I venture to say that with care and caution we can approach it. And I think today that we begin to understand more clearly what it was he sought to achieve and to appreciate more justly the ideals that inspired his work. The distance from his own times may be one of the reasons, and, paradoxically, the relevance of what he had to say for our own times may be another.

## Selected Bibliography

### EDITIONS

*Erasmi opera omnia.* Edited by Johannes Clericus. 10 vols. Leiden, 1703–1706.

———. Amsterdam, 1969– . A new critical edition still in progress.

*Erasmi opuscula.* Edited by Wallace K. Ferguson. The Hague, 1933.

*Opus epistolarum des. Erasmi Roteradami.* Edited by P. S. Allen, H. M. Allen, and H. W. Garrod. 12 vols. Oxford, 1906–1958.

TRANSLATIONS

*The "Adages" of Erasmus.* Translated by Margaret Mann Phillips. Cambridge, 1964. A study with translations of several important adages.

*Ciceronianus.* Translated by Izora Scott. New York, 1908.

*Collected Works of Erasmus.* Toronto and Buffalo, 1974– . An extensive edition of Erasmus' correspondence and writings.

*The Colloquies of Erasmus.* Translated by Craig R. Thompson. Chicago, 1965.

*Christian Humanism and the Reformation: Selected Writings of Erasmus.* Edited and translated by John C. Olin. New York, 1975. Contains *Compendium vitae,* the *Life of Erasmus* by Beatus Rhenanus, the *Paraclesis,* and several other important writings.

*The "Enchiridion" of Erasmus.* Translated by Raymond Himelick. Bloomington, Ind., 1963.

*The Education of a Christian Prince.* Translated by Lester K. Born. New York, 1936.

*Luther and Erasmus: Free Will and Salvation.* Edited and translated by E. Gordon Rupp et al. Philadelphia, 1969.

*The Praise of Folly.* Translated by Clerence H. Miller. New Haven, 1979.

*The Praise of Folly.* Translated by Betty Radice. Baltimore, 1971.

BIOGRAPHICAL AND CRITICAL STUDIES

Bainton, Roland H. *Erasmus of Christendom.* New York, 1969.

Bataillon, Marcel. *Erasme et l'Espagne.* Paris, 1937.

Chantraine, Georges. *"Mystère" et "Philosophie du Christ" selon Erasme.* Namur, 1971.

Huizinga, Johan. *Erasmus of Rotterdam.* Translated by F. Hopman. New York, 1952.

Hyma, Albert. *The Youth of Erasmus.* Ann Arbor, Mich., 1930.

Kohls, E.-W. *Die Theologie des Erasmus.* Basel, 1966.

Margolin, J.-C. *Erasme par lui-même.* Paris, 1965.

Olin, John C. *Six Essays on Erasmus and a Translation of Erasmus' Letter to Carondelet, 1523.* New York, 1979.

Phillips, Margaret Mann. *Erasmus and the Northern Renaissance.* London, 1949.

Reynolds, E. E. *Thomas More and Erasmus.* New York, 1965.

Smith, Preserved. *Erasmus.* New York, 1923.

Sowards, J. Kelley. *Desiderius Erasmus.* Boston, 1975.

Tracy, James D. *Erasmus: The Growth of a Mind.* Geneva, 1972

JOHN C. OLIN

# GUSTAVE FLAUBERT
## *(1821–1880)*

GUSTAVE FLAUBERT IS a writer of contradictory qualities and great complexities. He seems to be at once a romantic and a realist, an idealist and at the same time disillusioned, a writer of great emotion and a pure formalist. He is certainly one of the great proponents of art for art's sake, yet a generation of French writers—including Émile Zola, Guy de Maupassant, and the Goncourt brothers—considered him the father of neorealism and the social novel. Flaubert detested the mediocrity of French culture, but he spent most of his career writing about the stupidity of that world. He was not interested in politics, yet his *Éducation sentimentale (Sentimental Education)* is considered one of the best social documents on the revolution of 1848.

Of course, any writer can be said to embody contradictory impulses. But Flaubert's contradictions are fascinating precisely because they are specifically a reaction to the problems of the early modern world and the rise of modern culture. More than any other writer who preceded him, Flaubert detested not merely mankind but those particular changes that he imagined had come about as a result of the rising tide of industry and democracy. Being at once a critic and a part of that world, Flaubert, as did many later writers, found himself in an untenable and insoluble position. He saw his times as the nadir of civilization. As he puts it: "'89 destroyed royalty and the nobility, '48 the bourgeoisie, and '51 the people. There is nothing left but a bestial and imbecile rabble."[1] Although he believed that a writer should have "neither religion nor fatherland nor even any social conviction" (Steegmuller, p. 278), Flaubert still had social convictions about his own era. But though he detested his times, he was unable to suggest alternatives or how to achieve change, even in his art. His only recourse was to the power of art and description in the hope that these might make others share his beliefs and his pessimism.

Flaubert was born on 12 December 1821 at the hospital in Rouen, where his father was chief surgeon. He grew up in quiet comfort, performing plays, reading, and writing—always imagining an exotic and lush world that was the opposite of provincial Norman existence. It is hard to believe that one of the greatest writers in French sprang from this small-town life. If one tries to look for moments that led to the creation of Flaubert's genius, it is difficult if not impossible to discover anything remarkable or unusual in his childhood.

One event stood out in Flaubert's own imagination—and he wrote and rewrote this experience with such persistence that we must stop and take notice, although at first glance we seem to be dealing with a very common occurrence. At the age of of fifteen, Flaubert

[1]Francis Steegmuller, *Flaubert and Madame Bovary* (1977), p. 278. Further references to Steegmuller in the text are to this work.

saw a pretty woman nursing her baby on a beach. That woman—Élise Schlésinger—seized Flaubert's conscious and unconscious desires with such force that she shows up in one form or another in five novels that Flaubert wrote—*Mémoires d'un fou* (Memoirs of a Madman, written that year), *November,* the first *Sentimental Education* (all published posthumously), *Madame Bovary* (1857), and the final version of *Sentimental Education* (1869). Flaubert made friends with Élise Schlésinger and her husband and remained friends with them for most of his adult life. What this chance encounter triggered for Flaubert was an obsession with adultery and with women who were both lovers and mothers, as we will see.

A significant event, perhaps more significant than the first, took place in 1844. Flaubert was afflicted by a series of epileptic attacks when he was twenty-three years old. These attacks were a kind of visionary experience for Flaubert and were inspired by Saint Anthony, whose life Flaubert had read about and about whom he later wrote one of his major novels. In any case, these visions and attacks became the physical excuse for Flaubert to give up his law studies, which he detested, and to begin officially his career as a writer—a career in which he had previously only dabbled.

Flaubert's first significant novel was *November,* written when he was only twenty. It is a work of nostalgia for his own innocence, lost in a sexual sense only three years earlier. The novel recalls his first memorable sexual encounter. (He had apparently slept with his mother's maid earlier, but this adventure must not have struck him as particularly poignant or literary.) In the summer of 1839, when Flaubert was seventeen, his parents sent him on a trip to the south of France, Malta, and Corsica. On the trip, young Gustave met Eulalie Foucaud, a thirty-five-year-old Creole with an absent husband and a young daughter. Eulalie ran a hotel in Marseille and fell in love with the young tourist. For Flaubert, the experience was a triumphant entrance into a world of sexuality and voluptuousness that all his writing and reading had held out before him as a golden reward of life.

Flaubert's late adolescence, like that of most other people, was filled with thoughts of sexuality, but one might point to a special role that he gave to the sensual and the voluptuous that never left his work. Literature and sexuality were virtually inseparable. When Flaubert was not writing about sexuality, he was writing about superabundance, sensuality, hedonism, appetite, and depravity. His adolescent journals reveal this desperate yearning, to which he gave life in the fantasy world of Oriental courtesans, dancing girls, exotic prostitutes, as well as a world inspired by the marquis de Sade of murder, necrophilia, rape, and bestiality. Flaubert was at once attracted and repulsed by his own masturbatory vision, as a typical entry in his journal reveals:

> Oh flesh, flesh, that demon that keeps coming back incessantly, that tears the book from your hands and the cheerfulness from your heart, makes you somber, ferocious, selfish; you repel it, it returns; you surrender to it ecstatically, fling yourself at it, sprawl upon it, your nostrils flare, your muscle stiffens, your heart palpitates—and then you fall back moist-eyed, fed up, exhausted.
>
> (*Intimate Notebooks,* p. 29)

To this entry Flaubert added the comment "pitiable" in parenthesis to underscore his own repulsion for (and perhaps mastery of) his fantasies. Out of this desperation and ambivalence came *November.*

The novel derives much of its power from its youthful adoration of women and sexuality. The style is painfully intense, and words like "torment" and "yearning" are the building blocks of the book, as the following tribute to female tightrope walkers suggests: "I tormented my imagination dreaming of those strangely formed thighs so firmly encased in pink tights, those supple arms wreathed in bangles" (F. Jellinek trans., p. 8)

The novel chronicles the narrator's brief affair with a prostitute. The world created swells with polymorphous sensuality as the young narrator wanders through woods and fields—described as female and responsive. The narrator virtually makes love to the earth:

> I lay face downward on the ground in a place where there seemed to be the most shade, silence and darkness, the place that might best conceal me; and panting, I lunged into unbridled desire. The clouds hung heavy and sultry, they weighed on me, they crushed me as one breast crushes another. . . . I felt myself swooning with bliss beneath the weight of this amorous nature.
>
> (pp. 59–61)

Flaubert's youthful remaking of nature itself into his lover is important to his later work because it represents the way Flaubert ultimately saw his art as a transformation of mere reality. Obviously nature is a little more indifferent to most of us than Flaubert's narrator thinks. But writing and art can eroticize the world and in turn can eroticize the writing process so that fantasies become real, and the real can be incorporated into fantasy.

This eroticization of the world becomes so overwhelming in *November* that when the narrator enters the city from his erotic pastoral, every woman he sees wants him:

> Ladies in wraps bent from their balconies to see me and gazed at me, saying: "Love us! Love us!" . . . There was Woman everywhere: I rubbed elbows with her, I brushed against her, I inhaled Woman, for the air was redolent of her fragrance. . . . Not this woman nor that one, one no more than the other, but all of them, each of them, in the infinite variety of their forms and of my corresponding desire.
>
> (pp. 62–63)

Flaubert eroticizes every surface of reality—whether rural or urban landscape. In *November* the eros seems poignantly maternal. Nature is a huge and panting mother, and the city of women is in essence a projection of that desire for the mother. This early novel signals Flaubert's repeated obsession with the mother as sexual object. Although Marie, the prostitute who becomes the narrator's lover, frequently calls the narrator "child," she is described ambivalently as "serpentine, demonic," planting kisses in the way that "a beast of prey explores the belly of its victim" (p. 85). What is most interesting is the crossover in Flaubert's youthful mind between the mother as nurturer and the mother as predator. In Flaubert's work the erotic ultimately becomes crossed with the sadistic, and Marie's own biography sounds as though it came from a book by Sade, one of Flaubert's favorite authors. Marie, deflowered by an old nobleman, consorts with a variety of hunchbacks, dwarfs, and outcasts and is marked by perversions that "left upon her . . . the scent of a dying perfume, traces of vanished passions, that gave her a voluptuous majesty; debauch adorned her with an infernal beauty" (p. 117). In Marie, whose name must not be discounted as a reference to the Virgin Mary, Flaubert brings together for the first time the seemingly contradictory qualities he sought in women and in his female characters—the nurturing mother and the sadic lover.

*November* is not a fully realized novel, and one is tempted to agree with Flaubert's own assertion that the work is "a sentimental and amorous mishmash. . . . The action is nil. . . . Perhaps it is very beautiful, but I'm afraid it may be very false and rather pretentious and stilted" (p. viii). Flaubert tried to remedy this lack of action and characterization in his first version of *Sentimental Education,* written between 1843 and 1845. The word "sentimental" here is not used in our modern sense of "overly maudlin" and "melodramatic" but in the older usage denoting "of the feelings." Flaubert hoped to show how a young man's emotions were shaped and developed in an encounter with an older woman. The plot, while concerned with adulterous love and the fate of two young men, is quite different from the final version of the novel published years later. In the earlier work the story divides between two friends: Henri, who seeks romantic love and worldly power, and Jules, disappointed in love and fulfilled through suffering and art. In a sense the work is a kind of allegory about the inability of Flaubert to decide between these two ways of life, and the novel reveals this tension.

As Flaubert wrote in a letter to Louise Colet in 1852, the characters of Jules and Henri are two aspects of a vision:

> As far as literature is concerned, there are in me two distinct characters: one who is fond of declamation, of lyricism, of lofty flights, eaglelike, of the sound of sentences and the summits of thought; and the other who scrapes and digs out the truth as much as he can, who likes to stress the little facts as much as the big, and who tries to make you feel in an almost *physical* way the thing he reproduces. . . . The [first] *Sentimental Education* represented, without my knowing it, an attempt at fusing these two tendencies.

In this letter there is a deep perception of the dichotomy that haunts Flaubert's subsequent works—these two opposite views coexist and contradict one another in each of Flaubert's novels. Their unique and powerful quality springs from a tension between the lyrical descriptions of nature and life and the peculiarity of the quotidian physical details.

In the first *Sentimental Education* one sees this tension as well. Particularly, Flaubert glorifies femininity and the romantic love it offers at the outset only to tear down these ideals in the resolution of the book. The story opens when Henri Gosselin, eighteen years old, arrives in Paris to begin his study of law (as Flaubert himself had). Henri lodges at the home of Monsieur Renaud, who has an attractive wife named Émilie, with whom Henri falls in love. The first part of the book traces this infatuation and its consummation; this section prefigures the youthful longings in *November.* The characteristic contradictory themes of lyrical idealism and wallowing physicality dominate. This split is manifested in Henri's aesthetic of sexuality set against the mediocrity of life in Renaud's boarding house. Madame Renaud herself is a kind of goddess of sensuality and the romantic, and Henri places himself at her feet assuming that his adoration will free him from the bondage of student life, just as Emma Bovary will look to passion to free her from Yonville.

Émilie Renaud is another of Flaubert's maternal heroines "whose motherly ways had a certain tender, almost amorous quality." Her husband fits into a pattern of oafish older men and father types to be defeated—Messieurs Bovary and Arnoux included. Flaubert contemptuously referred to this type as the "Garçon"—the smug, self-satisfied shopkeeper, businessman, or professional. Monsieur Renaud is aptly described in this role:

> At the first interview he gave the impression of being shrewd, at the second, rather silly; he frequently smiled in an ironical way at the most insignificant things, but when you talked to him seriously he would stare at you over the top of his gold-rimmed spectacles with such profound intensity that it might almost be mistaken for subtlety. . . . The protuberant curves of his body, which was short and stocky, were covered with flabby, whitish flesh; he had a fat belly, weak, plump hands like those of an old woman of fifty, was knock-kneed, and always managed to get horribly muddy whenever he went out.

In contrast to the oafishness of the husband, Émilie is delightful and nurturing:

> She had such fine black eyes and handsome eyebrows, her lips were still so red and moist, her hands, in every action they performed, still moved with nimble grace. . . . If her bosom, which she was at little pains to hide, was perhaps rather full, on the other hand how sweet a fragrance it distilled when you came near her!
>
> (Garman, p. 15)

In *November* there was no rival to the young male protagonist, but in *Sentimental*

*Education,* as in his later works, there is a kind of savage competition against the Garçon, whether he is the husband of a desirable woman or the representative of middle-class society in general. While Émilie represents a flight from the ordinary and oppressive world through sensuality and love, the husband embodies the values of the society that traps and imprisons the hero and Flaubert himself. So this book begins a trend for Flaubert in which sensuality offers the possibility of revolt against the constrictions of life, and writing about that sensuality creates a method of revolt for Flaubert himself.

The divided consciousness of Flaubert holds out two possibilities of revolt for the characters of this novel. Jules, who begins in a secondary role, represents artistic isolation and suffering. At first he falls in love and fails with the woman in question. But his retreat from the pain of love leads to the painful but valuable existence of scholar and artist. Jules seeks solace in the world of Orientalism and the exotic, reading the novels of Sade, writing scholarly works on the "Asiatics," and in composing poems. His obscure existence is made to seem more important as the novel moves on, and eventually it is Jules's aesthetic and intellectual choice that is held out as the successful revolt.

The less successful revolt is the one followed by Henri—adultery and passion. This way comes to represent another kind of failure, since Henri and Émilie, once they become lovers, can no longer live in the oafish world of Monsieur Renaud's Garçon. Ironically, they make their way to America, apparently seen by Flaubert as the place of revolution and of anonymity. There they also run into financial problems and fall out of love. Once the power of adulterous revolt is ruined, both Henri and Émilie return to France—she to her husband and Henri to begin his spiral down to the abject mediocrity that Flaubert expands on in the later version of *Sentimental Education.* We seem to be told that the road of passion and love will lead to the palace of mediocrity, and by the end of the novel, Henri becomes a copy of the doltish Garçon. From his initial idealism he now moves to a "kind of lukewarm conviction and easygoing gusto that led him to fool himself and sometimes other people." We might see this conversion to oafhood as a statement by Flaubert that the quest for power and love will lead away from true revolt. Jules's conversion to scholarship and art thus becomes the right choice for Flaubert.

Following Henri's failed love affair, a certain formlessness in the novel signals Flaubert's abandonment of his protagonist Henri for Jules. Flaubert uses this part of the novel to make general statements about art, changes the form of the novel to a kind of theatrical dialogue, and shifts to Jules's life—but discusses it from Olympian heights of generalization. Gerhard Gerhardi has suggested that the reason for this decomposition of the narrative line is that Flaubert's famous quasi-epileptic attack near Pont L'Évêque intervened and not only changed the nature of his writing but also the artistic direction of the writer himself. This attack, in which Flaubert felt himself "carried off suddenly in a torrent of flames," is paralleled within the work by Jules's sudden insight into life that occurs after he has been hounded through the countryside by a mangy dog. Gerhardi notes that "it is hard to avoid the conclusion that Flaubert meant to dramatize his break with the world of contingency in the hallucinatory sequence . . . preceding Jules's entrance into the world of art." In his own mind, Flaubert had become, at this point, a writer to be reckoned with.

It was now that Flaubert decided to write a work he had thought about for some time—his "great Oriental tale." There was during the late eighteenth and nineteenth centuries a great fascination with the Middle East—a fascination that coincided with the European powers' exploration and colonization of the Middle and Far East. Literary intellectuals, among others, tended to think of these regions as romantic, mystical, erotic, and forbidden. Flaubert's decision to write *La tentation de*

*Saint Antoine* (*The Temptation of Saint Anthony,* published in revised form in 1874) was a logical consequence of this interest, which would combine his researches into ancient archaeology, his obsession with the Orient, and his reverence for mysticism. To prepare, he read widely in the sacred texts of Buddhism, Hinduism, Islam, and Confucianism, as well as Arabic, Indic, Japanese, and Persian folklore and poetry. He researched the writings of the Church fathers, the Acts of Council, the *Dictionary of Heresies,* and other religious works.

In the novel, Saint Anthony, a fourth-century monk, retires to a cave where he is tempted by a variety of demons and spirits. Flaubert's plan was to expand the list of tempters to include every mythological and heretical figure in all the civilizations of the world. Included are the Sphinx, the Queen of Sheba, the Chimera, the Marcionites, the Carpocratians, and every religious sect and religion that Flaubert had managed to study. There was no plot to speak of, and when the book was completed in September 1849, it was a huge mass of learning with little palpable interest for most readers. Maxime du Camp and Louis Bouilhet, two close friends, were called to Flaubert's home in Croisset, near Rouen, for a reading of the work, so far kept secret. As du Camp later wrote, "The hours during which Bouilhet and I, exchanging an occasional glance, sat silently listening to Flaubert . . . have remained very painful in my memory." After four days of listening to 541 large manuscript pages, du Camp concluded that he had heard

> words, words—harmonious phrases expertly put together . . . but often redundant, and containing whole passages that could have been transposed and combined without changing the effect of the book as a whole. There was no progression—the scene always remained the same. . . . We could not understand, we could not imagine, what Flaubert was driving at, and indeed he was arriving nowhere.
>
> (Steegmuller, p. 135)

Flaubert asked his friends for their opinion of his book and was told to "throw it into the fire, and never speak of it again."

After this crushing judgment Flaubert was unable or unwilling to write for several years. Yet he managed to change this failure to a kind of success. Du Camp and Bouilhet advised him to abandon his lyrical, idealistic, and romantic vision since these brought out the worst excesses of his style. They suggested that instead he write a realistic work that would anchor him to a more mundane, precise, recognizably novelistic technique. Honoré de Balzac was held up as an example of objectivity in narration to be emulated. For Flaubert, who valued the lofty and lyrical, Balzac represented among other things a descent to the cesspool of callous social climbers and aristocratic snobs.

Although Flaubert abandoned his project, he did eventually rewrite *The Temptation of Saint Anthony* twenty years later in a much abbreviated form. While du Camp and Bouilhet might have been correct about the ungainliness of the earlier draft, what they seemed to have missed was Flaubert's herculean effort to re-create the intellectual and philosophical moment of an age. This project, which seemed foolish and excessively arcane to them, was one that he repeated again and again in future works including *Madame Bovary, Sentimental Education, Salammbô* (1862), and *Bouvard and Pécuchet* (1881). Though Flaubert repeatedly emphasized that he was against politics and social novels, his interest in reproducing the ideology of a historical moment made him one of the predominant novelists we think of as cultural critics. What Flaubert realized following the debacle of *The Temptation of Saint Anthony* was that the depiction of his own time and thought, not that of the distant past, could best serve his purpose in creating art. As he later observes:

> To return to the antique in literature has been done already. To return to the Middle Ages has also been done already. The present is the only

> hope for literary subject matter. But the present offers an unstable foundation; at what point can one safely attach the first beams? But it is entirely on that the vitality and durability of modern literature depends; on being able to find a secure point of attachment in the present.
>
> (Steegmuller, p. 199)

But before Flaubert could divest himself of his own second-rate romantic illusions and heal the wounds inflicted by du Camp and Bouilhet's rejection of his work, he had to have a period of wandering in the desert. Such an occasion was provided by du Camp himself. He had once traveled through Asia Minor and now decided on an extended trip to the Middle East to photograph the great monuments of Egypt. He begged Flaubert to accompany him. After Flaubert secured the permission of his own mother, he agreed to go. In October 1849 they left for Egypt, where Flaubert was finally able to experience directly the Orient he had read about so assiduously in fantastic books like the *Arabian Nights* and Victor Hugo's *Les orientales* (1829)—a world he had known only through works of Western imagination.

Flaubert had always taken the Middle East rather personally. He imagined that he himself was part of antiquity, transposed to rural France by a kind of bad joke of fate. He wrote without much sense of humility of his desire to possess Cleopatra or Sheba as his mistress. And so this trip was to be a "purge of exoticism" that would flush the mundane from his psyche. His readings burst into life—transformed into material shape:

> Thus, as soon as I landed at Alexandria, I saw before me, alive, the anatomy of the Egyptian sculptures: the high shoulders, long torso, thin legs, etc. . . . Here the Bible is a picture of life today.
>
> (*Flaubert in Egypt,* pp. 75–79)

But Flaubert cared little for the massive pyramids and sculptures that still bring tourists to the Middle East and which du Camp had come to photograph. His interest was in the living examples of Oriental sensuality, sexuality, and sensibility that were so different from the habits of his Norman, or even Parisian, neighbors and friends. Flaubert dragged along with du Camp, but noted with amusement that most of the monuments he was forced to visit were covered with bird droppings. "Birdshit is Nature's protest in Egypt. . . . Nature has said to the monuments of Egypt: 'You will have none of me? You will not nourish the seed of the lichen? *Eh bien, merde!*' (well—shit!)."

Flaubert reveled in the exotic, bizarre, sexual, and excremental aspects of life in the Middle East. This world represented a living assault on the conventionality of the Garçon. Fascination ripples through the travel notes—there one sees syphilitic beggars, a hospital for venereal disease in which the patients exhibit their sores and lesions, dissected cadavers, camel urine, bird droppings, and the thousand natural and unnatural shocks that the European might receive in this most different culture. Flaubert's fascination with prostitution and sordid sexuality was fueled by nights spent with famous courtesans like Kuchuk Hanem and days engaged in pederasty at the baths. The Orient became a cavalcade of the bizarre, as one journal entry serves to indicate:

> To amuse the crowd, Mohammed Ali's jester took a woman in a Cairo bazaar one day, set her on the counter of a shop, and coupled with her publicly while the shopkeeper calmly smoked his pipe.
>
> On the road from Cairo to Shubra some time ago, a young fellow had himself publicly buggered by a large monkey—as in the story above, to create a good opinion of himself and make people laugh.
>
> A marabout died a while ago—an idiot—who had long passed as a saint marked by God; all the Moslem women came to see him and masturbated him—in the end he died of exhaustion.
>
> (*Flaubert in Egypt*, p. 44)

We might want to remember that while Flaubert was living this life counter to the metropolitan vision of Paris, he was gestating, as it were, his next novel, *Madame Bovary.* What Emma Bovary was unable to achieve in the way of sensuality and revolt in Yonville, Flaubert was permitted in the colonies. What Flaubert ultimately desired in sensual and literary life was a way of combining the fantastic and the earthly, the ideal and the excremental, the revolt against the Garçon's authority and the authority of his mother. The Orient provided a way for Flaubert to reconcile these contradictions. He could make love to a prostitute who evoked images of the *Arabian Nights* while breathing in the "smell of rancid butter." The contrast, what Flaubert frequently called the "bitterness" of this contrast, is what he most desired—and here one might refer to the scene in *Madame Bovary* in which love is pledged to Emma by Rudolphe amid a display of cattle and compost at the agricultural fair. The bedbugs on Kuchuk Hanem's mattress serve the same purpose:

> [They] were the most enchanting touch of all. Their nauseating odor mingled with the scent of her skin, which was dripping with sandalwood oil. I want a touch of bitterness in everything—always a jeer in the midst of our triumphs, desolation even in the midst of enthusiasm.
>
> (*Flaubert in Egypt,* p. 220)

The tension between the beautiful and the profane led Flaubert to books of antiquity like Apuleius' *Golden Ass* that combine "incense and urine, bestiality and mysticism," or to François Rabelais, whose use of excrement Flaubert sees as "lyrical." The Orient represented a vision of sensuality merged with a literary appreciation of the exotic—it was a world in which physical experience was a lesson in artistic and aesthetic sensibility.

Although he was close to writing *Madame Bovary,* Flaubert expresses in the travel journals a lack of interest in writing at all:

> At the present moment I see no reason whatever (even from a literary point of view) to do anything to get myself talked about. To live in Paris, to publish, to bestir myself—all that seems very tiresome, seen from this distance.
>
> (*Flaubert in Egypt,* p. 96)

Yet the suggestive quality of the Orient and of antiquity stood as silent lessons to Flaubert. When he saw the Parthenon, he could not help writing: "The Parthenon is one of the things that has most deeply penetrated my being in my entire life. Let people say what they will—Art is not a lie" (Steegmuller, p. 204).

Flaubert returned to Croisset in 1851, after twenty months of travel, and began to think once more of writing his realistic novel. Bouilhet suggested that he pattern the work after the life of a local health officer, Eugène Delamare, and his wife, who poisoned herself to escape a life of adultery and debt. This subject would allow Flaubert to combine his hatred for the mediocrity of contemporary life with his desire, expressed in *The Temptation of Saint Anthony,* to re-create in fiction the ideology of an era. Since Madame Delamare was reputed to have read and been corrupted by second-rate romantic novels, Flaubert would also be able to attack the inferior quality of modern literature in this new project.

Flaubert set to work with great difficulty, and in creating this great work of maturity, established certain hallmark practices and theories he would abide by most of his life. The first was a painfully slow period of composition. Unlike his writing of *The Temptation of Saint Anthony,* which proceeded rapidly, Flaubert found that the new fiction moved agonizingly slowly. It took him, on the average, four days to write one manuscript page, even though he worked between seven and twelve hours every day. He wanted a perfect style, and such perfectionism made speedy progress impossible. This painful trial of writing became the only way that Flaubert could ever write, suffering through art as did Jules in the first *Sentimental Education.* His frequent outbursts of frustration and rage became typical:

> I'm tormenting myself, scarifying myself. . . . My novel is having a frightful time getting started. I have abscesses of style, I itch with sentences that never appear. What a heavy oar the pen is, and what a difficult current ideas are to row in.
>
> (Steegmuller, p. 237)

He felt that writing was like "playing the piano with leaden balls attached to his fingers" (Steegmuller, p. 255).

This pain was a necessary counterpart to Flaubert's rather impossible aim of trying to create a style that would be objective, almost scientific, and that would eliminate any sense of an authorial presence in a novel. His style would eschew the language of romance and would present life as barely and sordidly as it could:

> I am trying to be impeccable, to follow a straight geometric line. No lyricism, no observations, personality of the author absent. It will be dismal to read: there will be atrocities in it—wretchedness, fetidness.
>
> (Steegmuller, p. 249)

In attempting this scientific style, Flaubert hoped to make his book focus more on method and style itself than on the story—which he hoped to make wretched and fetid. That is, his aim was to keep our sympathies away from the characters and focused on the *way* the story was told. In his view this method of narrating would elevate the project of novel-writing out of the trough of mere storytelling and into the higher realm of true art. Rather than using lyricism as a decoration, he would create a style so perfectly written and purely aesthetic that it would be lyrical and transcendent in and of itself.

In distancing his reader from the story, Flaubert thought he had done something rather new. He writes of *Madame Bovary,* "It will be the first time in any book, I think, that the young hero and the young heroine are made mock of. . . ." The point is not that the novel is a satire or a farce; it is among the first of a genre of writing that is now called the "anti-novel," in which our hopes and aspirations are not allied with those of the main characters. In this sense the reader is outside, looking in at the dissection of an aberrant and diseased human soul. Flaubert saw this distancing as part of the "scientific" nature of writing and reading that his work demanded.

Flaubert seems to be re-creating in words the dissections of cadavers that he watched his father perform at the Rouen Infirmary. Like the scalpel, writing was a scientific tool for observation—perhaps a better tool for understanding life than science could ever provide. Flaubert prided himself that his fiction was as accurate as science, and the following incident seemed to confirm this belief to him:

> I had great success today. You know that yesterday Rouen was "honored" by a visit from the minister of war. Well, I discovered in this morning's *Journal de Rouen* a sentence in the mayor's speech of welcome that I had written the day before, word for word, in my *Bovary* (in a speech by a prefect at an agricultural show). Not only were the idea and the words the same, but even the rhythm of the style. It's things like this that give me pleasure. When literature achieves the accuracy of an exact science, that's something!
>
> (Steegmuller, p. 282)

If writing were truly scientific, then Flaubert was not simply inventing the life of imaginary characters when he wrote novels; he was describing a particular set of circumstances that might create—according to the rules of logic and science—any number of Emma Bovarys:

> Everything one invents is true, you may be sure. Poetry is as precise as geometry. Induction is as accurate as deduction; . . . My poor Bovary, with-

> out a doubt, is suffering and weeping at this very instant in twenty villages in France.
>
> (letter to Louise Colet, 14 August 1853)

Fiction can be seen here as combining science and art, observation and creation, aesthetics and morality. The writer was no longer simply a storyteller but a kind of social psychologist—a scientist whose specialty was the human psyche and the environment that contained it. That Flaubert did not entirely accomplish this goal in attempting to fit his theories into practice is probably a saving grace. As Henry James pointed out, "The great good fortune of *Madame Bovary* is that the theory seems to have been invented after the fact."

Flaubert's aesthetic view was widely misunderstood when *Madame Bovary* was published. The novel received a great deal of notoriety, considering that it was the work of an unknown provincial. It was first published in serial form in du Camp's own *Revue de Paris,* but after several installments du Camp decided he had to edit the work to remove objectionable passages that might incur the Napoleonic censorship. Flaubert was furious over this violation of artistic integrity. Yet despite these bowdlerizations (the scene describing the curtained cab, among other episodes, was removed), the novel was brought to trial. Flaubert was vindicated, however, through the efforts of family and friends. The scandal of course helped to sell the book, as did the reputation of the work for explicit sexuality. What remains most remarkable is that *Madame Bovary* was widely condemned not for its lack of morality but for its dedication to realism.

Flaubert never thought of himself as a realist, though. As he writes: "Everyone thinks I am in love with reality when I actually detest it." The novelist Edmond Duranty, a professional realist, had written that the book "represents an obsession with description. Details are counted one by one, all are given equal value; every street, every house, every room, every brook, every blade of grass is described in full. . . . There is neither emotion nor feeling for life in this novel." Jules Barbey d'Aurevilly wrote that Flaubert was an "unwavering analyst . . . a describer of the minutest subtlety," but that a machine made "in Birmingham or Manchester out of good English steel" could have done the job just as well.

How could Flaubert have been considered a realist when he himself detested the realism of writers like Balzac? Perhaps the general reader simply found the inclusion of sordid detail—the dung outside Emma's father's farmhouse, the erotic implications of the wandering cab, the hideous, blind beggar, or the clinical description of Emma's death—to be a stinging reminder of what is "real" in life. Or the lack of any "virtuous character," as Sainte-Beuve bemoaned, might have created the impression of a radical attempt to undermine the traditions of romance.

But Flaubert was not merely interested in undermining tradition or poking his nose into the sordid. What he wanted to do was to link ideas and facts by instilling in material objects what other authors had often presented as abstract ideas and moral addresses put directly to the reader. Maurice Nadeau writes that "when Flaubert declared that 'ideas are facts,' he meant to reunite in a single whole the planes of imagination and dream and everyday life. . . ." (*The Greatness of Flaubert,* p. 139). Nadeau goes on to say that "it is amusing that Flaubert should be accused of 'realism' when he was the first to conjure up the total world of mingled consciousness and fact, through sensible appearances and with the aid of poetic language" (p. 142). What Nadeau does not say, though, is that such a technique could not help being considered "realistic" by a public who was used to the accepted conventions of eighteenth- and early-nineteenth-century novel writing. Of course Flaubert might be said to have redefined the world "realism" by combining the psychological and the imaginative with detailed physical descriptions of setting. Along with Balzac and to a certain extent Denis Diderot, Flaubert wanted to be so grounded in a materialist mode of writing that his scientific style would stand the traditional moralistic and idealistic novel on its head.

Let us examine his method by reading the famous description of Charles Bovary's hat at the opening of *Madame Bovary:*

> It was one of those headgears of composite order, in which we can find traces of the bear and the coonskin, the shako, the bowler, and the cotton nightcap; one of those poor things, in fine, whose dumb ugliness has depths of expression, like an imbecile's face. Ovoid and stiffened with whalebone, it began with three circular strips; then came in succession lozenges of velvet and rabbit fur separated by a red band; after that a sort of bag that ended in a cardboard polygon covered with complicated braiding, from which hung, at the end of a long, thin cord, small twisted gold threads in the manner of a tassel. The cap was new; its peak shone.
>
> (P. de Man trans.)[2]

Such a description, although tried occasionally by Balzac, was clearly an affront to most French readers, who had not usually been required by their novels to pursue such detail in a quotidian, albeit extraordinary, object. Even minutely detailed works like Daniel Defoe's *Robinson Crusoe* (1719) do not describe any one object in such length and certainly not at the opening of the narrative. The purpose of this paragraph may well have been to demonstrate symbolically in one object the entire range and mediocrity of Charles's personality, but the casual reader could only feel this section to be strangely without purpose. As Henry James wrote:

> To many people *Madame Bovary* will always be a hard book to read and an impossible one to enjoy. They will complain of the abuse of description, of the want of spontaneity, of the hideousness of the subject, of the dryness and coldness and cynicism of the tone.
>
> (*Madame Bovary and the Critics,* B. F. Bart ed., p. 63)

In some sense Flaubert's method was objectionable not so much because it chose the sordid but because it did so by placing greater emphasis on language and description than on the setting itself, as Paul Valéry and Gérard Genette have noted. The language draws attention to itself, so that the author is actually demonstrating *how* one writes *about* someone like Emma Bovary rather than actually *just writing* about her. Style triumphs over any mere subject.

> Style, as I conceive it, style as it will be realized some day—in ten years, or ten generations! It would be rhythmical as verse itself, precise as the language of science; and with undulations—a swelling of the violin, plumage of fire! A style that would enter into the idea like the point of a lancet.
>
> (*Madame Bovary and the Critics,* p. 37)

This adulation of style places *Madame Bovary* among the first novels to treat language as something unique in itself. And it is precisely language—or rather its misuse—that causes Emma Bovary's problem. Her tragedy is brought about by her mistaking the clichés of the pseudoromantic novels she reads for truths about the world. She is a character, like Don Quixote, who learns to see the world as if it were a romance. By mistaking the world for a literary construction, she inevitably places too great a premium on language and narrative—a misperception that ultimately destroys her. However, Flaubert's use of this misperception is much more scathing and all-encompassing than that of Cervantes. Cervantes allows a real world that can judge the foolishness of Quixote's mad quest, while Flaubert sees Emma's error as endemic, so

[2]Further references to *Madame Bovary* are to this edition.

that the readers of *Madame Bovary* themselves are doomed to repeat the heroine's logocentric misreadings. These readers, being no better or more perceptive than Emma, are strangely unsuited to understand the novel. Flaubert felt he had "torn out a bit of . . . [his] innards to serve up to the bourgeoisie" when he wrote his novel.

As a typical novel reader, Emma's first response to most situations is to place herself in a novelistic context. For example, after taking Rudolphe as a lover, she

> recalled the heroines of the books that she had read, and the lyric legion of these adulterous women began to sing in her memory with the voice of sisters that charmed her. She became herself, as it were, an actual part of these lyrical imaginings; at long last, as she saw herself among these lovers she had so envied, she fulfilled the love-dream of her youth.
>
> (part 2, ch. 9)

Emma transforms experience into narrative—choosing the second-rate narratives that had taught her how to interpret the world.

Flaubert's distance from the characters in the novel and his concern for style and method can be observed in the well-known scene at the agricultural fair when Rudolphe reveals his desire for Emma. The clichéd language of love culled from the popular romantic novels of the day is set against the awarding of prizes for farming accomplishments:

> "Take us, for instance," he said, "how did we happen to meet? What chance willed it? It was because across infinite distances, like two streams uniting, our particular inclinations pushed us toward one another."
>
> And he seized her hand; she did not withdraw it.
>
> "First prize for general farming!" announced the president.
>
> "—Just now, for example, when I went to your home. . . ."
>
> "To Mr. Binet of Quincampoix."
>
> "—Did I know I would accompany you?"
>
> "Seventy francs!"
>
> "—A hundred times I tried to leave; yet I followed you and stayed. . . ."
>
> "For compost!"
>
> "—As I would stay tonight, tomorrow, all other days, all my life!" . . .
>
> "But no, tell me there can be a place for me in your thoughts, in your life, can't there?"
>
> "Hog! first prize. . . ."
>
> (part 2, ch. 8)

The scene strikes one as rather comic, but Flaubert also shows how two forms of shallow language play off against each other. The language of the provincial fair and the inflated language of pseudoromanticism are equally devoid of the lyricism and transcendence that Emma expects to find through passion. These are words without the truth of real style.

One further scene that might illustrate the way Flaubert places his narrative and method in the foreground is the notorious cab scene in which Emma and her new lover Léon make love in a horsedrawn carriage while it wanders through the streets of Rouen. Flaubert deliberately leaves out any sexual description, and the reader merely gets a kind of guided tour of the city:

> "Where to, sir?" asked the coachman.
>
> "Anywhere!" said Léon, pushing Emma into the cab.
>
> And the lumbering machine set out.
>
> It went down the Rue Grand-Pont, crossed the Place des Arts, the Quai Napoléon, the Pont Neuf, and stopped short before the statue of Pierre Corneille.
>
> "Go on," cried a voice that came from within.
>
> The cab went on again; and as soon as it reached the Carrefour Lafayette, set off downhill, and entered the railroad station at a gallop.
>
> "No, straight on!" cried the same voice.
>
> (part 3, ch. 2)

Narrative style, the trick of presentation, is the subject of this scene, while the sexual action in the cab is secondary. Flaubert's brilliant way of depicting action by not describing it all brought the author as close as he might come to his ideal of writing about "nothing at all," and in effect makes his readers focus on the line between style and story.

Emma's attempt to escape from her small world is not so different from Flaubert's attempt to escape from his own culture through art. In fact her escape is only one of many attempted flights, including Saint Anthony's retreat to his cave, *November's* hero's escape to eroticism and then suicide, Henri's flight to Madame Renaud and America, Frédéric Moreau's move to the provinces, Bouvard and Pécuchet's rush to country life, Saint Julian's escape from his fate, and so on. None of these characters manages actually to disengage from the stagnation of his situation because no one chooses to escape through art. Flaubert offers no character the hope of the one mode that brought value to his own existence. In *Madame Bovary* escape from the world of the Garçon is impossible since all the characters are incarnations of this loutish archetype—from Monsieur Homais to the priest Bournisien. The Garçon is lauded at the end of the novel when Homais wins the Legion of Honor. The circle of entrapment is complete with Emma dead and Homais's mediocrity held aloft for commendation and memorialization.

After dwelling in the detail of provincial life, Flaubert decided finally to go ahead with his long-held wish to write a tale about the Orient. His obsession with this world, along with his practical experience, led him to create *Salammbô,* a work about as far from Yonville as he could go. The world was Carthage in the third century before Christ. As Flaubert wrote: "Few people will guess how sad one had to be to undertake to revive Carthage! It's a wilderness I was forced into out of disgust with modern life." Perhaps the choice to flee to antiquity was a mistake for Flaubert. "Hérodias" (1877), *Salammbô, The Temptation of Saint Anthony,* and "Saint Julian the Hospitaller"—all of which take place in the distant past—have failed to capture the imagination of the modern reader. They remain for the most part works that scholars will read for what they tell us about Flaubert, but are strangely stiff, remote, and bizarre. This is not to say that all these works are failures; certainly much brilliance erupts from the wealth of details, eroticism, and mystery that research and imagination produced. But these works fail to become stories so weighted are they with theory and scholarship. They are exemplary pieces, demonstration models, theoretical proofs that as experiments are fascinating but as narratives are often ponderous and leaden.

Flaubert's reasons for choosing the Orient are complex, as we have seen, but we cannot discount his cherished belief that he himself was actually reincarnated from the spirit of one long dead:

> It seems to me I've always existed, and I have memories going back to the pharaohs. I can see myself quite clearly at different ages in history, exercising different professions and with varying fortunes. . . . I have been a boatman, a *leno* [pimp] in Rome at the time of the Punic Wars, then a Greek rhetor in Suburrum eaten alive by bugs. I died in the Crusades from having eaten too many grapes on the coast of Syria. . . . Perhaps [I was] an eastern emperor. . . .
>
> (Nadeau, p. 161)

In a word, though Normandy was Flaubert's motherland, it was to the East that he traced the origins of his inspiration; though Croisset was his prison, Carthage was his land of freedom. His desire was therefore to apply to antiquity the scientific method he had evolved in writing *Madame Bovary.* Instead of the ordinariness of provincial life, he would now turn to the rich, lyrical, and superabundant world of Oriental opulence. These two novels that appear at first glance so different seem to come out of a similar desire: "I wanted to fix a mirage by applying to antiquity the methods of the modern novel."

The method of *Salammbô* is staggering.

Where in earlier works the profusion of sordid detail led to an oversupply of ordinary objects—in essence providing a counterbalance to the lyrical side of the narrative—in *Salammbô* the details themselves swell to a lurid and lyrical superfluity of lion skins, incense, jewels, flesh, spices, perfumes, tattoos, necklaces, rings, vermilion, and antinomy, piled on with the heavy strokes of a nineteenth-century harem painting. One thinks of the description of Hanno partaking of his favorite drink of weasel ashes and asparagus boiled in vinegar, or of the suggestive details of Salammbô's terrace:

> In the middle of the terrace was a small ivory bed, covered with lynx skins, with cushions of parrot feathers . . . and in the four corners rose four long burners full of spikenard, incense, cinnamon, and myrrh.
>
> (Krailsheimer, p. 51)

Or of the feast given for the barbarians in which

> oblong flames wavered over the bronze breastplates. The dishes encrusted with precious stones flashed and scintillated in sparkling profusion. The drinking bowls, rimmed with convex mirrors, multiplied the magnified reflection of things around. . . . the Greek wines that come in wineskins, Campanian wines kept in amphorae, Calabrian wines brought over in casks, as well as wines of cinnamon, jujube, and lotus. The wine spilled in slippery puddles on the ground. A cloud of steam from the hot food rose up into the foliage and mingled with the vapors exhaled by the crowd. One heard, at the same time, the noise of champing jaws, conversation, song, goblets, Campanian pitchers shattering into a thousand fragments, or the clear note of some great silver dish.
>
> (p. 19)

Such a description breathes excess—not only in the scene itself but in the scholarship that went into the making of the novel. Throughout *Salammbô* one is impressed and exhausted by the attempt to place into one book so much of the ancient world. Flaubert believed that for a book to exude truth "you have to be crammed up to the ears with your subject." And following his own advice, Flaubert claimed to have read more than fifteen hundred authors, ancient and modern, in preparation for the work. He even returned midway through the novel to the Middle East to steep himself in the past.

The danger of all this background is that it eclipses the main characters and makes them mere mannequins set against a display of archaeological artifacts. The beautiful and awesome virgin Salammbô is entirely without personality. She is a sculpted embodiment of the Oriental woman—the opposite in every extreme of the motherly Madame Renaud in the first *Sentimental Education.* In the story Salammbô, the royal devotee of the goddess Tanit, offers herself to the brutal warrior Matho in exchange for the goddess' holy veil, which Matho has stolen. Ultimately, Matho is dismembered and Salammbô dies on her wedding day in punishment for touching the veil.

Flaubert defended his desire to create a character without much depth by claiming that in effect he did not want to be precise about anything. He simply wanted to give an impression of the Carthaginian world. He defied anyone to "draw a Carthaginian chair or Salammbô's robe" since he had left everything purposely "indefinite." No one could dare call him a realist in this work.

Yet what is quite definite is an unleashing of sadistic violence unlike that in any of Flaubert's other works, with the exception of some youthful imitations of Sade. In *Salammbô,* mutilations, tortures, decomposing bodies, and infanticide are signposts along the Oriental way. One scene in which thousands of children are thrown into the burning mouth of an idol caused particular consternation to contemporary readers. Descriptions like the following are typical:

> the vermin could be seen leaving the dead, who were growing cold, to run over the hot sand.

> Perched on the top of boulders, crows stayed motionless, turned toward the dying.
>
> When darkness had fallen, yellow dogs, those filthy beasts that follow armies, softly came into the midst of the barbarians. First they licked the clotted blood from still warm stumps of flesh; and soon they began to devour the corpses, ripping them open at the belly.
>
> (p. 196)

Despite (or because of) protests against this lurid sort of description, *Salammbô* was quite a popular book and clinched Flaubert's reputation as a writer of note beyond the notoriety he had earned through a scandalous first novel. Appealing to the cult of Orientalism, Flaubert had written a work whose exoticism and morbidity sealed a pact between the readers and their escapist fantasies of harem nights and opiated days. If, as Edward Said has explained, the West had expropriated the Orient by re-creating it in the European imagination as a fantasy to be possessed, then Flaubert deliberately wrote a kind of viaticum that allowed novel readers to travel into that world collectively through an imaginative invasion and domination.

From this exotic past Flaubert moved again to the present and focused on his own generation. *Sentimental Education* is a continuation of the general project of depicting an age, an ideology, and a system of life. In *Madame Bovary*, it was provincial life; in *The Temptation of Saint Anthony* and in *Salammbô*, the mythic and religious world of antiquity; and in *Sentimental Education*, the life of young men in Paris at the time of the revolution of 1848. As Flaubert wrote:

> For the past month I've been hard at it on a novel of modern manners that will be set in Paris. I want to write the moral history of the men of my generation: the "sentimental" history would be more accurate.
>
> (Nadeau, p. 184)

In the first version of this book, written some twenty years earlier, the word "sentimental" seems to have been used fairly straightforwardly to signify "education of the feelings"; in this later work, however, one witnesses the obliteration of all sentiments, the denial of feeling, leading to the ultimate deflation and destruction of emotion.

This book is more mature and wide-ranging than the first *Sentimental Education*. In that earlier work we followed Jules and Henri as the former turned to art and the latter to disillusion. But in the second version a whole cast of characters proceeds through particular events of their time, absorbing the spirit of that age and changing their opinions as they develop. However, the net effect is that everyone becomes cynical, defeated, compromised, and without hope. While Jules was at least given the possibility of becoming an artist, his counterpart, Deslauriers, merely aims at power. No other character ever becomes even remotely admirable.

Flaubert was brutal toward his own era for many reasons, as we have seen, but this work is particularly bleak because he felt that his own generation had failed horribly through incompetence. His rage against French culture in general is made even more obvious by linking the love story of Frédéric Moreau and Madame Arnoux to the political and social convulsions of the time. The story begins during the declining reign of Louis Philippe, moves on to the revolution of 1848, and ends with the compromise and failure of that revolution in the coup d'etat of 1851. The state's trajectory of failure is mirrored in Frédéric's personal decline and ultimate failure. All the characters (with the exception of Dussardier, perhaps) are examples of compromised ideals, incompetence, inactivity, lack of imagination, and defeat.

The story of disillusion begins at the moment that Frédéric arrives in Paris to study law and fails his exams (as did Flaubert). In the beginning of Frédéric's listless drifting, he and his friend Deslauriers spin out fantasies of ideal careers. Frédéric wants to be the Sir Walter Scott of France; Deslauriers wants to be a philosopher. Frédéric changes his views and determines to become a follower of passion like Goethe's famous hero Werther; Deslauriers abandons philosophy for political economy. Frédéric then settles on painting, but immediately swerves again, deciding to write a history of aesthetics. In the same breath he fixes on the idea of dramatizing various periods of the French Revolution. This project metamorphoses immediately into a history of the Renaissance. Frédéric then tries to become a politician, promising if elected to destroy the rich. When he is defeated he concludes that the masses are cretins, and he becomes the lover of a wealthy woman, only to discover that she has no money. The movement here is from idealism to compromise and corruption. His mediocrity is manifest in his devotion to ideals and his absolute lack of interest in acting to uphold them.

In effect Frédéric is seduced by an ideology just as Emma Bovary was. Both these characters look to art as a salvation without realizing that they are incapable of living up to the ideals of even second-rate art. Aside from his artistic and scholarly aspirations, Frédéric actually has no career. "I have no profession; you are my exclusive occupation," he says to Madame Arnoux. In a novel devoted, in some sense, to the finding of a career, Frédéric proves the impossibility of his doing anything in life—and as with Emma Bovary, an obsessive passion holds out the only hope for salvation.

The decline of political ideas parallels the decline of all ideals in this work. Sénécal, the revolutionary who believes in the radical political theories of Charles Fourier and in the masses, becomes the harsh foreman in Arnoux's factory, and after that he is transformed into a policeman who kills Dussardier at a demonstration.

Art itself, Flaubert's one salvation, is also compromised in this commercial world. Monsieur Arnoux, the Garçon in yet another form, is the editor of the magazine *L'Art industriel*—an oxymoron if ever there was one for Flaubert. Arnoux's plan is to sell art at popular prices, and he accomplishes this goal by bestowing fame on second-rate artists whom he can control. Because Arnoux's view is that art is only a commodity, he delights in the market. In his next business venture, Arnoux runs a pottery factory that sells tiles with mythological designs in Renaissance style for the bathroom. Art has become merely utilitarian, and antiquity is deformed into mere decoration for that least revered of rooms. Mirroring the decline of art, the magazine *L'Art industriel* now becomes simply *L'Art,* run by a collective owned by shareholders, each of whom has the right to publish by virtue of the investment. Art for industry's sake now becomes art for money's sake. The same magazine is then transmuted into the revolutionary journal *Le flambard,* with its motto "Gunners to your cannon!" It treats "a book of poems and a pair of boots in exactly the same style."

Flaubert felt that political art was as much a travesty as industrial art. In the novel he has the artist Péllérin make revolutionary art ridiculous by painting a work showing "the Republic, or Progress, or Civilization, in the form of Christ driving a locomotive through a virgin forest"—an image all the more repulsive to Flaubert when one recalls that for him "modern stupidity and greatness are symbolized by a railroad." When Arnoux winds up setting up a patriotic music hall, and failing that a Gothic art shop specializing in religious knick-knacks, the failure of art is complete—the spiritual impulse merging with art in this world of compromised ideals can only produce worthless commodities.

The failure of projects and the compromise of ideals, of course, are not the only themes of *Sentimental Education.* There is also love. Frédéric plunges into an amorous obsession with Madame Arnoux after meeting her on a boat trip, an event paralleling Flaubert's own obsession with Madame Schlésinger. (Maurice Schlésinger, incidentally, was the prototype of Monsieur Arnoux in his various business enterprises.) Frédéric manages to find the Arnoux house and make himself a frequent visitor. Marie-Angèle Arnoux is a virtuous married woman, as her name perhaps exaggerates. Caught in this triangle, Frédéric suffers the torments of hating the husband (and liking him as well), desiring the wife, but being unable either to imagine her sexually or to exchange a word with her. The novel runs on this track for most of its plot, while Frédéric's fecklessness and paralysis reign.

Frequently Frédéric associates Madame Arnoux with his own mother, Madame Moreau. In fact the original name for Marie was supposed to be Madame Moreau, but Flaubert changed his mind and gave that name to Frédéric's mother—a fact that reminds us of Flaubert's own obsession with maternal women. The revolt through passion, a theme we have seen throughout Flaubert's writing, is not only ineffective but also is not even fully achieved. Frédéric never consummates his desire for Madame Arnoux, and his mistress is compromisingly also the lover of Monsieur Arnoux. Madame Arnoux remains chaste in body if not desire, and the final meeting of Marie and Frédéric is particularly touching and revealing because in it he realizes that her sexual aura consisted mainly of a maternal glow. When Frédéric meets her after several years have passed, enough time has elapsed to show him her true relation in his unconscious to his own mother. She removes her hat and lets him see her now-white hair, and Frédéric feels as if he were dealt "a blow full in the chest"; he also feels "repugnance akin to a dread of committing incest."

The book ends ambiguously when Frédéric and Deslauriers recall their childhood with longing and nostalgia. They remember one day in their adolescence when they naively went to the local brothel with bouquets of flowers for the whores, but had to flee from embarrassment. The men describe this act of ingenuous incompletion, incomplete as was Frédéric's passion for Madame Arnoux, as "the happiest moment of our lives." Failure to act is held aloft as a pleasure—the implication being that the adult world of sexuality is a deflation and a disappointment. Sexuality, along with art, politics, power, and ideals in general, turns out to be false.

In *Sentimental Education* sexuality is worked into the political arena in a way that no novelist before had done. The pyrrhic climax of Frédéric's infatuation with Madame Arnoux is set to take place on exactly the same day that the February revolution begins. Marie fails to appear because her son falls gravely ill, an act she sees as punishment for her adulterous desires. Frédéric, upset at her absence, plunges into the streets to "indulge in violent actions," including his first sexual encounter with his future mistress, who is Arnoux's at the moment. This development is particularly brilliant because the action of attempted adultery and then the placebo of fornication with Arnoux's mistress are linked to the overthrow of the king. The political and the erotic are set up by Flaubert to reveal a desire to replace the traditional old guard with a new order. But both attempts fail since Madame Arnoux does not show up and the revolution itself fails. The parody of Frédéric's appropriation of Arnoux's mistress rather than his wife is played out in the larger scene as the mob ransacks the royal palace:

> An obscene curiosity impelled the mob to ransack all the closets, search all the alcoves, and turn out all the drawers. Jailbirds thrust their arms into the princesses' bed, and rolled about on it as a consolation for not being able to rape them. . . . In the entrance-hall, standing on a pile of clothes, a prostitute was posing as a statue of Liberty, motionless and terrifying, with eyes wide open.
>
> (p. 289)

This pastiche of Eugène Delacroix's painting of Liberty leading the earlier revolution of 1830 is all the more telling since, as Flaubert's somewhat heavy symbolism implies, the people, like Frédéric, have accepted a prostitute for the real thing. The ideal easily becomes its opposite in this world.

Flaubert skillfully works the lives of his characters into the political world and the political world into the lives of the characters. Monsieur Dambreuse has a heart attack after the dismissal of General Changarnier; Frédéric's illegitimate child dies as the revolution fails; Monsieur Arnoux, the indomitable and indestructible father figure, easily becomes an officer in the revolutionary guard as he previously had been in the National Guard.

The complexity of this work, its attention to political and cultural history, its fatal and affecting love story, make it one of Flaubert's great works. Its special contribution to the history of the novel lies in the interconnecting of ideology, political event, psychological motivation, sexuality, and style into one seamless whole. All events are overdetermined, foreground and background are equally important, despite Flaubert's fear that he had made a work in which "backgrounds eclipse the foregrounds."

The oddity of this integration of elements is underlined by the contemporary critical response. Unlike *Madame Bovary* or *Salammbô, Sentimental Education* was generally reviled or ignored. It was considered too "stark," revealing an "intelligence that is all on the surface, with neither feeling, nor passion, enthusiasm, ideal, insight, thought, nor depth." One critic went so far as to say that the work was "not a novel" but merely a narrative that by being real "ceases to interest." What must have been difficult for contemporaries to accept was the strong attack on their generation and culture, the hopelessness of Flaubert's disillusionment.

But the most devastating aspect of Flaubert's critique was really structural. He implied, by linking background and foreground in this way, that the political and emotional were inseparable. This is to say, the failure of his characters was not the failure of an individual hero in a novel but of the entire social structure. France had become the character whose sentiments had not only failed to be educated but probably were never really there in the first place. We are not surprised to read another critic who complained that the colors of Flaubert's palette were "filth." Flaubert was never more correct than when he said that "the public only wants books that encourage its illusions, whereas *Sentimental Education*" clearly does not.

Flaubert's final works are a mixed grouping of tales, short stories, and long, strangely unnovelistic pieces. Flaubert published a reworked version of *The Temptation of Saint Anthony* and three short stories, all the while working on a final novel, *Bouvard and Pécuchet*, during the 1870's. *The Temptation of Saint Anthony,* a novel he described as "the work of my whole life," was the youthful work rejected by Flaubert's friends, reworked in middle age, and finally rewritten in 1872. As in the earlier versions and in the myth itself, Saint Anthony the Hermit is assailed by a variety of tempters who try to destroy his faith. In Flaubert's work, Saint Anthony cannot summon up refutations to this cumulative and powerful attack on religion, philosophy, and basic moral beliefs. The reader is ultimately placed on the side of the tempters, and the message of the devil seems to be the same as Flaubert's own bleak outlook on the impossibility of knowing or believing:

> All is illusion. Form may be an error of your senses. Substance an invention of your mind. Are you even sure you're alive? It may be that there is nothing.
>
> (ch. 6)

The work is pervaded by a profound negativity, all the more disturbing because of its all-inclusiveness. In early works Flaubert had attacked specific aspects of human life in particular epochs. Now he attacks the very enterprise of life itself, of consciousness, religion, and the necessity for morality.

In form, *The Temptation of Saint Anthony* is not a novel. It carries forward Flaubert's project of escaping the requirements of the traditional novel. There is barely a plot; the hermit merely sits in his cave and is assailed by each spirit in the manner of a medieval pageant play. The true subject of the book, as Michel Foucault points out in *Power/Knowledge,* is the history of books as repositories of cultural ideas and values. It is "a book produced from other books." In it we see the culmination of Flaubert's archaeological and scholarly modes of thought. The novel thus becomes a kind of encyclopedia or compendium that embraces all previous books, leaving aside the technology of fiction—character, plot, development—for a direct appropriation of knowledge.

*Bouvard and Pécuchet* was Flaubert's next project, and one he was to die before completing. It was a work intended to destroy once and for all the last remnants of the traditional novel, replacing them with the ultimate statement of encyclopedic form. *Bouvard and Pécuchet* supersedes *The Temptation of Saint Anthony* by concentrating not on the single focus of religion, but on the multitude of works that constitute all past and contemporary knowledge spewing out from "the unlimited proliferation of printed paper," as Foucault puts it. The story is simple: two middle-aged men meet by chance in a cafe in Paris and discover that they both are copyists—that is, the nineteenth-century equivalents of Xerox machines. They become fast friends, and when one of them inherits money, they decide to escape the oppression of city life to buy a country house. There they pursue nothing less than all the branches of human knowledge in a maniacally programmatic manner. They study agriculture, but fail to produce crops. They move on to another subject, devour every book, and then move on again—traversing philosophy, religion, history, science, medicine, cooking, and so on. The novel is often nothing more than a huge list of books consulted, with an occasional episode of sexual adventure or trouble with the neighbors.

Flaubert died before finishing volume 1, but the ending he envisaged would have had the two clerks renounce all learning and return to copying. The second volume of the work would be composed of all the quotations they had copied; it was to be Flaubert's grandest and final attack on human stupidity, containing verbatim the innumerable foolish things actually said or written by scholars and thinkers. This second volume was to serve "to spew out on my contemporaries the contempt they inspire in me, even if I break my ribs in the attempt." In keeping with the misanthropic tone, he adds that he wants to "exhale my resentment, spew forth my hatred, expectorate my spleen, ejaculate my anger, deterge my indignation." It seems fitting that he died in the attempt.

The third and final volume was to be a "Dictionary of Received Ideas"—the alphabetical compendium of the clichés and trite expressions of the Garçon and society in general. It would include "in alphabetical order and on every possible subject, all you need to say in public to pass for a decent, agreeable fellow." It goes without saying that Flaubert did not like decent, agreeable fellows. That third volume does exist in incomplete form and amounts to a powerfully funny satire of routinized thought, as trenchant as Jonathan Swift's *Polite Conversation* (1738).

The totality of the projected work amounted to nothing less than a cannonade on institutions, knowledge, systems, and the capacity of humans to help themselves through education. "I want to prove," Flaubert wrote to Maupassant, "that any education of whatever kind doesn't mean much, and that human nature means everything, or nearly everything." With this sweeping condemnation of education, Flaubert is left in a strange position. He still allows that the only escape from mediocrity—and mediocrity here includes the very enterprise of being human for the past two thousand years—is art.

Yet Flaubert's art by this stage had become merely a collection of lists about the mediocrity of life. The ultimate goal of his art—form—had become simply the walls of this warehouse of human stupidity. His prized form of expression—the book—could only condense and reproduce other books. Without a political critique like that of Zola, Dickens, George Eliot, or William Morris, Flaubert was unable to provide any alternative to humanity's stupidity. He was therefore caught in the paradox that his art—unless it lost itself in some Oriental reverie—was unable to create a vision of anything other than that stupidity he reviled.

Flaubert was aware of this impasse. He had heard enough criticism of his work to accept the charge that he was unable to create characters for whom one might have sympathy. His old friend George Sand made this very charge to Flaubert, and in response he wrote a short tale, "A Simple Heart," to balance out *Bouvard and Pécuchet,* which he was composing at the same time. "A Simple Heart" portrays a servant woman who lives, in Flaubert's words,

> an obscure life, the life of a poor country girl who is pious but faithful without fuss, and tender as new bread. She loves a man, her mistress's children, her nephew, an old man whom she tends, and finally her parrot. When the parrot dies she has it stuffed, and when she too dies she confuses the parrot with the Holy Ghost.
>
> (Nadeau, p. 252)

The story is written in a style that Flaubert emphasizes is "not ironical . . . it is very serious and very sad." His aim was "to move, to bring tears to the eyes of the tender-hearted; I am tender-hearted myself." This is Flaubert's genuine attempt to avoid the problem of encyclopedism and aestheticism, and it turns out to be a wonderfully moving work. However, it is so atypical of Flaubert that critics seem to have to apologize for its style or else insist on reading it in an ironic mode. In some way it is like the story of an Emma Bovary—but this one a provincial woman who has never read a novel, who accepts her lot in life, and who never has an ironic narrator to set her misery into folly.

Two other short stories of this period seem to partake of this exceptionally sympathetic writing—"Saint Julian the Hospitaller" and "Hérodias." The first story movingly recounts the legend of Saint Julian, detailing his miserable punishment for his sadistic attachment to hunting and his eventual salvation, as he floats heavenward on the body of Christ, who emerges from the body of a rotting leper. The second tale concerns the biblical episode of Salome and Saint John the Baptist. Here, in another atypical moment for Flaubert, redemption is offered at the end of the work when Herod weeps before the ghastly head of John, and the followers of Christ say, "Take heart! He has gone down to the dead to proclaim the coming of Christ." This is quite a different ending from Deslauriers and Frédéric's musings on brothels in *Sentimental Education.*

These stories, while they each pick up a thread of Flaubert's literary obsessions—provincial realism, myth, and antiquity—are essentially counterpoints to the direction of Flaubert's last major works. Those final novels reveal the truly unusual insights Flaubert had over his contemporaries. These radical experiments with narrative attempt to write about ideology, to contain within themselves the collected cultural monuments of the period, to become repositories of collected knowledge and at the same time showplaces for the futility of that knowledge.

Looking back on Flaubert's career, one notices a sweeping movement from romantic to nihilist, from lyrical to encyclopedic, from scorn for daily life to scorn for the very idea of life. In *Les romanciers naturalistes* (1893), Zola pointed out the effect of this change, attributing it in part to Flaubert's obsession with documenting through books the stupidity of humans:

> Note that his books are all there, that he had never done anything but study this imbecility, even in the splendid visions of *The Temptation of Saint Anthony.* He simply flung his admirable

> style over human folly, and I mean the lowest, the most vulgar, with occasional vistas of the wounded poet.

Indeed, Flaubert's critique, ungrounded as it was in any sense of history or explanation, grew more and more centered on folly and form—folly to keep the flames of savage indignation roaring, and form to elevate the attempt to the holiness of artistic style. Perhaps Zola understood this paradox best when he wrote that Flaubert's

> desire for perfection was, in the novelist, a real sickness that exhausted and immobilized him. If we follow him carefully, from this point of view, from *Madame Bovary* to *Bouvard and Pécuchet,* we shall see him gradually become preoccupied with form, reduce his vocabulary, increasingly limit the humanity of his characters. To be sure, this endowed French literature with perfect masterpieces. But it was sad to see this powerful talent relive the ancient fable of the nymphs who were changed to stone. Slowly, from the legs to the waist, then to the head, Flaubert turned to marble.

Ironically, it was in marble that Flaubert was immortalized by the world that had been the object of his intense and lifelong indignation. It is an irony Flaubert would not have failed to miss.

## Selected Bibliography


EDITIONS

INDIVIDUAL WORKS

*Madame Bovary.* Paris, 1857.

*Salammbô.* Paris, 1862.

*L'Éducation sentimentale: histoire d'un jeune homme.* Paris, 1869.

*La tentation de Saint Antoine.* Paris, 1874.

*Trois contes.* Paris, 1877. Contains "Un coeur simple," "La légende de Saint Julien l'Hospitalier," and "Hérodias."

*Bouvard et Pécuchet.* Paris, 1881.

*Premières oeuvres.* Paris, 1914–1920. Contains *Novembre.*

*La première Éducation sentimentale.* Paris, 1963.

*Dictionnaire des idées reçues, suivi des Mémoires d'un fou.* Edited by Claude Bonnefoy. Paris, 1964.

COLLECTED WORKS

*Oeuvres complètes.* 23 vols. Paris, 1910–1933. Includes thirteen vols. of letters.

*Oeuvres.* Edited by C. Thibaudet and R. Dumesnil. 2 vols. Paris, 1946–1948.

TRANSLATIONS

*Bouvard and Pecuchet.* Translated by A. J. Krailsheimer. New York, 1976.

*Dictionary of Accepted Ideas.* Translated by Jacques Barzun. New York, 1954.

*First Sentimental Education.* Translated by D. Garman. Berkeley, Calif., 1972.

*Flaubert in Egypt: A Sensibility on Tour.* Translated and edited by F. Steegmuller. Boston, 1973; Chicago, 1979.

*Intimate Notebooks, 1840–1841.* Translated by F. Steegmuller. Garden City, N.Y., 1967.

*Madame Bovary.* Translated by E. Marx-Aveling. New York, 1918.

————. Translated by F. Steegmuller. New York, 1957.

————. Translated by P. de Man. New York, 1965.

*November.* Translated by F. Jellinek, New York, 1932. The 1967 edition contains an introduction by F. Steegmuller.

*Salammbô.* Translated by A. J. Krailsheimer. New York, 1977.

*Selected Letters.* Translated and edited by F. Steegmuller. New York, 1953.

*Sentimental Education.* Translated by L. Hearn. New York, 1911. Edited by F. Carmody. Kentfield, Calif., 1974.

*Three Tales.* Translated by R. Baldick. Baltimore, 1961.

BIOGRAPHICAL AND CRITICAL STUDIES

Bart, B. F., ed. *Madame Bovary and the Critics: A Collection of Essays.* New York, 1966.

Levin, Harry. *The Gates of Horn*. Oxford, 1963.

Nadeau, Maurice. *The Greatness of Flaubert*. Translated by B. Bray. New York, 1972.

Sartre, Jean-Paul. *The Family Idiot: Gustave Flaubert*. Vol 1: 1821–1857. Chicago, 1981.

Spencer, Phillip. *Flaubert: A Biography*. New York, 1952.

Starkie, Enid. *Flaubert: The Making of the Master*. New York, 1967.

———. *Flaubert: The Master*. New York, 1971.

Steegmuller, Francis. *Flaubert and Madame Bovary: A Double Portrait*. New York, 1939. Rev. ed., New York, 1968, and Chicago, 1977.

LENNARD J. DAVIS

# SIGMUND FREUD

## *(1856–1939)*

IT HAS BEEN rightly said that we know more about Freud than about any other person in the history of mankind, and yet an extraordinary amount of primary material about him has not yet been brought to light. Freud's contemporaries had the advantage of listening to him, but it always remains for a succeeding age to be able to read more of his writings. Relative to Freud's contemporaries, we are privileged, even though a great part of Freud's works have still not been published. We may safely estimate that most of the unpublished writing consists of correspondence; indeed, Freud stands as one of the most prolific letter-writers in all of world literature.

No one else discovered so much about the workings of the human mind as did Freud. He gave us an unmatched method for studying the mind at its deepest levels; he explored and formulated the sexual complexity of individual and family life as no one else had previously done, and in so doing he revolutionized the entire field of psychopathology. It is one thing when a scientist invents a new instrument; it is quite another to proceed from that to make discoveries and construct a body of theory. Freud did both and more; with a knowledge that can be described as encyclopedic, he extended his findings in all kinds of directions in a profound way. He not only added considerably to the accumulated store of human knowledge but also radically altered the manner in which we look at our lives. Of all people living in our century, Freud was the one who most influenced it in various cultural ways. Such influence had both inspiring and unsettling aspects. Although Freud elaborated a dream theory that was a veritable rhetoric of the unconscious and that discovered poetry in each one of us, he also troubled the sleep of the world, ranking among the three men who have dealt severe blows to its narcissism. The first blow was a cosmological one administered by the sixteenth-century astronomer Nicholas Copernicus; he refuted geocentric theory and showed instead that we live on a relatively small fragment of matter revolving around the sun. Man's importance was next belittled by the biological findings of Charles Darwin, whose demonstration of evolution undercut our detachment from the animal world. Finally, Freud convincingly proved that man is not the master that he thinks he is over his own consciousness, rationality, and will.

Because of the particular nature of Freud's writings, they are still read as pertinent and timely classics in the field of psychoanalysis, which is thus singular among the sciences, whose founders are usually studied today merely for their historical interest. This fact, along with Freud's gigantic stature and the capital importance he ascribed to early development, helps to explain the surprising kinship between psychoanalysis and theology: they are both fields whose practitioners constantly have their originator in mind. It is certainly revelatory that a Jew, and not a Christian, discovered psychoanalysis; as Freud said in "Die Widerstände gegen die Psychoanalyse" ("Resistances to Psychoanalysis," 1925), it was his experience of social ostracism as a Jew and his consequent situation of solitary opposition that contributed to his founding a new science. Freud's discovery was facilitated because the prejudice of European Christians against the Jews placed the latter at a vantage point from which it was easier to examine the vicious irrationality of oppressors' self-justifying invocation of morality and supreme reason. The latter point may help to correct an all too common belief that the psychoanalyst's novel instruments are introspection and empathy—an injustice to mystical traditions that predate psychoanalysis by many centuries and that have formulated delicately honed procedures to refine one's introspection and empathy. Freud's contribution, in relation to these traditions, is to turn self-examination toward the unconscious traces of drive and defense. Freud's great historical innovation is to enhance introspection and empathy by self-analysis in its technical sense, that is, by the analysis of one's constellations of drive and defense.

In spite of his epochal brilliance as a scientist, the only prize Freud received while living was the Goethe Prize for literature. Albert Einstein's praise is confirmatory: "I do not know any contemporary who has presented his subject in the German language in such a masterly fashion." Other writers, such as Thomas Mann and Stefan Zweig, joined in the consensus that Freud was one of the exemplary masters of German prose. His writing shows a superb artistry in an astonishing number of different genres, from history, biography, autobiography, and letters to lectures, dialogues, case histories, and scientific treatises.

An account of Freud's life begins appropriately with his father. Jakob Freud (1815–1896) married his first wife, Sally Kramer, in 1831; they had two sons, Emmanuel (1833–1914) and Philipp (1836–1911). In 1852 Jakob's first wife died and it seems that he remarried, only to become a widower again not long afterward; then in 1855 he entered into marriage with Amalie Nathansohn (1835–1930). On 6 May of the next year Jakob and Amalie had their first child, Sigmund, who was born in Freiberg, a small Moravian village of less than five thousand people. (Today it is called Příbor and is located in Czechoslovakia.) In the next ten years Sigmund's mother had seven other children, five of whom were girls; one of her two sons, Julius, died at the age of eight months, when Sigmund himself was slightly less than two years old. Much has been said about the fact that Sigmund's uncles and half brothers, Emmanuel and Philipp, were approximately the age of his mother and that Sigmund was just a little older than his nephew John. This unusual familial entanglement undoubtedly influenced Freud's later explanation of the family romance, which is a child's fantasy that he is of noble lineage and that those claiming to be his parents are imposters. Before we follow Jakob Freud as he left with his family for Leipzig in 1859, we should mention another significant detail in the life of young Sigmund in Freiberg: he had an unforgettable Roman Catholic nanny who took him to mass and who talked to him of hell and heaven.

In 1860, after a short stay in Leipzig, Jakob took his family to Vienna, where he continued with his struggling merchant business. Not surprisingly, young Sigmund proved to be a brilliant student, usually coming out at the top of his class. In 1873 he enrolled for a medical doctor's degree at the University of Vienna, but because of his passion for research and for further study both inside and outside of medicine, he completed his medical training in eight years instead of the usual five. From 1876 to 1882 he worked in the physiological laboratory of the famous Ernst Brücke, who, along with Hermann Helmholtz, had propounded a biophysics and a mechanistic determinism of the human organism. Then Freud studied for a while under Theodor Meynert, the most famous specialist in brain anatomy of the day; thanks to Meynert's influence, Freud went on to become a neurologist (he was never a psychiatrist), eventually establishing himself as an authority on children's cerebral palsy. A third influential figure was Jean-Martin Charcot, at whose Parisian clinic Freud trained for several months during 1885 and 1886; there he became more alert to the psychological aspect of hysterical manifestations. When Freud returned from Paris, he married Martha Bernays, ending a four-year engagement.

A special place must be reserved for another of Freud's teachers, Josef Breuer. From 1880 to 1882 Breuer treated a woman now known by her pseudonym, Anna O. Breuer confided to Freud that he had hypnotized her, that she then recalled the original situations in which her several hysterical symptoms arose, and that her symptoms putatively disappeared when she expressed the suppressed emotion attached to the original causes. (Thus the term "cathartic therapy" was derived.) Gradually Freud became convinced of the far-reaching implications of this case. It was partly due to his own growing clinical convictions and partly due to Breuer's diminished objection to publicity that the case only appeared in print over ten years later (along with explanatory essays and other cases) in a collaborative work called *Studien über Hysterie* (*Studies in Hysteria,* 1893–1895). Despite their differences, Freud and the older Breuer agreed on two important notions that informed their coauthored venture: rather than being nonsensical, hysterical symptoms are fully meaningful and stand as substitutes for other mental acts, and as the patient discovers their meaning, the relevant symptoms disappear.

A key area of disagreement between Breuer and Freud concerned the importance of sexuality in the origin of neuroses. When the two went their separate professional ways, Freud felt more able to pursue his intuitions and observations about sexuality's decisive role. He became convinced that hysteria was traceable to a real sexual trauma experienced in one's life. (This theory is known as the seduction hypothesis.) But within a short time, Freud came to doubt this hypothesis and, after a period of self-doubt, proclaimed that fantasy might serve just as well as a trigger to neurotic formation.

As Freud's association with Breuer foundered, his friendship with Wilhelm Fliess intensified, so much so that Freud's semiofficial biographer Ernest Jones called it the only truly unusual experience in Freud's life. Freud found Fliess much more ready than Breuer to accord sexuality a central position, even though Fliess's approach to the subject was predominantly physiological rather than psychological. For a number of years Freud devalued himself in comparison with Fliess, whom he elevated unrealistically. Fliess acted not only as Freud's personal physician but also as a sort of personal savior. It was as though, in order to sustain the audacity of his originality and to alleviate his attendant guilt and shame, Freud had to cast Fliess in the role of supreme authority. By 1900 the intense friendship between Freud and Fliess was essentially over, after thirteen years. The split came as a result of Freud's growing independence and his skepticism about Fliess's powerful physiological theories.

During that friendship Freud started his self-analysis, which, from 1897 on, evolved into a systematic one. It was a heroic, painful experience, an unrepeatable one, for no one after Freud can be so innocent again; it was excruciating for a man of Freud's conservative background to acknowledge his murderous wishes against his deceased, beloved father and to confront in such solitude the longstanding variety and extent of his sexual longings. Besides improving his personal life in certain respects, the self-analysis facilitated his discovery of the importance of infantile sexuality, the functioning of bisexuality in neurosis, and some of the psychic significance of dreams.

From 1900 to 1905 Freud published a series of five distinguished works, which were influenced in various ways by his self-analysis: *Die Traumdeutung* (*The Interpretation of Dreams,*

1900), *Zur Psychopathologie des Alltagslebens* (*The Psychopathology of Everyday Life,* 1901), a case history of a female hysteric entitled "Bruchstück einer Hysterie-Analyse" ("Fragment of an Analysis of a Case of Hysteria," 1905), *Drei Abhandlungen zur Sexualtheorie* (*Three Essays on the Theory of Sexuality,* 1905), and *Der Witz und seine Beziehung zum Unbewussten* (*Jokes and Their Relation to the Unconscious,* 1905). Except for the case history, a common concern runs through the above texts. In the book on dreams Freud showed that although the technique of free association was first enlisted in relation to symptoms, it was potentially more revelatory when he applied it to dreams. Dreams were not pathological processes in themselves, and it was in interpreting those phenomena that Freud discovered the most about unconscious processes in normal as well as pathological psychic life. In *The Psychopathology of Everyday Life,* Freud investigated the unconscious processes underlying verbal slips, slips of the pen, and the like, committed by healthy people, thereby demonstrating again the continuity between normal and pathological mental events. In the *Three Essays,* Freud propounded a larger view of sexuality, one that established a continuity between infantile, normal adult, and perverse sexual life. Likewise, in the book on jokes, Freud demonstrated that the same processes that formed dreams went into the making of jokes.

In the opening years of the twentieth century, Freud was ending the period of his self-described "splendid isolation." The small group gathered around him slowly increased to include Alfred Adler, Karl Abraham, Sándor Ferenczi, Otto Rank, Carl Jung, and Jones. In 1909 Freud and Jung went to the United Sates, where they lectured and received honorary doctorates at Clark University. In 1910 the International Psychoanalytic Association was founded, and organizational splits soon followed—first Adler in 1911, then Jung in 1914, and Rank years afterward. Predictably, when World War I broke out, organized psychoanalysis suffered; yet it was precisely during that time that Freud wrote up his papers on metapsychology, which framed psychoanalytic theory in a highly abstract language dealing with conflict and psychic energy. Slightly later he delivered at the University of Vienna the *Vorlesungen zur Einführung in die Psychoanalyse* (*Introductory Lectures on Psycho-Analysis,* 1916–1917), a brilliant general presentation that still retains its usefulness.

When the war ended, Freud was over sixty years old, but that did not prevent him from entering into one of his most prolific periods. In 1920 he promulgated a new theory of the drives in *Jenseits des Lustprinzips* (*Beyond the Pleasure Principle,* 1920). In 1923 his *Das Ich und das Es* (*The Ego and the Id*) offered a novel picture of the mind according to which there are three agencies, the ego, the id, and the superego, the latter two threatening to overpower the ego. In 1926 Freud published his last major theoretical work, which he titled *Hemmung, Symptom und Angst* (*Inhibitions, Symptoms and Anxiety*). In it Freud revised his theory of anxiety, now seeing it as a signal by which the ego indicates some imminent danger; he also disputed Rank's idea that the trauma of human birth was the source of all subsequent anxiety. Then, in 1933, Freud published the *Neue Folge der Vorlesungen zur Einführung in die Psychoanalyse* (*New Introductory Lectures on Psycho-Analysis*), a supplementary series profitable to both the beginning and more advanced student and a locus of some controversial Freudian remarks on female psychology.

Starting in 1923, Freud was also preoccupied in another way—he had cancerous tumors in the palatal region, which necessitated over thirty operations before his death in 1939. Throughout this period, he tolerated the pain with an astounding courage, which even grew when he confronted the dispossessing Gestapo in 1938. Thanks to international cooperation, Freud was able to leave Vienna and settle down in England for his last days. It is entirely in keeping with Freud's strong moral personality that the last item he published in his lifetime—a letter that appeared in the review *Time and Tide* in 1938—dealt with anti-Semitism in England.

A further word might be said about Freud's character. Perhaps his most outstanding personal trait was his courage. It was that quality, along with his enormous intellectual powers of observation, analysis, imagination, and memory (photographic and phonographic), that enabled him to create the discipline of psychoanalysis. Overall, he was a rather stoic man of exceptional industry and determination; he also combined a revolutionary spirit with a firm belief in the triumph of reason and experiment. To family, friends, and needy visitors Freud repeatedly evinced extraordinary financial generosity, accompanied by his typical self-effacement, which partially explains why that quality of his has all too often gone unappreciated by commentators. On the other hand, if he was considerate, he could often be stern and harsh to a degree that intensified his problematic relationships with many of his male friends. Apparently Freud's relationships with women were not so affected by the deep-seated ambivalence revealed in his self-confessed need to always have both an intimate friend and a detested enemy.

Although Freud enjoys classic stature as a world writer, he is primarily important for having founded the psychoanalytic movement. Without understanding that, we hardly render appreciative justice to Freud, not only as the pioneer in a new science but also as a peerless expounder of that science.

The science Freud founded embodies more than a theory of the mind; psychoanalysis is a theory of repression and resistance as well as an explanation of the crucial role of sexuality and of the Oedipus complex. First, in conformity with its character as a depth psychology, traditional psychoanalysis considered the processes of the mind from three points of view: the dynamic, the economic, and the topographical (this triad constitutes Freud's so-called metapsychology). According to the dynamic standpoint, all mental processes—apart from the reception of external stimuli—interplay and form compromises with each other. The contents of these mental processes are governed by the compulsion to repeat and are represented as persistent images or ideas that are emotionally charged (e.g., the image of a hostile parent). In terms of Freud's final theoretical formulations, these investments derive from two possible drives: Thanatos, or the drive toward destruction and the dissolution of life, and Eros, the striving of all living things for closer union. (The manifestation of Eros as mental energy is called the libido.) In sum, the dynamic standpoint refers to psychic conflict that is based on the interaction of the two drives and their mental and affective derivatives.

From the economic point of view, the mental representatives of the drives are invested by the mind's instinctive tendency to reduce unpleasure and increase pleasure. The purpose of the mind or psychic apparatus is to keep the amount of excitation as low as possible in accordance with the pleasure principle, unpleasure being related to an increase of excitation and pleasure to a decrease. In the regular course of development, the pleasure principle is modified by its encounters with the external world and yields its place to the reality principle; according to the latter, the mind tolerates transient feelings of unpleasure in order to achieve the even greater, if delayed, pleasure of satisfaction.

We now come to the third or topographical point of view from which Freud theoretically considered the mental processes. Topographically, the mind is divisible into the conscious, preconscious, and unconscious. The great division here exists between the conscious and the unconscious, the latter consisting of repressed material and therefore incapable of being brought to consciousness by an act of volitional attention. On the other hand, the preconscious relates to those mental contents of which we are not aware at any particular moment but that are capable of achieving consciousness by an act of volitional attention.

Later, without abandoning the duality of the topographical theory of the mind, Freud proposed a tripartite categorization, generally known as the structural theory. In the structural sense, the mind is comprised of: the id, the repository of the drives, whose processes are fully unconscious; the ego, the site of reason, common sense, and perception of the external world, whose processes and contents nevertheless are mostly unconscious; and the superego, the site of self-observation and self-criticism, whose processes and contents are partly conscious but mostly unconscious.

There is finally the psychoanalytic theory of neuroses, which is founded on three cornerstones: the importance of repression, of the sexual drives, and of transference. Any attempt on the part of the psychoanalyst to dislodge the repressed from the patient's unconscious encounters resistance. At the same time, those unconscious impulses undergo what Freud described as "the return of the repressed" ("Weitere Bemerkungen über die Abwehrneuropsychosen" ["Further Remarks on the Neuropsychoses of Defence," 1896]). In such instances, the repressed material makes a compromise that alone allows it to enter consciousness. Neurotic symptoms, then, are compromise formations that stand as moderated satisfactions substituting for the full satisfactions that would result from an unconditional lifting of repression.

It is the sexual drive that is subject to the most repression throughout the various stages of life. Developmentally, psychosexual life is divisible into three stages: (1) the oral stage, extending into the second year of life and centering on the mouth and lips as erogenous zones; (2) the anal phase, lasting until the age of four, focusing on the anal erogenous zone, first in terms of pleasurable retention and later in terms of pleasurable elimination, and involving significant sadistic strivings and the voluntary control of the sphincter; and (3) the genital phase, beginning around the age of three and lasting approximately until the end of the fifth year, during which time there is a chiefly genital focus of sexual stimulation. Proper to this latter phase is the child's nuclear neurosis and most important conflict, the Oedipus complex, which consists of mainly unconscious ideas and feelings attending the wish to possess the parent of the opposite sex and to eliminate that of the same sex. (The term "Oedipus complex" applies to both sexes; the more accurate term for females, the Electra complex, has not gained wide currency.) In this Oedipal period the superego begins to assume its final form as the internalization of parental prohibition. Through internalization the superego becomes heir to the Oedipus complex; it forces the child to forsake certain gratifications and, in the case of violations of the internalized prohibitions, to be subject to self-guilt.

The so-called pregenital organizations, the oral and anal phases, are points at which the libido may become fixated and to which, if triggered by repression, it may regress; the form of any subsequent neurosis is determined by these infantile libidinal fixations. On the other hand, resolving the Oedipus complex involves the successful passage from autoerotic love to one capable of mature, true intimacy with another.

A further remark: transference is not restricted to the analytic setting; rather, being a universal phenomenon, it bears traces and patterns of the affectionate and hostile relationship that the child had with his parental figures and that he repeats variously with others in his later life.

Under the definition of psychoanalysis as a method of treating psychological disorders, it is appropriate to consider the evolution of psychoanalytic technique from its crude beginnings to its later refinements. Only toward the very end of 1887 did Freud try to treat patients with hypnosis; before that he used the standard techniques of massage, hydrotherapy, and electric stimulation. Although spurred on by Breuer, Freud gradually realized that using hypnosis to achieve catharsis did not produce the long-lasting desired results; that is, the catharsis or discharge of emotion attached to a previously repressed experience did not necessarily make symptoms disappear. Other factors involved in Freud's disillusionment with hypnosis were that not all patients could be hypnotized and that he himself was not a good hypnotist.

At this point Freud recalled that during his second stay in France, Hippolyte Bernheim had demonstrated that patients could be made to remember merely by the therapist's suggestion. Convinced, then, that patients really retained everything that was pathologically important and that it was merely a matter of obliging them to express it verbally, Freud commanded his patients to lie down, to shut their eyes, and, aided by the pressure of his hand on their foreheads, to communicate their emerging memories.

The next great technical step was the discovery of free association, which, according to many, ranks as the greatest of all Freud's discoveries. The endorsement of free association and the patient's attendant free choice to cooperate or not shows how far Freud moved away from the authoritarianism of hypnotic technique, which also had the disadvantages of concealing the patient's resistances and psychic processes from the therapist. With Freud's technique of free association, on the other hand, the patient was invited to put himself in a self-observing state and to say whatever came to him, even though he felt it to be disagreeable, reprehensible, nonsensical, trivial, or irrelevant. Freud called the reliance on free association the fundamental technical rule of analysis. He was not, however, oblivious to the paradoxical link between free association and determinism in that the ideas dredged up by the patient are really not free but are interconnected and linked in a determined way back to basic starting points. Such determinism permitted Freud to detect fundamental laws governing psychological life.

In this therapeutic venture, Freud proposed that the analyst be seated out of sight behind the reclining patient, maintaining himself in an evenly suspended attention in order to capture the drift of the patient's unconscious with his own unconscious. Aided by an *Einfühlung* (empathy) by which he would "feel" his way into the patient's psychic life, the analyst would present his interpretations; by means of them, he would explain the unconscious meanings found in the patient's symptoms, dreams, associations, and most important of all, the transference. It was in treating Dora that Freud learned that transference—the process by which a patient displaces onto his analyst his reactions to significant figures from his past life—is not only the greatest obstacle to obtaining a cure but also the analyst's most powerful therapeutic instrument. Transference functions ambiguously in the clinical working-through of the patient's resistances to the emergence of unconscious content into the conscious sphere. Looking back on Freud's technical evolution up to this point, we can see that he shifted his analytic focus from interpreting drive derivatives to interpreting resistances; concurrently, removing symptoms was no longer his primary aim per se, for overcoming a patient's resistances was thought to bring about the disappearance of symptoms as a secondary result.

Between 1910 and 1915 Freud introduced the notion of countertransference, i.e., the analyst's transference onto the patient ("Die zukünftigen Chancen der psychoanalytischen Therapie" ["The Future Prospects of Psycho-Analytic Therapy," 1910]), and also wrote six papers on technique. Though far from being a systematic elaboration of psychoanalytic technique, these papers give valuable guidelines about conducting a psychoanalytic treatment and understanding its phenomena. With notable emphasis, he pointed out that "every single association, every act of the person under treatment must reckon with the resistance," that transference emerges "as the most powerful resistance" ("Zur Dynamik der Übertragung" ["The Dynamics of Transference," 1912]) and is a piece of repetition, that a patient begins treatment by repeating instead of remembering, and that his ordinary illness acquires new meaning and is recapitulated as a "transference neurosis" whereby the analyst becomes the focal figure at whom the patient's conflicts are directed. By way of essential clarification, I should add that the foregoing remarks represent Freud's textual exposition but not necessarily his practice—how one theorizes and how one applies one's theories may be two different matters. In actual fact, despite his growing awareness of the transference, Freud continued to ascribe importance to memory retrieval and reconstruction of past events to a far greater degree than would many contemporary analysts, who ascribe greater importance to the transference and interaction in the current analytic setting.

We should not leave the consideration of psychoanalytic technique without trying to capture afresh some of its novelty. Due to many causes, including a benumbing popularization arising from the mass media, the originality of the psychoanalytic setting has been, in Erik Erikson's words, undercut and made subject to the "metabolism of the generations." But to realize the true meaning of that setting, we must appreciate the Renaissance openness of Freud—nothing alien was alien to him. Accordingly, he constructed a situation in which one was invited to complete freedom of expression without the constraints of criticism and condemnation; those who had previously risked being social outcasts for their bizarre, irrational, asocial behavior could now find out, in a context of cooperation and respect, that such behavior was indeed full of human meanings.

The undeniable value of psychoanalysis as a therapy, though, should not tempt us to neglect its pertinence to other fields. Indeed, a number of scholars specialize in what they call Freud's works of applied psychoanalysis, in which Freud applied psychoanalytic techniques to other disciplines. This descriptive epithet, however, is quite misleading. On the one hand, applied psychoanalysis is to be found in various remarks strewn throughout Freud's entire opus and hence is erroneously restricted to selected works. On the other hand and more significantly, the term "applied psychoanalysis" has a unidirectional, imperialistic note to it; more accurately and democratically, we ought to speak of psychoanalysis being variously co-involved or, better yet, coapplicable with a number of other disciplines.

This said, because of limited space, only the briefest mention can be made of some of Freud's writings in the fields of aesthetics, the social sciences, and religion. In *Der Wahn und die Träume in W. Jensens "Gradiva"* (*Delusions and Dreams in Jensen's "Gradiva,"* 1907), Freud showed how the structures of the dreams and delusions of the novel's protagonist correspond to those encountered in psychoanalytic practice. Turning to sculpture, Freud offered a fascinating, detailed study of the artist's conception in "Der Moses des Michelangelo" ("The Moses of Michelangelo," 1914). Freud's personal favorite among his works was his first elaborate psychoanalytic biography, *Eine Kindheitserinnerung des Leonardo da Vinci* (*Leonardo da Vinci and a Memory of His Childhood,* 1910). Freud examined the unconscious erotic ties that bind a group to its leader in *Massenpsychologie und Ich-Analyse* (*Group Psychology and the Analysis of the Ego,* 1921), his most outstanding contribution to social psychology. Two texts on religion may also be mentioned here. In *Die Zukunft einer Illusion* (*The Future of an Illusion,* 1927), Freud asserted that religion was an illusion arising from an infantile belief in the omnipotence of thought; and one of the highly contested claims Freud made in his *Der Mann Moses und die Monotheistische Religion* (*Moses and Monotheism,* 1939) was that Moses was really an Egyptian. In comparing the two latter works, Freud described himself as progressing from a conception of religion as sheer illusion to a conception of religion as embodying historical truth.

After the foregoing bird's-eye view of Freud's writing, we can move on to a more detailed study of five of his central works for the different blending of content and form in each. (One preliminary word of caution about the possibility of drawing inaccurate conclusions: the indication of multiple instinctual traces in Freud's writings does not necessarily disprove their propositions.) A masterpiece in psychoanalytic theory is *The Interpretation of Dreams,* by far the greatest of Freud's works, and a classic of world literature. The work is sui generis, blending autobiography, biography, literary analysis, history, and science, and brilliantly combining introspection, analysis, synthesis, imagination, and speculation. Starting from the tranquil assurance of the definite article in its title, *The Interpretation of Dreams* relentlessly overpowers the reader with insights and startling conclusions.

During the composition of his masterpiece, Freud was reportedly in a kind of waking dream state. To his friend Fliess, Freud confessed that when he sat down to write a paragraph he did not know where it would end. As a further illustration of his compositional freedom, he cited the joke about the horseman Itzig: "Itzig, where are you going?" "I don't know, but ask the horse." And yet, because of Freud's awesome intelligence, memory, and powers of concentration, there was an overriding expository control that counterpointed the oneiric, or dreamlike, drift of his work. Indeed, Freud's comment on *Oedipus Rex* in chapter 5 of *The Interpretation of Dreams* reflects also on his own writing:

> The action of the play consists in nothing other than a disclosure that is gradually increased and artistically delayed (a procedure comparable to psychoanalysis) telling us that Oedipus himself is the murderer of Laius and also that he is the son of the murdered man and Jocasta.
>
> (*Gesammelte Werke,* vols. 2–3, p. 268)

Parallel to the measured revelations of Sophocles is the incremental orchestration of Freud's theses. Thus his second chapter ends: "When the work of interpretation has been completed, we perceive that a dream is the fulfillment of a wish." The fourth chapter adds: "A dream is a (disguised) fulfillment of a (suppressed or repressed) wish." In the fifth chapter we read: "A succession of meanings or wish-fulfillments may be superimposed on one another, the bottom one being the fulfillment of a wish dating from earliest childhood." Then, in the final chapter, the simple formula is firmly fleshed out: "A wish that is represented in a dream must be an infantile one."

There is even a more striking organization to be found in the seven chapters of *The Interpretation of Dreams* when we realize that Freud associates the dream with a maternal identification. In chapters 2 and 7 Freud refers to the unfathomable core of the dream as its *Nabel* ("navel") and in the second instance it is further described as an inextricable point in a "tangle of dream-thoughts." Not only did Freud make an imaginative return to the womb in some particular dream or in his attempts to fathom it down to the navel, but he also arranged the book on dreams so that chapter by chapter he gets closer to understanding the navel. In the light of this maternal return, the book's whole is thus more than the sum of its parts.

Moreover, the nature imagery, which ranges from references to woods to references to high ground and which unifies *The Interpretation of Dreams,* symbolizes the body of a woman, precisely that of Freud's mother. Twice in his work Freud explicitly states that wood symbolizes the female, and in the *Introductory Lectures* he makes these pertinent statements about universal symbolism:

> The complicated topography of the female genital parts makes it understandable that they are very often represented as landscapes, with rocks, woods, and water. . . . "*Materia*" is derived from "*mater,*" "mother," and the material out of which anything originates is, so to speak, a mother to it. This ancient conception survives, therefore, in the symbolic use of wood for "woman" or "mother."
>
> (*Gesammelte Werke,* vol. 11, pp. 158–162)

Let us turn now to a well-known passage in Freud's letter to Fliess that imagistically describes the organization of the book on dreams:

> The whole thing is planned on the model of an imaginary walk. First comes the dark forest of authors (who do not see the trees), hopeless in a place where it is very easy to go astray. Then there is a ravine through which I lead the reader—my dream specimen with its peculiarities, its details, its indiscretions, and its bad jokes—and then suddenly the high ground and the view, and the question: "Which way do you want to go?"
>
> (*Briefe an Wilhelm Fliess,* p. 400)

Part of this passage is repeated verbatim in the initial lines of chapter 3 of *The Interpretation of Dreams,* where Freud and the reader suddenly emerge on high ground, and he proposes following one path among many. With chapter 5, he opens a new trail: "Now that we have reached our goal on this one path, we may return and choose a new starting-point for our rambles through the problems of the dream." At the opening of chapter 7, Freud looks back on the arduous journey: each path he has taken hitherto has led to light, but from now on every path will lead him back into darkness. It is highly meaningful that the dream's navel is mentioned in the seventh and last chapter for the second time. The previous chapters have prepared for an unprecedented theoretical examination of dream life in its depths.

Thus the journeying back and forth in the book on dreams involves Freud symbolically journeying inside and outside himself and his fantasized mother. In the specimen dream analysis in chapter 2, Freud associates his pregnant wife with the dream's heroine Irma and looks into her mouth-vagina. In an act of self-delivery, Freud emerges from this uterine chapter to the outer world, where he eventually encounters Oedipus in chapter 5. In terms of fantasy, then, *The Interpretation of Dreams* depicts a growing mastery over dreams and maternal figures and a development from the uterine to the pre-Oedipal and Oedipal stages of human maturation. All three stages figure imagistically in the final exploration of the mother's body in chapter 7, which, in the investigation of dream processes, reverts to their moment of inauguration, to the first memory trace and wish of the newborn child, and magnificently concludes that dreams of the future are molded by indestructible wishes into "a perfect likeness of the past."

To state it differently: dream processes are at once the book's subject and object, container and contained, form and matter. In composing this book, Freud confided to Fliess that he could make himself dream appropriate dreams—as if they were self-commanded performances. By the same token, he later recognized (as he wrote to Jung in 1911) a self-reflexiveness in what he himself censored and was defensive about: "The book proves the principles of dream interpretation by its own nature, so to speak, through its own deficiencies." The book on dreams not only describes but enacts what it describes. And it is this characteristic of enactive discourse that further ensures the unique position of *The Interpretation of Dreams* in the history of autobiography, and indeed in the whole of world literature, whether imaginative or scientific.

The foregoing examination prepares us to consider Freud's more strictly scientific analysis of dream formation. Within his enterprise of showing that dreams were anything but trivial and that they had profound meaning, Freud divides the dream into two basic parts, the manifest dream and the latent dream. The manifest dream is the dream dreamt, which the dreamer may be able to recall to various degrees in his waking state. The latent dream may draw upon nocturnal sensory stimuli, and more importantly, day residues, and most importantly, repressed infantile drives. The nocturnal sensory stimuli include such impressions as thirst and pain. For example, the dreamer may dream that he is slaking his thirst; in this sense, dreams may truly function as the guardians of sleep. Day residues are memory traces of experiences lived during the day or days prior to the dream; remaining active in the unconscious, they may, like the nocturnal sensory stimuli, appear in varying disguises in the manifest dream.

The core of the latent dream, however, is a wish or several wishes arising from the repressed infantile drives in the unconscious. The two qualifiers of the word "drives" must be seen in all their significance: the drives are repressed because the drive-related wishes were forbidden and therefore had to be driven away from consciousness; and they are infantile because the dream has a sedimented age, extending from the most recent to the most remote past. We might note that Freud insists that the repressed infantile wishes are not necessarily always of a sexual nature.

The manifest dream is the hallucinated expression of an unconscious wish or fantasy that is kept away from conscious waking life. The construction of the dream takes an appreciably longer period of time than the period of its actual staging—Freud makes the apt analogy of the relatively long preparation of fireworks and their short-lived explosion. Two other remarks are appropriate here: first, the "normal" hallucinatory nature of dreams in some ways is similar to the pathological thoughts of psychotic individuals in their waking state; and second, given the much lesser structuring in the child's mind in its process of development, the division of the dream into its manifest and latent parts is less pertinent for children's dreams than for adults'.

The passage from the latent to the manifest dream is effected by dreamwork, which Freud considered the quintessence of the dream. Even though sleep brings about a relaxation of repression so that unconscious wishes and fantasies may press forward for gratification, there is an alert censorship that ordinarily prevents their undisguised expression. It is here that the four principles of dreamwork come into play: displacement, condensation, symbolization, and representability. By virtue of the mechanism of displacement, affective energy formerly invested in a forbidden person is transferred onto a more neutral individual. Condensation, on the other hand, is the process whereby two or more images can be combined into a single image. (Conversely, a single latent wish may be distributed through several representations in the manifest content.) In symbolization, a fairly neutral object is substituted for one that is conflictingly charged and bears forbidden meanings. (For example, a tree stands for a penis.) Representability pertains ordinarily to the translatability of the latent content into the visual image of the manifest dream. (For example, the notion of understanding may be translated in the manifest dream as a person literally standing under something.)

To explain the effect of dreamwork, Freud invoked the military analogy of soldiers trying to pass beyond the enemy lines. Given the resistance at the line, the soldiers might well disguise themselves, preferably with the clothes of their enemy. Likewise, because of censorship, material cannot ordinarily pass into the manifest dream without undergoing various degrees of distortion. Thus the warded-off impulses may have recourse to the use of relatively neutral day residues and in that way pass into the manifest dream as compromise formations. Hence dream images are overdetermined in that they bear multiple meanings derived from multiple unconscious sources. A further difficulty in retrieving the original manifest dream is that sometime after it is dreamt, it is subject to what is called secondary elaboration, which imposes a logical coherence over the absurd and bizarre oneiric material. In the final analysis, then, the dream emerges as an extraordinarily complex phenomenon in mental life and testifies to the marvelous ways in which prohibited wishes may be fulfilled. In this regard, dreams of punishment do not really form an exception, for they may satisfy feelings of guilt and the attendant desire for reparative punishment.

Invaluable as what Freud called the royal road to the unconscious, the dream simultaneously manifests itself in three regressive ways: as a temporal regression from adulthood to childhood, as a topical regression from the conscious to the unconscious, and as a formal regression from the level of verbal language to the pictorial and symbolic representations proper to early life. In conclusion, we find it easy to agree with Freud's own estimate of *The Interpretation of Dreams:* "It contains, even according to my present-day judgment, the most valuable of all the discoveries it has been my good fortune to make. Insight such as this falls to one's lot but once in a lifetime."

*Totem und Tabu* (*Totem and Taboo,* 1913) comprises Freud's chief contribution to social anthropology, and it also constitutes a diptych with *The Interpretation of Dreams.* As Jones reports, Freud himself said that in the book on dreams he described the wish to kill the father, whereas in *Totem and Taboo* he portrayed the actual deed. It might additionally be noted that Thomas Mann admired the aesthetic quality of the prose of *Totem and Taboo,* and Freud held its fourth and last book to be the stylistic high point of his career.

Concentrating on the Australian aborigines, Freud makes conclusions about totemistic religion in general. For the aborigines, a totem, usually an animal, is venerated as the primeval ancestor of each entire clan. Where there are totems, there are usually interdictions against sexual or marital union among members of the same clan—thus the stricture to marry outside the totem (totemic exogamy) and thereby avoid group incest.

In its original sense, a taboo was an object or person who supposedly possessed mysterious powers and who was not to be touched—a situation provoking an ambivalent reaction of veneration and horror from tribal members. The principal prohibition regarding the taboo—that of touching—reminds us also of similar restraints in phobias and obsessional neuroses. By extension, taboos applied to actions, and even hostile thoughts about certain enemies, were gravely forbidden. If that hostility were carried to the point of killing an enemy, then the taboo broadened to include not only everything that came from the dead body but also its vindictive ghost. In the fear of that vindictiveness Freud sees the origin of conscience, for the death of the awesome other was both wanted and yet feared and not wanted. Sometimes, too, living rulers were the objects of the same ambivalence: if they were hated, they were also given mysterious powers; and if they were exalted above the lot of common mortals, they were also made to live a tormented, restricted existence tantamount to bondage.

But Freud's most daring hypothesis concerns the existence of the primal horde, and it is in the story of that horde that Freud first attempts to analyze the whole of man's social history. He sees totemism, therefore, as a decisive step in a hypothetical reconstruction linking the individual Oedipus complex and the prehistory of man. Indeed, Freud concludes that the origins not only of neurosis but also of religion, morals, society, and art converged in the Oedipus complex. Much of this is spelled out in Freud's famous and oft-cited passage about the primal horde:

> [In the primal horde] there was a violent, jealous father who kept all the females for himself and drove away his sons as they grew up. . . . One day the brothers who had been driven out came together, killed and devoured their father, and so made an end of the patriarchal horde. . . . The violent primal father had surely been the envied and feared model of each one of the company of brothers; and in the act of devouring him they accomplished their identification with him, and each one of them acquired a part of his strength. The totem meal, which is perhaps mankind's earliest festival, would be a repetition and a commemoration of this memorable and criminal deed, which was the beginning of so many things—social organization, moral restrictions and religion. . . . [Hence, according to what is now named deferred obedience, the sons] revoked their deeds in that they forbade the killing of the totem, the substitute for their father; and they renounced its fruits in that they resigned their claim to the women who were set free. They

> thus created out of their filial sense of guilt the two fundamental taboos of totemism, which on that very account had to correspond to the two repressed wishes of the Oedipus complex.
>
> (*Gesammelte Werke,* vol. 9, pp. 171–173)

My major concern is to show how the very writing of *Totem and Taboo* not only was retrospective but also acquired the value of a symbol of castration among the members of the growing psychoanalytic movement at the time. Awareness of the relevance of the treatise to Freud as father in relation to the surrounding analysts as sons is indispensable for any well-rounded appreciation of the treatise and accurately reveals it to be a current as well as retrospective reflection.

First of all, some dates are important. From 1910 to 1913 Freud wrote and completed *Totem and Taboo.* In the first of those years, 1910, Freud organized and chaired the international psychoanalytic congress at which the International Psychoanalytic Association was founded. In the last of those years, the rebellious Jung (whose name means "young" in German) resigned from the editorship of the main psychoanalytic journal and in 1914 resigned from the International Psychoanalytic Association. Those are the main temporal coordinates of the story Freud obliquely told about himself as the primal father of the psychoanalytic horde.

From early on, Freud's patriarchal role was explicitly acknowledged by his close followers, who proclaimed themselves to be his sons. By 1911 there was overt rebellion among the flock of Freud's disciples that he called "the wild hunt": Alfred Adler, Wilhelm Stekel, and Victor Tausk displayed their scientific and personal hostility. Meanwhile it was Jung whom Freud privately named as his successor. However, age, succession, and father-son rivalry were subjects that had haunted the relationship of Freud and Jung from its very beginning and that tolled like a ceaseless bell throughout their correspondence. Although Freud in fact nominated Jung in 1910 as the first president of the International Psychoanalytic Association, Freud—as his biographer Jones says—remained the real power behind the throne. Besides that, there is the little-known fact (radically distorted by Jones, a "faithful" son) that Freud had proposed that the president retain his title for life and be empowered to name or depose any analyst in the world; also, any speech to be given by an analyst or any article to be published by him would first have to be approved by the president. Fortunately, the Viennese analysts, mostly Jews, successfully rebelled against the transfer of presidential power, however token a power it was, to the Christian bastion of Jung's Zurich. Freud's outlook was broader than the sectarianism of his Viennese colleagues because he feared that his science would be labeled a Jewish discipline; yet, as history has shown, Vienna proved a better home for psychoanalysis.

Meanwhile, another story was emerging. Jung was contesting Freud's theory of the Oedipus complex and was writing *Wandlungen und Symbole des Libido* (*Psychology of the Unconscious,* 1912), a work that investigates the background of the mythological hero. Jung avowed that writing the last chapter, entitled "The Sacrifice," would involve the "sacrifice" of his friendship with Freud. Freud for his part was writing *Totem and Taboo,* thereby stepping into the field of anthropology and mythology, which he had formerly left to Jung.

Freud had unambiguously identified psychoanalytic doctrine as female ("Lady Psychoanalysis") and described his writing of *Totem and Taboo* as a casual liaison that turned into marriage; and he even dubbed the fourth book of his treatise a veritable "princess." Freud had also indicated that his working on the last part of *Totem and Taboo* was evidence that his death, impatiently awaited by his Viennese foes, was not yet realized. When Freud's opus was finally finished and published, some interpreted it also as a gesture of vengeance whereby Freud followed Jung into the domain of folk psychology and there annihilated him, symbolically castrated him, on his own ground. Thus the father killed the venturous son and kept Lady Psychoanalysis all to himself. Others among Freud's faithful followers—the self-styled "happy brothers"—formally celebrated the publication of *Totem and Taboo* by inviting Freud to a dinner, which they overtly called a totemic festival.

Thus *Totem and Taboo* is not merely a work of exposition or of self-reflection. Its very writing was a symbolic act in itself, castrating the "young" son who was not submissive; hence the work goes beyond description and stands forth as a piece of enactive discourse, performing the decisive role of restoring paternal authority in the psychoanalytic community of its time.

One of the most intriguing and fascinating texts in the whole of Freud's work is *Beyond the Pleasure Principle;* it is also Freud's most controversial text, repudiated by many of his faithful followers. Changing his former theory of drives, Freud made a new basic division between Thanatos and Eros. The latter is much more than the sexual drive Freud had identified earlier, for it exists in each cell and drives living substances to unite into larger entities, and in that way constitutes a flight forward. Ultimately, however, victory goes to Thanatos, which is the drive in all life to return to a previous inanimate state. Like Arthur Schopenhauer, Freud believed that the aim of life is death; this was a pessimistic view, to be sure, and one that undercut the romantic notion of the basic innocence of man and life.

Among the evidence for his theory of Eros, Freud cites the Upanishads and Plato's *Symposium.* Among the stronger evidence for the death drive is a phenomenon inferred from various clinical material: the compulsion to repeat (more ancient than the pleasure principle), as manifested in recurrent dreams proper to traumatic neuroses and in patients' tendency to repeat painful experiences in their lives.

We may now ask ourselves why it took Freud so many years to see aggression as a drive, especially since in the early 1890's Breuer had twice posited the aggressive drive in one of the sections he individually wrote for *Studies in Hysteria.* Searching for an answer to our question will also reveal that the delayed postulation of the death drive was a return to Freud's own repressed drives and that he wrote a text that proceeded as its own metaphor. The text not only described its subject but also enacted it.

To illustrate this, let us begin with the opening word of the text's title, "beyond," which means "farther on" or "on the other side" as opposed to "on this side." By the middle of chapter 1, Freud declares that the pleasure principle does not dominate the mental processes. Aided by various examples of repetition, the text gathers its own momentum, so that by the end of chapter 2 we read that there is something, yet nameless, that is "more primitive" than the pleasure principle. After naming the compulsion to repeat, Freud ends in chapter 3 by saying that we must further study the repetitive force, "which is more primitive, more elementary, more instinctual than the pleasure principle . . . to which . . . we have hitherto attributed dominance." By now, the "beyond" has clearly become "before" or "prior to" the pleasure principle. Freud's text is, like Eros itself, a series of progressive detours that eventually yield to a retrogressive direction. Freud's final arrival at a concept that is by definition retrogressive stands as a moment of irony as it refers us back to a radically progressive beginning. Such an expository gesture is paralleled by Freud's explanations of the origin of consciousness and of the compulsion to repeat, explanations that themselves are resumed and reexplained.

Consider Freud's *repeated* observation of his one-and-a-half-year-old grandson Ernst, who *repeatedly* played with a wooden reel and string when his mother was absent. Ernst would throw the reel away and cry "o-o-o-o," his way of saying the German word *fort* (gone); he then would retrieve the stringed reel and joyfully cry "da" (there), thus playing out his mother's absence and joyful return. Another game little Ernst played was to crouch below a full-length mirror that did not quite reach to the floor and periodically pop up to see his image in the mirror. Thus he was able to make his own image disappear from the mirror and return to it. We might remark that in writing this account, Freud (whose name means "joy" in German) twice inscribes his name in his grandson's game: Ernst's *freudig* (joyful) "da" was a substitute for his mother's *erfreulich* (joyful) return. Our reflection on the writing of this episode leads us to wonder about the autobiographical traces compulsively embedded in Freud's biographical account.

Another insightful example of Freud's multiple repetitions concerns the fact that *Beyond the Pleasure Principle* has seven chapters. Freud's preoccupation with numbers had the makings of a compulsive symptom: he had seven brothers and sisters; he thought that his life was characterized by seven-year cycles; and he associated the number seven with the prediction of death and the struggle of his seven internal organs to direct his life to an end. Freud's regular correspondence with his great friend Fliess lasted nearly fourteen years, and the correspondence with Jung nearly seven. There were exactly seven members of the Secret Committee (a committee ruling the International Psychoanalytic Association and unknown to its rank-and-file members until 1944). For years Freud felt strongly inhibited from visiting the forbidden city of Rome with its seven hills, and once he did, he returned for a sum of seven visits in all. Finally, there are other works in the Freudian canon that have seven chapters: *The Interpretation of Dreams, Jokes and Their Relation to the Unconscious,* the pivotal essay "Das Unbewusste" ("The Unconscious," 1915), *Die Frage der Laienanalyse* (*The Question of Lay Analysis,* 1926), and *New Introductory Lectures.* Moreover, the first two of the *Three Essays on the Theory of Sexuality* have seven parts each, as does Freud's own favorite among his writings, part 4 of *Totem and Taboo.*

I have left for the end one of the most significant details about *Beyond the Pleasure Principle:* although Freud repeatedly mentions Eros in it, he does not once use the term "Thanatos" to name the death drive, a significant omission in that the term had been used years before at the Vienna Psychoanalytic Society. A possible reason for Freud's omission is that he did not, consciously or unconsciously, want to have the name of his preferred child, Anna, formally inscribed in Th*ana*tos. For an explanation, we must return to Freud's unforgettable essay "Das Motiv der Kästchenwahl" ("The Theme of Three Caskets," 1913), which deals with the themes of love and death. Analyzing Shakespeare's *King Lear,* Freud asserts on the concluding page:

> Lear carries Cordelia's corpse on to the stage. Cordelia is Death. If one reverses the situation, it becomes understandable and familiar. She is the Goddess of Death, who takes away the dead hero from the battlefield, much as the Valkyrie do in German mythology. Eternal wisdom in the dress of primeval myth advises the old man to renounce love, to elect death and to make friends with the necessity of dying.
>
> (*Gesammelte Werke,* vol. 10, p. 36)

In a private letter to Ferenczi written around the time of "The Three Caskets," Freud acknowledged that its subject concerned his daughter Anna and death. These interconnections make it all the more significant that when Freud was composing *Beyond the Pleasure Principle,* he was at the same time attempting the impossible—he was trying to analyse his own daughter Anna. In that impossible adventure between father and daughter, the very oedipal drama of Eros and Thanatos could only be bizarrely repeated. Both Sigmund and Anna were caught in the progressive and retrogressive movements of striving for union and mortal dissolution, both of which were encapsulated orthographically by the palindrome "Anna," which reads the same backward and forward. As a self-defeating venture in which present and past were inevitably so fundamentally dislocated and distorted, this intrafamilial therapy was an *ana*chronism and a pseudo-*ana*lysis, yet it constituted the compulsive backdrop to *Beyond the Pleasure Principle,* which, in chapter 2, united grandfather Freud with one of his specifically mentioned daughters and grandchildren. The treatise is a repetitive exposition and enactment of an eternal return in autobiography and familial biography authored ultimately, according to the implications of the text, by an eternal ghostwriter in whom generations meet.

Freud wrote five great case histories, each of them unparalleled in psychiatric or psychoanalytic literature for analytic and literary power. Each of them also presents a rich mixture of clinical and theoretical material that never fails to offer a profound experience to the reader. The Schreber case is unique among these five cases in that Freud never saw its protagonist. Fascinated by the *Memoirs* of Daniel Schreber, a distinguished German judge whose serious illness had led to hospitalizations, Freud decided to write "Psychoanalytische Bemerkungen über einen autobiographisch beschriebenen Fall von Paranoia" ("Psychoanalytic Notes upon an Autobiographical Account of a Paranoid Case," 1911); Freud's account still remains a classic commentary on the psychodynamics of paranoia. Another case, "Analyse der Phobie eines fünfjährigen Knaben" ("Analysis of a Phobia of a Five-Year-Old Boy," 1909), deals with little Hans, whom Freud saw only once and otherwise treated through the reporting father. Thanks to the treatment of this little boy who so feared that a horse would bite him that he would not go outdoors, Freud for the first time directly demonstrated the existence of infantile sexuality and the Oedipus complex in a child. In "Fragment of an Analysis of a Case of Hysteria," Freud described his treatment of Dora, who suddenly and without explanation left him after the eleventh week of sessions. Although Freud admitted having realized the treatment's transferential implications too late, especially the negative paternal transference, he managed to use the case to write a remarkable, condensed synthesis of *Studies on Hysteria* and *The Interpretation of Dreams* that at the same time is a transitional piece anticipating some of the findings in *Three Essays on the Theory of Sexuality.*

The Rat Man figures as the subject of "Bemerkungen über einen Fall von Zwangsneurose" ("Notes upon a Case of Obsessional Neurosis," 1909). The case is singular in that it is generally alleged to be Freud's only complete one; it stands also as a matchless description of the phenomenology of obsessional neurosis and contains some theoretical statements on the neurosis that are still authoritative. Just before consulting Freud, the patient was on maneuvers, during one moment of which a "cruel captain" had told with relish the story of an oriental torture in which a pot of rats was affixed to the anus of the victim. Immediately the Rat Man (whence his name) fantasized that the torture was applied both to his beloved lady friend and to his long-deceased father. It was not long before rats began to symbolize many things for the Rat Man, including money, feces, gambling, penis, baby, and marriage.

At the center of the patient's pathology was a considerable unconscious hostility toward his father, whom he consciously loved. For some time after his father's demise, he refused to accept the death as fact; when he finally did, he manifested an intense ambivalence and pathological mourning in constantly visiting bereaved relatives to express his sympathy, for which he was nicknamed "carrion crow" in his family. Also, he habitually imagined people as dying so he could share heartfelt sympathy with the affected relatives. One classic obsessional gesture he directed to his lady friend was the following: after a serious disagreement with her, he happened to walk on a road over which the carriage of his departing lady was to pass, and he removed a stone that he felt to be lying dangerously in the middle of the road; next, overcome by hostility and thinking his action to be absurd, he went back and placed the stone in its original position.

Freud found that for the Rat Man, "looking took the place of touching" and carnal contiguity; his case involved an overdetermined use of the eye, for, as Freud stresses elsewhere, the optical zone is "perhaps the zone most remote from the sexual object." Also part and parcel of the Rat Man's obsessiveness was his reliance on defensive isolation. According to one of the meanings of this isolation, the Rat Man experienced ideas without the appropriate accompanying feeling, resulting in a severance of causal connections (contiguity) between ideas. According to another meaning of isolation, this time dealing with the articulation of ideas, the Rat Man inserted an interval of time between his utterances in order to lead astray any conscious investigation of their causal connections.

When we turn from the Rat Man as patient to Freud's exposition of the case as such, we come upon a surprise: the case is characterized by disconnectedness to such an extent that we must suspect some interference from Freud's unconscious and that we must finally identify the case not only as one of exposition but also as one of enactment. In this case, the gaps and disjunctions in Freud's text enact the discontinuities involved in the Rat Man's defensive isolation. Both in his correspondence with Jung and in the introduction to the case, Freud writes of its disconnected and aphoristic nature (aphorisms being broad statements that exist independently and have no ligatures or connections with other statements). And indeed, in the Rat Man case, instead of encountering the familiar Freud with his superb articulateness, we come upon a writer who, amid his many moments of brilliance, confuses the precipitating causes of his patient's illnesses, elaborates little on the links between the Rat Man's early and later loved objects, does not firmly correlate the clinical and theoretical considerations as he does in his other cases, and does not succeed in neatly tying together child and adult symptomatology. In sum, the isolation of causal connections, along with a theoretical doing and undoing (the alternating affirmation and withdrawal of propositions), punctuates Freud's text and exhibits its dual nature as subject and object, as exposition and enactment.

By general agreement, Freud's greatest case history is about the Wolf Man, the hero of "Aus der Geschichte einer infantilen Neurose" ("From the History of an Infantile Neurosis," 1918). The Wolf Man was a Russian patient whom Freud followed in treatment for four-and-a-half years; the Russian returned to Freud a second time, and then was treated afterward by others at irregular intervals for over fifty years. He literally became a ward of psychoanalysis.

The Wolf Man was twenty-three when he first consulted Freud for a psychoanalysis that in great part turned on a dream that the patient had had at the age of four:

> I dreamt that it is night and I lie in my bed. (My bed stood with its foot towards the window, and in front of the window was a row of old walnut trees. I know that it was winter and nighttime when I dreamt.) Suddenly the window opens by itself, and I see with great fright that on the big walnut tree before the window some white wolves are sitting. There were six or seven of them. The wolves were entirely white and looked like foxes rather than sheep-dogs, for they had large tails like foxes and their ears were pointed up like dogs when they pay attention to something. With great terror, obviously about being eaten up by the wolves, I scream and wake up.
>
> (*Gesammelte Werke,* vol. 12, p. 54)

Using other data arising from the analysis, Freud tries to trace the dream to a time two-and-a-half years earlier when the eighteen-month-old boy had witnessed his parents engaged in intercourse (the so-called primal scene). In the most audacious gesture to be found in his writings, Freud attempts to reconstruct a host of details attending that event: his patient's infantile age, his physical sickness at the time, the season of the year, the time of day, its general temperature, the place of the action, the state and color of his parents' clothes, the color of the bedclothes, the quality of the child's attention, his detection of his father's sounds and of the emotional expression on his mother's face, his observation of their genitals, their coital position, the number of occurrences of intercourse, the general nature of the witness's reaction, the specific manner in which the child interrupted his parents' lovemaking, and the tonal quality of his ensuing reaction. More specifically, Freud imagines the previous postulates to form the following scenario: one hot summer day, the eighteen-month-old boy, afflicted with malaria, was sleeping in a cot in his parents' bedroom, where the parents retired, half dressed, for a siesta; possibly at the height of a fever, at five in the afternoon the young child woke up and with strained attention watched his parents, half-dressed in white underclothes and kneeling on white bedclothes, engage in tergal coitus three times; while noticing his parents' genitalia, his father's heavy breathing, and his mother's facial expression of enjoyment, the generally passive baby suddenly had a bowel movement and screamed, thereby interrupting the young couple.

There are many reasons for distrusting the plausibility of Freud's reconstruction: to name but two, a young baby sorely afflicted with malaria and its distortion of the sensorium is incapable of prolonged, strained attention, and intercourse from the rear as a position precludes a child from seeing at any angle the genitalia of his parents. But what is so fascinating is that again and again Freud tries to "persuade" us of his interpretation. As a matter of fact, the word "persuade" occurs more frequently in the Wolf Man case than in Freud's other writings, and when one remembers what the term means in German, Freud's peculiar lexical insistence becomes clear. In German, the word is *überzeugen,* whose root, *zeugen*, means either to witness or to procreate. Those two actions, witnessing and procreating, constitute the two events of the primal scene—the witnessing of the child and the copulating of the parents. This, then, is but one indication—and there are others—that the subject of Freud's claims is intermingled with his strategy of rhetoric or persuasion. Once more, the division between subject and means, exposition and enactment, dwindles away. To put it another way, Freud's discourse is both a narrative of the past and a staging in the present, both a dramatic representation and a re-presentation.

A mention of the apocalyptic relevance of Freud will serve as a timely though uncomfortable conclusion. While creating a science that constantly distinguishes fantasy from reality in a variety of spheres, Freud enjoyed the painful distinction of living through a series of historical terrors: racial and religious persecution, the unscrupulousness of organized capitalism and Marxism, world war, the rise of Nazism, and so forth. One may wonder how Freud would have reflected on our nuclear era, which has its own ultimate distinction: namely, the psychotic-like fantasies of man's annihilating the universe might equally be sober considerations grounded in reality—for yesterday's nightmare is potentially today's reality. It was precisely within the legacy of the Freudian tradition that the British psychoanalyst Edward Glover wrote in 1946: "The capacity so painfully acquired by normal man to distinguish between sleep, hallucination, delusion and the objective reality has for the first time in history been seriously weakened."

## Selected Bibliography

### EDITIONS

INDIVIDUAL WORKS

*Studien über Hysterie.* Vienna, 1893–1895.

*Die Traumdeutung.* Vienna, 1900.

*Zur Psychopathologie des Alltagslebens.* Vienna, 1901.

*Drei Abhandlungen zur Sexualtheorie.* Vienna, 1905.

*Der Witz und seine Beziehung zum Unbewussten.* Vienna, 1905.

*Der Wahn und die Träume in W. Jensen's "Gradiva."* Vienna, 1907.

*Eine Kindheitserinnerung des Leonardo da Vinci.* Vienna, 1910.

*Totem und Tabu.* Vienna, 1913.

*Vorlesungen zur Einführung in die Psychoanalyse.* Vienna, 1916–1917.

*Jenseits des Lustprinzips.* Vienna, 1920.

*Massenpsychologie und Ich-Analyse.* Vienna, 1921.

*Das Ich und das Es.* Vienna, 1923.

*Die Frage der Laienanalyse.* Vienna, 1926.

*Hemmung, Symptom, und Angst.* Vienna, 1926.

*Die Zukunft einer Illusion.* Vienna, 1927.

*Neue Folge der Vorlesungen zur Einführung in die Psychoanalyse.* Vienna, 1933.

"Ein Wort zum Antisemitismus." In *Die Zukunft,* November 1938.

*Der Mann Moses und die Monotheistische Religion.* Amsterdam, 1939.

COLLECTED WORKS

*Sigmund Freud: Gesammelte Werke.* 18 vols. Frankfurt am Main, 1940–1968.

*Sigmund Freud: Studienausgabe.* 10 vols. Frankfurt am Main, 1969–1975.

CORRESPONDENCE

*The Freud–Jung Letters.* Edited by William McGuire and translated by Ralph Manheim and R. C. Hull. Princeton, N.J., 1974.

*Sigmund Freud: Briefe an Wilhelm Fliess (1887–1904).* Edited by J. Masson, M. Schröter, and G. Fichtner. Frankfurt am Main, 1986.

TRANSLATIONS

*The Freud–Jung Letters.* Edited by William McGuire and translated by Ralph Manheim and R. C. Hull. Princeton, N.J., 1974.

*A General Introduction to Psychoanalysis.* Translated by Joan Riviere. New York, 1952. Freud's *Introductory Lectures* also appear under this title.

*The Pelican Freud Library.* 14 vols. Translated by Angela Richards, James Strachey, et al. London, 1962–1985.

*Sigmund Freud: Three Case Histories.* Edited by Philip Rieff. New York, 1963. Contains case histories of Dora, the Rat Man, and the Wolf Man.

*The Standard Edition of the Complete Psychological Works of Sigmund Freud.* 24 vols. Translated by James Strachey, et al. London, 1953–1974.

BIOGRAPHICAL AND CRITICAL STUDIES

Andersson, Ola. *Studies in the Prehistory of Psychoanalysis.* Stockholm, 1962.

Anzieu, Didier. *Freud's Self-Analysis and the Discovery of Psychoanalysis.* Translated by Peter Graham. New York, 1986.

Bernheimer, Charles, and Clare Kahane, eds. *In Dora's Case: Freud—Hysteria—Feminism.* New York, 1985.

Blanton, Smiley. *Diary of My Analysis with Sigmund Freud.* New York, 1971.

Brenner, Charles. *An Elementary Textbook of Psychoanalysis.* New York, 1955.

Clark, Ronald W. *Freud: The Man and the Cause.* New York, 1980.

Eagle, Morris N. *Recent Developments in Psychoanalysis.* New York, 1984.

Eissler, Kurt R. *Medical Orthodoxy and the Future of Psychoanalysis.* New York, 1965.

————. *Talent and Genius.* New York, 1971.

————. *Victor Tausk's Suicide.* New York, 1983.

Ellenberger, Henri F. *The Discovery of the Unconscious: The History and Evolution of Dynamic Psychiatry.* New York, 1970.

Gardiner, Muriel, ed. *The Wolf-Man and Sigmund Freud.* New York, 1971.

Gay, Peter. *Freud, Jews and Other Germans: Masters and Victims in Modernist Culture.* New York, 1978.

Gilman, Sandra L., ed. *Introducing Psychoanalytic Theory.* New York, 1982.

Glover, Edward. *Freud or Jung?* London, 1950.

Hyman, Stanley Edgar. *The Tangled Bank: Darwin, Marx, Frazer and Freud as Imaginative Writers.* New York, 1962.

Janik, Allan, and Stephen Toulmin. *Wittgenstein's Vienna.* London, 1973.

Johnston, William M. *The Austrian Mind: An Intellectual and Social History, 1848–1938.* Berkeley, Calif., 1972.

Jones, Ernest. *Sigmund Freud: Life and Work.* 3 vols. New York, 1953–1957.

Kanzer, Mark, and Jules Glenn, eds. *Freud and His Self-Analysis.* New York, 1979.

————, eds. *Freud and His Patients.* New York, 1980.

Kardiner, Abram. *My Analysis with Freud: Reminiscences.* New York, 1977.

Kaufmann, Walter Arnold. *Discovering the Mind, Vol. 3: Freud Versus Adler and Jung.* New York, 1980.

Klein, Dennis B. *Jewish Origins of the Psychoanalytic Movement.* New York, 1981.

Kris, Ernst. *Psychoanalytic Explorations in Art.* New York, 1952.

Laplanche, Jean, and J. B. Pontalis. *The Language of Psychoanalysis.* Translated by Donald Nicholson-Smith. New York, 1973.

McGrath, William J. *Freud's Discovery of Psychoanalysis: The Politics of Hysteria.* Ithaca, N.Y., 1986.

Mahony, Patrick J. *Freud as a Writer.* New York, 1982.

———. *The Cries of the Wolf Man.* New York, 1984.

———. *Freud and the Rat Man.* New Haven, Conn., 1986.

Marcus, Steven. *Freud and the Culture of Psychoanalysis.* Boston, Mass., 1984.

Mehlman, J., ed. *French Freud: Structural Studies in Psychoanalysis.* Yale French Studies, no. 48. New Haven, Conn., 1972.

Meissner, W. W. *Psychoanalysis and Religious Experience.* New Haven, Conn., 1984.

Reik, Theodor. *From Thirty Years with Freud.* London, 1942.

Ricoeur, Paul. *Freud and Philosophy.* Translated by D. Savage. New Haven, Conn., 1970.

Rieff, Philip. *Freud: The Mind of the Moralist.* London, 1960.

Roazen, Paul. *Freud and His Followers.* New York, 1971.

Ruitenbeek, Hendrik Marinus., ed. *Freud as We Knew Him.* Detroit, 1973.

Schur, Max. *Freud: Living and Dying.* London, 1972.

Skura, Meridith Anne. *The Literary Use of the Psychoanalytic Process.* New Haven, Conn., 1981.

Spector, Jack J. *The Aesthetics of Freud: A Study in Psychoanalysis and Art.* London, 1972.

Stepansky, Paul E., ed. *Freud: Appraisals and Reappraisals.* Hillsdale, N.J., 1986.

Sterba, Richard F. *Reminiscences of a Viennese Psychoanalyst.* Detroit, 1982.

Sulloway, Frank J. *Freud, Biologist of the Mind: Beyond the Psychoanalytic Legend.* New York, 1979.

Wallace, Edwin R. *Freud and Anthropology: A History and Reappraisal.* New York, 1983.

Weber, Samuel. *The Legend of Freud.* Minneapolis, 1982.

Wollheim, Richard. *Freud.* London, 1971.

Wright, Elizabeth. *Psychoanalytic Criticism: Theory in Practice.* London, 1984.

PATRICK J. MAHONY

# FEDERICO GARCÍA LORCA

## *(1898–1936)*

HE WAS LOVED by intellectuals, who endlessly interpreted his poems, and by illiterate farmers, who sang them. Even Spanish officialdom for a long time tolerated his sexual and social viewpoints. His work could be oblique and obscure, but when he was playful or indignant, he was brilliantly clear. His voice could be subtle and soft, but about suffering it rang out as loud as the fascist guns that executed him.

In the thirty-eight years of his life, he wrote ten long plays, numerous one-act plays, six major books of poetry, over a thousand other poems, a book of narrations, and critical essays. Many of his works are still hidden. All this literary activity took place while he carried on as theater director, producer, and designer. He composed and arranged music, painted, and took a graduate degree in law. He lectured all over Spain, South America, Cuba, and the United States. A literary celebrity at home, he studied a year at Columbia University and wrote his excoriating *Poeta en Nueva York* (*Poet in New York,* published in 1940), which prophesied the fall of Wall Street in 1929 and the racial revolution of the 1960's.

His many letters reveal a man whose charm was justifiably legendary. He also could be coy, cajoling, exacting, cynical, silly, and impossible. A long-overdue letter of his begins, "Late, but on time." Still, no matter what he did, said, or wrote, he never lacked humor and intelligence. No one, friend or foe, denied his endlessly varied talents.

Lorca's work brims with sex, death, nature, unnaturalness, love, mysticism, spells, and cures for which there are no known diseases. He admits being influenced by nursery rhymes, lullabies, folk songs, peasant language, Eliot, Keats, Synge, Whitman, Góngora, Cervantes, and Quevedo. He beautifies a hunchbacked painter in his essay on her work; he writes a poem to the crazed daughter of Ferdinand and Isabella, Juana, who lived with her husband's corpse.

He was a traditional, classical, modern postmodernist. He was radical yet not political. He wrote, "I am an anarchist, communist, monarchist, socialist." His religion is "Muslim-Jewish-Christian-Atheist." He seems to have been everything but bigoted.

For sheer range of work, he rivals Bernard Shaw and Robert Graves. His appreciation is worldwide. Juan Ramón Jiménez was said to have received the 1956 Nobel Prize partly on behalf of Lorca. Critical and biographical works have never ceased appearing in the fifty years since his murder. A bibliography of translations alone would fill a volume.

As a child in Granada, Lorca entertained his family with imitations of the best show in town: the Mass. He would conscript his younger brother and sisters into the production by having them perform the roles of acolytes and confessors. The maid was his costume designer. His father, a cigar-smoking, macho farmer, spent long days on horseback overseeing his vast Andalusian holdings. His mother, a former schoolteacher, spent endless hours with Federico, who needed special care because of an infantile affliction (probably poliomyelitis) that left him weak for years to come. He also had another anomaly worthy of special handling: he was a prodigy.

His mother taught him the rudiments of literature, music, and painting. Before his feet could reach the pedals, he was composing simple tunes on the family piano. The great maestro Manuel de Falla (a Granadan) later encouraged his arrangements of the local folk songs that he took seriously the rest of his life, using them as the basis of three books: *Poema del cante jondo* (*Deep Song,* 1931), *Canciones (1921–1924)* (*Songs,* 1927), and *Romancero gitano* (*Gypsy Ballads,* 1928). As for painting, his exhibitions were taken quite seriously by the important artistic communities in Barcelona and Madrid.

Lucky poet, his family was not only well heeled but well situated. Lorca grew up in Granada, a collage of Muslim-Arab-Hebraic-Christian traditions in art and thought. Every famous artist passed through. Debussy and Ravel composed there. Intellectuals from all over the world came to sit in the çafé and join "the circle" to discuss art and ideas. And Granada itself is in the province of Andalusia, where Seneca and Martial lived during the Roman Empire; where Moses Maimonides and Averroës later produced secular and theological masterworks of philosophy.

Thus far Lorca does not make a very interesting protagonist: his warm, uncomplicated family life, the mutual love between himself and his siblings, their gruff but interested father, and the complete lack of financial difficulties do not make for exciting dramatic action, as drawing-room plays adequately demonstrate. But one day something so melodramatically symbolic occurred that no dramatist would sink to dramatizing it. Lorca himself tells about it in one of his lectures, "Charla sobre *Romancero gitano*" (Lecture on *Gypsy Ballads*). He recalls that one day in his childhood home of Fuente Vaqueros, where mountain-dwelling Gypsies rode down from caves, he looked up from his book to see a poor Gypsy glaring at him in his luxury. As Federico fled from the image, he heard someone calling "Amargo"—a name meaning "bitter." Amargo apparently never reappeared, but his look and the bitter taste it left stayed with Lorca. In many bristling poems later, he tried to decipher the encounter; he became obsessed with the figure, real or not, who "wanted to drown me with his hands." He began to write.

In the formative years of his creativity, he did not plunge unequivocally into poetry. His first published work, a book of his travels called *Impresiones y paisajes* (*Impressions and Landscapes*), sounds like a collection of paintings. Its publication date is 1918, when Lorca was twenty years old. The Baedekerian work is notable mainly as an attempt to exorcise the ghosts of writers past and sorrows present:

> It is frightening, a desolate orphanage with these sad and rickety children. It fills the heart with an immense weeping and a formidable yearning for equality. Maybe someday, when the children have suffered too much injustice, the meetinghouse will fall on the Municipal Board and flatten them into a big omelette, the kind the poor can't have.
>
> ("Galicia")

To understand completely Lorca's development, however, one must understand Spain's cultural crisis at the beginning of our era.

## *BACKGROUND*

Eighteen ninety-eight was a bad year for Spanish history. While the rest of Europe and America thrived, Spain had constant social, economic, and moral crises. It was rotten at its governmental core. Its colonial edges were eroding. The great Spanish Empire was a sliver of its former grandeur. When a disorganized United States Navy managed to win Cuba and the Philippines in a battle that sank the Spanish Armada, the Spanish ego went down with it. As if Spain was not in enough trouble, that year García Lorca was born.

Eighteen ninety-eight also gave birth to a movement known as the Generation of '98. This group of artists and thinkers questioned the conquistador legacy of a machismo that had founded and ruined a couple of civilizations and was about to ruin its own.

The Generation of '98 was centered mainly in Madrid. Its members were cosmopolitan, classically trained modernists who felt that the task of influencing Spain had fallen through the ages from the iron fist of the Inquisition into the hands of intellectuals and poets. Some important members were Ortega y Gasset, Unamuno, Valle-Inclán, Gómez de la Serna, Machado, Bergamín, and Jiménez. The last two were Nobel laureates.

By the time the Generation of '98 grew up it was a legitimate entity, if not assimilated, at least tolerated. It even had an innovative effect on education. The Residencia de los Estudiantes in Madrid was open to students of arts and sciences and to professionals in the experimental stages of their careers. In 1919 Lorca left his formal studies at the University of Granada to become part of the exciting body of experimentalists at the Residencia. Here a poet, a painter, a critic, or a physicist could obtain a room, domestic help, and food well served and prepared, and lead a life generally free from any cares that might detract from a busy creative day. A resident of the Residencia didn't have to worry about changing a sheet or a light bulb. He was not even required to attend a lecture, though the best minds of Spain and Europe shared their notions and theories with the eager "students."

Lorca was not one of these. He attended few lectures and fewer conferences. Instead he read the works of the most imaginative and idiosyncratic members of his generation and sought out their company in the cafés of Madrid. He began to carouse with Rafael Alberti, the openly leftist surrealist poet, and with Luis Buñuel, the moderately leftist surrealist film director and Salvador Dali's collaborator on *Un chien andalou,* a short surrealist film. Lorca worked on the scenario with them, but to what degree we do not know. Nor do we know how close was his collaboration with Dali.

From 1919 to 1928 Lorca enjoyed the cultural favors of the Residencia, had rich and riotous friendships, took prankish tours of high and low Madrid, drank deeply of the folklore of nearby villages (and of their grape production), recited his poems, often improvising them, to the delight of modern Madrid, and managed to write half a dozen major works. All in all, one can say that the educational experiment known as the Residencia de los Estudiantes, certainly in the case of Lorca, was a success.

The Generation of '98 proselytized. They spread the word that the word was with not God but creative man. Faith in the future of Spain would be restored by its writers. Designing the background, the artists of Catalonia built monumental prophecies to cubism, abstraction, and art deco. Picasso soon began carrying messages from Toulouse-Lautrec's Paris. Gaudi's churches featured ceramic shards, factory scrap, and sea conches in architectural collages that later affected the surrealists. Freud was showing the way to the distant landscape of the unconscious. In the secular religion of art, this became known as modernism. It was in this eccentric atmosphere that Lorca was born; when Dada began to flash its weirdness within, he did not avert his adolescent eyes.

Something was being said to someone. But what to whom? Ideas were coming down from the ether of the past to the air of fin-de-siècle Spain. It was not only the turn of a hundred-year gear, though; for the newly open-minded it was a rotation of the evolutionary wheel. They wanted the wheel to revolve smoothly, to make a comfortable cultural revolution.

Valle-Inclán, the W. C. Fields of Spanish literature, wrote, "Spain is a deformation of Europe." Gómez de la Serna's book *Senos*

(Breasts, 1917), a garden of mammary delights, indicates the kind of influence the writers of the Generation of '98 had on Lorca. They wrote and translated the literary and political manifestos that appeared constantly throughout the first quarter of the century. They hawked acmeism, bizarrism, ultraism, neosymbolism, and musical impressionism. If you ran short of inspiration one week, you wrote a manifesto. There was a mass marketing of these proclamations until surrealism knocked all other "isms" out of the box.

But the most powerful manifesto was not written; it was painted on canvas. The "ism" that endured was cubism. Cubism not only affected generations of painters, it had a great influence on writing, on the fractured imagery that mirrored the breakdown of European values and systems. Lorca was born into this. Gertrude Stein said, "Cubism could only come from Spain." It traveled well though. Cubistic imagery is Eliot's "pair of claws" crossing the ocean floor. Cummings represents cubistic syntax; Joyce, cubistic linguistics.

There is a moderate modernism perceivable through the gauzy gray of Lorca's first published poems, *Libro de poemas* (Book of Poems, 1921), which stretched from actual places to where the "indecisive phantasm / of an Augustive evening / shattered the horizon," with a bitter look that shadows most of his early poems.

In "El lagarto viejo" (The Old Lizard), "The oarless gondola of idea / crosses the tenebrous waters / of your burnt-out eyes." What can remain but sinister shade "when the sun is so sugary and soluble / it melts in the cup of the mountains" and the flocks, white as they may be, "muddy the road"? So:

> Do not bother looking
> for light in the dark.
> You will have a good place
> to look at the stars
> when the worms take their time
> to eat you . . .

> No one in the fields
> and the mountains extinguished
> and the road deserted . . .
> only from time to time
> the cuckoos sing to the darkness
> of the poplar trees.

But darkness does not prevent this "drop of crocodile," as Lorca calls the lizard, from

> . . . meditating
> in the green cutaway coat
> of the devil's abbot
> correct in his posture
> his collar starched
> with the very sad look
> of an emeritus professor.

Even in the dark, Lorca lets us know we should watch for a wink.

In 1924 André Breton announced in the *Manifeste du surréalisme* that through surrealism's eyes one's childhood and adulthood could be reexperienced. Lorca had de-dichotomized childhood and adulthood in this 1921 book of poems. In "Los encuentros de un caracol aventurero" (Encounters of an Adventurous Snail), a snail meets a colony of ants that has imprisoned one of its drones. The prisoner tells the snail he is being punished because he saw the stars. The other ants have stripped his antennae. What are stars, they demand. The captive ant replies:

> "I saw thousands of stars
> in my own darkness. Stars
> are lights on top of our head."
> "We don't see them," the ants retort
> and the snail, in all objectivity,
> must admit he cannot see
> above the grass.

This youthful book contains other poems of mysterious if naive charm, cunningly juxtaposed with Lorca's ever-present humor. His perverse, personal religion is heard in these first poems as well:

Christ held a reason
in evil hands
multiplying
his own specter.
Projecting his heart
into the black
gazes.
Believe!
("Símbolo" [Symbol])

We live
beneath a big mirror.
Man is blue!
Hosanna!
("El gran espejo" [The Big Mirror])

All is fair.
Brother, open your arms.
God is the point.
("Rayos" [Rays])

Adam and Eve.
The serpent
split the mirror
into a thousand pieces
and the apple
was the stone.
("Imitación" [Imitation])

He breaks the mirror, a faded symbol that has lost its vital quicksilver and only has behind it "a dead star . . . a mummy of the source, a conch of light / closed for the night." Official symbolism is beginning to wane. Soon González Martínez will revolt against Rubén Darío, the great symbolist idol, whose swan represented Romantic image play. Martínez writes, "Strangle the swan and its conniving plumage!" What is symbolism to one culture is, after all, reality to another. Lorca's Andalusia used the moon not as a symbol but as a calendar; the sun tells what time it is, and the sea is a washtub. Use of these as images by Andalusians was personal, experienced, unsymbolic. Lorca is in the above poem recognizing symbolism as a dim, limited reflection. He intuits symbolism's etymology: half a coin waiting for the other to give it value.

His next book, *Deep Song,* takes him toward the ultimate nonduality. Eliot's Sweeney says, "What's that life is? / Life is death." Lorca says, in effect, "Love is death." Therefore he not only endures but adores Death. Death is his natural leading lady who will remain with him until the end of the show. In "Malagueña" she is in what could be the setting of an O'Neill play:

Death
enters and exits
in this tavern.
Dark horse and sinister people
pass through the deep roads of the guitar.

There is a smell of salt
and of female blood
in the burning roses
of the navy.

Death
enters and exits
exits and enters
death
in the tavern.

Death, in the corner of the bar, sits down to watch us live it up. But her presence even in this atmosphere of sexuality makes clear that Death, Love's lover, is the star. Her dancing partner is the knife, equal in efficacy and beauty to any of man's or nature's instruments. In "Puñal" (The Dagger):

The dagger enters the heart
like the blade of a plow in the fallow earth,
like the rays of the sun setting
fire to the frightening gullies.

"Sorpresa" (Surprise) presents a street-beat, scenelike variation of the theme:

Stopped off on our street, dead
with a dagger in his breast!
Nobody knew nothing.

You should have seen the lamp post
shaking! Mother!
That little street lamp shaking!

It was dawn. Nobody
dared to see those eyes
open in the hard night air!

Yeh, death stopped off on our street
Yeh, the dagger in the breast
Yeh, nobody knew nothing.

These are done in the plaintive modality of the "deep song" of t he Andalusian Gypsies.

If Spain is the death capital of the western world, Andalusia is the Hollywood of funerals. Its dirge is the deep song, a primitive musical system originating in India and sung in Spain by Gypsies, who (Lorca tells us) brought it with them when Tamerlane raided India. In Andalusia the Gypsies combined the indigenous Iberian sounds and words with their own musical imports to give deep song its wailing, obsessive use of one note, destroying ordinary metrical rhythm. Lorca tells us this and more in "El canto jondo" ("Deep Song," 1922), an essay that reminds Spanish writers of their debt to the Gypsies for

> the creation of these songs, soul of our soul. . . . These lyrical channels through which all the pain, all the rites of the race can flow . . . and cross the cemetery of time. Deep Song comes from the first sigh. It is the living, eternal enigma posed by the Oriental Sphinx of Andalusia, an awesome riddle to be solved by death. Or Oedipus! Deep Song is a frightening blue archer who never runs out of arrows.

In short, deep song is death distilled into lyric.

Lorca's essay was written at the same time he was completing his book *Deep Song.* Here is a poem, "La Lola," that the great Gypsy singer Juan Breva could have sung. It is a woman, her past and her present:

Lola sings flamenco.
The little bullfighters
circle around her.
The little barber
from his doorway
follows the rhythms
with his head.

Between the sweet basil
and the mint, Lola sings
flamenco, that same Lola
who used to see herself
often in the puddles.

And a song about the maestro himself, in the same wistful modality:

Juan Breva had this body of a giant
and this little tiny girl's voice.
Nothing like his trill. It was
that same old song of pain
behind a smile that
made you think of lemon trees and
sleeping in the south of Spain.
And in his cry was the salt of the sea,
like Homer, singing,
blind. His voice had
that something of lightless ocean
and squeezed orange.

("Juan Breva")

Suddenly the singing stops. Amargo makes a bravura appearance with his silver dagger. Death, on a horse, approaches him, offering a trade:

> *Death:* What a beautiful knife you have. But gold knives go into the heart. Silver knives only cut the throat. Rather have mine?
> *Amargo:* Don't any knives cut bread?
> *Death:* A real man tears bread with his hands.

Amargo is reluctant to yield his dagger, which perhaps too clearly symbolizes life. So Death gives him his golden knife, the hard way.

> *Death:* Come on up! Quick! We can get to Granada before the dawn breaks. Here, take this knife I give you (stabs Amargo in the heart).

Amargo's mother sings his dirge:

They laid him out on my bedsheet,
on my oleanders and my palm leaves.
The twenty-seventh day of August
with a little knife of gold.

The cross! and it was all over.
He was brown and bitter.
Neighbors, give me a copper
pitcher of lemonade.

The cross. Don't cry anyone.
Amargo is on the moon.

The poetic alchemy of Lorca transforms the symbols; it blends the gold knife with the cross, blends Amargo with the moon—and all four with Death.

While Lorca still wears his symbolist cape in *Deep Song,* he also rolls up his political sleeves. A conscience stalks the book, exploding in a short ironic play about the arrest of a Gypsy. It seems to foreshadow the black New York that Lorca will later know. Brutalized, humiliated, unable to communicate adequately, a Gypsy stands before the audience, "small, with the look of a young mule casting a shadow on the officer's insignia."

*Lieutenant Colonel:* I'm the Lieutenant Colonel of the Civil Guard.
*Sergeant:* Yes.
*Lieutenant Colonel:* Nobody disobeys me.
*Sergeant:* No.
*Lieutenant Colonel:* I have three stars and twenty crosses.
*Sergeant:* Yes.
*Lieutenant Colonel:* The Cardinal Archbishop said "Hello" to me, in his purple tassle.
*Sergeant:* Yes.
*Lieutenant Colonel:* I'm the lieutenant, I'm the lieutenant, I'm the Lieutenant Colonel of the Civil Guard. (Indicates the manacled Gypsy.) What's that?
*Sergeant:* A Gypsy.
*Lieutenant Colonel* (to Gypsy): I am the Lieutenant Colonel of the Civil Guard.
*Gypsy:* Yes.
*Sergeant:* I found him and brung him in.
*Lieutenant Colonel:* Where was he?
*Sergeant:* The bridge of the river.
*Lieutenant Colonel:* What river?
*Gypsy:* All the rivers!

That is, the rebellion of the Gypsies lurks in all their haunts. But the nature of the rebellion is beyond the officer's understanding. The Gypsy's revolutionary crime is making revolutionary images:

*Lieutenant Colonel:* What were you doing there?
*Gypsy:* Building a cinnamon tower.
*Lieutenant Colonel:* Sergeant!
*Sergeant:* At your service, my Lieutenant Colonel of the Civil Guard.

The Gypsy's imagery keeps attacking, sabotaging. Each image is another blow:

*Gypsy:* I've invented wings to fly and I fly. With sulphur and roses in my mouth.

The sulphur of guns, the roses of sex, these are more than the Civil Guard can bear.

*Lieutenant Colonel:* Ay!
*Gypsy:* I really don't need wings. I fly without them. Clouds in my blood. And smoke rings.
*Lieutenant Colonel:* Ayyy! (The Lieutenant Colonel begins to have a heart attack.)
*Gypsy:* In January I have my orange blossoms.
*Lieutenant Colonel:* Ayyyyy!
*Gypsy:* And then it is *oranges in the snow.*

The rebel image is even subverting nature. It is too much for the Lieutenant Colonel, who dies. Romeo and Juliet appear:

*Romeo and Juliet:* We took his soul of tobacco and coffee "with" and flew it out the window—the soul of the Lieutenant Colonel of the Civil Guard.
*Sergeant:* Help!!

Lorca has dramatized the relationship of surrealism to revolution. What Breton, Aragon, and Picabia talked about in their manifestos, delivered successfully in Spain, he dramatizes through poetry. It is again Lorca's instinctive way of eliminating distinctions, this time between poetry, drama, and politics—a very uneasy triumvirate. But the subject and the forms here are joined as closely as lyric to song—deep song.

Death is more than subject matter for Lorca; from his developmental period onward, Death will stalk his pages until the day he joins "the southwind flame of evil skies."

> Every afternoon is Granada
> every afternoon a child is dead.
> (*Gacela* of the Dead Child)

Lorca is separated from death by "a wall of bad dreams." He writes that even the Spanish creative force, the Duende, is Death's male counterpart: "Duende serenades Death's house and doesn't arrive until he knows Death is in. The Duende loves the lip of the wound" ("Essay on Duende").

This liaison between death and the arts is possible only in Spain "because death is a national pastime." Lorca refers not only to the bullfight ("supremely civilized festival") but also to "the ice-moon heads painted by Zurbaran, the lightning yellow of El Greco, all of Goya. . . . The painting of Death with a guitar in Medina de Rioseco." These are artistic transformations of Spain's local saints' processions (where the bones play a prominent role) and the innumerable games and rites of Good Friday, "the one day the Spanish people win over Death." Elsewhere in the world death is a final curtain, elsewhere "the curtains are closed when someone dies," whereas "in Spain they open them. Most Spaniards stay home until their dying day, at which point they are taken out into the sunlight for the first time. [Spain is] a country open to death." The barren plains and surly mountains (in the second most mountainous country in Europe) allow little physical or social escape, so that "the dead are more alive in Spain than anywhere else in the world."

Each year yielded a new crop of manifestos. Lorca flitted among them like a bee with holes in its pockets. He himself never enlisted in movements of any sort. He used cubism, abstraction, and surrealism as bridges to poetry from his early love, painting, but he could not fully be identified with any style; or any art for that matter. The poet-critic Gerardo Diego wrote of Lorca's *Canciones,* "It is hard to say whether these are poetry, painting, or music."

> Cypresses
> (stagnant water)
> poplar
> (crystal water)
> willow
> (profound water)
> Heart
> (water of the eye)
> ("Remansos"
> [Puddles])

The poem's landscape is lined with trees. The waters (in parenthetical accompaniment) irrigate the poem harmonically, then modulate into tears. The trees in sudden syncopation take on the human beat of the heart that causes tears. The abstract flow of this poem is that of a painting and a musical composition. He is a bit less abstract about the mustache of a lover—"The puddle of your mouth / under the thicket of your kisses"—or about

> . . . moon rays beating
> on the anvil of the afternoon . . .
>
> If you come looking
> through the highways of the air
> (night is near)
> you'll find me weeping
> under the giant aspens,
> you beautiful brunette!

And there are images lying around such as "stars of lead revolve / upon a foot," and "Bee eater in your obscure trees . . . bee eater. / Eater eater eater eater. / Bee eater"—all in different media, but with Lorca's focus and stroke: "Black bodies hide / the shore of the sea / . . . your hips of Ceres in rhetoric of marble." And there are poems etched like modern Blake, even unto the titles:

He's looking for his voice.
(The king of crickets took it.)
In a drop of water
the boy is looking for his voice.

I won't use it to speak with! (I promise not
to speak with it)
I'll only make a ring of it
for my silence to wear
on its little finger.

In a drop of water
the boy looked for his voice.

(The captive voice was very distant,
wearing the robe of the cricket.)
("El niño mudo" [The Dumb Boy])

I said Good afternoon.
But it was not true.
Noon was another thing
and had disappeared.
And the light shrugs its shoulders
like a virgin.

Noon? Impossible. This
noon is untrue, this noon
has half a moon of lead.
The other half won't come.
And the light, it was plain to see,
was playing statues with the boy . . .
("El niño loco" [The Crazy Boy])

Then the concrete and the abstract meet:

Licorice, snake, and reed.
Aroma, Trace, and Penumbra:
air, land, and solitude
(the ladder reaches the moon)
("Nocturno esquemático"
[Schematic Nocturne])

Images like this unpeopled ladder standing by itself in the empty landscape wrongly relegated Lorca to the dream heap of surrealism. His talent was hospitable to any visual stimulus. He said a poet must be a professor of the five senses, "but it is sight that keeps an image in reality." Images of all sorts keep turning up in this interim period of his work. He even welcomes the insipid guest who tried to destroy modern painting—the Harlequin:

Red nipple of the sun.
Blue nipple of the moon.
Torso half coral.
Half silver and shadow.
("Arlequín")

But once he has the sad brat in his control, notice that Lorca dismembers him and transplants his parts to the sky, sea, metal, and darkness, using the scalpel of cubism.

*Canciones,* however, is not always all that serious. It also contains a delightful series of children's rhymes ("Through the highest corridors / comes a couple of señors,") and unrhymes:

Mama, I want to be of silver.
Son, you'll be very cold.
Mama, I want to be of water.
Son, you'll be very cold.
Mama, embroider me on your pillow.
That yes! Absolutely, this very minute!
("Canción tonta" [Silly Song])

Lorca understands a child's love of mystery. But who is this child making such sophisticated wishes? Or whose ear is pressed against the shell in "Caracola" (Sea Conch)?

They've brought me a seashell.
Inside, I hear the song
of an ocean of maps.
My heart fills with waters
and little fishes of shadow and silver.
They've brought me a seashell!

Who are "they"? Real children of a real mother who speaks in exaggerated wonderment? Or is it the honest amazement of a child given a seashell and hearing in it a sound he can describe only in terms of his geography book? Or is it the timeless yearning of both young and old?

Beware the small voice of these delicate poems; it calls you to a boundless space with answers to no known questions. Lorca explained the voice in an essay on Spanish nursery rhymes and lullabies (*nanas*):

> In the child-songs, the emotion of history's lasting light, without dates or facts, takes refuge. The love and breeze of our country inherent in the *nana* breathes life into dead epochs, the opposite of the stones, the bells, the people or even the language. . . . [Nursery rhyme] defines geographical character and etches a profile which time has rubbed out. . . . Its melody gives blood and palpitation and rigid erotic atmosphere to the characters in the songs.
>
> ("Essay on the Spanish Lullaby")

*Canciones,* like many later works, swings manic-depressively from the loving abandon of "Caracola" and "Canción tonta" to abandoned love. "Es verdad" (It's True) contains true pain:

> Why is it so much work to
> love you the way I love you?
> For love of you the air hurts me,
> my heart
> and my hat.

but humor is integrated even into this dark episode. Even the homosexuals he supported on and off the page receive an ironic verbal drubbing in "Canción del mariquita" (Song of the Sissy):

> The sissy combs his hair
> in his silken nightie . . .
> arranges his curls . . .
> sprays himself with jasmine

while the neighbors laugh and shout. But they, enviously, "spurt planets" when

> The evening disconnects itself
> from combs and entanglements.
> The scandal trembles
> striped like a zebra.
> The sissies of the South
> sing on the terraces.

What a deliciously carefree mix of abstract animal image and concrete human situation. It is in the *Canciones* that one of his most charming, disturbing poems appears. "Despedida" (Good-bye) refracts "Momento" (Moment) in *Deep Song.* In the previous volume he softly but certainly announced his burial wishes:

> When I die,
> bury me with my guitar
> beneath the sand.
> When I die,
> between the orange trees
> and the mint bushes.
> When I die,
> bury me, if you please,
> under a weather vane.
> When I die!

But by the time of "Despedida," he is not entirely certain death will affect him:

> If I die,
> leave the balcony open.
> The child is eating oranges.
> (From my balcony I see him.)
> The mower is mowing the field.
> (From my balcony I hear him.)
> If I die
> leave the balcony open.

Now it's "if" he dies, not "when." Perhaps he has received an intimation of immortality as his success has grown, and now he knows that something of him will never disappear entirely.

Death is always more than mere subject matter for Lorca; it will stalk his pages until it reaches him, as in "Canción de jinete" (Song of the Horseman), which has the brooding quality of Robert Frost:

> Cordoba.
> Far and lonely.
>
> Dark pony, big moon,
> and olives in my saddlebag.
>
> So what if I know the roads?
> I never will arrive at Cordoba.

Over the plain, through the wind
dark pony, red moon.
Death is watching me
from the towers of Cordoba.

Oh this road so long!
Oh my valiant horse
Oh to know Death awaits me
before I arrive at Cordoba.

Cordoba.
Far and lonely.

In "La imagen poética de don Luis de Góngora" (The Poetic Image of Luis de Góngora), Lorca writes:

> A poetic image is always a transference of meaning; Andalusian people call candy "Heaven's Bacon" and a cupola "Half-orange." Penetrating and sensitive imagery. I have heard a farmer in Granada say, "The rushes love to grow on the tongue of the river."

When *Gypsy Ballads* was published in 1928, it brought Lorca international acclaim. It was translated into English (by, among many others, Langston Hughes and Stephen Spender), French, Italian, German, and Esperanto. An Italian literary panel canonized it as one of the ten most important books of this century.

Spanish ballad literature from the Middle Ages is still extant. The ballad (in Spanish *romances*" is historically a miniepic, a few hundred lines of sixteen syllables divided into two equal verses, each ending feminine. Lorca used this same meter with minor variations. Generations were influenced by the ballad's dynamism, from the Golden Age of Spain through Góngora to Unamuno. The ballad is as vigorous as its heroic subjects—and as conservative. Yet this is the form Lorca found most convenient for his subversive purposes.

Lorca's use of this most traditional form in 1927 was a perverse, postmodernist slap at official modernism. (The ballads of Brecht didn't appear until after Germany had seen Lorca's ballads in an edition sponsored by Thomas Mann; Auden began writing ballads after driving an ambulance in 1936 in the Spanish Civil War.) In a letter (8 September 1928) Lorca tells of Dali's "harsh, arbitrary" criticism and of the "putrefactos" who don't understand the simplicity of his ballads, "although they say they do."

But the simplicity "died on my hands in the tenderest way. Now my poetry is on a sharper flight, more personal." Before *Gypsy Ballads* was completed, Lorca retailored this most nationalistic form to the style of the international avant-garde.

The "Romance sonámbulo" (Somnambulist Ballad) is the book's most frequently analyzed poem. The green in the line "Green I want you green" ("Verde que te quiero verde") has been taken to mean "fresh," "moonlit," "cadaverous," "lugubrious," "alive," and "dead." Take your pick of the myriad translations available. We might instead look at the more rarely translated works in the *Gypsy Ballads.* In "Reyerta" (Rumble), each line is like a camera shot in a poker scene:

Blades beautiful with avial blood
shine like fishes.
Sharp gloss of playing card
cuts through the citrus green,
horses bucking
and profiles on them.

Lorca's association with Luis Buñuel, the great surrealist filmmaker and his fellow student at the Residencia de los Estudiantes, bears fruit in this book. The judge surveys the bodies:

Gentlemen of the Civil Guard,
here it is again.
Four Romans dead
and five Carthaginians.

Lorca here intuits Heidegger's "destructive" principle of finding in an image the root that transcends time. He pans his camera past the local constabulary until it rests, transcending time and space, on an ancient battlefield where a similar battle was fought. Lorca often displays this instinct for mixing races and ages, an instinct not unrelated to the work of Eliot, who was being translated into Spanish at the time.

In "La casada infiel" (The Unfaithful Wife), "the starch of her petticoat / sounded in my ears / like a piece of silk / cut by ten daggers." The poem is a masterpiece of irony. A "Gypsy gentleman" makes fast love to another man's wife. It begins in the middle of a thought. Now or never!

> And so I took her down by the river
> believing she was a virgin,
> but she had a husband.

The preparatory scenes omitted, Lorca takes us to the climactic moment so quickly that the ballad becomes almost a skit. But the lines are lyrical, magical.

> The streetlights went out.
> The crickets went on.
> I touched her sleeping breasts
> and they opened to me pronto. . . .
> I scooped a little hollow in the sand
> for the bun on the back of her head.
> I took off my tie.
> She took off her dress.
> I took off my belt and revolver,
> she her four petticoats.
> Her thighs kept slipping away
> like fish caught unawares,
> one of flame, one of ice.
> That night I rode the best of all possible roads
> on a mare of mother-of-pearl. Bareback. . . .

But, being a "legitimate Gypsy gent," he gives her a sewing basket to remind her of her marital role. (It has been suggested that, to insult her, he pays her as a prostitute. What self-respecting prostitute would accept a sewing basket from a client?) His postcoital morality excuses him from falling in love with her because she was unfaithful to him when

> she had a husband
> and said she was a virgin
> when I took her to the river.

Numerical imagery generally delights Lorca; in the *Gypsy Ballads* it multiplies. The lover's wounds in "Romance Sonámbulo" are "three hundred dark red stains." In "La monja gitana" (Gypsy Nun), "five grapefruits sweeter . . . five slits in Christ . . . two riders riding" are in the sexually thwarted nun's sight and "twenty suns above" are burning into her. But the numbers soon become less arbitrary, more social.

To mine the politics embedded in these poems, they could be deconstructed into dramatic components, different voices playing lover, wife, narrator-chorus, townspeople, jury, judge, and so forth. In the three ballads to the patron saints (Raphael of Cordoba, Gabriel of Seville, and Michael of Granada), the characters in the poems help us understand Lorca's declaration that he is "Muslim-Jewish-Christian" (spoken like a devout atheist):

> St. Michael dressed in lace
> in the alcove of his tower
> shows his lovely thighs
> guided by the streetlight. . . .
> Women with hidden asses, big
> as copper planets, visit him,
> nostalgic for a yesterday of nightingales.

It is a yesterday of Arabic arithmetic elegance: "Three thousand nights old," St. Michael remains "King of worlds and odd numbers / in his Moorish finery."

By contrast, St. Raphael's numbers have cabalistic overtones: "Ten noises of Neptune." Ten, the size necessary for a synagogic congregation, where St. Raphael,

> The Jewish archangel in dark sequins
> leads the congregation of waves
> in search of sound and cradle.

The final saint, Gabriel, is decidedly Christian. A poor Gypsy virgin greets the saint of Cordoba "with three nails of joy." In a "little voice trembling with three green almonds," Gabriel promises her a son "with one mole and three wounds in his chest." Then he rises through the air with his "patent leather shoes and embroidered jacket" donated by the Gypsies.

In "Prendimiento de Antoñito el Camborio en el camino de Sevilla" (The Capture of Antoñito de Camborio on the Way to Seville) Antoñito wears "shoes the color of corinth / medallions of worry / and skin massaged with oil and jasmine." "Five Civil Guards" arrest him as "elegantly he strolls, curses between his eyes." His relatives accuse him of disgracing his family by not resisting arrest and not showering on the guards "five jets of blood." Instead, at "nine o' clock at night," he lets them "lock him in the calaboose" without a fight. He pays for his unmanliness in the next ballad, "Muerte de Antoñito el Camborio" (The Death of Antoñito de Camborio). His four cousins use four knives to kill him, and four angels mourn him while "two year old bulls dream / of bullfighting flowers." But suddenly, as in a group painting when Velázquez marks his presence with a self-portrait, Antoñito calls to his author:

> "Ah, Federico García,
> call the Civil Guard!
> They've broken me in two
> like a stalk of corn."
> He gave three blasts of blood
> and died in profile,
> a living coin never to be warmed,
> cushioned by a marching angel.

In "Muerto de amor" (Dead of Love), four lanterns are lit, the time is 11:00 P.M., one thousand dogs pursue a loveless lady as "seven cries, seven bloods, seven double poppies / make opaque moons break / into obscure salons."

In "The Ballad of One About To Be Executed," Amargo appears for the last time in Lorca's poetry. He must be killed again; this time the Civil Guard will do the job. The dying boy "dreams of thirteen boats of peace" as other boys unknowingly swim, like the oblivious skaters in the Nativity painting described in Auden's "Musée des Beaux Arts," or the oblivious farmer in Breughel's *Icarus* also mentioned in that poem. Lorca's imagery of the swimmers is worth noting for the originality with which he invests an old Andalusian expression: Dams, when opened, were called "bulls of the river."

> The dense bulls of water
> charged at the bathing boys
> with their waving horns.

The horns are graphic, rather than symbolic; they are the rushing reflections of the hornlike quarter moon in the waving water. In using the plural "bulls," Lorca makes it clear that the moon appears at one time in many rivers—that all things come from one source and, like Amargo, will return to it. De-symbolizing Lorca is a deepening process.

The poem that most appealed to liberal minds helped get him killed by fascists. "Romance de la Guardia Civil española" (Ballad of the Spanish Civil Guard) is a stripped account of a moment in the life of an oppressed people. As in Germany, it was Spanish policy to persecute the Gypsies. While any comment could violate its poignancy, the poem should be discussed in order to free Lorca's reality "from the shadows that blur the outlines." The poem tells of a raid on a Gypsy village by government-sanctioned vigilantes whose "capes in the moonlight glisten with stains of ink and wax" (of the candles by which they write their dread reports). Hollow as Eliot's men of straw,

> They have—which is why no tears—
> skulls of lead, souls of patent leather. . . .
> They order rubber silence
> and fears as fine as sand.
> Hunched and nocturnal,
> they go where they want
> and when they want.

Their minds have artillery instead of brains, says Lorca; they think in starless darkness

> and hide in their heads
> a vague astronomy
> of unconcrete pistols.

The Gypsy village with its moonlight and pumpkins is momentarily in focus:

O city of Gypsies
who ever saw you can forget?
City of musk and pain
and towers of cinnamon.

Then, raided by the Civil Guard, who "Nighten the night with their night" ("noche que noche nochera")

The Virgin and St. Joseph
lose their castanets
looking for the Gypsies
The Virgin is all dressed up
in a mayor's-wife outfit
of golden chocolate paper
and a necklace of almonds.
St. Joseph moving his arms
under a cape of silk. . . .
Two by two, moving
on the city in its joy,
a double nocturne of uniforms
craves and advances; the sky
is a showcase of spurs.

Even inanimate objects fear the looting of the law:

The city multiplies its doors,
the watches stop, and the cognac
disguises itself as November,
to avoid suspicion.

The town's shadowy streets become an arena of panic, as people die like saints:

The old Gypsy women flee
with their sleepy horses
and their jars of coins.
The parents of Christ
lose faith in authority.
St. Joseph, full of wounds,
shrouds a lady. . . .
The Virgin cleans the children
with a handkerchief spat on by stars. . . .
Rosa of the Camborio family
sits on her stoop and mourns,
her breasts cut off on a tray. . . .
Young women are pursued
by their own braids.

Nature itself capitulates to the gunfire:

Roses of black powder
blossom in the air.
Then the roofs are gullies.
Dawn shrugs its shoulders
wearing a profile of rock
until the Civil Guard
in a turmoil of silence
leave the flaming town.
O, city of Gypsies, who
of you has seen and forgot?
And if you have, you are free
to rummage through my mind—
play of moon and sand.

"Martirio de Santa Olalla" (St. Eulalia's Martyrdom) tells of the slicing off of the breasts of Eulalia (alluded to in "Romance de la Guardia Civil española") another joining of ancient and modern. The ballad of biblical incest, "Thamar y Amnón," recounts the lubricious tale of the virgin sister who "wants snow on her belly" while the brother watches with a "groin full of spume / his nakedness bright and extended / thin and concrete." He rapes her: "warm coral paints a brook on the map / till David cuts the harp."

Finally, a gem to end the discussion: "Preciosa y el aire" (Preciosa and the Wind) is based on Preciosa the Gitanilla (little Gypsy girl) of Cervantes' eponymous novel. Cervantes adored the character enough to write a sonnet about her:

When Preciosa touches her tambourine
Pearls fall from her fingertips;
Her sweet sound wounds the empty air,
And flowers say good-bye to her lips.
Souls are maddened and thought suspended
By her graces so superhuman,
So fresh, so simple, and so pure;
Her fame reaches up and touches Heaven.

Lorca transforms this into one of the most mysterious ballads ever written. Even for him it covers vast territory, from the religious to the sexual to the political. Eventually it arrives at mythic heights, bearing as well on simple adolescent sexual fear. It is the bad dream (or, worse, reality) of a young Gypsy girl caught between a brutish god (the big wind) and the English consul, who lives off the lean of the land, protected by the Civil Guard, seducing the impoverished Gypsies with exotic luxuries, like gin. "Preciosa y el aire" speaks for itself, here in its entirety:

Playing her parchment moon
Preciosa is coming
by an amphibian path
of laurel and crystal.
A starless silence fears
Preciosa's simple sound
falling into the roaring sea
with its song of a dark
night of fish.
On the mountain peaks
sleep the Civil Guard
guarding the white towers
where the English live.
And the Gypsies of the water
build, for a little fun,
arbors of white seashells
and branches of green pine.

Playing her parchment moon
Preciosa is coming.
The wind who never sleeps,
rises to take a look;
full of starry tongues,
peeks at the girl who plays
a sweet, absent song.
"My child, let me lift your dress.
Let me see! Let me see! Let me
open on my ancient fingers
the blue rose of your belly."

Throwing her tambourine, terrified
Preciosa runs, can't stop.
The god of the wind pursuing
with his red hot sword.
The sea muffles its roar.
The olive tree turns pale.
The flutes of shadow sing
to the smooth gong of snow.
Run, Preciosa, run,
the green wind will get you.
Run, Preciosa, run,
but watch him coming closer—
satyr of low stars
with his glittering tongues.

Preciosa, full of fear
runs into a house,
the high house in the pines
where the English consul lives.

Startled by her cries
three Civil Guard arrive
shrouded in capes of black,
hats down over their eyes.

The English give the child
a glass of lukewarm milk,
then a jigger of gin—
which Preciosa does not drink.

And she weeps and tells them all
her adventure in the night
while up on the roof the wind
is biting at the tiles.

The gate closes behind her, but this poem is left mysteriously ajar.

Ortega y Gasset, the internationally influential philosopher, published two of Lorca's elaborate odes in his magazine *Revista de occidente,* one a turbulent prayer for spiritual peace, "Oda al Santísimo Sacramento del Altar" (Ode to the Most Holy Sacrament), and one to the man who put him in the turmoil in the first place—Salvador Dali.

"Oda a Salvador Dalí" is rarely considered important because of Dali's later self-advertising eccentricity, which tended to erase the dazzling talent he displayed in his early work. But there is power and control of the difficult form in the long alexandrine lines Lorca chooses for these odes.

In a letter of 1928, Lorca wrote

> for discipline I'm doing these precise *academic* things now and opening my soul before the symbol of the Sacrament. . . . "Ode to the [Most Holy] Sacrament" contains great intensity. Probably the greatest poem I've ever done. The part on which I'm working now ("Devil, second enemy of the soul") is strong. This "Devil" is really a Devil. This part is obscure, metaphysical, until the extremely cruel beauty of the enemy escapes, a wounding beauty, enemy of love. . . . It's extremely difficult. But my faith will do it. . . . The verse "The unicorn seeks what the rose forgets" I like a lot. It has the indefinable poetic enchantment of blurred conversation.

In 1929 García Lorca was invited to visit Columbia University—the crown prince of European poetry on a graduate fellowship. Morningside Heights knew nothing of his genius; he was treated as another foreign student, just another Latino. His reaction was *Poet in New York,* a violent, indignant war cry and dirge.

Like any non–New York student in his first days in a Columbia dormitory, Lorca didn't feel very secure. He felt

> assassinated by Heaven
> between the forms that go toward the serpent
> and the forms looking for the crystal
> I'm going to let my hair grow.
> ("Vuelta de paseo" ["Back from a Walk"])

In a blur of exile, Lorca sees shapes and forms instead of people, a serpent instead of a river. In a letter he tells of "the loneliness a Spaniard feels, especially an Andalusian! If you fall they stomp you; fall into the harbor, they will drown you in lunch bags where sailors, women, pygmies, soldiers and policemen dance on a sleepy sea, a pasture for sirens, a promenade for morning bells and buoys." He despairs at the sight of New York's "little boys who squash little squirrels with a flush of stained frenzy on the saffron hills."

It seems Central Park wasn't safe then, either. Lorca nostalgically contrasts his own childhood,

> Those eyes of mine in 1910
> never saw a dead man buried
> never saw the weepers of the dawn feasting on garbage,
> nor hearts trembling, cornered like sea horses.
> Those eyes of mine in 1910
> saw the white wall where the girls went to pee,
> saw the muzzle of the bull, the poisonous mushrooms
> and a moon that for no good reason shone on the corners
> on pieces of dry lemon under the hard black of bottles.
> ("1910")

to growing up in New York:

> cigarette butts, bits of food, and shoes without heels. On its way home from the fair, the crowd sings and vomits in groups of hundreds over the railings of the boardwalk. In groups of thousands it urinates in the corners, on abandoned boats or the monument to Garibaldi or to the Unknown Soldier.
> (Charla sobre *Poeta en Nueva York* [Lecture on *Poet in New York*])

Some of his songs of the Gypsies make a safe journey from Spain to the United States: "Malagueña," for instance, with its image of death entering the tavern to the tune of a guitar, could have been set in a saloon near the Brooklyn Navy Yard, where, through mutual literary friends, Lorca met Hart Crane. Crane, surrounded by sailors all drunk on illegal beer, was in a stupor and barely knew who Lorca was. What could have been a literary moment in heaven is just another step down to a hell open twenty-four hours a night. Lorca, in raging reaction, watches sex addicts cruise for the grail of Genet, the lost and lonely of William Burroughs:

Human iguanas come to eat the sleepless men,
broken hearts meet crocodiles under the tender
protest of stars.
Nobody sleeps on this earth, nobody sleeps;
the boy they buried this morning wailed so
they sent out the dogs to silence him.

The past is dead; even Calderón, who wrote *La vida es sueño (Life Is a Dream),* is wrong:

LIFE IS NO DREAM. Watch out!
We will see another day of resurrection of
dried butterflies
and even in the landscape of gray sponges
we will see our gems brighten and roses flow
from our tongues.
But until then Watch out! Watch watch out.
You cannot ignore
that dead man with nothing on but a head and
a shoe.
You will go up against the wall [*llevaros al muro*];
no one asleep under the sky, because close one
eye, boys,
close one eye and hit 'em again, boys, hit 'em
again. . . .
No, nobody's asleep, I swear it
and by the light of the moon the fake drink
the poison and the skull of the theater.
("Ciudad sin sueño"
["The City That Never Sleeps"])

Lorca's natural ability to acquaint himself with a place, its underground, its secrets, its genius, its roots, its rot, was phenomenal. And it was this knack for locale that he displayed as no other poet during his stay in New York:

Under multiplication
there is a drop of duck blood.
Under division
there is a drop of sailor's blood.
Under addition, a river of young blood
a river that comes singing by
the dormitories and the shows,
and it is silver, cement and bronze
in the artificial dawn of New York.
The mountains exist. That I know.
I know. But I have not come to see the sky.
I come to see the oily blood
the blood that drives your car to Niagara
and your spirit to the cobra's gossip.
("New York, Oficina y denuncia"
["New York, Office and Denunciation"])

To escape his cultural isolation, Lorca often went a few blocks north for air, into Harlem. In Spain he had lived and written of the outcast Gypsies, the Andalusian dispossessed, written of them romantically, mystically. Now, he himself had been transformed into a displaced, Gypsy-like outsider in New York. Night after night he went to Lenox Avenue, walked 125th Street, visited the Apollo Theater and the clubs, and lived among the others, the blacks, Gypsies of New York. He began to see them from his underground vantage point, eye to eye, heart to heart.

He had to fashion an epic of the black race of North America, to sing the pain of the blacks in a white world, "slaves of all the white man's inventions and machines," who, as he said in his lecture on *Poet in New York,*

someday will refuse to cook for the whites, or drive their limousine, or button their stiff collar for fear of sticking a fork in their eyes. These inventions do not belong to them. The blacks live on credit, and the fathers have to maintain a strict discipline in their homes lest their women and children worship the phonograph record or eat the flat tires.

Lorca understood the spiritual roots of their politics: "The blacks long to be a nation." He notices how, in a club, an audience "black and wet as caviar, saw a naked dancer shimmying in a rain of invisible fire. But one could catch remoteness in her eyes—remoteness, reserve, the conviction that she was *not here* amid these applauding foreigners and Americans. All Harlem was like her."

Every day Lorca protested in verse. He protested to see "little black children guillotined by hard collars, suits, and violent boots as they emptied the spitoons of old men who walk like ducks." He protested to see "flesh kidnapped from Paradise" and displayed in the Cotton Club. He protested the saddest thing of all, that "the blacks did not want to be black, that they invent pomades to take away the delicious curl of their hair and powders that turn their faces gray and wither the succulent persimmon of their lips."

The "Danza de la muerte" ("Dance of Death") demonstrates his uncanny instinct for the source of suffering in others. Here he sees not only a political basis for black revenge, but a mystical one as well: the slaves were brought to America and deprived of their customs, languages, and religion when they were separated from their tribe. When a people is deprived of its gods, beware:

> Look at the mask, the mask coming
> from Africa to New York!
>
> Crocodile sand and fear upon New York!
> When the bank director watched the gauge
> and measured the cruel silence of coin.

The mask was heading for Wall Street; time for the crash, and then

> The mask will dance between columns of blood
> and numbers
> between hurricanes of gold and the moans of
> workers
> without work, howling in dark night at this
> lightless era
> of savage, impudent North America!

In the panic that is its revenge, the mask will go on dancing, but

> The Pope doesn't dance, nor the King,
> nor the blue tooth millionaire
> nor builders, nor emeralds, nor crazies, nor
> sodomites.
> Only the mask!

And the cobra, the recurrent image of uncoiling consciousness (*cf.* Eliot's *Rock*)

> . . . will hiss on the topmost penthouse
> and thorns will strike the patios and terraces
> and Wall Street will be a pyramid of moss.
> The mask, look at the mask,
> how it spits jungle poison
> into New York's unfinished anguish.

That is, New York's troubles are not over, and will not be over until we address the great cause of America's decline—racism. For though it only starts as a "black flush," the bloody revolutions will come. And they did. The famous one of the 1960's. The Harlem riot of 1943 received almost no attention until Ralph Ellison's *Invisible Man.* Lorca predicted it in 1930, in "Oda al rey de Harlem" (The King of Harlem). As the Mask represents the spirit of Africa, so the King embodies the lost dignity and power.

> Blood looking slow out of the corners of eyes,
> blood rusting the unguarded wind in its tracks,
> blood dissolving the butterflies at the
> windowpanes
> blood coming will come on the roofs and
> ceilings everywhere
> to burn the peroxide off blondes.

The white people must either understand, change, or

> escape to the corners, hide on top floors,
> because the heart of the jungle will crawl
> through the cracks
> and leave in your flesh a slimy trace of eclipse
> and a false sadness of faded love and plastic
> rose.
>
> In the most sapient silence
> the cooks and the waiters and those whose tongues
> clean the millionaire's wounds
> seek a king of the streets.
>
> Oblivion was expressed by three ink-drops on a
> monocle
> and love by a face, alone
> invisible to flowers of stone.
> Marrows and hearts of flowers under the clouds
> composed a desert of stubble, without one rose.

The tenses have gone berserk in the frenzy.

Black Black Black. Black.
No serpent or zebra or mule
even paled at death.
No woodcutter knows
when the thunderous tree he is cutting
will fall . . .

But the tree does, its black anger knows when the time will be right to crash down:

Wait in the shadow of your King
until the hemlock and thistle and thorn
rock the furthermost roofs.
Only then can you dance to the doubtless end
when flowers rise hard.

The endless clothing stores of Harlem were white owned. In them headless torsos of mannequins displayed clothes amid the music of the record stores blaring and the car horns and the wails of despair of a people whose royalty is lost in the crowds.

Oh Harlem in disguise!
Oh Harlem menaced by an army of suits without
heads!
Your noise has reached me
your noise has reached me past trunks and
elevators,
past the gates of gray.

With a spoon
the King of Harlem
gouged out the crocodile eyes
and beat the monkeys on the butt
with a spoon.

Even with so ineffectual a weapon, he must fight. Or make music with it among the smoking nightclub dwellers until dawn.

The flame of forever lurking in the flints,
the roaches drinking anisette
came to the black weeper's den.
The King was banging his spoon,
the tanks of garbage water arriving.

Time for the white people to try to understand the fury of Harlem:

Time to cross the bridges
and reach that black flush
and feel the breathing perfume
in its hot pineapple dress
knocking on our temples.

Time to kill the blonde bootlegger!
O Harlem Harlem Harlem
there is no anguish like your bloodshot
oppression,
your blood gushing in the eclipse of darkness,
your garnet violence deaf and dumb in the
half-light,
your great King prisoner, in janitor stripes!

But still, that night the King drummed away

with his hardest spoon,
gouged out the crocodile's eyes
and beat the monkeys on the butt
with a spoon.

Black Harlem was weeping, confused
beneath umbrellas and suns of gold,
high yellow women stretched gum
anxious for the white torso
and the wind was dusting the mirrors
and burst the veins of the dancers.

Black black. Black Harlem,
blood has no doors to your open-mouth night,
no such furious blood beneath the skin
alive in the spine of the knife.

Blood that searches through a thousand highways
dying of starch and ashes
among the beach's abandoned objects.

where cars float by with teeth sticking out.
past the dead horses and petty crimes,
past your great hopeless king
whose beard reaches down to the sea.

*Poet in New York* is an epic phantasmagoria of the reality lived mostly by New York City's unknown, uptown shadows. Through Harlem's eyes Lorca looked at all of America, what it was doing to its oppressed and depressed. The years were 1929 and 1930. To the weirdly gay songs of the Depression, he wrote a series of dark chords that foretold not only the riots of the 1960's but also the rot of the 1970's and the fall of United States power and esteem, especially in the Third World. *Poet in New York* is a miracle of political poetics.

The work has been called biographical, social, prophetic, mystical, surrealist; Lorca's *Waste Land,* his *Leaves of Grass.* The truth is that from all these seeds combined grew Lorca's anthology of New World flowers of evil that has puzzled many a critic (often needlessly: *Montaña del orso,* for instance, is not "mountain of the bear," but rather the very real Bear Mountain, up the Hudson River near West Point). The bibliography on this one book occupies at least ten pages. It has been the scene of many battles of ideology and the subject of as many revisionisms as has Marx himself. During the Franco regime Spanish critics treated it, like Lorca's murder, as a subject discreetly to be avoided. In the United States during the 1940's it was considered a social excoriation in verse. During the McCarthy era, it was either detoured or approached as a surrealist spiritual breakdown brought on by too much Freudianism and an affair with Salvador Dali. But his letters at the time reveal a depression, a desperation brought on by social and spiritual conditions in the United States that made peasant Spain look comparatively fortunate.

*Poet in New York* is an indignant, unsurrealist work of pure suffering for the nation he is calling out to, as in his "Pequeño poema infinito" (Little Infinite Poem):

> If you take the wrong way
> you get stuck in the snow
> and stuck in the snow
> you graze twenty centuries on graveyard grass.

In 1934 Lorca devoted his energy almost entirely to writing and producing plays. But he was driven by despair to write possibly the greatest elegy of the century. It was translated, sung, recorded, and subjected to constant critical examination. Everything about Lorca was becoming hyperbolic. *Llanto por Ignacio Sánchez Mejías* (*Lament for the Death of a Bullfighter,* 1935) is a four-part invention about the death of a great bullfighter. (In Spain not even artists root for the bull.) Sánchez was also a great patron of poets. He wrote poetry himself (not great). Most of all he was a great friend. Lorca saw in his death the fall of the courage and sensitivity of Spain. He mourned it in this harmonic masterpiece.

Part 1, "La cogida y la muerte" (The Wound and the Death), begins with a tympanic beat announcing the time of his death in the ring, "five in the afternoon." The famous "a las cinco de la tarde" refrain that keeps pounding through this section is like a human nailing a coffin:

> The rest of it was death and only death
> at five in the afternoon.
> The wind blew away the bandages . . .
> at five in the afternoon.
> And a thigh with a deserted horn
> at five in the afternoon.
> The bells of arsenic and smoke
> at five in the afternoon.
> And the corners group in silence
> at five in the afternoon.
> And only the bull's heart was high
> at five in the afternoon.
> When the sweat of snow was arriving
> at five in the afternoon.
> When the stadium was covered with iodine
> at five in the afternoon.
> Death laid eggs in the wound
> at five in the afternoon.
> At five in the afternoon.
> At exactly five in the afternoon . . .
> Bones and flutes sound in his ears. . . .

In Part 2, "La sangre derramada" (The Blood Flows), Lorca refuses to look, calling on history to help:

The cow of the old world
passed her sad tongue
over a snout of bloods
spilled on the sand,
and the bulls of Guisando,
almost death and almost stone,
mooed like two centuries
tired of trodding the earth.
No.
I do not want to see it.

In Part III, "The Body Laid Out," come long lines in a solemn cadence, enormous queues of imagery slowly passing a body lying in state:

Now noble Ignacio lies on the stone.
It's over. What happened?
look at his figure
covered with pale sulphurs
Death has given him a head of dark minotaur.

It's over. It's raining in his mouth.
The air, a fool, leaves his caved-in chest,
and Love, wet with tears of snow,
dries itself on the head of the herd.

What are they saying? The silent odors repose.
We are with a body in state vanishing.

In Part IV, "The Soul Not Here," Lorca knows his friend will be forgotten by most. But those who see the secret spirit of Andalusia escaping his body will not say that he died

like the dead of the Earth,
like the dead forgotten
in a mound of extinguished dogs.

They do not know you. No. But I sing you.
I sing your profile and grace, for *them.*
The stunning maturity of your understanding,
your appetite for death and the joy of its mouth.
The sadness your valiant gaiety had.

It will be a long time, or never, before
an Andalusian so true is born, so rich in motion.
I sing his elegance with sounds that moan,
and I remember a whimpering wind in the olive
trees.

There is an extant photo of Lorca swathed in an Arab's burnoose. In 1936 he published a book of poetry cloaked in Arabic sensibility, *Diván del Tamarit* (*Divan*). Some of his early poems have a transcendent, Semitic quality:

A book of poetry
is the death of Autumn.
The verses are the leaves.
Black on white earth.
("Prólogo" [Prologue])

But *Divan* has a fully Eastern, mystical feel

for imitating the races
beneath the ground; ignorant
of the water, I am in search
of a death of the light
that consumes me.

*Divan* displays Lorca's special gift for identifying with a distant poetics. It is not easy to distinguish between Lorca's original verses here and those of the Arabic poets to whom he paid the tribute of adaptation. But using Pound's "make it new" approach to translation, Lorca also made these *gacelas* very much his own, filling them with sensual surprises:

Nobody could understand the perfume
of the obscure magnolia of your belly.
Nobody knew you were martyring
a hummingbird of love between your teeth.

The following, "Gacela del mercado matutino" (Gacela of the Market in the Morning), is a lush example worth quoting in full to show how he treats a popular form.

I watch by the arch of the church of Elvira
for you to pass me by.
Then I hear them call your name
and I begin to cry.

What gray moon of the morning
sucks your blood as you pass?
Who's been reaping your seedling
that flamed in the snowy grass?

Who blew the little dart of cactus
into your heart of glass?

So go on under the arch of the church of Elvira.
I'll watch you pass me by.
I'll drink the look you do not give me
and begin to cry.

Why do you hit me on the street
with this voice of scorn?
What is a carnation like you
doing among alien thorns?
How near am I when you are gone,
how far when you and I meet!

Under the arch of the church of Elvira
I'll watch you pass me by.

But the time is 1936 and civil war approaches.

The wind is
a tulip of fear
and a very sick tulip
the dawn of Winter.

Sensing political danger, Lorca longs in these last poems

to be far from the tumult of cemeteries,
to sleep a while, a minute, a century only,
so everyone knows I have not died.

Still he plays dangerously; his homosexuality now politically overt, Lorca boldly states his desire "to live with that dark boy / who wanted to cut out his own heart at high tide." But darker trouble is coming.

## *THE PLAYS*

An account of Lorca's dramatic development must consider the forces that contributed to his complex theater aesthetic. Part of his avant-garde legacy was left to him by Spanish experimentalists, from the baroque Góngora to the expressionist Valle-Inclán; the rest came from Paris, which cultivated the intellectual fads that fed Europe's artists. Cultural France distributed German expressionism, Russian structuralism, and Italian futurism, to name just three. These were eagerly assimilated into modernist Spanish poetry, painting, and music (Machado, Gris, and Falla are examples).

As usual, the theater resisted change. Even the few Ibsenian modifications of the famous Jacinto Benavente were not welcome in the theater of rhetorical sentimentality that dominated the Spanish stage. Unfortunately, Benavente did not evolve beyond this minor realistic innovation; he soon bored even himself. His work degenerated into trite pleadings of honorable causes, and he received the Nobel Prize in 1922 (over Wedekind and Pirandello). Victory for the status quo! Spanish theater strove even harder for a new middle of mediocrity. Spanish playwrights and reviewers conspired to keep theatrical taste uncritically intact, managing to halt those hordes of "isms" at the Pyrenees and thus hold the theater in captivity. The result was that Spanish theater had little success, even commercially.

Lorca's first play, *El maleficio de la mariposa* (*The Butterfly's Evil Spell,* 1954), did not improve the situation. Only a claque of his fellow students at the Residencia remained after the first act for its entire run of one performance. This one-night last stand has all the lyric bravado of a young genius. The sudden appearance of a butterfly with a wounded wing among a colony of cockroaches alters the routine of their grubby lives. The suspicious roach colony, though, keeps the winged lady at a distance. She may be evil. The poetroach, an idealist among these dung dwellers, is mesmerized by the sunlit flier's blazing aura; he approaches her. She sings to him the wonders of sun and sky and tree, so inspiring the poetroach that he vainly tries to flap his rudimentary wings. But he cannot fly. Enamored, he begs her to stay. But her wing heals and she joyously flies from the soil, leaving the heartbroken roach behind. A sad shell of his former selflessness, he is unable either to accept the sunless conditions of his existence or to fly free into the sky.

While the plot is immature, there is the free-wheeling lyric invention here that characterizes Lorca's later works. He describes the work in its prologue as:

> a kind of defeated comedy about someone who, reaching for the moon, reached only his own heartbreak. Love . . . occurs in a deep meadow of insects where life is serene and undisturbed. They are content to drink dewdrops and bring up children. They made love out of habit. . . . Ah, but one day an insect tried to go beyond this love. Perhaps he had read a book with one of those poems that begin "O Woman, unrequited, I love you" and questions why stars move in their orbits. This is very harmful to souls not yet completely formed. Needless to say, the foresaken insect dies.

In Act 1, the witchroach, the poetroach's mentor, applies to the wounded butterfly (a common symbol for the soul) warm dew and a poultice of nettle paste:

> *Witchroach:* You know the secrets of waters and flowers
> How awful to see you dying in the dawn
> mourned by the prophetic nightingales.
> How lucky for us repugnant creatures
> to caress your silk-white wings
> and smell the sweetness of your dress.
> (act 1, scene 2)

The poetroach approaches with antennae brazenly painted with lily pollen. He sees the wounded butterfly:

> *Poetroach:* I've never felt such deep sorrow!
> *Sylvia* (A rich roach who loves poetroach in vain): He doesn't love me, mother.
> *Mother:* Just who does he think he is, all gussied up!
> *Witchroach:* Take a moonbath and a siesta, butterfly, in the shade of the ancient wood. Look at her! Isn't she gorgeous?
> *Poetroach:* I can't bear what my heart is going to feel.
> *Witchroach:* My poet, your destiny hangs on the wings of this great moth! Be loathe to love her, your old teacher tells you. Night will fall on your brow, night without stars. Meditate on it.
> (act 1, scene 6)

The poetroach does just that, wondering Don Juanesquely (Lorca's adverb):

> *Poetroach:* What love has the wind knit?
> The flower of my innocence gone
> and another grown.
> Who is she, come to rob my future,
> wings shining like ermine?

Two peasant roaches, one simple and one saintly, gossip about the effect the butterfly has had on the roach. It is an early indication of the sly wit lurking in Lorca's delicate verses:

> *Saintroach:* Did you see that poetroach declaiming away in the meadow?
> *Simpleroach:* That disgusts me. Singing, dreaming of not earning a living, the loafer.
> *Saintroach:* Ah, to quote the Allknowingroach in the Sky: "Dwell you not on the faults of others, for they in my kingdom who play and sing I value more than those who work all day."
> *Simpleroach:* The Allknowingroach never eats? Try telling that to the starving.
> *Saintroach:* Hunger is a demon with antennae of fire who must be driven out by—
> *Simpleroach:* Eating. Right?
> *Saintroach:* Wrong—praying!
> *Simpleroach:* The Allknowingroach in the Sky had some other life in mind. Do me a favor, dear. You're holy and wise. Tell the poetroach to get himself a job. He's going to die over that butterfly.
> (act 3, scene 1)

The poetroach, passing by, is in agreement:

> *Poetroach:* A presence of transparent snow has come to my door to steal my soul away . . .

There is a Krazy Kat quality to all this.

> *Simpleroach:* The poor thing is definitely out of his mind!
> *Poetroach:* What if I die
> and there is no Allknowingroach in the Sky?
> What if I sail beyond the trees
> and find nothing in the celestial seas?
> What if I go beyond above
> and find there is no higher love?

The poetroach is having a poetic breakdown. Meanwhile, the butterfly recovers; her departure is imminent. When the poetroach plights his troth, her only answer is a silent dance, her preparation to fly off among the trees.

> *Poetroach* (to the butterfly): Where do you want to fly to?
> It's night and your wing's still broken;
> I'll heal it with kisses. Marry me
> and an immense nightingale I know
> will fly us to the dawn.
> Don't fly in the dark; dark is so subtle,
> so confusing.
> Stay here and I'll catch a cricket
> to sing you to sleep.
> I'll feed you little sips
> of dewdrops from my nipping lips.
> (He embraces her.)
> Come, you're cold, my den is warm.
> (She withdraws.)
> Heartless butterfly! You go and who
> can I tell my sorrows to?

She is healthy now, ready to fly out of reach. He begins to wail:

> If the water in summer
> is cooled by the shadows,
> if the darkness at night
> is brightened by stars,
> by the endless eyes of the skies,
> why, why can't my soul find love?
> (act 2, scene 7)

He curses his body:

> Who put these sightless eyes on me?
> These handless feet
> cannot touch a love I cannot comprehend
> except to know that it will end my life?
> Why am I left in the darkness?
> Why can't a guy like me fly?

At which point, the Allknowingroach enters, in all his wisdom.

> *Allknowingroach:* What's happening?

This early manuscript ends here, abruptly but perhaps intentionally. It reveals all the passion of Lorca's later, less pastoral, plays, the subtleties of the poetroach lurking in its creator. There is more than promise in this patronized, patronless play. After some sixty-five years, it deserves a longer run than its last one.

The impressionistic one-act *El amor de don Perlimplín con Belisa en su jardín* (*The Love of Don Perlimplín for Belisa in His Garden,* 1938) is minimal by Anglo-American theatrical standards; the short play is to long plays as lyric poems are to epics. *Don Perlimplín,* a reworking of Lorca's own *La zapatera prodigiosa* (*The Shoemaker's Prodigious Wife,* 1938), is a transformation of the popular theme of the impotent husband and the sexy wife. Lorca's multilayered genius is never more evident than in this erotic staged poem. Absurd, touching, political, and musical, the tragic farce goes like this: Perlimplín, a rich, bookish, middle-aged nobleman, loves Belisa, who offstage sings:

> Love, love,
> between my locked-up limbs
> the sun swims like a fish.
> Warm water between the reeds,
> love, love.

But the song changes in its last lines to a warning of Perlimplín's advancing age:

> Cock of the dawn
> the night is moving on!
> Don't let it go,
> oh no!
> (Prologue)

Perlimplín's maid says, "Call her!" He does; she appears, seminude. Perlimplín asks for her hand. Belisa's mother enters, wearing an eighteenth-century wig full of birds and beads: "Mr. Perlimplín, you have the grace of your mother, whom I never had the luck to meet." Perlimplín thanks her. As in the absurdist plays, which had their debut a decade after Lorca's death, the characters do not talk to each other as in Ibsen, nor at each other as in Shaw, but rather through each other, addressing each other's unconscious while the outer selves ramble on, making do: business as usual. Note the nearness in tone to Wilde's *Lady Windermere's Fan,* another absurd precursor:

> *Maid:* We have decided—
> *Perlimplín:* We have decided—
> *Mother:* To enter marital negotiations, isn't that so?
> *Perlimplín:* That's so.
> *Belisa:* And me, Mama?
> *Mother:* And you agree, naturally. . . . Don Perlimplín has many lands; on these lands are many sheep. You take the sheep to market. In the market they give you money. Money gives you beauty. And beauty is coveted by all the other men . . . (To Perlimplín) You see her face, like a lily? (In a husky whisper) You should see what she's like on the inside! Like sugar! Forgive me. Why am I weighing you down with stuff like this, a person like you, so modern, so fantastically sophisticated . . .
> *Perlimplín:* I don't know how to express our gratitude.
> *Mother:* What charm! *Our* gratitude! The double thanks of your heart and your self. Not that I've had anything to do with a man for twenty years . . .
> *Maid:* What about the wedding?
> *Perlimplín:* Yes, the wedding . . .
> *Mother:* Name the day . . .

In the next scene Perlimplín wonders if Belisa has the strength to strangle him; she stands on the balcony, now almost entirely naked, the stage in semidarkness. Past the balcony flies a band of black paper birds.

With the bold syncopation characteristic of Lorca's poetry, the next scene lands us immediately in a nuptial bed that takes up almost the entire stage (like the one in Harvey Fierstein's *Torch Song Trilogy* fifty years later). The sun again "swimming like a fish in her thighs" can't get him over his cold feet. He shyly tiptoes out the door (to soft guitar music), leaving Belisa alone, naked, an enormous coiffure with lace cascading down her body.

> *Belisa:* Who looks for me with ardor will find me. My thirst is like the statues in the fountains who never get wet enough! O this music, o my God! Like the hot down of swans. God, is it me or the music?

She throws a great red velvet cape over her hot body. Suddenly five whistles are heard through five doors! Through a sixth appears Perlimplín with the good news: "I love you."

> *Belisa:* You little gentleman you, you're supposed to.
> *Perlimplín:* Yes?
> *Belisa:* Yes!
> *Perlimplín:* Why yes?
> *Belisa:* Because yes.
> *Perlimplín:* No . . . but when I looked through the keyhole and saw those men I felt love scalpel my throat.
>
> (scene 1)

Five whistles again. Belisa assures Perlimplín it is the clock. Time for bed. Lights out. Five whistles, louder. Two Sprites (Duendes) appear, played by children. Puckishly, they face the audience. They chat about how nice it is to hide the characters' failures:

> *Sprite I:* Because if things are not hidden with great care—
> *Sprite II:* They won't be discovered. And without this hiding and finding out—
> *Sprite I:* What would the poor audience do?
> *Sprite II:* So there mustn't be a hole in the curtain.
> *Sprite I:* Because the holes of today are darkness tomorrow.
> *Sprite II:* That's the fun of fuzzy things. People look into them for secrets they already know.

Here Lorca reveals the spine of the play by allowing two little ghosts to dangle the whole skeleton in front of us. Five balcony doors open, letting in men of five races, who whistle. Blackout.

The next scene, the morning after the wedding night, Perlimplín awakens. When he sits up in bed, a gorgeous rack of antlers has sprouted from his brow. The five open balcony doors have five ladders hooked over their edges, and a hat on each.

The next scene (2) is a week later. Perlimplín's dining table is set up like a distorted Last Supper. The skewed visual perspective prepares us for the juggling of time. The scene takes place shortly after the wedding night, yet there is a decade's worth of frustration in it. The maid weeps, telling Perlimplín not only of the European, Indian, African, Asiatic, and North American men who visited Belisa on her wedding night, but also that Belisa is waiting for a stranger who waves to her in her balcony. Belisa enters, fantasizing of the one whose "greeting makes my breasts tremble." A rock flies through the window; Perlimplín picks it up.

> *Belisa:* Don't read that rock!
> *Perlimplín:* Has he passed by today?
> *Belisa:* Twice, but he waved as if he didn't like me.
> *Perlimplín:* Never fear. I saw him! Never have I seen a chap in whom the virile and the delicate merged in a more harmonious manner.
> *Belisa:* He writes me letters.
> *Perlimplín:* Don't stand on ceremony. Tell your daddy.
> *Belisa:* His letters are about my body.
> *Perlimplín (stroking her hair):* Oh?
> *Belisa:* He writes: "Who the hell wants your soul? Beautiful souls are on the brink of death living in gray hairdos and bony hands." He wants my soft, white, quivering body!
> *Perlimplín:* What if I told you I know this beautiful young man? I am going to do for you what no one ever does for anyone. I am outside the world and its ridiculous moralities!

Don Perlimplín is about to watch his own cuckolding; he will summon the lover himself. We see the subtle satire of the voyeuristic master who cannot touch but who controls the touching, the old senator who sends the young soldier into battle. This play was, in fact, suppressed by General de Rivera, dictator and darling of the nobility.

In the final scene (3), Perlimplín instructs the maid to tell Belisa her mysterious lover will be in the garden that night:

> *Perlimplín:* I want her to love her lover more than she loves her own body. I have no pride, no honor. No honor, no pride.

The maid quits, protesting that while he may have neither honor nor pride, a servant has hers. He begs her to wait until the night is over. What can she do? As the master moves toward his own destruction, the servant must ready him. It is a deconstructive critic's dream play, full of mystical and social puns and psychoanalytical unzippings. Consider the ending itself: the lover, his face hidden in a red cape, returns to Belisa with an emerald dagger ("Green, green, I want you green") sticking in his chest. With his last breath he tells Belisa that Perlimplín thrust the dagger there shouting triumphantly, "Belisa has a soul now!" But the soul is "the booby prize of the weak!": He suddenly reveals himself to be Don Perlimplín; he calls out to himself, "You green, impotent phony! *You* could only enjoy Belisa's soul. *I* loved her body, nothing more! That is why you killed me with your fiery sapling of rare stones!"

> *Perlimplín:* Belisa, I am soul and you are body. (Belisa, half-naked again, embraces him.)
> *Belisa:* Why this deception? Why pretend you were my lover?
> *Perlimplín:* What lover? (He dies.)
> *Belisa:* I never realized he was so complicated.

On this monumental understatement the play comes to a close.

Lorca turns this slight romantic farce into a tour de force of poetry and humor, and in musical form: four balletic conversations replete with verbal pas de deux, pas de trois, and solos. Small, deceptively delicate, it is an erotic "Halleluia" (a Spanish Valentine's card for any occasion)—lacy, flowery, three dimensional. Francis Ferguson calls Perlimplín's deception "the triumph of Lorca's imagination." He had choreographed a dance for the body and the spirit and sent it swirling toward what Cocteau called a poetry of the theater, instead of poetry in the theater.

Still, director beware: one false move and the lace hides the complications—and the laughs. Luis Buñuel ran from a production of *Don Perlimplín* that confused the sentimental with the comical. Poetic theater is a dangerous game. Postmodern poetry, like painting, thrives not on drama but on theatricality. Lorca, as far back as 1929, was experimenting in just that direction.

Tragedy deals with superhuman forces that lead to an awesome comprehension by the human protagonist. In our century, however, poetic protagonists do not have to be human. They can be: History (Pound), Belief (Eliot), Society (Williams), Language (Joyce), or Idea (Stevens). The leading character in *Boda de sangre* (*Blood Wedding*), Yerma, and *La casa de Bernarda Alba* (*The House of Bernarda Alba*) is the spirit of the harsh land in which its author was born and murdered—Andalusia. It is the line that runs throughout the trilogy.

The Andalusians have no great love of this land, which even with irrigation is mainly scrub and cactus. It is ungiving, unworkable, and not their own; from ghettolike pueblos, impoverished commuters work the fields. The men come out early and go home late to a town that is an extended family. There is unity in their love of song and verbal irony. But the most unifying factor is the code. The code says a woman must have *vergüenza,* a sense of guarding the morality of the town. A woman must embody the principles of proper womanhood. She must never talk with a man who is not a blood relative. Even being alone by herself is not desirable. Adultery, of course, is the ultimate disgrace. The violent acts of *Blood Wedding* are not melodrama; they are merely an honest representation of the sheer reality of the Andalusian code.

The early sketches and puppet plays prepared the way for the mature comedies. The poems were a rehearsal for the tragic trilogy. Belief in teaching through poetic theater inspired this tragedy of Spain, a distillation of populist and poetic tendencies. The familiar themes are love and death, but they have a political shimmer. Having no right to freedom, the frustrated heroines of the trilogy are doomed either to give death or to receive it. While their sounds are suppressed, their silence calls to all of oppressed Spain.

*Blood Wedding* concerns the willing seduction of a bride by her former sweetheart, Leonardo. His family has killed the bridegroom's father and brothers. Leonardo abducts her and is pursued by the bridegroom into a forest. The two men kill each other; the groom's mother mourns the inevitable death of her last son. The bride, looking for love, instead causes death in the form of traditional honor.

In Granada's newspaper there was a story of a bride who ran off with a former lover on her wedding day. Following his own method of "letting a play write itself," Lorca kept the story in the fertile dark until, directed by its author in 1933, *Blood Wedding* was a critical and popular success. The title itself is a torn and bloody curtain that opens on an old family wound. As in the newspaper account, the bride runs off with her former lover on her wedding day. This is journalism at its most dramatic. But dramatically speaking, it is journalistic. Lorca heightens the conflict by having the bride come from a family in a lifelong blood feud with the family of the groom. The poet tosses the familiar cuckoldry theme (ordinarily the province of melodrama, or its kissing cousin, farce) into the ring of tragedy, resonating with the dry wind of a landscape as arid as its rules of honor. Blood only will feed the soil that produces wine, the sensuous grapes bursting in the mouth. The blood flows on, generation to generation, grave to grave, as man after man is killed in the population-control process known as vendetta.

The bride and groom have tried to cross impossible rivers of blood; they are a kind of reverse Romeo and Juliet, their marriage grudgingly ratified by two hated and hating families. But their love is unable to quiet the blood-hate rumbling through the family's veins. The Mother of the Groom personifies this. Try as she might to start off the wedding day with a smile, she does not fully share the joy. It reminds her of her days of fulfillment with a man who lay on her "smelling of carnation and strong as a bull," a man who was killed by

one of those little knives,
barely fits in the palm of the hand.
Makes you feel so grand—
it was one of those blades
that pierces the skin
goes all the way in
oh into the stream
it goes down through the blood
and it tickles
the root of a scream.

(act 3, scene 3)

This is the song she repeats when her dead son is carried in at the end. There is a self-fulfilling prophecy to her constantly recalling the blood images in her head, the arms flashing in the light, and her hate-lust. When, in fact, the blood spurts on the quivering air, it is as if she had been waiting to say, "I told you so!" She had lived this moment of her son's death from the day she buried her husband and put on the black costume she would never again remove. It would, she knew, come in handy all too soon in a way of life that flows with blood.

All the characters except Leonardo, the passionate, natural lover, are abstractions without personal names. They are Bride, Mother, Groom, Death—as though their human qualities disappear into the air and sink into the land, the real villain in the piece.

Catholicism in Andalusia is fervidly joined to faith in Gypsy fertility cures. Children are a godlike proof of moral evolution, as is characteristic of the Jewish and Islamic traditions that prevail in Moorish Andalusia. In *Yerma,* the trilogy shifts to the home of a morose, childless couple. Yerma believes she is barren. She goes "in a tide of fire" to a Gypsy conjurer who assures Yerma ("May my mouth fill with ants like the mouths of the dead if I lie") that she can have a child.

Yerma thirsts for a child at her breast "even if when he grows up he will drag me through the streets by the hair! Better to live with a son who'd kill me than with this vampire husband, year after year sucking my heart dry." In the code of the infertile Andalusian plain, an empty womb is like an open grave. The land must have sons who can force the dry soil to yield, who can husband it, make it give life. The woman's joy is to feed her man's appetites, but he must repay her with a child, or she becomes the walking dead.

Yerma's husband, Juan, forever works the land, "counts money at night after a day with his sheep, then covers [Yerma] with a dutiful belly as cold as a corpse." And he doesn't want children! All that matters is what he can hold, money and land, with no children to take them from him. In the last scene she wants to know what Juan wants with her.

*Juan:* I want you!
*Yerma:* You mean my cleaning, my cooking, my body!
*Juan:* I'm a man, like other men.

He forces her to the floor; she pleads with him, once and for all, to put life into her body. With his hands on her loins and his lips to her ear, he admits he is sterile.

*Juan:* Do I have to scream in your ear to make you understand? Now just lie back peacefully.

> *Yerma:* I should not hope for one?
> *Juan:* No.
> *Yerma:* Empty.
> *Juan:* Lie back, in peace, sweetly, you and I. Hold me!

He forces himself on top of her. She looks up at his face:

> *Juan:* In the moon you are so beautiful.
> *Yerma:* Hunting me like a pigeon to eat!
> *Juan:* Kiss me . . . like this. (Her hands grab his throat.)
> *Yerma:* Never.

She chokes him to death. In the background, a passing pilgrim sings a litany to her sacrifice for the sacrament denied her.

> I am alone for certain and I'll sleep with a dry body forever. I myself have killed my son, who might have announced to my blood new blood.
> (act 3, scene 2)

The tomb of her womb will be empty, but not because a son has risen.

This play is not a straightforward narrative; the wild dramatic leaps, the pregnant ellipses, and the sexual images are a fertile linguistic counterpoint to the barrenness of Yerma, our lady of the wasteland.

In a letter about *The House of Bernarda Alba,* Lorca wrote "My whole style must change. This is 1936. Just reality! I have no time for hallucination. Pure reality. A simple document. See? Not a drop of poetry! A photograph!" But, as photographer Garry Winogrand noted, there is nothing as mysterious as a fact clearly described. The decorum that Bernarda Alba's household projects to the rest of the town contrasts painfully to the reality of Bernarda's five frustrated daughters. The eldest (and richest) is engaged to Pepe el Romano. Pepe is prepared to marry the unattractive, thirty-nine-year-old Angustias. The youngest, twenty-year-old Adela, is furious. Pepe has made love to her. Though another sister, Martirio, denounces Adela's outspoken affections for Pepe, they all run to the window when he passes outside.

In act 2, Martirio steals Angustias' picture of Pepe. Adela is furious to discover her sister's hypocrisy, but she also admits having "had" Pepe the night before. Before Bernarda Alba can find out, there are terrible screams in the street. A woman who has had a child out of wedlock is being punished. Bernarda tells Adela, "They ought to shove a hot poker right where she sinned." The curtain falls on Adela feeling her stomach as Bernarda shouts to the women's tormentors, "Kill her!"

In act 3, as a stallion bucks against the wall from the stable next door, desire threatens to inflame the house. Angustias' impending marriage to Pepe is discussed with frightening calm. Martirio and Adela are insanely envious of Angustias and writhing jealously. When the rest of the household is asleep, Adela tries to leave to meet Pepe. Martirio catches her and they fight. Bernarda Alba awakens. Martirio tells of Adela's affair with Pepe. Bernarda leaves the house with a rifle. A gun goes off outside. Martirio tells Adela their mother killed Pepe. Adela kills herself. But Martirio was lying; Bernarda missed and Pepe was seen on horseback carrying his sexuality off into the night—as the horse keeps bucking against the walls of the house. Bernarda says Adela will be buried as a virgin.

The barren world of *Yerma* is developed further in this, Lorca's last play (*alba* in Latin means white, the absence of all color). There is a contrast between the women locked in the house and the men outside, trying to break through the wombish walls and enter. Even the stallion is trying to kick through its stall next door—a metaphor for the unbridled passion that takes the sisters from frustration to abandon. The house's eggshell-colored walls, blanched faces, and pallid lips are all the whiter against the black of the women's dresses. Sparse furnishings emphasize the virginal emptiness, again at odds with the passion of the daughters. The occupants of the house are in the grips of a great, corroding chastity belt.

Yet the playwright tells us these "walls are barren but for a few pictures of unlikely landscapes full of nymphs and legendary kings." The "art" on the walls strokes the consciousness of the spinster daughters (and the audience); an unconscious yearning for nymphlike freedom rests its eyes on a distant painted past when rulers cared and caressed. Representing a nondimensional hope, these men in the pictures are much like the photo of the missing husband in *The Glass Menagerie.* The difference is that in *Bernarda Alba* the painted men are the only ones we ever see. When an actual photo of Pepe el Romano is lost, it is enough to cause a quiet riot among all the sisters. All, including Bernarda Alba herself, treat the image as the man himself.

This is poetry converted into dramatic action: wordless provocation of ideas, a subliminal communication of the psychological, spiritual, sexual, and sociological interplay of the characters and forces that will justify the terrifying action in the last act. In this almost Beckettian emptiness, the women live their lives to the empty accompaniment of the town bells, which toll twice for a female corpse of a virgin, and the bucking of the stallion in the stable contiguous to the house, a part of their lives.

The set and sounds are two ways Lorca builds a nonverbal case out of the echoes and shadows of poetry. Though the verse form is lacking, the moments of poetry do not stop from the opening image to Bernarda's final exhortation: "No weeping! Death must be looked at face to face. Silence. We'll drown ourselves in the mourning of the Sea." The sea, the mother of all things, the dread sea of J. M. Synge (as translated by Lorca's early master, Jiménez).

Before we leave this trilogy that gives birth to nothing but death, we should look once again at the political criticism implied in such a house, where the children are so at odds with each other that they are dominated by one they could dethrone easily, if they could but unite. The varying factions on both the Left and Right at this time (1936) provide a link between Lorca's implicit comments on Spanish social life in the trilogy and the firing squad he faced for his efforts toward a political poetics.

*Doña Rosita la soltera* (*Doña Rosita, the Spinster,* 1938) has been called Lorca's Chekhovian play. There are shades of *The Cherry Orchard* and *The Three Sisters* in this pastel household's dissolution; all three acts deal with the passing of possibility as Rosita languishes over a lover who will never return. In the first act, youthful, delightful Rosita (little Rose) is happily engaged. Her fiancé, however, is needed to run his family's South American plantation. Rosita promises to wait; her lover promises to return. He never does—that is the plot, the skeleton of the play, as opposed to the story, which fleshes out the play with such details as the comically drawn aunt and uncle with whom she lives until the return of her absent lover. Her uncle discusses nothing but his roses. His favorite is Rosa Mutabile, a variety that blossoms, fades, and dies—all in one day.

> *Aunt:* Has the Rosa Mutabile blossomed yet?
> *Uncle:* Just beginning.
> *Aunt:* How long does it last?
> *Uncle:* One day. I intend to watch it all day long.
> (act 1)

In the first act, Rosita too is colorful in the dawn of her youth; in act 2 the empty age of thirty will blanch her skin; in act 3 the long night of her forties moves her toward despair. Others can do nothing but watch the flower of Rosita's youth decay:

> The Rosa Mutabile
> is blood red at dawn,
> coral, bursting. But
> when the afternoon faints
> the rose grows sallow
> like a cheek of salt. . . .
>
> and at the edge of darkness,
> her petals fall.
> (act 1)

The image is implanted in the play like a garden graft. As the plot develops, we look through a rose-colored veil, for the play is also implanted in the image. This is the dramatic imagery of a poet.

When, fifteen years after the time of act 1, Rosita receives a letter from her lover asking for her hand in marriage—by proxy—her uncle enters bearing the Rosa Mutabile "still red with the fire of its youth." But he has cut it by mistake before it has had a chance to mature. Rosita's memory is also cut; she has forgotten what her lover looks like.

The metaphor of roses is continued through act 2, but the housekeeper provides realistic comic relief when she wishes the roses were pears, cherries, or persimmons—traditionally, three sexual fruits. The aunt, mistress of the house, accuses the housekeeper of preferring food to beauty. The maid boldly replies, "I have a mouth for eating, dancing legs, and between them something else that likes to be fed." Lorca's maids are born in his political reality, unlike theater's customary wisecracking maid who seems never to have washed underwear for the household.

Lorca's humor can be satirical as well. Professor X, who speaks with the uncle, doubles as relief and chorus. The scene is set in 1900.

> *Professor X:* What progress!! Mr. Longoria of Madrid has just bought an automobile he can drive at the fantastic speed of twenty miles per hour, and the Shah of Persia, a very pleasant man, bought a Panhard Levassor, twenty-four horsepower.
> *Uncle:* The Paris-Madrid race was suspended because the racers all killed each other before they reached Bordeaux.
> *Professor X:* Count Zboronsky, dead in that accident, and Marcel Renault, or Renol, such in both fashions it can be pronounced, are saints of science who will be canonized as soon as we have a progressive religion.
> *Uncle:* You can't convert me.
> *Professor X:* A political science professor need not argue with a rose gardener. Such mystical practices are out, believe me! Nowadays, new paths are opened by Tolstwa, or Tolstoy, since in both fashions it may be pronounced. I myself live in the *polis,* not in *natura.*
> *Uncle:* One lives as one can.
> *Professor X:* If Santos Durmont, instead of studying comparative meteorology had dedicated himself to watching roses, the dirigible would be still in the bosom of Brahma.
> *Uncle:* Botany is a science.
> *Professor X:* But an *applied* science.
>
> (act 2)

This au courant, cosmopolitan, urbane buffoon has provided us with some laughs, but suddenly Lorca turns on a dime; the professor asks Rosita's hand in marriage. In an instant, we know what her matrimonial stock is worth: nothing.

The action of act 3 occurs ten years later. The uncle is dead, the house is sold. Aunt, Housekeeper, and Rosita are about to move. Rosita is urged to marry, but she won't abide the addlepated suitors who have appeared over the "years that fall like undergarments ripped from my body." Her lover has never again written. She is resigned, but she still speaks even of her betrayal in the pillowy murmurs of superannuated love; the maid and the aunt are more direct:

> *Aunt:* The false heart of the man! I'd like to take a boat, pick up a whip—
> *Maid* (interrupting): And take a sword and cut off his head and bash it with two stones and chop off that hand with its false lying letters of affection.
> *Aunt:* Ah, yes! Make him pay with blood what has cost blood. And afterward . . .
> *Maid:* Scatter the ashes over the sea, and
> *Aunt:* . . . revive him and bring him to Rosita with our honor satisfied.

The aunt and the housekeeper, in adversity, speak the same class of language. Rosita appears in a dress of light rose and doll-like long curls. She has aged much. Lorca's humor, though, remains unchanged.

> *Rosita:* What are you doing?
> *Maid:* Criticizing a bit.

An epiphanic moment that might well have influenced Tennessee Williams then occurs: a teenage boy arrives and tells Rosita that he put on his dead mother's dress for Carnival, but it scared him. As he leaves, the wind blows up "as if to make the garden ugly and lessen the pain" of leaving the place. The housekeeper comments, "Beautiful it never was." The three women leave the house—silent but for a door banging in the wind at the final curtain.

There are traces of allegory in the potency that leaves Spain for the New World, in people playing with gardens and tools while the freshness of Spain disappears like the Rosa Mutabile that dies in the short day that is a life, a century or two of a nation.

While in New York, Lorca somehow managed to find time between *Poet in New York* and a surrealist movie script, "Trip to the Moon," to work on what he called his impossible plays. They are highly innovative and not very original. Surrealistic hijinks poorly cover the thin themes of sexual freedom and artistic integrity.

*Así que pasen cinco años* (*If Five Years Pass,* 1937) is a complicated play about the simple idea of trying to stop time. Time is not only the idea but the device. Clocks strike but do not move, tenses collide in one sentence. The cast is multitudinous and miraculous. A cat talks, a mannequin walks, a football player produces endless Havana cigars from his knee pads. The Young Man (all characters in the play are abstractions) awaits his Betrothed, who runs and embraces the Football Player, her "dragon" who blows smoke in her face. An Old Man says she is only fifteen years old. The young man, still trying to destroy time, says, "Why not fifteen things old? . . . or Fifteen roses old?" Lorca specialists have found virtues in this play's early attempts at expressionism.

His play *El paseo de Buster Keaton* (*Buster Keaton's Promenade,* 1928) is a slapstick, surrealist piece that works on absolutely no level except that of fun. It contains stunning images and, small as it is, shows his genius for the consequential detail, bursting with energy, full as a tick. From the ending:

> *Buster Keaton* (surprised): I wish I could be a swan. But I can't although I want to. Where would I leave my hat, my bird collar, and my tie. What bad luck!
> (A young girl, wispy and tall, enters, riding a bicycle. She has the head of a nightingale.)
> *Young Girl:* To whom do I owe the honor?
> *Buster Keaton* (with reverence): A Buster Keaton.
> (The young girl faints and falls from the bicycle. Her striped legs tremble in the grass like two dying zebras. A gramophone announces in a thousand voices, "There are no nightingales in America!")
> *Buster Keaton* (on his knees): Excuse me for what I have been! Miss! (lower) Miss! (lower still) Miss! (kisses her).
> (On the Philadelphia horizon appear the brilliant stars of a police car.)

There are other romps impossible to describe, very arbitrary and obscure; some curiously funny, some daringly dull. *Retablillo de don Cristóbal* (*In the Flame of Don Cristóbal,* 1938) is a puppet-falsetto farce, simple and cunningly contrived, as true farces must be. Cristóbal is Lorca's commedia dell'arte hero, violently in love with his wife, Rosita (no relation to the spinster). She deceives him with every other man in the play, including its Director and Author; even the man he robbed and clubbed to death returns to enjoy her favors, all three beautiful feet of her.

In the prologue, the Author-Puppet assures the audience the earthy innocence of their charmingly free language will purify the commercial vulgarity entering the audience's home. The Director threatens to deprive the Author of his crust of bread if he doesn't cease blathering about good and evil. The piece continues in this slapstick folk form which Lorca considered to be the "temperature of a country's grace."

While in New York, Lorca worked on a play that was translated only recently: *El público*

(*The Audience,* 1934), meaning either the "public" or the "audience," an intentional ambiguity. It is about the audience and the public and their attitude toward individuality in art and sex. It is too complicated to reproduce here. In fact it has proven too complicated for any theater company to produce. By 1931, gravely affected by his stay in New York, Lorca was unambiguously favoring the public rather than the audience in terms of his work. He decided to take his work and the work of the early masters he loved and place them before the deprived, the assaulted, the illiterate populace.

Lorca left his family and the literary court of Madrid and bought two busses, which he filled with actors and students, intending to travel the countryside performing plays for "the forgotten." He produced the great works of Lope, Cervantes, and Calderón—productions that, Brecht-like, teach the illiterate through theater. He rolled happily through the peasant hills with his troupe of young artists and artisans of Spain, a kind of 1960's street theater engaged in the battle he first learned existed during that year-long lesson as a Columbia student.

It would have been difficult in the Spain of the 1930's to avoid the air of social change from South America. Spain's poor were changing. They no longer thought they were predestined by God to serve the nobility. The idea of possibilities for the next generation began to grow; the avant-garde endorsed it. Diego Rivera's murals pitted Lenin and Debs against Rockefeller and the czar.

The path to economic enlightenment was a labyrinth of Marxism, Leninism, Stalinism, and social democracy. But while liberals argued ideologies, Franco's vigilantes—equipped with Spanish zeal and German weapons—struck. They were the military arm of a crusade against Freud and Marx, against Gypsies, atheists, homosexuals, and democracy.

When official education fails, the task of educating often falls to the artist. Lorca, in this activist moment, determined to educate through his group of actors, students, and professionals. His poetic guerrilla theater was named La Barraca, after a novel by Blasco-Ibáñez about the Spanish peasants' plight. The name (The Barrack) obviously has a military connotation as well; Lorca was conscious of hermeneutics even as he was helping build sets and paint backdrops.

Lorca's La Barraca was the outcome of the bloodless revolution of April 1931 that banished Alfonso XIII from his throne and established a republic. The plan for La Barraca was presented by the Union Federal de Estudiantes Hispanicos, a students' coalition. Costs would be limited. The actors would all be students and professional friends. Lorca explained:

> La Barraca will be placed in a public park until the wandering *barraca,* the caravan theater, can go on wheels through the outskirts of Madrid on weekends and holidays. And in the summer we will tour Spain. Students in architecture will make the *barracas* and do the stage setting and assembling; students in philosophy will collaborate with the poets of the executive committee. I myself will be writing new things and helping with old ones.
>
> ("La barraca")

The new republican government approved money for the student actors and stage hands; busses were bought. La Barraca went on the road. Lorca produced his own version of Calderón's *Life Is a Dream* to celebrate the 400th anniversary of the play. He also adapted Lope de Vega's *Fuente Ovejuna (The Village of Fuente Ovejuna).* The plot: when a military commander sexually abuses the women of the town, he is flung from his palace balcony onto the prongs of the villagers' pitchforks. During the "trial" that ensues, the Inquisition tortures all the men and women of the village. They have agreed, however, not to name names. When asked who killed the commander, every citizen under oath and under the whip answers that the perpetrator was "the village of Fuente Ovejuna." The king and queen, Ferdinand and Isabella, with a wisdom Lope hints is divinely bestowed upon just rulers, decide to eliminate military rule in the town, avoiding further pollution of justice. The civilized, if not exactly civil, rule of Ferdinand and Isabella becomes abstract rather than historical in Lorca's hands. Look at production: the sets were contemporary; the medieval warlord of Lope's original became a contemporary landowner. The message was clear: peasants and bourgeoisie must never again be ruled by someone whose rape of the people is the only contact between ruler and ruled.

Following the populist footsteps of Lope (whose ars dramatica was "Damn the purists, full fun ahead!"), La Barraca presented Lope's classics on two nights—the first in the old version, the second simplified but stylized, "new as the latest experiment." Lorca charged little or no admission so that working people could attend. Lorca spattered the plays with verse set to popular melodies, like Lope, like the English Restoration ballad opera, and very much like Brecht's *Threepenny Opera.* Indeed, it seems the Brechtian commitment—already ten years on the boards—made its way across the Rhine and over the Sierras to land in Spain. Again, from "La barraca":

> The theater, in essence a part of the people, is almost dead, and the people are suffering accordingly, as they would if they had lost eyes, ears, or a sense of taste. We are going to give them back the very plays they used to love. Also, new plays in the modern manner, explained ahead of time, will be presented with the simplifications necessary to our plan.

They were in fine company. Brecht that same year turned *Richard III* into a Hitlerian Chicago gangster with *The Resistible Rise of Arturo Ui;* Lorca's Andalusian predecessor Seneca had transformed *Oedipus Tyrannus* into a moral Grand Guignol. It was "a way to educate the people of our beloved Republic, to take Good and Evil" in his bus around Spain.

La Barraca fell quickly in Spain. Conservatives in the shaky new republican government accused La Barraca of having moved politically left. They were right.

Expressionistic methods focused starkly on political implications. For instance, the lovers in Lope's *Peribáñez,* in their antisocial oblivion, reflect Unamuno's statement about Spanish intellectuals and the rise of fascism: "We never had any idea what was coming our way." So the unschooled, uncared-for audience at the dusty end of town found one place on a makeshift stage where ideas could be laughed at, applauded, and absorbed—where ideas had the floor. La Barraca toured in 1933 and 1934. While Hitler was mobilizing, Lorca's only weapon was Spain's Shakespeare, Lope.

Fifty years after Lorca's murder, it is still impossible to determine the accomplices. Several possibilities exist. In Granada a "Black Squad" of killers, whom the Civil Guard turned loose, terrorized the city. Apologists for Generalissimo Franco hoped these "uncontrollable elements" were at fault in Lorca's death. The varying factions of Spanish fascism blamed each other for the murder—and all blamed the Civil Guard. The buck was passed over Lorca's corpse writhing in an unmarked grave.

Gerald Brenan noted that the fascist journalist De Llano suggested the murder of Lorca was vengeance for the death of Benavente—a rather hysterical claim, considering Benavente lived until long after the war. A Lorchean twist.

Lorca was caught while hiding in the house of a literary Phalangist friend, Rosales. Members of the Rosales family were political and literary enemies of Ruiz Alonso, whose awful poetry had been rejected by Lorca and Rosales' magazine. It was he who turned in Lorca, according to Marcelle Auclair. Possible, Jean-Louis Schonberg suggested that the arrest was not strictly political but based on homosexual jealousy, with Ruiz Alonso again rejected by Lorca, this time personally.

Ian Gibson, after thorough research and consideration, concluded that Lorca was killed "not by any one man but by a group of ultra-Catholic members and the like-minded of *Acción Popular,* among whom Ruiz Alonso was most influential."

Of the three men who took Lorca from the Rosales' house, one, Trecastro, boasted of his part in the execution. V. S. Pritchett says we should take the words of this womanizing café hero with more than just one grain of salt, but there is no doubt Acción Popular hated Lorca for his contacts with the few liberal intellectuals in Granada. Granada was a deeply conservative city that had earlier resented the invasion of the Generation of '98. Now, with the beginnings of a peasant organization, the local establishment, traditional and intolerant since the Counter-Reformation, correctly saw liberal reform in education as a threat.

Lorca was too visible, dangerous, liberal. He was shot. Despite his literary victory over symbolism, his death had a symbolic significance; over four thousand people were shot by firing squad in Granada alone. While he had no defined political position, his death, as Pritchett noted, revealed "the ferocity which Franco awakened in a nation notoriously prone to violence."

While he was acquainted with left-wing politicians, his friends were Phalangists such as Rosales and José Antonio Primo de Rivera, the artistic dictator. What could have aroused such anger for him to be lined up one dawn in the first month of the war and machine gunned (some say through the anus)? The most significant answer comes from his betrayer, Ruiz Alonso: "He did more damage with his pen than others did with their guns."

## Selected Bibliography


### EDITIONS

#### INDIVIDUAL WORKS

*Impresiones y paisajes.* Granada, 1918.
*Libro de poemas.* Madrid, 1921.
*Santa Lucía y San Lázaro.* Madrid, 1927.
*Primer romancero gitano.* Madrid, 1928.
*Poema del cante jondo.* Madrid, 1931.
*Llanto por Ignacio Sánchez Mejías.* Madrid, 1935.
*Nocturno del hueco.* Madrid, 1935.
*Seis poemas galegos.* Santiago de Compostela, 1935.
*Diván del Tamarit.* New York, 1936.
*Primeras canciones.* Madrid, 1936.
*Poeta en Nueva York.* Madrid, 1940.

#### COLLECTED WORKS

*Obras completas.* Madrid, 1971. Contains bibliography.

### TRANSLATIONS

*Deep Song and Other Prose.* Edited and translated by Christopher Maurer. New York, 1980.
*Five Plays: Comedies and Tragicomedies.* Translated by James Graham-Luján and Richard L. O'Connell. New York, 1965.
*Impressions and Landscapes.* Translated by Lawrence H. Klibbe. Hanover, N.H., 1987.
*Poet in New York.* Translated by Ben Bellitt. New York, 1983.
*The Public and Play Without a Title.* Translated by Carlos Bauer. New York, 1983.
*Selected Letters.* Edited and translated by David Gershator. New York, 1983.
*Selected Poems.* Edited by Donald Allen and Francisco García Lorca. New York, 1955.
*Three Tragedies.* Translated by James Graham-Luján and Richard L. O'Connell. New York, 1947.

### BIOGRAPHICAL AND CRITICAL STUDIES

Adams, Mildred. *García Lorca: Playwright and Poet.* New York, 1977.
Aiken, Conrad. "Review of *The Poet in New York and Other Poems of Federico García Lorca.*" *New Republic* 103:309 (1940).
Alberti, Rafael, "García Lorca: *Poeta en Nueva York.*" *Sur* (Buenos Aires), 75:147–151 (1940).
Allen, Rupert C. *The Symbolic World of Federico García Lorca.* Albuquerque, N. Mex., 1972.
Butt, John. *Writers and Politics in Modern Spain.* New York, 1978.
Campbell, Roy. *Lorca.* New Haven, Conn., 1952.
Craige, Betty Jean. *Lorca's Poet in New York: The Fall into Consciousness.* Lexington, Kentucky, 1977.
Duran, Manuel. *Lorca: A Collection of Critical Essays.* Englewood Cliffs, N.J., 1962.
Frazier, Brenda, *La mujer en al teatro de Federico García Lorca.* Madrid, 1973.
Gabriel, Isidro. *Los mejores romances de la lengua castellana.* Buenos Aires, 1961.
Gibson, Ian. *The Death of Lorca.* Chicago, 1973.

———. *Federico García Lorca: A Life.* New York, 1989.

Gorman, John. *The Reception of Federico García Lorca in Germany.* Göppingen, 1973.

Higginbotham, Virginia. "Lorca's Apprenticeship in Surrealism." *Romanic Review* 61:109–122 (1970).

Honig, Edwin. *García Lorca.* New York, 1944.

Ilie, Paul. *The Surrealist Mode in Spanish Literature.* Ann Arbor, Mich., 1968.

Loughran, David K. *Federico García Lorca: The Poetry of Limits.* London, 1978.

Marcilly, Charles. *Ronde et fable de la solitude à New York. Prelude à Poeta en Nueva York de F. G. Lorca.* Paris, 1962.

Martínez Nadal, Rafael. *Federico García Lorca and the Public.* New York, 1974.

Ramos Gil, Carlos. *Ecos antiguos, estructuras nuevas, y mundo primario de la lírica de Lorca.* Bahía Blanca, 1967.

Rossi, Rosa. *Da Unamuno a Lorca.* Catania via Caronda, 1967.

ARNOLD WEINSTEIN

# ANDRÉ GIDE
## (1869–1951)

THROUGHOUT ALL HIS life and work André Gide searched for a plenitude that would balance and satisfy the needs engendered by various aspects of his personality: a persistent inclination toward mysticism and introspection, an ever-present temptation to indulge in pleasures of the flesh, and a need for rational testing and recording of experience. It took Gide the better part of eighty years to achieve some degree of fullness of experience and to reconcile antinomies within himself. He had progeny, he made peace with his God, he experienced the intensities of human existence, and he left behind him his complete works. As he wrote in *Thésée* (*Theseus,* 1946), "For the good of future humanity, I have done my work. I have lived."

If in eighty-two years Gide managed to accomplish so much, it took him at least the first twenty-four to formulate and to see the virtues of plenitude. Formed by the rigorous Protestant ethic, with its penchant for introspection, of his widowed mother and her companion, Anna Shackleton, Gide spent his early life attempting to enforce ascetic principles of behavior; he denied the sensual, the temporal, and the real in favor of the spiritual, the eternal, and the imaginary. He was ideally suited for the symbolist movement, or so it seemed from his first book, *Les cahiers d'André Walter* (The Notebooks of André Walter, translated as *The White Notebook,* 1891). But nothing human can be suppressed successfully, as Gide learned through experience. The more his hero tries to follow the ascetic path, the more he feels tempted by the scenic route; moreover, temptations overcome make him vulnerable to the sins of pride. Made distraught by his own ambivalent nature, by the evanescent world of his mind, by the ambiguity of his relationship with his cousin and intended wife, and by all sensual contact with the world, André Walter dies of brain fever and of the hallucinations he has learned to invoke with ease.

The first important result achieved by the publication of *The White Notebook* was to bring Gide into contact with Parisian literary circles. He met Maurice Barrès and Oscar Wilde, was introduced to most of the prominent symbolists, and frequented Stéphane Mallarmé's Tuesday evenings and José María de Heredia's Saturday afternoons. He decided to make a place for himself in the literary whirl. A first choice was to identify himself as a symbolist. The second was to justify this choice by composing a theory of the symbol, *Le traité du Narcisse* (*Narcissus,* 1891), and a symbolic travelogue, *Le voyage d'Urien* (*Urien's Voyage,* 1893). Although not the account of a real voyage, as the pun in the title suggests ("le voyage du rien" [the voyage of nothing]), the book represents nevertheless a timid step in the direction of a broader experience of life; Gide's imaginary travelers make their way through three landscapes suggest-ting as many responses to life: the sensual ("sur une mer pathétique" [on a sea of emotion]), the introspective ("la mer des Sargasses" [the Sargasso Sea]), and the ascetic ("la mer glaciale" [the Arctic Sea]). The last still best suits Gide's nature, and the second still tempts him, but he has grown enough to consider, however indirectly and negatively, the first and most troubling of his own interior landscapes.

But he evidently did not succeed in convincing himself of the evils of the flesh: he returned to the theme in his next work, *La tentative amoureuse* (*The Lover's Attempt,* 1893). Gide argues here that passion is self-consuming and hence destructive, that desire satisfied produces boredom, self-satisfaction, and complacency, and that the pleasures of the flesh can be addictive and dissolve the will. He presents the case in the form of a journey through the seasons of the year and in the persons of two young lovers, Luc and Rachel. Even before a year passes, both Luc and Gide become impatient with this love affair. Luc abandons Rachel in the hope of finding "new things"; Gide, abandoning both hurriedly, ends the story with similar aspirations.

Gide finished *The Lover's Attempt* during the summer of 1893, at about the time he and Paul-Albert Laurens decided to travel to North Africa to spend the year broadening their experience and fulfilling themselves. So radical a decision to explore the real world was prepared well in advance. For some time Gide had been gathering sufficient energy and arguments to break away from family, country, God, and his own pious impulses. During June 1891 he found in Jules Laforgue's writing a kindred spirit that encouraged him to develop a measure of objectivity flavored with irony; conversations with Wilde provoked a certain boldness in his thought and in the realization of his uniqueness; a visit to Munich in March and April 1892 affirmed his growing independence from his mother, as did the discovery of Johann Wolfgang von Goethe's plays, which he both read and saw there; and another experiment in independent traveling, in Spain during August 1893, further drew the young introspective out of himself and into the world of sensation. Finally, credit for Gide's gradual emergence is also due to the simple and sensual poetry of Francis Jammes and the pleasant summer months spent in the company and on the grounds of the Laurens family at Yport.

The *Journal* (1939) entries of 1893 document Gide's transformation. On 17 March, while visiting relatives at Montpellier just before leaving for Spain, Gide notes, "I love life and prefer sleep not because of its nothingness but because of dreams." A month or so later, Gide writes: "No longer read books by ascetics. Find exaltation elsewhere; admire the difficult joy of equilibrium, the joy of life's plenitude. May each thing offer all possible life it contains. It is a duty to make oneself happy." And, further expressing the attitude that was fully realized by the decision in October to leave for North Africa, Gide claims:

> I know that when I want to partake of those things which I had denied myself because of their beauty, it will not be like a sinner, in secret, with the bitterness of repentance; no, it will be without remorse, with force and joy. Leave the dream world at last and live a full and forceful life.
>
> (1:35)

Throughout the journal from April to October 1893 Gide rejects ever more boldly his former asceticism and pious yearnings for fulfillment in the kingdom of absolutes. He speaks of becoming robust, happy, and normal, of abandoning himself to life, and of putting the various aspects of his personality in equilibrium. He goes even further, seeing happiness and the highest form of originality in the absence of limits and scruples, in accepting, even seeking, all the sorts of experience that the human can possibly undergo. In the following years, after his trip to North Africa, Gide formulated this principle: "I am done with any system of morality that does not allow or teach the most noble, and most beautiful, and the most liberal use and development of our forces." Repeating later on in the 1894 journal entries other statements of this sort, he underscores the consciousness and deliberateness of his search for plenitude.

In North Africa Gide got more than he had bargained for and almost more than he could handle: an attack of tuberculosis and the subsequent slow convalescence in the desert town of Biskra intensified his physical reawakening and immersion in the world of sensations. Yet the first book Gide wrote and published after *The Lover's Attempt* and the first North African sojourn was not an ode to joy, but rather a mad piece of folly, the first sustained example of Gide's humor. *Paludes* (*Marshlands,* 1895) originated in early 1893 but was not composed until the fall of the following year, while Gide was continuing his cure in the cool mountain air of Neuchâtel. Because his reawakening was so recent and because he was anticipating returning to Biskra for the oncoming winter, it is not surprising that the "new" Gide should look back at his past nor that, fortified with newly won objectivity, he should treat this past with avenging irony. But even more interesting is that this first expression of the new Gide contains a sense of the comic that announces in many ways his subsequent work.

Gide himself has characterized his sense of humor as anchored in an inclination toward the bizarre, the illogical, and the unexpected. It expresses the mind's refusal to take seriously a suffocating world, suggesting that Gide's humor serves to mask problems that preoccupy him, enabling him to experiment with possible solutions casually and without the inhibiting effects of stage fright. From 1893 to 1895, when he was struggling both to free himself from his mother's moral influence and to define for himself the role and nature of the artist, he repeated on several occasions that everything in the truly original artist must appear new, that he alone has the key to a special world of his own. He wrote in his journal of this time: "He [the artist] must have a particular philosophy, aesthetics, ethics; his entire work tends only to result in revealing these. And that is what makes his style. I have also discovered, and this is very important, that he has to have a particular sense of humor."

Not all that is funny in Gide's writing and reported conversations can be classified under one type of humor or be made to fit within the category of his special sense of humor. In the journals, in much of the autobiographical material, and in some of the imaginative works, Gide's jokes range through most of the familiar categories, from low lusty humor to highbrow word and sound plays. Even within the framework of the *soties* (satirical farces), as he came to call his comic works, there is a variety of humor. Nevertheless, a point of view establishes a context of humor in the *soties* that is both peculiarly Gidian and rigorously consistent with the totality of Gide's world. On several occasions Gide uses the adjective *saugrenu* to describe his sense of humor. It means bizarre, absurd, or ridiculous, and tends to describe, in Gide's use, the vigorous but incongruent confrontation of two systems of thought or associations—that is, the confrontation of two or more words, ideas, or events, each of which suggests a frame of reference only apparently related to the others. At the basis of Gide's whimsy there is an eruption of illogic within a context promising logic or at least treated as logically coherent. Because the *saugrenu* operates on two levels, the level of incongruency and the suggested level of congruency, it is closely related to irony; it suggests what might be while falling short of the potential, remaining schematic, incomplete, or stunted.

There are many examples of this type of humor outside of the *soties,* in the *Journal,* in the memoirs, but none so succinct perhaps as two notations from the notebook of the hero of *Marshlands.* The first is "Lane bordered with birthwort," while the second reads, "'Why, dear friend,' said I, 'with a still uncertain sky, have you brought only one umbrella?' 'It's a parasol,' she answered." In the first example a lyrical description clashes with a cacophonous learned term and reveals a rather misguided eagerness for precision. In the second, a basically insignificant question is elevated to a level of serious and earnest inquiry by a vague preciosity of language; it is thereupon met with the same cuteness of formulation, which has a logic all its own, yet does not relate to the reality of the situation except on a purely linguistic level. Angèle, the narrator's interlocutor and companion, is perfectly rigorous in her logic of compromise: in the face of uncertain weather, rather than being caught with no umbrella at all or left carrying two to no avail, she compromises. Her choice is as logical as drizzle. But further rendering the exchange entirely nonsensical, the two major nouns (*ombrelle* and *en-tout-cas*) mean essentially the same thing: "parasol."

In his memoirs, *Si le grain ne meurt* (*If It Die . . . ,* 1926), Gide attributes the tone of these notations and his ability to sustain it to a mood he can describe only by the English word "estrangement." Because of his illness and his long-anticipated sensual reawakening in North Africa and because of his eagerness to return after his Swiss convalescence, Gide naturally felt dissociated from his erstwhile self and comrades. He was striving to live in the world, to absorb it and delight in it, while they persisted in rejecting it. But his feelings of estrangement were all too familiar to him and were an integral part of his personality. He confesses to a sort of dissociation from reality and to a disbelief in the reality of the world on numerous occasions throughout his life. Mentioned early in the *Journal* and frequently thereafter in various forms and recalled in *If It Die . . .* in several contexts, his difficulty again crops up at the very end of his life in *Ainsi soit-il ou les jeux sont faits* (*So Be It, or The Chips Are Down,* 1952), and is recorded succinctly in his journal: "I have never been able to *adhere* perfectly to reality." Such a handicap, better described as an inability to possess himself fully, to integrate a sense of self with emotion, thought, and sensation, explains the structure of his world view, his lifelong search for and idealization of plenitude and equilibrium as well as, eventually, his sense of humor. "What exalts us is the feeling of plenitude," Gide remarked in his journal shortly before his first voyage to North Africa. And in the same entry he articulated the opposite notion: "What makes us laugh is the feeling of atrophy in something capable of fullness. All things have within them the potential for plenitude."

It seems reasonable, on the basis of these and similar remarks made at so important a period in his life, to use them as guides for a discussion of his fiction. In addition to revealing the personal aspirations articulated early in life and maintained to its very end, these remarks suggest aesthetic analogues that, together with the problem of point of view, lie at the core of Gide's fictional technique. Atrophy in a personality fully capable of attaining fullness, traced from either a subjective or an objective point of view, yielded works of art Gide felt obliged to distinguish as either *récits* (tales) or *soties.* Viewed objectively, the results are comic; told from the vantage point of the victim, they are tragic. But in either case they record personality deformations that keep their victims from realizing the full measure of their potential.

## SOTIES

The main fault of his protagonist in *Marshlands,* which Gide in the preface called a sickness, is precisely his inability to ignore the stifling, swamplike world he lives in. He sees nothing but mediocrity all about him, in his friends, and in himself as well. But he is trapped in circumstances of his own making. The victim of an obsession that transforms his vision of the world and that in turn increases his feelings of "boredom, monotony, futility," he finds himself caught in an ever-narrowing spiral that brings the isolated fault of his personality to its conclusion in absurdity. The protagonist, potentially a full, round character, is flat, deformed, and atrophied by his obsession.

Gide's *Marshlands* is composed of the daily journal entries of a man of letters and excerpts from the book, "Marshlands," that he is busy writing. In the central episode, a mock symposium sponsored by his friend Angèle, he demonstrates his talent for transforming a variety of stimuli into terms consistent with his obsession. He describes his book in ways most appropriate to his interlocutors: for the physiologist, "Marshlands" is the story of animals whose eyes have atrophied as a result of living in the dark caves; for the critic, he quotes Vergil, and borrows Tityrus as his own hero; for the psychologist, the book is the story of the normal man, the protopersonality everyone takes as the point of departure for his own development; for the moralist, it is a didactic work intended to spur people to action; and for the group as a whole, "'Marshlands,' at this moment," he says, "is the story of Angèle's reception." He explains that the only way to tell a story so that everyone will understand it is to change its form in line with each new psychological and intellectual orientation. And, in fact, when he describes "Marshlands" to his very active friend Hubert, he recounts Tityrus' adventures—or non-adventures—day by day to the point of boring him. For the calm and delicate Angèle, his account verges at times on the tabloid human-interest story with interspersed discussions of fictional techniques.

Given the narrator's obsession, together with his lucidity and his desire to change, how does he break out of his distasteful situation? He cannot, of course, and every attempt to move, to change his ways, is frustrated, primarily by his own timidity and inertia. Nothing comes of his visits to the hothouses of the Jardin des Plantes except imagery for his book; his voyage to a suburban park aborts as well; he does not even finish his book but begins another with a similar paludal title, "Polders" ("Marshes"). It is not surprising, then, to discover, alongside the swamp image and the attendant ideas of immobility, images that suggest enclosure and confinement. Nouns such as "door," "gates," "windows," "curtains," "courtyards," and adjectives implying limitations, such as "small," "closed," "narrow," "circular," and so on, abound in the narrator's journal. The more obsessed he becomes, the more desperately he idealizes the contrary: the new, the unexpected, departures, voyages, action, freedom, and, especially, spontaneity.

Stagnancy horrifies him. At Angèle's banquet he informs the hostess that nothing irritates him more than "what goes round and round in place." Like the fan in her apartment, he and his friends are not truly immobile, yet they do no more than move about in place; they are stagnant. Their acts have become habits containing their personalities; they define themselves not by the style of an action, but by the action itself. But it is not only their own "normality" that encourages them along the easy path; everything urges them to lapse into a rut. The narrator proclaims: "And that's just what irritates me: everything outside, laws, customs, even the sidewalks seem to determine our lapses and ensure our monotony." That the narrator himself cannot avoid these setbacks is a point hammered home by the failure of his paltry little trip. He himself incarnates the stagnancy he cannot abide and, further, develops it to its extreme. In effect, Gide's narrator enacts in his own way the principle suggested in one of the "remarkable sentences" listed at the end of the *sotie:* "One must carry out to their conclusion all the ideas one has raised."

The major characters of *Le Prométhée mal enchaîné* (*Prometheus Misbound,* 1899) also bring to some sort of conclusion the ideas they raise, and, as a consequence, at least two of them emerge deformed. Gide's second *sotie* is made up of events that are as bizarre as the moods and futile gestures of his first. One May afternoon on the boulevards of Paris the "miglionnaire" banker, Zeus, delivers unsolicited and randomly a 500-franc bank note to an undistinguished person and, also at random, rewards another's kindness with a vigorous slap in the face. Meanwhile Prometheus, tired of his long sojourn in the Caucasian mountains, sheds his shackles and goes for a walk in Paris. At a café he meets Damocles and Cocles, the recipients of Zeus's largesse, who recount their stories and describe the transformations their lives have undergone since they were singled out. Damocles is obsessed by the sudden and inexplicable receipt of the bank note, while Cocles wins sympathy for his misfortunes. As his misfortunes grow (he loses an eye), Cocles continues to seek the others out, knowing he will profit from the sympathy of others. He receives the directorship of a large foundation to aid the blind. Damocles, on the other hand, cannot explain why he received the money and is tortured by the impossibility of finding its source and of repaying, or at least thanking, the unknown donor. Because of Zeus's gesture each has risen from the anonymous mass of people and has gained an identity. Because Damocles received money and can neither explain nor repay it, he discovers he has scruples; Cocles, unjustly victimized, becomes the underdog who seeks and attracts sympathy. Each nourishes his new identity with his whole being. Prometheus, the man with the eagle, recognizes himself in both the man with one eye and the man with the burden of debt. The eagle functions here as a symbol of an obsession that tyrannizes the person who nurtures it. Prometheus concludes that everyone must possess an identity to which he can devote himself: we must all have an eagle of our own that we can feed with our very substance.

But as Prometheus nourishes his eagle, he diminishes as it flourishes. Similarly, Damocles, so distraught by the dilemma that defines him, finally expends himself on it and dies of brain fever. Pondering these new developments, Prometheus reconsiders the substance of his first lecture, which he delivers near the beginning of the book, and, for Damocles' funeral oration, comes up with a parable that he hopes will clarify the tie between Damocles' death and his own decision to kill his eagle.

The parable has as its principal characters Angèle, Tityrus, and two more Vergilian figures, Meliboeus and Menalcas. Tityrus, surrounded by swamps and inertia, is prodded into activity by Menalcas, "who planted an idea in Tityrus' head and a seed in the swamp before him." The seed grows first into a plant and then into a gigantic oak to which Tityrus devotes himself and around which develops a settlement he eventually administers. Angèle, the librarian, invites the reluctant Tityrus to take a trip to Paris, from which place Meliboeus, the naked, Pan-like, flute-playing free spirit, takes Angèle with him to Rome. Tityrus, thus abandoned, finds himself once again at home, alone, and surrounded by swamps. The audience titters a bit, charmed by the humor in Tityrus' simplicity and circular busyness. But they do not fully grasp Prometheus' apparent reversal of position; the appearance itself of a sense of humor in one who had earlier claimed "an irremediably serious turn of mind" so disconcerts them that they laugh also, from nervousness. Happy that he has been able to please them, Prometheus admits that since Damocles' death he has found the secret of laughter. One cannot help trying to clarify this secret by resorting to Gide's own ideas on similar matters: laughter arises from atrophy and from the objectivity that permits the perception of a stunted growth as caricature.

Prometheus is astounded to discover that Zeus refuses to keep eagles, that he just distributes them. This revelation contradicts his basic precept and undermines his commitment to his own eagle. More damage is done to his original principle when he sees in Damocles the effect of excess devotion to one's eagle. Through Damocles' death Prometheus realizes that death is the limit beyond which one cannot develop an idea in oneself, that developing an idea to such an extreme is costly and prevents knowing other ideas. Prometheus realizes, in short, that unless he is careful, his eagle will end by devouring him completely. Such objectivity affords Prometheus a gauge to measure the excess of his beliefs and the degree of their complicity in Damocles' death. He now realizes that he need not forfeit all control to his eagle—that, although committed to an idea, he need not relinquish his autonomy. Before leaving the Caucasus, he had rid himself of "chains, tendons, straitjackets, parapets, and other scruples" that were petrifying him, and between four and five in autumn, he strolled down the boulevard that goes from the Madeleine to the Opéra; similarly, in his fable Tityrus, feeling that his "occupations, responsibilities, and various scruples held him no more than the great oak," smiled and left, "taking with him the money box and Angèle, and toward evening strolled with her down the boulevard that goes from the Madeleine to the Opéra."

Tityrus, too, discovers laughter when he discovers his freedom. It is neither futile nor tragic that the exercise of his new freedom ultimately leads him nowhere, that he has not progressed, that he returns to the neutral terrain he began on. Although abandoning himself to events, and ideas, and seeds, he does not abdicate his willpower and his control, so that when he needs them he can overcome his eagles and retain the potential to grow. The new Tityrus does not stagnate. "An idea," Gide says in the *Journal,* "continues to be a living force so long as all the nourishment in it is not used up in phenomena." Once it has been used up, it is abandoned. "Was it of no use, then?" his audience asks Prometheus after he has eaten the eagle. He answers: "Don't say that, Cocles! Its flesh has nourished us. When I questioned it, it answered nothing. But I have eaten it without rancor: had it made me suffer less, it would have been less fat; less fat, it would have been less delectable." Prometheus does not entirely reverse his previous position. Everyone must devote himself to his eagle; every idea must be brought to its furthest limit. But there are times when one must go beyond it, abandon it, or bring it to complete fruition outside of the self; otherwise one endangers one's health and full development. Prometheus survives the story in good health and spirits, feasts upon the eagle, and writes this book with one of its quills.

The work of art, precisely, allows the exceptional man to accomplish what he feels capable of without adverse consequences; it permits him a plenitude and an equilibrium that are, as Gide noted in 1897, "realizable only in the work of art." The mechanics of this procedure were outlined years later by Gide in an often-quoted letter to a critic who, in reviewing *L'Immoraliste* (*The Immoralist,* 1902), identified Gide with his hero: "How many buds we carry in ourselves, dear Scheffer, which bloom only in a book. . . . My recipe for creating a hero is quite simple: take one of these buds, put it in a pot—all alone—soon one has an admirable individual." Gide evidently permitted three unlikely characters to grow in his *sotie* along lines dictated by different approaches to a basic tenet of his early ethical code, which he imagistically synthesized in Prometheus' devotion to his eagle: in *The White Notebook* and in *Narcissus,* Gide formulated this tenet by saying, "We must all manifest, we must all represent"; he later developed it in a pamphlet, "Quelques reflexions sur la littérature et la morale" ("Some Thoughts on Literature and Ethics," published first in 1897 and again in 1899 as an appendix to *Prometheus Misbound,* and ultimately added to the *Journal* as "Literature and Ethics").

In *Les caves du Vatican* (*The Vatican Swindle,* 1914) the preoccupations of the earlier *soties* concerning action, freedom, and personal identity are brought into society. Despite the hubbub and social confusion of *Marshlands,* the prime concern is the point of view of the narrator and diarist. In *Prometheus Misbound,* too, Gide emphasizes the relationship of his caricatures to themselves. In *The Vatican Swindle* he is again concerned with man's relationship to himself and with the nature and function of identity, but here these preoccupations are placed in a social context; people interact with one another, and their actions have social consequences. This slight change in point of view is reflected in the very form of the novel. Like a blown-up philosophical tale in the manner of Voltaire, *The Vatican Swindle* is handled with the traditional narrative tools Gide had previously avoided: the third-person narrative with frequent plunges into the interior world of its characters; intrusion of the author's comments and opinions on the matter at hand; detailed, descriptive passages of places and persons; deliberate excursions into exposition of background and history of events and people; and, more subtly, a multiplicity of tones that coincide with the varieties of subject matter. *The Vatican Swindle* is essentially a traditional novel of adventure simplified and pushed to the extreme of parody.

The novel is divided into five parts, each bearing as its title the name of one of the major figures. Like Damocles and Cocles, each of the figures is so devoted to his eagle that he has atrophied and become one with it: Anthime Armand-Dubois, a behaviorist and mechanistic scientist, a pillar of the Society of Freemasons, and a militant atheist; Julius de Baraglioul, a traditionalist in politics, religion, and aesthetics, and a novelist convinced of the immutability of the novel of psychological analysis, of the consistency of human behavior, and of the inscrutability of the French Academy; Amédée Fleurissoire, a sincere and devoted believer, a manufacturer of religious articles, and a latter-day poor man's Parsifal or Sir Galahad. Even Protos (protagonist of the chapter entitled "Les mille-pattes" ["The Millipedes"], the name of the international organization of outlaws he leads), who is ever-present and constantly changing form and disguises and who advocates freedom and flexibility, is fixed by his need and program to oppose the staid members of the society he lives in. Only Lafcadio is free enough both socially and emotionally to be lawless and flexible like Prometheus. Although he too is a caricature, he becomes so enviable and attractive that Gide almost filled out his portrait with flesh and bone; at the end of *The Vatican Swindle* he is very nearly a round character, moving about in a two-dimensional world.

The people of *The Vatican Swindle* are divided into two groups, the select minority Protos calls "the subtle ones" and, by far the majority, "the crustaceans." To the first group belong only Protos and Lafcadio. But the qualities that make Lafcadio "a subtle one" serve no goal other than his own enrichment, whereas in Protos, who is as subtle and cunning as the devil himself, they are subservient to his need to dominate and oppose. Lafcadio was formed, without the rigors of family, by his courtesan mother and the talents of her successive lovers. Completely free and spontaneous, a creature of inconsistency, victim only of an insatiable curiosity that prompts him to act, Lafcadio lives heedless of consequences in a manner idealized by his complete opposite, the narrator of *Marshlands.* Capable of any action that tests and reveals him, Lafcadio feels his grip is "large enough to embrace all of humanity, or perhaps to strangle it." So far he has not committed a harmful act, but realizing that the difference between harmful and beneficial is slight for the man of action at the moment of action, he becomes interested in all the unforeseen elements in an act of violence. As a result he hurls Amédée Fleurissoire from the train compartment they are sharing while traveling between Rome and Naples.

The consequences of this act go beyond the exaltation surrounding the event and reach into the calm, lucid moments of his present life. "I lived oblivious," he tells young Geneviève de Baraglioul; "'I killed as though in a dream, a nightmare in which I've been floundering ever since.'" He was oblivious because he was unaware, as Protos informs him later, that one cannot live lawlessly, that even the millipedes have a rigid code and discipline, that one cannot "move out of one society so simply, without immediately falling into another," and that it is inconceivable "that any society can do without laws." Circumstances are so manipulated by Gide that the decision to accept responsibility for Fleurissoire's death depends on Lafcadio alone. At first he threatens to do so; by the end of the book, however, the narrator suggests that he will not give himself up so easily. Lafcadio can, like Prometheus, rise above a situation and continue to exercise his freedom.

This is not so for the crustaceans of the book, nearly all of whom exchange one eagle for another, one fixed identity for another, one society with its system of laws for another just as stringently legalized. Miraculously cured of rheumatism, Anthime becomes a Catholic, only to return to his old ways after Fleurissoire's death; Julius changes aesthetics and psychology based upon the example of gratuitous and inconsistent behavior offered by Lafcadio but reverts when he is elected to the Academy. Even in Fleurissoire a waning, pious fervor promises radical changes whose full development is cut short by Lafcadio's act.

In *The Vatican Swindle* Gide dramatizes the consequences of gratuitous acts as well as those arising from a change in identity. In the latter case he appears to test Prometheus' final hypothesis, concluding that, once atrophied by devotion to an idea, one is so deformed that atrophy remains even if the idea passes. Atrophy, as Gide means it, is the wasting away of a whole organism that results from improper nourishment or exercise of some of its important elements. He exemplifies it by fragmenting the human personality, exaggerating a few distinctive traits, and virtually excluding the rest. Depending upon the manner and the context in which these dominant traits are presented artistically, they become either exaggerations in caricature or tragic flaws.

A constant danger for Gide was too close identification with his characters. Understandably alarmed, he noted in a 1912 journal entry that his puppets in *The Vatican Swindle* were getting out of hand and rounding out with blood and bones: "They are forcing me to take them more and more seriously." Maintaining his characters at the level of caricature was essential to the free working-out of ideas he considered important. The obvious consequence of getting closer to his characters and treating them sympathetically would have been to undermine the whimsy of the *sotie* and inhibit his freedom. But even more dangerous, this seriousness would have transformed his work from caricature to tragedy. A key device, although not used in the first of the *soties,* is the objective third-person narrative, which gave Gide the distance from his characters that freed his whimsy and enabled him to see the ridiculousness in certain modes of seriousness and ultraserious behavior. Conversely, the first-person narrative presents a case subjectively and without the perspective that establishes some reasonable hierarchy of values. Unless this device is handled ironically, as Gide did in *Marshlands,* it lessens the distance between author or reader and the characters, evokes sympathy, and sets the scene for tragedy.

## RÉCITS

Jean Hytier noted that the *soties* are stories in which wisdom bears the mask of folly, while the *récits* reveal the folly under the appearance of wisdom. Essentially, then, the *récit* is the reverse of the *sotie,* distinguished by means of aesthetic devices alone. But the stuff each is made of is the same: deformation of the human personality presented either from the point of view of the victim or from some objective point of view.

All the *récits,* from *The Immoralist* to *Geneviève* (1936), tales recounted in the first person, are what Gide called critical or ironical books. *The Immoralist* is a book of warning, a critique of a certain form of individualism, characterized by a tendency to relinquish self-control to instincts. After the death of his young wife, for which his own selfishness and negligence were largely responsible, Michel finds himself alone, independent, and free. But after three months of abandon, he realizes that "knowing how to liberate oneself is nothing; what is difficult is knowing how to be free." He summons to his side several faithful friends, who sit and listen to him recount his life.

Brought up under the subtle limitations inculcated by his Huguenot mother, he transferred this severity and ascetism, upon her death, to the rigorous task of fashioning himself after his father. At twenty he was so skilled in philology and archaeology that his father farmed out research projects to him. Later, to satisfy his father's deathbed wish, he agreed to marry without quite knowing, at twenty-four, what marriage or life could entail. The first part of the book traces Michel's evolution from a concern with dead things to the discovery of a taste for life, from a vague awareness of his own sentiments to a need for sensation, and from a context of abstraction to a world of concrete things. Although he begins truly to see the world with the help of his wife, it is the severe attack of tuberculosis and subsequent slow convalescence in North Africa that reawaken him to life and to himself. In his search for health he establishes a simple and simplistic code that is finally carried beyond his convalescence: everything healthful and healthy is good while all else is evil. Because his early education and all the conventions of society it perpetuates offer resistance to his self-revelation, he brands them as evil and evolves an antisocial, anti-establishment doctrine that rejects artifice, culture, restraint, and intellect. He relinquishes his will and abandons himself to his instincts in the hope of casting off the new man and reaching the authentic, or "old," man the Bible speaks of.

Like Anthime Armand-Dubois, Michel falls into a system as rigid as the one he would escape. But he does not succeed in changing himself as thoroughly as he thinks. He carries over many intellectual needs: for strategy, for rational justification, and, mostly, for some authority against whom to react. Marceline, his wife, takes on this last role; she is his last tie to civilization and as such he has to destroy her. Ménalque, his friend and mentor, on the other hand, represents the ideal Michel has set for himself: the lucid, independent, and complete utilization of one's energies. Incapable of carrying out such an ethic, Michel simply abandons himself to sensation, attempting to justify and modify his behavior in reaction to the opposing ideals Ménalque and Marceline represent. Both realize, however, that Michel is eluding their influence. Marceline can do nothing to control her husband's growing selfishness. Ménalque, after noting the inconsistency in Michel's supposed disdain for property and his many possessions, finally urges Michel to keep his "calm happiness of the hearth." The last remark that Ménalque makes about Michel seems to sum up his evaluation of his would-be disciple: "One believes one possesses, and, in fact, one is possessed."

Possessed indeed to the point of dissolution of his willpower, Michel cannot abandon Marceline and live the life he dreams of all alone; he drags her back with him to North Africa, where she finally dies. Thereafter, unable to help himself, he needs others to tear him away from the small Algerian village he has settled in, to give him reasons for living, and to help him "prove to himself that he has not exceeded his rights."

If Michel's eagle is an obsession with sensations to the detriment of intellect and willpower, Alissa's, in *La porte étroite* (*Strait Is the Gate,* 1909), is made of other stuff. Where Michel dissolves willpower and exalts instinct, she denies instinct and tenses her will through continual self-abnegation. Alissa embodies the pious tendencies of young Gide, but allows them to grow independently of Gide's "grain of good sense." She chooses the narrow path of piety leading to God and ultimate self-denial in death. The more she effaces herself, the more she has to prove her worth by further sacrifices. God, of course, does not respond, and Alissa, in a moment of desperate solitude, cries out, "I should like to die now, quickly, before I understand once again that I am alone." Like Michel, Alissa is condemned to bring to conclusion one human tendency. As a consequence of her ascetic piety, she negates not only herself but also Jerome, with whom she could have enjoyed the calm happiness of the hearth. Like Michel, she lacks, as Gide notes in *Journal des faux-monnayeurs* (Journal of "The Counterfeiters," 1926), "the bit of good sense that keeps me from pushing their [the characters'] follies as far as they do." But Alissa lacks even more; beneath her intense piety she has a need to sublimate her fears and intensities into safe and traditionally respected channels. By striving for sanctity, she avoids having to create a personality of her own and to deal with instincts she fears are hers.

*Strait Is the Gate* is divided into two parts, or, rather, it is composed of two *récits:* Jerome's narrative of events and Alissa's record of her reactions in her journal. Although they represent two independent *récits,* the second narrative, along with Alissa's dialogues and letters quoted in the first part, is by far the more interesting and more important. Jerome's narrative exists only as a preparation and contextual explanation for the spiritual evolution traced in Alissa's journal. Jerome comes off as a rather docile and dependent man in whose literary style is reflected hesitation, self-righteousness, and fondness for constant qualifications. His style is flaccid, picky, Gide said on several occasions, but it is necessarily so. Jerome's narrative puts Alissa's journal and personality in relief by sparing her the need to recount facts and events that would normally weaken the intensity of her emotions and character development. Jerome acts as a possible and ever-ready solution to her dilemma but leaves any decision entirely up to her. His constancy and passivity are part of the décor in Alissa's world and exert upon her no pressure that she cannot easily combat.

Several other characters model for her the consequences of Jerome's offer. Tante Plantier, fertile, buxom, and devoted to her issue, as well as to that of her family, offers earthly wit, wisdom, and sound advice. Alissa's sister, Juliette, also counsels a less stringent path and acts upon her beliefs. Rather than waste her life pining for Jerome, with whom, unbelievably, she is in love, Juliette attempts by force of will to balance her needs and the possibilities of satisfying them. She marries another and settles down to some semblance of happiness.

After her sister's marriage, Alissa finds herself facing the still available Jerome and persists in not yielding. "An absolutely useless heroism," Gide said about her resistance. "Thought of her fiancé invoked in her, immediately, a sort of flush of heroism that was not voluntary, but practically unconscious, irresistible, and spontaneous." But this heroism is not entirely gratuitous. Jerome's presence immediately calls into play Alissa's sense of her own virtue, which is as strong as she fears her propensity to vice demands. In the closely knit world circumscribed by their families and the Protestant parish, only Alissa's mother, Lucile Bucolin, is an intruder. A Creole by birth and a courtesan by temperament, she flaunts herself with great glee in the ascetic environment she married into. While her children are still young and impressionable, she obtrusively takes a lover and finally disappears with him. It is apropos of this tragedy that the local pastor plants the justification of Alissa's and Jerome's withdrawal from life in a sermon based on Christ's words "Strive to enter through the narrow gate" (Luke 13:24). Sensitive to what she fears she inherited from her mother and aware that she resembles her greatly, Alissa early chooses to develop only the spiritual side of her nature, to which she directs all her intensity.

Alissa's choice of the narrow path is also strengthened by the numerous dead-end paths traced by those around her: examples of her unhappy father, of Jerome's widowed mother forever dressed in mourning, and of her lifelong companion, Miss Flora Ashburton, all encourage her to take any involvement other than a spiritual one as weakness or vice. But she is also trapped by a weak Jerome. Instead of helping her to integrate conflicting elements in her personality through his protection and understanding, he follows her lead and plays her game. "It is by being infatuated with his own weakness that man imitates," Ménalque tells Michel in a line eventually deleted from *The Immoralist.* In Alissa's case, it is through fear that she imitates the asceticism prevalent in her milieu, and it is because her intensity is frustrated by Jerome's weakness that she strives to realize what she feels is her noblest part by developing it to its extreme in death.

*La symphonie pastorale* (*The Pastoral Symphony,* 1919), like the other *récits,* is an ironic book. It criticizes self-deception of a kind to which Gide himself was particularly vulnerable: liberally interpreting the Scriptures to suit one's own needs and weaknesses. The pastor of La Brévine, a small mountain village in the Swiss Jura, recounts the development and education of a blind fifteen-year-old girl he had found two-and-a-half years earlier. Although not deaf, his young charge spent her first years in total silence and darkness because her aunt, whose death provided the occasion for the pastor's recovery of the child, was deaf herself. Moved by charity, the pastor decides to undertake the salvation of this soul lost in darkness, at great moral and physical expense to his wife and his own children. He soothes his disgruntled wife with arguments of charity and promises of help, although, in truth, his first impulse is to cite some of Christ's words. He says, "I kept them back, however, because it seems to me improper to cover my behavior behind the authority of the Holy Scriptures." But this is precisely what he does, increasingly and heedlessly, throughout the book. Moreover, as his wife seems to become more and more peevish toward him and as his own children interest him less, he becomes withdrawn and dependent upon himself to satisfy his intellectual, emotional, and spiritual needs. Because Gertrude, as he calls his charge, needs constant, patient attention and because she proves intelligent and responsive, he begins to fashion her as a complement to his own soul. Like an aging André Walter, he hopes to form the soul of his beloved so like his own that nothing can separate them. But soon love and charity change into something less generous and more earthy. When his wife chides him for spending more time with Gertrude than he ever spends with his own children, he hides behind the parable of the lost sheep. The more intense he becomes, the greater grows his dependence upon the Gospel as a source of sanctions.

But his dependence is selective. In the second notebook, where the narrative, rather than describing past events, yields to day-by-day journal entries, he immediately confesses his discovery of his true feelings after having reread his story. He had not previously realized that love was in question because he had felt no guilt. It is a small step, then, to defend the innocence of those feelings, and it is a step he takes blithely. The second entry of the notebook is laden with irony: "Gertrude's religious instruction has made me reread the Evangile with new eyes. It is more and more apparent to me that a number of notions that make up our Christian faith stem not from Christ's words but from St. Paul's commentaries." He proceeds to reconstruct standards of guilt by defining evil as any obstacle to happiness. The Gospels, he feels, teach principally "a method for attaining a life of happiness." The pastor concludes, "Gertrude's complete happiness, which shines out from her whole being, comes from her ignorance of sin." Moral strictures, he argues, invoking part of St. Paul's letter to the Romans, are dictated not by law but by love: "Nothing is unclean in itself; but it is unclean for anyone who thinks it is unclean" (14:14).

Gertrude's education makes her, in effect, a creature living in an illusory world of goodness, beauty, and eternal happiness. Into his world of harmony, indeed a pastoral symphony in its own way, the pastor allows no intrusion of reality. He rejects his son's interest in Gertrude and forbids him to court her, going so far as to accuse him of wanting to "take advantage of a disabled, innocent, and guileless person." When he is finally convinced of his son's honorable intentions, he can only ask for more time to think of a valid opposition to his proposed plan. "An instinct as sure as the voice of conscience warned me that I had to prevent this marriage at all costs." Later called upon to explain his reasons, he admits that he followed his conscience and not his reason, invoking Gertrude's innocence, impressionability, and lack of prudence. "It is a question of conscience," he concludes lamely.

Since the standard of judgement is his own conscience, his task is to ease this conscience. He immediately takes communion, surprisingly unattended—as though he would rebuke them—at the altar by either his wife or son. The son's abstention is clarified by the subsequent entries in the second notebook and puts into relief the exegetical clash that long interested Gide. His son, the pastor believes, feels doomed as soon as he discovers himself without props or authority to guide him. But Jacques insists upon facing the ever-present reality of sin, evil, and death by supporting St. Paul and accepting the necessity of commandments, threats, and prohibition. "In submission lies happiness," he says, and quotes a verse from Romans that his father had curiously overlooked earlier: "Do not let what you eat cause the ruin of one for whom Christ died" (14:15). The pastor remains absolutely impervious to the meaning of this verse by claiming fidelity to Christ and not to St. Paul; he is closer to Christ when he teaches that sin is only what disrupts the happiness of another "or compromises our very own." The example of his father, Jacques admits late in the book, has in fact guided him to understand the wisdom of converting to Catholicism.

Gertrude herself senses the incompleteness of the world view offered her by the pastor. In a tender scene near the end of the book, she acknowledges that her happiness seems to be based on ignorance. She would prefer lucidity to happiness, would prefer knowing what evil and ugliness there is about her just to be sure that she is not adding any of her own. The subsequent conversation suggests what she has on her mind; she wants reassurance from the pastor that her children will not inherit her blindness, that their love is real and passionate, although guilty. Finally, she admits that, although she ought to feel guilty, she cannot stop loving him. The pastor cannot respond, cannot reassure her one way or the other, cannot do more than wallow in his own lightheadedness. He is now thoroughly prepared to do what he feared Jacques had in mind, to take advantage of weakness, innocence, and ignorance.

The discovery that Gertrude's sight can be restored acts as a catalyst to the pastor's expression of his true feelings for her. Unable to refuse to do for her what must be a boon, he is still reluctant to break the news to her. On several occasions he tries and fails until finally he finds himself alone with her in her room: "I held her close to me for some time. She made no move to resist and, as she raised her face toward mine, our lips met." She enters the hospital the following day. After a successful operation and convalescence, she returns home and attempts suicide. When she sees the family, and especially Amélie, the wife, she realizes immediately that she has usurped the place of another; she sees her sin, her error. Now thoroughly familiar with St. Paul, thanks to Jacques's company during her convalescence, she quotes Romans: "I was once alive apart from the law, but when the commandment came, sin revived and I died" (7:9). She dies, in fact, shortly after, with a reproach on her lips; having seen Jacques she realized that it was he whom she loved and that it was he whom she could have married were it not for the pastor. Jacques, on the other hand, follows through to the end the path diametrically opposed to his father's: he accepts orthodoxy and converts himself and Gertrude to Catholicism.

Like Michel, the pastor, although with different emphases, if not different motives, refuses, at least in theory, to acknowledge any authority other than his own conscience, a conscience he claims thoroughly grounded in the words and example of Christ. In practice, however, he constantly passes off responsibility onto God, Christ, or the Scriptures, finding what he deems authorization for his own passion.

*Les faux-monnayeurs* (*The Counterfeiters,* 1926), the first and only book of his that Gide dared call a novel, had so long been on his mind that when he began writing it, in June 1919, he decided to record his progress in a special logbook, *Journal des faux-monnayeurs.* His timidity and reluctance with regard to the term "novel" can be explained by the rigor of his concept of the genre. The novel, for Gide, must of necessity present reality as seen from multiple vantage points; it must suggest the profusion and formlessness of the real world, while at the same time demonstrating a number of attempts to come to grips with it either artistically, psychologically, socially, or philosophically, and so that all points of view interact with one another. The first *sotie* and the *récits* present, at most, no more than two points of view whose consistencies of voice are not hindered by any external pressures. The main concern in these works is essentially the interior world of the protagonist—hence the first-person narrative. With *The Vatican Swindle* Gide begins to show an interest in the reciprocal influences of the interior and exterior worlds of a number of protagonists each in conflict with another. Its relation with the more sober *The Counterfeiters* is attested to by Gide's long-standing intention to use Lafcadio as a principal character of the later book; but even more convincing is the absolute identity of tone between the *sotie* and several chapters of the novel recounted in the third person. Particularly revealing is the second chapter, in which the two magistrates, Oscar Molinier and Albéric Profitendieu, stroll home at competitive paces and, puppetlike, parade for one another personalities atrophied not so much by their profession as by their own images of themselves. Both are as much caricatures as Anthime Armand-Dubois or Amédée Fleurissoire.

Significant, too, is the omniscient third-person narrative device used rarely by Gide, although insistently in both *The Vatican Swindle* and *The Counterfeiters.* But in the latter, the ominscient author surpasses the role of a technique or device: he himself becomes a character in the story he has invented not only by reacting to and commenting upon his people but also by illustrating still another point of view and still another attempt, this time successful, to make something of reality, to make a book out of the material the world offers. Like the omniscient author, Édouard is writing a novel also called "The Counterfeiters" and keeping a journal in which he notes all that can be of use for his book. Here he faces the same problems with handling events and incorporating them into meaningful experience suggested by Gide and the omniscient author he plays. Finally, through letters, but mostly through dialogue—since dialogue is an exchange of two or more points of view—reported either by the omniscient author or by Édouard, Gide succeeds in presenting still more points of view and efforts at fashioning a viable approach to reality.

In the novel, then, a number of people speak for themselves and reveal their efforts to reconcile themselves somehow to the world around them. Some have already erected a workable system and have settled themselves into it; for the most part these are members of the older generation: the magistrates; the pastors Azaïs and Vedel, who are Parisian equivalents of the pastor of *The Pastoral Symphony;* La Pérouse, who is painfully discovering the cruel trick God has played on him through the death of his grandson; Passavant, who like Baraglioul plays to the crowd; even Pauline Molinier, who spends the better part of her life covering up the inadequacies and hypocrisy of her husband. For the most part, adolescents or young adults—that is, those undergoing the dynamic process of "becoming"—understandably attract and retain most of the narrator's and Édouard's attention. And still a third group finds a voice in the novel: the young teenagers who are struggling not so much with the world at large as with the immediate social and cultural influences they are undergoing (Boris, George, Ghérandisol, and the vaguely suggested Caloub).

These three groups represent not only three major divisions of society but more significantly three stages in the struggle between atrophy and plenitude, or, in terms consistent with the novel's central image scheme, between the authentic and the counterfeit. The profound subject of the novel is precisely the many ways in which people choose to face the world, alternatives that are completely external to their personality and based on convention, revolt, or a simple lack of common sense. Gide's *Counterfeiters* is, in fact, a catalogue of the various ways in which one can live in a counterfeit life—but, especially, it is a catalogue of the various pressures that tend to divert those striving for plenitude.

In the very center of the novel two significant events take place: Édouard discusses the theory of the novel in general and of his own in particular, and Bernard uncovers a counterfeit coin. The two events are intimately related, especially in regard to the development of Édouard's character. One of his interlocutors finally asks him exactly who are the counterfeiters he proposes to write about. Like his predecessor, the narrator of *Marshlands,* Édouard gets tangled up in the exposition of ideas too close to him and in the description of work in progress. The bad impression he makes upon his friends is only partially atoned for by the narrator's intrusion and explanation of Édouard's thought. Édouard's use of the counterfeiters is purely figurative, we learn. At first the term designated certain of his colleagues:

> But the attribution broadened considerably; according as the wind of the spirit blew from Rome or elsewhere, his heroes became either priests or freemasons. If he let his mind go its way, it would soon capsize in abstraction where it would wallow comfortably. Ideas of exchange, devaluation, inflation were little by little overrunning his book as did theories of dress in Carlyle's *Sartor Resartus* where they usurped the character's roles.
>
> (Bussy trans., 1951, p. 176)

Although Édouard's title, "The Counterfeiters," refers to something quite concrete, he thinks of it in figurative and abstract terms. And it is precisely this mode of thinking that his young secretary Bernard objects to. Bernard shows him a false ten-franc piece and urges him to begin not with the idea of the counterfeit but with a fact, a false ten-franc coin, for example. He forces him to admit that such reality, although it does indeed interest him, basically troubles him. In fact, so deep is this trouble that only his diary and the processes of articulation it requires can give any semblance of reality to whatever happens to him. Or at least so he rationalizes in his journal. But he goes on to demonstrate a case in point. Recording the thoughts provoked by the false coin and his subsequent discussion with Bernard, he realizes that we create the drama of our lives by our attempts to impose upon the world our interpretation of it and by the way it resists:

> The resistance of facts invites us to transpose our ideal construction onto the world of dreams, of hope, of future life in which our belief is nourished by all our failures in this one. Realists begin with facts and adjust their ideas to them. Bernard is a realist. I am afraid I won't be able to get along with him.
>
> (Bussy trans., p. 189)

That is, unlike Bernard, Édouard will not adjust himself to facts but will adjust them, in his novel and journal, to fit his own ideals. With this admission, Édouard unwittingly classifies himself among the counterfeiters. Like Azaïs, the old pastor, and his son-in-law, Vedel, Édouard has constructed a world for himself frequently unencumbered either by fact or by reality. But even Edouard changes and leaves us with a slight hope; finally settled in a satisfactory relationship with his nephew, Olivier, he manages to write the first thirty pages of his novel.

However ambiguous Édouard's own status might appear at the end of the novel, that of most others who had been in flux throughout the novel seems clear. Those who had reached the final stage of development at the opening have failed and live counterfeit lives. What is worse, however, is that in persisting in their errors they force those around them either to imitate them or to reject their errors in favor of extremes just as false. Because of his fervor, sincerity, and simplicity, the old pastor, Azaïs, forces those he faces into playing roles, acquiescing, and being hypocrites as soon as they feel unable to share his conviction and enthusiasms. The hypocrisy of his son-in-law, Vedel, who continues to effect piety and devotion out of fidelity to an early enthusiasm, thickens the atmosphere of lies that his children have to grow up in. They are all pushed into making some sort of stand with regard to their upbringing; most of the children rebel and cynically project their rebellion into an ethic. An unnamed son leaves for Africa when he feels he cannot handle the rumblings of puberty; Laura goes off to England, marries a colorless French professor, commits adultery, and finds herself bearing her lover's child; Sarah ultimately goes off to England, thus proclaiming her independence after having exercised it promiscuously under the very nose of familial authority; and Armand, sensitive and troubled, becomes intellectually promiscuous and establishes cynicism and hypocrisy as the tenets of his behavior. Rachel alone stays at home; through total self-effacement she undertakes to deal with all the realities her father and grandfather do not acknowledge by keeping the household financially solvent.

Laura, after a bad start, seems to be heading toward a better future; she returns to her husband, who forgives all and promises to treat the child as his own. Under similar circumstances Albéric Profitendieu made a similar promise to Marguerite some nineteen years earlier. When Bernard discovers to his great relief that Profitendieu is not his real father and that he will not have the problem of resisting or submitting to the centripetal forces of heredity and early upbringing, he runs away from home seeking adventures that will enable him better to gauge his true potential. Like Michel, he dares free himself and follow his bent. Unlike his predecessor, however, he enters into a long struggle with himself from which he emerges, if not victorious, at least a bit more mature and endowed with that grain of good sense that so many of Gide's characters lack. Unlike Lafcadio, too, he learns that in this world it is not enough to dare: "He was beginning to understand that other people's happiness is often the price of daring." Learning that Profitendieu is alone and ailing, he returns home, not out of weakness, but out of the affection he had always felt for the man he had long taken for his father; he returns, too, because he has gained a feeling of freedom so profound that it frees him from the constant need to test and prove it. With Bernard and Laura, Olivier Molinier also promises to develop in the direction of authenticity. Unlike his brothers, he manages to escape the baneful influence of his complacent and hypocritical father and his well-meaning though no less hypocritical mother. Adopted by Edouard, his uncle, Olivier will live in an open atmosphere that will permit him to develop fully.

As sensitive and intelligent as his younger brother Olivier, Vincent Molinier falls into Michel's trap of illusory self-development and freedom. He seduces and then abandons Laura, is seduced, in turn, by Lady Griffith, and then exalts himself and her by exercising his will and strength, destroying first his more noble and generous instincts and finally his mistress herself. He abandons himself to his instincts, ignorant of the proviso in Édouard's often-quoted formula: "It is good to follow your bent, provided it moves upwards." George Molinier, although still a teenager, seems at first to have chosen the way of revolt and defiance. Like his classmate Ghérandisol, nephew and protégé of the novel's Protos-like figure, Strouvihou, George is in the process of fashioning himself into a "subtle one" and inadvertently falls into a system as rigid as the one he would escape. Through a suicide pact reserved for only a select few in their class, he and Ghérandisol provoke the suicide of another classmate, the timid and tormented grandson of La Pérouse, Boris. It is only with great effort that he finally comes to his senses and seeks the help of his mother. Ghérandisol, on the other hand, regrets only having lost his sangfroid by uncontrollably shuddering at the sight of the cadaver. Boris is a victim not only of his classmate's cruelty but also of his temperament, his early upbringing, and especially of Sophroniska, a sort of Freudian analyst into whose care Boris has been entrusted. Rigorously following certain psychoanalytic theories, Sophroniska so deforms facts to fit her interpretation of reality that she cannot realize the true causes of Boris' emotional improvement. Of far greater effectiveness for the young boy than her theories is the idyllic relationship between her charge and her daughter, Bronja.

In this one book, into which Gide wanted to pour all that life had shown and taught him, there is a catalogue of various types of counterfeit personalities and of the influences that force them to forsake authenticity. Essentially, the book is a study of the adolescent personality in its struggle and growth toward either a full or an atrophied maturity. But the book also contains aesthetic theories of fiction in the process of maturing in Édouard's mind, which are balanced against the logbook of Gide's own theories. Gide put much of his own thought into the mouth of Édouard; but the latter frequently develops his ideas to a point beyond logic or refuses to anchor them in reality. Reality bothers him, he tells Bernard during the long discussion of the novel, and for this very reason Bernard is quick to suggest that in his book Édouard begin right off with facts, with counterfeit coins. Although Bernard, the realist, introduces the false coins only in part 3, postponing these real facts forces them to act as concrete catalysts in a rather abstract system. As Édouard thinks first of the counterfeit only in a figurative sense, so, too, Gide's novel presents a series of people either living a lie or in the process of struggling with one. But these lives are viewed as counterfeit—that is, they earn the counterfeit label—only when the reality of the counterfeit coins intrudes into the orderly world of the novel. Similarly, the brutality of Boris' death intrudes into Édouard's consciousness and perception of the world:

> That is why I will not use Boris' suicide in my "The Counterfeiters"; I already have enough difficulty understanding it. And, then, I don't like "news items." They have in them a bit of the peremptory, the undeniable, the brutal, the outrageously real. . . . I allow reality to support my thought as a proof, but not to precede it. I don't like being surprised. I see Boris' suicide as an *indecency* because I didn't expect it.
>
> (Bussy trans., p. 363)

Boris' grandfather, La Pérouse, cannot assimilate this event either; plunged into a mystical despair that makes man the victim of a unified God and Satan, he cannot express his sorrow directly, a sorrow too profound, too "astounding," as Édouard observes, "to allow any steady contemplation."

After *The Counterfeiters,* Gide wrote nothing of the stature of his previous fiction unless it be *Theseus.* One can easily suppose that he literally used himself up on his novel just as he had foreseen in *Journal des faux-monnayeurs.* As he suggests on several occasions in his journal, were it not for an "undeniable diminution" in his creative prowess, his interest in social problems and in communism would not have usurped the place of his personal and moral concerns. But the lessening of his creative powers during the 1930's can be even further explained from another vantage point. Nearly all of his books up to and including *The Counterfeiters* answered a profound psychological need. The work of art provided him with a crutch thanks to which he was able to achieve "an equilibrium beyond time, an artificial health," as he says in the *Journal,* that he felt totally incapable of achieving in living. But as he grew older and more and more reconciled to his homosexuality, the stability obtained by composing works of art was slowly, imperceptibly transferred onto his person; he began to live by maintaining a balance of various contradictory forces of his personality. If, as Gide so often claimed, the spur of every impulse to social reform is an anomaly, an imbalance, a potential atrophy, his own deep-rooted perplexities dissolved as he exorcised the tyrannical potential of each of them. As he became well adjusted, he lost all desire to repeat reforms he had already worked out; by 1926 he had written cathartically of asceticism, of hedonism, and of a sort of romantic imagination; he had written a defense of homosexuality, a case study of himself, in the form of memoirs; and he had written the long-dreamed-of *summa, The Counterfeiters.*

In a journal entry for 19 July 1932 Gide stated, "Each of my books has, up until now, focused upon an uncertainty." A glance back at his work up to *The Counterfeiters* bears out the validity of this insight; supporting it, too, are the many statements Gide made in the *Journal* and elsewhere concerning the answers each of his works provided for his inner needs. In his attempt to achieve a fuller life, without the inhibiting consequences of real action, Gide relied upon his fantasy and made his protagonists act out to the fullest extent possible each of his own temptations. This explains the compensatory violence of a book like *Les nourritures terrestres* (*The Fruits of the Earth,* 1897), produced at the beginning of his career and certainly representing an epoch-making statement in the Gidian canon. It explains, too, why in 1927 Gide brought this book out of limbo and republished it; and finally, it explains why in 1935, at the peak of his political fervor, he returned to this same literary style and published *Les nouvelles nourritures* (*New Fruits of the Earth*).

As Gide knew long before he wrote the 1927 preface, *The Fruits of the Earth* was a book of convalescence, the fruit, as he wrote to Christian Beck—a young poet and philosopher also afflicted with lung problems—in 1907, of his tuberculosis: "There is in its very lyricism the excesses of one who clutches life as something he has almost lost." The scope of this statement should be extended to include the excesses of him who embraces life as something he has long denied himself. There is no fanatic like a new convert, and Gide consciously exorcised the extremes of hedonism and fanaticism in his song on the fruits of the earth. Conscious of the efficacy and psychic stability provided by a "system of compensations," and of the "usefulness of illness," as he noted in his *Journal* in 1896, he abandoned himself to extolling fervor, freedom, and joy. In abandoning himself—at least in literature—he both compensated for the effects of a cloistered youth and adolescence and let these "safe" compensations run their course. In this way he expended his hedonism, but he did not abandon his theory; he continued to praise the fruits of the earth and urged his fictional disciple Nathanaël, no less strongly at the end than at the beginning, to go his way alone, to rely on no one and nothing outside himself, to the point even of abandoning his master and this "manual of evasion."

*The Fruits of the Earth* has been taken most frequently as a panegyric of hedonism. It is true that those who speak in the "essay" tell of joy encountered and appetites satisfied, but the tone of voice in all cases is unique and uniform. Essentially, it is a hortatory tone, with Ménalque inviting his listeners and the narrator urging his readers and especially his young disciple, Nathanaël, to feed upon the fruits of the earth. In a very real sense, then,

*The Fruits of the Earth,* like an antidote to *Marshlands,* represents the aspirations of a long-sheltered and ascetic youth toward a full earthly experience and ultimately toward an equilibrium between the pleasures of the senses and those of the soul. But for the young Huguenot even pure hedonism was not easy to achieve without the essential condition so difficult for an introspective intellectual: the suppression of his thought and attendant self-consciousness. It is not surprising that the narrator feels obliged to reject speaking of himself, to defer "the ballad on the different forms of the mind," and to state, "Have you noticed that there is no one in this book? And even I am no more than a vision in it." Similarly, in the 1927 preface, Gide felt it necessary to point out that rather than hedonism his book glorifies destitution and, primarily, stripping oneself of one's ever-hovering intellect. In almost the same way as Gide condemned his own thought on a number of occasions, Ménalque in book 4 chides a comrade, who has wife, children, books, and a study, for expecting "to savor the powerful, total, and immediate sensation of life without forgetting what is extraneous to it. Your habit of thinking is a burden to you; you live in either the past or the future and you perceive nothing spontaneously. We are nothing except in the instantaneousness of life; the entire past dies in it before anything yet to come is born." And this Ménalque affirms after recounting how at fifty he sold "absolutely everything, not wanting to retain anything *personal* on earth; not even the slightest memory of yesteryear."

Book 4, which is nearly entirely devoted to Ménalque's autobiography, picks up and repeats the ideas and themes carefully suggested and developed in the first three books. The central idea developed by Ménalque revolves around his aversion to possessions of any kind for fear of possessing no more than that. Such a fear of property originally kept him from making any choices and ultimately from undertaking any action at all. But he finally understands that "all the drops from this vast divine source are equivalent; that the tiniest suffices to intoxicate us and to reveal the plenitude and totality of God." In effect, destitution provokes our thirst and hunger, incites our fervor, and enables us to receive and enjoy anything in our path. Ménalque rejects everything that might inhibit his receptivity to all sensations in their force and immediacy: he rejects family, institutions, hopes for the future, reliance on the past, everything but the slow, deliberate, and random cultivation of all his senses. He rejects, too, anything that stops challenging him to find and deploy new strengths; when people and things become familiar, he feels, they breed repose and reliance on past accomplishment. It is in this spirit that he concludes: "My heart without any attachment on earth has remained poor, and I will die easily. My happiness is made of fervor. Through all things indistinctly, I have adored intensely."

Fancy is bred not in the eye but in the mind, and therein lies the flaw in Gide's book and its ethics, a flaw that he was well aware of and casually exploits in the book itself. Fervor must be maintained at any price and by any means if the intensity of sensations is to continue as a cultivation of the self. This movement from the search for experience to the search for sensations and for ever-new sensations capable of maintaining fervor eventually degenerates into a frenzied hunt for stimulation. Finally there obtains a loss of the self so complete, a self so detached from past and future, that the narrator feels possessed: "What is called 'meditation' is an impossible constraint for me; I no longer understand the word 'solitude'; to be alone with myself is to be no longer anyone; I am inhabited."

In a letter to Marcel Drouin, his brother-in-law and a friend since adolescence, Gide wrote that he was concerned in *The Fruits of the Earth* with only one side of the coin, with the joy of desire and not the anguish and dissolution that it causes. But this in no way implies he was unaware of the other side; he dealt with it later, contenting himself for the moment with suggesting in the later books of *The Fruits of the Earth* possible outcomes of Ménalque's doctrine that call to mind *Saül* (1903) and *The Immoralist.* He felt that the importance of *The Fruits of the Earth* lay precisely in the full and unfettered exploitation of the sensual side of his personality. Letting it run its course, at least in the work of art, brought him to several other conclusions he later was able to verify in life. In "Le renoncement au voyage" ("Renunciation of Travel," included in *Amyntas,* 1906), Gide realized that his hypersensitivity stemmed mostly from his thirst for sensation so long repressed and not from a permanent physiological state. You cannot go back and find the same intensity of a former naive self, Gide says during his sixth visit to North Africa. And even in book 8 of *The Fruits of the Earth* the narrator nostalgically states the difficulty of becoming once again the young man he was in Biskra: "He who I was, that other one, ah! how could I become him again?"

Thus even in *The Fruits of the Earth,* where Gide planned to sing the joys of the flesh and fruits of the earth in compensation for the austere and cerebral side of his nature, he could not but indicate the deformed figure such a program can produce and by contrast suggest the ideal of equilibrium and plenitude. Here, already, are prefigurations of Michel and Saül, both dispossessed by the will-eroding power of their desires. And at last, even in his last *récit,* the long, happy life of Theseus, which he recounts with a measure of satisfaction and an abundance of detail, Gide cannot help confronting his pragmatic hero with the suffering inspired by Oedipus.

The long road traveled by Gide in search of tranquillity and plenitude is dramatically illustrated by the juxtaposition of these two books, *The Fruits of the Earth* and *Theseus:* the one an initial Dionysiac plunge into sensation doubled by a vague hesitation and anticipation of disaster, and the other no less intense sensually but set in balance by a taut, springlike willpower, a Corneillian sense of duty and service, and a devotion to a balanced exploitation of all his strengths. Theseus is a child of this earth, physically, intellectually, and emotionally agile; he is socially and sexually wily and adept, yet less given to indulgence of his pleasure than of his strengths and virtues.

The first great lesson Theseus recalls in his memoirs is a reliance on reason; the second is an exercise in strengthening his will. His father, Aegeus, one day told him that his pastoral life would have to come to an end: he was a king's son and would have to become worthy of succeeding his father on the throne. By a ruse, claiming that special weapons for Theseus were hidden by Poseidon beneath a stone, Aegeus succeeds in building up both Theseus' moral and physical strength; in his determination to find the weapons Theseus leaves no stone unturned, beginning even to tear apart the palace terrace. Aegeus gives his arms to Theseus, feeling that his son has amply shown a desire for glory that will not permit them to be used for any but noble end and mankind's happiness. In this manner Theseus developed a code that enabled him to overcome many monsters both within and without his personality; he strengthened his will, which enabled him to "stop living with abandon, however pleasing this freedom might have been." Although always ready for pleasure and never refusing to savor an amorous exploit, he never let himself be saddled by any and quickly went beyond them; in love, as in all else, "I was always less concerned and withheld by what I had accomplished than pulled by what still had to be done; and the more important always seemed to me still to come."

Theseus suggests that the hero is the one with an exceptionally strong will, the strength of which enables him to transcend the normal limits of good and evil and, for the greater glory of himself and future generations, to do, in fact, no evil, or at least to compensate for it. He embodies Gide's ethic in a curiously neo-

Leibnizian form: what is, is good, and what the hero does is good. A constant control and assurance is provided by his sense of duty and the full exploitation of his strengths and aptitudes. The hero ever strives to integrate within his experience the largest possible segment of reality about him, with its and his harmonies and dissonances.

The basis of the *récit* is a series of great encounters from which Theseus derives some personal benefit; two chapters are devoted to his early life and to the formative influences of his father and grandfather; eight chapters are devoted to Theseus' stay in Knossos, his encounters with Daedalus, Minos, and his family, particularly Ariadne, Phaedra, and the Minotaur; the final chapters revolve around the flight from Crete and the founding of Athens; finally, in an epilogue, Gide dramatizes a confrontation between Oedipus and Theseus. The confrontations with Daedalus and later with Oedipus are the key chapters of the narrative. As architect of the labyrinth, Daedalus is especially qualified to explain the subtle nature of his prison as well as to provide Theseus with a plan enabling him to enter the maze, accomplish his deed, and escape with little difficulty. To detain people in his labyrinth, Daedalus explains, it would be more effective to design a structure from which people would not want to escape. With this in mind, he fills the hallways and rooms of the maze with appetizers, incenses, and gases of all sorts that act upon the will: "Each person, following the inclination of his own mind thereupon prepares, loses himself, if you will, in his own private labyrinth." The way to overcome these subtle narcotics is to maintain a taut will, support it with a handmade gas mask, and guide oneself with reels of thread, firmly anchored outside the labyrinth. Daedalus calls this thread "a tangible symbol of duty" and says it is Theseus' bond to his past and to his future; without it, his life would become a hopeless imbroglio and a permanent immersion in the present and in the presence of sensations.

In the last encounter at Colonus, Theseus and Oedipus measure themselves against one another. By beginning the epilogue with an account of his own suffering, Theseus attempts to equate himself with Oedipus. Only in this area does there seem to be a common ground between the two. For Theseus had suceeded in all he had undertaken, whereas Oedipus had failed. "His misfortunes," Theseus writes, "could only enhance his grandeur in my eyes. No doubt I had triumphed everywhere and always, but on a level which, in comparison with Oedipus, seemed to me merely human, inferior, I might say." Here for the first time Theseus catches a glimpse of the infinite and has difficulty understanding. Why had Oedipus accepted defeat by putting out his eyes? Had he not even contributed to it? Oedipus gropes around for an answer likely to reach his interlocutor and convey some sort of meaning to him. He says he put out his eyes to punish them for not having seen the obvious, as an instinctive gesture, as an attempt to see his destiny through to the very end, or to destroy the false picture of the world of appearances in the hope of seeing into the "real, insensible" world beyond that is the realm of God. Theseus admits he does not quite fathom these explanations but does not deny the importance the spiritual world might have for some; yet he cannot accept the opposition Oedipus sets up between their two worlds. As in most of the book, in fact, Theseus' incomprehension and then final acceptance of Oedipus on Attic territory are the fruit of his constant attempt to contain all extremes and maintain them in equilibrium.

Like Theseus, Gide attempted to take into account as much of the world and as many ways of approaching it as possible. Theseus might not understand Oedipus' mystical impulse, but he certainly does make a place for Oedipus in his realms. So, too, Gide himself; but he went beyond each of his characters by balancing within himself both transcendental and terrestrial values. This attitude is evident in his memoirs, his journals, his travelogues, and especially in his criticism, where it becomes an aesthetic criterion. He saw himself as a modern counterpart to the classicists, in whom he valued above all else their modesty and its artistic analogue, litotes, as well as their stiving to take into account and maintain in harmony as much of reality as possible and to express the totality of their age. The limits of art, he said in a lecture titled "Les limites de l'art," written in 1901 ("The Limits of Art," undelivered but published in *Prétextes* [*Pretexts*, 1903]), like the limits of the human personality, are not external or legislatable but exist within the artist and within the human being. As such, they are not simply separate extremes but limits of a continuous extension. That is, Gide clarifies by quoting Pascal, "one knows one's greatness not by being at one extremity, but by touching both at the same time and filling in between them." Echoing this notion in the *Journal* of 1930, Gide remarks flippantly that he is ever conscious of his limits because he never occupies the center of his cage: "My whole being rushes toward the bars." The conclusion of the lecture rephrases an idea very dear to Gide: the artist must submit "to himself as much as possible, as much of nature as possible." This rewords an earlier idea often repeated in the *Journal* and elsewhere that Gide reprinted in capitals in *The Fruits of the Earth:* "Take to oneself as much humanity as possible."

Gide's unending search for harmony, for an equilibrium valuable only if attained with difficulty, lies at the heart of his ethic and aesthetic; works of different types, developing character traits to their extremes, represent less an exclusion by catharsis than an attempt to integrate these traits in the context of his whole personality. "Let's integrate, then," he tells his imaginary correspondent, Angèle, in a letter on classicism appearing in *Incidences* (1924). "Let's integrate. All that classicism refuses to integrate just might turn against it."

## Selected Bibliography

### EDITIONS

#### INDIVIDUAL WORKS


PROSE

*Les cahiers d'André Walter.* Paris, 1891.
*Le traité du Narcisse.* Paris, 1891.
*Le tentative amoureuse.* Paris, 1893.
*Le voyage d'Urien.* Paris, 1893.
*Paludes.* Paris, 1895.
*Les nourritures terrestres.* Paris, 1897.
*El Hadj.* In *Philoctète, Le traité du Narcisse, La tentative amoureuse, El Hadj.* Paris, 1899.
*Le Prométhée mal enchaîné.* Paris, 1899.
*L'Immoraliste.* Paris, 1902.
*Amyntas.* Paris, 1906; new edition, Paris, 1925.
*Le retour de l'enfant prodigue.* Paris, 1907. Includes *Le traité du Narcisse, La tentative amoureuse, El Hadj, Philoctète,* and *Bethsabé.*
*La porte étroite.* Paris, 1909.
*Isabelle.* Paris, 1911.
*Les caves du Vatican.* Paris, 1914.
*La symphonie pastorale.* Paris, 1919.
*Les faux-monnayeurs.* Paris, 1926.
*L'École des femmes.* Paris, 1929.
*Robert.* Paris, 1930.
*Les nouvelles nourritures.* Paris, 1935.
*Geneviève.* Paris, 1936.
*Thésée.* New York, 1946.

DRAMA

*Philoctète.* In *Philoctète, Le traité du Narcisse, La tentative amoureuse, El Hadj.* Paris, 1899.
*Le roi Candaule.* Paris, 1901.
*Saül.* Paris, 1903.
*Bethsabé.* Paris, 1912.
*Oedipe.* Paris, 1931.
*Perséphone.* Paris, 1934.
*Le treizième arbre.* Paris, 1942.
*Robert ou l'intérêt général.* Neuchâtel and Paris, 1949.

POETRY

*Les poésies d'André Walter.* Paris, 1892.

LITERARY CRITICISM, SOCIAL CRITICISM, AND TRAVEL WRITING

*Prétextes.* Paris, 1903.
*Oscar Wilde.* Paris, 1910.

*Nouveaux prétextes.* Paris, 1911.
*Souvenirs de la cour d'Assises.* Paris, 1914.
*Dostoïevski.* Paris, 1923.
*Corydon.* Paris, 1924.
*Incidences.* Paris, 1924.
*Voyage au Congo.* Paris, 1927.
*Le retour du Tchad.* Paris, 1928.
*Essai sur Montaigne.* Paris, 1929.
*L'Affaire Redureau suivie de faits divers.* Paris, 1930.
*La séquestrée de Poitiers.* Paris, 1930.
*Divers.* Paris, 1931.
*Retour de l'U.R.S.S.* Paris, 1936.
*Retouches à mon "Retour de l'U.R.S.S."* Paris, 1936.
*Attendu que . . .* Algiers, 1943.
*Interviews imaginaires.* Yverdon and Lausanne, 1943.
*Littérature engagée.* Paris, 1950.

AUTOBIOGRAPHICAL WORKS

*Numquid et tu.* Paris, 1926.
*Si le grain ne meurt.* Paris, 1926.
*Jeunesse.* Neuchâtel, 1945.
*Feuillets d'automne.* Paris, 1946.
*Et nunc manet in te.* Neuchatêl, 1951.
*Ainsi soit-il ou Les jeux sont faits.* Paris, 1952.

COLLECTED WORKS

*Oeuvres complètes.* Edited by L. Martin-Chauffier. 15 vols. Paris, 1932–1939.
*Théâtre.* Paris, 1942.
*Théâtre complet.* Edited by Richard Heyd. 8 vols. Neuchâtel, 1947–1949.
*Romans, récits, et soties: Oeuvres lyriques.* Edited by Y. Davetet and J. J. Thierry. Paris, 1958.

## JOURNALS

*Journal 1889–1939.* 4 vols. Paris, 1939.
*Journal 1939–1949. Souvenirs.* Paris, 1954.
*Journal des faux-monnayeurs.* Paris, 1926.

## CORRESPONDENCE

*Correspondance André Gide et Dorothy Bussy, Juin 1918–Janvier 1951.* 3 vols. Edited by Jean Lambert. Paris, 1979–1982.
*Correspondance Francis Jammes et André Gide, 1893–1938.* Edited by Robert Mallet. Paris, 1948.
*Correspondance Paul Claudel et André Gide, 1899–1926.* Edited by Robert Mallet. Paris, 1949.
*Correspondance Rainer Maria Rilke et André Gide, 1909–1926.* Edited by Renée Lang. Paris, 1952.
*Lettres de Charles De Bos et réponses d'André Gide.* Paris, 1950.
Marcel Proust. *Lettres à André Gide.* Neuchâtel, 1949.

## TRANSLATIONS

*Amyntas.* Translated by Villiers David. New York, 1958.
*The Correspondence Between Paul Claudel and André Gide.* Translated by John Russell. New York, 1952.
*Corydon.* Translated by Hugh Gibb. New York, 1950.
*The Counterfeiters.* Translated by Dorothy Bussy. New York, 1951. Includes *Journal of the Counterfeiters.*
*Dostoevski.* Translated by Dorothy Bussy. New York, 1926.
*The Fruits of the Earth and New Fruits of the Earth.* Translated by Dorothy Bussy. New York, 1949.
*If It Die. . . .* Translated by Dorothy Bussy. New York, 1935.
*The Immoralist.* Translated by Dorothy Bussy. New York, 1930.
*Isabelle.* Translated by Dorothy Bussy. In *Two Symphonies.* New York, 1931.
*The Journals of André Gide.* 4 vols. Translated by Justin O'Brien. New York, 1947–1951.
*The Living Thoughts of Montaigne.* Translated by Dorothy Bussy. New York, 1939.
*The Lover's Attempt.* Translated by Dorothy Bussy. In *The Return of the Prodigal.* London, 1953.
*Madeleine.* Translated by Justin O'Brien. New York, 1952.
*Marshlands and Prometheus Misbound: Two Satires.* Translated by George D. Painter. New York, 1953.
*My Theater.* Translated by Jackson Matthews. New York, 1951.
*Narcissus.* Translated by Dorothy Bussy. In *The Return of the Prodigal.* London, 1953.
*The Pastoral Symphony.* Translated by Dorothy Bussy. In *Two Symphonies.* New York, 1931.
*Pretexts: Reflections on Literature and Morality.* Edited by Justin O'Brien. Translated by Angelo Bertocci et al. New York, 1959.
*The Return of the Prodigal.* Translated by Dorothy Bussy. London, 1953.

*The School for Wives.* Translated by Dorothy Bussy. New York, 1950. Includes *Robert* and *Geneviève.*

*So Be It, or The Chips Are Down.* Translated by Justin O'Brien. New York, 1959.

*Strait Is the Gate.* Translated by Dorothy Bussy. New York, 1924.

*Theseus.* In *Two Legends: Oedipus and Theseus,* translated by John Russell. New York, 1959.

*Urien's Voyage.* Translated by Wade Baskin. New York, 1964.

*The Vatican Swindle.* Translated by Dorothy Bussy. New York, 1925.

*The White Notebook.* Translated by Wade Baskin. New York, 1965.

## BIOGRAPHICAL AND CRITICAL STUDIES

Brée, Germaine. *André Gide, l'insaisissable protée.* Paris, 1953. Revised and translated by Germaine Brée as *Gide.* New Brunswick, N.J., 1963.

Cordle, Thomas. *André Gide.* New York, 1969.

Delay, Jean. *La jeunesse d'André Gide.* 2 vols. Paris, 1956–1957. Translated by June Guicharnaud as *The Youth of André Gide.* Chicago, 1963. Abridged.

Fayer, H. M. *Gide, Freedom, and Dostoievsky.* Burlington, Vt., 1946.

Guerard, Albert J. *André Gide.* Cambridge, Mass., 1951.

Hytier, Jean. *André Gide.* Algiers, 1938. Translated by Richard Howard. Garden City, N.Y., 1962.

Ireland, G. W. *André Gide.* New York, 1963.

Martin, Claude. *La maturité André Gide: De "Paludes" à "L'Immoraliste" (1895–1902).* Paris, 1977.

Moutote, Daniel. *Le journal de Gide et les problèmes du moi (1889–1925).* Paris, 1968.

O'Brien, Justin. *Portrait of André Gide: A Critical Biography.* New York, 1953.

Rossi, Vinio. *André Gide: The Evolution of an Aesthetic.* New Brunswick, N.J., 1967.

*Yale French Studies* 7 (1950). Special issue devoted to Gide.

VINIO ROSSI

# JOHANN WOLFGANG von GOETHE

## *(1749–1832)*

WHEREAS OTHER AUTHORS in Western literature may appear to speak directly to their respective ages, Goethe seems to anticipate the future. There was a quality in the man that stood out in his own time and that was regarded as heathen or pagan. Such a perception was not negative, however. The quality of unreflective knowing, with its unique and inevitable freedom, was one that thinkers in the late eighteenth century sought to develop in their struggle against the restrictive rationalism of the Age of Reason. To Friedrich Schiller, his contemporary, Goethe was "the poet in whom nature functions more faithfully and purely than any other, and who, among modern poets, is perhaps least removed from the sensuous truth of things." Schiller thus admiringly relegated Goethe to the high poetic order of the ancient world and reserved for himself, as more typically a product of the modern era, the demanding task of regaining the artistic effect of immediate truth through unending conscious effort.

But neither Schiller nor the age foresaw the great schism with the past that inevitably resulted from the meeting of a truly open, unmediated sense of reality with the forces and ideas that were *of* the age, not merely *in* the age, as was its revolt against rationalism. For Goethe, that revolt came early and instinctively; but it meant little more than further reason to embrace the new concepts of organic growth, development, and process that were about to revolutionize science and philosophical thought, at least for a time. For Goethe, Gottfried von Herder was the most direct influence. Herder envisioned Earth as a planet among other planets, the things of Earth (nature) as interrelated in all their manifestations, and the things of man (culture and history) as comprehensive and cyclical. For Herder, everything had a universal context, not merely a universal meaning. The common event, like the individual human being, could be regarded no longer as simply representative of a higher abstract order, but rather must be seen as comprising a particular element in the order without which it could not be, nor in the past could have been, precisely the same. God became part of nature in the concept of pantheism, and in society the mass of men was absorbed into the body politic, though these developments were hardly related. In Germany political currents in no way kept pace with the intellectual and artistic achievements of the times.

Goethe went further than Herder. The same sense of openness that made Goethe so receptive to the new kept him open to its consequences. Where Herder promoted relativism as a natural result of his comprehensive view of the past (to know all is to forgive all), he stopped short of forgoing judgment in the present. Herder was a pastor. Goethe could say, also to a pastor, "All your ideals will not distract me from being true—good *and* evil, like nature." For all its *Sturm und Drang* (Storm and Stress) bravado, the remark remains fundamental to an understanding of his view of life. It is the outward expression of the inner sense of things that led him to note some thirty years later, as he made plans to write his autobiography: "As much false as good impulse, hence the eternal martyrdom." And, as much an experience of nature as a view of self is reflected in the earlier remark.

Nature for Goethe could be formidable, in its brightest and its darkest aspects. The vision of a harmonious universe that introduces the drama of *Faust* is immediately followed by a description of the tempestuous and destructive atmosphere that encloses the earth, the setting in which the hero, as man, must work out his moral destiny. Any glimpse of order or moment of peace in such a setting would be as rare as it would be desirable, and only the angels, who stand in eternity and praise the spectacle of Creation, seem far enough removed from the abundance to discern its patterns and grasp its meaning. Even the sun, which illuminates the whole, is so designed in the nature of things as to blind when looked at directly—as Faust learns when he resumes the journey in part 2, after the headlong experience of part 1; now with his back to the light, he seeks to understand through reflection.

Goethe took some sixty years to complete his *Faust,* and while his attention and energies were hardly consumed in this one undertaking during that long period, still it was not mere time, but rather a struggle with questions as yet unresolved, that determined the strange progress and the ultimately unique form of the work. (I leave a discussion of *Faust* to the end of this essay. Since the work spans the whole of the author's creative life, the discussion may serve more appropriately as a summary.) Conversely, since his other writings, including those in science, mark separately the artistic and intellectual stages through which the greater project passed in its development, they in turn anticipate and illuminate the parts from which the whole was made. We have in *Faust* not only the result of an unusual evolutionary process but its display as well.

Johann Wolfgang Goethe was born on 28 August 1749, in Frankfurt-am-Main, to a prosperous family. His father, a largely self-taught man, undertook the early education of the children and was the taskmaster. His mother, much younger, seems to have exerted the kind of influence that fosters freedom and a sense of self. Moreover, the city of his birth, Goethe said in later years, could not have been better suited to the interests and ambitions of a lively spirit; a city with a praiseworthy past, independence in politics, success in commerce, and advances in culture and social reform. In terms of enlightenment and early environment he was thus generally fortunate.

Goethe was thought dead at birth and was brought to life with great difficulty. He mentions the incident in his autobiography, *Dichtung und Wahrheit* (*Poetry and Truth,* 1811–1833), but in keeping with the detached tone of the narrative he notes it as the occasion for instituting better training for midwives, a reform his grandfather, as mayor of Frankfurt, subsequently effected. Of six children only he and one sister outlived childhood. Not that this experience, common at the time, upset the greater framework of security. Goethe singled out the devastating earthquake in Lisbon in 1755, which he heard of at age six (and Voltaire at age sixty), as the severest possible blow to a child taught to believe in a benevolent God and a universal order. The blow may have seemed more severe in retrospect, for we learn about it from him only much later, in the autobiography. But it would be wrong to assume that the reminiscence distorted the truth. More likely the opposite: hindsight rendered the truth more complete, more accessible to his own mind. The striking aspect of Goethe's life, and surely an element that contributed to its greatness, was his ability to comprehend (in the sense of taking in and holding firm) all the unbalancing, almost chaotic, but in any event continual, change that occurred in his development and that he actively sought out.

The early years were unsettling in that very way. The child of secure circumstances became the youth of extreme emotions, uncertainties, overcompensations, ups and downs. In school he ranked anywhere from first to seventeenth at any given time in his various subjects. Thomas Mann spoke of Goethe in this period as a "rearing, kicking thoroughbred colt." Yet for all the objectively dramatic or impressive content of his life—immediate success and fame, love affairs, meetings, correspondence and productive relationships with the great figures of the time, astonishing scope of interests and activities in science and human affairs—it was an inner need for change and growth that made the accomplishments possible. To the natural assumption that his *Faust* was based on a knowledge of the world gained by broad experience, he once said: "That may be. But had I not already carried the world within me through anticipation, with seeing eyes I would have remained blind, and all exploration and experience would have been nothing but a totally dead and vain endeavor." There was an immeasurable force in this development—whether one sees it in Goethe's terms or in less romantic, more psychological, realistic terms—that seemed to hold together his life and his understanding of life at its various stages, even while he was under the constant pressure of new experience and knowledge to change or redefine himself at the conscious level: whence the potential for growth; whence also the struggle. Goethe eventually came to regard the development of mankind in general in terms of change and redefinition.

He held his inner world intact in the early period mainly by a method close to hand, his poetic talent. He wrote as therapy. He developed the habit of transforming "whatever pleased or pained, or otherwise occupied" him into a fiction or a poem "in order to rectify my ideas of external things as well as to console myself inwardly." "All that I have published thus far," he wrote in 1812 in the second volume of his autobiography, "are only fragments of a confession." "If I did not write dramas now," he said, at a particularly low point, "I would perish." And although his earliest poems and plays surely served to balance the wild emotions resulting from the jealous love affair that was their subject matter, not until other influences and factors came into play did his confessional mode of writing begin to tell in his development, and bear upon the modern theory of literature and art. Again the important influence was Herder. He introduced Goethe to the poetry of early cultures, to Ossian (wrongly believed to be a Celtic bard), and to Shakespeare. The choice reflected not a preference but a philosophy. The view of history as the most essential human reality, a reality created by and for humankind, includes literature and art as the direct expressions of, not as mere supplements to, the truth history seeks to identify. The earlier the form the more immediate and true the expression. Poetry, in the view of Johann Georg Hamann, who in turn had taught Herder, was the mother tongue of humankind. Goethe responded avidly. The poet in this view stood above the philosopher, at least the rationalistic philosopher, as partaker of truth. Goethe, like a whole generation to come, relied on this new anatomy of genius that emphasized instinct and imagination over tradition and reason as the forces that create unerringly, much as nature does, without wholly conscious purpose.

Yet Goethe created for his own ends. Not that the distinction proved immediately important. The poetry that came forth as the first true expression of his genius need not be understood, nor is it better understood, by knowing its source in personal experience. His most significant poems are lyric poems, free in form, subjective almost by requirement. What "pleased or pained" Goethe in these poems would similarly affect many lyric poets for some time. His own poetry was in that sense itself an imitation, in the spirit of the direct response to nature that he found in the literature of ancient peoples. "May Song" (1771), which begins, "Nature comes to me/So splendidly," may stand as a single example.

The dramatic works into which Goethe poured his deepest and most immediate concerns at the time, in retrospect also seem more like anticipations of new dramatic forms than personal documents. *Götz von Berlichingen* (1773), for example, a historical drama in the Shakespearean vein, is so clearly the product of literary influence that Herder wrote to the young Goethe after reading the play: "Shakespeare has completely corrupted you." In this imitation of Shakespeare, Goethe succeeded in introducing native history into a German theater long dominated by foreign traditions, thereby meeting a need that Herder himself and Gotthold Ephraim Lessing before him had regarded as essential to the development of a national literature. But Goethe apparently made this important contribution with a different idea in mind. His drama was written, although it may not have been initially so conceived, to exorcise the guilt he felt in abandoning Friederike Brion, a young, pretty girl, the daughter of a pastor, who had been the muse of his joyous love poetry and whose memory now inhabited his first great work for the theater. The confessional mode began to tell. Still it was not its presence here, which Goethe specifically acknowledged in his autobiography, so much as its absence elsewhere that best reflected the process.

Of the dramas planned in this period in a vein similar to *Götz,* with a hero of deed or vision or revolt at their center—Caesar, Mahomet, Prometheus—none was completed. Perhaps the daring model of Shakespeare in *Götz* accounted for the dispatch with which this play was written. "Only a genius can influence a genius," Lessing had said. Yet the one other drama of substance that emerged at the time, *Clavigo,* shares with *Götz* the theme of ambition in conflict with loyalty—the essence of the Friederike experience—but in *Clavigo* it is the central theme, as appropriate to the form of popular bourgeois tragedy. Goethe reportedly wrote the play in a week.

If we can sense in these similarities and contrasts a clamoring to express many concerns, of which only those that would not be denied took form, we will have an understanding of both the origin and the nature of these early works of genius. For the main point about art as therapy in Goethe's case was its effectiveness. The artistic process demanded in its own right the very immediacy and truthfulness—as opposed to artfulness of expression—that were also demanded by the evolving style of the eighteenth and nineteenth centuries.

With *Götz von Berlichingen* began the revolutionary movement in German literature called Storm and Stress, a movement of youth, by youth, and for youth, which pressed the goal of individualism to the extreme of rejecting all forms of traditional and institutionalized order, in art as well as society. The teaching of Jean Jacques Rousseau lay in the background. There were heroes called "Wild" and "LeFeu" in plays with titles such as *Infanticide* and *Storm and Stress* (from which the movement took its name) and many versions of the Faust story. How far the young Goethe himself, in creating *Götz,* intended to go in this respect is a question that remains unanswered.

The important fact about the effectiveness of the therapy in Goethe's art is that it led to his development and was the instrument of development. To express his concerns, what pleased and pained him, was not the end he sought in his writings, but rather the means by which he discovered more truly what he thought and felt. If the creative process served at the same time to call forth from his inner world visions and images that seemed to reflect directly the imaginative and sensate world of the age, it remained a process and a means. The result, although not the conscious purpose, was constant change that required growth and growth that required change, over a lifetime.

Goethe rarely repeated himself. His mode of creating seemed not only to objectify his ideas about external and internal matters of the real world but also to force naturally a modification and development of his imaginary creations, his "poetic products" as he called them. The Storm and Stress as well as the romantic principles he appeared to espouse in his great early works gave way to more balanced, objective, and classical forms and styles in the middle years; these in turn—when ultimately confronted with evolution, the central, modern idea of the age—were compelled to develop further in order to reflect a new dynamics of perception and understanding. The confrontation occurred in *Faust,* part 2, which Goethe wrote toward the end of his life, after having experienced so much change and development in his times, his person, his character as thinker and poet, and in the very nature of the poem he had had for so many years in hand. Evolution formed the character of the work, in terms of its free and varied evolving form and style no less than in its theme.

We mention *Faust* again in passing, for the drama was begun in this period of Storm and Stress. *Urfaust* (*Ur* meaning original) is the most powerful exemplar of the movement, with the absolutist hero represented in a revolt that is metaphysical and not merely social, and the heroine in an abandonment that is morally harrowing and not merely unjust. The initial version remained incomplete. Again Goethe developed the theme of tragic love to its end, but hesitated to deal with the inner world of his formidable protagonist in other regards.

No such hesitation impeded the writing of the other work for which Goethe is perhaps best known in world literature, *Die Leiden des jungen Werthers* (*The Sorrows of Young Werther,* 1774). It was completed with the same dispatch as *Götz.* Whereas Shakespeare served as the model for *Götz,* Jean Jacques Rousseau, Samuel Richardson, and the epistolary novel directly influenced the conception of *Werther;* but Goethe used the form for a unique purpose. His novel is about suicide. The letters of Werther stand alone; those of his correspondent—and there is only one—are reflected but heeded less and less in Werther's own letters, as the objective world pales for him and his inner world—and by projection a life beyond—becomes seemingly more real. We are given this one side of the correspondence over the year and a half before his suicide, on Christmas Eve; a short, sympathetic note by the ostensible publisher of the letters, at the beginning of the novel; and a factual report of the death, at the end. The final sentence notes that no clergyman followed the coffin to the grave. "The worm of death was in him from the start," Goethe commented later, outside the novel.

Yet Werther is presented as unhappily in love, unto death. That his unhappy love was more truly the occasion than the cause of his suicide he could not have known and still performed the act. But his letters uncannily provide both the evidence, in terms of immediate sensation and circumstance, that motivates and justifies his action in his own eyes and the inversion of this evidence, the reader's sense of the growing unreality and extremity of Werther's position. Not that we read between the lines of his letters, which in his Hamlet-like intelligence and introspection he already does for us, as in "I laugh at my heart—and do its bidding." Rather we learn and know after the fact, as Goethe did, who in *Werther* drew on personal experience to such an extent that we can believe the novel's fictional pretense that no author exists outside the work. The intensity of feeling, the perceptions, the role of nature, the veiled contempt for society, the time made free by this contempt but unused—these reflect not merely an attitude toward life but an actual period in Goethe's life to which he gives direct expression, as in a poem. Hence the letter form.

Werther is a poet not in fact but in sensitivity; and he shares with Goethe not only the details of the unfortunate and unrequited love that the latter had felt for the betrothed of a friend and, in a similar setting, of the unwanted and idle occupation Goethe had taken up after his university years, but also the thought of suicide that had plagued him then. On completing the novel, in 1774, he felt free, "as if after a general confession," he says in his autobiography, appropriately titled *Poetry and Truth,* since it describes his life and art in the early period when they were so closely related. The impulse to write the novel came some time after Goethe's infatuation, upon the report of suicide by a young man with whom he had associated, a certain Councillor Jerusalem, who like himself had pondered the great question of existence, and, in the course of an unrealizable love for a married woman, had taken his own life.

The writing of *Werther,* Goethe suggests in the autobiography, saved him from the worst consequences of his relationship with Charlotte Buff, the original for the novel's Charlotte in situation, temperament, and character, as well as in name. But as there is therapy through the writing, there is also the thematic implication that the ability to express the self serves to balance and appease the unclear urges of the mind and soul. Werther is of artistic bent. Three times he attempts to paint a portrait of Lotte and three times, as he says, he "prostituted himself." This same Werther says earlier: "I could not, right now, draw, not a line, and I have never been a greater artist than in these moments." Goethe, on the other hand, in dedicating a poem to *Werther* some fifty years later, when he found himself as an old man seriously attracted to a young girl, could write as motto: "And where other men fall silent in their pain/A God gave me to tell what I suffer."

Goethe himelf had ambitions as a painter in the early period, and for all his efforts knew failure. Thus Werther's inability to express himself in art had some basis in Goethe's personal experience. We cannot properly tell where therapy ends in the novel and art as such begins. A romantic, tragic flaw is uncovered in Werther in the disproportion he experiences between imagination and realization, the sense, as Faust says later, that "The God who reigns within my breast . . . who moves me deeply inwardly/He cannot move the world without." Goethe's own failure in painting may well have been compensated by his writing, and may thus have contributed to the sheer expressiveness of his work.

*Werther* burst upon Europe in 1774 as *Götz von Berlichingen* had upon Germany the previous year; and the extent of its influence on both life and literature shows the depth with which the novel was generally understood. A Werther costume of blue frock coat and yellow vest became popular. Edition after edition of the work was published over a decade, even in countries well beyond Europe; and as an ultimate, startling proof of its effectiveness, the suicide in the novel became a model in life. Goethe moved to correct the impression that *Werther* had made as an apology for suicide, positively on the younger generation and negatively on the older, by adding to the frame of the novel the objective report at the end. He meant to counterbalance the overwhelmingly subjective content of the letters themselves.

Yet misunderstanding was inevitable. There is little in the artistic nature and intent of the novel to encourage reasoned response. Moreover, as Goethe himself notes in his autobiography, Edward Young's *Night Thoughts on Life, Death and Immortality,* so popular among German youth at the time, had laid the basis for a sentimental, romantic reading of *Werther.* Goethe's own omission of any moral pronouncement in the novel can only have furthered the sense that he had simply outdone his models, Rousseau and Richardson, in sentiment and feeling. He had in fact, though not in intent. For to have created in *Werther,* with its essentially lyrical and subjective form, the impression of a larger objective reality that could contain and account for the action, as in a drama or a novel, would have been to fill the vacuum in which the hero was meant to perish.

The larger reality for Werther is internal: "I look within myself and find a world." The objective realities that exist in his view—and there is no other view in the novel—are condemned by him, and his generation as a whole, as being without higher purpose and representing inherently compromised and false human values. Yet to the one true reality that seems to exist for him and his generation, the great attraction of nature and the response to it, he brings the same prohibitive anxiety that causes him to seek the unattainable in love. He wonders, for example, how many insects are trodden upon in the course of an innocent walk through nature. He allows Ossian to replace Homer as his one constant source of consolation, as if looking now in his reading for the same dark reflection of nature he experiences in his real world.

In a further evocation of the times in literature, a copy of Lessing's *Emilia Galotti* lies open on Werther's desk at the moment of his suicide, reflecting a touchingly misguided attempt to find an honorable parallel for his own action in the fate of a heroine who had wished her own death, to be sure, but for moral rather than emotional reasons. In point of fact, she did not die by her own hand. And in the natural religion he embraces, more fervently toward the end, Werther again shares with his generation, at least in Germany, a spirit diffuse and yet intense, a piety expressed by general sentiment rather than moral strictures and guidance. *The Sorrows of Young Werther* reflects its times but, through the subjective nature of its form, suggests the new spirit in the age as it came into being—undefined, as yet unreal, but immediate in feeling. The same immediacy of the unreal or unrealized serves the internal purposes of the novel for the resolution in suicide. No death in literature has been more persuasively motivated, through a joining of the individualistic form of the first-person narrative with the supremely private act of suicide. Here are a form and a content both appropriate to an individualistic, confessional mode of creating and definitive of a new movement in literature and the arts that stressed the personal and individual as opposed to the traditional and authoritative.

But the novel did not serve to define the author. *Werther* implies no alternative order of things that comprehends or underlies the disorder the novel describes. If the hero had not died of love, it would have to be said he died of life. Yet except for the viable principle of resolving inner conflict through expression in art—which Goethe demonstrated positively, Werther by default—no moral, social, or metaphysical resolution suggests itself in the work. None existed for Goethe himself at the time. *Werther* came at the beginning of a new age but also at the end of another, an age that in substituting the precepts of philosophy for those of religion had itself been challenged and had not as yet found a guide to the future through social revolution and social progress. This last option was never a real one for Goethe, despite the early evidence of *Götz* and the utopian vision at the end of *Faust,* and was hardly a thought in the mind of the apolitical Werther. The deepest sense that underlies the work, however, is that deed and action, expression in life or through art, persist.

Faust begins his translation of the Bible "In the beginning was the deed" ("Im Anfang war die Tat"). But the context in which this categorical imperative of life and development finds expression in human experience (as it had for Goethe in art) is not given. As a product of a new age such a context would long remain difficult to define. When Goethe in his own accomplishment of self-realization is accused of egotism (by Victor Hugo in *Les misérables*) or admired for the same characteristic (by Friedrich Nietzsche in *Human, All Too Human*), what is forgotten is his struggle to find a form of objective reality that would justify and generalize, make moral, his instinctive sense of truth. But that struggle was the cause and the definition of his accomplishment.

One year after the publication of *Werther* and the resounding success of the premiere of *Götz,* in Berlin in 1774, Goethe was invited to the duchy of Weimar by the eighteen-year-old ruler, Karl August, who had just assumed authority, married, and now intended to settle down. Goethe remained there for the rest of his life. The success of his writings was the direct cause for the invitation. But a secondary concern, that the young duke should have guidance from a companion of note, attached itself to the main thought of bringing prestige to the reign and proved indirectly of equal consequence. In his position Goethe was soon able to bring Herder to Weimar and, later, Schiller to nearby Jena to form a triumvirate of philosopher-poets, a genus characteristically German. A generation earlier Frederick the Great had invited Voltaire, not Lessing, to his court.

The undetermined nature of Goethe's position gradually translated itself into a succession of posts, from privy councilor through superintendent of mines and army recruitment to the directorship of the Weimar theater, from 1791 to 1817. In the beginning his advice was sought in almost all matters. He discharged his various duties with loyalty and in friendship and, if we believe those who praised him in his many capacities, with the ability of a great mind to grasp essentials even in unfamiliar disciplines. That was surely the case in science, to which he came untrained and yet to which he made measurable contributions.

Goethe's unofficial duties were virtually as extensive as his official ones. His early fame brought visitors to Weimar for the specific purpose of meeting the author of *Werther.* Then the regular flow of poetry, dramas, novels, minor pieces for the theater, and, periodically, the publication of collected works added to the merely curious two generations of writers and thinkers, often called the early and the later German romantics, who over the years felt they should come and pay their respects. These semiofficial duties were discharged, if we believe Goethe's detractors, sometimes with the barest tolerance, and it was from the critics of his public life rather than from his family and close acquaintances that there emerged the image of the man as severe and aloof. The scientific correspondence that soon developed along with the literary, as well as the reports of encounters and conversations (and the famous *Conversations with Goethe,* 1836–1848, by Johann Peter Eckermann, which covered the last years), have created an unprecedented volume of material in which the poet-thinker is reflected as if in a prism, and have come to seem an actual part of him, his own active rather than passive doing. Even the great seem to have been meaningfully aware of this presence. On arriving in Erfurt in 1808 and learning that Goethe was close by, Napoleon, who claimed to have read *Werther* seven times, arranged a meeting; on encountering the poet he reportedly said, "There is a man!" This impression of universality, the sense of the breadth of his interests and achievements as well as the depths of his humanity, persisted.

The security and responsibilities that Goethe found upon coming to Weimar might have affected his development quite differently had not order in some form been necessary to his life and his art. There had been a creative chaos in his writing. It abounded not only in multiple related themes but also in a variety of literary forms, some of which, such as the operetta (for example, *Erwin and Elmire* and *Claudine of Villa Bella,* both 1775), had no relation to the immediate expression of experience; and others of which, such as the delightful scatological fragment *Hanswurst's Wedding* (1775), had no pretensions to high art. The variety in his art derived from his life of travel, uncertainty of purpose, and romantic relationships. There was both a tragic and an almost absurd aspect to the confusion in his early development, from a collapse caused by the unrestrained activity of the first university years at Leipzig to the emotional pandemonium in his life just prior to the departure for Weimar. It was at this point that he said, "If I did not write dramas now, I would perish." The drama that he produced for the occasion, *Stella: A Play for Lovers,* indeed reflected his inner chaos; but unlike *Werther* it remained an artistic embarrassment, proving that although art served Goethe as therapy, the therapy did not invariably serve his art.

The Weimar experience provided limits and direction to the energies of Goethe's early years. It did not change or negate the first potential, as witness the variety that now emerged in new interests and forms of art, but it made possible the fuller realization of that potential, its "heightening," as Goethe himself might have termed the phenomenon. In the security of Weimar, Goethe could pursue this course and, as an instinctively unpolitical being, find no obstruction or contradiction outside the private struggle with his work. Yet it must be remembered that his security derived from an initial, almost consummate, success, which in freeing him from financial and everyday concerns also seemed to release him from the pursuit of literary fame. This should be noted in anticipation of the dilemma that later presented itself when he attempted to cast new truth and a new sense of reality in forms invented from an older view of the world; and when order and truth could no longer be united, he sided with truth. "Every form, even the most deeply felt, has something false about it," he later remarked.

Beauty and order, not surprisingly in the new, sheltered life in Weimar, replaced bold truth and nature as the conscious goals that Goethe sought in his art, and created for a time the classical stage of his development. The drama *Egmont* marked the transition. Begun in Frankfurt in the wake of *Götz,* it reflects the continued enthusiasm for Shakespeare that had led the young Goethe to honor his name day (William: October 14) "with great pomp" and a celebratory speech in 1771: "Nature! Nature! Nothing so like nature as Shakespeare's figures!"

In its setting *Egmont* resembles *Götz.* Although the historical background is Dutch rather than German, and the antagonistic force a foreign power, Spain, rather than an overarching political authority, its theme is the essential opposition of indigenous, natural, individual right to the traditional right of a preconceived higher order. That was likewise the theme of the fragmentary "Prometheus" (1772) and of *Urfaust,* and, when thought of in the same context, "Mahomet" and the establishing of a native religion. *Egmont* shares with *Götz* a continuing success as a work for the theater. By chance, the year 1787, when *Egmont* was finally completed after almost a decade, saw a new revolt against authority in Brussels, and the play's parallels to the situation were not lost on the contemporary public. Count Egmont has the characteristics of a popular hero: zest for life, congeniality, and a politically tragic fate that he resignedly, almost indifferently, meets.

Goethe reveals in his autobiography the reasons why he wrote. How he wrote also proved a question of importance, which *Egmont* in its protracted development raised for the first time. With the exception of *Faust,* which Goethe created in a kind of subterranean recess of his mind, no work shows better than *Egmont* the often unusual process of his art: those writings destined for completion were soon completed, those not, immediately abandoned; and in rare cases, successful parts, such as the great odes from "Prometheus" and "Mahomet," were salvaged for the future. Goethe identified the difficulty with *Egmont* as the "annoying fourth act," the high point of the dramatic action, where the central political issue had to be explicated, joined, and resolved in effect, if not in final word. The political context may have given pause to the unpolitical author, but the solution he found not only disguised any original difficulty but resulted in a presentation of historical forces in a dramatic conflict lending tragic seriousness and authority to the play.

The greater underlying difficulty with *Egmont* resulted from its having been begun in one period and completed in another. *Egmont,* in the company of *Götz* and *Faust,* was originally conceived as a drama of character, not of history, and, it may be assumed, conceived in a form as free and expressive as other German works from the Storm and Stress period. In Egmont, Goethe said, he wished to represent a strangely vital human force that he termed "daemonic." The force was commonly perceived in animals, he believed, but was almost frightening when found in human beings. A strange power emanated from such persons, who were not always exceptional in terms of intellect or human qualities, yet who exerted an incredible influence on others. They seemed to be engaged in a battle with the universe itself, which might be their only equal.

In his autobiography, where he expressed these ideas many years later, Goethe sees Napoleon as the contemporary figure who most clearly exemplifies the darkly charismatic quality of the daemonic; he also mentions Lord Byron in the same regard. The task, and the difficulty, was to externalize this inward, yet unselfconscious quality in the hero of a drama, traditionally the most objective of literary forms. Its historical display might have been empty and its physical expression unlikely, given the confines of the stage, as well as the order and restraint toward which Goethe was striving when he took up the theme again. What resulted was not a lesser work than might have been accomplished in a freer form. Rather Goethe's commitment to nature, as opposed to idea, in his art (from which the strength of his lyric poetry derives), led him to create such a natural and immediate background for his central figure that the character refuses to stand out.

The historical context in *Egmont* is more concrete in terms of place and persons than in *Götz,* in which the action sprawls over time and place in epic exuberance. But the figure of Götz absorbs the exuberance; it does not create it. The figure of Faust in the early version seems to find unhampered expression in the great stylistic freedom of the work, yet the theme itself—magic and the atmosphere of the occult—and the poetry lend as much intensity to his being as what he says and does.

The balancing provided by the context or background in *Egmont* is therefore not new, merely different; and while it serves to diffuse the aura of the daemonic personality that Goethe created for his hero, at the same time it makes clear the implications of the action that Egmont himself expresses at the end of the play: "We think we are free, and ourselves guide our lives, and in our inmost being we are drawn to our fate." These words are not the verbal residue of a war once undertaken against the universe and lost, as with Faust or with Egmont as originally conceived. Rather they reflect the tragic recognition by a historical figure that his role in events has been determined less by his designs than by the use to which the events have put him, through his own natural instincts. Here the designs of fate are toward freedom from oppression; and Egmont serves well. Goethe designated the play a tragedy, but the closing stage direction calls for a "victory symphony," which Beethoven composed.

*Egmont* is a work of transition, not one of contradictions resolved. If it had been the latter, it would be hard to understand why *Iphigenia in Tauris,* the next major work for the theater that Goethe undertook after settling in Weimar, underwent no similar struggle for development. *Iphigenia* not only represents a step forward in order and beauty in art but came to stand as the single highest achievement of Weimar classicism, as the new form of literature and philosophy of life would later be known. But to presuppose simple progress in the achievement, as we almost inevitably would in comparing Goethe with the past, would be to overlook the more important process that again took place.

*Iphigenia,* the epitome of classicism, emerged from the same creative context that produced *Werther,* which is the epitome of romanticism. The one was a confession of what pleased, the other of what pained, the author; the one all but a direct copy of an experience, the other a distillation of its essence; yet both have identifiable characters and circumstances from real life. Not that *Iphigenia* shows the dispatch of composition of some of the early writings. Goethe's new duties and interests in Weimar (his studies in science began during the first years there) allowed few extended hours for creative literary work. But a version of *Iphigenia* was duly completed and staged in 1779, with Goethe himself in the role of Orestes. In contrast with *Egmont,* the fourth act of this play was written in a single day.

At the center of the Weimar experience for Goethe, at least in the years 1775 to 1786, when he left for Italy, was his relationship with Charlotte von Stein. As she was seven years his senior and married to Baron von Stein, the love Goethe felt for her could neither be happy nor remain simple. Yet its importance for his life was clear. He said many years later, "I thank [her and Shakespeare] for what I am." Her moderating influence paralleled that of his new environment, as the new surroundings perhaps led him to seek and find in the maturer woman the settling, quieting, and guiding power he did not himself possess. The "eternal feminine," of which in the last lines of *Faust* the Chorus Mysticus speaks, surely invested this relationship that was for Goethe a heightened form of love. "In another life/You were my sister or my wife," he writes in the poem that begins "Why were we given to see so clearly?" (1776) and that marks the beginnings of his devotion to Frau von Stein. Many poems were inspired by other love relationships, each poetic cycle unique in its feeling, for Goethe did not love one woman over the years or many women in one way. Love, like nature, was a subject of the greatest inspiration for his lyric genius and also had its evolution in his life and work.

The poem to Charlotte von Stein suggests her relation to the classical figure of Iphigenia in the mind of the poet. The relation is abstract. Yet Iphigenia was the sister of Orestes, who in this modernized version, through the purity and beauty of her spirit rather than the bidding of an oracle (as in the legend), helps to free her brother from his tormented wandering—the outward expression of the guilt he carries within him. The internalization of the Furies had been all but accomplished by Euripides in his version. The originality of the new interpretation lies elsewhere, in the internal means by which the Furies, which exist only in Orestes' mind, are expelled. In the middle of the play, after Orestes has met and discovered the identity of the priestess of Tauris, who is Iphigenia, no joyous recognition scene occurs. Rather, Orestes, who has heard that human sacrifice is still practiced on the island, sees the possibility of his own death at the hand of his sister as an end whose tragic irony befits his life and his accursed heritage. He falls unconscious. Awaking from his unconscious state, he envisions, as in a dream, his own descent into Hades. There his family greets and welcomes him, themselves freed of their ancient enmity; and in their welcome they seemingly free him. He can say to his mother, whom he had murdered, "Here is your son!" In the *belief* that he has died, he has atoned for the crime. "The curse is lifting. . . . The Furies are departing." Not until this point can he truly recognize, and come to see by, the moral radiance that Iphigenia sheds.

Had the play not continued beyond this point, it might be argued that this beautiful, classical *Iphigenia* represents little more than a sublimation of sexual qualities in the idealized portrait of a woman. The married Charlotte von Stein was not far removed in time from the betrothed Charlotte of *Werther.* Also, at the beginning of his relationship with Frau von Stein, Goethe had written a short play, "The Brother and Sister," in which at the end the couple who have been living together discover they are in fact not related and can be married. The "sister" is free to become the wife. Since literary history has not answered the question of whether Charlotte von Stein and Goethe consummated their love, the negative assumption would support the contention of Goethe's empty idealization of her. But if Goethe originally conceived *Iphigenia* as a means of resolving a personal dilemma (and both the time of its conception and its theme would support this), in the process of writing he developed the implications of the action to include a moral frame of reference that encompassed and transcended any initial subjective or therapeutic intent.

It is as if the play effectively begins after the redemption of Orestes. He and Iphigenia are now made to leave the island, not deceitfully but by a means more befitting the spirit in which Iphigenia has already begun to exert her influence, a spirit that pervades the whole play. The actual escape in the ancient legend is effected in the modern version on a spiritual plane: Iphigenia persuades Thoas, the ruler of the island, to abandon the rite of human sacrifice and to release her and Orestes. Just as the goddess Athena in Aeschylus' *Oresteia* casts the decisive vote to establish the new rule of law in Athens against the earlier, primitive form of justice, Iphigenia moves to humanize law as such, as if in yet a further stage of evolution. If not in its popularity, then in its deeper meaning, the play was of the late eighteenth century in seeking a new moral order through the dictates of feeling and rejecting the older dictates of both religion and reason. When Iphigenia obtains from Thoas not merely his permission to return home with her brother but also the blessing of his final "Lebt wohl!" we sense that not only these two characters but all human beings should "fare well."

*Iphigenia* brought to a high point the humanistic ideal that had its beginnings in German literature in Lessing's pleas for religious tolerance, and that Schiller in his turn would develop in the political and social realms. Yet *Iphigenia* remains an idealization, and not simply in its insular setting, which may well have been abstracted from the duchy of Weimar or at least from Goethe's own sense of life in his new surroundings after his own spiritual and geographical wanderings. In Aeschylus' play the Furies are not cast out, but taken up and integrated into the new order. When Goethe himself later pronounced his *Iphigenia* "so damned humane," the remark may have stemmed from thoughts of his *Faust,* where not only man's primitive urges but evil itself are absorbed in the human condition with great moral pain and little idealization.

In the next major drama Goethe undertook in this period, *Torquato Tasso* (1789), the humanistic ideal was not presented but presupposed. It formed the background for the play, a background particularized, however, with a more immediate purpose in mind. The court of Ferrara, which had housed the great Italian poet Tasso under the patronage of the noble family of Este, was to reflect the court of Weimar, in a tribute to Goethe's benefactors. In the foreground is the theme of the artist in relation to society, with the important difference, in contrast to the thought of today, that the social order is presumed benevolent and presented in a positive light.

Goethe approached the problem generically. The play was to depict the "disproportion of talent to life," he said. The Tasso whom Goethe imagined is neither the deranged figure of popular legend, the mad artist, nor the artist warped in his social being by surroundings indifferent and covertly antagonistic to his values and concerns—the artist of modern legend. His Tasso is presented sympathetically, with the characteristics that Goethe once recognized in himself and perhaps still acknowledged at the deepest level: erratic emotions and behavior, rash decisions, and living ahead of reality, as perhaps an artist must in order to create. *Tasso* was not a confession for Goethe, although he said that the work was of his "very flesh and bones." He said the same of *Götz* without necessarily implying that all details in the play corresponded to concrete experience. Life and art were now so little at odds in Goethe that in the same period in which he wrote *Tasso* he began the *Roman Elegies,* the fifth poem of which contains the celebrated motif of the poet composing his verse in his mistress' arms, counting the hexameters on her spine.

A writer "depicts a whole character as it appeared to him in his soul; such a complete character no single person possesses alone," Caroline Herder felt it necessary to say about *Tasso* (letter of 20 March 1789) when many at court, rightly seeing Weimar in the setting of Ferrara, looked for particular resemblances to themselves, after the precedent in *Werther.* Goethe contrasts his poet, a man of extremes, to the figure who represents, equally abstractly or generically, a different mode of being: Antonio, the man of affairs and the world. "They have become enemies," it is observed in the play, "because nature did not form one person from the two of them." I do not believe that Goethe intended this remark to suggest that within himself these preternatural enemies had been reconciled. The psychological tension between Tasso and Antonio, which persists to the end of the play, implies that these opposite forces will never be found at rest. The drama has been criticized for its seemingly abrupt and ambiguous ending, in which the hero clings to a resolute Antonio—whether in a demonstration of feeling he would later, as so often, regret, or in a recognition of his ultimate dependence on the objective world that Antonio represents, remains unclear.

Tasso has received the blessing of art; he says, "And where other men fall silent in their grief, a God gave me to say how I suffer." A man of the world would seem in need of no such gift. Yet Antonio's worldly way of living—in which he is a success, and as deserving of success as Tasso is with his genius—isolates him from the life of feeling and leaves him no time for thought or pain. He remains, in spite of himself and his concern for others, somewhat cold. Like Tasso, he is presented as a living figure, and each of them has his own special blindness.

The work was titled a play, not a tragedy—instinctively right, as it proved not to be Goethe's last word on the subject. At age seventy-two, in love with a girl of seventeen, and remembering from *Werther* his salvation in art from pain and confusion, Goethe wrote "Trilogy of Passion," affixing as a motto to the second poem, "Elegy," the lines of Tasso quoted above but significantly changing the "how" to "what" in "A God gave me to say what I suffer." The general development that Goethe underwent from a romantic to a more classical approach in creating and understanding art has often been tellingly illustrated by this subtle change of detail. But there was development yet to come.

Goethe's trip to Italy in 1786, a decade after his arrival in Weimar, had a profound, measurable influence on his life, thought, and art. He describes that influence in his *Italienische Reise* (*Italian Journey,* 1816–1829) in a notation for 6 March 1787: "What I have always told myself has occurred—that only in this land would I understand certain questions about nature and the confusion surrounding them." Here the scientist speaks, albeit the still enthusiastic scientist who would ultimately have to abandon his spectacular thought of finding in Italy a specimen of the plant that represented all plants, his plant primeval or *Urpflanze.* But he never forsook the spirit that prompted the search: "to recognize the essential form with which nature always toys and toying brings forth manifold life." This scientist-poet made three consecutive visits to Mount Vesuvius, the scientist recording geological observations and the poet, who had found lyric inspiration so often before in settings of night and storm, noting his fascination with a "formless mass that time after time consumed itself and has declared war on all sense of beauty.'' This in contrast to the artist Johann Heinrich Tischbein, his companion at Vesuvius, who painted the famous portrait of Goethe posed before the Roman countryside, and whose aesthetic sensibilities were, in Goethe's view, justly offended by the volcanic slag heap. Goethe the novelist described the people, landscapes, cities, and customs; and when particularly struck, as in his experience of carnival in Rome, he wrote with a concreteness and power that raised the reporting of fact to the level of art. He published the carnival piece separately.

Above all, and not surprising in that setting, Goethe's persona as student of art and architecture predominated, but less as an enthusiast than as a scholar intent on gaining firsthand a full and detailed knowledge of traditions that he would develop in his works. The history and appreciation of art—whether his role in furthering art was as editor, critic, or theoretician—became for Goethe an interest and occupation rivaling that of science and literature on his return from Italy. And since objective clarity was the object and the ideal of his research in both art history and science, the two endeavors not only complemented each other but promoted and heightened the tendency toward order in his life and work already begun in Weimar.

Italy for Goethe was the land of clarity and light, in contrast to his motherland of gloom in spirit as well as climate. In a tangible, almost demonstrative commitment to his new understanding and way of seeing the world, he took the prose version of *Iphigenia* completed earlier and turned it into measured verse. *Tasso,* begun in prose, was similarly given a new form while he was in Rome. The *Roman Elegies* and the *Venetian Epigrams* (1790), conceived during the sojourn in Italy, reflect the new climate of his thought.

The unusual way in which Goethe developed as writer and thinker, or perhaps our unusually great knowledge of the details of that development, permits us to regard the Italian experience as both a culminating achievement and a belated end. The years in Weimar were in a sense an interruption: Goethe had been ready to leave for Italy when he accepted Karl August's invitation. The thought of Italy had long been in his mind, instilled early by his father's enthusiasm for that country, kept alive by his own study of art, and finally matured through the descriptions by Johann Winckelmann of its treasures from the ancient world, which were uppermost in importance to any young artist and writer of the time. Goethe had anticipated and then found the ''noble simplicity and quiet greatness'' in classical art that Winckelmann had originally described.

On his return from Italy to Weimar in 1788, however, he did not pursue that ideal in his own works for long. Instead, he recovered his earlier beginnings. Except for the uniquely charming, idyllic epic poem *Hermann and Dorothea* (1797), and a poem in similar form but with less original content, *Reynard the Fox* (1797), he completed little of any length in the classical vein, although fragmentary undertakings abounded. The most important of the latter is ''Helena'' (1800), which was conceived in the strict form of ancient Greek tragedy and became the greater part of the third act of *Faust,* part 2. In *Die natürliche Tochter* (*The Natural Daughter*, 1798), a drama set during the French Revolution and written in its wake, he carries his urge for generalization and universalization to the point of using abstract designations for all roles except the heroine, and creates a form that is incongruous with the literary tradition born of that historical event. *Iphigenia* and *Tasso,* though rendered formally classical in their measured lines, had already been so conceived in their settings of stable but isolated worlds.

On the other hand, when Goethe resumed work on *Wilhelm Meisters Lehrjare* (*Wilhelm Meister's Apprenticeship,*1795), which he had also begun during the first years in Weimar, he expanded the action, which had been limited in the early version to the world of theater, to include society as a whole. Thus he provides an outer world of realistic persons and events, which had been missing in *Werther,* to contain the hero and serve as a measure of his deeds. In his choice of worlds—that of the middle class—he returns to a contemporary setting and to his own social beginnings.

Even broader in implication, the nature poetry that Goethe continued to write gained a dimension beyond the earlier context of the poet responding to his surroundings. Perhaps owing to the influence of scientific observation of the physical world, such poems as "Song of the Spirits Above the Waters" (1779), "The Limits of Man" (1781), and "The Divine" (1780) entertain no thought of consolation or rest for man in his natural state. His instinct to strive upward brings attendant loss of equilibrium, "And with him play/The clouds and the wind." In the second poem the opposite urge, to secure himself on solid ground, keeps him at heights not "comparable/Even to the tree or the vine." And in "The Divine," in a world in which "The sun will shine/Alike on good and evil," a human being may be exhorted to be "noble/Helpful and good" and so separate himself from the seemingly indifferent laws of nature. But Goethe's larger question of humankind's place in the scheme of creation, which would form a basis for his morality, remains unanswered.

These poems were written relatively early, and of course in no way represent the full range of the constantly varying forms of verse that Goethe employed over a lifetime as most amenable to a certain mood, occasion, whim, thought, or experiment. The ballads he wrote together with Schiller or the whole book of verse, the *West-East Divan* (1814–1818), which was composed in imitation not only of the formal values of Persian poetry but also of an ancient cultural mode of thinking, suggest the inclusiveness of his lyric talent. And he could no more keep his science from informing his literary works than he could keep his "realistic tic," as he called it, from reducing theoretical ideas to their palpable demonstrability in the real world. He conceived his *Wahlverwandtschaften (Elective Affinities,* 1809) in order to illustrate a bizarre connection between chemical processes and human relationships.

This tension between the concentrated objectivity of science and the urge to comprehensiveness in art, this "breathing in and breathing out" of the human spirit, to use an analogy that Goethe applied to the laws of nature, had reached a high point in the works conceived after Italy. Begun late, *Wilhelm Meisters Wanderjahre* (*Wilhelm Meister's Travels,* 1807–1821) failed to be completed. It is as if Goethe, with his new insights into science, had grown impatient with the slow processes of reality that a novel must describe.

Upon introduction an aristocrat is asked, "Who are you?" But "What do you do?" is asked of a member of the middle class. Goethe made this telling point in *Wilhelm Meister,* but with no intent to criticize, let alone satirize. He accepted the distinctions between the classes, in his writings and in life. But the differences between the classes anticipate the theme and reflect the new form in *Wilhelm Meister.* The nobility is; the middle class does. And although Goethe was concerned not with the nobles, in their pursuit of happiness, but only with the middle class, the contrast between their modes of living was implicit in the social changes in the late eighteenth and early nineteenth centuries. He himself had risen, had become "von Goethe"; he could be rather than do in his art and his life. "The highest respect an author can have for his public is that he never offers what is expected but what he himself at the respective stages of his own development considers good and useful," he writes in *Maximen und Reflexionen* (*Maxims and Reflections,* 1833). It is precisely with those who are forced to do, however, that he is concerned in this novel—perhaps out of instinctive loyalty to his own beginnings; in any event in keeping with the movement toward realism in the novel of the period.

Yet the realism in *Wilhelm Meister* is only apparent. The characters from the theater world, the personalities and incidents from common life, even the poetic and haunting figures such as the alcoholic suicide and the strange orphan girl Mignon, are not there as parts of a real world reflected in the novel. Nor is the world there as a background to a single-minded action that assumes dramatic proportions and comes to a conclusion. *Wilhelm Meister* reflects development, as in the designations drawn from the guild system—"apprenticeship" for the first part, "travels" for the second, and the implied and eventual "master." The hero would grow into his name, Meister, in this form of novel, which came to be known as the bildungsroman, or novel of development.

Thus in addition to their being in their own right, which would justify their existence in a realistic novel, the characters surrounding the hero function as influences on him. The hero in turn, with his receptive nature and urge toward good, absorbs or instinctively resists the qualities of persons and forces with which he is not so much confronted—for confrontation denies his nature—as simply presented by circumstance.

The novel of development is not a novel of education. The characters in its world have their own lives to live, so that their influence is mainly indirect and rarely disinterested, as in life. The realism in *Wilhelm Meister,* as well as in the general tradition of the bildungsroman, derives from the essentially undramatic character of its events and mode of narration. Given the extensive development in German of the shorter realistic form of the novella, which Theodor Storm characterized as "the sister of the drama," there seems to have been less need for prose fiction in German literature to develop along the lines of the great European tradition, and more opportunity for it to pursue a unique course. Goethe himself saw no contradiction in the concept of a passive hero. In fact, in a discussion of the difference between the novel and drama in *Wilhelm Meister* itself, he defines the hero or heroine in a novel as suffering, in the sense of accepting the world; and in a drama as actively exerting influence on the world. The one was "leidend" (passive in the sense of "suffer unto me") in his role, the other "wirkend" (active).

In the novel of development at least, the central figure gains little by resistance and self-assertion, for the author's purpose is first to create a self that can gainfully resist and assert in a given social context. What the hero seeks is not a set of rules of behavior or morality, but simply the opportunity to realize the potential of his own nature, which, as Wilhelm Meister says, "was denied me by my birth." The danger for the middle class, which had freed itself from the predetermined roles and norms of privileged society, was that it would misuse its new freedom in a desperate pursuit of goals identified with the older order, such as status and wealth. "Remember to live" is the conclusion of the *Apprenticeship.* How one is to live is a question for the individual. When the novel was welcomed in its time with the sense that "everyone will see in Wilhelm his own apprenticeship," it was not with the conviction that a norm had been established for a class, but in recognition of shared progress among individuals.

Yet it was the tone of the novel more than its content that struck the times as new. Friedrich Schlegel, in his essay on *Wilhelm Meister,* identifies Goethe's supremely detached attitude toward his characters and his work as the truly modern element, which Schlegel describes as romantic irony and warns against mistaking as want of seriousness. Goethe said of his position in relation to his novel, "I placed myself, as it were, between myself and my subject." The detachment serves the pedagogical stance in the work, but also reflects a stage in his development, which had moved from Storm and Stress immediacy through the objectivity of the dramas in classical form to a style just beyond objectivity. In *Elective Affinities*, a product of the later period, the choice of a chemical process as the basis for a story of male and female relationships already committed the work to a kind of in-between seriousness. The affinity of A for B and C for D upon contact becomes a relation of A to D and B to C, then reverts to the initial partners and preferences, as in a quadrille. The conservative dignity of the narration further sharpens the irony without recourse to humor. Only in that tone, indeed, is the tragic motif, the unrelieved seriousness at the end of the novel, possible.

On the other hand, where the irony and the interpolated author are absent in the writings of this period, the seriousness seems to lose life and become pedantic. There was in the older Goethe a tendency to pronounce on life that is not attributable to age. The singular lack of pronouncements in *Faust,* part 2, completed in the last years, has been traditionally the stumbling block for those who initially view the work as a philosophical poem only to discover that it represents thought reduced to true poetry—thought in process, not in conclusion. But where conclusion is demanded, as in *Wilhelm Meister's Travels,* the author appears to conclude before the fact. The novel abounds in observations on human experience (many of them recovered for *Maxims and Reflections*), but fails to re-create the realities that substantiate or, better, cause the observations; for typically, thought and experience were one in Goethe. Paradoxically, in his scientific work *Theory of Color* (1810) he appears to have failed in reverse, in that in a realm where an abstract approach to his subject might have been more suitable, he persists in the pragmatism that served him so well in his descriptive scientific research and was ignored by the scholarly community. The poetry of the late period, to the extent that it remains lyrical, does not, of course, reflect the problem, and in the great philosophical, or oracular, poems such as "Urworte. Orpheus" ("Primal Words. Orphic," 1817–1818) the language is at a level that transcends style and tone. Yet a pedagogical, almost pedantic, tendency is recognizable in the Goethe of later years, and was duly, perhaps unconsciously, recorded by the young Eckermann in his *Conversations.* That Goethe resisted that tendency in *Faust* redounds greatly to his importance, but also increases our difficulty with him as a figure in world literature.

If the best explanation of an idea is its history, as Novalis said, the best explication of *Faust* is its development. The sixty years that Goethe took to complete the work already suggest the part that development and change played in its composition, as if the author had carefully and deliberately remade the whole at each stage of its growth—which he did not. Rather he took what he had written as it was written, with few minor changes (though some changes are obvious), and subsumed it into broader frames of comprehension, broader poetic visions. *Urfaust* was made understandable in part 1, and then part 1 was treated similarly in part 2. *Faust* thus existed first and had meaning second.

Yet its very being proved disturbing, and so its meaning was and is thought confusing, especially in the latter part. The great tradition in European literature had been built, and continued to insist, on order—if no longer in fixed terms, at least in consistency of form. It was with this tradition that Goethe broke in *Faust,* of necessity. The tradition had not created a form, at least in drama, that could contain and reflect the new sense of life and the new awareness of life's relation to the laws of nature—a new morality, in short, not asserted but experienced and stated as art. The dilemma of expressing a newly envisioned reality in older, inherited forms had not been faced in the literature of the age. Either freer forms were developed for the new purpose, such as the lyric poetry that was the strength of the modern movement as a whole; or the implications of the new mode of thought and feeling were restricted to their effects within the social realm—the province of the novel and the drama—in which they were artistically manageable. In his choice of theme, however, as well as in his choice of the dramatic form, Goethe committed himself to a course that was bound for contradiction and radically new development when he decided to save his Faust. There is no salvation without a justification, and not merely within the social order, which the Faust theme transcends. And although at some point Goethe must have become fully aware that the spirit of the age had found reasons—unconsciously—for the salvation of the legendary figure once thought damnable, these reasons had never before been presented poetically. Lessing's redeemed Faust had never come to be.

We know that when Goethe was confronted with the alternative of presenting the intent of his work in clear but artificial terms—"I have ideas, too," he once said—or trusting his poetic imagination to render his meaning, he deliberately chose the latter. In a plan for part 2, after he had already struggled with his unwieldy subject in part 1, he writes: "Formless content to be preferred to empty form." He had often referred to his project in such terms as "this barbaric composition" and "this poetic monster." Not that the decision resulted in a kind of chaos fraught with meaning, but the underlying tension did determine the ultimate nature of the work.

Yet *Faust* was begun relatively simply. We suppose that Goethe had the beginnings of a Faust drama already in mind when the occasion presented itself for his further developing the legendary theme with equally charged content from contemporary life. In Frankfurt in 1772 an unwed mother, Susanna Margaretha Brandt, killed her child in desperation and was put to death for the crime. Not only his own outrage at the injustice, which he shared with his Storm and Stress generation, but his personal relation to the fate of an abandoned young woman prompted Goethe to set down an early version, *Urfaust,* or, as it is called in the context of the final version, the Gretchen tragedy. Even the name Margaretha, both the proper and the diminutive forms of which (Margarete-Grete-Gretchen) Goethe employs for his heroine in *Urfaust,* suggests a closeness to the actual event, although the antecedent in his private experience was probably his relationship to Friederike Brion.

Goethe immediately developed not merely the intensely romantic aspect of his tragedy that Gounod made famous in his opera, but the intense realism as well. Goethe's Margarete, insane and imprisoned at the end, remains lucid enough to relive her drowning of her child, and yet is deranged enough to believe that the reality can be reversed. To Faust she cries: "See it struggle! Save the poor little thing, it's still struggling! Just across the way, into the woods, to the left of the pond, where the plank is. Save it! Save it!" The one example stands for many. Even in the later version, where Goethe attempts to "mute," as he says, the starker prose passages in *Urfaust* by rendering them in verse, in this passage he allows the poetic form to break down. It is significant that he does not simply remove the motif, as Gounod had. *Faust* is a work of retention, and Goethe did not easily reject as wrong what he had once felt true, by reason of the truth it possessed for having been. In that, Goethe is faithful in his art to the philosophy of his teacher Herder, who also saw the past as a part of the present not to be ignored.

The retention of the old within the new continued in the composition of *Faust* at its various stages. The Faust theme proper was not developed in the first version. There was no pact with the Devil, for example. But what was developed is of greatest importance. Goethe himelf claimed that everything in his play followed from Faust's wager with the Devil, but it would be more true to say in the light of the completed work that everything grew from the first lines he wrote. He had taken from the medieval legend and the puppet play, and probably also from his Storm and Stress attitudes at the time, the motif of dissatisfaction with knowledge and frustration with life as the incentive for seeking truth through magic. (The age itself looked to poetry for truth.) Faust seeks to know "what held the world together in its innermost core." Magic immediately supplies an answer: first, in the vision of the macrocosm that beautifully displays the order and harmony in the universe but appears to Faust an empty thing: "a mere display"; and, alternately, through the Earth Spirit, which seems to draw Faust closer and closer by its emanations of activity and vitality but proves terrifying in its manifestation: "Frightful image!" This is the spirit of "Birth and grave/An eternal sea/Ever changing" that "worked the fabric of life/On the rushing loom of time." Faust feels not only repelled but demeaned by the spirit. "You are like the spirit you resemble/Not me," he is told, and he has to conclude: "I who was created in the image of God/Am equal not even to you!"

Only when these alternate visions are subsumed into the broader frames of references that Goethe placed in and around *Urfaust* in creating part 1, do they gain their true importance, "like the prophecy through the fulfillment," as Goethe says in a different context. The "Prologue in Heaven" contains the visions in its own view from eternity. The archangels praise Creation both for the astonishing beauty and harmony that it still possesses "as on the primal day" and for the formidable alternately storming and brightening atmosphere surrounding Earth, itself spinning at the greatest speed. It is in this atmosphere that the action in the drama takes place. The view is that of *Urfaust,* from the opposite end of the telescope, ordered at a great remove, confusing in close proximity. Only from a perspective outside of time and beyond nature can the ultimate design in the universe be understood, although such understanding would then serve no purpose. The vision of God and Creation gives the angels "strength/*Since* none may fathom thee" (italics added). The view from eternity at the beginning and end of *Faust* neither contradicts philosophical pragmatism, the system of knowledge that underlies the work, nor mocks the Christian imagery drawn from the legendary setting. The pragmatism is that of a poet, not a philosopher. Goethe rejects metaphysical speculation as a source of knowledge, as does Faust in the end, but he respects living religious symbolism as one form of poetic imagination among others. He accepts religion generally, though not for himself. "If you do not have art you should have religion" is his position.

Similarly, the figure of the Devil that appears in *Urfaust* is given further definition in the new context. Mephistopheles is presented in *Urfaust* as a wryly humorous cavalier—cynical, but with little suggestion of evil in him except for his cold delight in Gretchen's tragedy: "She is condemned!" These are the last words of the original version. Nor is evil in the conventional sense intended to be his realm or his function. He is a gadfly, a spirit who perpetually and instinctively "denied," and in his negation arouses humankind, who might otherwise "too much relish ease," to positive action; thus he is welcome in the design of things. The Lord: "Of all the spirits who negate,/The rogue is least offensive to me." The humor Mephistopheles employs on earth in *Urfaust* he also employed in heaven; his roguish cynicism is directed now against the species rather than individual human foibles. The human species in its endless endeavors to conquer and achieve reminds him of "the longlegged grasshopper/Who for all its flighty jumps/Ends again in the grass, singing the same old song." And the humor of this spirit—who always, not selectively, negates—turns itself of course upon the work in which it exists, to deny the work's seriousness. As "the heavens close" at the end of the prologue, Mephistopheles, alone on the stage, addresses the audience with a typically flippant remark: "It's nice of such a great lord [God]/To speak so socially even with the Devil." The audience is returned to its time and place; the theatrical illusion is broken. Yet this return from illusion to reality, this romantic irony, or, as we might say today, alienation effect, is in *Faust* not an artistic device but one more aspect of the play of oppositions that informs the work.

What is given and repeated in nature is reflected in thought and in art. If evil no longer represents the opposite but the obverse of good—whence the welcome for Mephistopheles in heaven—humor represents not the destruction of seriousness but a necessary element in the process of human thinking. There could be no comprehensive truth without it, any more than without what we term "evil" in the context of our present stage of evolution, as part 2 makes clear. More important for the understanding of this unique work as a whole, the destroyer of illusion, in the philosophical and artistic sense, is the role Goethe instinctively assigned to Mephistopheles in *Urfaust* long before he "continued" the part in the "Prologue in Heaven"; thus his function and meaning, becoming clear only later, remained indistinguishable from his simple being, as in nature, even if it is nature conceived as evolving in its own right and not as the expression of a higher idea. Again, the one example stands for many and indeed epitomizes the character of the work itself in its development and resolution, since, like Wilhelm Meister growing into his name, both the work as a whole and the character of Mephistopheles grow into their meanings. Faust, originally conceived as a Storm and Stress figure, comes to represent humankind when in the "Prologue in Heaven," composed some twenty-five years later, God allows Mephistopheles to tempt Faust, thereby placing him in the position of Job. This was the first step toward a new Faust saved, the representative of a modern humanity redeemed in action, not in suffering.

From the individual to the generic describes the development that *Faust* underwent from its initial stage to the completion and publication of part 1 in 1808. The suicide Faust is made to attempt in the first important extension of the action reflects that development, more clearly so because of Werther's being in the background. In his frustration with life and his rejection by the Earth Spirit, and in the hope that he can simply escape the confines of earthly existence and find expression for his boundless energies "in a new day beckoning to new shores," Faust places the vial of poison to his lips. At that moment, from outside the study in which he has despondently spent the night, church bells ring and there sounds a choral song celebrating Easter morning. Childhood memories thus hold him back from "that last, earnest step." Yet it is the natural process of things—day following night and spring following winter—that accounts for the hope emerging at the extremity of despair as much as does the more symbolic representation of Christian rebirth following crucifixion. If the worm of death is in Werther, the force of life is in Faust, necessarily if he is to stand for humankind. That his Christian childhood also evokes these forces does not, however, make the forces themselves Christian. Neither should the "two souls" that Faust finds within himself, which are chosen by Goethe as a poetic formulation relevant to his theme in the next extension of the action in "Easter Promenade," be understood in the traditional sense of higher and lower urges. The image is conceived within the same larger framework of the phenomena and laws of nature that the drama has now established as its ultimate point of reference. In the vision of a new humanity the soul in Faust that "clings to the world with urgent feeling" is no longer to be classed lower than the soul that "lifts itself from earth/ Toward the realm of lofty endeavor"; instead it must be seen as separate but equal. Faust, who continues to think in terms of hierarchy and dichotomy rather than concentricity and the interrelatedness of opposing forces—he is not given the view from eternity that we are allowed—suffers from the opposition of his two souls, as his assistant, Wagner, does not. Wagner, the symbol of the Enlightenment, knows only one urge, which

Faust, with a touch of self-pity, tells him is the better state; and he "should never come to know the other."

At this point the drama takes its most radical turn, in the reuse and reinterpretation of the pact with the Devil. The reuse is important in that it again reflects Goethe's tendency to absorb the old in the new, not in supercession but in reconstitution. The young Goethe had rejected the pedantic, rationalistic philosophy of Wagner out of hand in *Urfaust;* but, although he still regards it as naive in its single-mindedness, he now gives it a more sympathetic treatment. It is after all one of Faust's own souls, as the Enlightenment itself remains a part of the humanity he is intended to represent. But neither is the sensuously existential soul in Faust to gain sway, in a reverse imbalance of instinct or feeling. Nor, however, are the two souls brought into harmony, as the Renaissance attempted but, to judge from subsequent history, did not securely accomplish.

The radical departure in *Faust* is to look to nature and discover that balance is struck in life precisely through the play of oppositions and extremes, but not in rest, which nature does not know. Goethe simply applies this principle, which in his scientific thought he calls "polarity," to the moral realm. He defines good as the productive and life-affirming, and evil as the negating force. Mephistopheles says: "[I am] of that power a part/ That always wills evil and ever causes good." The only pact that might be negotiated between a Faust possessed of two souls and a Devil who in his very commitment to evil promotes good cannot be a pact in which either might see his own fixed advantage; hence, the pact as wager, as a matter contingent on development, as a product wholly of the work that produces it. Faust in his despair at ever finding peace or happiness challenges Mephistopheles to provide him with a perfect moment of experience to which he will say: "Stay! Thou art so beautiful! . . . Then may the clock stop, the hands fall,/And time be no more for me!" The foregone conclusion in the traditional pact (with its predetermined time and set conditions) might appear here to be supplanted by an open-ended agreement that more truly reflects the dynamic sense of life in the new age. Yet the old was comprehended in the new. It was also a foregone conclusion that no moment in the ceaselessly evolving world (of the modern conception) would stop in any real sense, except outside of time, in eternity, in death: "and time be no more for me." This agreement is in effect a non sequitur, which Faust in his skepticism and hopelessness accepts, and the Devil in his ignorance of human time (for he is immortal) does not reject. The difference, of course, is that the one foregone conclusion is damnation and the other salvation. In this view, humanity is not merely redeemable but already redeemed by its will to life.

Part 1 is comprehended in part 2. The first part displays the broad patterns of nature in which humanity has its being, and the second part attempts to justify these laws and ways of nature to man. A justification is necessary, for the ways are painful. What distinguishes Faust from the Earth Spirit, to whom he felt so close in essential being, is that he experiences as pain and frustration the constant change and flux in things that the spirit experiences simply as process. What we as readers might gradually recognize as rhythmic cycles are undergone by Faust as vicious circles. The inability to reach perfection within time (for the horizon recedes when one approaches it in a world that is round), though all-saving in the species (for it prompts further endeavor) is yet tragic in the individual. To have the central figure understand and accept this tragic component in the human condition, which component alone renders the natural philosophy in *Faust* moral, is the task of part 2. Yet the best, indeed the only, explanation of the condition is its history. The antecedents to the present are therefore now displayed, not as historical reality, which would have been impossible within the confines of a drama, but in an imaginative, poetic, colorful, at times consciously symbolic representation.

Goethe proceeds as follows. (We give here only the barest outline, not that there are details of plot and character development to describe; rather, the whole was presented from a myriad of sides, as in the prism of science or in a kind of literary cubism.) The pursuit of the perfect moment is not forgotten and emerges centrally in the Helen of Troy episode that constitutes act 3, then definitively, and once again dramatically, in the final act. But this single concern is placed within contexts that are allowed to develop in their own right as much as in relation to the whole, so that a "world poem," a *Weltgedicht,* to use Schlegel's term for the challenge of the modern movement, all but comes into being. This is not Goethe's design, however. It is the result of his abiding faith in the natural and his concomitant suspicion of purely logical and abstract relations in thought. The Helen episode, for example, had been written separately in 1800, and then was incorporated years later into the greater work, where it retains its original form and being, including its Greek hexamaters, while gaining new meaning. Goethe had taken the path of least resistance, for the Helen motif was a part of the Faust legend. He had taken that path from the beginning when he retained older material. It *was* the path of nature.

Yet, generally, he was more deliberate in his approach to part 2. He seized any opportunity to join the separate parts, which threatened to move as far apart artistically as they were moving in time. Thus the opening scene constitutes in effect a Prologue on Earth, or better, a Prologue in Nature. The great healing powers of nature in the form of sleep are now evoked to "bathe [Faust] in forgetfulness," to "remove the bitter arrow of reproach," to "cleanse him from the horrors lived" and restore him to the energies of life within which there is no continuing. The "horrors lived" are those of part 1 as a totality, but, specifically, the Gretchen episode. Gretchen is saved within the *supernatural* frame of the first part, when in the final version a "voice from above" answers Mephistopheles' judgment, "She is sentenced!" ("Ist gerichtet!") with "She is saved!" ("Ist gerettet!"); within the new poetic framework of part 2 Faust is restored in nature. The God who saves Gretchen by his grace becomes in this pantheistic view the God who saves by natural cause. Faust now arises at dawn and, as if repeating the error he makes throughout part 1 of attacking truth frontally, gazes directly into the new day and is "blinded." But here he is made to turn his back to the sun, so that he can see by its reflection: "We are given the world in colorful reflection."

In its form part 2 makes that simple but radical reversal and assumption. Its content, one is always surprised to discover or recall, remains traditional. Faust's activity at an imperial court is requisite to the theme and here comprises acts 1 and 4. The creation of a human being in a test tube, which forms the content and theme of act 2, is not an integral part of the legend but is directly related to alchemy, the "white magic" that Faust practices as a science. The Helen episode, in one form or another, was included in every Faust puppet play, and so it is here as act 3. Act 5 is wholly original with Goethe; necessarily so, for once the antecedents to the present are displayed, the present itself, the new, has to be addressed. But since outward display is impossible, an expansion ad absurdum in the theater, the play must create worlds within itself, implode in "colorful reflection" rather than expand as it might have done in another form.

Act 1, for example—which has the task of evoking the world of the legend as a cultural and social milieu as well as a political and historical arena, and of suggesting the abuse of life's abundance—introduces a carnival ball, a "masque," which functions poetically as a background to the drama in the foreground;

that is, the interaction of personages at the imperial court, Faust and Mephistopheles included. Act 4, the pendant act to act 1 both thematically and dramatically, suggests the aggressive compensation for the "too much relishing of ease" (against which the Lord has warned in the "Prologue in Heaven") in a war between emperor and anti-emperor, and the forces underlying the war in figures such as Bullyboy, Havequick, Holdfast, and Instant Plunder.

The light satirical humor of act 1 led Goethe on one occasion to describe the whole of part 2 as "these very serious jokes." The description also fits act 2, in which is created Homunculus, a creature who is endowed with speech, intelligence, and wit, but who—in a reversal of the Frankenstein legend and, perhaps, of the science of the eighteenth and nineteenth centuries—needs a body in order "to come into being." The search for this body takes Homunculus into a fantastic "classical Walpurgis night," where amid a panorama of human and animal beings at various stages of development he vainly seeks information about the nature of material reality. Finally at a loss, he is forced to return to the sea so that he will come into being by due natural process.

The same theme of necessary progression is further developed on a cultural plane in act 3. The union of Faust and Helen of Troy, of contemporary man and the ancient ideal of beauty, though it teaches the visionary Faust to seek the eternal in the living moment, is yet the result of magic, of a disjoining of time, and is doomed in the real world. The attempt to make real in the present what was, and could only have been, true in the past is symbolized in the figure of Euphorion, the fruit of that union of past and present in whom Goethe saw Lord Byron, the younger contemporary poet he admired and to whom he felt akin. Euphorion, climbing to ever greater earthly heights, finally attempts to fly and perishes. In 1824, when Goethe was at work on this part of *Faust,* Byron died in Greece, in a foreign land and for a cause that was not his own. There was something unnatural and forced in his death, Goethe observed.

Act 5 concludes within an evolutionist framework of continual change. To have had Faust recognize that a perfect moment is unattainable in time would have been simply to confirm the skepticism with which he initially entered the pact: the Devil's loss would not have been his own gain. To have had him resign himself in this way would have been to effect by negative means what would have been accomplished positively in reaching perfection—that is, rest and stagnation. The theme of resignation that emerges most prominently in *Wilhelm Meister's Travels* I see as a last temptation to escape the implications of the greater work; and the former, as if in a symbolic gesture, was never completed. Faust would enjoy, just before his death and "in anticipation," a perfect moment born of the vision of a new humanity that had "its life and its freedom/ By gaining them anew each day." This life was to be a living neither *for* the moment, the results of which were on display at the imperial court, nor *in* the moment, as in an earlier innocence not to be regained, but rather *toward* the moment conceived as continuous, as in evolving nature.

Yet the vision is a delusion. The busy workers with their spades whom Faust assumes are breaking ground for his great project of reclaiming land from the sea for his new society are in fact preparing his grave. With this final tragic irony, this negation of the positive, which Faust himself is not made to know, we, who are also comprehended in the drama, are in turn confronted with the challenge of ourselves continuing in apprehensive hope, with only a sense of positive necessity. For there is no ending, no concluding, except in death. Only from outside of time, where negation does not obtain, can Goethe offer hope. The Chorus Mysticus at the end of the play celebrates permanence in change itself: "Everything transitory/ Is only a symbol." In its final words the chorus speaks strangely of the Eternal Feminine, which will "draw us onward" and which seems to encompass the mother in nature as well as the revitalizing and yet tempering powers of love.

We have described Goethe in his development, not in his accomplishments. The accomplishments are indeed great, and might have been recounted in their own right. He did in fact move through and beyond his era as thinker and poet, until in *Faust* he created a culminating masterwork that presaged the future. But to describe in terms of progress what was more important as process would have been not only to repeat a common error, but to repeat it in the instance and at the expense of a writer and an age that made such a distinction effectively relevant for the first time.

## Selected Bibliography


EDITIONS

*Goethes Werke.* 143 vols. Weimar, 1887–1919. The standard German edition.

————. Edited by Erich Trunz et al. 14 vols. Hamburg, 1948–1964. Revised ed. 1981. The most widely used scholarly edition, with index, periodically updated notes, and bibliography.

TRANSLATIONS

*The Autobiography of Johann Wolfgang von Goethe.* Translated by John Oxenford. London, 1872. Reprinted 1969.

*Goethe: Conversations and Encounters.* Translated and edited by David Luke and Robert Pack. Chicago, 1966.

*Goethe on Art.* Edited and translated by John Gage. Berkeley, 1980. New but badly flawed translation of the essays on art.

*Goethe: Selected Verse.* Translated by David Luke. Baltimore, 1964. Prose translations.

*Goethe's Italian Journey.* Translated and edited by W. H. Auden. New York, 1963. Reprinted 1982.

*Goethe's Wisdom and Experience.* Translated and edited by Hermann Weigand. New York, 1949.

*Goethe's Works.* Edited by Victor Lange et al. Boston, 1982– . Vol 1: *Selected Poems.* Translated by Christopher Middleton, John Frederick Nims, and David Luke. 1982. Vol. 2: *Faust. Part I and Part II.* Translated by Stuart Atkins. 1984.

*Goethe's World: As Seen in His Letters and Memoirs.* Edited by Berthold Biermann. Freeport, N.Y., 1949. Reprinted 1971.

See also B. Q. Morgan, *A Critical Bibliograhy of German Literature in English Translation.* 3 vols. New York, 1932, 1965. Second supplement, edited by Murray F. Smith. Metuchen, N.J., 1972. Patrick O'Neill, comp., *German Literature in English Translation: A Select Bibliography.* Toronto, 1981. Includes mainly works in print.

BIOGRAPHICAL AND CRITICAL STUDIES

Atkins, Stuart. *Goethe's "Faust": A Literary Analysis.* Cambridge, Mass., 1964.

————. *The Testament of "Werther" in Poetry and Drama.* Cambridge, Mass., 1949.

Baldensperger, F. *Goethe en France.* Paris, 1920. Reprinted 1973.

Bergstraesser, Arnold. *Goethe's Image of Man and Society.* Chicago, 1949.

Bielschowsky, Albert. *Goethe.* Translated by William A. Cooper. 3 vols. New York, 1905–1908. Reprinted 1969.

Blackall, Erich. *Goethe and the Novel.* Ithaca and London, 1976.

Brett, G. S. "Goethe's Place in the History of Science." *University of Toronto Quarterly* 1:279–299 (1932).

Bruford, Walter H. *Theatre, Drama and Audience in Goethe's Germany.* London, 1950.

Butler, E. M. *Byron and Goethe: Analysis of a Passion.* London, 1956.

————. *The Fortunes of Faust.* Cambridge, 1952.

Carlson, Marvin. *Goethe and the Weimar Theater.* Ithaca and London, 1978.

Carré, Jean-Marie. *Goethe en Angleterre.* Paris, 1920.

Cassirer, Ernst. *Rousseau, Kant, Goethe.* Translated by James Gutmann et al. Princeton, 1945.

Dieckmann, Liselotte. *Goethe's "Faust": A Critical Reading.* Englewood, N.J., 1972.

Eckermann, J. P. *Conversations with Goethe.* Edited by Victor Lange and translated by Gisela O'Brien. New York, 1964. Selections.

Eissler, K. R. *Goethe: A Psychoanalytic Study, 1775–1786.* 2 vols. Detroit, 1963.

# JOHANN WOLFGANG VON GOETHE


Eliot, George. "The Morality of Wilhelm Meister." In *Essays*. London, 1963.

Fairley, Barker. *Goethe as Revealed in His Poetry*. Chicago, 1932.

————. *Goethe's "Faust": Six Essays*. Oxford, 1953.

————. *A Study of Goethe*. Oxford, 1947.

Frantz, A. *Half a Hundred Thralls to Faust: A Study Based on the British and American Translations of Goethe's "Faust."* Chapel Hill, 1949.

Friedenthal, Richard. *Goethe: His Life and Times*. London, 1965.

Gearey, John. *Goethe's "Faust": The Making of Part I*. New Haven and London, 1981.

Gillies, Alexander. *Goethe's "Faust": An Interpretation*. Oxford, 1957.

Gray, Ronald. *Goethe, the Alchemist*. Cambridge, 1952.

Gronicka, André von. *The Russian Image of Goethe*. Philadelphia, 1968.

Hammer, Carl. *Goethe and Rousseau: Resonances of the Mind*. Lexington, Ky., 1973.

Hartner, Willy. "Goethe and the Natural Sciences." In Victor Lange, ed., *Goethe: A Collection of Critical Essays*. Englewood, N.J., 1968.

Hatfield, Henry. *Aesthetic Paganism in German Literature: From Winckelmann to the Death of Goethe*. Cambridge, Mass., 1964.

————. *Goethe: A Critical Introduction*. Cambridge, Mass., 1963.

Heller, Erich. "Faust's Damnation." In *The Artist's Journey into the Interior, and Other Essays*. New York, 1965.

————. "Goethe and the Idea of Scientific Truth." In *The Disinherited Mind*. New York, 1965.

Heller, Otto. *Faust and Faustus*. St. Louis, 1931.

Jackson, Naomi. "Goethe's Drawings." *Harvard Germanic Museum Bulletin* 1, nos. 7 and 8 (1938).

Jantz, Harold. *Goethe's Faust as a Renaissance Man*. Princeton, 1951. Reprinted 1974.

Lange, Victor, ed. *Goethe: A Collection of Critical Essays*. Englewood, N.J., 1968. Includes the editor's essay "Goethe's Craft of Fiction."

Leppmann, Wolfgang. *The German Image of Goethe*. Oxford, 1961.

Lewes, George Henry. *The Life of Goethe*. 2 vols. London, 1855. Reprinted 1973.

Lukács, Georg. *Goethe and His Age*. Translated by R. Anchor. New York, 1968.

Magnus, Rudolf. *Goethe as a Scientist*. Translated by Heinz Norden. New York, 1949.

Mann, Thomas. "Fantasy on Goethe." In *Last Essays*. New York, 1966.

————. "Goethe and Tolstoi." In *Three Essays*. New York, 1929.

————. "Introduction." In Thomas Mann, ed., *The Permanent Goethe*. New York, 1948.

Mason, Eudo. *Goethe's "Faust": Its Genesis and Purport*. Berkeley, 1967.

Nisbet, H. B. *Goethe and the Scientific Tradition*. London, 1972.

Palmer, P. M., and R. P. More. *The Sources of the Faust Tradition*. New York, 1965.

Peacock, Ronald. *Goethe's Major Plays*. Manchester, 1959.

Pochmann, H. A. *German Culture in America: Philosophical and Literary Influences, 1600–1900*. Madison, Wis., 1957.

Reiss, Hans. *Goethe's Novels*. Coral Gables, Fla., 1969.

Robertson, John George. *The Life and Work of Goethe*. London, 1927. Revised ed., 1932. Reprinted 1973.

Robson-Scott, W. D. *The Younger Goethe and the Visual Arts*. Cambridge, 1981.

Salm, Peter. *The Poem as Plant: A Biological View of Goethe's "Faust."* Cleveland, 1971.

Santayana, George. "Goethe's *Faust*." In *Three Philosophical Poets*. Cambridge, Mass., 1910. Reprinted 1953.

Seidlin, Oskar. "Iphigenia and the Humane Ideal." In V. Lange, ed., *Goethe*, above.

Stawell, F. M., and G. Lowes Dickinson. *Goethe's "Faust."* London, 1928. Reprinted 1978.

Steiner, Rudolf. *The Theory of Knowledge Implicit in Goethe's World View*. Translated by O. D. Wannamaker. New York, 1940.

Sternfeld, Frederick William. *Goethe and Music*. New York, 1954.

Strich, Fritz. *Goethe and World Literature*. Translated by C. A. Sym. Westport, Conn., 1971.

Swales, Martin. "*Wilhelm Meister's Apprenticeship*." In *The German Bildungsroman from Wieland to Hesse*. Princeton, 1978.

Thomas, Calvin. *Goethe*. Philadelphia, 1917. Reprinted 1973.

Trevelyan, Humphrey. *Goethe and the Greeks*. Cambridge, 1941.

Urzidill, Johannes. "Goethe and Art." *Germanic Review* 24:184–189 (1949).

Viëtor, Karl. *Goethe, the Poet.* Translated by Moses Hadas. Cambridge, Mass., 1949.

———. *Goethe, the Thinker.* Translated by B. Q. Morgan. Cambridge, Mass., 1950.

Weinberg, Kurt. *The Figure of Faust in Valéry and Goethe.* Princeton, 1976.

Wells, George. "Goethe and Evolution." *Journal of the History of Ideas* 28:537–550 (1967).

Wilkinson, E. M., and L. A. Willoughby. *Goethe: Poet and Thinker.* London, 1962.

See also the extensive and useful introductions to the American editions of *Faust* by S. Heffner, H. Rehder, and W. F. Twadell (Lexington, Mass., 1954–1955) and by Calvin Thomas (Boston, 1892–1897), as well as the materials, notes, and commentary by Cyrus Hamlin in the edition of the English translation by Walter Arndt (New York, 1976).

## BIBLIOGRAPHIES

Pyritz, Hans. *Goethe-Bibliographie.* 2 vols. Heidelberg, 1965 and 1968.

*Goethe Jahrbuch.* A yearly bibliography published in Weimar.

See also the publications of the *Goethe Society of North America* (1982– ) and the *English Goethe Society.*

JOHN GEAREY